The Economics of International Integration

Својим синовима Јовану и Николи

Στους υιούς μου, Γιάννη και Νικόλαο

Ai miei figli, Jovan e Nikola

To my sons, Jovan and Nikola

The Economics of International Integration

Miroslav N. Jovanović

Economic Affairs Officer, United Nations Economic Commission for Europe, Geneva, Switzerland

Edward Elgar

Cheltenham, UK • Northampton, MA, USA

Published by
Edward Elgar Publishing Limited
Glensanda House
Montpellier Parade
Cheltenham
Glos GL50 1UA
UK

Edward Elgar Publishing, Inc.
136 West Street
Suite 202
Northampton
Massachusetts 01060
USA

A catalogue record for this book
is available from the British Library

Library of Congress Cataloguing in Publication Data

Jovanović, Miroslav N., 1957–
The economics of international integration/Miroslav N. Jovanović.
p. cm.
Includes bibliographical references and index.
1. International economic integration. 2. Customs unions. 3. Monetary policy. 4. Space in economics. 5. International economic integration—Case studies. I. Title.
HF1418.5.J678 2006
337.1—dc22

2005049824

ISBN-13: 978 1 84542 271 4 (cased)
ISBN-10: 1 84542 271 6 (cased)

Printed and bound in Great Britain by MPG Books Ltd, Bodmin, Cornwall

How good and pleasant it is when brothers live together in unity.
Psalms 133:1

Contents

Foreword

The pursuit of economic integration has been one of the most important economic developments over the whole of the sixty-year period starting with the end of the Second World War. Integration has been attempted at various depths, running from tariff reductions under the GATT and the WTO, through full preferential elimination of tariffs in various customs unions, through various levels of deeper integration, to the type of economic union envisaged by the EU, although set back (possibly temporarily) by the recent rejections of the European constitution by voters in France and the Netherlands. It has also been pursued at various geographic coverages, running from all the members of the WTO, down to the plethora of bi-national trade liberalising agreements currently being established between the US and several of its neighbours in the Western Hemisphere.

Over this whole period, the many issues and problems raised by the various forms of integration have been an ongoing concern of both theoretical and applied economists as well as policy makers. I first encountered the theoretical problems when, as a graduate student at the London School of Economics in 1953–54, I read Viner's path-breaking book, *The Theory of Customs Unions*. Shortly after that, I made my own small contribution to the early development of this literature by arguing that, important though they were, Viner's concepts of trade creation and trade diversion concentrated solely on the production side, studying the effect on producers of the changes in relative prices brought about by the union, while tariff reductions also had an effect that works through the consumption side by changing the relative prices to which consumers respond. During the second year of my graduate studies, I made early contact with the applied side of integration when I attended the Council of Westminster, which was held in London as one of the early stages in the movement towards the European Economic Community. The Canadian government wanted to be represented, but not thinking it worthwhile to send a delegation from Canada, they sought out Canadians already in the UK, choosing three, Robert M. Clark, a UBC professor on sabbatical at Manchester, Harry Johnson, then a fellow of King's College Cambridge, and myself, a PhD student at the LSE. I knew some trade theory but little about trade policy and nothing about diplomacy or the formation of the EEC, so this was pretty heady stuff.

Although working in many other fields, I maintained an interest in integration over the subsequent years. Then as Senior Economic Adviser for the C.D. Howe Institute, a Toronto think-tank, I took part in the great Canadian debate over the proposed free trade area with the US and later, as chairman of a Federal government subcommittee overseeing that agreement, I played some part in Canada's decision to insinuate itself into the US Mexican FTA negotiations, thereby turning a proposed bilateral US–Mexican FTA into the NAFTA.

During that time, I taught one course on economic policy at Queen's University and met Miroslav Jovanović, who was the outstanding student in my class. Since that time, I have followed his career and welcomed the first edition of his book *The Economics of International Integration*. Its success is now attested by this, its third edition, in which he has improved and elaborated on his already comprehensive work on all aspects of the economics of integration.

The most distinctive aspect of his treatment continues to be his own creative union of theory and applied material. For him, the major interest always resides in the problems created by the working out of various forms of integration in real situations. He uses theory but no more than is needed to act as a tool for enlightening our understanding of what we see in the world around us.

For those who want a comprehensive survey relevant for understanding the issues surrounding economic integration, this is an excellent book. For those who wish to go in more depth into the theories that deal with these issues, this book establishes a set of signposts that can provide guidance when more formal and specific theoretical treatments are studied in detail.

A wholly new introduction discusses the splintering of the multinational trading system and the rapid rise of regional trading arrangements, often involving bilateral arrangements. One of the most important issues in economic integration today is how the plethora of regional, often bilateral, agreements will affect the evolution of multinational economic integration. After the conclusion of the US–Canada FTA and NAFTA, I was optimistic that these regional agreements could solve problems that seemed intractable in more multinational contexts; that they would not inhibit multinational negotiations in the WTO; and that some of them would grow to become much wider regional agreements – in the case of NAFTA evolving into a Western Hemispheric FTA. Now, I am not so sure and I welcome the extensive treatment given to such issues by Dr Jovanović.

The book's much updated Chapter 2 on customs unions sets the tone for the whole volume. It selects topic areas one after another; it reviews the relevant theory of each, on the assumption that the reader already has some acquaintance with it; it then goes on to consider a host of important applied issues in the area under consideration. The reader wanting to know the relevant theory and the main applied issues that have arisen around any topic relating to customs unions will find that this chapter provides excellent source material as well as a valuable consideration of most of the issues. The chapter concludes with a new section asking why countries continue to press for integration when the measured effects of the resulting resource reallocations seem small. The discussion covers many possibilities, of which my own answer is twofold. First, policy makers continue to believe that the dynamic effects are larger than any measurement exercise has been able to establish and, second, institutionalising trade liberalisation is seen as an effective defence against the rise of sentiments for trade restrictions, such as can be seen sporadically in many countries, not the least of which is the US.

Chapter 3 does the same for common markets. Chapter 4, on economic union, is by far the longest chapter, which is as it should be, since economic union is the final goal of many of the looser associations. Sometimes this is their stated goal, and sometimes forces unleashed by looser forms of integration push their members in that direction. Dr Jovanović's treatment of these issues verges on the exhaustive. The chapter covers the important monetary, fiscal, industrial and regional policies. New discussions under monetary policy of the Stability and Growth Pact and sterling and the Euro are timely, as is the discussion of the Lisbon Agenda under industrial policy. The updated section in Chapter 5 on regional schemes also has timely discussions, this time of the enlargement of the EU in general and the inclusion of Turkey in particular. The consequences of the current round of EU enlargement, and the desirability of further rounds, are almost sure to be some of the most hotly debated issues over the next decade, making the book's discussions valuable.

Dr Jovanović devotes considerable space to the important topic of industrial policy, which is occupying much government attention. Governments are concerned about footloose, knowledge-intensive industries, both when they have them (lest they lose them), and when they do not have them (in the hope of attracting them). Rightly or wrongly, new industrial policies are key issues in many countries today, and harmonising them poses major problems for jurisdictions that belong to economic unions. In view of the vast complexity of the subject, Dr Jovanović's treatment must be sketchy in places. He does, however, touch on virtually all of the important issues that might need further, in-depth study by those seeking a detailed appreciation.

Regional policy poses even more vexing problems than does industrial policy. Over the years, and in most countries, regional policies have had much more uniformly disappointing results than industrial policies – perhaps because regional policies have so often concentrated on supporting sunset industries and on establishing isolated new enterprises with no consideration of the need for clusters of related firms if genuine competitive advantages are to be created. Dr Jovanović deals with key issues of regional policy in general and then illustrates them with the experience of the EU.

Readers who set out on these pages have a rich and varied experience awaiting them. The coverage is remarkably comprehensive, considering that it is all condensed into around 800 pages. For every reader, there will be things to agree with, and things to argue with – as is to be expected in so rich a survey. But there is much to be gained in both cases. Finally, the main text is followed by a list of research topics, many of which should be on a list of completed researches ten years from now.

Richard G. Lipsey
Vancouver, BC
2005

Preface

The traditional theory of international economic integration is an elegant and quite convincing academic exercise. Its conclusions are straightforward and offer useful insights into the incentives for and the general consequences of integration. With that in mind, the first objective of this book is to introduce the reader to the area of international economic integration. The other goal, equally important, is to extend the traditional theory of integration by addressing issues that were ignored in the neo-classical model. These include market imperfections such as economies of scale, foreign direct investment and an evolutionary approach to the spatial location of firms and industries. This reflects the modern research attitude to trade, competition, investment and spatial location and distribution of production. The analysis is supplemented by numerous examples from the real world in order to provide support for theoretical statements. A quantitative approach to analysis is kept at the minimum; thus, it is hoped that the book will be readily accessible to a wide audience.

A presentation of a general theory of international economic integration is not (yet) possible. This is due primarily to the absence of generally applicable theories of international trade and spatial location of production. The neo-classical theory has looked at comparative advantages; hence, the standard theory of regional economic integration has largely been presented in such a framework. A modern theory and policy on trade, investment and spatial location of production cannot be separated from competition and industrial policies. New research models identified other determinants of countries' trade, investment and patterns of location of production. In a world of imperfect competition, various externalities and economies of scale, there are many reasons for trade, foreign direct investment, geographical location of industries and integration, even if countries are identical in their factor endowments, size, technologies and tastes. In such a situation, there are a number of second-best choices about economic actions. This book considers both theoretical and practical economic choices linked with international economic integration.

The analysis acknowledges the importance of the traditional, neoclassical theory of trade: countries trade because they are differently endowed with resources, technology and/or predilections. None the less, such a trade model is more appropriate to trade in simple goods such as wheat, wine or iron ore, while the new theory is better suited as a theoretical tool for the analysis of trade in goods such as aircraft and pharmaceuticals, as well as services such as marketing or financial analysis.[1] The new theoretical model supplements the traditional one with innovative qualities, that is, the consideration of market imperfections, in particular, economies of scale, externalities, foreign direct investment and spatial location of businesses. Because they are inconsistent with perfect competition, these issues were omitted from the picture in the traditional model. The new model questions the conventional argument that free trade is always an optimal economic strategy. When a particular situation is compounded with market imperfections, economic integration/regionalism can sometimes make sense.

Once trade and competition take place in an imperfect economic environment, solutions to economic problems are no longer unique. The outcomes of economic games depend on assumptions about the past, present and expected future complex behaviour of players. In these circumstances, economic policy (intervention in the form of integration) may simply add an adjustment mechanism to the already highly imperfect and suboptimal market situation. Economic policy and integration may also be abused by those who rely on certain (incomplete or distorted) economic facts in order to pursue rent-seeking objectives. When the economic situation is not simple and straightforward, many outcomes become possible, but not equally desirable. Therefore, the new model of economic integration is a mix of various theoretical approaches to trade, competition, investment and spatial location. The new theory does not argue that the classical model is wrong, but rather that it is not necessarily correct. Market imperfections need not be rectified by new barriers to trade, factor mobility and foreign investment, but rather by domestic policies that alleviate the problem (of competitiveness) at its source, such as the supply of certain types of labour (education) and venture capital.

Contrary to widespread belief, the new model does not give *carte blanche* to medium- and long-term protectionism, because a cycle of retaliation and counter-retaliation makes everybody worse off.[2] Intervention may be employed under certain conditions as a handy short-term economic policy tool. All developed countries have used it at some crucial point in their past. They use it or threaten to use it even at the present time, for example in the textile industry. However, governments do not always have all the necessary information and tools for intelligent intervention, but nor do free markets always bring desirable solutions. The new model argues that with a bit of astute intervention, under certain conditions, economic policy may improve a country's national and international economic position.

Treatment of the theory of international economic integration has been basically Eurocentric, because integration had its deepest meaning there. However, there are no big theoretical differences between integration among industrialised and among less-developed countries. The arguments in favour of integration are the same. What may differ are the intentions and ambitions of countries, as well as the starting base. In spite of the poor achievements of previous integration efforts by the developing world, those countries may still wish to employ international economic integration as a part of their development strategy, but perhaps by no longer following the south–south integration path as in the past, but rather trying north–south integration as exemplified in the case of Mexico's 1994 free trade agreement with the United States and Canada, as well as the 1995 customs union deal between Turkey and the European Union.[3]

The book is organised as follows. After the Introduction, which presents the basic notions related to integration (Chapter 1), Chapter 2 deals with preferential trade issues related to customs unions and free trade areas, which is the most rigorously developed part of the theory of international economic integration. The analysis is carried out in static and dynamic models, as well as in partial and general equilibrium frameworks. Increased competition on a secured and enlarged market by means of integration, specialisation and returns to scale receive special treatment, as they are the most important dynamic effects. A discussion of adjustment costs suggests that they do not always represent a serious barrier to integration, especially in the medium and long runs.

Chapter 3 is devoted to common markets. Factor (labour and capital) mobility lies at the heart of the analysis. Labour migration, including a number of controversies surrounding this issue, particularly which country (sending or receiving) benefits more from integration, is outlined in the context of Europe. Prospects for increased foreign direct investment activity and operations of transnational corporations are analysed with respect to integration arrangements of both developed and developing countries. Discussion is supported by statistical data on foreign direct investment in the European Union.

Chapter 4 examines economic unions. Monetary, fiscal, industrial and regional (spatial location of firms/industries) policies are considered in turn. The point is that all these policies in an economic union can be defended by the same arguments that are used to justify similar policies in a single country consisting of several regions. Monetary policy is the area where the effects of integration are felt first. Fiscal policy refers to taxation and budgetary problems among countries. The creation of comparative advantage and wealth is considered in the discussion of industrial policy in manufacturing and services. The geographical location of business and the distribution of wealth is emphasised in regional policy, which is used as a buffer against the potentially negative consequences of other economic policies.

Past, present and emerging integration schemes and their experiences are examined in Chapter 5. Integration deals are arbitrarily distributed on the basis of geography. Appendix 5A1 supplements these considerations by giving an overview of the defunct Council for Mutual Economic Assistance, while Appendix 5A2 examines the issue of the eastern enlargement of the EU. It demonstrates ways, means and first achievements of larger-scale integration between developed and some less-developed countries in Europe. There are also references to the possible entry of Turkey into the European Union.

Chapter 6 deals with the measurement of the effects of international economic integration. There are serious methodological limits to the quantification of these effects, as well as interpretations of the results of studies. Most importantly, it is not yet possible to create a reliable counterfactual situation which would simulate the scenarios occurring with or without integration. It is stated that the end result of estimations is an amalgam of various effects, some of which have nothing to do with integration. Hence, the theory of international economic integration is in certain dimensions more intuitive than conclusive.

Chapter 7 concludes the book and argues that regional economic integration is now here to stay.[4] Even though the results of the Uruguay Round provided a major impetus to multilateral solutions in international trade, regional trade arrangements (mainly free trade areas) continue to proliferate. Multilateral liberalisation and regionalism could be mutually reinforcing, provided that the regional integration schemes adopt a relatively liberal external trade and investment policy, and that they cooperate. On those grounds and if these elements are true, integration arrangements may be a favourable development for the world economy. It is important to bear in mind that countries grow richer in the medium and long terms together, not at each other's expense.

I hope that the book will be of interest to economists specialising in international economics, international trade and integration, spatial economics and European studies. However, if it also attracts the curiosity and attention of those studying economic development, international business and policy makers, then this is to be welcomed.

Notes

1. One may even argue that both the classical and the new theory of trade and spatial economics are limited to a few special cases. None the less, one should not disregard the consideration of extreme cases, as many useful things may be learned from the analysis of such examples.
2. Intervention in the field of education may be an exception. Forward-looking countries may and do subsidise the education of their labour and management. Retaliatory measures and sanctions for subsidies to education and training have not (yet) been invented and applied. The reason is that the effects of such subsidies are slow in coming and become apparent only in the long term.
3. The term European Union (EU) is used throughout the book as the organisational habitat for the European integration that took place over time in the European Economic Community, the European Community and the EU.
4. There are also various issues with regard to the disintegration of countries, for example, as experienced by the Soviet Union, Czechoslovakia, Yugoslavia or Ethiopia (Eritrea) in the early 1990s. In addition, there are strong, long-term and sometimes even violent regional autonomy (and more than that) movements in many countries including France (Corsica), Spain (Catalonia and the Basque region), Britain (Northern Ireland, Scotland, even Wales), Belgium (the Flemish region), Italy (the northern 'Padania'), Russia (Chechnya), Turkey (Kurdistan).

Acknowledgements

My involvement in international economic integration began when I was studying European integration at the Europa Institute of the University of Amsterdam during the 1980/81 academic year. However, the pivotal event that led to the writing of this book was my study and research programme at Queen's University, Kingston, Ontario, during the 1986/87 academic year. I continued working and publishing on the subject at the University of Belgrade, the United Nations Centre on Transnational Corporations in New York and the United Nations Economic Commission for Europe in Geneva.

I have benefited from human capital and discussions, as well as delightful and advantageous contacts with many friends and colleagues over the years. There are, however, several to whom I owe a special debt of gratitude for various kinds of valuable inspiration, encouragement, comments and assistance in the preparation of this book. Je tiens à remercier tout particulièrement Marinette Payot qui m'a beaucoup aidé sans que je le sache. Un ringraziamento va a Marina Rossi che mi ha aiutato senza saperlo. I also extend my thanks to Marc-Aurel Battaglia, Lisa Borgatti, Eric Fiechter, Eckhard Freyer, Dragoš Kalajić, Oskar Kovač, Richard G. Lipsey, Alexandar Rado, Joël Robichaud, Rolf Traeger, Hélène-Divna Tzico Stefanesco, Joanna Wheeler and James Wiltshire. Jovan and Nikola Jovanović assisted greatly with the graphics. The UN library in Geneva, particularly Anthony Donnarumma and Cristina Giordano, provided me with most of the sources. Margaret Pugh edited the text superbly, while Sheila Milne proofread the final version. Finally, Luke Adams of Edward Elgar encouraged this project from the outset, while Caroline Cornish efficiently prepared the text for print.

I am grateful to all of them. The usual disclaimer, however, applies here: I bear sole responsibility for all shortcomings and mistakes. In addition, the expressed views are my own and are not necessarily those of the organisation in which I work.

Miroslav N. Jovanović
Geneva, 2006

Abbreviations and Acronyms

APEC	Asia Pacific Economic Cooperation
ASEAN	Association of South-East Asian Nations
CACM	Central American Common Market
CAP	Common Agricultural Policy
CEAO	Communauté Economique de l'Afrique de l'Ouest (West African Economic Community)
CEFTA	Central European Free Trade Agreement
CER	Closer Economic Relations (Australia and New Zealand)
CFA	Communauté Financière Africaine (African Financial Community)
CMEA	Council for Mutual Economic Assistance (Comecon)
COCOM	Coordinating Committee on Multilateral Export Controls
COMESA	Common Market for Eastern and Southern Africa
DG	Directorate-General (in the European Commission)
DISC	Domestic International Sales Corporation
DTI	Department of Trade and Industry (UK)
EAC	East African Community
ECB	European Central Bank
ECOFIN	Economic and Financial Committee
ECOWAS	Economic Community of West African States
ECU	European Currency Unit

EEA	European Economic Area
EFTA	European Free Trade Association
EIB	European Investment Bank
EMI	European Monetary Institute
EMS	European Monetary System
EMU	economic and monetary union
ERDF	European Regional Development Fund
ERM	Exchange Rate Mechanism
EU	European Union
EURES	European Employment Services
FDI	foreign direct investment
FIRA	Foreign Investment Review Agency (Canada)
FSC	Foreign Sales Corporation (United States)
FTAA	Free Trade Area of the Americas
GATS	General Agreement on Trade in Services
GATT	General Agreement on Tariffs and Trade
GDP	gross domestic product
IBEC	International Bank for Economic Cooperation
IIB	International Investment Bank
IIT	intra-industry trade
IMF	International Monetary Fund
LAFTA	Latin American Free Trade Area
LAIA	Latin American Integration Association
Mercosur	Mercado Común del Sur (Southern Common Market)
MFN	most favoured nation
MITI	Ministry of International Trade and Industry (Japan)
NAFTA	North American Free Trade Agreement
NAIRU	non-accelerating inflation rate of unemployment
NATO	North Atlantic Treaty Organisation
NGO	non-governmental organisation
NMS	new member state
NTB	non-tariff barrier
OAU	Organisation of African Unity
OECD	Organisation for Economic Cooperation and Development
PHARE	Poland, Hungary: Assistance for Economic Restructuring
PPS	purchasing power standard
PTA	Preferential Trade Area for Eastern and Southern African States
R&D	research and development
SACN	South American Community of Nations
SACU	South African Customs Union
SADC	Southern African Development Community

SCP	structure–conduct–performance
SITC	Standard International Trade Classification
SME	small and medium-sized enterprise
TNC	transnational corporation
TRIM	trade-related investment measure
TRIPS	trade-related intellectual property rights
UDEAC	Union Douanière et Economique de l'Afrique Centrale (Central African Customs and Economic Union)
UN	United Nations
UNCTAD	UN Conference on Trade and Development
UNCTC	UN Centre on Transnational Corporations
UNECE	UN Economic Commission for Europe
US	United States
VAT	value-added tax
VCR	video cassette recorder
WAEMU	West African Economic and Monetary Union
WAMU	West African Monetary Union
WAMZ	West African Monetary Zone
WTO	World Trade Organisation

My people perish for lack of knowledge.
Hosea 4:6

1 Introduction

1.1 Issues

The importance and influence of international economic integration is well recognised.[1] The existence of various preferential trade agreements and their proliferation shape the form, nature and often the direction of the world trading system. Integration has affected most of the countries in the world. It has also become an unavoidable and powerful element in most national and international economic policy decisions. In fact, most of the countries throughout the world have either attempted to enter or entered into a trade liberalisation or integration agreement with others.[2] Therefore, the character of and relation between regional integration and a multilateral trading system continues to be at the heart of the trade and investment policy debate. Some of the biggest achievements in integration, however, have been among the developed countries, in particular the European Union (EU). Integration both deepened and widened in Europe. Countries in other parts of the world have attempted to emulate some of the integration methods and achievements that took place in the EU, but with varying degrees of success.

Many policy makers generally had a favourable view of integration. They attempted to use economic integration as a means of securing access to a wider market and reinforcing growth in order to attain a higher level of national welfare. The degree of success in integration, however, has varied between regions. In the EU, following the elimination of tariffs and quotas in 1968, a deepening of integration covered areas such as competition, public procurement and services, thus preceding, even provoking, multilateral negotiations and agreements on these issues.[3] Developing countries have changed their inward-looking integration strategies of the 1960s to ones of improved economic ties with the developed north from the 1990s. However, because of changed aspirations, past experiences in integration in the developing world are not always very useful guides for future integration policy. None the less, international economic integration has remained an attractive economic strategy in the developing world. This is because integration can serve as a reliable 'insurance policy' against sudden changes in the trading behaviour and policy of partner countries. 'Dividends' from a policy of integration include an increase in business predictability which has a potentially positive impact on domestic and foreign investment.

In spite of past experiences with integration, which may have been quite negative in certain developing-country groups, there are continuing opportunities and challenges. These have been prompted by several developments since the mid-1980s, including:

- deepening and widening of integration in the EU and North America;
- integration between developed countries such as the United States (US) and Canada, on the one hand, and a developing one such as Mexico, on the other;
- economic transition in the formerly centrally planned economies in central and eastern Europe and the 2004 EU entry of eight of these countries (with the prospect of others following in the future);
- a change in economic policies in the developing countries towards more outward-looking and liberal models;
- change in the structure of production (the move towards knowledge-based goods and services and operations of transnational corporations: TNCs);
- the changing character of protectionism ('voluntary' export restraint deals, harassment by countervailing measures and so on;) and
- weakening confidence in the multilateral trading system since 1995.

A response to these challenges was often found in trade liberalisation agreements and deeper integration. For example, the EU Single Market Programme (1985–92) was an agreement to coordinate policies that historically have been regarded as domestic.

The basic argument in favour of trade liberalisation is that it improves the allocation of resources. As such, it contributes to efficiency in production and to economic growth. In order to introduce and enforce the principle of multilateral trade liberalisation, the founders of the General Agreement on Tariffs and Trade (GATT) (1948) introduced the most favoured nation (MFN) treatment. According to Article I, 'any advantage, favour, privilege or immunity granted by any contracting party to any product originating in or destined for any other country shall be accorded immediately and unconditionally to the like product originating in or destined for the territories of all other contracting parties'. The consequence is that if a country opens up its market to another country, it must also open it to all other GATT member countries. The MFN treatment was supposed both to prevent the return of mercantilist trade policies (of the 1930s) and to introduce order in and expansion of the process of multilateral trade liberalisation.

The basic principles of the GATT are:

- non-discrimination;
- reciprocity;[4]
- transparency;
- enforcement; and
- the impartial settlement of disputes.

These principles were originally conceived to ameliorate international trade at the border. At the time of the creation of the GATT, border measures were, perhaps, the most important protectionist instruments. As tariffs were reduced over time, grey-area measures (non-tariff barriers: NTBs) expanded, and transformed protectionist techniques. Protection now takes place not at the border, but within the domestic market once goods and services cross the border. The Uruguay Round was a sign that the multilateral trading system was seeking ways and means to address these new challenges.

This chapter is structured as follows. Section 1.2 questions whether the multilateral trading system is falling apart, and Section 1.3 discusses interdependence. Sections 1.4 and 1.5 clarify definitions and types. Finally, Section 1.6 examines sovereignty.

1.2 Is the multilateral trading system falling apart?

The GATT recognised the importance and value of economic integration between countries. That process can have the same economic rationale as integration within a single country that has different regions. Hence, regional economic integration, according to GATT Article XXIV, does not pose an inherent threat to global trade liberalisation. None the less, the GATT constrains the level of the common external tariff and other trade measures in customs unions. On the whole, these trade measures should not be higher or more restrictive than those of the member countries prior to the integration agreement. The General Agreement on Trade in Services (GATS) (Article V) has a similar attitude regarding regulation of trade-liberalising agreements in services between member countries.

In spite of a declared official interest in the success of the Doha Round (2001–05?) of multilateral negotiations under the auspices of the World Trade Organization (WTO),[5] there is considerable uncertainty regarding the future and relevance of the multilateral trading system. These problems are embodied in obvious, serious and repeated troubles (Seattle in 1999 and Cancun in 2003)[6] within the ongoing Doha Round of multilateral trade liberalisation negotiations. This is all compounded by the ambiguous attitudes of many negotiators from both the developed and the developing world concerning the real success of the Doha Round.[7] Such developments cast some doubt on the future of the multilateral trading system. In the meantime, economic integration deals are proliferating worldwide. Compared with a 'clean and lean' multilateral trading system and rules, the existing trading system creates and maintains a complex labyrinth of international trading rules and relations, which is an additional reason for studying international economic integration.

While international trade has grown faster than income over the past decades, there are questions and doubts about the role and influence of the GATT/WTO in these developments. Could this be attributed to the GATT/WTO? 'Who knows? But there are plenty of other candidates. Higher rates of productivity in tradables, falling transport costs, regional trade associations, converging tastes, shift from primary products towards manufacturing and services, growing international liquidity, and changing endowments are all possibilities' (Rose, 2004, p. 112).

Between 1947 and 2005 a total of 300 integration agreements had been notified to the GATT and WTO.[8] The founding fathers of the GATT (which is part of the WTO) exempted free trade areas and customs unions from the MFN clause, but they did not predict a proliferation of these agreements in such a way that the world trading system would be fragmented.[9] Over 150 of these agreements are in force (Figure 1.1).[10] However, only one, the Czech and Slovak Customs Union (1993), was 'cleared' by the GATT Working Party as fully consistent with the conditions laid out in Article XXIV. For all the others, including the 'clearance' of the Treaty of Rome, which established the European Economic Community in 1957, the result was inconclusive. The reasons why there was no definite and clear

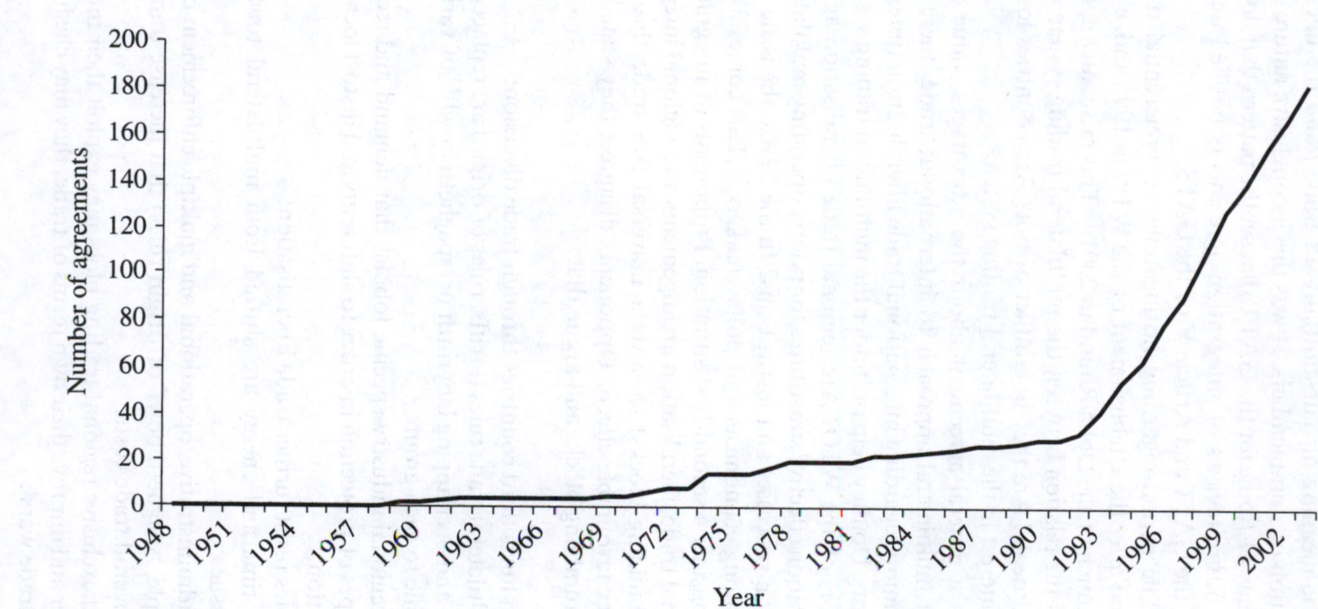

Source: WTO (2004).

Figure 1.1 Regional trade agreements in force by year of entry into force

agreement in the working party were the ambiguous interpretations of Article XXIV (the meaning of 'substantially all trade') and the unclear effects of integration on non-members. It was this inconclusive nature and impact of the Treaty of Rome for the GATT that set the pattern that dominated nearly all future reviews of integration agreements notified under Article XXIV of the GATT and Article V of the GATS.

The most prolific period regarding notifications of preferential trade agreements started *after* the establishment of the WTO in 1995 and, especially, after the launch of the Doha Round in 2001.[11] This raises an important issue: what is the relation between the multilateral trading system and these preferential deals? Are they in conflict or not? Are countries losing confidence and interest in the multilateral trading system?

While there is a general agreement about the advantages, value and importance of a multilateral approach to international trade, there are differences in opinion regarding international trade liberalisation (integration) arrangements. Do they help or hinder the multilateral trading system under the auspices of the WTO? Are regional trade liberalisation agreements and integration effective substitutes for poorly operating multilateral trade liberalisation processes and institutions? In the 1990s, the issue was hotly debated among economists and policy makers.[12] This comes as no surprise as we consider a second-best situation. Proponents of integration argue that regional trade liberalisation arrangements and regional integration are steps (building blocks) towards a universal free trade through growth and other favourable effects. Opponents disagree; they state that these deals are stumbling blocks and argue that:

- integration hurts third countries through trade diversion;
- simple multilateral trade rules (tariffs, rules of origin) are replaced by a complex and overlapping labyrinth or 'spaghetti bowl'[13] of various rules specific to each group;
- there are regional industry-specific lobbies that demand and receive various types of protection in order to shift rents and distort location of production;
- these lobbies resist further trade liberalisation;
- resources, time and energy are shifted from multilateral towards regional issues;
- there are administrative, operational and multiple enforcement costs (for example, 'spaghetti bowl' of origin rules) that increase transaction and overall trade costs;
- strong and exclusive regional trading blocs may exploit their monopoly power and improve their own terms of trade; they may clash and provoke 'trade wars';

- deeper integration may introduce protection in previously unprotected business areas;
- major players in multilateral trade liberalisation negotiations, the US and especially the EU, are bound to specific trade liberalisation (discrimination) agreements (the EU has never been too enthusiastic about free trade, the Common Agricultural Policy being the prime example); and
- regional trade arrangements may slow down and postpone progress on the multilateral plane as there are gainers from the existence of deals that discriminate in trade who may not welcome the arrival of a new multilateral deal.

In spite of the hot debate and concerns among economists and politicians, the hard empirical evidence about the effects of preferential trade on multilateral trade liberalisation was rather slim. In an analysis of the effect of preferential trade deals on the US stance on multilateral trade liberalisation, Limão (2005, p. 19) found the stumbling block effect. This was based on the discovery that the US multilateral tariff reductions for goods traded under preferential trade agreements were smaller than those in similar goods not imported from partners in preferential trade deals.

Testimony given on 8 May 2001 to the US House Committee on Ways and Means (Subcommittee on Trade) regarding a future Free Trade Area of the Americas provides an example of the stumbling block effect in multilateral negotiations on liberalisation of trade. Several countries from the Caribbean region have produced rum for centuries. In some of them, such as the US Virgin Islands, only tourism is a more important national industry. These countries export low value-added bulk and bottled rum to the US. This product, one of the major export items, enters the US duty free under the Caribbean Basin Initiative.

> The unique and critical role of rum in the Caribbean region – and the importance of maintaining preferences for low-value rum – was most recently affirmed in a landmark 1997 understanding between the United States and the European Union. In WTO tariff negotiations in 1996, U.S. and EU negotiators had initially agreed to phase out all tariffs on rum and other 'white spirits' by 2000. This unexpected development was met with alarm by Caribbean governments, Administration officials and Members of Congress. They emphasized to the trade negotiators that such a drastic change in the tariff structure for rum would deal a severe blow to the economies of the USVI, Puerto Rico, and the Caribbean.
>
> In response to this outcry, U.S. and EU negotiators, as well as Caribbean governments and producers, revisited rum tariffs in complex and delicate discussions aimed at addressing the special role of rum in the Caribbean region. These discussions, which involved officials at the highest levels of the various

> governments, resulted in a carefully constructed compromise for rum. Under this compromise, the United States agreed to substantially *liberalize* duties on expensive rum. However, to protect the interests of the USVI and other Caribbean island producers, the United States also agreed to *maintain* existing MFN duties on low-value bottled and bulk rum.[14]

Figure 1.2 presents graphically the web of the EU's passion for trade liberalisation deals as it stood in 1996. The EU became a regional hub, while most of the other partners were the 'spokes'. This 'spaghetti bowl' of relations in trade was further 'seasoned' with a formidable entry process of transition countries from central and eastern Europe and deals with Mediterranean, Latin American and African, Caribbean and Pacific countries. The figure does not capture the fact that each deal has its own rules of origin. If this all looks complicated, difficult and confusing, that is because it is. Therefore, such a complex, overlapping and even chaotic structure distorts investment decisions and allocation of resources. It may seem to be an unlikely vehicle to take countries towards a simple non-discriminatory universal (multilateral) free trade system. As a result, the EU MFN trade regime applies to only nine WTO member countries[15] which account for about 36 per cent of its merchandise trade. But the EU is not the only contributor to this messy situation in international trade relations. Figure 1.3 presents a similar shambles in the Pacific region.

The EU has many preferential trade agreements with most developing countries that have been in operation for decades. However, 'the empirical literature supports the broad conclusion that trade preferences have had little beneficial impact beyond the obvious rent transfer accompanying duty-free entry of goods' (Panagariya, 2002, p. 1426). Earlier, Whalley (1990, p. 1319) commented:

> [T]he available quantitative studies, limited as they are, seem to point to the conclusion that special and differential treatment has had only a marginal effect on country economic performance, especially through GSP. And in the more rapidly growing economies, such as Korea, Taiwan, Turkey and others, there is little evidence that special and differential treatment has played much of a role in their strong growth performance.

Preferences offered to one group of developing countries might have been to the detriment of others. These favours could have reduced domestic demand for reform in the beneficiary countries. They felt less pressure for reform (because of the secure foreign market) than was the case in countries that did not have preferential trade deals.

If there are so many serious objections to regional trade agreements and little hard quantitative evidence about their clear beneficial effects, what is

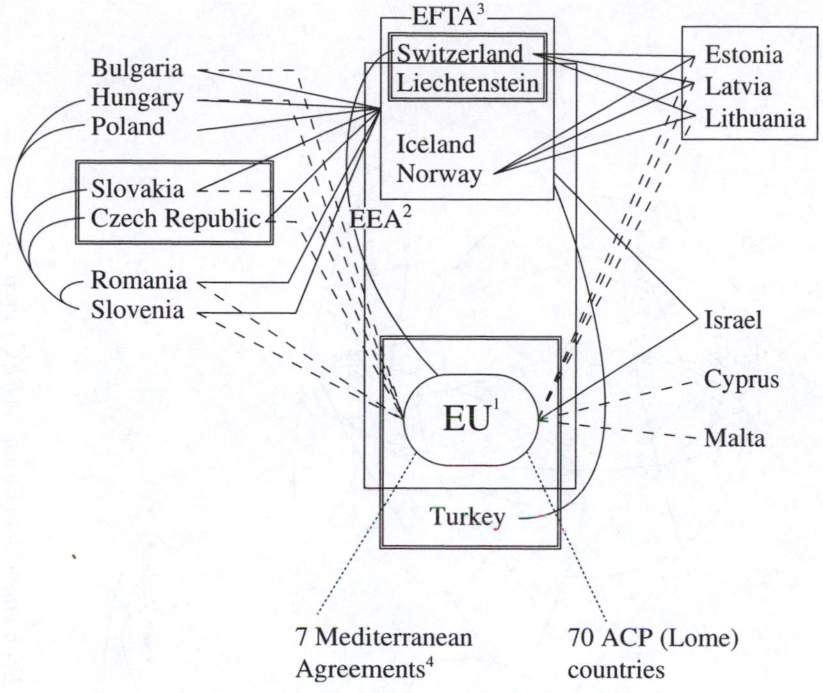

Notes:
Does not include countries of the former Soviet Union other than the Baltic countries.

1. European Union: Austria, Belgium, Denmark, Finland, France, Germany, Greece, Ireland, Italy, Luxemburg, the Netherlands, Portugal, Spain, Sweden and the United Kingdom.
2. European Economic Area.
3. European Free Trade Area.
4. Algeria, Egypt, Jordon, Lebanon, Morocco, Syria and Tunisia.

EU Single Market
Customs unions
Free trade areas
EU association agreements
Non-reciprocal agreements

Source: Snape (1996, p. 392).

Figure 1.2 Preferential trade agreements of the European Union, 1996

their fatal fascination and justification? Why do they proliferate? In the real world, bilateral or regional trading agreements may be a response to tremendous and uncertain resource costs related to multilateral negotiations and deals. It may be simpler, faster, cheaper and more tangible to put into practice a regional integration deal, than to wait a very long time for an

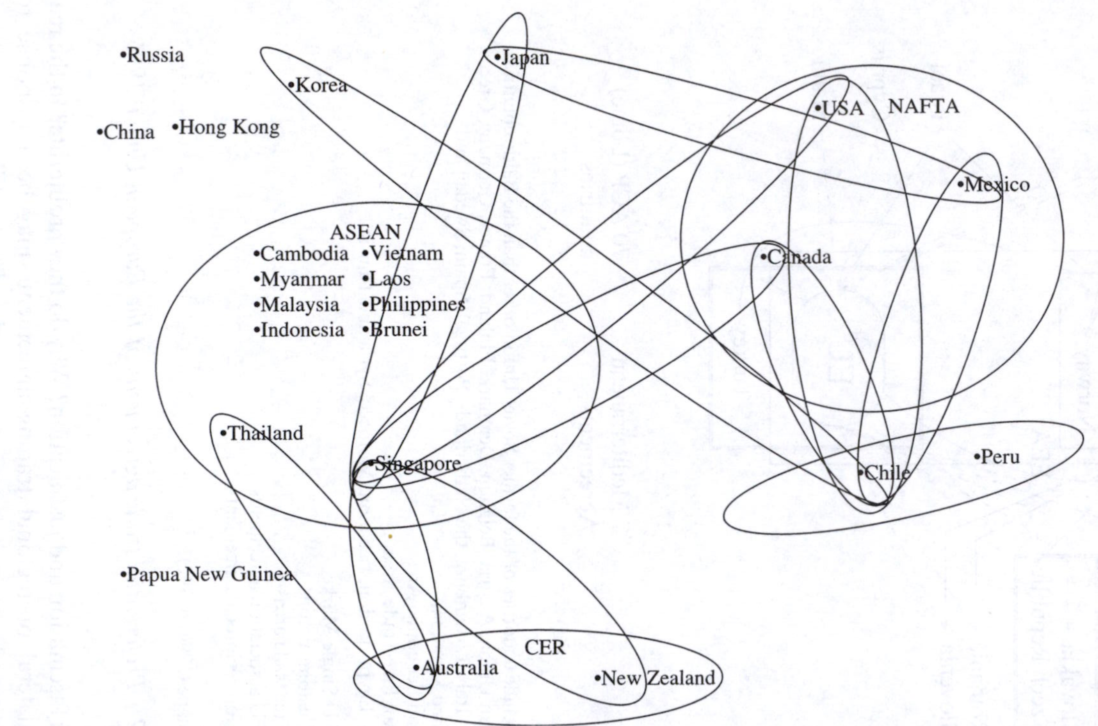

Source: Lloyd and MacLaren (2004, p. 460).

Figure 1.3 Regional trade agreements in the Asia Pacific Economic Cooperation (APEC) area, 2004

uncertain multilateral trade arrangement and its benefits. Static and usually short-term costs in terms of trade diversion do not give the full picture of the costs of regional deals for third countries.[16] Long-term dynamic effects may be much more important and beneficial for everyone. The choice that policy makers face is not between multilateral agreements and economic integration, but rather between a potentially beneficial economic integration with select partners (now) or no such arrangement at all.

Whether regional economic integration results in multilaterally liberal trade cannot be proved. However, integration may start this process. The bottom line may be uncertain: are the new integration programmes the outcome of the success of multilateralism or its failure?

One should not forget important ideological factors and political, especially security, gains that integration agreements bring. Some of them, the EU being one example,[17] were created primarily to ensure that war between France and Germany would be impossible. Economic integration was simply a vehicle towards that objective. Politics and strong and sustained commitment (or a lack of it) according to the letter and spirit of the agreed goals are often the primary reason for the success, slow progress or failure of an integrating group. In addition, many integration deals go well beyond mere trade, so that arguments concerning the costs of integration are not necessarily the whole story.[18] Many quantitative studies about the effects of integration on world welfare have questionable and ambiguous results.

Could the GATT really have done much better in the absence of moves towards regional free trade areas? 'This did not seem too plausible . . . the situation would not be better, and could easily have been worse, had the great free trade agreements of recent years never happened' (Krugman, 1995b, pp. 181–2).[19]

Each notified regional trade agreement was examined during the GATT years by an individual working party. In 1996, the WTO General Council established the Committee on Regional Trade Agreements, whose task was to examine individual agreements and to ascertain the implications for the multilateral trading system. This forum failed to produce a report because of the lack of consensus.[20] Reasons include the long-standing disputes about the interpretation of WTO rules against which deals are assessed; the uncertain effect of integration on non-members; institutional problems arising from the absence of WTO rules (on preferential rules of origin); and the potential links between the consistency judgement and the possible future dispute settlement process.[21]

Big countries such as the US may further their own political objectives by offering agreements on bilateral free trade. Such deals may break down coalitions in the developing world.[22] Bilateral or regional deals may divert attention and energy from the multilateral path. However, the US entered into free trade deals with Israel, Canada and Mexico during the Uruguay Round (1986–94) without losing sight of the final multilateral deal. Similarly, the US entered into free trade arrangements with Chile and Singapore in 2004 during the Doha Round. None the less, it is feared that regional trading blocs may turn hostile and destabilise the world economy because of various conflicting interests, including pressure from the well-entrenched special rent-seeking lobbies. What if simple non-discriminatory multilateral trade rules are replaced by complex rules of origin (internal to each group) that are not in accord with each other?

1.3 Interdependence

The interdependence of economic life among countries created a situation in which national economic problems increasingly become a matter of international concern. The predominant way of solving these international problems is at the national level, where the most decisive influence is wielded by a small number of large and highly developed countries, as well as a few oil-exporting ones. While free market competition can create a situation in which large firms can absorb their small competitors, such an analogy is not possible when dealing with sovereign countries. Large and developed countries cannot always behave like firms (Panić, 1988, p. 284).

Statements from prominent public figures, in particular from the larger nations, often make headlines and can have an impact on the currency market, trade policy and investments. Therefore, such remarks need to be treated with caution. A statement by the (former) US President Bill Clinton that each nation is 'like a big corporation competing in the global marketplace' is like saying that the US and Japan are competitors in the same way as Coca-Cola competes with Pepsi (Krugman, 1996b, p. 4).[23] Firms are rivals for a limited pool of potential profits. What distinguishes states from firms is that one firm may absorb another, which is not possible in normal circumstances in the case of states.[24] In addition, states may introduce protectionist measures (international disintegration). Such an option is not open to firms. Countries are not firms. They cannot be driven out of every business.[25] However, countries can be driven out of some lines of business, which may have permanent effects on trade. States produce goods that compete with one another, but more importantly states are one another's export markets and suppliers of useful things. David Ricardo taught us in 1817 that international trade is *not* about competition, *but rather* about mutually beneficial exchange. The purpose of trade is imports, not exports. Imports give a country the chance to get what it wants. Exports is a toll that a country must 'suffer' in order to pay for its imports. Those ideas by Ricardo were as much misunderstood two centuries ago as they are today.

Coordination of economic policies and international economic integration may alleviate and even solve a number of international economic problems. Economic nationalism, as opposed to coordination and integration/regionalism, has always been quite an appealing economic strategy in certain circles. This is because the tools for protection from the unfavourable effects of integration/regionalism and trade liberalisation, which have a basically short-term nature, are not fully developed. In any case, this book argues that countries integrate:

- to secure access to markets of partner countries;
- to secure and cement domestic market-orientated reforms;
- to adapt trade barriers according to preferences of the involved countries;
- because of trust among the participating countries;
- because a very large group of countries may have many conflicting objectives and interests;
- because integration potentially weakens and shrinks the power of vested interests and monopolies;
- because integration agreements can be employed as a bargaining tool with third countries;
- because terms-of-trade effects and gains to exporters provide benefits from preferential trading agreements that are not available from unilateral trade liberalisation policies;
- because in the long run the benefits of integration may be felt by all;
- because the long-term dynamic benefits are greater than the possible short-run static costs; and
- because international economic integration is a desirable strategy, at least for small and medium-sized countries.

In theory, economic efficiency can be fostered by a policy of free trade which stimulates competition. It rationalises production of goods and services and provides conditions for a higher average standard of living and greater welfare in the future. The adjustment to free trade, at least within the integrated group, should not be traumatic at all. There is substantial evidence of this in the relatively frictionless overall adjustment to the successive reductions in tariffs under the GATT/WTO and the system of transparent rules for trade, as well as the smooth transition to the creation and enlargement of the EU. Similar stories may be told for the cases of the European Free Trade Association (EFTA) and North American Free Trade Agreement (NAFTA).

Large and developed countries depend to a lesser degree on external relations than do small countries. In theory, these countries may have a diversified economic structure which provides the opportunity for an autarkic economic policy, while such a policy for small countries in a situation of economies of scale and other externalities does not have a long-term economic rationale. Without secure and free access to a wider market, a relatively limited domestic market and demand in small countries often prevents the employment of the most efficient technology, even if trade barriers are prohibitive. If certain production takes place, the consequences include short production runs, high prices and a lower standard of living. The efficient operation of many modern technologies requires secure access to the widest market which does not exist in small, and sometimes medium-sized, countries. Elimination of tariffs, NTBs, restrictions on factor mobility, as well as international coordination of economic policies and integration can be solutions to this problem of country size. The goal is to increase, improve and secure access to the markets of the participating countries.

A liberal trade and flexible adjustment policy for a small country may be a superior alternative to the policy of long-term protection. The competitive position of small countries can be jeopardised if protection increases the price of inputs. Moreover, protection can provoke retaliatory measures from trading partners. It can also inhibit the adjustment incentives of the protected industry with an overall negative long-term impact on the whole economy. While having a limited influence on the events in the world economy, small countries can have leverage over their own competitive future by means of a liberal economic policy and/or international economic integration.

Global negotiations over tariff reductions were organised by the GATT/WTO with a certain degree of success. Consecutive rounds of negotiations have, however, significantly reduced tariffs on selected manufactured goods. Until the Uruguay Round (1986–94), little was done to liberalise trade in agriculture, services, textiles and clothing, or to lower NTBs which have mushroomed as tariffs were dismantled. The Doha Round intends to build on these achievements and to include in the negotiations issues such as agriculture, services, intellectual property rights, trade and investment, competition rules, public procurement, electronic commerce and the environment.

Due to different economic, political, climatic, cultural and other features, it is unlikely that countries around the world would readily offer universal concessions in trade. One can easily imagine a case in which those concessions can be exchanged within a smaller and closely knit group of countries with significantly less effort than on a universal scale. In addition, monitoring the implementation of the arrangement and resolution of disputes is simpler within a relatively smaller and (presumably) cordial group of countries. There are also fewer incentives and opportunities to cheat. Hence, a regional integration arrangement is more credible and the potential for cooperation within the group is improved.

Free trade and the unimpeded movement of factors is the first-best policy in a world which does not have any distortions. This is only a hypothetical situation. The rationale for international economic integration may be found where there are distortions. When one distortion (such as a universal tariff of a country) is replaced by another (for example, a common external tariff of a customs union), the net welfare effect may be unchanged, positive or negative. The theory of international economic integration is the analysis of a second-best situation and it is not surprising that general principles cannot be found. What matters, however, is not only the prediction of theory, but rather what happens in real life.

This book shows that, despite the second-best character of international economic integration in theory, in practice integration/regionalism may, under certain conditions, be a workable and acceptable economic strategy. A policy recommendation for small and medium-sized countries is that in a world of continuous technological and market changes, when there are risks and uncertainties, integration may expand and secure markets for the greatest variety of a country's goods and services in the future and, hence, mitigate the costs of the necessary and inevitable adjustment.

1.4 Definitions

The main objective of economic activities is an increase in welfare. The approach towards this goal deals with the organisation of the human community because players have various and often conflicting interests and potentials. The organisation should allow agents to maximise their utility in the pursuit of their own ends and expectations, subject to the limitations presented by the environment and their capabilities.

International economic integration is one of the means for an increase in welfare: countries can increase the welfare of the integrated group, or of some countries within the group, or of the world as a whole. Machlup (1979, p. 3) stated that the term 'integration' in economics was first used in industrial organisation to refer to combinations of firms. Horizontal integration referred to linkages of competitors, while vertical integration referred to the unification of suppliers and buyers. As a term, the integration of economies of separate states was not found anywhere in the old, chiefly historical, literature on the economic interrelationship between states, or in the literature about customs unions (including the German *Zollverein* of 1834–71), or in the literature on international trade prior to the 1940s. Viner (1950) was the first to lay the foundation for the theory of customs unions which represented the core of the traditional theory of international economic integration.

International economic integration does not have a clear-cut meaning for all economists. One of the first definitions of integration was given by Tinbergen (1954, p. 122). He defined, on the one hand, *negative* integration as the removal of discriminatory and restrictive institutions and the introduction of freedom for economic transactions. On the other hand, the adjustment of existing and the establishment of new policies and institutions endowed with coercive powers was identified as *positive* integration. This introduced some confusion since freedom was described as 'negative', while coercion was regarded as a 'positive' move! Experience teaches us that it is easier to advance in the direction of 'negative' integration (removal of tariffs and quotas) than towards 'positive' integration (introduction of common economic policies) because the 'positive' approach deals with sensitive issues of national sovereignty. None the less, Anderson and Blackhurst (1993, p. 1) define regional economic integration in a 'negative' dimension as 'the process of reducing economic significance of national political boundaries within a geographic area.' A 'positive' introduction of a common currency may escape this definition.

Pinder (1969, pp. 143–5) cites the *Oxford Dictionary* which described integration as the combination of parts into a whole. Union is the outcome of the combination of these parts or members. He concluded that integration was a process towards union and defined economic integration as the removal of discrimination between the economic agents of the member countries, as well as the creation and implementation of common policies.

Kahnert et al. (1969, p. 11) understand integration as a process of the progressive removal of discrimination that exists along national borders. That is, however, only a part of what integration brings. Other components of integration, such as a common policy in trade or factor mobility, were left out of the definition.

Mennis and Sauvant (1976, p. 75) consider integration as a process whereby boundaries between nation-states become less discontinuous, thereby leading to the formation of more-comprehensive systems. They believe economic integration consists of the linking up and merging (not the abolition) of the industrial apparatus, administration and economic policies of the participating countries.

Pelkmans (1984, p. 3) defines economic integration as the elimination of economic frontiers between two or more economies. An economic frontier is a demarcation line across which the mobility of goods, services and factors is relatively low. The potential mobility of certain factors was the criterion for economic integration according to this passive definition of integration. There is no indication that such a policy actively promotes mobility and cooperation. The mere removal of 'economic frontiers' does not necessarily offer either a carrot or a stick to factors to move. There are many non-economic obstacles to mobility which include language, custom, the propensity to stick to place of birth and the like for labour, while political and other risks inhibit capital movements.

Balassa (1973, p. 1) defines economic integration both as a process and as a state of affairs.[26] As a process (dynamic concept), integration meant the removal of discrimination between different states, while as a state of affairs (static concept) it meant the absence of different forms of discrimination. The Achilles' heel of this definition is its restriction in concentrating only on the process or state of affairs among the countries that integrate. One can distinguish among intra-national (inter-provincial), international and world (universal, global) integration. Agreements among states about adjustment or coordination of some economic areas could be called integration, so one could deal with sectoral and general integration. Balassa's definition did not say whether economic integration was the final goal or a point on the way towards some target. This ambiguity could be avoided by making a distinction between complete and partial integration.

Swann (1996, p. 3) describes economic integration as a state of affairs or a process that involves the combination of previously separate economies into larger arrangements. Lahiri (1998) defines regionalism as a tendency towards preferential trading arrangements among 'countries belonging possibly to a particular region' (p. 1126). Would this definition of regionalism be adequate for the free trade area between the US and Israel?

Maksimova (1976, p. 33) argues that economic integration was a process of developing deep and stable relationships concerning the division of labour between national economies. That is, a process for the formation of international economic entities, within the framework of groups of countries with the same type of socio-economic system, which are consciously regulated in the interests of the ruling classes of these countries. It is true that international economic integration is a highly politicised process, but this definition excludes the possibility of integration even by means of preferential agreements between countries that have different political systems. This is important in practice as there has been a whole spectrum of preferential agreements between the EU and developing countries which have the widest range of political systems. None the less, the EU requires that applicant countries for full EU membership have a stable democratic political system comparable to those in the current EU member countries.

Holzman (1976, p. 59) states that economic integration was a situation in which the prices of all similar goods and similar factors in two regions were equalised. This made the two regions in essence one region or market. This definition implies that economic integration was the realisation of factor price equalisation between two regions. It implicitly assumes that there are no barriers to the movements of goods, services and factors between the two regions and that there are institutions that facilitate those movements.

Marer and Montias (1988, p. 156) point out that economic integration has traditionally been equated with the division of labour in a geographical region, although it was usually not made clear what minimum level of trade would justify speaking of integration. Recently, economic integration was assumed to consist of the internationalisation of markets for capital, labour, technology and entrepreneurship in addition to markets for goods and services. Marer and Montias argue (p. 161) that the necessary and sufficient condition for complete integration is the equality of prices of any pair of goods in every member country (adjusted for transportation costs). The same remark as that made with regard to Holzman's definition applies here too.

Drysdale and Garnaut (1993, p. 189) look at integration only as a movement towards one single price for a good, service or factor of production. If one wants to encompass the term 'integration', then one needs to refer also to policies that make that movement happen. In addition, if integration refers to issues such as social policy including education, then it includes more than a 'technical' move towards equalisation of prices.

Panić (1988, pp. 3–5) distinguishes between openness, integration and interdependence. An economy is open if it has few barriers to international trade and factor movements. Because an economy is open does not necessarily mean that it is integrated in the international economic system. International integration has its full meaning only when it describes an active participation in the international division of labour. Two or more economies are said to be interdependent when they are linked to such a degree that economic developments in each of them are significantly influenced by the economic situation and policies in the partner country.

Molle (1991, p. 5) equates economic integration with the progressive elimination of economic frontiers between countries. As a rule, the process of elimination of 'economic frontiers' is gradual. The transition period for full adjustment to the new situation usually takes, in practice, at least five to ten years. However, following the establishment of the European Economic Area (EEA) in 1994 between the EU and most of the EFTA countries, the participating EFTA states had to apply the *acquis communautaire*[27] immediately, except in a few specified cases. There was no transition period. When central and east European countries negotiated their entry into the EU, the timing of the entry depended primarily on their ability to accept, implement and enforce the *acquis communautaire* in order to eliminate the need for derogations and transition measures (European Commission, 1997a, pp. 51–2).

El-Agraa (1985, p. 1) refers to international economic integration as the discriminatory removal of all trade impediments between participating nations and the establishment of certain elements of coordination between them. This definition implies the removal of barriers to trade in goods and services, as well as freedom of movement for factors of production. Hence, this definition only partly covers free trade areas and customs unions as types of integration. Later, El-Agraa (1988, p. xiii) takes international economic integration to mean an act of agreement between two or more nations to pursue common goals and policies. This is an 'active' definition of integration.

Robson (1987, p. 1) notes that economic integration was concerned with efficiency in resource use, with particular reference to the spatial aspect. He defines full integration as freedom of movement of goods and factors of production and an absence of discrimination. Freedom of movement for factors is not allowed for in some types of international economic integration, hence this definition cannot be applied to all arrangements. Later, he defines international economic integration (often termed 'regionalisation') as 'the institutional combination of separate national economies into larger blocs or communities' (Robson, 1998, p. 1). This definition refers to the institutional (presumably public) combination of national economies. What if two different firms in two different countries integrate on their own? Is this included in the definition or not?

The European Commission (1997c, p. 23) defines market integration 'as a state where the outcomes of economic decisions are independent of national frontiers'. While this definition may be relevant for the decisions of certain international firms, national frontiers are relevant for the introduction and management of a common currency in an integrated area.

There is also an identification of international economic integration with globalisation. Wolf (2001) states that 'Globalisation is no more than an (admittedly ugly) name for the process of integration across frontiers of liberalising market economies at a time of rapidly falling costs of transport and communications.'[28]

All these definitions of international economic integration reveal that integration is a complex notion which must be defined with care. Definitions are often vague and do not offer adequate tools for the easing of the process of integration among countries. Integration means different things in different countries and at different times. In the developed market economies, integration is taken to be a way of introducing the most profitable technologies (often linked with economies of scale), allocate them in the most efficient way and foster free and fair competition; during the period of central planning in central and eastern Europe it meant the planning of the development of certain industrial activities; while in the developing countries, integration was one of the tools for economic development. At the time of the German *Zollverein* the grouping of countries meant the development of economic interdependence, nation-building and self-reliance. Today, international economic integration refers to an increase in the level of welfare.

Machlup (1979, p. 24) states that one of the most obvious signs of international economic integration is the non-existence of customs posts between integrated countries. Total economic integration among countries with market economies is not achieved until these countries know the level of their mutual trade. There are no statistics to show the volume of trade between Pennsylvania and Ohio, for instance.

There is an unresolved question about what is to be integrated. Is it to be citizens, markets, production, consumption, commodities, services, regions, factors, money, resources, something else, all of this together, or just some of these components? What are the measures for the advance, stagnation or decline of international economic integration? What is the essence of international economic integration and what are the criteria for the appraisal of this process? Machlup (ibid., p. 43) argues that trade is the quintessence of economic integration and the division of labour its underlying principle. If one ignores transportation and other trade-related costs, then the basic principle for the appraisal of international economic integration is equality of prices for comparable goods and services in all integrated countries.

Machlup's test is much easier for standardised goods and services than for differentiated ones. A meaningful comparison of the price gap of a good in different markets should take into account not only the transport costs but also, and more importantly, the consumption patterns in different countries. This is an extremely difficult exercise, even in monetary unions. Income, tastes, preferences, traditions and climate may be homogeneous in relatively small areas, sometimes even within a single country. The more homogeneous are the countries, the easier the test.

What is usually omitted from definitions of international economic integration is any consideration of foreign direct investment (FDI) and integrated international production. Compared with mere trade, FDI introduces a more profound and longer-term dimension into integration among countries. However, if foreign-owned production is to take place, an integration scheme has to provide freedom of establishment.

Finally, we can conclude that international economic integration is a process and a means by which a group of countries strives to increase its level of welfare. It involves the recognition that a weak or strong partnership between countries can achieve this goal in a more efficient way than by unilateral and independent pursuance of policy in each country. Integration requires at least some division of labour and freedom of movement for goods and services within the group. Relatively 'higher' types of integration arrangements also require a free mobility of factors of production within the integrated area, as well as certain restrictions on these movements between the integrated area and countries outside of it.

The essential point is that the countries that integrate adopt a kind of inward-looking approach and take more care about what happens in the group than about what happens outside of it. In addition, at least some consultation, if not coordination of competition, monetary, fiscal and regional development policies is a necessary condition for the success and durability of integration, as is the case in federal states. This is to be supported by an effective dispute settlement mechanism. The process of integration may be practically unlimited, just as is the continuous integration of various regions within a single country. From a 'technical' point of view, international economic integration can be a finite process, that is, the elimination of tariffs and quantitative restrictions, as well as the introduction of rules of competition and common external protection in a customs union. However, new dimensions of competition, NTBs, standards, new technologies, as well as changes in the market, require continuous adjustments of individual countries and the group as a whole. This all makes integration more an evolving and continuing process than a limited one. International economic integration is a process by which the firms and economies of separate states merge in larger entities. Such a definition of integration, incorporating the ideas in this paragraph, will be maintained throughout this book.

1.5 Types

If trade is impeded by tariffs, quotas, NTBs and obstacles to factor mobility, then consumption in an integrated area is potentially higher than the sum of the consumption of individual countries which are potential partners for integration. International economic integration removes, at least partly, these and other distortions to trade, competition, investment and, possibly, factor mobility. In this sense, international economic integration between at least two countries can be of the following seven theoretical types:

- A *preferential tariff agreement* among countries assumes that the tariffs on trade among the signatory countries are lower in relation to tariffs charged on trade with third countries.
- A *partial customs union* is formed when the participating countries retain their initial tariffs on their mutual trade and introduce a common external tariff on trade with third countries.
- A *free trade area* is an agreement among countries about the elimination of all tariff and quantitative restrictions on mutual trade. Every country in this area retains its own tariff and other regulation of trade with third countries. The bases of this agreement are the rules of origin. These rules prevent trade deflection, which is the import of a good from third countries into the area by country A (that has a relatively lower external tariff than the partner country B) in order to re-export the good to country B. None the less, production deflection is possible if the production of goods that contain imported inputs is shifted to countries that have lower tariffs if the difference in tariffs offsets the difference in production and trade costs.
- In a *customs union*, participating countries not only remove tariff and quantitative restrictions on their intra-group trade, but also introduce a common external tariff on trade with third countries. The participating countries take part in international negotiations about trade and tariffs as a single entity.
- In a *common market*, apart from a customs union, there is free mobility of factors of production. Common regulations (restrictions) on the movement of factors with third countries are introduced.
- An *economic union* among countries assumes not only a common market, but also the harmonisation of fiscal, monetary, industrial, regional, transport and other economic policies.
- A *total economic union* among countries assumes union with a single economic policy and a supranational government (of this confederation) with great economic authority. There are no administrative barriers to the movements of goods, services and factors, hence prices are equalised net of transport costs.

Table 1.1 presents select theoretical types of international economic integration arrangements. The process of integration does not necessarily have to be gradual from one type to another. The establishment of any of these types depends on the agreement among the participating countries.

Table 1.1 Theoretical types of international economic integration

Policy action	Type				
	Free trade area	Customs union	Common market	Economic union	Total economic union
Removal of tariffs and quotas	Yes	Yes	Yes	Yes	Yes
Common external tariff	No	Yes	Yes	Yes	Yes
Factor mobility	No	No	Yes	Yes	Yes
Harmonisation of economic policies	No	No	No	Yes	Yes
Total unification of economic policies	No	No	No	No	Yes

Spontaneous or market integration is created by actions of TNCs, banks and other financial institutions, often without the involvement of their parent governments, while formal or institutional integration seeks an official agreement among governments to eliminate either some or indeed all restrictions on trade and factor movements in their economic relations (Panić, 1988, pp. 6–7). There is substantial historical evidence to support the argument that the formal (*de jure*) approach to integration seeks a spontaneous (*de facto*) way, and vice versa.

The decision about entering into a customs union or any other type of integration has always been primarily political, but economic considerations usually play a very important role (as already seen above). The question to abandon part of national sovereignty regarding taxation of trade (all in a customs union, a part of that in a free trade area) is generally made by politicians. The EU was, after all, not established in 1957 in order to liberalise trade, but rather to exclude the possibility of war between France and Germany. Economic integration was just a means for the achievement of that political goal.

An interesting case occurred following the establishment of a free trade area between Canada and the US in 1988. There were moves to include Mexico in the NAFTA. If the US were to enter into a bilateral free trade deal with Mexico and, then, conclude similar bilateral arrangements with other (Latin American) countries, that would create the 'hub-and-spoke model' of integration (which was undesirable for Canada and other countries involved). The US, as the regional hub, would have a separate agreement with each spoke country. As such, the US would have great advantages of negotiating individually with each partner country, as well as being the only country with a tariff-free access to the markets of all participants. This would further enhance the US locational advantages for FDI. Therefore, Canada decided to be involved in the free trade deal with Mexico in order to avoid the negative consequences of the hub-and-spoke model of integration.

1.6 Sovereignty

International economic integration is popularly criticised on the grounds that it reduces a country's national sovereignty (undisputed political power). When two or more sovereign countries sign a treaty, they agree to do and/or not do specified things. Therefore, it is not a valid criticism of any international treaty to say that it entails a loss of national sovereignty. All treaties do so in one way or another. The real issue is: do the countries' concessions constitute a mutually beneficial deal? Is the surrender of sovereignty justified by the results? Consider, for example, the Canadian debate leading up to the Canada–US Free Trade Agreement in Lipsey and York (1988).

Canada is a relatively small (in economic terms) and open economy. The competitive future of this country has been seriously jeopardised by the uncertain future of the relatively liberal international trading system. So, Canada negotiated and subsequently signed a free trade agreement with the US in 1988. Negotiations and the pre-election period at that time were subject to one of the greatest debates in Canadian history. The opponents of the agreement tried, with initial success, to persuade a majority of Canadians that the deal would significantly reduce Canadian sovereignty and distinctiveness. The fuss created by opponents of the deal was perhaps one of the greatest in the history of international economic integration. Giving their vote to the Conservatives, the Canadians, however, supported the agreement.[29]

There was a fear that Canada would need to harmonise a range of economic policies with the US. If experience is a reliable guide, then this fear is not relevant. The Netherlands has a developed and costly social policy while Belgium spends relatively less in this area. Yet, these two countries have been in a free trade area for more than half a century without harmonising their social policies. As for other economic policies, pressures for harmonisation do exist. If tax rates differ among countries and if factor movement is allowed, then, other things being equal, factors will move to countries where the tax burden is lower. But note: these harmonising pressures exist even in a situation without integration! For example, within a common market, apart from the agreed-upon matters, countries will have to give each other 'national treatment'. This means that countries can adopt any policy they wish, even those that are completely different from policies in the partner countries with just one important proviso: the country should not use these policies to discriminate among partner countries on the basis of their nationality. International economic integration is not the enemy of diversity in many economic policies. In other cases, such as EU monetary policy within the eurozone, integration reduces the diversity of the main policy instruments. This issue raises all sorts of problems when economies at various levels of development, facing different problems, become integrated. Such policies should be coordinated, or even harmonised.

If a small country (such as Albania or Cuba) accepts and pursues a long-term policy of protection and isolation, as opposed to liberalisation, openness or international economic integration, it chooses a long-term deterioration in its international economic position. This is coupled with a reduction in living standards in relation to countries which do not employ protectionism as their economic strategy. Can a country preserve its sovereignty and the welfare of its citizens in the face of a long-term declining trend in the standard of living?

The expectation of a net economic gain compared with the situation without international economic integration is the most fundamental incentive for such integration. Anticipated gains from secure access to a larger market include an increase in the efficiency in the use of factors due to increased competition, specialisation, economies of scale, increases in investment (domestic and foreign), improvements in terms of trade, reduced risk and equalisation of factor prices. Integration will be beneficial when cooperation and coordination of policies takes place instead of the disintegrated exercise of sovereign economic power through conflicting policies. National sovereignty is pooled, rather than given up. Small and medium-sized open countries need to realise that it is much less a choice between national sovereignty and international economic integration, and much more a choice between one form of interdependence and another. If one's goal is to increase the competitiveness of goods and services produced in a small country and secure the widest markets for its output in the future, then international economic integration is a serious alternative to the national freedom to implement and continue with damaging economic policies.

Notes

1. Haberler noted as early as 1964 that 'We live in the age of integration' (Haberler, 1964, p. 1).
2. Preferential trade agreements and integration are progressively taking place among countries that are not spatially near each other. Therefore, the term international

(regional) economic integration is wider than regional trade integration and liberalisation. None the less, these terms may sometimes be used in this book interchangeably.

3. It is widely accepted that the Dillon (1959–62), Kennedy (1963–67) and Tokyo (1973–79) Rounds of trade negotiations were attempts by the US and other developed market economies to reduce the discriminating effect that came from the creation and enlargement of the EU.
4. The developed market economies granted the developing countries an exemption from reciprocity. Although this might have been seen as a concession to the developing world, in some cases, indeed, this 'concession' excluded developing countries from negotiations about certain trade issues. As these countries 'graduate' in their development process, as the newly industrialised Asian countries have done, there is an understandable demand for an exchange of concessions between the developing countries and the developed market economies. This has, in fact, taken place, during the Uruguay Round.
5. The Uruguay Round deal established the WTO in 1995. The WTO is the only multilateral institution that can curb the operation of large trading blocs. It is an 'umbrella' organisation for the GATT, GATS and the Agreement on Trade Related Intellectual Property Rights (TRIPS).
6. Another failure could potentially make the WTO a marginal international institution.
7. The interim agreement reached in Geneva in 2004 committed the 147 WTO member countries to continue negotiations about further multilateral liberalisation of trade. The bases for talks include issues such as eliminating almost all farm-export subsidies by the developed countries, and the need for developing countries to cut their tariffs on imports, and to make customs clearance procedures simpler and easier.
8. Of the 300 notified agreements, 150 are currently in force. These include notifications under GATT Article XXIV, GATS Article V, accession to the existing agreements, as well as the Enabling Clause (adopted in 1979 to enable developing countries to reduce tariffs on trade among themselves). Most of the deals in force are free trade areas (70 per cent), partial scope agreements account for 23 per cent and customs unions account for 7 per cent (WTO, 2003, p. 4). WTO (2004) Regional Trade Agreements. www.wto.org/english/tratop_e/region_e/region_e.htm.
9. The number of preferential trade deals is not the issue that matters most. What is more important is the share of international trade of each deal, as well as its impact and importance for world trade. Internal exports in goods within the North American Free Trade Agreement (NAFTA), for example, accounted for 10 per cent of world exports, while intra-NAFTA imports of goods accounted for 9 per cent of world imports in 2002 (WTO, 2003, pp. 2–3).
10. The EU enlargement from 15 to 25 member countries in 2004 ended 65 preferential trade agreements.
11. The greatest concentrations of preferential trading agreements are in the Euro-Mediterranean area and in the Asia-Pacific region.
12. For the debate on whether regional arrangements are building or stumbling blocks on the road towards universal free trade, see Lipsey and Smith (1989), Krugman (1991c, 1995b), Bhagwati (1995), Snape (1996), Frenkel (1997), Bagwell and Staiger (1998), Bhagwati et al. (1998), Ethier (1998), Baldwin et al. (1999), Krueger (1999), Laird (1999), Panagariya (1999, 2000), McLaren (2002) and Limão (2005). The answer to the dilemma is likely to be found in the middle ground between those two extreme positions.
13. Bhagwati (1995, p. 2).
14. Emphasis added. http://waysandmeans.house.gov/legacy/trade/107cong/5-8-01/5-8chri.htm.
15. Australia, Canada, Chinese Taipei, China, Japan, Republic of Korea, New Zealand, Singapore and the US (WTO, 2004, p. 22).
16. Lowering of tariffs under the auspices of GATT/WTO reduced large-scale opportunities for trade diversion.
17. The Association of South-East Asian Nations (ASEAN) is another example.
18. Recall the distorting effects of the EU's Common Agricultural Policy on international trade.

19. Renato Ruggiero, Director-General of the WTO, wrote in a comment to the *International Herald Tribune* (28 November 1996) that 'regional agreements have been a generally positive force for liberalization'.
20. The 'clearance' of the preferential trade agreements under the GATT working parties was almost always inconclusive. This includes the Treaty of Rome.
21. WTO (2004). Regional Trade Agreements: Work of the Committee on Regional Trade Agreements. www.wto.org/english/tratop_e/region_e/regcom_e.htm.
22. The EU may do exactly the same. Russia may also try, to an extent, to integrate with certain countries that emerged from the former Soviet Union.
23. Even though international trade is more extensive than ever before, national living standards are chiefly determined by *domestic* economic factors, rather than by competition for world markets. After all, the 'globalised' US economy trades only about 13 per cent of its GDP, roughly the same as a century ago. In addition, at least 70 per cent of employment and value added in the US is in 'non-tradable' industries that do not compete on world markets.

    The rate of growth in the standard of living in large developed countries depends on national productivity growth. Period. A comparison of the productivity growth in other countries does not matter for domestic living standards. If domestic productivity growth is 1 per cent a year, the national income of that country grows roughly 1 per cent a year, even though productivity growth elsewhere is 0 or 4 per cent (Krugman, 1996c).

    There is always rivalry for status and power between states. Hence, it is interesting to compare them. But asserting that Japanese growth diminishes US status is far different from saying that it reduces the US standard of living. 'So let's start telling the truth: competitiveness is a meaningless word when applied to national economies' (Krugman, 1996b, p. 22).
24. There are, however, unfortunate examples as when the US absorbed Hawaii or Turkey took over northern Cyprus. One may also hesitate to define in this light the *Anschluss* of East Germany by West Germany in 1989.
25. There are strong equilibrating forces that can ensure that a country sells goods in world markets. David Hume pointed out two centuries ago that in the case with the gold standard a country that imports more than it exports has a drain on gold and a fall in the money supply. Prices and wages fall, hence the goods and labour in that country become cheap so that they grow attractive to foreign buyers. The deficit in trade is corrected. In the modern world without the gold standard, deficits are not usually corrected by the depreciation of prices and wages, but rather through the depreciation of national currencies.
26. Balassa kept the same definition of economic integration in *The New Palgrave Dictionary of Economics* (1987, p. 43).
27. The existence and operation of the EU is based on law. The whole body of the established EU laws, policies and practices are called the *acquis communautaire* or the EU patrimony. It is widely estimated that the *acquis* consisted of about 80 000 pages of legal acts in 2005. The ever evolving and expanding *acquis* was enlarged by 2279 new regulations in 2004 alone. However, most of the regulations have a limited time duration.
28. M. Wolf, 'How trade can help the world', *Financial Times*, 3 October 2001, p. 15.
29. It is interesting to note that there was neither great nor heated public debate about the eastern enlargement in the EU(15) countries when eight central and east European countries plus Cyprus and Malta joined the EU in 2004. Even though this enlargement would provoke seismic changes in the EU (general institutional organisation, allocation of common funds and farm policy), the general public in the EU(15) were apathetic about the enlargement. The eastern enlargement (like many EU-related issues) was regarded as a done deal by the European elite behind the backs of its citizens, just as was the case with the Maastricht Treaty and the introduction of the eurozone. The European elite needs to win the hearts and minds of the people for the integration project. If it continues to disregard the public, results that come from ballot boxes may easily slow down and fragment the whole integration process in Europe, as was the case with the failed referenda on the European Constitution in France and the Netherlands in 2005.

Anyone who hears and obeys these teachings of mine
is like a wise person who built a house on solid rock.
Rain poured down, rivers flooded, and winds beat against that house.
But it did not fall, because it was built on solid rock.
Matthew 7:24–5

2 Customs Unions

2.1 Introduction

All types of international economic integration have always provoked interest because they both promote and restrict trade at the same time. Trade is liberalised, at least partly, among the participating countries, while it is also distorted with third countries as there are various barriers between the integrated group and the rest of the world. On these grounds the analysis of international economic integration including preferential trade agreements is delicate, complex and often speculative. It is a set of theoretical experiments that try to simplify and portray the economic process. However, this ought to be tested against evidence. A customs union is the type of integration that has received the most attention in research and is the most rigorously developed branch of the neo-classical theory of economic integration and preferential trading areas.

The tariff system may discriminate between commodities and/or countries. *Commodity discrimination* takes place when different rates of import duty are charged on different commodities/goods. *Country discrimination* is found when the same commodity is subject to different rates of duty based on country of origin. Lipsey (1960, p. 496) defined the theory of customs unions as a branch of tariff theory which deals with the effect of geographically discriminatory changes in trade barriers. However, while this is true in the static sense, in a dynamic setting a customs union may be, among other things, a means for economic development.

The efficiency criterion used most often in economics is that of *Pareto optimality*. An allocation of resources is said to be Pareto optimal if no other feasible allocation exists in which some agents would be better off (in a welfare sense) and no agents worse off. By a judicious definition of welfare, the Pareto-optimal allocation is the one that best satisfies social objectives. Pareto optimality is achieved exclusively in the state of free trade and free factor mobility (the first-best solution), so that other states, in which there are distortions (tariffs, subsidies, taxes, monopolies, externalities, agglomerations, differentiated goods, minimum wages, local content requirements, to mention just a few), are suboptimal.

It is highly likely that the Pareto-optimal allocation cannot be achieved because of one or several distortions. Can a second-best position be attained by satisfying the remaining Pareto conditions? The theory of the second best answered in the negative (Lipsey and Lancaster, 1956–57). In the presence of distortions, if none of the conditions for Pareto optimality can be satisfied, then the removal of some of the distortions does not necessarily increase welfare, nor does the addition of other distortions necessarily decrease it. One suboptimal situation is replaced by another suboptimal situation. Welfare may remain unaffected, or be increased or decreased.[1] This implies that there can be no reliable expectation about the welfare effect of a partial change in the current situation. The theory of the second best has a disastrous effect on welfare economics. In most circumstances, people (economists included) disregard the second-best character of the situation and concentrate on direct effects.[2]

In spite of its second-best character,[3] Lipsey (1960) was not discouraged enough to be prevented from writing a seminal article on the theory of customs unions. It is often forgotten that the theory of the second best does not render welfare economics totally powerless, it only warns economists and policy makers that there cannot be a unique set of policies that is best for the entire economy.

> [There are] two key points that apply when technology is changing endogenously. First, comparative advantage is not given exogenously. It is changed by the actions of innovating agents and their actions can be influenced by public policy. So the policy advice 'allocate resources so as to exploit current comparative advantages' is not obviously better than the advice 'allocate resources so as to create new comparative advantages that will make use of natural advantages that are available'. Second, as we have already noted, the groping behaviour under uncertainty and the endogeneity of choice sets that results when technology is changing endogenously implies the absence of a unique, welfare-maximizing

> equilibrium. If such an equilibrium does not exist, there can be no unique optimal allocation of resources, even in the absence of all other 'distortions'. It follows that the allocation resulting from free trade cannot be shown to be superior to all other allocations. (Lipsey et al., 2005, p. 509)

The intuition behind the neo-classical theory of customs unions is the proposition that the potential consumption of goods and services in a customs union between countries A and B, respectively, is higher than the sum of the individual consumptions in these two countries in the case when trade between them is distorted by tariffs and quotas. In this situation one should, at least partly, remove these impediments.

This chapter is structured as follows. It starts with a consideration of the static model of customs unions (Section 2.2). This includes a number of restrictive assumptions, partial and general equilibrium, effects of protection and conditions for a welfare-improving customs union. Section 2.3 examines the dynamic model, and discusses monopoly, market structure, innovation (technology performance), specialisation and returns to scale, terms of trade, as well as adjustment costs. The following sections consider optimum partners for a customs union (Section 2.4), free trade areas (Section 2.5) and distribution of costs and benefits of integration (Section 2.6). Non-tariff barriers are analysed in Section 2.7 and Section 2.8 concludes. Let us begin with the static model.

2.2 Static model

2.2.1 ASSUMPTIONS

A static model of the theory of customs unions considers the impact of the formation of a customs union on trade flows and consumption in the integrated countries. The classical (orthodox or static) theory of customs unions is burdened by 'excess luggage' of explicit and implicit assumptions. This model makes theoretical consideration easier, but it also simplifies reality to the extent that the policy recommendations should be considered with great care. None the less, many useful things can be learned from the consideration of extreme cases.

Assume that there are only three countries. Country A, a relatively small country in relation to the other two, forms a customs union with country B. Country C (which may represent all other countries in the world) is discriminated against by the customs union by means of a common external tariff. A relatively small number of states in this abstract model provides the possibility of a relatively higher analytical power in the model. Tariffs are levied on an *ad valorem* basis in all countries. Rates of tariffs are the same both for final goods and for inputs, so that the rate of nominal protection equals the rate of effective protection. The assumption of equal rates of tariffs prior to integration removes the possible dispute about the initial level of the common external tariff. Tariffs are the only instrument of trade policy and there are no non-tariff barriers (NTBs). The price of imported goods for home consumers (P_{mt}) is composed of the price of an imported good (P_m) and tariff (t):

$$P_{mt} = (1 + t)P_m \tag{2.1}$$

where $t \geq 0$. State intervention exists only at the border and trade is balanced. Free or perfect competition exists in markets for goods, services and factors. Perfect competition (or complete equality of opportunity) exists in all economies, but for the existence of tariffs.

Production costs per unit of output are constant over all levels of output. To put it more formally, production functions are homogeneous of degree one, that is, to produce one more unit of good X, inputs must be increased by a constant proportion. Costs of production determine the retail prices of goods. Producers in an industry operate at the minimum efficient scale at the production possibility frontier. Countries embark upon the production of certain goods based on the difference in prices (relative abundance or scarcity) of home factors.

The theory of customs unions refers to the manufacturing sector: a fixed quantity of factors of production is fully employed. There are no industry-specific factors such as special human and physical capital, entrepreneurship and the like. In a dynamic model, these specific factors can be transformed in the medium and long runs, but this would require adjustment costs which are ruled out in the static model. Mobility of factors is perfect within their home country, while goods are perfectly mobile between the integrated countries. This means that transnational corporations (TNCs) are ignored. There are no trade costs, that is, all costs linked with getting the final good to the consumer (tariffs, transport, storage, distribution, information, marketing, contract enforcement, insurance, exchange and banking).

All countries have access to the same technology and differ only in their factor endowments. Economies are static with constant expectations. This is to say that rates of growth, technologies, tastes and propensities to consume, save, import and invest, are given and unchangeable. This avoids the problem of explaining external shocks which introduce irreversible path-dependent changes. There are no new goods, and there is no innovation or depreciation of the capital stock. All goods and services are homogeneous, that is, consumers do not prefer the consumption of goods and services from any particular supplier. They decide upon their purchases exclusively on the basis of differences in price. All goods and services have unit income elasticities of demand, that is, every increase or decrease in income has a proportional change in demand for all goods and services in the same direction. This means that demand is 'well behaved'. Non-tradable goods do not exist. There is no intra-industry trade or 'cross-hauling': a country cannot both export and import identical goods or close substitutes. There are no inventories. All markets clear simultaneously. Such equilibrium must be both sustainable and feasible, that is, firms can neither profitably undercut market price nor make losses.

In this model there is no financial, technical or social uncertainty. This is a handy assumption, as in the reverse case one may not be very sure about what to maximise. Firms and resource owners are perfectly informed about all markets while consumers are fully familiar with goods and services. This assumption was relevant in the past, but the development of the Internet brought economies close to a situation of full, timely and perfect information. Fiscal (taxes and subsidies) and monetary (rates of exchange, interest, inflation and balance of payments) operations are ruled out. Finally, a country that is not included in a customs union is assumed not to retaliate against the integrated countries.

The above assumptions are highly restrictive. However, they greatly simplify the analysis so that the essential properties of the model can be easily understood. A simple story told within this model does not necessarily mean that it is a naive story. The objective of the following analysis is to make a point, rather than to be realistic.

2.2.2 PARTIAL EQUILIBRIUM MODEL

International trade comes as a response to causes that are based on national differences in the following essentials:

- factor endowments (factor proportions);
- demand (size, sophistication and fickleness);
- home market effect;[4]
- production functions (technology and efficiency);
- economies of scale;
- growth rates and increase in income;
- income distribution;[5]
- market structure and competition;
- production and factor taxes;
- rates of exchange;

- change in tastes;
- agglomeration and clustering of production;
- trade costs; and
- demographic factors.[6]

These basic reasons for trade are tackled in economic theory in several ways, but there are two principal models: the classical (or neo-classical) and the new (strategic) theory of trade. The basic features of these two models are briefly outlined in Table 2.1.

The partial equilibrium model of trade deals with the market for a single good. Suppose that three countries produce the same good, but with varying levels of efficiency: their production functions differ. This model is described in Table 2.2.

Country C has the lowest unit cost of production, hence this country will become the world supplier of this good in the free trade situation. Suppose now that country A wants to protect its inefficient domestic producers from foreign competition for whatever reason. Tariffs are an available means of protection which have distortionary effects.[7] The most important effect is that they move the country away from free trade towards autarky. Gains from specialisation are sacrificed because resources are diverted away from the pattern of comparative advantage. In addition to reducing potential consumption, tariffs redistribute income in favour of factors which are used in production in the protected industry and decrease the possibility of their more efficient employment elsewhere in the economy. If country A wants to protect its home production of this good, it must levy a tariff. This tariff of, for example, 100 per cent not only increases the price of the imported good to country A's consumers but, more importantly, it shifts consumption away from imports towards country A's domestic production. In these circumstances, country A could increase domestic consumption of this good if it enters into a customs union with either of the countries in this model. Table 2.3 presents prices of the imported good with the tariff on country A's market.

If country A forms a customs union with country B, then consumers in country A could import the good from country B at a cost of €50 per unit, rather than buy it from domestic suppliers at the cost of €60 as before. Hence, they are better off than with a non-discriminatory tariff. If country A creates a customs union with country C, then country A's consumers are in an even better position compared to a customs union with country B. Now, they purchase the good at a unit price of €35. In both cases, consumers in country A are better off than in the situation in which they were buying the domestically produced good. The final effect in both cases is welfare-increasing trade creation as the cost of trade is reduced.

Table 2.1 Trade theory models

Aspect	Classical trade theory	New (strategic) trade theory
Assumptions	Given factor endowments Technology given No entry barriers Static model Maximisation under certainty Trade based on costs, that is, supply potentials Considers trade in goods Factors are mobile within a country, but not between countries Tariffs may be the only trade-related costs Equilibrium is unique and optimal Theoretical ideas: sound, clear and straightforward	Economies of scale High fixed costs (entry and exit barriers) Innovation in production, organisation and control Technology constantly changing Trade is based on demand, that is, 'love of variety' Intellectual property Dynamic and evolutionary model Accumulation and upgrading of factors which magnify output potential (cumulative causation) Path dependence and non-ergodicity Considers trade in goods and services Both national and international mobility of factors is constrained The target of the theory is moving (nature of production and trade changes fast because of multiple equilibria) Existence of trade cost Multiple and potentially non-optimal equilibria Seeking, selection and adaptation under uncertainty Theoretical ideas: an incomplete and unsystematic collection of various ideas and common themes that discount the weight of tariffs and trade creation and trade diversion effects
Trade barriers	Transparent Tariffs and quotas	Non-transparent Standards and their implementation Customs and administrative procedures Government intervention: NTBs, public procurement, taxes, subsidies, public monopolies, local content rules, and so on

Table 2.1 (continued)

Aspect	Classical trade theory	New (strategic) trade theory
Specialisation	Absolute advantages Comparative advantages Homogeneous goods	Man-made comparative advantages (periodically short-lived) Goods and services are differentiated Widening in varieties of goods and services High-quality goods with after-sales service Clusters and agglomerations
Competition	Perfect Many small suppliers First-best situation Prices End-state equilibrium	Imperfect A select number of suppliers that may influence prices within their (narrow) market niche Second-best situation Price and non-price Continuously evolving process
Trade policy	Liberal Exceptionally 'infant industry' protection	Interventionist, but selective and (presumably) diminishing over time
Trade pattern	Inter-industry Highly specialised Set of traded goods is both complete and fixed	Intra-industry Not totally specialised (full specialisation is only within a given and narrow product niche) Trade pattern in developed countries is as wide as ever
Adjustment costs	In theory: none (all markets clear at once) In practice: significant	Weak if related to product differentiation and changes in varieties within the same commodity group Significant if related to economies of scale, innovation, launching of an utterly new production or a cluster
Welfare effect of trade	Favourable for all participants Higher steady-state comes instantly	Highly uncertain Some may gain a lot, others may lose a lot Always changing Higher steady state comes after unpredictably long time

Table 2.2 Unit cost of production of a good in euros

Country	A	B	C
Unit cost of production	60	50	35

Table 2.3 Price of an imported good in euros with the tariff in country A

Import duty (%)	Price of a good from	
	Country B	Country C
100	100	70
50	75	52.5

The formation of a customs union encourages *trade creation* as the result of a shift from a dearer to a cheaper source of supply. Other things being equal, this is a potential move towards free trade because a less efficient protected domestic supplier is replaced by a more efficient foreign one. Country A gives up the production of a good in which it has a comparative disadvantage in order to acquire it more cheaply by importing it from a partner country, so trade is created. This welfare-improving effect depends also on the assumption that the freed domestic resources can find alternative employment elsewhere in the economy. If, in addition to trade creation 'internal' to the customs union, there is an increase in imports from third countries ('external' to the customs union) due to increased growth, as was the case in the EU, the situation is described as *double* trade creation.

Suppose now that, prior to the formation of the customs union, the duty on imports was 50 per cent in country A. Table 2.3 shows that in this case the supplier of country A would be country C. Country A's domestic industry offers this good at a unit price of €60, country B at a price of €75, while country C is the cheapest source of supply at €52.5. If, instead, country A enters into a customs union with country B and if the common external tariff for the good in question is 50 per cent, then country A would purchase this good from country B. In this case, country A pays €50 per unit to country B, while at the same time a unit of the good from country C costs €52.5. The outcome in this case is *trade diversion*.

Trade diversion works in the opposite way from trade creation. The cheapest foreign supplier is replaced by a relatively dearer customs union partner. Due to the common external tariff, business is taken away from the most efficient world manufacturer, so production and trade in this good are reduced. This creates a global welfare loss. Trade within a customs union takes place at a protected (higher) level of prices. A higher union level of prices relative to the international one brings benefits to internal exporters. Importers lose as they pay the partner country suppliers a higher price per unit of import and their country forgoes tariff revenue which is not levied on intra-union imports. Trade creation and trade diversion are often called 'Vinerian effects' after Jacob Viner (1950), who first introduced the terms and provoked discussion and research into the issues of customs unions and international economic integration.

The net static welfare effect on the world depends on which of the two Vinerian effects dominates. It may be positive, negative or neutral. There is no a priori general statement about the final effect. The second-best nature of preferential trading and the creation of customs unions makes it hard to gauge the final welfare effect. Some consider regional preferential trading to be stepping stones (building blocks) towards universal free trade, while others worry that they embody stumbling blocks on the same route. Hence, the favourable attitude of the GATT (Article XXIV) towards customs unions and free trade areas as trade liberalising moves cannot be accepted without reservation.

The principal economic policies in the EU such as the Common Commercial Policy (customs union) or the Common Agricultural Policy (CAP) were mostly shaped according to the interests of the domestic producers. The interests of consumers were largely neglected. Hence, the possibility of a potentially trade-diverting bias in the EU should not come as a surprise. None the less, the mounting role of the European Parliament in the EU structure may increase the influence of consumers in the EU decision-making structure.

Trade diversion may be more beneficial than trade creation for consumption in country A, which gives preferential treatment to select suppliers. This is because country A does not sacrifice home production. The source of benefits is anticipated trade creation since, by assumption, bilateral trade flows must balance. The comparison here is between trade creation and the autarkic volume of domestic production. An integrating country will not benefit from trade creation unless it increases its exports to the partners (as compared to the pre-union level) which from a partner's point of view can represent trade diversion (Robson, 1987, p. 52).

Suppose that country A and country B form a customs union and that trade flows among countries A, B and C have the following patterns:

- If country A alone produces this good, but does so inefficiently, then the choice between domestic production and imports from country C depends on the level of the common external tariff.

- If both countries in the customs union produce the good, but inefficiently, then the least inefficient country will supply the customs union market subject to the protection of the common external tariff.
- If neither country in the customs union produces the good, then there is no trade diversion. The cheapest foreign supplier supplies the customs union.
- If only one country in the customs union produces the good in question, but in the most efficient way, then this country will supply the market even without a common external trade protection.

By offering a joint level of protection, the common external tariff may promote a more efficient allocation of resources within the customs union from its internal point of view.

The influence of international economic integration on trade flows is illustrated here by two examples. When Britain joined the EU in 1973, the share of its imports from other EU partner countries increased significantly over a decade. Trade between Mexico and the US doubled over the five years that preceded the creation of the North American Free Trade Agreement (NAFTA) in 1994. Even the announcement and preliminary negotiations about a serious integration deal had a positive impact on the volume and direction of trade in the region and prompted an increase in foreign direct investment (FDI) towards Mexico. A similar example could be found in the case of Slovakia before it joined the EU in 2004.

The position of Turkey in relation to the EU could be similar to that of Mexico *vis-à-vis* the US in NAFTA. Turkey created a customs union with the EU in 1995. Unlike Mexico, Turkey failed to attract large-scale FDI principally because of corruption, red tape and lack of protection of intellectual property rights. Hence integration is a welcome but only a supporting policy instrument. Many exclusively domestic policy areas need to be in place in order to have the proper environment for the favourable operation of integration.

Patterns of consumption change following the creation of a customs union (see Figure 2.1). *Inter-country substitution* occurs when one country replaces the other as the source of supply for some good. *Inter-commodity substitution* occurs when one commodity is substituted, at least at the margin, for another one as a result of a shift in relative prices (Lipsey, 1960, p. 504). The latter occurs, for example, when country A imports from the customs union partner country B relatively cheaper veal which replaces at least some of the pork produced in country A and at least some of the chicken which is imported from country C, and when consumers in a customs union replace part of the demand for theatre and opera by relatively 'cheaper' stereo, video and other entertainment equipment.

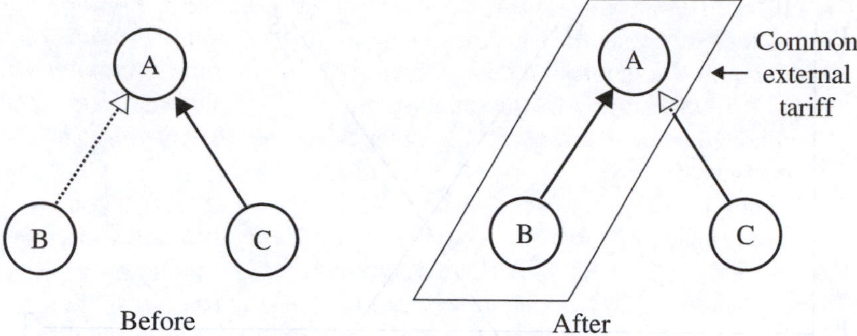

Figure 2.1 *Flows of imports of a good to country A, before and after the creation of a customs union with country B*

Figure 2.2 illustrates the effects of a tariff and a customs union on economic efficiency for a single good in country A's market. SS represents country A's domestic supply curve; similarly, DD shows the domestic demand curve. Country B's supply curve is BB, while country C's supply curve for the same good is CC. Both foreign countries can supply unconditionally any quantity of the demanded good at fixed prices. Both foreign supply curves are flat (perfectly elastic). It is a consequence of the smallness of the country in our example. This country cannot exert influence on its terms of trade, but in a customs union with other countries this is likely to change. Prior to the imposition of a tariff, at price 0C home demand for the good is $0Q_6$. Domestic producers supply $0Q_1$ while country C supplies Q_1Q_6.

Suppose that country A introduces a tariff on imports such that the price for domestic consumers is 0T. Now, country A can expand domestic production from $0Q_1$ to $0Q_3$ and curtail home consumption of the good from $0Q_6$ to $0Q_4$. The government collects tariff revenue equal to $CT \times Q_3Q_4$.

Let us assume that country A, which imposed a non-discriminatory *ad valorem* tariff on imports, enters into a customs union with country B. The price of imports from country C with a common external tariff of CT is 0T. Country B will supply country A's market. Country A's inefficient production contracts from $0Q_3$ to $0Q_2$ while consumption increases from $0Q_4$ to $0Q_5$. *Trade expansion* due to the creation of the customs union equals the sum of the reduction in home production Q_2Q_3 and the increase in home consumption Q_4Q_5. Country A's government does not earn any tariff proceeds from imports of the good from the customs union partner, country B. Trade expansion inevitably affects rationalisation in production. This takes place through an improved deployment of existing factors, increased size of

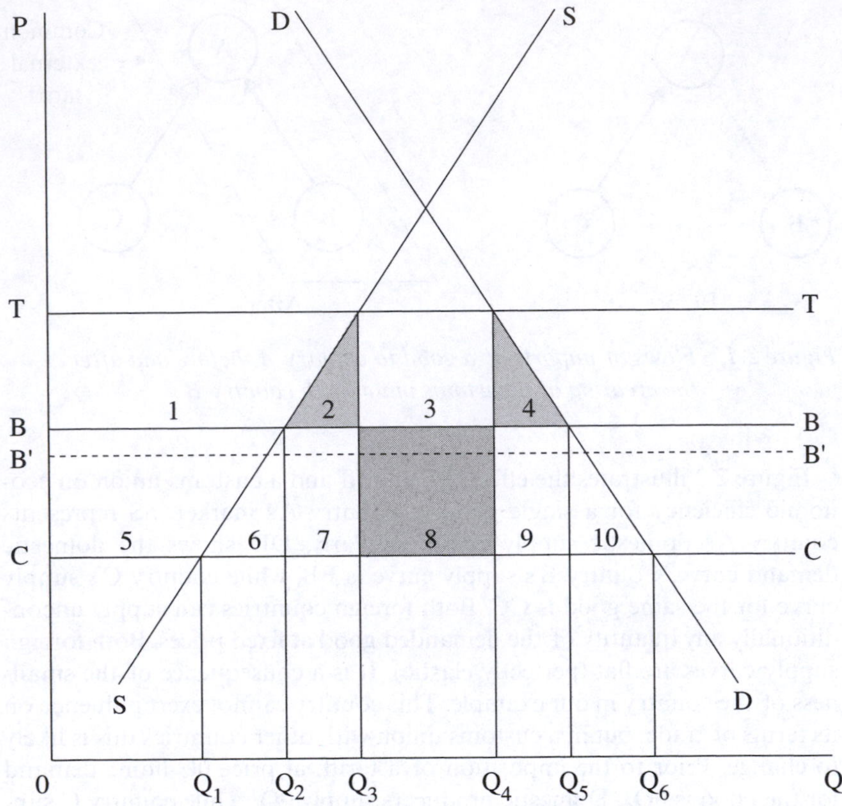

Figure 2.2 Effect of a tariff and customs union on production and consumption in country A

production units (reallocation of resources within sectors). One of the responses of firms in the EU to the Single Market Programme was a big wave of mergers and acquisitions around the year 1990. The consequences of these rationalisations are in theory expected to be decreased unit costs of goods and services, as well as increased standards of living on average.

Trade expansion effects, however, should not be overemphasised. The downward adjustment of domestic tariffs to the common external tariff need not result in an increased trade expansion effect in a customs union. This alignment will first lead to a reduction to 'normal' levels of the profit margins of the protected domestic producers. If there is excess capacity in the protected industries, a possible increase in the domestic demand which comes as a consequence of the fall in price will be met first by the country's own production (if it exists), rather than through imports. Thus, the trade expansion effects due to the creation of a customs union will not be as large as would be suggested by the difference in tariffs before the creation of a customs union and after it. Therefore, the scope for trade diversion is, indeed, smaller than it may first appear. It is simply the potential for an expansion in trade and competition that immediately does this good work for consumers, as well as for producers in the long term.

Consumers' surplus is defined as the difference between the consumers' total valuation of the goods consumed and the total cost of obtaining them. It is represented by the area under the demand curve and above the price that consumers face. Any decrease in price, other things being equal, increases consumers' surplus. Country A's consumers benefit when their country enters into a customs union with country B in relation to the situation with an initial non-discriminatory tariff. Their gain is given by the area 1 + 2 + 3 + 4 in Figure 2.2. These consumers are, however, worse off in comparison to the free trade situation in which country C is the supplier. This loss is given by the area 5 + 6 + 7 + 8 + 9 + 10. Domestic producers lose a part of their surplus in a customs union compared to the situation with a non-discriminatory *ad valorem* tariff (area above SS up to the price 0B which they receive). This is represented by area 1. From the national standpoint, area 1 nets out as part of both the consumers' gain and the producers' loss. Country A loses tariff revenue (area 3) which it collected in the initial situation. Hence, the net gain for country A is area 2 + 4.

The formation of a customs union has increased trade and consumption in country A in comparison to the initial situation with a non-discriminatory tariff. In the situation prior to the formation of a customs union, country A imports the good from country C, pays for it an amount equal to $Q_3Q_4 \times 0C$ and collects revenue equal to the area 3 + 8. After the formation of a customs union, area 3 is returned to consumers in the form of lower prices for the good, while area 8 represents a higher price charged by the customs union partner country. The return of area 3 to the consumers may be regarded as Hicksian compensation. When tariffs change, compensation is seldom paid. Hence, demand curve DD may be regarded simply as an approximation to the compensated Hicksian demand curve. It is important to note that country A pays, for the same amount of imports Q_3Q_4, a higher price to the customs union partner ($Q_3Q_4 \times 0B$) than was paid to the country C suppliers prior to the customs union formation. The country has a greater outflow of foreign exchange and does not collect revenue which it had done when it had imposed a non-discriminatory tariff on imports from country C. The outflow of foreign exchange from country A was equal to $Q_3Q_4 \times 0C$, while area 3 + 4 illustrates the transfer from consumers to producers within the home country.

The net welfare effect of the creation of a customs union in country A depends on the relative size of the Vinerian effects: trade creation (area 2 + 4) minus trade diversion (area 8). Instead of a *revenue-generating* obstacle to trade (tariff) a government may introduce *cost-increasing* barriers (various technical standards and tests) whose effect may be a reduction in trade. (Let the effect of the NTBs be BT in trade with country B.) If the set of NTBs is removed, the effect on domestic consumers and producers would be the same as in the situation when the tariff was removed. The government, which has never earned direct revenue from the set of non-tariff regulations, would lose nothing. The social gain from reducing these barriers is area 2 + 3 + 4. This *internal market opening* took place in the EU under the Single European Market Programme.

If one introduces dynamics into this model, in the form of increasing returns to scale, country B, as the customs union supplier of the good, faces an increased demand. Production would become more efficient and the price might fall from 0B to 0B′. This enhances trade creation and decreases the size of the trade diversion effect.

Figure 2.2 belongs to the family of standard microeconomic partial equilibrium analytical tools. Unfortunately, they all deal with only a part of the business cycle, that is, with the first third of the cycle when demand rises. Other cases, such as stagnation or reduction in demand, are seldom considered.

2.2.3 PROTECTION

The choice by country A to protect its industry may be questioned from the outset. There are at least two good reasons to object to trade restrictions in the medium and long terms in particular in the developed countries:

- First, new barriers to trade can provoke retaliation from foreign countries where domestic exporters already have an interest or intend to penetrate.[8]
- Second, and more subtly, if intermediate goods exist, all trade barriers raise the price of imported inputs. Therefore, they act as a tax on exports.[9] With the tariff, country A employs more resources in an industry in which it does not have a comparative advantage (although it may develop it).

Bearing in mind the assumption that the amount of resources is fixed and moving away from the partial equilibrium model, the fact is that resources are diverted away from business activities in which this country may have a comparative advantage. If a home industry is not competitive, a tariff may save jobs in this business in the short term. This may, however, lead to reduced activity in other home industries. If the uncompetitively produced home good is an input in other industries, their export performance may be at risk and investment reduced. The overall end result is increased unemployment and a lower standard of living in the longer term.

Policy makers can easily identify jobs that are saved by various forms of protection, but do not easily recognise the adverse consequences of this protection, hence the need for a general equilibrium model. Long-term protection wastes resources on inefficient production. Everybody loses except the government (because of increased revenues) and the protected industry in the short term. The problem in the short run is that the general equilibrium consequences of a given policy cannot be easily quantified. This policy of import substitution as opposed to a policy of export promotion and openness may be substantiated on the grounds that foreign markets for country A's exports are closed.

The national security argument for tariffs can also be questioned. Trade-affected industries lobby for protection. This plea does not take into account the fact that industrial decline rarely, if ever, implies the actual demise of an industry. Possible nuclear warfare, long-range cruise missiles and 'smart' bombs remove a part of the classical national security argument for protection. Risk-averse governments may consider stockpiling and/or guaranteeing supplies of goods and services from allies before imposing a tariff (Tyson and Zysman, 1987a, p. 41). Apart from security of supply, there are other reasons why a country may wish to preserve at least part of a (declining) domestic industry which is exposed to international competition. The opportunities for domestic production increase bargaining power in negotiations about the long-term supply contracts with foreigners. In addition, if the cost situation changes in the future, some domestic research and development (R&D), as well as production capacity, may be a good starting point for regaining competitiveness.

The infant industry and similar arguments of learning by doing for protection state that entrants to an industry suffer losses while they acquire know-how, suppliers, customers, trained labour and the like in the period of infancy, so they need protection. It takes time for a firm to become profitable. Everybody knows that. If bankers, investors and entrepreneurs are not prepared to accept short-term losses as their investment towards long-term gains without government intervention, this is a clear indication that the market does not consider the enterprise to be viable, and so does not deserve tariff protection.

A free trader would argue that every firm profitable by market criteria does not need to be protected. If the infant industry argument is to make sense, then there must be some evidence of market failure, either in capital markets (entrepreneurs cannot obtain adequate loans), or labour markets (such as inadequate training or fluctuations in the labour force) or some evidence that the production structure warrants protection. For example, increasing returns to scale or other positive externalities that require a certain level of protection during the initial, but limited time. These market failures may be corrected by economic policy (intervention). However, there are many old infants. What starts as an infant industry argument for protection turns into an employment protection argument. Finally, old infants are often nationalised at continuous cost to the taxpayers (Brander, 1987, p. 19). If a government bails out a declining industry and/or firm and creates a precedent, this produces expectations that the cost of poor business management will be socialised. This may be one of the main sources of the adjustment difficulties in the 'problem' industries in the developed countries.

The infant industry argument for protection was examined by Lipsey et al. (2005, pp. 510–12). They stated:

> As it is usually presented in modern textbooks, it is a static argument that assumes given technology. A product has a falling cost curve that has a very large minimum efficient scale (MES), and production costs are the only relevant costs. All firms face the same cost curve wherever they are located. Established firms are at their MESs but new ones have to start high up on their long-run cost curve and need assistance to exist long enough to move along and down it. If the potential new entrants are in one country and the established firms in other countries, the objective can be achieved through tariffs. The argument clearly applies only to non-price-taking firms since with price-taking, and many existing firms each operating at its MES, a new entrant could go all the way to its own MES immediately.
>
> This argument never seemed convincing to theorists. They argued that with perfect capital markets, a new entrant could borrow enough to go to its MES immediately. If it could not do so, they asked why some private sector agent would not bankroll the firm to get to the MES if the firm would be viable thereafter. Supporters claimed, among other things, that capital rationing was common in less developed countries.
>
> But standard Industrial Organisation (IO) and structuralist-evolutionary (S-E) theories suggest that this version of the infant industry defence is wide of the mark. First, IO theory shows that in any manufactured commodity, selling, distribution, design, product quality, after-sales servicing, maintenance, and other similar costs are at least as important as direct production costs. Some of these are once-for-all entry costs while others persist. The former can create powerful barriers to entry. Second, S-E theory suggests that the technology of production is not costlessly transferable among agents. A new start-up firm has to undergo much learning by doing and by using in order to accumulate the requisite tacit knowledge. So, it cannot go to its MES immediately. The extra costs incurred until the learning is completed, which may last for years, can be thought of as yet another entry cost. Third, when an industry's technology is

> continually changing endogenously, a new firm does not face a given static cost curve. The firm does not know in advance how long it will take to get to the cost level currently achieved by those already in the industry – or if it will ever be able to do so given local limitations. But this is not enough to guarantee success since existing oligopolistic firms are continually engaging in competition to lower their costs and improve their products through R&D. So the new entrants are pursuing a moving target rather than shooting at a stationary one. Fourth, it follows from the above points that there is much uncertainty in trying to enter a market in which costs and products are constantly changing. Private investors may take a different, more conservative view on accepting uncertainty than does the state, and that view may differ among nations according to their different social values.
>
> Thus, the simple text book cost curve, which is assumed to be available to any new entrant anywhere in the world, and which is the one that will be operated on when entry is completed, is a misleading fiction. It results in a misstatement of the infant industry problem as one of moving along a pre-existing, negatively sloped, long-run cost curve, whereas the real problem is to develop an industry whose rate of technological progress – progress that shifts cost curves downwards and develops new products – compares favourably with those of its foreign competitors.
>
> When technological change is endogenous, the encouragement of a successful infant industry can *shift* the local cost curve downwards as new technologies are developed that produce at lower cost than anything previously in existence. This is not an easy thing to do, as is attested by countless failures to develop such industries through public policy. But neither is it impossible, as is attested by some of the major successes reviewed below. . . .
>
> So much for the theory. The other major input into policy judgment is evidence. In the trade policy debate there is ample evidence of the power of *appropriately used* trade restrictions and infant industry assistance. As a general observation, not a single country in the west industrialized under completely free trade. The closest was probably Britain. But that country gave key protection to its textile industry in the eighteenth century when it banned the importation of Indian cotton goods. It also placed a series of restrictions on manufacturing activity in its colonies, and forced exports from its colonies bound for anywhere in Europe to flow through English ports. Virtually all other countries including Germany, France, the USA, and the former British Dominions sheltered their emerging manufacturing industries behind trade restrictions. These were eventually reduced, and some were lifted completely, but only *after* the industries had developed for at least several decades and often for more than a century.

Lipsey et al. (2005) also mentioned examples of successful altering of comparative advantage through government policy. These cases were found in modern growth experience of Asian countries which include the Japanese car industry, electronics in Taiwan and computer-related production and services in Singapore.

2.2.4 IS THERE A SUPERIOR POLICY TO THE CREATION OF A CUSTOMS UNION?

One ought always to ask whether there are superior alternative policies for a country to the creation of a customs union. Unilateral, non-discriminatory reductions in import tariffs may look to be a better policy than the formation of a customs union. It seems preferable to obtain trade creation exclusively as a result of unilateral tariff reductions, rather than to create a customs union which causes both trade creation and trade diversion (Cooper and Massel, 1965, pp. 745–6). Such an argument cannot be accepted without serious reservations. A customs union offers something which is not offered by a unilateral reduction in tariffs. That is, an elimination of tariffs in customs union partner countries. A unilateral reduction in tariffs exaggerates the price reduction effects on consumption, while it eliminates the possibility of penetration into the markets of customs union partners.

The necessity of tariff bargaining with foreigners, so important to domestic exporters, was left out of the picture in the earlier analysis. In addition, various barriers to trade with the non-union member countries were ignored (for example, transport costs). If such barriers are present, then a redirection of trade towards customs union partners in the region may not introduce (large extra) costs. On the contrary, it may bring certain savings in the form of lowered transport charges. Hence, this model questions, from an efficiency viewpoint, the desirability of a wide preferential-trading system such as the old British Commonwealth, where transport costs downgraded the commercial opportunities that were offered by preferential trade. Given the elimination of tariffs in the markets of a customs union among partner countries and reduction in obstacles to trade such as transport costs, the gains that come from the non-preferential unilateral tariff reduction need not be greater than the beneficial effects that arise from the creation of a customs union (Wonnacott and Wonnacott, 1981). Reciprocal deals draw in obligations of several countries; hence they may have greater standing than mere unilateral concessions.

Bilateral trade deals can offer returns that might not be realistically expected through multilateral negotiations. In the case of the free trade deal between Canada and the US, these gains include (Lipsey and Smith, 1989, pp. 319–21):

- the complete elimination of tariffs on goods that meet the stipulated rules of origin;
- a number of NTBs are eliminated, while the use of the rest is seriously restricted;
- most commercial services are covered by the agreement;

- a number of specific trade disputes were settled;
- there is a liberal and stable bilateral FDI regime;
- any US legislation that concerns Canada must be discussed bilaterally before it is passed; and
- if there is a dispute, the complaining country may elect to use either the GATT/WTO or the bilateral mechanism.

The likelihood that Canada would obtain such path-breaking and powerful trade-liberalising measures through multilateral negotiations in the foreseeable future is very slim. Therefore, this bilateral deal was chosen as a much faster path to achieve this goal.

In spite of the trade diversion costs of a customs union, the terms of trade of member countries might turn in their favour, so that, on balance, each member country may be better off than in the unilateral tariff reduction case. The classical approach to the theory of tariffs is mistaken. This approach, on the one hand, finds gains in the replacement of domestic goods for cheaper foreign goods, while on the other, the expansion of domestic exports does not bring gains in this model to the exporting country (except possible improvement of the terms of trade), but rather to the foreigners (Johnson, 1973, p. 80).

Suppose that compensatory payments between countries are allowed for. Then any customs union (or preferential trading area) is potentially favourable for all countries that consider participation, since they can be compensated for losses when they join. This means that a customs union among countries can be extended to $n+1$ countries. By expansion, this implies that there is an incentive to extend the customs union until the whole world is included, until free trade prevails throughout the world. Preferential trade blocs can be constructed in such a way that welfare of the outside countries is unaffected (Kemp and Wan, 1976). For example, a 'deeper' integration within the EU caused 'wider' integration in Europe. A market-deepening Single Market Programme triggered membership requests from European countries that were previously happy to be outside the EU. Once a group enlarges, the cost to non-members of staying out of the club may increase. Hence, there is a *domino effect* (Baldwin, 1995a, p. 46). If there are no entry costs and no strong political objectives, this process may lead to universal free trade.

Interest in joining a customs union or any other type of preferential trade or integration agreement may exist even without compensatory payments ('bribes'). In fact, these 'compensations' are never paid in practice. The reason for this is simple. The larger the integrated bloc, the greater the internal trade. Hence, there is an increased possibility that the group may have an influence and turn terms of trade with third countries to its advantage.

If others things such as productivity in the outside world remain unchanged, the countries that are left outside the group may lose in the long run. Therefore, every new country that joins the integrated group creates additional push motives for other countries to join the group (even if there are no compensatory payments at all).

While Viner questioned the overall welfare effects of the creation of a customs union, Kemp and Wan seem to bring back the pre-Viner perception that customs unions are always welfare-improving devices. The Kemp–Wan smooth scenario, perhaps among the most elegant reasoning in international economics, is often interpreted in a way that relates to two post-integration elements:

- the level of tariffs and
- the volume of trade with outsiders.

If both are unaffected by integration, or better, if these tariffs are in the post-integration period at a lower level, while trade and investment with outsiders increase, it is supposed that integration was globally beneficial and welcome. While such interpretations may make certain sense in the short run, if one wants to get a fuller picture about welfare effects, then one must consider changes in terms of trade between the customs union and the non-members.

The general Kemp–Wan argument hinges on the supposition that the integrated countries are open and that they welcome new entrants, and it also rests on the absence of political obstacles to integration. The possibility of either blocking any new enlargement or making the entry costs excessive (without full, direct or indirect compensation) puts this neat scenario into question.

Incentives to join a free trade agreement exist even without compensatory transfers among the participating countries. The reason is that the group may turn its terms of trade with the rest of the world towards its own advantage (against the non-members). Third countries may face shrinking markets, hence their domestic producers lobby to join the group. As the group enlarges, this provides inducements to others to join. The bigger the group becomes, the stronger the influence it may exert on its terms of trade with the rest of the world. In theory, the group enlarges until it covers the whole world.

Such reasoning may lead to the classical pre-Viner proposition that a customs union is a step towards free trade. This conclusion depends on the existence of inter-country transfers within the customs union. This is a severe restriction and the greatest weakness of this approach. The more countries there are in a customs union, the greater will be the potential demand and need for compensation. If certain adjustment schemes are adopted in reality, they are often the products of political bargaining, not purely the outcome of the economic impact of integration. These schemes are too complicated and they never compensate in full (compensation schemes are never perfect), which limits the actual size of a customs union. This leads to the conclusion that non-economic reasons play a prominent role in economic integration. The experience of the EU, its creation and enlargements illustrate that political considerations play a major role in integration.

2.2.5 TARIFFS AND SUBSIDIES

Consideration of the impact of tariffs on imports would be incomplete without comparing them to production (and export) subsidies ('corporate welfare'). The effect of a tariff on imports of a good is equivalent to a combination of a tax on domestic consumption and a subsidy on home production of the same good. Tariffs and subsidies are close substitutes. A reduction in one of them may be compensated for by an increase in the other. The existence of tariffs permits the domestic producers to charge higher prices on the local market than would otherwise have been the case. Unlike the 'direct' payment from consumers to producers in the case of tariffs, a subsidy goes from taxpayers to the government, and then to the protected industry. The transfer technique is different, but the policy goal is the same.

Various types of intervention including subsidies (production, location, export, investment, marketing, even some types of R&D) may provoke retaliation. In addition, they are not generally recommended by major international economic organisations or developed countries to developing countries as trade, industrial or development policy instruments. The WTO 'disciplines' the use of subsidies and regulates the actions that can be taken to counter their effects.[10] In addition, subsidies are alleged to be costly for the budget, difficult to administer, subject to rent-seekers and they have a weak impact on exports. None the less, the fact remains that advanced countries reached their level of industrial development partly because of protection at some time in the past. They took over and established value-adding economic activities with important externalities. Their firms adjusted to market competition and reduced demand for protection in certain lines of production. However, special interest groups such as firms whose business is in textiles, apparel or shoes (or industries in trouble) still lobby hard for protection from competition that comes from developing countries. Even in aeronautics, there is a long and ongoing row between

Boeing (US) and Airbus (EU) which revolves around heavy and long-term subsidies on either side.

A domestic tariff increases prices of both imported goods and home-produced protected goods (at least in the short run). This distortion has as its cost the losses of gains from exchange and from specialisation, as well as a loss in domestic consumption. One cost of subsidies is a loss of gains from specialisation, however domestic prices and consumption remain unchanged.[11] Thus, at least in the long run, a restriction of imports is equal to a reduction in potential exports when a fixed amount of resources is fully employed prior to the introduction of distortions. Resources are being shifted out of exports into import-substituting industries. However, in the short run (before elections), authorities might be more concerned about the level of (un)employment than about income transfers which both tariffs and production subsidies imply.

Tariffs are more readily 'supplied' by governments because of at least two internal factors. First, they do not pose any short-term burden on tight budgets and, second, tariffs may be introduced in such a way that they cannot easily be labelled as firm specific, which is not always the case with subsidies. Although subsidies may sometimes be a preferred trade instrument in theory, they are not without flaws. Subsidies provide certain opportunities for a fast aggregation of skills within an industry (firm), but they lower the level of competition and ease the market pressure to create a bond between learning, doing, expanding and competing.

If country A is subject to subsidised supplies of good X from country B, country A should consider the consequences of such circumstances. Subsidies are based on the potential to earn economic rents from foreign consumers and producers in the future (beggar thy neighbour). *Economic rents* refer to the proceeds of the producers and exporters which are in excess of what is necessary to cover the costs of production and trade, and to yield an average return on investment. These rents represent super-normal profits that are returns to scarcities such as unique capabilities of firms or individuals.[12]

The potential to get these rents in evolutionary economics represents the strongest economic motive, not only for innovation and introduction of new technologies, but also to combat and reduce high risk and uncertainty. Subsidies will improve the social welfare of the exporting country only if profits of the exporting industry exceed the cost of the subsidy to the taxpayers. If country A consumers obtain the good X at a lower price from country B than from its domestic producers, then domestic consumers are better off, although its home producers of good X are worse off. All this is at the expense of country B's taxpayers. If country B is willing to supply country A with the subsidised good X indefinitely, then a wise policy for country A is to accept these supplies and shift domestic resources to business activities where the return is higher in relation to the return on the home production of the good X. If country B, however, subsidises its exports of good X in order to discharge cyclical surpluses or in order to prevent the entry of country A's firms into the market of good X or to drive them out of it in the long run in order to charge monopoly prices later, then country A need not accept this offer as the only source of supply.

Although tariffs and subsidies have similar effects on trade and production, the GATT does not prohibit tariffs, while its Code on Subsidies and Countervailing Duties (1979) prohibits export subsidies (with the exception of certain primary products) if such subsidies cause material injury to the importing country's firms.[13] The injury must be proved prior to the introduction of a countervailing duty and its objective has to be to offset the effect of foreign subsidies on domestic business. Of course, the maximum countervailing duty permitted by the GATT is limited by the amount of subsidy embodied in imports of the country that introduces the duty. The effects of such a policy are restricted only to the competitive situation in the home market of the country that introduces the countervailing duty. Similarly, in the situation of a balance of payments deficit, the International Monetary Fund (IMF) recommends a tariff, but does not advise the use of export subsidies.[14]

Foreign subsidies may induce countervailing duties by the 'injured' countries. If these countries do not either produce or have some potential for the production of a good, then there are no grounds for the imposition of these duties. The relative size of trading partners and their relative openness to trade play a crucial role. Relatively small countries are more reliant on external trade than larger ones. A small subsidy to an import-competing industry in a large country may have a more distorting impact than a large subsidy applied to a small country's exports.

Preferences for tariffs are often due to compelling political realities. People are used to tariffs, while subsidies typify unfair competition. One country cannot force foreigners to eliminate tariffs on exports, but it may, if it identifies their subsidies, make them remove these by threatening to impose countervailing duties.[15] An international abolition of tariffs would be ignored, while a prohibition of export subsidies legitimates retaliation by means of countervailing duties (Wonnacott, 1987, pp. 86–7). There are, of course, other incentives for the introduction of subsidies. Let us consider them in turn.

Firms invest because of the anticipation of profits in the future. Investments are undertaken because markets are foreseen, costs of production make profits possible and funds, at acceptable rates, are available. If profit opportunities are fading away, then unemployment may rise.

Governments are reluctant to accept such a state of affairs, so they offer subsidies (investment, employment, R&D, production and/or export), among other things, to firms, in order to alter unfavourable trends. If a country wants to protect all the firms in an industry, then an outright subsidy may be a better alternative to reduced tax rates. A subsidy may help all firms in an industry, while reduced tax rates may help only those that are profitable. Reduced taxes may be preferred if the policy goal is to remove the lame ducks.

A valid case for subsidies can be made if there are market imperfections. Unemployment was a cyclical phenomenon in the past. Nowadays, its nature is different. In many cases labour needs retraining in order to be hired, and needs constant upgrading of skills in order to be kept employed. Vocational training is a valid case for subsidies. In addition, there are no countervailing duties for grants to students to study engineering (that will shape the comparative advantage and competitiveness of a country in the future).

A special type of subsidy may be present in government procurement policies. By discriminating in the award of public contracts, a government may sharpen the competitive edge of an economy. That is very important during the first tentative steps in the development of an industry, good or service. A firm's shareholders thus receive income transfers from home taxpayers. If the industry is successful and if sunk costs are high, then latecomers may not enter the market. This strategic pre-emption of the market may provide the firm with super-normal profits (rents) from sales on foreign markets. One example is the purchase of defence equipment as a subsidy to high-technology firms. This is the case in the US aircraft industry which has been receiving indirect subsidies. In Europe, the Airbus industry is (in)directly subsidised by participating governments. It is very hard, even impossible, for potential investors in other regions of the world to compete with firms that combine forces with national governments in this industry. In general, if firms notice and expect an increase in demand and enlargement of the market (which are the effects of integration or preferential trade), 'it will *always* pay existing firms to pre-empt the market by establishing new plants before the time when it would first pay new firms to enter' (Eaton and Lipsey, 1979b, p. 149; original emphasis). However, these first firms may often make costly mistakes.

If one ignores the possibility of retaliation, intervention can make a country better off. When super-normal profits (rents) from export to foreign countries exceed the cost of subsidies (production and/or export), the exporting country obviously increases its wealth in the short and medium terms. National 'profits' from subsidies need not be measured only in pecuniary terms. By supplying energy to the countries in the former eastern bloc at prices that were below those on the international market, the former Soviet Union was able to wrest many political advantages from the region.

A special type of subsidy may also be present in goods and services supplied to firms and citizens by the government. These goods and services are offered in certain cases at lower prices by public enterprises than would be the case if private firms (which must pay taxes) provided such output. When managers of companies start spending more time lobbying for government grants than worrying about the actual operation of their companies, taxpayers and consumers should start getting nervous (Brander, 1987, p. 28).

The long-term prosperity of a country cannot be promoted by subsidies to rent-seeking inefficient firms, whereby no additional new wealth is created, but an extra tax is imposed on the prosperous. This corrodes the operation of a market economy and slows down innovation. In services that are provided by the government and not by private firms, there can easily be some subsidy element. For example, in Brussels, the seat of the European Commission and a number of other international organisations, there were several thousand interest (pressure) groups. These rent-seekers employ around 15 000 lobbyists[16] with the number rising together with the expansion of the Commission's authority and enlargements of the EU. This is roughly one lobbyist (representative of special interest) per employee of the European Commission.

An output subsidy may be 'preferable' to an export subsidy. The rationale is that an output subsidy does not necessarily lead to higher domestic prices of differentiated products, as is the case with a tariff or an export subsidy (Flam and Helpman, 1987, pp. 94–5). Output subsidies are often tacitly accepted, while export subsidies are often subject to countervailing duties. An R&D subsidy always expands these activities: more varieties appear on the market and more firms enter the industry. The price of differentiated goods may increase or decline, as an enlarged number of firms may result in lower output per firm. This R&D subsidy may, therefore, improve or reduce welfare, or leave it unchanged.

One of the most obvious expressions of subsidies was the 1971 US Domestic International Sales Corporation (DISC) Act which enabled American exporters to shelter part of their foreign income from taxation. Initially, the DISC allowed exporters an indefinite postponement of the payment of about a quarter of the income tax on their export profits. This acted as a direct subsidy to capital used in the production of exports. In 1976, the GATT Panel found the DISC to be a direct export subsidy programme in conflict with the GATT rules. The US replaced the DISC with the Foreign Sales Corporation (FSC) Act in 1984.[17] This scheme provides benefits to some 6000 American-owned firms (subsidy seekers) among which are giant producers and exporters.

According to the WTO Panel findings in 2001, the FSC is an illegal US export subsidy scheme, which has to be changed or abolished. It provides tax relief for income earned abroad by a subsidiary of an American TNC. This benefits big exporters such as Boeing, Caterpillar, General Electric, Intel, Microsoft and Motorola. The US claimed that the FSC tax exemption was to avoid double taxation. This was not upheld as FSCs are typically established in tax havens such as Barbados, Guam and the Virgin Islands where no income tax is paid at all.[18] The WTO authorised the EU to introduce annual trade sanctions against imports from the US worth $4 billion. This is the biggest ever retaliation authorisation by the WTO. In 2003, the WTO approved a list of 1800 US products targeted by the EU for retaliation. The EU hit list selected American products that would be hurt most in electorally sensitive areas. Tariffs would be imposed on products from textiles (hitting North Carolina) to Tropicana juice (wounding the electorally swing state of Florida).

The EU wanted to apply these approved sanctions from March 2004 to give America time to arrange for the necessary legislation. This pressurised the US Senate Finance Committee into passing legislation in 2003 that would abolish the FSC and replace it with a 3 per cent tax cut for producers located in the US.[19] This bill was unacceptable to the EU as it had a three-year transition period to enable the gradual withdrawal of existing tax breaks. In addition, a new bill would replace the FSC with nearly $140 billion in new tax breaks to US firms. The principal provision is a reduction in the top corporate tax rate from 35 to 32 per cent.[20]

For the first time in the history of transatlantic trade relations, the EU imposed trade sanctions on US goods on 1 March 2004. The EU chose to be cautious with the application of sanctions (in the form of tariffs) so as not to antagonise the US. Sanctions were not applied on politically sensitive products such as citrus fruit or textiles. Instead, they were applied on fairly 'inoffensive' goods such as jewellery, honey, paper, nuclear reactors, roller skates, toys and refrigerators. The EU sanctions affected US exports worth €290 million in 2004. However, the tariffs were designed to rise gradually by 1 per cent each month (to increase the economic pain for US exporters) until they affected US exports worth €533 million a year (which is far below the WTO approved volume of imports eligible for sanctions).[21] The EU lifted these sanctions in January 2005.

The new theory of strategic[22] trade and industrial policy (a refined variant of the optimum-tariff theory) has identified areas where government intervention can 'correct' certain market imperfections.[23] Among the available policy instruments for 'massaging markets' (intervention) are subsidies. This policy instrument, however, must be financed either by taxes or by borrowing. Taxes produce distortions because they affect the supply of labour, wage costs and/or discourage consumption. Government borrowing increases interest rates and tends to crowd out private investment. These welfare losses are not necessarily larger than the welfare gains obtained from the same subsidies. Governments often prefer to subsidise inputs. This may cause X-inefficiency problems such as a wasteful use of the subsidised resources and protection of firms from competition, which reduces pressure on firms to minimise costs. None the less, there is no presumption that the reduced costs from learning by doing and economies of scale are more important than the increased costs resulting from the X-inefficiency induced by subsidies. The new trade theorists have chosen to ignore these problems and biased their conclusions in favour of activist industrial and trade policies.

To complete the discussion of subsidies, reference has to be made to the reasons why administrations tend to avoid them. Governments dislike direct subsidies because they place the cost within the government's budget, while regulatory measures transfer the cost to the private sector. If a government subsidises then it must tax, borrow and/or reduce current expenditure. Subsidies are readily measurable and receivers identifiable. Costs incurred by a tariff are spread over numerous consumers and its effects cannot be measured with a high degree of accuracy. A subsidy may be offered on a 'one-off' basis, but often it becomes an ongoing commitment which may end up in the nationalisation of a bankrupt firm because of various 'strategic' or employment considerations. In addition, with budget deficits, governments cannot easily find the necessary funds for subsidies. Therefore, one of the choices for the subsidisation of exports may be a depreciation of the exchange rate.

The costs of financing and disbursing subsidies may be quite high, whereas the administrative costs of the implementation of tariffs are relatively low and the proceeds are easy to collect. Administering the distribution of subsidies may be a formidable task and quite difficult to handle. Sometimes these subsidies are not necessary. If the handling of this instrument is easy, then too many marginal firms will receive support. If a private investment would have been made in any case, then a subsidy for it would be regarded as no more than the replacement of private money by public (corporate welfare).

Research and development in the EU information technology industry was both undertaken by firms on their own and subsidised by the public. That industry is interesting, as over 40 per cent of all strategic technology alliances took place there during the 1980s. Apart from these private cooperative deals, cost-sharing technology partnerships developed with the involvement of governments and the EU. The two networks operated side by side. R&D that was subsidised by the EU was found to resemble the 'private' one and simply reproduced the basic 'private' network of cooperation of large EU firms. Strong oligopolistic lobbies were able to lure the EU into giving subsidies. One now wonders if the EU-funded R&D network was necessary at all (Hagedoorn and Schakenraad, 1993).

Yet another reason which prevents the introduction of subsidies is international commitment such as membership of the GATT/WTO. Subsidies may lead to foreign retaliation which would make the trade balance even worse. Some countries may enter into subsidy warfare in order to attract FDI. This action may induce greater distortions than arise with tariffs.

Both tariffs and subsidies, as policy instruments, introduce distortions. Therefore, any policy that involves either instrument should be carefully considered and crafted. In comparison with free trade, the situation involving imperfections in either of these instruments is suboptimal. If a country subsidises, then it might gain an advantage, but only temporarily. Anything that provides a country with a disadvantage in exporting in the short run will cause the adjustment of the exchange rate or factor prices in the long run (Johnson and Krauss, 1973, p. 240). The new theory of trade and strategic industrial policy questioned such a view. It stated that intervention matters a lot as there are certain irreversibilities that can perpetuate themselves (clustering of related firms with economies of scale). Protection also distorts market signals. However, even though protection is a second-best strategy by economic criteria relative to a liberal trade regime, it is a workable, well accepted and often superior political strategy.

2.2.6 GENERAL EQUILIBRIUM MODEL

A partial equilibrium model considers the market for a single good. It assumes that all prices other than that of the good in question are fixed. A general equilibrium model considers all markets. All prices are variable and competitive equilibrium requires that all markets clear (everything fits at once). All markets are connected by a chain of inputs and substitutes, information technology, mobility of factors and goods, income (if one spends more on something, less will remain for other things) and so on.

Consideration of the general equilibrium model will start with the 3×2 model. In this case there are three countries, A, B and C, as well as two goods (markets) X and Y, respectively. Lipsey (1957 and 1960) was the first to study these cases in a customs union framework. The model included full specialisation and constant costs. A small country A imports good X from country C which is the foreign supplier with the lowest price.

Consider a case illustrated in Figure 2.3, where substitution in consumption is allowed for by smooth and convex indifference curves. There

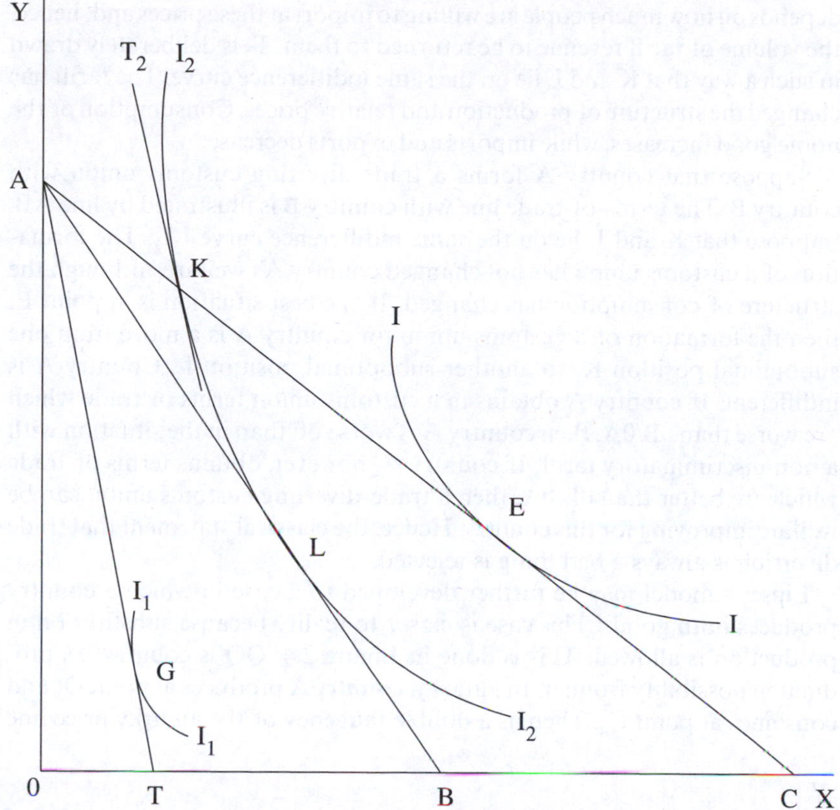

Figure 2.3 Welfare in a trade-diverting customs union

are three countries, A, B and C, and two goods, X and Y, respectively. In the free trade case, country A trades with country C and achieves indifference curve II. Suppose now that country A introduces a non-discriminatory tariff on imports. The relative price in country A is now AT.

Suppose that this tariff does not give enough incentive to home entrepreneurs to embark upon production of good X. Country A achieves the indifference curve I_1I_1 with equilibrium at point G. If the government either returns all tariff proceeds to consumers or spends the entire amount in the same fashion as the consumers would otherwise have done, then the equilibrium should be on line AC (as country C is the best foreign supplier). The equilibrium point is at point K, which is the point where the line T_2 (parallel to AT which illustrates compensation of consumers) intersects with terms-of-trade line AC. The extent of the rightward shift in the terms-of-trade line depends on how much people are willing to import at these prices and, hence, the volume of tariff revenue to be returned to them. T_2 is deliberately drawn in such a way that K and L lie on the same indifference curve. The tariff has changed the structure of production and relative prices. Consumption of the home good increases, while imports and exports decrease.

Suppose that country A forms a trade-diverting customs union with country B. The terms-of-trade line with country B is illustrated by line AB. Suppose that K and L lie on the same indifference curve I_2I_2. The formation of a customs union has not changed country A's welfare, although the structure of consumption has changed. If the best situation is at point E, then the formation of a customs union for country A is a move from one suboptimal position K, to another suboptimal position L. Country A is indifferent. If country A obtains in a customs union terms of trade which are worse than 0B/0A, then country A is worse off than in the situation with a non-discriminatory tariff. If country A, however, obtains terms of trade which are better than 0B/0A, then a trade-diverting customs union can be welfare improving for this country. Hence, the classical statement that trade diversion is always a bad thing is rejected.

Lipsey's model may be further developed to a case in which a country produces both goods. This case is closer to reality because substitution in production is allowed. This is done in Figure 2.4. QQ is country A's production possibility frontier. In autarky, country A produces at point Q_a and consumes at point C_a. There is a double tangency of the autarky price line

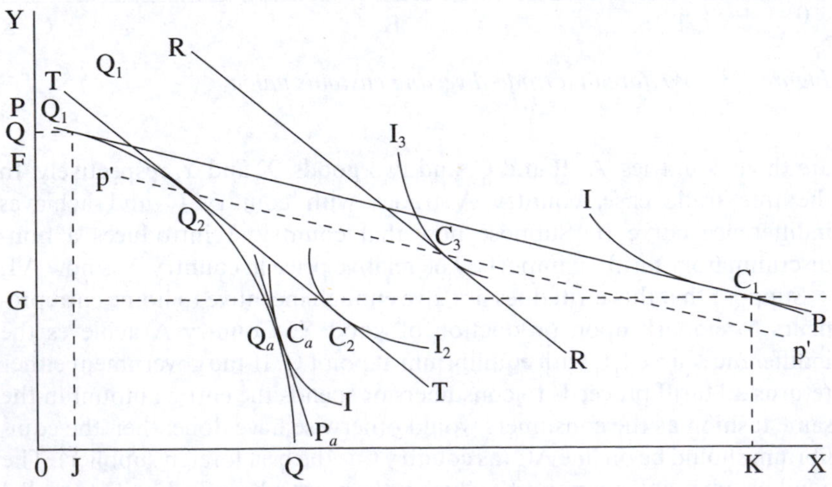

Figure 2.4 Production and consumption in country A before and after a tariff

P_a with the production possibility curve QQ and indifference curve I at a single point. Suppose now that this country opens up for international trade. It is a small country, so it faces a given price ratio PP between good X and good Y. Country A then produces at point Q_1 and consumes at point C_1. The double tangency of production point Q_1 and consumption point C_1 is not required to be at one point. Country A exports quantity FG of good Y and imports quantity JK of good X from country C.

Suppose, now, that country A imposes a non-discriminatory tariff on imports. With the new price line, TT, country A's production is at Q_2 and consumption is at point C_2. Both production and consumption points are closer to the autarkic levels. If home consumers are compensated (all tariff proceeds are returned to them), then there will be additional imports. This is shown by the line RR which is parallel to line TT (the distance between the two lines equals tariff revenue) and consumption is at C_3. Now, suppose that country A enters into a trade-diverting customs union with country B which is a less efficient supplier than country C. If country A achieves a lower indifference curve in this customs union than I_3, then country A is worse off than in the pre-customs union situation. If country A, however, achieves in the customs union a higher indifference curve than I_3, then this trade-diverting customs union is increasing its welfare and is beneficial to this country.

In order to be closer to reality, higher dimensional models are necessary. Consider a 3×3 model in which country A produces good X, while it imports good Y from country B and good Z from country C. Table 2.4 states three optimality conditions between country A's domestic($_d$) and

Table 2.4 Prices in country A and their relation to prices on the international market

Free trade	Non-preferential *ad valorem* tariff	Customs union with country B
$\frac{PA_d}{PB_d}=\frac{PA_i}{PB_i}$	$\frac{PA_d}{PB_d}<\frac{PA_i}{PB_i}$	$\frac{PA_d}{PB_d}=\frac{PA_i}{PB_i}$
$\frac{PA_d}{PC_d}=\frac{PA_i}{PC_i}$	$\frac{PA_d}{PC_d}<\frac{PA_i}{PC_i}$	$\frac{PA_d}{PC_d}<\frac{PA_i}{PC_i}$
$\frac{PB_d}{PC_d}=\frac{PB_i}{PC_i}$	$\frac{PB_d}{PC_d}=\frac{PB_i}{PC_i}$	$\frac{PB_d}{PC_d}<\frac{PB_i}{PC_i}$

Source: Lipsey (1960).

international($_i$) prices for this model. In free trade all three conditions are fulfilled. Price ratios for the same goods in country A and abroad are equal. If country A imposes a non-preferential tariff on all imports, then optimality will be achieved only in the price ratio between the imported goods. A customs union with country B shifts country A from one suboptimal position to another, since optimality is satisfied only in one case (between country A's good X and country B's good Y).

Apart from Lipsey (1960), 3 × 3 models of customs union were initially studied by Meade (1968), Berglas (1979), Riezman (1979) and Lloyd (1982). In the model by Meade, each country exports one good while it imports the other two from other countries. Riezman's model permits each country to export two goods and import only one good. The model by Berglas is more complicated. Country A and country B have only one export good each. Both countries import two goods. Country A exports its good X to both country B and country C and imports good Y from country B and good Z from country C. Country B exports good Y only to country A and imports good X from country A and good Z from country C. Figure 2.5 illustrates trade flows in these three models.

The models by Meade and Riezman have very different trade flows, but the two are symmetric as opposed to Berglas's model which is asymmetric (Lloyd, 1982, p. 49). Patterns of trade may be different and more complicated than those illustrated in Figure 2.5. Asymmetry in trade patterns prior to the formation of a customs union has an important impact on the welfare between the countries that form a customs union. The extension from three- to n-good models ($n > 3$) permits introduction of a greater number of trade patterns, but it does not significantly affect the results (Berglas, 1979, p. 317).

Higher dimensional models of trade such as the 3 × 3 model, and even more complex ones, are necessary because they offer an important advantage: substitution effects. In a two-good model, one must be an export and

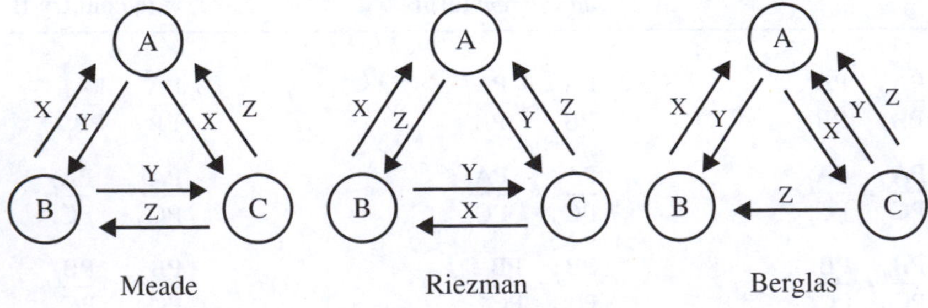

Figure 2.5 Trade flows among countries in models by Meade, Riezman and Berglas

the other an import good in each country. Higher dimensional models permit various restrictions on trade among different countries. The weakness of the models is that they assume that the goods are final goods. Any reduction in impediments to trade on semi-processed goods may have a different impact on national production from a reduction of barriers to trade on final goods. A relatively high tariff on imports of final goods encourages this kind of production domestically. However, a relatively high tariff on imports of final goods in country B induces country A to expand the production and export of semi-processed goods.

The intuition behind gravity models of trade is found in physics. Attraction or gravity force (total trade) between two objects (countries) depends on their respective masses (size of their economies) and the spatial distance between them. These models use factors that include country size, income and population to mirror demand and supply (the bigger the country, the smaller the interaction with the outside world); common borders and physical distance to reflect transport costs; common language (to describe cultural affinity); and artificial trade barriers. Some explain regional pattern and concentration of trade and integration as a result of low transport costs (low natural obstacles, hence they are 'natural' trading partners such as the US and Canada), while others argue that they are the outcome of discriminatory (preferential) trading deals. In general, gravity models give us little guidance about the suitability of preferential trade. The spaghetti-bowl mix of preferential trade relations may provide certain incentives to veer towards a simple and lean multilateral liberalisation of trade.

2.2.7 CONDITIONS FOR A WELFARE-IMPROVING CUSTOMS UNION

In a world with distortions in trade, any customs union is just a second-best solution. On these grounds, a prescription for a welfare improvement is not possible. None the less, foreigners would find it harder to compete in an integrated area. This is not because common trade barriers are increased relative to the individual trade barriers prior to integration. In fact, these barriers may be lowered on average. However, major difficulties in penetration may come from the enhanced market competitiveness of the goods produced in the integrated area.

Each of these conditions tends to make trade creation and welfare improvements more likely:

- The lower the demand for country C's exports and the greater the demand for goods produced by partner countries in a customs union, the greater the likelihood of an improvement in welfare due to trade creation.

- The higher the trade barriers in third countries, the higher the trade creation in the customs union.
- The level of tariffs (as well as other impediments to trade) typifies a country's lack of competitiveness. In an extreme situation when country A has a prohibitive tariff and if domestic production is impossible, then there will be no home consumption of the good in question. Any reduction in this tariff has a potentially beneficial welfare effect on consumers in country A. Figure 2.2 illustrates the case in which the higher the pre-customs union tariff in country A, the higher is the trade creation in a customs union with country B. Of course, the common external tariff must be lower than the pre-customs union tariff. The lower the tariffs in country C on exports from country A, the lower will be the export diversion towards country B. The lower the common external tariff, the smaller is the probability that the union partner will replace the most efficient supplier, which is country C. A relatively low common external tariff permits some competition from countries which are outside the customs union. A partial reduction in tariffs potentially brings greater benefits than the creation of a customs union, because it inhibits trade diversion. The lower the pre-customs union tariffs, the lower the potential benefits from a customs union. All these effects, however, depend on the elasticity of trade flows to the change in tariffs.
- The 'flatter' the demand and supply curves in relation to the quantity axis in Figure 2.2 (elasticity must be greater than unity), the greater the areas 2 and 4 which embody trade creation.
- The larger the number of countries that participate in a customs union, the smaller the probability of trade diversion. An incentive to form and enlarge a customs union persists until the entire world becomes a customs union, that is, until the introduction of universally accepted free trade. A customs union among all countries of the world would have only trade creation as a consequence.
- If integration takes place between neighbouring countries, the lower the transportation costs and the greater the gains from integration. That is why free trade deals between the US and Israel (1985) or Canada and Israel (1997) had only a very limited impact on integrating the economies of the countries concerned.
- The more inelastic the supply from third countries, the more these countries lose, while the customs union partner countries gain. Trade diversion is preferable to trade creation for the preference-granting

country, for it does not entail any sacrifice of domestic industrial production (Johnson, 1973, p. 89).[24]

- Goods of different countries are competitive if these countries have similar costs of production for the same good. Integration of countries with such a production structure produces, potentially, the greatest gains. If the same countries have different costs of production for the same good, they have a complementary economic structure. Integration in this case may also produce gains, but perhaps not as big as in the former instance.
- The larger the number of (small) firms in the same industry, the smaller the potential resistance of vested interests that can oppose integration and a 'painful' adjustment to the new situation, with more competition on an integrated market.
- The less developed the economies prior to integration, the higher the potential opportunities for benefits from (planned) specialisation.

Trade among countries with different costs of production for similar goods and different factor endowments may often be characterised by inter-industry trade, while trade among countries with similar costs of production for similar goods, with similar factor endowments and similar consumer preferences (tastes) may be characterised by intra-industry trade. Competition between countries with complementary economic structures in a customs union will ensure that the most efficient producer supplies the customs union market, which secures a welfare gain. In a multi-country and multi-good case, however, country A may be the most efficient producer of good X, while country B is the least efficient producer of the same good. In addition, country B may be the most efficient producer of good Y, while country A is the least efficient producer of this good. So, regarding goods X and Y, these two countries have complementary production structures. A customs union between these two countries, which covers just two industries that produce goods X and Y, may be welfare improving only for them.

If countries that contemplate the creation of a customs union have competitive structures prior to integration, but achieve complementarity after entry into the customs union, then an increase in welfare might be the outcome. All these (im)possibilities represent another reinforcement of the theoretical second-best character of customs unions.

The introduction of terms such as complementarity and competitiveness are not necessary. The most important condition for a welfare-improving outcome from the creation of a customs union is that a customs union stimulates competition within its boundaries and that the common external tariff is not erected primarily for protection against imports from outside countries (Lundgren, 1969, p. 38).

2.3 Dynamic model

2.3.1 INTRODUCTION

The old, static, neo-classical rules of economics require significant modification. Information technology, the rapid pace of innovation, fast-changing technology and market uncertainty generally characterise the modern economy. A fast, cheap and easy information flow has reduced many of the past barriers to business. In addition, innovative activity has significantly changed the extent and character of the modern economy. The Middle Ages in Europe (5th to 15th centuries) offered only a few, but important, inventions that found practical application.[25] These included: cement, inventions in metallurgy (improved production of iron), horse-shoes, the horse collar (that is, one that did not half-throttle the animal as soon as it started to pull with any significant force), the heavy plough (and the consequent development of the three-field system), windmills, the spinning wheel, the printing press, the mechanical clock, spectacles, the astrolabe, the fork, glass mirrors and underwear. The only constant feature in the modern, dynamic economy is an ever-accelerating pace of innovation and change, in particular in the improvement of and reduction in the price of already existing goods and services.

The classical theory of customs unions assumed that the static effects of resource reallocation occurred in a timeless framework. If one wants to move the theory of customs unions towards reality one must consider dynamic, that is, restructuring, effects. Many accept the proposition that markets are imperfect and that there are externalities such as economies of scale and product differentiation that make competition imperfect. When market structure is like this, regionalism/integration can be justified, as markets may be extended, deepened and secured, and because the market power of individual firms may be reduced. This may have a positive impact on competition, productivity, innovation and a reduction in prices.

Instead of considering only the possibility of trade in goods, dynamic models analyse the possibility of resource allocation across time. The static effects of international economic integration have their most obvious and profound influence in the period immediately following the creation of, for example, a customs union.[26] Gradually, after some years of adjustment, the dynamic effects will increase in importance and become dominant. These dynamic influences, which also include accumulation effects, push technological constraints further and provide the group with an additional integration-induced 'growth bonus'.

Trade flows do not remain constant. In fact, they evolve and alter over time. Changes in the equilibrium points in, for example, Figure 2.2 are described as instantaneous. Such shifts in equilibrium points, however, may not always be possible. Delays in reaction on the part of countries and consumers in a customs union could be caused by their recourse to stocks. Hence, they do not immediately need to purchase those goods whose price has decreased as a consequence of the formation of a customs union. They may also have some contractual commitments that cannot be abandoned overnight. Finally, buyers may not be aware of all the changes. Up to the 19th century, state intervention was negligible, but markets remained disconnected because of imperfect information and relatively high transport costs. The Internet has, however, eliminated the constraint of the lack of timely information. A time lapse between the implementation of a policy change (the creation of a customs union) and its favourable effects may include an initial period of economic deterioration in certain industries which may be followed by improvements due to the J-curve effect.

Consideration of dynamic, that is, restructuring effects is done in terms of effects of increased competition, specialisation and economies of scale, terms of trade and so on.

2.3.2 CHANGE IN THE EFFICIENCY IN THE USE OF FACTORS DUE TO INCREASED COMPETITION

Introduction

One of the most important functions of competition is the exchange of information. In theory, free market competition provides everyone with the widest opportunities for business and produces the best sectoral and spatial allocation of resources. By so doing, competition both improves efficiency in the use of factors because of their constant reallocation and, something which is often forgotten, introduces a permanent instability into the system. This conclusion has been accepted by neo-classical economic theory as a truth. It has provided the intellectual backing for competition (antitrust) policy. However, while competition may create lucrative opportunities and gains, it may also be the source of problems and concerns such as risk and uncertainty. The objective of this policy is that markets attain and maintain the flexibility needed to promote initiative, innovation and constant improvement in the allocation of resources. The final intention and goal is, of course, to maintain and raise living standards. Hence, what matters in theory is how to play the competition game, rather than who wins or loses. In practice, however, politicians, members of the public, firms and lobbies are quite concerned about the winners.

Competition policy is a combination of two irreconcilable forces. On the one hand, there is an argument for the (spatial) concentration of business, which rationalises production and enables economies of scale. On the other hand, there is a case for an antitrust policy,[27] which prevents monopolisation, protects individual freedom and rights and, through increased competition, increases welfare. The challenge for governments is to achieve and maintain a dynamic balance between these two tendencies. They need to keep the best parts of each of the two opposing tendencies, profit from the harmonious equilibrium between the two, avoid excessive regulation that interferes with the freedom to contract which may impair competitiveness, and employ competition policy as a tool to increase the standard of living.

As a term, free market is almost an oxymoron. Such a system may operate 'as is expected' even in theory only if there is a system of well-developed, accepted and enforced rules, regulations, codes and conventions.[28] Even a self-declared, smug, free market-prone, democratic and liberal government such as the one in the US has awesome power, as they have no qualms about reminding everyone both at home and abroad. In any case, a relatively 'free market' has been so far the most efficient economic organisation model. However, there are a number of admirable types. One size does not fit all here and at all times. It cannot be mechanically and swiftly transplanted elsewhere with success like flu. Apart from the American model,[29] there are others which include those in the Scandinavian countries,[30] France, Germany, Switzerland, Canada or Asia. Both pluralism and specific discipline operate in each of these market systems. All of them slowly evolved over many centuries and shaped the form, significance and influence of national political, economic and social institutions through providing opportunities, learning, imitation, selection and reward. These cannot be mechanically and swiftly transplanted.

Regional integration arrangements widen markets for the participating countries, hence one of their first dynamic effects is in the field of competition. Therefore, the EU has its own rules for market behaviour. They refer to the restriction of competition, abuse of the dominant position and state aids. The importance of the competition policy was enhanced by the Single European Market Programme, completed in 1992.

Monopoly

In a perfectly competitive market, the marginal revenue (MR) curve of a firm is a straight line (Figure 2.6). No firm can influence the market price. Each firm is a price taker.[31] Hence, the MR curve of every firm equals the market price. In a simple model with linear demand, cost and revenue curves, the MR curve passes through the horizontal axis 0Q (representing

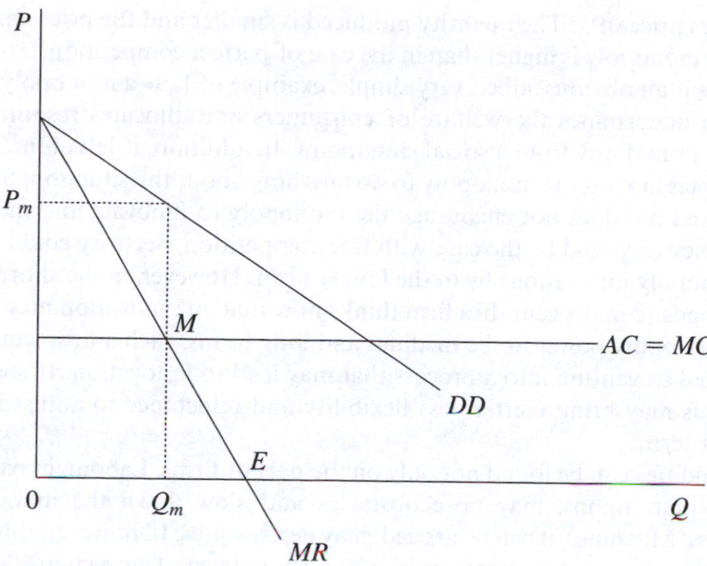

Figure 2.6 Welfare effects of a monopoly

the quantity produced) at point E. At this point, MR is zero. To the left of E on the horizontal axis, MR is positive and in moving from 0 to E, total revenue increases. To the right of E on the same axis, MR is negative, and in moving from E to Q, total revenue decreases. At E, total revenue is at a maximum.

The market structure of a monopolistic industry is at the opposite extreme from perfect competition. Entry into such an industry is costly, risky and time-consuming, although potentially highly profitable in the short and medium terms. Whereas in a state of perfect competition no firm has any power whatsoever over the market price, a monopoly (exclusive) supplier has the power to influence the market price of a good or a service if there are no substitutes. To counter such conduct, governments may choose to intervene and prevent/rectify such non-competitive behaviour. This can be done by regulation of the behaviour of monopolies and/or by liberalisation of imports.[32] A monopolist which wanted to maximise total revenue would never supply a quantity bigger than 0E.

With constant returns to scale, average costs are constant, hence the average cost (AC) curve is horizontal. The consequence of this simplification is that marginal costs (MC) equal AC. This enables the point to be found at which profit is at its maximum if demand curve is DD. It is maximised at point M, where MR = MC. At that point, a monopolist produces $0Q_m$ and charges price $0P_m$. The quantity produced is smaller and the price charged by the monopoly is higher than in the case of perfect competition.

This is an obvious, albeit very simple, example of how a monopoly (or a cartel) undermines the welfare of consumers and allocates resources in a suboptimal way from a social standpoint. In addition, if left alone, there is no pressure on the monopoly to do anything about the situation. Such a sheltered life does not encourage the monopoly to innovate and increase efficiency as would be the case with free competition. Security could make a monopoly innovation shy in the longer term. However, in the short term the opposite may occur. If a firm thinks now that an innovation may bring it a monopoly power in the medium and long terms, such a firm would be tempted to venture into a process that may lead to innovation. If successful, this may bring inertia, less flexibility and reluctance to adjust in the longer term.

Rigidities can be found not only on the part of firms. Labour, in particular labour unions, may pose obstacles and slow down the innovation process. Machines, it can be argued, may destroy jobs. If, however, this were ever true, it may be correct only in the short term. The response of the Luddites in the early 19th century to the introduction of looms and spinning jennies was to destroy them. Technological progress, increased productivity and alternative sources of employment, often requiring a superior skills profile, more than compensate for any supposed short-term social loss. Only those who are reluctant to adjust to the new situation suffer. Although technology has advanced rapidly in recent centuries, unemployment has not risen with it. Increases in productivity, output and job openings have risen together over the long term.

If a monopoly exists, one should not rush to the conclusion that its presence per se leads to economic inefficiency. It is possible that in industries with high entry barriers, enormous sunk costs and economies of scale (for example, the aerospace industry) a single efficient producer may sell the good or a service at a lower price than would be charged by many inefficient producers in the same industry. In such cases it may not be a smart move to break up a concentrated industry. The authorities would be better taxing the excessive profits of firms in such industries and/or making sure that they are reinvested. If the market grows sufficiently, then the authorities need to encourage other, potentially efficient and profitable, producers to enter the same kind of business.

More than a century ago, it was feared in the US that the concentration of economic influence could create possibilities for strengthening political power as well. The industries in question were steel, oil and tobacco. The Sherman Act of 1890 was a reaction to such fears. This act forbade monopolisation of any business in the US. Its intention was not only to prevent political influence by the business, but also to ensure that there was rivalry in innovation and opportunities for new firms. However, one has to note that under President George W. Bush the political power of big firms has never been greater in the US than it is today.

Policies intended to increase competitiveness sometimes produce unexpected results. During the 1950s, the US government wanted to break up large and powerful corporations. One such corporation was AT&T. Little attention was paid during the debate to the position of Bell Labs and the fact that it had played the major part in innovation in telecommunications over the preceding century. Deregulation of the industry prohibited the US telephone operating companies from making phones or switching equipment. As a result, US exports grew moderately, while imports exploded (Lipsey, 1992b, p. 295).

From the above examples stem arguments in favour of a competition policy. The intention of this policy is to improve efficiency in the use of factors with the objective of increasing welfare. However, in a real market situation that is full of imperfections (economies of scale, externalities, sunk costs, innovation, asymmetric information and so on) one may easily find arguments in favour of a certain concentration of production (mergers) and protection of intellectual property rights.[33]

Five computer companies accused Microsoft of unfair business practices in the US in 1998. The court found in 2000 that Microsoft, the world's biggest software company, was guilty of antitrust violations and of monopolistic behaviour in the software market. This is another case that has generated a lot of hot air. The judge decreed that Microsoft should be split into two companies: one to develop and produce the operating system (Windows) and the other that would be involved with the application packages (Office, Internet Explorer and so on). The real outcome could be the creation of two monopolies instead of one!

At the heart of the debate is the issue of capacity to innovate. There was a risk that Microsoft would limit the ability of third parties to innovate. The problem with splitting the company is that numerous operating systems and applications may emerge. However, the potential for customer confusion that could result may be exaggerated, as there is a strong commercial incentive to maintain compatibility. In addition, Microsoft was charged with exhibiting monopolistic behaviour such as operating exclusion contracts, as well as increasing sales by raising the price of older versions of software after the launch of a new version.

Microsoft duly appealed against such a judgment and argued that regulators have no right to meddle or determine which features software companies should bundle into their products in order to increase their functionality. This is particularly important in a dynamic and highly innovative industry. While bundling may bring certain gains, it also makes it harder for competitors to offer innovative services. Several questions immediately come to mind:

- Is it smart to allow (or drive) an innovative firm such as Microsoft to spend as much on legal issues as it spends on R&D?
- In the 'new economy' based on and driven by knowledge, a firm that innovates gains a temporary monopoly power. Another firm with a superior product that creates a new temporary and 'fragile' monopoly replaces this firm. Hence, the new economy may have more (fragile) monopolies than the 'old economy'. If such dynamics encourages innovation and improvement, consumers can benefit. Should one encourage such market dynamics or not? When should regulation step in? How?
- Where is the balance between innovation and standardisation (which may stifle innovation)?
- Where is the balance between intellectual property rights and the wider public interest?
- How does all this affect the long-term interests of the consumers?

There are no sound data for a thorough cost–benefit analysis in such cases. Data are also missing to assess long-term interests of consumers in an industry that is at the frontier of innovation. This requires a very fine judgment and anyone who is confident of providing a clear-cut answer risks ridicule. Solving such issues may not easily fit into predetermined charts and models. Those that handle competition policy should also rely on their finer instincts. In any case, the basic principles and instincts in this area should include a preference for competition over monopoly, pluralism and spread over concentration, as well as new entrants over incumbents.

The appeals court in the US confirmed the earlier ruling that Microsoft was a monopoly, but it rejected the remedy of breaking up the company. A settlement was reached with the Department of Justice in 2001. Microsoft had to: allow PC makers to replace some parts of Windows by alternatives made by other firms; reveal certain codes to ensure that software written by other firms operates smoothly; and have its operation monitored by an (enigmatic) three-man committee of experts.[34] As a declared monopoly, Microsoft is vulnerable to legal actions in the future.

The US case against Microsoft was brought because the company wanted to do away with competitors such as Netscape (does anyone still remember it?). The European Commission is also investigating Microsoft. The case is linked with the bundling of Media Player in the Windows XP operating system, as well as the smooth/rough link between PCs and servers that run Windows (users have to make a choice regarding which server to install). Microsoft's position is that consumers want products with more features. This brings improved interoperability, and also, Microsoft may argue, lower prices. In addition, if Media Player is unbundled from Windows, then this may raise queries such as whether one should take out printer drivers, graphics, spellcheckers, Internet browsers and so on. On the other hand, if Microsoft produces all that is required, where does that leave other firms?

When the European Commission found in 2004 that Microsoft abused its near-monopoly market position, the company faced a fine of €497 million (one of the biggest ever imposed on a single company) and a request to separate Windows from Media Player software. Some allege that this initial fine took into account Microsoft's global operations.[35] Microsoft's legal battle against this ruling could last about five years, so some Microsoft competitors may not survive to see its conclusion. In the meantime, the market situation may change, hence there may be serious doubts and little evidence that the case against Microsoft could have favourable effects on competition and on consumers. It is also a difficult task to provide evidence on what would have happened had the European Commission let Microsoft enjoy its near-monopoly position.

The American procedure in antitrust cases is carried out in courts that permit open challenge of the arguments. The same procedure (at least initially) in the EU takes place behind closed doors in the European Commission, which acts as prosecutor, judge, jury and executioner. The complex history of the Microsoft case in the US courts reveals that there is no consistency in the principles applied even without a single legal system. Therefore, if there are various regulators throughout the world, this should facilitate a harmonisation of principles and practices. Even a global competition authority may be a good option to be considered.

The obvious causes of ineffectiveness of antitrust policy include the following (Crandall and Winston, 2003, p. 23):

- The excessive duration of court cases. The particular issue that is focused on may easily evolve into something different over time. By the time the case is resolved, it may be of little relevance.
- Difficulties in formulating effective remedies.
- Difficulties in ascertaining which potentially anticompetitive act or instance may jeopardise consumer welfare.
- Rapid change in technology, intellectual property and dynamic competition relentlessly increase challenges of formulating and implementing effective antitrust policy.

- Political influences about which antitrust cases are initiated, settled or dropped.

It is sometimes argued that it is quite costly to trade intangible technology assets at arm's length because 'it is a combination of skills, equipment and organisation embodied in people and institutions as much as in machinery and equipment' (Sharp and Pavitt, 1993, p. 147). If an inventor fears that his/her patent rights[36] are not sufficiently protected (enforcement, length of the patent right, level of penalties), he/she will keep the innovation secret or be disinclined to participate in R&D in the future. Once created, certain types of knowledge can readily be passed on to others at sometimes little cost. If this innovation cannot be protected, it cannot be sold. For example, Albert Einstein (1879–1955), an ordinary clerk at the Zurich Patent Office and a sloppy student at Eidgenössische Technische Hochschule Zürich (ETHZ) (the Swiss Federal Institute of Technology Zurich), devised with his senior fellow student Mileva Marić (who became his first wife from 1903 to 1919) the general theory of relativity. He was awarded the Nobel Prize in 1921 (he kept the honour, but gave the money to Marić). 'This led to the university appointment that had previously eluded him, and thereafter Einstein worked in universities. Einstein was honored wherever he went. But he never became a rich man' (Kay, 2004, p. 266).

A part of the innovation process may lean towards outcomes that may not be easily imitated. A conflict between static and dynamic efficiency in production, as well as between the welfare of producers and consumers, is obvious. As technology becomes older and is no longer at the core of the business activities of the innovator, it becomes more likely that the innovator will disseminate the technology, intellectual property rights, goodwill and know-how through licensing.

The appropriation of returns from innovation is not a major problem if the innovator is a non-profit institution such as a research institute, university or government. Non-profit-making innovators are most likely to make their findings public and, in fact, these may be disseminated immediately. OECD countries allocated about $680 billion (about 2.2 per cent of overall GDP) to R&D in 2003. The US accounted for 42 per cent of the OECD total. This represented about the same as the combined total of the EU (30 per cent) and Japan (16 per cent). The business community was the principal source of finance of R&D in OECD countries in the same year. Its contribution was 62 per cent of the total (most of the balance came from the government).[37] However, this contribution varies among countries. The private sector financed 73 per cent of R&D in Japan, 63 per cent in the US and 55 per cent in the EU. Most of the R&D activity in the OECD countries, about 70 per cent, takes place in private firms (OECD, 2005). R&D

expenditure as a share of the GDP in the EU(15) was 1.92 per cent in 1999, which increased to 1.99 per cent in 2002. In spite of this increase, the gap between the US and Japan on the one hand, and the EU on the other, was not narrowed. The US devoted 2.80 per cent of its GDP to R&D in 2002, while Japan allocated 2.98 per cent in the same year.[38]

The problem of appropriation arises when there is a conflict between public interest in the spread of information and knowledge, and private interest in holding and employing that knowledge for lucrative purposes. If private knowledge acquired through risky investment of resources is not protected, at least for some period of time, there will be little incentive to generate innovations that drive efficiency and, hence, contribute to future growth. A sound knowledge-based economy demands strong protection of intellectual property.

An analysis by Levin et al. (1987) of alternative ways of protecting the competitive (monopolistic) advantages of new and improved processes and products found that patents are the least effective means for appropriating returns. Lead time over competitors,[39] a fast-track learning curve (unit costs of production fall as output increases over time) and sales/service effort were regarded by the surveyed firms as providing better returns than patents. Firms may sometimes refrain from patenting products or processes to avoid revealing the facts or details of innovation because of the possible disclosure of information to competitors and imitators. At the same time, firms have every incentive to advertise the benefits of new or improved products and disseminate them to consumers. Therefore, secrecy about innovation is both difficult and undesirable. It may be better to be concerned about the creation of future business secrets than to worry about the protection of existing ones.

Additional profits can accrue from the production of complementary assets (cameras and films; recorders and tapes/discs). Therefore, not only innovation and manufacturing (technological leadership), but also, and equally important, distribution and after-sales service (commercial leadership) are of great advantage in capturing markets and profits.[40] In the fields of cameras, audio and video goods (and some segments of the car market) Japanese companies have virtually ousted most of their international competitors and changed the international geography of production in these industries[41] through an uninterrupted tide of technical improvements and distribution/service networks.

The benefits of increased competition will materialise only if firms compete and do not collude to avoid competition. Competition stimulates innovation. It may, in turn, bring new technologies with large sunk costs, geographical concentration of production and other entry barriers. If this is the case, then neither unfettered markets nor monopolies (oligopolies) should be ignored. Otherwise, consumer welfare would be distorted and allocation of resources may take place in a suboptimal way from a social standpoint. Hence, there is a need for a competition policy, not only in the market of a single country, but also in a much larger area. This area is generally limited by the geographical space where economic cycles are in step. The rule of law, based in part on economic theory, may modify market distortions both in single countries and in integration groups.

Concept

One of the most obvious initial effects of international economic integration is the improvement in efficiency in the use of factors due to increased competition in the geographically enlarged and secured market. In this context, competitiveness of firms has two aspects: national and international. In both cases, a competitive firm is one that is able to make a profit without being protected and/or subsidised. This means that the output of a firm (goods and/or services) is in demand and is produced at the right time, in the right quantity and quality, as well as being superior to the output of most of its competitors. The goods and services of a country are internationally competitive if they are able to withstand free and fair competition on the world market while, at the same time, the country's inhabitants maintain and increase their standard of living on average and in the long term.

There are three concepts related to competitiveness:

- *Cost competitiveness* addresses the difference (that is, profit) between the price at which a good is sold and the cost of its production. If a firm is able to reduce the costs of production by reducing input prices, innovation and/or organising production and marketing in a more efficient way that is not available to its competitors, it may improve its relative profit margin.
- A firm has a *price-competitive* product if it matches other firms' products in all characteristics, including price. This type of competitiveness can be improved if the firm unilaterally reduces the price of its good (other things being equal) and/or upgrades its attributes and provides a better service.
- *Relative profitability* exists when there is the possibility of geographical price discrimination (for example, between domestic and foreign markets). The different profit margins in these markets indicate relative profitability.

The measurement of the competitiveness of an integrated group of countries includes the intra-group trade ratio (intra-group export/intra-group import) and extra-group trade ratio (extra-group export/extra-group import). In addition, the competitiveness of an integrated country's economic sector (or industries within it) may be measured in the following two ways.

First, the *trade specialisation index* (TSI) provides details about the integrated country *j*'s specialisation in exports in relation to other partner countries in the group. If this index for good *i* is greater than 1, country *j* is specialised in the export of good *i* within the group. TSI (equation (2.2)) reveals country *j*'s comparative advantage within the group. The conceptual problem with this approach is that the structure of exports may vary because of a change in domestic consumption that may not alter either the volume or the composition of domestic output.

$$\mathrm{TSI} = \frac{(X_{i,j}/X_{\mathrm{ind},j})}{(X_{i,g}/X_{\mathrm{ind},g})} \tag{2.2}$$

where:

$X_{i,j}$ = export of good *i* from country *j* to the partner countries in the integration group;
$X_{\mathrm{ind},j}$ = total industry exports to the group from country *j*;
$X_{i,g}$ = intra-group exports of good *i*;
$X_{\mathrm{ind},g}$ = total industry exports within the group *g*.

Second, the *production specialisation index* (PSI) is identical to the TSI, except that export (X) variables are replaced by production (P) ones. PSI shows where country *j* is more specialised in production than its integration partners. This index reveals country *j*'s production advantage as well as its domestic consumption pattern. Interpretation of both the TSI and the PSI may be distorted if the production and export of good *i* in country *j* is protected/subsidised. The revealed 'advantage' would be misleading, as in the case of exports of farm goods from the EU because of the CAP.

Goods that are produced and traded by a country may be categorised by their economic idiosyncrasies. There are five, sometimes overlapping, types of goods (Audretsch, 1993, pp. 94–5):

- Ricardo goods have high natural resource content. These commodities include minerals, fuels, wood, paper, fibres and food.
- Product-cycle goods include those that rely on high technology and where information serves as a crucial input.[42] This group includes chemicals, pharmaceuticals, plastics, dyes, fertilisers, explosives, machinery, aircraft and instruments.

- R&D-intensive goods include industries where R&D expenditure is at least 5 per cent of the sales value. These are pharmaceuticals, office machinery, aircraft and telecom goods.
- High-advertising goods are the ones where advertising expenditures are at least 5 per cent of the sales value. These include drinks, cereals, soaps, perfumes and watches.
- Goods that are produced by high-concentration industries include tobacco, liquid fuels, edible oils, tubes, home appliances, motor vehicles and railway equipment.

Audretsch (ibid., pp. 95–6) made a geographical comparison of these five types of goods. The comparison was for the 1975–83 period among the rich western countries (mainly the OECD), poor western countries (mainly the south European countries) and then the centrally planned countries of central and eastern Europe. The findings were as follows:

- In 1975, western countries had a comparative disadvantage in the Ricardo goods while the other two groups had a comparative advantage. By 1983, central and east European countries, together with the rich western countries, were exhibiting a comparative disadvantage in Ricardo goods, reflecting their inability to compete with resource-rich developing countries.
- The rich western countries have a constant comparative advantage in product-cycle, R&D-intensive and advertising-intensive goods over the other two groups of countries.
- Rich western, as well as central and east European, countries have a competitive advantage in highly concentrated industries over the poor western nations.

Whereas competition in goods is more or less global, competition in many services is localised. A large part of competitive activity in manufactured goods has a price component; competition in many services has, predominantly, a non-price dimension. Reputation and past experience of services often play a crucial role in choosing a supplier for a certain type of service. Local providers of some services and those with a recognised (international) reputation have a specific market power. Local market influence on producers of goods is in most cases non-existent as goods may be (easily) traded across space. Because the service industries are generally subjected to a lower degree of competitiveness than the manufacturing industries and as a result of legislation designed to protect consumers, administrative regulation in the services sector is quite high.

The competitiveness of a country's goods and services may be increased through depreciation of a home currency and/or by a reduction in wages. The best way to increase competitiveness, however, is to increase productivity. Developing, intermediate and advanced countries trade more or less successfully all over the world, but their standard of living depends on their productivity. However, the ability to trade depends only on the ability to produce something that is wanted by consumers, while the rate of exchange ensures that exports can be sold. This was Ricardo's message in the early 19th century and it is as important (and as little understood) today as it was in his time (Lipsey, 1993c, p. 21).

The new theory of trade and strategic industrial policy (initiated in the early 1980s) argues that, with imperfect competition, there are no unique solutions to economic problems.[43] The outcome depends on assumptions about the conduct of economic agents. There is a strong possibility that in a situation with imperfect competition, firms are able to make above-average profits (rents). Intervention in fields of trade, competition and industry may, under certain conditions, geographically redistribute these rents in favour of domestic firms. This rent shifting is the main feature of strategic trade and industrial policies. Hence, there is an assumption about the 'strategic interdependence' among firms. This means that profits of one firm are directly affected by the individual strategy choices of other firms and such a relation is understood by the firms (Brander, 1995, p. 1397). The strategic trade policy of beggar thy neighbour ('war' over economic rents) does not occur in the situation of either pure monopoly or perfect competition. This policy may look like a zero-sum game, where many lose in the long term through a chain of retaliations and counter-retaliations. However, 'countries that would otherwise compete with each other at the level of strategic policy have an incentive to make agreements that would ameliorate or prevent such rivalries' (ibid., pp. 1447–8).

There is, potentially, at least one good reason for intervention.[44] With externalities, spillovers and geographical clustering of production, governments may find reasons to protect initially some growing, often high-technology industries that depend on economies of scale. These are the industries for which accumulated knowledge is the prime source of competitiveness and whose expenditure on R&D, and employment of engineers and scientists, is (well) above the average for the economy. Sunk costs and R&D may be funded by governments, as the positive effects of introducing new technology are felt throughout the economy and beyond the confines of the firm or industry that introduces it. The whole world may benefit, in some cases, from new technology whose development was supported by government intervention. For example, spaceships had to be equipped with computers, which needed to be powerful, small and light.

A spillover from the development of this kind of equipment was the creation of personal computers. Therefore, the new theory goes, with externalities and under certain dubious conditions (no retaliation, well-informed governments[45]), intervention may be a positive-sum game where everyone potentially gains in the long run. Critics of the new theory have not been able to prove it wrong, but argue that it is not necessarily correct. In fact, what is not understood is that the new theory provides only a programme for research, rather than a prescription for policy (Krugman, 1993b, p. 164).

Market Structure

A market for a good or a service is said to be contestable if there is a smooth entry and exit route for a firm. The number of firms in the market should be 'sufficient' to prevent a single firm or group of firms from increasing prices and making rents (super-normal profits). Relative ease of entering the business would prevent the incumbent firms from charging exorbitant prices. The opportunity of making high rents would immediately attract new entrants. Geographical extensions of the market (economic integration) reinforce potentials for pro-competition market behaviour.

Imagine a situation with two identical countries A and B, one good X and no trade. Assume also a monopoly in country A, and free competition in country B in the market for the same good. One can reasonably expect that prices for good X are lower in country B. If one now introduces free trade between the two countries, country B would export good X to country A. This example shows that a pure difference in market structure between the countries may explain the geographical location of production and trade, even though the countries may have identical production technologies and factor endowments. This crucial aspect has been overlooked by the classical theory of spatial economics.

Competition policies may be classified according to the structure–conduct–performance (SCP) paradigm. The thrust of the SCP paradigm is that performance in a defined market depends on the interaction between the structure of the market and the conduct of buyers and sellers in it.

- *Structure* refers to the organisation of production and distribution, that is, which enterprises are permitted to enter into which business activities. It determines the number and size of buyers and sellers; product differentiation; and relationships (horizontal and vertical integration) between buyers and sellers.

- *Conduct* describes how firms behave in their business. This refers to the competitive strategy of suppliers such as (predatory) pricing, innovation, advertising and investment.
- *Performance* refers to the goals of economic organisation such as efficiency, technological progress, availability of goods and full employment of resources.

The most common indicator of market structure or the degree of competition is the proportion of industry output, sales, investment or employment attributable to a subset (usually three to ten) of all firms in the industry. It shows the force of the competitive pressure on the incumbents. If this ratio is relatively high, then it illustrates that market power is concentrated in relatively few firms.

It is, however, important to be cautious when dealing with these ratios. While an employment concentration ratio may indicate a monopoly situation, a sales concentration ratio may not. Competitiveness is linked not only to market shares, but, as a dynamic phenomenon, to the relative growth of productivity, innovation, R&D, size and quality of the capital stock, mobility of resources, operational control, success in shifting out of declining lines of business, education of management, training of labour, incentives and so on. These ratios do, however, provide a useful, if second-best, barometer of the oligopolistic restriction of competition.

The Hirschman–Herfindahl index (HHI) is an alternative and more complete measure of market structure than the concentration ratio. It is increasingly being used in the public fight against oligopolies.

$$\mathrm{HHI} = \sum S_i^2 \times 100. \qquad (2.3)$$

The HHI (equation (2.3)) is the sum of squared market shares of each firm in the defined market. It is between 0 and 100. The index is 100 when there is a monopoly, while it is relatively small in competitive industries. The HHI takes account of all firms (that is, both their absolute number and relative difference in size) in the defined market, whereas the concentration ratio accounts only for a select number of firms in the same market. Antitrust lawyers still place much weight on the HHI. However, economists are increasingly sceptical about its value. Although some economists use the HHI as an initial screening tool, it is more useful to consider how easy it is for new and potentially efficient firms to enter the target market. New firms are attracted to enter an industry by the potential for new profit lures. Estimates of the ease and likelihood of new firms entering an industry are inevitably highly speculative.

Integration may provoke several scenarios regarding market structure. On the one hand, an increase in industrial concentration may arise from firms' decisions to take advantage of economies of scale and intra-industry production linkages. Economies of scope[46] may also increase geographical concentration because they favour diversified firms which are often large. On the other hand, smaller firms may benefit, as in Japan or in Germany, because they may be included in the network of large ones. In addition, reduced trade costs make it easier for smaller firms to penetrate into the markets of partner countries. This may reduce concentration.

Firms compete through product differentiation, innovation, quality, R&D, advertising and special close links with suppliers, clients and various institutions, as well as on price. The exceptions are, of course, raw materials and certain standardised semi-finished goods. In spite of trendy talk about the 'global economy' and the diminishing role played by specific geographical locations for business, competitive advantages are often heavily local. These gains come from the clustering of highly specialised knowledge and skills and the existence of rivals, sophisticated customers and institutions in a specific geographical area (Porter, 1998a). Even though many of these advantages are external to individual firms, they are internal to the cluster in which they locate their operations.

Major changes in the capacity of a firm that are linked to high sunk costs do not take place frequently. However, it is more difficult to test the impact of non-price rivalry such as competitors' R&D, innovation, design activities and non-technical matters such as management and marketing than their prices. It also takes longer to retaliate in these areas than to change prices (Schmalensee, 1988, p. 670).

Innovation

The process of technological change is driven by several factors, including the following five:

- The existence of unexploited lucrative opportunities for the solution of problems such as the transformation of electricity into sound or light into electricity.
- Changes in government regulation such as changes in technical and safety standards (including concerns about the environment) and trade policy.
- The change in prices (relative scarcity) of raw materials, energy, labour or transport and communication.
- Clients with the toughest demands may set in motion the innovation process. Search for a challenge and rivalry, rather than staying away

from them, inspires innovation. The same holds for regular contacts with research centres.

- A change in consumers' needs, tastes, sophistication and fickleness. Increases in income and decreased working time increase the demand for leisure and entertainment. At the same time, more stressful work takes its toll on workers' health, increasing demand for medical and rehabilitation services.

Innovation is the principal activity for economic growth. It brings new ideas and enlarges the stock of knowledge that in turn enhances productivity. Patents are linked with innovation as they provide the means to reward someone who comes up with a worthy commercial idea.

The innovation process has four distinct but interrelated phases:

- *invention*: discovery of something new which can 'work';
- *innovation*: translation of invention into commercial use;
- *spread*: diffusion in the market; and
- *absorption*: learning from clients and conversion into a public good.

If, because of a change in circumstances (for example, integration), firms innovate (that is, realise their technological, organisational and control potentials and capabilities to develop, produce and sell goods and services) and introduce new technologies and new goods/services in order to maintain or improve their market position, then efficiency overall may increase. From a given set of resources one may expect to achieve more and/or better-quality output. This directly increases national welfare on average. In fact, for a small or medium-sized country, integration enables economic development and progress at a lower cost than does autarky.

There is, however, an opposing force. When there are market imperfections, such as economies of scale and externalities, firms make rents. Free competition leads to concentration and agglomeration, which may reduce competition in the future. The new theory of trade and strategic industrial policy holds that there may be fierce competition even among a few firms. Examples include the aircraft industry, the long-distance telephone call market and the Japanese market for electronic goods (largely confined to half a dozen domestic conglomerates). Technical innovations prompt legal and policy innovations. The telephone business, for example, was for a very long time considered to be a 'natural monopoly'. Nowadays, it is a highly competitive industry.

Innovation changes the mix of factors that are used in the production and/or consumption of goods and services. Usually, an innovation brings a reduction in the quantity of factors needed to produce a good or service,

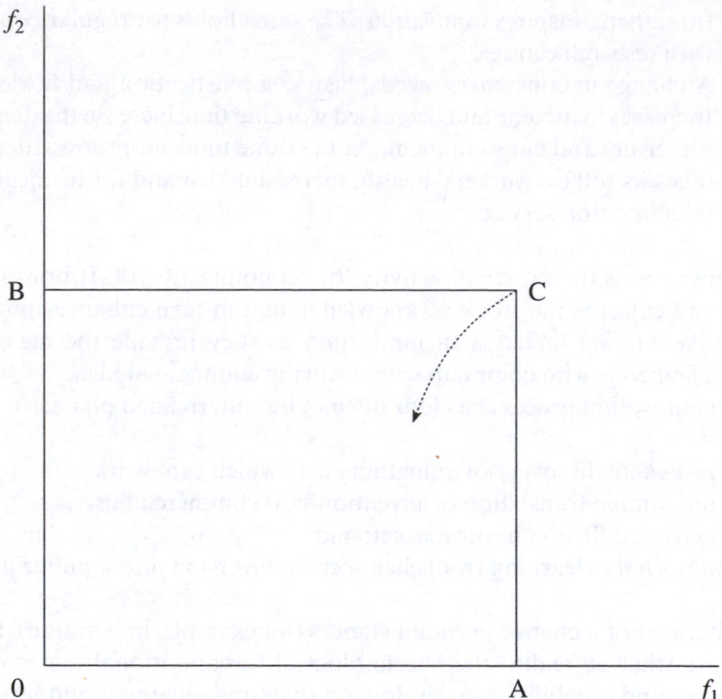

Figure 2.7 Effects of innovation on the use of factors

as shown by an arrow in Figure 2.7. This makes output cheaper and, consequently, more competitive. Suppose that the production of a good requires two factors, f_1 and f_2. If production requires, per unit of output, 0A of factor f_1 and 0B of factor f_2, then the resource required to produce the good is represented by rectangle 0ACB. Innovation normally reduces the area of rectangle 0ACB (note the direction of the arrow). However, the market receptiveness to take up new products depends on the cost, convenience in use, as well as culture. If, however, one factor, such as oil or some other raw material, suddenly becomes scarce, innovation may reduce the consumption of that factor, but disproportionally increase (at least temporarily) the requirement for the other factor. Hence, in such a special case, the area of the rectangle 0ACB may increase as the result of innovation.

Economic integration opens up and secures the markets of the integrated countries to local firms. It is reasonable to expect competition to have a positive effect on innovation, but what are the effects of such a process in the long term?

- If innovation *spreads* geographically, and if it increases competition, then competition and innovation reinforce each other.
- If, however, innovation becomes *centralised* over time and space because it is costly, uncertain and risky so that only a few large firms can undertake it, then geographical extension of markets would have a positive effect on innovation only in the short term.

It is therefore necessary to ensure that immediate positive effects continue in the long term (Geroski, 1988, pp. 377–9). In order to maintain the 'necessary' level of competition within the integrated area, the countries involved may decide to reduce the level of common external tariff and NTBs.

The impact of competition is not restricted to prices and costs. Competition also yields other favourable effects. It stimulates technical progress, widens consumer choice, improves the quality of goods and services and rationalises the organisation of firms. It is important to remember that firms seldom lose out to competitors because their product is overpriced or because their production capacity is insufficient; rather, they lose because they fail to develop and/or introduce new products and production processes as well or as quickly as their competitors (Lipsey, 1993a, p. 18). If a firm does not make its own product obsolete through innovation, some other entrepreneur will. The 'prospect theory' of psychology explains that individuals are more hurt by a loss than they are encouraged by gains of equal size, that is, fear of loss is often more powerful than the expectation of gain.

The innovation process is sometimes accidental, but always uncertain and risky. It is often linked with serendipity.[47] For example, in 1970, Spencer Silver, a research chemist at 3M, was working in the area of adhesive technology. His goal was to produce the strongest glue on the market and his reputation was ruined when he developed a product that was quite the opposite. He did, however, discover that his new glue could be used again and did not leave any traces on the surface to which it was applied. He tried for a decade to find an application for his glue, but there was no interest at 3M. However, Silver had a friend, Arthur Fry, who was a singer in his local church choir. Every Sunday he inserted slips of paper into his hymnbook to mark the pages of the hymns to be sung during the service. And every Sunday the slips would fall out as he opened the book. Fry remembered Silver's 'futile' invention and applied it to the slips of paper, which stayed in place. A year later, in 1981, 3M started producing the now omnipresent 'Post-it' notes (Hillman and Gibbs, 1998, p. 183).[48]

As a result of relentless innovation, techniques that are used in the production process change constantly. But innovation changes not only the method of production of goods and services but also our values and the way we live. For example, Hollywood films changed how we lived and worked, how we saw the world, even how young people courted (in cars, away from the eyes of parents and chaperones). Or the short-message system (SMS) on mobile phones and e-mail altered the nightlife of the young, as well as single persons throughout the world. These changes can be minor or revolutionary. Lipsey (1993b, pp. 3–4) described four levels of innovation:

- *Incremental innovation*: a series of changes, each small, but with a large cumulative effect.
- *Radical innovations*: major but discontinuous changes such as the development of a new material (for example, plastic), a new source of power or new products (aircraft, computer or laser).
- *Changes in the technology system*: changes that affect an economic sector and industries within it, such as the changes that occurred in the chemical and related industries in the 19th century.
- *Technological revolution*: innovations that change the whole techno-economic paradigm.[49]

Innovation is an important economic driver. It will be the basis of competition in the future and will continue to affect the location of production. Production and use of electricity, as well as information technology are probably the most important invented general purpose technologies. Electricity is universally accepted and applied. Its effects are known. The same is not yet fully the case with information technology.

In the field of personal computers, for example, the greatest competition is no longer between assembly companies such as Compaq, IBM, Toshiba and Dell, but between companies operating in the area of added value, such as microprocessors, dominated by Intel, and operating software, where Microsoft, through its Windows program, reigns supreme. Market advantage for critical elements of the system is often held in the form of intellectual property (Borrus and Zysman, 1997; Zysman and Schwartz, 1998, p. 409).

There is, however, no simple answer to the question of whether international economic integration (extension of the market) stimulates or prevents innovation. There are two opposing views. First, a monopoly organisation has a secure market for its output. It can anticipate reaping normal or supernormal profits (rents) from any innovation. It is therefore easier for such a firm to innovate than one that does not have such market security. On the other hand, with no competitive pressure, a monopolist company may not feel the need to innovate. The sense of long-term stability fosters a conservative way of thinking that may restrict innovative activity. Monopolists may not wish to 'rock the boat' and can prevent or delay the implementation of innovations of their own production or developed by others.

The huge increases in income and living standards that have been seen over the past 250 years, particularly in the western world, are the consequence of several factors. At the end of the 17th century there was a strong convergence between the theoretical understanding of science and the application of that knowledge. A critical mass of knowledge in the fields of mathematics and mechanics was accumulated and applied to the understanding of atmospheric pressure and the invention of the steam engine. This provided the foundation for a technological revolution that resulted in a 150-year period of radical innovation in the areas of transport (rail and water), textiles, mining, tools, metallurgy and food processing.

Most inventions originated in a small group of countries, and this group has remained relatively stable over a long period of time. There is a clear geographical localisation of innovation activities. During the Industrial Revolution, Britain led the way, joined by Germany, the US, France, Switzerland and Sweden in the second half of the 19th century. Membership of this select group of countries has been stable for over a century. The only major newcomer to the group was Japan just after the Second World War, although a few newly industrialised countries, such as South Korea and Taiwan, also joined this exclusive club.[50]

Patents may be used as a helpful proxy of innovation and technological performance. However, one needs to keep in mind the limitations and weaknesses of patents as markers of innovatory activity. There are a number of inventions that are not patented; many patents do not have any commercial application; and there are also differences in national patent rules which impede comparisons. Out of almost 100 000 patent applications to the European Patent Office in 1999 (Table 2.5), 47 per cent of the total originated in the EU, 28 per cent came from the US and 18 per cent from Japan. The biggest part of the EU patents, 21 per cent, came from Germany, which contributed more than Britain, France, Italy and the Netherlands together. Relative to population, the highest number of patents came from Switzerland, Finland, Germany and Sweden (in that order). The available data from the US Patent and Trademark Office reveal that more than half of all patents granted in the US (1977–2001) were domestic in origin.[51] According to these gross data, this means that the US is the most innovative economy in the world. It attracts and rewards creative individuals. The rest of the patents are highly concentrated in a relatively small group of 11 countries which comprises in descending order: Japan, Germany, France, Britain, Canada, Taiwan, Switzerland, Italy, Sweden, the Netherlands and South Korea.

A warning sign for the EU about a serious brain drain is that '40 per cent of the research community in the US are European graduates'.[52] The US looks after their talents well and rewards their originality and creativity.

Table 2.5 European Patent Office patent applications by priority year and by inventor's country of residence

	1991	1995	1999	Average annual growth rate (%)	Share in OECD applications to the EPO (%)			Number of EPO patent applications per million population		
				1991–99	1991	1995	1999	1991	1995	1999
Canada	548	805	1 493	13.3	0.93	1.19	1.50	19.6	27.4	48.9
Mexico	14	24	40	14.1	0.02	0.04	0.04	0.2	0.3	0.4
United States	17 401	21 005	28 109	6.2	29.45	30.98	28.32	68.7	78.9	100.7
Australia	399	487	885	10.5	0.67	0.72	0.89	22.9	26.8	46.4
Japan	11 804	12 191	17 454	5.0	19.98	17.98	17.58	95.3	97.1	137.8
Korea	168	453	972	24.6	0.28	0.67	0.98	3.9	10.0	20.9
New Zealand	44	64	135	15.2	0.07	0.09	0.14	12.5	17.5	35.5
Austria	655	670	1 043	6.0	1.11	0.99	1.05	83.9	83.2	128.9
Belgium	596	803	1 277	10.0	1.01	1.18	1.29	59.6	79.3	124.9
Czech Republic	28	19	60	9.9	0.05	0.03	0.06	2.7	1.8	5.8
Denmark	364	486	802	10.4	0.62	0.72	0.81	70.7	92.9	150.7
Finland	417	698	1 367	16.0	0.71	1.03	1.38	83.1	136.6	264.6
France	4 961	5 115	7 050	4.5	8.40	7.54	7.10	84.9	86.1	116.9
Germany	11 285	12 953	20 397	7.7	19.10	19.10	20.55	141.1	158.6	248.5
Greece	25	27	48	8.7	0.04	0.04	0.05	2.4	2.5	4.4
Hungary	56	54	107	8.4	0.09	0.08	0.11	5.4	5.3	10.5
Iceland	10	10	35	16.5	0.02	0.01	0.04	39.7	38.0	125.6
Ireland	64	96	216	16.5	0.11	0.14	0.22	18.1	26.6	57.5
Italy	2 285	2 468	3 638	6.0	3.87	3.64	3.67	40.3	43.1	63.1

Luxembourg	30	32	60	9.0	0.05	0.05	0.06	77.4	79.0	138.5
Netherlands	1 439	1 724	2 873	9.0	2.43	2.54	2.89	95.5	111.5	181.7
Norway	173	235	356	9.4	0.29	0.35	0.36	40.6	54.0	79.7
Poland	19	13	32	6.4	0.03	0.02	0.03	0.5	0.3	0.8
Portugal	10	14	36	16.7	0.02	0.02	0.04	1.1	1.4	3.5
Slovak Republic	0	7	15	–	0.00	0.01	0.02	0.0	1.3	2.9
Spain	322	386	714	10.5	0.55	0.57	0.72	8.3	9.9	18.0
Sweden	923	1 514	2 119	11.0	1.56	2.23	2.13	107.1	171.5	239.2
Switzerland	1 593	1 679	2 424	5.4	2.70	2.48	2.44	234.3	238.5	339.2
Turkey	4	5	22	22.8	0.01	0.01	0.02	0.1	0.1	0.3
United Kingdom	3 452	3 769	5 492	6.0	5.84	5.56	5.53	60.1	65.0	93.8
European Union	26 827	30 755	47 130	7.3	45.40	45.36	47.48	73.0	82.4	125.0
OECD Total	59 089	67 806	99 268	6.7	100.00	100.00	100.00	56.0	62.2	88.4
World	60 020	68 993	101 731	6.8						

Source: OECD, Patent database, May 2003.

The European Council in Lisbon (2000) declared a new strategic goal for the EU to become 'the most competitive and dynamic knowledge-based economy in the world capable of sustainable economic growth with more and better jobs and greater social cohesion'[53] by 2010, which seems to be quite a challenging and ambitious task. There are a few tough competitors for this position.

Why is innovation so concentrated? Europe was technologically backward and 'uncivilised' around the 11th century both by Chinese standards and by those in the Islamic world. What happened in these European countries in the 17th century and was allowed to continue undisturbed? Why did it not happen before? What prevented the Islamic world from continuing its innovative course after the 13th century or what prevented China from doing so after the 15th century? Evidence to support theories about these issues is still imperfect and controversial.[54] None the less, several overlapping factors may, in combination, provide a partial explanation.

- Willingness and readiness to accept and live with the change and adaptation (*values and culture*) are one element. Continuous change and self-reinforcing adaptation is essential to make a population and state wealthier. However, this needs to be coupled with investments and displacement of the mentality of self-sufficiency. Social institutions ought to be in place to streamline certain behaviour, even to interfere with our freedom of choice: to tax the consumption of things that many consider to be harmful such as spirits, tobacco and gambling; to prevent and outlaw production, trade and consumption of drugs; and to subsidise education, libraries and culture-related activities and institutions such as museums, operas and ballet.
- *Politics and vested interests* are often linked with resistances to change. All societies have tried to resist change at one time or another, but this is inevitably self-damaging and in vain in the long term. For example, ancient China looked with suspicion at new ideas introduced by foreigners. Indeed, the country's rulers often banned such innovations. In Florence, in 1299, bankers were forbidden from using Arabic numbers. And in Danzig (Gdansk) Anton Müller invented the ribbon loom in 1529. This invention, which produced six pieces of cloth at the same time, proved fatal for the inventor. The City Council, fearing the unemployment and pauperisation of a large part of the workforce, suppressed the use of the loom and ordered that Müller be secretly drowned. Elsewhere, Galileo Galilei (1564–1642) made discoveries with his telescope in 1610 that overturned the comprehension of the world. However, he could not persuade the inquisitors to take a look through his telescope. The inquisitors' ideology

persuaded them that what Galileo claimed to see was, according to their doctrine, not there. Some 350 years after Galileo's death, in 1992, Pope John Paul II gave an address on behalf of the Catholic Church in which he admitted that errors had been made by the theological advisors in the case of Galileo. He declared the Galileo case closed, but he did not admit that the Church was wrong to convict Galileo on a charge of heresy because of his belief that the earth rotates round the sun.

- In the successful countries, *institutions* that provided a favourable environment for innovation and growth were created. In Britain, for example, the Magna Carta of 1215 gave subjects the right to their own property. They were protected from the Crown, which until then had been entitled to seize property at random. In contrast, arbitrary confiscation continued to be common in the Muslim world and in Asia. In the western world, rulers quickly learned that a tax on property was more profitable than random confiscation, as tax proceeds continue to accrue indefinitely. In addition, there ought to be institutions that can accumulate, store, teach and extend scientific knowledge. Medieval universities in Europe, their libraries, scholars and teaching methods provided this relatively independent institutional framework. Even though China and the Muslim world had superb innovations and knowledge, they lacked such an institutional framework.[55] The outcome of all this was a social system in Europe that promoted innovation and growth more than any previous system. Britain was the leader in the actual commercialisation of scientific achievements and the first Industrial Revolution (roughly between 1750 and 1850). The reason was the understanding and application of Newtonian experimental and mechanical science (elsewhere in Europe science was more deductive and mathematics oriented at that time). In any case, in modern times the new institutions have almost eliminated the gap between frontline science and applied technology.
- The size of the *local market* (remember that integration increases the size of the market),[56] competition and supply of skills are important ingredients in the complex links between technological opportunities and entrepreneurial decisions. R&D plays a crucial role in the innovation process as it sustains a supply of knowledge.
- Another possible explanation for the relative constancy of countries that innovate most is that innovation reflects the *cumulative* and interrelated nature of acquired knowledge. Once it exists, knowledge does not cease to exist, and discovery builds on discovery. Knowledge has a non-rivalrous property. If someone uses it, it does not prevent others from using it. Innovation also reflects a change in technological

> capabilities and economic incentives.[57] It is related not only to the creation and absorption of new knowledge, but also to its adaptation, extension and control within an innovation-friendly environment. All in all, this provides strong grounds for the creation of dynamic comparative advantages, certain irreversibilities[58] and economic growth[59] of firms and nations as success breeds the potential for further success. The higher the levels of accumulation of knowledge and capital stock, the greater are the benefits of technological progress[60] and vice versa. 'Thus, the accumulation of knowledge, with labour and capital constant, is not subject to decreasing returns in the same way as is the accumulation of capital, with ideas (technological knowledge) constant. This is due largely to the characteristic of knowledge that it can be combined and recombined with other pieces of existing or yet-to-be created pieces of knowledge to form new technologies, which in turn creates even more opportunities' (Lipsey et al., 2005, p. 431). This is also reflected in the export performance of countries, as well as in differences in labour productivity. Innovation is concentrated in a few firms in industries with high entry barriers such as aerospace, chemicals, automobiles, electric and electronic industries, while it is spread among many firms in machinery and the production of instruments (Dosi et al., 1990).

Empirical studies show that monopolisation or concentration is not the main reason for innovation. Cumulative (clustered) knowledge enabled Germany to excel in the fields of chemicals and high-quality engineering, Britain in pop music and publishing, Italy in fashion and design and the US in computer software, aeronautics and the cinema. But innovation is also to be found in industries that are less concentrated and where there are no significant barriers to entry. New entrants may have greater motivation to test and develop new products and technologies than well-established firms.

In many industrialised countries, the average size of firms is becoming smaller, not bigger. This reflects increased demand for more custom-made goods, produced in smaller batches, utilising production factors that can be readily switched to various alternative uses. But this is only on average. The industries with the most advanced technology are frequently the most geographically concentrated, highly profitable and often the largest. Modern technology is increasing the importance of capital, especially human capital.[61] Krugman (1996a, pp. 13–14) found statistical evidence from the US economy that the 'really high value-added' industries (in relation to the number of employees) are cigarette manufacturing and petrol refining, whereas the so-called 'high-technology industries' such as aircraft and electronics were about average. However, one has to remember that high-technology industries have important externalities and linkages for the whole economy. Although the number of computers a nation has is somewhat less important than how and for what purpose they are used, for example playing Tetris or Solitaire or organising inventories, production, transport and distribution. Another problem is that most computers are used in the services sector (finance, accounting and health care) where it is hard to measure output.

It is one thing to invent or discover new or improved goods or services (product differentiation) and/or uncover a new way to produce or market already existing goods and services and quite another to exploit that success commercially. The electric dynamo was invented in 1881, but it took firms four decades to reorganise plants to take advantage of the flexibility in production offered by electric power. The basic videocassette recorder (VCR) technology was the result of an invention by Ampex in the US in the 1950s. When Ampex started selling VCRs in 1963 the retail price was $30 000 a piece. No wonder that only a few were sold over several years. Philips, a Dutch company, produced the first VCR aimed at the consumer market in 1971, several years before Sony introduced its Betamax model. Soon after, other Japanese manufacturers entered the market, and before long they came to dominate the international market for (home) video equipment. To avoid a repeat experience, Philips took a different tack after inventing compact discs and developed the final technology jointly with Sony. Hence, the geography of innovation and the geography of production need not coincide. The microprocessor was invented in 1971, but firms are still learning how to make best use of it. One of the reasons for this situation is due to Moore's law,[62] which refers to the doubling of chip performance about every 18 months.

In a similar vein, commercial jet technology was a British invention. Rolls-Royce was the first producer. This led to the production of the first jet transport aircraft. Later, the US took the lead (with Boeing and McDonnell-Douglas), which was, subsequently, seriously challenged, even overtaken in some market segments by the European Airbus (a consortium of government-supported British, German, French and Spanish firms). Government support of the Airbus provoked a sharp reaction from the US (which ignored the fact that US aircraft producers were generously subsidised through defence contracts). This led to the GATT Agreement on Trade in Civil Aircraft (1979). While 'supporting' the civil aircraft programmes, the signatories 'shall seek to avoid adverse effects on trade in civil aircraft' (Article 6.1). This is a statement that offers a number of different interpretations.[63] As such, it was insufficient to calm down tensions in the aircraft trade. A Bilateral Agreement (1992) between the US and the EU was supposed to introduce a framework for all government 'involvement' in the development of commercial aircraft with 100 seats or more. However, it did not take account of past damage. The deal did not eliminate, but merely constrained, subsidies (for innovation and R&D). It set quantitative limits on both direct and indirect (military) subsidies for the development of new aircraft. The permitted limit for the direct subsidy for the development cost of a new aircraft was set at 33 per cent. Identifiable benefits from indirect subsidies were limited to 4 per cent of each firm's annual sales (Tyson, 1992, p. 207).

The US unilaterally withdrew in 2004 from the 1992 Bilateral Agreement and initiated the WTO procedure concerning the alleged illegal ($15 billion) launch subsidies that Airbus received. At the same time, the EU filed a counter case claiming that Boeing was given $23 billion illegal aid through R&D assistance and lucrative government contracts. While Boeing has to compete with other companies such as Lockheed-Martin for such favours, Airbus is receiving them directly from the EU member governments. An important reason behind this case and its timing is that Airbus overtook Boeing and captured 54 per cent of the global market for large aircraft in 2003. The US claims that this is due to subsidies.[64] The WTO should make a ruling on this case between two trading giants which both profited from subsidies. However, there is a possibility of a bilateral diplomatic solution of the issue.

A new agreement that would regulate trade in this duopoly market for civil aircraft is necessary. This industry and market is so important that it should not be left to the vagaries of market forces. New parties such as Japan, even Brazil, Russia and China, may need to enter into any new agreement as there is a lot of outsourcing in this business. Accounting rules ought to be transparent, in particular in the post-Enron and post-Parmalat world. Perhaps there ought to be a cap on allowed direct and indirect subsidies and a timetable for their reduction. There should also be a mechanism for the oversight of the business with certain and meaningful justice.

A positive effect on innovation (creation of technology) in the EU was expected to come from the operation of the Single European Market. A deepened regional market would stimulate competition and provide an incentive to innovation that would further promote competition for the benefit of the consumers. If corrective measures (in support of trade, competition or industrial policy) were added, they would not necessarily violate a liberal trading system in the long term. They would simply add an adjustment mechanism to the already highly imperfect and suboptimal market situation.

Perfect competition (perfectly contestable market) is based on zero entry and exit costs in an industry. This eliminates inefficient firms from a market, but at the same time rewards the efficient ones. Joseph Schumpeter called this process 'creative destruction'. Competition is not driven by changes in prices, but rather by innovation and introduction of new products. If equilibrium is ever achieved, it is at best a short-term and temporary event. If inter-country factor mobility is allowed for, the supply of factors (labour, capital, land, technology, organisation and entrepreneurship) increases. This 'pluralism' backs innovation in technology, goods, services, organisation and control. Competition probably operates best when a firm believes that it is in a process that is leading it towards becoming a monopolist (at best) or an oligopolist (at least). However, consumers may suffer in a monopolistic or oligopolistic industry structure. This can be redressed somewhat if oligopolistic firms introduce the most efficient innovations as rapidly as perfectly competitive firms would and if governments prevent such a market structure from behaving in a non-competitive way.

Small open economies inevitably have to rely on various foreign technologies. Such countries often do not have the necessary resources and need to develop basic technologies for all lines of production. If this situation is regarded as detrimental, then economic integration may increase the pool of resources (human, technological and financial) for innovation and the development of new technologies, products and inputs, which may mitigate the potential disadvantage of smallness and isolation. Such pooling started in the EU in the mid-1980s with a series of R&D programmes.

In a relatively well-integrated area such as the EU, one would expect the prices of similar goods in different countries to be similar, owing to competition and trade. The stronger the competition and the larger the volume of trade, other things being equal, the smaller the price variation. Pre-tax prices of the same good would be expected to vary only as a result of differences in the cost of transportation, handling, insurance and, to some extent, marketing between countries. However, this expectation is not borne out in reality. The EU was aware of the barriers to competition other than tariffs and quotas (NTBs), so it created the Single European Market in 1993.

Various regional factors prevent full equalisation of prices. Some geographical areas may have small markets for certain goods and services (for example, parasols in Finland and antifreeze in Greece). So, in order to do business and make some profit there, firms may price their goods relatively higher. In this case market presence may be a much more important public policy and private business objective than requiring price homogenisation in all markets. Or, for example, differences in taste or special requirements regarding the basic ingredients of a product (for instance, chocolate) may cause the price of a good to vary. And, if there are local substitutes, foreign suppliers may modify the price of their goods. Some goods (such as wine) may be regarded as luxuries in one country and taxed accordingly, but regarded as basic necessities in another country. This widens the price gap for the same good in different countries, and sometimes even in different regions of the same country. In a perfectly competitive market (with free entry and exit) for a good, free competition ensures equality of prices and drives profits to zero. In imperfectly competitive markets there is scope for price variation and, therefore, for profits.

The problem of innovation and new technology not resulting in an obvious and measurable increase in output is known as the 'productivity paradox'. Some argue that there is no technological revolution and that computers are not productive: a personal computer that is 100 times more powerful than one made 10 years ago is not proportionately more productive. Others argue that decades must pass before the fruits of technological breakthroughs can be discerned. Yet others insist that there are benefits, but that standard statistical tools are inadequate to measure them. This is most obvious in the services sector. How can the output of a bank be measured? Has the economy become so complex and fast-changing[65] that it has become unmeasurable? If this is so, it is increasingly difficult to regulate it, and to tax it.

Intra-industry Trade

Although increased competition offers potential gains from both more efficient industrial and geographical allocation of resources in production and increased consumption, there is no guarantee that these gains will be achieved in practice. If a government takes this view and believes that domestic production will be wiped out by foreign competition, then it may pursue a policy of protection on the grounds that it is better to produce something inefficiently at home than to produce nothing at all. This disastrous scenario has not been borne out in reality. The very existence of the EU, which has continued to expand in size, as well as in scope and depth, is the best example of a positive scenario. Most firms in the EU countries have not been put out of business because of competition from firms in partner countries. Instead, many of them have continuously increased their business in the long run. They have specialised in lines of production that satisfy distinct demand segments throughout the EU. This fact cannot be explained by the classical theories.

The 'awkward fact' is that trade takes place in differentiated products (Eaton and Lipsey, 1997, pp. 228–9). Strong advertising campaigns create awareness about 'differences' among what are basically very similar and easily substitutable goods (for instance, cars, printers, fax and photocopying machines, T-shirts, skis, soaps, toothpastes, TV sets, painkillers, breakfast cereals, refrigerators, trainers, cigarettes, bicycles or audio-, video- or DVD-recorders and discs). This phenomenon is known in theory as intra-industry trade.[66] It is the result of both the desire by consumers to have a wide choice of goods and economies of scale at the level of firms. Generally, product differentiation tends to dominate product specialisation in the internal trade of the EU.

There are also other examples that support the thesis of a smooth intra-industry adjustment in trade and geography of production. Successive rounds of negotiations within the GATT reduced tariffs. The ensuing intra-industry adjustments in trade and specialisation among developed countries were relatively smooth. Contrary to the expectation of the factor endowment theory, intra-industry adjustment prevailed and carried fewer costs than would have been the case with inter-industry adjustment. If it is feared that foreigners will eliminate domestic firms through competition, exchange rates can act as an important safety-valve to prevent this happening and ease the process of adjustment to the new situation.

Inter-industry trade between countries basically reflects differences in national factor endowment. This type of trade brings efficiency gains through resource allocation, as well as benefits that come from the supply of a new set of different products. Intra-industry trade, on the other hand, is associated with product differentiation. Consumers benefit from this type of trade through increased variety of closely substitutable goods and services, as well as through increased competition of products made with increasing returns of scale.

As incomes have risen, consumers are no longer satisfied with identical or standardised goods. They demand and pay for varieties of the same basic good, often tailored to their individual needs and tastes. The larger the variety of demanded and available goods and services, the smaller is the importance of economies of scale. Intra-industry trade refers to trade in differentiated goods. It occurs when a country simultaneously exports and imports goods (final or semi-finished) that are close substitutes in consumption. Differentiation of goods begins when various characteristics are added to the basic good or component, backed up by strong R&D and advertising campaigns. Thus, gains from trade in differentiated goods may arise through an increase in consumer choice (not necessarily through lower prices only).

The variety of goods produced in a country, the new theory suggests, is limited by the existence of scale economies in production. Thus, similar countries have an incentive to trade. Their trade may often be in goods that are produced with similar factor proportions. Such trade does not involve the major adjustment problems that are commonly found with more conventional trade patterns (Krugman, 1990a, pp. 50–51). In fact, one of the most distinctive properties of the liberalisation of trade in the EU was an increase in intra-industry trade coupled with modest adjustment costs (Sapir, 1992, pp. 1496–7).

At the heart of neo-classical international trade and customs union theory is the analysis of two goods only. Therefore, it cannot satisfactorily account for preference diversity and intra-industry trade. The neo-classical theory's 'clean' model of perfect competition is not applicable here. The potential for intra-industry trade increases with the level of economic development, similarity in preferences (tastes), openness to trade and geographical proximity, which reduces the costs of transport, marketing and after-sales service.

A significant portion of trade among developed countries is intra-industry. In this case, variety may be preferred to quantity, so that some proportion of trade is attributable not only to differences in factor endowment, but also to different national preferences (tastes). This is the case in the EU. The response of successful firms to such business challenges is to find a specialist market niche and to employ economies of scope, rather than scale.

In an 'early' example of intra-industry trade, Linder (1961, p. 102) noted that ships that brought European beer to Milwaukee took American beer back to Europe. Although lacking a formal theory, the examination of international trade flows by Grubel and Lloyd (1975) noted that an important part of these flows was within the same industry classification group.

Finger (1975) believes that intra-industry trade is an anomaly due to the definition of new products and processes and statistical sorting of data. However, Loertscher and Wolter (1980, p. 286) demonstrated that intra-industry trade between countries is not a statistical fabrication, but a real phenomenon. This type of trade between countries is likely to be strong if:

- they are both relatively highly developed;
- the difference in their level of development is small;
- they have large national markets;
- the barriers to trade are low;
- there is a high potential for product differentiation;
- entry in narrow product lines is obstructed by significant barriers (sunk costs); and
- transaction costs are low.

Research shows that incentives to intra-industry trade are similar levels of per capita income and country size, product differentiation, participation in regional integration schemes, common borders, as well as similar language and culture. Negative influences on this type of trade are exerted by standardisation (reduction in consumer choice), distance between countries (which increases the cost of information and services necessary for trade in differentiated goods) and trade barriers that reduce all trade flows (Balassa and Bauwens, 1988, p. 1436).

Intra-industry trade is relatively high among developed countries. It refers to trade within the same trade classification group. One may, therefore, wonder whether intra-industry trade is a statistical aberration rather than an authentic phenomenon. In addition, it may be argued that two varieties of the same product are not always two distinct goods. The criteria for data aggregation in the Standard International Trade Classification (SITC) are similarity in inputs and substitutability in consumption. These criteria often contradict each other. Many of the three-digit groups in the SITC include heterogeneous goods. For example, SITC 751 (office machines) includes typewriters, word-processing machines, cash registers and photocopying machines, whereas SITC 895 (office and stationery supplies) includes filing cabinets, paper clips, fountain pens, chalk and typewriter ribbons. On these grounds one could conclude that intra-industry trade is a pure statistical fabrication. However, this is not so in reality. If one studied trade groups with more than three digits, differences could and would appear. The index of intra-industry trade (IIT) in a country is represented by the ratio of the absolute difference between exports and imports in a trade classification group to the sum of exports and imports in the same classification group:

$$\text{IIT} = 1 - \frac{|X_j - M_j|}{X_j + M_j} \tag{2.4}$$

The intra-industry trade index (equation (2.4)) is high and is equal to 1 for complete intra-industry specialisation (a country imports and exports goods in a group in the same quantity). This is a sign of a geographical spread of an industry. The index is low and equals zero for complete inter-industry specialisation. Such spatial concentration of production is usually the result of high entry barriers and economies of scale. However, the index does not distinguish between cross-hauling of final output and intra-industry trade that is the consequence of production sharing within an industry. It does not distinguish between quality-differentiated trade in goods either. In any case, intra-industry trade increases welfare because it extends the variety of available goods to the consumers. As there is no evidence of large adjustment costs to this type of trade, one may conclude that intra-industry trade makes everyone better off.

The *ex ante* expectation that trade liberalisation and integration could shift the IIT index closer to 1 (suggesting a geographical spread of production) in the case of developed countries has been investigated in numerous studies.[67] Among the EU countries, the IIT index was highest in 1987 for France (0.83), Britain (0.77), Belgium (0.77), Germany (0.76) and the

Netherlands (0.76) and lowest in Portugal (0.37) and Greece (0.31), implying that these two countries had a high inter-industry specialisation (*European Economy*, 1990b, pp. 40–41). None the less, various statistical results regarding the significance of intra-industry trade may be called into doubt. For example, if there are strong centripetal (agglomeration) forces in high-technology or chemical industries because of economies of scale and production linkages, the IIT index should be low. However, 'average intra-EU IIT in high-tech products has been higher than the overall mean for most of our sample period, which indicates above average geographical dispersion of these sectors' (Brülhart, 1998b, pp. 328–9). This is an indication that additional theoretical and empirical work needs to be done in this field (Brülhart, 1998a, p. 790).

Some goods belonging to the same classification group may be perfect substitutes and have identical end uses (for example, plates). However, plates can be made of china, glass, paper, plastic, wood, metal or ceramic. Every type of this end product requires totally different and unrelated factor inputs and production technology. Other examples include tableware, furniture, clothing and so on. These differences among goods that enter a single SITC group may not be important for statistical records, but they are often of crucial importance to consumers. Demand for a variety of products increases with a rise in income. Higher income gives consumers the opportunity to express variety in taste through, for example, purchasing different styles of clothing. Economic integration may change consumers' preferences as the choice of goods available before the formation of a customs union or reduction in tariffs may be quite different.

Market integration in the EU increased intra-industry trade within this group of countries, whereas planned integration in the former Council for Mutual Economic Assistance (CMEA) had as its consequence greater inter-industry trade (Drabek and Greenaway, 1984, pp. 463–4). Preferences in the centrally planned economies are revealed through plan targets and are different from those in economies in which market forces demonstrate consumer preferences. In market economies, competition takes place among firms, whereas in centrally planned economies competition occurs among different plans offered to the central planning body. A free trade area between the US and Canada (1987) was not expected to alter crucially the pattern of trade between these two countries. One reason was that the last step in the reduction in tariffs agreed during the Tokyo Round of the GATT negotiations took place in 1987. After this reduction, trade between the US and Canada became largely free: 80 per cent of all trade was duty free, while a further 15 per cent was subject to a tariff of 5 per cent or less. Another reason was that consumer tastes are more similar in North America than between countries in the EU.

The fact that a large part of trade among developed countries is intra-industry may lead to the conclusion that the Heckscher–Ohlin (factor proportions) theory of trade is not valid. Intra-industry trade is not based on differences in factor endowments among countries. Countries tend to specialise and export goods that are demanded by the majority of domestic consumers. It is this demand ('home market effect') that induces production, rather than domestic factor endowment. Countries have a competitive edge in the production of these goods and thus gain an advantage in foreign markets, while they import goods demanded by a minority of the home population (Linder, 1961). The US, Japan and Germany have the greatest comparative advantage in goods for which their home market is relatively big. These are standardised goods for mass consumption. There is, however, one major exception. The major market for German dyes is the British textiles industry (and to a lesser extent that in the US). The German domestic market for dyestuffs is relatively small (Nelson, 1999, p. 12). Toyota has achieved world leadership in passenger cars, even though its domestic market is smaller than that of General Motors. The size of the domestic market in this case became less significant than the technological competitive advantage.

An important analytical question is whether factor proportions (Heckscher–Ohlin) or economic geography (determined by economies of scale and market access) is more important to predict trade within industries. Limited research found that in the case of Sweden the answer was both. A large domestic market, as well as plentiful endowment of human capital, increases the quality of exports (Greenaway and Torstensson, 2000, p. 277).

Petrus Verdoorn suggested that the principal difference in manufacturing between US and European firms is not so much the size of firm/plant as the length of the individual production run. The range of processes carried out in the same factory is much smaller in the US than in Europe (Hague, 1960, p. 346). Compared with plants in the same industry, production runs in the US are several times larger than in Europe, even when the plants are owned by the same TNC (Pratten, 1971, pp. 195, 308–9; 1988, pp. 69–70). On the other hand, even in the most efficient developed countries, manufacturing is often carried out in factories of quite moderate size. Differences in plant productivity are best explained by (1) inappropriate labour relations, in particular where many thousands of workers need to be employed together; (2) inadequate level of technical training; and (3) an unsatisfactory incentives structure (Prais, 1981, pp. 272 ff.). In support of one of these arguments (1), it has been found that the number of strikes increases exponentially with plant size (Geroski and Jacquemin, 1985, p. 174).

Because of a larger and more homogenised market, which required large production runs, labour productivity in the manufacturing industries in

1986 was some 50 per cent higher in the US than in Germany. This figure may overstate the difference in productivity between the two countries as it makes little allowance for the high quality of German manufactured products (Pratten, 1988, pp. 126–7). For example, a preoccupation with large quantities of output and economies of scale rendered the taste of standard American chocolate, for a European, appalling.

Intra-industry trade may be described in terms of monopolistic competition and product differentiation. Perfect competition is not a realistic market structure, so perfect monopolistic competition is the most perfect market structure in a situation with differentiated goods (Lancaster, 1980). Armington's assumption states that products in the same industry, but from different countries, are imperfect substitutes (Armington, 1969, p. 160). In other words, buyers' preferences for different(iated) goods are independent. Armington's assumption, however, overestimated the degree of market power of a particular producer.

Three main findings stem from the data presented in Table 2.6. First, intra-industry trade is relatively high in the EU. Second, there was a convergence of levels of intra-industry trade across countries between 1961 and 1990. The countries with the lowest initial levels of intra-industry trade experienced sharp increases over this period. Third, intra-industry trade in manufactured goods in the EU grew consistently in the 1960s and early 1970s and

Table 2.6 Intra-industry trade within the EU by member country, 1961–92

Country	1961	1967	1972	1977	1985	1988	1990	1992
Belgium–Luxembourg	0.51	0.56	0.49	0.57	0.56	0.57	0.58	0.60
Denmark	0.30	0.37	0.41	0.44	0.42	0.44	0.43	0.47
France	0.60	0.69	0.67	0.71	0.68	0.67	0.67	0.72
Germany	0.47	0.56	0.57	0.57	0.60	0.59	0.61	0.68
Greece	0.02	0.06	0.08	0.10	0.15	0.15	0.16	0.15
Ireland	0.22	0.28	0.36	0.45	0.40	0.38	0.38	0.41
Italy	0.44	0.56	0.57	0.56	0.52	0.51	0.51	0.51
Netherlands	0.54	0.57	0.59	0.59	0.60	0.62	0.61	0.67
Portugal	0.04	0.10	0.13	0.14	0.24	0.25	0.30	0.31
Spain	0.10	0.16	0.29	0.38	0.47	0.56	0.57	0.60
UK	0.51	0.67	0.65	0.71	0.62	0.59	0.64	0.68
EU	0.48	0.56	0.57	0.59	0.58	0.58	0.59	0.64

Notes: Unadjusted Grubel and Lloyd indices calculated from SITC five-digit statistics from OECD for SITC sections 5–8. Average of 11 countries, weighted by values of intra-EU manufactured imports and exports.

Source: Brülhart and Elliott (1999, p. 106).

then stabilised, but it resumed its increasing trend between 1988 and 1992. However, it is important to bear in mind that the SITC was revised twice in this period, in 1978 and in 1988. Thus, it is not possible to conclude that the upward trend in intra-industry trade in the EU is slowing down. In addition, it appears that the Single Market Programme, contrary to the *ex ante* predictions, 'did not entail an increase in inter-industry specialisation' (Brülhart and Elliott, 1999, pp. 106–9). It could be concluded that the increase in intra-industry trade in the EU is evidence that economic integration did not produce a geographical concentration of production in select EU regions or countries.

'So with integration, specialisation may initially fall during structural adjustment and then increase. This would explain why Spain, Portugal, and the UK, which were all late joiners to the EU, show a fall in specialisation when comparing 1968–1990, and an upward trend starting in the late 1970s and early 1980s' (Amiti, 1999, p. 579). The most likely explanation is that, before joining the EU, these countries had relatively high trade barriers that protected production for which there was no national comparative advantage. Entry into the EU eliminated administrative trade barriers and reduced trade costs. However, in all countries, specialisation increased over the 1980–90 period.

Each country's geography of production became different from the rest in the group. Although this reallocation of resources has obvious benefits that come from specialisation, the snag is that specialised countries may react in a different way to asymmetric shocks and require diverse policy instruments to counter them. Therefore, in the light of the eurozone and eastern enlargement, there is a strong need for the creation of EU policy tools to counter such obstacles to the smooth operation of the Single European Market.

Instead of taking goods themselves as the basis for analysis, 'address models' of goods differentiation take characteristics that are embodied in goods as their starting point (Lipsey, 1987a). A computer is a good that can be considered as a collection of different attributes, such as memory, speed, printing, graphics and the like. Figure 2.8 illustrates two characteristics of a set of goods (computers).

Each good (computer), A, B or C, has a certain combination of characteristic S (speed) and characteristic M (memory). Each good is defined by its location in the continuous space of characteristics, hence it has a certain 'address'. Consumer preferences are defined by characteristics, not goods. Some consumers prefer memory over speed, whereas others prefer the opposite. Under the assumption that all three goods in Figure 2.8 have the same price, let a consumer have tastes embodied in the indifference curve II. This consumer maximises utility by purchasing good B. Each

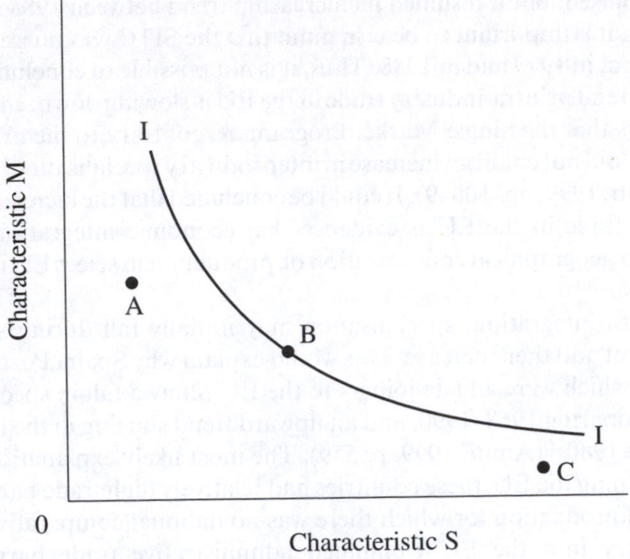

Figure 2.8 Characteristics of computers

good in this model has close and distant neighbours. There are many goods and many consumers. Every consumer attempts to attain his or her highest indifference curve. This gives rise to intra-industry trade. Address models of localised (monopolistic) competition can be an important factor in explaining intra-industry trade and, hence, contribute to the explanation of the location of production.

All general explanations of trade in differentiated goods refer only to final goods traded among developed countries. In addition, intra-industry trade is affected by imperfect product markets (monopolisation) and by consumer demand for a variety of goods. Economies of scale can be another important factor in explaining trade in differentiated goods. Countries with a similar endowment of factors will still trade. Imperfect information about goods on the part of consumers might have had an impact on intra-industry trade in the past, but this aspect is rapidly diminishing as the Internet, global advertising and other methods of disseminating information worldwide gain importance.

The Heckscher–Ohlin theory gives students the impression that the factor proportions theory of trade is orthodox. Linder's theory tends to be less rigorous and thus has not made the same impression on students. None the less, Leamer (1984) found evidence which supports the classical theory, while Greenaway and Torstensson (2000) found that both factor proportions and economic geography variables appear to be important in determining trade within industries. Linder's research does not reject the factor proportion theory, but rather it asserts that factor proportion is not the only cause of trade. One may conclude that the factor proportions theory determines geographical location of production (specialisation) and trade *among* different SITC classification groups, while economies of scale and diversity in tastes determine the geography of production and trade *within* SITC classification groups. As most changes in demand take place within certain clusters of goods, this is a sign that changes in technology are important driving forces of trade and (re)allocation of production.

European Union

Introduction

Competition policy is one of the foremost economic policies of the EU. It is also an area where centralisation of authority makes full sense. The European Commission has special responsibility for the proper operation of competition in the EU because it 'handles' a much larger number of firms than any member country. The European Commission's approach to this policy is based on strict rules. Basic rules (including exceptions) in EU competition policy can be found in the Treaty of Rome and the rulings of the Court of Justice.

In essence, there should be no barriers to internal trade and competition in the EU. Freedom of movement for goods, services, people and capital (four freedoms) are contained in Article 3(c) of the Treaty of Rome.[68] The EU does not tolerate any discrimination on the grounds of nationality[69] (Article 12). 'The internal market shall comprise an area without internal frontiers in which the free movement of goods, persons, services and capital is ensured' (Article 14). This provision was intended to abolish NTBs on internal trade and ensure the most liberal competition rules for EU residents. Freedom of movement of goods is elaborated in Articles 23–31.[70] Free movement (and establishment) of persons, services and capital is regulated by Articles 39–60. As for national tax provisions, they must not discriminate against goods that originate in other member states of the EU (Articles 90–93). In addition, Article 157 requires both the EU and its member states to ensure the necessary conditions for the competitiveness of EU industry.

Competition rules are founded on the assumption that the concentration of (private) economic power within monopolies, oligopolies, cartels or other market structures that have similar negative effects on consumers need to be outlawed and/or regulated and monitored. Individual economic freedom needs to be fostered through the rules of market competition. The objective of this approach is to allocate factors among sectors and space according to the criterion of efficiency and, hence, contribute to an increase in the average standard of living.

In 1985, the EU accepted a technical blueprint, known as the Single Market Programme,[71] which outlined 282 measures for the attainment of the genuine Single European Market by the end of 1992. Its founding principle was the removal of NTBs to internal trade in the EU. The move from a fragmented to a genuinely integrated market can produce some of the most striking results of economic integration. The programme was meant to intensify competition and increase the competitiveness of EU goods and services compared with exports from the US, Japan and the newly industrialised countries. It removed border controls, introduced mutual recognition of standards, established a single licence and home-country autonomy over financial services and opened national public procurement contracts to suppliers from other EU member countries.

The principal gains of the Single European Market come not from the reduction in the costs of internal EU trade, which is a result of the removal of NTBs, but rather from the longer-term dynamic benefits of increased competition on the expanded internal market. This was supposed to stimulate economies of scale, removal of X-inefficiency, exit of the weakest and growth of the strongest firms, innovation and breakdown of collusive behaviour. The anti-competitive market behaviour of various local monopolies is largely checked. Competition in the EU could, however, be furthered if EU internal liberalisation were coupled with external trade liberalisation. There are at least two arguments for additional external opening of the EU in order to deepen competition. First, intra-EU trade is mostly in differentiated products (intra-industry). Second, an element of intra-EU trade takes place between subsidiaries of a single TNC. Extra-EU competitive pressure is necessary to ease such an oligopolistic structure and increase the competitiveness of both traditional and new-growth industries (Jacquemin and Sapir, 1991).

Monetary union is expected to help businesses to eliminate the risk and costs associated with currency fluctuations. The elimination of this distortion of competition, trade and investment will contribute to the reduction in intra-EU trade costs. The existence of the euro will guide the EU economy towards a greater price transparency that will ease and motivate expansion in intra-EU trade. The whole process will lead towards a downward convergence in prices.

Here we shall concentrate on the rules that govern the actions of both firms and governments to prevent them from reducing competition in the Single European Market and, hence, have an impact on spatial distribution of production. Two articles of the Treaty of Rome govern the actions of *firms*. Article 81 refers to restrictions on competition, while Article 82 prohibits the abuse of a dominant position. *Governments* may also jeopardise the process of competition. This is the case with state aids (subsidies). Article 87 regulates this issue. The European Commission must be notified of all cases of aid above a certain level so that it can examine their legality and compatibility with the goals of the EU.

There were 262 new cases of breaches of Articles 81 and 82, respectively (Figure 2.9), in 2003. The volume and dynamics of closed cases are presented in Figure 2.10. It is obvious that a vast majority of the cases are solved through informal procedure. In addition, there were 552 new cases[72] of violation of Article 87 (state aid) that were referred to the European Commission in 2003. This all indicates that the European Commission is quite active in the policy area of market competition.

In order to implement its duties as the guardian of the Treaty of Rome, the Council of Ministers issued Regulation 17/62 (1962). The European Commission has the right to request relevant information from all enterprises, their associations and member states. If the information is not provided, the Commission may impose a daily fine of up to €1000 until the information is provided. The European Commission is also empowered to investigate the case. This includes 'dawn raids' (unannounced early-morning visits) to the premises of the parties involved in a case. For example, the European Commission inspectors 'raided' mobile phone companies in Britain and Germany as a part of an investigation into price fixing on international charges in both countries in 2001. The same happened in

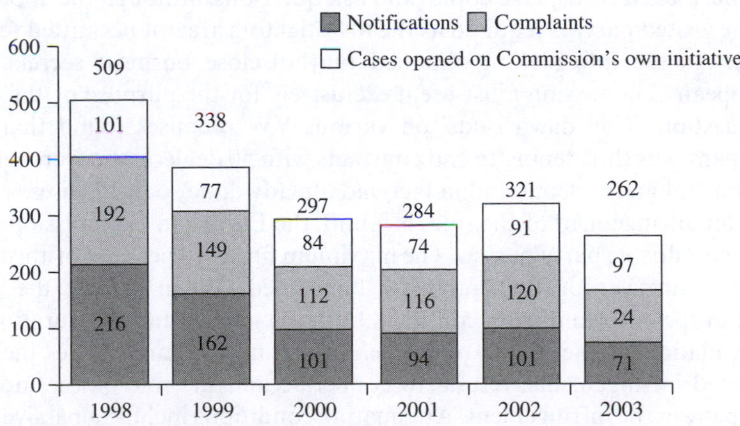

Source: European Commission (2004a).

Figure 2.9 New competition-related cases, 1998–2003

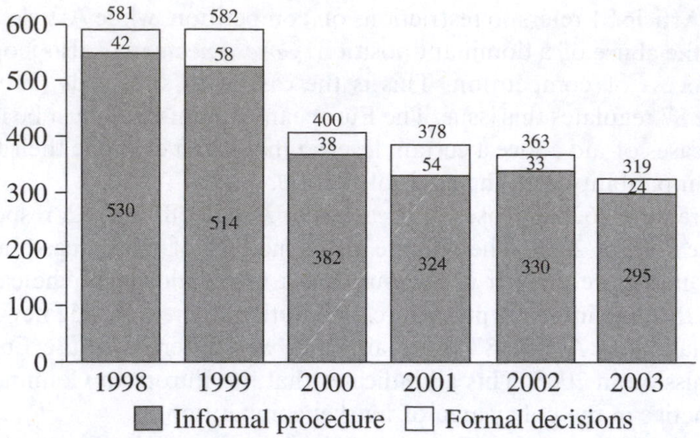

Source: European Commission (2004a).

Figure 2.10 Closed competition-related cases, 1998–2003

2005 when the inspectors raided the offices of glass manufacturers in six EU countries. The police may also raid the European Commission's premises without warning. This happened in the price fraud, corruption and insider trading in cereals markets case of 15 October 2003.

One of many examples occurred in 1995, when inspectors raided the offices of Volkswagen and Audi in Germany, as well as the premises of their Italian distributor Autogerma. Inspectors may examine books, accounts and business records, take copies and ask questions, although the approval of the visited party is required as the investigators are not permitted to use force. As the information obtained may disclose business secrets, the European Commission must use it exclusively for the purpose of the case in question. The 'dawn raids' on various VW premises found that the company was threatening to end contracts with 50 dealers who were selling to non-Italian residents, and in fact had already done so in 12 cases.

If an infringement of the rules is found, the European Commission may fine the culpable party/parties. The maximum fine is 10 per cent of the total annual turnover of the enterprise concerned. When setting the fine, the European Commission considers both the gravity and the duration of the violation of the Treaty of Rome. Aggravating circumstances include repeated infringements, refusal to cooperate and the role of the mother company in the infringement. Attenuating conditions include a passive role in the infringement, cooperation in the proceedings and termination of the infringement following the intervention by the European Commission. In 1998, the Commission fined VW €102 million. The size of the fine reflected the duration of the felony (which began in 1987 and continued until 1993 in spite of repeated warnings). A look at the fines imposed by the European Commission shows that these have been increasing over time. The guilty parties may appeal against decisions of the European Commission to the Court of First Instance. A further appeal may be brought before the Court of Justice.

The European Commission found that 13 manufacturers of vitamins participated in cartels that allocated sales quotas, fixed and increased prices, and set up a system to monitor and enforce their agreements. Eight companies, led by Hoffmann-La Roche and BASF, were fined €855 million in total in 2001. The Hoffmann-La Roche portion of the fine, €462 million, was one of the biggest ever imposed on a single company by the European Commission.

Restriction of competition

It is increasingly risky and costly to develop a new good, service, technology or organisational and control competence. The same is often true for entering a new market. Thus, sharing costs and risk, as well as achieving economies of scale, is a major incentive for firms to form various types of partnership. Article 81 of the Treaty of Rome prohibits 'as incompatible with the common market' all explicit or implicit, as well as horizontal or vertical agreements (collusion) among firms that may have a negative impact on internal EU trade 'and which have as their object or effect the prevention, restriction or distortion of competition within the common market', unless authorised by the European Commission. Private practices that restrict competition according to this article include:

- direct or indirect fixing of prices and other trading conditions;
- limitation or control of production, markets, technical development or investment;
- sharing of markets;
- application of dissimilar conditions to equivalent transactions with different clients; and
- tying unconnected transactions into contracts.

It has been recognised for quite some time, at least in the smaller countries in Europe, that there is a need for some spatial concentration of business. Hence, Article 81(3) itemises the exemptions from the general EU rules of competition. Its application is often based on political compromises, hence the potential danger (uncertainty) that comes from the lack of transparency. An agreement, decision or practice may be declared compatible with the common market if it contributes to an improvement in the production or distribution of goods, or to the promotion of economic or technical progress, 'while allowing consumers a fair share of the resulting benefit'. In addition, to be exempt from the standard rules of competition, the restrictive agreement must be necessary for the accomplishment of the desired business end (the appropriateness principle).

If some kinds of business practice occur frequently and are generally compatible with the rules of competition, if certain conditions are fulfilled, the European Commission may grant a block exemption. For example, Commission Regulation 2659/2000 block exempts categories of R&D agreements between competing firms. It belongs to a new type of block exemption regulation that moves away from the former approach of looking primarily at contractual clauses in favour of a greater regard to the actual market power of the parties. The block exemption therefore works with a market share threshold that is set at 25 per cent (combined market share of all parties to an agreement). Beyond these market shares, R&D agreements are not automatically prohibited, but have to be assessed individually. In this context, the Commission guidelines on horizontal cooperation agreements provide orientation to undertakings. However, 'hardcore' restrictions (price fixing, output limitation or allocation of markets or customers) remain prohibited. Regulation 358/2003 provides a block exemption to insurance companies for certain kinds of deals for the 2003–10 period. The insurance companies are allowed, among other things, to jointly calculate risks, jointly study future risks and establish non-binding standard policy conditions. Other areas where block exemptions are in place include specialisation agreements, vertical restraints (distribution agreements), technology transfer agreements, employment aid for the creation of new jobs or recruitment of disadvantaged or disabled persons, aid for training of personnel, as well as a certain number of sector-specific block exemptions.

Manufacturers in the EU constitute a powerful lobby with a large influence on economic policy. For example, car producers have been exempt (Article 81(3) of the Treaty of Rome) from the full rigour of competition since 1985 (Regulation 123/85). The rationale put forward by the car lobby, and accepted by the European Commission, was that cars are a unique type of consumer good: they are specialised items that require individual attention and after-sales service, and there is an impact on the environment and road traffic safety. Thus, cars are sold through tightly controlled exclusive dealerships and, as far as possible, serviced using only original spare parts (consumers benefit from the specialised knowledge of dealers and service engineers, which should improve safety). In addition, producers control geographical market segmentation and regulate the quantity and prices of cars sold. Although there is little competition between retailers of the same type of car, there is still solid competition among different producers of cars. Despite receiving such preferential treatment from the European Commission, car manufacturers have failed to fulfil their part of the bargain, that is, to allow consumers to shop around within the EU for the best deals. There are still significant differences in prices for the same type of car among the member countries of the EU and guarantees are not honoured throughout the region. The consumers pay the cost of this uncompetitive behaviour in higher car prices and reduced choice.

In 1995, for instance, prospective buyers from Austria flooded into Italy to buy cars because identical models were as much as 30 per cent cheaper there (partly due to the depreciation of the lira). The Italian car dealers refused to sell cars to non-nationals. In other countries, dealers also often refuse to sell cars to non-nationals or discourage them from purchasing cars by quoting excessively long delivery times, various surcharges or warnings that after-sales service would not be honoured abroad. In spite of all these problems, in 1995 the block exemption was extended for a further seven years (Regulation 1475/95). The new terms allowed multidealership as a means of avoiding 'exclusive' dealership. However, this is a largely futile gesture as the second franchise had to be on different premises, under different management and in the form of a distinct legal entity. The British Consumers' Association sent a protest to the European Commission signed by 20 000 people saying that they were being 'ripped off' by the dealers.[73] This is not easily ignored as the exemption has not brought tangible benefits to the consumers.

The European Commission changed the car dealership regime from October 2002. Under the new regime (valid until 2010) car dealers, even supermarkets, may sell cars from any manufacturer, negotiate and offer service with any service provider of their own choice, as well as open sales outlets anywhere in the EU. Car services may order spare parts from any supplier, not only from the ones that are selected by the car manufacturer. The new regime was founded on worthy intentions, as it is supposed to have some influence on the shape of the EU car market and bring certain gains to the consumers. However, massive changes in the market are not expected. The entrenched local dealers and their knowledge of local clients' needs would still provide an effective entry barrier to the local market. Compounded with differences in taxes, the homogenisation of car prices in the EU will remain a pipe-dream.

Although there has been some reduction in price differentials for the same model of car in the EU since the establishment of the Single European Market, price differences for the same model of new car among EU member countries remain and are unlikely to disappear soon. The 'normal' rules of competition do not apply in this important market, which remains a 'black hole' in the Single European Market. However, the introduction of the eurozone contributed to increased price transparency, while easy access to data about car prices provided consumers with better information. The average standard deviation of prices between the eurozone countries fell from 4.9 to 4.4 per cent between 2003 and 2004. Although the gap in pre-tax prices for new cars has narrowed somewhat, it is still considerable. Out of 90 surveyed models of new cars in the eurozone countries in 2004, 25 models still have a difference that exceeds 20 per cent on average. For the best-selling models in the medium-sized car market segment, price differentials can be as much as 28 per cent for a VW Golf in 2004. On average, Germany has the highest prices in the eurozone, while Finland has the lowest (on average about 10 per cent lower than in Germany). In the EU(25), pre-tax prices for new cars are lowest in Poland, about 9 per cent less than in Finland. However, this depends on the model of the car (luxury cars and sports utility vehicles are more expensive in Poland than in the eurozone). Hence, cross-border shopping still provides opportunities for certain savings.[74]

Examples of uncompetitive behaviour may be found elsewhere. Perfume producers have a similar right to license only upmarket shops to sell their products. And, after all, could or should competition laws force Burger King outlets to sell McDonald's hamburgers and vice versa?

A 1998 study of 53 homogeneous products in the eurozone by Lehman Brothers found that, on average, prices varied among countries by 24 per cent. This is twice as much as in the US.[75] Regional tastes differ. The Dutch eat much more yoghurt than others do in the EU. Hence, the price of the same type of yoghurt is relatively lower in the Netherlands than in other EU member countries. Marketing methods and client convenience also have an impact on prices. Hence, ice cream or a soft drink may cost twice as much at a petrol station or on a beach than if bought in a packet of six in a supermarket. Prices will always differ by a margin that may include transport costs and differences in tax rates, but consumers tolerate small differences. The single currency (the euro), as well as Internet shopping and the competition that it introduced, are expected to lead to a convergence of prices, and those sellers that do not adjust will lose business. However, those that cater to the local market with specific regional tastes and preferences may not be affected to a large extent by increased competition.

There are objective factors that may explain a lack of full price convergence and price disparities among different markets in an integrated area. They include the following:

- *Structural factors*: transport costs, type of good (perishable or not), consumer preferences, quality of good and the existence of branded and own-label products.

- *Behavioural factors*: business strategies of firms such as running distribution or market-sharing agreements.
- *Policy factors*: taxes, subsidies, permissions, quotas, standards that favour local firms, as well as other NTBs.

The EU ousted most of the policy-related factors from the Single European Market and it monitors and manages the behavioural ones. None the less, there are still differences in taxes and structural factors that will continue to have a negative impact on price convergence in the Single European Market even of homogeneous products (for example, sugar, washing powder or certain dairy products) which is entirely based on differences in prices.

The merger/acquisition control procedure of the EU has seven, often overlapping, steps: pre-notification discussions, notification, investigation, negotiation, decision, political evaluation and judicial scrutiny. The strength of the EU procedure in comparison with the past and with other jurisdictions is that it is:

- fast (the majority of cases are resolved within a month);
- flexible (pre-notification discussions resolve the question of the necessary background information for the decision); and
- a 'one-stop shop' (the European Commission is the single body in charge of receiving notifications, investigations and decisions).

The European Commission may approve a merger, clear it with conditions or block it. Although the EU procedure is simple, it has (at least) one major weakness: its lack of transparency. The European Commission has considerable discretionary room for manoeuvre in the decision-making process.[76]

Exemptions from the competition rules of the EU are possible under Article 81(3) of the Treaty of Rome. To obtain an exemption, the firms involved need to demonstrate that the benefits of the deal outweigh the anti-competitive effects. The firms need to prove to the European Commission that the deal improves production and/or distribution of goods/services and that it promotes technological progress. In addition, a 'fair share' of the resulting benefits must be passed on to consumers.

In the past, the procedure for clearance was quite long, typically taking up to two years to obtain an exemption. However, since 1993, in the case of any deal (principally, but not exclusively, joint ventures) between firms that has implications for the structure of an industry, the parties must receive a consenting or a warning letter within two months of the mandatory notification of the European Commission about such an agreement. The first examples included an approved joint venture between Olivetti and

Canon (1987) for the development and production of printers and fax machines. The justification for this exception was the avoidance of duplication of development costs and the transfer of technology from Canon (Japan) to Olivetti (Italy). The joint venture by Asea Brown Bovery (ABB) for the development and production of high-performance batteries was also approved on the grounds that it brings innovation, reduces dependence on imported oil and, indirectly, improves the quality of life of consumers. In 1991, however, a merger between Aérospatiale and Alenia/de Havilland was prohibited on the grounds that the merged company would enjoy a dominant position in the worldwide market for medium-sized (40–59 seats) turbopropelled aeroplanes.

Competition rules apply not only to the written and enforceable deals among undertakings, but also to tacit ones such as concerted practices. The 'dyestuffs' case (1969) is an example of this. On three occasions in the 1960s (1964, 1965 and 1967), the biggest EU producers of aniline dyes increased their supply prices by identical margins with a time lag of only a few days. Professional organisations from the textile and leather industries complained to the European Commission. The 10 firms charged denied the existence of any gentleman's agreement and argued that in a closely knit industry each producer follows the price leader. None the less, the Commission had enough circumstantial evidence of collusion to find the parties involved guilty of price fixing and to fine them a total of €0.5 million. The firms involved in this case were BASF, Bayer, Hoechst and Cassella Farbwerke Mainkur (Germany); Francolor (France); ACNA (Italy); ICI (Britain); and Ciba, Sandoz and Geigy (Switzerland). The Court of Justice upheld the decision of the Commission on the grounds that the national markets for dyestuffs were fragmented and that synchronised price rises did not correspond to the normal conditions of the market. One of the important issues that came out of this anti-cartel case was that the Commission and the Court applied the EU competition rules on an extraterritorial basis. British and Swiss enterprises were party to the gentleman's agreement and, although at that time neither Britain nor Switzerland was a member of the EU, the companies involved were fined for non-competitive market behaviour. The principle that was established in this case was that each firm must independently determine its business policy in the common market.

EU competition legislation may be applied to firms that are located and/or do business anywhere in the world. Acceptance, adoption, implementation and enforcement of the EU competition rules is one of the key conditions that must be accepted by any country that wants to join the EU. In order to avoid a potential problem regarding competition in the EU market, two Swiss companies, Ciba-Geigy and Sandoz, requested that the European Commission 'clear' their domestic Swiss merger to form Novartis.

The Commission considered over 100 affected markets. As this extraterritorial merger was predominantly of a complementary nature, it was approved in 1996. And in 1998, the Commission approved the merger of two Swiss banks, UBS and SBS. These cases provide further proof that there is a need for an internationally or, perhaps better to begin with, regionally accepted common set of minimum rules in the area of competition policy. These rules would oust, or reduce, the use of unilateral and extraterritorial competition policy instruments.

There was a big fuss in the EU about a purely American acquisition when Boeing bought McDonnell-Douglas in 1997.[77] Although the American authorities and the European Commission investigated the same market, they came to different conclusions. This was in spite of the bilateral European Commission/US Government Competition Agreement (signed in 1991, approved in 1995) to exchange information, coordinate procedures and consult on cases and remedies. The limits of bilateralism were exposed by this case. *The Economist* reported that there was 'the lethal cocktail of politics, national champions and defence interests' (26 July 1997, p. 62). In addition, the two competition regimes have different economic rationales, principles, legal forms and institutional contexts. They are not likely to see all cases in an identical way (Cini and McGowan, 1998, p. 207). None the less, Boeing recognised the jurisdiction of the European Commission when it filed details of the merger. The European Commission accepted the deal subject to some minor concessions by Boeing. However, there are encouraging examples of cooperation between the EU and US authorities, such as a joint investigation of Microsoft in 1995.

Competition policy requires skilful handling in any scheme that integrates countries. Breaking up a price-fixing cartel is obviously a competition issue. However, deciding how many large chemical or car companies the EU should have is also a political question which shapes the national geography of production. There ought to be some control over mergers with an EU dimension. All industries in the EU use mergers and acquisitions in their business strategy. This was most pronounced in the second half of the 1980s when firms were faced with the possibility of a genuine Single European Market from the early 1990s.[78] One tool of the programme was the elimination of unnecessary regulation (NTBs) that was splintering national markets for goods, services and factors in the EU. The business community responded to this challenge with mergers, acquisitions, strategic alliances, joint ventures and networking, all with the aim of consolidating their position in the new, frontier-free and highly competitive market. Such a business policy had an indirect positive effect on standardisation. The European Commission tolerated it because it believed that it would increase efficiency.

Table 2.7 Mergers and majority acquisitions, 1987–1993

Year	National mergers[a]	EU internal[b]	EU international[c]	International EU[d]	Outside EU[e]
1987/88	2110	252	499	160	114
1988/89	3187	761	659	447	310
1989/90	3853	1122	655	768	356
1990/91	3638	947	550	729	376
1991/92	3720	760	497	605	326
1992/93	3004	634	537	656	381

Notes:
[a] Deals among firms of the same country.
[b] Deals involving firms from at least two different member states of the EU.
[c] Deals in which EU firms acquire firms of non-EU origin.
[d] Deals in which the bidder is from outside the EU and acquires one or several EU firms.
[e] Deals in which there was no involvement of EU firms.

Source: *XXIIIrd Report on Competition Policy 1993* (Brussels: European Commission, 1994).

After a flurry of merger activity in the second half of the 1980s, reaching a peak in 1989/90 (when much restructuring took place), concentration activity decelerated (Table 2.7). By late 1992, when the Single European Market was operational, the business structure and operation had been clarified. The volume and dynamics of merger notifications and final decisions during 1996–2002 is given in Figure 2.11.

Most mergers and acquisitions occurred around 1990 in the manufacturing industry and, especially, in paper manufacturing, followed by the food and drink,[79] sugar-based production and chemicals industries. This is explained by the removal of NTBs in internal trade. The metal-based production industries (mechanical and electro-based engineering and vehicles) also experienced a relatively high level of concentration activity. Suppliers of public goods in these two industries consolidated with the intention of sharing R&D costs and thus withstanding potentially strong competition. Wholesale distributors reacted to the elimination of NTBs by concentration of their activities. The same was true for the providers of financial services.

The major motive for mergers and acquisitions throughout the period of observation was to strengthen market position, followed by the development of commercial activities (market expansion) and rationalisation of business (*European Economy*, 1994a, p. 20). The objective was to prepare for intensive competition in the Single European Market. Companies in Britain, Germany[80] and France were the most favoured targets for intra-EU

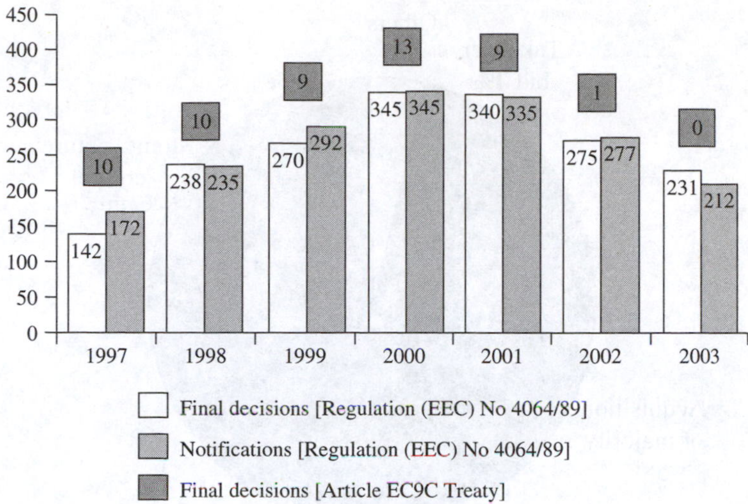

Source: European Commission (2004a).

Figure 2.11 Merger control: number of notifications and of final decisions, 1997–2003

mergers. At the same time, firms from these three countries were the most active buyers of companies in the EU. None the less, the EU concentration in manufacturing was still 12 per cent below that in the US in 1993 (*European Economy*, 1996, p. 119). Parent companies from Britain, Germany and France (the 'trio') were also active in purchasing non-EU firms. While British firms preferred to purchase companies in North America, German and French parent firms distributed their non-EU purchases evenly among North America, western (non-EU) and eastern Europe. As for non-EU acquirers of EU firms, North American buyers were most active in the EU trio, followed by Switzerland, Sweden and Japan.

A new trend in inter-firm relations that has emerged is that firms operating in the low- and medium-technology sectors use mergers and acquisitions in their business strategy, whereas those in high-technology industries employ cooperation and collaboration (joint ventures). This is a divergence from the historical pattern of inter-firm relations, as firms have traditionally tried to protect their knowledge and experience in manufacturing and marketing. The high costs of developing new and upgrading existing technologies has made it pragmatic to share the high costs of R&D. As far as the actual type of merger operation was concerned, majority acquisitions (49 per cent of cases) and joint ventures (33 per cent of cases) were practised most in the EU in the 1994–2003 period (Figure 2.12).

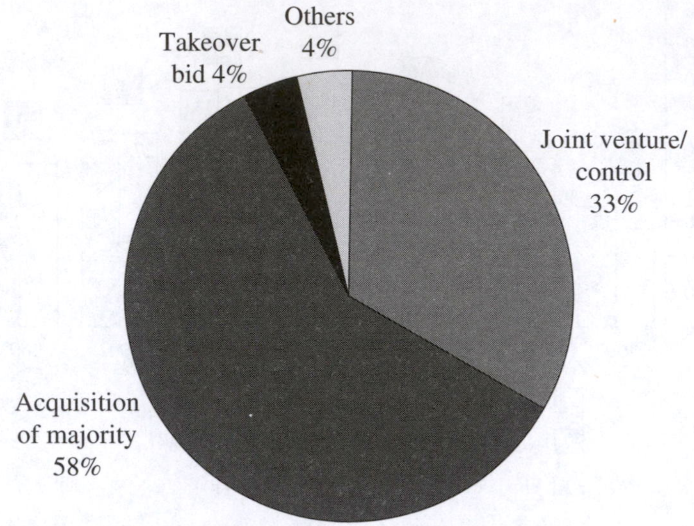

Source: European Commission (2004a).

Figure 2.12 Mergers: breakdown by type of operation, 1994–2004

In a competitive market, mergers and acquisitions are thought to bring at least two efficiency gains: a reduction in management costs and a reduction in transaction costs. These benefits need to be weighed against the possible costs that accrue from the potential inefficiencies that may be the consequence of concentration. If the expected efficiency gains are not realised and do not outweigh the disadvantages, the new merged enterprise may suffer as a result of differences in corporate cultures (in Germany engineers run firms, in Britain accountants, in Italy designers), inflexibility and poor coordination of business functions.

A number of studies examining full legal mergers in various countries in the EU have found no evidence of substantial efficiency gains. Nor were economies of scale significant. Mergers had little or no effect on post-merger profitability. There was no significant difference in the returns per share three years after the merger.[81] The costs of changes in business organisation were often greater than the benefits claimed by the promoters of takeovers. The main reasons for these disappointments include the high prices paid for target firms as managers often overestimate their own ability to run them or they pursue personal reasons other than maximisation of shareholder value, overestimation of the business potential of the acquired firm and mismanagement of the integration process with the acquired firm.[82] This is most obvious in the cases of mergers of firms in the production of steel or cars, as well as in airlines.

McKinsey, a management consultant company, reviewed 160 mergers in the 1992–99 period and discovered that only 12 of the merged groups succeeded in lifting growth above the trends before the merger; the other 148 failed.[83] Other studies, such as Dickerson et al. (1997, p. 359) found no evidence that acquisition in Britain had a net beneficial effect on company performance if measured by profit criteria. In fact, this impact was detrimental and systematic. Perhaps company growth through internal investment, rather than a merger, may offer a superior profit growth rate. In a study of Fortune 500 takeovers (1981–95) in the US, Trimbath (2002) found that most of them (more than two-thirds) resulted in increased efficiency measured by cost per unit of revenue. The editorial article in the *Financial Times* 'Merger mania' (29 October 2003) stated:

> The prospect of investment bankers pocketing millions for 'advising' clients to do what turns out to be a very lousy deal is unappetising. Several academic studies published in the past couple of years have suggested that two-thirds of deals fail. The criteria include revenue growth, share price performance and meeting the targets set when transaction was announced.

With this in mind, further research, analysis and evaluation are required in the area of mergers and acquisitions.

In general, shareholders in acquired firms are likely to benefit from a merger, but investors in the acquiring firms are likely to lose out. There are also problems in creating a new management culture in the merged company, whereas cost savings and new economies of scale can be negligible. This does not mean that all mergers and acquisitions have been failures, but it does mean that all claims about the splendid future of the merged company need to be taken with a pinch of salt. Business gurus, management consultants and investment bankers have reached the same conclusion: less than half of all mergers add value in the medium term.[84] Thus, some conglomerates sell off parts of their business that are not at the core of their activity in order to raise money for acquisitions in their main business area and to simplify their operations. Others expand and diversify their business activities and brands.

Examples of diversification include cases where chocolate bar companies enter the ice-cream market. Harley-Davidson and Levi's entered the after-shave lotion market. Easy Jet went from cheap air transport to businesses that include rent-a-car, Internet cafes, holidays, gifts and insurance. Virgin expanded from low budget air transport to entertainment, clothing, drinks and books. McDonald's is varying its normally uniform menus to meet national tastes. Benetton, a clothing chain, took control of Autostrade, operator of highways in Italy, once they were privatised in 2000. Coca-Cola was founded as a company in 1892, and remained a one-product company for almost a century. Now it manages a portfolio of over 200 brands, most of them local.[85] Smith & Wesson (the US producer of the most powerful handgun, the Magnum) started offering on its online catalogue[86] items that include furniture, salsa bowls, bed and bath items, as well as ice buckets. Smith & Wesson targets, apologies, directs a part of its business strategy towards middle-aged homeowners. Enron, an energy company, went into telecommunications and water. This just contributed to the failure of the company on a grand scale. In any case, diversification, mergers and acquisitions are not necessarily wrong business strategies, but they are very risky.[87]

Despite promises of reduction in costs, economies of scale and the creation of 'champions' to counter foreign rivals, mergers were used as defensive business policy instruments. The rationale that led to the large wave of mergers in the US (and Britain) during the 1960s and 1970s proved to be unfounded. Instead of supporting adjustment, mergers obstructed it by protecting firms from competitive pressure. This was reflected in the relatively slow response of some US firms to oil crises and to Japanese competition in certain industries during the 1980s, as well as competition from China from the start of the new millennium. Firms in the EU would be wise to avoid any repetition of the US experience. The presence in the EU of Japanese and US TNCs with their advanced technology and business organisation and control in some lines of manufacturing industry, as well as the 'flight' of certain domestic firms towards China, may be the principal motivators to the EU domestic firms to restructure their business and become more competitive.

A tidal wave of mergers and acquisitions in the EU was prompted by the need to restructure segmented industries and liberalise capital markets (exploiting restructuring and financial know-how from the US), as well as by the Single European Market. The volume of mergers and acquisitions relative to start-up investments raises serious questions regarding competition (because of the reduction in the number of independent firms and an increase in the potential for collusion) in the Single European Market. Mergers and acquisitions are a global phenomenon. However, so is competition, so anxieties about the effect of the location and structure of merged businesses on competition is to some extent offset by the expansion of 'global' over regional or national competition, as well as by the fact that there has been some restructuring of the business of the acquired firms (European Commission, 1998, pp. 144–5).

One result of the numerous mergers and acquisitions is that the degree of concentration in the EU has risen compared with the pre-Single Market

Programme era. This may *increase* price competition on the internal EU market and abroad through rationalisation of production and economies of scale. At the same time, an increased concentration (oligopolies) of business may *restrict* competition. Therefore, the EU introduced an important legal instrument for the *ex ante* control of mergers in 1990.[88]

The EU needs a sound competition policy to prevent pan-EU oligopolies (corporate fortresses) replacing national ones and eliminating the competitive pressure that comes from open markets. Revised merger legislation (designed to simplify the regulatory burden on merging companies) that came into force in 1998 gives the European Commission a say in any merger with an EU dimension (smaller mergers are under the control of national competition authorities). This is the case if:

- annual worldwide turnover of the new (merged) company is above €2.5bn (the general threshold);
- in each of at least three member states the combined turnover of all of the companies concerned is above €100m;
- in each of these three member states the aggregate turnover of each of at least two companies involved is over €25m;
- the aggregate EU-wide turnover of at least two involved firms is more than €100m.

The decisive determinant according to these thresholds is *turnover*, not the country of domicile/nationality of the parent enterprise.[89] If the proposed merged company could occupy a dominant position that would restrict competition (the new firm could, for example, increase prices by 10 per cent without losing market share), the European Commission has the authority to stop the deal. However, the European Commission has not so far blocked any deal that would result in the merged firm having a market share of less than 40 per cent. Thus, the purpose of the Merger Control Regulation is to prevent *ex ante* the creation of unwanted market behaviour that comes from the abuse of dominant position in the Single European Market. The implementation of the policy has, however, some arbitrary aspects such as estimating the market strength of potential entrants or remaining competitors, determining substitutes and defining the product or geographical market. In any case, the refusal rate of mergers and acquisitions by the European Commission has been less than 1 per cent of the total notified deals.

A number of firms do have as their aim worldwide market dominance and, as a result, merger and acquisition deals are getting bigger and more complex. This increases the workload on the European Commission's limited resources to the possible detriment of the merits of the system: predictability and speed. That the system needs to be reformed is obvious; the question is should the time allowed for decisions be extended, thus compromising a basic tenet of the system, or should the European Commission be empowered to handle only the biggest deals and leave the rest to the national courts (and 'punish' smaller merger deals with a set of national jurisdictions)?

In the light of the eastern enlargement and with the intention of reducing bureaucracy and increasing the effectiveness of enforcement action concerning agreements between undertakings that restrict competition, as well as abuses of dominant positions, the EU implemented in 2002 the most comprehensive antitrust reform since 1962. The Council's Regulation 1/2003 is applied from May 2004 (it replaced Regulation 17/62). The substance of Rome Treaty Articles 81 and 82, respectively, is unchanged. The reform simplified the way in which the antitrust rules are enforced in the EU. The compliance burden for firms is reduced, as the notification system for agreements between firms to the European Commission no longer exists. The European Commission and the national competition authorities are able to focus their resources in the new situation on the fight against those restrictions and abuses that are most harmful to competition and consumers.

The reform places a greater responsibility on firms. They will have to assess themselves whether their deal restricts competition and, if so, whether it fulfils the conditions of the exception rule in Article 81(3). This may create some uncertainty. However, this task for enterprises is alleviated by block exemption regulations (regulations introducing a presumption of legality for agreements that fulfil the specific conditions set out therein) which are maintained in the new system. The European Commission has also published extensive guidelines on the application of Article 81. Where unusual questions arise, firms may ask for guidance from the European Commission in individual cases.

Guidance from the European Commission together with the body of case law of the EU Court of Justice and the European Commission's case practice should also give sufficient substance to the national competition authorities and national courts to apply the EU antitrust rules in a consistent way. The national courts may always ask the European Commission for information or for their opinion. The national competition authorities are linked to the European Commission through a newly created network of authorities (European Competition Network). Where they apply Articles 81 or 82 they are obliged to inform the Commission at different stages of the procedure. In addition, the investigation powers of the European Commission are extended, as the Commission may interview any person who may have useful information for the case under investigation, and it may also enter any premises where business records may be kept (including private residences).

Dominant position

If a firm has or achieves a dominant market position, it may significantly affect competition and the geography of production. The dominant market position may be secured in several ways, including the following five:

- Firms may have innovative skills and competences not only in products (goods/services) but also in management, control and firm-level planning. They may make risky investments in R&D, production and/or marketing that their competitors do not have the nerve for. Such first-mover advantages that are in line with the rules may result in dominance of the market and supernormal profits (Microsoft's MS-DOS and Windows, Sony's Playstations, as well as Nintendo's Game Boy are obvious examples). The life cycle of products is shortening all the time, hence the importance of innovating. In fact, most firms compete by continually assuming quasi-monopolistic positions that are based on innovation of various kinds.[90] In spite of continuous innovations by Microsoft, the most valuable user assets (personal files) are transferable from one Microsoft system to another. Apple, a competitor, failed to realise this in time, allowing Microsoft to achieve a near-monopoly. The classical view that firms are only an input conversion mechanism does not reflect the contemporary world. In addition to their input conversion and value-adding functions, firms are also involved in learning-by-doing and innovation activities. Geographical concentration in industries with various entry barriers may occur as a direct consequence of a firm behaving efficiently. A policy that promotes R&D among firms in the EU may provide them with a better basis for oligopolistic competition at home and abroad and to face up to foreign rivals, mainly from Japan and the US.
- The dominant position in the market could be attained through mergers and acquisitions. This is typical in English-speaking countries.
- A firm may achieve or protect its dominant position through anti-competitive business practices. Examples of this include exclusive dealerships and predatory pricing. However, exclusive dealerships do not always reduce welfare; for example, compared with the situation of free entry and exit among dealers/retailers, permanent and exclusive dealership (including after-sales service) might be a superior and welfare-increasing solution for certain complex goods and services.
- The dominant position can be captured and maintained through a competitive and risky pricing policy. If economies of scale and learning result in a significant fall in prices as output increases over time, a risk-loving firm (for example, Texas Instruments in the 1960s and

1970s) may choose to set current prices on the basis of the expected (low) unit costs of production in the future. Alternatively, prices may be based on the average cost of production over the life cycle of the product.

- Yet another way in which firms come to dominate a market is through the granting of a licence by public authorities. Examples can be found in 'natural' monopolies such as public utilities (water, gas, electricity, rail transport, postal services and the local telephone service). In these industries, the minimum efficient scale is so large that a single firm is necessary to serve the entire national market.

From the outset one should be less concerned about the existence of a dominant firm (Microsoft) than about how the dominant firm 'plays the game'. Many people forget that Microsoft competes with Microsoft (Windows XP competes with Windows Millennium Edition, which competes with Windows 98, which competes with Windows 95). If the price of the new version is too high, consumers will stick to the old computer software. However, Microsoft may increase the price of the old versions when the new one is launched on the market in order to boost sales of the new version.

Article 82 of the Treaty of Rome refers to the issue of the dominant position in a market. It does not prohibit a dominant position (monopoly or monopsony) *ex ante*, but rather forbids the *abuse* of it. This has only an *ex post* effect. In order to determine whether an infringement of the EU market has taken place, the European Commission looks at three factors:

- the existence of the dominant position;
- its abuse (in pricing or control of production, distribution or servicing); and
- the negative effect on trade among the member countries.

Large firms are permitted by the Treaty of Rome to enjoy market dominance, but they are forbidden to exercise it. This is somewhat naïve. Whoever yields the power will behave as a monopolist; the temptation is irresistible. In any case, the legal framework recognises that there is a need for some level of concentration in some industries for reasons of efficiency. It is inevitable for the attainment of the efficient scale of production, in both home and foreign markets. Otherwise, protected and inefficient national firms, which have higher production costs than foreign competitors, would continue to impose welfare losses on consumers. This is why many/most European countries have relaxed their antitrust policies. Otherwise, small domestic firms could be protected only at a high cost and with a diminution of production efficiency. Concentration (geographical agglomeration) of production is a potential barrier to foreign competition on the home market and a springboard for penetration into foreign markets.[91]

A five-year-long dominant position case was closed in 2004 by a written agreement between the European Commission and Coca-Cola. The latter promised that it would change its marketing practice in the EU. In return, it will not be liable to pay a fine for breaking EU competition law. Coca-Cola promised not to force retailers into exclusive deals, not to offer rebates that would give incentives to retailers to stock only Coca-Cola, as well as to give 20 per cent of the space in Coca-Cola's freezers to products made by its competitors. As a result of the Commission's action, consumers can benefit on several counts. They will be able to choose carbonated soft drinks in pubs, cafés or shops on the bases of price and personal preferences, rather than take Coca-Cola because it is the only one available there.

The growing concentration of the semiconductor equipment and materials industries by a few Japanese enterprises created a strategic threat to both commercial and defence interests. For example, because of the concerns of the socialist members of the Japanese Parliament in 1983, the Ministry of International Trade and Industry (MITI) reportedly ordered Kyocera (a domestic manufacturer of high-technology ceramic products) not to take part in contracts to sell ceramic nose cones to the US Tomahawk missile programme (Graham and Krugman, 1995, p. 118). In another example, Nikon, one of only two Japanese suppliers of some kinds of semiconductor-producing machinery, withheld its latest models from foreign customers for up to two years after making them available to Japanese clients (Tyson, 1992, p. 146). The 'explanation' put forward was that the 'regular' customers needed to be served in a better way and before the others. The behaviour of IBM was similar. This firm has also refused to sell its components to other clients (Sharp and Pavitt, 1993, p. 144).

State aid

In the neo-classical economic model, perfect competition can be undermined by protection and subsidies. The distinction between the two distortions is subtle. On the one hand, tariff and non-tariff *protection* allow protected suppliers to charge higher prices in the local market than would be the case with free imports. Such protection provides an 'implicit subsidy' paid directly from consumers to producers. On the other hand, *subsidies* go to domestic producers not directly from consumers, but rather from taxpayers to the government and then to producers. The two types of 'support' have the same objective: to support a certain national (inefficient) production geography as resources are kept in or shifted into import-substituting industries. Where the two instruments differ is in transparency and the method of supplying funds to the selected industries or firms within them.

Those who accept that the market functions efficiently use this argument as a case against subsidies (state aids). Although such an argument applies in many instances, there are other situations in which the neo-classical theory does not hold. In a situation with imperfections such as externalities (R&D or pollution), economies of scale, multiple equilibria, path dependence, imperfect mobility of factors and sunk costs, intervention may be justified. Therefore, industrial and regional policies may be used as justifications for the existence of state aids.

One of the key elements in the EU competition policy is a unique supervision and control of state aids. Subsidies may distort competition and efficient allocation of resources (geography of production). Article 87 of the Treaty of Rome recognises this issue and regulates it.[92] It prohibits any aid that distorts or threatens to distort competition among member countries. This means that Article 87 does not apply to aid given as support to firms or for the production of goods and services that do not enter intra-EU trade (local consumption), or aid for exports outside the EU (regulated by Article 132).

The European Commission accepted and applied a transparent approach to subsidies. It published *Surveys of State Aid* biennially until 2001, when it was replaced by *State Aid Scoreboards*. This provides an overview of state aids in the EU and an opportunity to inspect the underlying trends based on the most recent data. The Commission also expects its trading partners, particularly candidate countries, to follow suit.

There are, however, a few exceptions to the general rule of incompatibility of state aid with free market competition. Article 87 states that aid that is compatible with the treaty is of the kind given on a non-discriminatory basis to individuals for social purposes, as well as aid to regions affected by disasters. Aid that can be considered compatible with the treaty is the kind given to projects that are in the EU's interest and aid for regional development in the 'areas where the standard of living is abnormally low' (for the purpose of social cohesion in the EU). The Council of Ministers (based on the proposal from the European Commission) has the discretionary right to decide that other aid may be compatible with the EU rules. This includes aid to small and medium-sized enterprises (SMEs),[93] conservation of energy, protection of the environment, promotion of national culture and alleviation of serious disturbances in a national economy. If an industry comes under competitive and/or restructuring pressure, the European Commission considers the social, environmental, human capital development (especially relevant after

Lisbon 2000) and other impacts of such an adjustment. The European Commission may permit aid under conditions that are based on principles that include:

- temporariness (a clear time limit);
- transparency (the amount of aid has to be measurable);
- selectivity (aid is supposed to be given to firms and industries that have a reasonable chance of standing on their own after the restructuring period); and
- appropriateness (aid has to match the basic needs of the assisted firm/industry to operate during the restructuring period,[94] after which the assisted firm/industry has to become economically viable on its own).

In order to ease the workload and concentrate on the large and potentially the most damaging cases, the European Commission introduced a *de minimis* rule in 1992. According to this rule, governments are not required to notify the Commission of aid that does not exceed €100 000 over a period of three years. It is supposed that such aid does not distort competition within the meaning of the Treaty of Rome. In addition, aid linked to environmental issues may be allowed if it enables an improvement in conditions beyond the required environmental standards. The Commission takes the same favourable view regarding aid to SMEs as long as they contribute to social stability and economic dynamism.

Article 87, as well as EU court practice, provides the European Commission with a wide discretionary margin in the decision-making process. None the less, the Commission employs two criteria:

- *Compensatory justification* To be 'cleared' as compatible with the rules, aid has to conform with goals set out in Article 87 and it must be proved that, without state aid, free markets would not be capable of accomplishing the same end.
- *Transparency* Each aid programme has to be justified and its effects measurable. Member states must notify the Commission about the form, volume, duration and objectives of aid.

If, two months after the notification, the European Commission has not made an explicit decision, aid is regarded as tacitly accepted. The European Commission may decide 'not to raise objections', which means that the application is preliminarily approved, but the Commission needs further information in order to reach a final decision. The Commission can open up the procedure (Article 88) and ask the parties concerned to submit their comments. The European Commission then makes a final decision on the compatibility of aid with the EU rules.

Article 87 defines state aid as any measure that distorts or threatens to distort competition on the common market. The European Commission and the Court of Justice interpret this broad definition of state aid in a rather open way. They take aid to mean any favour given by a government to promote a certain economic activity: some economic agents or activities are treated more favourably than the others. Hence, this distorts competition because of favouritism regarding the ones that receive assistance and others that do not.

Services of general economic interest present a special area of attention. Many of those services may not be commercially viable without public aid. This is most obvious in the area of transport, railways in particular. The *Altmark* case (C280/00) concerned state aid to the bus service in the rural district of Stendal in Germany. The European Court of Justice ruled in 2000 that compensations to firms that perform services of general economic interest do not represent state aid that distorts competition on the Single European Market. Hence, public authorities are allowed to support firms that provide public services with funds necessary for the operation of their business. However, any compensation over and above this (vaguely defined) norm is incompatible with Article 87. If there is an overcapacity, such as in certain types of road transport, in principle no aid is permitted for the purchase of vehicles. However, it is possible to grant aid if its objective is to increase safety in traffic or the protection of the environment.

State aid can be provided in a form that includes subsidies, tax concessions, special public guarantees, supply of goods or services on preferential conditions and favours regarding credit terms offered to one or more firms or their associates. Loans and guarantees given by the state or its agency do not necessarily constitute aid. The aid element exists only when such injections of funds are offered on conditions that are superior to the ones prevailing on the market.

Some governments still attempt to disguise industrial aid as regional aid. This is difficult to detect if the aided company makes a loss. R&D support can similarly be abused. 'Support' to the manufacturing and services sectors needs to be in the R&D stage otherwise foreign competitors, mainly from the US, would complain that EU subsidies are distorting international competition. Any EU member state can finance basic and applied research in the private sector according to agreed sliding scales.[95] The Commission's framework on state aid for R&D of 1995 outlined several criteria for the compatibility of such aid with the Single European Market. They include the following:

- There is a distinction between 'industrial research' and 'pre-competitive development activity'. The closer to the marketplace for final goods, the more aid is likely to distort competition.
- State aid for R&D should create an incentive for the recipient firm to carry out R&D in addition to what it would undertake in the normal course of its business operation. (Now, prove that?)
- Aid for 'industrial research' may be up to 50 per cent of the cost, whereas aid for 'pre-competitive development' may be up to 25 per cent of the cost. None the less, there are special additional bonuses of 10 per cent for projects that involve SMEs, of 15 per cent if the project is a priority under the EU R&D programme and up to 10 per cent if R&D is undertaken in regions eligible for regional aid.
- Maximum aid for R&D in the EU (allowable under the GATT Agreement on Subsidies and Countervailing Measures) is 75 per cent for 'industrial research' and 50 per cent for 'pre-competitive development activity'.
- Member states have to notify the European Commission about all individual aid packages for projects exceeding €25 million in which aid exceeds €5 million.

The State-aid Department of the European Commission has a staff of about 80 officials responsible for monitoring state aid and carrying out other tasks in the field. They cannot be expected to examine every instance of state aid, especially as every region in each member country has staff (which often significantly outnumber the Commission's) to dispense aid. Therefore, the European Commission's priority is to prevent anti-competition aid programmes.[96] The Commission has to ensure that aid is given to the most disadvantaged regions and that it is compatible with Treaty rules. If it is not, then it may demand that such aid is repaid to the state. This was the case in 2003 when the European Commission decided that Electricité de France (the state-owned power group) must repay about €1 billion. All these formidable issues linked to competition are increasingly becoming a paradise for lawyers.

A general EU aid policy intention is to reduce the volume of aid and reduce public meddling in business. However, there are two general reform priorities. One is to support the Lisbon objectives and EU cohesion, while the other is to consolidate and simplify rules wherever possible. Aid will be authorised if it assists the Lisbon strategy especially in private R&D; if it helps the lagging regions to increase the competitiveness of their firms (rather than to aid inefficient businesses); and if it assists SMEs to train and employ labour, as well as to access capital.

The new multisectoral framework on regional assistance for large investment projects entered into force in 2004. This included a limited notification

Table 2.8 Public aid scale

Size of the project	Adjusted aid ceiling
Up to €50 million	No reduction. 100% of regional state aid ceiling
For the part between €50 million and €100 million	50% of regional state aid ceiling
For the part exceeding €100 million	34% of regional state aid ceiling

Note: For example, in an area with a regional aid ceiling of 20 per cent, a project with an eligible investment cost of €80 million can obtain up to €13 million in aid; that is, €10 million for the first €50 million of investment, plus €3 million for the remaining €30 million of investment.

obligation for large projects balanced by a significant reduction in tolerable aid levels. According to this framework, the actual aid that a large project can receive matches the aid ceiling set in the regional aid maps, which is then automatically reduced in accordance with the scale set in Table 2.8.

A 'cohesion bonus' can be granted to large projects co-financed by the EU structural funds. For such projects, the acceptable aid intensity calculated under the above scale will be multiplied by a factor of 1.15. In so doing, this system will take into account the significance of these large co-financed projects for the economic and social cohesion of the EU. In any case, firms that receive regional aid must maintain their business activity and remain in the same location for at least five years, otherwise the received funds must be repaid.

Any project still has to be notified and assessed individually if the intended aid in that project is higher than could be obtained by a €100 million project. If such a project reinforces a high market share (less than 25 per cent), or increases capacity in a non-growing sector by more than 5 per cent, aid will not be authorised.

The European Commission has approved public aid (subsidies) for many purposes. This was usually the case when they serve the common interest of the EU. Such derogations from Article 87 include support to regional development, R&D, creation of human capital, SMEs, savings in energy and protection of the environment. Table 2.9 presents the dynamics of state aids in the EU(15) in the 1992–2002 period. State aid peaked (€75 billion) during the 1993 recession (the year when the Single European Market started its first year of operation). From then, aid slowly but surely declined as the eurozone set strict limits on public expenditure[97] for the participating countries. The sharpest annual decline in aid was from €60 billion in 1998 to €52 billion in 1999 when the eurozone started its first year of operation.

Table 2.9 *Trend in the annual level of state aid in EU(15), 1999–2002*

	1992	1993	1994	1995	1996	1997	1998	1999	2000	2001	2002	Average 1998–2000	Average 2000–2002
Total state aid less railways (€bn)	70.4	75.2	72.4	71.0	71.5	67.1	60.5	52.5	50.9	49.5	48.8	54.6	49.7
Total state aid less agriculture, fisheries and transport (€bn)	54.4	60.2	55.4	52.6	54.2	50.2	46.4	37.6	36.6	35.4	34.0	40.2	35.4
Total aid less railways (% of GDP)	1.09	1.18	1.11	1.00	0.98	0.88	0.77	0.64	0.59	0.57	0.56	0.67	0.57
Total aid less agriculture, fisheries and transport (% of GDP)	0.85	0.95	0.85	0.74	0.75	0.66	0.59	0.46	0.43	0.41	0.39	0.49	0.41

Source: European Commission (2004). *State Aid Scoreboard*. Brussels, 20 April 2004, COM(2004) 256 final.

After this, total aid continued to decline by about €1 billion a year. None the less, the volume of granted aid remained massive: €49 billion at the end of the period of observation.

State aid as a share of GDP in 1998–2002 is given in Figure 2.13. State aid in the EU(15) accounts for about 0.4 per cent of GDP. Britain and the Netherlands are the least interventionist states by this measure, while Portugal and Denmark were the most interventionist ones during the period of observation. Average EU(15) state aid per capita in purchasing power standard (PPS) during the same period declined from €107 to €94 (Table 2.10). Large disparities among countries can easily be discerned. Britain was the most 'liberal' country (€36 per capita), while Denmark (€228 per capita) intervened more than six times as much as Britain during 2000–02.

The manufacturing sector received half of the total aid, while agriculture received more than a quarter during 2000–02 (Table 2.11). State aid represented more than 1.5 per cent of the value added in the EU(15) manufacturing sector during 1998–2002. The highest share was in Denmark, while the lowest was in Britain (Figure 2.14). Among the horizontal EU objectives in 2002, regional aid, environment, R&D and SMEs (in this declining order) received most aid. There are still large disparities among the EU member countries regarding priorities that they accord to different target objectives for aid. For example, the Scandinavian countries assist the environment-related activities more than the others (Table 2.12).

The 'price' (aid) for maintaining certain production geography in the national economies of the member countries was predominantly paid in terms of grants (59 per cent) and tax exemptions (24 per cent) during 2000–02 (Figure 2.15). However, there are differences among the EU countries. While Austria, Belgium, Denmark, Spain and Sweden provided over 80 per cent of aid in the form of grants, Germany (38 per cent), Ireland (67 per cent) and Portugal (74 per cent) preferred tax exemptions.

A general downward trend in state aid in the EU(15) reflects several issues, including: the application of competition rules in the EU; a reduction in public expenditure and budget discipline 'forced' by the Maastricht criteria for the eurozone; and a political commitment to reduce state aid as a percentage of GDP in order to increase the competitiveness of EU goods and services along the lines of the Lisbon declaration (2000). Overall reduction in state aid is a pro-competition move in the EU. In addition, if aid is channelled towards innovation and acquisition of human capital, this may only assist the process that started in Lisbon. This is an encouraging trend as this type of assistance to businesses and regions is one of very few policy instruments available in the eurozone. Reliance on competition policy within the Single European Market will continue to stimulate market-led

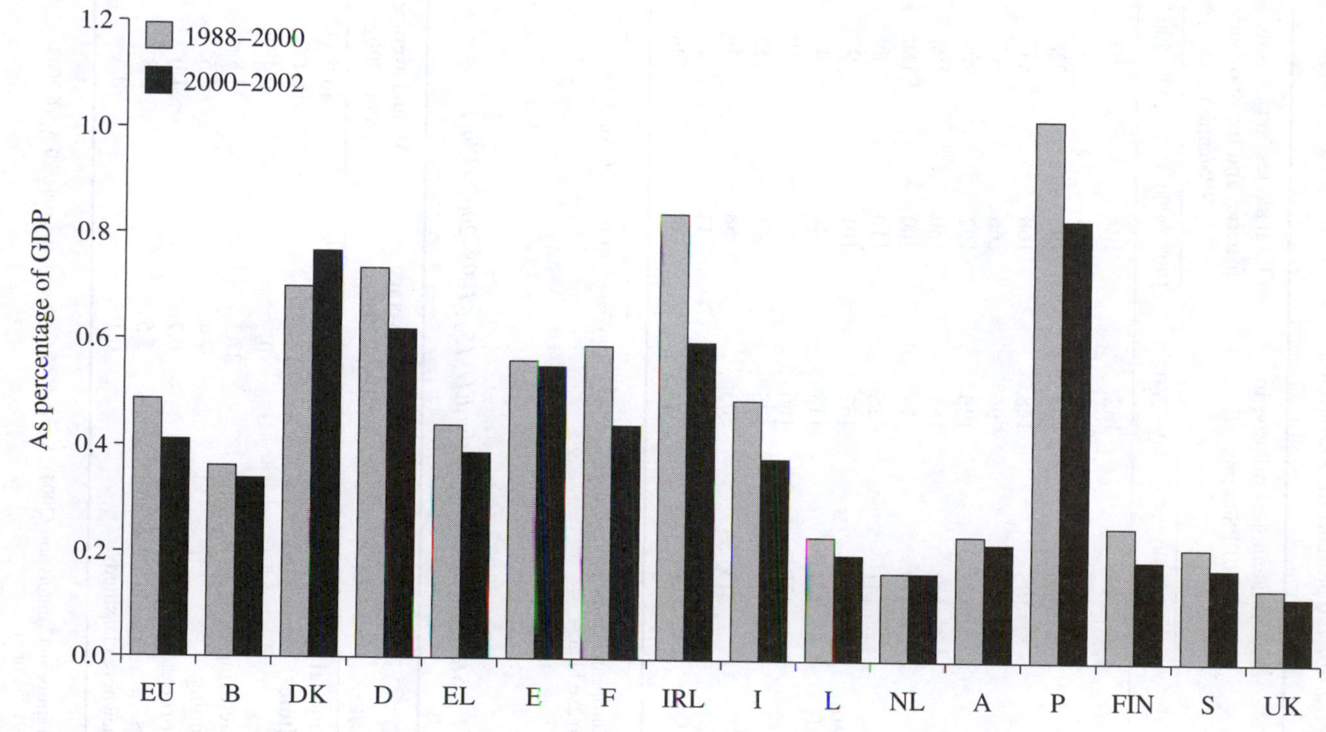

Source: European Commission (2004). *State Aid Scoreboard*. Brussels, 20 April 2004, COM(2004) 256 final.

Figure 2.13 State aid (less agriculture, fisheries and transport) as a percentage of GDP, 1998–2002

Table 2.10 State aid per capita, 1998–2002

	Total aid less railways in PPS/capita		Total aid less agriculture, fisheries and transport in PPS/capita	
	1998–2000	2000–2002	1998–2000	2000–2002
EU	146	132	107	94
Belgium	115	125	84	83
Denmark	260	294	197	228
Germany	185	168	168	147
Greece	101	96	66	60
Spain	125	130	102	104
France	178	161	130	108
Ireland	313	278	200	160
Italy	141	115	110	89
Luxembourg	175	167	101	93
Netherlands	134	118	44	43
Austria	170	166	58	59
Portugal	211	176	161	130
Finland	313	303	58	46
Sweden	100	102	53	47
UK	57	55	35	36

Source: European Commission (2004). *State Aid Scoreboard*. Brussels, 20 April 2004, COM(2004) 256 final.

Table 2.11 State aid by sector in the EU(15), 1998–2002 (€bn)

	Annual average 1998–2000	Annual average 2000–2002
Overall national aid of which:	54.6	49.7
Agriculture	13.4	13.1
Fisheries	0.3	0.4
Manufacturing	27.3	24.8
Coal mining	7.4	6.5
Transport exl. railways	0.7	1.0
Services	5.5	3.8
Not elsewhere classified	0.1	0.3

Source: European Commission (2004). *State Aid Scoreboard*. Brussels, 20 April 2004, COM(2004) 256 final.

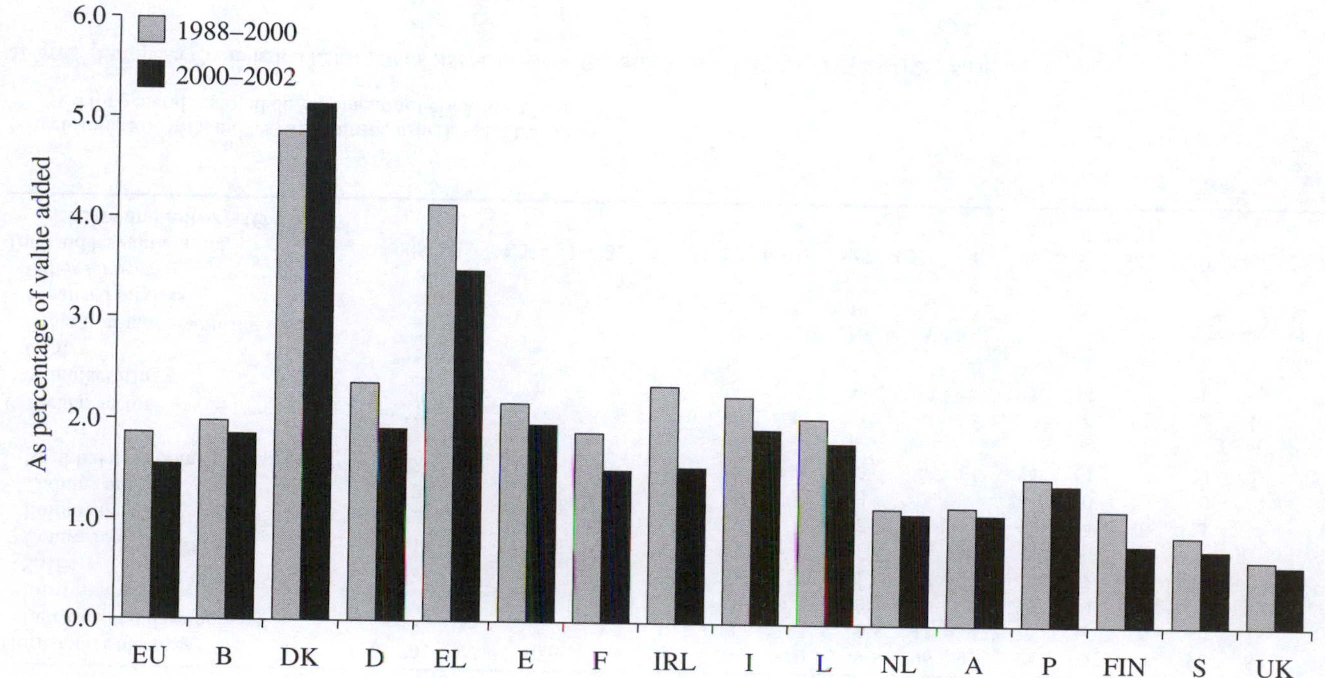

Source: European Commission (2004). *State Aid Scoreboard*. Brussels, 20 April 2004, COM(2004) 256 final.

Figure 2.14 *State aid (less agriculture, fisheries and transport) to the manufacturing sector as a percentage of value-added, 1998–2002*

Table 2.12 *State aid for horizontal objectives and particular sectors in EU(15) in 2002**

	EU	B	DK	D	EL	E	F	IRL	I	L	NL	A	P	FIN	S	UK
Horizontal objectives	73	97	10.0	66	100	67	60	49	96	92	98	95	39	98	84	70
Research and development	15	15	5	14	10	12	18	8	13	9	26	33	5	0	18	27
Environment	15	0	53	30	–	4	3	0	0	0	39	19	5	38	39	5
SMEs	14	20	1	6	15	20	17	2	33	21	4	17	15	12	5	15
Commerce	1	0	–	0	–	0	2	–	2	1	5	–	0	7	–	0
Employment aid	2	7	34	0	–	3	0	8	1	–	0	4	6	11	–	0
Training aid	2	2	3	0	–	8	0	4	1	–	–	10	5	0	1	2
Regional development n.c.c. (**)	23	52	3	16	74	19	18	26	46	61	24	14	3	29	21	21
	–	–	–	–	–	–	–	–	–	–	–	–	–	–	–	–
Particular sectors	27	3	0	34	0	33	40	51	4	8	2	4	61	2	16	30
Manufacturing	3	–	0	4	0	5	2	35	3	–	2	4	4	0	–	1
Coal	15	–	–	30	–	28	16	–	–	–	–	–	–	–	–	1
Other non-manufacturing sectors	2	–	–	–	–	0	0	–	0	–	–	0	–	–	–	28
Financial services	5	–	–	–	–	–	22	14	–	–	–	–	57	–	–	–
Other services	0	3	–	0	–	0	–	3	–	8	–	–	0	2	15	–
Total aid less agriculture, fisheries and railways (€bn)	34.005	933	1.274	11.431	410	3.503	6.197	525	4.528	56	780	453	649	231	406	2.629

Notes:
* Percentage of total aid less agriculture, fisheries and transport.
** Aid for general regional development not elsewhere classified.

Source: European Commission (2004). *State Aid Scoreboard*. Brussels, 20 April 2004, COM(2004) 256 final.

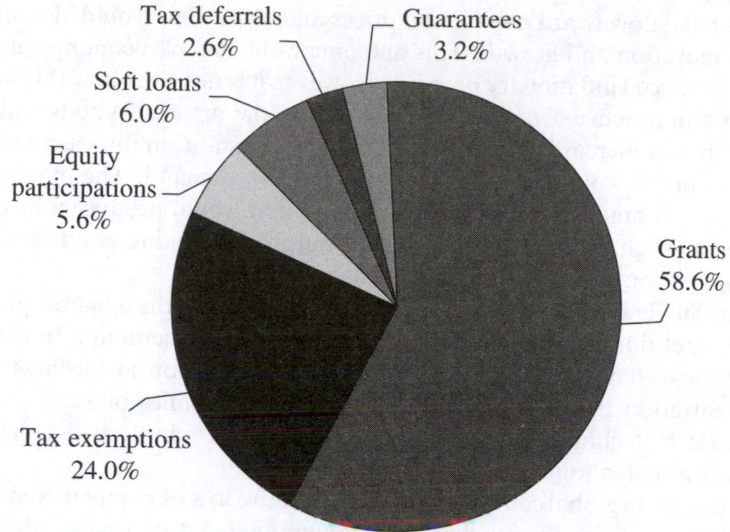

Source: European Commission (2004). *State Aid Scoreboard*. Brussels, 20 April 2004, COM(2004) 256 final.

Figure 2.15 Share of each aid instrument in total aid for manufacturing and services in the EU(15), 2000–2002

restructuring and more efficient spatial allocation of resources. However, this has important policy implications for the central and east European EU member countries, as they still need substantial assistance to catch up with the ever-expanding *acquis communautaire*. Budgetary restrictions could provoke internal EU(15) political problems. One can already hear voices saying: 'Why should we subsidise the new member countries when we have unresolved domestic issues and when we are making unprecedented efforts to reduce our domestic expenditure still further because of the eurozone?'

Conclusion

Relatively small countries that are in the process of development employ industrial policies that may not always be competition friendly. Even large and now developed countries used this type of policy at one time. Relatively large and developed countries claim that they now value the benefits of competition.[98] As concentration of business in certain industries increases, there is a trend to tighten antitrust policy and maintain a certain level of competition in the internal market. Increased competition would in most cases put a downward pressure on prices and costs. This would also stimulate innovation and growth. This outcome would enable economic growth with a reduced inflationary pressure. However, it is not clear how this would happen in practice. Competition may reduce the prices of goods and services. It may increase output, but keep prices constant. In this case a reduction in prices would be offset by an increase in demand. The most likely outcome in practice would be that competition would produce a blend of benefits which accrue from increase in output of existing goods and services, creation of new ones and decrease in prices.

The Single European Market Programme enhanced the dynamic process of competition through an easing of the market segmentation in the EU and, somewhat paradoxically, increasing concentration in business. This concentration permitted the employment of economies of scale and an increase in technical efficiency in production. In addition, it enhanced R&D through a joint sharing of high costs.

A change in global competition and the relative loss of competitiveness by the EU in comparison with the US in the computer and aerospace industries, Japan in cars and consumer electronics, and developing countries in textiles and clothing, as well as a potential loss in a number of other industries, were among the driving forces that brought about the Single European Market in 1993. Businesses reacted to this internal market deepening by consolidations through mergers and acquisitions, as well as joint ventures. An increase in internal EU competition that came through the elimination of internal barriers gave the EU the chance of benefiting from the unexploited economies of scale that reduced, over time, costs of production and increased the global competitiveness, not only of manufacturing (aircraft or mobile telecom products), but also of services. All this would provide an additional bonus to investment and the growth of the EU's economy. Hence, not only innovating firms and those that use state-of-the-art technologies but consumers too are able to reap rewards from the opportunities provided by increased competition. The dynamic segment (at least) of labour might gain from the integration process, as trade and competition do not determine whether there are jobs, but rather what kind of jobs are available.

2.3.3 SPECIALISATION AND RETURNS TO SCALE

Returns to scale refer to the relation between input requirements and output response with its impact on costs. Economies of scale comprise a number of things, from simple technical scale to phenomena such as processing complex information; direction, control and improvement of independent activities; and experience. If a firm's output increases in the same proportion as its inputs, then that firm's technology exhibits constant returns to scale, or, one may say, a firm has constant marginal costs. If a firm's output increases by a greater proportion than inputs, then this firm's technology has increasing returns to scale or it enjoys decreasing marginal costs (or increasing marginal product).[99] If a firm's output decreases by a smaller proportion than input requirements, then the firm suffers from decreasing returns to scale or increasing marginal costs.

Suppose that a firm uses a set of inputs X in the production of a good Y. Constant, increasing and decreasing returns to scale may be defined for homogeneous production functions. A function is homogeneous of degree k if:

$$f(tx_1, tx_2) = t^k f(x_1, x_2) \tag{2.5}$$

where $t > 0$ and k is constant. If the set of inputs X is increased by t, output is increased by t^k : $k = 1$ implying constant returns to scale; $k > 1$ increasing returns to scale; and $0 < k < 1$ results in decreasing returns to scale.

These can also be presented graphically. Figure 2.16 depicts technologies with various returns to scale. A firm's technology has constant returns to scale in case (a) where isoquants for output of quantities 1, 2 and 3, respectively, intersect the path from the origin at equal distances, making 0A = AB = BC. In the increasing returns to scale (case b), isoquants are closer together, 0A > AB > BC. The third case (c) describes decreasing returns to scale. Isoquants are farther away from each other, 0A < AB < BC.

Figure 2.17 illustrates the cost behaviour of different technologies. With constant returns to scale, marginal cost per unit of output Y is unchanged. With increasing returns to scale, as output increases, costs per unit of output are decreasing; while with decreasing returns to scale as output

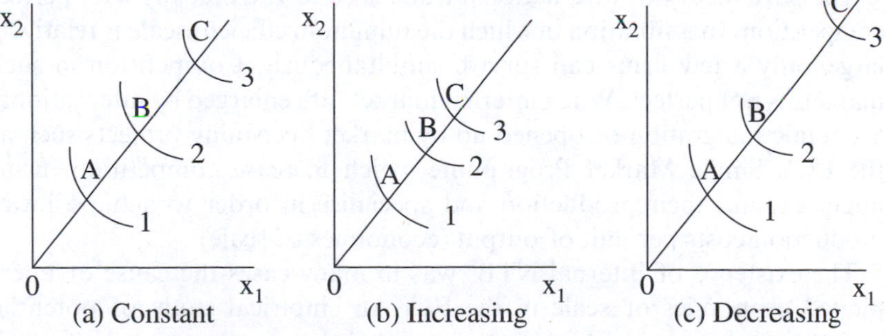

Figure 2.16 Technologies with constant, increasing and decreasing returns to scale

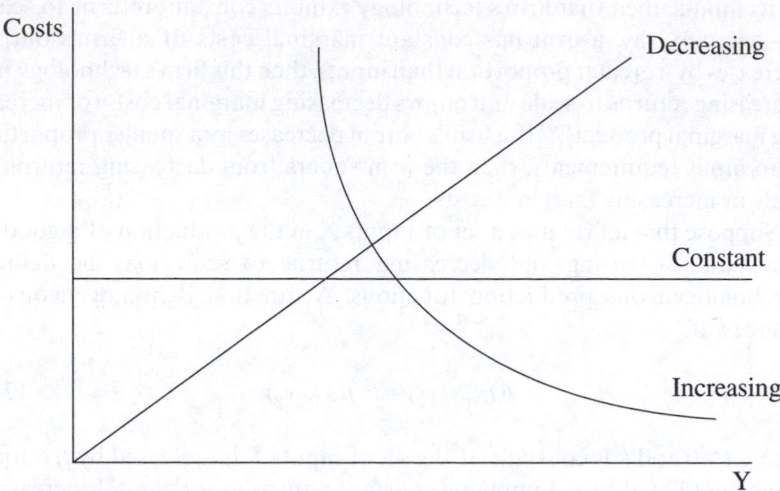

Figure 2.17 Cost curves with constant, increasing and decreasing returns to scale

increases, costs per unit of output are also increasing. Decreasing returns to scale describe a situation in which there are some inputs (such as land) in fixed supply. With increasing returns to scale in industry Y, the ratio at which the two goods exchange in the market differs from the ratio in which they can be converted into one another through production. When factors are shifted to the increasing returns to scale industry, the gain in production in that industry is greater than the loss of output in the other, so there is a net increase in output. This increases real wages, average standards of living and GDP.

The pure theory of international trade is concerned mostly with perfect competition. In a situation in which the minimum efficient scale is relatively large, only a few firms can survive simultaneously. Competition in such markets is not perfect. When internal markets are enlarged by international economic integration or opened up by market-deepening projects such as the EU's Single Market Programme which increase competition, firms might expand their production and specialise in order to achieve lower production costs per unit of output (economies of scale).

The existence of internal NTBs was in many cases the cause of unexploited economies of scale in the EU. An empirical study of potential economies of scale in EU industry reported that in more than half of all manufacturing industries 20 firms of efficient size could co-exist in the EU, whereas the largest national markets can support only four each. The EU internal market offers the potential for efficiency and competition. Twenty efficient firms are more likely to ensure effective competition than only four firms (Emerson et al., 1988, p. 18). This finding ignored the logic behind the role of concentration in modern industries and the contribution which a few oligopolies, exploiting economies of scale and carefully monitored by appropriate regulatory authorities, can and do make to economic welfare. Besides, there may be fierce competition even among these four firms. Just take a look at competition in the EU and US long-distance telephone-call business or the fierce competition among a few Japanese electronic conglomerates in both the domestic and international markets. In addition, relatively high diversity of tastes in EU countries can make the achievement of output in very large production runs unnecessary and unprofitable, contrary to the US where the internal market is very homogenised.

The approach to economies of scale does not have to be mechanical. Successful managers of firms must know where to find economies of scale so that a firm may lower its minimum efficient scale of production by buying certain components from outside. Take, for example, car production and assume that each car consists of three equally important components (X, Y and Z, respectively) plus the assembly. In addition, the annual production of the following quantities of components is necessary to achieve the minimum efficient scale: X = 800 000; Y = 500 000; Z = 250 000; and assembly 100 000. If all inputs are produced internally, then the firm must produce 800 000 cars in order to reach the minimum efficient scale in production in X. However, if the firm buys X and Y from other firms that are specialised in the production of these components and that are sold to various car manufacturers, then it only needs to produce 250 000 cars to achieve the minimum efficient scale in the production of Z. Technological change has reduced the minimum efficient scale of production, but the firms tend to increase the value of just-in-time operation and minimisation in stocks. Although the example is rather simplistic, in reality Volvo could be an example of a car producer that fits such a category. Even though the production run of Volvo is significantly smaller than, for example, Toyota or Volkswagen, Volvo has often been a highly profitable car manufacturer.

The US economic system is created in such a way that it is open to internal competition. Antitrust legislation is very strong. None the less, the President's Commission on Industrial Competitiveness (1985, vol. 2, pp. 192–3) recognised the potential efficiency gains which may come from the concentration of business in certain industries. Without the prospective reward of temporary monopoly, firms may not have big incentives to innovate. 'A nation that sacrifices a particular high-technology industry will gradually sacrifice many of the local technological capabilities nurtured by it. And the ultimate loss is likely to be even greater, since without these capabilities the nation will find it difficult to exploit the footloose technological knowledge created abroad' (Tyson, 1992, p. 42). A temporary departure from free competition may be desirable, in the sense that it is better to allow the establishment of temporary monopolies as a way of inducing innovation than to seek static efficiency at the cost of technological progress (Krugman, 1990a, p. 173). If the American firms fail to withstand international competition over a wide range of industries, then the US approach to competition in a situation with imperfect markets, rapidly changing technology and expanding exchange of information (both by volume and by speed) could consign the American example to the history books.

Changes in technology exert a continuous pressure on plant efficiency. Hence, the minimum efficient plant size changes over time. Large-scale production is attractive and profitable only if there is secure access to a wide and growing market. It is reasonable, therefore, to assume that firms which operate on a wide market are more likely to be closer to the minimum efficient plant size than those which act within a more restricted framework. However, recent developments in technology are diminishing the classic scale economies associated with mass production in large plants. In response to an increase in income and to changes in demand, modern technology increases the role of smaller, but highly specialised or flexible, plants.

Economies of scale are largest in transport equipment, electronics, office machines, chemicals and other manufactured products. These are the industries in which demand has the highest growth and where technology changes rapidly. The common element in these industries is the vast investment required to produce even a small amount of output.[100] Advanced technology is not necessarily based on increasing returns to scale, but such returns are frequently found in high-technology industries. In addition, these industries are under continuous pressure from international competition. Industries with relatively smaller returns to scale are those with a stagnant demand and relatively low technology content. They include the food, textile, clothing and footwear industries. The problem with the EU's manufacturing sector is that a significant part of its export specialisation has for a long time been in industries with relatively stagnant or declining demand and relatively weak economies of scale, while the US and Japanese producers and exporters have specialised in goods produced by industries with strong economies of scale. This was especially true during the 1980s.

Adam Smith pointed out that specialisation is limited by the extent of the market. A customs union increases the market area for firms in the participating countries, hence it opens up opportunities for specialisation. A country may gain from economies of scale which form an independent source for trade. If countries trade, they may gain not only from the exchange of goods and services but also from specialisation and a wider choice of goods. Trade increases the bundle of available goods and services in relation to what is available in autarky. Specialisation and alteration in the output mix in a country may take full advantage of its factor endowment. This holds not only for economic integration but also for strategies to open up and deepen the internal market, as was the case with the Single European Market Programme. It was hoped that the long-term impact of the programme, together with additional instruments, would rectify the EU's comparative disadvantage in comparison with the US, Japan and a few other countries in certain industries. Later on came the Lisbon (2000) declaration to make the EU 'the most competitive and dynamic knowledge-based economy in the world capable of sustainable growth with more and better jobs and greater social cohesion' by 2010.[101]

Economies of scale may be internal to individual firms. They may also be external to these firms when the whole industry grows and when all the firms in that industry enjoy the fruits of such growth. For example, networking (phones or cyberspace exchange of data) is the consequence of economies of scale. The peculiarity of economies of scale is that they are not consistent with perfect competition. With imperfect market structure all welfare outcomes are possible (but not necessarily desirable). A perfectly competitive firm takes the price for its output as given. A firm with increasing returns to scale in such a market will find it profitable to produce one more unit of output since it can do so at less than the prevailing price. Thus, it would tend to increase output until it dominates the market, while efficiency may set the price for its output.

Consider the case in Figure 2.18 which illustrates the impact of economies of scale on price in the exporting country A. The vertical axis shows the price in country A for good X. Increasing returns to scale are implied by the downward-sloping AC_a curve. The producer of this good has a monopoly position in the domestic market. There is no producer in country B, but this country has a tariff on imports of good X for fiscal reasons. Domestic demand in country A is represented by the curve D_a and the demand for the product in country B is represented by the curves D_b and $D_{b'}$. The former is the demand curve incorporating a tariff in country B on imports of good X, while the latter reflects demand for this good if no tariffs were levied.

The initial equilibrium in this market is represented by the intersection of the joint demand curve D_{a+b} and the AC_a curve as implied by the monopoly position of the country A producer. If countries A and B enter into a customs union, then the tariff on imports of good X into country B will be eliminated, increasing the demand for this good. Thus, the curve representing demand in country B is $D_{b'}$ and the joint demand in the customs union is $D_{a+b'}$. Faced with this increased demand the producer in country A will expand output. With increasing returns to scale this output expansion lowers the marginal

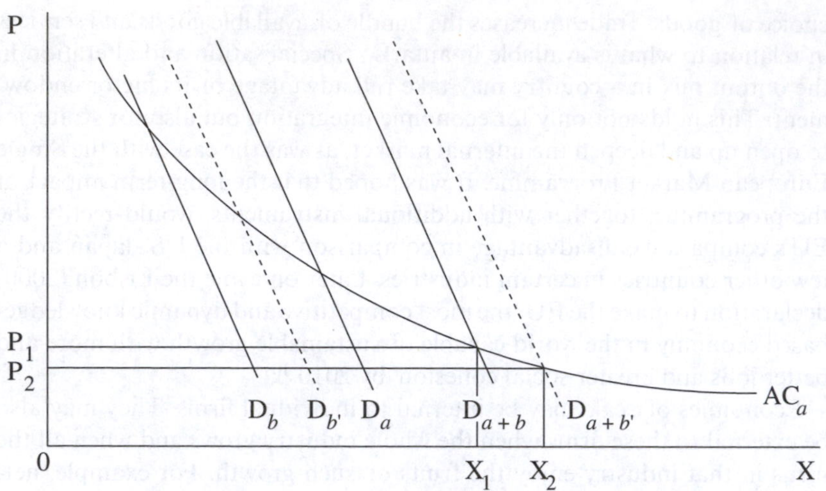

Figure 2.18 Economies of scale and their impact on price in the exporting country

and average costs of production and leads to a fall in the equilibrium price from P_1 to P_2. The elimination of the tariff has an unambiguously positive effect: all consumers can purchase a greater quantity of good X at a lower price and profit to the producer has increased.

The above result is called the 'cost-reduction effect' (Corden, 1984, p. 123). It is distinct from trade creation since the existing supplier reduces the price for the good X. There is an additional effect: suppose that there was an initial tariff on imports of good X but it was insufficient to induce domestic production of X in country A. After the creation of a customs union with country B, the market area for country A is increased. Costs of production may fall, hence production of good X may begin in country A, replacing imports into both customs union partners from country C. For country A this is *trade suppression*, while for country B it represents *trade diversion*. While learning by doing, country A may become a more efficient producer of good X than country C, so in the longer run this policy may pay off. The country in which production with increasing returns to scale occurs gets double gains (employment and increased production). Governments in the customs union may cooperate in order to evenly distribute the industries with increasing returns to scale, otherwise they may end up in an investment subsidy war to attract such industries.

At the start of the Single European Market Programme the estimate was that the opening up of public procurement contracts in the EU would save the local taxpayers €20 billion. Bids that come from third countries could be rejected if the non-EU content is more than 50 per cent (unless there is a reciprocity treaty with the third country) and if the non-EU bid is up to 3 per cent cheaper than the best bid coming from the EU. Such a system could cause losses to taxpayers. For example, they would have to pay higher prices for Greek or Portuguese supplies of tinned food consumed by different armies than would be the case if they were purchased in a third country. In addition, prior to the 1990s, Greece and Portugal were buying electrical turbines from Switzerland as there was no domestic production; following the establishment of the Single European Market in 1993, the supplies would come from relatively less efficient (more expensive) providers in the EU. Those extra outlays could add to the budget deficits the governments want to curb. As the Swiss and other non-EU producers are subject to economies of scale, a reduction of sales/output in the EU will tend to increase their prices. The Single European Market system benefits Greek or Spanish ship builders and ship repairers relative to Japan and the developing world (Tovias, 1990).

In perfectly contestable markets, price equals marginal cost (firms just cover production costs of the last unit and profits are zero). Economies of scale introduce imperfection into the market system, since firms set prices at average cost and make profits. Therefore, economies of scale lead to more specialisation compared with the situation with constant returns to scale. Barriers to entry and exit protect the existence of these firms with economies of scale. These barriers increase risk, costs, uncertainty and delays to a newcomer relative to the incumbent.

The definition of entry barriers is important for court antitrust cases. However, this definition has a long, rich and confused history.[102] Inability by lawyers and economists to reach a broad consensus about the definition of entry barriers introduced debates about the desirability of certain mergers and acquisitions. If a merger or an acquisition creates barriers to entry, it may not be socially desirable. For our purposes, we shall take an entry barrier to mean an advantage that the incumbent firm enjoys over potential new entrants. This advantage permits the incumbent firm to increase prices of output above the equilibrium level at least for a certain period of time without attracting the entry of new firms. Entry barriers create a rent from previous investment that provided the firm with incumbency. Social welfare is reduced because of no or because of delayed new entry of firms into this market.

Barriers to *entry* in an industry include:

- high human and capital requirements (sunk costs necessary to achieve minimum efficient scale of output);
- product differentiation and consumer preferences and brand loyalties;

- indivisible production technology (a strong close spatial presence of suppliers and consumers is necessary);
- externalities (linkages);
- R&D;
- regulation (environment, product quality, permissions, accounting, standards, intellectual property rights);
- marketing (access to distribution network, exclusive dealership);
- advertising needs and costs;
- reaction by market incumbents (predatory pricing and excess capacity in the existing firms to discourage any new entry);
- trade and industrial policies (tariffs, quotas, domestic content requirements, NTBs);
- organisational complexity; and
- availability of staff.

Barriers to *exit* include:

- past sunk costs (not yet depreciated);
- durable specialised assets that cannot be sold easily;
- regulation (bankruptcy law, labour settlement, cost of dismantling facilities, for example, nuclear power plants);
- public bailout (otherwise medium-sized towns may disappear);
- new trade protection;
- strategic business decision by a diversified firm to save the facility for the future; and
- emotional attachment to the facility by the managers and owners.

Predatory behaviour is a medium- or long-term business strategy that aims to eliminate an existing or potential future competitor from a market. A firm that employs this strategy wants to preserve its (monopoly or oligopoly) market position by three general means:

- below-cost pricing of output (charging unprofitably low prices at the present time);
- restriction of access to assets (refusal to supply inputs, exclusive dealings, excessive charges to enter marketing network, fidelity rebates that reward clients not to purchase from competitors or new entrants); and
- building a much larger output capacity than current and expected demand. If there is a potential entrant, the predator may slightly increase output and lower prices. This would discourage certain potential entrants from entering the market and starting production.

The predatory strategy may be backed either by the home government's support or by charging the domestic consumers high prices in a protected market. In addition, a risk-loving firm may price its current output on the bases of the expected future lower costs of production and expanded demand, rather than on the current costs that may be higher (and low current demand). This was the practice of Texas Instruments during the 1960s and early 1970s in order to build volume of production, gain market share and move down the learning curve. It was Texas Instruments and not the Japanese producers of semiconductors that pioneered this strategy of 'pre-emptive price cutting' (Tyson, 1992, p. 89).

Sometimes it may be hard to distinguish predatory pricing from vigorous price competition. Predatory pricing is seldom a winning strategy in the long term. When a predator raises prices again, this tempts new competitors to consider market entry. The predator's losses may exceed the prey's since the prey can shut down temporarily and 'mothball' output potential while the predator must make substantial sales to keep prices low. If the prey goes bankrupt, the predator may need to acquire its assets in order to prevent a new rival from buying them up. It would often be less costly to merge with the prey at the outset than to drive it out of business by a predatory strategy (Schmalensee, 1988, p. 665). In addition, 'price wars' may have negative consequences for productivity growth in the longer term. This is because firms will have to reallocate resources from investment to cover the expenses of a 'price war'.

AKZO, a Dutch-based chemical TNC, charged different prices to buyers of comparable size. These differences in prices were not based on differences in the quality of products or changes in production costs. Therefore, the EU Court (Case C-62/86 *AKZO v. Commission*, 1991) concluded that this type of pricing behaviour by AKZO was not to pursue a general policy of favourable prices, but rather to adopt a strategy that could damage ECS, a small British competitor. AKZO was subsequently fined for this type of market behaviour. In 2003, for example, the European Commission imposed a fine of €10 million on Wanadoo, a French telecom company,[103] for abuse of a dominant position in the form of predatory pricing in ADSL-based Internet access services for the general public. Wanadoo was found to have charged prices below cost in the period from March 2001 to October 2002. This practice restricted market entry and development potential for competitors. This damaged the interests of consumers on a market which is key to the development of the information society.

Retaliation against predatory pricing can be done by means of antidumping duties. The existence of this kind of dumping is not that easily proved in practice. Even the GATT/WTO rules do not take into account volatile exchange rates, continuous shortening in the life cycle of high-technology goods and the complexity of modern marketing arrangements.

Investments in market penetration and some of the investments in plant and R&D are not recoverable. They also often have little market value. Large sunk costs make firms reluctant to enter an industry if long-term access to wide markets is not secure. Expectations about the future demand and profit play a key role in the decision-making process. This restricted or blocked entry results in a smaller number of firms in the industry than would be the case under free entry. Sunk costs provide advantages to the first entrants. Substantial rents may be earned from being at the forefront of technological change, where standards are set for future products and processes, and where, once standards are established and industries have matured, new entry becomes difficult (Tyson, 1987, p. 74). A defensive strategy to counteract such developments would be to respond to the competitor's action in order to retain market share, while an offensive strategy would be the development of improved or new goods or services in order to enter new market segments and/or to weaken the competitor.

Market pre-emption and moving early may create a market position and profits that may be sustained for a very long time. The Swiss firms in pharmaceuticals and watches, the German chemical companies, Procter & Gamble in detergents since the 1930s and Microsoft in computer software since the 1990s are obvious examples. They were among the first to move, they learned 'how to do it', exploited economies of scale, influenced standards, formed marketing networks, created brand names and established consumer loyalty. If imitation is slow, hard, costly and risky, such developments place potential competitors at a disadvantage. The longer the time lag for imitation, the greater the possibility for the firm to reap rents as the reward for risk and the right choice of investment. This increases the possibilities for rents obtained by first movers, but also opens up a great risk of failure and of falling into a trap of rigid specialisation that prevents them from adjusting to changes or moving further or elsewhere in production. New technologies might not remain clandestine forever. If a monopolist makes a profit, other firms will try to enter the industry. Imitators could appear so that the firm's advantage and rents would be eroded. This is why IBM, with an 'open' PC system, had a greater longer-term worldwide success than Macintosh with its 'closed' system.

A mature technology means that factories for standardised goods are often similar in size, hence countries may differ in the number of plants because of variations in the size of the market. This is a lesson for small and medium-sized countries, as well as for the developing ones. They should pool their markets and resources in order to overcome these barriers to entry and to reap the benefits of economies of scale.

Above a certain level of output some costs, such as depreciation of equipment, can increase disproportionally in relation to output. For example, the ends of the blades on a very large turbine move at a speed that can be close to that of sound. At such a speed, 'metal fatigue' increases disproportionally in relation to a turbine's capacity. Beyond a certain level of rotation speed, the costs in all engines based on revolution increase more than the returns. Or small and light aeroplanes can endure a 'hard landing' that would wreck a jumbo jet. Physical relations limit speed, size and weight. In addition, a strike in a firm with increasing returns to scale technology may have a profound impact on the profitability of the firm. However, the threat of competition or of removing barriers to imports may mitigate the distortion imposed by trade unions.

From the vantage point of production, economies of scale might require some level of standardisation which could restrict product variety and consumer choice. Standardisation started with the Industrial Revolution in western Europe (roughly between 1750 and 1850). Standards are technical regulations which specify the characteristics of goods. They can be quite different among countries. To harmonise them in a customs union for trade and competition purposes would be difficult. Mutual recognition of standards can be an attractive strategy in the short term. This places traders in different countries on an equal footing and eliminates disadvantages which accrue to some of them from NTBs. However, trade in general, and intra-industry trade in particular, could increase product variety in relation to autarky. Product differentiation could reduce export opportunities for small open economies such as Austria, Belgium or Switzerland. These countries have little influence on foreign tastes and tend to enjoy comparative advantages in semi-manufactured goods (Gleiser et al., 1980, p. 521).

The US and Japan, for example, have a market for durable consumer goods sometimes dominated by a single brand which takes advantage of economies of scale. The situation in EU countries is different. Almost every country has its domestic producer. But the American or Japanese formula cannot easily be replicated in Europe. This is due to diverse and deeply rooted national preferences. While the British want to load their washing machines from the front, the French prefer to do so from the top. The Dutch like high-powered machines which can spin most of the moisture out of the washing; the Italians prefer slower-spinning machines, leaving the southern sun to do the drying. This situation has its impact on the protectionist pressure against third-country suppliers, but also against suppliers from within the EU as they are prevented from following a pan-European production strategy. Yet, there are other (relatively new) goods where preferences among countries are identical. It is likely that French cheese producers will look for the same qualities in a photocopier or a fax machine as would Italian wine exporters. Common accounting and company or banking laws, therefore, could be quite useful in the EU.

If the EU approximation of standards takes place upwardly, the overall level of regulation and costs of production will increase and south and east European countries will find it increasingly difficult to withstand international competition and will grow at a slower pace than the rest of the EU. As growth falls, demand for protectionism increases. If, however, various types of, for instance, labour regulation are left to member states and the framework of mutual recognition is kept, then the northern and western EU countries could get rid of certain laws and south and east European countries would grow rapidly. The EU would expand at a substantial rate which would permit the implementation of a liberal trade policy. The ultimate irony is that only the latter course would allow northern and western EU countries to pay high wages and sustain a heavy social expenditure (Curzon Price, 1991, p. 124).

Although the Single European Market removed many NTBs to internal trade in the EU, there are others that still persist, making the single internal market imperfect. Prior to the period when the single-market initiative was applied (1985–92), major obstacles to internal trade included physical border controls, technical barriers (standards and product/service regulations), public procurement, different intellectual and industrial property laws, state aid, fiscal barriers, as well as obstacles to the mobility of labour and capital. The Single European Market made a distinction between what was essential to harmonise, and what could be left to mutual recognition. While EU standards are still being developed, the guiding principle should be mutual recognition of national standards. EU standards are being developed on a large scale, approximately 1000 a year. However, too many national regulations are still being produced, making it as hard as ever to achieve and maintain a truly homogeneous single market (Curzon Price, 1996a). It seems that regulation keeps on reinventing itself.

Various attempts to harmonise diverse goods at the EU level created a public furore in many countries. Examples include fuss about prawn cocktail crisps in Britain; the permissible level of bacteria in cheese in France; undersize apples in Denmark; the use of other than durum (hard) wheat for pasta in Italy; the application of other than the *Reinheitsgebot* (of 1516) purity rule for brewing beer in Germany; or the removal of the tilde (˜) from computer keyboards in Spain. Each year every EU country produces thousands of new regulations on new technologies and products. Every one that relates to the smooth operation of the internal market must be submitted to the European Commission. As each one carries a possible seed of conflict, it must be treated with caution. Unless it is subject to regular monitoring, the genuine Single European Market could ultimately disappear. Thus, Decision 3052/95 (adopted in 1995 and implemented in 1997) provides an improved procedure to deal with the remaining obstacles to the free movement of goods in the single market. The decision obliges member states to notify the Commission of individual measures preventing the free movement of a model, type or category of a product that has been made or sold legally in another country. The purpose of the measure is to encourage member states to think twice before making any exceptions to the EU system of mutual recognition.[104]

The neo-classical theory of international trade argues that countries should specialise in the production of those goods for which they have a comparative advantage. Modern theories are questioning this line of reasoning. International specialisation and trade are due to other factors as well. Economies of scale stimulate specialisation in production for a narrow market niche, but on a wide international market. This may entail only the reallocation of resources within the same industry or sometimes within a single company. Modern footloose industries are not linked to any particular region by inputs such as iron ore or power. So, a country's comparative advantage can be created by deliberate actions of firms, banks and/or governments.

Any consideration of returns to scale would be incomplete without mentioning services. The impact of returns to scale on costs in the manufacturing sector is obvious indeed. It is less capable of significantly reducing costs in the services sector, although experience and competition can increase productivity in this sector too. Banking, insurance, advertising, transport and shipping are the industries that are most affected by international competition. However, there are serious methodological limitations in the quantification of returns to scale in the services sector (for example, how does one measure the output of an insurance company?).

Returns to scale have not been thoroughly studied in the theory of customs unions because it is difficult to model them. Therefore, one should be very careful about using classical theory either as a description of what is likely to happen in a customs union or as a guide to policies that will ensure that such a union fulfils its expectations. Another important fact is that a substantial part of production is linked with economies of scope rather than scale. While economies of scale imply a certain level of standardisation in tastes and production, economies of scope deal with product or process diversity. Economies of scope allow firms such as Benetton to respond swiftly to changes in the supply of inputs and shifts in demand because they come from the common control of distinct, but interrelated, production activities. For example, the same kind of fabric can be used in the production of various goods.

Economies of scale are coupled with market imperfections which allow various welfare outcomes. Distortions, such as deviations from marginal cost pricing or the existence of barriers to entry and exit, mean that the creation of a customs union (or for that matter any other type of international economic integration) does not necessarily either improve or worsen welfare. With economies of scale and other distortions, the welfare effects of customs union creation and pattern of trade are much more affected by government policy than they are in the neo-classical theorists' world of pure clean and lean comparative advantage and factor proportions.

2.3.4 TERMS OF TRADE

A number of people commonly and intuitively worry that the emergence of new competitors can reduce real income in the incumbent economies. Others argue that this is a positive development, as an expansion of markets brings success and wealth to everyone. Both of these intuitions are mistaken. Growth in other countries may either aid or hurt the home country. This effect depends on the home country's bias in terms of trade:

$$T = \frac{P_x}{P_m}. \tag{2.6}$$

The terms of trade (T) are the price of a good a country exports (P_x) divided by the price of a good it imports (P_m). It is the ratio of the quantity of imports that may be obtained in trade for a certain quantity of exports or, alternatively, it is the relative price of imports to exports.[105] An increase in the terms of trade increases a country's welfare, while a decrease in this ratio reduces welfare. If a country experiences growth strongly biased towards its export good X, then, if other things are equal, the relative price of good X is decreasing. In this situation, the country has to export more of this good X for the same quantity of imported good Y. Export-biased growth tends to worsen a growing country's terms of trade to the benefit of the rest of the world. The reverse is true for the import-biased growth.

Although terms of trade provide an intellectually 'justified' basis for intervention, this has not featured significantly in many integration arrangements. If home demand for good X is elastic, then the home country's tariff on imports may reduce both consumption and imports of this good. If this country can act as a monopsonist it may turn prices on the international market in its favour, which improves its terms of trade (at least in the short term). The same powers may be wielded by a customs union. Third countries may lose on two counts: first, there is a loss in exports through trade diversion; and second, third countries have to increase their effort in exports to the customs union in order to mitigate the impact of adverse terms-of-trade changes.

If a customs union is large enough to influence its terms of trade on both the export and import sides (externalisation of integration), then the customs union sets the international prices for these goods. Other countries, supposedly small ones, which are price takers for the standardised goods, must accept prices which prevail in the customs union less the common external tariff and less the cost of transport if they want to sell in the customs union market. However, even relatively small countries are able to influence their terms of trade if they have specialisation in industries that are monopolistically competitive. A big customs union may exercise its monopoly and monopsony powers at the expense of third countries' consumers who pay domestic tariffs and producers who pay the customs union's external tariff if they want to export there.[106]

Monopoly power is not without its disadvantages. If a customs union is large enough to influence prices on international markets then, in the absence of offsetting changes in the rest of the world, an increase in the customs union's supply of good X simply decreases the price of that good. On the side of the customs union's demand for good Y from abroad, an increase in demand will increase the price of good Y. The greater the demand in the customs union for good Y and the greater the supply of good X and the greater the trade of the customs union, the greater will be the deterioration of the customs union's terms of trade. With both monopoly and monopsony powers, and without changes in the outside world, the customs union is made worse off by its desire to increase trade with third countries. This situation may be called an 'immiserising customs union'.

The terms-of-trade effects of a customs union have not only an external dimension – there is also an internal significance: trade flows among the member countries are affected too. The integrated partners are not only allies in their relations with third countries but also competitors in the customs union's internal market. The elimination of tariffs and quotas on trade in a customs union has a direct impact on internal trade and prices. A union member country may gain from an improvement of customs union terms of trade with third countries, but this gain may be reduced by worsened terms of trade with the customs union partner countries. The countries that are in a customs union may experience a shift in productivity due to increased competition and the rapid introduction of new technologies. If one excludes all demographic changes, then any increase in labour productivity has the direct effect of increasing real income under the assumption of unchanged quantity and velocity of money. This has a direct impact on the terms of trade because prices of home goods fall.

The bargaining power of those countries that have entered into a customs union is greater than the power they exert as individuals prior to entering the customs union. The EU countries use this 'weapon' in trade relations and negotiations with both the US and Japan and others. The Association of South-East Asian Nations (ASEAN) is another example of an 'integrated' group that is able to extract concessions in trade from foreign partners that are superior to those that would be available to the individual member countries. What matters, however, is not the absolute but rather the relative size of the union against its trading partners.

The improvement in the terms of trade is not only the principal effect but also one of the major goals of the integration of trade in manufactures in western Europe. The reason for the official silence on the issue is the possible charges by the injured trading partners (Petith, 1977, p. 272). The statement that improvement in terms of trade (beggar thy neighbour) is the major goal of integration in trade in manufactures in western Europe is hard to reconcile with what is happening in practice. Neither firms nor governments think in these terms, although the potential for the employment of a 'fortress' mentality as a bargaining chip is there.

The EU is often advised by third countries, especially the US, to adopt more liberal trade policies and to resist the temptation to create a 'Fortress Europe'. This was most obvious during the years of the formation of the Single European Market (1985–92). The capacity and willingness of the EU to accept such advice depends, at least in part, on similar actions by its major trading partners: the US, Japan and, increasingly, newly industrialised countries such as South Korea, China (and Taiwan), as well as Brazil.

2.3.5 OTHER EFFECTS

Increase in Earnings from Exports

Suppose that countries A and B form a customs union and that country B imports good X from country A. Country A exporters may expect an increase in export earnings from trade with the customs union partner because tariffs are no longer applied to their internal trade. Under similar assumptions country B firms may expect an increase in their export earnings from trade with country A. The assumption made is that the adjustment is cost free. Whether this short-term increase in export earnings would be sustained in the long run depends on the shift in the pattern of consumption in both countries. If one introduces costs of adjustment, then in the long run both countries have to generate income and production that would continue the short-run pattern of trade. It also depends on the development of substitutes and the level of the common external tariff which may (not) prevent imports from the outside world.

Public Goods and Services

So far we have referred to the effects of the formation of a customs union on final private goods. Let us introduce public goods which are consumed by everybody in a country, and which enhance welfare just as the consumption of private goods does. Those who want to consume many of these goods may not be prevented from doing so, nor will they be forced to pay the full price for these goods or services. There are many free riders.

Without government support, free markets would provide few public goods and services such as: defence; flood, fire and police protection; R&D (without the protection of the private appropriation of benefits); a system of contract law and a mechanism for its enforcement; arts; parks; statistics; air force acrobats; weather forecasting; and the like. Many countries generate public pride by developing the production of something that others do not make or something that they have previously imported (but without mentioning either the cost involved or the final good's import content). The Americans put a stop to their Moon landings once the former Soviet Union had pulled out (to some extent) of the space race. Such activities contribute to the 'psychological income' of a nation. Income maintenance and the provision of private goods and services, such as education and health care, at prices below costs still constitute a significant part of the activity and expenditure of every state.

Precise information on the direct and indirect costs of every public good and service are not readily available to each consumer. If consumers and taxpayers were fully aware of the total cost, they may be less keen on supporting their massive production. If there are similar propensities for the production and consumption of these goods in the countries in a customs union, then the cost per unit of the public good or service can be reduced by integration if countries can produce and consume these goods and services jointly.

In a situation where there is a preference for public goods (for example, a kind of industrial and/or agricultural production) the creation of a customs union may be a more efficient way of satisfying this preference than a country's individual non-discriminatory tariff protection. Neoclassical theory suggests that a direct production subsidy, rather than a customs union, is the most efficient protective means. The rationale for this suggestion is that this policy avoids the consumption costs which are the consequence of a tariff. On these grounds, the economic rationale for a customs union can be established on a public goods basis only if political or other constraints rule out the use of direct production subsidies (Robson, 1987, p. 53).

A country's international commitments (for example, membership of the GATT/WTO) preclude or severely restrict the use of subsidies or discriminatory tariff treatment, and expenditure from the national budgets is frequently curtailed. In this case the formation of a customs union seems to be the only feasible way of reaping the benefits of increased economic freedom created within the group. In most cases, international schemes that integrate countries occur among countries whose preferences for public goods are similar (ibid., p. 54). However, the fact remains that non-economic reasons often play a very prominent role during the creation of actual customs unions, as was the case in the EU and its subsequent enlargements.

Reallocation of Resources and Adjustment Costs

Economic integration increases individuals' welfare through increases in product variety and consumption. The neo-classical model assumes that adjustment of production (shifts from unprofitable into profitable activities) is instantaneous and costless. This is a significant weakness of the model. The immediate effects of external shocks such as changes in technology, trade liberalisation and economic integration are increases in efficiency and income. Increased employment comes later. Adjusting to such shocks may require time, resources and government intervention. Gains from shifts in production and trade as a consequence of integration should be set against the cost of adjustment in order to determine the net welfare effects of integration.

Adjustment costs (the social price of change) may be quite high in uncompetitive economies. Consider the length of time needed for the transition economies of central and eastern Europe to change to a market-type economic system. However, countries' failure to engage in external trade for a long time can become an additional obstacle to adjustment. Adjustment costs are borne both by individuals and by society. Private adjustment costs include a reduction in wages, losses in the value of housing and a depreciation of the value of firms' capital. Social costs include lost output from unemployed capital and labour.

Common external protection may discriminate against imports from outside countries in such a way that these external economies may adjust more swiftly than would otherwise be the case. To circumvent common external protection, the governments of excluded countries may respond by, among other things, shaping their geography of production and utilising their comparative advantage in higher-level manufacturing to gain a competitive edge in advanced products and export them to the integrated group of countries. Dynamic models are not as straightforward as classical models of trade and investment, but they are much closer to real life.

Experience in the EU, the EFTA and successive rounds of tariff reductions under the GATT/WTO has shown that geographical and industrial adjustment takes place relatively slowly but smoothly over a long period of time. In the case of the EU, the adjustment costs were much smaller than expected, so the elimination of tariffs was able to proceed at a faster pace (after 10 and a half years) than anticipated in the Treaty of Rome (12 years). Adjustments took place within industries, rather than between them. The disastrous scenario of firms going out of business in the EU on a large scale has never materialised. The reason for this, and for the mitigation of adjustment costs, may be found in increased capital mobility and flexible rates of exchange, although the relatively high growth rates and near full employment of the 1960s helped the adjustment process. One should not ignore the importance of having selective and achievable strategic goals. For example, the shipbuilding industry in Britain and Spain declined because it failed to specialise in the same way as the Finnish industry (in icebreakers), it was not able to match the production costs in South Korea and it lacked the potential for diversification that existed in Japan. But this is the story of only one industry. One should never generalise the situation in the whole economy based on a single-industry case study.

There is no gain without pain. If the pressure and adjustment costs that result from a relaxation of trade restrictions do not hurt someone somewhere in the economy, then they probably produce no overall benefit either. The 'compulsory' reallocation of resources is a source of gains. The adjustment cost is a finite, one-off investment. The gains accruing from improved resource allocation are ongoing. Thus, there are reasons to believe that the 'pain' is much exaggerated (Curzon Price, 1987, p. 16). Trade liberalisation accelerates competition in participating countries. For this reason, the expectation that international economic integration is beneficial in the long term can be accepted with considerable confidence. Economic adjustment and changes in the geography of production are essential for countries that want continued economic growth in the face of fast-changing technology and markets when all decisions are high-risk ones. It is necessary to learn how to live with change in order to reap gains from such a strategy.

Adjustment costs associated with shifts in economic activities include a need for a reallocation of labour. Jobs will be lost in some business activities and geographical areas, while they will be created in others. Structural funds for social, regional and industrial issues can act as built-in stabilisers that help the initial losers to recover.

An economic policy of non-interference with market forces has obvious advantages because competition and efficiency are stimulated, consumers' tastes are satisfied and there is a reduction in the costs of government administration and intervention. On the other hand, government intervention may be necessary because markets are imperfect, firms seldom take into account the social costs of production (externalities) and adjustment and market forces may increase inequality through the regional distribution of income. However, intervention intended to ease the pain of adjustment can evolve into deeply rooted protectionism that eventually increases costs for everybody. Hence, neither a pure market system nor excessive government intervention can account for all the private and social costs and benefits of adjustment. While intervention may solve major economic issues, market forces may be more successful in fine-tuning the economy.

A country's comparative advantage and geography of production are dynamic concepts. They change their character and significance over time. Countries cannot be certain that their current production advantages will remain unchanged in the future. International economic integration may be a reliable way for a country to secure wide markets for home goods/services and to obtain sources of supply in the future. Geographical proximity of the partner countries ensures that gains from trade, specialisation and a wider choice of goods are not wasted on transport costs.

2.4 'Optimum' partners for a customs union

International economic integration has been exercised in all parts of the world. There is hardly any country that is not touched by this process. However, since the Second World War many of these attempts have failed or achieved very little. The reasons for this include:

- overdependence on trade with countries outside the group (as is the case for all schemes that integrate developing countries);
- an internal market that is too small to support more than a modest degree of industrialisation and economies of scale (the Central American Common Market);
- high costs of transportation and poor communications (the Latin American Free Trade Association; integration schemes in Africa); and
- a central planning system of economic integration, as was the case in the former CMEA, which ignored market signals and prevented spontaneous fine-tuning of the economy.

A large volume of trade between countries is a condition that may induce countries to contemplate integration. If trade is of minor importance for country A, this country may not have a deep economic interest in entering a discriminatory trade arrangement with another country. The US and Canada entered into a free trade deal with Mexico (NAFTA) primarily for political reasons.[107] The 2004 eastern enlargement of the EU was also primarily motivated by political considerations. Although it was obvious what the EU may contribute to the transition countries in central and eastern Europe in economic terms, it was much less obvious what these eight countries could contribute to the EU. Their combined market size measured by the GDP at the time of eastern enlargement in 2004 was 'only' 4 per cent of the EU(15).

The creation of the German *Zollverein* integrated 39 German states in 1834. They were different sizes and they were at a diverse level of development. Bavaria's economy was principally based on agriculture. Other partner states in the *Zollverein* were lagging behind the British level of industrial development, but were far ahead of Bavaria. Towards the end of the 19th century, Bavaria attracted low technology manufacturing that profited from the local low wages. However, during the early 20th century, when the second industrial revolution took place (principally the production of vehicles), Bavaria became the heart of German car manufacturing. Bavaria's current high level of development should not be attributed exclusively to German integration. Investments in the education of engineers, researchers and managers, training of labour, capable public administrators and private managers, as well as entrepreneurship are the principal explanations for this development. However, none of these factors would have brought about the scale of success had Bavaria stayed out of the *Zollverein* and, later, the EU, and remained a relatively small and poor farming-based economy.

A costly trade policy of a customs union among partners that have a different production structure may trigger tensions, even its break-up. For example, the northern states in the US produced industrial goods which they sold to the southern states. The southern states produced cotton which they exported to Europe. The US Congress, dominated by the northern states, sharply increased import duties for manufactured goods in 1828. The result was that the north could charge higher prices for its goods on the entire domestic market. A massive additional transfer of income took place from the south to the north. South Carolina was against this tariff policy and threatened to secede unless it was revoked. The Federal government sent troops southwards, but Congress backed down. As the north could gain so much from high tariffs, it tried to introduce them again in 1860. This time Congress had the upper hand. 'This (perhaps as much as slavery) was the issue that led the Southern states to try to quit the Union' (Schiff, 2000, p. 18). Eleven southern states tried to secede from the Union, and the subsequent American Civil War lasted from 1861 to 1865.

Common and widely used technical standards in the areas of transport, telecommunications, data processing and electronics produce a relatively efficient operation of international networks without any form of economic integration. So, if this operates smoothly, the potential partner countries could look for other economic fields that may operate as well, but which require preferential trade or some other type of formal international economic integration arrangement.

Consider two countries, A and B. Country A is large and country B is small. Assume next that country A is diversified in production. If both countries are at the same level of economic development as measured by income per capita, then it is likely that the structure of imports of country B consists of a larger number of items than the structure of imports in country A. Country A may satisfy most or all of its demands from domestic sources, and this may influence its terms of trade. These assumptions hinge on the existence of important economies of scale that permit firms in the larger country to have lower costs of production. Country B has to accept the world market prices (country A's) for all goods and services other than those in which it efficiently specialises. Country A sets most of the international prices. If small country B wants to sell a standardised good in country A's market, then country B has to accept country A's domestic price less the tariff and other costs of trade. Hence, large country A's tariff may bring greater welfare cost to small country B than are the benefits from country B's own tariff on imports.

In Figure 2.19, QQ′ illustrates country B's linear production possibility frontier. The price line coincides with the production possibility frontier in autarky. With the indifference curve I, home production and consumption is at point C. If the price line moves to P_1 because of trade, then the corner solution results. Country B becomes completely specialised in the production of good Y at point Q. With the indifference curve I′ consumption is at point C_1, that is, the point where the indifference curve is tangential to the price line. If the price line changes so that production and consumption points meet, the result is offer curve QCB for country B with a kink. The construction of the offer curve for country A is similar, but the production possibility frontier for this country is shifted outwards from QQ′ and it also has a different (flatter) slope.

Consider the situation in Figure 2.20 with trade in two goods, X and Y, and two countries, A and B, where country A is large and country B is small. 0A represents big country A's offer curve, while 0B represents small country B's offer curve. The offer curves for both countries are constructed

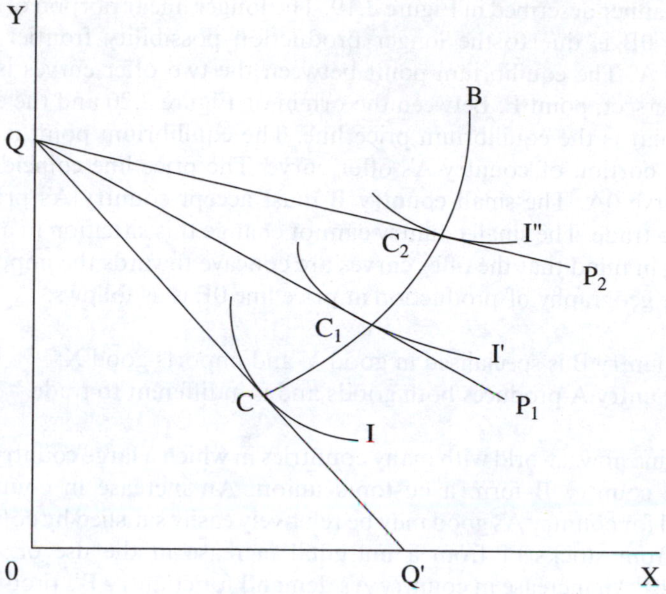

Figure 2.19 Offer curve in country B with linear production possibility frontier

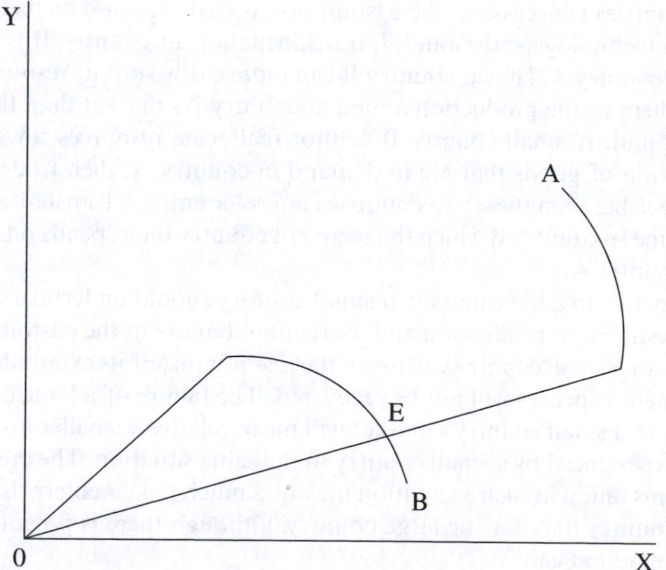

Figure 2.20 Terms of trade between a big and a small country

in the manner described in Figure 2.19. The longer linear portion of 0A relative to 0B is due to the longer production possibility frontier of big country A. The equilibrium point between the two offer curves is where they intersect, point E. Between the origin of Figure 2.20 and the equilibrium point is the equilibrium price line. The equilibrium point is on the straight portion of country A's offer curve. The price line coincides with offer curve 0A. The small country B must accept country A's price if it wants to trade. The small country cannot change this situation in any way. Bearing in mind that the offer curves are concave towards the import axis, then the geography of production at price line 0E is as follows:

- country B is specialised in good Y and imports good X;
- country A produces both goods and is indifferent to trade.

Imagine now a world with many countries in which a large country A and a small country B form a customs union. An increase in country B's demand for country A's good may be relatively easily satisfied by country A, either from stocks or from a marginal increase in the use of existing resources. An increase in country A's demand for country B's product may not be satisfied immediately if country B does not have free capacity or stocks. Country B's capacity may be limited by non-specialised, short production runs. If some reallocation of resources in the economies of these two countries is necessary, the assumption is that, because of its less specialised technologies, the rate of transformation in country B is smaller than in country A. Hence, country B can more easily shift its resources and direct them to the production aimed at country A's market than the other way around. If small country B cannot reallocate resources towards the production of goods that are in demand in country A, then trade cannot take place between these two countries unless country A transfers a part of its income to country B which the recipient country then spends on imports from country A.

To operate in a large market, a small country should undertake substantial investment in production and marketing. Failure in the customs union market for a small country will mean the loss of most of its external market. Investment expenses will not be recovered. The failure of a large country's exports to a small country's market will mean relatively smaller losses than those experienced by a small country in the same situation. The creation of a customs union in such a situation may be a much riskier enterprise for the small country than for the large country, although there is potential for a larger marginal gain.

There is an argument advanced in many new trade theory models that when two economies of unequal size enter into a trade liberalisation deal or when they integrate, industry will be attracted to and clustered in the larger market and more developed economy (centre) and away from the smaller country (periphery). A case in point is the former East African Community (1967–77) in which Kenya benefited to the detriment of Uganda and Tanzania. More recently, there is a concentration of businesses in relatively more advanced (larger) economies of the Economic Community of West African States in Senegal (Dakar) and Ivory Coast (Abijan). These centripetal forces may predominate when the initial pre-liberalisation or pre-integration barriers are at high and intermediate levels. This also may explain in part why the US and especially the EU have a passion for preferential (that is, discriminatory hub-and-spoke) trade agreements, rather than multilateral trade liberalisation deals. Within a bilateral deal, the EU has the position of a hub. As such, it may gain more (or lose less) than in a multilateral deal. However, 'at very low trade barriers, factor price differences can overturn these effects' (Puga and Venables, 1998, p. 239). Remote places do not necessarily need to be poor locations for firms as their remoteness is already reflected in their factor prices (Venables and Limão, 2002, pp. 260–61). Ireland and Finland are obvious examples from the 1990s of how small and peripheral countries may adjust and expand, attracting foreign companies and developing their own firms and industries, and thereby profit from integration with a large group of advanced countries.

During lean times, government intervention in the form of subsidies is often needed for the start and operation of some industries. When a small country subsidises an economic activity, it most often has exports in mind. When a large country subsidises home production it has in mind import substitution and employment. On these grounds, part of the small country's exports may be subject to countervailing duties by country A. Owing to the asymmetric size of their markets, the large country may not regard the opening of the small country's market as an 'adequate economic compensation' for the opening of its own larger market. If there are many countries, and if country B trades heavily with country A, then trade relations with the external world for country B are almost bilateral. The trade relations of country A may be more evenly distributed among various countries. On these grounds, country A would request further concessions from country B.

A sad example of 'integration' between a big and a small country is the US annexation of Hawaii. It all started with sugar. Very sweetly. Sugar was grown in Hawaii and exported to California as early as 1827. Exports grew continuously. Hawaii initiated a treaty on reciprocal trade with the US in 1848. The treaty was signed in 1855, but the US Senate did not ratify it. The same thing happened with another treaty in 1867. Finally, in 1875 a new treaty was signed and approved by the US Senate. It provided reciprocal duty-free trade. The treaty was supposed to be an economic success for Hawaii, in particular, for its sugar exports. In 1890, the US passed a Tariff Bill that removed US duties on sugar from all other countries. Thus, Hawaii lost its privileged position in the US market. In this situation, annexation could have been the solution. In addition, Hawaii had political problems. The taxation system was inequitable and the government did not fully represent the will of the people. Various machinations, including a small revolution, ensued, with the objective of annexation. However, these efforts failed. Nevertheless, by virtue of a resolution of the US Congress in 1898, Hawaii became part of the US. The Hawaiians were given no vote in the matter, and the change caused little disturbance in Hawaii – after all, by this time the country was so dependent on the US that annexation seemed to be the best way to have continued free access to the US market (Wilkinson, 1985).

Following the break-up of the former Soviet Union (1992), some newly independent states (such as Belarus) have found it hard and costly to 'go it alone' with respect to both internal and external matters, and are exploring ways to re-establish the broken ties with Russia. Others, such as the five central Asian former Soviet republics (Kazakhstan, Kyrgyzstan, Tajikistan, Turkmenistan and Uzbekistan) are exploring the 2005 idea of the creation of a Central Asian Union, modelled on the example of the EU.

A big country may have several negotiating ploys in dealings with a small country. Wilkinson (1997, pp. 46–8) lists the sequence of US negotiating techniques. First the US openly voices an interest in negotiating a trade liberalisation agreement with a select partner country. When this has aroused a certain enthusiasm in the country, the US backs off. Then, in order to revive its own interest in negotiations, the US sets preconditions to start negotiations. However, such conditions now become part of actual negotiations (something that the country needs to give in return for the US concessions). When negotiations start and the negotiating country is enthusiastic about the deal, the US applies car dealer tactics: it now demands new (sometimes unreasonable) concessions; it lists the benefits that the country may obtain from the deal with the US; discussion is delayed, then extended without any real concession offered until the very last moment (deadline for the final conclusion of the deal). It is well established in theory that a small country can gain a lot from a trade liberalisation deal. However, when one takes account of differences in the bargaining power between the prospective partners, the conventionally accepted theoretical truth may need modifying.[108]

The position of small countries in negotiations about economic integration is often weak, but it is not hopeless. Of course, factors other than the relative size of countries influence negotiations. If it has a choice, then a small country has some negotiating power. It may look for partners elsewhere and/or leave the integration deal if it thinks that the arrangement with the large country will bring losses. If a small country has a genuine resource, a strategic geographical location and/or if it specialises in certain production niches (Austria, Belgium, the Netherlands, Switzerland[109]) then it may influence negotiations and its terms of trade with a large country. Economic integration reduces the importance of the limited size of the domestic market. As such, it is more favourable to relatively small countries that lack access to the larger market. Hence, small countries can benefit more from integration than large ones. This is true not only on the production side because of economies of scale, but also on the consumption side because of the relatively larger change in relative prices and because of the increased variety of the available goods and services. The small Benelux and Scandinavian countries, as well as Greece and Portugal, and later the Baltic and central and east European states found sound economic grounds for integration with the rest of the EU. Canada and Mexico have done the same in integration with the US.

In an analysis of the 1986 enlargement of the EU (a large partner) when Spain and Portugal (small partners) joined the group, Casella (1996) found that the smaller EU member countries could gain more than the large ones. Countries with a large domestic market already profit from economies of scale. Integration (enlargement of the market) allows small countries to profit from economies of scale, something that was not available earlier. After 1986, France and Britain lost export market shares in Spain and Portugal to smaller EU countries. However, such a theoretical expectation was not confirmed in the case of Germany and in particular Italy (in fact, Italy increased exports). A continued empirical examination of the issue is necessary to draw more reliable conclusions regarding the problem. However, it is clear from the theory and data that larger countries do not gain asymmetrically more from integration (or an enlargement of the existing group) than smaller countries.

The greater the similarity between the countries that contemplate integration, perhaps the easier the negotiations and the smoother the adjustment and operation of the final arrangement. Optimum partners for negotiations about the creation of a customs union are those of equal economic size, such as France, Germany and possibly Italy were at the time of the establishment of the European Economic Community (1957). This theoretical condition of optimum partnership (political conditions aside) does not offer any country the chance to blackmail other countries on economic grounds and creates a more egalitarian relationship. Integration of partners of unequal size such as Switzerland and Liechtenstein, Belgium and Luxembourg, or any enlargement of the EU forced the smaller country to accept *acquis helvétique*, *acquis belge* or *acquis communautaire*, respectively, in full. Major negotiations were about the length of the transition period, not about the substance of the *acquis*.

The (intra-industry) adjustment to the new circumstances is easier and smoother in countries that are similar in terms of income levels and factors of production. Inter-industry adjustment in different economies is relatively hard. The existence, however, of relatively small and 'backward' countries in the EU is evidence that there are various possibilities and positive interests for countries to participate in international economic integration.

Medium-size countries such as Canada (wheat), Saudi Arabia (oil) and Brazil (coffee) may influence the price of their primary products. Although income elasticities of demand for manufactured goods (traded on the oligopolistic markets of developed countries) are relatively high, the elasticities for primary goods (traded on competitive markets) are relatively low. Hence, smaller countries which are major exporters of primary goods generally have weaker bargaining positions than countries whose products are sold in oligopolistic markets.

The removal of tariffs on trade among countries may have substantive effects only if the integrated countries have or can create a base for the production of various goods and services that are in demand in the partner countries. This is of particular importance for developing countries. These countries have relatively low levels of income, many of them have a similar structure of production (often goods and services for subsistence which do not enter into international trade) and frequently production and export is concentrated on one or a few goods. These countries do not have much to integrate in such a situation. The production structure of such countries (together with poor infrastructure) often does not permit them to trade even on a modest scale. The volume of internal trade within the groups that integrate developing countries seldom exceeds 10 per cent of total trade (a notable exceptions is ASEAN) as is obvious from Table 2.13. These countries compete on the same international markets with primary goods and often do not have many different goods and services to offer each other. As such, the developing countries have a structural bias against trade and, hence, benefit less from integration.

Reallocation of home resources in these countries, including upgrading of human capital, together with the discovery and commercial use of raw materials coupled with foreign aid and loans, may help developing countries to produce differentiated output and offer a variety of goods and services to an enlarged number of partners in trade. A simple liberalisation of trade alone, within a group of developing countries, as the neo-classical

Table 2.13 *Intra-trade of regional and trade groups*

Trade group	Value of intra-trade (exports in millions of dollars)						Intra-trade of groups as percentage of total exports of each group					
	1980	1990	1995	2000	2002	2003	1980	1990	1995	2000	2002	2003
EUROPE												
EFTA	524	782	925	831	879	1072	1.1	0.8	0.7	0.6	0.6	0.6
EU (25)	483 141	1022 932	1 385 805	1 618 929	1 732 227	2 063 450	60.9	67.1	66.1	67.2	66.7	67.2
EU (15)	456 857	981 260	1 259 699	1 420 090	1 491 272	1 767 282	60.8	65.9	62.4	62.1	61.1	61.4
Eurozone	306 473	669 971	860 976	946 891	1 006 699	1 226 917	51.4	55.1	52.1	50.8	49.7	50.8
AMERICA												
ANCOM	1 161	1 312	4 812	5 116	5 070	4 781	3.8	4.1	12.0	8.5	9.5	7.4
CACM	1 174	667	1 594	2 418	2 598	3 288	24.4	15.3	21.8	14.8	11.0	11.9
CARICOM	599	456	877	1 076	1 252	1 538	5.4	8.0	12.2	14.4	12.5	12.5
FTAA	167 719	300 700	525 346	857 839	797 612	841 264	43.4	46.6	52.5	60.7	60.9	59.8
LAIA	11 192	13 350	35 986	44 241	37 154	43 103	13.9	11.6	17.3	13.1	11.4	11.8
MERCOSUR	3 424	4 127	14 199	17 910	10 573	13 383	11.6	8.9	20.3	20.0	11.3	11.8
NAFTA	102 218	226 273	394 472	676 441	626 985	651 213	33.6	41.4	46.2	55.7	56.7	56.1
OECS	4	29	39	38	43	54	9.0	8.1	12.6	10.0	3.8	6.9
AFRICA												
CEPGL	2	7	8	10	12	15	0.1	0.5	0.5	0.8	0.7	1.2
COMESA	555	890	1 027	1 281	1 465	1 812	5.7	6.3	6.0	4.9	5.4	5.8
ECCAS	89	163	163	196	193	236	1.4	1.4	1.5	1.1	1.1	1.1
ECOWAS	661	1 532	1 875	2 811	3 192	3 541	9.6	8.0	9.0	9.5	11.5	9.8
MRU	7	0	1	5	5	6	0.8	0.0	0.1	0.4	0.2	0.3
SADC	108	1 058	4 124	4 453	4 240	5 345	0.4	3.1	10.6	12.0	9.3	10.0
CEMAC (UDEAC)	75	139	120	101	120	157	1.6	2.3	2.1	1.0	1.4	1.4
UEMOA	460	621	560	741	857	1 043	9.6	13.0	10.3	13.1	12.1	12.8
UMA	109	958	1 109	1 112	1 243	1 553	0.3	2.9	3.8	2.3	2.8	2.7

Table 2.13 (continued)

Trade group	Value of intra-trade (exports in millions of dollars)						Intra-trade of groups as percentage of total exports of each group					
	1980	1990	1995	2000	2002	2003	1980	1990	1995	2000	2002	2003
ASIA												
ASEAN	12413	27365	79544	98060	91765	102281	17.4	19.0	24.6	23.0	22.7	21.2
Bangkok	783	2429	21728	37765	50901	75258	1.7	1.6	6.8	7.6	9.3	10.6
ECO	392	1243	4746	4473	4955	6696	6.3	3.2	7.9	5.6	5.9	6.0
GCC	4632	6906	6832	7218	6905	7864	3.0	8.0	6.8	4.5	4.6	4.2
MSG	11	5	18	22	27	34	0.7	0.3	0.4	0.6	0.8	0.7
SAARC	613	863	2024	2593	2998	3869	4.8	3.2	4.4	4.1	4.2	4.5
INTERREGIONAL GROUPINGS												
APEC	357697	901561	1688707	2283093	2168694	2463981	57.9	68.3	71.8	73.3	73.4	72.7
BSEC	1190	1229	25505	24747	27348	34668	5.9	4.2	18.1	14.2	14.1	14.3
CIS	–	–	31529	28760	29517	37625	–	–	28.6	20.0	19.6	20.0

Notes:

EFTA	European Free Trade Association
EU	European Union
ANCOM	Andean Group
CACM	Central American Common Market
CARICOM	Caribbean Community
FTAA	Free Trade Area of the Americas
LAIA	Latin American Integration Association
MERCOSUR	Southern Common Market
NAFTA	North American Free Trade Agreement
OECS	Organisation of Eastern Caribbean States
CEPGL	Economic Community of the Great Lakes Countries
COMESA	Common Market for Eastern and Southern Africa

ECCAS	Economic Community of Central African States
ECOWAS	Economic Community of West African States
MRU	Mano River Union
SADC	Southern African Development Community
CEMAC	Economic and Monetary Community of Central Africa
UEMOA	West African Economic and Monetary Union
UMA	Arab Maghreb Union
ASEAN	Association of South-East Asian Nations
Bangkok	Bangkok Agreement
ECO	Economic Cooperation Organisation
GCC	Gulf Cooperation Council
MSG	Melanesian Spearhead Group
SAARC	South Asian Association for Regional Cooperation
APEC	Asia-Pacific Economic Cooperation
BSEC	Black Sea Economic Cooperation
CIS	Commonwealth of Independent States.

Source: UNCTAD *Handbook of Statistics*, 2004. New York: United Nations. UNCTAD Secretariat computations based on International Monetary Fund, Direction of Trade Statistics.

school suggests, has not been enough. A more interventionist approach in the shaping of comparative advantage, imports of technology and capital from outside the group will be needed.

A necessary condition for successful international economic integration is a certain minimal level of economic development. It is assumed that an increase in development of developing countries will lead to an increase in product variety in the national output mix. This may give an impetus to trade. This minimum level of economic development depends on the ambitions of the countries involved. Do these countries want to form a customs union to increase their bargaining power or do they wish to use it as a means to increase or foster economic prosperity? The latter requires a higher level of economic development than the former.

The actual timing of integration plays an important role. During periods of economic prosperity it is easier to find gains for the participants than during a recession. Prosperity makes negotiations easier because every participant may expect to gain. Very high rates of growth, however, are not necessarily ideal for international economic integration. On the one hand, entry into a customs union introduces changes that do not necessarily have to be efficient because there is not sufficient capacity in the economy to accept them. The economy may be 'overheated' and integration may increase production (marginally), but it may also increase inflation. On the other hand, during a recession economic integration may mitigate the effects of economic crisis.

International economic integration is not suitable for all countries at all times. Certain types of integration are more attractive than others to different countries. There are, however, several conditions for the success of integration, including:

- relatively large size of the group;
- low level of protection (tariffs and NTBs) before and after integration;
- geographical proximity of countries;
- a certain (already achieved) minimum stage of development;
- market structure (complementary or competitive);
- achievement of the dynamic effects;
- distribution of costs and benefits; and
- system for the settlement of disputes.

The potential partners for integration should check whether they meet these conditions or whether they can achieve them by means of international economic integration.

2.5 Free trade areas

Both free trade areas (or, better, *preferential* trade areas) and customs unions yield similar results for an economy and the integrated group and differ only in detail. Free trade areas tend to result in more trade creation and less trade diversion than a tariff-averaging customs union. This detail has often been forgotten in discussions about international economic integration (Curzon Price, 1997, p. 182). A tariff-averaging customs union increases the level of protection of those countries that previously did not have tariffs or whose tariffs were below the level of the common external tariff, as was the case when relatively liberal-trading EFTA countries joined the EU. As such, free trade areas place a much lower cost on third countries than tariff-averaging customs unions.

If one assumes that the level of the common external tariff is equal to the lowest tariff of a member country in a customs union, then there is no theoretical difference between a free trade area and a customs union. The effects of both types of integration arrangements are identical. Of course, countries in a free trade area still take part in international negotiations about trade and tariffs on their own behalf, whereas countries in a customs union negotiate as a single unit. As there is no common commercial policy relative to third countries in a free trade area, countries (such as Canada or Switzerland) that value their sovereignty highly have the formal chance to go it alone in trade matters. Free trade areas in practice usually include manufactured goods, but exclude agricultural ones. This is because many countries want to preserve independence in national agricultural policies. The wisdom (depending on values and priorities) of this policy choice is quite another matter.

Rules of origin (preference) are the basis of a free trade agreement, as well as other preferential trade deals with the exception of a customs union. These rules prevent geographical *trade deflection*. This effect of a free trade area refers to the import of goods from third countries into the area by country A (which has a relatively lower tariff than the partner country B) in order to re-export the goods in question to country B. These speculations depend not only on the difference in the level of tariffs, but also on transport, storage and insurance costs, as well as on the quality (perishability) of goods. Without rules of origin in a free trade area, only the lowest tariffs would be effective. In fact, a free trade area would be equal to a customs union in which the lowest tariffs of a member country would apply. Trade deflection problems do not exist in customs unions because of the existence of the common external tariff.

The proliferation of discriminatory, that is, geographically preferential, trading agreements increased the importance of the rules of origin.

Foreign exporters seek to avoid the payment of customs duties, while the protection-seeking domestic competitors endeavour to prevent them from evading those requirements. Rules of origin are required especially in free trade areas in order to determine which goods are entitled to enjoy those trade preferences. Apart from tariff discrimination, other purposes of rules of origin include the determination of eligibility for quotas and informing consumers that have a preference for goods of a certain geographical origin. There are four different methods for the determination of these rules (Palmeter, 1993; 1995):

- *Substantial transformation* Geographical origin is determined by the country in which the good underwent the last substantial transformation (the one that gave the good a new name, a new character and a new use). Critics say that this is an imprecise and subjective method.
- *Change in the tariff heading* Even if the good made/assembled in country A has imported components, that good can be regarded by foreign countries as a good that originated in country A if that was sufficient to change the tariff classification heading of the imported materials. Opponents of this system say that the flaw is that the existing tariff schedules were not designed to determine the origin of the goods and that the system may be abused by strong industrial lobbies.
- *Value-added method* A certain minimum added value must be incorporated in the good in country A in order to enable foreigners to regard the good as originating in country A. The trouble is that the method depends on controversial accounting systems and even a slight change in the exchange rate may produce a different result. The minimum area content requirement can also be criticised on the grounds that it shifts the production factor mix away from the optimum, it reduces rationalisation in production and can reinforce market rigidities.
- *Specified technological processes* A good must pass through a certain technological transformation in country A in order to be regarded by foreign countries as having been produced in country A. The problems here are that technology changes rapidly and that it is impossible to draft and keep updated internationally agreed classification systems and records on processes for all goods that enter into international trade.

The trade-diverting effects of the rules of origin could be mitigated by the elimination of quotas and multilateral tariff reductions.

The Kyoto Customs Convention (1973) states that, unless a good is wholly produced in a country, what determines the geographical origin of a good is the country where the 'last' substantial process took place. Packaging and dilution with water do not change the essential features of a good, so they are not taken as important elements that change the origin of goods.

Rules of origin can be restrictive or liberal. If the required value added within the area is, for example, 90 per cent, then very few goods would qualify for duty-free treatment. Liberal rules of origin require that only a minor part of the value of goods should be added within the area. Commonly, rules of origin require that 50 per cent of value added should be within the area in order that goods receive a tariff-free status (for example, EFTA or the Canada–US Free Trade Agreement). In the case of NAFTA, Mexico and Canada were in favour of relatively liberal rules of origin because of the positive impact of such rules on the Japanese FDI in the two countries and the potential exports of goods to the US. Initially the required local content of goods for liberal treatment in NAFTA was 50 per cent, but gradually increased to 62.5 per cent from 2002.

An important issue is the basis for the application of, for example, a 50 per cent value-added rule. The choice is between the application of this rule to direct manufacturing costs or to invoice values that include overheads. Consider the following example. The direct cost of manufacturing good X in country A is \$75, while overheads and profits are \$25, making a total invoice value of \$100. For good X to be exported without tariffs to the free trade area partner country B, the 50 per cent direct cost rule allows \$37.50 worth of imported components, while the 50 per cent of invoice value rule allows \$50 worth. The former rule offers a higher protection against the use of out-of-area inputs than does the latter. The Canada–US Free Trade Agreement uses the direct cost rule (as does the free trade deal between Australia and New Zealand). However, EFTA uses the invoice value rule (Lipsey and York, 1988, pp. 31–3).

Rules of origin can be criticised on the grounds that they are open to much abuse (for example, a simple change of packing), that they can be avoided by unscrupulous traders (for example, fake origin statements and marks on the goods) or that the costs of monitoring the system are too high. The experience of the British Imperial preference scheme offered evidence that the operation of the system may be smooth. But in this case the parties were geographically separated, whereas it would be difficult to prevent smuggling along a reasonably open continuous land frontier (Curzon Price, 1987, pp. 22–3). As regards the EU system of preferences offered to the Lomé group of developing countries, the older and more complex the system becomes, the more administrative resources it absorbs. Many working hours were lost by firms, by customs, by forgers of origin certificates, by checkers of these forgeries and so on. If those countries had been offered the most favoured nation (MFN) treatment, this would have been more efficient from the resource-allocation point of view, as well as cheaper to run (Curzon Price, 1996b, pp. 73–4).

Elsewhere, certificates of origin may be easily abused. For example, according to the *European Voice*, the volume of Israeli orange juice imported into the EU at preferential rates was in 1993 three times this country's production capacity.[110]

Free trade in manufactured goods between the EU and EFTA countries operated easily. This was due to similar and low tariff rates between the parties. None the less, the rules of origin were quite costly to apply. They may require complex, troublesome and costly accounting methods for both inputs and for finished goods. The cost of formalities to determine the origin of a good was between 3 and 5 per cent of the value of shipment. Many exporters did not find it worthwhile to make use of the origin rules at all and opted for paying tariffs on their exports (Herin, 1986, p. 16). The WTO stated that the cost to collect, manage and store information needed for administration and verification of origin in Europe was about 3 per cent of product prices. 'Such high cost could lead traders to abandon the idea of claiming preferences after having weighed the net benefit to be negligible if not negative' (WTO, 2004, p. 51).

Preferential trade deals are common in north–south trade relations. The EU has a 'passion' for and a plethora of those arrangements with the developing countries. The problem is that they are complex and incoherent. Therefore, they make compliance demanding and costly. This erodes the benefit of the accorded preferential trade access offered to the southern countries. In the case of the US trade preference offered to Mexico within NAFTA, Anson et al. (2004) state that this was 4 per cent on average in 2000. The estimated total compliance costs were 5 per cent (almost a half was attributable to administrative costs). Hence, rules of origin largely 'undid' preferential tariff access. NAFTA offered little real market access to the southern partner.

Additional evaluation of rules of origin and paper-based certificates reveals that they do not fit into current economic reality. These rules were designed in the past when they reflected protectionist policy objectives. Hence, such rules do not take into account integrated international ways of (global) production. They also do not make allowances for the new flexible production and distribution technologies. Their complexity increases trade costs and demands rationalisation and simplification.

It is difficult to assess whether a free trade area is preferable to the formation of a customs union without knowing at least two elements: the tariff levels in the participating countries, and the limits and controls that provide rules of origin. In general, a customs union with a low common external tariff is much simpler to administer and is preferred to a free trade area with numerous complicated rules of origin that increase compliance and administrative costs (Clausing, 2000, p. 433).

Hitherto, the analysis has dealt with tariffs on final goods. If tariffs are introduced on raw materials and semi-manufactured goods, and if one supposes that production functions are identical in all members of a free trade area, all other things being equal, production will be located in the member country that has the lowest tariffs on inputs. Such a situation results in the creation of 'tariff factories', which distort investment decisions and introduce geographical deflection in production. Once established, the producers would resist liberalisation of trade. All this increases both the prices paid by consumers and the possibility of retaliation from abroad. A solution to the problem may be found in liberal rules of origin that encourage trade creation and reduce misallocation of resources, rather than in restrictive rules which generate trade diversion.

2.6 Distribution of costs and benefits

A reasonable expectation is that the welfare of the participating countries may change following economic integration. Exactly what and how much of that can be measured is the issue encountered in Chapter 6. Market forces will not necessarily result in politically acceptable changes in the geographical, industrial or social distribution of the costs and benefits of integration. Some member countries may reap, or may be perceived by partners to get, more benefits than others. This can introduce tensions, even the demise of certain integration groups as happened with the East African Community in 1967.

The general problem is similar to the issue of income distribution in a single country between owners of assets, industries, classes, regions, the sexes and so on. The most efficient producers in some member countries may increase sales, employ more factors, introduce large-scale production and generate government revenue. Other countries in the group purchase from their partners, who may not be the most efficient suppliers in the world but who are protected by the common external tariff in a customs union. These importing countries lose tariff revenue and they pay a higher price for the goods that their partners produce less efficiently than third-country suppliers. These countries, whose destiny would be to lose from integration without being compensated in some way, would never enter into such an arrangement. Although the establishment of a customs union can make some countries worse off than before, compensation of losers by gainers may ensure that everybody is better off. For a successful integration scheme, member countries must be satisfied, at least in the medium term, with the distribution of the costs and benefits.

There are three possible theoretical cases of geographical distribution of costs and benefits in a customs union:

1. All countries in a customs union reap equal benefits which accrue from integration.
2. All countries gain from a customs union, but benefits are distributed disproportionately.
3. Some countries gain, while others lose.

If the criterion for the distribution of benefits in a customs union is equality of income per capita, then there are various options as solutions to the issue. In the first case above, no action is required because everybody increases their income in proportion. The second case is more problematical. Is compensation necessary? Countries may want to assess whether some might gain more than others, and under what conditions, before the creation of a customs union. In the third case, if gains are larger than losses, compensation is necessary in order to convince the losers to take part or continue in a customs union. It is important to remember that just because one country gains from integration this does not mean that other countries in the arrangement will lose out to a similar extent. The question is: up to what point should one compensate? Should one compensate only up to the point where losses are covered and give the rest of the benefits to the gainers? Should one compensate only up to the point at which losers can be convinced to participate?

Venables (2003) argued that integration among high-income countries (north–north integration) may produce convergence of their per capita incomes, while integration among low-income countries (south–south integration) may produce divergence among their per capita incomes. Participating countries in the north–north case may successfully specialise within their market niche advantages. In the south–south case, the location of the production for the group market may move to the richer countries at the expense of the others in this group of low-income countries. Therefore, north–south integration may in these circumstances serve the low-income countries better. In this arrangement, a low-income country may expect high export demand for its output from the north. This may improve the southern country's terms of trade which would give it a larger share of gains from integration. Mexico initially benefited from these integration-related developments with the US and Canada within NAFTA. However, the EU–Turkey customs union and the Cotonou Agreement between the EU and developing countries still need to prove themselves.

If a move (integration) increases welfare then those who gain from this move may compensate those who lose. This is the compensation test. The second, the bribery test, is one in which the potential losers remain better off by bribing the potential gainers not to make the move. If the gainers are allowed to make the change, the move will take place, unless the potential losers are able to persuade the potential gainers to stay where they are. Any change which passes the compensation test increases the size of the economic pie. If these moves are continuous, the pie grows continuously. With compensation, it is unlikely that a player's share will always go on falling. On the other hand, changes that do not pass the compensation test reduce the size of the economic pie, so in the long term everyone is worse off.

Compensation to the losers may be *ex ante* or *ex post*. In the former case, the unequal results of international economic integration for the member countries are foreseen in advance, while the latter method of compensation is necessary if compensation is to be in full. There is always a danger of systematic losses. The losers may blame integration for their troubles and seek compensation. The successful entrepreneurs may be discouraged from continued participation as endless transfers to the losers may reduce their profits.

Compensation to the losers may be paid in different ways. It may be a mere transfer of funds. If unconditional, this transfer may destroy the recipient's incentives to adjust. Alternatively, compensation may take the form of development of infrastructure, education and training of labour and marketing studies that promote a local spirit of enterprise, a learning culture and adjustment.

One criterion for fiscal compensation that is often put forward in the case of integration arrangements among the developing countries is the loss of customs revenue as a result of the creation of a customs union and the purchase of goods from the partner countries (at higher prices than prevail on the external market). Direct transfers of funds from supplier countries' treasuries to buyer countries' budgets may solve this problem. A country that receives full compensation for customs revenue losses has the same level of government proceeds that it had before integration. This country can shift its resources to the profitable production of goods that are in demand in partner countries and achieve production gains. However, full and exclusively fiscal compensation is not generally accepted as the sole means of compensation to countries that 'appear to lose' in any type of international economic integration. In fact these compensations are hardly ever paid.[111]

If FDI is a possibility, the welfare and gains accruing to a country can be divided into two components: 'national' welfare, which accrues to national factors of production, and 'domestic' welfare, which accrues to national and foreign-owned or controlled assets (Bhagwati and Tironi, 1980). A question often asked in Latin America during the 1970s and 1980s was 'who gains and how from economic integration?' There was concern that foreign TNCs were the major beneficiaries of integration to the detriment of the countries in the region (Vaitsos, 1978; UNCTAD, 1983).

Proceeds from the common external tariff should belong to the customs union. The size of the proceeds depends not only on the volume and value of external trade, the relative level of the common external tariffs and the type of traded goods, but also on the preferential trade arrangements of the customs union with external countries and groups. The distribution of these proceeds may be a complex problem. Countries that trade with many partners and which obtain an important part of their revenue from tariff proceeds (Britain before it joined the EU in 1973) do not have the right to dispose of these funds freely in the customs union framework. In the developing countries, tariff revenue is an important, sometimes principal, element of public proceeds. If integration reduces them to any great extent, then there may be internal pressures to increase the level of the common external tariff. In any case, there are several ways of distributing common proceeds. The revenue may be spent on the common activities of the customs union, distributed to the member countries, given to third countries as compensation for trade diversion, saved as a reserve or any combination of these.

Manipulating the level of the common external tariff may also be of interest. It may be set as the average rate of tariffs of the customs union member countries before integration. However, to eliminate some internal monopolies, a customs union may set the common external tariff at a lower level in order to allow a certain degree of foreign competition. If the level of the common external tariff does not reduce trade with the rest of the world, then there will be no trade diversion.

The system for the distribution of costs and benefits of integration is often controversial. One must, however, remember that economic integration is not about clear balances and *juste retour* from the common budget, but rather about a joint enhancement of opportunities for business and growth in the group in the medium and longer terms. However, some politicians do not readily accept the argument that integration is not a zero-sum game.

A reduction in the level of the common external tariff and NTBs may be not only the most elegant but also the least harmful way of compensating those who are felt to be losers (consumers, external countries) from trade diversion in a customs union. If fiscal transfers are required between countries in a common market or economic union, these transfers may be carried out through regional, social and cohesion policies. Economics is the academic field that (among other things) studies the reasons for differences in efficiency among various agents. The distribution of the results among (un)equal players is a matter to be studied in politics.

2.7 Non-tariff barriers

2.7.1 INTRODUCTION

The GATT was quite successful in achieving a continuous reduction in tariffs on industrial goods during the post-Second World War period. Unfortunately, at the same time, NTBs have flourished and eroded the beneficial liberalising effects of tariff cuts. NTBs are all measures other than tariffs that influence international trade. They affect trade and the geography of production. Some of them are overt (quotas), while others fall into a grey area such as the application of technical standards or rules of origin. Although they are costlier in terms of resource efficiency and they do not create customs revenue, they have increased because the GATT/WTO do not permit a unilateral introduction of new tariffs, while at the same time domestic pressure groups and vested interests may be quite successful in eliciting protection. NTBs are strongest in the 'sensitive' groups of goods and services. In fact, the use of NTBs may determine which groups of goods are sensitive. The implementation of the Treaty of Rome eliminated tariffs and quotas on internal trade in the EU in 1968. The elimination of NTBs, was the task of the Single European Market Programme (1985–92).

Whereas tariffs, like transport costs, increase the price of a good, NTBs act like import quotas, but do not generate revenue for the government. Currently, NTBs present the most important and dangerous barriers to trade, fragmenting markets and production more severely than tariffs have ever done. Tariffs were, on average, reduced under the auspices of the GATT/WTO to relatively low levels, so that they now play a relatively minor role in the protection of the economic inefficiency of a country. None the less, national administrations try to obtain short-term political gains through protectionism at the expense of long-term economic benefits. Hence, NTBs are and will be high on the agenda for all future international moves to liberalise trade.

The inclusion of general and social issues such as the environment, labour standards and human rights in trade liberalisation negotiations and deals may generate unwanted and harmful effects on trade in the longer term. No matter the nobility of intentions, hard reality may ensure that these issues may be used in the future as handy tools for protectionism.

Perhaps such important general and social areas may be better dealt with outside trade deals and the WTO.

Consideration of NTBs has always been difficult. One reason for this is the creativity of their instigators, but another, more important, reason is the lack of data. Administrations either do not record the use of NTBs, or do so only partly. It comes as no surprise that the reported impact of NTBs can lead to considerable underestimations. Our classification of NTBs is presented in Table 2.14.

Table 2.14 Non-tariff barriers

Principal group	Type
1. Government involvement in international trade	Subsidies (production, exports, credit, R&D, low cost government services)
	Public procurement (local, regional, central)
	State monopoly trading
	Exchange rate restrictions
	Embargoes
	Tied aid
2. Customs and administrative entry procedures	Customs classification
	Customs valuation
	Monitoring measures (antidumping and countervailing duties)
	Rules of origin
	Consular formalities
	Trade licensing
	Deposits
	Compulsory insurance with the local insurers
	Compulsory unloading and storage
	Calendar of imports
	Administrative controls
	Inadequate institution to appeal against decisions by the customs
3. Standards	Technical
	Health
	Safety
	Environment ('green standards')[a]
	Lack of recognition of international standards
	Inspection, testing and certification
	Abusive sampling practices
	Packing, volume, weight and labelling[b]
	Registration of patents and brand names (and lack of it)
	Pirated goods

Table 2.14 (continued)

Principal group	Type
4. Others	Quotas (tariff-free ceilings) Local content and equity rules Tax remission rules Variable levies Bilateral agreements Buy domestic campaigns Voluntary export restriction agreements Self-limitation agreements Orderly marketing agreements Multifibre Agreement Lack of transparency and ambiguous laws Cartel practices Precautionary principle Permission to advertise

Notes:

a. Recycling at least a part of the product (e.g. paper, plastic, glass, electrical appliances or computer hardware) may be a 'green' requirement. However, recycling paper requires a lot of chemicals (which are partly released into the environment) and energy. Would a request to plant more trees be a superior choice?

b. Labelling in itself is not a panacea. It ought to have an easily understandable message. But, should that be a positive or a negative statement? For example: 'meat from an animal that *was* fed with genetically modified organisms' *or* 'meat from an animal that *was not* fed with genetically modified organisms'?

The greatest criticism of NTBs is their lack of transparency. Hence, they are prone to abuse and need to be monitored closely, which increases firms' administrative costs. As an economic policy instrument, tariffs are a blunt weapon against which markets can defend themselves through adjustment measures. In contrast, NTBs circumvent market forces and, hence, introduce greater distortions, risk and uncertainty. NTBs therefore prevent efficient spatial and industrial location of resources, investment and specialisation.

2.7.2 ANTIDUMPING

If a government observes that a good is or is likely to be suddenly imported into its country in large quantities, it may introduce an antidumping tariff. Foreign exporters can circumvent this barrier by changing the geography of production. For example, they may move the final stage of production to the tariff-imposing country. To counter this action, the home authorities may request that goods produced domestically must have a certain local content in order to obtain preferential treatment. Once the original supplier of the good meets this requirement, the local authorities may go further, as was the case with the EU control of imports of Japanese integrated circuits (microchips). Chips that are only assembled in a country are not considered to originate in that country. The EU non-preferential rules of origin link the origin of microchips to the place where the diffusion process takes place. Assembly and testing come after the diffusion process and they add to the final value of the chip about as much as diffusion.

There are two reasons for this decision by the European Commission regarding rules of origin for integrated circuits. First, the rules demand that a part of the manufacturing process takes place in the EU, which requires an inflow of FDI and the creation of high-quality local jobs in the EU. Second, the intention was to support EU producers of microchips, some of whom practise diffusion in the EU while assembly and testing takes place in non-EU countries where labour costs are lower. In this case, the EU defined the origin of the good as the place where the 'most' (rather than the 'last') substantial production process took place. Origin is determined by where R&D takes place and by the location of capital equipment used in the production of such goods, rather than by the place of transformation of goods. According to these rules, Ricoh photocopiers, which are made (well, assembled) in California, originate not in the US but rather in Japan because that is where essential parts such as drums, rollers, side plates and other working equipment originate. Having declared the origin of these machines to be Japan, the EU has an arsenal of NTBs to curtail imports of these goods from the US. This has provoked tensions in EU trade with the US.[112]

The EU has a so-called 'sunset' clause that applies to antidumping duties. Antidumping measures apply for 'only' five years unless there is a review in which dumping and injury are again established. There is no sunset provision in US antidumping laws, which can last almost indefinitely, as exemplified by the fact that they have been applied to Japanese colour TV sets for 30 years. In addition, the scope of the measures has been expanded to cover liquid crystal display, as well as projection television (Belderbos, 1997, p. 425).

A firm may avoid antidumping actions by changing production geography (relocating production). A new plant may be located either in a third country or in the country that has imposed antidumping duties (tariff jumping). However, the European Commission and the US Department of Commerce have the right to include third-country exports within the scope of an antidumping measure. For example, during 1989–90, nine Japanese fax-producing plants were established in the EU even though there were no antidumping investigations. Some of these firms explicitly stated that fear of antidumping measures was their major reason for investing and location in the EU (ibid., pp. 434–4). Once established in the EU, these firms can sell at any price they want (below the production costs or below the prevailing prices on the local market). They are not allowed to discriminate or segment the market and they may not follow predatory pricing policies. The EU rules on competition may prevent this.[113]

After virtual elimination of tariffs and quotas through multilateral negotiations, the GATT-sanctioned antidumping trade protection devices are becoming the principal barriers to trade at the start of the 21st century.[114] If a firm sells a product abroad at a price that is below that at which it sells in its home market, this constitutes dumping. The injured country may introduce a duty. Both dumping and injury are necessary conditions to impose an antidumping duty. This idea seems neat in theory, but to apply it in practice may be difficult and controversial.

- *Dumping* What if a country produces and exports a good that is not sold at home? How should this principle be applied if, say, the Chinese produce and export each year millions of artificial Christmas trees for the EU and US markets and do not sell these products at home because there is no market there? What arbitrary method should be used to determine the domestic Chinese price for Christmas trees?
- *Injury* To determine injury to the domestic industry may be even more open to random whims and abuse by the 'injured' industry and investigating government. What measure should be used? An increase in the volume of imports? Changes (reduction) in the domestic production? Market share? An increase in the domestic unemployment? All of these? In what proportion?

Ambiguity of rules and discretion in determining injury present considerable problems. The most contentious issue relates to cumulation whereby the investigating authority adds all imports from all countries under investigation and assesses their combined injury impact on the domestic industry. This cumulation is in use in the EU, as well as in the US, Canada and Australia. In the EU, in 45 per cent of cases in which defendants agreed to increase their prices in order to bridge the dumping (injury), no injury would have been found if the European Commission had not aggregated imports from the countries under investigation (Tharakan et al., 1998, p. 335).[115]

The number of antidumping duties or antidumping cases (there are hundreds of them, mainly in the developed countries although India and China also use them) is not something that matters most as an NTB. The biggest problem and discouragement to trade, investment, innovation, economies of scale and reduction in prices to consumers may result from the serious *possibility* of being harassed by the authority of a country that imports the good in question. A country may apply ambiguous rules and use them in an unorthodox way with the intention of sheltering inefficient domestic producers. The exposure to such risk cannot be fully quantified. The investigated suspect (foreign producer or exporter) has, at his/her own expense, to provide the inspectors with all operating details, including a full list of the costs of production. The result is that the 'injured' country's industry obtains all important details about foreign competitors for free. Importers also face costs, risk and uncertainty as, once the antidumping procedure is completed, they may need to pay backdated antidumping duties.

The existence of antidumping measures may endanger and reduce all expected gains that may result from multilateral free trade. This situation in international trade may prevail for quite some time. The solution may be to create, apply and enforce multilateral rules to determine dumping and injury. With such rules it may be possible to construct a counterfactual situation of a case to try to ascertain and separate effects. In addition, cumulation may be eliminated, save for the case where there is collusion among exporters.

The Byrd Amendment was enacted in the US in 2000. This is a law that requires the US customs administration to directly distribute antidumping and anti-subsidy proceeds to the company(ies) that initiated the case. This has encouraged antidumping complaints by the American firms (producers of shrimps, candles, furniture and other goods) that were seeking windfall profits. The WTO ruled in 2003 that the US policy was illegal. As this amendment was not repealed, the EU and Canada were allowed to introduce sanctions on imports from the US from May 2005.[116]

2.7.3 PUBLIC PROCUREMENT

Government at all levels (local, regional and central) is an important consumer of goods and services. It can use its procurement policies either to protect home business (SMEs in particular, as is the case in Germany) and employment or to influence the geography of production and support young industries during their first tentative steps in order to help the creation of a country's comparative advantage. Public procurement can also be employed as an instrument to apply regional policy and aid to the advantage of certain population groups (for instance, women and minorities).

An open public procurement market in the EU is seen to be one of the major potential benefits that EU firms may exploit. The EU-wide competitive tendering directives require the publication of all tender notices above a certain (rather low) financial threshold in the *Official Journal of the European Community*.[117] Coupled with compliance with EU technical standards and a reasonable time for the submission of the offer, together with transparent award criteria, this increases the fairness of the bidding and award procedure. The low threshold is intended to avoid understating the value of the contract in order to evade open tendering. The threshold may need to be increased. On the one hand, it may not be attractive enough for the non-national companies, while on the other, it is quite costly for local authorities to put work out to tender.

The European Commission may exclude foreign firms from the public procurement market if EU enterprises do not have reciprocal access to public contracts in the countries from which these firms originate. In spite of this, there is a chance of inertia (read 'buy domestic'). A public authority could subdivide a large public contract into a series of small ones and thus avoid the obligation to advertise and award the business locally.

The annual EU(15) public procurement market for goods and services was 16 per cent of the combined GDP of member countries or over €1493 billion in 2002. A common procurement vocabulary, introduced in 2002, is a tool to modernise, simplify and increase the flexibility in the EU public procurement market. The share of the total number of public procurement contracts openly advertised in the *Official Journal* (a sign of market transparency) was 8.4 per cent in 1995. This share gradually increased to 16.3 per cent in 2002. The *value* of these advertised contracts was 'only' 2.65 per cent of total EU(15) GDP in 2002. Even though this may seem like a rather low share, competition in this market has been steadily increasing from 1995 when the same share was 1.44 per cent. Smaller countries that lack domestic industrial capacities seem prepared to source more from outside their domestic economies. Greece, for instance, advertised 46 per cent of its public purchases contracts (this represented 5.8 per cent of the GDP), while Germany did so only in 8 per cent of cases (this represented 1.3 per cent of the GDP) in 2002 (WTO, 2004, pp. 66–9).

2.7.4 TECHNICAL STANDARDS

Goods eligible for tariff and quota-free trade in all integration arrangements are those that are produced by countries within the group. The exceptions are the products that endanger public morality, public security and order, as well as human, animal or plant life or health. An important NTB can be found in the guise of technical standards (a set of specifications for the production and/or operation of a good). Technical standards are different from tariffs in that they increase production and operation costs, while tariffs have an additional revenue-generating effect for the government. The real intention of these standards as hidden barriers to trade is in many cases to protect the national producer despite the long-term costs in the form of higher prices that come from lower economies of scale, poorer technical/energy efficiency and reduced competition.

One of the best-known examples of an NTB operating within an integrated group arose in Germany in 1979. Germany banned the importation of a French fruit-based liqueur, *Cassis de Dijon*, on the grounds that liqueurs consumed in Germany should have an alcohol content of at least 25 per cent, and that of Cassis de Dijon was 5 per cent less than this norm. The German administration wanted to protect its domestic consumers on the grounds that they may buy this 'weaker' drink thinking that it is 'strong'. In addition, weak spirits may be better tolerated by consumers. Hence the administration wanted to reduce consumption in order to protect public health. This case was considered by the European Court of Justice, which ruled that the ban on liqueur imports was not legitimate. The implications of this ruling are of paramount importance: any goods legally produced and traded in one member country cannot be banned from importation in partner countries on the grounds that national standards differ. The ruling opened the way to competition in all goods manufactured in the EU, with the exception of those that could jeopardise an important national interest.

Where differences in national standards do exist, consumer protection is assured by the addition of a warning on the product. However, this ruling is not in itself sufficient to guarantee a uniform market throughout the EU and a concomitant increase in competitiveness. To achieve a uniform market requires harmonisation, with all its attendant disadvantages of excessive regulation, reduction in choice and the long time required for its implementation. The *Cassis de Dijon* case was cited as a precedent when the EU forced Germany in 1987 to open its market to beers from other EU countries despite the fact that some beers do not comply with the German beer purity law, *Reinheitsgebot* (1516), which specifies that beer must be composed only of water, barley, hops and yeast. This decision has not, as feared, endangered Germany's beer production. Many other national laws define, in particular countries, what, for example, can be sold as pasta, sausage or lemonade. In any case, since the *Cassis de Dijon* case in 1979, mutual recognition (and standardisation) has been the cornerstone of the Single European Market.

Following a six-year legal battle, the European Court of Justice ruled in 2003 in favour of the *Associazione Prosciutto di Parma* in the case against British ASDA Stores Ltd (owned by the US retail giant Wal-Mart). The judges upheld the *Associazione*'s request to stop slicing and packing the hams in-house and selling the result as Parma ham. The ruling does not affect Parma ham sold at delicatessen counters, which is sliced in front of the client. The pre-packed and sliced ham sold on supermarket shelves must be cut in the region of origin, otherwise the reputation and authenticity of the ham may suffer. The *Associazione* has about 200 producers of ham in Parma. It controls the whole process of production including slicing and packaging. This guarantees the quality and genuineness of this popular and expensive product.[118] The ruling also applies to *Grana Padano* (Parmesan) cheese, another prime gastronomical product. Italian cuisine is highly appreciated and is becoming hugely popular throughout the world. However, this great popularity and market created a fertile ground in which many cheap imitations may flourish. There are about 600 foods and 4000 wines that enjoy the protection of EU law. In order to be protected against cheap imitations, they must pass rigorous checks to maintain quality. These goods may be luxuries, but their annual market is €40 billion. Consumers are also interested in the protection of originality and quality of food. A carefully regulated, enforced and supervised system would eliminate a host of food scares from dioxin in chicken to 'mad cow disease' (BSE).

The European Commission drafted a plan in 2004 to introduce a 'Made in the EU' label on all products. This is supposed to promote European origin as a mark of distinction. In addition, the specific origin mark ignores the existence of global production chains. Brand experts criticised this plan on the grounds that consumers have few positive associations with the EU. Some governments asked the Commission to abandon the proposal. Distributors and consumers rightly want specific information about the origin of goods they sell, buy and consume. In this regard, they prefer to see, for example, a 'Made in Germany' stamp on tools or 'Made in Italy' label for clothes or shoes. Or, if they buy whisky, they think of Scotland, not of the EU.[119]

Many examples of NTBs arise from the application of standards, and this has a direct impact on the spatial location of production. Belgium allows margarine to be sold only in oval containers, while square ones are reserved for butter. The standard width of consumer durables in the EU countries is 60 centimetres, but in Switzerland it is a few centimetres less. A bylaw of the City of London stipulates that in taxis gentlemen must be able to sit comfortably in an upright position with their hats on. While in Britain it is illegal for lifts to have a stop button, the same button is obligatory in Belgium. In the Netherlands, beer can be sold only in returnable bottles, whereas the German standard for a beer container is non-returnable bottles. None of these technical specifications has a crucial impact on the protection of life and health. Their final effect is to reduce competition and increase prices to the consumers. Trade and industrial policy may well escape the scrutiny of voters but small, well-organised manufacturing lobbies can wield a strong influence on government attitudes.

In order to protect the integrity of the French language against an invasion of foreign words, the French government tried to insist that a French word should be used on the packaging of a particular good that is sold in France: *pétales de maïs* instead of 'cornflakes'. However, according to the 1995 EU law, if a good that is legally sold on the Single European Market has a clear and unambiguous photograph together with a name in an 'easily understood language', it is not necessary to translate the name of the good into the language of the country in which the good is sold.

In order to deal with various standards, the EU has adopted three different approaches:

- *Mutual recognition* National regulation in other member states is recognised as equivalent. This can work only when there is a similarity among national standards.
- *Harmonisation of standards (old approach)* Various technical standards for vehicles, food or chemicals had to be harmonised in detail and were mandatory. It is not surprising that this was a rather slow approach, not only because of the thorough technical work involved, but also because of the required unanimity in the Council of Ministers.
- *The new approach* The EU sets only the essential characteristics of the good (minimum important requirements). The industry can have a greater degree of freedom to satisfy it and to be innovative.

Harmonised standards are essential in some areas, such as safety,[120] health and the environment, whereas mutual recognition (an agreement to acknowledge diversity) may be an interim solution for traded goods until harmonisation is carried out. In any case, a long-term advantage of harmonisation is that firms will have to comply with only one set of rules instead of up to 25 different sets. This may increase the gains that can be achieved from economies of scale. However, this only makes sense when the market for a good or a service extends to more than one member state. For example, although consumer preferences for relatively new goods such as VCRs, fax and photocopying machines, printers, CD-ROMs, computers and mobile phones are similar throughout the EU, there are widespread differences in the markets for foodstuffs and beverages, with preferences often strictly local.[121] In such cases, a potential EU standard that does not embrace these distinctions may do more harm than good. The member states of the EU are, however, obliged to notify the European Commission in advance about all draft regulations and standards. If the Commission or other member states find that a new standard contains elements of a barrier to trade, they may apply remedial action as allowed under Articles 30 or 94 of the Treaty of Rome.

EU member states may legislate in the non-harmonised areas, provided that they previously notify the European Commission about draft regulations and standards. This is important because of the mutual recognition principle. The Commission is quite satisfied with this system of previous notification because it avoids the creation of barriers to the free movement of goods and services. However, the European Commission estimated that the non-application of the mutual recognition principle cut intra-EU trade by €150 billion in 2000 (WTO, 2004, p. 61).

2.7.5 RED TAPE

Another imaginative NTB is illustrated by the *Poitiers* case. In autumn 1982, the French government wanted to protect the home market from imports of Japanese VCRs. There was, however, no domestic production of VCRs. The home manufacturer, Thomson, simply imported Japanese VCRs and distributed them under its own name. Just before Christmas 1982, the French government decreed that all Japanese VCRs should undergo a customs inspection in the town of Poitiers in order to ensure that instruction manuals in French accompanied them. Poitiers is in the middle of France, far from all main ports of entry for these goods; its customs post was staffed by only eight officers and was not well equipped. This decision increased costs (transport, insurance, interest, delays) and reduced the quantity of imported and sold VCRs to 3000 units a month.

Such a measure might make some sense in a situation where a government wanted to restrain rising consumer expenditure that was causing a short-term drain on the balance of payments. In such instances, however, a more appropriate measure might be an excise duty or high sales tax. The moral of this tale is that the time to protect against the importation of goods whose efficient manufacturing depends on economies of scale and a steep learning curve is before external suppliers have captured most of the domestic market. The attention that this case attracted in the media was considerable, leaving the French government 'no other choice' than to revoke the measure. After Christmas, of course! A supplementary tax 'replaced' the Poitiers customs clearance procedure in January 1983.

2.7.6 JAPANESE CARS

Following the Second World War, Japan wanted to enter into a large-scale production of passenger cars (non-military vehicles). The MITI introduced high tariffs and quotas on imports of cars from the US and Europe, hindered FDI into the car industry, as well as scaled down the number of home manufacturers of cars from a dozen to three. Japan also feared in 1952 that small Italian cars would make substantial inroads into its market. Therefore, Japan initiated an import quota deal. According to this arrangement, the number of Japanese cars that could be imported from Japan directly into Italy was set at 2800 passenger cars and 800 all-terrain vehicles per year. When the situation changed and the Japanese became highly competitive in the production of cars, this NTB rebounded on Japan.[122]

Since 1987 the European Commission has refused to support Italy's attempts to invoke Article 134[123] to block indirect imports of Japanese cars through other EU countries. Hence, imports of Japanese cars have soared.[124] Other EU countries had annual 'caps' on the imports of Japanese cars. For example, the 'cap' for Japanese cars in the French market was about 3 per cent, while in Britain it was about 10 per cent of domestic sales. A tacit limit to the market share achieved by Japanese car producers in the German market was about 15 per cent. The result is a lose–lose situation. On the one hand, consumers lose as they have to pay more for both domestic and imported cars and, on the other, the location of the EU car industry is postponing its inevitable structural adjustment and potentially losing its competitive edge relative to the Japanese. The governments of the EU countries simply bow to the short-term interests of powerful domestic manufacturing lobbies.

The EU and Japan concluded a 'car deal' in 1991. The EU offered the Japanese an increase in market share from 11 per cent in 1991 to 17 per cent (including Japanese cars manufactured in the EU) until 2000, when all quotas disappeared. Unfortunately, the parties placed different interpretations on the deal. The EU argued that the maximum number of Japanese cars either imported from Japan or produced in Japanese plants in the EU is based on forecasts of market growth and, if the market grows less than forecast, it had the right to renegotiate the deal. The Japanese interpretation of the deal was that the EU has committed itself not to restrict the sale of Japanese cars in the EU. In any case the accord shows that the EU is keen to increase competition and efficiency in the EU car industry. Another accord between the EU and Japan in 1995 is intended to simplify EU exports of cars and commercial vehicles to Japan through the mutual recognition of vehicle standards, as well as allowing Japanese inspectors (who issue certificates to imported cars) to work in Europe. From 2000, the EU protection of its car industry relied mostly on tariffs, standards, as well as market entry and distribution costs.

2.7.7 PRECAUTIONARY AND PREVENTION PRINCIPLES

As already stated, all goods legally produced in the EU may be freely traded throughout the EU unless they endanger public morality or the life or health of humans, animals and plants. This freedom may be challenged in practice by two principles that can sometimes act as NTBs:

- *Precautionary principle* refers to a proactive regulatory method. According to this principle, there are specific cases that are linked to a certain exposure to danger and risk. They concern products, technologies or activities. Although a hazard may not yet be scientifically documented beyond reasonable doubt, it can plausibly be anticipated in the light of accumulated experience. Even though there is a lack of definitive scientific knowledge, one must react now (prohibit or regulate heavily), before the arrival of a potential hazard. Although it may have certain justification following grave hazards and dangers such as BSE, this principle may be badly manipulated and abused by rent-seeking vested interests. The principle has been on the books since 1958 when the US Congress enacted an amendment to the Food, Drug and Cosmetic Act. Any new additive to food is presumed unsafe until its safety had been demonstrated through scientific procedures: 'The US statute places the burden of proof on the manufacturer and requires that foods containing new additives be presumed unsafe until proven safe. But in the case of GM foods, the US turned the law on its head and insists they must be presumed safe until proven not to be.'[125] From the 1980s, Germany was very active in introducing environment-related legislation based on this principle. The French court invoked the principle in 1998 when it suspended the sale of three genetically modified corn varieties. The EU may apply this principle in practice, but action should be proportional[126] to the potential risk and non-discriminatory, as well as subject to review and change in the light of new scientific findings. The EU lifted this six-year-long ban in 2004 because of pressure from the US through the WTO.
- *Preventive (reactive) principle* applies in the situation when the mischief has already occurred and when there is a need to prevent or curtail the repetition of the known type of harm and damage.

France invoked the precautionary principle in 1999 to maintain its unilateral ban on the imports of beef from Britain. This was a direct challenge both to the principle of the free movement of goods and to the authority of the European Commission, which after several years had lifted its ban on exports of British beef, which had been imposed because of BSE.

The precautionary principle touches on several sensitive and emotional issues (health, food safety, environment) and can provoke fierce protests from consumer groups. Although the precautionary principle is not (yet) enshrined in EU law, its political significance is that it may be applied at any point. If the application of the principle were to proliferate to any great extent, this would signify the end of the Single European Market for the goods involved.[127] The goal of the newly established European Food Safety Authority (2002) is to provide scientific input into the EU decision-making procedure.

2.7.8 RULES OF ORIGIN

Liberalisation of trade and FDI with third countries potentially increases both trade with those countries and the share of foreign inputs in domestically produced 'hybrid' goods.[128] Rules of origin in general, and the minimum local content requirement in particular, are used as NTBs to prevent goods with a high external content from receiving preferential treatment in the internal trade of the EU. However, it is increasingly difficult to determine the 'nationality' of some goods, for example, cars. Countries throughout the world are free to use rules of origin as policy measures, as they are not yet regulated by the WTO. As a result, practice varies considerably, causing difficulty for both producers and traders.

The present EU rules of origin are based on the Community Customs Code (CCC) established in Regulation 2913/92 and its implementing provisions established in Regulation 2454/93. Article 23 of the CCC relates to goods produced in a single country. According to Article 24, goods whose production involved more than one country are deemed to originate in the country where they

- underwent their last substantial processing or working,
- provided that this processing or working was economically justified,
- that it took place in an undertaking equipped for that purpose, and
- that its working or processing results in a new product or represents an important stage of manufacture.

The following list presents some examples about ascertaining the origin:

- *Unrecorded diskettes* (Code no. 8523.20) If neither the disk nor upper and lower shells are manufactured in the country where assembly of the diskette takes place, the diskette shall have the origin of the country where the components representing the highest percentage of the ex-works price originated. Assembly and packing alone shall not confer origin.

- *Television receivers* (Code no. 85.28) The 45 per cent value-added rule. When this rule is not met, the apparatus shall be treated as originating in the country of origin of parts whose ex-works price represents more than 35 per cent of the final ex-works price. When the 35 per cent rule is met in two countries, the apparatus shall be treated as originating in the country of origin of parts representing the greater percentage value.
- *Photocopying apparatus* (Code no. 90.09) Change of tariff heading or 45 per cent value-added rule, except assembly of photocopying apparatus accompanied by the manufacture of the harness, drum, rollers, side plates, roller bearings, screws and nuts.

The WTO intends to draft new standards for the determination of origin that would be universally applicable. Until it does so, the EU will continue to determine the origin of the goods according to the above legal provisions and in accordance with the Kyoto Convention (except for the provisions on which a reservation has been expressed by the EU).

Yet another complication in the calculation of added value and the shares of different countries in the final origin of a good is presented by fluctuations in the rates of exchange. For example, what rate of exchange should be used to calculate added value: the rate prevailing on the date of importation of inputs or the rate on the date when the final good is exported to the EU? A case in point arose in the export of ballpoint pens (made from American components) from Switzerland to France in 1983. The European Court of Justice decided in favour of the date of importation.

Controversies about origin were for a long time confined to trade in goods, but are now relevant to trade in services too. What determines the 'nationality' of traded services? Many are based on wide international networks. None the less, certain criteria are emerging, including place of incorporation, location of headquarters, nationality of ownership and control, and the principal place of operation and intellectual input.

Rules of origin are responsible for many controversies, heated debates and tensions in international trade. In a supposedly 'globalised' international economy where TNCs are increasingly involved in foreign production, rules of origin make less and less sense. They are associated with distortions in investment decisions and reduction in international production and trade, and generally do more harm than good.

2.7.9 TRADE-RELATED INVESTMENT MEASURES

A trade-related investment measure (TRIM) is a new name for the 'old' performance requirement. UNCTC (1991a) provided a survey of TRIMs. It was found that local content requirements are more common than regulations regarding exports or employment. Although TRIMs exist in both developed and developing countries, they are more common in the developed world. They are usually concentrated in specific industries, such as car-making, chemicals and computers. This study of 682 investment projects found that in 83 per cent of cases TRIM requirements (such as local sourcing, exporting) would have been undertaken anyway; that is, not only were TRIMs intruding in the mix of inputs in the production process, but they were also redundant. In any case, the WTO outlawed these measures in the Agreement on TRIMs.

The Agreement on TRIMs, negotiated during the Uruguay Round, applies only to measures that affect trade in goods. This agreement states that no member country shall apply a measure that is prohibited by the provisions of GATT Article III (national treatment) or Article XI (quantitative restrictions). Examples of inconsistent measures, as spelled out in the Annex of the agreement, include local content or trade balancing requests. The agreement contains transitional arrangements that allowed countries to maintain notified TRIMs for a limited period of time following the entry into force of the WTO (two years in the case of developed countries, five years for developing countries and seven years for least-developed countries). The agreement also established a Committee on TRIMs to monitor the operation and implementation of these commitments.

2.8 Conclusions or why countries integrate

Economic integration may increase the average welfare of consumers in the involved countries in many different direct and indirect ways. The problem is that the benefits accrue to everyone in relatively small instalments and only in the medium and long terms. Another issue is that there are serious problems and limitations regarding measurement of these gains. Some of these gains include:

- secure access to the market of partner countries;
- increased investment opportunities as expectations may be established with an increased degree of security;

- an elimination of trade barriers reduces the cost of trade;
- competition forces firms to apply new ideas and technologies;
- increased competition on internal market puts a downward pressure on prices;
- facilitation of exchange of technical information;
- due to the enlarged market, producers may better exploit and benefit from economies of scale;
- improved efficiency in the use of resources;
- potential for coordination of certain economic policies in order to increase their effectiveness;
- improved and strengthened bargaining position with external partners;
- research and innovation may be stimulated because of tougher competition on a larger market and a possibility of sharing fixed costs in such a market environment;
- the market of the integrated group provides more opportunities for a wider range of goods and services that can be offered to consumers, hence there is an improvement in individuals' utility function; and
- reduction in X-inefficiency which moves the production activities of firms closer to best-practice business organisation.

However, one must always bear in mind that international economic integration is never more than a useful *supporting* tool that increases the intensity of sound domestic macro- and microeconomic policies but cannot act as their replacement. If these domestic policies are not healthy, integration by itself cannot be their substitute.

The traditional (static) model of customs unions considered the effect of a reduction in tariffs on trade and welfare. It concluded that the lowering or elimination of tariffs increased competition which could lead to an improvement in welfare. The new theory pays attention to the dynamic effects of integration. With economies of scale and imperfect competition, there are no unconditional expectations that all countries will gain from integration, even less that they will gain equally. In the absence of adjustment policies, such as industrial, regional, cohesion and social policies, integration may impose net costs on some countries, rather than give them net benefits. It may take decades to achieve a new, higher and stable steady state. Therefore, cooperation among countries regarding the distribution of gains and losses is a necessary condition for successful integration. In any case, integration profoundly changes the economic structure of participating countries which must modify, and even abandon, the established domestic monopolies and autarkic traditions.

The theory of a customs union is based on a large number of restrictive assumptions, so the technical modelling may be far from realistic. Various restrictions in a customs union, such as the prohibition on factor movements or coordinated fiscal and monetary policies, can be overcome in common markets and economic unions.

The theory of customs unions studies extreme cases and is intuitive in nature. All analyses are suggestive rather than definitive and conclusive. Yet another difficulty stems from the fact that this theory includes simultaneously both free trade within a customs union and protection against third countries in the form of the common external tariff (and NTBs). A customs union reduces tariffs on trade among some countries, so it may seem beneficial in relation to a situation where each country applies its own system of tariffs. In a customs union, tariffs are removed on the internal trade, but a common external tariff is erected. One distortion is replaced by another, so regarding the final effect on welfare, all outcomes are possible. If free trade is the first-best policy, then a customs union is, at best, a second-best situation. A universal prescription for the success of a customs union may not be found. Free trade is only first best in an imaginary first-best world with no 'distortions'. We do not live in such a world. Instead, free trade and customs unions are just two different second-best policies. One cannot draw any conclusion about the real world from what is true in an ideal world that is quite different from the real one. None the less, our effort was not in vain, as many useful things may be learned from the analysis of extreme and second-best cases, even though there is no unique set of policies that is always best for the entire economy.

Dynamic effects are extremely hard to model and quantify rigorously. For example, it is difficult to predict the exact impact of competition on technological innovation. Modern trade barriers are more obscure and complicated to negotiate and to enforce by agreement than was the earlier case with pure tariffs and quotas. Although these are intuitive issues, they are important for economic integration and its direction.

There is still the question of why integration takes place in reality. Estimates of trade creation and trade diversion that could contribute to the explanation of why integration takes place at all have been disappointingly small in most studies. In addition, the literature has been slow to develop quantification of dynamic effects of integration. Hence, the hard quantitative explanations for economic integration were missing. The rationale for the creation of integration schemes in real life was often found in non-economic motives. Europe (no more wars in Europe) is an example of this idea. However, there is another, different explanation about the grounds for integration in general. Practical people think the economic gains (listed two paragraphs below) are large, in spite of the inability of economists to measure them. This may be valid for the US–Canada free-trade deal and the NAFTA. The smaller integration deals between the US and other Western hemisphere countries may be explained by non-economic motives on the part of the US, but this does not apply to the smaller partners of the US, who are almost exclusively concerned with economic gains.

One has to recall two things. First, the principal goal of European integration was to protect peace by ensuring, through economic means, that war between France and Germany would be impossible. Integration was a tool, not an objective in itself. Second, the important wave of theoretical contributions to the theory and measurement of international economic integration came only *after* the signature of the Treaty of Rome (1957).

Why do international economic integration and preferential trading agreements take place at all? The answer to this question has several components and dimensions:

- First and foremost, countries integrate in order to secure access to markets of partner countries and to protect important trade relations against disruptions.
- They also want to secure and consolidate domestic market-oriented reforms.
- Trade barriers can be adapted according to the preferences of the involved countries.
- Trust among the participating countries is important. A relatively small number of participants may create cosy relationships, and make monitoring and enforcement of the deal easier, while friendly positive cooperation within the group may potentially help the exchange of favours, mutual agreement and perhaps settle disputes more quickly and efficiently than is the case in multilateral institutions.[129] A large group of countries may have many conflicting objectives.
- Opening up for trade is about greater competition which weakens and reduces the power of vested interests and monopolies. This gives opportunities to many firms, rather than to a select few. This, in turn, creates additional opportunities for growth.
- Integration agreements can be employed as a bargaining tool with external countries.
- Terms-of-trade effects and gains to exporters provide benefits from preferential trading agreements that are not available from unilateral trade liberalisation policies.

Given these motives, it is not necessary to resort exclusively to non-economic reasons for economic integration.

International economic integration increases the potential for significant international improvement in economic welfare. The countries have to organise themselves, that is, adjust individually and collectively, to reap these gains. Specialisation and increase in the export potentials in order to pay for the imports are necessary conditions for success. In addition, adjustment policies must be well thought out. Unfriendly policies can cancel out all the beneficial effects which accrue from improved access to a larger market.

In the world of rapid change in technology and conditions in the market, a country may not be sure that its current comparative advantages will be safe in the future. So, a country may wish to secure markets for the widest variety of its goods and services as a hedge against abrupt changes in the trade policy of its partners. International economic integration is an uphill struggle, but may be an attractive solution to such a problem.

Integration can be a risky enterprise for a small country in relation to protectionism in the short run. However, a defensive policy of protection may generate the economic decline of a small country in the long run. Few countries could accept this as their long-term goal. Integration may be a solution to this scenario. A willingness to cooperate with partner countries on the issue of the distribution of costs and benefits that accrue from the creation of a customs union and the settlement of disputes is of great importance for the smooth and beneficial operation, as well as for the survival, of a customs union. International economic integration may be subject to various disputes. Most of them stem from the existence of NTBs. An effective dispute settlement mechanism is a necessary condition for the survival of the scheme.

An inevitable question has always been: are regional trading arrangements good or bad for world welfare? The answer to this question depends on the answer to a related question: is regional economic integration assisting (building block) or damaging (stumbling block) the multilateral trading system? Some reply yes, others reply no. This is the consequence of the value judgements within the 'second-best' world. Even though most of the past international integration schemes were on a rocky road (indeed, many of them disappeared, particularly in the developing countries), in general terms they tended to increase trade, rather than to restrict it. Hence, this may be taken at first sight to be an economically beneficial effect.

Discrimination in trade has not gone away. There is still a long way to go before genuine multilateral liberal trade is achieved. Integration may assist, complement and ease multilateral trade:

- if trade and investments are free within the group;
- if common external barriers to trade are made transparent and not increased relative to the pre-integration situation (GATT Article XXIV);

- if the group reduces its external barriers to trade, investment and factor mobility;
- if the group is not closed and if it expands;
- if the internal rules (competition, origin and so on) are clear and trade friendly (not bureaucratic); and
- if there is an effective and reliable dispute settlement mechanism.

Integration is a tool that only supports (rather than replaces) a sound domestic macroeconomic economic policy and structural reforms. Inappropriate domestic fiscal (taxation that distorts the economy), monetary and exchange rate policy will prevent the domestic private sector from being internationally competitive.

The current wave of interest in integration which started in the 1990s is different from the largely unsuccessful attempts to integrate countries during the 1950s and 1960s, with a notable exception in Europe. The new integration initiatives are founded on a different basis:

- Almost all countries credibly decided to accept and apply market-based reforms and outward-oriented economic policy. They opened up and welcomed FDI.
- Integrated international production created and extended by TNCs and huge international flows of FDI are features of the modern economy. This was the case to a very much lower degree during the 1950s and 1960s.
- The successive GATT/WTO rounds of trade negotiations have almost eliminated tariffs and quotas as important obstacles to trade on a multilateral basis.
- There has been slow, cumbersome, half-hearted and uncertain progress in the Doha Round of WTO negotiations.

It is, however, true that, on the negative side, the new regional integration initiatives may generate trade diversion. The founding fathers of the GATT/WTO exempted free trade areas and customs unions from the MFN clause, but they did not predict a proliferation of these agreements that may fragment the world trading system. Big countries such as the US may break coalitions in the developing world by offering bilateral trade deals. Bilateral or regional deals may divert attention from the multilateral path. However, the US entered into free trade deals with Israel, Canada and Mexico during the Uruguay Round (1986–94) without reducing its commitment to the final multilateral deal. Similarly, the US entered into free trade arrangements with Chile and Singapore in 2004 during the Doha Round.

It is feared that regional trading blocs may turn hostile and cause splintering, even a collapse, in the liberal- and multilateral-minded world trading system because of various conflicting interests, including pressure from the well-entrenched rent-seeking special national and regional lobbies. What if the simplicity of non-discriminatory multilateral trade continues to be replaced by complex internal rules of origin that are not in accord with the others?

In the real world, bilateral or regional trading agreements may be a response to tremendous and uncertain resource costs related to multilateral negotiations and deals. It may be simpler, faster, cheaper and more tangible to put into practice a regional integration deal, than to wait an interminable time for an uncertain multilateral trade arrangement and its benefits. The choice that policy makers face may often not be between multilateral agreements and economic integration, but rather between a potentially beneficial economic integration with select partners and no such arrangement at all. Whether regional economic integration can evolve into multilateral liberal trade is not yet known. Integration may, however, start this process. The bottom line may be uncertain: are the new integration programmes the outcome of the success of multilateralism or its failure?

Notes

1. There are difficulties in explaining to the public that half a loaf of bread in certain cases may be worse than none.
2. Some argue that the Kaldor–Hicks compensation test may be a more practical analytical tool to ascertain net social benefits than is Pareto optimality. According to the Kaldor–Hicks test, a change from state A to state B is socially welfare improving if those that gained from the move to B can compensate those that lost and still be better off than in state A. The measurement and comparison of total social costs and total social benefits is the foundation of cost–benefit analysis.
3. When there is a discriminatory trade liberalisation arrangement, then, in static terms, a country gains from the opening up of partners' markets and 'loses' from its own trade liberalisation.
4. Countries tend to specialise and export goods for which they have a relatively large domestic market. It is this domestic demand or home market effect (Linder, 1961; Krugman, 1980) that induces production, rather than domestic factor endowment. The response by firms to strong local demand for a product is so powerful that it leads this country to export that product. Countries have a competitive edge in the production of these goods and thus gain an advantage in foreign markets, while they import goods demanded by a minority of the home population. The factor endowment or comparative advantage model would not predict the home market effect. However, economic geography would predict it. The US, Japan and Germany have the greatest comparative advantage in goods for which their home market is relatively big. These are standardised goods for mass consumption. Empirical investigation by Davies and Weinstein (2003) found support for the existence of home market effects, as well as for the role and importance of increasing returns in determining the production structure for the OECD countries.

5. Income may be distributed to a small part of the population (landowners or owners of capital), who may spend it on imported luxury goods and services. This may prevent the establishment of industry in their area or country. If income is predominantly distributed in favour of a large number of families who demand home-made goods and services, this may have a strongly positive impact on the location of firms in the domestic market.
6. Ageing population and retirement patterns influence trade. The old demand health-related goods and services. A significant number of retired Germans move to Spain to enjoy a milder climate and a lower cost of living. They have specific demands that have a partial influence on trade.
7. Quotas are another instrument, but one that makes it pointless for producers to compete against each other. Quotas are more harmful than tariffs because their impact on rising prices to consumers is hidden. Hence, they may spread without check.
8. In general, EU integration has benefited third countries. The major exceptions are the countries that specialised in temperate agricultural goods covered by the CAP (Sapir, 1992, p. 1503). The Single European Market has been trade creating both for the EU and for external producers (European Commission, 1997d, p. 3). Hence, there was no need for retaliation.
9. This is part of the reason why highly protected countries, such as those in Eastern Europe before the transition period at the start of the 1990s had, in general, a poor export performance in western markets.
10. Uruguay Round Agreement on Subsidies and Countervailing Measures (1994).
11. The problem with the subsidies is that all taxpayers contribute to them, not just those who are consumers, as is the case with tariffs.
12. Rents are due to barriers to entry such as large sunk costs, economies of scale, externalities, advertising, regulatory policies, distribution and service networks, asymmetric information, as well as consumer loyalty to a certain brand or a person (a singer, actor or sportsman).
13. Article VI of the GATT permits countries harmed to levy countervailing duties (unfair trading practice) in order to offset the impact of injurious foreign subsidies. Article XVI calls on member countries to observe self-restraints relative to export subsidies.
14. 'Free trade' cannot easily be fostered without reference to exchange rates. A depreciation in the value of the national currency in country A helps exporters, while local competitors in the importing country B may regard such a change as a 'subsidy' received by exporters in country A. The US dollar sometimes fluctuates ±20 per cent within one year relative to other major currencies. Fluctuations in exchange rates in the domestic currencies of the countries in the EU can jeopardise competition in the internal market. That is one of the reasons why the EU was pushing for the establishment of the monetary union.
15. As a general rule, antidumping and countervailing duties in the EU expire after five years.
16. M. Karnitschnig, 'Berlin Scandals Highlight an Absence of Regulations; Fancy Addresses for Parties', *Wall Street Journal*, 10 February 2005.
17. The subsidy scheme works like this: any US firm whose exports have at least 50 per cent of US content can create an FSC in a tax haven. Most of these 'letter box' companies are usually located in Barbados, Guam or the Virgin Islands. The US parent firm 'sells' its goods to its FSC which afterwards 'exports' them further. There is no physical transaction of goods as the FSC subcontracts the whole deal back to its parent. Up to 65 per cent of the FSC's income is exempt from US taxation. The remainder of the income is taxed (minimally) by the tax haven. Dividends paid by the FSC to its parent are not taxed. Using an FSC may reduce the US company's tax bill by 15 to 30 per cent (F. Williams, 'Trade ruling takes WTO into realm of domestic taxation', *Financial Times*, 25 February 2000, p. 7).
18. Boeing's financial statement for 2001 shows that the FSC benefit amounted to $222 million which represented about 8 per cent of Boeing's net earnings in the same year (European Commission, 2002b, p. 45).

19. The bill is complicated by a provision that the US companies may repatriate as much as $400 billion of foreign earnings at a corporate tax rate of 5.25 per cent instead of the normal 35 per cent (*Financial Times*, 27 October 2003).
20. H. Yeager, 'Corporate tax breaks approved by Senate', *Financial Times*, 11 October 2004.
21. T. Buck, 'Sad day as EU puts sanctions on US goods', *Financial Times*, 1 March 2004.
22. 'Strategic' does not have any military connotation here, but rather it refers to an industry with significant externalities (economies of scale or linkages with the rest of the economy).
23. The problem is that there may be costly errors in judgement; foreign retaliation may be provoked with the consequent undermining of the multilateral trading system.
24. This is another reinforcement of the theoretical second-best character of customs unions.
25. There were many more inventions, for example by Leonardo da Vinci, that were put into practice with a delay of several centuries.
26. For countries that enter an already existing customs union, this effect starts the moment there is a serious indication of full entry.
27. Competition policy does not protect individual competitors, but rather the process of competition.
28. If one had to negotiate a contract each time one buys apples, orders a meal or purchases a train ticket, without the existence of such rules, a very long period of time would be required for each transaction. Apples would rot, the meal would arrive next month, while trains would leave empty (provided that they were running on time).
29. The American business model is based on four principal ingredients: material self-interest governs our economic lives (greed is good, nice guys finish last); markets should operate freely; the size and influence of the state administration should be kept at a minimum; and taxation should be low, just sufficient to cover the minimum state functions (Kay, 2004, p. 313). This model 'is deficient for its naive approach to issues of human motivation, its simplistic analysis of structures of property rights, its inability to maintain efficiency in the face of imperfect information, its misleading account of markets in risk, its glossing over problems of cooperation and coordination, and its failure to describe the generation of new knowledge on which its very success depends' (ibid., p. 320).
30. The World Economic Forum states that the Scandinavian model produced and fostered highly competitive economies with exemplary R&D, education, social care and stability. This was achieved without the cruel social inequalities that are the outcome of the American model. Critics state that the Scandinavian model is based on heavy public expenditure. Even though this may be true, an overlooked fact is that EU countries such as France, Germany or Italy have a similar public expenditure, but these funds were used less efficiently than is the case in Scandinavia.
31. Hayek criticised the neo-classical model, which is based on perfect competition, in the following way: 'But I must be content with thus briefly indicating the absurdity of the usual procedure of starting the analysis with a situation in which all the facts are supposed to be known. This is a state of affairs which economic theory curiously calls "perfect competition". It leaves no room whatever for the activity called competition, which is presumed to have already done its task' (Hayek, 1978, p. 182).
32. Liberalisation of imports has the strongest impact when exchange rates are stable. Volatility in the exchange rate market may loosen the grip of this policy instrument.
33. Intellectual property rights are those that come from patent, copyright and trademark rules.
34. These three men will be software experts, not lawyers. The Department of Justice and Microsoft would each select one member, and those two would select the third. Their role is to notify only the Department of Justice (not the public or the industry) about their findings. The Department may use the dossier compiled by this committee to initiate another court case.
35. *Financial Times*, 22 March 2004.

36. *Patent* rights exist to protect an individual's codifiable innovation and knowledge, whereas *trademarks* protect the reputation of a firm. Other knowledge that comes from learning through trial and error is largely unprotected because it may not be 'blue-printed'.
37. Foreign funding of R&D has continued to be an important source of financing. Belgium, Hungary and the Netherlands received more than 10 per cent of their R&D from abroad, while the same share in Austria, Britain and Greece was more than 15 per cent.
38. Eurostat (2003). 'R&D expenditure and personnel in the EU', *Statistics in Focus*, Theme 9–8/2003, p. 1.
39. Lead-time advantages over competitors was the most frequently used protection method in the EU (Eurostat, 2004, 'Innovation output and barriers to innovation', *Statistics in Focus*, Theme 9–1/2004, p. 3).
40. The importance of after-sales service varies depending on the good. This service is non-existent for soaps and detergents, but it is essential for printing presses, on-line printers or photocopiers.
41. Self-satisfaction and a lack of real local competition contributed to the German camera-producing industry being driven out by the Japanese (Porter, 1990a, p. 169).
42. Timely, correct and cheap information is becoming a crucial input in the decision-making process. A banker who is handling large funds over his PC terminal is a long way from the British general, Sir Edward Pakenham, who lost the battle of New Orleans and his life on 8 January 1815, fifteen days after the Treaty of Ghent ended the war, but several days before the frigate arrived at his headquarters with the news about the end of the war (Lipsey, 1992b, p. 288).
43. The neo-classical doctrine relies on an elegant, but unrealistic, assumption that markets are perfect. Without such a hypothesis, there is no case for optimality in resource allocation.
44. If there is no retaliation, the 'optimal tariff' may be another reason for intervention. This is the case when a (large) country (or a group of countries) is strong enough to influence the world prices of the goods it trades. This country can reduce the world demand for the good in question by imposing or increasing tariffs. The price of the affected good falls, hence the tariff-imposing country tilts the terms of trade in its favour.
45. Because of asymmetric information, firms may have certain incentives to mislead the government.
46. Economies of scope are the outcome of the need for flexible (innovation-driven) methods of production. This is because the total production costs of manufacturing two separate goods may be higher than the costs of producing them together. A single firm can reduce average costs of production of two or more goods or services that share a common input without complete congestion. Identical technology can be employed for the production of differentiated output.
47. Serendipity is the faculty of making happy and unexpected discoveries by accident.
48. Viagra, the most widespread medicine used to treat male impotence, is another example of serendipity. Dr Ian Osterloh experimented with this medicine during the early 1990s with the aim of finding a painkiller for those suffering from angina pectoris. This is a dangerous disease, characterised by sudden and severe pain in the lower part of the chest, towards the left side, and a feeling of suffocation and fear of impending death. Pfizer, the pharmaceuticals company, was ready to give up on the project. However, certain male patients who were using this medicine during the research phase reported that following its consumption their virility was boosted. The rest is generally known. A medicine sought after for four millennia was found thanks to serendipity.
49. 'Schumpeterians' point to five long waves in modern history: (1) 1780–1840, steam power drove the Industrial Revolution; (2) 1840–90, the introduction of the railways; (3) 1890–1930, the introduction and production of electric power; (4) 1930–80, cheap oil and cars; and (5) information technology.
50. While R&D and innovation activities in the US are mainly led by the military and double-use industries where demand is limited, these activities in other countries are

more consumer related, that is, they are directed towards the development of goods and services for which demand exists everywhere. In addition, R&D is chiefly mission oriented towards big problems in countries such as the US, France and Britain. In countries such as Germany, Japan, Sweden or Switzerland, R&D is directed more, but not exclusively, towards the solution of practical problems.

51. Regarding the industry structure, patents are concentrated in pharmaceuticals, chemistry, molecular biology, semiconductor device manufacturing, optics, measuring and testing related devices, as well as telecommunications.
52. G. Parker, 'Brussels points the finger at lax states', *Financial Times*, 21 January 2004.
53. European Council, Lisbon 2000, Presidency Conclusions, § 5.
54. For a discussion of this issue, see Lipsey et al. (2005).
55. China lacked the institutions of higher learning that would house the collective memory of scientific discoveries and look after scholars. Everything was highly centralised in China and done in the name of the emperor. Secrecy also worked against the spread and accumulation of knowledge, mathematics in particular. The purpose of the 15th-century Chinese fleet of 2100 ships was to spread the fame of the emperor and Buddhism to the barbarians (goods, not commerce, were carried principally as presents). This fleet was far superior to anything in Europe at that time. The next emperor disdained commerce and opposed contacts with the barbarians. Hence, in 1525 all ocean-going ships were destroyed and their owners arrested.

    Gunpowder, a Chinese invention for example, was used in China as a toy, while it was an industrial tool and a part of war technology in Europe. In addition, ignorance of Newtonian mechanics put China at a big technological disadvantage *vis-à-vis* Europe in the 18th century.

    'The Islamic authorities resisted the use of printing because they saw it as encouraging ordinary people to interpret the holy writings for themselves rather than as dictated by the clergy, a fear shared by the Catholic church. European Protestants, on the other hand, embraced printing for the very same reason. . . . So the decline of Islamic science can be traced to a number of developments that were different from those in the West, many of them due to historical accidents: a theocracy with no concept of degrees of jurisdiction or of a developing code of laws; religious hostility to established science and free enquiry; no major institutional innovations such as the corporation – in the form of guilds, universities, independent cities, and business organizations. In short, while the West was developing a pluralistic society, Islam was solidifying a monolithic, relatively rigid, theocratic society' (Lipsey et al., 2005, pp. 275–6).
56. Apart from the integration of separate markets, other supporting adjustment devices include deregulation and privatisation.
57. The era of imaginative individuals as major sources of innovation was the 19th century and earlier. To fly to the Moon and return safe and sound involves the work of a large team of experts.
58. These irreversibilities include savings in factor (including energy) inputs per unit of output.
59. Economic growth may be propelled (among other elements) by the following three components (or by their combination): investment in capital and/or human resources, trade and technological change.
60. The time it takes for national income per capita to double in the early stages of industrialisation has fallen dramatically. In Britain it took around 60 years to do so after 1780, in Japan some 35 years after 1885, in Brazil 18 years after 1961 and in China 10 years after 1977. The main reason is technological progress. Countries are able to purchase foreign technology to make their home factors more productive. There is also another dimension to new technology. While it was an increase in the physical capacity to influence the environment and to produce goods that brought about the Industrial Revolution in the 19th century, the current industrial revolution has a more qualitative dimension. Lipsey sounded a note of caution when he compared present-day England with that in the Elizabethan era: 'It took 400 years for England to develop from that

stage to its present one. To do the same elsewhere in half of the time of 200 years would be a tremendous achievement; to aspire to do it in 25 or 50 years may be to court disaster' (Lipsey, 1992a, p. 755).

61. 'The great majority of innovations did *not* come from formal R&D (even in organisations such as Du Pont . . . which had strong in-house R&D facilities). Most . . . came from production engineers, systems engineers, technicians, managers, maintenance personnel and of course production workers' (Freeman, 1994, p. 474, original emphasis).
62. Gordon Moore was the co-founder of Intel.
63. International agreements are usually ambiguous. This allows diplomats to interpret them at home in their own favour. Conversely, constitutions and other domestic laws are (supposedly) transparent. This is because domestic politicians want the voters to understand them in order to win their votes.
64. E. Adlen and C. Daniel, 'US files WTO case against Airbus subsidies', *Financial Times*, 6 October 2004; E. Adlen and R. Minder, 'Airbus and Boeing pose huge test for EU–US relations', *Financial Times*, 6 October 2004.
65. 'The idea that we are living in an age of dramatic technological progress is mainly hype; the reality is that we live in a time when the fundamental things are actually not changing very rapidly at all. . . . The slightly depressing truth is that technology has been letting us down lately' (Krugman, 1998b, p. 104). This may be the truth if one remembers the constant maintenance necessary for PCs. The only new good that altered life for people on a larger scale during the 1990s was the mobile phone. The Internet is the only major service that has done the same in the same period. However, there is a continuous stream of small improvements in already existing goods.
66. A large part of intra-industry trade is in parts and components.
67. See the surveys by Greenaway and Milner (1987) and Greenaway and Torstensson (1997).
68. The original Treaty of Rome (1957) has been altered by the Single European Act (1987) and the treaties of Maastricht (1992), Amsterdam (1997) and Nice (2001), respectively. Throughout this book reference is made to the latest consolidated version of the Treaty of Rome (2002) available at the following web address: http://europa.eu.int/eur-lex/pri/en/oj/dat/2002/c_325/c_32520021224en00010184.pdf.
69. This refers to those who belong to the EU.
70. An exception to the general freedom of movement of goods is possible only in the case when such movement jeopardises public morality, security and the health of humans, animals or plants (Article 30).
71. This programme is also known as the White Paper, the Cockfield Report or the 1992 Programme.
72. This number does not include cases that relate to agriculture, fisheries, transport and coal.
73. *Financial Times*, 12 May 2000, p. 1.
74. Europa – Rapid – Press Release, IP/04/1003, 29 July 2004; and MEMO/04/202, 29 July 2004.
75. *The Economist*, 28 November 1998, p. 87.
76. A special and still unresolved issue refers to takeovers by foreign firms. If the foreign buyer comes from a country with relatively cheap capital (low rate of interest) relative to the country of the target firm, such an acquirer has an advantage over other potential buyers that have access to financial markets that charge higher interest rates. If the authorities in the country of the target firm want to retain domestic ownership of such a business, they could restrict takeovers by foreign firms and/or give subsidies to the domestic acquirers. A much more effective policy than such direct interference in business would be to keep the domestic macroeconomic policy in order and, hence, have a domestic capital market competitive with the international one.
77. At the beginning of 1997, Boeing's share of the world market was 64 per cent, Airbus's was 30 per cent and McDonnell-Douglas's was 6 per cent. In Europe, the corresponding figures were Boeing 31 per cent, Airbus 37 per cent and McDonnell-Douglas 2 per cent (*Bulletin Quotidien Europe*, 23 May 1997).

78. If to start a business requires overcoming substantial sunk costs, then mere deregulation and the Single European Market may not be enough. Further measures (such as subsidies) may be necessary to provide an investment impetus to firms.
79. The degree of concentration was much lower in the food and drink than in the chemical industry. It was higher at the national than at the EU level because of the barriers to trade (European Communities, 1991, p. 227).
80. Privatisation in the former East Germany accounted for part of the merger and acquisition activity in Germany.
81. This result was similar to the one reached in many studies on mergers in the US.
82. Jacquemin, 1990a, pp. 13–14; 1990b, p. 541; Jacquemin and Wright, 1993, p. 528; UNCTAD, 2000, p. 138; Pautler, 2001, p. 53.
83. W. Hutton, 'What Europe can teach Uncle Sam', *The Guardian*, 29 April 2002.
84. *The Economist*, 9 January 1999, p. 13.
85. *Financial Times*, 27 March 2003, p. 13.
86. www.crossingsbysw.com/pages/home_decor.
87. Europe has 40 battery producers compared with five in the US, 50 tractor makers while America has four and 16 firms building railway engines, whereas the US has two (*The Economist*, 23 January 1999, p. 67). Some firms think that they may prosper better if they become huge through mergers and acquisitions.
88. Another important tool for the control of dominance in the EU market and for enhancing competition was the conclusion of the Uruguay Round in 1994. After ratification, this deal further liberalised international trade, increased competition and, hence, modified/limited the non-competitive behaviour of the concentrated EU industries.
89. These thresholds also apply to firms that originate outside the EU.
90. If competitive firms want to keep their lead, they need to follow developments not only in their own industry but also in unrelated, but potentially competing, ones. Examples of 'learning-by-watching' may be found in the disappearance, almost overnight, of the market for cine cameras after the appearance of video cameras, the seismic shift in the market for mechanical watches after the invention of digital ones, and the move from dot matrix to laser printers or fibreoptics that evolved independently of the telecommunication technology.
91. A refusal to supply goods or services was taken to be an infringement of Article 82. In the *United Brands* case (1976) the European Commission found that United Brands, the major supplier of (Chiquita) bananas to most of the EU countries, abused its dominant position by refusing to supply green bananas to Olesen, a Danish ripener and distributor. Although Olesen had taken part in an advertising operation with one of United Brands' competitors, the Court found that the reaction of United Brands to a competitive threat was excessive and, hence, abusive. The refusal to supply bananas was a significant intrusion into the independence of small and medium-sized enterprises. United Brands was fined €1m by the Commission. The Court reduced the fine to €0.85m.
92. This article, however, neither outlaws nor discourages state ownership of enterprises.
93. The EU guidelines for state aid for small and medium-sized enterprises (1992) state that these firms (defined as having fewer than 50 employees) may receive support of up to 15 per cent of their investment cost. Enterprises with 50 to 250 employees may receive the same aid up to 7.5 per cent of their investment cost, while larger firms may get the same only in the assisted regions of the EU.
94. In the case of steel, shipbuilding or textiles, restructuring often means a reduction in production capacity.
95. A special type of public aid is in the form of public purchases. In Italy, for example, a law required that 30 per cent of contracts be awarded to firms based in the southern part of the country. The EU Court of Justice ruled in 1990 that such a law violated the public procurement directives. In other countries such as France or Germany there is no explicit buy-national law. None the less, publicly owned enterprises (railways, PTT) are 'expected' to prefer home-made goods and services to foreign ones.
96. The biggest state-aid case that came before the European Commission was the $9.4 billion rescue package for Crédit Lyonnais, the French state-owned bank. It was

approved in 1995 (*Financial Times*, 27 July 1995, p. 13). The cost soared to $16.9 billion in 1998 (*Financial Times*, 7 May 1998, p. 2), while the total cost of the cleanup to French taxpayers was $30 billion (*Stratfor*, 16 July 2002). The overall impression is that the approval by the European Commission had political motivations. In addition, the Commission failed an important test. It should have demanded a bigger reduction in the bank's business.

97. The largest reductions in expenditure affected domestic aid to the regions of Germany and Italy.
98. That is what they claim, when it suits them. What they do is another matter – just think of the US and EU trade policies in agricultural goods, cotton, textiles or subsidies to the aircraft industry.
99. When there are significant scale and learning economies, risk-loving firms have incentives to set current prices not on the basis of current costs, but rather on the costs they expect to achieve in the future once full economies of scale are reached.
100. The first disk produced by Microsoft with Windows 2000 cost Microsoft about half a billion dollars. The second disk cost them three to four cents, just the cost of reproducing the first one. The cost of the third was three to four cents, and so on. Start-up costs are immensely high (Arthur, 2002, p. 2).
101. European Council, Lisbon 2000, Presidency Conclusions, § 5.
102. See McAfee et al. (2004).
103. At the time of this case, Wanadoo was 72 per cent owned by France Télécom.
104. If a country such as Germany set higher standards than other EU countries, it could have carried on enforcing those standards with trade restrictions. The purpose of Decision 3052/95 is to prevent such behaviour.
105. *Barter* terms of trade are measured by how many units of domestic good have to be exported to pay for one unit of imports. *Factoral* terms of trade are measured by how many hours of foreign labour can be paid for by exporting the output of one hour of domestic labour.
106. Alternatively, the government may offer subsidies. In this case foreign taxpayers foot the bill.
107. The US also has free trade agreements with Chile, Israel, Jordan, Morocco and Singapore, basically for political reasons. Australia and New Zealand may join this group soon on economic and political grounds. There are also negotiations with Bahrain, Panama and Thailand. The US wants to further its political goals and rewards cooperative countries by free trade agreements. The countries that are in the queue for a free trade deal include smaller states such as Tunisia, Georgia, Uzbekistan and Kyrgyzstan. However, countries such as Egypt, Turkey or Pakistan, even though they are cooperative in the US war against terrorism, have relatively large economies that rely heavily on textiles exports. It would be tough for the US economy to adjust quickly and easily to this type of import within a free trade area.
108. For example, Singapore had a strict anti-chewing gum policy. 'Singapore was tragically forced into a limited retreat from its brave anti-gum stance by its recent bilateral trade agreement with the US. Dastardly American negotiators, under pressure from US chewing gum manufacturers ("pushers" would be more accurate), bulldozed through a partial relaxation of the ban' ('A sticky problem', *Financial Times*, 3 November 2004).
109. Swiss companies accounted for a third of the world's production of textile machinery in 1997 (*Financial Times*, 26 February 1998, p. 8).
110. 'Warning of increase in VAT fraud', *European Voice*, 20 November 1997, p. 7.
111. A rare, perhaps the only, example of a kind of compensation in an integration group can be found in the EU. When the Conservatives took office in Britain in 1979, they made a big to-do about the disproportionate British contribution to the EU budget which was a result of the workings of the CAP. The argument was that Britain failed to get a 'fair share' of the EU budget because of its small domestic agricultural sector. Margaret Thatcher said: 'I want my money back'. After a long hostile process, Britain obtained an annual 'rebate' (abatement) at the meeting of the European Council in Fontainebleau (1984). It was calculated on the basis of a formula related to the EU

expenditure in Britain and the VAT-based portion of the British contribution to the EU budget. This abatement was paid each year in the form of reduced VAT contribution in the following year. This settlement was advantageous to the Council of Ministers because the European Parliament is not involved in the revenue side of the picture. The Parliament has authority only over the expenditure part of the EU budget and the overall size of the EU budget.

112. Canon invested over $100 million and located a new production facility for photocopiers in the US, rather than building it in China or Malaysia where production costs are lower. The reason was a special NAFTA rule of origin for copiers which requires 80 per cent of local value added (UNCTAD, 1999b, p. 15).
113. A comparative study of antidumping actions in the US, the EU, Canada and Australia concluded that 90 per cent of imports that were unfairly priced according to antidumping rules would be found to be fairly priced under corresponding domestic rules of competition (UNCTAD, 1999b, p. 17).
114. If a government of one country subsidises exports, then another country has the right to introduce *countervailing duties*. As governments of at least two countries are involved, this dispute often becomes quite visible.
115. Another complication arises from the practice of 'zeroing'. Goods priced above home market prices are ignored for the calculation of average dumping margin. Therefore, the final antidumping duty is inflated.
116. R. Minder and E. Alden, 'EU and Canada retaliate against US imports', *Financial Times*, 31 March 2005.
117. The directives give many different thresholds. For example, the threshold for public works is €5 million; supply contracts for various goods and services all have different thresholds which are about €0.2 million. There are, of course, loopholes. For example, certain public works may be split into a number of smaller ones that are below the limit. Another way of avoiding EU scrutiny is to underestimate the value of the procured goods and services.

    The supply of military goods is excluded from rules on competition for national security reasons. This makes the military equipment market one of the most fiercely protected national markets in the EU. Its annual volume is about €30 billion. A proposed voluntary code regarding this segmented market could reduce duplication of R&D and lower the high cost of equipment produced in relatively low series (G. Parker, 'EU poised to increase competition in military contracts this year', *Financial Times*, 29 March 2005).
118. The *Associazione* exported to Britain more than 6 million packets of pre-sliced Parma ham in 2002 (P. Popham and S. Castle, 'The "barmy Parma drama" is over', *The Independent*, 21 May 2003).
119. *Financial Times*, 11 January 2004 and 4 February 2004.
120. 'Dutch window cleaners were outraged to discover that their standard ladders were too long to comply with EU health-and-safety regulations' (*The Economist*, 'Outgrowing the Union' A survey of the EU, 25 September 2004, p. 15).
121. In 2001, non-harmonised products in trade accounted for about 21 per cent of the total tariff lines (WTO, 2004, p. 60).
122. It was the US demand to exclude agriculture from the agreement that resulted in the formation of the GATT. This resulted in a later backlash against the US in farm trade with the EU and Japan.
123. Old Article 115.
124. Between 1989 and 1991, the annual imports of Japanese cars into Italy more than doubled from 10 000 to 22 000 (*Financial Times*, 5 August 1991).
125. S. Druker, 'America's hypocrisy over modified produce', *Financial Times*, 18 May 2004, p. 19.
126. Yes, proportional. This may be perfect in theory, but how to ascertain that in practice?
127. There was little that the European Commission could do against the French unilateral action. This was not because of the fear of protests in France, but because it would take up to two years to settle the dispute in the European Court of Justice. 'If the Commission

cannot bring the "offenders" into line fast, its confidence can be seriously damaged. Therefore, a change in the EU rules is necessary that would provide the Commission with the necessary instruments for a quick reaction' (*European Voice*, 28 October 1999, p. 11).

128. An example is cars produced by Nissan in Britain. France limited imports of Japanese cars to 3 per cent of the domestic market and claimed that the Nissan Bluebird cars produced in Britain were Japanese in origin. An earlier informal guideline stated that Japanese cars produced in the EU would receive preferential (domestic) treatment in the EU market if local EU content was at least 60 per cent. In 1988, France proposed an increase in this threshold to 80 per cent. Currently, in order to qualify for national treatment in the EU, the produced (assembled) cars must have 60 per cent of local (EU) content.

129. Countries like to be a member of a select 'club'. Alan Winters put this succinctly by comparing preferential trade deals to street gangs: 'you may not like them, but if they are in your neighbourhood, it is safer to be in one' (Mansfield and Reinhardt, 2003, p. 857).

I pray that in all respects you may prosper and be in good health,
just as your soul prospers.
3 John 2

3 Common Markets

3.1 Introduction

The entire analysis of customs unions applies to common markets too. Due to the free mobility of factors of production in a common market, the effects of a customs union are, however, substantially enriched. The scope and size of effects on a more efficient allocation of resources and capabilities (improvements in the locational advantages for business) are due to the free factor flow from low to high productivity businesses and geographical locations within the common market.

Apart from free factor mobility within the group, a condition for the integration of factor markets is the non-discrimination of factors originating in the partner countries. In this situation, factors respond to signals and incentives which include demand, higher productivity and returns within a common market. Integration of factor markets will be encountered as mobility of labour and capital. Thus this chapter is structured as follows. Following the introduction, Section 3.2 discusses labour mobility and Section 3.3 investigates capital mobility.

3.1.1 EQUALISATION OF FACTOR PRICES

Let us start by assuming a model that consists of two countries A and B, two final goods X and Y and two factors of production K and L. Suppose further that factor mobility is perfect within each country, but prohibited between countries. If there are no barriers to trade and no distortions, if technology is the same and freely accessible to both countries, if production functions are completely homogeneous, if both goods are produced in both countries and isoquants intersect only once (there is no factor intensity reversal), then free trade in goods will in theory equalise both relative prices in goods and relative factor prices and their returns in each country.[1] This stringent situation is illustrated in Figure 3.1.

In the figure, X_a represents the unit isocost line (the combination of factors which keeps output constant) for good X in country A (production of which is relatively labour 'intensive'), while X_b describes the same cost line for good X in country B, where its production is relatively capital 'intensive'. Equilibrium occurs at point E, where factor prices are equalised through trade at levels $0r_e$ for capital and $0W_e$ for labour. In this model trade is a substitute for factor mobility.

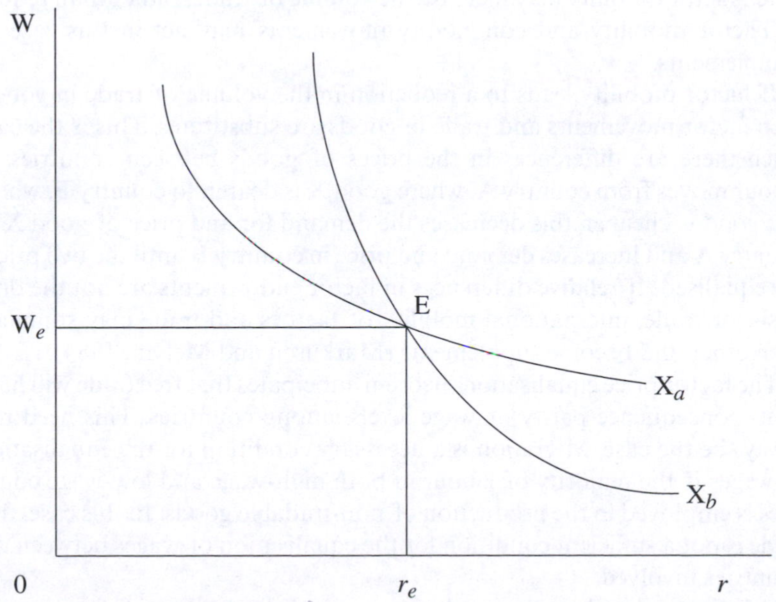

Figure 3.1 Equalisation of factor prices

The exclusion of balance of payments adjustments from comparative statistics implies that the adjustment process between the two distant points in time has worked well and that the balance is in equilibrium. However, in reality, such a process may last about a generation (recall the eastern enlargement of the EU). Thus, a static model, which usually ignores the adjustment process, can hardly be justified. If capital accumulation, economies of scale, path dependence and economic growth are included in the consideration, they produce different results in the long term from the straightforward static model.

Free international trade in goods and factor movements are prevented by the existence of various barriers. In this framework, according to one view, commodity movements are still a substitute for factor movements. An increase in trade restrictions stimulates factor movements, while an increase in barriers to international factor mobility enhances trade in goods (Mundell, 1957, p. 321).

So far it has been assumed that technology is the same in both countries. However, this is not always the case. Differences in technologies among countries enhance, rather than reduce, the opportunities for international capital mobility. Some developing countries export raw materials in return for foreign direct investment (FDI), which enables them to produce and later export manufactured goods (Purvis, 1972, p. 991). When technologies differ, factor mobility may increase the volume of trade, rather than reduce it. Factor mobility and commodity movements may act in this case as complements.

If factor mobility leads to a reduction in the volume of trade in goods, then factor movements and trade in goods are substitutes. This is the case when there are differences in the prices of goods between countries. If labour moves from country A, where good X is dearer, to country B, where this good is cheaper, this decreases the demand for and price of good X in country A and increases demand and price in country B until the two prices are equalised. If relative differences in factor endowments are not the only basis for trade, international mobility of factors and trade may stimulate each other and become supplements (Markusen and Melvin, 1984).

The factor price equalisation theorem anticipates that free trade will have as its consequence parity of wage levels among countries. This need not always be the case. Migration is a necessary condition for the equalisation of wages if the majority of labour in both high-wage and low-wage countries is employed in the production of non-tradable goods. In this case, free trade is not a sufficient condition for the equalisation of wages between the countries involved.

Substitutability between trade in goods and mobility of factors (the Heckscher–Ohlin model) may be the exception, rather than the rule. If countries are quite different in relative factor endowments and have weak economies of scale, then individuals who draw their income from factors that are relatively scarce end up worse off as a result of trade. If countries are similar and trade is mostly motivated by economies of scale (intra-industry trade), then one might expect to find that even scarce factors gain (Krugman, 1990a, p. 80).

If there is a free geographical mobility of factors, then countries become relatively well endowed with the factors used 'intensively' in the production of export goods (Markusen, 1983, p. 355). International mobility of factors and trade are often taken to be complements, rather than substitutes. A high mobility and concentration of factors (designers in northern Italy, chemical engineers in Basle, financial experts in London and New York or computer scientists in California or Boston) will create an additional comparative advantage, which will, in turn, enhance trade. 'Globalisation' of international business and the integrated international operations of transnational corporations (TNCs) contribute to this situation. This is most obvious in the EU, where an expansion of intra-group FDI and TNC operations has accompanied a high level of intra-group trade.

In the manufacturing industry, access to foreign markets by horizontal TNCs is a choice between exporting and investing abroad. The decision depends on factors such as economies of scale, the cost of the project, trade costs, trade regime, competition and the like. In this case, trade and FDI (foreign production) are substitutes. Vertical TNCs, by contrast, aim to profit from location of plants in different countries. Depending on local circumstances, these affiliates specialise in different phases in the production process and send (sell) each other inputs, components and final goods. In this case, FDI and trade are complements. In services, however, trade and FDI can be expected to have a complementary dimension. A foreign presence (right of establishment) in the services sector is normally expected to increase trade.

If FDI is a response to trade barriers, then it acts in a trade-replacing way. If, however, FDI is an efficiency-seeking investment (developing natural resources), then it operates in a trade-promoting way. In any case, there is some evidence that FDI has increased trade in the EU (van Aarle, 1996, p. 137). An extensive survey of the impact of the Single Market Programme on FDI in the EU found strong evidence that FDI and trade are complementary (European Commission, 1998, p. 1).

Theoretical considerations about substitutability or complementarity between trade and FDI lost their significance in the light of new considerations about the spatial location of firms. This is reinforced by the fact that high-technology exports are the principal foreign exchange earners for the developing countries.[2] The issue is: what are the underlining conditions that make specific locations advantageous for particular business activities? This holds for both domestic and foreign firms.

A study of relative differences in labour rewards in the EU found that there was a convergence in labour costs between the mid-1950s (that is before the EU was created) and the mid-1960s. From 1968 onwards the trend was reversed. The reasons for convergence may be found in free trade in goods and more liberal movements of capital and labour which came from the Mediterranean countries that were not members of the EU (Tovias, 1982).

This approach was disputed as it did not provide an explanation for the converging trend in wages before the creation of the EU or the divergent trend after 1968. There is not even a single wage level within a country because of heterogeneous qualifications and employer demand in each sector. Due to imperfect mobility of labour, trade may be expected to lead to a convergence in prices of goods and wages in industries that are involved in trade. A correlation should exist between the liberalisation of internal trade and changes in the level of wages (Gremmen, 1985). In testing this idea a few errors were made, the most important being the expectation of an insignificant coefficient on the capital–labour ratio. Wage differences between the north and the south of Italy or the US reveal that this expectation is not correct. The results of the re-estimation found that the relation between the level of wages and trade intensity (the sum of countries' marginal propensities to import each other's goods) is not as direct as Gremmen assumed. In addition, it was found that the capital–labour ratio remains an important determinant of factor prices even if international economic integration has advanced as far as it has in the EU. This is not to deny that increasing trade relations lead to decreasing wage differentials, but rather to say that trade intensity must be considered in conjunction with differences in the capital–labour ratio (van Mourik, 1987).

Free mobility of factors in a common market and an expectation of equalisation of factor prices may be an attractive incentive for countries to close the gap in the levels of income and development within the integrated area. How this works in practice is not quite clear. The experience of the EU presented evidence that some corrective measures were necessary, such as social and regional funds.

Economies of scale make specialisation more likely. Every technology requires different types of labour, so complete factor price equalisation seems unlikely. Distortions such as tariffs, subsidies, taxes or costs of transport make equalisation of factor prices real only in a strict model. In the real world there may appear only a tendency towards the equalisation of factor prices.

Lord, we do not know where You are going,
and how can we know the way?
John 14:5

3.2 Labour mobility

3.2.1 INTRODUCTION

A customs union involves product market integration. A common market adds to that development the potentials for integration of factor markets within the group. It is expected in theory that the free intra-group flow of factors will improve the allocation of resources over the one achieved in either a free trade area or a customs union. The neo-classical Heckscher–Ohlin trade theory concludes that a country with a rich supply of labour may either export labour-intensive goods or import capital and export labour, under the assumption that technology is the same in all countries at all times. In either case the country is equally well off.

This section is structured as follows. The next subsection (3.2.2) presents a brief background. Subsections 3.2.3 and 3.2.4, respectively, consider the costs and benefits of labour migration for countries of origin and countries of destination. Subsection 3.2.5 deals with labour mobility in the EU (legal framework, migration data and waves, and the EU response). The final subsection (3.2.6) concludes that labour migration, in particular immigration, will be high on the EU agenda of priorities over the coming decades because of demographic trends in the EU and imminent labour shortages that may last for several decades.

3.2.2 BACKGROUND

Mobility of labour or labour responsiveness to demand has long been a significant facet of economic life. Labour has moved not only in space among regions and countries, but also among economic sectors and different professions.[3] In the late 1950s, agriculture employed about 20 per cent of the labour force in most industrialised economies. Half a century later, agriculture employs about 4 per cent of the labour force in these countries.

The theoretical assumption that labour has a greater degree of mobility within a country than among countries may not always be substantiated. A century ago inter-country mobility of labour between Ireland and other developed English-speaking countries was, perhaps, much greater than internal Irish labour mobility. None the less, labour mobility should not always be taken in its 'technical' meaning of pure movements of persons from place A to place B. One has to bear in mind that these people are taking with them their skills, knowledge, experiences, culture and organisational competence.

Outside of common markets, international labour migration is characterised by a legal asymmetry. The Universal Declaration of Human Rights (1948), Article 13, denies the right to the country of origin to close its borders to bona fide emigrants. This country may not control the emigration flows according to its interest. The country of destination, however, has an undisputed right to restrict the entry of immigrants, although this is not explicitly mentioned in the Declaration. In these circumstances migration flows are primarily determined by demand in the receiving countries. So, the personal will and readiness to move is a necessary condition for labour migration, but it is not a sufficient one.

3.2.3 COUNTRY OF ORIGIN

If political instability and economic problems (push determinants) overcome the propensity to stay in the homeland (pull factors), then there are several reasons for the international migration of labour. The most significant include the possibility of finding a job which may be able to provide conditions for better living, as well as improved conditions for specialisation and promotion. Most immigrants to the EU worked prior to migration, although unemployment was a factor that influenced 'push' towards emigration.[4] In these complex conditions, migrants act as utility-maximising units subject to push and pull forces.

In general, an emigration pattern has a few phases. Initially, men migrate individually in search of a (better) job and education or in order to escape persecution. Then, gradually, comes a phase which involves women because of family reunification.

The migration of labour has its obstacles. They can be found both in receiving countries and in countries of origin. Socio-psychological obstacles to migration can include different culture and languages,[5] national historical experiences (wars, occupation), rules for the recognition of qualifications, as well as variations in climate, religion, diet and clothing. Such barriers to migration were high in the 19th century for intra-European mobility of labour, which was one of the reasons why Europe was a source of significant emigration at that time. In addition, socio-psychological obstacles may be part of the reason why Japan has almost closed its borders for legal immigration. Economic obstacles include lack of information about job openings, conditions of work, social security, legal systems, systems of dismissal (last in, first out) and the loss of seniority. During recession and unemployment periods there may be nationalistic, racial and religious tensions between the local population and immigrants. Some political parties and certain trade unions may lobby against immigration, as well as for driving immigrants away.

Countries of origin have significant losses in manpower. Migrants are usually younger men who are prepared to take the risk of moving. These regions may then be left with a higher proportion of women and older people. Potential producers leave while consumers remain behind. Countries of origin lose a part of their national wealth which was invested in the raising and education of their population. If the migrants are experienced and educated, then their positions may often be filled by less sophisticated staff. The result is lower productivity and lower national wealth.

The brain-drain argument is not always convincing. Many of those who migrate cannot find appropriate jobs in their home countries. The physician who leaves Malawi is one thing, as Malawi needs more medical services.[6] An astrophysicist from Congo is quite another. Congo has few laboratories, radio-telescopes or powerful computers; expertise in this field cannot be employed and so it makes sense for this skilled person to go abroad and possibly send some money back to his country of origin. However, if computer engineers emigrate from Mozambique, there is no point in this country importing computers, and without the import of new technology it will remain backward indefinitely. If migrants return after a (long) period abroad, some of them may be old and/or ill, so they become consumers, which will reduce the local tax base and increase the cost of social services to the remaining population.

Apart from these costs, countries of origin can obtain certain short-term gains from emigration. This movement of labour reduces the pressure which is caused by unemployment and reduces the payment of unemployment benefits (if they exist). Possible remittances of hard currency can reduce the balance of payments pressure, and if migrants return they may bring with them certain new skills and (hard currency) savings which will help them to obtain or create better jobs. This can help the development efforts of the country. One should not forget a potential inflow of pension funds.

If countries do not produce exportable goods, then they have to export labour services (if other countries want to accept them) in order to pay for imports. However, there is an asymmetry in the perception of labour mobility. When the rich north wants to send workers abroad, then that counts as trade in 'services'. When the poor south wants to do the same, it is regarded as 'immigration'.

The volume of possible remittances depends on the number of migrants, the length of their stay, and incentives. It is estimated that the annual volume of remittances in the world by migrants to their families at home is more than $120 billion.[7] Mexican migrant workers sent home $16.6 billion in remittances in 2004. This accounted for more than 2 per cent of Mexico's GDP and brought in more hard currency than tourism.[8] The shorter the stay of migrants abroad, the higher the probability that they would transfer or bring back all their savings to their home country. During short stays abroad, their aim is to earn and save as much as possible. If they stay abroad for a longer period, then they may wish to enjoy a higher standard of living than during relatively short stays, thus reducing the volume of funds which may potentially be remitted to their country of origin. If the country of origin offers incentives for the transfer of these funds by way of attractive rates of interest, rate of exchange, allowances for imports and investment, and if there is an overall stability, then there is a greater probability that some funds will be attracted.

3.2.4 COUNTRY OF DESTINATION

The supply of local labour and the level of economic activity determine the demand for foreign labour in the country of destination. A country may permit an inflow of foreign labour bearing in mind, first and foremost, the welfare of its own citizens. That is always the starting point in the creation of all policies. Others count too because of possible retaliation and for other reasons, including moral ones, but the country's own citizens come first. There has always been an excess demand for a particular labour segment. This could be either for cyclical and seasonal reasons or for structural ones (new professions). A normal market response to such labour shortages has been to increase wages in this segment of the labour market and to increase demand for education and training. Firms resist the demand for higher wages and instead seek immigrant labour. Hence, there is always a demand for immigration at any level of population and rate of unemployment. This is a self-defeating immigration policy as it perpetuates a never-ending demand for more immigration.

The country of destination must be aware that people arrive with all their virtues and vices. Foreign workers may face both open and hidden conflicts with the local population. The host-country population may dislike foreigners because they take jobs from the domestic population,[9] they bring their own customs, increase congestion, depress wages and send their savings abroad, to mention just a few reasons. In certain cases, such as the migration of retired persons from Scandinavia to Spain or from Canada to Florida, this should not be regarded as migration that is in response to wage differentials. These migrants do not work; they spend and enjoy their life savings, and create a permanent demand for certain services and jobs for the locals.

The country of destination gains obvious benefits from immigration.[10] Migrants are a very mobile segment of the labour force. Once they enter a country, they are usually not linked to any particular place. Mobility of local labour in the EU is quite low.[11] There are various reasons for this low labour mobility in the EU, including: relatives and friends living nearby; spouses with jobs that they do not want to leave; children being well settled in local schools; and people enjoying living in their home, which may still be mortgaged.

In general, the country of destination may acquire labour which is cheaper and whose training has not been paid for by the domestic taxpayers. Migrants increase the demand for housing and goods and they pay taxes which may exceed what they receive in transfer payments, public services and other benefits. Temporary migrants are most likely to be employed. If they are highly paid, the net present value of the balance of the stream of public receipts from them and expenditures on them tilt in favour of the country of destination. With the selfish beggar-thy-neighbour policy of immigration, it pays the country of destination to extract human capital from the rest of the world, particularly through a selective immigration policy based on temporary entry.

If migrants have relatively low education and experience, they take jobs that are unattractive to the domestic workforce at the offered rates. These jobs include low-paid and often tedious work in mines, foundries, construction, garbage collection, cleaning, hotels, restaurants and so on. Migrants compete for these vacancies with the local youth and women who may have reduced opportunities for work. While offering lower wages for these jobs, countries of destination may partially reduce the price of inputs (labour) and partially increase the competitiveness of their tradable goods and services, at least in the short run.

There are no language barriers to the movement of local labour within the home country. Migrant workers may not know the language of the host country, making it difficult for them to participate in the local social life. The only place where they can express themselves as creative beings is in production, with the result that these workers may sometimes work more quickly and efficiently. This may provoke clashes with the local workers as new production norms may be increased. Migrants may leave after a while, while the locals may be tied by those norms for a long time. Employers may sometimes prefer to conclude direct agreements with migrant workers rather than employ local labour. Not only may migrant workers be working for lower wages than the domestic labour in the absence of legal protection, but also they can be dismissed with fewer repercussions for the employer. Alternatively, the permits of foreign workers might not be renewed.

The mobility of migrant labour within the country of destination has an impact on the national equalisation of wages. Of course, every new wave of immigration depresses the wages offered to earlier immigrants. Foreign labour that is legally employed need not necessarily be cheaper than local labour as there is legislation requiring the payment of fair wages to all. However, foreign labour is more easily controlled and manipulated by management.

The impact of labour immigration on the local labour market in the destination country has always provoked a certain amount of interest. This is particularly true for the traditional destination countries such as the US, Canada and Australia.[12] For example, there is a well-known case of a sudden inflow of refugees from the Cuban port of Mariel to Miami (Florida) in 1980. Within just a few months 125 000 people arrived, increasing Miami's labour force by 7 per cent. However, employment and wages among the local population including the unskilled labour remained virtually unaffected.[13] Surveys of studies about the relation and impact of immigrants on the wage rates and native unemployment in the US found no significant effects (Leamer and Levinsohn, 1995, p. 1360; Simon, 1996, p. 130). Such findings question the widely held view that wages, like almost everything else on the American market, are flexible. Analyses of similar effects in Europe are rather limited. A study of the impact of immigrants on local wages in Britain,[14] the Netherlands[15] and Norway[16] found very small effects (Hartog and Zorlu, 2002, p. 25). This finding would also support the widely held view that wages are quite rigid in Europe.

One line of reasoning says that if allowed to work, immigrants may be putting into the local public funds more than they take out. They arrive when they are young, healthy and productive. They pay taxes and other contributions for many years before they are entitled to collect pensions and receive medical care. This argument does not take fully into account the following issues: the ageing of immigrants themselves, the length of their stay and the impact of their families. Calculations of the benefits of working immigrants to the economic growth of the country of their destination ought to be discounted by the effect that their families have on the population growth in that country. The families, particularly if they are large, capture many social benefits at the local level. If the working immigrants are in the low-paid labour segment, the net effect on the host-country exchequer may easily be negative.

Table 3.1 The net fiscal externality of a migrant to Germany in euros per year

In Euros per immigrant and year	Length of stay in years		
	0–10	10–25	25+
Balance of state revenues/expenditures			
Health insurance	−590	−43	49
Pension insurance without child effect	1376	1606	2148
Nursing insurance	95	117	176
Unemployment insurance	127	217	−519
Taxes and tax-financed benefits	−3375	−3227	−1001
Total balance*	**−2367**	**−1330**	**853**
Full child effect on pensions	1126	1314	1757
Total balance with full child effect	−1241	−16	2610

Note: Using the socio-economic panel (6810 surveyed households in Germany) the stock of immigrants in west Germany was surveyed in 1997; it consists of those persons of non-German citizenship who live in west Germany, naturalised persons and persons with mothers of non-German citizenship excluding immigrants of German descent. * Cash value of payments made and received excluding any child effects.

Source: Sinn (2004, p. 14).

Table 3.1 presents data on the net fiscal externality of an immigrant to Germany. Sinn (2004) argued that migrants who stayed in Germany for more than 25 years made an annual net contribution to the public funds of €852. If the child effect is included, this contribution was €2610. However, unlike permanent migration to the US, Canada and Israel, migration to Germany is typically a 'return migration'. A large majority of immigrants (about 80 per cent) return to their home countries after about a decade. They do not stay long enough in Germany to become net fiscal contributors. If the migrants bring their sometimes quite big families along with them and stay less than a decade, they receive annually on average €2367 more from tax-financed welfare benefits and public infrastructure services than they contribute to the German funds. The second generation of immigrants remains typically in the group of below-average wage earners, hence it becomes a net 'burden' on the public funds.

There is anxiety in Germany that relatively generous welfare benefits may act as a magnet for migrants[17] from central and east Europe. It has been suggested that the rules for non-Germans to access welfare benefits should be tightened (Sinn, 2004). This may be understandable in the short run because of the unemployment and fiscal deficit problems in Germany. There are at least two adjustment mechanisms in the medium term regarding this problem. First is the adjustment period for the free movement of labour in the EU from the new member countries in central and eastern Europe. This freedom will be granted from 2011. Second, by that time, central and east European EU countries will be touched by the same demographical trends. There will be a shortage of labour in those countries, hence there will be fewer people interested in migrating than was the case when these countries joined the EU in 2004.

Some immigration will always be necessary. This relates to specific skills, knowledge and experience that are either rare or costly to create on a smaller scale, but are valuable for the economy of the country of destination. In addition, the knowledge of foreign languages or certain cultures may be acquired in this way. However, the claim that immigration is (net) beneficial for the country of destination should be tested and proved in each situation.

3.2.5 EUROPEAN UNION

Legal Framework

The original Treaty of Rome had only a few provisions that related to immigration. Article 39 provides for the freedom of movement of workers within the EU. It also abolishes any discrimination among workers who are citizens of the member states. In addition, Article 18 provides EU citizens with an unrestricted right to move and reside within the territory of the EU. Title IV Visas, Asylum, Immigration and Other Policies Related to Free Movement of Persons was introduced into the original Treaty of Rome by the Treaty of Amsterdam (Articles 61–9 of the Treaty of Rome). There is a requirement to establish progressively an area of freedom, security and justice; to introduce common measures for controls while persons are crossing external borders of the EU; and to eliminate all such controls for people (be they EU or non-EU nationals) crossing internal borders within the EU. Britain and Ireland got an opt-out from this provision (Article 69). There is also a requirement for the harmonisation of measures regarding legal and illegal immigration, refugees and asylum.

Migration Waves

Following the Second World War, the migration of people in Europe was characterised by several distinct phases:

- The first phase was the period from 1945 to the early 1960s. People moved because of the adjustment to the situation following the end of the war, as well as because of the process of decolonisation. For example, 12 million ethnic Germans were forced to leave central and eastern Europe. Most of them settled in Germany. Colonial powers such as Britain, Belgium, France and the Netherlands were affected by return migration from European colonies and the inflow of workers from former overseas territories. More than a million French residents of Algeria resettled in France during and after the Algerian war of independence.

- The second phase overlaps the preceding one. It lasted from 1955 to 1973. Labour shortages in some EU countries led to openness for immigration. Labour from Italy, Spain, Portugal, Greece, Turkey, former Yugoslavia, Morocco and Tunisia was migrating northwards, mainly, but not exclusively, to Germany and France.[18] About 5 million people moved northwards during this period.
- The third period from 1973 to 1988 was characterised by restrained migration. Following the first oil price shock and the related economic crises and social tensions, the recruitment of foreign labour stopped abruptly. Policies that encouraged return migration were not working. However, the foreign population in the EU was increasing as family members were joining workers who were already in the EU. In addition, these new residents had high fertility rates.
- The fourth phase started in 1988. It was linked with the dissolution of socialism, economic transition and ethnic wars. Hundreds of thousands of refugees and asylum seekers, as well as economic migrants, moved to the EU countries. Germany alone received 1.5 million new immigrants in 1992 (Zimmermann, 1995, pp. 46–7).
- A fifth stage of labour movement may start around the year 2010. Demographical trends and imminent labour shortages in the EU may provoke labour migrations towards the EU for decades to come.

Consequences

Conventional wisdom states that an abolition of barriers to international migration of labour would bring an increase in labour flow. This hypothesis could be tested in the case of the EU. The total number of intra-EU migrants of the original six member countries was about half a million prior to 1960, which increased to a little over 800 000 in 1968. This volume of migrant workers remained almost constant until the early 1980s and since then it has decreased to 650 000 migrants. All other intra-EU migrations were national (from southern to northern Italy or from western regions of France into Paris), rather than inter-state. The inevitable conclusion is that the creation of the EU has not significantly changed intra-EU labour migrations. While intra-EU trade increased, the intra-EU migrations decreased. Trade and the migration of labour were substitutes (Straubhaar, 1988).

The explanation for a greater migration of labour from third countries rather than within the EU can partly be found in the differences in production functions and barriers to trade among countries. The more similar the structure and the level of development between countries and the lower the barriers to trade, the greater will be the substitution effect between trade and labour migration. This also explains the migration of labour from Italy just after the creation of the EU, as well as the subsequent reduction in this flow.

The explanation for the decline in intra-EU labour mobility during the 1980s can also be found in significant improvements in the state of their local economies. Labour migration from Italy has slowed down since 1967. The same has happened in Greece since the early 1970s. Similar tendencies can be observed in the cases of Spain and Portugal since the mid-1980s. In addition, traditional countries of emigration such as Italy or Greece became targets for significant legal and illegal immigration. North Africans and Albanians were entering Italy clandestinely, while Greece was a target for a similar migration by the Albanians. A number of Bulgarians, Serbs, Poles and Russians entered Greece legally, but stayed on after their permits expired.

An interesting fact is Italy's transition over the past three decades from a net exporter to a net importer of non-European, mainly Mediterranean, illegal labour. Illegal immigrants work in and contribute to the growth of the informal economy. Costs of labour are both lower and more flexible in the black economy. This encourages firms to shift resources from the legal economy to the informal one. However, the technology available is less efficient in the underground economy. Hence, illegal immigration makes possible a transfer of capital (and labour) towards the informal economy. This may be favourable for the firms that avoid tax obligations, but it is damaging for the economy as a whole (Dell'Aringa and Neri, 1989, p. 134).

Recessions now rarely affect only one country. During times of economic slowdown the unemployed in the EU stayed in their country of origin. This was because the chances of finding employment abroad were smaller than at home. If there were some gaps between supply and demand in the labour market, labour migration from third countries was closing them, rather than internal EU flows. Reduced EU internal labour migration was due to a trend which was evening up the income and productivity levels among the original six member countries, as well as the growth in the other EU countries that created domestic demand for labour. Hence, the expectation that the creation of a common market would significantly increase long-term intra-group migrations of labour was refuted in the case of the EU.

There is also a special type of international mobility of labour which is often overlooked. Many TNCs stipulate that their employees must circulate and spend time in various affiliates in order to maintain integration both at the international and personal levels. Staff often move at regular intervals. Although this is recorded in statistics as international mobility of labour, it occurs within the same firm.

Data and Trends

Exact data on the flow of migrants are deficient. A conservative estimate puts the number of illegal immigrants into the EU(15) at 500 000 a year.[19] Therefore, Table 3.2 presents an approximation about stock data of the labour force by broad groups of citizenship in the EU in 2002. The table reveals that the majority of migrants in the EU were non-EU nationals. Migration of labour can be a significant feature even if countries are not formally integrated.

Immigration into the EU has been the principal source of population growth over the 1990s. In absolute terms migration is highest in recent years in Italy, Britain and Germany. These countries together accounted for more than 60 per cent of the total net immigration in the EU.[20] The net inflow of migrants added 0.2 per cent a year to the EU population during the second half of the 1990s. Most of the immigrants were non-EU nationals. The vast majority of them (about 40 per cent) were young, under the age of 30. The non-EU nationals that were emigrating from the EU were older than those immigrating into the EU. This could be expected as the former were returning after working or studying in the EU. Given the low and declining rate of natural increase in the EU population, net immigration added about 80 per cent to the population growth. Immigration could assume rising importance in the years to come as the growth of the working-age population in the EU slows down and comes to a halt around 2010. Given the persistent slowdown in the rate of natural increase of the population, the population growth in the EU over the coming 10–20 years is likely to be determined almost entirely by the scale of immigration.[21]

Non-EU nationals represented about 4 per cent of the population living in the EU in 2000. EU nationals living in another EU member state accounted for an additional 1.5 per cent of the EU population.[22] Migrants from central and eastern Europe were concentrated principally in the EU countries that are bordering their country of origin. Migrants from Africa represented about a quarter of non-EU nationals living in the EU. People from this region accounted for more than two-thirds of immigrants in France and Portugal. Asians and immigrants from the Caribbean accounted for almost half of non-EU nationals living in Britain.

Non-EU nationals (in 2000) represented 9 per cent of people residing in Germany (this share includes those born in Germany) and 7 per cent in

Table 3.2 Estimates of the labour force (employed plus unemployed populations) in EU countries by broad groups of citizenship, 2002 (thousands)

Citizenship	B	DK	D	EL	E	F	IRL	I	L	NL	A	P	FIN	S	UK
Nationals	3 754.0	2 662.8	33 225.6	3 739.5	15 819.8	22 562.4	1 653.5	–	107.8	7 838.8	3 383.5	5 016.2	2 375.0	4 164.8	27 025.3
Other EU nationals	231.5	28.3	1 022.4	5.3	83.2	575.2	56.5	–	71.6	124.1	59.9	12.2	8.5	86.6	501.5
Non-EU nationals	67.0	49.4	2 027.0	204.1	337.7	747.5	39.9	–	8.9	156.8	291.0	104.4	22.8	95.7	810.9
No answer	–	–	–	–	–	–	–	21 756.8	–	56.7	–	–	0.1	0.7	0.5
Total	4 052.5	2 740.5	36 275.1	3 948.9	16 240.7	23 885.1	1 749.8	21 756.8	188.2	8 176.4	3 734.4	5 132.7	2 406.4	4 347.9	28 338.3

Source: Eurostat (2003), Labour Force Survey.

Austria. Non-EU nationals in Spain, Italy, Ireland and Finland accounted for less than 1 per cent of the total resident population.

As far as the level of education is concerned, non-EU nationals living in the EU in 2000 had, on average, lower levels of education than the EU nationals. Forty-six per cent of men of non-EU nationality in the 25–39 age group had no educational qualifications beyond compulsory schooling, compared with 29 per cent of the EU nationals. Only 17 per cent of non-EU nationals had tertiary or university education, while the share of EU nationals in this group was 24 per cent. The unemployment rate among men who were EU nationals in the same age group was 6.5 per cent, which was significantly lower than the 15 per cent rate among the non-EU nationals. As far as women are concerned, their unemployment rates were 10 and 19 per cent, respectively. These differences in unemployment rates need not be seen primarily as the reluctance by non-EU immigrants to work compared with the EU nationals. It reflects, in part, problems regarding access to jobs that face non-EU nationals. In addition, non-EU immigrant women are faced with cultural differences and difficulties in affording childcare.[23]

Demographical trends in the EU(15) reveal that Europeans are living longer, but they are not having enough children to keep the working-age population stable between now and 2050. This is particularly relevant for the ratio between workers and pensioners. In order to maintain this balance, the EU(15) would need to 'import' about 1.6 million migrants a year.[24] The current political (and economic) situation may not easily tolerate such a development.

According to certain scenarios presented in a UN study,[25] France would need an average of 136 000 immigrants per year in the 2010–50 period; Germany alone would need 458 000 migrants a year in the 1995–2050 period; while Italy would need to have an annual net immigration from 75 000 in 1995–2000 to 318 000 in 2045–50 with a peak of 613 000 immigrants between 2025 and 2030. There is a slight downward longer-term trend in unemployment rates in the EU countries. EU nationals may become increasingly choosy about the jobs they are prepared to do. If nothing is done, the EU(25) population of about 450 million in 2004 would drop to fewer than 400 million in 2050 without immigration.[26]

No matter how selective immigration policy may be, it may not solve demographical problems, but it may be a part of the solution. A growing number of potential immigrants may be found in the Middle East and north Africa; however, the fact that they are Muslims may cause friction in the receiving countries. Austrians still have a strong collective memory of hardships suffered during the Turkish sieges of Vienna (1529–1683) and fear that this may be repeated. They might well wonder whether the 1683 victory over the Muslims (the Ottoman Empire) was in vain.

In theory, all EU citizens have the freedom to travel, stay and work in other partner countries. This will also apply to the 10 countries that joined the EU in 2004. This eastern enlargement is expected to have only a transitory impact on migration flows towards the EU(15). The annual flow of these migrants is estimated to be about 300 000, which represents 3 million people over a decade. They will go mainly to Germany and Austria (OECD, 2003c, p. 85). However, in practice, with the exception of Britain and Ireland, in 2004 all EU(15) member countries applied their right to impose transitional arrangements which restrict these freedoms for nationals from central and eastern Europe until 2011. Interestingly, this is the time when the central and east European countries will also be influenced by the general EU(15) demographical trends. In addition, the cases of Spain and Portugal, and earlier Greece and Italy, show that migrations flows ceased once the domestic economic situation had improved following EU entry.

Response

The reality is that geographical mobility of EU nationals within the EU is very low, with the exception of certain border regions. Cultural obstacles, including language, are very important in this domain. In order to ameliorate this problem, the European Commission coordinates the European Employment Services (EURES), which is a European labour market network for cooperation among public employment services, trade unions and employers' associations. Its goals are:

- to inform and counsel mobile workers about vacancies and living and working conditions elsewhere in the EU;
- to assist employers who wish to recruit workers from other EU countries; and
- to guide and ease the free movement of workers in the EU.

The connected job databases within EURES provide greater opportunities for job seekers, as well as a greater transparency in the EU labour market. The EU member countries realised that if they act together they may become more efficient. Hence, they try to engage in a convergence process regarding national employment policies.

According to one proposal, an efficient EU immigration policy needs to be regulated by economic instruments. This may be based in future on two possible pillars (Straubhaar and Zimmermann, 1993, p. 233):

- The labour market should determine the volume of labour migration. There should be no legal restrictions for economically motivated migration. As soon as the migrant has a job, he or she should be allowed to enter the EU country. If the person is out of a job for a specified period (such as 6 or 12 months), the local authority may withdraw the residence permit from that person. Migrants may be invited to purchase citizenship and pay for it over a fixed period of time.

- The authorities need to set quotas for non-economically motivated (mass) migration such as refugees and asylum seekers.

The European Commission is aware of the demographical changes and realities regarding the imminent labour shortages. Following the requirement introduced by the Treaty of Amsterdam, the common legal framework concerning the admission and conditions of stay of non-EU nationals has been put in place. The European Commission set out its strategy related to immigration, integration and employment in its Communication (2003).[27] It is expected that immigration or internal EU migrations involving the central and east European countries will be from moderate to limited. In order to fulfil the objectives set in Lisbon, the EU should first mobilise its internal resources. Recruitment of suitable migrants may help to reduce labour shortfalls in the short term. Even certain types of 'green cards' may be considered. In the longer term (2010–30) immigration may help to ease the effects of the demographic transition. In addition, an enhanced, structured and quality dialogue ought to be developed with the countries that may be the source of immigrants. Immigration is not the only solution to all the effects of an ageing population. Incentives to EU nationals to have more children should also be introduced.

The attempt to create a common immigration policy aroused mixed reactions in 2005. Spain and Italy favour such a policy (presumably to an extent liberal), while countries such as Germany and Austria oppose it. Spain offered an amnesty in 2005 to the roughly one million illegal immigrants (mainly from Latin America and Africa) who had and continue to have a job contract. The intention was to prevent exploitation of these migrants and increase social security and tax revenue. Germany, the Netherlands and other EU countries that take a tough stand on immigration were dismayed. Their concern is that the Spanish policy could encourage immigrants to enter Spain illegally, stay there five years to receive a residency permit and subsequently move elsewhere in the EU.

Countries are beginning to break their silence on the issue of immigration. France sent a signal in the form of denying headscarves in state schools. The Danish government has courted popularity by restricting immigration. The Dutch, a nation with a long history of welcoming foreigners, are planning to tighten immigration rules: before permanent residency is granted to someone from outside the EU, that person has to pass an examination on Dutch culture and the language. In a similar vein, Britain also intends to tighten immigration from non-EU countries; it aims primarily to encourage immigrants who may contribute to the British economy, for example, doctors, finance experts, engineers and information technology specialists. A 'point system' that is based on the age of the potential immigrant, level of education, work experience and earning power is in preparation. It is also proposed that immigrants should sit language and general knowledge tests about Britain, as well as wait five years before they obtain permanent residency and another five before they can bring family members to Britain. National, not EU, law covers immigration policies. Bearing in mind such divergent immigration policies, the European Commission proposes that member states should hold consultations (an early-warning system) about national immigration policy initiatives.

EURES should investigate how to contribute to the job mobility of non-EU nationals within the EU. Non-EU nationals will need to be more firmly integrated in the EU social inclusion process.[28] In any case, many European countries have a long history of assimilating immigrants. However, this process has been neither fast nor smooth.[29] The European lesson is that it took generations to accept 'outsiders' as 'insiders'. In spite of this social 'resistance', over time European countries have also developed formal rules to include immigrants into their society.

In spite of privatisation, the government is still an important employer in all EU countries. Therefore, many jobs may be closed to foreigners even if they are citizens of the EU partner countries. This potential obstacle to employment has been removed by the European Court of Justice ruling that only those positions that are linked with national security may be reserved for domestic labour. It would be absurd to argue that a person loses skills, experience and knowledge simply by crossing a border. In order to facilitate labour mobility, in particular highly educated labour, the EU sets qualitative (content of training) and quantitative (years of study, number of course hours) criteria which must be met in order that courses should be accredited and mutually recognised.

The Bologna process on the creation of a European area for higher education started in 1999 when 29 countries signed a declaration to reform their national higher education systems. This reform should be such that an overall convergence in education emerges at the European level. The principal commitments are: to have university courses organised in two cycles (bachelors and masters); to promote mobility of lecturers and students (to use credit transfers); and to work towards a mutually acceptable quality assurance in education. The resulting debate and reform process has moved with surprising speed, and a number of signatories have already started to overhaul their own national system of higher education. Many other countries, impressed by the declaration and the reform process, have also started to sign up.

The free movement of people is one of the cornerstones of the single market in the EU. It is also one of the visible symbols for ordinary people that European integration actually works. Therefore, most EU countries signed an accord on the free circulation of people in the small Luxembourg village of Schengen in 1985 (the deal was revised in 1990). The nub of the Schengen Agreement was to shift passport controls from internal frontiers to external EU borders, to set a uniform visa policy, to increase cooperation among the national authorities that deal with these issues, as well as to coordinate asylum policies.[30] Once in, everyone can move freely within the Schengen zone countries. However, non-EU nationals can work only in the country from which they obtained a visa. The curious feature regarding the Schengen deal is that until the Treaty of Amsterdam (1997) it was a convention outside the remit of the EU treaties.

The Schengen Agreement was put into effect in seven[31] EU countries in March 1995. In practice the introduction of the deal was coupled with many delays which included, for example, the creation of the Schengen Information System, a common database for wanted people and for stolen goods. Once initiated, the system soon ran into difficulty. Faced with a wave of Islamic terrorist attacks, France effectively pulled out of the main commitment of the deal in June 1995. It introduced land-border controls because of the fear of terrorism,[32] which was the same reason why Britain stayed out of the arrangement in the first place. Subsequently, France returned to the fold. None the less, many of the EU countries had voiced their increasing concerns about immigration, legal or otherwise, even before the 11 March 2004 bombing of trains in Madrid. This is compounded by relatively high and persisting unemployment figures.

No matter how genuine these fears of terrorism, drug smuggling and illegal immigration are, the truth is that, as a rule, terrorists and drug smugglers with their illicit cargoes are not caught on borders, but rather in the actual country after tip-offs. Another setback to the spirit of Schengen came when Spain threatened to suspend the key provisions of the agreement when a Belgian court failed to authorise the deportation of two suspected Basque terrorists to Spain in 1996. In spite of these initial difficulties, the Schengen zone operation developed satisfactorily. Other countries joined the group, and by 2005 it had 15 members. Of the EU(15) countries, Britain and Ireland chose to stay outside the Schengen zone; however, two non-EU countries (Iceland and Norway) joined the group.

3.2.6 CONCLUSION

Major labour movements took place from the Mediterranean countries into the EU during the 1960s and early 1970s. The exception was Italy which had been in the EU since its establishment. Internal labour mobility in the EU has not played a significant role in European integration in spite of relatively important differences in average wages (and productivity) among countries.

The experience of EU countries with a tradition of being the source of emigration, such as Italy, Greece, Spain and Portugal, is revealing. During the initial period following EU entry there are waves of emigration to the EU partner countries. However, once the economic situation improves in the sending countries, emigration slows down and eventually ceases. Meanwhile, a new type of temporary human mobility has emerged in the EU, involving students, lecturers and research staff supported by the EU.

The stagnating population level, combined with prosperous economic conditions in comparison with adjoining regions, will continue to create strong economic incentives for migration into the EU, especially from the year 2010.

The EU is aware of the demographical changes and realities regarding the looming labour shortages and it is anticipated that immigration into the EU will be one of its principal challenges in the coming decades. Another and perhaps more important challenge is to increase the productivity of the existing stock of the population. This would decrease demand for immigration into the EU and ease problems and tensions with immigrants as experienced throughout France in November 2005. Jobless growth may do the trick.

Does the eagle mount up at your command,
And make its nest on high?
Job 39:37

3.3 Capital mobility

3.3.1 INTRODUCTION

The spatial distribution of production is shaped not only by actions of national firms and governments, but also by decisions, customs and practices of foreign-owned (controlled) firms, as well as organisations that impose international rules. Some preferential trading or integration agreements such as common markets permit the free movement of factors among member countries on the condition that factors originating in partner countries are not subjected to discrimination. The promotion of geographical and sectoral factor mobility results in more efficient allocation of resources from the group's standpoint. These improvements in the locational advantages of the group for business are due to the free internal factor flow from low- to high-productivity locations, businesses and professions within the common market. In this situation, factors respond to signals that include demand, higher productivity and higher returns within the group.

This section is devoted to the mobility of capital and is structured as follows. Subsection 3.3.2 considers the principal issues related to FDI. The following sections examine TNCs (3.3.3), intervention (3.3.4) and TNCs and international economic integration (3.3.5). Subsection 3.3.6 discusses the nature, evolution and significance of flows in the EU, and Subsection 3.3.7 concludes.

3.3.2 FOREIGN DIRECT INVESTMENT

General Considerations

The theory of preferential trade explores the effect of integration on the location of production, structure of trade and changes in welfare. Little attention has been devoted to the geographical origin of ownership of firms.

This gap is bridged by the theory of FDI, which studies locational advantages for investment in different countries, competitive advantages of firms that originate in different countries, as well as the interaction between firms, local natural and government resources and capabilities in the contexts of spatial distribution of economic activities and economic integration.

Entrepreneurs view a country's preferential trading and integration arrangements as long-term economic signals and firm facts, unlike changes in prices, which may reflect only a temporary situation on the market. Entrepreneurs can form expectations with a higher degree of certainty. Hence, TNCs may locate a part of their production in such an expanding area and increase FDI by the creation of 'tariff factories'.

The creation of tariff factories within an integrated area is a strategy that TNCs pursue, not to take advantage of their efficiency or to employ a foreign resource (resource efficiency), but rather to benefit from (or avoid) the shield provided by the common external tariff and non-tariff barriers (NTBs). This could be one of the reasons why Japanese TNCs were eager to establish a presence in the EU prior to 1993 and the full implementation of the Single European Market. They wanted to become EU residents and thus circumvent the potential threat of a 'Fortress Europe'. In addition to such an 'investment creation effect' (a strategic response of foreign firms to potential trade diversion), new prospects for improved business without tariffs and quotas on trade within the (protected) region may prompt local firms to rearrange production facilities within the group. This may produce an 'investment diversion effect'. This strategic response of firms to trade creation may have as its effect an increase in FDI in some countries in the group and a decrease in FDI in others.

Capital moves among countries in the form of portfolio and direct investments. Portfolio investment is most often simply a short-term movement of claims that is speculative in nature. The main objectives include an increase in the value of assets and relative safety. This type of capital mobility may be prompted by differences in interest rates. The recipient country will probably not wish to use these funds for investment in fixed assets and structures that must be repaid in the long term, so these movements of capital may be seen by the recipient country as hot, unstable and 'bad'. Volatility of portfolio investment complicates their analysis. The large number of portfolio investments, made in many cases by brokers, obscures who is doing what and why.

Foreign direct investment reflects the goal of an entrepreneur from country A to acquire a lasting interest (including management and control) in an asset in country B. FDI is much more than plain capital. It includes technological, managerial, marketing and control knowledge and capabilities; and it also includes a network of contacts that may be available only internally through TNCs. One should bear in mind that more than a third of world trade today is within the same company. In principle, FDI asks for freedom of establishment and, if possible, national treatment in foreign markets. This distinct type of international capital flow has a strong risk-taking and, often, industry-specific dimension. FDI is often the result of decisions by TNCs. Therefore, it may be a part of a proxy for the investment and location activities of TNCs (bearing in mind that TNCs may control operations abroad simply by issuing licences).

International Firm: Theory

Ownership and control of the firm was neglected in the analysis by an implicit assumption that these do not matter or by the supposition that all assets and structures are domestically owned. The presence of TNCs increases the mobility of capital, expands the availability of information and new products, widens marketing and trade networks, changes competition structure and alters substitution of labour for capital. A TNC has different locational considerations from a comparable national firm engaged in the same type and scale of activity. A tendency is that strictly national firms expand where they already are, while TNCs enter where they think they may profit from access to the largest and growing market, availability and favourable costs of inputs, transport and/or taxes and subsidies. TNCs have 'organisational capital', that is, a special culture, a common set of rules, practices, routines and values, which help them overcome various barriers through an internal network while operating in different geographical, social, legal and other environments.

There are at least eight basic theories that explain certain aspects of why firms engage in trans-border business activities and become TNCs.[33] First, the motivation to control foreign firms may not come from the need to employ assets and structures in a prudent way in foreign markets, but rather to remove competition from other enterprises. Hymer (1976) advocated such a *market-power* approach by TNCs. Reuber (1973, pp. 133–4) argued in a similar vein that long-term strategic factors for FDI include the desire to eliminate competitors from foreign markets, to be within a protected foreign market, to secure a low-cost source of supply and to lock in the target country to a specific technology for a long time. Such a longer-term strategic view overshadows possible short-run variations in the profitability of FDI.

The problem with this argument is that most of the TNCs (measured by their number) are small and medium sized. There were about 61 000 parent firms with about 900 000 foreign affiliates in 2003 (UNCTAD, 2004, p. xvii). This shows that to become a TNC, a firm need not be a monopolist or an oligopolist at home and try to exercise that power abroad. If there is strong competition in the market for differentiated goods and services and if there is a high degree of substitutability between products (perfumes, soaps, watches, clothing, vehicles, passenger air transport on certain lines, to mention just a few examples), then the market-power argument for the transnationalisation of business is weakened.

Second, while the market-power model excludes potential rivals from competition, the *internalisation* theory holds that an arm's-length relation among individual firms is in some cases less efficient (for example, trade in technology) than an intra-firm cooperative association. Intra-firm trade is trade between enterprises that belong to the same group, but are located in different countries. Profits may be maximised by means of an efficient and friendly intra-firm trade in intermediaries that eliminates sometimes excessive transaction costs (middlemen, exchange rate risk, infringement of intellectual property rights, bargaining costs) which occur when the business is conducted through the market. In these circumstances a hierarchical organisation (an enterprise) may better reward parties in the longer term, as well as curb bargaining and incentives to cheat, than markets and external contractors.

The share of intra-firm exports in the total exports of manufacturing affiliates under foreign control is in the range between 15 and 60 per cent in the OECD countries. This proportion held steady at about 50 per cent throughout the 1990s in the US, Canada and the Netherlands, but rose sharply in Sweden (from 35 to 75 per cent) and declined in Japan (from 35 to 15 per cent) (OECD, 2005, p. 138). In addition, more than a third of world trade in 2003 was within the same company.[34] Payments of about 80 per cent of fees and royalties for technology 'take place between parent firms and their foreign affiliates' (UNCTAD, 1997, p. 20). Royalty receipts by the US TNCs were $35 billion in 1999 alone (UNCTAD, 2004, p. 113). This is an indication that TNCs play a key role in disseminating technology around the world (at least in the locations where they operate). These enormous intra-firm dealings across many countries require delicate and high-quality company governance. In certain cases this requires strong and unified lines of command, in others there is a need for decentralisation and flexibility. In any case, there is always at least subtle overall company supervision and control.

The importance and volume of intra-firm trade and various special alliances among firms indicate that markets are (becoming) incomplete. As such, it may be difficult to put these markets 'in order' according to free trade principles and objectives. Therefore, absolute advantages of a country or specific locations within it (clusters) may dominate and outweigh comparative advantages in their relevance for the location of production, FDI and, consequently, structure, volume and direction of trade.

While Reuber and Hymer conceive TNCs as vehicles for reaping monopoly profits and for the internalisation of pecuniary externalities, the internalisation model looks at TNCs as a mode of business organisation that reduces transaction costs and internalises non-pecuniary externalities. This model of FDI may be convincing in some cases, but it may not explain the structure and location of all FDI flows. In addition to the internalisation possibilities, there ought to be ownership-specific and locational advantages for FDI.

Excessive internalisation leads firms to diversify into unrelated technologies. This may provoke an increase in costs of production as they venture into businesses that are outside their core competence. Mastering new technologies diverts time, efforts and funds from further specialisation in the core business competence. Therefore, buying from other specialised firms (outsourcing), rather than producing certain goods and services in-house, may be the preferred course of business action to achieve and maintain a greater degree of competitiveness.

Markusen (1984) tried to integrate TNCs into general equilibrium trade models and locational patterns of firms that horizontally or vertically integrate across national borders. Intangible assets, as sources of multiplant economies, are often firm, rather than plant specific. They include organisation, management, control, R&D, advertising, marketing and distribution. Many of these activities are centralised (finance) and present a 'joint input' across all production units. A TNC avoids replication of these activities that would be necessary if these units operated as independent national firms. This brings a 'technical' advantage to a TNC. However, if these advantages are transformed into market power, then the welfare effects of TNCs may not be clear. In any case, a firm will operate in two or more countries and become a TNC if trade costs are sufficiently higher relative to the disadvantage that comes from fixed costs that are linked to the operation of two or more plants that serve two or more local markets in different countries (Markusen and Venables, 2000, p. 221).

Third, the *eclectic paradigm* (Dunning, 1988, pp. 42–5; 1999, pp. 1–3) explained the trans-border business activities of TNCs as a joint mix and interaction of three independent factors:

- In order to locate production abroad and be commercially successful, a TNC must have or control internationally mobile income-generating *ownership*-specific (O) advantages, assets, structures, capabilities or skills. These firm-specific advantages include tangible and intangible advantages such as better technology, brand name, access to wide markets, monopoly, competence of managers, ability to innovate and so on that are superior to the ones that are available to local firms (including other TNCs) in the potential target country. That is, a firm needs to operate either on a different production function from other firms or at a different point on the same function.

- *Locational* (L) (non-mobile) advantages refer to the comparative or location-specific advantages of the target country. They refer both to the geographical distribution of resources and to those created by the government.[35]
- There must be opportunities for the *internalisation* (I) of ownership-specific advantages (management and quality control, protection of property rights, avoidance of uncertainty of buyers and so on). It should be in the interest of the firm to transfer these advantages abroad within its own organisation, rather than sell the right to use them to other firms located in the country of intended production. Fixed exchange rates or a single international currency provide a degree of stability necessary for longer-term business planning with a high degree of confidence.

The eclectic paradigm claims that the exact mix of the OLI factors facing each potential investor depends on the specific context. If a firm possesses or controls ownership-specific advantages, then it may use licensing in order to penetrate foreign markets. If it has both ownership-specific and internalisation advantages, such an enterprise may use exports as a means of entering foreign markets. Only when a firm is able to take *simultaneous* return of OLI advantages will it employ FDI as a means of locating and operating in foreign markets. This model, however, does not apply to diversified and vertically integrated TNCs (Caves, 1996, p. 5).

Fourth, the *product-cycle* model reasons that mature (and, perhaps, environmentally unsound) lines of production of goods (there is no explicit reference to services) are passed on to developing countries (Posner, 1961; Vernon, 1966). Such spatial reallocation of production is based on the experience of Anglo-Saxon firms and depends a lot on low factor costs.

The product-cycle argument as the major explanation for the location of business abroad and with a rather vague timetable for this spread of production cannot pass the test of recent developments. Asian firms, however, do not replicate this pattern of location of production abroad on a large scale. The Japanese auto companies invested at home and in the US and Europe at about the same time for a similar type of production. There is a heavy concentration of FDI in developed countries, while the majority of developing countries are relatively neglected in FDI flows. In addition, countries start investing abroad at a much earlier stage of their development than before. The newly industrialised countries and many other developing countries are already investing abroad. In many cases these investments are in the developed world. Such developments may be prompted by the desire:

- to be present in the developed countries' markets (closer to wealthy customers);
- to be near the source and cluster of the principal technological developments in manufacturing, distribution, management and already existing infrastructure (to have a foreign 'listening and learning post');
- to participate in R&D programmes;
- to avoid the dangers of protectionism in target countries;
- to win public contracts; and
- to exploit the strength of the host country's domestic currency.

Fifth is the *follow-your-leader* ('me-too') hypothesis. Oligopolists are risk minimisers. They would like to protect their own market position and avoid destructive competition. Therefore, they typically try to minimise risk and follow each other into the new (foreign) markets (Knickerboker, 1973, p. 100). A study of timing of FDI by US TNCs in manufacturing seems to support this 'snowball' or 'herd' behaviour. The Japanese TNCs in automotive and consumer electronic industries were 'following their domestic leader' when they located their manufacturing facilities in the EU and the US during the 1980s and 1990s. This type of investment location behaviour is quite relevant during the opening phases of new markets. If a TNC has no previous experience in a certain new market, then the actions of competitors in that market may be quite informative. Examples of this herd behaviour are the actions of TNCs in China especially after 1997 (Asian financial crisis) and to an extent in eastern Europe from the start of the 1990s.[36] In addition, the mergers and acquisitions[37] 'mania' of the 1990s in the EU and the US shows how asset seeking by one TNC may be followed by others.

Such 'catastrophic' relocation of industry as a result of the predicted behaviour of rival firms is one feature of the core–periphery model, one of the key economic geography models. It is postulated that when trade costs lie in a certain range all firms in an industry may relocate en masse, although this would not be the optimum strategy for an individual firm were it to relocate on its own.

While relatively low labour costs in China could have been the reason to start to locate certain operations there at the start of the 1990s, things have changed. It was reported that China's Pearl River delta attracted $1 billion of FDI a month. Microwave ovens are produced in Shunde. Just one of its giant factories produces 40 per cent of the global output. Shenzhen produces 70 per cent of the world's photocopiers and 80 per cent of the artificial Christmas trees. Dongguan has 80 000 people working in a single factory making running shoes for the world's teenagers. Flextronics is a Singapore electronics maker that produces for Microsoft, Motorola, Dell and Sony. The manager of its Chinese plant in Doumen said: 'It is a myth that companies are coming here just for the cheap labour. It is the efficiency of the supply chain that drives them here as more and more of worldwide demand is consolidated in this area.'[38]

Sixth, the competitive international industry model for the location of business abroad refers to oligopolistic competition and rivalry within the same industry. This is basically *exchange of threats* (tit-for-tat strategy) regarding business moves by foreign rivals (Graham, 1978). Large firms keep an eye on the actions of their rivals, that is, they act strategically (pay attention to the likely reaction of their competitors to their own actions). What Texaco does in Europe, Shell will (try to) do in the US. Competition is not 'cut-throat', but rather 'stable' among several oligopolies. Other examples of this rivalistic trend include FDI in the manufacturing of cars and tyres or supply of services such as hotels and advertising. Small and medium-sized enterprises (SMEs) such as gas stations in the middle of nowhere may act independently in their business. However, SMEs in a cluster keep a vigilant eye on the actions of their competitors.

Seventh is the *diversification of portfolios* model of foreign investment (Brainard and Tobin, 1992). This approach considers uncertainty. Fluctuations in the rates of return on capital invested in various countries introduce an element of risk. This inconvenience may be reduced by a diversification of portfolios.

Firm-specific assets and exchange rates may be the eighth basic reason for FDI. Suppose that there is a target firm in the US with an innovation (a firm-specific asset) that can make the acquiring firm's assembly line 10 per cent more productive (10 per cent more output for the same level of input). If a US firm wants to acquire the target firm, then a change in the rate of exchange makes no difference as its gains will continue to be denominated in dollars. If, however, the acquiring firm is in Japan, the gains will be denominated in yen. A depreciation of the dollar relative to the yen would increase the Japanese firm's reservation bid, while the US firm's bid would remain unchanged. It is more likely that the Japanese firm would acquire the asset in this situation.

The actual evidence about this taking place is rather mixed. The price of US assets need not matter, only the rate of return: when the dollar depreciates, both the price of a US asset and its rate of return will go down. Blonigen (1997) found a connection between exchange rate movements (weak dollar) and higher levels of Japanese acquisitions in the US in industries which involve firm-specific assets. This refers to the Japanese acquisitions in the US during 1975–92. However, in their analysis of relations between exchange rate movements and FDI flows from the US to 20 countries during the 1980–95 period, Chakrabarti and Scholnick (2002, p. 19) found that devaluation in the preceding year does not have a robust positive impact on FDI flows.

In addition to the above basic theories on why firms locate abroad, three other dimensions are relevant for coming to grips with the issue: cost minimisation, available technology and taxes. First, Kravis and Lipsey (1982, p. 222) argued that the location of foreign affiliates of TNCs is decided on the basis of *cost minimisation*. However, the intensity of this determinant varies from industry to industry.

Second, Yamawaki (1993, pp. 19–20) did not dispute the importance of a relative difference in factor costs, but the *availability of technology* in the target country is an additional and equally important factor for the location of Japanese FDI in the EU. A Japanese TNC from a certain industry decided to locate in the EU country which has a certain advantage over other EU countries in the same industry. Britain is preferred by the Japanese TNCs for the location of production of cars and electrical/electronic equipment, Germany for precision instruments and machinery, Belgium for stone, glass and clay products, while TNCs from the chemical industry prefer Germany, the Netherlands, Spain and France.

Third come differences in *taxes and fiscal incentives*. While there are many 'tax havens' that attract quite a few firms (mainly from finance) and many countries offer different fiscal incentives to firms in order to attract them, is this enough by itself? Are tax incentives a bit more than 'corporate welfare'? Should countries enter into a 'locations tournament'? Politicians usually use only three reasons to justify a local incentive programme: jobs, jobs and jobs!

The evidence about the importance and influence of taxes on the location of firms is still controversial. Certain investors may avoid locations that offer financial incentives as evidence of a region's non-competitiveness. Limited survey information reveals that fiscal variables matter little regarding business location. However, business executives often lobby hard for fiscal incentives. One can understand that attitude as firms have no incentives to forgo such direct and indirect subsidies, even if they do not affect location decisions to a significant degree (Wasylenko, 1991). This was a confirmation of the results of an earlier study by Carlton which found that tax variables usually have a 'very small and always statistically insignificant' (Carlton, 1983, p. 447) impact on locational choice.

Mody and Srinivasan (1998, p. 795) found that corporate tax rates do not have a major influence over FDI either by the American or by the Japanese

TNCs. Devereux and Griffith (1998) found that agglomeration effects were important for the US TNCs that invested in Europe, while the effective tax rates played a role in the choice between locations, but not in the decision of whether to locate a subsidiary in Europe. Moss Kanter (2003) argued that contrary to common belief, the prime reason for FDI in South Carolina was not low wages and tax incentives, but rather the competence of its workforce. In another case in France, Crozet et al. (2004) found that foreign investors were not sensitive to investment incentives. In addition, French and EU regional policy investment incentives did not have any significant impact.

A study of the effect of the elimination of a tax on paper for printing news (which accounted for about half of the production costs) in the Netherlands in 1869 revealed that this assisted in the creation of new newspaper firms. Two-thirds of these new entries took place in cities that already had other newspapers, while the other third occurred in provincial towns that previously did not have a newspaper. Even though a tax cut played an important role, the principal reason for this type of location of firms was the size and growth of the local market. Hence, there is no basic difference in the rationale for a firm's location between a century and a half ago and now (Pfann and van Kranenburg, 2002).

Although many surveys give state and local taxes a low ranking on the list of location determinants, many locations in various states within the US can be close substitutes. In such a situation, even a small difference in production costs can play a key role for a particular decision concerning the location of business (Bartik, 1991, p. 8). American firms became more sensitive to differences in host-country taxes towards the end of the 1984–92 period (Altshuler et al., 1998). As part of its policy to lower company taxes prevailing in the east of the EU(25), Austria reduced company taxes from 35 to 25 per cent in 2005. This strained relations between Austria and Germany, and in Bavaria in particular, because of the 'exodus of jobs to Austria'.[39] To counter the move, in March 2005, Germany proposed a cut in company tax rate from 25 to 19 per cent.[40]

The issue of the impact of taxes on the location of TNCs continues to be a controversial research area. There is a lack of consensus as results cited in academic literature are still mixed. High(er) taxes may be preferred to low taxes by firms if the tax proceeds are used to finance local services and infrastructure useful for the business sector. In any case, high-quality infrastructure is preferred by foreign investors to tax incentives. Transfer pricing and tax deductions in the home country provide other ways to minimise the tax burden on profit (Wheeler and Mody, 1992, pp. 71–2).

The issue of tax competition and incentives for the location of FDI is open. The relevance of taxes and subsidies to the attraction of FDI depends on the objectives of TNCs. If the goal of a TNC is to serve the market of the target country, then these concessions do not matter for FDI in that country. If a TNC intends to serve the international market, all things being equal, various fiscal allowances do play a role in attracting footloose industries. However, a much superior policy to a special tax treatment has always been to ensure better domestic infrastructure and continuously improve the supply of domestic human capital through education and training. This could enhance the domestic absorptive capacity as perhaps the principal vehicle to transfer potential spillovers to the local economy.

'The economic desirability of locational incentives is not clear, particularly if they detract from building competitive capabilities and encourage bidding wars' (UNCTAD, 2003, p. 126). Tax incentives for investment, in particular FDI, are conventionally not recommended. This is also the stance taken by the World Bank, the IMF and other international bodies that advise on tax matters. Tax incentives are bad in theory and bad in practice. They are bad in theory as they introduce distortions. Investment decisions by entrepreneurs are made differently from the case without the special tax stimulus. They are bad in practice because of their ineffectiveness: tax considerations are rarely the principal determinant for the location of FDI. They are also inefficient as their cost may well exceed any benefit that they may bring.[41] They are difficult to administer as there is a lack of transparency and they are subject to abuse and corruption[42] by the 'old boys' club'. Finally, they are not equitable as they benefit certain investors, but not others (Easson, 2001, p. 266). If various incentives are offered only to foreigners, then there is a possibility of 'round-tripping'. Domestic capital leaves the country in order to return in the guise of FDI, so as to profit from better treatment in the home country. This has been the case in Russia from the early 1990s.

In spite of the above arguments, tax considerations have recently become an increasingly important factor for the location of investment. Why is this so? Why are tax incentives becoming more and more generous? Tax considerations do not feature highly in the initial strategic decision by TNCs to invest abroad or not. However, once the decision to go abroad is reached, differences in taxes between regions in the target country or differences among countries tend to play a significant role.

More than 100 countries worldwide offer tax incentives for FDI. The type of incentive that is most commonly employed is the tax holiday, which is the worst in almost every respect. Administration of these incentives is amazingly complicated; there are opportunities for abuse and avoidance; they may attract only short-term FDI to benefit from the tax holiday while it lasts; and (particularly in the developing countries) they are often beyond the capacity of tax administrations to manage and monitor. Therefore it is not surprising that tax incentives are often inefficient and ineffective (Easson, 2001, p. 375; Tanzi and Zee, 2000, p. 316).

The optimal solution to the issue of these enticements may include an international agreement among countries to eliminate all tax incentives for investment (or to limit them in a uniform way). In the absence of such an agreement, and according to the prisoner's dilemma concept, few countries would risk acting in this way unilaterally.

In the situation with market imperfections there is no single theory or model that can provide a completely satisfactory answer to each issue related to trans-border investment activities of firms. Motives for foreign investment and production are different, complex, multifaceted and not always consistent. They change over time in response to changes in the market, technology, needs, tastes, sophistication, management strategy, actions of rivals and economic policy. However, if taken together, these theories may provide useful elements for an understanding of the issue.

Globalisation

Liberalisation in the national and international economy is a policy choice of *governments*, primarily in the developed world. It is linked with privatisation and downsizing of the activities of the public sector and the expansion of the activities of the private sector. *Globalisation* of the economy and production is a fact. It is the outcome of the behaviour of *firms* (TNCs), their organisation, changing technology in production and distribution, control and finance, as well as economies of scale and takeovers. In part, it is also the consequence of a change in the behaviour of consumers (fickleness and declining loyalty to national producers and certain national products)[43] and liberalisation of national and international economies for trade, production and finance.

As a process primarily driven by technology and actions of TNCs (power is shifted from states to firms),[44] globalisation lacks two important components: transparency and accountability.[45] Many are suspicious about corporations and their increasing power over everybody's life. An obvious example is the influence of large pharmaceutical TNCs on governments and the WTO (trade-related intellectual property rights).

The process of globalisation deals with the change in the geography of (integrated international) production and consumption as it reduces the importance of proximity to inputs or markets. It widens boundaries and deepens space for the geographical location of production and consumption because of the declining costs of getting goods and services to the market. A rapid expansion of FDI is the key component of this process.

Capital market liberalisation and increased capital mobility have radically reduced the influence of governments in the monetary sphere. However, governments have gained increased control in other areas. For example, computers and information technology have greatly increased potential for data collection and processing, and consequently control over firms and citizens, which is relevant for tax and other purposes.

Regionalisation is increasing in importance in the world economy. This was exemplified in the inability of 135 member countries of the WTO to agree even on the agenda for the 'Millennium Round' of global trade negotiations that took place in Seattle in 1999. Well-organised, vociferous and strong worldwide protests by environmentalists, farmers, enemies of genetically modified food and big business, human rights activists, labour unions, anti-capitalists and animal rights activists exacerbated the problems of that meeting and many others that followed. There are deep divisions about the nature and extent of globalisation as shaped and conducted by the instruments of global control such as the WTO, the World Bank, the IMF and TNCs. Therefore, the creation of integrated global economic policies is likely to be a very hard task for quite some time to come. It seems that the regional approach to economic problems will call the tune at least in the medium term.

The rapid international expansion of TNCs made them the most visible feature of globalisation. Being foreign, sometimes making visible and highly publicised mistakes and often being big, TNCs are easy targets for non-governmental organisations (NGOs) which can run successful campaigns to disgrace a mighty TNC. A number of NGOs are relatively small players who would like to 'punch above their weight' because of the urgency of the matter.[46] Examples of their campaigns include valid targets such as land mines, HIV/Aids or poverty and third world debt. NGOs increased public awareness and pushed through agreements on the control of 'greenhouse gases' in the United Nations Conference on Environment and Development, the 'Earth Summit' in Rio de Janeiro in 1992. They also helped in torpedoing the Multilateral Agreement on Investment in 1998 and created much ado in Seattle in 1999 (and many other subsequent meetings), which contributed to the failure to start a new WTO round of global trade negotiations before the meeting in Doha in 2001. No matter how justified the reasons for the campaign, these 'civil society' protestors against global capitalism demonstrated that the tide of globalisation could be checked and even turned back.

The anti-globalisation movement is moving beyond its radical, protest-driven even anarchist legacy (which might have worked against it) towards a movement with a concrete agenda. Rock-throwers, like the Luddites (1811–16) who destroyed factory machines, were ineffectual and irrelevant in the long term. The strategy of the anti-globalisation movement is to address four weaknesses of the globalisation process:

- a lack of legitimacy,
- a lack of accountability,[47]
- a lack of organisation and
- a lack of transparency.

The idea is not to be against globalisation as it may contribute to the maximum viable economic activity that may create resources necessary to achieve other social goals. The idea is to put limits on it. The question is what kind of 'globalisation' is desirable and how to achieve it? The World Social Forum (Porto Alegre, Brazil) has made valiant attempts to put hundreds of disparate groups under one umbrella. These groups all use global communication networks to push for their particular cause. The forum recommends a range of activities from limiting the power of TNCs to adding new responsibilities and regulatory powers to the established international organisations such as the UN, the International Labour Office and the World Health Organization. In this way the anti-globalisation movement may be able to gain more leverage on the national and international scene.

The anti-globalisation campaigners have shown that governments are not powerless. The authorities can just as easily dismantle old trade and investment barriers as they can introduce new ones. New technology, in particular the Internet, telecommunications, computing and data processing can offer some of the greatest economic opportunities ever for increasing living standards in all countries. Governments and the national elite in all countries (due to incompetence or indifference) have failed to explain this. However, the process needs to be coupled with balanced policies both in the rich and in the poor world. Even though global economic integration may be the best end point for the future of the world economy for the proponents of globalisation, it is more likely that other outcomes may be chosen in the future. Globalisation may be favourable for economic efficiency, but it can be harmful for social goals.

Apart from a partial integration of international production, globalisation brings risks and disruptions. Volatile capital flows, speculative attacks on currencies, financial crises and unpredictable reallocation of jobs are obvious examples of the increased economic and social vulnerability of many countries, in particular in the developing world. To wrap up the issue, Henry Kissinger called globalisation 'another name for the dominant role of the United States'.[48]

The vogue term 'globalisation' has not yet been well or clearly defined. Hence, this fuzzy but powerful metaphor is overused, often abused and very often misleading. For some it basically refers to the choices and strategies, as well as the shape, extent, direction and significance of activities of TNCs. 'Globalisation has been defined in business schools as the production and distribution of products and services of a homogeneous type and quality on a worldwide basis. Simply put – providing the same output to countries everywhere' (Rugman and Hodgetts, 2001, p. 333).

'Thanks' to al-Qaida many realised that globalisation goes well beyond links that bind TNCs, producers, traders and bankers. For others, globalisation is linked with and invigorated by new technologies in communications and information processing. It is a sum of techniques that are at the disposal of private players and states. Yet for others, globalisation is an incentive to the reform process in economic strategy in many countries as outward-looking economic models replace inward-looking and TNC-hostile economic policies. So globalisation is openness to trade and investment with foreign and more and more geographically distant countries. Others look at globalisation as a process that alters interactions among agents across space; still others equate globalisation with economic integration.[49] Anne Krueger defined it as 'the increasingly rapid exchange of ideas, people, and goods made possible by falling transport costs and technological advances, all leading to the closer integration of the world including – but not limited to – the economy'.[50]

Uniformity and homogeneity in the modern world may be a heavy price to pay for new or 'better' standardised things that we consume. This introduces an ever present potential for the neo-communist danger that everyone eats and drinks the same, is dressed the same, shops in the same way, uses homogeneous (perfectly substitutable) goods and services and finally may even, or is forced to, perhaps, think 'the same'. If someone is not 'in step' with these global developments (regardless of their democratic appearance and sugar-coating), well, then . . . he or she may 'court trouble' from the central 'politburo'!

The ease, convenience, high speed and low cost of communication via the Internet and other means are well recognised and appreciated. The same holds for the participation of an increasing number of countries that take part in global production and exchange. However, in the process, companies such as Microsoft have gained an enormous power over our work and lives. This is amplified by similar possibilities by governments, thugs and computer hackers. They can intrude into our databases related to work, finance, leisure, emotional relations, thoughts, ideas, privacy, habits, voting intentions, movements, conversations, addresses . . . and messages. They can steal our passwords, impersonate us, misuse our data and commit fraud without us being aware of it until it may be too late. They can oversee, control and even direct and manage parts of our lives. Some anti-globalisation activists appreciate the potential benefits of globalisation, but all campaigners are in favour of strict limitations and control to curb the possible excesses.

The Internet symbolises the borderlessness brought about by globalisation. Physical presence in a specific location is not necessary. In the invisible continent of cyberspace, the users are 'everywhere and nowhere' at once. They use the Internet as a meeting place, a market, a distribution device, a library, and the like. This alters the geography of production, at least for certain goods and services. People spend more time working at home or 'on the road', hence certain office space (in congested cities) is vacated. However, one does not need to give an absolute value to globalisation. In spite of this process, localisation and clusters still matter. Firms that went furthest in 'globalisation' report that face-to-face contact is essential for the smooth organisation of business within the firm and marketing outside it. In addition, just try telling someone who wants to enter the EU or North America from outside that this is a 'borderless world'. Borders continue to matter a great deal as people from different locations are prevented from crossing them without a cumbersome, costly and uncertain administrative procedure.

The Internet is based on communication and data that are located in computers that exist in the real world. Initially, this parallel universe of pure data existed everywhere freely in a 'lawless' world. The Internet is breaking down barriers and eliminating physical distance. However, computers exist in an identifiable geographical space. If they can be located together with their users, then they are subject to law. Now governments are increasing their control over cyberspace. For example, France prohibited the sale of Nazi memorabilia on the Internet; Iran banned access to immoral or anti-Iranian information; while South Korea prohibited access to gambling websites. There is also increased international police cooperation in combating child pornography, or computer viruses and hackers that attack major computer networks. Hence, borders are being created in the Internet. Even though the economic impact of geographical distance is being reduced, the local economic geography is retaining its strength.

The imposition of 'global' standards may have its justification for relatively new and standardised goods and services such as copiers, fax machines, computers, mobile phones or better medicines, otherwise communication and exchange of information might be difficult and costly. However, the imposition of such standards for traditional goods (for example, food) with the exception of health and the environment may not be easily justified. If needs, choices and tastes for certain types of food are strongly locally specific (even the thickness of pizzas throughout Italy differs) why should one favour or impose global Pizza Hut type standards?

John Gray of the London School of Economics claimed that people are losing faith in globalisation, and that:

> [L]ed by the United States, the world's richest states have acted on the assumption that people everywhere want to live as they do. As a result, they failed to recognise the deadly mixture of emotions – cultural resentment, the sense of injustice and a genuine rejection of western modernity – that lies behind the attacks on New York and Washington . . . The ideal of a universal civilisation is a recipe for unending conflict, and it is time it was given up.[51]

It is not that the people who live outside the western world cannot adopt a liberal attitude, rather that there are social, cultural and institutional barriers that prevent a fast transfer of western standards, values, culture and institutions elsewhere. One must also consider the choices of the 'recipients'. Do they really want and need what is exported or 'imposed' on them? Local conditions may not support the one-size-fits-all approach. Globalisation may be less rewarding to firms than ambitiously predicted and expected. Consumers often demand many niche goods that detach them from the crowd.

There was a faulty premise and a vision that all people are culturally homogeneous in that they think, act and most of all, shop alike (or like Americans); that there exist institutional bases for political democracy; and that citizens are aware of their duties to one another and to the state. Checks and balances are mixed; there is mistrust *vis-à-vis* the government and state administration which is often deeply rooted in dictatorship, authoritarian and bureaucratic conduct, as well as in corruption. Without very long-term reform, education and trust-building, any attempt to transfer 'global' (social) standards quickly would fail, and fail miserably, in many parts of the world. It should not be forgotten that 'it took 400 years for England to develop from that stage to its present one. To do the same elsewhere in half the time of 200 years would be a tremendous achievement; to aspire to do it in 25 or 50 years may be to court disaster' (Lipsey, 1992a, p. 755).[52] Local differences tend to be stubborn. Until the world becomes homogeneous, adaptation towards local preferences and capabilities will be necessary. Globalisation problems, which appeared in the form of concerns over progress in the WTO or in the Multilateral Agreement on Investment illustrate signals of regional (triad: US, EU and Japan) or even local power.

It is true that the greatest and matchless advantage of free markets and globalisation is that they give free choice to consumers. Economic interactions are voluntary, so consumers are free to choose, for example, between local and global goods and services. But, this is only on the surface. If global products are advertised aggressively by large TNCs,[53] including campaigns that are often beyond the financial capacity of local competitors, then the 'free choice' by consumers may be restricted and the local producers (and certain dimensions of the local culture) may be damaged. Critics of such unchecked global capital movements say that global TNCs put 'profits before people'. When these TNCs 'start talking about how they will no longer put profits first, people (rightly) think they are lying'.[54]

The critics of globalisation have certain valid points. Paul Krugman wrote: 'The promise of export-led growth has failed in too many places. In particular, Latin America has signally failed to replicate Asia's success: Latin nations have liberalized, privatized and deregulated, with results ranging from disappointing (Mexico) to catastrophic (Argentina)'.[55] However, John Kay argued: 'The essence of economic globalisation is specialisation by function and skill on an unprecedented scale. I cannot tell you how to get rich but I can tell you how to stay poor. Do not become involved in the global marketplace.'[56] In any case, a large part of modern trade is intra-industry. This is the outcome of specialisation.

Another cost of globalisation can be found in the examples of countries such as Mexico, Thailand, Indonesia, South Korea and Russia, which suffered financial crises in the second half of the 1990s. Without the exposure to global capital markets, the crises would not have developed as they did. Critics of this view argue that these countries would not have experienced such rapid development prior to the crisis without such exposure. In any case, one ought to be fair and observe that certain 'global tendencies' were already present, well before the current wave of globalisation. For example, there was (for whatever reason and by whatever means) a spread of certain European languages outside Europe; a spread of Islam in Africa, Asia and Europe; and a spread of Christianity in Latin America.

Trade and foreign investments (globalisation) are partners, not adversaries, of social agendas, but they ought to be coupled with effective national and international institutions that ease adjustment problems (such as the polluter-pays principle). Globalisation may bring adjustment costs in the affected industries and labour markets, but this may be only transitory. The gradual opening up of markets in Japan during the 1970s, and later in south-east Asia during the 1980s, eastern Europe from the early 1990s and in China from the second half of the 1990s, demonstrates that as a country grows wealthier it ceases to be competitive in the production of labour-intensive goods. Such a country becomes at a later stage an importer of some of these goods and concentrates its production on higher value-added activities.

Child labour, begging, theft and prostitution in poor countries would certainly decline if globalisation opened advanced countries' markets to the products made by the children's parents. Even though globalisation spreads symbols of highly dubious value such as Coca-Cola, McDonald's, MTV, Halloween and chewing gum,[57] it also spreads basic values such as the rights of women and children. However, it is unfortunate that the latter takes place at a much slower pace. A still unresolved problem is that under globalisation, human rights may sometimes be more important than state sovereignty.

The debate about globalisation is often about jobs (social dimension). Supporters argue that it is beneficial and that it creates jobs, while critics argue the opposite and say that jobs migrate to trading partners and competitors. Certain segments of labour in all countries are suspicious of globalisation, as they no longer perceive the national government as a guaranteed protector of their concerns against external threats. To counter these fears, the best long-term policy response may be to advance the possibilities for education and training, as technical progress has a strong bias against unskilled workers.

As far as firms are concerned, efficiency-seeking enterprises, particularly some TNCs, search for seamless and wide international markets regarding trade and investment. On the one hand, the *globalisation* of economic activity is making national frontiers less divisive than ever before.[58] Such worldwide economic integration and integrated international production of goods and services whereby competitors are in one another's backyard are made possible by the expansion of information and telecommunication technologies.[59] This process is sometimes inverted, on the other hand, by the wide spread of *regionalism* sometimes pushed by relatively inefficient firms and governments that are driven by short-term election interests, even though the conditions for a relatively successful integration process, such as that in western Europe, may be largely absent.

Regional integration (a second-best solution) may be a promising form of supranational governance in areas where there is a strong case for coordination and harmonisation of national policies. Integration may resolve conflicts through positive cooperation within a cosy group but, if pushed to the limit, it may undermine multilateral (first-best) trade and investment systems and fragment the world economy into conflicting regional blocs. Regionalism and multilateralism (globalisation) need not necessarily conflict. If the regional blocs cooperate and if they adopt liberal external trade and investment policies, the outcome may be an overall welfare improvement. The pace of international trade liberalisation since the 1960s, as well as the extension of the GATT into new areas such as services and agriculture, might have been much slower in the absence of challenges posed by the progress in integration in the EU. The debate should not be between regionalism and multilateralism, but rather between liberalism and interventionism (Blackhurst and Henderson, 1993, p. 412).

It is often forgotten that the spirit of 'globalisation' does not bring anything essentially new. The need is for more freedom for trade in goods and services and for capital mobility (FDI). The economic role of national frontiers declines as national economies merge in a single 'global' unit. In a nutshell, the idea is to return to the essentials of the system that was prevailing during the first wave of globalisation (1850–1914). 'Re-globalisation' may be a more appropriate term for the second wave that started and continued from the 1960s.

The spirit of globalisation might remain the same in both globalisation waves, but there are important space-related differences in their actual attainment. During the first wave the north (Europe and the US) industrialised, while the south (especially China and India) deindustrialised. There was an expansion of trade and factor movements (both labour and capital), while incomes between the two regions diverged. In the second wave of globalisation, it was the south (east Asia) that industrialised, while the north deindustrialised. Trade and capital mobility expanded (mass labour migration was small by the first-wave standards), while incomes between the two regions generally converged. Urbanisation remained an important feature in both north and south during both waves of globalisation (Baldwin and Martin, 2004, pp. 2707–8).

An enlarged market is an important gain for efficiency-seeking firms in a small country. In a situation without integration, foreign countries can simply threaten a small country that they will introduce protectionist measures or 'sanctions' against it (the US frequently makes such threats to many countries). Such a warning can seriously undermine the quality of all economic decisions in a small country. Integration enhances and secures market access for partner countries, as well as increasing the potential for long-term competitiveness of a small country's goods and services. A common market may eliminate or harmonise national incentives to foreign TNCs to locate in partner countries (which were previously subject to countervailing duties). It also mitigates non-economic considerations, such as political pressures on third-country investors to locate in a particular country.

Transnational corporations behave like other firms: they primarily follow the opportunities for maximising profit while staying within the law. With the exception of resource-oriented FDI, the size and growth of the local market, including privileged access to international markets (instead of mere differences in the cost of labour), are the most prominent motivators for their trans-border business operations. In addition, in a situation where market liberalisation became a widely accepted policy choice, there is an increase in the importance of created assets and structures (technology and ability to create it, business culture, capability to organise and control production and marketing, communications infrastructure, marketing networks) as determinants for FDI. This is why 69 per cent of the activities of TNCs were located in developed market economies (measured by the stock of FDI in 2003) (UNCTAD, 2004, p. 376). In spite of the talk about 'globalisation', on average, a significant part of the output of affiliates is still sold on the local market.[60] In this situation the developing countries and those in transition face very tough competition to attract TNCs.

The relation between social spending and competitiveness of a country's goods and services is complex. Some argue that TNCs rush to locate in countries with low social spending to save on costs. However, de Grauwe and Polan (2003) found evidence that wealthy countries that spend most on social needs, on average rank highest in terms of competitiveness. Countries with highly competitive output generate extra income. They can afford generous social outlays. But there is also a reverse causality. Competitiveness depends on an absence of prolonged social conflicts, superb human capital and the quality of the government. People would be prone to take a risk if they knew that they would not be condemned to poverty if they fail. One of the principal roles of an efficient government is to transform social security contributions into energies for social value added. Those that manage this conversion well are likely to benefit in terms of enhanced competitiveness.

Foreign investors will locate their activities in a country that offers the most favourable cost mix of operation (production and marketing), provided that this factors well into the longer-term vision of potential profit. FDI can be made simpler by regionalisation of the world economy and international economic integration. However, integration/regionalisation is only a supporting tool for the tendencies that bring about international business globalisation. Modern competitive firms are usually TNCs that 'globalise' their business in the search for seamless and extensive markets. Therefore, an increasing share of domestic output even in the developed countries is under the control of foreign TNCs. The same holds for an increasing share of foreign output of domestic TNCs. Strong FDI relations may exist even though the countries or groups of countries are not formally integrated. Just take a look at the example of two-way FDI flows between the US and the EU.

The glue that binds transatlantic relations together is not principally trade, but FDI. Large global interpenetration of FDI reduces the possibility that regional arrangements may become closed blocs. A 'hostage population' of TNCs may reduce the fear of retaliatory measures. Extensive FDI links between the US and the EU have helped to reduce any potential conflict between the two partners regarding market access. The same is not yet true of Japan. It is hoped that Japan will mature as a foreign investor in future and that potential conflict with that country will be defused.

Trans-border Business Activities

There are four main types of trans-border business activities that are conducted by TNCs: market seeking, resource based, rationalised and strategic asset seeking (Dunning, 1999, pp. 3–4):

- *Market-seeking* (demand-oriented) investments search for new markets, but they replace trade. They are influenced by the relative size and growth of the foreign market in which the investment is made, the relative costs of supplying that market through imports or local production, as well as the relative advantage of engaging in direct local production or licensing.
- *Resource-seeking* (supply-oriented) FDI is motivated by the availability and cost of both natural resources and labour in the target location. As the products of such investments are often exported abroad, the economic climate in foreign markets, changes in technology, transport costs and barriers to trade influence the attractiveness of such investment to TNCs.
- *Rationalised investments* seek efficiency. Like resource-based investments, they are complementary to trade. Their attractiveness is found in cost considerations. They are influenced by the ease with which intermediate or final products (linked to economies of scale and specialisation) can be traded on the international market. A case in question is the US loss of competitiveness as a site for labour-extensive production. The domestic US enterprises from this area of manufacturing locate abroad (Mexico, China and elsewhere in Asia).
- *Strategic asset-seeking* FDI is aimed at protecting and augmenting the existing ownership-specific advantages of the investing firm. Alternatively, such FDI may be aimed at reducing the advantages of competitors.

3.3.3 TRANSNATIONAL CORPORATIONS

Introduction

Any firm that owns, has a lasting interest in or controls[61] assets and structures in more than one country can be called a TNC. It is a wider concept than FDI since it includes non-equity business participation in another country. FDI is often the result of decisions by TNCs. Therefore, FDI may be a relatively good proxy for the investment activities of TNCs. A note of caution has to be added, however. TNCs may control trans-border business

Table 3.3 FDI inward stock in the world, the EU, the US, central and eastern Europe, developing countries, Japan and China, 1990, 1995 and 2000–2003 ($bn)

Host country/region	1990	1995	2000	2001	2002	2003
World total	1950.3	2992.1	6089.9	6606.8	7371.5	8245.1
EU(15)	748.3	1136.0	2257.7	2418.1	2899.8	3335.4
US	394.9	535.5	1214.2	1321.1	1505.1	1553.9
Central and eastern Europe	2.8	39.5	138.3	155.7	228.2	263.3
Developing countries	547.9	916.7	1939.9	2173.8	2093.6	2280.1
Japan	9.5	36.5	50.3	50.3	78.1	89.7
China	20.7	134.9	348.3	395.2	447.9	501.5

Source: UNCTAD (2004).

operations by non-equity involvement such as licensing. In the case of licensing, a TNC must be assured that the goods or services provided conform with the original quality standards.

Investment activity is one of the most sensitive indicators of a country's economic climate. What exactly it indicates, however, is not always clear. Increases in investment may indicate the emergence of new business opportunities, interest in the future, reactions to international competition and response to increasing cost pressures. In any case, sluggish investment activity, as during the 1970s, is an indication of rough economic times (Schatz and Wolter, 1987, p. 29).

The stock of FDI in a national economy indicates what proportion of the home economy is owned/controlled by foreign firms. The total world inward *stock* (the production potential) in 2003 was estimated to be over $8 trillion (Table 3.3). The spatial distribution of the stock of FDI is asymmetrical. In 2003, 69 per cent of FDI stock was located in developed countries. This is confirmation that FDI activity is strongest among comparable, mainly highly developed, countries.[62]

Inflows of FDI reflect the ability of a country to attract FDI (national location-specific advantages). The EU was the major target for FDI. Worldwide *inflows* of FDI in 2003 were $559 billion. This was 'only' half of the flows in 2000, when they had a peak of $1.4 trillion (Table 3.4). The principal factor behind this decline was slow economic growth throughout the world, as well as weak prospects for recovery in the short term. FDI flows are a strongly cyclical phenomenon. The remarkable exceptions to the generally declining tendency were China (huge and growing potentials of

Table 3.4 Annual FDI inflows in the world, the EU, the US, central and eastern Europe, developing countries, Japan and China, 1997–2003 ($bn)

Host country/region	1997	1998	1999	2000	2001	2002	2003
World total	481.9	690.9	1086.7	1378.9	817.6	678.7	559.5
EU(15)	127.9	249.9	479.3	671.4	357.4	374.0	295.1
US	103.4	174.4	283.4	314.0	159.4	62.1	29.7
Central and eastern Europe	19.0	24.3	26.5	27.5	26.3	31.2	21.0
Developing countries	193.2	194.0	231.9	252.4	219.7	157.6	172.0
Japan	3.2	3.2	12.7	8.3	6.2	9.3	6.3
China	44.2	45.5	40.3	40.7	46.9	52.7	53.5

Source: UNCTAD (2004).

the local market and possibilities to export to third countries) and to an extent central and east European countries (imminent entry of the EU). China became the principal single FDI recipient in 2003. It overtook the US, traditionally the prime target for FDI.

Outflows of FDI mirror the willingness and capacity of a country's firms to enter and stay in trans-border business activities. The principal world sources of FDI during 1997–2003 were the EU countries (Table 3.5). One may expect increased FDI outflows from China, which aims to establish and maintain efficient distribution, marketing and service networks for its goods; to exploit its growing financial potential; to be closer to the leading R&D resources elsewhere in the world (IBM in the US); to transfer the lower end and mature manufacturing production to less-developed countries (bicycle production to Ghana); and to invest in the production of resources (China's economic Achilles' heel) to secure their supply (Latin America, Middle East, Africa).

The sectoral distribution of FDI reveals that the industries that are absorbing the largest slices of FDI are those dominated by high-technology and highly qualified personnel. They also have higher than average expenditure on R&D relative to sales. The reasons for such a distribution may be found in the excessive transaction costs of arm's-length contacts through the market, so internalisation of these links within a firm seems to be a better business choice. In addition, they include those that benefit from strong economies of scale in the production of (sophisticated) intermediary goods; their output of final products is highly differentiated; and their production is sensitive to information.

Table 3.5 Annual FDI outflows in the world, the EU, the US, Canada, Japan, Switzerland, China and Hong Kong, 1997–2003 ($bn)

Host country/region	1997	1998	1999	2000	2001	2002	2003
World total	477.0	683.2	1092.3	1186.8	721.5	596.5	612.2
EU(15)	220.9	415.4	724.3	806.1	429.2	351.2	337.0
US	95.8	131.0	209.2	142.6	124.5	115.3	151.9
Canada	23.1	34.5	17.2	44.6	36.1	26.4	21.5
Japan	26.0	24.1	22.7	31.5	38.3	32.2	28.8
Switzerland	17.7	18.8	33.3	44.7	18.2	7.6	10.9
China	2.6	2.6	1.8	0.9	6.9	2.5	1.8
Hong Kong (China)	24.7	17.0	19.3	59.4	11.3	17.5	3.8

Source: UNCTAD (2004).

A possible EU drive towards a reciprocal treatment of FDI with Japan (or any other country) may not be highly productive. It is generally accepted that TNCs bring benefits that potentially more than compensate for the possible costs and concerns. The EU is, after all, the major world source of FDI, so the demand for a bilateral reciprocal treatment may be counterproductive. The principle of reciprocity in FDI often means the aligning of regulations upwards (reciprocal treatment in trade is often different as it sometimes levels down trade provisions).

Determinants

Large companies are in most cases TNCs. They are not directly or completely accountable to any government, but rather have their own ethos. Chauvinism regarding the location of business (personnel matters are a different issue) is alien to international firms, for their business decisions are not likely to be based on either ideological or nationalistic grounds (Rubin, 1970, p. 183). The most crucial determinants of FDI are the relative difference in returns and profit maximisation in the long run, market presence, availability of resources, expectations of growth in demand and political stability. These determinants for the location of an affiliate may be more important than a country's participation in a regional economic bloc.

Table 3.6 summarises investors' motives and determinants for FDI in the target location. It is obvious that the issue is rather complicated. Therefore, forecasting FDI flows is difficult and uncertain, as determinants are complex, highly changeable from case to case and not always measurable.

Transnational corporations behave like other market-oriented firms: primarily they look for opportunities to make a profit. Thus they compare

Table 3.6 Investors' motives and determinants for FDI in the target location

Investors' motives	Determinants in the target location
1. Market	Size of private and public demand Its growth (current and prospective) Access to regional (integration) and global markets Local, regional and country consumer needs, tastes, sophistication, preferences and fickleness Market structure (competition, openness, protection) Entry barriers Scope to exercise market power (becoming a monopolist) Actions by competitors: follow your leader ('snowball', 'me-too', or 'herding' behaviour) or exchange of threats (tit-for-tat strategy among oligopolists) Demanding clients
2. Resources	Mobility of resources Raw materials (availability, prices) Skilled labour and educated management System of education Brain drain Unskilled labour (low cost) Available technology (production functions) Innovation and R&D capabilities and potentials Infrastructure Inputs including supporting services Available capital at favourable rates Organisation of labour (voluntary or mandatory labour unions) Work habits (Japanese TNCs sometimes prefer to locate in rural areas as they mistrust urban workers because of their 'different' work habits and mobility)
3. Efficiency	Cost of resources (listed under No. 2) adjusted for productivity where appropriate Cost and easiness of operation (transactions, trade, transport, communication, and so on) Efficiency of the supply chain Trade and marketing networks Logistics Points at the product cycle and production function
4. Others	Existence of clusters Macroeconomic and other stability Incentives (subsidies and taxes) and concessions

Table 3.6 (continued)

Investors' motive	Determinants in the target location
	Rules, regulations and policies (FDI entry and protection, mergers and acquisitions, competition, labour, tax, subsidy, trade, NTBs, and so on)
	Pressure by the government in the target country to locate there
	Movements in exchange rates
	Investment promotion and friendliness (helpfulness during considerations about FDI, entry, operation and exit)
	Dispute settlement system
	Establishment of a listening, learning and monitoring post
	Culture (way of doing business, openness, corruption, red tape, languages spoken, and so on)
	Quality of life

current and expected profits at home and abroad. The principal motivators for FDI and trans-border business activity are summarised in Table 3.6, and just a few will be mentioned here. The size and rate of growth of a local market in the target country is approximated by income, its growth and by privileged access to regional and international markets. This was the most prominent general motivator for trans-border business operations. Depending on the industry, the availability of resources (including the cost of labour adjusted for productivity) were relevant too. Other motivators, although recognised, were less important. This is because of the strong impact of the real market size on the minimum efficient scale for production.

As the general level of protection of the national market declines due to liberalisation (there is no need to jump over national tariff barriers) and as various types of economic integration proliferate around the world, the mere size of the national market continues to be important, but other motivators are gaining in significance and strength. The local availability of technical, managerial and organisation (networking) knowledge, capabilities and competences including innovation together with the existence of clusters, become principal motives for FDI. Seeking, enhancing and protecting such strategic assets and structures became a prominent motivator for FDI. This is linked with high skills, education and experience of labour in the target location. Such labour and management is expensive everywhere. This means that low wages (adjusted for productivity) cease to be a sufficient determinant for FDI.

Where market liberalisation is a widely accepted policy choice, created assets (technology and ability to create it, business culture, capability to organise and control production and marketing, communications infrastructure and marketing networks internal and external to firms) are increasingly important determinants for FDI. This is why most activities of TNCs are geographically located in developed market economies (measured by the stock of FDI).

Neo-classical theory cannot predict with absolute certainty the geographical location of activities resulting from capital mobility within a common market. TNCs that use complex technologies do not worry about tariffs and quotas. They are concerned, rather, with domestic regulations such as environmental standards.[63] A degree of government intervention may influence the spatial location of TNCs, with important implications for the future distribution of output and trade.

Some goods and services must be adapted in order to meet local needs and preferences (for example, food). Locating at least a part of the production process near the place of consumption may do this more cheaply. Other reasons for FDI instead of, or together with, exporting include taking advantage of a range of the host country's incentives such as financial incentives (subsidies, reduced taxes), tariff protection, exemption from import duties, public purchases and granting monopoly rights. Other motives include market pre-emption, increase in market power, as well as the empire-building ambitions of firms.

The literature based on surveys and case studies suggests that government strategies such as tax incentives and industrial policies have little, if any, effect on the location of industry. All studies are aware of the difficulties in ascertaining the impact of public policy measures on the location of production. Public policies have mixed effects on the location of firms: on the one hand, higher taxes increase the operating costs of firms; on the other, higher taxes in some areas may be used to pay for better public services, such as education or infrastructure, that support the operation of firms (Smith and Florida, 1994, p. 31).

In a survey of 30 TNCs covering 74 investment projects concerning cars, computers, food processing and petrochemicals, many TNCs revealed that government incentives were not an issue and, where they existed, simply made an already attractive country for the location of business operations even more attractive. Investment decisions were made on the grounds of economic and long-term strategic conditions regarding inputs, costs and markets. Overall, incentives are not an important factor in the set of elements that determine inward FDI. Once the decision is made to invest in the target country (or region), the incentives may have an impact on the exact choice of location within the target country (UNCTAD, 1998, pp. 103–4).

As for geographical origin, most TNCs originate in countries with decentralised political systems such as the US, Britain and the Netherlands, which have the longest history of transnationalisation of national economic activity. In these countries, the TNCs and the state foster relations of complementarity. In centralised states, the administration does not want to share power with any enterprise; however, this has changed in past decades, particularly in France and more recently in 'communist' China.

If producers and government in a big country A make a credible threat to close its market to exporters from a small country B, then one of the options for country B is to establish 'fifth column' production in country A. This would preserve country B's market share in country A's market. If overheads are covered in country B's home market, then its firm in country A may sell on a marginal cost basis. Many European and Japanese TNCs have concentrated on breaking into the US market and become 'US nationals' in order to avoid unilateral and whimsical US economic sanctions and changes in the American trade regime. Making immediate profit from such an investment has played a secondary role, at least in the short term. A similar observation in the EU was the flurry of non-EU TNCs that settled in the EU prior to the full implementation of the Single Market Programme at the end of 1992.

The success of Japanese firms in reducing the labour content of the final output is one of the factors contributing to the expansion of their FDI into relatively high labour cost areas such as North America or the EU. High labour productivity can make up for higher wages. This is why the most significant part of all activities by TNCs takes place in a select group of developed countries. Relatively low nominal wages do not necessarily equal low labour costs – labour productivity should be taken into consideration. In addition, low or declining wages may mean a (local) shrinking market. If this were the case, and if TNCs are interested in the local market, this may act as a deterrent to FDI. Despite the advantage of cheaper labour in Italy, Greece and Portugal, relative to the central and northern EU countries in the 1960s, labour outflow from, rather than capital inflow to, southern Europe was the equilibrating force at that time.

Foreign direct investment is a tool used by enterprises that want to exploit long-term profit-making opportunities abroad. Before embarking upon FDI, an enterprise compares alternative geographical locations at home and at various places abroad. If investing abroad seems to be the more promising option, then the enterprise has to make sure that it possesses or can obtain certain mobile income-generating firm-specific advantages in production or transactions that could enable it to operate profitably in the foreign environment. These advantages include exclusive or privileged access to specific assets and structures, as well as better organising and control capabilities for both production and transactions.

Local firms have several advantages over foreign ones, for example:

- they have a better knowledge of local consumer and supplier markets;
- they do not have the costs of operating at a distance;
- they often receive favours from the government;
- they do not operate in a different, often hostile, language, tax, legal, exchange rate, social and political environment; and
- TNCs may have some disadvantages in the eyes of certain local politicians in target countries as they are foreign and, often, relatively large.

Therefore, TNCs bear these elements in mind when deciding on the location of their affiliates. They weigh up whether they have enough advantages over other firms or whether they can create the capacity to overcome these obstacles.

A difficulty for TNCs may be that they have to attract key managers and technicians from the headquarters to a foreign subsidiary. This may require both higher wages for such personnel and higher allowances for their families. TNCs that extract and export natural resources are at risk of becoming a target for nationalisation. If a TNC wants to operate in such a geographical and social environment, it must have or control special advantages. These special and mobile advantages over its domestic competitors include a superior production technology and management technique (a TNC ought to operate on a different production function or at a different point on the same production function than domestic firms), a well-known brand name or, especially important for services, access to markets and quality control. For these reasons, it is no surprise that TNCs are often more profitable and successful than local competitors in the same industry.

While firm-specific income-generating and mobile advantages are a necessary condition for FDI, they are not a sufficient condition. If trade were free, firms could simply use their advantages by exporting instead of producing abroad. Various market imperfections limit the size of the market for free trade and, hence, justify FDI. These include tariffs and NTBs, differences in factor prices, sunk costs and after-sales service. Therefore, an enterprise with a specific and mobile income-generating advantage considers a number of different possibilities and restraints at various foreign locations before settling abroad.

Linkages, Externalities and Spillovers of Transnational Corporations

Targeting some key productive activities that have significant linkages with the rest of the economy requires some form of government intervention.

Japan's decision to target steel, shipbuilding and toys in the 1950s and 1960s was highly profitable. This choice turned out to be questionable in the 1970s, so Japan turned to cars and machine tools. In the 1980s and 1990s, the Japanese chose electronics as their target industry (Tyson, 1987, p. 70). This target became obsolete from the 1990s as software overtook hardware in importance, and in this industry the US leads.

In the past the selected industries have had important spillover effects throughout the economy. Henry Ford's assembly line production technology from the 1920s spread to all manufacturing industries in the US and elsewhere. Telecommunications affect the dissemination of information, computers have an impact on data processing, while transportation equipment and logistics affect the size of the market. As a result of these linkages, private returns from these industries are smaller than social returns. The targeting and location, in a common market or any other type of integration, of key industries that may have significant linkages with other industries or partner countries may have important and long-term beneficial spillover effects on the group. Various potential linkages between the operation of TNCs and the growth process are presented in Figure 3.2.

To understand and capture spillovers in general and in irreversible time, one needs a definition of externalities. Carlaw and Lipsey (2002, p. 1306) define externalities as follows:

> Externalities are unpaid for effects conferred by the *continuing* and *potentially variable* actions of one set of agents (who we call 'initiating agents') on another set of agents (who we call 'receiving agents') who are not involved in the initiating agent's activity, and for which the receiving agents would be willing to pay.
>
> Externalities typically prevent the fulfilment of optimality conditions since there will be too much of activities that produce negative externalities and too little of the activities that produce positive externalities. (Original emphasis)

The existence, quality and strength of links between a TNC and the local environment depend in part on the objectives of the TNC. If it wishes to minimise costs of production, then the relation with the local business environment may have a hierarchical form and relatively low local embeddedness. However, if the TNC pursues a policy of cooperation, rather than arm's-length hierarchy, the linkages with the local businesses may be deeper. This may take the form of technology transfer, training of labour, sharing information about future production demands and the like. But these linkages and spillovers on the local economy also depend on the ability of the local businesses to adjust, absorb and apply knowledge from TNCs and serve as their reliable partners. In Ireland, for example, an economy with a high level of involvement by TNCs, spillovers were noted in domestic plants that operate in high-technology industries. No evidence

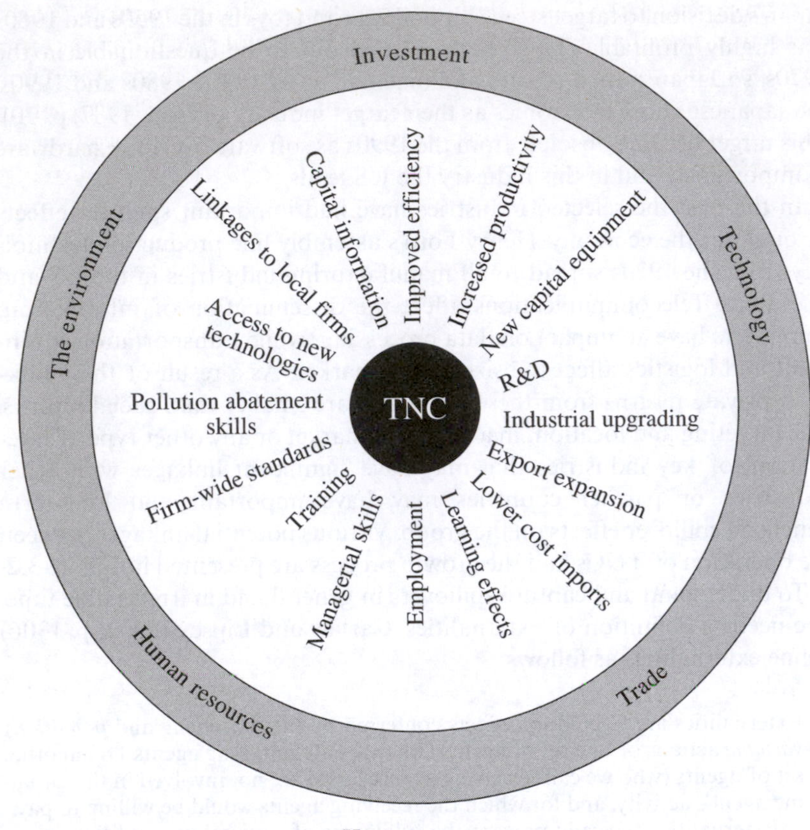

Source: UNCTAD (1992, p. 247).

Figure 3.2 Transnational corporations and the growth process

of such spillover was found in the low-technology industries (Görg and Strobl, 2003, p. 593).

Spillovers on the local economy may sometimes take the form of imitation. Bangladesh did not have a developed textile industry before the end of the 1970s, while this industry is now the country's principal exporter. Desh Garments, for example, was a small Bangladeshi firm established in 1977. It sent 130 of its production and management staff for training in Daewoo's state-of-the-art factories in South Korea. Following a six-month training period, they returned to Bangladesh to start a shirt-making company. The most useful part of the training was not how to operate the technical side of the textile machinery, but rather how to transfer the

Korean experience to Bangladesh with regard to exchange controls and the protectionist trading system. A year after a successful collaboration, Desh cancelled the cooperation agreement with Daewoo. 'Of the 130 Desh workers trained by Daewoo, 115 of them left during [the] 1980s to set up their own garment export firms. This explosion of garment companies started by ex-Desh workers gave Bangladesh its textile industry, currently responsible for three-quarters of its exports' (Margalioth, 2003, p. 175).

When a firm wants to locate and produce abroad it does not necessarily need to export capital. A firm may rent capital abroad rather than purchase or build a production unit. Instead of using its own funds, a firm may borrow in its home, host country's or a third country's financial market. In the case of fixed exchange rates, countries may enter into an 'interest rate war' in order to attract capital into their economies. Integrated capital markets with harmonised rates of interest and mobility of capital may prevent this outcome. While labour markets are most often regional (in Europe), capital markets are national and, with liberalisation, they are becoming international.

Neither firms nor governments depend on savings in their home markets. Interest rates and demand for funds in one country are affected by money (short-term) and capital (long-term) markets in other countries because of the links among financial markets. Of course, this holds if there is confidence in foreign borrowers. Small countries are interest rate takers, so that even the national housing (non-traded good) market feels the impact from foreign markets through changes in interest rates. Free international mobility of capital prevents the independent conduct of monetary policy. If a country lowers interest rates in relation to third countries, then capital will flow abroad. This also destabilises the exchange rate if all else is equal. In addition, if a country increases interest rates (in relation to foreign countries) in order to curb domestic inflation, if other things are constant, capital will flow into the country. The supply of money increases, and inflation is the consequence. Free international mobility of capital introduced during the 1990s, at least among the developed market economies, is a self-policing international market device that controls the 'correctness' of national monetary policy and its conformity with the 'best practice'. In this situation, the role and the existence of the IMF became largely unnecessary and irrelevant, and, in the case of IMF loans that kept certain corrupt and bankrupt regimes in the developing countries afloat, this role could easily have been harmful.

Financial markets may sometimes favour large companies and countries and discriminate against small ones. Large companies and countries provide apparently greater security that the funds will be returned and interest paid. A large stock of assets lends weight to this confidence. These markets may discriminate against risky investments such as seabed research, new sources of energy or materials and the like. By integrating capital markets, small countries may mitigate the effect of their relative disadvantage.

The electronics industry in Taiwan has benefited from a geographical variety of foreign investors (mainly from the US and Japan). These TNCs provided education for managers and training for workers, improved the efficiency and quality of production and created stable markets and production and marketing links with local suppliers. These initiatives provided a solid foundation for the creation of an indigenous electronics industry in Taiwan, which evolved with global standards. Mexico's misfortune in the electronics industry was that it received FDI only from declining US component makers and assemblers. This was coupled with a lack of integration with the domestic Mexican electronics industry. Crediting the Taiwanese government for the success of its industry and blaming the Mexican government for its failure would be too simplistic (Lowe and Kenney, 1999, p. 1439).

Economic and business intuition, as well as theory, accepts the existence of favourable spillover effects of TNCs on local businesses. *Ex ante* expectations are that TNCs would increase local employment, exports and tax revenue and that some knowledge would spill over into the local economy through movement of labour or by means of purchase orders. However, clear empirical evidence about the actual nature and magnitude of these effects is still to be ascertained. This throws doubt on the wisdom of offering (financial) incentives to TNCs to locate in a specific area.

Görg and Strobl (2001, p. F724) found that the results of studies about the presence of spillovers were mixed. Hanson (2001, pp. 14 and 23) reported only weak and mixed evidence that FDI brings positive spillover effects for the host country. Görg and Greenaway (2004, pp. 187–90) surveyed a body of the existing literature on the benefits of FDI on the host economy. They mentioned that theory points to the reasons why spillovers may arise, but they found little robust empirical evidence on the actual existence of spillovers.[64] Are TNCs protecting their assets for themselves (preventing horizontal spillovers)? Or are researchers looking for spillovers in the wrong place with incorrect research tools? Empirical studies generally look at cross-section effects on industries. An increasing availability of plant-level data makes even firm plant-level analysis feasible.

In a similar survey of spillovers in the host economies, Blomström and Kokko (2003, p. 14) found that the results from a number of case studies about the presence of spillovers seem to be mixed. If these spillovers have an impact on the adjoining firms, these effects depend on the adequate, even comparable, technological level of local firms to absorb them and on host-country policies. Mody (2004, pp. 1209 and 1218) found little evidence that

FDI speeded up productivity growth and improved corporate governance. He argued that the domestic absorption capabilities appear to be crucial for the spillover effects to take place. Rodrik (2004, p. 30) mentioned 'very little systematic evidence of technological and other externalities from foreign direct investment'. R.E. Lipsey (2004, pp. 365 and 371) reported only mixed evidence about the existence of (positive) spillovers on the local economy. Where they existed, the domestic firms did not lag far behind the technology employed by the subsidiary of the TNC. Spillovers were largely in the form of transfer of knowledge (particularly knowledge of demand in the world market) and knowledge about the ways and means of fitting national production into the global production network. This is, however, neither immediately obvious nor easy to measure.

As there is little or no convincing evidence that FDI brings positive spillovers for the host economy, there is little support for the idea that promoting FDI is justified on welfare grounds. What is the reason for such weak or neutral effects regarding spillovers? Answers to this question can be found in the fact that affiliates of TNCs may outcompete the domestic firms and shift demand away from the local competitors; there are time lags in the learning process by the domestic firms and adjustment to the presence and demand of TNCs; and TNCs may guard their internal advantages and prevent leaks to local firms. Even though there is controversy about spillovers, there is a consensus in the literature in this respect: the national economic policy regarding investment should be general and available to all firms (notwithstanding their origin), rather than specific and targeted towards a select type of investment. So why is there a special treatment of TNCs by countries even in the absence of firm evidence about spillovers on the local economy? Politicians want to do 'something' for certain constituencies in return for votes. They try to attract TNCs that will offer new jobs. In addition, governments try to lure TNCs into competition with other potential locations that offer allowances notwithstanding the obvious costs and uncertain and illusionary benefits.

Transfer Pricing

Foreign ownership and control of domestic output potentials is often seen by the general public as a burden on the domestic economy that is brought by TNCs. A more serious argument against the operation of TNCs is that they behave in the market of the host country in an anti-competitive way through various business practices such as predatory pricing, monopolisation or transfer pricing.

One argument against TNCs used by host countries concerns their internal (transfer) pricing system.[65] TNCs internalise intermediate product and service[66] markets. Prices in trade among different sister enterprises are arrived at by non-market means.[67] For example, GlaxoSmithKline develops, produces and sells drugs in a global market. It conducts R&D in seven countries, manufactures in 38 and sells in 191. It may not be meaningful to ask what part of its worldwide profits is made in Britain, as if the same profits were made in transactions among independent national firms. TNCs prosper precisely because this is not the case.[68] In addition, if transfer of technology is measured by international payments of royalties and fees, then about 80 per cent of payments are undertaken on an intra-firm basis (UNCTAD, 1997, p. 20). By doing so, TNCs may shift profits out of countries with relatively high taxes to those with the lowest corporate taxes (tax avoidance)[69] or they may oust competition by cross-subsidising product lines.

In order to shift profits from relatively high-tax countries such as Britain, Spain or the US, vertical TNCs may overprice imports of inputs (including intra-group borrowing) and underprice exports.[70] The world's largest TNCs such as General Electric of the US, Toyota of Japan or Nestlé of Switzerland have paid little or nothing to the British tax authorities in the most recently reported financial years. The same holds for British subsidiaries of foreign-owned investment banks such as Goldman Sachs, Morgan Stanley, Merrill Lynch and Credit Suisse.[71] Does this mean that there is one set of rules for the big guys, and another for the small ones? It is, however, true that 'corporate giants' contribute a lot through personal taxes and VAT, but it may be surprising to find their reported 'low' profitability in Britain. Even though the share of the collected revenue by means of corporation tax is on the decline because of reduction in tax rates and 'financial engineering' (transfer pricing), the national tax authorities still get their cut by other means. They do not always squeeze firms too much as they do not want them to go and settle elsewhere.

The situation that permits transfer pricing and global tax arbitrage arises from possibilities brought by globalisation. It stimulates purely domestic firms to internationalise their business operations. A TNC locates costs, revenue, borrowing and profits in the most favourable tax jurisdiction for overall group profit. An estimate for the US found that tax loss from artificial transfer pricing was $53 billion in 2001.[72]

Tax inspection, even academic enquiry of transfer pricing, is often difficult. Comparison with competitors is obscured by a different mix of products and corporate structures. The ownership of a TNC such as Procter & Gamble, for example, changed hands just four times between January and May 2003.[73] In any case, the pricing system, internal to TNCs may distort both the efficient spatial location of production (resource-wise) and flows of finance and trade.

One way to control operations of the TNCs in the host country could be to ask that the internal pricing system treats the parent and its subsidiary as if they were two separate companies. The enforcement and control of such a requirement may be seriously endangered if there are no substitutes for these internally traded goods and various (headquarters) services. Another solution may be to harmonise fiscal systems and their enforcement in countries where TNCs operate. None the less, a note of caution needs to be added. Transfer pricing is probably used much more commonly than TNCs are willing to admit, but much less frequently than is supposed by outsiders (Plasschaert, 1994, p. 13). In any case, transfer pricing is not widespread in small and decentralised TNCs or in TNCs that operate in competitive markets.

Internalisation of intermediate goods or services markets within TNCs is not always done with the primary goal of avoiding taxes on corporate profits. Another possible reason is to maintain high quality in the supply of goods and services, as local or external suppliers may not necessarily be able to maintain the high quality and timely delivery standards required by the TNC. None the less, fiddling with transfer pricing is more widespread in the developing countries than in the developed world. The balance of payments position of developing countries often drives them to control flows of foreign exchange. Strict controls may induce TNCs to manipulate the internal pricing in order to protect and/or increase profits. The developing countries are not well equipped either to detect or to control manipulation of the internal prices of TNCs.

Research and Development

A potential case in the host country against TNCs is that TNCs rely heavily on the R&D of their parent companies and that their head office charges for its central services in a way that might not be supervised or controlled by the host country, which can make both subsidiaries and host countries too dependent on foreign R&D and technology. Is this really the case?

When General Electric acquired Tungsram, a huge and renowned Hungarian light bulb company in 1990, it closed down Tungsram's R&D department. However, when it was realised that light source research was so strong in Hungary, General Electric resumed and reinforced this Hungarian research in 1994. Elsewhere, empirical research in Canada found that the subsidiaries of TNCs undertook more R&D than domestic Canadian firms (Rugman, 1985, p. 468). In another example, European lift manufacturers decided to carry out their R&D of lifts for tall buildings in their US subsidiaries because there are so many skyscrapers there.

While there is historical evidence that most R&D took place in the headquarters of TNCs, this is no longer necessarily the case on a large scale. There are many instances of foreign subsidiaries developing technologies that have benefited the parent firm, especially from the mid-1980s. For example, a US TNC such as IBM had research breakthroughs in superconductor technology in Switzerland; Hoffmann-La Roche (Switzerland) developed important new pharmaceuticals such as librium and valium in New Jersey (US); Toshiba made advances in audio technology in its British laboratory; and Matsushita's R&D facilities for air-conditioners are in Malaysia. However, in order to arrive at a solid conclusion, more evidence at a much more disaggregated level is needed. Affiliates of foreign TNCs in the US look much like the domestic US firms: there are no particular signs of headquarters effects (Graham and Krugman, 1995, pp. 73–4, 119).[74] There is a trend, based on the evolutionary view of economics, for TNCs to create and promote networks of internal and external innovation (Cantwell and Piscitello, 2005, p. 3).[75]

Foreign affiliates hold an increasing share of R&D. In this internationalisation of technology, they account for between less than 5 per cent in Japan and over 70 per cent in Hungary and Ireland. Foreign affiliates' share of over 30 per cent is undertaken in Australia, Britain, Canada, the Netherlands, Portugal, Slovakia, Spain and Sweden (OECD, 2003c).

The geographical spread of R&D activities carried out by TNCs and the selection of the actual location for this activity is driven by several factors, including:

- the available sophisticated and experienced local R&D staff;
- a desire to enhance the existing and acquire new competences;
- the need to adapt output to the needs, preferences and requests of the local market;
- subsidies or pressure from the host government to establish local R&D facilities;
- the possibility of establishing a 'listening and learning post' in the host country; and
- the prospect of capturing spillovers.

However, an international spread of locations for R&D does not mean, as seen in the discussion on competition policy, that the innovation process has also followed this 'global' trend.

A small country often does not have the necessary resources for large-scale basic research compared to a big and developed country. By importing technology a small country may have access to the results of a much larger volume of R&D wherever it is carried out. It can be both complementary and supplementary to R&D already undertaken in the domestic economy. Relying on the domestic operation of foreign-owned TNCs may be a superior economic policy choice for a risk-averse (poor and small) country than being dependent on foreign supplies of the same good produced elsewhere. Technology transfers from abroad and domestic efforts in education and endeavours to master new technology are like scissor blades: their joint effect is greater than the impact of either one alone (Pack and Saggi, 1997, pp. 94–5).

Inter-firm strategic alliances in the development of technology in the EU increased sharply during the 1980s. In addition, the European Commission became heavily involved in projects on a cost-sharing basis. Over 70 per cent of private (largely non-subsidised) strategic technology alliances were related to joint R&D of new core technologies in the fields of informatics, new materials and biotechnology. A major field of co-operation was in information technologies, as over 40 per cent of all strategic technology alliances were in this field (Hagedoorn and Schakenraad, 1993, p. 373).

A comparison between established 'private' cooperation in R&D and cooperation sponsored by the EU found that these two forms are very similar in the case of leading enterprises. In fact, 'subsidised R&D networks add to already existing or emerging private networks and merely reproduce the basic structure of European large firm co-operation' (ibid., p. 387). This being the case, it is difficult to understand why leading and large firms in the EU need subsidies! If the 'official' (EU-sponsored) spatial network largely reproduces the already existing 'private' one, then it may be redundant. Financial resources could have been used elsewhere (for instance, to fund programmes that are not in the field of informatics, such as biotechnology or education or infrastructure). Is such replication of R&D networks the outcome of the lobbying power of powerful firms or is it necessary to accelerate R&D in the private sector because of significant externalities?[76] Perhaps such waste of scarce public money will be checked in the future by WTO rules on subsidisation.

There is a tendency to reduce the risks and costs of R&D within TNCs. Over 70 per cent of international strategic technology alliances between companies from the EU and NAFTA are focused on R&D (Hagedoorn, 1998, p. 184). This may be an important incentive for mergers and acquisitions in the pharmaceuticals industry (the major reason is still the very fragmented nature of the pharmaceuticals industry compared with car manufacturing). High risk and uncertainty, as well as excessive R&D costs, drive firms to centralise these functions (usually in their country of origin). Another reason is the exploitation of host countries' incentives to R&D (subsidies, tax breaks, secure contracts). In this case, the basic research remains in the headquarters, while subsidiaries undertake applied development according to local demand, regulations and incentives. It is often forgotten that many firms that create knowledge are neither TNCs nor large (for example, in the areas of computer hardware and software). The only condition for their creation in certain locations is that they operate in a competitive environment, which is often lacking in small countries.

Host Countries and Transnational Corporations

The greatest power of TNCs stems from their high international mobility to enter and exit from an industry or a location.[77] TNCs can act as spatial capital arbitrageurs. They may borrow in countries where the rate of interest is lowest and invest in countries where they expect the highest returns. TNCs may spread overheads and risk among their subsidiaries. These enterprises also extend control over international markets. If a subsidiary is producing final goods, then other parts of a TNC may increase export components to this subsidiary.

Many TNCs create sophisticated and complicated technologies. They avoid the transfer of this technology through the market in order to prevent competitors from copying it. The longer the technology gap with imitators lasts, the longer the TNC can behave like a monopolist. Thus, a TNC usually transfers technology first among its subsidiaries.

Relations between TNCs and host countries may sometimes be quite tense. Mining is an industry that requires a huge amount of investment before commercial exploitation can begin. Different countries often compete and offer incentives for FDI and effectively engage in a 'locations tournament' (David, 1984). At this stage a TNC has the strongest bargaining position. When TNCs locate their operations in host countries they may, for example, react to changes in the host country's tax system or interest rates quite differently from domestic firms, which may not be able to withdraw from the home market. Thus, TNCs may become a threat to the host country's national economic policies. To counter this danger, the common market member countries should coordinate and harmonise their policies regarding competition, capital mobility and TNCs.

If TNCs produce final goods in host countries and if they import raw materials and components from countries which are outside the common market instead of purchasing them from the local suppliers, then they may jeopardise the process of integration within a common market. The external dependence of the area may increase instead of being reduced. Where the member countries of a common market or other type of international economic integration compete among themselves for FDI in the absence of an agreed industrial policy, it is unreasonable to expect the operation of the

TNCs to result in an optimal spatial allocation of resources (Robson, 1983, p. 32). This has happened in the Caribbean region.

A large amount of investment may, however, keep a TNC as a hostage of the host country. These sunk costs with limited or no 'salvage value' may represent a barrier to exit from the host country. In this case, the host-country government can show the TNC who is boss. The host governments may renegotiate the deals with the TNCs. This kind of danger may induce the TNCs to borrow predominantly on the host-country's financial market and transfer from elsewhere only the technical and managerial expertise. A possible closure of a subsidiary in the host country would be at the cost of some local jobs in both the subsidiary and supplying firms. The affected local workers and their families may lobby in favour of the interests of the TNC, which may find allies among industries in the host country. As long as TNCs purchase from them, both subsidiaries and local firms may work together in lobbying the government for protection, subsidies, tax breaks and procurement agreements.

The distinctiveness of national character and, hence, social value systems may have a certain impact on the attraction of FDI. For instance, Yutang Lin (1935) in his famous discussion of the Chinese character remarked (p. 58):

> . . . the Chinese are a hard-boiled lot. There is no nonsense about them: they do not live in order to die, as the Christians pretend to do, nor do they seek for a Utopia on earth, as many seers of the West do. They just want to order this life on earth, which they know to be full of pain and sorrow, so that they may work peaceably, endure nobly, and live happily. Of the noble virtues of the West, of nobility, ambition, zeal for reform, public spirit, sense for adventure and heroic courage, the Chinese are devoid. They cannot be interested in climbing Mont Blanc or in exploring the North Pole. But they are tremendously interested in this commonplace world, and they have an indomitable patience, an indefatigable industry, a sense of duty, a level-headed commonsense, cheerfulness, humour, tolerance, pacificism, and that unequalled genius for finding happiness in hard environments which we call contentment – qualities that make this commonplace life enjoyable to them. And chief of these are pacificism and tolerance, which are the mark of a mellow culture, and which seem to be lacking in modern Europe.

If this were true and acceptable, try to replicate it outside China!

A serious threat to the market structure of a host country may be introduced by a TNC. It may monopolise the whole domestic market and by predatory pricing prevent the entry of domestic firms to the industry. It may introduce technologies that use relatively more of the resources in short supply (capital) and relatively less of the component that is abundant (labour) in the host country.

As far as wages are concerned, there is overwhelming evidence that TNCs in all kinds of countries pay relatively higher wages to labour of a given quality than local firms do. The reasons for such a wage policy include the following elements (R.E. Lipsey, 2004, pp. 346, 351):

- TNCs may be forced to offer higher wages by host-country regulations or by home-country pressures about 'fair pay'.
- Local labour may prefer domestic firms and it ought to be compensated to overcome this preference.
- If TNCs bring certain proprietary technology, they may wish to reduce labour turnover. By offering higher pay they may retain labour, hence they may reduce technology leaks to domestic firms.
- TNCs may wish to find and attract better workers and managers. More knowledgeable local firms may identify, get and keep these workers without this wage premium.
- Certain TNCs operate in higher-wage industries of the economy. They hire highly educated managers and sophisticated workers.

Differences in wages may also be due to the fact that the home firms do not value sufficiently a resource that is in short supply. Vacancies in the domestic firms may be filled by less-well-trained labour, which may have an adverse effect on the growth of production in the host country. Although technologies used by the TNCs in the host countries may not be the most up to date, they can be superior to those which are currently in use in developing countries (environmentally sound technologies are an obvious example).

Transnational corporations may have an adverse impact on the allocation of resources in the host country if their operation accounts for a significant proportion of production, employment, purchases and sales. Thus, the operation of TNCs may have a greater influence in certain segments of industry in developing countries than in developed countries. This state of affairs demands a coordinated approach towards TNCs by the regional groups in the developing world, as was the case with the controversial Decision 24 (1970) in the Andean Pact.[78] It also requires the establishment and enforcement of a common industrial policy. This can be supported by the regional development banks and/or by joint planning. Openness to and participation in an integrated network of international production of TNCs will contribute to the growth potential of the developing countries.

This analysis suggests that the TNCs do not pay much attention to the overall needs of the host countries. This is true. However, it is not a duty of TNCs to meet the social needs, including the infrastructure needs, of the host country. Nobody forces host countries to accept TNCs. The fulfilment of these social demands is the role of the host country's government. In the presence of unemployed resources, inflation, foreign and budgetary debt, famine and underdevelopment, any hard currency investment is welcome. Any attempt by the host government to restrict the entry and operation of TNCs may dry up this trickle of capital inflow. Host countries sometimes behave (or used to) as if they want FDI funds, but not the foreign investor to handle them. Unfortunately, the developing countries are those that most need these investments. TNCs often ask what will happen after they invest and start production: will the utility companies increase prices? Will the employees request an immediate increase in wages? Will the consumers demand bigger loans as the TNC is a large, successful and rich company?

In order to increase local embeddedness, some TNCs involve themselves in local communities through sponsorship of local sporting and cultural events, and even education and training. Whether this is a calculated public relations ploy (as in the case of some Japanese and German TNCs that operate in Britain) to avoid criticism or a real and deep commitment towards the local communities remains unanswered (Dicken et al., 1995, p. 41).

Economic adjustment in the developing world may be facilitated by the presence of TNCs. These corporations have the know-how, the ability to raise funds and the widespread marketing channels that help export growth. They may create and maintain relevant spillover effects such as linkages with local firms that may prompt the creation of new local firms and the restructuring of existing ones.

The local content[79] requirements for locating FDI in a particular country may be criticised on the grounds that they distort investors' input choices, stimulate suboptimal input mixes and potentially increase prices. In a survey of 682 projects, it was found that in 83 per cent of cases in which there was a requirement to accomplish the objectives of trade-related investment measures (TRIMs) such as local sourcing and exporting, the firms planned to do so anyway (UNCTC, 1991a, p. 4). That is to say, TRIMs were redundant.

Certain companies, such as Nike and Wal-Mart, have sourcing structures that are more geographically spread than their sales. Nike, for example, sources 99 per cent of its products offshore (principally from China and south-east Asia). However, most of its sales (52 per cent) are in its home US market (Rugman and Verbeke, 2003, p. 14).

Local content requirements were often used in the past as means to promote, even force, linkages between TNCs and local firms. Others with the same policy objective included trade (export performance) and foreign exchange balancing demands. However, over the past few decades, most countries have strategically altered their economic policies from the general protection of domestic firms to widespread openness. In addition, the WTO 1995 TRIMs Agreement (Article 2) requires the phasing out of TRIMs.[80] While there might be certain initial successes in the forging of linkages with the local suppliers, forced requirements on a TNC's affiliate may jeopardise the efficient technology mix in the production. As such, this can easily endanger the efficiency in the production process, lower competitiveness and reduce incentives for other TNCs to come and locate in that country. A far superior and more sophisticated policy that can be employed by governments to foster links and spillovers between the local industry and affiliates of TNCs is to provide information about the local business environment, to act as a matchmaker with the local firms and to upgrade the technology level of the local firms through education, training and finance.

In many developing countries, mineral resources, including oil, are the property of the state. It is the government that negotiates terms of entry with TNCs. In manufacturing, the role of the government is somewhat less pronounced. In this case, the government usually sets general terms of entry, performance and exit from an industry. While the developing countries, as a rule, regulate the conditions for entry of TNCs with greater scrutiny, developed countries control their exit and the possible consequences regarding job losses and the environment.

It is popularly argued that TNCs invest most often in fast-growing manufacturing industries such as electronics and medicine-related industries. These industries thus 'fall into foreign hands', possibly giving foreigners undue influence in the host country and interfering with sovereignty.[81] One example was when the US introduced a ban on the export of technology for the gas pipeline from the then USSR to western Europe in the early 1980s. Many subsidiaries of US TNCs in western Europe were affected by this decision. It is much harder for a host country to influence the parent country of a TNC through a subsidiary.

In spite of allegedly lower environmental standards in the developing countries, a massive transfer of polluting business activities to these countries has not taken place, at least not on a large scale. This is the consequence of the constant focus of TNCs on the developed countries and the adherence of TNCs to the unilateral application of environmental standards (often the same as in their home country) that are superior to those prevailing in the host developing country. TNCs fear legal challenges in their home countries for damages done abroad.

As noted earlier, modern technologies complicate the employment impact of FDI. Modern technologies substitute capital for labour. A *greenfield* investment (building a new factory) is an attractive business option when blending existing assets and structures with others is undesirable, risky and costly. Investors can tailor-make the production site, and manufacturing and management techniques, to suit their particular needs. Previous management habits and labour relations are not inherited. This type of investment increases employment in the host country if it does not put domestic competitors out of business.

A *takeover* (merger and acquisition) of an existing firm is a preferred business choice if the cost of a greenfield entry exceeds the cost of a takeover. The investor may immediately start production, but this does not add to the national output capacity in the host country at the time of entry (this is just a transfer of ownership). This is a fast way to enter rapidly changing markets, and hence, in general, a more common way to enter foreign markets than through a greenfield investment. This holds particularly for entry into the developed market economies. Takeovers do not necessarily increase employment and may reduce it if the merged firm rationalises the existing activity. A foreign-located subsidiary may begin as a unit for marketing of the final good. If it develops further, it may become a product specialist, which may increase employment (direct and indirect) of a particular type of labour. However, one has to remember that employment is determined by demand for final goods and services.

Takeovers (mergers and acquisitions) provide means for the 'external' growth of TNCs. They are attractive to TNCs that have wide international marketing networks and are tempting to sellers who are interested in penetrating the widest possible market. This is enhanced if the acquired (or merged) enterprise is not linked to any industrial group, which helps to avoid conflicting interests. This is why the Anglo-Saxon enterprises dominate cross-border mergers and acquisitions in Europe. TNCs may also grow 'internally' through subsidiaries. Mergers and acquisitions are, however, virtually unknown in Japan.

Transnational corporations treat their business in different countries as a single-market operation. Therefore, their financial service is always centralised (or confined to a very limited number of locations) as this may best meet the needs of the corporation as a whole.[82] The financial service represents the backbone of the control of overall corporation operation and efficiency. This is most pronounced in the case where ownership-specific advantages of a TNC are generating high returns. Other operations such as employment, wage and labour relations are always decentralised within TNCs. Labour markets are local and often highly regulated, so decentralisation of these issues is the optimal policy for TNCs. Rapid international mobility and multiplant coordination and control of a growing part of business activities are among the greatest advantages of TNCs over other firms. For example, Nike (an American 'producer' of sports goods) keeps its R&D in Oregon, but subcontracts the actual manufacturing of clothes and shoes in more than 700 factories in 50 countries, principally in Asia.[83] If wages increase in one country, Nike simply moves production to another.

Benefits and Concerns

Estimates of the potential gains from economic integration and operations of TNCs are generally based on the classical assumption that the set of traded goods is both complete and *fixed*. In such a case, the gains from trade and FDI appear to be quite small. Prices in the economy could be changed by government (tariff) intervention, so the quantity of produced and traded goods would change, but the list of the manufactured and traded goods would remain the same.

Suppose now that the list of goods is *expandable*. The neo-Schumpeterian economic model assumes that there are no limits for the introduction of new goods and services in an economy. Let us assume, in addition, that the introduction of a new commodity requires a large amount of fixed costs.[84] This is especially true in the case of the developing countries. Perfect competition and free trade exclude (major) fixed costs from consideration. Once the fixed costs are included in the picture, their presence is often used as a justification for government intervention. When important fixed costs enter the model, a substantial volume of the good needs to be sold in order to make a profit. In such a case, a tariff on the good in question may reduce demand. If this reduction in (international) demand is important, then the commodity may never appear on the market. Losses from such a development or gains in the reverse case may not be easily estimated, at least not for the time being. In any case, if the new goods are left out of consideration, then this kind of analysis can bring substantial underestimates of the welfare cost of trade restrictions (Romer, 1994). These new goods and services are usually brought (to the developing countries) by TNCs.

Integrated countries may obtain certain benefits from the trans-border business activity of firms. These gains, specific to the operation of TNCs within the area, include not only *tangible* resources (for example, transfer of capital on more favourable terms than could be obtained on capital markets, tax receipts, economies of scale, sourcing of inputs from local suppliers and employment) that are provided at lower cost than through the market, but also various *intangible* assets and structures. These intangible assets include new technologies in production, management and control of assets and structures that make the existing resources more productive; positive externalities in production through linkages;[85] international marketing networks that can overcome barriers for exports into foreign markets; new ideas; clustering of related firms; training of labour; and competition. The pecuniary element of these spillovers is quite difficult to measure and could easily escape the attention of a non-economist. Other issues include monopolisation, restrictive business practices, increased sourcing from the parent country with a negative impact on the balance of trade, transfer pricing, transfer of profits abroad and spatial polarisation of economic activity. All these elements affect the spatial allocation of resources in a way that is not always favourable to either the integrated country or the whole group.

Despite a relative academic hostility, public sensitivity, polemics against foreign firms that export home resources and some official anxiety about the operation of TNCs, the situation has changed since the 1980s. All countries in the world welcome TNCs. There is a tendency towards convergence in the national rules regulating FDI. Apart from some screening, these countries provide TNCs with various incentives which include the provision of infrastructure, subsidised loans, tax exemptions, export incentives, opportunities for complete ownership and exemptions from duties. However, these countries have to bear in mind that they compete with other possible locations (and countries), hence there is a tendency towards liberal and converging national systems relating to TNCs. The growing and wide markets in the US and EU are still the most preferred locations for TNCs. If other regions want to attract TNCs, then, ideally, they should have some 'unique selling point' that TNCs cannot find in Europe or North America. Or in China.

Apart from these drawbacks, host countries experience significant gains and thus welcome the arrival and operation of TNCs. These corporations may bring in new technology that is superior to existing domestic technology. This has the effect, in the host country, of increasing output capacity, jobs and tax proceeds, as well as resulting in savings in unemployment benefits and perhaps also creating exports. TNCs enter into growth industries and provide technological expertise that would otherwise be missing. Some TNCs produce brand-name drinks or cigarettes, whose consumption is subject to excise duties. Governments may need or want these proceeds and therefore become an ally of the TNCs. Barriers to entry, such as huge initial capital investment in an industry, can be overcome with TNC input. When the host country's policy is to promote exports or substitute imports, then TNCs may fill part of this role.

One major incentive to persuade TNCs to locate their operations in a country or an integrated region is to offer them a stable macroeconomic environment and a growing market. International economic integration provides certain conditions for this opportunity. Other carrots include tax holidays, subsidies, tariff protection and secure public purchases. In the medium and longer terms, the best policy is to influence the supply of educated local labour (a created factor) as an additional incentive to TNCs to select the country for the location of their operations.

Potential benefits and concerns from the location of TNCs in a national economy may not be measured directly and in the short term. None the less, many of them can be listed as in Table 3.7.

Table 3.7 Potential benefits and concerns that bring TNCs to the target country/location

Benefits	Concerns
Investment may add to the capital formation and production capacity of the country. This may stimulate growth of the target country	• Flow of FDI is volatile • Capital may be raised on the local market so there is no inflow of fresh capital • Mergers and acquisitions relate only to the transfer of ownership. Only greenfield investment adds to the capital formation • If higher productivity of a TNC affiliate is achieved at the expense of lower productivity of domestic firms, there may be no implications for aggregate growth • Most of FDI goes into financial services (the EU case). This does not bring a direct and large-scale improvement in the manufacturing industry in the target country • TNCs may exert strong lobbying pressure and may request incentives such as subsidies and tax holidays. Such benefits and 'location tournaments' among countries may introduce important opportunity costs, unnecessary waste of scarce public funds and serious distortions in the national economy regarding spatial and industrial location of resources. This creates disadvantages to local firms. Incentives to TNCs may be difficult to administer • Foreigners own and control domestic assets and structures. The domestic industry falls into the hands of foreigners. Because of their high international mobility, TNCs may behave in a different way from the domestic firms in identical situations.

Table 3.7 (continued)

Benefits	Concerns
	• TNCs repatriate profits abroad instead of reinvesting them in the location where they were made
TNCs may transfer new technology, knowledge, experience, skills and ideas in production, management and control (human and organisational capital embedded in TNCs). This is also linked with economies of scale and improved efficiency. TNCs may also develop local or transfer innovation activities and certain R&D activities if there is local knowledge, experience, skills and/or subsidies	• TNCs may transfer out-of-date and polluting technologies • TNCs may close local facilities and concentrate R&D activities in their headquarters. The country in which the affiliate is located may be put in a long-term dependency position regarding technology • TNCs may introduce technologies that use more resources that are in short supply (capital) in the target country and relatively less of the locally abundant resource (labour) • TNCs may develop and employ sophisticated technologies in order to prevent easy copying. They may keep this technology internal to the firm to retain as long as possible their position of monopolists in their respective businesses. Spillovers to the local industry do not take place • TNCs pay higher wages in order to attract and keep better workers. The domestic industry is left with other workers. There is no transfer of knowledge to local firms • Excessive internalisation of business may diversify the affiliate into unrelated technologies (outside the core competence). This may reduce the competitiveness of its output
TNCs may create, develop, expand and upgrade spillovers and links with the local economy	• Spillovers and links depend on the technological capacity of the local economy to accept them. The closer the technological capacity of the local firms to a TNC affiliate, the greater the potential spillover • Literature surveys such as Görg and Strobl (2001), Hanson (2001), Blomström and Kokko (2003), Görg and Greenaway (2004), (Lipsey, R.E., 2004) and Rodrik (2004) found only mixed

Table 3.7 (continued)

Benefits	Concerns
	evidence about the existence of positive spillovers on the local economy
TNCs employ local labour and contribute to an increase in the local skills	• A takeover (merger or acquisition) of a local firm transfers only the ownership. There is no immediate change in employment. If the new owner rationalises production, employment may be reduced • A greenfield entry may increase employment, but if the affiliate puts local competitors out of business, the level of employment may change in the target country • TNCs often offer higher wages, hence they attract the best workers and managers. The local firms may remain with a lower quality of labour • TNCs pay higher wages to keep the best workers and managers to prevent the leakage of knowledge to the local economy • Local trade unions may request higher wages throughout the economy. These increases may be over and above productivity. This may jeopardise the competitiveness of the country's output • TNCs may use technologies that employ factors that are in short supply locally (capital) • If labour unions demand 'too much', a TNC may threaten to move its affiliate elsewhere
TNCs may stimulate competition and force local competitors and suppliers to upgrade their business	• Restrictive business practices such as monopolisation of the market and predatory and transfer pricing may hamper the expansion of existing and development of new local firms • TNCs may crowd out local firms from the local capital market • Various public concessions and subsidies offered only to TNCs create distortions that damage local firms • Unethical and criminal practices (for example, bribery, 'campaign contributions',

Table 3.7 (continued)

Benefits	Concerns
	improper accounting, false billings and statements) may create huge corporate failures and scandals such as Enron (2002) in the US or Parmalat (2003) in Italy with business consequences that reverberate throughout the world
TNCs offer access to a wide international manufacturing, marketing and trade network. They bring the target country into this well-established network that may stimulate exports. More than a third of world trade today is within the same company. Some of these important 'internal' TNC markets may be infiltrated only through affiliates	• Affiliates may produce only for the local market at a suboptimal scale of production • Affiliates do not buy inputs in the local market, but import them from other affiliates. This may increase imports (rather than exports). Transfer pricing may jeopardise the balance of payments position
TNCs pay taxes and contribute to the tax revenue in the host country	• Transfer pricing may diminish local tax receipts • Tax avoidance may do the same • Various tax incentives may degrade the effect of taxes collected

National and International Regulation

The basis of the OECD Declaration on International Investment and Multinational Enterprises (1976) and the OECD Guidelines for Multinational Enterprises (1986) (both revised in 2000) is the principle of national treatment of foreign companies. This principle means that, provided national security is not jeopardised, TNCs have the same rights and obligations as domestic companies in similar situations. This does not put all foreign suppliers on an equal footing in the importing country market (which is what the MFN clause does); rather it refers to the treatment of foreign suppliers in comparison with domestic ones.

Resource-rich[86] and prosperous countries such as Canada may exercise the greatest leverage on TNCs. Canada's experience is one of the most interesting examples of control of TNCs. It is relevant, as a significant part of the economic integration between Canada and the US has an FDI dimension.

Both Canada and the US are signatories to the OECD Declaration. In 1973, a few years before this declaration was delivered, Canada established the Foreign Investment Review Agency (FIRA) to survey inward FDI. This move was a reaction to a relatively large share of foreign ownership of Canadian industry. One could argue that much of the foreign ownership of the host-country industry can be attributed to the level of the host country's tariffs, taxes, subsidies and other incentives. TNCs overcome tariff obstacles by locating 'tariff factories' in the host country. FIRA's intention was not to stop FDI in Canada, but rather to allow it only if it resulted in beneficial effects to Canada. The criterion upon which FIRA evaluated both the takeovers of existing Canadian firms and the establishment of new businesses included expanded exports, use of Canadian resources, increase in investment, employment and productivity, as well as compatibility with the national industrial and other economic policies.

FIRA's rejection rate of 20 per cent was an important barrier for certain investors and was high compared with rates of some 1 per cent in other countries that used a similar screening process (Lipsey, 1985, p. 101). This caused many firms to withdraw their requests in order to avoid uncertain and costly application procedures, while other firms that might have been potential investors have not even applied. At the beginning of the 1980s, FIRA's rejection rate was reduced. The Conservative government transformed FIRA from a nationalistic authority aimed at increasing Canadian ownership in domestic industry into an organisation for the attraction of FDI and in 1984 renamed it Investment Canada. The fear of too much foreign capital had given way to a fear of too little (Lipsey and Smith, 1986, p. 53).

Access to growing national and international markets and a stable macroeconomic environment are major incentives for locating of FDI in some geographical areas. However, a stable, predictable and transparent legal situation also encourages FDI as it lowers risk and potentially increases profits. There are global rules that regulate international trade in goods (WTO), but as yet there are no such rules regarding FDI. A complex set of bilateral[87] and some regional treaties regulate FDI, but coverage of these rules is not complete. In addition, many governments offer incentives to attract FDI. Diversity in the treatment of FDI in bilateral deals and the possibility of a sudden reversal in the liberalisation trend in times of crisis (Asia 1997–98) create a need for a multilateral treaty. This is in theory. In practice, Mody (2004, p. 1211) gave evidence that in the 1982–92 period, US TNCs carried out less (not more) FDI in countries with which the US had recently concluded a bilateral investment treaty. Tax treaties reduce chances for tax evasion and transfer pricing. Where there are no such treaties, TNCs profit from loopholes in foreign tax systems and various concessions that are offered to their own advantage.

The OECD drafted a Multilateral Agreement on Investment (MAI) with the aim of providing a sound legal environment, including open markets, based on the principle of non-discrimination between domestic and foreign investors. In addition, there would be instruments for dispute settlement among all involved parties (various combinations of public and private players) and enforcement of decisions.

In spite of grand expectations, the MAI project got into serious trouble and was shelved in 1998. The critics argued that the exclusive OECD 'club' of then 29 countries did not take into account the needs of the developing countries. Another criticism was that the MAI gave excessive power to TNCs regarding protection of the investment, transfer of funds, right of establishment and MFN treatment. These criticisms are relevant if one bears in mind that India still remembers the moment when the first ships of the East India Company arrived at the port of Surat. The company came to India as a trader in 1608 and ended up virtually owning it.

The national legal system that regulates FDI in most OECD countries is well developed. Hence, the MAI was of little real significance for these developed countries, even though most of the FDI activity in the world is within the OECD group. The drafters' intention was to lure the emerging players in the FDI flows to join the agreement. However, few developing countries were ready and willing to sign a deal that they did not shape (exchanging concessions such as domestic market opening for FDI in return for the opening of OECD markets for agricultural goods and migration of labour). Some critics saw the MAI as a tool of neo-colonialism. However, the work on the MAI was not in vain since it raised an important issue. Perhaps it will have better luck in the future – possibly within the WTO, which has a wider membership (about 150 countries), dispute settlement instruments and experience in handling difficult negotiations.

3.3.4 INTERVENTION

If market imperfections permit rents (above-average profits), then the governments of the integrated countries may wish to intervene. The larger market of an integrated area may be better able to absorb the cost of intervention owing to the spread of such costs than would be the case for individual countries acting alone. For instance, a simplified example based on the metaphor of a prisoner's dilemma is presented in Table 3.8.

Suppose that there are just two firms capable of producing aircraft: British Aerospace in Britain and Aérospatiale in France. Assume also that,

Table 3.8 Profit in the aircraft industry without intervention

Britain / France	Production	No production
Production	−3; −3	10; 0
No production	0; 10	0; 0

because of sunk costs, R&D and economies of scale, only one firm can produce aircraft efficiently (profit-wise) within the EU and that public authorities prefer to purchase domestically made goods. The figures in Table 3.8 then show the profit of the two firms. If there is no intervention by the government, the firm that moves first captures the market and makes a profit. If both produce, both lose; if neither produces, there is neither gain nor loss. If only one country has the ability to produce aircraft, the government of the other may then try to persuade a foreign TNC to locate its production within the confines of its borders, thus putting the potential competitor from the partner country out of business. This possibility for a geographical location of production is a strong case for a joint treatment of TNCs by the integration groups.

Now suppose that there is no domestic producer of aircraft in Britain and that the domestic government decides that it may be sensible to have aircraft production located at home and to move first to strategically and irreversibly pre-empt any other player.[88] The reasons may include employment, export and prestige, but also, and more importantly, various externalities, including obtaining the leading edge in one of the high-technology industries and also national pride. Some early movers sustain their position for decades. For example, Procter & Gamble, Unilever and Colgate have been international leaders in washing powder production since the 1930s. With this in mind, the government decides to invite Boeing to come and locate its production in Britain. As bait, it offers various subsidies and protection to capture the aircraft market in the integration arrangement with France. The major reason for the subsidy is not simply to increase export sales, but rather to improve the terms of trade and secure rents for the home firm, a cluster of related domestic enterprises and, finally, for the country itself. Of course, such a policy may have a significant balance of payments effect in the medium and long terms. Hence, the structure of markets and the operations of TNCs matter for the spatial distribution of production.

The neo-classical model deals with the given and perfect resources and capabilities, whereas the new theory studies market imperfections, multiple equilibria, path dependence and government intervention in a dynamic set-up. This new approach tries to suppress market constraints and to push

Table 3.9 Profit in the aircraft industry with intervention

France \ Britain	Production	No production
Production	−3; 2	10; 0
No production	0; 15	0; 0

economic frontiers outwards. It considers economies of scale, externalities, differentiated products, changing technology and FDI. These are all features of modern manufacturing. The new theory questions the proposition that free markets may successfully take advantage of the potential benefits in the new situation. Such an approach is different from the neo-classical one, in which TNCs were, by definition, excluded from consideration. The assumption in free markets is that there are no grounds for trans-border business activities as the spatial and sectoral allocation of resources is perfect and full (first-best solution). The new theory explains why countries can trade not only when their resource endowments and production capabilities are *different*, as in the neo-classical situation, but also when their resource endowment and production capabilities are *identical*. The case in question is the intra-industry trade (that is, intra-EU trade) in cars.

One thing, however, ought to be clear from the outset. The new theory does not replace the neo-classical one. It considers only market imperfections that can be mitigated by intervention, which may introduce an adjustment instrument into an already highly imperfect situation. Table 3.9 shows what would happen to the profits of the two aircraft producers if the British government subsidised its (foreign owned/controlled) firm with monetary units that equal 5. If the firm located in Britain decides to produce, it will always have an advantage over its non-subsidised French rival.

When market imperfections exist, the British government can influence the geography of production (spatial location of resources and specialisation). None the less, if the choice of national champions is to be a good one, the government should be competent and well informed, otherwise the result may be costly commercial failures, such as the Franco-British Concorde project or computers in France. Many governments in east Asia have intervened successfully in their economies. However, governments in many east European and developing countries have intervened much more, and yet have singularly failed to achieve the economic successes seen in east Asia. In any case, intervention is facilitated when the number of potentially competing firms is small and production output is standardised.

Engineered comparative advantages of countries and firms are becoming more important in modern footloose industries and are tending to erode inherited comparative advantages. For example, trade within the EU is to a large extent of an intra-industry character. It is driven much more by economies of scale than by the 'classic' comparative advantages of those countries. If pushed to the limit, a national reaction to a monopoly in a foreign country is the creation of a national monopoly. That is fighting fire with fire (Curzon Price, 1993, p. 394).

In order to intervene/subsidise in an intelligent way, governments need a great deal of information that is quite costly to obtain: information not only about current and potential future technology and demand, but also about the strategies of other governments and TNCs. If they choose wisely, strategic policy can be a superb device. In practice, a subsidy in one country may provoke retaliation in another in the form of a subsidy or a counter-balancing duty. The retaliation and counter-retaliation cycle makes everyone worse off. Integration may offer some advantages to developing countries in such a situation. It may inspire these countries to negotiate the distribution of strategic industries within the area or attract TNCs in order to maximise positive externalities and reduce unnecessary subsidies. The basic argument for the government's involvement may be that without intervention in the area, and owing to imperfections, there may be *underinvestment* in a strategic industry. If, however, intervention is not well managed, *overinvestment* may be the consequence.

The simple model of strategic investment, industrial and trade policy is based on the expectation that the subsidised home production of a tradable good or service shifts monopoly profits (rents) to the home country and to the firms owned/controlled by it. These profits should be over and above the cost of the subsidy. If the domestic firms are affiliates of foreign TNCs, then the effect on the home country's welfare may be uncertain. No matter what the circumstances are, the expectation that profit shifting may enhance the home country's welfare holds only when foreign countries do not retaliate against domestic subsidies. A cycle of retaliation and counter-retaliation would make everyone worse off. In addition, when there is a liberal treatment of FDI, bilateral trade deficits may give off misleading signals. For example, if Japan (or any other country) invests in China in order to take advantage of relatively low labour costs and to export output to the US, the bilateral deficit in trade between the US and Japan may shrink, but the overall US trade deficit may increase because of extra US imports from China.

Governments need to bear in mind that general favours (subsidies) handed out to domestic firms may trickle down to foreign beneficiaries located within the confines of the jurisdiction of the government. A more effective policy may be to use subsidies to develop and upgrade the skills of domestic human capital as footloose capital is increasingly attracted by, among other factors, created factors such as the local availability of skilled, highly trained and experienced labour and management.

In advanced and integrated countries such as the US, the constituent parts may compete with one another by offering substantial grants (and grant equivalents) in order to attract world-scale manufacturing projects. The size of these grants is increasing. In 1984, Michigan offered state and local incentives worth $120 million (equivalent to $14 000 per job) to attract Mazda; in 1986, Indiana offered $110 million ($51 000 per job) to Subaru-Isuzu; in 1989, Kentucky offered $325 million ($108 000 per job) to Toyota (UNCTC, 1991a, pp. 73–4); in 1983, Alabama gave $252 million ($168 000 per job) to Mercedes-Benz; and North Carolina handed out $130 million ($108 000 per job) to BMW. In spite of strict rules of competition, countries in the EU are sometimes allowed to dispense 'incentives' to TNCs to settle within their confines. Britain gave $89 million ($29 675 per job) to Samsung in 1994, while France granted $111 million ($56 923 per job) to Mercedes-Benz and Swatch in 1995 (UNCTAD, 1995a, p. 18). In 1996, Dow Chemicals received a subsidy of $6.8 billion for an investment in the petrochemical industry in Germany ($3.4 million per job), and in 2000, Alabama gave an incentive package worth $158 million to Honda to locate a $400 million assembly plant that would employ 1500 workers ($105 333 per job) (UNCTAD, 2002, pp. 204–5). These kinds of subsidies and participation in 'location tournaments' are well beyond the financial capabilities of developing countries.

The self-reinforcing aspect of FDI begins to operate only after a certain level of development. The developing countries 'which are already doing well in these categories do not need location tournaments. The others are not likely to profit from them' (Wheeler and Mody, 1992, p. 72). The ability of the developing world to attract FDI depends on many factors that these countries cannot control. There are, however, certain elements that can be controlled by the developing countries. These countries need to try to stabilise their macroeconomic and political situation, improve the quality and quantity of human capital and infrastructure, liberalise trade and investment policies, actively promote their advantages to the business community and study potentials for integration or preferential trade with other (neighbouring) countries. Such a policy approach would stimulate domestic private investment and growth. It could also be argued that they might wish to pursue such policies even if they had little effect on FDI.

In an examination of annual FDI flows (1960–90) towards the major integration groups in the developing world, Jovanović (1995) found no difference in FDI flows before and after the creation of the integration group. The national economic (and political) situation played a much more important role for the attraction of FDI than did participation in the integration deal. This conclusion was later reconfirmed by Blomström and Kokko (1997, p. 39). In considering the situation in Ireland, it was found that 'recent FDI growth has taken place at a time when the relative value of Ireland's incentives has been eroded. This erosion stems both from domestic reductions in incentives and from the increasing use of regional incentives elsewhere in the EU. This may suggest that incentives are necessary, but not sufficient to attract internationally mobile investment' (Braunerhjelm et al., 2000, p. 85).

3.3.5 TRANSNATIONAL CORPORATIONS AND INTERNATIONAL ECONOMIC INTEGRATION

Many business activities entail high costs, uncertainties and risk as they face rapid changes in technology, demand and needs, so the operation of such activities in relatively small markets may not be commercially viable from an efficiency point of view. Worldwide free trade may not be achieved in the short or medium term (if ever), so international economic integration or preferential trade may be an attractive second-best policy option. Such integration, although to an extent an inward-looking strategy, widens/pools the markets of the participating countries. Larger and growing markets provide greater confidence than relatively smaller ones to both domestic and foreign investors.

Domestic markets in most countries are so small that even a high degree of protection of growth-propelling manufacturing industries and services aimed at supplying the local market may not be viable in terms of efficient employment of resources. By supplying a larger market provided by the integration arrangement, participating countries may increase production, capacity utilisation, employment and investment; reduce vulnerability to external shocks; capture economies of scale; improve bargaining positions in international markets; and increase average standards of living. These results should be viewed in comparison with the situation in which all countries act alone under heavy domestic protection.

The production and distribution of goods and services in an integrated area is not the sole prerogative of domestic firms, but can also be carried out by TNCs and their affiliates. This consideration adds an extra element to the theoretical analysis that brings it closer to the real world, but it also introduces some analytical drawbacks to the pure and simple theoretical models. In an early work, Mundell (1957) argued that, within the Heckscher–Ohlin theoretical model, trade in goods and trade in factors may substitute for each other. Markusen (1983) has shown that the operations of TNCs (flow of factors) are complementary to international trade, rather than substitutes, and that Mundell's proposition may describe only a special case.

Foreign direct investment is the result of market imperfections, as in a free trade situation the spatial and sector-wise allocation of resources is perfect and there are no grounds for FDI. None the less, TNCs are a source of powerful internal enterprise-created links that may contribute to the integration of national economies. Countries should aim to set realistic objectives in relation to integration or preferential trade: to determine how TNCs fit into the picture, to structure their entry, operation and exit and to negotiate deals. In addition, if the integrated countries master the production of goods and services to such an extent that it increases their international competitiveness, then firms within the area may expand abroad and themselves become TNCs. They may increase the employment of home resources and enter new markets beyond the confines of the market of the integrated area.

Suppose that a monopolist TNC exports a good to a group of integrated countries protected by a common binding quota. If the TNC also decides to locate within the integrated area, it may choose to produce there any quantity of the good it wishes. In such a case, the integration scheme (as a whole, but not necessarily every part of it) may benefit significantly as there is additional employment of domestic factors and domestic consumers also gain because the price of the good may fall. In another case, if local firms are competing with a TNC in the home market, the location of the TNC within the integrated area may benefit both consumers (price falls) and resource utilisation as domestic firms must become more competitive if they want to remain in business. If such a process works well, then there is no justification for restrictions on the operation of foreign TNCs in an integrated area (be it in the developed or developing world).

An arrangement that integrates countries may improve the terms of trade of the group with the rest of the world. If the price of a good or service that is imported to the group falls after integration, then such an arrangement increases the rents of the scheme to the detriment of those previously made by foreign firms. Suppose that country A and country B integrate. If a TNC outside the integration scheme that produces good X is located in country B prior to integration and continues to operate there after the regional arrangement is formed, then the price of good X may fall as a result of either competition in the integrated market or the increased efficiency that comes from economies of scale. If country A starts importing good X from country B, then country A experiences other benefits in addition to the stimulation of trade. The rents of the TNC dwindle, whereas the surplus of country A's consumers rises. In this case country A experiences the so-called 'foreign profit diversion' effect. If another TNC in country A were to produce good Y, which is then exported to the partner country B after integration, country A experiences the opposite effect of 'foreign profit creation' (Tironi, 1982, pp. 155–6).

Foreign profit creation/diversion effects are of vital importance to integration schemes whose economic structures are dominated or influenced by TNCs. This may be the case in countries that are involved in the 'globalisation' of international business, as well as in many developing countries. If such countries integrate, then TNCs are mostly interested in favourable foreign profit creation effects. Consider two countries contemplating integration, each of which has in its market a TNC that manufactures the same undifferentiated good. If the leverage of the two TNCs on decision making is significant in the two countries, then the TNCs may collude and undermine the integration efforts.

Governments usually respect the opinions of the business community, especially if the business has a significant effect on the welfare of the country. Hence, in some cases, TNCs may even play off one government against another and continue with an inefficient (from a resource allocation point of view) but, for them, profitable production.[89] This is one reason why the integration arrangements of developing countries may include provisions that refer to TNCs. None the less, the policy of an integrated area towards TNCs depends on the basic objectives of the group. If the basic objective of the group is an increase in *employment*, then ownership of the firms is irrelevant. FDI is, after all, an investment. If the goal of the group is to *shift rents* towards the integrated countries, then it matters who is the owner of the manufacturing and services production and marketing units.[90] In reality, however, governments are not totally indifferent to who owns 'national' assets and structures.

If the integrated market of the (developing) countries is still small enough for the establishment of a cluster of related suppliers, then the major beneficiaries may be TNCs that assemble goods and/or perform only limited (usually final) manufacturing operations. Such a tendency may be enhanced when the integrated countries have relaxed rules of origin for goods that qualify for liberal treatment in internal trade. Although the internal trade of the group increases, so does the extra-group import content of the traded goods. Broad regional deepening of production linkages does not take place. Estimates of the potential increase in trade should refer to the dual pattern of trade (imports of components from abroad and export of finalised goods within the group) and discount the gross increase in internal trade of the region. Instead of the expected relative reduction in the dependency on external markets, integration on such terms may have the completely opposite effect.

The governments of potential host countries may compete with one another in offering subsidies to TNCs to entice them to invest and locate in their country. In this game, the principal winners may be the TNCs themselves as their bargaining power is enhanced. One outcome may be that TNCs locate in more than one country, supply the local protected market and engage in parallel production on a scale that is suboptimal from a resource allocation point of view, while these countries lose interest in the integration process. Such a strategy requires a common competition policy, a joint industrialisation programme and coordinated treatment of TNCs by countries in the group, otherwise the links with the suppliers from the local economy and integration partner country may be superficial. Integration may lead to a production structure that is dominated by firms alien to the integrated group and in which potentially positive absorption and spread of changes in the market (created by the involvement of TNCs) by the local enterprises fails to take place.

Transnational corporations have an interest in promoting integration among developing countries with small markets, but only in countries where they have not been involved before integration. In medium-sized and large developing countries, the position of TNCs may be quite different. TNCs may in fact attempt to prevent integration among countries of this size. The primary concern of TNCs may not be efficiency in production, but rather the likely reactions of other TNCs, as well as the avoidance of conflicts (UNCTAD, 1983, p. 12).

3.3.6 EUROPEAN UNION

Issues

Free capital mobility largely results in the loss of national monetary independence. For example, all else being equal, an increase in a member country's interest rate relative to those in the outside world, intended to slow down the economy and curb inflation, would have the result of increasing the domestic money supply. Many TNCs would invest funds in that country in order to profit from higher rates of interest. The reverse situation, of a country lowering its interest rates with the intention of stimulating economic activity by cheap loans, would lead to a decrease in available funds as TNCs would transfer financial resources to countries with higher rates of interest (Panić, 1991, p. 212). It is unlikely that national firms would be able to influence exchange rate policy to the same degree and as fast as TNCs. However, this does not mean that TNCs render government policies irrelevant. The governments of large countries still have significant autonomy to pursue policies in the national interest for two reasons. First, they have more self-sufficient economies than small countries and, second, the size of their market is such that TNCs do not want to be excluded from it. Hence, TNCs will be careful not to irritate the host government (Panić, 1998, pp. 273–4).

The establishment of the European Economic Community, as phase 1 in the integration process, stimulated TNCs from the US to invest and later expand activities in this region during the 1960s and 1970s. The implementation of the Single Market Programme (phase 2) and the completion of the Single European Market was expected to increase investment of Japanese TNCs in the EU. However, the realisation of this expectation also depended, in part, on the evolution of the tariffs and NTBs in the EU. The establishment of the eurozone in 1999 as phase 3 may reinforce the attractiveness of the EU as a location for FDI. This expectation was initially supported by a relative decline in the value of the euro relative to the dollar in the first year of its operation and the start of the Lisbon Agenda plan.

While phase 1 eliminated (among other things) tariffs on internal trade, the objective of phase 2 was to eliminate NTBs on internal trade, which was expected to increase efficiency of production (rationalised investments), reduce transaction costs, increase competition and demand and harmonise standards. This required some adjustments of internal production in the EU. The rationale for the existence of 'tariff factories' was removed. Thus, investment in production that avoided internal EU barriers was significantly reduced or even eliminated.

Phase 2 was expected to increase the operation and investment of TNCs originating in the EU, as well as cooperative agreements and strategic alliances between them. An additional effect would be investment creation. In the longer term, it was thought that European TNCs could become like those in the US and take full advantage of economies of scale. Europeans generally have more demanding and sophisticated tastes than American consumers, and demand differentiated goods (one need go no further than Italy for examples of this behaviour). Hence, large-scale production of homogenised goods, as occurs in the US, has never been expected in the EU.

The objective of phase 3 is to 'level the monetary playing field' for the countries that take part in the eurozone and to remove all exchange rate risks that jeopardise competition, trade and investment. Eastern enlargement (phase 4) widened the EU market to cover 25 countries and potentially made the EU a more attractive location for FDI.

Foreign TNCs initially feared that the EU would create a 'Fortress Europe' whose aim would be to protect the home market through the Single Market Programme. Some of them rushed to establish themselves in the EU before the potential 'discrimination' took place. Target enterprises in the EU became overvalued to the extent that other locations, most notably in the US, began to appear more attractive. Despite this, the EU continued to be an interesting location for FDI, as foreign TNCs were also hoping to enter into strategic alliances with EU firms.

Fragmentation of production in various EU countries had as its result a replication of various group functions. The primary impact of the Single European Market on TNCs located in the EU was through increased competition. TNCs were led to coordinate production in their subsidiaries in order to profit from economies of scale. Horizontally integrated TNCs such as 3M responded to the deepening of integration in the EU by specialisation of production in their plants. 'Post-it' notes are made in its British plant, while Scotch tape is produced in its German unit. Previously, 3M produced a wide range of 'sticky' goods in each country in order to serve predominantly the local market. Vertically integrated TNCs such as Ford responded to the new opportunities by vertical specialisation. Differentials and gearboxes are produced in France, while engines are made in Spain. A further restructuring of the company, announced in 2000, ended production in Belarus, Poland and Portugal, and concentrated output in Germany, Spain and Belgium.[91] In addition, there emerged a special kind of relation among the competing firms. A removal of NTBs on internal trade and liberalisation of public procurement 'forced' inter-firm specialisation in similar goods. For example, ICI (Britain) specialised in marine, decorative and industrial paints, while BASF (Germany) did the same in automobile paints (Dunning, 1994a, pp. 296–7).

In spite of the potentials for the concentration of production that were provided by the Single European Market, the Japanese (and the US) car-producing TNCs continue to broaden locations for production in the EU, rather than simply concentrate production to employ economies of scale (Ando, 1998, p. 23). Although the Japanese began by assembling cars in Britain, they spread their new production activities elsewhere in the EU (Toyota plant in France).

Evolution

The Defense Production Act (1950) in the US and its amended Section 721, known as the Exxon-Florio amendment (1988), give the US president the right to block mergers, acquisitions or takeovers of domestic firms by foreign TNCs when such action is likely to jeopardise national security. If a merger, acquisition or takeover has security implications, it has to be notified for clearance with the Committee on Foreign Investment in the United States (CFIUS) which applies the Exxon-Florio provisions.

Japan has few formal barriers to inward FDI. None the less, the real obstacles to FDI in Japan are not found in the legal sphere. They exist as a cost of 'doing business in Japan', such as close and strong informal links among businesses, tight labour markets, language barriers and difficulties in obtaining the necessary data.

Unlike the US, the EU does not have a common policy regarding FDI. Only Article 43 of the Treaty of Rome gives the right of establishment to businesses throughout the EU for the nationals of any member state. Of course, articles that refer to the issues that include competition, taxation, environment, industry and social issues also refer to FDI. In any case, the EU has the lowest barriers in the industrialised world to inward FDI (OECD, 2003b, p. 169). The obstacles mainly included personnel restrictions, local content requirements and government procurement.

The impact of the creation of the EU on the attraction of FDI from the US was at the centre of early studies of the relationship between integration (or, as it was then called, 'tariff discrimination' introduced by the EU and EFTA) and FDI. The expectation was that the spatial location of FDI would be influenced by integration, and in particular that the establishment of the EU would lure TNCs there. Scaperlanda (1967, p. 26), in examining the American FDI trend in Europe between 1951 and 1964, found that the formation of the EU(6) did not attract a large share of American FDI. FDI from the US to the EU(6) since 1958 has amounted to \$3.5 billion, compared with \$4 billion to non-EU European countries over the same period. Factors such as familiarity with the country in which the investment was to be located, differences in the application of technology and the financial liquidity to fund foreign investment had a greater effect on the spatial distribution of FDI than the creation of the EU(6). In addition, the American TNCs were more interested in the French market than in the EU(6).

Instead of calculating the FDI trend for the whole 1951–64 period, merging 'before' and 'after' EU effects (as did Scaperlanda) and masking investment shifts rather than revealing them, Wallis (1968) divided the period of analysis into two subperiods. The share of the American FDI in the EU(6) moved along a continuous and increasing path in the 1951–64 period with a kink in 1958. Before 1958, the EU(6) share increased by 0.7 per cent a year, whereas after 1958 the average annual increase was 2.7 per cent. An increase in the US FDI in Europe was also observed in the following way: 'Fifteen years from now it is quite possible that the world's third largest industrial power, just after the United States and Russia, will not be Europe, but *American industry in Europe*. Already, in the ninth year of the Common Market, this European market is basically American in organisation' (Servan-Schreiber, 1969, p. 3; original emphasis).

D'Arge (1969, 1971a, 1971b) attempted to determine the impact of European integration on American FDI in the EU and EFTA. The effect of the formation of a trading bloc on the location of FDI may follow three patterns:

- a one-off (intercept) shift in trend;
- a gradual increase in trend (slope shift); or
- a combination of the other two.

The data showed that, in the case of EFTA, there was a positive intercept shift (a one-off effect), while in the period following the creation of the EU(6) there was a combination of shifts in both slope and intercept.

Scaperlanda and Reiling (1971) found that European integration had no significant effect on US FDI flows in this region: FDI flows to the EU(6) and EFTA were similar after 1959, although it had been expected that the EU would attract more FDI than EFTA did. However, it is important to remember that at that time the major location for the American FDI in Europe was the UK, which was a member of EFTA, but not the EU(6). Thus, early studies of the impact of integration on FDI do not give a clear picture of the effect of integration on FDI.

Clarification of the situation came later with evidence that, in the case of American FDI in the EU(6), size and growth of the market played an important role (Goldberg, 1972, p. 692; Scaperlanda and Balough, 1983, p. 389). However, Culem (1988) argued that FDI is not in direct competition with domestic investments. A foreign country may be desirable in its own right because it has a specific factor (not available at home) that is necessary for the production process, or because an external outpost may be better placed to monitor developments in foreign markets or because the foreign government has exerted political pressure to locate there. Culem found that 'the size of the European market does not appear to exert any attraction on U.S. direct investments' (p. 900).

Econometric modelling of FDI is a formidable task as FDI flow is a cyclical phenomenon, while determinants are complex, changeable over time and space, and not always measurable. The results of models depend greatly on the assumptions made, so the conclusions can only be tentative. None the less, there is general support for the hypothesis that tariff discrimination, regionalism and integration influence FDI to some extent. However, this cannot be translated into a statement that an *x* per cent change in tariffs will induce a *y* per cent change in FDI. Therefore, strong policy recommendations on the basis of such models would be reckless (Lunn, 1980, p. 99).

Recent studies report that the net effect of integration has been to increase both internal EU and third-country investment in the EU. The elimination of import duties on internal EU trade encouraged non-EU investors to locate in the EU (Dunning and Robson, 1987, p. 113), while the elimination of NTBs (Single Market Programme) and widening of the internal market prompted both EU and third-country TNCs to invest.[92] An increase in FDI activity following the start of the Single Market Programme in 1985 has been confirmed not only by Eurostat statistics but also by several other studies.[93]

The Single Market Programme prompted TNCs to rationalise their operations in the EU. Hence, the absence of any reference to TNCs in the influential official reports generated by the Single European Act, such as Emerson et al. (1988) and Cecchini (1988), comes as a surprise. The assumption in those reports seems to be that international specialisation and trade is carried out by firms whose operational facilities are confined to a single country. The growth and predominance of TNCs in most areas of economic activity made this kind of analysis inappropriate (Panić, 1991, p. 204).

Britain has always been a relatively attractive location for TNCs, although its economic performance relative to other EU major economies has at certain times been poor. What is the reason for this interest? Regional incentives are no more generous there than in the rest of the EU.[94] One reason for its appeal that is often cited is the commonality of the English language, although large TNCs are able to afford to ease and overcome the language barrier.[95] Another reason that is sometimes put forward is that a presence in Britain can serve as a springboard to the rest of the EU, but this could equally apply to other EU member states. Britain scores well in the following essentials:

- the labour force can be highly competent and experienced, but relatively low paid (compared with other major EU countries, in particular during periods when the pound is low as was the case at the end of the 1970s) and because of relatively low add-on costs (social charges);
- a relatively large and open domestic market;
- a favourable industrial and educational infrastructure;
- social and political stability; and
- once clusters of TNCs were established, they started to act as a magnet for other TNCs to locate in Britain ('snowball effect').

Japanese TNCs have not been reluctant to invest in Britain. However, they prefer to build new factories in rural areas rather than take over existing plants. They also prefer takeovers to joint ventures. In industries in which Japanese TNCs have a clear comparative advantage, 'greenfield' entry is their preferred way to locate. One advantage of this is that previous managerial habits and labour relations are not inherited. In addition, such sites are often in depressed areas which attract subsidies. Greenfield locations enable Japanese TNCs to introduce their own technology, work practices and management style, with high productivity (Ford and Strange, 1999, p. 124). In Britain, Japanese TNCs were not always attracted to existing clusters, but created new ones. In industries where their comparative advantage is weaker, Japanese TNCs are more likely to form alliances and joint ventures.

In the US, Japanese investors tend to prefer locations (states) where labour unionisation is low. This has less to do with saving on labour costs and more to do with the Japanese organisation of production. Japanese manufacturing plants often require fewer job categories than is the case in their American counterparts. Labour unions are perceived as impediments to flexible production practices. In some cases, Japanese TNCs prefer to locate in rural areas as they mistrust urban workers because they perceive that these workers have developed 'bad work habits' and because they have greater mobility (Woodward, 1992, pp. 696–9). In addition, Japanese TNCs in the car industry offer relatively high wages in order to ensure the development of higher levels of human capital and workforce stability. This is in sharp contrast to the hypothesis in the earlier literature that TNCs predominantly seek locations for their investment in the areas where they can profit from low wage costs (Smith and Florida, 1994, pp. 29–30, 39).

Yamawaki (1993, pp. 19–20) argued that the decision about the location of production depends not only on factor costs, but also on comparative advantage in technology in the target country. A Japanese TNC from a particular industry invests in the country that already has a comparative advantage in the same industry over its counterparts in the EU partner countries.

Spatial choice of location of Japanese TNCs has the following policy implications for the countries that consider the location of these TNCs as an astute policy choice (Ford and Strange, 1999, pp. 133–4):

- Japanese TNCs are attracted to areas with a cluster of manufacturing industries in which they operate and where there exists a high density of previous Japanese FDI.
- A highly educated and innovative workforce attracts Japanese TNCs, with consequent policy implications for education and R&D.
- Labour market flexibility and a low level of labour unionisation are preferred by the Japanese TNCs. This may be a stimulus to labour market reform.
- Relatively low wages are also an attractive factor for Japanese TNCs.

Flow of Foreign Direct Investment

Table 3.10 summarises internal EU FDI outflows per investor country during the 1992–2003 period. EU(15) FDI outflows were steadily increasing from €48 billion in 1992 to a peak of €692 billion in 2000. As was the case with the global world FDI flows, owing to the economic slowdown internal FDI flows declined to €258 billion in 2003. The principal intra-EU investors were Germany, Belgium/Luxembourg,[96] France, the Netherlands and Britain.

The destination of internal EU FDI flows is given in Table 3.11. These flows were concentrated in Britain, Belgium/Luxembourg (BLEU), France, Germany, Ireland, the Netherlands, Spain and Sweden. Apart from Ireland and Spain, these countries were at the same time major internal investors in the EU. Internal flows of FDI in the EU, therefore, suggest a trend towards agglomeration. The central and east European member countries exhibit a growing attraction as locations for FDI, especially following favourable trade and cooperation, as well as serious chances that they would join the EU.

Before the start of the Single Market Programme, endogenous EU firms generally had a primarily national orientation, whereas foreign-owned TNCs (mainly American) had a pan-European business perspective. The removal of NTBs that came with the Single Market Programme was, among other things, aimed at addressing this disequilibrium in European business operations. It had an obvious and positive impact on internal FDI flows from 1985. Save for 1997–98, EU internal FDI flows were more important than outflows from the EU to third countries. Another interesting observation is that the southern countries such as Greece and Portugal were initially left out of the internal EU flows of FDI, but slowly began to catch up in the course of the 1990s.

The EU countries were investing not only within their group, but also outside of it. Data on external EU FDI outflows are given in Table 3.12. The US and EFTA countries have always been both major locations (targets) for FDI from the EU and, at the same time, major sources of FDI coming into the EU (Table 3.13). This evidence supports arguments about agglomeration tendencies in FDI.

In general terms, the EU, together with the US, was the major target for the location of FDI from third countries. The principal foreign (third-country) investor in the EU was the US followed at a distance by EFTA. Japan also invested in the EU, but its investment was much less than FDI by EFTA. Yamada and Yamada (1996) reported that the principal goal of Japanese investors in the EU was to avoid emerging protectionism. The EU candidate countries invested modestly in the EU, predominantly in trade-related services.

Earlier data on FDI flows demonstrate that intra-EU FDI flows became very important from 1989. Previously, European integration was only one factor that influenced FDI flows from the EU countries within and out of the EU. While the liberalisation of internal EU trade had a strong impact on trade integration, a study of FDI flows shows that before 1989 and during 1997–98, integration was stronger on the global plane than within the EU.

Thomsen and Nicolaides (1991, p. 103) argued that the Single Market Programme had its greatest influence not on the quantity of FDI in that period in the EU, but rather on its timing. Such an argument should be viewed with caution. The Single Market Programme has the potential to affect (enhance) the long-term growth prospects of the EU. In addition, the programme changed the EU business regime and created advantages additional to the already existing EU specific locational advantages. Hence, the long-term level of inward FDI in the EU is higher than it would have been otherwise (European Commission, 1998, p. 96).

It has already been mentioned that there was a degree of concentration of FDI in the 'core' EU countries. This was in spite of the fact that these countries did not (always) have the highest rates of growth. Greece, Ireland and Portugal had higher rates of growth than Britain. However, in spite of this growth and increasing integration, the size of an individual country market may still be a very important determinant for the location of FDI. The highest-growth countries are not always the principal locations for FDI.

Jovanović (2005a, pp. 735–8) discussed data on the industry distribution of intra-EU(15) FDI in the 1992–2001 period. Internally, EU investors were interested primarily in finance-related services, transport, telecommunications, real estate and business-related services. Within the non-services side of the economy, they were also interested in general manufacturing, petroleum, chemicals, transport equipment and mechanical products.

As for the distribution of incoming FDI from third countries among sectors and industries in the EU(15) in the 1992–2001 period, EU services received by far the largest share of FDI from third countries. Finance-related services, real estate, transport and trade were the principal target industries for this type of FDI. Office machinery and transport equipment were the major targets for FDI within the manufacturing sector.

These data permit only cautious conclusions about the impact of the Single European Market and the eurozone on the spatial concentration of extra-EU FDI in EU manufacturing. In the car-making industry, Britain became a less attractive proposition for FDI, while Spain became more so. In the electrical equipment manufacturing industry, Germany became the preferred location for FDI, in particular for the higher-value-added operations.

Table 3.10 Intra-EU direct investment outflows reported by EU member states, 1992–2003 (€m)

	1992	1993	1994	1995	1996	1997	1998	1999	2000	2001	2002	2003
EU (15 countries)	48 222	40 711	53 593	61 781	74 274	96 771	149 443	427 314	692 711	337 611	355 007	258 431
Belgium	n.a.	n.a.	n.a.	n.a.	n.a.	n.a.	n.a.	n.a.	n.a.	n.a.	8 903	25 650
BLEU	7 332	2 675	866	6 671	2 347	5 930	16 778	112 942	158 640	67 730	128 883	n.a.
Czech Republic	n.a.	n.a.	n.a.	n.a.	n.a.	n.a.	n.a.	n.a.	−24	67	241	192
Denmark	1 460	297	2 212	998	1 614	2 459	3 734	7 142	n.a. (c)	7 045	n.a. (c)	927
Germany	9 853	9 720	9 851	17 420	19 345	14 643	24 246	61 396	5 709	−8 671	19 009	−5 036
Estonia	n.a.	n.a.	n.a.	n.a.	n.a.	2	−1	−2	25	223	125	108
Greece	n.a.	n.a.	n.a.	n.a.	n.a.	n.a.	n.a.	n.a.	1 932	n.a.	n.a.	−316
Spain	234	1 584	474	827	1 634	3 826	5 241	10 983	23 683	21 265	18 033	14 486
France	11 891	6 012	10 345	9 014	11 626	19 542	26 101	74 443	108 752	72 083	25 560	37 528
Ireland	n.a.	n.a.	n.a.	n.a.	n.a.	n.a.	1 126	823	−23	n.a.	2 141	2 712
Italy	2 464	4 732	3 201	3 601	3 732	5 667	5 183	3 563	8 985	20 704	15 595	6 050
Cyprus	n.a.	n.a.	n.a.	n.a.	n.a.	n.a. (c)	n.a. (c)	n.a. (c)	n.a. (c)	227	418	377
Latvia	n.a.	n.a.	n.a.	n.a.	n.a.	n.a.	n.a.	n.a.	4	12	0	8
Lithuania	n.a.	n.a.	n.a.	n.a.	n.a.	0	0	0	0	n.a.	n.a.	14
Luxembourg	n.a.	n.a.	n.a.	n.a.	n.a.	n.a.	n.a.	n.a.	n.a.	n.a.	128 368	58 116
Hungary	n.a.	n.a.	n.a.	n.a.	n.a.	n.a.	n.a.	102	230	42	199	455
Malta	n.a.	n.a.	n.a.	n.a.	n.a.	n.a.	n.a.	n.a.	n.a.	n.a.	n.a.	n.a.
Netherlands	n.a.	4 832	9 059	5 803	10 694	8 800	18 724	32 213	29 064	24 399	24 955	16 069
Austria	n.a.	n.a.	n.a.	326	499	814	1 329	1 013	3 068	1 666	3 577	5 584

Poland	n.a.	n.a.	n.a.	n.a.	n.a.	n.a.	n.a.	−30	−22	−140	258	125
Portugal	462	84	163	410	182	825	1 160	−1 716	3 560	7 248	3 723	−779
Slovenia	n.a.	n.a.	n.a.	31	−22	4	35	14	17	86	131	23
Slovakia	n.a.	n.a.	n.a.	n.a.	n.a.	n.a.	n.a.	n.a.	0	n.a.	n.a.	13
Finland	−677	1 190	3 430	1 092	2 196	3 195	15 411	4 003	12 849	n.a.	n.a.	−809
Sweden	−69	1 192	2 655	1 214	663	1 305	9 519	13 224	n.a. (c)	1 936	5 326	n.a.
United Kingdom	6 364	7 886	10 664	11 411	16 505	25 087	16 940	58 933	204 378	20 112	41 315	16 370

Note: n.a. not available; [c] confidential.

Source: Eurostat (2005).

Table 3.11 Intra-EU direct investment inflows reported by EU member states, 1992–2003 (€m)

	1992	1993	1994	1995	1996	1997	1998	1999	2000	2001	2002	2003
EU (15 countries)	32714	37231	39358	46358	48741	74635	135847	376057	786658	406066	319434	214209
Belgium	n.a.	n.a.	n.a.	n.a.	n.a.	n.a.	n.a.	n.a.	n.a.	n.a.	13911	26091
BLEU	6737	6302	5357	6489	7943	7866	12229	118447	201185	65881	107638	n.a.
Czech Republic	n.a.	n.a.	n.a.	n.a.	n.a.	n.a.	n.a.	n.a.	4333	5575	8460	1160
Denmark	541	843	3053	2587	208	1857	1053	7426	n.a. (c)	7169	n.a. (c)	1440
Germany	1248	541	3045	4278	3148	7187	19610	41610	202298	14825	31559	9323
Estonia	n.a.	n.a.	110	118	68	149	488	240	376	488	259	669
Greece	n.a.	n.a.	n.a.	n.a.	n.a.	n.a.	n.a.	n.a.	1155	n.a.	n.a.	853
Spain	4300	6963	5446	3784	3590	4719	9493	7551	27807	26650	20743	16368
France	8212	7803	9341	11646	13152	16053	22458	35973	41215	53434	39820	30210
Ireland	n.a.	n.a.	n.a.	n.a.	n.a.	n.a.	4647	6307	40936	n.a.	14426	18601
Italy	1501	2528	1467	2567	2274	2224	2117	4310	10346	13100	12155	13213
Cyprus	n.a.	n.a.	n.a.	n.a.	n.a.	196	n.a. (c)	211	408	463	452	539
Latvia	n.a.	n.a.	n.a.	n.a.	n.a.	n.a.	n.a.	n.a.	202	75	169	150
Lithuania	n.a.	n.a.	n.a.	n.a.	n.a.	161	634	277	287	n.a.	474	79
Luxembourg	n.a.	n.a.	n.a.	n.a.	n.a.	n.a.	n.a.	n.a.	n.a.	n.a.	105089	44228
Hungary	n.a.	n.a.	n.a.	n.a.	n.a.	n.a.	n.a.	1331	1381	3159	2034	2278
Malta	n.a.	n.a.	n.a.	n.a.	n.a.	n.a.	n.a.	n.a.	n.a.	n.a.	n.a.	n.a.
Netherlands	n.a.	5869	1692	5055	3479	8637	13222	25001	35276	30581	19554	17515
Austria	n.a.	n.a.	n.a.	840	3020	1486	4342	2093	7747	5681	−264	4513

Poland	n.a.	n.a.	n.a.	n.a.	n.a.	3286	4485	6119	9575	5857	4236	2788
Portugal	1191	1062	681	390	1075	1672	1196	1233	7085	6312	1665	52
Slovenia	n.a.	n.a.	n.a.	262	252	285	342	347	422	276	645	233
Slovakia	n.a.	n.a.	n.a.	n.a.	n.a.	n.a.	n.a.	n.a.	1928	n.a.	n.a.	619
Finland	59	512	981	481	999	1480	10332	4131	9230	n.a.	n.a.	2184
Sweden	196	1264	2378	853	2205	5092	12950	50450	n.a. (c)	10475	7744	n.a.
United Kingdom	3011	2037	4337	4289	5742	9974	16863	60231	85965	28155	30226	5266

Note: n.a. not available; c confidential.

Source: Eurostat (2005).

Table 3.12 EU direct investment outward flows by extra-EU country of destination, 1992–2003 (€m)

	1992	1993	1994	1995	1996	1997	1998	1999	2000	2001	2002	2003
Ten new member states	n.a.	n.a.	n.a.	n.a.	n.a.	n.a.	n.a.	n.a.	n.a.	19418	6697	6544
Czech Republic	764	812	952	1944	1155	1592	1670	3485	2897	4772	−196	−2536
Estonia	n.a.	n.a.	n.a.	n.a.	72	88	384	331	276	343	402	203
Cyprus	n.a.	n.a.	n.a.	n.a.	n.a.	n.a.	n.a.	n.a.	n.a.	235	571	−413
Latvia	n.a.	n.a.	n.a.	n.a.	23	53	63	115	435	326	70	−77
Lithuania	n.a.	n.a.	n.a.	n.a.	64	61	433	241	211	379	346	412
Hungary	989	1217	849	2378	1442	1768	2705	608	4875	4460	−501	4207
Malta	n.a.	n.a.	n.a.	n.a.	n.a.	n.a.	n.a.	n.a.	n.a.	−34	−2218	431
Poland	230	759	641	1153	2424	2420	4218	7662	10568	6806	2529	2005
Slovenia	n.a.	73	55	81	85	164	168	481	126	582	1145	1114
Slovakia	n.a.	243	116	108	278	275	307	347	1366	1550	4546	1195
Extra-EU-25	n.a.	n.a.	n.a.	n.a.	n.a.	n.a.	n.a.	n.a.	n.a.	286352	127746	126229
Extra-EU-15	17670	24377	32386	62407	68665	109802	218754	320307	435676	305772	134441	132776
Extra-eurozone	n.a.	n.a.	n.a.	77527	86118	132807	258179	516886	531044	380567	176117	179664
Extra-EU-15, not allocated	n.a.	n.a.	n.a.	n.a.	n.a.	591	489	11959	26406	2727	4482	−32
Bulgaria	9	32	67	10	55	153	168	155	402	408	1088	485
Croatia	n.a.	31	72	187	94	199	190	1315	529	1122	667	1261
Romania	−12	25	48	81	103	364	394	653	530	1010	620	933
Turkey	367	279	389	350	405	425	1013	944	1424	2978	984	948
EFTA (CH, IS, LI, NO)	1525	1692	8265	3362	5574	10901	24019	13967	69217	10393	28883	10431
Norway	299	360	1259	1330	1141	3321	3412	4366	8262	2733	1401	−329
Switzerland	1176	1327	6953	1913	4385	7704	20512	9475	61034	7591	27510	10707
Russian Federation	n.a.	122	376	314	576	1699	254	1315	2000	2619	1295	8085
Canada	278	−157	586	1520	765	1405	4594	3916	38541	7221	839	2550
United States	6956	13856	9772	33138	25824	49033	128679	191437	182111	139184	−8875	53720

Latin America	945	841	3 573	3 566	8 727	17 785	26 253	37 539	41 919	29 088	8 976	3231
China (excluding Hong Kong)	113	181	548	787	1 654	1 816	435	2 196	2 181	2526	3 213	3 079
Hong Kong (CN)	−300	130	−303	1 393	1 247	−68	2 519	1 971	−3 853	48 571	2 832	1 729
Japan	420	−1 172	735	1 378	2 474	1 297	696	8 698	6 729	−9 417	10 191	736
Petroleum Exporting Countries (OPEC)	551	859	446	1 057	3 613	3 642	1 847	−116	4 259	5 654	13	1 404
African, Caribbean and Pacific countries, signatories of the Partnership Agreement (Cotonou agreement) (77 countries)	826	−125	826	1 110	1 922	2 394	3 190	5 138	10 362	9 697	2 811	7 264
All countries of the world	66 371	65 428	85 728	124 099	143 393	206 573	368 197	747 623	1 128 387	624 535	484 130	385 993

Note: n.a. not available.

Source: Eurostat (2005).

Table 3.13 EU direct investment inward flows by extra-EU investing country, 1992–2003 (€m)

	1992	1993	1994	1995	1996	1997	1998	1999	2000	2001	2002	2003
Ten new member states	n.a.	n.a.	n.a.	n.a.	n.a.	n.a.	n.a.	n.a.	n.a.	2226	2665	1325
Czech Republic	−7	0	125	33	−17	−8	26	82	63	125	354	403
Estonia	n.a.	n.a.	n.a.	n.a.	−1	1	−2	16	29	37	145	−70
Cyprus	n.a.	n.a.	n.a.	n.a.	n.a.	n.a.	n.a.	n.a.	n.a.	591	501	−143
Latvia	n.a.	n.a.	n.a.	n.a.	4	1	−7	3	117	−70	70	144
Lithuania	n.a.	n.a.	n.a.	n.a.	2	3	−7	4	14	16	23	32
Hungary	−23	0	169	136	38	92	220	303	401	1080	415	−86
Malta	n.a.	n.a.	n.a.	n.a.	n.a.	n.a.	n.a.	n.a.	n.a.	123	149	−70
Poland	14	6	153	35	−18	88	45	−2	256	249	489	766
Slovenia	n.a.	41	−0	−1	−7	−14	−9	19	92	36	233	13
Slovakia	n.a.	0	−6	−1	5	−4	−9	−11	−4	37	282	343
Extra-EU-25	n.a.	n.a.	n.a.	n.a.	n.a.	n.a.	n.a.	n.a.	n.a.	120058	139793	113222
Extra-EU-15	22907	20775	22132	42464	36509	50160	96432	122764	180101	122282	142456	114547
Extra-eurozone	n.a.	n.a.	n.a.	55995	48906	71012	135511	276124	455052	247942	188916	145327
Extra-EU-15, not allocated	n.a.	n.a.	n.a.	n.a.	n.a.	1814	1519	8865	20021	−2476	−458	281
Bulgaria	1	2	12	3	−4	14	2	4	64	18	22	68
Croatia	n.a.	1	1	3	−33	−20	14	9	−24	5	−9	−3
Romania	0	0	7	6	1	−4	−6	5	3	20	5	48
Turkey	44	39	−121	22	98	114	230	128	275	404	−243	1627
EFTA (CH, IS, LI, NO)	3309	1913	5450	7838	6887	6911	18765	9767	26597	9355	13177	21042
Norway	470	462	608	1757	2741	1718	1613	462	6593	1427	5232	2156
Switzerland	2827	1606	4861	5956	4474	5241	17301	9060	19768	7442	7643	18576
Russian Federation	n.a.	−207	38	63	27	280	−285	131	374	663	210	499
Canada	359	674	−394	742	−300	1406	8954	2160	14623	7250	2467	8203
United States	12424	10886	11722	28760	23760	28068	54931	76016	79906	61143	52148	50364

Latin America	105	798	−50	−7	226	675	568	2	594	2 649	3 962	187
China (excluding Hong Kong)	31	3	11	18	17	−368	34	228	208	326	−120	137
Hong Kong (CN)	313	252	70	22	386	381	18	309	1 985	5 891	2 539	1 025
Japan	1 858	1 599	1 340	1 040	305	2 603	2 091	3 404	17 127	8 290	8 804	4 696
Petroleum Exporting Countries (OPEC)	673	384	426	398	−199	630	17	299	1 148	761	2 078	−310
African, Caribbean and Pacific countries, signatories of the Partnership Agreement (Cotonou agreement) (77 countries)	178	355	386	−152	343	390	1621	−54	784	4 250	1 889	−8 771
All countries of the world	55 702	57 934	61 505	88 379	86 705	124 795	232 279	498 819	966 760	544 994	480 274	336 181

Note: n.a. not available.

Source: Eurostat (2005).

However, it is still a moot analytical point whether inward FDI brings to the EU high-value-added employment and technology or low-level, tariff-jumping assembly work (European Commission, 1998, p. 141). In addition, a high concentration of FDI on finance provokes a question: how big an impact has FDI had on the EU manufacturing industry?

As for the outflow of FDI from the EU(15) to third countries in the 1992–2001 period, finance-related services, real estate and business-related services were the principal targets for EU investors in third countries. There was also interest in general manufacturing, as well as in electricity, gas and water. Again, there is a certain clustering of FDI on select industries within the services sector.

3.3.7 CONCLUSION

As FDI touches issues such as ownership of land and real estate, direct employment and taxes, it is a more politically charged issue than trade. A popular perception, based on shoddy economics, is that the export of goods is beneficial for a country and, therefore, needs to be supported, whereas (some) imports are perceived to be dangerous as they might jeopardise the national output and employment potential.[97] However, FDI is treated in a different way. Outflows are being deterred, as there is a fear that exporting capital means exporting exports and exporting jobs, while inflows are welcomed.

With protection and subscale operations by TNCs, the host country may end up worse off than if it had never received FDI. Such a situation may create a vicious circle of adverse signals and harmful incentives. The penalties in terms of lost opportunities are high, but so are rewards for successes in attracting TNCs into well-structured projects. If TNCs operate at full scale in a reasonably competitive environment, they may provide the host economy with the 'usual list' of benefits such as capital, technology and management know-how (Moran, 1998, pp. 155–6).

Capital mobility has its costs and benefits. If these effects are desirable, they should be stimulated, otherwise they should be regulated, controlled and taxed. Simultaneous inflow and outflow of FDI in integrated countries is possible and quite likely. This was confirmed in the case of the EU. However, FDI flows and the consequent geography of production may be significant even without formal integration and specific trade preferences – just look at transatlantic FDI flows. TNCs primarily follow the opportunities for making profits in large and growing markets in the long term. Therefore, economic integration (at least in Europe) is *a*, rather than *the*, cause of FDI.

The relative loss of the international competitive position of the EU in relation to the US, Japan and the newly industrialised countries (in several lines of production) in the 1970s and 1980s have increased both interest in and the need for strengthening the competitiveness of output of EU companies. These TNCs are the key actors in improving the international competitiveness of goods made and services provided in the EU. Ambitious and well-funded public research programmes in the EU may assist the domestic firms to lead or to catch up and later to improve their position *vis-à-vis* their major international competitors if astutely linked with the production resources and potentials, as well as current and future domestic and foreign demand.

American investors in the EU were market seeking in the 1950s and 1960s. The same was true of Japanese FDI in the 1970s and 1980s. As EU consumers were not able to purchase what they wanted because of NTBs, Japanese TNCs invested in the EU in order to satisfy an existing and growing local demand. TNCs from both source countries have generally looked at the EU market as a single unit. Their advantages over local EU enterprises included, in some cases, not only a superior capability to innovate products and technologies and manage multiplant production and supply, but also a willingness, experience and ability to serve consumers from a local base, rather than through exports, which was the favourite method of operation of many national firms in the EU.

There is, however, at least one difference between Japanese and American FDI in the EU. Nearly half of Japanese FDI was concentrated in banking and insurance in the early 1990s. At the same time, more than half of American FDI was in the manufacturing industry, while about a third was in financial services. Therefore, Japanese FDI has relatively less impact, at present, on EU manufacturing industry than the American TNCs (Buigues and Jacquemin, 1992, p. 22; European Commission, 1998, p. 3). This focus by Japanese investors may come as a surprise as Japan has the advantage in electronics and cars. A concentration of Japanese FDI in financial services (relying on human, rather than physical, capital) both in the EU and the US is, however, a partial reflection of Japanese balance of payments surpluses and the appreciation of the yen at that time. However, from 1994, the interest of the Japanese TNCs shifted predominantly towards the Pacific Rim countries.

In order to avoid weakening the competitive position of EU firms in global markets, the EU may follow two courses, although employing a mix of the two has its attractions. First, the EU may increase protection of domestic firms against foreign TNCs through various NTBs (although the use of TRIMs is outlawed by the 1995 WTO Agreement). Second, the EU may open its domestic market and encourage foreign, in particular high-technology, TNCs to locate their manufacturing operations in the EU. As widely argued, EU firms in certain manufacturing industries are less efficient than their counterparts in the US and Japan. If the EU were to adopt and maintain a liberal economic policy and EU firms were to adjust and withstand competition from foreign TNCs, then they may, in relative terms, gain more from market liberalisation than their foreign competitors.

The incomplete internal market in the EU was the major cause of a sub-optimal production structure in the region prior to 1993. All economic agents, including TNCs, behave as welfare-maximising units in the long term, subject to the prevailing conditions. These private agents should not be criticised for actions that may be in conflict with public objectives. The start of the Single European Market, which included the removal of NTBs, assisted in a rationalisation of production and enhanced the location-specific advantages of the EU. The introduction of the eurozone in 1999 removed internal EU exchange rate risks and consolidated earlier achievements in integration, at least for the participating countries. Coupled with eastern enlargement (2004), this will continue to contribute to an increase in both the size and the growth of the EU market, which could, in turn, further increase investment expenditure in the region in the longer term.

An extensive survey of the impact of the Single European Market on FDI found strong evidence that FDI and trade are complementary (European Commission, 1998, p. 1). Concerns that the Single European Market would lead to a concentration of general economic activity into the 'core' EU countries were not justified. In fact, there has been a limited spread of economic activity to the 'peripheral' EU countries which enjoy certain cost advantages (ibid., p. 145).

As one of the major players in the international capital mobility scene, the EU would like to see multilateral rules for FDI. Even though there are multilateral agreements that deal with specific 'technical' FDI issues such as TRIMs or dispute settlements or with sectoral matters such as services (GATS), there is no overall multilateral agreement on investment. However, FDI issues are discussed within the WTO. The future multilateral agreement may include the following elements:

- Foreigners would have the right to invest and operate competitively in all sectors of the economy; only a few exceptions to the general rule may be allowed.
- There should be no discrimination against foreign investors based on their origin. A 'standstill' commitment would prevent the introduction of new restrictions.

- There should be a 'roll-back' principle to gradually eliminate national (or group) measures that run counter to the liberalisation of FDI rules.

Notes

1. Various regional factors prevent full equalisation of prices. Recall the example about parasols and antifreeze in the EU from Chapter 2.
2. Exports of high-technology products by developing countries in 2000 amounted to $450 billion. This is $64 billion more than exports of primary products or $140 billion more than medium-technology exports (UNCTAD, 2002, p. 145).
3. One also needs to recall migrations in Europe in the past centuries. 'Immigration hovers in the penumbra of official European history. If anything, Europe has traditionally thought of itself as a continent of emigration, not of immigration. Yet immigration is part of the landscape. In the 18th century, when Amsterdam built its polders and cleared its bogs, it brought in northern German workers. When the French built their vineyards, they employed Spaniards. When London built its water and sewerage infrastructure, the Irish provided the labour. In the 19th century, when Baron Haussmann rebuilt Paris, he brought in Germans and Belgians. When Germany built its railways and steel mills it used Italians and Poles.

   'This was not immigration on a small scale. Europe – not the Americas, as is usually thought – was the main destination for Italians in their century of emigration from 1876 to 1976. About 12.6m Italians went to other European countries, 1m more than emigrated to non-European countries. And while the US was the country that received the largest number of Italians – with 5.7m – France was not that far behind, with 4.1m. Switzerland, smaller still, received 4m, Germany 2.4m and Austria 1.2m' (S. Sassen, 'The migration fallacy', *Financial Times*, 27 December 2004).
4. Eurostat (2001). 'Why do people migrate?', *Statistics in Focus*, Theme 3–1/2001, p. 2.
5. Different languages are not always an insurmountable problem for big TNCs. Philips, ABB and SKF use English as their corporate language, rather than Dutch, German or Swedish.
6. 'It is said that there are more trained Malawian doctors in Birmingham than there are in Malawi. This is insane. Malawi needs them far more' (Q. Peel, 'A dynamic Europe needs immigrants', *Financial Times*, 3 March 2005).
7. R. Lapper, 'LatAm and Caribbean migrants send home $45.8bn', *Financial Times*, 21 March 2005.
8. J. Authers, 'Mexican migrants send $16bn in remittances', *Financial Times*, 1 February 2005.
9. In a static world, free immigration of labour lowers (or prevents the increase of) the real wages of certain wage earners in the receiving country. The idea that there is a fixed amount of work to be done in the world is known as the 'lump of labour fallacy'. According to this suggestion, if one worker increases the amount of work he/she does, this reduces the work and job opportunities for others. Such ideas have provoked many misguided policies. In France, for example, the socialist governments sought to initiate job creation by reducing the length of the working week, by early retirement schemes and by the extension of vacations. The Luddite 'lump of labour' idea soon reappears whenever there is a recession. If jobs cannot be created because of inappropriate policy, it is easy, politically effective and cheap to blame foreign competitors for domestic problems and failures. Hence, protection may be sought against goods that are imported from China or other countries.
10. There is a fine difference between immigration and immigrant policy. The former refers to the admission of foreigners into the receiving country. An immigrant policy deals with the treatment of resident foreigners.

11. It is estimated that labour is almost three times more mobile among the federal states in the US if compared with labour mobility within individual EU states. There are good reasons for the American geographical rootlessness. The US is a very homogenised country. If one pushes this to the limit, no matter where you go within the US, the structure of the supply of goods and services is almost identical. Language is the same, while most American cities, towns and villages look similar. This may be one of the most important reasons why the majority of Americans move so readily and so often.
12. Israel is an interesting example of a country that absorbed a large number of immigrants during the 1990s when the population of the country increased by a quarter (immigration principally from the former Soviet Union).
13. *The Economist*, 1 November 1997, p. 98.
14. Immigration from the Caribbean countries and south Asia.
15. Immigration from Indonesia, Suriname, Antilles, Turkey and Morocco.
16. Immigrants from other Scandinavian countries, Britain and the US were employed in oil and gas exploration and production. Immigrants from Turkey, Morocco, India and Pakistan sought unskilled manual jobs.
17. New York City mayor John Lindsay wanted to remove the poor and homeless from the streets. To this end he increased welfare benefits in 1968. As a consequence, the poor from all over the US flocked to New York City, claimed welfare benefits and drove the city to near-bankruptcy. The banks refused to extend loans to the city in 1975, hence harsh welfare benefit rules were introduced (Sinn, 2004, p. 19).
18. Immigration from the developing countries since the 1960s has changed the composition of parts of France, Belgium, the Netherlands and a few other EU countries. For example, the estimated number of Muslims in France is over 7 per cent of the population or about 4.5 million (*The Economist*, 'A survey of the European Union', 25 September 2004, p. 16).
19. *The Economist*, 16 October 1999, p. 20.
20. Eurostat (2002). 'Migration keeps the EU population growing', *Statistics in Focus*, Theme 3–7/2002.
21. Eurostat (2003). 'Women and men migrating to and from the European Union', *Statistics in Focus*, Theme 3–2/2003, p. 2.
22. Eurostat (2003). 'Women and men migrating to and from the European Union', *Statistics in Focus*, Theme 3–2/2003, p. 4.
23. Eurostat (2003). 'Women and men migrating to and from the European Union', *Statistics in Focus*, Theme 3–2/2003.
24. *The Economist*, 6 May 2000, p. 21.
25. United Nations (2000). 'Replacement migration: is it a solution to declining and ageing populations?' ESA/P/WP.160, 21 March 2000.
26. Kofi Annan, 'Migrants can help rejuvenate an ageing Europe', *Financial Times*, 29 January 2004.
27. Communication from the Commission to the Council, the European Parliament, the European Economic and Social Committee and the Committee of the Regions on Immigration, Integration and Employment. Brussels, 3 June 2003 COM (2003) 336 final.
28. Certain EU countries such as Britain, France, Ireland and Italy allow dual citizenship. Others, such as Germany or Denmark, require that people relinquish their old citizenship when becoming German or Danish. If a Turk gives up his/her citizenship, he/she has to forgo rural property rights in Turkey. This is one of the reasons why Turks in Germany are very cautious about becoming German.
29. 'Following five centuries of intra-European migration, Europeans are a rather mixed people: one-quarter of French people, for instance, have a foreign-born parent or grandparent; in Vienna, the figure is 40 per cent' (S. Sassen, 'The migration fallacy', *Financial Times*, 27 December 2004).
30. The Dublin Convention (1990) of the EU(12) provided for a joint procedure for asylum seekers. The Convention has reconfirmed the Schengen Agreement on this issue. A common asylum procedure would apply from 2010.
31. Benelux, France, Germany, Portugal and Spain. Other countries joined later.

32. The French refused to implement the agreement, using the argument that terrorists might escape the vigilance of some of their co-signatories.
33. In an early study, Weber (1909) offered two basic reasons why firms 'go to produce abroad'. The primary determinant is the achievement of lower labour and transport costs, while the secondary element is the benefit of large-scale production.
34. G. de Jonquières, 'Battles among regulators could damage trade', *Financial Times*, 25 May 2003.
35. For example, over a certain period of time governments may change the availability, quality and cost of the domestic factors. The disposable tools for this policy include training of labour and education of management, R&D, science, transport and communication infrastructure and tax policies.
36. 'Japanese companies follow each other' said a senior adviser at the Czech investment promotion agency. 'As soon as there is a big famous investor, the others start to consider the possibilities.' The principal reason for the location in the Czech Republic is geography (rather than relatively low wages). Another important reason for the Japanese TNCs is tradition in technical universities and the electronic industry ('Electronic giants go for Czech launchpad', *Financial Times*, 10 June 2003).

    Car manufactures adopted a similar attitude in Slovakia, where Volkswagen established its subsidiary in 1991. After a successful and huge increase in production, Volkswagen became the biggest company in Slovakia. Peugeot decided to locate in Slovakia in 2003. This was followed by Hyundai's decision to invest in a car assembly plant too in 2004.
37. In a *merger* two or more firms decide to pool their assets to form a new company. In this process one or more companies disappear completely. An *acquisition* does not constitute a merger if the acquired company does not disappear. Mergers are relatively less frequent than acquisitions.
38. J. Kynge and D. Roberts, 'The Pearl river delta is attracting $1bn of investment a month amid one of the fastest bursts of economic development in history', *Financial Times*, 4 February 2003.
39. H. Simonian, 'EU tax row set to grow over Austria investor data', *Financial Times*, 17 January 2005.
40. This cut would affect only public limited companies. SMEs, often family owned, make up 85 per cent of German firms that pay income tax where rates rise progressively to 42 per cent ('No flat tax', *Financial Times*, 18 May 2005).
41. How should one measure these benefits? What should be measured? Should it be done in fiscal terms? Or in social terms?
42. 'Jack Straw, foreign secretary, has let it be known that he intends to turn a blind eye to some of the requirements of two-year-old legislation banning UK businesses from bribing foreign officials. . . . From one perspective, his stance can be viewed as pragmatic realism. So-called facilitation payments are exempted by the US Foreign Corrupt Practices Act, a model of its kind, and are not explicitly outlawed by the anti-bribery convention negotiated by members of the Organisation for Economic Co-operation and Development. . . . the borderline between "facilitation" payments and bribes aimed at winning business by underhand means is only loosely defined legally and fuzzy in practice. . . . Nonetheless, his partial and retrospective interpretation of the law sounds curious from a politician who, as home secretary, boasted of being "tough on crime"' ('De minimis non curat Straw', *Financial Times*, 20 February 2004). The IMF estimates that more than $500 billion are laundered in the global financial system each year. 'Official estimates put the UK share at £25 billion' ('London's dirty secret', *Financial Times*, 29 October 2004).
43. One should not accord an absolute value to the decline of consumer loyalty to local brands. Regional rather than 'global' strategies in certain food and health-care products may offer a superior business outcome. However, there was a certain 'global success' by, for example, Coca-Cola, which succeeded in replacing a part of the consumption of milk and healthy natural fruit juices by an artificial and sweet liquid that has a questionable impact on health and weight.

44. It was the church that once determined our life, then the state and now it is corporations. Governments court firms (TNCs) to come and locate within the confines of their control. Critics say that the protection of the vulnerable in society or safeguarding of the environment is weakened, even that it is left to the mercy of big businesses. This may be the case in certain lines of production, but it all depends on specific circumstances. In some cases the regulatory framework facing TNCs was strengthened, while in others it was loosened.
45. The same holds for the increase in the power of special influence groups such as NGOs. Do these unelected groups of people with sometimes questionable accountability represent a risky shift of power towards special vested interests? Or do they represent a move towards the new 'civil society' (indeed, can anyone define this type of society)? Why does the general public sometimes believe more in these organisations that often lack resources for rigorous analysis than in the government?
46. NGOs often consider that it may be better to be just about right and make a fuss now in order to put an issue on the policy agenda, than to wait for firm scientific evidence and miss the political boat.
47. See note 45, above.
48. H. Kissinger, 'Globalisation: America's role for the millennium', *The Irish Independent*, 13 October 1999.
49. 'Globalisation is no more than an (admittedly ugly) name for the process of integration across frontiers of liberalising market economies at a time of rapidly falling costs of transport and communications' (M. Wolf, *Financial Times*, 3 October 2001, p. 15).
50. A. Krueger, 'Educating globalisation's Luddites', *Financial Times*, 16 April 2004.
51. *The Economist*, 29 September 2001, p. 14. The reference here is to the attacks of 11 September 2001.
52. Institutional elements such as clear property rights are very important for foreign investors. However, the mere transfer of these solutions from the developed countries elsewhere is not a sufficient condition for successful economic performance. For example, while Russia has introduced a system of private property rights, China has retained the general socialist legal system. None the less, domestic and foreign investors regarded China as a promising location for investment and this country became one of the prime locations for investment. There was a strong credibility that investments would be protected. In contrast, this credibility was lower in Russia in spite of the property rights system, which is one reason why Russia continued to score much lower than China as a location for FDI.
53. Apart from Russians and Poles, few people cared much about vodka prior to the early 1980s. Then a Swedish firm, Absolut Vodka, launched one of the most successful advertising campaigns in the US. Following that, vodka became one of the most popular spirits in the world.
54. *The Economist*, 'A survey of globalisation', 29 September 2001, p. 4.
55. P. Krugman, 'The Good News', *The New York Times*, 28 November 2003.
56. J. Kay, 'Global business deserves a peaceful May Day', *Financial Times*, 28 April 2004.
57. One thinks of the particular consequences of chewing gum, which pollutes lifts, pavements, and the underside of desks and chairs.
58. Increased international mobility of factors, increased international intra-firm transactions, expanding international cooperative arrangements between firms, the increasing importance of knowledge, as well as a reduction in transport and communication costs, support the process of globalisation and are constituent parts of it. In these circumstances, individual actions of national governments may not increase global welfare (pollution is an example) and certain supranational rules may be necessary in order to deliver more beneficial outcomes.
59. Trade is relatively more concentrated within regions than FDI. This suggests that trade plays a more prominent role in intra-regional integration arrangements, while FDI has a greater influence on global integration (UNCTAD, 1993, p. 7).
60. 'Over 90 per cent of products produced in each of the triad regions is sold within that region. There is no global car. . . . well over 90 per cent of MNE manufacturing is intra-regional rather than global' (Rugman, 2002, p. 5).

61. Control may not be easy to define in all circumstances. A 51 per cent ownership of a firm is a clear sign of full control. However, in some cases 20 or even 10 per cent ownership is sufficient for the control of a firm if other shareholders are widely dispersed and unorganised.
62. FDI stock in 'small' Ireland was $193 billion in 2003. This was more than twice the same indicator in Japan in the same year.
63. According to research carried out by the location division of Ernst & Young, firms now appear to accept higher costs of production in return for high environmental standards. 'Regions that sell themselves on the basis of relaxed environmental legislation may soon find their approach counterproductive' (*Business Europe*, 12 March 1997).
64. Smarzynska Javorcik (2004) found data in the case of Lithuania that confirm evidence consistent with positive productivity spillovers. These were brought by links between affiliates of TNCs and their local suppliers (vertical links). At the same time, Sabrianova Peter et al. (2004) reported negative spillovers from FDI on the domestically owned Czech and Russian firms. They have not been converging to the technological frontier set by foreign-owned firms. However, foreign-owned firms had positive spillovers on other foreign-owned firms in both the Czech Republic and Russia.
65. Intra-company pricing refers to transactions among related units of the same firm. Not every manipulation of transfer prices increases the overall profits of the entire company, as these extra revenues stem from sales to outside customers (Plasschaert, 1994, p. 1).
66. Trade in services is expanding. Monitoring internal prices for services is a much more complex task than inspecting the same prices for goods by the employment of free market criteria.
67. Firms are reluctant to comment and release data on their internal prices. Hence, there is a black hole in this area of research.
68. S. Bond, 'The Kafkaesque charade of corporate taxes', *Financial Times*, 26 January 2004.
69. Tax avoidance, unlike tax evasion, does not involve breaking any laws, but rather making the best use of positive regulations. In practice, the difference between the two is often ambiguous.
70. Transfer of profits out of the country takes place when TNCs do not find the country in question a promising location for the reinvestment of earnings. Such a transfer may send a warning signal to the local government that something is wrong in the economy and that something needs to be done about it.
71. J. Plender, 'Top banks pay little tax to the UK exchequer', *Financial Times*, 20 July 2004.
72. J. Plender and M. Simons, 'A big squeeze for governments: how transfer pricing threatens global tax revenues', *Financial Times*, 22 July 2004.
73. Ibid.
74. TNCs that come from the US and operate in the EU reported an annual R&D of almost $2500 per employee in 1989. In contrast, Euro-affiliates of Japanese TNCs reported R&D per employee of around $725 in the same year (Gittelman et al., 1992, p. 18). The reasons for the difference include a relatively strong headquarters effect, as Japanese FDI in Europe is a fairly novel phenomenon compared with FDI from the US. American TNCs have been present in Europe on a larger scale since the 1950s. In addition, Japanese TNCs may be more involved in the EU in relatively mature manufacturing industries and services where R&D expenditure is not as high as in other activities.
75. 'The recent emergence of internationally integrated MNC networks is best observed in Europe, where the contribution of foreign-owned MNCs to national technological capabilities is much greater than elsewhere. About one-quarter of large firm R&D carried out within Europe has been conducted under foreign ownership, while the world average is only just over one-tenth' (Cantwell and Piscitello, 2005, p. 11).
76. Decisions taken at the EU level are easy targets for special lobbies as they are made far from the public gaze. The co-decision procedure between the Council of Ministers and the European Parliament introduced by the Maastricht Treaty tried to ameliorate this shortcoming. This is a step forward compared with the past, but there is still a danger that EU technology policy may become a sophisticated new form of protectionism.

77. TNCs are sometimes more economically powerful than certain countries. To support this view, 51 out of the world's 100 biggest economies are corporations (*Finance & Development*, September 2004, p. 52).
78. Issues related to Decision 24 are discussed in Chapter 5.
79. Local content usually means 'national content' (value added within a country) or value added within the group such as the EU or NAFTA.
80. Article 4 of the same agreement allows only temporary derogations from this obligation to developing countries.
81. Mitsubishi bought a well-known American symbol, the Rockefeller Center in Manhattan, in 1989. Many Americans felt uneasy about that 'national loss' and feared that the domestic 'silver' was being taken, sorry purchased, by foreigners. However, this purchase turned out to be a financial disaster for the Japanese, and they quit the building in 1995.
82. For example, Pirelli (Italy) coordinates and guarantees its global financial duties from a Swiss affiliate which is in charge of finance for the whole corporation. The US affiliate of Siemens (Germany) transmits daily financial data to headquarters, which is in charge of global financial management (UNCTAD, 1993, p. 124).
83. *Financial Times*, 7 March 2002, p. 8.
84. The introduction of a new good depends not only on the fixed costs and expected benefits, but also on substitution and complementarity with the goods that already exist on the market. Of course, there must be or needs to be created real demand for the new good or service.
85. Linkages with the local suppliers (local embeddedness) depend on the choice of the TNC and the existence of the suitable local firms with which a TNC can do business.
86. Investment in natural resources has three distinct features. First, the geographical location of non-renewable resources is not mutable; second, investments require huge amounts of capital which is linked with significant economies of scale; and, third, processing of minerals is linked with a considerable consumption of energy.
87. By the end of 2003, 2265 bilateral investment treaties and 2316 double taxation treaties had been signed (UNCTAD, 2004, p. xvii).
88. According to an influential view, no matter what a government does to influence competitiveness and increase exports in the short term, the exchange rate and factor prices would still have to be adjusted in the long term (Johnson and Krauss, 1973, p. 240). The new theory disputed such an approach and argued that, in the presence of increasing returns to scale, externalities and the economies of learning, the policy of the government does matter. Such a policy may, if handled properly, bring irreversible advantages for the country in question.
89. In the situation where TNCs do not dominate in the economy of a country or an integrated group of countries, then, of course, their impact may be marginal. The situation, however, in virtually all present-day regional groupings of developing countries is that TNCs play a dominant role (Robson, 1987, p. 209).
90. Educated management and a trained labour force (domestic human capital) is what matters for the country, rather than ownership of the business (Reich, 1990). Tyson (1991) disagreed with such a view and argued that ownership still mattered. This view is, however, opposed to the traditional and declared US stance that favours free trade and free flow of capital.
91. *Financial Times*, 13 May 2000, p. 1.
92. Yannopoulos (1990) surveyed the diversity of views expressed in the debate on the effect of European integration on FDI.
93. These studies include Aristotelous and Fountas (1996, p. 579), Dunning (1997, p. 13), Jovanović (1997a, pp. 324–9; 1998a, pp. 158–64; 2001a, pp. 239–52), European Commission (1998) and Clegg and Scott-Green (1999, p. 612).
94. Government incentives influenced TNCs such as Ford to make new investments in the north-west of the country and Wales. Honda, Nissan and Toyota benefited from public grants as they settled in regions with unemployment problems. However, those allowances were equally available in Britain to other firms from the EU or third countries, whether they were from car production or other industries.

95. Siemens of Germany, for example, made English its main corporate language in 1998.
96. One has to be careful when interpreting the data for a country such as Luxembourg (or Switzerland). Such countries often act only as intermediaries for the inflow and outflow of funds.
97. Through trade a country acquires useful things from abroad. Therefore, imports are a gain, rather than a cost. To pay for imports, the country has to 'send' its useful goods and services abroad. In these terms exports are a cost, rather than a gain!

So he who had received five talents came and brought five other talents, saying,
'Lord, you delivered to me five talents;
look, I have gained five more talents besides them.'
His lord said to him,
'Well done, good and faithful servant; you were faithful over a few things,
I will make you ruler over many things. Enter into the joy of your lord.'
Matthew 25:20–21

4 Economic Union

4.1 Introduction

None of the types of international economic integration can exist in its pure theoretical form. A customs union deals not only with the elimination of tariffs and quotas and the introduction of the common external tariff, but also with industrial policy and specialisation. It may also deal with non-tariff barriers (NTBs) and foreign direct investment (FDI) from partner countries, as well as from outsiders. Free mobility of labour in a common market requires not only the elimination of discrimination against labour from partner countries, but also some degree of harmonisation of social policy (social security, unemployment benefits, pension funds, vocational training). Without harmonisation of these issues, distortions may be created which may induce labour to move in response to signals other than its relative abundance/scarcity and returns. The buffer against unacceptable costs which accrue from the free migration of labour and flow of capital can be found in regional policy. Therefore, common markets may have some elements of economic unions. In addition, an economic union need not be complete. The principal argument in favour of an economic union is found in its potential to increase the efficiency in the allocation of resources in relation to a common market.

The creation of an economic union can be defended by the same arguments which are used in favour of the creation, implementation and protection of a single general economic policy in a country which has different regions. It can also be challenged by the same arguments that say that one policy for different regions does not make sense (as often heard in Canada and elsewhere: one size does not fit all, even less so all the time).

This chapter is structured as follows. Section 4.2 deals with monetary policy because that is the field where the impact of international economic integration is quickest and most obvious. Section 4.3 examines fiscal policy, which is necessary for the proper operation of an economic union. Industrial and regional policies (Sections 4.4 and 4.5, respectively) have a strong impact on an economic union. While industrial policy is directed towards the creation of new wealth, regional (and social) policies are turned towards the distribution of wealth that is already created.

For wisdom is a shelter as money is a shelter,
but the excellence of knowledge is that wisdom
gives life to those who have it.
Ecclesiastes 7:12

4.2 Monetary integration

4.2.1 INTRODUCTION

Monetary policy is central for overall economic strategy in an economic and monetary union (EMU) because of its control over the money stock. The control over the rate of inflation contributes to the creation of conditions necessary for sustained economic growth. As monetary policy is one of the most sensitive economic policies, the treaties establishing the EU made special reference to these issues. In fact, the Maastricht Treaty is almost entirely about the EMU. This is because integration of monetary policies in the EU is necessary not only for the stability of rates of exchange and prices (and their transparency), balance of payments and investment decisions, but also for the protection of the already achieved level of integration, as well as for the motivation for further integration in the future.

Relatively small countries may have, in certain cases, an incentive to integrate their money in order to avoid the monetary domination of large countries. The joint money may overcome the disadvantage (vulnerability to external shocks) of atomised currencies and under certain theoretical conditions it may become a rival to the money of larger countries in international currency markets. A common currency among the integrated countries may become an outward symbol, but it is not a necessary condition for a successful EMU.

A *monetary system* between countries should be distinguished from a monetary union. Countries in a monetary system link their currencies together and act as a single unit in relation to third currencies. A *monetary union* among countries is an ambitious enterprise. It exists if there is either a single currency (*de jure* EMU) or an irrevocable fixity among the rates of exchange of the participating countries together with a free mobility of goods, services and factors (*de facto* EMU). This prevents any alterations in the rates of exchange as indirect methods of non-tariff protection or as a subsidy to exports. It also means that the member countries should seek recourse to the capital markets in order to find funds to cover their budget deficit. Within an EMU, it should be as easy, for example, for a Frenchman to pay a German within Europe as it is for a Welshman to pay an Englishman within the United Kingdom (Meade, 1973, p. 162).

In theory, an economic and monetary union requires the following elements:

- centralisation of monetary policy;
- a single central bank or a system of central banks that control stabilisation policies;
- convertibility (at least internal) of the participating countries' currencies;
- unified performance on the international financial markets;
- capital market integration;
- identical rates of inflation;
- harmonisation of fiscal systems;
- replacement of balance of payments disequilibria with regional imbalances;
- similar levels of economic development or a well-endowed fund for transfers of real resources to the less-developed regions and those under external shocks; and
- continuous consultation about and coordination of economic policies among the participating countries, as well as the adjustment of wages on the union level.

There may also exist a pseudo exchange rate union (Corden, 1972). In this kind of union, member countries fix the exchange rates of their currencies and freely accept each other's money. However, since there is no pooling of foreign reserves and no central monetary authority, such a union is not stable. Since there is no mechanism to coordinate national policies, an individual member country may choose to absorb real resources from the union partners by running a balance of payments deficit with them. In addition, such a country may change the effective exchange rates of other members by creating a deficit in the union's balance of payments with the rest of the world. A full EMU is not vulnerable to such instability. Foreign exchange rates are pooled and monetary policy is operated by a single monetary authority. In a pseudo exchange rate union, there is imperfect coordination of national monetary policies, but in a full EMU the problem is solved by policy centralisation (Cobham, 1989, p. 204).

This section is structured as follows. It starts with the traditional single-criterion theory of monetary integration (4.2.2). A superior, that is, cost–benefit model, further develops these theoretical concepts (4.2.3). Parallel currencies (4.2.4) are presented before the analysis of the past monetary arrangements in the EU (4.2.5). The eurozone, that is, monetary unification based on the Maastricht Treaty, is the subject matter of the next subsection (4.2.6), followed by an examination of the achievements, problems and outlook for the eurozone (4.2.7). A separate subsection (4.2.8) deals with the British quandary regarding the eurozone. Monetary integration in the West African Economic and Monetary Union is then presented (4.2.9). The conclusion (4.2.10) is that the creation of the eurozone is the greatest achievement in the history of European integration. However, we should sound a note of caution. Since the whole enterprise is primarily based on political considerations, it needs to pass the test of time.

4.2.2 TRADITIONAL MODEL

Exchange Rate Regimes

Both flexible and fixed exchange rates have their virtues and vices. The benefits of a flexible exchange rate include their free floating according to demand and supply. This improves the spatial and industrial allocation of resources and in liberal societies removes the need for government interference. There is no need whatsoever for foreign currency reserves, because balance of payments disequilibria are adjusted automatically. A country is free to pursue independently its national priorities regarding inflation, employment and interest rate targets. Any possible mistake in economic policy may be straightened out by continuous and smooth changes in rates of exchange. If there is an external shock, flexible exchange rates offer a fast short-term adjustment policy instrument.

There are, of course, several arguments against free floating. The most serious one is that this rate of exchange divides the economies of different countries. As such, it reduces the benefits of economies of scale and lower costs of goods and services, and also influences spatial location of firms in a suboptimal way. The floating rates of exchange stimulate speculation, uncertainty and instability. All the alleged criticisms about a smooth adjustment without the need for changes in reserves were disproved during the 1970s. Any change in the rate of exchange would have an impact on home prices. Its repercussions would be swifter in the countries which have a relatively greater degree of openness. There is, however, another problem with the floating rate of exchange: overshooting. Although some changes in economic policy have been announced but not yet applied, the floating rates of exchange move and overshoot their long-run equilibrium.

The objections to fixed exchange rates are a mirror image of the virtues of the flexible rates, and include the following. Fixed exchange rates do not permit every country to pursue independently its own policy choices and goals regarding employment and inflation. Countries have to subordinate their monetary policy to the requirements of the external balance. When the time comes for adjustment in the rate of exchange, it may be relatively large and disruptive in relation to the smooth, potentially frequent and small changes in the exchange rate in the case of the free float. The system of fixed rates of exchange requires reserves of foreign currencies for intervention in the currency market in order to defend the fixed parity. These funds may be derived from alternative productive uses.

The arguments in favour of fixed rates of exchange are those which justify the introduction of a single currency in a country. This system stimulates cooperation and integration among countries and under certain conditions contributes to an efficient spatial distribution of resources, as opposed to floating rates which encourage 'economic nationalism' and disintegration. The most important feature of fixed rates of exchange is that they bring stability; prices are less inflationary and more transparent and comparable; the spatial allocation of resources is improved because decisions about investment are not delivered exclusively on the basis of short-term market signals; uncertainty is reduced and trade flows are stabilised. All this stimulates economic integration among countries, which is why the establishment of the Single European Market in 1993 'needed' to be followed and supplemented by a monetary union.

There is no general rule about which system of exchange rates is better. If a country has a balance of payments deficit, then it has to restore competitiveness. This can be done by a reduction in private and public consumption, so it requires cutting wages directly, or devaluation, which in turn cuts wages indirectly. But the choice of the exchange system here plays no role at all. Reductions in real income are necessary under either exchange rate system.

It is a formidable task to offer a definite conclusion about the 'correct' system of exchange rates. The above choices contrast costs against benefits of a particular system. In practice, the choice may often be between the costs of one system and the costs of another. In such a situation it comes as no surprise that economists cannot be unanimous. In an EMU, small countries can overcome the disadvantage that stems from their relatively small economic size and thus these countries can create an area of economic stability. They may also reap the fruits of economic cooperation in an area where expectations may have a significant degree of accuracy.

Discussion about the exchange rate regimes (fixed, floating or managed), sheds light on only one side of a country's monetary policy in an international context. The other side deals with domestic monetary policy and market rigidities or flexibility. Linkages between national money supply and rates of interest, as well as price levels and price control, factor mobility and flexibility in wages, must also be considered. Otherwise, the debate may be pointless.

In its highest form, monetary integration means that everybody within an EMU is free to use their own currency for any kind of payment to partners. The minimum definition of monetary integration is absence of restrictions, while the maximum definition requires the use of a single currency (Machlup, 1979, p. 23). Monetary integration may exist even without the integration of markets for goods (and services) and the integration of goods markets may exist without monetary integration. The former case is exemplified by countries in the West African Monetary Union which have a single currency, the CFA franc (*Communauté financière africaine franc*), and a similar monetary policy to France (their former colonial master), but there is little real integration of markets for goods, services and factors among them. An example of the latter case is EFTA, where member countries have integrated their markets for manufactured goods, but there is no formal integration of the monetary policy among them.

Factor Mobility

The traditional single criterion model of monetary integration started with the theory of optimum currency areas. This theory was a purely academic exercise during the 1960s, and interest in it was not revived until the early 1990s. This was prompted by the intention to bolster the European Monetary System (EMS) introduced in 1979, as well as by the break-up of formerly federal states in central and eastern Europe, in particular the former Soviet Union. These developments created problems of how to handle the new and separate currencies in most of the newly independent or newly created states which are 'small' and have their own national currency, in some cases, for the first time in their history.

The theory of optimum currency areas was started by Mundell (1961). Economic adjustment can take place on international and national levels. On the international level, the basic issue of adjustment is whether the countries with trade deficits will accept inflation or deflation in their respective economies. On the national level, the pace of inflation in countries that have a single currency, but several regions, is regulated by the desire of the central authorities to permit unemployment in regions with a deficit. If the objective is the achievement of a greater degree of employment and stable prices in a world where there is more than one currency area, then this requires floating exchange rates based on regional rather than national currencies. For Mundell, a region is the optimum currency area as people and factors move easily within it. Factor mobility is the criterion that determines a region. Within the currency areas factors are mobile, while between them factors are immobile. Fluctuating rates of exchange are, according to Mundell, the adjustment mechanism between various currency areas, while factor mobility and flexible labour markets are the equilibrating mechanism within them.

Factor mobility as the criterion for an optimum currency area should be considered carefully. The difficulty with this model is that a region may be an economic unit, while the domain of a currency is an expression of national sovereignty which seldom coincides with a region.[1] In addition, factor mobility may change over time. Strong integration of goods and factor markets can tighten the budget constraint. Borrowing today implies higher taxes tomorrow. If factors (labour and capital) are free to move, this may give incentives to mobile factors to move to lower-tax jurisdictions which would erode the tax base in a high-tax country. Investors know that today's ability to borrow from a government is limited by its capability to tax tomorrow, and also its ability to tax tomorrow is restricted by factor mobility. Hence, investors will reduce or refuse their lending to governments threatening to exceed their borrowing capacity. The higher the integration of factor markets, the sooner this takes place (Eichengreen, 1993a, p. 1335). The governments also know the likely reactions of firms (and workers) and are therefore careful not to run large public deficits. Otherwise, they risk the departure of both firms and employable labour elsewhere.

Mobility of capital is sensitive to the degree of economic activity and the outlook for economic prosperity. In the 19th century, labour and capital were flowing towards the Americas and Australia as the areas of promising development which needed those factors most. During the 'golden' 1960s, however, labour and capital were flowing towards the growing developed and relatively rich regions and countries.

Labour is not a homogeneous factor. Its full mobility may exist only in relatively small geographical areas or within a very specialised professional category. The experience of the EU(6) provides the best proof of this. The flow of labour in the EU in the 1960s and up to the mid-1970s came mostly from workers from Mediterranean countries that were not members of the EU (with the exception of Italy). Those labour flows may not be taken as intra-EU labour mobility. In addition, migration rates are lower in Europe than they are in the US or China.[2] This is not only between European states, but also within them. 'The elasticity of migration with respect to interregional wage differences is at least five times as large for the US as for Britain' (Eichengreen, 1993b, p. 132). The gap in this type of responsiveness between the US and China on the one hand and other European countries on the other is bigger. The implication is that labour mobility is a less powerful labour market stabiliser (adjustment mechanism) in Europe than is the case in the US or China. In addition, EU governments may tax personal income at high(er) rates without any great danger that this would provoke emigration.

Regions within a single country grow at different rates. The same holds for countries in an EMU. These developments cause tension which is exacerbated if there are fewer opportunities for adjustment, such as factor mobility and fiscal compensations. Some argue that it would not have been sensible for northern Italy (for example, Padania) to have a separate currency, thus creating a separate economy from the southern (Mafia-ridden, subsidy-consuming and Vatican-dominated) part of the country. The cost of such monetary disintegration could be relatively high. However, quite a number of 'Padanians' have a very different opinion about the issue.

At the start of the 1960s when Mundell wrote his article there was relatively little free international mobility of capital. A decade later he (1973) published another, little-known article on common currencies. That was at a time when large-scale international mobility of capital was starting to emerge, which had seemed a remote possibility at the beginning of the 1960s. In this situation the exchange rate ceased to be a factor of stabilisation because of speculative attacks and exchange market disturbancies. Thus, Mundell's earlier suggestion to use the exchange rate to stabilise the economy should be abandoned. Exchange rates are inefficient stabilisation mechanisms. This is a view contrary to that presented in 1961. Mundell's (1973) argument is that capital markets may be fully integrated only within a monetary union. Countries that are outside the monetary union are exposed to asymmetric external shocks that come from instability in international capital flows, as those countries do not have an insurance cushion that is provided by the monetary union. Hence, Mundell became the promoter of widespread monetary unions. 'The optimum currency area is the world' (ibid., p. 125). Even though Krugman (1998b) labels economics a 'dismal science', it nevertheless has its own seductive charm and attraction: one may be awarded the Nobel Prize for saying totally opposite things (Mundell received the prize in 1999).

Opponents of monetary unions find support in the early Mundell (1961). Every country is special in some way and it ought to preserve its monetary independence. These arguments are flying high in Britain, Denmark, Sweden and Switzerland, the countries that have been quite successful in maintaining monetary stability. Elsewhere, southern and eastern European countries remember periods of monetary instability. A monetary union with principal trading partners that can provide a stable and credible currency anchor may be a vehicle for these countries to import and secure monetary stability. The later Mundell (1973) was their bible. Monetary union was expected to bring gains such as reduction in exchange risk, lower transaction costs, price transparency and expansion in trade that would act as an additional engine of growth (de Grauwe and Kouretas, 2004, pp. 681–2).

An economic entity may pass the criteria for an optimum currency *ex ante*, but may fail the same criteria *ex post*. Krugman (1993d, p. 260) suggested:

> Theory and experience of the US suggests that EC regions will become increasingly specialized, and that as they become more specialized they will become more vulnerable to region-specific shocks. Regions will, of course, be unable to respond with counter-cyclical monetary or exchange rate policy . . . In the US the heavily federalized fiscal system offers a partial solution to the problem of regional stabilization. Unless there is a massive change in European institutions, this automatic cushion will be absent.

Productivity gains from increased regional specialisation and a secure enlarged market are most probably the principal reasons for creating an economic and monetary union. Does Krugman share the same fine-tuning fallacy as Mundel (1961)? If one takes into account risk-sharing through portfolio diversification in bond holdings, the case for a monetary union among specialising entities may become even stronger (McKinnon, 2004, p. 705).

Openness

The second major approach focused attention on the degree of openness of a country (McKinnon, 1963). Commodities in a country may be distributed between tradables and non-tradables. The ratio between these goods determines the degree of its openness to trade. As a rule, the smaller the country, the greater the relative degree of its trade interaction with other countries. A high degree of openness embodies relatively high specialisation of a country and it may be taken as the criterion for the optimum currency area.

When the tradable goods represent a significant part of home consumption (unless most of the consumer's goods are imported), then changing the rate of exchange would not change a country's real wages. Such a country (presumably small) is advised to enter into an EMU for it may not be an optimum currency area as a single unit (Corden, 1972). The greater a country's openness, the smaller the chances for the effective independent use of exchange rates as an instrument for economic stabilisation.

Relatively small economies are advised to link their currencies with the currency of their major trading partner. This is the case when the former colonies link their currency to that of their former master (for example, the CFA franc zone) or when some of the transition economies of central and eastern Europe linked their currencies to the German mark as was the case during the 1990s. The second piece of advice to small economies which conduct a significant part of their trade among themselves is to link their currencies together. In the case of a single currency all financial dealings may be simpler. This is part of the reason why the 50 federal states in the US may not be able to separately issue and operate their own currencies in an efficient way.[3] A similar observation may be applied to the 16 federal states in Germany or the 23 Swiss cantons. Further evidence can be found in the serious problems in handling monetary affairs in most of the independent states that emerged from the former Soviet Union. Whether such advice is unconditionally applicable to all EU countries is debatable among economists.

If small open economies operate near full employment, then internal fiscal measures are advised for the adjustment of the balance of payments. Fixed exchange rates will be more productive in this case than flexible ones as they would have a less damaging effect on prices. A variation in the exchange rate will elicit a small response to the change in the level of imports because of high dependency on imports. Therefore, a variation in the rate of exchange should be much higher than in those countries which are relatively less open.

An alteration in the exchange rate will have a direct and significant impact on real income. Consumers and trade unions will demand indexation of wages with a resulting change in prices and the exchange rate. If money illusion exists, the impression that changes in nominal (money) wages are identical to changes in real income, then a change in the exchange rate may be an effective means for adjusting the balance of payments. However, money illusion is not a long-term phenomenon. It is no longer even a short-term event. An alteration in the exchange rate may not be effectively employed for the adjustment of balance of payments independently of other instruments. Flexible rates of exchange may be an efficient means for the adjustment in relatively large economies which are linked by small trade relations.

The assumptions in this model are that the equilibrium in the balance of payments is caused by microeconomic changes in demand and supply and, also, that prices in the outside world are stable. The argument about the relative stability of prices in the outside world cannot be substantiated for the period lasting for about three decades since the early 1970s. When prices in the outside world are fluctuating, this is directly conveyed to home prices through a fixed exchange rate. The openness of an economy may be the criterion for an optimum currency area if the outside world is more stable than the economic situation in a small open economy. Fixed exchange rates may force small open economies to pursue a more rigorous economic policy than under the fluctuating exchange rate regime which permits a policy of monetary 'indiscipline'. If money illusion does not exist, then the possibility of altering the exchange rate as an adjustment instrument becomes meaningless.

The Benelux countries and Denmark have participated in the EMS since its creation. Other small European countries (for example, Austria, Finland, Norway, Sweden and Switzerland) initially decided to stay out of the EMS and manage their exchange rates unilaterally, although these countries paid close attention to the developments in the EMS. The argument of openness fails to explain why small EU countries such as Denmark and Sweden still have national control over their exchange rate in spite of strong trade relations with the member countries of the EMU (introduced into the EU in three stages by the Maastricht Treaty). In addition, it fails to explain why relatively large countries such as Germany and France opted for the EMU and the euro, while Britain is still out of it. The basic flaw of the optimum currency area theory is that it fails to distinguish between the case for fixed exchange rates and the situation when separate states join together in a common currency (McKinnon, 1994, p. 61).

Diversification

The third major contribution stated that countries whose production is diversified do not have to change their terms of trade with foreign countries as often as the less-diversified countries (Kenen, 1969). An external shock in the form of a reduction in foreign demand for a country's major export item may have a relatively smaller impact on the diversified country's employment than on a specialised country's economy and employment. Finally, links between home and foreign demand, as well as export and investment, are weaker in the diversified country than in a specialised one. Large and frequent exchange rate changes are not necessary for a diversified country because of the overlap in the reduction and increase in demand for various export goods. This overlap may keep the proceeds from exports at a relatively stable average level. In conclusion, Kenen suggested that fixed rates of exchange are suitable for diversified countries. Diversification is his criterion for the optimum currency area.

Diversification helps the stabilisation of home investment and adjustment of the economy to external shocks. The US may be the closest example of such an economy. The continued wide acceptance and use of the US dollar as an international currency reflects in part the essential structural properties of the US economy that change slowly over time.

These include the size of the US economy and its diversification and openness. Countries with specialised economies and relatively low levels of diversification have a need to belong to currency areas with flexible rates of exchange. Such countries are more vulnerable to external shocks than are diversified economies. Examples may be found in Denmark, Iceland, New Zealand and most of the African countries.

Regarding the EU, one may note and expect that the structure of the economies of the member countries may change, even radically alter, as the result of the EMU (and eastern enlargement). If transactions costs and exchange rate risk are important for commerce, then the EMU would promote competition and trade. This would also influence specialisation and spatial location of firms and industries. Hence, at least in theory, the past structure of the national economies and historical data may not be appropriate benchmarks for the comparisons of future business cycles and industry-specific external shocks. Empirically, Frenkel and Rose (1998, p. 1023) found that 30 years of data from 20 industrialised countries provide a strong positive relationship between the degree of bilateral trade intensity and the cross-country bilateral correlation of business cycles.

While McKinnon deals with internal shocks to an economy, Kenen considers external ones. Kenen's argument may be weakened in the situation where the reduction in foreign demand occurs during a general fall in demand during recession. This reduces total demand, so a country's diversification does not help much in mitigating the fall in the demand for exports.

Other Strands

Coordination of economic policies can be a criterion for an EMU (Werner, 1970). Economic policies which are not coordinated among countries may be a major reason for the disturbance in the equilibrium of the balance of payments. Coordination of economic, in particular, monetary policies, from a supranational centre requires political will on the part of the participating countries. A declaration towards such an objective was made in the Maastricht Treaty.

One criterion for monetary integration may be a similar rate of inflation among the potential member countries (Fleming, 1971). Diverging ratios of employment to inflation among these countries will cause hardship and lead to disagreements about the necessary policy tools. Countries with a balance of payments surplus would be driven to accept a higher rate of inflation than when they are free to choose this ratio. Conversely, countries with deficits may be asked to tolerate a higher rate of unemployment than they would be willing to accept if they were free to choose it.

An optimum currency area may be defined as a region in which no part insists on creating money and having a monetary policy of its own (Machlup, 1979, p. 71). A monetary union which imposes minimum costs on the participating countries may be called an optimum currency area (Robson, 1983, p. 143). An optimum currency area may be alternatively defined as an area in which the net benefits of integration (for example, increase in welfare in the form of greater stability in prices and smaller disturbances coming from abroad) outweigh the costs (restraint to individual uses of monetary and fiscal policies) (Grubel, 1984, p. 39). This is to say, 'the last recruit conferred more benefits than costs on existing members, but the next one will do the reverse' (Maloney and Macmillen, 1999, p. 572).

An optimum currency area aims at identifying a group of countries within which it is optimal to have fixed exchange rates while, at the same time, keeping a certain flexibility in the exchange rate with the third countries (Thygesen, 1987, p. 163). Very small currency conversion costs and openness are likely to make the EU an optimal currency area, while high levels of government spending will make it less likely (Canzoneri and Rogers, 1990, p. 422). An optimum currency area may also be defined as one that attains the macroeconomic objectives of internal balance (low unemployment and inflation) and external balance (a sustainable position in the balance of payments) (Tavlas, 1993a, p. 32). Mongelli (2002, p. 7) defines an optimum currency area as the optimal geographical domain of a single currency which may include several currencies irrevocably linked by a fixed rate of exchange.

In the initial phase during the 1960s, discussions about optimal currency areas emerged from the debate about fixed and flexible exchange rates. The properties or criteria for an optimum currency area include: flexible prices and wages; high factor mobility; strong financial integration to overcome financial disequilibria; fiscal integration to provide transfers to those adversely affected by asymmetric shocks; openness of the economy of the integrated group to cushion the impact of changes in prices in the external world; a high diversification of the economy to mitigate the impact of external shocks; similarities in national rates of inflation; and political integration to facilitate loyalty to the common commitments in the monetary sphere, and also to increase the credibility of the scheme and avoid cheating.

It is very difficult to measure these elements and assess their impact. Therefore, the notion of an optimum currency area is more theoretical than practical. An eternal trilemma (impossible trinity) in open economies is how to solve three basic issues. One cannot have perfectly mobile capital, monetary independence and a fixed exchange rate all at the same time (although it is possible to have any two of these elements). If a government or a monetary authority of an EMU wants free capital mobility and fixed exchange rates, it has to give up monetary autonomy. If it wants monetary autonomy and free capital mobility, it has to have a floating exchange rate. If it wants fixed exchange rates and monetary autonomy, it has to restrict capital mobility.

A region may be an economic unit which does not necessarily coincide with the domain of a currency. An optimum currency area may be able to sustain itself. Its definition may demand liberalisation of all economic activities within it and its protection against the outside world. Despite their relevant arguments, these definitions can hardly be applied to countries in the real world, since the states are constituted in a suboptimal way, such that full economic efficiency (regardless of the external world) can seldom, if ever, be achieved.

The EU may not be an optimum currency area according to these criteria. There is a relatively low labour mobility and wages are quite rigid if there is a need and pressure to move downwards. If this is what really matters for the success of an EMU, then the cost may be unacceptably high. A single criterion theoretical model has a narrow scope. Therefore, it is unable to present the costs and benefits of an EMU. The next task is to amend this shortcoming.

4.2.3 COSTS AND BENEFITS

Issues

A more practical and fruitful method of analysing an EMU is to study the optimum economic policy area, rather than the optimum currency area. A single state becomes increasingly ineffective as an independent policy-making unit in modern times of continuous changes in technology, relatively easy and cheap dissemination of information and frequent market changes. This is true for all countries in the world, but it is not true for all of them equally. Therefore, not all of them seek international solutions to their national problems. In a situation where economic problems assume global proportions there is only one optimum policy area: the world (Panić, 1988, pp. 317–30). The most pressing international economic problems cannot be solved by countries acting in isolation. The solutions to these problems can be found in coordinated national economic management. A system of safeguards which would include assistance in the form of transfer of (real) resources to the countries which experience temporary difficulties, is an essential feature for the survival of an efficient multilateral system of trade and payments.

The shortcomings of the traditional single-criterion and optimum-currency model of international monetary integration may be overcome by the 'new theory' of monetary integration that relies on the cost–benefit model. This model offers more satisfactory policy implications. The costs which may be incurred by a country's participation in monetary integration may be traced to the losses of a country's right to alter independently its rate of exchange, its ratio between inflation and unemployment, its ability to handle regional development policy, as well as its seigniorage. Monetary integration brings a number of benefits. These include a dismissal of the exchange problems within the group of countries in the arrangement, an increase in influence in monetary affairs and an increase in monetary stability. The larger the integrated area, the larger the gains. We now turn to the analysis of the costs and benefits of monetary integration.

Costs

First, the creation of a supranational body to conduct monetary policy (money supply, rate of interest and rate of exchange) in an EMU may be perceived as a significant loss of the participating countries' national *sovereignty*. This is the first cost, which may provoke adverse political as well as psychological consequences in countries that take part in the arrangement. The most sensitive issue may be the loss of the right to alter independently the rate of exchange. The loss occurs fully against the currencies of partner countries and partially against other countries. A right, often used selfishly, is lost. However, the gains here come from the pooling of the monetary policies of the member countries that can exercise a much greater leverage over their monetary policy in comparison to the situation prior to monetary integration.

When policy makers want to adjust the balance of payments by means of alterations in a country's rate of exchange, then the most critical issue is the fall in real wages. Labour may accept a fall in real wages under the condition that the other alternative is (longer-term) unemployment. A reduction in the rate of exchange introduces an increase in the price for imported goods, as well as for some home-produced goods and services. The impact of the devaluation depends on the openness of a country. A reduction in real wages brings an advantage in the cost of labour and a relative decrease in the price of export goods and services in the short run. This classical scenario may be seriously questioned. Money illusion no longer has a significant impact on labour. Every increase in inflation and corresponding fall in real wages, under the assumption that there is no change in productivity, encourages labour and concerned trade unions to demand an increase in wages. The short-term cost advantage of devaluation is eroded by such increases.

Devaluation as an instrument of economic policy may not alone eliminate deficits in the balance of payments. The government may state that its policy objective is not to use devaluation in the fight against inflation. Such a policy goal may act as an important incentive to firms to resist higher costs because their goods and services would become uncompetitive on the foreign and, potentially, home market, if trade were free. A recession may be another, although less desirable, cure for inflation. Shrinking markets give firms incentives to keep prices low, while rising unemployment forces trade unions to resist increases in wages.

Exchange rates started to float in the early 1970s and did so for a decade. The experience has provided sufficient evidence that a country's autonomy in a situation of floating exchange rates is overstated. The reason is that a majority of countries are small and open. This leads to the conclusion that the sole use of the exchange rate as the adjustment mechanism of the balance of payments is of limited significance. Fiscal policy[4] and labour mobility are necessary supplements. The devaluation of a national currency is a sign of failure to manage the economy soundly and carefully according to stringent, but widely accepted and applied international standards. The standards of international economic prudence show that it is the national bureaucracy which is the only loser from the deprivation of the right to devalue the national currency. Therefore, the loss in autonomy in the management of a country's rate of exchange as a policy instrument is of little real significance.

If, however, the rate of exchange of a group of countries such as the EU is fixed to an anchor currency such as the German mark, as was the case in the EMS until August 1993, the situation can change. If international capital markets are free, the loss of autonomy in the fixing of the exchange market does not matter as long as the business cycles match one another. If the cycles differ, as has been the case in the EU, partner countries may be reluctant to follow the monetary policy of the anchor currency, since it may not match the necessary policy actions of the other participating countries.

The correlation of business cycles among countries depends on the depth of their economic integration, particularly integration in trade. If a common currency among countries assists in promotion of trade, as it is widely claimed, then this may contribute to synchronising business cycles.

Second, it was argued that floating rates of exchange permit unconstrained choices between unemployment and inflation in a country. On these grounds, countries may seem to be free to pursue their own stabilisation policies. An EMU constrains the independent national choice of the inflation, unemployment and interest rates. This national choice, as a second cost of monetary integration, is constrained by the choice and influence of other partner countries. A loss of the right to deal independently may significantly jeopardise national preferences regarding the possible choices. A country with relatively low inflation and a balance of payments surplus may, in accordance with its economic and political strength, impose its own goals on other partner countries, because it has much less pressure to adjust than the other countries.

A common currency levels the competitiveness of the group in the monetary field. If a region's factor productivity is lower than the average in the group, then the regional/country authorities will have to 'tolerate' unemployment. Labour mobility (outflow) may be a solution to the problem. The higher the labour mobility, the more diversified the output pattern, and the more flexible prices and wages, the smoother the adjustment. Applied to the EU, only the relative diversification of the economic structure may pass the test for a smooth adjustment. Other macroeconomic criteria (labour mobility and flexible wages) do not fare well at all.

This consideration has been examined with geometric rigour by de Grauwe (1975). It was proved that countries differ regarding the position of their Phillips curves, rates of productivity growth and the preferences of governments between unemployment and inflation. These are the differences that explain why, in the absence of an EMU, rates of inflation among countries will be equal only by accident. For a smooth operation of an EMU, the condition is not only balanced growth, but also equal unemployment rates, otherwise the EMU may not survive without intercountry compensatory transfer of resources. The mere integration of economic policy goals may not be effective without agreement on the means to achieve the agreed targets. If countries cope with a common problem and employ different tools, the outcome of harmonisation of economic policy objectives may only do more harm than good.

The Phillips curve suggests that there is a measurable, inverse relation between unemployment and inflation (for example, see Figure 4.3, p. 371). The government could reduce unemployment by means of a demand stimulus such as an increase in the budget deficit, while the price for this policy is increased inflation. In Milton Friedman's model, the rate of unemployment is independent of the rate of inflation. The followers of this school criticise Phillips curve theory for not seeing that continuous inflationary policy provokes changes in expectations about future inflation. They argue that there is only one rate of unemployment at which prices (inflation) and wages are constant: the natural rate of unemployment or the non-accelerating inflation rate of unemployment (NAIRU).

No matter what a government does, the rate of unemployment may not fall below the national NAIRU. It is like a speed limit for an economy. However, this rate is not constant over time. It is determined by real factors which include minimum wage legislation, tax policy, dole money, labour mobility, the level of education and impetus for vocational training, demographic factors, payroll taxes and various add-on costs,[5] as well as the choice between work and leisure. In another words, the NAIRU is determined by the structure of the labour market, rather than by the amount of demand. Most of these factors are influenced by economic policy. Every attempt to lower the rate of unemployment below the NAIRU by means of monetary expansion would only accelerate inflation. Hence, the loss of this economic policy choice is also of limited significance.

The main way to reduce unemployment is to reduce the NAIRU. This can be done by reducing the social security benefits below the minimum wage for unskilled labour, shortening the time during which these benefits apply, providing incentives for vocational training and controlling the demands of trade unions. Economic policy should be active in combating unemployment. The long-term unemployed have obsolete experience and training which makes them less attractive to potential employers. Those who are unemployed compete less vigorously on the labour market and put less downward pressure on wages. The NAIRU increases with the expansion of the long-term unemployed. Economic policy should withdraw social benefits from those who refuse vocational training and/or jobs with the exception of anyone beyond the agreed age. The problem of the EU and its member countries is that they have not dealt with the issue of the long-term unemployed, but have continued to hand out relatively generous benefits for long periods. Almost half of the unemployed in the EU are out of work for over a year, while in the US the proportion is about 10 per cent.

The Canadian experience during 1950–62 with a fluctuating rate of exchange is illustrative. Canada wanted monetary independence in relation to the US. Theoretical arguments (illusions) about greater national independence and freedom regarding employment policy in a flexible exchange rate situation seemed attractive. Canadian hopes were high. At the end of this period a mismanaged government intervention succeeded in destabilising prices in Canada and growth stagnated. The decision to abandon flexible exchange rates showed that the benefits in the stability of employment and economic independence are smaller than the cost paid in economic instability and efficiency. Given the contemporary capital market integration among open economies, significant differences in real interest rates among different countries may not exist. Hence, an open economy may not rely independently on this instrument of economic policy. In a situation where two or more currencies are close substitutes and where there exists free capital mobility, the central banks of these countries cannot conduct independent monetary policies even under fluctuating exchange rates. Small open economies may be advised to link their monetary policies to those of their major partners in trade and investment.

Third, a serious problem in a monetary union may be traced in the inflow of capital into the prosperous regions. The regions losing this capital expect a compensatory public action including transfers from the prosperous ones. Those countries which feel that their destiny is to be losers from an EMU would not enter into such an arrangement. The system of transfers may be a bribe to these regions/countries to participate. When there are budget deficits and expenditure cuts, the funds for transfers may not be found easily. None the less, the gainers may be quite happy to compensate the losers and protect the net gains from integration.

Fourth is the loss of seigniorage. This comes from the national currency held abroad (also called the inflation tax).[6] Instead of selling debt, a government may print money and, hence, raise revenue in order to cover its budget deficit. The government taxes (inflation tax) the holders of cash held by the public and the commercial banks' low-interest-bearing deposits/reserves held at the central bank.[7] In an EMU, inflating a national way out of economic crisis is not possible. Therefore, a country in need is supposed to reduce its debt or sell more reserves, or both.

Fifth includes changeover costs from switching to a new currency. These are administrative, technical printing and distribution costs of the new currency such as the adaptation of money distribution and vending machines. Unscrupulous traders may use the confusion linked with the introduction of the new numéraire to increase prices (as happened during the introduction of the euro in 2002).

Southern European countries that have a history of monetary instability were enthusiastic about the introduction of the euro. However, once the euro was introduced, it became quite unpopular in Italy and Greece. Prices increased. Table 4.1 shows price increases in select food items in Italy in the period from November 2001 to November 2002. Each family purchases food on an almost daily basis. Consumers could observe and feel the continuous dwindling of their purchasing power. The official explanation was that these food prices do not greatly affect the general rate of inflation. This gave 'little comfort for consumers who have experienced price increases of 30 per cent on goods and services they buy daily' (de Grauwe and Kouretas, 2004, p. 682).

No one expected such a price increase. How did this happen? A possible explanation may include the following elements. Food is sold on a relatively competitive market. However, price elasticity of demand for food is low. It may be hard for an individual seller to exploit this low price elasticity of demand, since he/she would be 'punished' by competitors and clients, and he/she would lose business. Collective action by sellers is necessary to exploit this situation. Such action is not easy in a normal situation. However, the opportunity does arise occasionally – the introduction of the

Table 4.1 Price increases of food products in Italy, November 2001–November 2002 (%)

Food	Price increase
Breakfast (bread, snacks)	23.3
Pasta, bread, rice	20.1
Beverages	32.9
Meat, eggs and fresh fish	22.1
Cold cuts	27.5
Canned food	30.9
Fruit and vegetables	50.8
Frozen food	23.6
Total	29.2

Source: Eurispes according to de Grauwe and Kouretas (2004, p. 683).

euro opened a window of opportunity that was abused by sellers. The lesson was learned. When another country adopts the euro, the initial period should be followed by certain temporary price control (ibid., p. 683).[8]

To sum up, an EMU introduces significant losses in the constitutional autonomy of participating states, but real autonomy to conduct independent monetary policy for a small open country in the situation of convertibility, synchronised economic cycles and openness for trade and investment will remain almost intact.

Benefits

The benefits of monetary integration are numerous, but generally intuitive in their nature. They are barely quantifiable and non-economists have difficulty in comprehending their character and significance. The principal gains from monetary integration are the following:

- The most important benefit that an EMU brings to its participants is an improvement in integration of markets for goods, services and factors.
- Prices are transparent and directly comparable. This boosts competition and specialisation in tradable goods and services. Spatial and industrial location of resources is improved.
- In a situation of stable prices, interest and exchange rates, internal trade and investment flows are not volatile, as there is no exchange rate risk and uncertainty.

- Transaction[9] and hedging costs are significantly reduced.
- There are gains from additional trade.
- Investors may decide with a high degree of long-term confidence. There are no intra-union controls for direct investment. For example, without a single currency, a German investor may regard an investment project in Belgium as riskier than the same project in Germany.
- By unifying monetary and coordinating fiscal policies, the participating countries are led to fewer distortions while combating macroeconomic disequilibria. This introduces both a greater internal monetary stability and an increase in influence in international monetary affairs. This contributes to economic growth and dynamic gains.
- The pooling of national reserves of foreign currencies is also advantageous for the members of an EMU. By internalising their 'foreign' trade, these countries reduce their demand for foreign currency reserves. Such reserves may not be necessary for trade within the group, but they may still be needed for trade with third countries. Anyway, there are certain economies in the use of reserves. Their level is reduced and overhead costs are spread throughout the participating countries. These funds can then be spent on or invested in alternative and more productive uses.

This is an expectation in theory. A single currency in the EU was likely to save on the exchange reserves of the member states.[10] In practice, countries still hold official reserves, which may be a hangover from the Bretton Woods system of fixed exchange rates. However, that system fell apart three decades ago. Therefore, the need to hold reserves ought to be reduced, perhaps significantly. None the less, global foreign exchange reserves still exist without a declining tendency. The reason is that countries still need such reserves to close transitory gaps in the demand and supply of foreign exchange.

The net effect of monetary integration may not be easily and directly quantified. Let us assume the reverse case. There were tremendous costs as a result of the monetary disintegration of countries such as the former Soviet Union or the former Yugoslavia. Just imagine the losses of the monetary disintegration of the US or Germany where each federal state independently handles its own currency. If there is no control group of similar non-integrated countries, then there is no yardstick against which one may compare the relative performance of the countries which created an EMU.

The costs which may be brought by monetary integration in the form of an increase in prices or unemployment are relatively easy to identify, borne by the few and perhaps short term. If they are not short term, then an indefinite intra-union system of transfer of resources is a necessary condition for the survival of the scheme. The benefits which accrue from monetary integration are long term, they come in small amounts to everybody and they are hard to quantify with any precision. Moreover, these benefits create the potential for new capital formation (a permanent growth bonus) which may accelerate growth of output in the long run.

The 'new theory' of monetary integration suggests that there are somewhat fewer costs (loss of autonomy to handle domestic macroeconomic policies) and somewhat more benefits (gains in credibility in the combat against inflation) associated with monetary integration (Tavlas, 1993b, p. 682). The benefits of an EMU are larger the greater the intra-union factor mobility, the more diversified the economies, the higher the flexibility of wages, the greater the internal trade and the higher the synchronisation of economic cycles among the member countries. The EU can pass most of these tests, except for labour mobility and flexibility of wages.

4.2.4 PARALLEL CURRENCIES

Is an irrevocable fixity of exchange rates a sufficient condition for monetary integration or is the introduction of a single currency necessary in an EMU? Suppose that there are various currencies in an EMU which are tied by a fixed exchange rate. If there is an increase in the supply of any of these currencies, then convertibility may be maintained only by intervention, either in the form of the absorption of this currency by the monetary authorities or by a reduction in demand (restriction in transactions). The first method represents monetary expansion, while the other is an act of disintegration.

A common currency may be an outward symbol, but is not a necessary condition for a successful EMU. Capital mobility and irrevocably fixed exchange rates of currencies in an EMU may create a single currency *de facto* in everything except, possibly, in name, while a single currency will create a monetary union *de jure*. Ultimately a single currency will be necessary, because it makes the irrevocable fixity of exchange rates of the participating currencies completely credible. Many international pledges towards fixed exchange rates have broken down.[11] As soon as markets question the promise of the participants in the deal, this leads them to start speculating. In addition, a single currency will eliminate possible conversion charges; prices in the area will be fully transparent and comparable; and there will be external benefits (such as the introduction of a 'better' symmetry in the international monetary system). Individual participating countries will not have even the remote possibility of finding their way out of economic difficulties by using the means of devaluation and/or inflation.

An evolutionary approach to the introduction of an EMU may be that a common currency exists side by side with currencies of the member countries. Once agents are used to dealing with the common currency, it may gradually replace the money of the participating countries. This is the case with parallel currencies. An important issue here is that the new, parallel currency ought to be linked to the pace of economic activity, otherwise price stability can be threatened. In addition, it may bring an extra complication in the monetary affairs of the integrated countries. A gradual convergence among the currencies will cause the participating currencies to yield an identical return. They will become perfect substitutes. A full monetary unification can take place.

Gradual monetary integration suffers from a serious flaw: a lack of credibility. During the transition phase, participating countries may find a way to step out temporarily from the arrangement. A system that permits some, even though remote, autonomy in the national monetary policy in a situation of free capital mobility is subject to speculative attacks (the most obvious example in the EU took place in July 1993). On the one hand, the longer the transition to a single currency, the greater the fragility of the system. On the other, a quick acceptance of a single currency can provoke harsh regional disequilibria for which the countries may not be prepared (for example, a lack of stabilisers such as well-endowed regional funds). Policy makers need to balance the two sides before they decide. They also have to take into account the German experience. Unemployment increased in the former East Germany after reunification with the western part of the country in 1990. It resulted directly from an instant merger of two economies that were on a very different level of development before they were ready for a full EMU. Should the same be repeated in the EU? If one member country is in a process of economic expansion, while the other one is in recession, they need different monetary policy countermeasures. How to reconcile this in the absence of effective built-in stabilisers or automatic transfer of sufficient funds?

The above theoretical model about parallel currencies has two caveats: it ignores network effects and switching costs (Dowd and Greenaway, 1993a, p. 1180). For example, after the break-up of the former Soviet Union (1992), the rouble was a currency which did not fit well into the new realities. Certain newly independent states continued to use the rouble because of the network effects, that is, because it was used by most of their trading partners. In addition, the switching costs from one currency to another are quite high. Thus, it can be better to use only one currency because of the network effects, conversion charges and switching costs. If the benefits of a single currency outweigh these costs, welfare is maximised and it is justified, from the economic point of view, in switching to a single currency. According to a view from the start of the 1990s, in the case of the EU, the German mark would be the best option as the EU common currency. The mark had the biggest existing network, while the Bundesbank had greater credibility than any of the existing central banks in the EU (Dowd and Greenaway, 1993b, p. 243).

The currencies of member countries in an EMU are perfect substitutes. On the one hand, it would be meaningless to talk in this context about a parallel currency, since any such currency would be indistinguishable from national currencies in everything but name. The concept of a parallel currency becomes meaningful only in the intermediate stage of an EMU, when different currencies are not perfect substitutes because of transaction costs and/or exchange rate expectations. Reductions in exchange rate variability diminish the usefulness of a parallel (basket) currency as an instrument for risk diversification, unless transaction costs in the parallel (common) currency decline by more than those in the component currencies. On the other hand, a parallel currency is unlikely to develop in a case where national currencies are only very imperfect substitutes, because of high conversion costs. Widespread use of a parallel currency alongside national currencies can therefore be expected only under a high degree of monetary integration (Gros, 1989, p. 224).

A common currency may replace national currencies after some period of adjustment. Stability in the monetary sphere may be a result. However, the new and single currency in the area would not solve the problem of the budget deficits of member countries that would be revealed, in part, as regional disequilibria.

Gresham's law says that in a situation of two currencies (in his example, gold and silver coins) circulating side by side in the economy, then 'the bad money will drive out the good', except where there is a fixed exchange rate between the two currencies. This result has not materialised in certain instances.[12]

4.2.5 EUROPEAN UNION

Background

Integration in the EU has advanced at a pace faster than envisaged in the Treaty of Rome. The customs union was fully established among the founding member countries in 1968, a year and a half ahead of schedule. This was one of the most significant initial achievements of the group.

After the initial success in the establishment of a customs union, the EU contemplated the establishment of an EMU. There were two schools of thought about how to apply this idea. They were the 'monetarists' and the 'economists'. The first school (Belgium, France and Luxembourg) argued that a promising EMU requires an irrevocable fixity of exchange rates of the participating countries from the outset. The member countries will, then, be driven to coordinate their economic policies in order to mitigate and, eventually, eliminate the discrepancies in their economies, necessary for a full EMU. They also argued in favour of a well-endowed fund for the support of adjustments of the balance of payments. Complete freedom of capital movements should be permitted only after the establishment of a full EMU. Finally, they felt that supranationality should be on a relatively low level.

The school of 'economists' (Germany and the Netherlands) argued that fixed exchange rates for a group of countries that are on relatively different levels of development is a formidable task. They argued that the coordination of economic policies should be the primary task, because it would bring economic harmonisation among the participating countries. They argued in favour of a free movement of capital from the outset and felt that fixed exchange rates could be introduced only after the fulfilment of the above conditions.

The Werner Report (1970) was offered as the blueprint for EMU in the EU. The report required fixed exchange rates and free mobility of capital. Thus, it represented a compromise between the two schools. Super-optimism (EMU by 1980) was not rewarded because the report overestimated the will of the member states to abandon their monetary authority in favour of a supranational body, in particular in the light of the turmoil on the currency markets during the 1970s. This approach may also have failed because it wanted to fix rates of exchange without prior monetary reform among the member countries.

European Monetary System

The early 1970s were characterised by significant turbulence on the international monetary scene. Currencies were fluctuating, so this state of affairs endangered the functioning of trade flows in the EU. The Council of Ministers asked the member governments not only to follow the ±2.25 per cent margins of fluctuation in relation to the dollar, but also to reduce the level of fluctuation among their respective currencies. This created the 'European snake' (common margins of fluctuation). If the daily fluctuations of the currencies of the EU member states were plotted, the result would be a snake-like ribbon. The width of the snake depended on the fluctuation of the strongest and the weakest currencies, remaining always within the ±2.25 per cent fluctuation margins of the dollar tunnel. The creation of the snake was mainly a European reaction to the erratic behaviour of the dollar on the international money market.

The main feature of the snake was intervention. When the sum of the fluctuations exceeded the margins, intervention was supposed to take place (the strongest currency should purchase the weakest one). The dollar tunnel disappeared in 1973, so the snake found itself in the lake. The currencies in the snake were entering and leaving the system quite often. This introduced uncertainty in trade relations in the EU. Apart from external pressures which the snake was unable to resist, an internal shortcoming (different national monetary policies) also played a role. Something should have been done about that.

The member countries of the EU wanted not just to preserve the already achieved level of economic integration, but also to add to it. A further step was the creation of the EMS. The approach was completely different from the one which established the snake. Instead of preparing various economic plans for political consideration, the EU member countries first delivered their political decision about the establishment of the system, and then reached agreement about the technical/operational details of the system. The EMS was introduced in 1979, and its objectives were:

- to stabilise exchange rates through closer monetary cooperation among the member countries;
- to promote further integration of the group; and
- to contribute to the stabilisation of international monetary relations.

The key role in the EMS was played by the European Currency Unit (ECU). The ECU was basically a 'cocktail' of fixed proportions of currencies of EU member countries. The share of every currency in the ECU depended on the economic potential of the country (aggregate GDP), its share in intra-EU trade and the need for short-term monetary support. The composition of the ECU is presented in Table 4.2. Alterations in the composition may occur every five years or when the share of each currency changes by at least 25 per cent in relation to the originally calculated value. In addition, it can be changed when the currency of a new member country enters the 'basket'. The currency composition of the ECU was 'frozen' by Article 118 of the Treaty of Rome (as revised by the Maastricht Treaty), which is why the currencies of Austria, Finland and Sweden are not included in the basket.

The Exchange Rate Mechanism (ERM) of the EMS has been at the centre of controversy since its inception. Every currency in the EMS had its own central rate versus other partner currencies and the ECU. In relation to the partner currencies in the system individual currencies could fluctuate within a ±2.25 per cent band. The exceptions were the Italian lira, the Spanish peseta and the British pound, which were permitted to float

Table 4.2 Composition of the ECU (%)

Currency	Weight in the 'basket'			
	1979–84	1984–89	1989–94	1995
1 German mark	33.0	32.0	30.1	32.7
2 French franc	19.8	19.0	19.0	20.8
3 Pound sterling	13.3	15.0	13.0	11.2
4 Dutch guilder	10.5	10.1	9.4	10.2
5 Belgian franc	9.3	8.2	7.6	8.4
6 Italian lira	9.5	10.2	10.15	7.2
7 Spanish peseta	–	–	5.3	4.2
8 Danish krone	3.1	2.7	2.45	2.7
9 Irish pound	1.1	1.2	1.1	1.1
10 Portuguese escudo	–	–	0.8	0.7
11 Greek drachma	–	1.3	0.8	0.5
12 Luxembourg franc	0.4	0.3	0.3	0.3
Total	100.0	100.0	100.0	100.0

Source: European Monetary Institute (1996).

within a ±6 per cent limit.[13] When a currency reaches its limit (upper or lower) of fluctuation in relation to another EMS partner currency, then intervention in the national currency of one of the two central banks is compulsory. Intervention within the margins of fluctuation may be either in the national currency of the EMS members or in dollars.[14]

The fluctuation of each EMS currency against the ECU was slightly stricter. The Commission has individualised each currency's margin of fluctuation. It was strictest for the German mark ±1.51 per cent and widest for the Irish pound ±2.22 per cent (the currencies under the 'special treatment' had wider margins of fluctuation than the standard ones in relation to the ECU).

There was an implicit objective behind the relatively strict margins of fluctuation for currencies in the EMS: to drive member countries to accept similar economic policies and to converge. This convergence does not necessarily aim at averaging out the economic performance criteria. Although the EMS has not produced full convergence of the macroeconomic indicators of the member countries, it seemed for quite some time that it was heading towards the desired outcome. The best signal was that most member countries remained in the EMS despite strains.

In order to prevent frequent interventions, the EMS has introduced an early-warning system in the form of a divergence indicator. The divergence threshold was ±75 per cent of a currency's fluctuation in relation to the ECU. The role of this indicator was ambiguous. As soon as the divergence threshold was reached, the countries in question were not formally required to do anything, even to consult. Therefore, this innovation has not played an important role in the EMS. None the less, consultation and cooperation of the monetary authorities of the EU member countries have compensated, at least in part, for this shortcoming.

The strongest arguments for the non-participating countries to join the ERM seemed to be predominantly political. It was not conducive to integration for them to remain aloof from one of the most significant achievements of the EU at that time. In addition, and more importantly, the creation of a genuine internal market for goods, services and factors would be incomplete without a single market for money.

The EMS funds for exchange market interventions were relatively well endowed. The very short-term financing facility for compulsory interventions provides the participating central banks with an unlimited amount of partner currency loans. None the less, in practice the Bundesbank did not accept intervention without limits. The short-term monetary support disposed of ECU14 billion for the finance of temporary balance of payments deficits, while the medium-term support facility disposed of ECU11 billion (but the use of this mechanism was subject to certain conditions).

A country with a better performance in inflation, balance of payments, employment and growth than other countries has least pressure to adjust and, in relation to its size and weight, it may call the tune in the shaping of other countries' economic variables. Hence, Germany was able to dominate within the EMS. The system operated asymmetrically in formulating the monetary policies of other member countries as they had to bear the adjustment burden. Since inflation was reduced and other monetary variables were generally aligned among most member countries, the EMS operated in a more symmetric way before the reunification of Germany in October 1990.[15]

The EMS could sometimes slow down the rate of economic adjustment of a member country. When countries borrow on the international financial markets, such markets do not consider exclusively the creditworthiness (reserves, deficits, experience in adjustments and outlook) of the borrowing country. These markets also consider membership of the EMS and its possibilities for financial support. In this indirect way, financial markets take into account the reserves of other EMS countries. The markets believe that the partner countries will help the borrowing country to resolve its financial difficulties. This was a recognition of the relative success of the EMS. However, it may prevent a country from accepting greater monetary discipline. A government may employ a more ruthless method of eroding the real burden of debt and use inflation. In any case, a country which follows a policy of a relative monetary undiscipline will reduce domestic reserves and lose creditworthiness in the long run. Foreign creditors may reasonably demand higher interest rates which usually deter investment and, hence, reduce the future economic potential of the country. An agreed limitation for national borrowing needs to be a part of an EMU.

Apart from funds for exchange market interventions, other EMS adjustment mechanisms include home price and income alterations, rates of interest and control of capital flows, as well as increased cooperation and exchange of information. Controls of internal trade flows are, of course, prohibited.

The rates of exchange in the EMS were semi-fixed. The EMS did not have as its goal the petrification of exchange rates among member countries. The adjustments of the central rates may take place either every five years or according to needs. When all other mechanisms for intervention were used up, the country in question could ask for permission to change the central rate of its currency. The Council of Ministers usually decided about these changes during the weekend (when the financial markets are closed). The effects of realignments (or devaluations) may be eroded by inflation. So, the best and, surely, the hardest way for the stability of the system is that the deficit countries increase productivity above the EU average.

In spite of its relative rigidity, the EMS made the rates of exchange quasi-flexible. If a currency was experiencing difficulties that could not be solved by intervention, then the system permitted adjustments (revaluations and devaluations) of the central rate of exchange. This kind of adjustment happened relatively often during the first years of the existence of the EMS.

A change in the central rate of a currency (devaluation) was still a permitted means for the restoration of competitiveness among EMS member countries. In a distant scenario without national currencies, even *de facto*, the restoration of national competitiveness could be achieved by an increase in productivity, reduction in wages or by labour migration to the advanced regions or all of these. The US is an example where wages are flexible and labour is highly mobile. At the same time a single currency has a smooth internal performance. The US interregional adjustments are eased by a system of implicit federal government transfers of real resources. The federal government spends much and taxes little in the backward or ill-performing states/regions, while it does the reverse in the advanced states/regions.[16] A similar mechanism does not (yet) exist in the EU, which, with its vast internal market, does not yet have economic stabilisers on the American scale that are intended to ease the adjustment troubles of both countries and regions within them. There are, however, growing structural funds in the EU. The adjustment requires not only the transfer of real resources, but also measures to enhance mobility of factors from low- to high-productivity regions. On this count, the EU has so far failed. Hence, because of relatively low labour mobility, EU countries will be able to sustain relatively high taxes on people's income.

All member countries of the EU have exchanged for ECUs 20 per cent of their gold reserves (the role of gold was partly reaffirmed)[17] and 20 per cent of their dollar reserves with the European Monetary Institute (EMI) (until 1994, the European Fund for Monetary Cooperation). These assets were swapped on a revolving quarterly basis for ECUs. Hence the ECU was not a newly created reserve asset which was an addition to the existing stocks of reserves such as the special drawing rights. The creation of the ECU transformed a part of the existing reserve assets into another asset. The amount of ECUs issued changed every quarter in relation to the changes in member countries' volume of reserves, the price of gold and the dollar exchange rate.

The ECU was used as:

- an accounting unit for intervention;
- a means of settlement among central banks;
- a part of international financial reserves;
- a basis for the calculation of the divergence indicator;
- a unit for the store of value (because of its relative stability); and
- a unit for financial transactions and statistics of the EU administration.

There were, also, ECU-denominated bonds. Many banks opened personal accounts in ECUs and offered an interest rate which was a weighted average of interest rates of the participant countries in the ECU. They also offered travellers' cheques denominated in ECUs. Interest rate differentials reflect mainly differences in the national rates of inflation. Once the exchange rates start to move with inflation differentials, the profitability of holding ECUs was expected to diminish.

The ECU used by the monetary authorities was the official ECU, while businesses and the public used the private or commercial ECU. Nevertheless, the ECU market was not fragmented. All dealings were in a single ECU, as the definition of both was the same. A central bank could hold ECUs. If the national currency came under pressure, the bank could sell ECUs and purchase the national currency. This might be a cheaper and less notable way of intervention than a direct borrowing of other currencies to buy domestic when the exchange rate was falling. The major reason for the relative spread in the use of private ECUs was the demand of business for simplifying transactions and, possibly, avoiding capital controls where they existed. The ECU was attractive because of its greater stability in relation to its components. Apart from the intra-firm trade, firms did not have great incentives to use the ECU when the rates of exchange were not stable (since they may have wished to exploit the difference in prices). Non-EU investors preferred to deal in a single currency rather than several different ones. The market value of the ECU was not directly influenced by the value of the dollar as it was not incorporated into the ECU basket as is the case with the special drawing rights. Therefore, dollar holders could buy ECUs and hedge against the dollar exchange risk.

A shock came on 16 September 1992. The demand for funds to cover the excessive costs of the reunification of Germany put pressure on its budget. In order to contain this inflationary pressure, Germany raised interest rates. At about the same time, the US wanted to revive demand by cutting interest rates. The dollar became cheaper, while the German mark became dearer. The divergency prompted speculation that hit the weaker currencies hard in the EMS. Currency market speculation forced Britain, and then Italy, to suspend their membership of the ERM. According to documents released for the first time in 2005, in the exercise to support the exchange rate of the pound, Britain spent £27 billion.[18] The net cost of the expulsion from the ERM to the British taxpayer was £3.2 billion.[19] This had a disastrous long-term effect for the then ruling Conservative party and contributed to the suspicion about the future monetary integration projects. The EMS was also on the brink of a breakdown. In this situation, some would argue, a single EU currency would evade such a crisis.

Britain failed to foresee (i) the effects of the recession that was provoked by the German unification, (ii) its impact on the adjustable-peg exchange rate in the situation of high international mobility of capital and (iii) underestimated the determination of EU partners to enter into a monetary union. There was also a pledge to respect and maintain the exchange rate of DM 2.95 to a pound. 'But such a system is always likely to evince promises that cannot be kept.'[20]

Britain, however, gained certain benefits from the 25 per cent depreciation in the value of the pound in the following months. For example, by February 1993, Philips moved the manufacturing of cathode tubes from the Netherlands to Britain. Likewise, Hoover also relocated the production of vacuum cleaners from France to Scotland (Eichengreen, 1993a, p. 1329).

Adjustments in the rates of exchange together with capital controls were used by some countries in the EMS, for example Italy and France, to control the domestic monetary system more easily than through other, relatively harsh means, such as recession. They were able to follow, to an extent and for some time, a different course in the national macroeconomic variables from their foreign partners. Capital, one of the major lubricants of the economy, was 'forced' to remain at home. In addition, an outflow of capital pushes up interest rates. This slows down the economy, perhaps at a moment when it needs to grow. However, the problem is that capital controls retard structural adjustments that need to take place in any case. Although a short-term effect of controls may bring certain policy successes, the long-term costs of the structural transformation increase, which is why an interest rate policy may be preferred.

Capital controls are effective ways to manage monetary affairs in a situation where money markets expect adjustments in the exchange rate.[21] Then, controls ensure that holders keep (in the country) the currency that is about to be devalued. Controls may be permanent or temporary (as emergency measures to prevent speculative capital flows). In the absence of capital controls, devaluation of weak currencies cannot be postponed; however, controls make the delay of devaluation possible. None the less, delays increase uncertainty about the rate of exchange in the future and, hence, jeopardise investment decisions. With capital controls, a relatively modest increase in the national rate of interest will achieve the desired monetary policy effect. Without capital controls, the only instrument that can be used with the same effect is a sudden and, usually, large increase in interest rates. The main defence of capital controls is not found in the fact that they are cost free, but rather that they are less costly than the movements of exchange and interest rates that would occur without these controls (Folkerts-Landau and Mathieson, 1989, p. 8).

The removal of the remaining capital controls in the EU in 1995 was one of the notable achievements of the Single Market Programme. It made residents of the EU sensitive to differences in interest rates. Transnational corporations (TNCs), including banks, as major beneficiaries of the dismantling of capital controls, could effortlessly change and diversify the currency composition and maturity of their financial portfolios. By doing so, TNCs and other money holders may jeopardise the objective of monetary policy of individual member countries in a situation with easy and cheap currency substitution. An increase in the national rate of interest in order to reduce the supply of money and 'cool' the economy will have the opposite effect. Increased interest rates will attract a sudden inflow of foreign capital and increase the national supply of money. Such swift changes are not very likely in the flow of goods (and services). Conversely, if the intention of the national government is to stimulate home economic activity by a reduction in interest rates, the effect of such a policy will be the opposite from the one intended. Capital will fly out of the country to locations where rates of interest are higher.

Without capital controls, investors speculate about which currency is to be devalued next. Enormous capital flows can destabilise exchange rates.

With a daily trade of about $1.2 trillion on international foreign-exchange markets and with more than one currency in the market, it is possible to gamble. No national intervention can triumph over the speculators. This happened in the EU in the summers of 1992 and 1993. The grand dreams of an EMU in the relatively medium term were, in fact, pushed further into the future.

In the situation with huge and rapid capital movements, a monetary union with the major trading partners may offer a promising degree of insulation against harmful features of international capital mobility. A separate currency and independent setting of the rate of exchange may move in a way obstructive to the economy. As such it may become in itself a source of shocks to the economy.

Without capital controls, large differences in the rate of interest among the EMS countries cannot be sustained. In the new situation, the EU member countries have no other rational choice but to pool their national monetary policies and cooperate. Any increase in monetary instability among EU currencies will provoke the mobility of funds in the search for a greater profit in the short run or a greater security in the long run, thus making it impossible to maintain EMS parities without even greater harmonisation of national monetary policies (Panić, 1991). The Bundesbank was calling the tune in the EMS. In that situation a pooling of monetary policies among the countries of the EU could increase the sovereignty of smaller countries because they would, in the new situation, have some say in the EU monetary policy-making process from within. Although national central banks may become increasingly independent from their national governments, they need to enhance their reliance on other national central banks in the EU.

A reduction in the variance of economic indicators among countries may illustrate their economic convergence. The narrowing of the differences in the performance criteria among countries does not necessarily mean that their standards of living are becoming more equal. Membership of the EMS may be used by the national government as a convincing argument during the pursuance of a prudent national economic policy in the fight against any opposition. The EMS has introduced convergence in domestic monetary policies and inflation rates, but it has not been fully backed up by corresponding progress in the fiscal sector and external balance.

A mere convergence in the rate of inflation and other monetary variables may not be enough for the smooth operation of the single EU market. The EMS was not able to increase significantly the use of the ECU, the role of the European Fund for Monetary Cooperation was marginalised and the present form of the system was unable to bring about spontaneous monetary integration. Those objectives might be achieved if there were a common European central bank, a system of central banks or a common monetary authority. This did not happen before the implementation of the Maastricht Treaty because of a fear that the monetary issues would be dealt with by a remote bureaucracy. Every government was afraid of losing monetary sovereignty: the right to cheat on its citizens, firms and other holders of its money without a promise to convert paper money into gold. Another fear was that they might not be able to pursue their own stabilisation policy. These anxieties were not well founded. In order to carry on with national stabilisation, balance of payments, regional, industrial and other policies, governments still have at their disposal taxes, subsidies, some procurement and certain budget deficits. The only (severe) restrictions on their sovereignty to choose stabilisation policies were that they could not employ exchange rate changes and have a different rate of inflation from their partner countries.

It must always be borne in mind that in an EMU, the national governments still have the opportunity to tax and spend in the way they think is most appropriate. Budget deficits are still possible, subject to only one condition: expenditure must be financed by borrowing (on commercial terms) rather than by printing domestic money. For example, borrowing and expenditure of the cantons in Switzerland and provinces in Canada are not subject to constraints. The *Länder* in Germany restrict borrowing only to the extent that it is necessary to finance investment. The federal states and local governments in the US are not allowed to run deficits (this is an American version of the Stability and Growth Pact). Only in Australia does the federal government continuously supervise state debts.

The freedom to tax and spend in an EMU, however, is not absolute. As soon as a country's national finances jeopardise the stability of the union, such as excess imports that depress the value of a common currency, the union's authority may intervene. It may impose limits on the borrowing from the central bank and other sources, ceilings on the budget deficit, a request for non-interest-bearing deposits and fines. In a single-currency area, foreign debt has to be serviced by export earnings. The national debt, however, does not present an immediate real burden on the economy because it represents a transfer between present and future generations.

There may be a temptation for a country in a monetary system to run a budget deficit for quite some time according to current needs. Although governments are often safer borrowers in relation to private ones,[22] capital markets will increase interest rates to heavy borrowers when their creditworthiness is jeopardised. Big budget deficits keep long-term interest rates on a higher level than would otherwise be the case. This reduces the size and effectiveness of the cuts in short-term interest rates. The governments of the

EU countries generally failed to do this during the 1980s, hence the lack of power in employing fiscal policy to prop up recovery in the 1990s. If a state in federations such as the US and Canada increases its borrowing, then the value of government bonds falls throughout the country. In this case, the federal government can step in to correct the distortion. However, such a well-developed corrective mechanism does not yet exist in the EU.

4.2.6 EUROPEAN MONETARY UNION

Monetary unions were often, but not always, created as a part of the process of political unification among countries.[23] Economic reasons for an EMU include enhanced monetary stability, improved spatial and industrial allocation of resources, boosted competition because of transparent prices, deepened integration, reduced transaction costs, access to wider markets, gains from economies of scale and from trade, as well as gains that come from harmonisation of policies. Non-economic reasons such as geographical proximity, common language, culture, history and religion contributed to monetary unification. The break-ups of monetary unions are often found in political factors. Once the political unity among the participating countries dissolves, it is most likely that the monetary union will vanish (Bordo and Jonung, 1999, pp. 24–5). Hence, the political will and the firm promise and determination to respect fully a common currency system explains the rise and fall[24] of monetary unions. Interestingly enough, the Irish break with sterling had no noted effect on trade between Britain and Ireland.

The main argument in favour of a common central bank is that it reduces uncertainties and conflicts about and among national monetary policies. It does so by providing a forum in which national views can be represented and problems resolved. In the absence of a common central bank, national conflicts are resolved by market forces with adverse externalities for efforts to promote greater stability of exchange rates (Folkerts-Landau and Mathieson, 1989, p. 15). Therefore, within a common central bank, national sovereignty may be increased in comparison with the previous situation. Independent central banks, such as the judiciary, are constitutional institutions since they are not accountable to the elected government or parliament. Their autonomy comes from a general consensus about long-term economic objectives and from the fact that their instruments may be badly abused by the political majority of the day (Vaubel, 1990, p. 941).

Even though the experts are not subject to great political pressure to court popular opinion, a question still remains: do the appointed central bankers (a part of the elite) possess a knowledge about the country's long-term needs that is superior to that held by the governments that represent the voting public? The same question also applies to the entire national elite. Does it foster the necessary dialogue and cooperation with the general public? Does the general public have the relevant information and clarification by the experts and by the elite to understand and evaluate how a certain decision factors into the national interest? Does the general public have the knowledge to identify and assess the importance and character of crucial decisions for the shape and direction of the national interest? Does the general public have the time and interest to bother with these issues? Voter apathy is becoming common. Is this a reaction to being treated with disdain by the remote and arrogant elite? Or is this situation created deliberately? People need to hold on to their jobs, to have two part-time jobs because of the general uncertainty (possible unemployment or terrorist attacks), because of their mortgages, savings for their old age and/or the education of their children. Hence, they pass on these decisions to the elite. They know that the elite will get what it wants in the end. And all this has a democratic sugar-coating.

During the discussions that led to the Maastricht Treaty, there were two extreme possibilities for the final shape of the EU Central Bank and a number of intermediary ones. One extreme was the model of Germany's Bundesbank. It was independent from the government in the conduct of monetary policy and possibly, therefore, quite successful. The Bundesbank ensured stable prices, high employment, balanced foreign trade, as well as a constant and reasonable economic growth. The other extreme was the Bank of France, in which the government had a full stake. Thus France wanted to see a kind of 'accountability' (transparency in operations and reporting) of the EU Central Bank to public bodies. As Germany was the engine of EU monetary stability until 1992–93, the Maastricht Treaty opted for this kind of central bank for the EU. Many EU member countries preferred to see a 'German-influenced' EU bank, rather than the continuation of the prevailing system that was 'German controlled'. In the system with binding rules and procedures, the smaller EU countries may be represented on the bank's board where they could, at least to an extent, shape policy from within.

The Delors Report (1989) gave an impetus to the creation of the EMU. It envisaged the EMU in three stages. Its wise approach was not to state any specific date apart from mid-1990 for the beginning of the first stage. During this stage, the member countries would strengthen the coordination of their economic and monetary policies. The removal of the remaining capital controls would require this in any case. All countries would enter the ERM of the EMS. Stage two would be marked by the creation of the European Central Bank (a system of central banks or a monetary authority). The major macroeconomic indicators would be set for all member countries including the size and financing of the budget deficit. In addition, the margins of fluctuation in the ERM would be narrowed. The first two stages would not be fully stable, as there would be the potential for speculative attacks. In the last stage of the creation of the EMU, a common central bank would be the only authority responsible for the conduct of monetary policy throughout the EU. Exchange rates among the national currencies would be permanently fixed without any fluctuations. A single currency would emerge. It may be a necessary condition for a genuine single market where national competitiveness would not be influenced by the individual alterations in exchange rates. This was the blueprint for the finalisation of the Maastricht Treaty.

In 1990, the British proposed an alternative plan that would introduce a 'hard ECU' as the 13th currency at that time, in stage two, as a parallel currency. It would be an additional anti-inflationary control on governments that aim to ease national monetary policy. It would be issued by the central bank in exchange for deposits of national currencies. The 'hard ECU' would be managed in such a way that each national central bank would compensate the EU's central bank for any losses caused by devaluation of its currency and that any inflating national central bank would buy back its national currency with, for example, dollars or yen. Wide acceptability of the 'hard ECUs' would prevent national central banks from inflating. The problem with this plan was that the British saw it as an end in itself, not as a vehicle towards a single EU currency. This plan received little support during negotiations over EMU.

After the currency disturbances of September 1992 when Britain and Italy left the ERM, a new and bigger shock took place at the end of July 1993 with its actual demise. Germany's need to obtain funds to finance the reintegration of its eastern region increased interest rates. The country placed its national interest ahead of the concerns of the EU by refusing to cut interest rates.[25] This produced a currency crisis. To ease the strain, a way out was found in an increase in the margins for the fluctuations of the currencies participating in the ERM. They were widened from ±2.25 per cent to ±15 per cent from the central parity. The 'dirty float' began. The EMS revealed its fragility. However, a step back from the EMU path was a preferable action to total suspension of the EMS. The widening of opportunities to fluctuate within the ERM increased the scope for differences in the national economic policies. Even though this was a possibility, it was not exercised. Countries endeavoured to keep the exchange rate of their currencies within the 'old' margins of fluctuation. None the less, the mere existence of the permitted wider margins for fluctuations introduced an element of uncertainty.

A condition for the establishment of the EMU is that 'normal' (without a definition) fluctuation margins for currencies need to be observed for at least two years. However, what was 'normal' in the situation when the ERM remained only in name? The wide increase in fluctuation margins made a mockery of the Maastricht Treaty's intentions to introduce a single currency in the relatively near future. One needs to remember, however, that annual exchange rate movements of ±15 per cent or more are quite common outside the EU (for example, the dollar).

The Maastricht Treaty is in essence mostly about the EMU. This is voiced both in the Preamble and in Article B, as well as in Articles 2 and 98–124, respectively, of the Treaty of Rome (as amended by the Maastricht Treaty). This was an expected step after the establishment of a free internal market in 1993. For a free flow of goods and services, as well as for an efficient sectoral and geographical allocation of resources, a necessary condition is a degree of stability in exchange rates and a removal of conversion costs.

According to the Maastricht Treaty, EMU was to be achieved in three stages. During the first, there was a reinforcement of coordination of economic and monetary policies of the member countries. The second stage started in January 1994 with the establishment of the European Monetary Institute in Frankfurt. This took place in an unsettled exchange rate environment. The EMI was to coordinate the EU members' monetary policies and prepare the conditions for the final stage. The central banks of the member states needed to become independent before the end of the second stage when the EMI would be transformed into an independent European Central Bank (ECB). In fact, there would be a European System of Central Banks, which would be composed of the ECB and the central banks of the member states (Article 107 of the Treaty of Rome).

The ECB is supposed to be very tough on inflation. However, this policy could cost the EU countries hundreds of thousands of existing and new jobs. Perhaps this may be partly true, but the primary source of the EU unemployment problem is not necessarily in a looser monetary or fiscal policy (although both of them were made inflexible by the Maastricht criteria for EMU), but rather in reforms of labour markets and the welfare system. Politicians might have realised somehow belatedly that the only 'soft' option for economic adjustment needs to come from flexibility in national labour markets.

According to the Treaty of Rome (Article 105 as amended by the Maastricht Treaty) the ECB has to:

- keep prices stable;[26]
- define and implement the monetary policy;

- conduct foreign-exchange operations;
- hold and manage official foreign reserves of the member states; and
- promote the smooth operation of the payments system.

There was a chance that Frankfurt would take the major part of trade in the EU single currency if the pound stayed out of this project. Having an EMU whose major financial markets are off-shore would be, on the surface, an unusual arrangement. However, London had already become the market where trading in the German mark, Europe's most important currency (before the introduction of the euro), took place. Hence, its position on the financial markets should not be seriously threatened.

The siting of London as the principal European financial market need not be jeopardised by the location of the ECB in Frankfurt. The US Federal Reserve is based in Washington, DC, while the principal financial centre is New York. London continues to have big advantages over Frankfurt. The chief institutional investors are located in London; regulation is rather light; and there is a cluster of accumulated talent, knowledge, experience and expertise in finance. More people work in the City of London in finance than constitute the entire population of Frankfurt.[27]

The Council of Ministers was supposed to decide by a qualified majority whether a majority (at least eight) of the EU countries fulfil all of the following five necessary criteria for the third stage of the EMU (Article 121 of the Treaty of Rome and Protocol on the Convergence Criteria of the Maastricht Treaty):

- a high degree of price stability (inflation within the margin of 1.5 per cent of the three best-performing EU countries);
- sound public financial position (budget deficit of less than 3 per cent of GDP);[28]
- a national debt of less than 60 per cent of GDP;[29]
- the observance of the 'normal' fluctuation margins (no devaluation within the EU exchange rate mechanism for at least two preceding years); and
- the durability of convergence of economic policies, which should be reflected in the long-term interest rate levels (interest rate has to be within the 2 per cent margin of the three best-performing EU countries).

The final decision about the eligibility of the countries was to be taken in 1998. If a country fails one (or, perhaps, two) conditions but makes good progress on these issues, it may be allowed into the EMU. If the Council is not able to decide about the beginning of the third stage, the Maastricht

Treaty stipulated that it would begin on 1 January 1999 for the countries that fulfil the necessary conditions for the EMU. These countries would irrevocably fix their exchange rates and the ECU would subsequently replace the national currencies by the 'euro'. This was expected to unleash the full potential of the genuine Single European Market. The ECB would follow its primary commitment of price stability and, consequently, set interest rates and conduct foreign-exchange operations. In addition, the ECB would support economic growth and employment. The ECB would report regularly to the EU finance ministers (meetings of the Economic and Financial Committee (ECOFIN) which would issue broad economic policy guidelines) and to the European Parliament. In any case, the application of the five criteria for the third stage of the EMU, if carried out strictly, would have a certain deflationary effect on the economy of the EU.

There are two theoretical types of deflation (a general fall in the level of prices):

- The 'good deflation' is the consequence of improvements in technology (faster computers or more fuel efficient engines) as this permits the production of better new goods at lower costs.
- The 'bad deflation' is the one that creates production overcapacity: the market is flooded with goods that it cannot absorb. Prices fall, but producers neither hire new workers nor invest in new equipment. Consumers are accustomed to falling prices and postpone purchases. Hence, producers have even less revenue. The breakdown of the relation between supply and demand is at the heart of bad deflation.

The immense analytical and policy problem is that the two types of deflation often take place at the same time and within the same industry. Signals can be mixed, so policy advice and actions may be confused and damaging. The way to tackle the deflationary economy is to ensure a sustained demand (consumer spending). Leapfrogging in technology and/or expansion in demand can tackle this problem. With its 'culture' of relentless innovation, the American economy has a degree of resistance to deflationary pressure.

Deflation may easily be cured if the central bank prints more money and passes it to the banks. With this extra cash, banks issue more loans, the rate of interest falls, there is more investment by firms and spending by the population, the economy picks up and the price level stops falling. That is how it works in theory. Suppose now that the economy is in such bad shape that a decline in interest rate towards zero is not enough to revive the economy and to push it towards prosperity. This situation is known as a liquidity trap. There is extra money in the economy, but these funds rest idle. There is no point in lending money if there is no reward (profit) for doing so. Hence, the monetary policy becomes ineffective. If the expectation is that prices will fall further in the future, then consumers will postpone their purchases. This will further depress the current demand.

Falling prices also mean falling incomes and capacity utilisation, as well as rising unemployment. Firms may find that they have to pay their fixed interest rates from a dwindling cash flow, while families have to pay a fixed mortgage out of shrinking income (the real value of debt rises). The indebted cut their spending. All this further discourages both borrowing and spending by the private sector. In order to balance its books, the government may borrow until the investors have faith in the government's ability to repay its debt. At the point at which debt grows faster than revenue and when there is no credible scenario that the budget can be brought under control, creditors will not lend money. Then, the government may both increase taxes and cut social spending; this became a well-accepted way of life (pensions, health care and education) and a part of the social contract in Europe, which would hit hard the middle class and those most in need.

One strategy to fight deflation can be to announce an inflation target by a credible[30] central bank and to flood the economy with money. A certain, but small, inflation may always be welcome in the countries that have adopted the euro. The reason for this type of controlled inflation is simple: it is the inflexibility in prices and nominal wages to downward pressure. If inflation is non-existent or if it is very low, real wages and prices in weak industries will remain high. This will trigger bankruptcies and job losses.

Germany and France are the main victims of very low inflation. The employed in these two countries have relatively high wages and high prices prevail in the production of non-tradable goods and services.[31] Labour market reforms, including a reduction in the welfare benefits are also one of the policy choices. However, the political process for this is thorny and highly uncertain.[32] None the less, France made moves in 2005 to introduce a certain flexibility in the 35-hour working week rules. The leitmotif was 'earn more by working more'. The earlier policy of sharing work (lump of labour fallacy) has proved to be illusory. The root of the problem ought to be tackled: over-regulation. Hundreds of thousands of new jobs could be created by a deregulation of protected markets (loosening of criteria for issuing licences). This is most obvious in services ranging from hotels, shops and taxis to accounting and hairdressing.

The Maastricht convergence criteria for the eurozone are arbitrary. Economic theory suggests other conditions for an EMU. These include flexibility in labour markets, factor (labour) mobility, openness, diversification and fiscal transfers. The Maastricht criteria could be met once the countries are *in* the EMU; however, *before* such union takes place this may be extremely hard to achieve. 'The Maastricht treaty has it back to front. . . . On balance the Maastricht convergence criteria are *obstacles* to a monetary union in Europe' (de Grauwe, 1994, pp. 159–61; original emphasis). The question is whether the difficult journey towards a durable EMU as structured by the Maastricht Treaty is becoming impossible.[33]

In the rush to meet the Maastricht criteria for the third stage of the EMU, governments introduced additional (temporary) taxes, took on austerity measures and, consequently, restrained flexibility of fiscal policy. The consequences were numerous industrial actions, as well as high taxation as an obstacle to employment.

The 1998 decision was that Austria, Belgium, Finland, France, Germany, Ireland, Italy, Luxembourg, the Netherlands, Portugal and Spain satisfied the Maastricht criteria for the EMU. Even if some countries such as Belgium and Italy (later, also, Greece) had excessive public debt, they were judged to have made sufficient progress towards the satisfaction of these criteria. Greece subsequently fulfilled the same conditions and joined the eurozone group in 2001 (even though it was revealed in 2004 that the officially reported deficit figures were falsely deflated). Britain, Denmark and Sweden chose not to participate in the eurozone.

A single currency is favourable for the US economy, as there are no harmful effects in the sense of restraints on the national macroeconomic policy obvious in the eurozone. This is because the American economy has three features that are still missing in the EU:

- (alleged) wage flexibility;
- relatively high mobility of labour; and
- automatic fiscal transfers from the central government.

As shown in Figures 4.1 and 4.2, respectively, the Maastricht convergence criteria for the EMU were applied in a relaxed way. If the EMU took place only among the select group of countries that strictly fulfilled the Maastricht criteria, the excluded countries would face divergence rather than convergence in certain macroeconomic variables, because they have been left out of the arrangement. Exchange rates between the full eurozone countries and those that are outside could be volatile.[34] This would have an adverse impact on trade flows in the Single European Market.

As so much political capital had been invested in the EMU, it took place as planned in the Maastricht Treaty, but it was based on a flexible and generous interpretation of the Maastricht criteria. Hence, there may be certain doubts about the stability and endurance of the system. Policy makers should always consider a contingency plan in the event of tensions and if

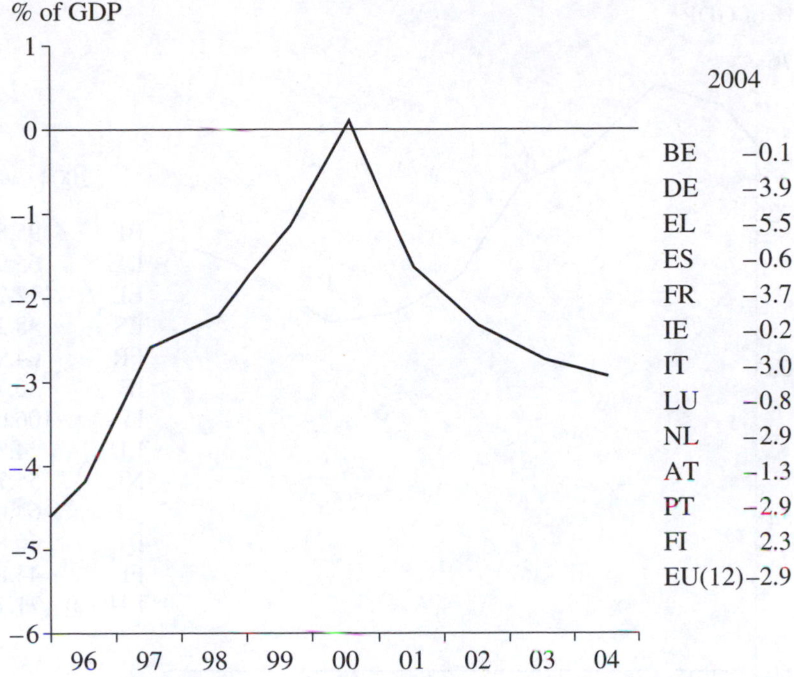

Source: European Commission ECFIN (2005).

Figure 4.1 General government balance as per cent of GDP, 1996–2004

things go wrong or, indeed, very wrong with the EMU in the years to come. However, this has not taken place and there are no contingency plans.

4.2.7 ACHIEVEMENTS, PROBLEMS AND OUTLOOK

The officially declared and planned schedule for the introduction of the euro as a new European *über*-currency followed the expected timetable:

- *February 1996*: start of the banknote competition;
- *December 1996*: winning design selected;
- *mid-1998*: start of printing;
- *January 1999*: scheduled start of the EMU (stage three); one-for-one conversion of the ECU into the (virtual currency) euro; irrevocable fixation of the rate of exchange of the currencies in the EMU;
- *mid-2001*: currency delivered to EMU central banks;

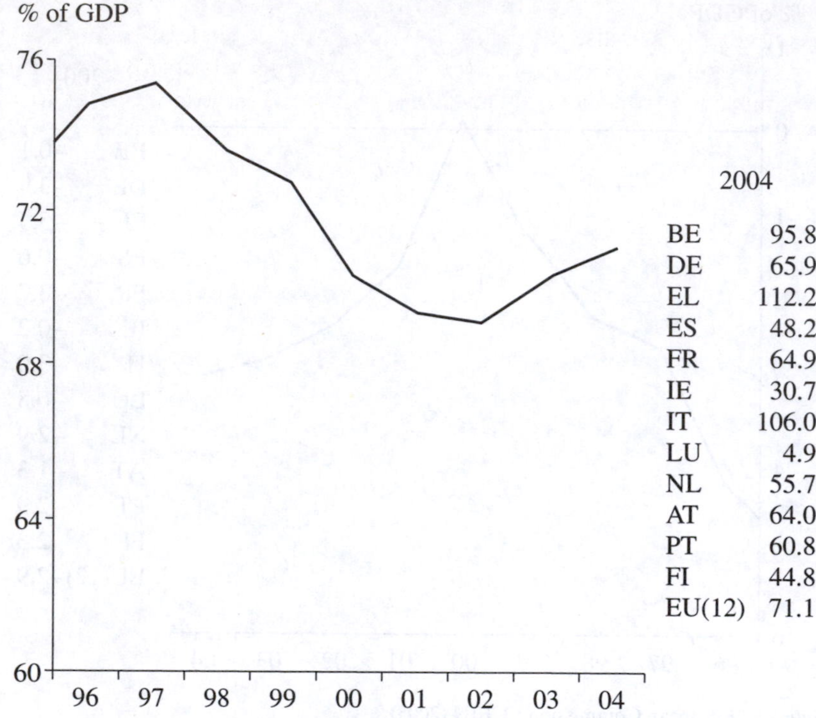

Source: European Commission ECFIN (2005).

Figure 4.2 General government debt as per cent of GDP, 1996–2004

- *January 2002*: euro notes and coins (real currency) enter circulation *alongside* national currencies which will no longer be legal tender six months after the introduction of the euro;[35] and
- *July 2002*: the euro is the only legal tender in the eurozone countries.

Although many had serious doubts not only about the EMU but also about its timetable, the implementation of the eurozone among the 12 EU member countries was, indeed, the greatest achievement in EU history. In addition, it was one of the greatest monetary achievements since the existence of written history, in particular because it involved paper money and the whole enterprise took place without political integration among countries.

The objective of the Stability and Growth Pact (1997) was to keep the EMU on track by means of a sustainable fiscal policy. The legal basis for this agreement was in Articles 99 and 104 of the Treaty of Rome. The pact was needed to stabilise the debt/GDP ratios at reasonable levels following years of rising public debt. If one or several governments borrow recklessly, no limits on borrowing would give them a chance for a free ride in the eurozone. As a result, all eurozone countries would pay a price for such irresponsible national policy as interest rates would increase throughout the zone. Therefore, the reasoning behind the pact was to shield the ECB from national pressures to reduce debt through inflation.

The EU politicians generally accepted the German-inspired idea of the Stability and Growth Pact. To put it bluntly, Germany mistrusted Italy in monetary affairs. The pact was disputed only when its application brought national economic pain. The pact limits the eurozone member country's deficit to 3 per cent of GDP and threatens any member country that exceeds this limit with relatively heavy fines. Germany wanted to have automatic fines imposed on any eurozone country with a budget deficit of over 3 per cent. However, France argued that sanctions for excessive borrowing by member states must be a political matter. The final agreement was that the Council of Ministers (excluding the country being hit) may penalise the country with a fine of up to 0.5 per cent of its GDP by a qualified majority vote. Countries in deep recession are exempt from a fine, with the proviso that their economies shrink by more than 2 per cent within a year.

Even though the threat of fines exists in theory, it was hard to imagine that they would be applied in practice (indeed, sanctions were only an empty threat). One cannot fine a state as if it were a tipsy driver. States must never be humiliated. This stance is something that questions the credibility of the system. Perhaps certain non-pecuniary sanctions such as a reduction in the voting right or weight for a limited period of time may need to be considered.

When a country's budget is in the deficit zone covered by the Stability and Growth Pact, the European Commission has the option of three types of involvement (see also Articles 101 and 104, respectively, of the Treaty of Rome):

- If a country deficit moves towards the 3 per cent limit, the European Commission may just note the problem.
- If it comes close to the 3 per cent limit, it may warn the government of the country in question.
- If the limit is broken, a complicated fining procedure may begin.

The European Commission issued its first warning to a eurozone country on 30 January 2003. This was to Germany, the biggest European economy and, ironically, the country that insisted on the introduction of the pact. Subsequently, the Commission also issued warnings to France, Italy,

Greece and Portugal (see data in Figure 4.1). While Germany and Portugal made rigorous spending cuts in order to try reduce their budget deficit below 3 per cent in 2004, France was facing falling government revenue and rising unemployment. Hence, to reduce the budget deficit below the 3 per cent norm would have been a tough task for some years to come.

The European Commission's president, Romano Prodi, told *Le Monde* (17 October 2002): 'I know very well that the Stability Pact is stupid, like all decisions that are rigid. The Stability Pact is imperfect, we need a more intelligent mechanism and more flexibility'. This gave certain hints that the European Commission may yield to the demands of big countries (Germany, France and Italy which together account for three-quarters of the eurozone economy), even though the (small) countries that have taken unpopular and strict macroeconomic measures are reluctant to give Germany and France a 'get out of jail free' card.

Most of these deficits arose because of cyclical factors (growth rates were lower than expected), rather than because of reckless national spending. Hence, revenues were falling and were not meeting the budgetary outlays. The growth prospects are such that Germany cannot expect to balance its budget by 2006 as requested by the Commission. This means that the 3 per cent limit could be breached (with impunity) for four or five years in a row. This is adding to the strain in the Stability and Growth Pact. Is a solution to the problem to relax the 3 per cent limit? Would this introduce a precedent: when the rules governing the eurozone become inconvenient, should they be rewritten? Would this put at risk the credibility of the eurozone?

Eurozone finance ministers (ECOFIN) breached the Stability and Growth Pact in November 2003 by voting not to impose sanctions on France and Germany for continually breaking the 3 per cent deficit cap. This would be bad enough even in a simple free trade area. But recall that the eurozone is a currency union. France and Germany tried to avoid the rules without incurring any penalty. Because of this, the European Commission took ECOFIN to the Court of Justice in January 2004.

The issue in this case was not whether the pact with an empty threat of sanctions is sensible or not (it isn't), but whether the Council of Ministers has the right to abandon a procedure which is necessary for legal certainty. This is not only a legal but also a political question about who runs the EU – the national governments (through the Council of Ministers) or the European Commission which represents the common EU interest? The power struggle and worsening atmosphere between the two EU institutions was obvious. The July 2004 ruling of the Court of Justice was to nullify (not overturn) ECOFIN's decision. This means in practice that no matter what the European Commission may recommend, it is the Council of Ministers that ultimately makes the decision.

The Stability and Growth Pact created a source of conflict within the EU. In reality, national borrowing on the capital market may not significantly increase interest rates for all countries. Hence, this may be a weak argument against the pact. However, a stronger argument against it is this: if a country is experiencing slow growth or is in recession and if its budgetary deficit is close to 3 per cent of the GDP, the pact may force that country to tighten its budgetary policy and restrain the economy at the very time when it needs loosening. Some argue that the pact has been a 'stupid idea' as markets could offset the profligate spenders by charging an extra premium on loans without damaging the others. Others say that the pact is necessary to enforce fiscal rigour. Is the construction of an EMU to be a learning-by-doing process? Or is this type of learning more appropriate for a primary school? The markets and voters may exact swift retribution for unwanted experiments and painful errors.

Modern nations have many (social) responsibilities towards their citizens, which are stretched during recessions when there is a greater expectation and demand for the social system to operate. The Stability and Growth Pact was blind to this issue. The new altered arrangement should treat countries in a different and more flexible way. A budget deficit should be treated as a target over the business cycle that allows certain flexibility on both sides. If a country's target is a 50 per cent debt to GDP ratio, then simple maths implies that this country can maintain an average annual budget deficit of 2 per cent (assuming that the nominal annual average GDP growth rate is 4 per cent).[36]

Since its introduction, the operation of the pact has been marred by three problems: countries failed to adjust their fiscal balances during 'good times'; growth slowed down; and the Byzantine procedure for dealing with countries that breached the agreed fiscal margins. Some may argue that the pact was acting as an alarm bell that many (big countries) wanted to mute. There was also a risk of ending up with a pact that nobody respects, and another that the pact would be weakened by so many exceptions and flexible rules that it would be of little real value. After a protracted controversy and debate, the European Council in Brussels (23 March 2005) endorsed the ECOFIN report of 20 March 2005 regarding the Stability and Growth Pact.[37] Among a maze of legal terms and literary sugarcoating in Annex II of the Presidency Conclusions is the following statement: 'The aim is not to increase the rigidity or flexibility of current rules but rather to make them more effective.'[38] So, the goal is to have a more effective pact (with rules as quoted above). And then, to achieve the stated aim, the Conclusions continue:

> The Stability and Growth Pact lays down the obligation for Member States to adhere to the medium term objective (MTO) for their budgetary positions of 'close to balance or in surplus' (CTBOIS).

> In light of the increased economic and budgetary heterogeneity in the EU of 25 Member States, the Council agrees that the MTO should be differentiated for individual Member States to take into account the diversity of economic and budgetary positions and developments as well as of fiscal risk to the sustainability of public finances, also in the face of prospective demographic changes.
>
> The Council therefore proposes developing medium-term objectives that, by taking account of the characteristics of the economy of each Member State, pursue a triple aim. They should firstly provide a safety margin with respect to the 3% deficit limit. They should also ensure rapid progress towards sustainability. Taking this into account, they should allow room for budgetary manoeuvre, in particular taking into account the needs for public investment.
>
> MTOs should be differentiated and may diverge from CTBOIS for individual Member States on the basis of their current debt ratio and potential growth, while preserving sufficient margin below the reference value of −3% of GDP. The range for the country-specific MTOs for euro area and ERM II Member States would thus be, in cyclically adjusted terms, net of one-off and temporary measures, between −1% of GDP for low debt/high potential growth countries and balance or surplus for high debt/low potential growth countries.[39]

Translated into plain English this means that the Stability and Growth Pact rules were changed (loosened) in order to make them compatible with economic cycles. According to these reforms, budget deficits that are in excess of 3 per cent of the GDP are allowed, provided that this overdraft is small (up to 4 per cent), temporary and acceptable to other member countries and the European Commission. The finance ministers and the European Commission should give (ill-defined) 'due consideration' to the EU policy goals and unity, as well as to a country's net contribution to the EU budget and international aid expenditure.[40] Hence, the pact, buried in November 2003, received official confirmation and is more in line with reality. Escape clauses had made it toothless. It is hard to imagine how a fiscally profligate government can be punished.

These changes have been welcomed by a number of EU countries as many of them had experienced difficulties in abiding by the earlier pact rules. Central and east European EU member countries were also positive about the revisions as they hope to join the eurozone by the end of the decade. However, others have expressed concerns that the pact is no longer worth the paper it is written on. The ECB worries that these changes may influence and damage the international standing of the euro. An introduction of country-specific fiscal targets, excluding expenditure such as pensions and public investment even in part, may introduce the potential for everlasting manipulations and 'creative accounting'.

Prodigal members of the eurozone may be able to free ride on the back of others. Earnings spreads among bonds issued by the eurozone member states are negligible. Eurozone countries treat bonds of the partners as equal when they are accepted as collateral. Banks can always liquidise 'lower-quality' bonds with the ECB without incurring any loss. In the new situation, while accepting lower-quality bonds, the ECB should consider curtailing such an operation. A small, but differential, charge may send a signal about the potential risk. This would then spread to the private banking sector, which could also 'punish' the profligate country.

Although the original pact reduced the room for manoeuvre for autonomous national budgetary policy, this might be the price to be paid, at least at the beginning, for the credibility of the new common paper *über*-currency. Lest it be forgotten, this credibility is based on a promise, a credible promise for the time being, to pay. But it is still an international promise which ought to be tested over time and, especially, during lean times. History is full of such promises that were not honoured straight away: for example, the Latin Monetary Union (1865–1927) included Belgium, France, Italy and Switzerland (Greece joined in 1868); while Denmark, Sweden and later Norway belonged to the Scandinavian Monetary Union (1873–1914). Apart from insufficient economic convergence among the economies of the involved countries, high and diverging rates of inflation, the domino effect in banking crises and a lack of political union that could enforce policies were always among the principal causes for their demise. The same holds for the Austro-Hungarian, Soviet and Yugoslav economic unions towards the end of their existence. The real problem for governments is related to the issue of how to honour international promises and, at the same time, to please the domestic voters. As long as governments are sovereign (no political union), the EMU will be capable of breaking up.

The eurozone countries have few instruments to combat recession. There are no ample, automatic and preset funds at the EU level to act as anti-recession stabilisers, while member government expenditure is severely limited by the Stability and Growth Pact. The MacDougall Report (1977) suggested that a workable EMU may need a common budget equal to 7.5 per cent of the EU's GDP. The usual annual EU budget is about 1 per cent of the EU's GDP and is too small to act as a real and effective built-in stabiliser.

While all countries occasionally face the same problem in recessions, none of the developed countries imposed a numerical target for its budget deficit. Why should the eurozone be an exception? The reason is the risk of default (and the consequent massive capital outflow). However, in mature democracies such dangers are remote. The political cost of governments failing to maintain solvency is high. Voters would quickly oust such governments. In addition, huge debts are not created out of 'thin air'. It takes years to accumulate them. The members of the eurozone have solid political institutions that would steer them away from budgetary disasters. Viewed in a political light, the Stability and Growth Pact is a vote of no confidence by the EU regarding the strength of the democratic institutions in the member states.[41]

Doubts have been raised as to whether market forces can replace fiscal policy in an EMU. That is, whether citizens of the participating countries can diversify their risk in such a way that their consumption patterns are non-stochastic. The view that the EMU can provide a consumption smoothing by way of private capital mobility and that no fiscal intervention is necessary presupposes the existence of two conditions (Demopoulos and Yannacopoulos, 2001):

- *Capital markets are efficient*: that is, all agents cannot simultaneously improve their welfare.
- *Risk sharing is complete*: this means that agents can transfer their wealth across all states so that their consumption levels are identical in all of them.

Markets are, however, incomplete. Asset holders may diversify their risk through stock markets, but wage earners cannot do that. In addition, information is asymmetric. Not everyone can understand and appreciate the properties of all goods, and there are also transaction costs. This all limits the ability of agents to transfer wealth across markets. Optimum allocation of risk without a matching distribution of wealth may benefit the rich who hold well-diversified assets, but not the poor who have no such distribution. Therefore, in a world of perfect markets, equal probability beliefs by agents and equitable distribution of income, all risks can be shared through markets. Fiscal transfers of funds across regions are not required. In all other cases, consumption cannot be equalised by markets alone. Therefore, a transfer of funds is necessary for the survival of an EMU.

The great problem and a serious test, even a time bomb, that is looming in Europe is linked to pensions. Chancellor Otto von Bismarck first introduced the prevailing pay-as-you-go pension system in Germany in 1889. This system can work nicely as long as the number of active workers greatly outnumbers the retired. This was the case during the Bismarck days: at that time the retirement age was 70 years, while life expectancy was 48.[42] Nowadays, the idea and promise by pension schemes that 40 years of working life can fund 30 years of retirement no longer holds water, particularly at the current level of contributions and rate of return on investment.

The vast majority of pension liabilities are unfunded.[43] Current pensions come out of current tax income (pay-as-you-go system). This level varies from around half in Britain (with a highly developed privately funded pension system for households) to over 90 per cent in Italy.[44] The ongoing burden on taxpayers is immense, which is an alarming fact for public spending.

Demographic trends show that the 'baby-boom' generation will retire en masse around the year 2010. The pressure on the pension funds will significantly increase for several decades to come. This important and expanding imbalance will put a strain on EMU rules.[45] Certain countries will find it impossible to pay state guaranteed pensions without raising budget deficits or raising taxes to insupportable levels. However, this is only half of the problem. The other half is that governments are unable to do anything substantial about this! At least not at the moment. Alain Juppé lost his job as French prime minister in 1997 because of the reform of pensions that provoked a wave of strikes in 1995, the worst since 1968. The same thing happened earlier to the first government of Silvio Berlusconi in Italy: pension reforms provoked strikes, so the government left office in 1994. Strikes, for example, those that brought French cities to a virtual standstill in May and June 2003, illustrated trade unions' determination to resist changes in the pension system.[46] Similar reforms were also bitterly resisted in Germany, Italy and Austria.

Pensions have a vital role in the social protection system. Expenditure on pensions involves about 50 per cent of total social benefits. The national annual public expenditure on pensions as a share of GDP in the EU(25) countries is high. Although this ratio was the highest in 2001 in Italy and Austria (14.7 and 14.2 per cent, respectively) followed by Greece, France and Germany, and lowest in Ireland and Slovakia (3.7 and 7.2 per cent, respectively), most of the other EU countries have a ratio of about 12 per cent of GDP.[47] Even if an additional increase in public expenditure on pensions of 3 to 5 per cent of GDP is spread over several decades, it would create a serious challenge for the sustainability of public finances.[48] However, this is only part of the story. Another additional difficulty and, perhaps, greater demand would come from the expenditure for health care and other old-age-related outlays. This risk has not yet been fully realised or explained – perhaps because there are no sweet and easy answers to this problem. Hence, an additional 'danger' is in a liberal complacency which comes from a lack of insight as to how dire the fiscal outlook actually is. The profound crisis that is looming may challenge, destabilise and damage the very values on which the contemporary quality of life in Europe is based.

So what is to be done in a situation in which the population is ageing, while there are falling birth rates? Possibly there are measures such as various types of direct and indirect subsidies to people to have more children; raising the age for regular and early retirement; incentives to those who want to continue to work after the retirement age; encouragement to participate in private pension schemes; larger worker and employer contributions; an increase in taxes; subsidies for savings for old age; allowing the retired to become poorer relative to the rest of society; and selective immigration. Some of these measures are highly unpopular, politically explosive and strongly resisted.

When given an opportunity to vote on the crucial issue of their country's participation in the eurozone, Swedish voters did not approve entry in a 2003 referendum. The voters did not primarily reject the euro as such, but they declared the case unproven, in particular regarding rigidities that impede the national economies.

4.2.8 BRITAIN AND THE EURO

The issue of whether Britain should join the eurozone and accept the euro causes much political controversy and is a great research challenge. On the technical side, economists examine the pros and cons of the issue, which will have profound consequences for the shape and direction of the British economy. Eurozone entry would represent the end of 1000 years of British monetary independence. Politicians must grasp the strength and depth of these (often ambiguous) arguments, and then evaluate and select the desired, preferred or possible course of action. However, there are no clear-cut answers for Britain regarding the eurozone.

One of the first questions to ask in this long and heated debate is what is in the national interest of Britain – growing together (deeper integration) with EU partners or drifting apart from them?

- If a deeper union with EU partners is in the British interest, then 'growing together' is the outcome of common policies with EU partners, including monetary policy. In this case, it may be a smart move to join the eurozone as soon as possible and to abandon the pound.
- If it is in the British interest to join the eurozone, but in some undefined time in the future, then the policy of staying aloof may carry a significant cost. As with any new policy, eurozone participants are still formulating the rules. From the outside, Britain and its Bank of England would have little influence on the ECB. However, if Britain were an insider, it would have a direct and significant weight and influence in the shaping of eurozone events. An obvious example is a possible revision of the Stability and Growth Pact. Here, public spending on long-term investment projects should be looked at in a different light from other public expenditure. This would resolve the controversy between a short-run need for flexibility and a longer-run

demand for fiscal discipline. If Britain continues to 'wait and see', the eurozone rules will be shaped and consolidated without a British input from within. This could make British entry into the eurozone much harder in the future.[49]

- If it is in the British interest not to join, the situation resolves itself. The pound will continue to be independent.

Could Britain live in a larger family of countries with a single monetary policy? Is the British economy so very different from others in Europe? Could a one-size-fits-all interest rate be acceptable in and favourable for Britain? The British economy has some important particularities:

- Shocks such as those in 1979–80 (oil prices) and around 1992 (recession) were relatively better absorbed by Britain than by the other major EU economies such as France and Germany (Figures 4.3–7, respectively). Basically, the first consequences of these shocks were the acceleration in the rates of unemployment and inflation everywhere. Over time, Britain, France and Germany were all able to decelerate inflation to very similar rates. However, regarding unemployment, the situation is different. Unemployment was only a transitory event in Britain, which was able to reduce the unemployment

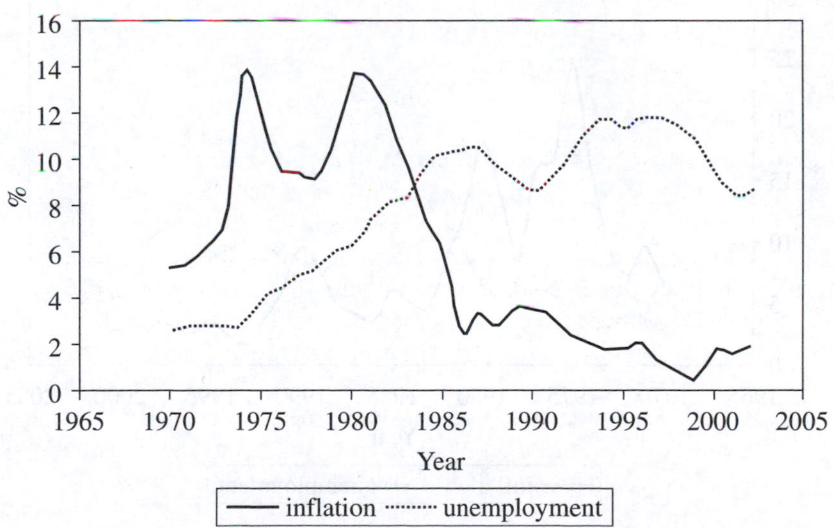

Source: UNECE, Eurostat (2005).

Figure 4.3 Inflation and unemployment in France, 1970–2004

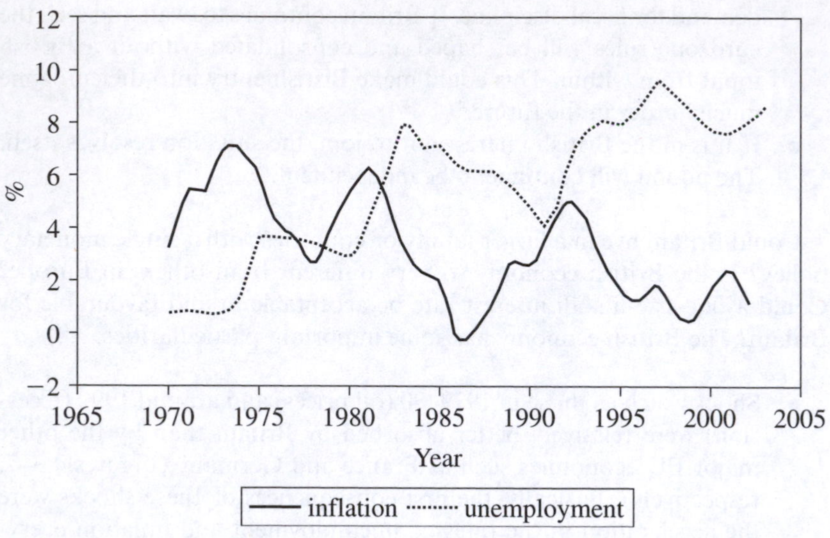

Source: UNECE, Eurostat (2005).

Figure 4.4 Inflation and unemployment in Germany, 1970–2004

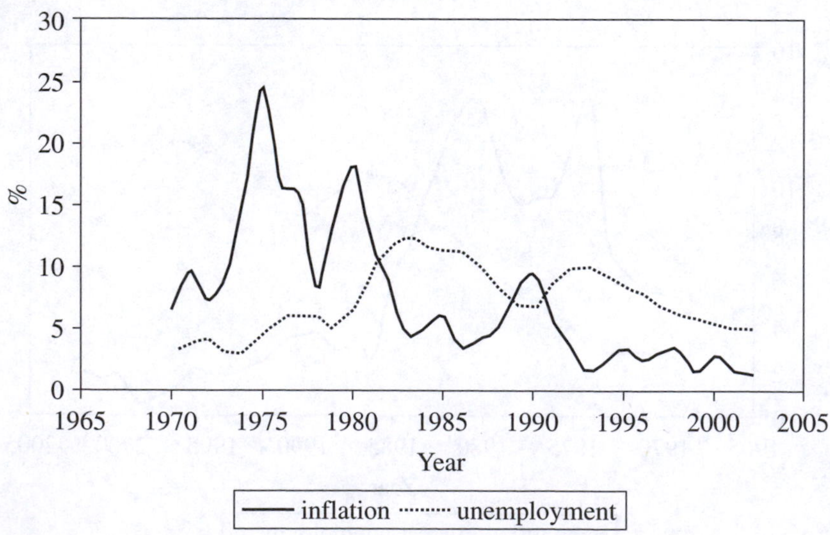

Source: UNECE, Eurostat (2005).

Figure 4.5 Inflation and unemployment in the UK, 1970–2004

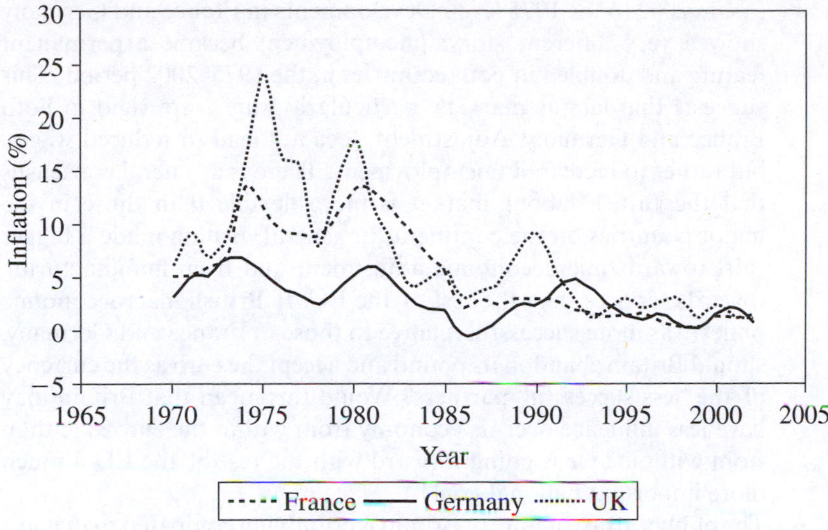

Source: UNECE, Eurostat (2005).

Figure 4.6 Inflation in France, Germany and the UK, 1970–2004 (%)

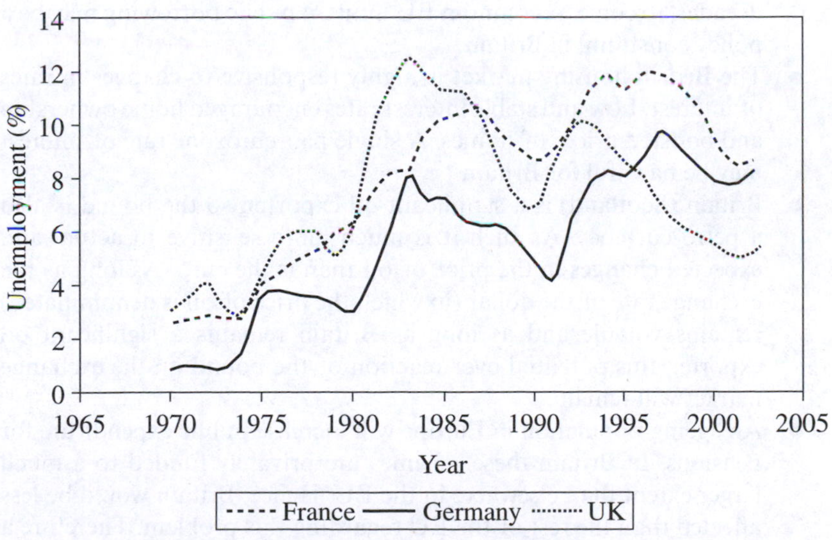

Source: UNECE, Eurostat (2005).

Figure 4.7 Unemployment in France, Germany and the UK, 1970–2004 (%)

rate in 2002 to the 1975 level. Developments in France and Germany show a very different story: unemployment became a permanent feature and doubled in both countries in the 1975–2002 period. This suggests that labour markets, particularly wages, are rigid in both France and Germany. Adjustment does not lead to reduced wages, but rather to increased unemployment. There is a general consensus that the British labour market is more flexible than those in the major countries on the continent. In general, Britain made a bigger shift towards microeconomic adjustment and from manufacturing towards services than the rest of the EU. If British macroeconomic policy was more successful relative to those in France and Germany, should Britain abandon its pound and accept the euro as the currency of the 'less successful' partners? Would this mean that Britain may have less influence over its economy from within the eurozone than from without? Or is going forward with the rest of the EU a much more important national goal?

- The public infrastructure in Britain is crumbling compared to that in a number of EU countries, and a doubling of public investment in infrastructure may be necessary. Borrowing these funds may be a fairer way to finance projects than through current taxation. Borrowing spreads the cost to the people who will benefit from them in the years, even decades, to come. A common EU limit on public borrowing may be a policy constraint in Britain.
- The British housing market is highly responsive to changes in rates of interest. Low and stable interest rates encouraged home ownership and boosted prices of homes. A single pan-eurozone rate of interest may be harmful for Britain.
- Britain (Scotland) is a significant oil exporter, so the pound is also a petro-currency. As such it is much more sensitive to actual and expected changes in the price of oil than is the euro. As long as the exchange rate of the dollar (in which the price of oil is denominated) remains volatile and as long as Britain remains a significant oil exporter, this potential over-reaction of the pound on the exchange market will remain.
- An ageing population in Europe will increase public expenditure for pensions. In Britain these schemes are privately funded to a much larger extent than elsewhere in the EU. Hence, Britain would be less affected than the rest of the EU regarding this problem. Therefore a one-size-fits-all monetary and fiscal policy may be problematic for Britain.
- At the heart of the eurozone policy is a single basic target: low inflation. It is difficult to coordinate national policies in order to achieve and

sustain this policy goal. All other desired objectives such as reduction in unemployment, economic stability, investment and growth are supposed to come about as side-effects. They are subject to 'soft' coordination. It may be quite demanding and problematical to coordinate national macroeconomic policies with the demands of the ECB. These difficulties would be amplified because the participating countries have different sizes and causes of budget deficits, diverse priorities and policy targets, as well as distinct ideas about the causes of and remedies for their economic problems.

- Asymmetric transmission of shocks within the eurozone may remain a common factor for quite some time in the future. This may hit certain regions particularly hard as there are no (or if there are, they are weak and slow) automatic stabilisers. Perhaps one should consider more carefully before entering into a monetary union with countries in which there is a wide discrepancy in the above elements. This is very important not only for Britain, but also for the countries in central and eastern Europe.
- But what are the real and significant costs of remaining outside the eurozone? Are they in lost additional trade, reduced competition and slower growth? Frenkel and Rose (1998) argued that currency unions expand trade. Prices are becoming transparent, competition intensifies, there is more specialisation and productivity increases. 'Countries that use the same currency tend to trade disproportionately . . . *countries with the same currency trade over three times as much as countries with different currencies*' (Rose, 2000, p. 17; original emphasis). If this were true, then the eurozone countries should have improved their performance since the introduction of the euro in 1999. However, this has not yet been observed to any significant degree. In fact, 'productivity growth has deteriorated substantially in the EU since 1995, precisely when one would have expected the looming currency union to have had a powerful positive effect'.[50] If large currency areas are so important, then one may expect to find that larger European countries are richer per capita than the smaller ones. The evidence, however, does not support such an expectation. Subsequent research pointed out that Rose's estimates relied overwhelmingly on currency unions that involve small and/or poor countries. Other econometric methods give positive estimates on the impact of the euro on trade within a range between 4 and 16 per cent (Micco et al., 2003, p. 318).

Bearing all this in mind, Britain may perhaps face less integration and more asymmetric shocks in the eurozone. Therefore, costs of eurozone membership may be potentially high for Britain (de Grauwe, 2002, p. 8). However, one may credibly argue that each and every country has its peculiarities and that there are important costs and significant benefits (see Section 4.2.3, above) that come from monetary integration. In any case, 12 EU countries took a *political* decision to take part in the eurozone. It is up to the other EU countries to evaluate whether it is a shrewd move to join the 'innermost core' of EU integration or to stay in the 'outer circles'.

In order to assess the possibility of joining the eurozone, as well as the costs and benefits of such a policy move, in 2003 the British government devised five 'tests':

- economic convergence with the eurozone;
- sufficient flexibility to adapt;
- impact on jobs;
- effect on financial services; and
- influence on FDI.

After publishing 18 detailed studies and a lengthy assessment on British membership of the eurozone in 2003, the Treasury's answer was 'not yet'. Martin Wolf wrote 'Never in human history can so many have written so much for so small a result.'[51] If only Britain had approached the CAP with such rigour before it joined the EU in 1971. If Britain retains these five tests for future reference and use regarding the eurozone, these criteria would become a barrier to eurozone entry – implying that Britain is not serious about joining.

Long-term potentials and gains such as lower currency volatility, deeper capital markets, price transparency, greater competition and increased trade, should be compared with the costs of a partial loss of monetary sovereignty to set short-term interest rates. This would affect the influence on the level of output, in particular if the national cycle is out of step with the rest of the eurozone. The British economy is stronglly linked with the rest of the EU economy. More than half of its trade is with the eurozone countries (there may be savings in transaction costs). Eurozone entry may be a favourable move to reinforce these ties, and national trade, productivity and wealth may increase.

Whether to join the eurozone is a tantalising issue for Britain. If the prize in the form of a more dynamic and stable economy that attracts FDI is tempting enough, then the government should commit itself to overcoming obstacles as soon as possible, but perhaps without a fixed timetable. Obviously, the decision to join the eurozone is linked with as many risks as there are in the choice to stay outside it.

4.2.9 WEST AFRICAN ECONOMIC AND MONETARY UNION

The West African Monetary Union (WAMU)[52] consists of seven west African states: Benin, Burkina Faso, Ivory Coast, Mali, Niger, Senegal and Togo. Membership of WAMU has varied over time. Mauritania participated in WAMU from its inception in 1962, but withdrew in 1972; Togo joined in 1963; Mali withdrew, but rejoined in 1984. WAMU has provided these countries with a freely circulating common currency, the CFA (*Communauté financière africaine*) franc, since its inception. This currency was linked by a fixed rate of exchange to the French franc without any changes from 1948 to 1994 at the rate of 1 French franc = 50 CFA francs. The CFA franc is issued by a common central bank which pools the member countries' reserves. France is very involved in this system because of guarantees of an unlimited convertibility of CFA francs into French francs at the fixed exchange rate. Such free and unlimited convertibility contributed to the capital drain and added to other causes which culminated in a devaluation of 50 per cent in January 1994.

WAMU's role was passive in the first decade of its existence. The WAMU central bank was charged with the maintenance of liquidity (money supply/GNP) and not with responsibilities for maintaining monetary and price stability and balance of payments equilibrium (Robson, 1983, p. 150). Its monetary policy was centralised in the Paris headquarters although WAMU kept agencies in each member country. WAMU's monetary policy was not coordinated with the fiscal policies of the member countries. At the beginning of the 1960s these countries were heavily dependent on France for all external economic affairs. The WAMU countries became linked to the EU by the Yaoundé and, subsequently, the Lomé conventions which provide trade preferences and aid from the EU. They also joined the IMF and the World Bank, thereby increasing the number of external economic partners. Anyway, France has preserved its dominant position in the region. The WAMU countries hoped to reduce the strong French influence and increase their autonomy in the monetary sphere. This brought certain reforms in 1974.

Reform was founded on the grounds that a monetary union among the member countries was necessary for faster economic development, but that the monetary arrangements should be organised differently from before. The most important changes occurred regarding the rediscount facilities. Instead of the 10 per cent annual increase in the money supply, the reform allowed a 45 per cent annual increase in each country (this amount would be rediscounted by the WAMU central bank). This has increased the power of the national credit committees. Foreign reserves of the member countries may be diversified, but at least 65 per cent of them should be in French francs.[53] The WAMU countries align their exchange rate policy with France while, in return, France guarantees free convertibility of CFA francs. The site of the central bank was transferred from Paris to Dakar. Prior to the reform, central bank decisions were made by a two-thirds majority where France had half of the bank's board membership. After the reform the decisions were made by simple majority. Two directors represent each member country (France included) on the board.

It is difficult to create a counterfactual world in which one may evaluate the degree of success of any monetary union. However, there is one important benefit of being linked in a monetary union. Some of the poorest countries in a volatile area have low monetary credibility. Being involved in a monetary union prevents governments from printing money willy-nilly in order to finance deficit.

The relative economic performance of the CFA franc zone countries can be compared to other developing countries. The performance of the CFA franc countries was relatively poorer than that of all other developing countries in the 1960–73 period, while their economic performance was significantly improved during the 1974–82 period. A more suitable 'control group' of developing countries can be taken for comparison. This group can be found among other sub-Saharan countries which are much more similar to the CFA franc countries in climate, endowment of factors and other elements. The WAMU countries grew significantly faster than the group of other sub-Saharan countries (Devarajan and de Melo, 1987, p. 491). This result may support the view that participation in a monetary union and its 'discipline' was much more helpful for the economic adjustment of countries during the period of floating and sharp increases in prices than the free and uncoordinated float of other sub-Saharan countries. Although it was possible to change the parity of the CFA franc, WAMU has maintained a fixed parity with the French franc. Such exceptional stability has been a major factor in the creation and maintenance of confidence in the CFA franc (Guillaumont and Guillaumont, 1989, p. 144).

Following the demise of the trade arrangement at the end of the 1980s, the WAMU countries changed the name of the monetary union to the West African Economic and Monetary Union (WAEMU)[54] in 1994. Guinea Bissau joined the group in 1997. As the earlier monetary arrangements were not changed (there is the same single currency), WAEMU had a reliable base on which to build fresh trade, compensation and fiscal harmonisation arrangements. The CFA franc became automatically linked to the euro at a fixed rate of 1 euro = 656 CFA francs in 1999 and France continued to guarantee its convertibility. The WAEMU countries have a grand vision of introducing mobility of goods, services, capital and persons, free of all tariffs and NTBs, and coordinating and harmonising national economic policies, as well as introducing common policies. To this end, the WAEMU set up a customs union in 2000 (the common external tariff ranges between 0 and 20 per cent, depending on the good).

The 1994 devaluation brought one-time positive benefits regarding the regional balance of trade, but competitiveness in trade in this region is not a monetary phenomenon. The roots of the problem are in the structure of the economy and political organisation of the countries. This cannot be solved permanently by devaluations. The reforms in the structure of regional economies are not taking place at a satisfactory pace.

The future of WAEMU may be uncertain. Other African countries have devalued their currencies, so the share of WAEMU countries in the continent's exports may be threatened. The smuggling of goods from weak currency countries into WAEMU is common. The relative strength of the euro and a fall in the prices of primary commodities, except oil, require another devaluation and possibly a loosening of the link with the euro.[55] A slump in commodity prices in the early 2000s made growth in WAEMU slower than in the rest of sub-Saharan Africa. This may lead to misalignment in exchange rates between WAEMU and other countries in the region.

The Economic Community of West African States (ECOWAS) includes the WAEMU members and other, predominantly English-speaking countries in the region. The two groups decided in 1999 to converge their economic policies. ECOWAS is considering the possibility of creating a monetary union. If this ambitious project gets off the ground, then which is the currency to link to? Some ECOWAS countries are not keen to link their currency to France, that is, to the euro. They view such a move as potentially neo-colonial. If there were a link to the euro, then this would require agreement with the eurozone countries. This may be quite challenging, as certain eurozone countries are leery of granting such an accord as a number of ECOWAS countries have a history of monetary indiscipline. If this does not end the ECOWAS dream of a monetary union, then it may herald the end of the CFA franc zone.

4.2.10 CONCLUSION

The rationale for common economic policies exists in the case where the EU is better placed to do certain things than are the member countries (subsidiarity). There is scarcely a better example of this than the cases of monetary and trade/competition policies. An EMU promotes and strengthens integration. The politicians in the eurozone countries succeeded in creating the EMU with the euro as an *über*-currency that could rival the dollar. This introduced both monetary stability in economic relations among the participating countries and rigidities regarding monetary and fiscal policy. The whole project is based on two political premises: policy coordination and irreversibility. Therefore, mere economic and monetary union is not the end of the story. Fiscal harmonisation and budgetary coordination could be the next step, as this would contribute to the full effectiveness of the stabilisation and growth policy. The problem is that Europe has a history of monetary unions that initially were greeted with enthusiasm, but subsequently fell apart.

Monetary integration is a field where genuine economic integration among countries is tested.[56] Hence, the creation of the eurozone among the 12 EU countries is not only great, it is the greatest achievement in the history of the EU. The EU countries supplemented the customs union and the Single European Market with the EMU,[57] which would secure and enhance growth and trade flows. Policy priority in the eurozone is to keep inflation very low. All other beneficial outcomes (investment, employment, growth) are implicitly supposed to come as a byproduct of stable prices.

Even though the creation of the eurozone is a very important step towards completing the Single European Market, the eurozone has always been an essentially political, rather than a predominantly economic project. Never before have so many countries entered into a monetary union with so little progress towards a political union. As long as governments are sovereign (no political union), the eurozone will be capable of breaking up. Therefore, the eurozone is indeed the greatest achievement, but it is also the biggest risk the EU has ever taken. It is also a mission that may transform both the political and economic scenery of Europe.

As was the case with many other major projects, the eurozone was conceived by the EU elite. It is the most ambitious project in Europe since the Bolshevik revolution (1918). No currency has circulated in Europe so widely since the Roman Empire. The introduction of the euro in January 1999 was the biggest currency innovation since the introduction of the US dollar in 1792. However, unlike in the US, there is no fiscal element in the deal: automatic fiscal transfers as built-in stabilisers are absent. The 12 eurozone countries had a cap on the national budget deficit of only 3 per cent of GDP. This has been a serious limitation for the conduct of macroeconomic policy in both Germany and France from 2002. The Stability and Growth Pact was too rigid for the stabilisation policy over an economic cycle, hence certain rules were formally relaxed in 2005.

Although the EU does not have either high mobility of labour or flexibility in wages (this may provoke high adjustment costs and unemployment), an EMU is welcome not only because of the Single European Market, but also because of external factors. There are serious doubts about the future stability and value of the dollar because of the rising American foreign debt (over $2.3 trillion or over a quarter of total US GDP in 2003). The US has huge and growing budget and trade deficits, the biggest in the history of the planet. Projections are that such deficits will continue as far as the eye can see. The officially projected budget deficit for 2004 is $521 billion (the 2002 official projection for 2004 was $14 billion). Increased spending, primarily for defence and homeland security, contributes to this deficit. But the biggest reason is the fall in revenues that come almost entirely from personal income tax and corporate profit tax (mostly paid by the richest 5 per cent of families). This plunge in tax collection from the wealthy is partly due to the Bush administration's tax cuts and probably also due to tax avoidance and evasion. Even a severe reduction in the non-defence and homeland security related spending would not make a significant reduction in the deficit. The government cut taxes and then used the resulting deficit to argue in favour of slashing public spending (on social security and Medicare) as an increase in taxes would jeopardise economic growth. The middle class will not give up programmes that are essential for its financial security, while the wealthy and neo-conservatives will not abandon tax cuts. Foreign investors have been financing the US deficits. Until when?[58]

The growing US reliance on short-term borrowing from the rest of the world must be closely watched. The US needed about $3 billion of foreign capital a day to finance its current account deficit and maintain the stability of the dollar in 2004. These funds were principally coming from Asia, Japan and China in particular, but Europe and the Middle East also had a share.[59] In this situation, the value of the dollar needs to fall now *vis-à-vis* Asian currencies if a sharper fall in the future is to be avoided. A strong rival currency such as the euro (if it is credible and widely accepted) is most welcome.[60] Portfolio switching into the euro may keep its value high. If this happens, or better, once this takes place, there will be considerable fluctuations in the exchange rate between the dollar and the euro.

The current strength of a currency on the international market is not a sign of national economic virility.[61] A superior and more sophisticated measure is how the economy responds and adjusts to changes; how it reforms its structure; how it overcomes rigidities; and how this affects prospects for future growth. A reduction in the value of a currency on the currency market may concern the national economy only if it pushes up prices of imported goods and services to the extent that this translates into domestic inflation. A currency's long-term value is based on economic fundamentals and the political stability of the issuing country.

The reunification of Germany was the major instigator of the Maastricht Treaty, as well as the reason for the treaty's good and bad implementation points. The eurozone became too rigid to adjust to disequilibrating shocks such as the reunification of Germany and the consequent budget deficits. The high German interest rates (because of the decision to pay for the reunification[62] by borrowing, rather than by raising taxes) and the need of other EU economies in recession to get cheap loans produced the upheaval that speculators desired. The exchange rate crisis of 1993 was a good reminder to policy makers that markets cannot be avoided. Capital markets will always test the resolve of governments to defend the narrow bands of the exchange rate. While economies are in recession, governments will not enter such a contest. The wreckage of the ERM is one of the symbols of the evident 'weakness' of governments and the power of markets.

The eurozone is and will be subject to institutional tests. The ECB will be tested in times of economic difficulty as there may be a perception that it is not able to act decisively because it has to be mindful of each component nation. In addition, budget deficits in the major eurozone countries will challenge the rules and the credibility of the zone. This will be compounded by a severe test around the year 2010 when there will be an increased demand for pension funds. The eurozone should pass the hardest test of all: that of time. There are a number (particularly in America) who question the long-term viability of the scheme.

Intra-eurozone exchange rate risk is eliminated, but a single European capital market is not guaranteed. National government bonds (for example, German and Italian) in euros may not become perfect substitutes. Differences in default risk and national tax treatment mean that the bond market will remain fragmented, although less than was the case before the introduction of the euro.

One of the expected consequences of the creation of the eurozone is that member countries have similar prices for traded goods. However, there are still large differences in prices for non-tradable goods and services (rents, catering, building materials). The primary reason is a difference in wage levels which reflects different levels in development. Economic convergence over the coming decades will have a certain impact on the convergence of prices in industries that produce non-tradable goods and services.

Increased heterogeneity in the EU(25) following the eastern enlargement can be one of the big tests for the coordination of EU policies.[63] Half of the EU is inside the eurozone, while the other half is outside. The structure of the economy in Britain and countries in central and eastern Europe is such that they may easily be subject to asymmetric shocks relative to the eurozone. Different national conditions and pressing problems can make policy coordination issues formidable.

Render therefore unto Caesar the things which are Caesar's,
and unto God the things that are God's.
Matthew 22:21

4.3 Fiscal integration and the common budget

4.3.1 INTRODUCTION

It is a common assumption in the standard theory of customs unions that, by the elimination of tariffs and quotas, trade within an integrated area becomes free (except for the existence of the common external tariff). It is also commonly assumed that foreign trade is fostered by relative differences in national production functions and resource endowments. This is just an illusion. Tariff and quota systems are not the only obstacles that distort the free flow of trade in goods and services (as well as factor mobility). Fiscal measures such as taxes and subsidies also create distortions in trade and competition, and they influence spatial and industrial allocation of resources. The focus of the White Paper (1985) and the Single Market Programme was mostly on the elimination of frontier controls. After the creation of a genuine Single European Market in the EU in 1993 and the EMU (achieved in 1999 for the 12 eurozone countries), attention needs to be directed towards tax issues.

The basic questions in this process include the following: what are the taxation principles? What is the historical experience in tax harmonisation? What is economically necessary and politically feasible? Should taxes and subsidies be identical throughout the EU? Should they be set independently by each country and markets allowed to equilibrate trade flows and allocation of factors and, supposedly, introduce approximation in taxes at the end of the process? Should national preferences arising from a variety of geographical or social reasons be reflected in tax diversity among the EU countries? What are the lessons to be learned from fiscal federalism?

This section deals with fiscal policy and the budget of the EU and is structured as follows. It starts with fiscal policy issues and principles (4.3.2). The next subsection (4.3.3) outlines the tax history in federal[64] states such as Switzerland, Germany, the US and Britain. Direct and indirect taxes are the subject matter of the next two subsections (4.3.4 and 4.3.5), respectively. Future challenges are then discussed (4.3.6), followed by a brief concluding comment (4.3.7). The final subsection (4.3.8) gives a brief analysis of the EU budget. The overall conclusion is that there is considerable room for improvement in the field of fiscal and budgetary issues; however, deeply rooted national interests, preferences and practices will prevent any rapid and large-scale moves in this area.

4.3.2 FISCAL POLICY

Introduction

The right to tax is at the very heart of a country's national sovereignty. Certain government revenue is always necessary for the operation of the state administration and for the conduct of select policies. The fiscal policy of a country deals with the influence and consequences of the demand, size, revenues and expenditure of the public sector. Taxation and fiscal policy are often used to affect and shape the basic economic variables, including:

- setting the stage, rules and incentives for the 'economic game' (permissions, bans, competition, taxes, subsidies, corporate governance, intellectual property, dispute settlement and so on);
- achieving and maintaining macroeconomic and political stability and having a long-term vision and programme on how to reach this goal and maintain it over time;
- affecting economic stabilisation (reduction in the fluctuation of macroeconomic variables around desired, planned or possible levels) and combating cyclical disturbances;
- having an effect on equity in the distribution of national wealth and income among regions, sectors, firms, classes, age groups, family status groups and persons;
- influencing allocation of resources (spatial and sectoral; investment and organisation of firms);
- supervising and directing the volume and composition of expenditure, consumption and investment;
- motivating and sustaining savings;
- improving general microeconomic capacity (education, infrastructure, information, forecasting, institutions);
- influencing the provision of a range of goods and services;[65]
- managing the pattern and extent of employment of resources;
- reflecting strategic behaviour of national government;[66]
- reducing and eliminating tax evasion and tax fraud;

- initiating certain actions; and
- owning and using certain assets.

As such, the fiscal policy shapes and directs the level and form of operation of markets for goods, services and factors.

Fiscal policy is concerned with the creation and adjustment of a system of taxes that is required to finance the necessary and chosen level and direction of public expenditure (intervention). This system should be equitable and efficient. Ideally:

- it ought to keep the budget in balance over an economic cycle;
- it ought to interfere as little as possible with the private sector business decisions in normal situations; and
- it ought to be in harmony with basic international tax standards.

As one of the oldest sovereign rights, fiscal policy is deeply entrenched in the state structure. It is a long-drawn-out and difficult process to alter fiscal policy in a democratic society. Fiscal, including budgetary, procedures are lengthy and complex.

A prudent fiscal policy ought to ensure that all levels of government (local, regional and central) are involved in and spend on only those activities where they can use resources in a better way than the private sector. Taxes ought to be high enough to cover that cost, but levied in a way that distorts the economy as little as possible. However, there are some valid social cases for distortion such as conservation of energy and control of pollution. The problem that must be avoided is the burdening of too narrow a tax base, otherwise tax rates would be high and distorting.

Fiscal policy has a direct (blunt) effect on income, as well as on the consumption of goods and services. This is in contrast to monetary policy, which does the same thing, but in an indirect (fine-tuning) way through financial markets. By a simple change in transfers and rates of taxes and subsidies, the fiscal authority may directly affect expenditure and consumption. However, the problem with fiscal policy is that its impact is gradual. In normal circumstances, this policy has to pass through a long and rigid parliamentary procedure. Therefore, fiscal policy changes may take place once (or only a few times) a year. Monetary policy may do the same job as fiscal policy, but in a discreet manner and, potentially, much faster. By changing interest or exchange rates, a government may react swiftly to emerging crises and opportunities. Such a quick reaction is not always possible with fiscal policy. 'Fiscal policy is like a tanker, it changes course very slowly' (Baldwin and Wyplosz, 2004, p. 382). Hence the need for the coordination of fiscal and monetary policies in an EMU. If they work one against the other, neither will be effective and the result may be damaging.

A tax ratio relates tax revenues to the GDP of a country. It is taken to be a measure of the general tax burden in the economy. Table 4.3 presents the share of total taxes including social charges as a share of GDP in the EU(25) in the 1995–2002 period. The highest tax ratio is found in Scandinavia and Belgium, while the lowest is in Ireland, the Baltic states, Cyprus, Malta, Greece, Spain and Britain. Figure 4.8 compares tax to GDP ratio in the EU(25), Norway, the US and Japan in 1995, 2000 and 2002. It shows that this ratio is higher in European countries (often more than 10 per cent) than is the case in the US or Japan.

In some cases, the tax ratio has been changing, even increasing over time as was the case in the EU(15) from 40.6 to 42 per cent in the 1995–2000 period. There are at least three reasons for this:

- the welfare state has changed, often increased social care transfers, which are financed mostly by social security levies;
- economic development and an increase in opportunities have had their impact on the growth of taxable incomes. Taxpayers have been climbing into higher brackets, so these proceeds have increased; and
- inflation has increased nominal tax revenues and undermined their real value.

However, in the 2000–02 period, there was a reduction in this ratio. Economic downturn reduced the collection of taxes sensitive to fluctuation in economic activity.

These trends in the EU may change around the year 2010 and beyond when the baby-boom generation starts to retire. An ageing population and the related needs and social obligations (pensions, health and other care) will increase the demand for such types of transfer over the coming decades. Tough budgetary rules in the eurozone may alter (perhaps reduce) certain transfers for social care. At the same time, enlarged demand for social services would exert a strong opposite pressure. In addition, the introduction of the euro and monetary stability with a very low inflation rate is reducing the devaluation of the real value of tax revenues.

Taxation Principles

In designing tax systems, governments customarily consider three basic indicators of taxpayers' ability to pay (wealth): what people and firms own; what they spend; and what they earn. The traditional principles of taxation deal with fairness, certainty, convenience and efficiency. They were

Table 4.3 *Total taxes including social charges as a share of GDP in the EU(25) and Norway, 1995–2002 (%)*

	1995	1996	1997	1998	1999	2000	2001	2002	Average 1995–2002	Change[1] 1995–2002	Difference[2] 1995–2002
BE	45.1	45.3	45.7	45.4	46.0	46.0	46.2	46.6	45.9	0.4	1.5
CZ	39.9	38.7	37.9	36.5	37.3	34.4	34.3	35.4	36.8	−2.0	−4.5
DK	49.3	49.9	49.8	50.1	51.5	49.5	49.9	48.9	49.9	0.0	−0.4
DE	40.8	41.6	41.6	41.6	42.3	42.5	40.8	40.2	41.4	−0.2	−0.7
EE	–	–	–	–	–	–	–	35.2	35.2		
EL	32.6	33.0	34.2	36.3	37.3	38.8	37.0	36.2	35.7	2.0	3.6
ES	33.4	33.8	34.2	34.5	35.1	35.6	35.5	36.2	34.8	1.1	2.7
FR	44.0	45.0	45.2	45.1	45.7	45.2	45.0	44.2	44.9	0.1	0.2
IE	33.4	33.5	32.8	32.1	32.1	32.1	30.5	28.6	31.9	1.9	−4.8
IT	41.2	42.8	44.7	43.2	43.3	42.7	42.5	41.7	42.8	−0.1	0.6
CY	–	–	–	29.2	29.5	31.4	32.7	32.5	31.1		
LV	37.2	34.3	35.6	37.3	35.6	33.1	31.8	31.3	34.5	−2.2	−5.9
LT	28.6	28.1	29.8	32.2	32.4	30.4	29.1	28.8	29.9	0.3	0.2
LU	42.3	42.4	41.5	40.2	40.4	40.7	40.7	41.9	41.3	−0.4	−0.4
HU	–	–	–	–	–	–	39.4	38.8	39.1		
MT	27.7	26.2	27.9	26.2	27.4	29.1	30.4	31.3	28.3	2.1	3.6
NL	40.6	40.8	40.7	40.3	41.7	41.5	40.0	39.5	40.6	−0.2	−1.1
AT	42.3	43.7	44.5	44.3	44.3	43.5	45.3	44.4	44.1	0.5	2.1
PL	34.3	38.7	37.9	37.0	37.0	36.2	41.2	39.1	37.7	1.3	4.8
PT	33.6	34.4	34.7	34.9	36.0	36.4	35.6	36.3	35.2	1.1	2.8
SI	41.3	40.0	38.9	39.6	40.0	39.4	39.4	39.8	39.8	−0.3	−1.5
SK	41.5	40.3	38.0	38.3	35.9	34.3	32.9	33.0	36.8	−3.6	−8.5
FI	46.0	47.3	46.5	46.4	46.8	48.0	46.0	45.9	46.6	−0.1	−0.1

Table 4.3 (continued)

	1995	1996	1997	1998	1999	2000	2001	2002	Average 1995–2002	Change[1] 1995–2002	Difference[2] 1995–2002
BSE	49.5	51.9	52.5	53.1	53.8	53.9	52.2	50.6	52.2	0.3	1.1
UK	35.4	35.0	35.6	36.6	36.9	37.5	37.3	35.8	36.3	0.7	0.5
NO	42.6	43.0	42.7	42.7	43.0	43.1	43.7	44.2	43.1	0.5	1.6
EU25	40.5	41.3	41.5	41.4	41.8	41.7	41.1	40.4	41.2	0.0	−0.2
EU15	40.6	41.4	41.6	41.6	42.0	42.0	41.2	40.5	41.4	0.0	−0.1
Euro12	41.0	41.8	42.2	42.0	42.4	42.4	41.5	41.0	41.8	0.0	0.1
NMS10	36.5	38.3	37.5	36.6	36.6	35.4	38.3	37.3	37.1	0.0	0.8
EU25 (arithmetic average)	39.1	39.4	39.6	39.2	39.5	39.2	39.0	38.5	39.2	−0.2	−0.6
EU15 (arithmetic average)	40.6	41.4	41.6	41.7	42.2	42.3	41.6	41.1	41.6	0.2	0.5
Euro12 (arithmetic average)	39.6	40.3	40.5	40.5	40.9	41.1	40.4	40.2	40.4	0.2	0.5
NMS10 (arithmetic average)	35.8	35.2	35.1	34.6	34.4	33.5	34.6	34.5	34.7	−0.6	−1.3
Ratio at dev. and mean in %[3]	15.0	16.0	15.3	15.7	15.8	15.5	15.4	14.9	–	–	−0.1
Difference max. and min.[3]	21.8	25.7	24.5	26.9	26.4	24.9	23.1	22.0	–	–	0.1

Notes:

1. Estimated annual average growth ratio in %.
2. in % points of GDP.
3. for EU15

BE: Belgium; CZ: Czech Republic; DK: Denmark; DE: Germany, EE: Estonia; EL: Greece; ES: Spain; FR: France; IE: Ireland; IT: Italy; CY: Cyprus; LV: Latvia; LT: Lithuania; LU: Luxembourg; HU: Hungary; MT: Malta; NL: Netherlands; AT: Austria; PL: Poland; PT: Portugal; SI: Slovenia; SK: Slovakia; FI: Finland; SE: Sweden; UK: United Kingdom; NO: Norway; NMS: new member state.

Source: European Commission (2004b).

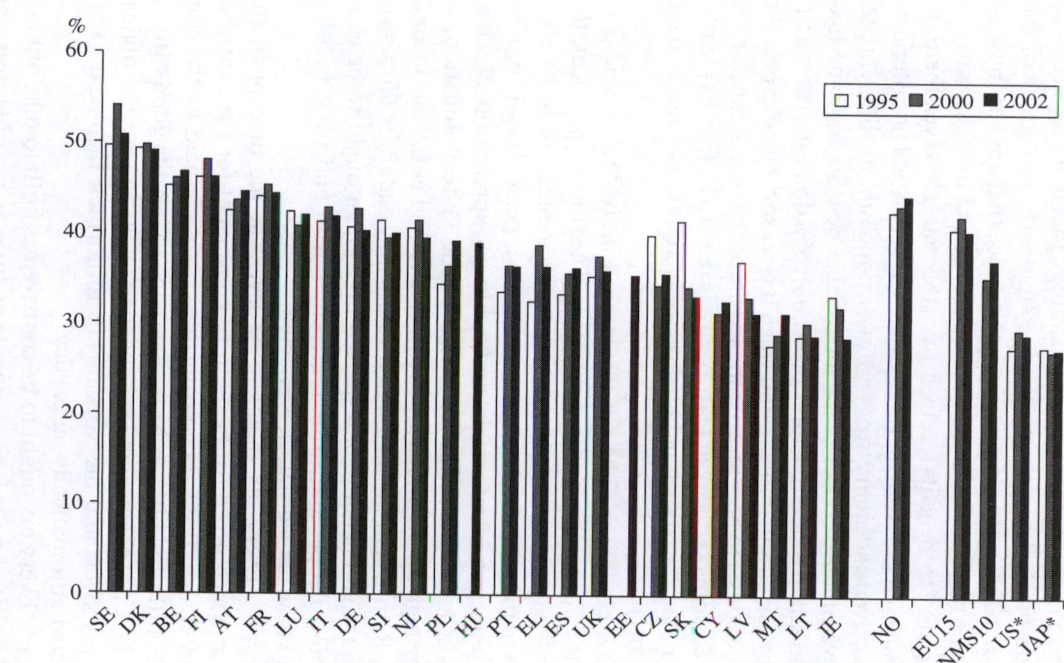

Note: For abbreviations, see Table 4.3.

Source: European Commission (2004).

Figure 4.8 Tax to GDP ratio in the EU(25), Norway, US and Japan in 1995, 2000 and 2002 (%)

established by Adam Smith (1839, pp. 371–2) and have stood the test of time remarkably well.

- *Fairness (equality or inequality)* 'The subjects of every state ought to contribute towards the support of the government, as nearly as possible, in proportion to their respective abilities; that is in proportion to the revenue which they respectively enjoy under the protection of the state' (ibid., p. 371). It is of primary importance that any tax must be fair. Citizens ought to be taxed both in proportion to their ability to pay and relative to 'benefits received' from the state. However, there are widely dispersed government services such as security. The criteria of benefits received and ability to pay are often impossible to differentiate. When government services grant identifiable benefits to some taxpayers and not to others (customs protection of a domestic car manufacturer by tariffs and quotas), and when it is reasonable to expect the user (monopolist) to bear an acceptable part of the cost, financing the benefits (customs service), at least partly, is seen to be fair. Evidently, this does not apply to such public services as welfare assistance to the poor and needy.
- *Clarity and certainty* 'The tax which each individual is bound to pay ought to be certain and not arbitrary. The time of payment, the manner of payment, the quantity to be paid, ought all to be clear and plain to the contributor, and to every other person' (ibid., p. 371). The consequence of uncertain and arbitrary application of taxes produces a lack of confidence in the public system. Inflation, in particular high inflation, may move people to higher taxable income brackets. Rising tax bills on inflated values may endanger fairness in imposing taxes. Therefore, a respected tax system ought to be clear and certain. People and firms must know who and what is being taxed and how tax legislation is enacted.
- *Convenience* 'Every tax ought to be levied at the time or in the manner in which it is most likely to be convenient for the contributor to pay it. . . . Taxes on consumable goods . . . paid by the consumer . . . little and little, as he has occasion to buy the goods' (ibid., pp. 371–2). Convenience and compliance ought to ease the obligations of taxpayers and the work of tax authorities. Income tax may be deducted automatically on payday.
- *Efficiency* 'Every tax ought to be contrived as both to take out and to keep out of the pockets of people as little as possible over and above what it brings into the public treasury' (ibid., p. 372). Levying may require a great number of officers; frequent visits and intensive investigations may create unnecessary trouble and officers' salaries

may eat up much of the collected taxes. The fiscal system should not impede the free flow of goods, services and factors, domestically or internationally.

Further basic principles have been added to the Smith list over time:

- *Source* Smart taxes ought to be other than taxes on trade and company profits. These two types of tax are the most distorting. Unfortunately, they are also the most common in the developing world. Taxes on trade (both export and import) prevent specialisation, while loophole-ridden taxes on company profits distort investment decisions. Sales taxes (for example, value-added tax) may be the most attractive alternative.
- *Tax elasticity* This deals with an automatic response of taxes to changing economic conditions without adjustments in tax rates. High elasticity, however, creates inequities during periods of rapid inflation by pushing people into higher tax-rate brackets, although the real value of their income is falling because of rising prices. The large nominal revenues then encourage government spending just when the growing tax burdens discourage taxpayers from working, saving and investing. This situation may worsen a state of economic stagnation accompanied by inflation. In such instances, the tax levy has become too elastic.
- *No retroactivity* Taxpayers must have confidence in the law as it existed at the time when they entered into a transaction.
- *Neutrality* The primary purpose of taxes is to raise revenue, not to micromanage the economy with subsidies and penalties. A tax should not cause economic agents to change their economic behaviour. Suppliers and buyers of a good or service ought to be indifferent about being taxed in any of the integrated countries.

Fiscal Federalism

Harmonisation of the fiscal system among countries has two meanings. First, the lower form of fiscal harmonisation may be equated with cooperation among countries. These countries exchange information and/or enter into loose agreements about ways and types of taxation. Second, in its higher meaning, fiscal harmonisation means the standardisation of mutual tax systems regarding methods, types and rates of taxes and tax exemptions (Prest, 1983, p. 61).

Fiscal federalism deals with the design of an agreed and optimal system of cooperation, coordination and sharing fiscal rights and responsibilities between different levels of local, regional state and federal governments. At the EU level, it may also imply the creation of a supranational fiscal authority (subsidiarity). However, this should be measured and adjusted to the merits and costs of economies of scale in joint action, as well as the availability of information and their understanding on different levels of government.

Revenue decentralisation favours a smaller size of (central) government proceeds. This shifts public revenue from taxes to user charges. The advantage of such a policy choice is that users may choose to use or not to use certain services. If users decide to use those services, they have to pay for them directly. Switzerland provides an interesting case for consideration of this issue: it has 23 decentralised cantons which enjoy a large degree of fiscal autonomy, but have a legal demand to balance their budgets over time. The Swiss system of direct democracy and fiscal federalism can effectively restrain government spending. Although this may contain public deficits, such a set-up may not prevent them. Institutional constraints are necessary for this control (Feld and Kirchgässner, 2004).

The integration of fiscal policies in an EMU refers to the role of public finance and the part played by the budget. It studies the rationale, structure and impact of fiscal (tax and budgetary) systems of the integrated countries. Integration of fiscal policies implies not only a harmonisation of national systems of taxes and subsidies, but also issues such as public expenditure, transfers (redistribution) within and between countries, regions, economic sectors and individuals; combat of cyclical disturbances; stabilisation policy; and tax evasion. The highest type of fiscal integration among countries represents a unified system of taxes and subsidies, as well as the existence of a single budget that is empowered to cope with all economic issues of common concern. This has, however, only been achieved in centralised federal states.

In the general case, fiscal federalism is complicated by the existence of different currencies that take part in the venture and that are not irrevocably linked through the fixed exchange rate. If an EMU is to conduct an effective stabilisation policy it should be endowed with the power to tax and borrow, as well as to spend. This implies that its budget may be not only in balance, but more importantly, in temporary deficit or surplus over an economic cycle. An EMU may not necessarily directly tax firms and individuals, but it may tax member governments. In order to maximise welfare, the EMU needs to decide about the preferred distribution of functions among distinct governments (principles of subsidiarity, cooperation or competition). It should also act upon that decision and divide public goods and services into those that ought to be provided commonly, and those that should be supplied at a national or local level. In addition, applied to an EMU, fiscal federalism needs to take care of a certain transfer of resources from prosperous countries/sectors to needy ones, as well as to promote mobility of resources.

Fiscal neutrality among the integrated countries refers to a situation in which a supplier or a consumer of a good or service is indifferent about being taxed in any of the integrated countries. This is an important prerequisite for the efficient spatial and sectoral allocation of resources and for the operation of an EMU.[67] The fiscal authorities should be quite cautious while assessing taxes and spending tax receipts. If they tax a significant part of profit or income, then they may destroy incentives for business, work, savings and investment. They may stimulate factors to move to geographical or professional locations where they can maximise net returns. Taxation can, however, be a powerful tool for the direction of certain business activities towards desired spatial or professional locations, but there may also be a capital flight towards tax havens. A high tax policy may find a certain social justification (for example, equity), although it may be questionable from an efficiency standpoint. The above scenario depends on the sensitivity of factors to taxation. If this sensitivity and responsiveness is relatively low (as is the case with the mobility of labour in the EU), then the local authorities may tax income at higher rates in the knowledge that this is unlikely to provoke large-scale emigration.

The member countries of an EMU may basically finance a common budget according to the principles of benefit and ability to pay. First, the principle of benefit is based on the rule of clear balances or *juste retour* (a fair return). Those who obtain concessions from the budget expenditure ought to contribute to these public funds in proportion to the benefits they receive. Second, economic benefits of integration accrue to the participating countries not only through the transfers of (common) public funds. The most important gains come from a secure long-term freedom for intragroup trade and investment, mobility of factors, specialisation, acceleration in economic activity and the like. Such a neo-classical expectation may not require 'corrective measures' since all countries and regions benefit from integration in the medium and long terms.[68] However, in the case with imperfect markets and economies of scale, this expectation may not materialise. In this situation, the principle of the ability to pay features highly. Individual contributions and receipts from the common budget in a given period do not have to be equal. Net contributions reflect a country's ability to pay. However, a nominal net contributory position of a country can well be more than compensated by various spillovers that stem from membership of an EMU. Therefore, the *juste retour* principle may get a new dimension: it is a discreet, but continuous economic growth throughout a group with a certain flow of resources from the rich and thriving to the less-well-off member countries and those in (temporary) need.

4.3.3 A BIT OF HISTORY

The purpose of this subsection is to refer briefly to a few historical examples that relate, in part, to the issue of international tax harmonisation which may have a federal dimension. Some of these stories refer to a 'forced' imposition of taxes by foreigners. Some of them may seem (indeed they are) extreme. The reason why they were selected was simply to make a point for a group such as the EU. These examples may provide a part of the answer to the question of why tax harmonisation or unification among countries that integrate is a very delicate and difficult matter. For example, the Duke of Alva (Fernando Álvarez de Toledo), the Spanish governor-general, was the last foreigner to try to impose a tax on the Dutch. That was in the 16th century. His action, together with the Roman Catholic Inquisition, provoked an 80-year war (1567–1648). The following examples relate to Switzerland, Germany, the US and Britain.

Switzerland

Around the 10th century, the area that is now known as Switzerland consisted of a collection of small states ruled by dukes, counts, bishops and abbots, as well as a number of independent small city-states. The Holy Roman Emperor Rudolf I of the Habsburg dynasty attempted to claim feudal rights in Switzerland in 1276. His authority would present a threat to the traditional liberties of the Swiss. To resist Rudolf's aggression, the three central forest cantons (Uri, Schwyz and Unterwalden) concluded a secret deal concerning mutual defence in 1291 'to last, if God wills, for ever'. During the 14th century, Zurich, Glarus, Bern, Lucerne and Zug entered this league. Other cantons joined later.

Although nominally under the Habsburg family early in the 14th century, the Swiss opposed the Habsburgs in the Welf-Waiblingen disputes. The Habsburgs sent punitive expeditions into the mountains and triggered nearly a century of warfare. Unable to cope with the freedom-loving, strong and belligerent Swiss mountaineers, the Habsburgs abandoned their attempts to acquire the region in 1474. However, in 1499 the Holy Roman Emperor Maximilian I attempted to cancel various Swiss rights and to tax them. A war followed and the mountaineers defeated him. The subsequent Treaty of Basle (1499) gave Switzerland virtual independence.

New cantons continued to join the confederation. There was no chief of state or attempt by any one canton to impose authority on another, even though there were religious and other differences.[69] The Helvetic[70] confederation was loose, but its army was one of the strongest in Europe at that time. Because of their skill and bravery in war, Swiss mercenaries became famous throughout Europe.[71] Their services were in demand, appreciated and well paid and occasionally they were even on different sides of the same conflict. In the course of the wars between Italy and France in the early 16th century, Swiss troops, fighting with the French as mercenaries, were able to annex the Italian districts and towns that later formed the canton of Ticino. The Swiss troops then fought against the French, but were defeated in 1515. This prompted Switzerland to follow a neutral policy in international affairs.

Swiss bank secrecy has been protecting deposits for over three centuries. Geneva bankers were known as the French king's bankers. The first known text on bank secrecy dates back to 1713. The Great Council of Geneva adopted banking regulations which stipulated the bankers' obligation to 'keep a register of their clients and their transactions. They are, however, prohibited from revealing this information to anyone other than the client concerned, except with the expressed agreement of the City Council.' Switzerland then became and remained a political and financial asylum for those fleeing the political upheavals that have been present in Europe since 1789.

The first big clients in Swiss banks were the kings of France, who greatly valued the discretion of their money lenders. The Geneva bankers were actually Protestants. Many of them were French citizens, chased out of France following the repeal of the Edict of Nantes by Louis XIV in 1685. Putting behind them the discrimination and bullying they suffered in France, they financed the French kings from Geneva. The French kings were the best clients for loans at the time – they were fund hungry, but they had the ability to repay loans. Discretion was of the utmost importance in these delicate matters. It should not be known publicly that the French Roman Catholic king borrowed money from 'heretic' Protestants. Business is business – on both sides.[72]

The Great Depression led to stricter foreign exchange controls in Germany in 1931. Hitler introduced a law whereby the penalty for any German with capital abroad was capital punishment. The Gestapo began to spy on Swiss banks, and when three Germans who had deposits in Switzerland were sentenced and executed, the Swiss government was persuaded to reinforce bank secrecy. The federal banking law (1934) stated that bank secrecy fell within the criminal domain, and any banker who infringed this law was thereafter punishable by imprisonment. Clients' secrecy and banking prudence and discretion was reinforced.

Switzerland did not have a direct tax on revenue until the time of the Second World War. That event was dramatic enough to justify the introduction of the much resisted Federal Tax for Defence (*Impôt pour la Défense Nationale*). Solidarity during times of war has been one of the principal integration factors in Switzerland since the creation of the country in 1291. It was envisaged that the newly introduced tax would stay only until the end of the war. However, as time passed, the population became accustomed to the tax (which is still a solidarity tax since two-thirds are redistributed to the Cantons according to their needs) and accepted its renewal when the government decided to call it the Direct Federal Tax (*Impôt fédéral direct*) after the war, provided that it would remain limited in time. This limitation to 10-year periods is still in force, and despite the government's wish to abolish it, it is most likely to be retained indefinitely. It was renewed in 2005.

Before the Direct Federal Tax was introduced, the Swiss cantons and communes were the only administrations that had the power to tax. They levied independently direct local taxes on persons and firms (the communal tax is a percentage of the cantonal tax, but each commune is free to set that percentage). The Swiss federation did not aim to restrict the freedom of the cantons. One of the objectives was to be rid of the burden presented by any emperor who tried to squeeze a share of their gains in businesses through various tolls. The Swiss were and remained businessmen who wanted to see value added to anything they were paying for. Apparently, creating an association among the cantons was economically more efficient than depending on an emperor for security. This type of democracy seemed cheaper and more effective.

Thus, it is not difficult to understand why the Swiss continue to value highly their tax, banking and other national legacies and why it was hard to enter into a deal with the EU (or anyone else) concerning taxation of non-resident deposits. In addition, a fact often overlooked by certain politicians and commentators is that value-added tax (VAT) rates in Switzerland are lower than in the neighbouring EU states. This may continue to stimulate individual shopping for select goods in Switzerland from EU countries.

Germany

It took many centuries to unify the German nation and state. Larger-scale unification was started by Charlemagne (742–814), King of the Franks (768–814) and Emperor of the Romans (800–814), whose empire was inherited by his successors from Saxony. What we now call Germany first existed as the Holy Roman Empire (800–1806) (the First Reich). This was a loose confederation of mini-states. The borders of this empire shifted greatly throughout its history because of wars, alliances and marriages, but its principal area was always that of the German states. Even though its character and population were German, its aspirations were a universal rule in the west. Germany became a 'belated nation' because of internal quarrels and rivalries not only among kingdoms, principalities and a number of free cities, but also because of religious tensions. All in all, this prevented German integration. From the 10th century the rulers of the Holy Roman Empire were elected German kings, who usually sought, but did not always receive, imperial coronation by the popes in Rome. In any case, before the French Revolution, the Germans never had a unified state of their own.

Friedrich Barbarossa (1122–90) saw himself as the successor of the Roman emperors who claimed to be the 'lords of the world'. As such he considered that he had an absolute right to levy taxes. His grandson, Friedrich II (1194–1250), had his court in Palermo (Sicily). He was a powerful promoter of Roman law, and took a different approach to taxation from his grandfather. He applied the Byzantine emperor Justinian's (483–565) principle '*Quod omnes tangit, ab omnes approbari debet*'[73] (what concerns all should be approved by all). This meant that the royal families in various German states were not allowed to levy taxes without the consent of the nobility.

Modern absolutism in Europe started at the end of the 15th century and did well for more than two centuries. It marked the emergence of nation states and brought, at the time, modern principles of sovereignty. Its best example was the French King Louis XIV (1643–1715). His declaration '*L'état, c'est moi*' (I am the state) sums up the concept neatly. Bavaria, Brandenburg, Hanover and Saxony started to develop into centres in their own right in Germany. The family of Hohenzollern[74] was granted Brandenburg (Berlin) in the 15th century, and they acquired a number of additional, geographically unconnected territories to the west. Eastwards was Prussia, which they inherited as a Polish duchy in 1618 and transformed into an independent kingdom in 1701. Gradually, all the Hohenzollern lands together became known as the kingdom of Prussia.

The origin of German patriotism (some call it nationalism) can be traced to the Romantic Movement in the late 18th century. It was a response to the export of French Enlightenment ideas and invasions by Napoleon. Over a period of 16 years (1799–1815) the German states fought five wars against the well-trained and integrated armies of revolutionary and Napoleonic France. As there had never been a unified German state, the Germans experienced in practice the French example of what a unified state can achieve. As far as Austria is concerned, it was relatively sizeable as a state, but largely un-German. Marriages and wars caused Austria to include 'states' and territories that were not German speaking. The only large 'German' state was Prussia.

The Congress of Vienna (1815) replaced the Holy Roman Empire of more than 240 squabbling states by the German Confederation. This was a loose association of 39 sovereign states. Many Germans hoped for a free unified nation state and liberal type of government similar to the British model. They wanted a constitution guaranteeing popular representation, trial by jury and free speech. These ideas also appealed to the various peoples incorporated in the Austrian Empire. Austria, Britain, Prussia and Russia formed the Quadruple Alliance to suppress, by force if necessary, any threat to the Vienna arrangement. However, later on Prussia outsmarted the others, principally Austria, by instituting a customs union among most of the German states apart from Austria.

Friedrich List (1789–1846) was a prominent intellectual and practical proponent of the economic unification of Germany. In 1820, together with Frankfurt merchants and industrialists, he founded the German Trade and Business Union, which strived for the abolition of the 39 tax (customs) frontiers that existed among the German states and for the introduction of a unified German customs area. On the basis of this intellectual input, Prussia encouraged neighbouring states to join this low-tax alliance which gradually developed into a customs union, the *Zollverein* (1834–71). List also planned a train network for all of Germany and in 1834 founded the Leipzig-Dresden Train Company which started providing rail transport services a year later. In theoretical terms, he put forward the 'theory of productive forces', which defended infant industry protection. List saw this to be an element leading to a free trade (no-duty) area in *Mitteleuropa*.

This all had a strong impact on economic development. Germany's industrial output, principally in Prussia, was lower than that in Britain in the 1850s, but its rate of growth was faster. Prussia wanted to secure the new German lands along the Rhine. This was done by a carefully crafted major tax reform and by lowering customs duties. Karl Friedrich von Stein, Karl August von Hardenberg and Wilhelm von Humboldt, together with List, influenced reforms in Prussia. They sought to crack the old feudal intra-German barriers and to create a modern society of free citizens. Strong cultural, linguistic and patriotic feelings about unifications were always present, but it was principally the economic interest that was at the very heart of German unification.

The *Zollverein* was the principal factor that brought the 39 German states closer together. It allowed trade among them by lowering taxes. These were originally set by each country at a very high rate. Before 1848 the Austrian emperors (but not their foreign minister, Clemens von Metternich) did not conceive that the *Zollverein* could lead to a larger political role for Prussia. However, Metternich and his successors pushed for Austria to join the *Zollverein* in order to dominate the group and to turn it into a high tariff area, but Prussia prevented this on economic and political grounds. In addition, Prussia concluded a free trade agreement with

France in 1861. Austrian products made behind a high tariff wall could not compete easily on such a large 'liberal' trading market.

In 1861, the Prussian parliament granted the government additional funds for reforms, but a year later it refused to do so without a reduction of compulsory military service from three to two years. King William I would not yield to that request as he feared that conservative values would be insufficiently inculcated in the recruits. For the very same reason, the liberal-dominated parliament insisted on shortening the term of military service. As a compromise deal, they named Otto von Bismarck (1815–98) as prime minister. Bismarck proceeded to collect the additional taxes on the basis of the 1861 budget, arguing that the constitution did not provide for the case of an impasse, hence he would have to apply the preceding year's budget.[75] To justify the increase in the army, he warned that 'the great questions of the day [German unification] will not be settled by speeches and majority decisions . . . but by blood and iron'.

Public opinion began to shift to Bismarck's side in 1864, when he used the expanded Prussian army, in alliance with Austria, to annex the provinces of Schleswig and Holstein from Denmark. In 1866 he intensified a Prusso-Austrian quarrel over the abysmal running of these territories by Austria. This escalated into a brief and victorious war with Austria. Some smaller German states that allied with Austria were also crushed. Bismarck incorporated Schleswig-Holstein and Hanover into Prussia. During the same year, he also united all north and central German states into the North German Confederation which was under the Prussian leadership. Faced with these achievements, the Prussian parliament bowed to Bismarck and retroactively sanctioned his financial improvisations of the past four years.

Not sufficiently pleased with these accomplishments, Bismarck's next ambition was to make Prussia the great power in Europe. In order to do this, it would be necessary to defeat France, a feat that was accomplished in 1870.[76] He wanted to use the strength of the consequent national enthusiasm to bring the reluctant south German states into a united Germany. Bismarck had not only established Prussia as the great continental power, but also provoked patriotic enthusiasm and attracted the southern German states to join the North German Confederation, thus forming the German Empire (*Deutsches Reich*). On 18 January 1871, King William I of Prussia was proclaimed in Versailles by all the states of Germany to be their emperor. Germany was a united country on a federal basis and the Second Reich had been created. The German area had changed beyond recognition in a matter of decades.

Having sufficiently enlarged Prussia, the Iron Chancellor, as Bismarck was called, worked for peace. During his 19 years of governing, Bismarck continued to encourage the Industrial Revolution through technical universities and tax incentives. Advanced industrial technology was applied from 1850 in the iron production in the Ruhr and Saar regions and stimulated through tax incentives. Regarding social care, Bismarck introduced the prevailing pay-as-you-go pension system in 1889.

United States

At the end of the Seven Years' War (1756–63) France was expelled both from North America and from India. In both regions Britain became the pre-eminent power and supreme on the high seas. However, the war left Britain with a sizeable debt and costly responsibilities to govern the newly gained land in North America. Parliament decided that the crest of the Appalachian Mountains was the end of the line. Lands to the west were declared off limits to new settlement. The area would be too sparsely populated for their own safety. Young colonists felt cheated, but the vastly expanded area would have to pay someone to defend it. London gave the colonists a stark choice: either raise your own troops to patrol the frontier or pay for a force of 10 000 to do it for you. The colonists would not accept either solution and they did not propose any alternative. So parliament passed the *Stamp Act* (1765) without any debate. The colonists had to buy and use specially stamped paper for all official documents and newspapers. This act provoked strong opposition throughout North America. The colonists regarded this as a violation of their right not to be taxed without representation: no representation, no taxation! The protest, which included a boycott of British goods, was so strong that trade between Britain and North America came to a halt. The British parliament rescinded the Stamp Act in 1766, not because of the North American protest to taxation, but rather at the request of the economically depressed British traders.

Well, if the colonists did not want to pay internal taxes, then they could be forced to pay 'external' ones on the goods (such as tea) that were imported from abroad. The objective of the *Tea Act* (1773) was to rescue the British East India Company from bankruptcy and to demonstrate the power of the British parliament to tax the colonies. Every American knows that the United States of America was founded on a revolt over taxes. They tend to forget that this was not linked with a tax hike, but rather with a tax cut (which removed commercial middlemen). The tax on tea shipped to the colonies in North America was reduced so that the East India Company's tea could be sold there at a lower price than was the price of smuggled tea. The colonists, however, refused to buy the English tea. They viewed the Tea Act as a violation of their constitutional right not to be taxed without representation. In addition, this would likely lead to the monopoly of the

East India Company as local traders could be put out of business. This led a group of Bostonians to protest against the tea tax, and they prevented the unloading of 342 chests of tea from three British ships that arrived in Boston in November 1773. However, the royal governor of Massachusetts, Thomas Hutchinson, would not permit the ships to return to England until the duty had been paid. On the evening of 16 December 1773 a group of Bostonians boarded the ships and dumped the tea into Boston Harbour (the 'Boston Tea Party'). When the government of Boston refused to pay for the destroyed tea, the British closed the port until compensation was paid. In addition, the British parliament passed the *Coercive Acts* (1774), a series of laws designed to punish the province of Massachusetts and to demonstrate parliament's sovereignty. This led to the first armed conflicts and, eventually, to the American War of Independence (Revolution) (1775–83).

The US federal law of 1791, sponsored by the head of the federalists and secretary of the treasury Alexander Hamilton, imposed an excise duty on whisky. This provoked a number of riots in 1794 known as 'the Whiskey Rebellion'. The burden of this excise duty fell largely on western Pennsylvania, which was at the time one of the chief whisky-producing regions of the country. Many grain farmers were also distillers. They depended almost totally on whisky as a source of income. They considered the law to be an attack on their basic economic interest and liberty. Their resistance to the collection of excise duty assumed grave proportions. The federal authorities issued arrest warrants for a large number of non-compliant distillers in the spring of 1794. The riots that followed brought damage to property and the death of one federal officer. In August 1794, President George Washington ordered the insurgents to disperse and requested the governors of Pennsylvania and a few other states to mobilise their troops. There were also negotiations with representatives from western Pennsylvania. However, all was in vain, and Washington ordered a military action in October 1794. The operation was swift as there was almost no resistance. The Whiskey Rebellion is interesting and important as it reflected the strong local preferences and because it provided a test (the first of its kind in the US) of the strengths and limits of the federal government's authority.

Britain

Imposition of new taxes in our times, even within a single complacent democratic country or a federation, is neither easy nor trouble free. The British government under Margaret Thatcher introduced a 'poll tax' (the community charge). As a government with a free market ideology, the rationale for the poll tax was found in the argument that people do not pay for goods on the market in proportion to their income and wealth. There is a strong market tendency to have the same price for an identical good or service throughout the market: one good, one price. Therefore, it would be a market-neutral policy for each person to pay the same tax, rather than pay in proportion to his/her income or wealth. Hence, according to this ultra-liberal doctrine everyone should pay an equal tax – equal voting weight, equal taxation – regardless of income. It was dubbed the poll tax.

The poll tax is not only economically flawed, but also socially unjust. The purchase of goods and services on the market is, under normal conditions, voluntary. However, the payment of tax is obligatory. The government has coercive powers to charge a tax on a person's very existence regardless of the need of that person for the public service. This regressive tax had not been seriously considered in London for over 600 years. One of the reasons was that a similar tax in 1381 sparked the Peasants' Revolt. In order to calm the insurgence, King Richard II promised to end the repression of peasants by the nobility. Once the menace had passed, the king reneged on his promise and commented: 'Villeins ye are, and villeins ye shall remain'; that is, promises to little people do not count.

The poll tax was supposed to be the flagship of Mrs Thatcher's government. It was first introduced in Scotland in 1989 and a year later in England. There was a strong 'don't pay' campaign in Scotland even though this was punishable by law. The Scots felt that the poll tax was anti-Scottish and that it had been imposed on them by the English majority in London. It was outrageous and in breach of the Treaty of Union which was supposed to ensure that no taxes were imposed on Scotland which were not also levied on England. In addition, large-scale but peaceful protests in Scotland were ignored by the government in London. However, the 'don't pay' campaign later inspired about 15 million British people to refuse to pay the tax. Many people switched to supporting Labour because they detested the tax, even though senior Labour politicians did little to oppose it. The violent and widespread anti-poll tax riots, particularly in Trafalgar Square in London, forced the government to abolish the poll tax on 21 March 1990 and this contributed to Mrs Thatcher's resignation six months later.

Models of society differ among countries. These national choices need not be transposed to others, particularly not by bullying. These models depend on habits, mentality, history and social priorities, choices and values. Citizens in some countries hold the usefulness and efficiency of the government in high esteem, while in others this respect is much lower for various reasons, for example, corruption. Thus, it is little wonder that Britain insists that unanimity in EU tax matters should be preserved. According to Britain (and some other countries, such as Austria and

Luxembourg, which do not express themselves as forcibly) there should be no changes whatsoever in EU tax matters without the full consent of all EU member countries. Therefore, it is not surprising that the EU has no power to levy taxes.

4.3.4 DIRECT TAXES

The issue that needs to be addressed next is the classification of taxes. According to their base, taxes may be levied on income and wealth (direct taxes) and consumption (indirect taxes). *Direct taxes* are charges on the income of firms and individuals (factor returns), as well as property ownership, and are effective at the end of the production process. They have an impact on the mobility of factors and any change has a direct impact on taxpayers' purchasing power. They include corporation tax, income tax and tax on wealth. The share of direct taxes in total taxes in the EU(25) is about one-third. However, the central and east European member countries had a lower share, about 22 per cent (Table 4.4). *Indirect taxes* are applied to consumption. They affect movements of goods and services. Any alteration of these taxes changes the price of goods and services. Local governments traditionally depend most heavily on property taxes, while state governments rely on sales and income taxes. In addition and depending on constitutional arrangements, a federal or central government in a country that has full sovereignty over its domestic monetary affairs can create money. It does not have to raise enough from the domestic tax system to balance its budget.

Corporate Taxes

The international aspect of corporate taxation refers to the taxation of TNCs. Differences in corporate taxes among countries in which a free capital mobility is permitted may endanger the efficient spatial and sectoral allocation of resources if capital owners tend to maximise their net profits in the short run. Other things being equal, capital would flow to and locate in countries or regions with a relatively low level of corporate taxes (although this is only one, allegedly minor, variable that influences investment decisions). TNCs decide on their trans-border location not only according to the production-efficiency criteria, but also according to others that include differences in market growth, trade regime, competition, tax rates, subsidies, general stability and so on.

There are two key issues. The first one deals with high taxes. If this type of tax burden shows that there is a high-quality infrastructure, trained labour and educated management, this may be an indication that the location may

Table 4.4 Total direct taxes as a share of total taxes in the EU(25) and Norway, 1995–2002 (%)

	1995	1996	1997	1998	1999	2000	2001	2002	Average 1995–2002	Change[1] 1995–2002	Difference[2] 1995–2002
BE	37.9	37.6	38.1	38.9	38.1	38.7	39.2	38.8	38.4	0.5	1.0
CZ	25.1	23.8	22.7	24.0	23.2	24.4	25.8	26.2	24.4	1.1	1.1
DK	62.1	61.8	61.3	60.1	60.2	60.3	60.5	60.5	60.8	0.4	−1.6
DE	27.5	27.9	27.2	28.0	28.4	29.8	27.6	27.1	27.9	0.2	−0.4
EE	–	–	–	–	–	–	–	24.4	24.4	–	–
EL	23.8	22.5	23.9	27.0	27.2	28.8	26.7	26.9	25.8	2.7	3.1
ES	31.3	31.4	31.6	30.6	30.2	30.5	30.4	31.3	30.9	0.4	−0.1
FR	20.6	20.9	22.3	27.0	27.8	28.4	29.0	27.6	25.4	5.3	7.0
IE	41.1	42.5	43.3	43.4	43.4	42.7	43.1	40.8	42.5	0.0	−0.3
IT	37.4	36.7	37.7	34.5	35.3	34.7	35.7	34.5	35.8	−1.1	−2.9
CY	–	–	–	35.3	38.2	36.7	36.2	35.8	36.4	–	–
LV	23.2	24.5	26.9	27.2	27.1	27.2	28.2	29.9	26.8	3.0	6.7
LT	30.7	29.4	21.9	28.3	28.6	27.9	27.1	26.2	27.5	0.9	−4.4
LU	41.6	42.5	42.2	41.1	39.2	38.3	38.5	39.3	40.3	−1.5	−2.3
HU	–	–	–	–	–	–	26.7	26.9	26.8		
MT	31.4	29.7	30.7	31.4	32.4	33.3	33.7	36.1	32.3	2.2	4.7
NL	31.2	32.3	31.3	30.9	30.0	30.0	30.6	31.3	30.9	0.5	0.1
AT	28.4	30.1	30.4	30.8	30.3	30.6	33.4	31.6	30.7	1.5	3.2
PL	33.2	29.9	30.3	29.5	20.6	21.0	19.6	18.7	25.4	−9.0	−14.4
PT	26.6	27.8	27.9	27.0	27.5	28.8	27.9	26.9	27.6	0.3	0.3
SI	17.5	18.8	19.7	19.7	19.3	20.2	20.2	20.2	19.5	1.7	2.7
SK	27.9	26.1	26.6	25.2	25.3	22.1	22.6	22.6	24.9	−3.3	−5.3
FI	38.2	40.7	40.2	41.3	40.9	45.3	43.0	42.9	41.6	1.7	4.7

SE	40.8	40.7	41.2	40.5	41.5	41.9	39.1	36.8	40.3	−1.0	−3.9
UK	42.6	42.8	43.0	45.1	44.5	45.0	45.6	44.2	44.1	0.8	1.6
NO	37.9	39.5	39.5	37.2	39.3	46.8	46.5	46.4	41.6	3.3	8.4
EU25	31.5	31.8	32.5	33.4	33.5	34.3	33.9	33.1	33.0	1.0	1.6
EU15	31.5	31.9	32.6	33.6	33.8	34.6	34.4	33.5	33.3	1.2	2.0
Euro12	27.0	27.6	28.0	28.7	29.1	29.7	29.4	28.8	28.5	1.1	1.7
NMS10	29.1	27.2	27.3	27.5	22.2	22.5	22.5	22.5	25.1	−4.2	−6.6

Notes: For abbreviations, see Table 4.3.
1. Estimated annual average growth rate in %.
2. in % points of total taxation.

Source: European Commission (2004b).

be attractive for a TNC. If low taxes mean that these services are at a low level then, depending on the industry and strategic goals of a TNC, foreign and domestic investors may not find this an attractive location to go to or to be in. The second issue concerns subsidies. If in a free market situation a firm, domestic or foreign (TNC), finds a location in geographical space or in an industry to be attractive profit-wise, then it will locate there without any subsidy. Subsidies to firms to locate in an already determined place are not necessary. If public subsidies are offered at all, are they a sign of a lack of business appeal (lack of competitive attraction) of the location in question? However, the empirical evidence about the impact of taxes and subsidies on the geographical location of firms is still inconclusive.

Corporate taxes may be collected according to various methods: the classical, integrated, dual and imputation systems. Their basic features are as follows:

- A *classical* (or a *separate*) method represents one extreme. According to this method, a firm is taken as a separate entity, distinct from its shareholders. Corporations are taxed irrespective of whether profits are distributed. At the same time, shareholders' income is taxed notwithstanding the fact that the corporation has already paid taxes on its profit.
- An *integrated* method represents another extreme which is relevant for theoretical considerations. Here, a corporation is viewed as a collection of shareholders. Corporate tax is eliminated while shareholders pay tax on their portion of corporate profits. Hence, personal income tax and corporate tax are integrated in full. However, it is difficult to apply this system because of the practical problems of allocating corporate income to possibly thousands of shareholders.
- The *dual* (two-rate, split-rate) method falls between the two extremes. A corporation pays tax at a lower rate if profits are distributed than in the case when they are not.
- *Imputation* is another intermediate system for taxing corporations. In contrast to the dual system, however, relief is provided here at the shareholder level. Corporations pay taxes just as in the classical system, while shareholders receive credit, usually in the year they receive dividends, for the tax already paid by the corporation.

Computation of corporate profits has provoked much controversy. The authorities of several states in the US[77] apply a *unitary* (formulary apportionment) method for the taxation of TNCs. This arbitrary and controversial method was inspired, in part, by the problem of transfer pricing (manipulation of the cost of imported inputs and exported output).

A TNC derives its income not only from the place of its residence, but also from the operation of its subsidiaries. The rationale for the unitary method of taxation is that profits of the TNC accrue from its global operations, so that a TNC needs to be taken as a single unit. The tax authorities, in particular in California, extend beyond the confines of their state's geographical jurisdiction. Because of an increasing diversity and volume of international transactions and the globalisation of business activities, it is hard to assess exactly the individual affiliate's contribution to the overall profit of a TNC (UNCTAD, 1993, p. 209).

If the unitary method is applied, then the tax authorities relate sales, assets and/or payroll expenditure of the affiliate under their jurisdiction to the TNC's worldwide sales, assets and/or payroll outlays. The business community adamantly disputes such a mechanical view that averages the global operations of a TNC across the board. Profit uniformity at all stages of production and trade, as well as at all international locations, does not prevail. The cost-plus or resale-minus method of taxation that exists elsewhere may be a superior tax choice.

In a 'globalised' international economy there may be continuous multi-jurisdictional conflicts regarding the taxation of TNCs. The national tax authorities take a semi-arbitrary unitary method and assess the share of global profits of the TNC that should be taxed within the confines of their jurisdiction. This approach contrasts sharply with the traditional separate accounting rules (arm's-length method) of tax assessment among distinct fiscal authorities because it is not (necessarily) arbitrary. Although the unitary method has elicited support from certain intellectuals, the business community is adamantly opposed to it. This opposition not only comes from the increased administrative costs for the TNCs, but also runs contrary to the US constitutional provision that the federal government (not the ones in the constituting states) is in charge of foreign commerce.

If the unitary principle is applied in only one or a few (but not all) locations where a TNC operates, the following two cases are possible. First, if the operation of the affiliate is more profitable than the average overall profitability of the TNC, then the local authority that applies the unitary method of corporate taxation would collect less tax than it could by the application of the cost-plus method. Second, if business operations of the affiliate are less profitable than the average universal profitability of the TNC, then the local tax office will collect more tax than under the alternative collection method. The second case directly harms the profitability of the affiliate, reduces the corporate funds for the potential investment and, hence, undermines the long-term interests of the host country. In 1994, after 17 years of legal battle, the US Supreme Court decided in favour of California with respect to the unitary method of taxation (Barclays Bank lost the case). The Court held that unitary taxation did not violate the foreign commerce clause. The implications of the decision are not fully clear. If profitability of a TNC is higher in California than elsewhere in the world, that company may benefit from unitary tax assessment. As of 1986, California allowed taxpayers to choose between unitary tax assessment and the 'water's edge' method (taxation of income within the confines of the US, rather than worldwide income). This is a system close to the universally accepted arm's-length method.

Unitary taxation offers the advantage of being location neutral. It also discourages tax evasion and flight. The problem and difficulty is, however, how to arrive at the unitary taxation in practice? The problems of technical tax assessment and tax base determination are formidable. The first victim in this process may be tax autonomy. Hence, changes in any tax system are very slow indeed. If a 'correct' unitary taxation is the final goal, then it should be arrived at multilaterally by all tax authorities.

The principal disadvantages of the unitary method of taxation are the following:

- The *method of calculation* is the most significant objection.[78] The formula used to determine the allotment of profit to be taxed by a specific tax authority could easily have certain arbitrary elements. The main distortion that is brought by unitary taxation is that it is different from the standard arm's-length taxation principle. In addition, states using the unitary method adopt a formula favourable to themselves. Many states use different formulas (more distortions) and the outcome is the creation of a potentially higher aggregate taxable income than the total business income.
- *Data* that use tax authorities to assess the portion of the global profit that ought to be taxed within their tax jurisdiction may be neither sufficient nor fully reliable. Collection of data and reporting obligations may easily be (very) different among different countries. In these circumstances, it may be difficult to assess the 'global business' and the 'local profit' of a company to be taxed.
- An *international consensus* in these matters is necessary. Unfortunately, this is very difficult to achieve and would involve a lengthy consultation period. A predetermined global formula for taxation may be a possible solution to this problem. However, these prearranged formulas have flaws as they do not pay attention to the specific facts, circumstances, merits, business efficiency and risks in each particular case and location.[79] The result is that in many cases there could be overtaxation, while in others there could be undertaxation (Sadiq, 2001, p. 283).

The arm's-length method of taxation is the accepted international norm even though it may not be the most astute approach. This is because such a method creates a simulated world in which each and every transaction is treated as if it were between independent firms. The argument for a unitary method of taxation is based on the idea that a TNC is one company. Therefore, it ought to be taxed in that way. Internal transactions, including transfer pricing within a TNC, need not be made in an arm's-length way (that is, as if the transaction was between independent firms).

The main goal of corporate taxation is not to increase the price of goods and services, but rather to capture a part of the firm's profit. Frequent changes in the corporation-tax systems should be avoided, because they increase uncertainty and the administrative burden on firms. Unless they are favourable for business, these variations distort the decision-making process concerning investment and may have a long-term negative effect on capital that would withdraw or reduce investment in these geographical locations.

A firm may pass on the tax burden to consumers in the form of higher prices for its goods and services or to its employees, by reduced wages, or a combination of the two. By passing on the tax burden, it may reduce, in part or in full, the impact of the tax on its profit. The possibility for the passing on of the tax burden depends on the idiosyncrasies of the goods/ services and the labour market. If a firm is free to set its prices, then it depends on competition as to whether this passing on is possible. If prices are regulated, then the way of passing on the tax burden is different. Suppose that the prices do not rise. A firm may reduce the quality of its output in order to save profits. In the opposite case when prices do not fall, a firm may improve the quality of its output and after-sales service in order to increase its competitiveness and save or increase its market share.

The importance of the distribution of the tax burden between individuals and firms may be analysed in the following example. Suppose that P_d stands for the price paid by consumers. If one imposes a tax of t dollars per unit of output on the suppliers (firms), then the price P_s which they receive is:

$$P_s = P_d - t. \tag{4.1}$$

The condition for equilibrium is:

$$P_s(q) = P_d(q) - t. \tag{4.2}$$

Assume that one imposes the same tax of t dollars per unit of purchased good on the buyers. The price paid by consumers is:

$$P_d = P_s + t. \tag{4.3}$$

The condition for equilibrium in this case is:

$$P_d(q) = P_s(q) + t. \tag{4.4}$$

Note that the two conditions for equilibrium, (4.2) and (4.4), are the same. Thus the quantity P_s and P_d in equilibrium is independent of whether the tax is levied on demanders (individuals) or suppliers (firms). The volume of government revenue does not change. What changes is the composition of the revenue, which may provoke heated political debate. Many tax authorities obviously do not understand these simple and straightforward equations.

The integrationist school argues that income has to be taxed as a whole in spite of differences in its source, and that all taxes are ultimately borne by the people. In contrast, the absolutist school argues that firms are separate legal entities that need to be taxed in their own capacity (under the assumption that they do not pass on the tax burden either to their employees or to consumers). Another reason for the separate treatment of corporations is that they use government services without fully paying for them. This has an impact on the reduction of costs of operation. Tax authorities can use their policy to regulate investment by firms and to control their monopoly position. On these grounds, tax instruments can influence the behaviour of the business sector.

If private capital flows are a significant feature of economic relations among countries, some of these countries may find an incentive to negotiate tax treaties in order to avoid double taxation and, possibly, achieve tax neutrality. Tax neutrality between investment in home country A and foreign country B is achieved when firms are indifferent (other things being equal) between investing, producing, buying and selling in either country. This means that a tax should not cause firms and people to change their economic behaviour. In this case, the foreign country's tax equals the corporate tax plus the *withholding tax* (tax on the transfer of profits). If under a condition of free capital mobility country A's firm finds country B's taxes equal to country A's, then there is tax neutrality between these two countries.[80] If this is not the case and if other conditions are equal, investment may flow to the country that has relatively lower taxes.

Capital flight may be mitigated and eliminated if the authorities remove distortions that initially provoked this exodus of capital. For those who want to send capital back home, a certain tax amnesty needs to be considered together with a low rate of penalty payments. Evening out of taxes (certain harmonisation of tax rules and rates) within a wider international area and cooperation among tax authorities may discourage tax dodgers and illegal capital flight, but this may not be an appropriate solution for all regions (one size does not fit all).

Cooperation among the tax authorities in partner countries may be necessary for the smooth operation of the economies of the integrated countries. This demand is amplified if the desired goals are free mobility of capital, free competition, efficient spatial and sectoral allocation of resources, 'fairness' in the distribution of revenues among the member countries and the elimination of administrative difficulties. This is of special importance in a situation of fixed exchange rates and free capital mobility. Measures to reduce the risks of tax evasion can take the form of a generalised withholding tax for all EMU residents and/or a commitment of banks to disclose information about interest received by the union residents. Therefore, the need to create conduit companies, as intermediary subsidiaries that take advantage of tax treaties in order to reduce withholding taxes, can be eliminated. As tax harmonisation deals with difficult and deeply rooted national customs and preferences, the EU has not put the harmonisation issue aside, but it did not press member countries on this issue in an aggressive way. The Single European Market and the eurozone are expected to exert the sophisticated, behind-the-scenes market-led pressure on countries to approximate taxes, as the high-tax countries, other things being equal, would lose market competitiveness of their goods and services, and also be less attractive geographical locations for FDI.

Tax competition may be an effective tool to promote economic development. The 23 Swiss cantons have competing tax systems that ultimately support economic expansion. Harmful tax competition exists, in general, when only select activities are promoted. This distorts the allocation of resources. In broad terms, tax competition lowers taxes, while tax harmonisation may make them rise. If let alone, tax competition may provoke a 'race to the bottom' in order to attract business to locate in specific places and countries. However, this scenario depends on the assumption that the firms care only about taxes when they select the location for their operations. In addition, low taxes may be too low from both the business and the social standpoints. Business and the social infrastructure may be poor and unattractive. Hence, relatively higher tax locations may be preferred by firms to low tax areas. At the same time, authorities in these locations may safely presume that the majority of firms may not go elsewhere only because of high(er) local taxes. If there are benefits in the agglomeration of businesses and clustering of firms (strong functional intra-industry production links), then tax rates may safely be different between the cluster (centre) and its periphery. If, however, taxes are harmonised between the two regions or countries, then both may suffer. The centre would have to reduce taxes and, consequently, social and business services. The periphery would need to increase taxes and bankrupt many local firms. The tax base would shrink further.

Competition between countries to attract TNCs to locate within their confines is driving down tax rates.[81] However, this has a side-effect. Governments find it increasingly difficult to raise revenue from businesses. Hence, there is an intensified pressure to increase taxes on individuals in the same locations, particularly if they are not mobile. Otherwise the social programmes may not continue.

Capital income has a high degree of mobility. This has become more pronounced since the introduction of the euro in 1999. However, the taxation of income from savings is a sensitive issue. The European Commission would like to reduce 'harmful' tax competition among the EU member countries regarding income from non-resident savings. A withholding tax may find a certain rationale as Germany[82] and Scandinavian states forgo quite a bit of tax revenue as their wealthy citizens and institutions (pension funds) save in non-resident accounts, primarily in Luxembourg and Britain. However, an argument against this tax cites the logistical nightmare of administering it and distributing proceeds. In addition, it would give incentives to place holdings in non-EU financial centres such as the Channel Islands (UK), Switzerland and elsewhere. Jersey, Guernsey and the Isle of Man are not members of the EU. They have no obligation to align their fiscal system with that of the EU. Therefore, Luxembourg would never accept an accord which excludes the Channel Islands. A common tax of, for example, 20 per cent in the EU would mean an immediate capital flight from Luxembourg to the Channel Island banks.

After a 14-year process of negotiations (horse-trading and blackmailing[83]) over the taxation of income from savings, the EU agreed on rules to crack down on tax fraud and tax evasion in 2003. According to this deal, 12 EU countries would start exchanging information on the savings of non-residents from mid-2005. Hence, each EU member country will be able to tax its citizens on non-resident savings in the EU. Austria, Belgium and Luxembourg were exempt from the obligation to exchange information because of the secrecy provisions in their banking systems, but they will have to levy a withholding tax instead. Three-quarters of these proceeds are to be transferred to the saver's country of origin, while the rest would remain in the country in which the funds were saved. The tax rate would rise from 15 per cent in 2005 to 35 per cent in 2010. In order to prevent capital flight from the EU to 'easier' tax regimes such as Andorra, the Channel Islands, Liechtenstein, Monaco and Switzerland[84] will have to either exchange information or impose a tax. Switzerland agreed to apply the same withholding tax as sharing account information violates clients' right to secrecy.[85] However, this may play into the hands of tax evaders, money launderers, arms traders, drug and human smugglers and terrorists who need to hide their money. If the elimination of tax evasion and money laundering are the principal policy objectives, it seems that cooperation, even some exchange and sharing of information on bank accounts among governments, may be the most effective policy tools.

Corporate Taxes in the European Union

The basic treaties of the EU are relatively short on tax provisions. There are just a few articles in the Treaty of Rome that refer to the general issue of taxation. Article 90 stipulates that imported products from the partner countries may not be taxed more highly than comparable domestic goods. This has introduced the principle of destination for VAT, as well as non-discrimination in the EU internal commerce. Article 91 introduced tax neutrality. It states that any repayment of tax on goods exported to the EU partner countries may not exceed the taxes actually paid on the goods in question. Article 93 requires unanimity in harmonisation of indirect taxes (there is no specific call for the harmonisation of direct taxes). This harmonisation of taxes may go only as far as 'is necessary to ensure the establishment and functioning of the internal market'. Article 94 authorises the Council of Ministers to approximate laws that directly affect the establishment or operation of the common market. The decision about this must be unanimous. Article 95 §2 excludes fiscal matters from the majority voting procedure. The unanimity principle has prevented rapid progress in the approximation of fiscal matters in the EU.

Effective top statutory tax rates on corporate income in the EU(25) have been changing over time in the EU (Table 4.5). Figure 4.9 shows the evolution of effective top statutory tax rates on corporate income in the EU(15) and new member states in the 1995–2004 period. Two trends are obvious from these data: there is a strong tendency to reduce tax on corporate income and the new member states have always had this tax rate at least 10 per cent below that in the EU(15). Figure 4.10 gives the situation in 2004. These data shows that there is tax competition between the EU(15) (Ireland apart) and the new member states. While this may have a certain influence on the location of tax-sensitive firms towards the eastern part of the EU, this indicator does not specify what the location offers businesses in return for the collected (lower) taxes.

Table 4.6 illustrates, in a simplified way, differences in corporate tax systems in the EU, candidate countries, Switzerland, the US and Japan. The table does not take into account any of the complex and different surtaxes, surcharges, local taxes, credits, exemptions, special treatment of the small and medium-sized enterprises (SMEs) and the like that apply in nearly all countries. The differences in systems and rates of corporate taxes point to the distortions of tax neutrality for investment in the EU (and outside it).

Table 4.5 Effective top statutory tax rates on corporate income in the EU(25), 1995–2004 (%)

	1995	1996	1997	1998	1999	2000	2001	2002	2003	2004	Difference 1995–2004
BE	40.2	40.2	40.2	40.2	40.2	40.2	40.2	40.2	34.0	34.0	–6.2
DK	34.0	34.0	34.0	34.0	32.0	32.0	30.0	30.0	30.0	30.0	–4.0
DE	56.8	56.7	56.7	56.0	51.6	51.6	38.3	38.3	39.6	38.3	–18.5
EL	40.0	40.0	40.0	40.0	40.0	40.0	37.5	35.0	35.0	35.0	–5.0
ES	35.0	35.0	35.0	35.0	35.0	35.0	35.0	35.0	35.0	35.0	0.0
FR	36.7	36.7	36.7	41.7	40.0	36.7	36.4	35.4	35.4	35.4	–1.2
IE	40.0	38.0	36.0	32.0	28.0	24.0	20.0	16.0	12.5	12.5	–27.5
IT	52.2	53.2	53.2	41.3	41.3	41.3	40.3	40.3	38.3	37.3	–15.0
LU	40.9	40.9	39.3	37.5	37.5	37.5	37.5	30.4	30.4	30.4	–10.5
NL	35.0	35.0	35.0	35.0	35.0	35.0	35.0	34.5	34.5	34.5	–0.5
AT	34.0	34.0	34.0	34.0	34.0	34.0	34.0	34.0	34.0	34.0	0.0
PT	39.6	39.6	39.6	37.4	37.4	35.2	35.2	33.0	33.0	27.5	–12.1
FI	25.0	28.0	28.0	28.0	28.0	29.0	29.0	29.0	29.0	29.0	4.0
SE	28.0	28.0	28.0	28.0	28.0	28.0	28.0	28.0	28.0	28.0	0.0
UK	33.0	33.0	31.0	31.0	30.0	30.0	30.0	30.0	30.0	30.0	–3.0
CZ	41.0	39.0	39.0	35.0	35.0	31.0	31.0	31.0	31.0	28.0	–13.0
EE	26.0	26.0	26.0	26.0	26.0	26.0	26.0	26.0	26.0	26.0	0.0
CY	25.0	25.0	25.0	25.0	25.0	29.0	28.0	28.0	15.0	15.0	–10.0
LV	25.0	25.0	25.0	25.0	25.0	25.0	25.0	22.0	19.0	15.0	–10.0
LT	29.0	29.0	29.0	29.0	29.0	24.0	24.0	15.0	15.0	15.0	–14.0
HU	19.6	19.6	19.6	19.6	19.6	19.6	19.6	19.6	19.6	17.7	–2.0
MT	35.0	35.0	35.0	35.0	35.0	35.0	35.0	35.0	35.0	35.0	0.0

PL	40.0	40.0	38.0	36.0	34.0	30.0	28.0	28.0	27.0	19.0	–21.0
SI	25.0	25.0	25.0	25.0	25.0	25.0	25.0	25.0	25.0	25.0	0.0
SK	40.0	40.0	40.0	40.0	40.0	29.0	29.0	25.0	25.0	19.0	–21.0
Mean EU-15 (arithm.)	38.0	38.1	37.8	36.7	35.9	35.3	33.8	32.6	31.9	31.4	–6.6
Mean EU-NMS10 (arithm.)	30.6	30.4	30.2	29.6	29.4	27.4	27.1	25.5	23.8	21.5	–9.1

Note: For abbreviations, see Table 4.3.

Source: European Commission (2004b).

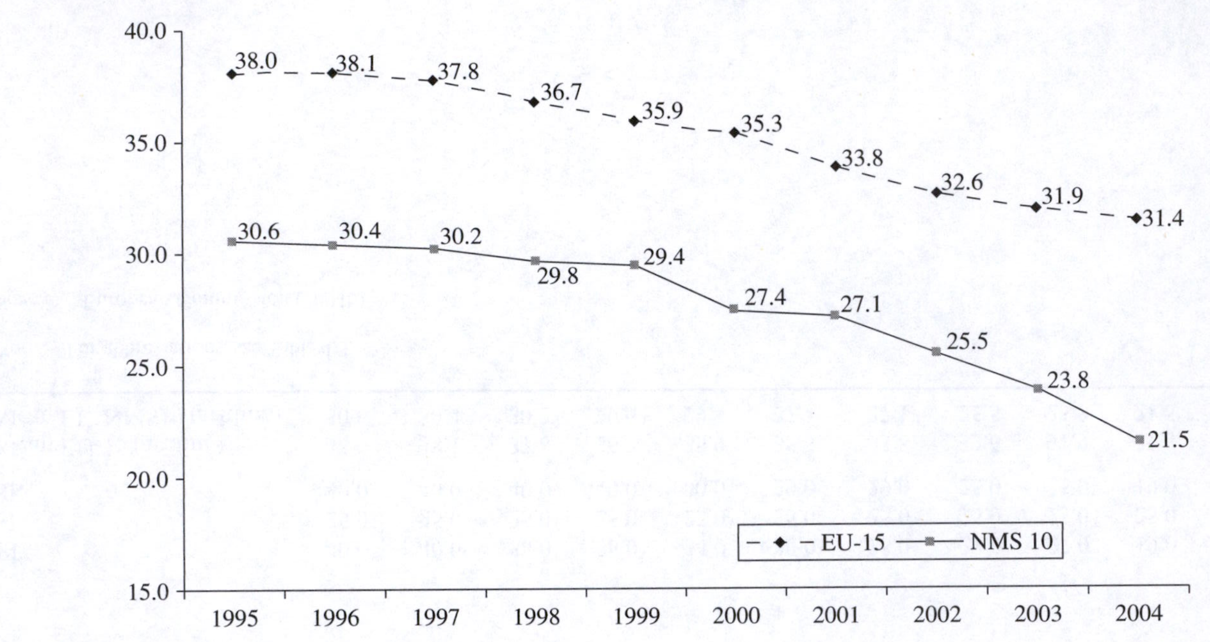

Note: NMS: new member states.

Source: European Commission (2004b).

Figure 4.9 Development of effective top statutory tax rates on corporate income in the EU(15) and new member states, 1995–2004 (%)

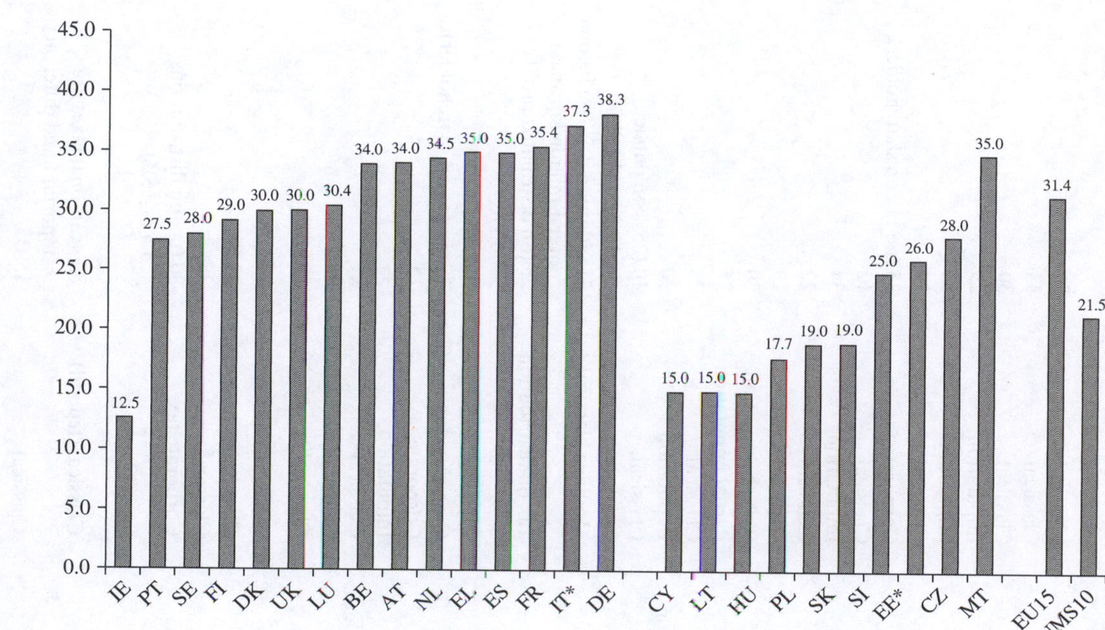

Note: For abbreviations, see Table 4.3.

Source: European Commission (2004b).

Figure 4.10 *Effective top statutory tax rates on corporate income in the EU(25) in 2004 (%)*

Table 4.6 Systems and rates of corporate taxes in EU(25), candidate countries, Switzerland, the US and Japan in 2003

Country	System	Rate (%)
EU(25)		
1. Austria	Classical	34
2. Belgium	Classical	33
3. Denmark	Classical	30
4. Finland	Imputation	29
5. France	Imputation	34
6. Germany	Classical	25
7. Greece	Corporate tax	35 (no tax on shareholder)
8. Ireland	Classical	12
9. Italy	Imputation	34
10. Luxembourg	Classical	22
11. Netherlands	Classical	29
12. Portugal	Partial exemption	30
13. Spain	Partial imputation	35
14. Sweden	Classical	28
15. United Kingdom	Imputation	30
16. Cyprus	Classical	10 (25% on public corporate bodies)
17. Czech Republic	Modified classical	31 (additional 5% on income over 1 million korunas)
18. Estonia	Tax on distribution	26 (on distributed profit only)
19. Hungary	Classical	18
20. Latvia	Corporate tax	15 (no tax on shareholder)
21. Lithuania	Corporate tax	15
22. Malta	Imputation	35
23. Poland	Classical	27
24. Slovakia	Classical	25
25. Slovenia	Classical	25
Candidate countries		
26. Bulgaria	Classical	23.5
27. Romania	Classical	25
28. Turkey	Corporate tax	30 (tax on distributions 5.5 or 16%)
Other		
29. Switzerland	Classical (federal)	8.5 (cantonal taxes are important and different)
30. United States	Classical	15–35
31. Japan	Classical	28–37.5

Source: International Bureau of Fiscal Documentation (2004).

Therefore, the European Commission considered proposing a single corporate tax rate for the EU, but stepped back from the idea. A special committee proposed a minimum tax rate (30 per cent) and a maximum rate (40 per cent) that could be introduced in the EU countries. The proposed rates may be meaningful only if the tax base is also harmonised.[86] The problem has been identified, but a solution that could be transformed into EU law is not always easy to find. In theory, a TNC is ready to pay relatively higher corporate taxes in country A if it supplies the business sector with educated labour, infrastructure, lower social contributions, even trade protection, relative to country B where the corporate tax rate is lower.

The objective of tax harmonisation or equalisation of corporate tax rates in the EU is to introduce an identical 'tax distortion' across the EU. The idea to 'level the playing field' may have justification in win–lose (zero-sum game) contests. In sports, for example in boxing, one sportsman wins, while the other loses a match. It makes sense to have the rules that stipulate that each of them has roughly the same weight just before the match. However, this idea is problematic from the outset in other circumstances. In business, for example, both buyer and seller gain. This is a win–win situation (positive-sum game). Differences in national taxation reflect a variety of national circumstances, choices and objectives. Why should fresh garden tomatoes cost the same in Italy and in Finland? If pushed to the limit, if taxes level the playing field, there would be no trade, no specialisation and little growth.

The corporate tax distorts another important variable for firms, related to the form and level of financing. A corporate tax 'punishes' enterprises that raise their capital through equity, rather than debt. This is because interest payments can be deducted from taxable profits, while the return on equity cannot. Possibly the best solution would be to eliminate corporate taxes. Taxes on corporate profit could be collected from shareholders' income and/or on corporate cash flow before the interest is paid (not as now, after the deductions for the interest payments). This would be in line with a tendency to avoid taxes that hurt capital formation and investment. In addition, if dividends get special tax treatment, then wealthy people who get most of their income from dividends may easily end up paying lower tax rates than ordinary people who work for a living.

Differences in corporate taxation may distort investment and location decisions by firms. Therefore, this may introduce distortions into the operation of the Single European Market, hence there is a need for an EU action towards the convergence of corporate taxes. The Ruding Committee (1992) reaffirmed this observation, but recommended that the existing system of corporate taxation be retained. That is to say, the state in which profits of a TNC originate should continue to tax them in full (that is, both distributed and retained profits should be taxed). If the profits are transferred to the parent country, this state should exempt them from taxation or allow a tax credit for the taxes already paid in the country where they were made. This reflects the difficulty of harmonising taxes on the international level. It seems that tax reform within countries needs to precede tax reform between them.[87]

Juridical *double taxation* arises when a single economic income is taxed twice. If a firm (TNC) operates in two countries, its profit may be taxed by the two national tax authorities. It is often forgotten that what matters for TNCs is not the fact that profits are taxed twice, but rather the level of total taxation. If the profit of country A's TNC earned in country B has been taxed by country B, then country A may exempt this TNC from taxes on that part of its income earned in country B. Another method of solving this problem is that country A provides credit to its TNCs on taxes paid in country B. In this case the tax burden on country A's corporation operating in country B is the same as that made from purely home operations in country A, provided that country B's taxes are lower than or equal to those in country A.

The solution to the double taxation problem may also be found elsewhere. One possible solution is the unitary method of collection of corporate taxes (with all its controversies). A second is the profit-split method. Income of the distinct affiliates of a TNC is split in relation to the functions they perform and in relation to the associated risk. The difference between the profit-split and the unitary methods is that the former applies a functional analysis that is unique to each transaction, while the latter averages out all transactions. A third potential solution is the mutual agreement procedure where the national tax authorities discuss and try to correct tax discrepancies. In fact, they try to find an acceptable way of applying an existing method. The EU Arbitration Convention provided for binding arbitration related to the adjustment of profits of associated enterprises. A fourth answer may be found in advance-pricing agreements. Again, this is the application of an existing method. A TNC may acquire an advance agreement from the tax authority on the system for the allocation of its profit. This method represents a departure from the usual tax procedure (tax audits may take place even a few years after a transaction has taken place) since it refers to unknown future evolution (UNCTAD, 1993, pp. 207–10).

The Arbitration Convention

The objective of the 1990 EU Convention on the Elimination of Double Taxation in Connection with the Adjustment of Profits of Associated

Enterprises (90/436/EEC) (or the EU Arbitration Convention) is to eliminate double taxation of profits in connection with the adjustment of transfers of profits between associated enterprises. The convention came into force in January 1995 for a period of five years.

Transnational corporations operating within the Single European Market need to know that their profits will not be exposed to double taxation. The Arbitration Convention provides for independent arbitration (dispute resolution) where two EU member states are unable to resolve a disagreement as to the proper allocation of taxable profits in transfer pricing cases. It will help to ensure that enterprises doing business within the Single European Market are not exposed to double taxation of their profits. Such disagreements can arise from differing interpretations of the 'arm's-length principle', the internationally agreed tax standard for determining prices at which associated enterprises (TNCs) transfer goods, services, finance and intangible assets from one to another.

Double taxation hinders a free flow of trade, capital and investment, so it is desirable to avoid it wherever possible. When the double taxation problem arises, the firm affected presents its case to the tax authorities concerned. If these authorities cannot solve the problem satisfactorily, they endeavour to reach mutual agreement with the authorities of the member state where the associated firm is taxed. If no agreement can be reached, the authorities present the case to an advisory commission, which suggests a way of solving the problem. Although the tax authorities may subsequently adopt, by mutual agreement, a solution different from that suggested by the advisory commission, they are bound to adopt the commission's advice if they cannot reach agreement. The commission consists of a chairman, two representatives from each of the tax authorities concerned and an even number of independent members.

In 1999, before the expiration of the convention, the EU member states signed a protocol for an automatic extension of the convention for five-year periods, unless contracting countries oppose. According to a survey prepared by the EU Joint Transfer Pricing Forum, several states have accepted a taxpayer request to initiate a mutual agreement procedure under the Arbitration Convention (which expired in 2000) and were willing to participate in the arbitration procedure, provided that there is agreement with the other member state involved in the dispute. Countries finally ratified the protocol only in 2004 and the convention re-entered into force retroactively from 2000.

Parallel to the process of ratification of the extension protocol, the EU member states have, within the framework of the EU Joint Transfer Pricing Forum, agreed to give the highest priority to finding practical solutions for a more uniform application of the convention. The aim is to work on the basis of consensus to reach non-legislative improvements to practical procedural problems such as deadlines, suspension of tax collection, interest charges and advisory committee establishment and operation.

Personal Income Tax

Differences in personal income taxes between countries and different regions within them may have effects on the mobility of labour. This tax difference in the EU(25) in 2004 is given in Figure 4.11. Tax competition between the EU(15) (higher taxes) and the new member countries (lower taxes) is obvious. Actual labour mobility depends on a number of factors that include the chances of finding employment, improved standards of living, social obstacles, social security benefits and immigration rules. Differences in personal income taxes may be neither the most decisive nor the only incentive for labour to move. This is generally the case throughout the EU. As labour has a very low propensity to migrate, the local authorities can retain rather high taxes on personal income without fearing that this would create incentives for a massive emigration from the region. The difference in personal income tax rates has a certain sway only for the migration of the upper-middle class and the rich.

It is a generally accepted principle that taxes are applied in those countries in which income originated. In addition, most countries tax the global income of their residents, but with foreign tax relief. A person originating in country A who works for part of the year in country B and the rest of the year in country A would pay income tax on pay earned in country B and ask for tax credit while paying income tax in country A for the rest of the taxable income. This person's tax payment would be the same as if the whole income had been earned in country A, unless country B's income tax is higher than that in country A.

Personal income tax is taken to be one of the most genuine rights of a state. There is little chance of this tax being harmonised in either the eurozone or an EMU. The EU is fully aware of this issue, so it has few ambitions in the sphere of personal income taxation. On the one hand, a potential for free mobility of labour in the EU may provide a behind-the-scenes pressure for harmonisation of national personal income taxes. On the other hand, such pressure is not great because of the still considerable social obstacles[88] to moving from one country to another. In addition, free labour mobility in the EU for citizens of the central and eastern European member countries will apply from 2011.

A notable exception has often been the taxation of income of frontier and migrant workers. Tax agreements generally avoid double taxation, both in the country of destination (where the income was earned) and the

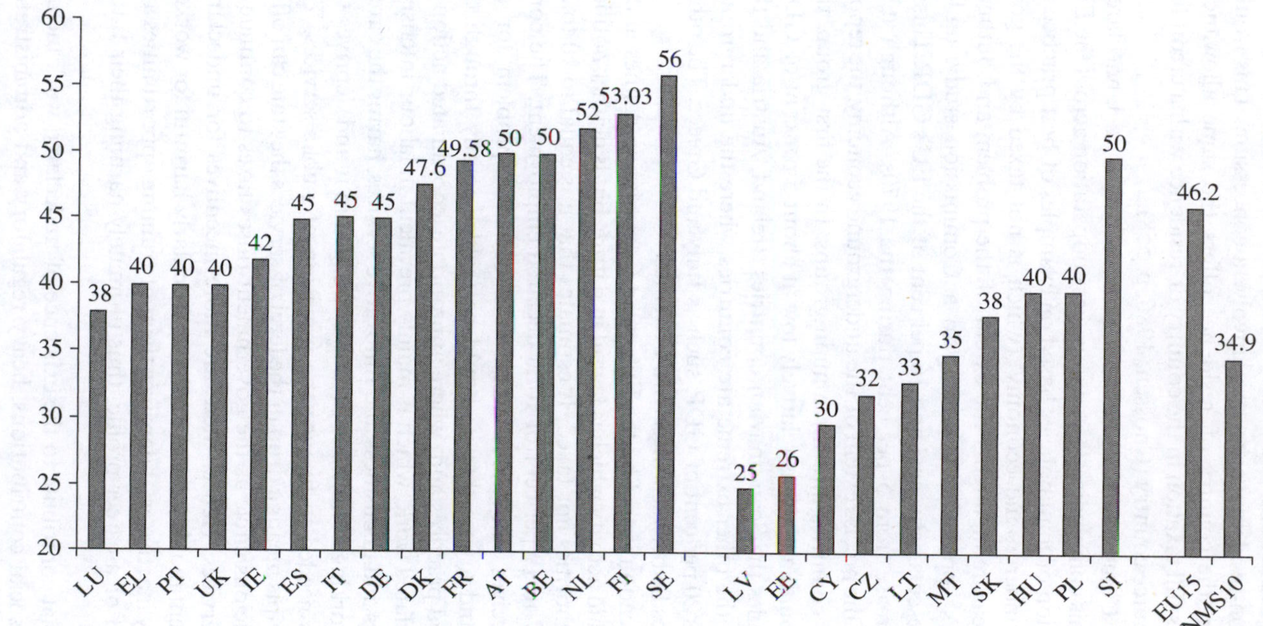

Note: For abbreviations, see Table 4.3.

Source: European Commission (2004b).

Figure 4.11 Top statutory personal income tax rate in the EU(25) in 2004 (%)

country of origin (where the income maker resides). Troublesome issues remain regarding deductions, allowances and applicable rates. Granting an allowance to a non-resident worker may involve a concession. This would be the case when the country of residence offers the same allowance. Generally, there is full taxation in the country of residence with a credit for tax paid in the source country (Cnossen, 1986, p. 558).

The European Commission adopted a Communication on Undeclared Work in 1998. This communication encourages cooperation across the EU and the formulation of joint policies based on examples of best practice in combating the 'underground economy' (which is not taxed by the government). This feature highlights the extent of the problem and outlines the Commission's approach. According to a Commission study, undeclared work represents between 7 and 16 per cent of the EU's GDP. This is a significant increase from 5 per cent during the 1970s. Although it is difficult to assess the precise extent of the underground economy, the report classifies the EU countries into three main groups. In the first group, the level of underground activity is relatively low at about 5 per cent of GDP. This group includes the Scandinavian countries, Ireland, Austria and the Netherlands. At the other extreme are countries where the underground economy exceeds 20 per cent of GDP, such as Italy and Greece. The other member countries lie between these two extremes.

The communication issued by the European Commission defines undeclared work as paid activity which is lawful in nature, but is neither notified to the public authorities nor taxed. It estimates that it is equal to 10 to 28 million jobs or 7 to 19 per cent of total declared employment. The communication perceives undeclared work as a common problem for all member states and argues that it should be tackled jointly through the exchange of good practices and, where appropriate, coordinated action at EU level. Undeclared work, which is mainly prevalent in labour-intensive, low-profit sectors and in business and innovative services, harms the career prospects and working conditions of those engaged in it and deprives the state of receipts needed to finance the provision of public services. The reduction in receipts means a drop in the level of services the state can offer. This creates a vicious circle as the government raises taxes to continue to provide these services. Hence, there are more incentives for undeclared work. Engagement in undeclared work is particularly harmful for workers who are officially inactive, as it deprives them of training opportunities and the development of a career profile, thus ultimately harming their future employability.

The factors that contribute to the existence of undeclared work include high taxes and social contributions, heavy regulatory and administrative burdens, inappropriate labour market legislation, cultural acceptance and the existence of easy opportunity. What is necessary to combat this situation is a combination of measures aimed at reducing the advantages of being in the undeclared economy, such as awareness-raising campaigns, tighter controls and stronger sanctions, as well as the adaptation of inappropriate legislation and the reduction of burdens on and obstacles to business.

The level, nature, consequences and causes of undeclared work have also been the subject of European Commission reports in the past. There are still difficulties in reaching a common definition and obtaining reliable data on the level of undeclared activity and the individuals involved in it. The wide margin in the estimated size of the underground economy as a percentage of GDP bears witness to these difficulties. Undeclared work is of particular concern because it is particularly prevalent in the sectors which the Commission seeks to target for job creation (labour-intensive services such as domestic services). It causes possible distortions of competition in the internal market and the loss of revenue to the state, thus reducing the ability to provide services. Undeclared work is particularly difficult to combat, because it is often either based on a consensual exchange of the two parties involved or perceived as a matter of economic necessity. The European Commission is now hoping to build on the exchange of best practice in order to design measures to help combat this problem.

One idea for consideration is the introduction of a flat-tax system. On the one hand, this tax scheme does away with the complicated system of brackets, exceptions and allowances, while on the other, low-income earners do not pay any tax. If the tax rate is set relatively low, this may bring two generally beneficial effects. First, a high degree of compliance may be assured and second, entrepreneurship, risk taking and extra work effort by taxpayers is rewarded (they can keep more of what they earn). Expanded economic activity together with higher compliance widens the tax base to which a low tax rate is applied. A lower tax rate is applied to more income that comes from reinvigorated economic activity.

4.3.5 INDIRECT TAXES

Indirect taxes are levied on the production and consumption of goods and services. They influence the retail price, and hence affect patterns of trade and consumption. Indirect taxes are ultimately paid by the final consumer. Sales and turnover taxes, excise duties and tariffs are the basic indirect taxes. The share of these taxes in total taxes in the EU(25) is about a third (Table 4.7).[89] In contrast with direct taxes, indirect taxes are seldom progressive. The principles for the levying of these taxes will be considered before the analysis of indirect taxes.

Table 4.7 Total indirect taxes as a share of total taxes in the EU(25) and Norway, 1995–2002 (%)

	1995	1996	1997	1998	1999	2000	2001	2002	Average 1995–2002	Change[1] 1995–2002	Difference[2] 1995–2002
BE	29.5	30.2	30.3	29.9	30.7	30.6	29.5	29.7	30.1	0.0	0.3
CZ	34.7	34.5	34.5	33.4	34.4	33.5	32.3	31.3	33.6	–1.3	–3.3
DK	34.8	35.0	35.6	35.8	35.6	35.1	35.0	36.1	35.5	0.2	1.3
DE	30.1	29.3	29.3	29.4	30.3	29.9	30.5	30.5	29.9	0.5	0.4
EE	–	–	–	–	–	–	–	40.1	40.1	–	–
EL	44.1	44.8	43.5	41.4	42.3	40.9	41.6	40.5	42.4	–1.3	–3.6
ES	32.6	32.4	32.7	34.2	35.1	34.6	33.8	33.6	33.6	0.7	0.9
FR	36.8	37.2	37.0	36.9	36.2	35.5	34.7	36.2	33.2	–1.0	–1.6
IE	43.9	43.7	43.4	43.5	43.1	43.4	42.0	43.7	43.3	0.3	–0.2
IT	30.9	29.1	28.9	36.7	36.0	36.3	35.3	35.9	33.7	3.2	5.0
CY	–	–	–	39.9	36.1	41.5	41.9	42.7	40.8	–	–
LV	40.7	40.3	39.9	40.9	40.2	39.6	39.9	37.7	39.9	0.7	–3.0
LT	43.0	42.2	49.2	43.5	42.7	41.2	42.1	43.5	43.4	0.6	0.6
LU	31.9	31.6	32.7	33.5	35.2	36.1	34.4	33.4	33.6	1.3	1.4
HU	–	–	–	–	–	–	39.5	39.2	39.5	–	–
MT	46.0	45.7	44.8	45.2	45.3	44.5	43.9	42.5	44.7	0.9	–3.5
NL	29.3	29.9	30.7	31.1	31.5	31.4	33.7	33.5	31.4	1.9	4.2
AT	35.9	35.3	35.5	35.2	35.6	35.3	33.9	35.2	35.2	0.4	–0.7
PL	37.5	39.0	37.8	37.9	39.3	40.3	38.9	40.4	38.9	0.9	2.9
PT	43.5	42.7	41.8	43.0	43.0	41.4	41.2	42.1	42.3	0.5	–1.3
SI	39.5	41.3	41.5	42.3	43.5	41.8	41.3	41.9	41.7	0.5	2.4
SK	37.7	38.5	37.7	35.0	36.3	37.9	35.8	36.4	36.9	0.6	–1.3

FI	31.0	30.4	32.1	31.5	31.6	29.5	30.0	30.6	30.8	0.5	–0.4
SE	32.8	32.2	32.4	33.4	35.2	31.4	32.6	34.3	33.0	0.4	1.4
UK	39.9	39.8	39.4	38.1	38.7	38.1	37.4	38.9	38.8	0.7	–1.1
NO	38.8	38.1	37.9	38.6	37.1	32.4	32.3	31.2	35.8	3.4	–7.6
EU25	33.5	33.2	33.4	34.5	34.8	34.4	34.3	34.8	34.1	0.5	1.2
EU15	33.5	33.1	33.2	34.4	34.7	34.2	34.1	34.6	34.0	0.6	1.1
Euro12	31.3	30.9	30.9	32.5	32.6	32.3	32.2	32.5	31.9	0.7	1.1
NMS10	37.2	38.2	37.8	37.5	38.6	39.1	38.2	38.7	38.2	0.5	1.5

Notes: For abbreviations, see Table 4.3.
1. Estimated annual average growth rate in %.
2. in % points of total taxation.

Source: European Commission (2004b).

Principles of Destination and Origin

Tax authorities are aware of the possible impact that indirect taxes have on trade in goods and services. Therefore, they introduced a safety device in the form of the destination and origin principle for taxation. This is of great importance to those countries that integrate. According to the principle of destination, taxes on goods are applied in the country of their consumption. This is the norm accepted in the WTO. However, according to the principle of origin, taxes apply in the country of their production.

The *destination principle* states that consumption of all goods in one destination should be subject to the same tax, irrespective of the origin of their production. This principle removes tax distortions on competition between goods on the consuming country's market. The goods compete on equal tax conditions. This principle does not interfere with the location of production. It is widely accepted in international trade relations even though it requires the existence of fiscal frontiers among countries. The problem is that this principle may give the illusion that it stimulates exports and acts as a quasi-tariff on imports. This issue will be discussed shortly.

The *origin* or *production principle* asserts that all goods produced in one country should be taxed in that country, despite the possibility that these goods may be exported or consumed at home. If the production tax on good X in country A is lower than the same tax on the same good in country B, then if exported at zero transport and other costs, good X produced in country A will have a tax advantage in country B's market over country B's home-made good, X. This introduces a distortion that interferes with the spatial location of production between the countries. For allocational neutrality, a harmonised rate of tax between countries is a necessary condition.

Even within a customs union or a common market, there may exist fiscal frontiers if the member countries accept the principle of destination. The fiscal authorities of each country should know where and when they are entitled to tax consumption of goods or services. The origin principle may have an advantage, for it does not require fiscal frontiers. This conserves scarce resources.

Taxes levied according to the destination and origin principles differ regarding their revenue impact. These two principles determine to which government the proceeds accrue. A full economic optimisation cannot be achieved if there are different tax rates levied on various goods. Suppose that country A levies a VAT at the rate of 25 per cent on cars only, while the partner country B applies a uniform tax at the rate of 10 per cent on all goods. Suppose that both countries apply the destination principle for tax collection. In this case, the production in either country would be maximised because it would not be affected by the tax. Consumption would, however, be distorted. The relative consumer prices would be distorted because cars are dearer relative to clothes in country A than they are in country B. Consequently, country A's consumers buy fewer cars and more clothes than they would do otherwise. The opposite tendency prevails in country B. In this case, trade between the two countries would not be optimal. Conversely, suppose that the two countries collect taxes according to the origin principle. In this case, trade would be optimised for the relative consumer prices would be the same in each country. So, although trade is optimised, tax would still distort the maximisation of production. This is because producer prices, net of tax, would be reduced in a disproportionate way. Country A producers would be stimulated to produce clothes, rather than cars, while the opposite tendency would prevail in country B. Once indirect tax is not levied at a uniform rate on all goods, the choice is between the destination principle, which maximises production but does not optimise trade, and the origin principle, which optimises trade but does not maximise production (Robson, 1987, pp. 122–3).

The principle of destination offers an opportunity for tax evasion that is unavailable (if the records are not faked) with the origin principle. If taxes differ, then a consumer may be tempted to purchase a good in the state in which the relative tax burden is lower and consume it in the country where the tax burden is relatively higher. Consumers may easily purchase goods in one country and send or bring them to another one, or order these goods from abroad. This tax evasion depends on the differences in taxation, cost of transport and cooperation of buyers and sellers who do not inform the tax authorities if they know that the objective of certain purchases is tax evasion. The revenue effect of a standard tax at a rate of 40 per cent in a country where tax evasion is widespread (for example, the 'olive-oil belt' or Club Med countries of the EU) may be much smaller than the revenue impact of the same tax at a rate of 10 per cent in a country where tax evasion is not a common practice.

The tax system in the US relies on corporate and personal income taxes applied according to the origin principle. The tax authorities in the EU countries rely upon consumption taxes with the application of the destination principle.[90] If the Europeans export goods to the US, they may have an advantage embodied in the difference in the tax systems. The US may contemplate the introduction of a border tax adjustment. This step may involve an addition to or reduction in the taxes already paid in Europe. The objective would be to keep competition in the US market on the same tax footing.

While the origin principle does not involve visible border tax adjustment, the destination principle includes it to the full extent of the tax. The long-run effect of either principle is, however, the same. In general equilibrium, any short-run advantage to one country will be eliminated in the long run by changes in the rate of exchange and domestic prices (Johnson and Krauss, 1973, p. 241). The US is a net importer of manufactured goods from Europe and Japan. It is advantageous, however, for the US to have these two exporting countries administer taxes on a destination, rather than origin basis (Hamilton and Whalley, 1986, p. 377). This is correct in the short run. In the long-run general equilibrium, the operation of exchange rates and factor prices (Johnson–Krauss law) would, presumably, eliminate any short-run (dis)advantage to these countries.

The new theory of trade and strategic industrial policy disputes the Johnson–Krauss argument. In a real situation with imperfect markets (increasing returns to scale, externalities and the economies of learning) and when the economic system is non-ergodic, once the production of, for example, aircraft or fast trains starts at a very restricted number of locations in the world, it perpetuates itself at those few locations. There is no room in the world even for three producers of the wide-body passenger aircraft. In this case, the exchange rate argument (Johnson–Krauss) is of little help for small and medium-sized countries.

Both the destination and the origin principles are imperfect. The destination principle for taxation is able to accomplish efficiency in the location of production, but not efficiency in trade. The origin principle has an inverse effect. If taxes are applied according to this principle, then trade may be efficient, but the location of production may not be efficient.

Sales and Turnover Taxes

Sales and turnover taxes are payments to the government that are applied to all taxable goods and services except those subject to excise duties. Turnover tax is applied during the process of production, while if the tax is applied during sales to the final consumer it is called a sales tax. There are two methods for the collection of the sales tax: the cumulative multistage cascade method, and VAT. Apart from these two multiphase methods for the collection of the sales tax, there is also a one-stage method, applied only once, either at the stage of production or at the wholesale or retail sales phase. The following analysis will deal with the multiphase methods.

Cumulative multistage cascade method

According to the cumulative multistage cascade method for the collection of sales tax, the tax is applied every time goods and services are transferred against payment. The tax base includes the aggregate value of goods that includes previously paid taxes on raw materials and inputs. The levying and collection of this tax is relatively simple, the tax burden may appear to be distributed over a larger number of taxpayers and the rate of sales tax applied by this method is relatively lower than the rate applied by the VAT method.

Firms may be stimulated by this method of collection of sales tax to integrate vertically in order to pay tax only at the last stage of the production process. This may have a favourable impact on the expansion of the business activities of firms (diversification). It may, however, cause a misallocation of resources. This artificial vertical integration may erode the advantages of specialisation and the efficiency of numerous SMEs if the vertically integrated firm ceases to use their output or if it absorbs them.

Value-added tax

This method of collection of sales tax is applied every time a good or service is sold, but it applies only on the value that is added in the respective phase of production, which is the difference between the price paid for inputs and the price received for output (hence, value added). The application of VAT starts at the beginning of the production process and ends up in the retail sale to the final consumer. VAT avoids double or multiple taxation in the previous stages of production (addition of value). Every taxpayer has to prove to the tax authorities, with an invoice, that the tax has been paid in the previous stages of production. Hence, there is a kind of a self-regulating mechanism.

In the early stages of economic development, countries have relatively simple tax systems which apply only to a few goods and services. As countries develop, they tend to introduce a tax system that is more sophisticated, with a wider and more neutral tax base and coverage, and more efficient. Taxes on international trade (exports and imports) should be replaced by sales taxes that are collected by the VAT method. A relatively low rate of tax applied according to this method can raise a high return. It does not distort the economy, because it is neutral to the production mix of home and imported factors. In addition, it does not discriminate between production for home and foreign markets. VAT is neutral regarding the vertical integration of firms, so specialised SMEs may remain in business. If sales tax is collected according to the VAT method, then it is harder to evade it in comparison to the situation where tax is collected only at the retail stage.

VAT based on the principle of destination is accepted in the EU as the method for the collection of sales tax. The method is harmonised, but there is a wide range of differences in the rates of this tax among EU countries. If the objective is to have a single rate of this tax, then there is considerable room for improvement in the future. The elimination of fiscal frontiers in the EU in 1993 and the creation of the Single European Market placed a certain market pressure on tax authorities to 'align' the national VAT rates and prices, otherwise firms would lose business, in particular, in the frontier regions. The creation of the eurozone (1999) and the introduction of the euro into circulation in 2002 added to this pressure.

The White Paper (European Communities, 1985) proposed the setting up of the EU Clearing House System. Its role would be to ensure that the VAT collected in the exporting member country and deducted in the importing member country was reimbursed to the latter. The crucial feature in this system would play across EU bookkeeping and computerisation. This system would, in principle, create a situation for taxable persons within the EU identical to the one that prevails in the member countries. In spite of the potential benefits of such a tax system, it was criticised on the grounds that it would be bureaucratic and costly.

In practice, however, the existence of widely diverging rates of tax and tax exemptions may expose the system to the risk of fraud and evasion. The EU was aware that some fraud and evasion already existed, but the scale of such distortions after the removal of fiscal frontiers and the introduction of the euro, would increase without tax harmonisation. Therefore, a minimum standard VAT rate of 15 per cent on most goods became a legal obligation in the EU from October 1992.

It is relatively understandable for Britain (as well as Ireland and Greece) to oppose this type of tax alignment since cross-border shopping is not a common feature in those countries as they have no common land frontier with the rest of the EU. However, for Austria, the Benelux countries, France and Germany, where cross-border shopping is common, it is easy to accept such arguments.

A move towards the origin principle (collection of tax during production) would require a system for redistribution of revenues (refunds) from the country where the goods were produced and taxed to the one where they are consumed. The effect of such a system would be as if the tax had been levied on consumption. Although there were concerns in some member countries because of the need to find alternative employment for thousands of customs officers, the fiscal frontiers between EU countries were removed in 1993. This was the most visible benefit of the implementation of the Single European Market.[91] Consumers are now free to purchase goods in any EU country and bring them home with very few restrictions, provided that the imported goods are only for their personal consumption. There are, of course, exceptions, but only two: the purchase of new cars is taxed in the country of registration, while mail-order purchases are taxed either at the rate applying in the country of destination or at the rate in the seller's country (depending on the seller's annual sales volume in the country of destination).

Border tax adjustment without border controls was preserved in the EU. The former border controls were shifted by the interim system (introduced in 1993) to exporting and importing firms (centralised costs were replaced by decentralised costs in firms). The transitional system was extended in 1997 for an indefinite period, because EU countries were and still are unable to agree on the final shape of the VAT system based on the principle of origin. This system replaced time-consuming tax controls and payments at the EU internal borders with a demanding centralised reporting system carried out by the companies themselves. The final system will allow firms to pay VAT in the country of origin, as if all EU member countries were a single country. The burden of redistribution of VAT revenue will then fall on the member states. This would be advantageous to businesses as they would not have to differentiate between domestic and intra-EU sales. None the less, there will be two problems. First, a clearing-house system will have to redistribute revenue around the EU as countries that export a lot will benefit from the system, while those that import a lot will lose. Second, the origin-based tax system will enhance the need for a higher harmonisation of VAT rates. In the meantime, the current transitory system seems to be operating quite well. This will, of course, be taken into account during the reassessment of the tax system.

This gradual approach was extremely difficult to apply. EU member states showed little enthusiasm in practice for the move towards the origin system. There is a reluctance to move towards a greater degree of harmonisation of VAT rates even though this is a precondition for the definitive system. Bearing in mind the potential and actual resistance concerning tax harmonisation, the European Commission has a patient long-term goal of origin-based taxation based on small steps, relating simplification, modernisation and administrative cooperation among member countries.

Table 4.8 illustrates differences in VAT rates in the EU, candidate countries, Switzerland, the US and Japan. The lower rates apply to food, clothing and other essential items. Portugal has lower rates in its autonomous regions. Ireland and Britain use the zero rate for food, books and children's clothing. The other countries generally apply an exception with credit (which comes down to the same thing as a zero rate) to exports and supplies assimilated to exports, such as supplies to embassies, to ships leaving the country and the like. In Ireland and Britain these supplies are also covered by the zero rate.

The EU rules assert that goods should be taxed at between 15 and 25 per cent, except for a series of commodities that carry reduced rates. In order to simplify the EU's maze of VAT rates, the European Commission

Table 4.8 VAT rates in the EU, candidate countries, Switzerland, the US and Japan in 1990, 1997, 2003 and 2005 (%)

Country	1990	1997	2003	2005
1. Austria		10, *20*	10, *20*	10, 12, *20*
2. Belgium	1, *6*, 17, *19*, 25, 33	1, *6*, 12, *21*	6, 12, *21*	0, 6, 12, *21*
3. Denmark	*22*	*25*	*25*	1, *25*
4. Finland		6, *12*, *17*, *22*	8, 17, *22*	0, 8, 17, *22*
5. France	2, *5.5*, 13, *18.6*, 25	2.1, *5.5*, *20.6*	2.1, 5.5, *19.6*	2.1, 5.5, *19.6*
6. Germany	7, *14*	7, *15*	7, *16*	7, *16*
7. Greece	3, *6*, *16*, 36	4, *8*, *18*	4, 8, *18*	4, 8, *18*
8. Ireland	*0*, 2, 5, *10*, *23*	*0*, 3.3, 12.5, *21*	4.3, 13.5, *21*	0, 4.8, 13.5, *21*
9. Italy	4, *9*, *19*, 38	4, *10*, 16, *19*	4, 10, *20*	4, 10, *20*
10. Luxembourg	*3*, *6*, *12*	*3*, 6, *12*, *15*	3, 6, 12, *15*	3, 6, 12, *15*
11. Netherlands	*6*, *18.5*	*6*, *17.5*	6, *19*	6, *19*
12. Portugal	*8*, *16*, 30	5, 12, *17*	5, 12, *19*	5, 12, *19*
13. Spain	*6*, *12*, 33	*4*, *7*, *16*	4, 7, *16*	4, 7, *16*
14. Sweden		6, 12, *25*	6, 12, *25*	6, 12, *25*
15. United Kingdom	*0*, *15*	*0*, *17.5*	5, *17.5*	0, 5, *17.5*
New member countries				
16. Cyprus			5, *15*	0, 5, *15*
17. Czech Republic			5, *22*	5, *19*
18. Estonia			5, *18*	5, *18*
19. Hungary			12, *25*	5, 15, *25*
20. Latvia			9, *18*	0, 15, *18*
21. Lithuania			9, *18*	5, 9, *18*
22. Malta			5, *15*	5, *18*

23. Poland	3, 7, *22*	0, 3, 7, *22*
24. Slovakia	14, *20*	*19*
25. Slovenia	8.5, *20*	8.5, *20*
Candidate countries		
26. Croatia		22
27. Bulgaria	20	20
28. Romania	19	9, 19
29. Turkey	1, 8, *18*	1, 8, *18*
Others		
31. Japan	5 (including local tax)	5 (including local tax)
32. Switzerland	2.4, 3.6, *7.6*	2.4, 3.6, *7.6*
33. United States	No VAT, state and municipal taxes approximatively 4–19	

Note: Standard rates italicised.

Source: International Bureau of Fiscal Documentation (2005).

proposed a plan (in 2003) that would require Britain and Ireland, which have zero VAT rate on children's clothes and shoes, to apply VAT on these goods. Otherwise, this would distort the Single European Market. The British Treasury declared that it would use the veto to block this plan if necessary as one of the election promises was to keep a zero rating on these goods.

A broad-based VAT can be criticised on the grounds that it is regressive. The reason for the regressive impact of VAT in the EU can be found in the structure of national demand. Consumption to which VAT applies usually embraces a relatively higher proportion of the GDP in the less-advanced member countries than in the richer ones. Other components of demand, such as investment, which is presumably higher in the more advanced countries, is not burdened by VAT. The low-income segment of the population can be helped by transfer payments. This can make VAT directly progressive. Zero rating, exemptions and multiple rates do not always directly assist the low-income group, which is the target population.

The EU conducted a wide-ranging survey in the second half of the 1980s. About 20 000 businesspeople from 12 EU countries were asked to rank the biggest barriers to free trade. The most damaging of all were overt obstacles. Different national technical standards, administrative and customs formalities were at the top, while differences in rates of VAT and excise duties were at the bottom of the list of eight barriers (Emerson et al., 1988, pp. 44–6).

Excise Duties

Excise duty is a type of indirect tax that is levied for the purpose of raising public revenue. It is applied in almost every country to tobacco, spirits and liquid fuels. Excise duties are also applied in some countries to coffee, tea, cocoa, salt, bananas, light bulbs and playing cards. These duties are levied only once, usually at the stage of production or import. Another property of excise duties is that they are generally high in relation to other taxes.

While the VAT is proportional to the value of output, an excise duty may either be based on the *ad valorem* principle (retail or wholesale price) or it may be a specific tax. Within the EU, tobacco products are subject to both. There is a specific tax per cigarette and an *ad valorem* tax based on the retail price of the cigarettes concerned (Kay, 1990, p. 34).

Table 4.9 presents excise duties in the EU(15) member countries. The table shows that there is a wide variety in charges among the countries. This difference is due to the various choices of fiscal and health authorities. If the difference in excise duties among countries exceeds the costs of the reallocation of resources or transport, it will have a distorting effect on the

Table 4.9 Excise duties in the EU(15) countries at the end of 2003 (€)

Country	Beer (/hl/°alc. or /hl/°Plato)		Wine (/hl)		Intermediate products (/hl)		Ethyl alcohol (/hl)		Petrol and gas oil (1000 lit)		Liquid petroleum gas (LPG) and methane (/1000 kg)		Heavy fuel oil and kerosene (/1000 kg)		Cigarettes (/1000 pieces)
	min	max	min	max	min	max	min	max	min	max	min	max	min	max	
B	1.5	1.7	14.9	161.1	74.4	161.1	1660.9	1660.9	5.0	551.8	0.0	37.2	0.0	551.8	18.7
DK	0.0	68.7	60.6	189.2	60.6	142.0	2019.6	2019.6	281.7	626.2	356.8	468.5	281.3	405.8	65.9
D	0.4	0.8	0.0	136.0	102.0	153.0	730.0	1303.0	61.4	721.0	60.6	161.0	25.0	654.5	61.7
EL	0.6	1.1	0.0	0.0	0.0	45.0	454.0	908.0	21.0	337.0	0.3	100.0	19.0	245.0	4.5
E	0.0	0.8	0.0	0.0	29.7	49.5	647.5	739.0	84.7	428.8	0.0	125.0	14.4	315.8	3.9
F	1.3	2.6	3.4	8.4	214.0	214.0	835.0	1450.0	54.9	636.7	39.4	100.2	16.8	571.0	7.7
IR	19.9	19.9	91.0	546.0	273.0	396.1	3925.0	3925.0	47.4	553.0	35.9	104.7	13.45	325.2	133.4
I	1.4	1.4	0.0	0.0	49.6	49.6	645.4	645.4	121.0	541.8	16.0	284.8	63.8	337.5	3.9
L	0.4	0.8	0.0	0.0	47.1	66.9	1041.2	1041.2	5.0	424.1	0.0	101.6	0.0	295.0	11.9
NL	5.5	31.4	29.5	201.2	72.9	201.2	1775.0	1775.0	46.6	703.7	0.0	78.9	15.5	337.3	55.5
A	1.3	2.1	0.0	144.0	73.0	73.0	540.0	1000.0	69.0	479.0	43.0	261.0	36.0	282.0	21.4
P	3.0	21.3	0.0	0.0	51.3	51.3	440.3	880.5	87.9	548.7	7.5	100.0	13.0	264.3	40.7
FI	1.7	28.6	4.5	235.5	428.9	706.4	168.0	5046.0	70.6	676.2	0.0	0.0	59.6	319.4	15.1
S	16.1	16.1	0.0	242.4	279.5	464.1	5505.2	5505.2	317.7	592.9	145.2	291.9	317.7	409.5	22.0
UK	0.0	19.5	77.9	351.4	252.8	337.1	3116.1	3116.1	67.2	895.3	0.0	143.4	0.0	848.7	154.3

Note: B: Belgium; DK: Denmark; D: Germany; EL: Greece; E: Spain; F: France; IR: Ireland; I: Italy; L: Luxembourg; NL: Netherlands; A: Austria; P: Portugal; FI: Finland; S: Sweden; UK: United Kingdom.

Source: DG General Taxation and Customs Union, Excise Duty Tables, December 2003.

geographical location of resources or pattern of trade. The difference in the maximum excise duty on 1000 litres of petrol of €242 between high-duty Germany and low-duty Austria is significant when one bears in mind that it costs just a few euros to transport this amount of fuel by pipeline.

The VAT is calculated on the price of a good that includes the excise duty. Any change in the excise duty will produce differences in the VAT revenue. Hence the need for a certain harmonisation of excise duties too. In the US, each federal state has its own liquor duty. Liquor and cigarettes should bear the national tax authority stamp. Only the nationally stamped goods can be purchased legally within a state. In the EU, import for personal consumption is unlimited, while bulk intra-EU commercial transport and trade in these goods without the proper tax clearance is forbidden and punishable. The harmonised rates proposed by the European Commission should be viewed only as a yardstick, as it would be extremely difficult to try to unify excise duties throughout the EU member countries (it would be like 'waiting for Godot').

The goods that are subject to excise duties are normally stored in bonded warehouses that are controlled by the public authorities. Once the goods are taken out for consumption, the excise duty is levied. If the goods are exported, the excise duty is not charged upon presentation of a proof of export. The importing country of these goods controls the import at the frontier where it establishes liability for excise duty. This ensures that excise duty is charged in the country where the goods are consumed. After the creation of the Single European Market, which removed tax and other internal frontiers, the wide divergence in excise duties would distort trade, because of a real danger of fraud and evasion. The White Paper proposed as a solution a linkage system for bonded warehouses for products subject to excise duties and the approximation of these charges in the EU.

4.3.6 FUTURE CHALLENGES

Indirect taxes are already aligned to an extent within the Single European Market. Direct tax systems, on the other hand, require only limited harmonisation and can generally be left to individual EU countries. However, there is a consensus in principle across the EU that cooperation is needed to remove harmful tax competition.

The full impact of the potential tax competition, high international mobility of capital and certain TNCs, and integrated international production has not yet been fully grasped by many tax authorities. Divergent tax rates on highly portable luxury and expensive goods may not be sustained. Hence, there is a trend away from taxing these goods and towards taxing the consumption of petroleum, spirits and tobacco. However, different taxes and their rates may remain on non-tradable goods and real property.

In order to deal with harmful tax competition, the European Commission proposed several measures that may introduce certain bases for increased tax coordination between the member countries. These include the following:

- a code of conduct for business taxation, in parallel with a European Commission notice on state aids in the form of taxation measures;
- the elimination of distortions in the taxation of capital income;
- the elimination of withholding taxes on cross-border interest and royalty payments between companies that belong to the EU member states; and
- the elimination of significant distortions in the area of indirect taxation.

The European Commission's strategy for the future was revealed in a Communication (COM(97) 464) which was approved by the Council of Ministers in 1997. The Commission has a code of conduct for business taxation. It seeks to introduce a coordinated approach to harmful tax competition and to promote a system of employment-friendly taxation. This was important as there was a trend which revealed an increasing tax burden on labour (particularly the least skilled and the least mobile). In addition, larger firms were better placed and equipped to take advantage of tax competition between countries.

Even though the code of conduct for business taxation is not a legally binding document, it has political force. The code is a rather comprehensive document as it includes a review and monitoring process. When the Council of Ministers adopted the code, it recognised the positive general effects of fair competition. In this spirit, the code was designed to spot actions and tools that affect the location of business in the EU by targeting non-residents and by providing them with more favourable tax treatment than that which is generally available in the host member state. The code sets out the criteria that may ascertain harmful actions and tools. These criteria include:

- an effective level of taxation which is significantly lower than the general level of taxation in the country concerned;
- tax benefits reserved only for non-residents;
- tax incentives for activities which are isolated from the domestic economy and therefore have no impact on the national tax base;

- tax advantages even in the absence of any real economic activity;
- the basis for profit determination for branches of a TNC departing from internationally accepted rules, in particular those approved by the OECD; and
- lack of transparency.

The member states are supposed to roll back the existing tax measures that represent harmful tax competition and to refrain from introducing any such measures in the future ('standstill'). The Code of Conduct Group has been monitoring the rollback and standstill provisions. The group sends its reports to the Council of Ministers on a regular basis. The code helps to prevent and overcome economic distortions and an erosion of tax bases within the EU.

A number of disparities in the area of VAT and the tax treatment of energy products ought to be removed in order to prevent the risk of harmful tax competition. Among the changes proposed, the European Commission aspires:

- to modify the status of the VAT committee (regulatory committee);
- to exempt from VAT those transactions in gold that are made for investment purposes (such transactions are still taxed when used for industrial purposes);
- to review the taxation of passenger transport;
- to revise the rates applied to energy products; and
- to establish the FISCALIS programme of cooperation between member states against fraud in the area of indirect taxation.

In 2000, in order to remove the competitive disadvantage of EU firms involved in e-commerce[92] relative to foreign (principally US) competitors, the European Commission proposed a set of ideas. These include a request to a foreign supplier with annual sales of over €100 000 in the EU to be registered in an EU member country; sales by EU firms abroad would be VAT free; sales within the EU to consumers would be according to the principle of origin (does not need trans-border tax adjustment), while on-line sales among EU firms would be according to the principle of destination. As of 2002 and regarding e-commerce and radio and TV broadcasting, VAT is collected at the place the service is consumed (recipient destination).

The case for the unitary method of taxation may gain certain additional support in the future. The expansion of integrated international production (TNCs) and an increased international mobility of factors, capital in particular, are reaching the point at which the taxation of business founded on the unitary method may be superior to the arm's-length method of taxation. This topic could be discussed interminably. Progress in international tax matters, including attempts to approximate, harmonise or unify tax systems, takes a very long time indeed. The reason for this is simple: the jealously protected sovereign national tax privileges.

There is a pressing need to make progress in the field of taxation and to ensure more effective coordination of tax policies. This is relevant for further development of the Single European Market, ways and means to enable industry to compete on the world market, the need to reduce the level of unemployment and challenges brought by e-commerce. The issue of harmful tax competition, which threatens to reduce revenues, to distort tax structures and to interfere with spatial and sectoral location of investments, should be kept relatively high on the EU policy discussion agenda. Additional challenges in the tax field refer to taxation in the light of an ageing population, the social expenditure necessary for the care of the aged and the fight against fraud and irregularities.

4.3.7 CONCLUSION

Most national tax systems are deeply rooted in an era when economies were largely closed and when international capital movements were small or non-existent. The national tax authorities could tax income and business with little regard for what goes on in other countries. The contemporary system of integrated international production, economic integration, a high degree of capital mobility and 'globalisation' changed all that. Increasingly, it matters what is going on at home, as well as abroad. There are at least three reasons for this:

- *Income of TNCs* A large part of trade within many TNCs represents intra-firm trade. TNCs may manipulate (transfer pricing) the costs of their intra-firm transactions in order to have their income taxed where it is most favourable for the corporation. Certain TNCs may be sensitive to tax and subsidy incentives, hence they may move the location of their business.
- *Personal income* It is estimated that income earned from foreign investment and savings (profit, dividends and interest) is growing exponentially. National tax authorities are not always able to track this individual income as much of it may come from tax havens. This income tends to be unreported or under-reported to the national tax authorities. Recent moves towards the exchange of information among EU countries may significantly reduce tax evasion.

- *Sales taxes* Open borders, advertising, access to information, the internet, mail ordering, electronic payments, smaller size of many goods, lower cost of transport, increased travel and the like all increase international purchasing, especially of goods that are expensive and easily portable. Lower sales taxes and the refund of paid taxes on these goods if exported add to the consumer's decision to purchase internationally.

The benefits that accrue from the elimination of fiscal frontiers in the EU refer to the following gains. The investment decisions of firms are improved as the tax system increases the degree of certainty in relation to the situation where every country manages its own taxes. A removal of tax posts at frontiers saves resources and, more importantly, increases the opportunities for competition and, consequently, improves prospects for a superior spatial location of production. Of course, some facilities for random anti-terrorist, health, veterinary and illegal immigration checks may be necessary. Finally, harmonisation of the tax system would enhance the equalisation of prices and lower the distortions due to different systems and rates of taxation. However, the matter is complex and difficult as we have already seen that one size does not fit all regions well.

Tax competition may tempt governments to offer tax concessions (lower taxes) and provide tax incentives (subsidies) in order to lure TNCs to relocate their operations. Potential (short-term) losses in tax revenue may be compensated or more than compensated in the medium term. The expectation is that if 'all goes well', TNCs can employ local labour and purchase locally produced inputs. Salaries of the employed will be taxed, as well as goods and services purchased by these salaries, and there will be less expenditure on unemployment benefits and so on.

A country (or group of countries) that frequently changes its (their) fiscal systems may be regarded as potentially risky locations for investment. This may provoke a reduction in the inflow and an increase in the outflow of capital to the relatively more politically stable and economically growing destinations. The European Commission's tax policy strategy set out in a Communication on Tax Policy in the European Union – Priorities for the Years Ahead (COM (2001) 260) of 23 May 2001 recognises that a complete unification of fiscal systems need not be a prerequisite for the smooth functioning of an EMU or a single market.[93] The US is the best example in support of this argument. The federal states in the US have differences in their respective tax systems. This system has functioned relatively satisfactorily without any tax posts between the states for a number of decades. However, these differences in the tax systems are relatively minor (Table 4.10). There is a significant degree of harmonisation among tax

Table 4.10 Sales taxes in the United State in 2005 (%)

State	State tax	Local tax
Alabama	4	1–5
Alaska	No	1–6
Arizona	5.6	0–3
Arkansas	6	0.5–5.5
California	6.25	1–2.5
Colorado	2.9	1–5
Connecticut	6	No
Delaware	No	No
District of Columbia	5.75	No
Florida	6	0.5–1
Georgia	4	1–3
Hawaii	4	No
Idaho	6	0–2
Illinois	6.25	0.25–3
Indiana	6	No
Iowa	5	0.5–1
Kansas	5.3	0–3
Kentucky	6	No
Louisiana	4	2–6.25
Maine	5	No
Maryland	5	No
Massachusetts	5	No
Michigan	6	No
Minnesota	6.5	0–1
Mississippi	7	No
Missouri	4.225	0–4.5
Montana	No	No
Nebraska	5	0.5–1.5
Nevada	6.5	0–1
New Hampshire	No	No
New Jersey	6	No
New Mexico	5	0.125–2.25
New York	4.25	2.75–4.625
North Carolina	4.5	2.5–3
North Dakota	5	1–2.5
Ohio	6	0.5–2
Oklahoma	4.5	1–6
Oregon	No	No
Pennsylvania	6	0–1
Rhode Island	7	No
South Carolina	5	0–2
South Dakota	4	1–4

Table 4.10 (continued)

State	State tax	Local tax
Tennessee	7	1.5–2.75
Texas	6.25	0.5–2
Utah	4.75	1–2.75
Vermont	6	No
Virginia	4	1
Washington	6.5	0.5–2.4
West Virginia	6	No
Wisconsin	5	0–0.6
Wyoming	4	0–2

Source: International Bureau of Fiscal Documentation (2005).

systems in federal units. The US also has high labour mobility. If certain local or state taxes change (increase), this may easily provoke an outflow of labour and management from that location. Such a swift response does not exist in Europe. Therefore, the local European or state authorities could 'comfortably' retain relatively high and distinct taxes without fearing that people (but not companies) would go elsewhere. In addition, the operation of firms within clusters makes firms relatively less sensitive to taxes. This provides the local authorities with opportunities to tax them more heavily than would otherwise be the case.

A genuine Single European Market requires a certain degree of harmonisation of indirect taxes among its member countries. Otherwise, member governments would have to accept substantial diversions in revenues. It is widely believed that a difference in sales tax of up to 5 per cent can introduce distortions that may be acceptable among the integrated countries and that these differences would not bring unbearable budgetary problems. However, the problem arises when the national budgets have different trends regarding their deficits. Alterations in the national tax systems in such situations can bring serious political difficulties.

As for the possibility of a significant degree of harmonisation (or, in an extreme case, unification) of fiscal systems in the EMU, there are certain grounds for pessimism. A tax policy is one of the most fundamental national sovereign rights. Recall Britain's vigorous opposition to the inclusion of fiscal matters in the majority-voting issues in the Single European Act and onwards. The achievement of national goals within a fiscal policy does not necessarily coincide at all times with those of other partners. Although the eurozone may agree on the basic objectives, their achievement may be left to the member countries which may sometimes wish to use different and potentially conflicting instruments. None the less, the sophisticated market-led approach (bottom-up) to integration in tax matters that came from the Single European Act (a removal of fiscal frontiers) might compel national tax authorities to align their tax rates and systems. Otherwise, other things being equal, businesses that are sensitive to taxation may move to and settle in the countries where the tax treatment is most favourable. This bottom-up approach by the EU is a significant shift from the earlier policy proposals that argued in favour of full tax harmonisation (top down).

The public is sensitive to general changes in tax systems. Full fiscal harmonisation in the EU may require an increase in taxes in some countries (for example, Latvia and Lithuania) while it may require their decrease in others (for example, Austria and Spain). In the low-tax countries there is opposition to tax increases, while in the high-tax countries there is a fear of revenue losses. Therefore, a partial fiscal harmonisation (only agreed taxes) might be a good first step for those who argue in favour of harmonisation. One of the issues not dealt with in the Single Market Programme was that very little has been done in the area of tax approximation. Harmonisation of fiscal systems of the countries that are in the EU, and especially in the eurozone, requires caution, gradualism and, more than anything else, the political will which economic theory cannot predict.

Tax harmonisation (averaging) may not bring gains either to developed or to backward regions or countries. While this harmonisation may reduce the tax revenue of the authorities in the former group, at the same time it makes backward regions less attractive for investment. As this provides certain arguments in favour of tax competition, one must note the effects of harmful tax competition for internationally mobile business activities. If there is a lack of transparency regarding tax provisions and in their application (in favour of non-residents), and if there is a lack of exchange of information between national fiscal authorities, then such tax competition may have a harmful effect on the allocation of resources. The role of international agreements is to prevent and end such practices.

There is also the ever-important question: why are taxes in general not coming down in the EU? There are several possible answers. First, economic integration is not yet complete. This situation may remain for quite some time to come. Second, technology has improved, and made trade in goods, communication and transport cheaper. However, there are still costs involved in overcoming the problems of distance. The third aspect may be linked with ideology. The end goal of the radical right may include the objective to end taxes on all income that comes from capital (ownership) and to replace them with taxes on wages (earned income) only. Such an approach to taxes is resisted in Europe.

To add to the confusion about policy advice and direction, there are dilemmas in theory too. In principle, taxes ought to be as low as possible and distributed among a wide constituency of taxpayers. Many agree that VAT has important advantages over other tax collection methods. However, the VAT advantages conceal two important and often disregarded issues. The first is the resource cost of tax collection and control. Administrative and time-related costs linked with VAT are not always and fully understood and appreciated. Second, the collection of sales tax by means of VAT gradually obfuscates the link between the taxpayer and the government. Taxpayers may not have such an obvious and strong link with the public authorities as is the case when they pay income tax. Once they pay income tax, they may become much more aware of and interested in what they give and what they may demand and expect in return.

There are also certain ideas about a transfer of another part of the overall tax burden from direct taxes (33 per cent of total taxes in the EU) to indirect (consumption) taxes (34 per cent of total taxes in the EU). Indirect taxes may need to rise to about 40 per cent of the total tax burden. The reasons are that these taxes do not increase production costs, they do not hamper exports and competitiveness of domestic output, and they have the same effect on domestic and imported goods. If such ideas are accepted, then they ought to fly in unison in all EU countries. Otherwise, depending on the goods in question, consumers would shop around the EU wherever the tax burden is lowest. Generally, however, there are various difficulties and weaknesses to be resolved. Direct taxes have a progressive dimension, while indirect taxes do not consider social aspects such as the wealth of a consumer and the standard of living. It may not be an election-winning strategy to argue in favour of a transfer of the tax burden from direct to indirect taxes.

Another debate raging is on the merits and vices of the flat tax system applied in a uniform way on personal income, corporate profits and VAT. Advocates argue that a single flat tax with one rate applied on a broad base simplifies tax administration, improves the understanding of tax matters, broadens the tax base, reduces tax avoidance, discourages tax evasion, attracts FDI, boosts the economy and increases tax revenue. Critics oppose this type of taxation as it shifts the tax burden from the wealthy to mid- and low-income groups.

A gradualist type of tax integration that allows for a certain degree of competition (public choice approach) may be politically preferred to a holistic unification or harmonisation. In any case, tax issues are very sensitive and many may agree, overtly or covertly, that tax matters should be resolved unanimously in the EU in spite of the fact that this may require many years of arduous work.

4.3.8 BUDGET OF THE EUROPEAN UNION

Introduction

Together with the law and its enforcement, the budget, its revenue and expenditure, is one of the most essential instruments that an economic and/or political organisation may employ to fulfil its role. The budget should not only cover administrative costs, but also dispose of funds for intervention in the economy. Otherwise, the role of such an organisation may be limited to mere consultation and, perhaps, research of certain issues. The budget of most international organisations covers only their administrative expenses. A rare exception is the EU, which returns and redistributes about 95 per cent of its receipts to the member countries. The budgets of the member countries reduce their expenditure for their own interventions in the fields where the EU has competence and where it intervenes.

In 1970 the EU budget amounted to €3.6 billion or €19 per inhabitant. In 2003, the EU budget stood at €98 billion or €258 per inhabitant or €0.7 per day. Yet, this is 'only' 1.1 per cent of the combined GDP of the 15 member countries of the EU. Following enlargement in 2004, the EU(25) budget of €105 billion means an EU expenditure of €232 per inhabitant a year or €0.6 a day.

Principles

The EU budget is subject to certain general principles. All EU expenditure must be presented in a single document (principle of *unity*). According to the principle of *annuality*, the budget operations relate to a given budgetary year which coincides with the calendar year. This facilitates the control of the work of the EU executive branch. The principle of *equilibrium* requires that the budget must be in annual balance (Article 268 of the Treaty of Rome) and must be wholly financed from its own resources (Article 269). Deficit financing or taking loans to finance the possible deficits are outlawed. Specific budgetary revenue may not be assigned or linked to a particular expenditure (principle of *universality*). Finally, the principle of *specification* requires that expenditure has to be specified. A precise purpose has to be given to each outlay in order to prevent any confusion between appropriations.

As already seen in Section 4.2, the objective of the Stability and Growth Pact (1997) is to keep the eurozone on track by means of a sustainable fiscal policy. This was needed to stabilise the debt/GDP ratios at reasonable levels following years of rising public debt. If one or several governments borrow recklessly, no limits on borrowing would give them a chance for a free ride in the eurozone. As a result, all eurozone countries could pay a price for such irresponsible national spending policy, as interest rates could increase throughout the zone. Therefore, the reasoning behind the pact was to shield the ECB from national pressures to reduce debt through inflation.

The absolute and relative size of the EU budget is, however, quite small in relation to its share of the joint GDP of the member states, as well as in relation to the potential impact on the large-scale macroeconomic life of the EU. As such, it differs from the national budgets since the EU budget plays a significant role neither in economic stabilisation nor in allocation of resources (apart from agriculture). In addition, its potential stabilisation role is jeopardised by the annuality principle.

Even though there is a principle of annuality, the EU sometimes engages in multiannual financial operations. These operations are continuously expanding. Therefore, the dual requirements are reflected in the advent of two distinct appropriations:

- The *payment* appropriations cover expenditure (to the limit entered in the current annual budget) that result from the commitments undertaken in the current financial year and preceding financial years.
- The *commitment* appropriations refer to the total cost (ceiling) in the current financial year of the obligations that are to be carried out over a period of more than one financial year. The commitment appropriations are larger than payment appropriations.

The Treaty of Rome (Article 272) sets two types of EU budgetary outlays: compulsory and non-compulsory expenditures. The distinction between the two is basically political, so it was often a source of conflict between the European Parliament and the Council of Ministers. A vague definition of the two kinds of expenditure was drafted in 1982 by a joint Declaration of the European Commission, the Council of Ministers and the European Parliament, which stated that compulsory expenditure from the budget is obligatory for the EU in order to meet its obligations. This refers both to the internal and external tasks that stem from the treaties and other acts. All other expenditure is non-compulsory.

The Council of Ministers has the last word on compulsory expenditure, while the European Parliament decides on the non-compulsory outlays. The Parliament may increase the amount of non-compulsory expenditure by amending the draft budget. The maximum rate of increase in relation to the preceding fiscal year depends on the trend of the GDP increase in the EU, average variation in the budgets of the member states, and trends in the cost of living, as well as on the approval by the Council. Before the drafting of a new budget, the presidents of the three institutions have a 'trialogue' meeting to determine the grouping of the new budget chapters and the ones for which the legal basis might have changed.

Procedure

Article 272 of the Treaty of Rome lays out the budgetary procedure (sequence of steps and deadlines) that should be respected by the European Commission, the Council and the European Parliament. The prescribed budgetary procedure begins on 1 July and ends on 31 December of the year preceding the budget year in question. In practice however, from 1977, the procedure starts much earlier. The sequencing of the annual budgetary procedure is as follows:

- The European Commission is to prepare and send to the Council and Parliament the *preliminary draft budget* by 15 June. It does so by compiling the requests of all spending departments according to the EU's needs and political priorities for the coming year. The Commission also arbitrates between conflicting claims on the basis of the priorities set for the year in question. The preliminary draft budget can be amended in order to allow for the inclusion of new information that was not available prior to June.
- The Council conducts its first reading of the preliminary draft budget and on this basis and after a conciliation meeting with the Parliament establishes the *draft budget* before 31 July. This draft budget is sent by mid-September to the Parliament for the first reading.
- The European Parliament conducts its *first reading* of the draft budget during October. It may amend the non-compulsory expenditure by the absolute majority of its members. Modifications in the compulsory expenditure require an absolute majority of votes cast. The Parliament is supposed to pass the amended draft back to the Council by mid-November for the second reading.
- After the conciliation meeting with the Parliament, the Council conducts its *second reading* of the draft budget during the third week of November. The draft budget is altered following the amendments (for the non-compulsory expenditure) by the Parliament or proposed modifications regarding compulsory expenditure. Unless the entire budget is rejected by the Parliament, this is the stage when the Council determines the final amount of the compulsory expenditure. The amended draft budget is returned to the Parliament around the last week of November for the second and final reading.
- As the Council decides on compulsory expenditure, the Parliament spends most of its time in reviewing the non-compulsory outlays.

For that part of the budget, the Parliament may accept or refuse the proposals by the Council. The budget is *accepted* (before the New Year) and could be implemented when the Parliament approves it by a majority of its members. Three-fifths of the votes cast must be in favour.

- As certain unforeseen and exceptional events may take place during the year when the budget is implemented, the European Commission is entitled to propose *amendments* to the ongoing budget. These changes are subject to the same procedural rules as the general budget.

Expenditure

The budgetary crises of the 1980s prompted the EU institutions to reconsider budgetary procedure and discipline. The budget was sometimes balanced by accounting tricks dubbed 'creative accounting'. Certain payments were deferred until the following year, when it was expected that the financial conditions would improve. As part of the reform in 1988 and in order to ensure budgetary discipline and to improve the budgetary procedure, the European Parliament, the Council and the European Commission ought to agree in advance on the main budgetary priorities in the forthcoming medium term. The objective is to institute a binding medium-term financial framework for the EU expenditure known as the 'financial perspective'.

The financial perspective shows both the maximum amount and the structure of foreseeable EU outlays. A reference point for the budgetary expenditure was the financial perspective from 1988 to 1992. The subsequent agreements covered seven-year periods, 1993–99 and 2000–06. Tough negotiations started on the post-enlargement financial perspective, 2007–13, even before the eastern enlargement in 2004.

The financial perspective differs from indicative financial programming in that the ceilings are binding on the parties to the Interinstitutional Agreement. The financial perspective marks the maximum amount of payment appropriations for the various chapters of EU expenditure. It is not a multiannual budget. The reason is that the usual annual budgetary procedure still applies in order to determine the actual level of expenditure (but up to the ceiling provided by the financial perspective). The three institutions agree to respect the annual expenditure ceiling for each expenditure item. The ceilings, however, need to be sufficiently high in order to allow for the flexibility necessary for the budgetary management. The ceiling may be revised in either direction, but that depends only on unforeseen events (such as German reunification, the violent disintegration of the former

Yugoslavia or aid to Rwanda) that took place after the Interinstitutional Agreement was signed.

The 1988 reform of the budget had three additional aspects:

- The total own resources of the EU budget were not linked to the VAT contribution. Instead, resources needed to cover the budgetary expenditure had a ceiling in appropriations for payments. This overall ceiling was fixed for each year from 1988 to 1992 as a percentage of the Union's GDP (for example, 1.15 per cent in 1989 and 1.2 per cent in 1992). The new ceilings gradually increased from 1.20 to 1.27 per cent in the period which ended in 1999.
- The budgetary discipline, as a shared responsibility of the European Commission, the Council and the Parliament, was increased. Its major objective was to check farm expenditure. The means to achieve this is a guideline whereby it may not increase by more than 74 per cent of the annual rate of growth of EU GDP.
- The coordination and increase in effectiveness of the three structural funds (the European Agricultural Guarantee and Guidance Fund: EAGGF; the European Regional Development Fund: ERDF; and the European Social Fund: ESF). The objectives included the adjustment of regions whose development was below the EU average, structural conversion in the regions hit by industrial decline, the fight against long-term unemployment, the occupational integration of young people, the adjustment of the farming structure and the development of rural areas.

The European Council in Berlin (1999) decided to keep the EU budget ceiling at a level that does not exceed 1.27 per cent of the total EU GDP in the period of the new financial perspective, 2000–06.[94] This means that the enlargement-related expenditure must fit within this limit set for 'own resources'.[95] This (or any other) fixed rate may be disputed as it may not fulfil the allocation, or the stabilisation or the redistribution tasks in an EMU. As for the total annual aid that the member country may receive from the EU budget, this was limited to 4 per cent of the national GDP.[96] This was a political compromise as are most solutions in the EU. In addition, the Council decided to link the national contribution to the EU budget to the member country's ability to contribute (GDP).[97] Economically successful EU members would have to pay more as they can afford more.

A new emphasis in expenditure includes the financing of the trans-European transport, telecommunications and energy networks. Priority would be given to the cross-frontier links between the national networks.

As for external action, the EU will pay attention to emergency aid (primarily to the countries in the vicinity), as well as loan guarantees.

Outlays from the EU budget have expanded and diversified remarkably since its inception. Table 4.11 presents the financial perspective for 2000–06. As far as the annual expenditure is concerned, the Common Agricultural Policy (CAP) disposes of half of the entire budget. Hence, in relative terms, expenditure on all other various economic activities and policies may not be highly concentrated. Structural funds of the EU include the ERDF, the ESF, the Guidance Section of the Agricultural Fund and, from 1993, the Cohesion Fund. Outlays on transport and fisheries are also included in this chapter. The share of structural funds in 2003 is 33 per cent of the budget. A notable feature of the components of this chapter is that their shares are continuously rising in the general budget over time. The (ab)use of structural funds may become a serious stumbling block in the future, just as agricultural expenditure has continued to be for decades.

Administrative operations cost the EU only 5 per cent of its budget, while the rest of the budget is redistributed mostly to the member countries. This distinguishes the EU from other international organisations, since elsewhere the budget is used mainly for administrative expenditure.

The total size of the EU annual budget may not be all that large if compared with the annual national government expenditure on particular activities. For example, the EU budget in 2003 was €98 billion. During the same year, out of its annual budget of €659 billion (£456 billion), the British government spent €104 billion (£72 billion) on the National Health Service and €85 billion (£59 billion) on education. At the same time, out of its budget of €272 billion, the French government spent €69 billion on national education, research and the young. The German federal government in the same period spent €82 billion on health and social security out of its budget of €248 billion.

Audit of EU expenditure has been provoking a number of controversies. In 2005, for the eleventh year in a row, the Court of Auditors was able to certify that only 5 per cent of EU expenditure was legal and regular (this concerns mainly internal administration). The remaining 95 per cent of outlays did not receive a positive statement of assurance 'due to the incidence of errors found'.[98]

Revenue

The EU budget was financed by the national contributions of member states until 1970. After that year, the EU got its 'own' resources, including customs duties, agricultural levies and a budget-balancing resource of up to 1 per cent of the VAT base (the base was increased to 1.4 per cent in

Table 4.11 EU budget according to the financial perspective, 2000–06

Appropriations for commitments	Current prices				2003 prices		
	2000	2001	2002	2003	2004	2005	2006
1. AGRICULTURE	41 738	44 530	46 587	47 378	46 285	45 386	45 094
Agricultural expenditure (except rural development)	37 352	40 035	41 992	42 680	41 576	40 667	40 364
Rural development and supporting measures	4 386	4 495	4 595	4 698	4 709	4 719	4 730
2. STRUCTURAL OPERATIONS	32 678	32 720	33 638	33 968	33 652	33 384	32 588
Structural funds	30 019	30 005	30 849	31 129	30 922	30 654	29 863
Cohesion fund	2 659	2 715	2 789	2 839	2 730	2 730	2 725
3. INTERNAL POLICIES[1]	6 031	6 272	6 558	6 796	6 915	7 034	7 165
4. EXTERNAL ACTION	4 627	4 735	4 873	4 972	4 983	4 994	5 004
5. ADMINISTRATION[2]	4 638	4 776	5 012	5 211	5 319	5 428	5 536
6. RESERVES	906	916	676	434	434	434	434
Monetary reserve	500	500	250				
Emergency aid reserve	203	208	213	217	217	217	217
Guarantee reserve	203	208	213	217	217	217	217
7. PRE-ACCESSION AID	3 174	3 240	3 328	3 386	3 386	3 386	3 386
Agriculture	529	540	555	564	564	564	564
Pre-accession structural instrument	1 058	1 080	1 109	1 129	1 129	1 129	1 129
PHARE (applicant countries)	1 587	1 620	1 664	1 693	1 693	1 693	1 693
APPROPRIATIONS FOR COMMITMENTS – Total	93 792	97 189	100 672	102 145	100 974	100 046	99 207

Table 4.11 (continued)

Appropriations for payments	Current prices				2003 prices		
	2000	2001	2002	2003	2004	2005	2006
APPROPRIATIONS FOR PAYMENTS – Total	91 322	94 730	100 078	102 767	99 553	97 659	97 075
Appropriations for payments as % of GNI	1.10%	1.10%	1.12%	1.10%	1.04%	1.00%	0.97%
Available for accession (appropriations for payments)			4 397	7 266	9 626	12 387	15 396
Agriculture			1 698	2 197	2 652	3 172	3 680
Other expenditure			2 699	5 069	6 974	9 215	11 716
CEILING, APPROPRIATIONS FOR PAYMENTS	91 322	94 730	104 475	110 033	109 179	110 046	112 471
Ceiling, payment as % of GNI	1.10%	1.10%	1.17%	1.18%	1.14%	1.12%	1.12%
Margin for unforeseen expenditure	0.17%	0.17%	0.10%	0.09%	0.13%	0.15%	0.15%
Own resources ceiling	1.27%	1.27%	1.27%	1.27%	1.27%	1.27%	1.27%

Notes:
1. In accordance with Article 2 of Decision No. 182/1999/EC of the European Parliament and of the Council and Article 2 of Council Decision 1999/64/Euratom (OJ L 26, 1.2.1999, pp. 1 and 34), €11 510 million at current prices is available for research over the 2000–02 period.
2. The expenditure on pensions included under the ceiling for this heading is calculated net of staff contributions to the pension scheme, up to a maximum of €1100 million at 1999 prices for the period 2000–06.

Source: European Commission (2000).

Table 4.12 The EU(15) budget revenue in 2002 and 2003

Type of revenue	2002		2003	
	€ million	%	€ million	%
1. Agricultural duties and sugar levies	1 419.4	1.5	1 426.4	1.5
2. Customs duties	10 300.7	10.7	10 713.9	11.0
3. Regularisation of collection costs for 2001	–2 037.9	–2.1	–	–
4. VAT	22 601.2	23.6	24 121.3	24.7
5. Fourth resource	46 605.0	48.7	59 403.9	60.9
6. Miscellaneous and surpluses from previous years	16 768.0	17.6	1 837.4	1.9
Total	95 656.4	100.0	97 502.9	100.0

Source: European Commission, General Budget of the European Union for the Financial Year 2003.

1985). While customs duties are an obvious revenue item of the EU budget, the rest comes from the national treasuries according to a formula which is beyond most human understanding.

Own resources of the EU budget represent a one-time tax revenue allocated to the EU. They accrue automatically to the EU without any need for additional decisions by national governments. A reform of finances in 1988 changed and expanded own financial resources of the EU. These resources are:

- customs duties;
- agricultural, sugar and isoglucose levies;
- VAT resources;
- the fourth resource; and
- miscellaneous revenue.

Table 4.12 presents the EU budget revenue in 2002 and 2003:

- *Customs duties* and agricultural levies are the 'natural' proceeds of a customs union. Customs duties that are applied on imports of goods from non-member countries represent 11 per cent of revenue. Their relative impact is diminishing over time because of EU enlargements, preferential trade agreements and continuous reduction of tariffs by the GATT/WTO. This trend may be partly compensated by an increase in the volume of trade with external countries, but recession can reduce the level and scope of economic activity and, consequently, reduce imports.

- *Agricultural levies* (1.5 per cent of the budget revenue) are variable charges applied on imports of farm goods that are included in the CAP and imported from third countries. They are a changeable source of revenue for they depend on the volume of imports, which relies in part on weather conditions and partly on the trade concessions that the EU offers to foreign partners. Another element in this fluctuation is that world market prices for agricultural goods frequently change. The EU is becoming increasingly self-sufficient in a number of agricultural products of the temperate zone, hence there is a reduction in demand for imported farm goods from this geographical zone. Sugar and isoglucose levies are charges on producers that are supposed to make them share the financial burden of market support for production and storage.
- *The VAT contribution* includes 25 per cent of the revenue. It is calculated for each member country by the application of a uniform rate of 1.4 per cent to the national VAT base. This base for calculation may not exceed 55 per cent of the national GDP.
- *The 'fourth resource'* is closely related to a country's ability to pay. This revenue item provided 61 per cent of the EU budget. Together with the VAT resources, it is the only dynamic component of the budgetary revenue as it is derived from the application of a rate to the GDP of each member country. It is an additional source as it is calculated during the budgetary procedure in order to top up the difference between the budgetary expenditure and (insufficient) revenue that accrues from other sources.
- The fifth revenue item is negligible relative to the total budget. It covers *miscellaneous revenue* such as deductions from the salaries of the EU civil servants, fines and possible surpluses from preceding years.

Challenges

The EU budget expenditure and revenue were not related either to the EU need to influence economic life in the EMU (agriculture is the only exception) or, until recently, to the relative economic wealth of the member countries. Instead of singling out economic areas that need to be influenced at the EU level, and then creating the necessary funds, the EU still continues to pick up economic policies (areas for intervention) that can fit into these limited funds.

It should never be forgotten that it is neither the absolute nor the relative size of the budget that matters. What matters is the size of funds that are necessary to change certain behaviour in the desired direction. In some cases, the amount of funds can be tiny. For example, in the development of SMEs, a simple freedom of establishment, certain tax incentives and loan guarantees (underwriting risk) can do the job. In others, such as agriculture, infrastructure or adjustment out of obsolete industries, the amounts required to change behaviour in the desired way can be enormous.

When the member countries of the EU agree to pursue a common policy, one can also expect that the means for carrying out that policy may also be transferred upwards towards the EU institutions. The problem is that the member countries take the EU as the appropriate plane for the conduct of common policies in certain cases, but they are quite unyielding (Britain is not an exception here) when new funds have to be created. Reforms of the EU budget were resisted by the regions and countries that benefit from the present structure (mainly the agricultural regions in the north and the less-developed ones in the south). An increased expenditure on economic activities (other than agriculture), without extra funds, can jeopardise the current distribution of costs and benefits. Without the ability to increase or substantially reorganise spending, the EU should continue to endeavour to coordinate its own expenditure with that of the member countries.

The European Council in Copenhagen (2002) and previously in Brussels (2002)[99] reconfirmed its Berlin (1999)[100] decision that the ceiling for enlargement-related expenditure set out for the years 2004–06 must be respected. That is to say that the total EU expenditure must fit into own resources, which are limited to 1.27 per cent of the combined EU GDP of all member countries. Therefore, the EU has very limited room for manoeuvre to enlarge its funds.

Sapir et al. (2003) proposed that the EU has to use its funds in a more astute way than was the case in the past. Around a half of the EU budget should be spent on growth-stimulating activities such as research, higher education, infrastructure projects and institution building in the new central and east European member countries. The only way to do this and to remain within the current budgetary limits is to scrap the CAP and regional funds. No wonder that such suggestions were highly controversial and were subsequently rejected. In any case, these thoughts contributed to a wide-ranging debate about the future direction of the EU.

A formal obligation to contribute to the EU budget exists for every member country. The disequilibrium between the payments to and receipts from the EU budget created tensions between Britain and the rest of the EU for quite some time.[101] These issues may have certain nominal relevance for the day-to-day (unpleasant) political debates. None the less, it must be remembered that economic integration is not an enterprise with short-term or, even, long-term clear financial balances (*juste retour*). Rather, integration is an undertaking that offers a longer-term security promise to employ resources and potentials of the participants in a superior way than would be the case otherwise. Therefore, a country that is a net contributor to the budget should not be seen as a loser from the integration venture (for example, Germany), but rather as a participant that is gaining elsewhere: secure, unrestricted and long-term free access to partner-country markets for its goods and services. These are the principal gains from country integration.

The EU budget started to be financed from 'own resources' in 1970, three years before Britain joined the group. As a country that had a significant part of its foreign trade with the non-EU countries, Britain was an important contributor to the EU budget (customs proceeds). Britain had a very small agricultural sector, hence it was not a significant receiver of EU funds. In addition, certain British regions were below the EU average level of development. Once all this was compounded, Britain emerged as a significant net contributor to the EU budget. The ERDF was created in 1973, partly in order to direct certain EU funds to Britain. None the less, the British net budgetary position continued to worsen.

The Conservative party took office in 1979 and made a big to-do about this disproportionate contribution to the EU budget as a result of the workings of the CAP. The argument was that Britain failed to get a 'fair share' of the EU budget because of its small agricultural sector. Mrs Thatcher said: 'I want my money back.' After a long and acrimonious process, Britain obtained an annual 'rebate' (abatement) at the European Council in Fontainebleau (1984).[102] This was a recognition of the relative poverty of Britain at that time and that a high proportion of the EU's budget expenditure was on the CAP. The rebate was calculated on the basis of a formula related to EU expenditure in Britain and the VAT-based portion of the British contribution to the EU budget. This rebate was paid each year in the form of a reduced VAT contribution in the following year. This settlement was advantageous to the Council of Ministers because the European Parliament was not involved with the revenue side of the picture (recall that the Parliament has authority only over the expenditure part of the EU budget).

The British rebate is worth an average of €4.6 billion a year.[103] Britain, a country that was by all measures above the EU(15) and EU(25) average GDP per capita in 2004, could not even dream that two decades after the Fontainebleau deal this rebate would be partly funded by the poor countries from central and eastern Europe. The EU expenditure on the CAP will most likely continue to fall in the future. The British rebate cannot be justified for much longer, hence this issue will be tackled in negotiations about the new financial perspective (2007–13).

Conclusion

The EU budget absorbs only slightly more than 1 per cent of the combined GDP of its member countries. Compared with the national budgets (with the exception of agriculture) it plays only a minor role in the redistribution of income and allocation of resources. Its role in economic stabilisation has never existed. The influential MacDougall Report (1977) noted that in federal states such as the US and Germany, federal spending was in the neighbourhood of 20–25 per cent of GDP. Such an increase in EU spending cannot reasonably be expected in the near future. In the pre-federal stage of the EU, a budget that absorbs 5–7 per cent of the combined GDP (without transfers for defence) could have an impact on economic stabilisation and an evening of regional disparities. Such a budget might be able to influence social (unemployment, education, health, retirement), regional and external aid policies in an EMU. Resources might be found either in the transfer of funds from the national budgets and/or in an increase in the 'fourth' budgetary resource. The problem is that the member countries are still very reluctant to increase the budgetary powers of the EU. The controversial Stability and Growth Pact is institutionally preventing them from increasing expenditure beyond prescribed and monitored limits. If the EU gets more resources for its budget, the total public expenditure in the EU, compared with similar uncoordinated outlays of member states, may be reduced because of the economies of scale. A budget with increased resources may represent a built-in stabiliser for macroeconomic management. In addition, transfers among regions may enhance economic convergence and strengthen the cohesion of the EU.

In contrast to a variety of revenue sources employed to fill the national budgets, the EU budget is financed from a narrow range of sources. On the expenditure side, there is a high concentration of resources in one area: agriculture. This contrasts with the much-diversified public expenditure in member countries. However, the possibility of changing such a pattern of EU revenue still remains in the hands of member countries and it is left to their (un)willingness to enhance the powers of the EU. If there are no rapid changes in the structure of national and EU expenditure, the EU Lisbon (2000) aspirations to become 'the most competitive and dynamic knowledge-based economy in the world capable of sustainable economic growth with more and better jobs and greater social cohesion'[104] by 2010 will be a forlorn pipe-dream.

The EU has a strong indirect means of controlling a significant part of public expenditure in all member countries: EU competition policy. State aids absorb a sizeable chunk of the national budgets. Control of these outlays does not require extra expenditure from the EU budget.

One may expect that the EU(25) budget will remain at the heart of interest and controversy in the future. What may take place is reform, or rather restructuring (in relative terms), within the framework of the existing budget. Increased contributions to the EU budget according to the level of national wealth or the principle of ability to pay should be further encouraged.

Even before the eastern enlargement in 2004, very tough, complicated and controversial negotiations and horse-trading started to define the new financial perspective for the 2007–13 period. The European Commission proposed to spend €1000 billion over the seven-year period (1.24 per cent of the EU GDP). Major increases in spending would be in areas such as research and transport and other networks in order to boost the competitiveness of EU output and meet the Lisbon target by 2010. The net contributors to the EU budget (France, Germany, Austria, Britain, Sweden and the Netherlands) argue in favour of a budget equal to 1 per cent of the EU(25) GDP. In any case, in 2004 the EU entered into a much more difficult and complicated phase of integration than most people imagine.

> But this I say: He who sows sparingly will also reap sparingly,
> and he who sows bountifully will also reap bountifully.
> 2 Corinthians 9:6

4.4 Industrial policy in manufacturing and services

4.4.1 INTRODUCTION

Explicit industrial policy as a part of overall economic policy did not attract the attention of research interests in the industrialised countries with market-based economies until the mid-1970s. This can be explained by the underlying economic developments. During the 1960s and early 1970s the industrialised countries experienced relatively fast economic growth with low rates of both inflation and unemployment. The prices of raw materials were stable and relatively low, while labour was able to move without major disturbances from agriculture to the manufacturing and services sectors. Excess demand for labour was met by a steady inflow of labour from abroad. This period was also characterised by sporadic government intervention to influence the national geography of production in the manufacturing and services sectors. Relatively free markets were operating smoothly without significant disruption. During this period, the GATT was active in the lowering of tariffs.

The 'golden 60s' were followed by a period whose principal characteristics were the result of a sharp increase in the price of oil in 1973. This triggered rises in inflation, unemployment and a deceleration in the rate of growth throughout the world. International competition increased sharply because suppliers were fighting in shrinking markets. It seemed that the free market system and the entrenched geography of production were not capable of coping satisfactorily with this situation. There developed an awareness of a need for alternative strategies (that is, based on intervention in manufacturing, services and trade) to handle the new situation. Industrial policy, an actively researched area during the 1980s, could be seen as a supply-side response to market imperfections. Discussion was less about the formation of capital and more about its sectoral, industrial and geographical allocation and use. It was also more about economic adjustment policy than industrial policy (a term disliked by both politicians and neo-classical economists).[105] None the less, the gloves were off in the debate about industrial policy in the developed market economies.

This section is structured as follows. First, various industrial policy issues such as its definition, its rationale, intervention, instruments, selectivity and small and medium-sized enterprises (SMEs) are discussed (4.4.2). This is followed by a consideration of the underlying principles of EU industrial policy, its evolution, importance and variety, technology policy and possible ways ahead (4.4.3). Additional analysis (4.4.4) is devoted to the character and significance of services in general and in the EU in particular. The conclusion (4.4.5) offers a list of factors and means that should be included in any respectable industrial policy.

4.4.2 INDUSTRIAL POLICY ISSUES

Meaning

An industry is usually taken to mean a group of firms that produce the same or similar kinds of good (or service) and which compete in the same market. The literature on modern industrial policy started its development in the early 1980s, and various definitions of industrial policy were proposed. Before surveying a selection of these, it is helpful to recall the difference between competition and industrial policy. The former is directed towards the freeing of market forces, while the latter seeks to channel them (Geroski, 1987, p. 57). In addition, industrial policy may sometimes have strong anti-competitive results, such as the need for the functional and spatial concentration of business to achieve economies of scale and a reduction in trade costs.

Some definitions of industrial policy are specific and selective. Industrial policy can be defined as coordinated targeting. This is the selection of parts of the economy, such as firms, projects or industries, for special treatment (targeting), coupled with a coordinated government plan to influence industrial structure in defined ways (coordination) (Brander, 1987, p. 4). Industrial policy implies policies that relate to specific industries, such as the correction of restrictive business practices (Pinder, 1982, p. 44). Industrial policies can be those government policies that are intended to have a direct effect on a particular industry or firm (McFetridge, 1985, p. 1). Industrial policy is aimed at particular industries (and firms as their components) in order to reach ends that are perceived by the government to be beneficial for the country as a whole (Chang, 1994, p. 60). This definition does not, however, distinguish between the short- and long-term perspectives. Different policies need to be employed to achieve efficiency in the timescale changes.

Other definitions of industrial policy are broad, often overloaded, and include many areas of public policy. For example, 'industrial policy includes all government actions that affect industry such as domestic and foreign investment, innovation, external trade, regional and labour policies, environmental features and all other aspects' (Donges, 1980, p. 189). 'Industrial policy can be any government measure or set of measures used to promote or prevent structural change' (Curzon Price, 1981, p. 17). Industrial policy may mean all measures that improve the economy's supply potential: anything that will improve growth, productivity and competitiveness (Adams and Klein, 1983, p. 3).

Another look at industrial policy can take it to mean a government policy action that is aimed at or motivated by problems within specific sectors. These 'problems' presumably occur in both declining and expanding (manufacturing or service) industries. The solutions to these problems are not necessarily sector specific, although that is a possibility (Tyson and Zysman, 1987a, p. 19). Industrial policy is the initiation and coordination of government activities in order to influence and improve the productivity and competitiveness of particular industries or the whole economy (Johnson, 1984, p. 8). It can be defined as the set of selective measures adopted by the state to alter industrial organisation (Blais, 1986, p. 4). Another definition states that its focus has been on the ideal relation between governments and markets. 'Industrial policy need not be equated with national planning. It is, rather, a formula for making the economy adaptable and dynamic' (Reich, 1982, pp. 75–9). 'The term industrial policy describes that group of policies whose explicit objective is to influence the operation of industry' (Sharp and Shepherd, 1987, p. 107). 'An industrial policy implies intervention by a government which seeks to promote particular industries in some way. This may be either to stimulate production and growth of an industry's size or to promote export sales' (Whalley, 1987, p. 84). This definition does not, however, include government influence on the decline of and exit from an industry. 'Industrial policy may be equated with intervention employed to cope with market failures or a price system that affects the allocation of resources' (Komiya, 1988, p. 4). 'All acts and policies of a government that relate to industry, constitute industrial policy' (Bayliss and El-Agraa, 1990, p. 137). The World Bank defines industrial policy as 'government efforts to alter industrial structure to promote productivity-based growth' (World Bank, 1993, p. 304). It is not clear whether this means that aid to ailing industries lies outside the scope of industrial policy. 'Industrial policy includes all actions that are taken to advance industrial development beyond what is allowed by the free market system' (Lall, 1994, p. 651). Industrial policy may also mean 'a set of public interventions through taxes, subsidies and regulations on domestic products or factors of production that attempt to modify the allocation of domestic resources that is the consequence of the free operation of market forces' (Gual, 1995, p. 9).

Industrial policy may mean different things for various countries at different times. Developing countries look at industrial policy as a means of economic development. They may favour some industries over others. Once these countries become developed, industrial policy may be directed towards fostering free competition. In the former centrally planned economies, industrial policy meant planning and imposing production and investment targets in each sector and industry within it.

Industrialised countries have had implicit industrial policies for a long time. They are embodied in trade, competition, tax, R&D, standardisation, education, regional, transport, environment, public procurement and other policies that have derived effects on the industrial structure. This is due to the interdependence of economic policies within the economic system. Therefore, some countries have joint ministries of industry and international trade. This is the case, for instance, with the British Department of Trade and Industry (DTI) and the Japanese Ministry of International Trade and Industry (MITI), although there are differences in the powers and role in the economy between the two ministries.

In the most-developed countries, the period after the Second World War was characterised by reductions in tariffs, as well as measures to prevent the demise of declining industries. However, governments' industrial policies may be a simple continuation of the old protectionism by more sophisticated means (Pinder et al., 1979, p. 9). Governments' tax and transfer policies have their impact on demand. This affects the structure and spatial location of manufacturing production, that is, where new employment is created, attracted or kept. By direct production and supply of public goods and services, as well as through public procurement, governments influence, at least in part, the geography of production of their economies. Other government policies, such as foreign policy, have no direct effect on the size of the economic pie in their country. However, they can influence industrial structure, its geographical distribution and employment. This is the case when governments ban the export of (high-technology) goods abroad.

Three (non-mutually exclusive) broad types of industrial policy are macroeconomic, sectoral and microeconomic orientation. Macroeconomic orientation is least interventionist because it leaves the operation of industries and firms to market forces. Policy orientation simply improves the general economic climate for business. Sector-specific orientation becomes relevant when market failures affect certain industries. It tries to amend the particular market shortcoming. Microeconomic orientation of industrial policy may direct a government to act directly towards specific firms or industrial groups (Jacquemin, 1984, pp. 4–5).

There are another three broad types of industrial policy: market oriented, interventionist or mixed. The first type (market oriented) fosters competition and free markets. The second (interventionist) policy may be conducted as in the centrally planned economies. In practice, industrial policy is most often a mixture of the first two. Most countries may be classified as 'massaged-market economies'.[106] The issue that most often differs between countries is not whether or not they intervene, but rather the degree, form and impact of intervention in industry.

Industrial policy may also be described as adjustment prone or adjustment averse. Adjustment-prone industrial policy stimulates adjustment of various industries to enter into new production, remain competitive or ease the exit from selected lines of production. Adjustment-averse industrial policy is the policy of protection, which impedes changes in an economy by preserving the status quo.

The level of industrial policy can be general or specific. The choice is between discrimination and non-discrimination. The degree of intervention should be as high as possible. This means that it needs to be general, that is, available to every industry and enterprise. Once the policy is put in place, the market is perhaps the best tool to fine-tune the economy, to create and to exploit unforeseen opportunities, as well as to select the firms or industries that should take advantage of the employed policy instruments. Market forces may divert players from the inefficient employment of resources. The policy should be tailored to suit local needs (industry or firm) in cases where there are no externalities. In addition, it should be used with care because governments are not infallible and may well make the wrong commercial choice, as was the case with the French and British Concorde project.

A critical definition of industrial policy states that it is 'the label used to describe a wide-ranging, ill-assorted collection of micro-based supply-side initiatives that are designed to improve market performance in a variety of mutually inconsistent ways. Intervention is typically demanded in cases with market failures and where major changes need to be effected quickly' (Geroski, 1989, p. 21). To formulate a definition of industrial policy may be as difficult as describing a Chinese dish: 'One US Supreme Court Justice tried to find a definition of pornography and said: "You know it when you see it, but you can't define it"; so it may be with industrial policy' (Audretsch, 1989, p. 10).

Various economic policies have their impact on industrial policy. Not only trade policy, but also competition, social, education, regional, energy, transport, health, environment and other policy areas all have a strong spatial and industrial impact. Hence, most definitions of industrial policy include, at least implicitly, the need for a stable economic environment and coordination of various economic policies. Only then can specific targeting of industrial policy make its full contribution to economic growth and improvement in productivity and competitiveness, the final objective being an increase in the standard of living. On such grounds, broad definitions of industrial policy may embrace all of these facets. Hence, industrial policy is an economic policy that shapes a country's comparative advantage. Its objective is to influence the change in national economic structure (reallocation of resources among sectors, industries, professions and regions) in order to enhance the creation and growth of national wealth, rather than to distribute it.

Rationale

The classical economic model based on free trade and perfect competition predicts that *laissez-faire* is universally beneficial and costless. However, the new theory of strategic[107] trade and industrial policy has shown that intervention can sometimes play a useful role in mitigating the shortcomings of market imperfections and can alter the national and international geography of production. In general, economic adjustment (industrial, sectoral, professional and geographical reallocation and use of resources) is prompted by factors that include an increase in GDP and its distribution, as well as by changes in demand, technology, market structure, tastes, needs, prices, foreign competition and marketing, all of which contribute to a potential increase or loss in current competitiveness. In addition, environmental constraints and a rapidly ageing population also contribute to economic adjustment. This process is not smooth, or easy or costless or fast, hence the need for an industrial policy.

Abundant natural resources may often be a problem for a country, not a benefit. A discovery of resources attracts gamblers, opportunists and crooks such as Francisco Pizzaro (Latin America), Robert Clive (East India Company) or Cecil Rhodes (South Africa). These resources provoke or contribute to civil wars: Angola, Congo or Nigeria. Elsewhere, abundant natural resources may harm economic development because they introduce severe distortions in the structure of the economy. Plentiful oil reserves and exports as is the case in Saudi Arabia, Bahrain or Kuwait keep local wages too high to permit a relatively balanced local development of the manufacturing industry. Foreigners from less-well-off countries fill jobs in services in these countries. However, certain countries that are exceptionally poor in natural resources such as Switzerland, Austria or Japan are highly developed and among the wealthiest in the world. They 'benefited' from the absence of such resources. These countries base their prosperity on the most important resource: human capital. Elsewhere, in Iceland and Norway for example, ample natural resources were managed rather well. However, a certain level of previous economic and political development helped considerably in the building of a national consensus on the management of those resources.

The creation of wealth used to depend in the distant past to a large extent on the local availability of natural resources. As the economy evolved, wealth creation started to depend more on physical assets (mainly equipment and finance). Prosperity of the modern economy and competitiveness of output depend not only on the physical, but also and increasingly on intangible assets such as knowledge and information processing, as well as on organisational and control potentials and capabilities.

Instead of relying on inherited and natural advantages, industrial policy may help in the conscious shaping of a country's comparative advantage through the supplies of trained labour and educated management with a specific profile (engineers versus ethnographers), tax, infrastructure, public purchase and R&D policies. However, it is important to note that both intervention (action) and *laissez-faire* (non-intervention) have an impact on the structure of industry and, hence, on the geography of production. The challenge for a government is to achieve, maintain and profit from the best balance between the two approaches. But this is not at all easy.

Countries in the EU and the US responded to the circumstances prevailing during the 1970s primarily by protectionism. Along with other industrialised countries, they realised that the solution to lagging productivity, recession, deteriorating export performance, increasing market penetration for manufacturing goods from developing countries and reallocation of some manufacturing activities outside the developed world may be found in policies that affect the structure and development of national industry. None the less, inadequate economic performance is not a sufficient condition for the justification of industrial policy. The question is not whether the economy is operating (un)satisfactorily, but rather whether an industrial policy might have achieved a better result than a free market system (Adams, 1983, p. 405). Any policy has to be tested according to the gains and losses that it creates in a dynamic context.

Once free markets lose credibility as efficient conductors of an economy, the introduction of intervention (various economic policies) seems inevitable. The question then is 'How can the government intervene in the most efficient and least harmful way?' The choice might be between leaving the economy to imperfect entrepreneurs and the possibly even riskier strategy of having it run by imperfect governments (Curzon Price, 1981, p. 20). However, there is no strong a priori reason why an economy run by imperfect governments should be at greater risk than one run by imperfect entrepreneurs. Both of these are second-best (suboptimal) solutions.

Risk taking (entrepreneurship) has always been a significant engine of economic growth albeit the benefits achieved are accompanied by attendant dangers. The costs of adjustment are borne principally by those who are weak or powerless. Thus, governments have often followed a defensive policy with the objective of securing employment in the short term and evading social tensions, at least during their term in office. The socialisation of risk in the form of various economic policies may make life safer in the short run, but it also prevents both free operation of individual entrepreneurial activity and an even greater increase in the economic pie in the future. This process may be seen as bowing to the public's desire to see a happy marriage between progress and stability (Blais, 1986, p. 41). Interestingly, however, in Britain rescuing a declining industry (coal) to protect jobs proved not to be the safe route to re-election for the government during the 1970s. Taxpayers and consumers are not unaware of the costs of such a rescue. However, in many countries strong trade unions in declining industries can still mobilise a strong lobbying influence. Those who have full confidence in the operation of a free market system would say that the market will take care of itself. Why bother to change those things which will happen anyway? This school of thought fails to take account of a number of serious market imperfections.

The most influential reasons for intervention may be found in the loss of a competitive position, the management of the expansion of new and the decline of old industries, the handling of industries subject to scale effects and externalities, and attracting footloose industries (Lipsey, 1987b, p. 117). Fostering strategic manufacturing and services industries with strong forward and backward links to the rest of the economy can be a very attractive policy goal. These industries supply external or non-priced gains to the rest of the economy. Growing industries such as semiconductors, electronics or telecommunications have a much more profound spillover effect on the economy than do the furniture or clothing industries.

Technologies that are 'critical' for a large country's competitiveness and/or defence include those that deal with new materials, energy sources and the environment; biotechnology and pharmacy; manufacturing, including production of tools; information gathering, communications, data processing and computers; and transportation and aeronautics, including navigation. Because of large sunk costs and economies of scale, small and medium-sized countries do not have the means, or indeed the necessity (if they can acquire them through trade), to develop all or most of these technologies and make them commercially viable. What these countries may do instead is to select a 'critical mass' of 'critical' technologies or parts of them (for example, components, basic chemicals) and try to excel in those market niches, as is the case with Switzerland, Austria, and the Benelux and Scandinavian countries.

Another classification of the reasons for an industrial policy groups them into three broad categories: respectable, false and non-economic (Curzon Price, 1990, pp. 159–67):

- *Respectable arguments* include market failures because, in practice, a perfect competition model does not always lead to a stable equilibrium. However, the problem is that a market failure such as wage rigidity or monopolies can frequently be traced to a previous intervention by the government. Another pretext for intervention is domestic distortions. A uniform rate of VAT would have a neutral effect on the consumption of goods or services in a country, but a reduction in VAT on food, for example, may cause some resources to shift to that industry at a time when the telecommunications or data-processing industries could have made better use of them. Infant industries provide a good excuse for intervention, but the problem is that there are many old 'infants' that may never become self-sustaining. One can also build an intellectually respectable case for industrial policy based on positive externalities and spillover effects (Krugman, 1993b, pp. 160–61).[108] These include benefits arising from the establishment of common technical standards for the production and/or operation of goods, for example, in the telecommunications industry. However, mistakes can be costly if governments target the wrong industry, for example, computers in France (Bull) or Britain (ICL), Concorde (Britain and France) and petrochemicals and aluminium in Japan before the first oil shock.[109] The process may become overpoliticised and subject to strong lobbying as in the case of public goods that everyone wants and consumes, although these goods may be produced at a loss.
- The first *false argument* in favour of intervention is the issue of employment. Employment subsidies used to prolong the life of jobs in declining industries are often implemented at the expense of growing industries that may need them to expand operations and which could provide more and better jobs in the future. Likewise, proponents of the balance of payments argument for intervention tend to forget that resources that move into the protected industries may come from those industries with better export opportunities. Hence, a drop in imports may provoke a fall in exports.
- *Non-economic arguments* may be quite strong. It is often hard to dispute the issue of national security. This is a political process that confounds the predictive abilities of an economist. The problem is that it may be pushed to the limit in the case of industries that can be labelled as essential for national defence. In general, 'smart bombs'

> and electronic and nuclear weapons counteract the national security argument for intervention. Long-term supply contracts with allies and stockpiling may be considered prior to intervention. Social arguments for intervention, focused on the redistribution rather than the creation of material wealth, such as regional development or the protection of the environment and culture, may have some non-economic weight in any discussion about intervention.

The relative shares of the manufacturing industry and agriculture in GDP and employment have been declining continuously in industrialised countries over the past decades. In 2003, the GDP of the EU(15) was accounted for predominantly by services (70 per cent), with the rest distributed between manufacturing (27 per cent) and agriculture (3 per cent).[110] Hence, the process of deindustrialisation leads countries to a post-industrial society. These countries are better called service rather than industrialised economies, because manufacturing industry is a statistically 'shrinking' sector in relation to services. Some manufacturing jobs from developed countries have geographically relocated to the developing world.

One has to be very cautious with generalisations. Services contribute about a quarter of total intermediate consumption by the manufacturing sector in large economies (OECD, 2003c, D.8). Many services are directly linked to the manufacturing of goods, such as transport, finance, telecommunications, maintenance and other business services including everything from cleaning offices to business consultancy and advertising. Such services are not directly aimed at individuals for their personal consumption. If they are included in manufacturing and agriculture, then the relative share of these sectors in the national economy is significantly increased. In fact, they are most intimately linked with each other. In regions with few services, manufacturing industry performs below its potential. Hence, the relation between manufacturing and services is not one-way. New manufacturing technologies require new, better and/or more services, while services (such as R&D) may create new manufacturing technologies that may, in turn, create demand for services and so on. Profound changes in the structure of manufacturing and services have blurred the distinction between the two economic sectors.

A relative increase in the demand for services and growth in this sector was made possible by an increase in the productivity of the manufacturing sector. This has made more resources available for the services sector of the economy. Increased productivity results in a reduction in the price of manufactured goods, leading to an increase in disposable funds for the consumption of services. This makes industrial policy in manufacturing and services interesting for consideration.[111]

The MIT (Massachusetts Institute of Technology) Commission on Industrial Policy studied the importance of manufacturing during the 1980s. From a study of the US economy, the Commission drew the following conclusions (Dertouzos et al., 1990, pp. 39–42):

- In 1987 in the US, imports of goods and services were 10 times higher than exports of services. It is necessary to manufacture and export goods in order to pay for imports. The more resources are reallocated to services, the lower the chance of balancing the balance of payments.
- Moving resources from the manufacturing industry into services causes a shift from a sector with relatively high productivity growth to one with lower growth.
- Almost all R&D is carried out in the manufacturing sector.
- National defence depends on the purchase of a great amount of manufactured goods. If a country starts to depend on foreign suppliers, national security may be placed in jeopardy.

The Role of the Government

The standard comparative advantage and factor proportions theories of international trade may be satisfactory for the explanation of trade in primary goods. However, they are less satisfactory in explaining trade in industrial goods. Manufacturing can be seen as a collection of industries with no factor abundance base. On those grounds it is difficult to explain why the US exports computer software, why France exports perfumes while Japan exports copiers, cameras and DVDs, why the Swiss export chocolate, chemicals and watches or why Pakistan exports soccer balls.

A country's comparative advantage not only depends on its geographical resource endowment, but is also shaped over time by the actions of both businesses and government. Government economic policies may affect comparative advantage over time by influencing the quantity and quality of labour, capital, incentives and technology. Comparative advantage in manufacturing industries is not an unchangeable condition of nature, but often the outcome of economic policies that affect incentives to save, invest, innovate, diffuse technology and acquire or 'import' human capital (as was the choice during the 1960s and may be the case from 2010 for several decades).

Until the 1970s, market imperfections and multiple equilibria were at the margin of orthodox economic analysis, but these imperfections are at the heart of the analysis of the new theory of trade and industrial policy. A country's size, regional disequilibria, skill, mobility and unionisation of labour, R&D, sunk costs, economies of scale, competition and bankruptcy laws are just a few imperfections. To ignore them is to fail to realise that their effects can be mitigated by economic policy (Tyson, 1987, pp. 67–71). In the field of manufacturing, a government has at its disposal several policy instruments. These include trade policy (tariffs, subsidies and NTBs) that may reduce competition and antitrust policy that increases it; preferential tax treatment; non-commercial loans and loan guarantees as a support to risk capital; exports, insurance and other subsidies; public procurement; support for education and vocational retraining; assistance to workers to improve their professional and geographical mobility; and the provision of public or publicly financed R&D.

Free competition within an economic union brings costs of adjustment to which governments, voters and citizens are not indifferent. It is often forgotten that increased competition brings benefits in terms of economic restructuring. The costs of adjustment are often highly concentrated on the (vociferous) few and are usually temporary, whereas the benefits are dispersed over a long period of time and throughout society, but in relatively small instalments to everyone. In the real, second-best and imperfect world, there may be enough scope for both market mechanism and select intervention (economic policy).

The role of governments as organisers of national economies is coming under increasing inquiry. Governments can play several roles in economic activity, including:

- setting up general economic, legal and political stability;
- initiation;
- supervision;
- ownership of assets; and
- arbitration.

In spite of general agreement about the need to reduce the extent of public intervention in the allocation of resources in a national economy, it is a fact that the countries that have had the most impressive economic achievements during the past two decades are those whose governments exerted a strong and positive influence over all facets of commercial affairs (Dunning, 1994b, p. 1). The actions of governments, markets and firms are not substitutes for one another, but they do need to be mutually supportive. Instead of being obstacles, they need to be structured in such a way as to support and facilitate the actions of the others. This is a formidable task indeed.

A general reduction in tariffs and NTBs, as well as economic integration, may increase a country's market. However, free markets often fail to take a long-term view of society's needs when making structural adjustments.

Such adjustment (the transfer of resources from declining to growing industries) is not necessarily a swift, cheap and smooth process. In addition, it is a risky operation, as the future of expanding industries is not secure in the long term. If (a big if) astute adjustment policies (intervention) can facilitate these shifts and if this stimulates the new use of resources by providing incentives and support to the private businesses to adjust to the new situation, then intervention may have a certain justification.

One can make predictions about the model of economic adjustment based on the characteristics of a country's financial system. First, if this system relies on capital markets that allocate resources by competitively established prices, the adjustment process is company led. The allocation decisions are the responsibility of firms, as is the case in the US. Second, in a credit-based financial system where the government is administering prices, the adjustment process is state led (such as the past experiences of Japan and France). Finally, in a credit-based system where price formation is dominated by banks, the adjustment process can be considered as negotiated. An example can be found in Germany (Zysman, 1983, p. 18).

A common view of the world holds that firms play Cournot–Nash games against all other players (each firm decides on a course of action, for example, optimising output, on the assumption that the behaviour of the other firms remains constant), whereas governments play the Stackelberg game (the agent knows the reaction functions of all others) against firms and Cournot–Nash games against other governments (Brander and Spencer, 1985, p. 84). Unfortunately, these are all games that can produce relatively unstable equilibria and fluctuations in prices. In contrast, collusion among the players would lead to a relatively stable (Chamberlin) solution.

Justified Intervention

The key question in the debate on industrial policy (the relationship of states and market) still remains: can imperfect governments manage the shift of resources any better than imperfect markets? The answer is 'generally not', but this does not mean that market solutions are always superior to other ones. Just as the dangers of market failure are often exaggerated, so are the competencies of governments. All agree, however, that the state is needed to guarantee property rights. There are, none the less, some cases when a government's intervention (policy) may fare better than a free market solution. Here are some examples of situations in which intervention may be justified.

First, the time horizon in which private markets operate is relatively short. They may not foresee countries' long-term needs in the face of changing circumstances, capabilities and opportunities with a high degree of accuracy. Market prices cannot signal the profitability of future allocation of resources and production of goods and services that are not yet invented. Japanese manufacturing is financed to a large extent by bank credits, whereas US industry uses this source of finance to a much lesser extent. This means that managers of Japanese firms who ask their bank manager for a loan can justify the request on the grounds of the profits that will accrue 'when their ship comes in'. Managers in a comparable American firm in a similar situation must be sure that they can see the funnel of the ship in the distance. Hence, US industrial production is in general much more affected by the short-term interests of shareholders than is Japanese industry. The major goal of Japanese and German bank and enterprise managers is to try to ensure a firm's long-term competitive position in the market and thus some of them tend to look favourably on risky investments such as the commercialisation of new technologies. In contrast, the US system favours readily measurable physical assets (mergers and acquisitions) over intangible assets such as education or R&D. In spite of such a theoretical observation, the US is in practice the world leader in new technology and its application.

Government policy can shift this short-term perspective towards longer-term economic considerations. However, less than perfect foresight can lead banks into bad loans, which can culminate in financial crisis, as occurred in the developing countries during the 1980s or in Japan at the end of the 1990s. Japan and the newly developed countries such as Korea had been held up as examples of a successful manufacturing-led development path based on intervention. These Asian countries were delivering 'good news' for a long time over the 1970s and 1980s. Much of the credit for these achievements went to government planners who 'knew what they were doing'. However, when serious regional crises emerged in the late 1990s (essentially because of lightly regulated banking, which was subject to severe moral hazard problems), the truth was revealed: they didn't know. Sceptics argue that Japan and Korea would have had an even steeper growth curve had it not been for selective intervention. Given macroeconomic stability, equilibrium and a stable exchange rate, high and stable savings and investment rates, an enterprising spirit, a respectable level of education, relatively competitive labour markets and a relatively liberal trading system were more than enough to stimulate even faster growth. The contribution of selective intervention was negligible or harmful (Pack, 2000, p. 51).

Second, in a different case, risk-averse governments may countenance stockpiling in order to cushion the effect of a possible crisis. Private markets may not have the inclination and/or funds to do the same in the long term. A government may estimate the cost of this kind of risk in terms of GDP that would be sacrificed in the case of an unexpected reduction in the availability of certain inputs.

Third, governments may wish to keep some facilities for the home production as a bargaining chip to use with foreign suppliers while negotiating prices of long-term supply contracts. This should deter foreign monopolies from charging monopoly prices.

Fourth, market forces are quite efficient in allocating resources among producers and allocating goods and services among consumers in simple and static settings. Much of the power of markets in these circumstances emerges from the fact that prices convey all the necessary information to participants in the market. This enables them to act independently, without explicit coordination, and still reach a collectively efficient solution. It is possible that markets can, at least in principle, solve simple and static problems in a remarkably efficient way, but it is not entirely surprising to learn that the free market game is less successful in more demanding circumstances with market imperfections. Adjustment problems occur because of the unsatisfactory operation of the market/price game viewed from the long-term vantage point. It is the aim of forward-looking intervention to set the economy on the road towards the desired long-term equilibrium.

Fifth, basic research provides significant positive externalities (spillovers) throughout the economy. These social gains are in most cases difficult for private markets to grasp because the private risks and costs may be very high and the benefits uncertain. In addition, without interventions such as patents and other intellectual property rights, free markets cannot guarantee sufficient pecuniary returns to the private risk-taking innovator. The outputs of successful basic research fuel technological progress in the country. In most countries, such research is funded in full or in part by the government either directly (subsidy) or indirectly (tax relief). Governments and private businesses share the risk.

Sixth, industrial policy may ease economic adjustment in a more efficient and equitable way than free market forces. This policy may provide support for R&D, education and training, support for geographical and professional mobility of labour, investment subsidies, protection and other support such as that for the improvement of infrastructure during the early vulnerable period of a new industry. Free market forces fail to do so. As for adjustment and exit from ailing industries, government policy may offer unemployment benefits, vocational training and early retirement schemes. Industrial policy can, to an extent, both anticipate and shape these changes. It can be involved either directly in picking the winners/losers or indirectly by creating the business environment in which firms can make choices in a potentially successful and desirable way.

Seventh, agriculture is a sector in which every government intervenes. Because of the impact of weather conditions and biological cycles, free market forces cannot achieve the reliability of supply and stability of incomes of the farm population relative to the labour force in other sectors. In addition, governments seek to secure the domestic supply of farm goods in circumstances of war, as well as protecting the landscape and environment.

Finally, the eighth reason for the introduction of an industrial policy is that this policy may be able to respond, with various internal and external (retaliatory) measures, to the economic policies of other countries. Left alone, market forces may take advantage of foreign policies in the short term, but if the long-term strategy of foreign competitors is to undermine the importing country's home production by means of predatory pricing in order to create an international monopoly, then the long-term effect may be detrimental to the importing country's welfare. An industrial policy may be a suitable response because it can change the possible free market outcome.

Instruments

Tariffs (trade policy) have historically been the most important instrument of industrial policy. After a number of rounds of multilateral reduction in tariffs under the auspices of GATT/WTO, the use of this instrument has been restricted in scope and reduced in power. However, other methods and instruments of intervention have developed. Some of these represent protectionist pressures against adjustment, while others are adjustment oriented. They include:

- subsidies for exports, production, R&D, education, employment and investment;
- NTBs;
- tax, exchange rate and credit policy;
- public purchases;
- price and exchange controls;
- regulation of the market (such as licensing);
- technical and other standards;
- direct production by the state;
- provision of infrastructure; and
- competition and concentration policy.

The most benign intervention is the kind that does not harm other businesses and sectors. The most effective instruments of such an industrial policy include macroeconomic stability, education and the provision of infrastructure. Low inflation, a stable exchange rate, slightly positive real rates of interest and protection of intellectual property may be the best tools of such an industrial policy. Savings will increase and entrepreneurs will have the chance to observe and shape their future with a relatively high degree of accuracy. Well-educated managers and a well-trained workforce (investment in human capital as a created factor) provide the economy with the most valuable assets capable of solving problems. Moreover, in many cases, private businesses are generally not interested in investing in long-term infrastructure projects (sewage systems, roads, bridges and so on), so the government needs to step in.

Subsidies may be a distorting instrument of industrial policy. They may diminish incentives for the advance of profitable firms if these firms are always taxed in order to provide the government with revenue to subsidise inefficient enterprises. A subsidy that stimulates the introduction of new capital may distort a firm's choice of technologies. This is relevant for firms that use capital and labour in different proportions. If a firm has to pay the full cost of capital it might choose another technology. A one-off subsidy to investment may help a firm buy time and adjust to an unexpected change in technology or demand (its fickleness and sophistication). If the value of subsidies and other favours is smaller than the value added in the given industry, then subsidisation may be justified (but determining this can be quite difficult and uncertain). If subsidies are provided to an industry or firm on a permanent basis for the protection of employment, then there is no incentive for the management to perform as efficiently as in those enterprises or industries where market criteria dominate. A permanently subsidised industry or firm is a very likely candidate for nationalisation.

Sufficient subsidies will always maintain output (in ailing industries) at a level that would be unsustainable in free market conditions. Emerging industries, where investment risk is quite high, have to offer the prospect of relatively higher rewards than elsewhere in the economy in order to attract factors. Gains in productivity in these new businesses may be able to cushion increases in pecuniary rewards to investors without increases in prices. However, faced with the possibility of higher wages in one industry, trade unions may press for increases in wages elsewhere in the economy. Without increases in productivity, the result may be an increase in prices throughout the economy. None the less, the industries that use new technologies and in which productivity is higher than elsewhere in the economy may be one step ahead of other businesses in this race.

The policy of shoring up a 'dying' industry for an excessively long period of time is like moving forwards, but looking backwards. It may be preferable to compensate redundant labour rather than continue to shore up ailing firms. Compensation to redundant labour needs to be provided by the public authorities because the whole society benefits from the process of industrial change and adjustment. Shareholders of dying firms should not be compensated for the depreciation in the value of their shares. They should channel their funds into the growing businesses that need fresh capital for expansion, not to those that are declining and do not need it according to free market criteria (Curzon Price, 1981, pp. 27–9).

In contrast to industries that use ageing technologies, emerging ones require venture capital: they may be quite small, numerous, unstable and have an uncertain future. When they are in trouble their voice may not be heard as loudly as that of declining industries. Investment in emerging firms is risky because many of them collapse before they reach maturity. However, these firms are the greatest propelling agents of a modern economy. Although many of them disappear from the market, many others stay to grow and new ones are created. The OECD survey of nine European countries found that from 12 to 19 per cent of all non-agricultural firms entered or exited the market every year in the 1997–2000 period. Entries represented between 7 and 11 per cent of all active firms and exits averaged about 8 per cent in 1999 (OECD, 2003c, D.10). A high birth rate of new firms is the best indication of the vitality of a system which creates opportunities, so that many new enterprises may be started and the risk accepted. Alfred Marshall drew an analogy between the forest (industry, sector or the whole economy) and the trees (individual firms). Trees may grow and decay for individual reasons, but what is important for the economy is that the forest is there and that it continues to grow.

Entrepreneurs (sometimes seen as 'maniacs with a vision') often have genuine ideas, but many of them do not have the necessary knowledge about how to run a business. Some of them may have the knowledge, but cannot persuade those with funds to support their projects. Why is this so? Reasons include a number of cultural factors (risk-loving or risk-averse investors) and the lack of knowledge and understanding to recognise and seize the opportunity. For example, a century ago a man went to a Belfast bank and asked for a loan to start a company. He explained to the bank managers that his invention was a highly productive mechanical device that would replace horses in ploughing. This was too risky for the bank as it could not foresee that the enterprise would be a commercial success. Hence this man, whose name was Ferguson, went to Canada. He met another man by the name of Massey, they teamed up, and the rest is history. Massey Ferguson became one of the major world producers of tractors and agriculture-related machinery. The moral of this story is that one needs to recognise and seize the opportunity. *Carpe diem*. 'John Gutfreund, chairman of Solomon Brothers, one of the most aggressive investment banks of the 1980s, said successful traders must wake up each morning "ready to bite ass of a bear" ' (Kay, 2004, p. 315).

All protectionist measures offered to an industry should be conditional, otherwise the problems of the industry can be exacerbated. If the protected industry is a declining one, then its adjustment may be postponed or reversed by production or employment subsidies. This increases costs to society in the long term because the desired change (transfer of resources from low- to high-profit industries) does not take place. The adjustment policy needs to be of limited duration. It should involve both public funds and private capital, as well as make the cost of action as transparent as possible. In addition, the recipients of assistance should be expected to develop comparative advantages prior to the termination of that help. Market processes should be encouraged and managerial practices improved.

It has been argued, not without dispute, that protectionism did not cost the US economy any more than the trade deficit did. The real harm done by protectionism (reduction in the efficiency of production because of a fragmentation of markets, as well as prevention of specialisation and economies of scale) is more modest than was usually assumed in the case of the US. The major industrial nations suffer more, in economic terms, from the relatively unattractive problems for economic analysis such as 'avoidable traffic congestion and unnecessary waste in defence contracting than they do from protectionism. To take the most extreme example, the cost to taxpayers of the savings and loan bailout alone will be at least five times as large as the annual cost to US consumers of all US import restrictions' (Krugman, 1990b, p. 36). The reasons why protectionism features relatively highly on the public agenda can be found in politics and symbolism. Politically, free trade offsets economic nationalism, while symbolically free trade is a cornerstone of liberal democracies. In addition, those involved in protected businesses, such as agriculture and manufacturing industries that employ ageing technologies, tend to vote in large numbers, unlike the rest of the population.

Direct subsidies for R&D or indirect subsidies in the form of public procurement are powerful instruments for the support of industries that introduce new technologies or new goods and services. The volume of demand and its structure provides the most important incentive for production. This is also crucial for the strategic industries, whose activities provide external and non-priced gains through linkages and externalities to the rest of the economy (examples include the machine-tool industry, biotechnology, pharmaceuticals, computers, telecommunications and data-processing).[112] If start-up costs create a barrier to entry into a strategic industry, the government may step in and help out. If the governments of other countries are subsidising their strategic industries, the case for intervention by the domestic government can look very persuasive. In the early unstable phase of the introduction of a new production technology, good or service, a secure government demand provides a powerful impetus for the firm to develop the product and open new markets. If this production does not become self-sustaining within a specified period of time, then it may never become profitable and resources that may be allocated for protection may be used elsewhere in the future with a greater efficiency in improving competitiveness.

The costs of subsidies need to be considered before intervention. A subsidy to one firm is a tax on others. If there is the chance of high returns in the future, such a tax might be worth bearing, but the gains are impossible to judge in advance. Once a government starts handing out subsidies, demands for more aid may go on expanding without end. At that point, political power, rather than 'economic sense', determines who gets what and where. The long isolation of an industry from market forces may remove the incentive to respond swiftly to signals that come from competition in international markets.

When affording protection to an industry, it must be on the condition that the schedule of protection/intervention will be revised downwards over time. Protection that is not temporary and selective may create serious adjustment problems and increase costs in the future. The strategy of selection and the transitory nature of protection may provide a limited adjustment period to an industry by mitigating the full impact of international competition. This programme does not ensure the existence of inefficient industries and firms, but rather their adjustment and exit from declining industries. The self-liquidation of protection is perhaps the only way of keeping up the incentive to adjust. If adjustment programmes offer funds to firms, then this must be on the condition that these funds are spent on specified activities. Technical advisory boards that represent a wide community should oversee adjustment programmes (Tyson and Zysman, 1987b, p. 425).

Public intervention in many countries has primarily, but not exclusively, been directed towards 'problem' industries such as agriculture, coal, steel, textiles and footwear. However, there appears to be growing interest in intervening in emerging industries where technology changes fast. Intervention in this case takes the form of providing or subsidising innovation and R&D, special tax treatment of new technologies (tax holidays and subsidies), training of labour, education of management, government procurement and provision of infrastructure, as well as more general instruments such as planning, policy guidelines and exchange of information.

Many of these instruments may be applied to a single target simultaneously, and may sometimes be in conflict. If the objective is to increase efficiency, then competition and concentration may be conflicting. Many industries may not operate efficiently without a certain degree of concentration dictated by minimum efficient economies of scale. So, this has to be accepted. Small countries usually do not have very restrictive anti-monopoly laws, because efficient production in the home (unprotected) market and possibly even abroad often allows the existence of only one efficient production unit. Countries such as France foster a policy of concentration and efficiency, whereas others such as the US, because of the huge home market, have strong anti-monopoly legislation that favours free (internal) competition. Inward-looking industries whose production technologies are in the declining phase of their life cycle traditionally lobby in every country for protection, whereas the emerging industries, which are oriented to the widest international market, support free trade.

Small and Medium-sized Enterprises

It was a strongly held belief in Europe during the 1960s that large American-style companies were the key factor in the economic growth of a country. These enterprises may, among other things, spend substantial funds on R&D and increase the international competitiveness of their output. Hence, mergers and acquisitions were encouraged. That policy left Europe with a number of slumbering industrial giants, ill-equipped to face the challenges of the 1970s and 1980s (Geroski and Jacquemin, 1985, p. 175). However, experience has shown that those countries that spend most on R&D do not necessarily have the highest rates of growth. It was also realised that SMEs,[113] largely forgotten or pushed to the outskirts of traditional economic analysis, are important players in economic revival and employment. Subsequently, the policy that strongly encouraged mergers and acquisitions was abandoned. It is recognised that, per unit of investment, more jobs are created by SMEs than by large companies. This may be one of the outcomes of the business policy of (large) firms that want to avoid conflicts with organised labour. Product differentiation demands production on a smaller scale and decentralisation of business. This is radically different from the prevailing theoretical expectations during the 1960s.

An expansion of SMEs started after the first oil shock (1973). However, jobs created by SMEs often have the disadvantage of being relatively less secure than those in large firms. Being small, these firms need to be flexible if they want to withstand competition. Flexible SMEs often use hit-and-run tactics in their business, linked with low sunk costs, as they can react faster to new business opportunities than more rigid, large firms. 'Small is beautiful' when one wants to move and change, but it is not so 'beautiful' when you want to attract a risky investment. SMEs are often less able than large companies to behave 'strategically' and do not have as much lobbying power. This is because SMEs are vulnerable to the actions of large firms and government policy. Large firms may also have a much larger capacity to deal with uncertainties and international crises than SMEs. Despite this, SMEs are necessary for the balanced growth of an economy, as they provide links among various subsectors. In general, neither large businesses nor SMEs can be efficient in isolation. They both need each other. Big businesses may use specialised SMEs as subcontractors and buffers against fluctuations in demand.

Whereas industrial policy deals with selected industries, policy on SMEs deals with firms of a specific size in all industries. The aim of SME policy is to rectify market imperfections that may work to the disadvantage of smaller firms (uncertain future, high risk, potential isolation, low asset value although not necessarily of 'low quality'). This policy also exploits the positive aspects of relative smallness, such as organisational flexibility, fast and smooth flow of information, product differentiation and custom-made goods and services.

When a large corporation operating in a declining industry closes down a plant in a city dependent on that industry, the first reaction of the government is often to offer subsidies to large new corporations to settle there. However, industrial rhinoceroses attracted by such subsidies usually remain loyal to the area only as long as the incentive lasts. If it is not certain that the incentives (subsidies) will last until the end of the investment/production programme, firms will not be attracted to the area. Risk-averse enterprises may in this situation request larger incentives and/or invest only in projects with relatively high rates of return.

Locally created jobs can be found in the development of SMEs. Of course, SMEs may not create enough jobs in the short term to make up for the loss of jobs in a geographical area where a large corporation has closed down. However, in the past ten to twenty years, SMEs have accounted for more than half of new jobs in some countries, such as the US. In the EU, SMEs are expected to flourish. About 20.5 million SMEs in 2000 were employing about 80 million people (two-thirds of all those employed) in the EU.[114] SMEs are often very efficient because, in spite of their size, they can achieve economies of scale by specialising in a very specific market segment and addressing the entire EU rather than a local or national area (assuming demand for their output exists there). Large Italian firms such as Fiat, Olivetti and Pirelli dominate the domestic market in their industries, but outside Italy these firms have a (very) modest share of world markets. In contrast, Italian firms in industries dominated by SMEs, such as footwear and clothing, are often world leaders (Porter, 1990a, p. 445).

A policy of support for SMEs is quite different from one that fosters the development of a few national champions that are easy to control. Until the 1980s, the EU countries generally regarded SMEs as unstable and marginal firms. Although it is true that many SMEs have a much shorter life-span than large firms (many SMEs disappear from the market before they reach maturity), new ones are continually being created. This is not a worrying sign, but rather an indicator that the economic system is healthy and conducive to trying out new business opportunities. Since the mid-1980s, the EU approach towards SMEs has changed. Many industrial policy programmes now support this type of enterprise. SMEs are of vital importance when a market is in the process of opening and deepening, as was the case with the Single Market Programme. Euro-Info centres act as 'marriage' agencies for SMEs, brokering the establishment of business networks among such firms. This evolutionary and cumulative process needs for its sustenance an educational system that supplies businesses with employees proficient in the skills required. None the less, the EU needs to be much more explicit in its industrial policy towards SMEs. Hence, it has been decided that the European Investment Bank (EIB) should in future support SMEs to a much greater degree than in the past.

Spain has traditionally been a relatively closed economy; hence, it is interesting to explore the impact of the Single Market Programme (market opening) on Spanish SMEs. Although the economy was protected, exporting was widespread among Spain's SMEs even before Spain joined the EU in 1986. Jarillo and Martínez (1991) surveyed a sample of SMEs three years after Spain's entry into the EU, by which time the Single Market Programme was in full swing. They found that:

- almost all SMEs were exporters even when the Spanish economy was still relatively isolated from the rest of the world;
- the costs of production were declining as a competitive advantage, whereas design, style and superior technology were assuming increasing importance;
- two-thirds of the SMEs were exporting to the EU even before 1986; and
- some SMEs saw the Single Market Programme as a threat (the group of firms for which international activities were secondary to their main business in Spain), while none saw it as a new opportunity as access to the EU market had been almost free since the mid-1970s.

Hence, the Single Market Programme was perceived by Spanish SMEs as a 'bad thing' or as a non-event! In spite of that conclusion, there is a large gap in our knowledge of the relationship between economic integration and the behaviour of SMEs.

The opening up and deepening of the internal EU market prompted by the Single European Market brought several advantages to SMEs, including:

- the rationalisation of distribution networks;
- cheaper and fewer inspections of conformity standards;

- diversification of suppliers;
- more efficient stock controls; and
- savings in time and cost of transport.

In addition, the European Council in St Maria di Fiera (2000), Annex III, accepted the European Charter for Small Enterprises. According to this charter (which supports the Lisbon strategy for the future of the EU economy), SMEs must be considered as a main driver for innovation and employment as well as social and local integration in Europe. Policy action towards SMEs should include:

- education and training for entrepreneurship;
- cheaper and faster start-up;
- better legislation and regulation;
- availability of skills;
- improving online access;
- more benefits from the Single European Market;
- taxation and financial matters;
- strengthening the technological capacity of small enterprises;
- successful e-business models and top-class small business support; and
- development of a more effective representation of SMEs' interests at EU and national levels.

However, not everything in the garden is rosy. Many SMEs do not fully understand the operation of the Single European Market. They may be familiar with the concept, but relatively few understand the conditions under which they can use the 'CE' (*conformité européenne*) mark, which shows that the good was produced in the EU and that it meets EU standards. Future EU policy regarding SMEs needs to take account of the following issues:

- easing access of SMEs to financial resources (this was the major weakness of SMEs and is supposed to be mitigated by the new policy orientation of the EIB);
- incentives to individuals to become entrepreneurs;
- a simple and clear regulatory climate in which to start up small business;
- opening up of public contracts to SMEs;
- incentives for advice and technology transfer to SMEs;
- stimulation of innovation in SMEs; and
- modification in education and training beyond primary level in order to assist the unemployed to become entrepreneurs.

Diversification and Reallocation of Resources

The promotion of adjustment of some industries does not always go smoothly. Some ailing industries are well-established, relatively large employers of labour with a strong political lobby. This is often the case with the steel industry. However, some steel firms undergo adjustment quite successfully. Such was the case with the US Steel Company, which closed 13 steel-making units and diversified out of steel. The company invested funds in a shopping centre in Pittsburgh, Pennsylvania, and a chemical business in Texas. Steel-making came to account for only 11 per cent of US Steel's operating income (Trebilcock, 1986, p. 141). Other steel companies prefer a quiet life. They neither innovate nor compete, but they are able to mobilise powerful political forces and government policy instruments (for example, tariffs, quotas, NTBs, subsidies) in order to resist adjustment (contraction in output and labour redundancies).

The response of a number of US firms to shocks such as an increase in labour costs during the 1970s and 1980s was to stick to the same technology, but to invest abroad where labour costs are lower. In contrast, the response of Japanese firms to the same shock was to change technology and increase productivity. In addition, some Japanese TNCs operating in the US increased the US content of their goods over and above the domestic content of their US counterparts in the same industry. A number of US firms wanted to compete with Japanese TNCs in the home market, not necessarily on the basis of productivity, but rather on the grounds of low labour costs. Thus, many US firms started either to source heavily from abroad (developing countries) or to geographically relocate their labour-intensive operations there or both. Japanese TNCs operating in the US increased productivity, so that, for example, by the mid-1980s colour TVs sold in the US by domestically owned firms had less local content than those made by Japanese competitors. In 1987, cars produced in the US by Honda had a local content of over 60 per cent. This was expected to increase to 75 per cent over the following 10 years (Graham and Krugman, 1995, pp. 79–80).

The newly industrialised countries have substantially increased their competitiveness in traditional industries such as steel, shipbuilding and textiles. China has become highly competitive in certain parts of mass market electronics. Their output position is irreversible in the medium and, perhaps, long term. These industries cannot be recovered in the developed market economies on the grounds of reductions in wages. Such a policy would involve a waste of resources, as trade unions would resist cuts in wages to meet the level of wages prevailing in the newly industrialised countries which have productivity at a level similar to that in developed market economies.

When economic adjustment is spread over a number of years, it may appear to be easier and less costly per unit of time. Some 'breathing space' for structural change (slowing down the attrition or keeping ailing industries alive) may be achieved, but this argument is not always valid. First, the damage to the rest of the economy is greater the longer a depressed industry is allowed to last and, second, there is no evidence that prolonged adjustment is any easier to bear than quick surgery. Even direct costs may turn out, in practice, to be higher (Curzon Price, 1981, p. 120).

Picking the Winner/Loser

The new theory of trade and strategic industrial policy found, in contrast to neo-classical theory, that some manufacturing and service industries may be relatively more 'important' to an economy than others. These are the industries with economies of scale, numerous forward and backward linkages and non-priced spillover effects (externalities) on the rest of the economy. Privileges granted to these industries *may* create a new irreversible competitive advantage for a country.

The findings of the new theory are not prescriptions for economic policy, but rather an agenda for further research (Krugman, 1993b, p. 164). A selective industrial policy goes hand in hand with a policy of picking a winner (creating a national champion) or a loser (bailing out). Industries are established or maintained in or removed from certain geographical locations. This process has always been difficult and risky and has demanded considerable and costly information. If this were not so, then you would probably not read this book, but rather look at the stock market report, and invest and increase the value of your assets by several zeros daily. Today's winner, if wrongly chosen and requiring permanent subsidies, may become tomorrow's loser. When intervening, it is important to have reasonable aims and it is preferable to use policy tools in an indirect way and be ready to withdraw from the project if undesirable events occur, in order to prevent even greater damage and losses.

The preference for picking the winner most often occurs in those countries whose domestic market is small and unable to support the competition of several firms operating at the optimum level of efficiency. In theory, national free market policies can be fostered in large countries, such as the US, which can leave market forces to select the best suppliers. Smaller countries usually have to rely on selective policies, which are potentially riskier. They have to make the best use of the limited amount of available resources. These resources have to be concentrated on selected industries (specialisation). Such an industrial and trade policy may be termed 'cautious activism', which should not be taken to mean protectionism.

Whereas France relies on a relatively centralised model of the economy, Germany has fostered a decentralised model. However, these two countries have achieved a similar level of economic success (de Ghellinck, 1988, p. 140). When picking the winner, a government chooses between supporting emerging industries and propping up ailing ones (protection of the existing structure which is adjustment averse). The balance between the two depends upon both the power of the industries involved and the aims of the government.

The policy of singling out certain industries or firms for special treatment inevitably means ignoring the problems of all the others. This policy support of national champions, which was in vogue during the 1970s, includes showering them with taxpayers' money. The background idea is that 'size equals power'. The 'neglected' businesses are at a relative disadvantage because they cannot count on direct support from the state if they happen to be in need. In addition, they are taxed in one way or another in order to provide funds for the public support of the 'privileged' businesses. This drains funds for investment in the promising enterprises. Such a policy has a strong impact on the geography of production.

Neglecting emerging and expanding industries with strong positive externalities can reduce the inclination of entrepreneurs to take risks and jeopardise the growth of the economy in the future. If a government cannot formulate the basic structural objectives of national economic policy, then the politically strongest segment of business will seize it.[115] Policy will be formulated in a hurry in response to the political pressures of the moment, with the likely outcome of protecting troubled industries. Independence, resistance to business pressures and clear economic objectives on the part of government remove extemporisations in economic policies. If this were not the case, a country's industrial policy would be an instrument for supporting obsolete industries and a brake on expanding ones (Tyson and Zysman, 1987a, p. 22). The history of trade and industrial policy (just look at the GATT rounds of negotiations) reveals how hard it is to combat the entrenched interests of producers.

Output grows fastest in *emerging* industries, which do not necessarily create a significant number of direct jobs but, as a result of linkages and other externalities, have good potential to create indirect jobs. There has, however, been a notable technological improvement in *declining* industries such as textiles and steel. Thus, the distinction between the two kinds of industry is mostly for analytical purposes, as there are no industries with obsolete production technologies, but rather firms (within those industries) that employ ageing technology.

An astute government may note that the industries are no longer sharply divided into 'good' and emerging industries such as electronics, and 'bad' and declining ones such as shipbuilding, as was the case in the 1970s and 1980s. In fact, it has become apparent that there is to a large extent a 'global' structure of manufacturing, whatever the industry. In these circumstances and if other factors are the same, the law of supply and demand will always locate the lowest value-added part of the production chain in the geographical area with the lowest wages. In these circumstances, a smart option for the risk-averse developing country may be to choose first to establish a 'good declining industry', rather than an uncertain expanding one. Of course, the potential consequence of this type of expectation and choice may be a decline in the standard of living relative to countries that have adopted a different development model and are successful (?!) in its implementation.

Targeting (selection or welfare ranking) is linked to four basic issues:

- *which* industries or firms should receive support;
- *what* kind of support should be provided;
- *where* they are located; and
- *how long* the assistance should last.

The industries that are singled out for 'special treatment' are usually those that are significant employers and those that have important externalities or strong lobbying power. In addition, if private markets do not favour risky investments, such as the development of alternative sources of energy, then governments may also single out such investments for special treatment.

If domestic regulations regarding safety standards are stricter and more costly to apply at home than abroad, then, other things being equal, this may place home firms at a disadvantage relative to foreign competitors. Such a case may be used as an argument for demanding some national public 'support' and international involvement in these affairs in order to force foreign competitors to adhere to a similar level of environmental protection. This issue was important during the eastern enlargement of the EU.

Political reasons such as national defence and pride may influence decisions about support for certain industries. Assistance should cease as soon as the beneficiary becomes profitable; or once it becomes obvious that this will never happen (governments are on the whole known to be unwilling to slash subsidies when there is evidence of failure as happened during the Concorde project); or after the expiration of the specified period of assistance. Governments may not know which choice would become a winner. However, they need to know when they have a loser that ought to be eliminated.

Japan is thought to be an example of a country that has reaped the fruits of conscious targeting of certain manufacturing industries for several decades. As a result it has stayed one step ahead of its competitors regarding new technologies in the targeted industries.[116] During the 1960s, the target industries were steel and shipbuilding because of their externalities and economies of scale. Even though Japan is short of natural resources, cheap sea transport was able to offer advantages over other countries that had resources at home, but had to transport them overland at higher cost. All this could provide sources of competitiveness for Japan. Another target was the production of cheap and shoddy goods such as toys.

The energy crises and vulnerabilities of the 1970s shifted Japan's manufacturing emphasis away from the polluting and resource-intensive production of steel towards machine tools and cars. The target for the 1980s was R&D-based electronics (photocopiers, computers, audio and video equipment and consumer electronics). R&D-based production was the target for the 1990s, principally in the semiconductor and information technology industries. However, instead of making adaptive efforts as in the past, Japan had to undertake original R&D activities.[117] This may be taken as an example of the shaping of comparative advantage in a dynamic context for a specified, relatively limited, period of time.

Japanese 'targeting' was first and foremost an information-collecting, interpretation and transmission process which helped individual firms to make investment decisions. Japan emphasised intervention in technological areas that created a large bilateral trade surplus with the US, rather than intervention in firms. However, in spite of the success in high-technology industries, average living standards in Japan are below those in the US or the EU. Part of the explanation may be found in the relatively high proportion of Japanese national resources that are devoted to stagnant industries compared with the US.

Japanese industrial targeting has not always been successful, for a variety of reasons. During the 1960s, MITI selected steel and shipbuilding as the 'winners'. Intervention (support) was quite substantial. At that time, Japanese corporations faced an identical business choice and also opted to invest in these industries, although this would have happened even without government intervention. Japan then targeted the production of aluminium and petrochemicals, a choice that was subsequently proved by the first oil shock to be a mistake. MITI tried to reduce the number of car manufacturers (electronics was not on the priority list) during the early 1960s as the US and Europe were at that time ahead of Japan in this industry.[118] In spite of official opposition to expansion, net entry took place including Honda, Mazda and Subaru (Porter and Sakakibara, 2004, p. 39). Private enterprises continued to invest independently, and were successful without public support (if one leaves aside the relatively closed domestic market). The private policy was right and yielded positive results for some decades to come.

If left alone, private businesses may sometimes find highly successful solutions. Throughout the 1990s and beyond, Microsoft (which ended up as a global monopoly) was the prime example of such development in the US. However, it is impossible to know in advance which company from which industry and in which location will replicate the success of Microsoft.

During the 1990s, Japanese industrial policy was transformed. Increased emphasis was given to deregulation and privatisation in the economy together with safeguarding the traditional consensus-building spirit. As for the targeting of 'high-growth industries', the evidence that is emerging does not reveal Japanese success in this area. 'Targeting was actually more prevalent in the uncompetitive Japan, while a large proportion of the competitive industries had no government targeting' (Porter, 1996, p. 88).

From the mid-1990s, China has fostered a policy of big national champions in certain areas of manufacturing. These champions (for example, TCL in television sets and mobile phones) dominate the domestic market and try to capture a share of the global one.

Elsewhere in the developed market economies, the policy of targeting has not always gone so smoothly. After the Second World War, industrial policy relied partly on the unorganised labour that was flowing from agriculture and abroad into the manufacturing industry. This situation has changed. Trade unions try to organise labour. This may influence (that is, postpone) economic adjustment, even though it may be to the long-term detriment of the economy.

France is keen to create large and efficient firms that can compete in international markets. It is less concerned with domestic competition. France's Interministerial Committee for the Development of Strategic Industries decides on the key industries, defines the strategy and chooses a firm to be national champion to implement that programme. The implementation method takes the form of a contract between the government and the designated firm. Unfortunately, however, the French government has not always had perfect foresight. Misjudgements were made in very costly projects such as Concorde and computers during the 1960s. The Concorde project was a technological success and an engineer's delight. The project started in 1962 when fuel was cheap and when air travel was for the elite. However, Concorde consumed a large amount of fuel, it was too noisy and there were trade-offs between speed and passenger comfort. The air travel market has changed significantly over the past four decades. Flying is a mass market. Most passengers travel for pleasure and fun, not for business. Hence, Concorde was a commercial failure and was finally grounded in 2003.

The French strategy for computers was to try to build large mainframes in order to compete directly with IBM, rather than to begin with small computers or peripheral equipment and learn by doing over time. This was too ambitious for the relatively undeveloped French firms to cope with, so the effort failed. The mistake might have been avoided if government industrial policy makers had consulted more with private experts. Private firms also make mistakes, but they are less likely to ignore market forces (and the various choices that they offer, in particular when using their own or shareholders' funds) than government officials who use taxpayers' money and who are often subject to various political pressures and their own re-election goals.

The early French mistakes, however, were not in vain. During the Airbus[119] project, the government learned to select the segment of the market for which demand would be high. It also tied customers by early purchasing of aircraft parts in exchange for orders (Carliner, 1988, p. 164). This is the most, and perhaps the only, successful example of overt targeting in Europe.

Chile can offer an example of successful targeting with its salmon industry. Until the mid-1970s, Chile exported hardly any salmon, but during the early 1980s it adopted and modified fish-farming technology from Norway and Scotland. The success was such that Chile entered the league of major world exporters of salmon.

Leyland is an example of failed targeting in Britain. The government's intention was to consolidate domestic car companies under the leadership of Leyland. The result was the destruction of the united company. However, Britain acquired a dynamic and fragmented car manufacturing industry and market from the 1980s. It is dominated by the Japanese TNCs that transferred into Britain the industry lesson from Japan: domestic competition is the key element for global competitiveness. Italy's Fiat is struggling because of the long-term damage caused by its status as national champion. French and German car manufacturers, however, provide examples of how firms can compete internationally with success without constant government intervention.

Direct targeting of particular industries or firms has not been a striking feature of US industrial policy. The American system was conceived and established in such a way as to foster, in principle, individual freedom, not to discriminate among firms or industries. The only exceptions are agriculture and steel, as well as sporadic bailouts of firms such as Lockheed (1971) or Chrysler (1979). Government consumption on all levels, however, creates a big overall demand pull to the economy owing to a huge general expenditure and the budget deficit. As a part of public expenditure, defence-related[120] and selective public procurement indirectly influences the development and expansion of high-technology industries with a significant long-term impact on private consumption. For example, from the early 1960s NASA (US National Aeronautics and Space Administration) began to demand computers for spaceships that had to be small, light and powerful. The industry provided such computers, and once they were commercialised, personal computers (PCs) flooded the global market.

The American software industry was a spillover from the US public procurement policy that imposed uniform standards. This was essential for the industry's subsequent commercial development and success. Hence, the argument that the US government does not intervene in the economy does not hold water. In special situations (for example, during the Second World War), the US had an explicit industrial policy.[121] In addition, the US has become the major producer of food in the world as a consequence of calculated economic and other policies that embraced various subsidies.

Other success stories in the developed countries reflect the period of protection in every country in this group. Each of them substantially protected its home market during early stages of development. Even a few generations ago, the Japanese car industry developed after the Second World War behind a big protective wall. Without protection, the industry would probably have become an outlet of the US TNCs. The development and expansion of the aeroplane manufacturing industry in the US and Europe was based on significant government intervention. Public intervention was also valuable in establishing the computer industry in Taiwan, which is now the world's largest supplier of computer monitors, motherboards and various PC peripherals. A similar example can be found in intervention by the government of Singapore to opt for the production of hard discs.

Human capital and human resource management are key factors in increasing a country's comparative advantage in a situation of rapidly changing market conditions and technology (which reduces the need for unskilled labour). Basic choices, such as the education of ethnologists or engineers, singers or mathematicians, lawyers or designers, influence a country's geography of production and the competitiveness of its goods and services. Macroeconomic policy may support, in an important way, the creation of comparative advantage, but it is human capital (properly organised, valued and continuously educated) that presents the major lever in the enhancement of a country's competitive advantage.

One has to bear in mind that there is a big redistribution of income: from those less skilled (or less fortunate) towards those with many skills. This takes place among regions within each country, but also on an international scale.[122] 'Old' rules, where real wages go hand in hand with an increase in productivity, no longer apply. High productivity no longer warrants high wages. With high international mobility of goods and capital there is always somebody elsewhere in the world willing to do the same job for less money (Krugman, 1996b).

During the 19th and early 20th centuries, bright British pupils were steered towards the classics in Oxford and Cambridge, while technical subjects were reserved for the less gifted. The situation was the reverse in France, Germany and Japan. After the Second World War, British industry began to recruit widely from the universities. A career in industry, even if a fifth choice after callings to the Foreign Office, the BBC, academia or the Church, became socially acceptable for the sons (and increasingly the daughters) of the Establishment (Sharp and Shepherd, 1987, pp. 83–4; Porter, 1990a, p. 115).

Some may argue that government planners and other public officials in France,[123] Germany and Japan may be more competent and sophisticated than managers in private firms in these countries. The best and most ambitious students aspire to government service. In North America, society has a different attitude. Many people look on government jobs as inferior to those in the private sector because, among other things, they are less well paid. It is not surprising to find that Japan, France and Germany have an 'open and direct' industrial policy, while the US and Canada do not, at least not overt industrial policies. Nevertheless, shoddy economic policies in these two countries might be easily amended if civil servants were given a freer hand by the system (Brander, 1987, p. 40).

4.4.3 EUROPEAN UNION

Rationale

The grounds for the introduction of an industrial policy in the EU can be identified in at least seven related areas:

- If uncoordinated, national policies introduce a wasteful duplication either of scarce resources for R&D or investment in productive assets of suboptimal capacity. If minimum efficient economies of scale demand access to a market that is wider than the national one, then there is a case for a common EU approach to the issue. Some competition in the diversity of R&D, ideas and production is necessary because it can be a source of creativity. None the less, the authorities need to strike a harmonious balance between competition and coordination, in order to profit from both of them. Hence, a certain degree of coordination of industrial policies at the EU level contributes to the efficiency of the policy.

- A common or a coordinated industrial policy in a large and expanding EU market may wield a deeper (positive or negative) impact on the economy than any isolated national policy can, no matter how big the national market of a member country.
- With free mobility of factors in the EU, any disequilibria in a national economy may first provoke an immediate and massive outflow or inflow of capital and, afterwards, of other factors if the disequilibria are not corrected. If a government wants to cool down the economy by increasing the rate of interest, the result may be the opposite from the desired one. High rates of interest will provoke a large inflow of foreign hot capital and the economy may become 'overheated'. The eurozone eliminated this danger for the participating countries. Therefore, the deeper the integration in the EU, the less effective are national macroeconomic policies that are pursued in isolation. A common or coordinated EU policy in such circumstances is more effective than the sum of national ones.
- Although EU firms are rivals on the EU internal market, they are allies in competition against firms from third countries both in the world and in the Single European Market. If national economic policies used to tackle the same problem are different and have undesirable and unwanted spillover effects on the EU partner countries, then there are grounds for the introduction of a common industrial policy.
- Another argument may be found in the 'unfair' trade and industrial practices of foreign rivals. An EU industrial policy may act as a countermeasure.
- No matter how disputed in theory, concern about employment always carries weight in daily politics.
- Last, but not least, there is a case for externalities that create market failure (the difference between private and social benefits). When there are undesired spillover effects across the frontiers of a single country from, for example, large investments in certain businesses that pollute, then the appropriate response to such events can be found in a common EU policy.

In spite of the arguments in favour of an EU industrial policy, one should not be misled into thinking that this is a substitute for national policies. On the contrary, national and EU policy should be complementary. In fact, EU policy should apply only to those areas where it has the potential to be more beneficial than national policies (the principle of subsidiarity). In general, policies at EU level need to be as general as possible, while those with a local dimension need to be custom-made and specific. There has to be coordination between the EU and national/local policies in order to avoid the implementation of conflicting instruments even when there is agreement about the major goals to be attained.

One of the principal aims of the Treaty of Rome was to increase the competitiveness of output of domestic firms relative to the US at the time of the creation of the EU (1957). The intention was to locate new and expand existing industries in order to take advantage of the economies of scale that would be provided by an enlarged EU market. It was primarily the expansion of domestic demand that stimulated the development of both the US and, later, Japan. Competitiveness was created in these two countries on the basis of the secure, even protected, large domestic market. In comparison with the US and Japan, no member state of the EU could claim to have a very large domestic market. The EU was conceived, among other things, to redress this 'disadvantage'.

Before the establishment of the EU, small European countries' industrial policy was often defensive (for example, subsidies to protect employment) rather than aggressive (for example, risky entry into new industries). In the 1960s, relatively weak anti-merger laws created the potential for the establishment of large European corporations which could, it was thought at that time, successfully compete with their US and Japanese rivals. However, the problem was not merely in the size of firms in the EU. Fragmented by NTBs, the internal market of the EU had as a consequence economic rigidity that shielded many national firms from both EU internal competition and the necessary adjustment. The outcome at that time was that in certain manufacturing industries, relative to the US and Japan, the EU came close to being a 'manufacturing museum'.

Protectionism has been the instrument of EU industrial policy in spite of the costs and postponement of adjustment. Resistance to abandoning obsolete technologies and industries permitted others, most notably Japan, to gain the competitive edge and penetrate the EU market with many high-technology goods. This was pronounced during the 1980s. All trade measures that protect the textile industry in the developed world were scrapped from 2005. This was the consequence of the 1995 Uruguay Round WTO deal. The textile industry in the EU and US had a 10-year 'advance notice' to adjust to this competition from other countries, particularly from China. As the textile industry in the developed world has largely failed in this endeavour, one wonders just how much longer it (or any other industry) needs to adjust to a change?

Without domestic restructuring, and with the exception of German and Dutch firms and some from a few other countries, foreign TNCs that are located in the EU and that operate in the expanding industries may be among the first major beneficiaries of the Single European Market. If the instruments of protection and cartelisation (for example, in the coal and steel industry) are not coupled with other tools of industrial policy (for example, contraction of obsolete industries or assistance for a limited time for the introduction of new technologies), then such a policy will be ineffective from the resource viewpoint. It may be pursued by those who choose to do so and who can afford to be wasteful.

Evolution

The first attempt to introduce a 'real' industrial policy in the EU dates back to 1970. The European Commission's *Memorandum on Industrial Policy* (the Colonna Report) aimed to shape the structure of EU industry and to set priorities for common action. As there was no strong legal basis for the introduction of a common industrial policy in the Treaty of Rome, the report restricted itself to ambitious general statements and five recommendations:

- The report foresaw the creation of a single EU market (such as the US) based on the abolition of internal barriers to trade.
- It required the harmonisation of legal and fiscal rules that would ease the establishment of enterprises throughout the EU.
- It envisaged the creation of a European Company Statute. Although the EU had existed for more than a decade, firms were very slow to merge businesses across national boundaries. As TNCs were perceived to be important vehicles for improvements in competitiveness and technology relative to foreign rivals, there was a need for the support (intervention) of intra-EU mergers and acquisitions. The absence of EU corporate law presented a serious problem. Large national corporations that tried to merge at the EU level, such as Fiat-Citroën, Agfa-Gevaert, Dunlop-Pirelli or Fokker-VFW, soon gave up. A notable exception is Airbus (set up in 1970). The pan-EU TNCs that survived to 'adolescence' were those (Philips, Shell, Unilever) that had existed long before the establishment of the EU.
- Changing demand conditions create a need for economic adjustment. This adaptation could be achieved smoothly if there was an encouragement of geographical and occupational mobility of labour and upgraded business management.
- The final recommendation was an extension of the EU solidarity regarding foreign competition, R&D and finance.

Consideration of the report ran into difficulty, as there were two opposing views. On the one hand, Germany did not want any interference in industrial policy at either the national or the EU level. On the other hand,

France was in favour of coordinating national economic policies. Other countries sided with one or other of these views.

The next step in the shaping of EU industrial policy was a *Memorandum on the Technological and Industrial Policy Programme* (the Spinelli Report) in 1973. Basically, it was a scaled-down version of the Colonna Report. The new report argued in favour of the exchange of information, the coordination of national R&D policies, joint R&D projects and the elimination of national technical barriers. The broad strategy did not fully succeed because of different economic philosophies among the member countries. After the oil crisis the member countries pursued nationalistic industrial policies and were not very interested in a joint approach to the issue. In fact, they passed on to the EU the adjustment of the problem industries (steel, shipbuilding, textiles and in some cases even cars) via trade, social and regional policies, while keeping the management of expanding industries under national control. During this period there was only some coordination of technical standards and joint actions in R&D.

A profound step towards the elimination of NTBs in internal trade, competition and, hence, industrial policy came with the introduction of the 1985 programme *Completing the Internal Market* (the Cockfield Report). This supply-side-oriented 'technical' programme had 282 industry-specific legislative proposals for the elimination of NTBs, as well as a timetable for their implementation by the end of 1992. The adoption of the Cockfield White Paper (1985) and the Single European Act (1987) provided the EU with the means to apply the Single European Market programme. The objective was the achievement of a genuine single internal market through the adoption, implementation and enforcement of 282 measures (directives). This was the outcome of the political determination of the member states to eliminate NTBs on internal trade and change their 'atomised' industrial policies. The EU tried to employ its resources in a more efficient way by a reduction in physical, technical and fiscal barriers to internal trade (elimination of X-inefficiencies).

The classical integration method (elimination of tariffs and quotas) in the EU exhausted its static effects at the end of the 1960s. A new approach, the ousting of NTBs, favoured full factor mobility. It was implemented in order to create a genuine frontier-free internal market in the EU. The stress was on a change in the rules, rather than on additional funds. The creation of a homogeneous internal market, such as that in the US, which benefits from enormous economies of scale, was not expected. The Europeans have, on average, far more refined and deeply rooted tastes, hence they value and benefit from variety and wide choice. They demand and are often ready to pay for superior quality and diversity. The aim of the Single European Market was simply to improve competition and market access to diverse national, regional and local markets, as well as to introduce flexible and large-scale modes of production where appropriate.

The abolition of customs duties and quotas in the EU benefited only those industries that serve private consumers. There is also another market, that for goods and services consumed by governments. Industries that employ new technologies failed either to serve the entire EU market for these goods and services, or to profit from economies of scale because of the existence of NTBs. These national industries compete for public funds and orders, which is why EU firms tended to cooperate more with partners in the US or Japan than among themselves. By entering into a joint venture with a Japanese firm, an EU enterprise made up for its technological gap without forgoing the protectionist shield and/or privileges in the form of public procurement, major export contracts, tax relief and R&D accorded by the state (Defraigne, 1984, p. 369). Another explanation of these developments is that EU firms were interested in forming partnerships with firms that were market or technology leaders regardless of their nationality, origin or geographical location (Narula, 1999, p. 718). The outcome of such a policy was that EU standards for high-technology goods were non-existent, and relatively large and protected national corporations, which were not very interested in intra-EU industrial cooperation, were created. These firms were unable to respond swiftly to changes in the international market. An obvious example of this sluggishness was the relatively slow adjustment to the oil shocks.

EU company law was required to help meet the objectives of the Treaty of Rome regarding the harmonious development of economic activities in the EU. Thus, the European Commission proposed the European Company Statute in 1989. The arguments in favour of the statute include the elimination of the difficulties that come from the current national tax systems for those firms that operate in several EU countries. Business in the entire EU market would be made simpler and less costly if the firms were incorporated under a single code of law. The absence of this statute was estimated to cost the business community €30 billion a year.[124] The statute was adopted in 2001 and entered into force in 2004. It offers a possibility for firms that operate in more than one EU country to be established as a single company under EU law. This allows business operations throughout the EU under one set of rules and a unified management and reporting system, rather than under different national laws of each member state where they operate. The case against the statute is that increased interference by the EU may jeopardise national sovereignty.

The European Commission was not without further ideas on industrial policy. The 1990 Bangemann Communication, *Industrial Policy in an Open and Competitive Environment*, had, basically, the following three proposals.

First, industrial policy needs to be adjustment friendly. This has to take place within the framework of a liberal trade policy. Second, EU industrial policy has to be in accord with other common policies. They need to reinforce one another. Third, difficulties within industries or regions need to be settled by the employment of horizontal measures. The means for the achievement of these ideas should include an improvement in the operation of both the internal market and the international market, as well as the creation of an investment-friendly environment for risk taking in the EU.

The 1993 Delors White Paper, *Growth, Competitiveness, Employment*, aimed to prepare the EU for the 21st century. Its major stated goal was a reduction in unemployment. This was to be achieved, among other means, by an ambitious wave of investment from various sources into the following areas: €400 billion over 15 years into transport and energy in trans-European networks; €150 billion until the year 2000 into telecommunications; and €280 billion over 12 years into environment-related projects. The Council of Ministers did not support the project and it was shelved because of budgetary austerity measures.

Following a Council of Ministers resolution (1992) calling for an overall analysis of the effectiveness of measures taken while creating the Single European Market, the European Commission undertook a comprehensive analysis of the entire set of economic policies in the EU. The Monti Report (1996) was followed by 39 volumes of background studies published by Kogan Page in 1997–98 under the title *The Single Market Review* (European Commission, 1997c). They were split among six headings: manufacturing, services, dismantling of barriers, trade and investment, competition and economies of scale, and aggregate and regional impact of the Single European Market. The full impact of the Single European Market could not be fully predicted as the effect of the removal of some NTBs (non-technical barriers) on the geography of production and welfare would be fully felt only in the longer term. However, the report gave directions for the preservation of the Single European Market and the implementation of the eurozone from 1999.

The impact of the Single European Market is most obvious in highly regulated (and hence fragmented) industries such as pharmaceuticals. A major regulatory change in the EU took place with the establishment of the European Agency for the Evaluation of Medicinal Products in 1995. As a result, this traditionally local government-controlled industry changed significantly. The Single European Market altered the business practices of firms in the pharmaceuticals industry in seven ways:

- *Market authorisation* National regulatory authorities that control the introduction of new products at different rates affect not only the location of production and trade, but also the health and life of patients. To change this, the European Agency for the Evaluation of Medicinal Products became the single decision-making body in the EU in 1995. However, pharmaceutical firms still have the choice of following a centralised procedure that leads to a single authorisation for the entire EU (this procedure is mandatory for products derived from biotechnology) or a decentralised procedure based on mutual recognition of national marketing authorisations. It seems obvious that firms will tend to locate in the country with the least regulatory delay and then make use of the principle of mutual recognition to market their products throughout the EU. The result is that pharmaceutical companies are no longer required to follow the sometimes archaic regulations of a single authority, but can 'shop around' to find the most flexible one which will give the fastest approval and enable a speedy market launch of the products. Biotechnology, an area that arouses tremendous hope for the future expansion of business and at the same time fear of the new and unknown, is unified at the EU level. This gives security to customers in the Single European Market.

- *Dependence on domestic market* Before 1995, more than 60 per cent of pharmaceuticals produced in France, Germany, Greece, Italy, Portugal and Spain were sold on the domestic market. This was the consequence of preferential government procurement from local firms, insistence on local R&D and local content requirements. Since the opening up of the EU market, firms selling primarily to their national markets have been in jeopardy: in the pharmaceuticals industry it is no good being a large fish in a small pond. Even in the US, large domestic manufacturers have experienced a dramatic fall in their market share, and in the EU 'globalisation' is the only means of survival. This can be achieved by internal growth, alliances and cooperation with other firms or through acquisitions. A lack of preferential treatment (market deepening that came from the Single European Market) was a wake-up call to these companies to start sharpening their competitiveness, which had suffered from earlier government protection.
- *Parallel trade* In 1974, the EU Court of Justice ruled in favour of parallel importation (*Centrafarm* v. *Sterling Drug*), that is, the purchasing of drugs in a low-price market and their repackaging and diversion to other markets. The principle is that medicinal drugs are permitted to move freely from one country to another if the importing country provides a marketing authorisation. As long as drugs are priced differently in different EU countries, this type of trade will

continue to exist. This 'temporary situation' will disappear with full market unification. With rising pressure on their health budgets, governments are encouraging these forms of competition and 'price reduction'. At present, prices in southern European countries are usually lower, hence most of this trade is going northwards. The introduction of the euro in 1999 marked the beginning of the process of a greater price transparency. Combined with Internet shopping, consumers can find out almost instantly where to buy the cheapest medicines. There is great potential for parallel imports. However, an emerging trend is for TNCs to treat the EU as a unified market and to sell new drugs at the same price throughout the EU.

- *Regulated prices* The price of drugs varies between EU countries for many reasons: price control schemes, variation in the costs of production, variable exchange rates, differences in reimbursement systems, transfer pricing, patent status, package sizes, rebates and taxes. The difference in price between the cheapest and most expensive country may be as much as tenfold. The Single European Market is bringing a slow convergence in drug prices, but progress is slow and many of the distortions mentioned will continue to be present for some time. The introduction of the euro has been the principal factor in bringing price harmonisation throughout the EU. New drugs are registered centrally and are sold at the same price across the Single European Market. Previous obstacles such as exchange rates are disappearing and firms look at the EU member countries as one economic entity. This is the only weapon in the business community's armoury if it wants to enjoy undisturbed presence in all regions.
- *Expenditure for R&D* Competition will stimulate innovation. R&D for new drugs directed at the regional and global market will increase. R&D in the pharmaceuticals industry has always been mission oriented, regardless of integration.
- *Rationalisation of operation* Producing a drug involves the manufacture of the active substance and, subsequently, the conversion of this ingredient into different dosage forms. The former has been centralised in the EU, whereas the latter has been decentralised. Many plants are not benefiting from economies of scale as they are operating at between one-third and one-half of their capacity. Overcapacity in the pharmaceutical industry is estimated to be 40 per cent worldwide. Plant closures and alteration in the geography of production are imminent, partly because of new manufacturing methods and partly as a consequence of market opening in the EU, which will bring benefits in the form of economies of scale. At the same time, firms are being attracted to move location within the EU by regional benefits

(subsidies) aimed at reducing unemployment in the subsidy-giving region. It is fast becoming irrelevant in certain cases whether company headquarters or manufacturing capacities are based in Germany, France or Spain, for example. Aventis, the largest European pharmaceutical company, formed by the merger of Hoechst and Rhône-Poulenc Rohrer, has its headquarters in Strasbourg and has adopted English as the common language of communication across the company.

- *Mergers and acquisitions* There are still many opportunities for consolidation in the pharmaceutical industry when compared with, for example, car manufacturing. Consolidation of the industry is expected to accelerate in the next few years. During the mid-1990s the largest pharmaceutical company in the world commanded less than 5 per cent of the total world market. Expect to witness in the coming years fast growth of companies in this industry as they strive to achieve synergies, cut costs, obtain bigger R&D budgets and reach a bigger 'critical mass'. Examples of this trend so far include the purchase of Syntex by Hoffmann-La Roche and the mergers of Hoechst and Rhône-Poulenc Rohrer into Aventis, Ciba Geigy and Sandoz into Novartis, Astra and Zeneca, and Glaxo Wellcome and Smith Kline Beecham. This trend will continue and, in addition to major US mergers, such as that between Pfizer and Warner Lambert, one may expect to see more transatlantic mergers, such as that between Pharmacia and UpJohn. This consolidation is resulting in R&D departments big enough to develop new drugs, as well as the ability to produce medicines in the most efficient way unhindered by local differences that were previously limiting factors in the growth of the pharmaceutical industry in the EU.

Competitiveness, as the ability of the economy to provide its population with high and rising standards of living and high rates of employment on a sustainable basis, is at the very heart of the ambitious goals set for the EU by the European Council in Lisbon (2000). The Lisbon Agenda was an attempt to introduce a new integration and growth vigour into the EU following the introduction of the Single European Market and the creation of the eurozone (for the select group of EU countries). This agenda was intended to unlock the EU's growth potentials, in particular regarding the limp performance compared with the American economic virility.

Achieving the demanding Lisbon goals depends in large part on the ability of the EU to foster and exploit new profitable competences and, where it already has them, they should be maintained and developed. There are a few tough competitors for the position of 'the most competitive and dynamic knowledge-based economy in the world'.[125] The EU has to innovate, but the omens are not very encouraging. Political declarations must be translated more forcefully into action in the EU member countries. In order to achieve the Lisbon objectives, the following shortcomings must be addressed:

- While 'grand projects' such as the Single European Market from 1993 or the eurozone (1999) were achieved through legal means, the ambitious and far-reaching Lisbon Agenda is an intergovernmental project that lacks an enforcement mechanism. The European Commission was engaged in its creation only as a minor partner.
- Regarding the 'transposition deficit', what is agreed at the EU level needs to be applied at the national level. This 'open' method of coordination is not binding enough. Member states often fail to meet deadlines (particularly if the implementation of the decision is costly). This may reflect either certain 'technical difficulties' or a lack of enthusiasm about the project or both. Enforcement mechanisms are weak. The European Commission cannot force a member state to implement the Lisbon Agenda.
- An important part of the Lisbon Agenda deals with a change in rigid labour markets. However, the reform of this area is in the hands of national governments which face tough resistance to changes in this field.
- Yet another part of the problem is that the EU budget is ill-equipped (small and skewed towards farming) to promote growth.

Important barriers to entrepreneurship in the EU do not come mainly from the barriers to entry, although administrative obstacles are present. To start up a firm in the US, time is counted in days. To do the same in the EU countries, it is counted in months. Key administrative barriers in the EU countries come from impediments to adjusting and expanding businesses. Job-protection laws discourage firms from new hiring.

So, is the implementation of the ambitious and demanding Lisbon strategy a semi-failure or a semi-success? Were expectations about long-term benefits 'oversold'? Was comparison with the US economy wide of the mark? Shouldn't the EU try to emulate the 'household' Scandinavian, rather than the ill-fitting American, economic model and best practice? Has there been too little investment in the instruments (information and communication technology; R&D; reform of the labour market) to achieve results? A few issues may have been dealt with by the mid-term review. To achieve more in a better and more efficient way with ever-decreasing prices is important. However, that is not all. The EU is clearly reminded of this in the field of agriculture. The lesson should also be learned in other areas of economic activity. Important obstacles for the faster achievement of the Lisbon objectives include the still fragmented service markets. There are also measures which are still firmly in the hands of national governments. These include labour markets and pension reform. The only difference in the policy tools for tackling each of these issues is in the degree of bitterness and discontent that they bring. Should Europe follow the American model, then – a model in which there is highly uneven distribution of welfare, including health care? This may not wash in Europe unless the politicians convince the voters that the long-term Lisbon-related 'gains' can more than compensate for the current 'sacrifices'.

In February 2005, the European Commission prepared a communication, 'Working Together for Growth and Jobs: A New Start for the Lisbon Strategy',[126] as a background document for the mid-term review of the Lisbon process by the European Council. The Commission recognised that progress has been at best mixed. The Commission did not intend to rewrite the Lisbon Agenda, but rather to give it a new start. The Commission wanted to make the EU a more attractive area in which to invest and work. Knowledge and innovation should be the 'beating heart of European growth'. General policies are needed to enable the business sector to create more and better jobs. Failure to achieve the Lisbon objectives has a cost in the widening gap in the EU's growth potential compared to other economic partners. The future implementation of the Lisbon Agenda should also be reflected in the new financial perspective (2007–13) and in an overall increase in R&D spending by a third, to reach and stay at the level of 3 per cent of GDP.

One of the proposed actions related to an improvement in the governance of the Lisbon process. This is because the division of responsibilities between the EU and member countries was not clear – there were too many overlapping reporting and listing procedures with little 'political ownership'. The EU's role appeared to be that of a think-tank.

According to the 2005 communication, member states are expected to adopt national action programmes for growth and jobs with clear commitments and targets. They also need to appoint a focal person, a 'Mr' or 'Ms' Lisbon at government level and to simplify reporting. There should be only one Lisbon report for the EU and for each country on the progress made. This would repair the existing weakness of the whole process: delivery. As such, this would assist the European Council to give guidance each spring and the European Commission to monitor the process.

One of the statements in the communication (p. 13) is striking: 'Productivity growth and increased employment must go hand in hand. We need to avoid the type of jobless growth that has marred the performance of the US economy in the past years.' There is much talk and concern about the imminent shortage of labour in the EU from around 2010 because of the demographical trends. There are also serious anxieties and doubts about the negative effects that could lead to more immigration, in particular mass immigration. Perhaps the elimination of such a stated policy goal from the communication could provide a solution to the problem. The answer may be to foster jobless growth based on an increase in productivity of the existing workers built on knowledge and innovation in the EU.

The European Council had a mid-term review of the Lisbon Agenda in March 2005 in Brussels. It concluded that the achievements were mixed after five years, and that the Lisbon strategy should be relaunched. In general terms, there are three actions that could have been taken in this situation:

- create a strategy that would reduce national budget deficits in the medium term;
- adopt a directive on the creation of single market in services; and
- scale down the wide Lisbon Agenda and focus more specifically on growth and employment.

However, the European Council did just the opposite: the eurozone budgetary rules were relaxed and the work on the single market in services (the expected principal contributor to growth and employment) was scaled down. On the one hand, France and Germany welcomed the idea about the single market in services, but on the other they were reluctant to accept the consequences of such a market: an inflow of low-cost labour from central and east European member countries. They wanted deeper integration, but without any adjustment problems. It is unlikely that the EU can make more progress towards the stated goals without a greater degree of flexibility in the labour market. It is little comfort that the Council broadly supported the ideas presented in the communication by the European Commission: an increase in funds to achieve the stated Lisbon objectives; emphasis on learning and R&D; and an improvement in the governance of the process (every spring the European Commission is to present a report to the European Council on the progress made).

At the end of 2002, in an earlier step in the development of its industrial policy, the European Commission had approved a communication, 'Industrial Policy in an Enlarged Europe'. This was an attempt to define this important policy area in the light of eastern enlargement. EU industrial policy must take into account the requirements of other policies (economic, social and environmental), but it should also attend to the needs of the manufacturing industry itself. It is not easy to reconcile the consistency, dynamic interaction and balance among these policies and their objectives as there are no magic solutions. The document recognises the importance and weight of the services sector in the economy, but it acknowledges that the manufacturing industry is the source of EU prosperity. It also rejects the flawed view that manufacturing will no longer play a key role in the knowledge-based information and services society.

In many segments, the EU manufacturing industry is modern and competitive – in spite of a slight relative reduction of EU manufacturing products in world trade over the past decade (the principal rivals suffered even more from the arrival of new actors such as China and other newly developed countries). The weak element in EU manufacturing *vis-à-vis* principal rivals is productivity. Even though investment in computers and information technology was substantial, productivity gains are still slow in coming.

Two key factors of industrial competitiveness deserve particular attention in the EU according to the 2002 communication:

- *Knowledge and innovation* There is a need for improved efforts in education, vocational training and R&D to put the available accumulated knowledge at the disposal of industry. This is nothing new, but it has to be signalled repeatedly. New technologies, including electronics, bio- and nanotechnology, have to be developed, as do the skills and know-how to use them. The number of patents in the EU is much smaller than is the case in the US. However, the EU fares very well in other industries. In order to counter the negative developments, the European Commission is addressing one of the roots of the problem: a lack of investment in R&D. It wants to increase the current average level of investment of 1.9 per cent of GDP to 3 per cent in order to match the US and Japanese investment of 2.7 and 3 per cent, respectively. One area where the EU lags behind particularly is R&D financed by the private sector.[127] Every sector and activity should be constantly initiating, refining and improving its products, services and processes. The conditions to stimulate vigorous innovation have to be in place.
- *Entrepreneurship* This is the capacity and will to take risks and establish new, improved or different businesses. A (large) number of Europeans are too reluctant to bear entrepreneurial risk, too readily satisfied with limited business growth and unwilling to acknowledge and reward the social contribution of risk takers. They should be encouraged to change this behaviour.

A recent attempt to regulate a part of the manufacturing industry concerned chemicals. The European Commission maintains that various chemical substances are responsible, at least in part, for the increase in the number of allergies and other illnesses over the past decades. These chemical substances range from ingredients in cosmetics to flame retardants in furniture. Therefore, in 2003 the Commission proposed an overhaul of the way in which the chemical industry is regulated, by shifting the burden of safety testing from governments to the industry. A single integrated system, REACH (Registration, Evaluation and Authorisation of Chemicals), would replace over 40 directives and regulations, and would treat existing and new substances equally. The objectives are to protect health and the environment, as well as to stimulate innovation and competitiveness.

About 30 000 chemicals that already existed before 1981 and that were unaffected by various subsequent directives will have to be tested for their safety. (Intermediate chemicals that do not leave factories are exempted.) The industry strongly objects to such proposals, which would cost it €2.3 billion according to the European Commission, and more than 10 times that amount according to the industry itself.[128] Animal rights campaigners also protest against this proposal as millions of animals would be killed needlessly since companies would have to replicate tests to obtain approval for the same product. It is doubtful whether such ambitious proposals will be furthered in the immediate future, even though the European Commission claims that total health benefits of the legislation may be as high as €50 billion over 30 years.[129] The question is how to handle older chemicals (and assure everyone that they are safe) in a way that does not jeopardise one of the best-performing EU industries.

Technology Policy

Since the 1960s, some of the major factors determining industrial structures in the developed market economies have included changes in technologies, foreign competition, environmental issues, changing employment patterns and an ageing population. With this in mind, the European Commission was initially more concerned with industries in crisis. However, from the 1980s it started to become more involved with the industries and technologies of the future: those that have strategic importance for the competitiveness of goods (and services) in the internal, as well as external, markets. Therefore, during the mid-1980s the EU introduced various technology-push programmes with the aim of creating and sustaining leadership in the market. In designing these programmes, the European Commission has to balance the interests of the DG Competition, which advocates *laissez-faire*, and the other DGs, which favour policy intervention. These programmes have (indirectly) resulted in the technology policy of the EU. The technology policy is necessary because of significant technological spillovers throughout the economy.

Until the mid-1980s, the form and direction of R&D in the EU fell within the remit of national governments (with the notable exception of the European Atomic Energy Community: Euratom). The model for the national approach was to some extent the Japanese experience of public support to industries from MITI in the form of exchange of information, cooperation and partial funding of R&D projects. A change came with the Single European Market Programme. The legal basis for the EU action in R&D came in 1987 via the Single European Act (Title VI). Although there had been previous initiatives, the member governments decided for the first time to contribute significant funds for R&D to EU programmes. According to the revised Treaty of Rome, the EU will strengthen its scientific and technological bases and encourage competitiveness at the international level (Article 163). The European Commission and the member states are supposed to coordinate policies and programmes carried out at the national level (Article 165). The EU needs to adopt a multiannual framework programme for its R&D projects (Article 166). The EU may cooperate with third countries or international organisations to implement its long-term R&D programme (Article 170).

One goal of the EU is to strengthen links between research institutes and entrepreneurs throughout the EU in order to transform the long-held perception in Europe that science (that is, R&D) is culture, whereas in the US it is business. However, in the US there is another factor that encourages a fast reaction to changing technologies. Vigilant financial markets in the US often look favourably on certain risky (short-term) investments by innovative firms. This ethos of support for such innovation, still missing in Europe, forces American firms to adjust rapidly to shifting markets and changing technology. This explains a sizeable part of the difference between the US and the EU in terms of commercial exploitation of the results of R&D.

In circumstances in which strong national elements still dominate, the EU should endeavour to coordinate national policies, promote cooperation in R&D and production, and support the flexibility of the industrial structure. Coordination of national policies regarding declining industries should avoid an integration-unfriendly beggar-thy-neighbour mentality. In the light of the (irreversible) changes brought about by the Single European Market and the eurozone, expanding industries (those in which production technology is changing) should introduce common EU standards that facilitate large-scale production and an increase in competitiveness. The objective is to avoid the creation of incompatible standards, as happened with the PAL and SECAM television systems. During the 1990s, the European Commission and national governments spent heavily (in the event, wastefully) on the development of analogue high-definition television (HDTV), which was rendered obsolete by the advance of digital technology. It would have been far more preferable for the Commission and governments to improve the R&D environment than to target possible technology winners.

There are several reasons for the EU's dependence on third-country suppliers of high-technology goods. On the supply side, EU investment in R&D is lower than in the US and Japan; the EU also allocates fewer human resources to R&D and there are often delays in putting into production and marketing the results of R&D. On the demand side, national 'attitudes' (for example, buy domestic) may limit the potential demand for high-technology products in EU countries, making it difficult for EU high-technology manufacturers to achieve the necessary economies of scale. European firms are less receptive to new products than their US and Japanese rivals, there is a lack of strong links between producers and consumers, and there is inadequate training in new technologies (Jacquemin and Sapir, 1991, pp. 44–5).[130] Various EU technology programmes are intended to redress this situation.

Philips and Thomson led the lobby of EU companies in the early 1980s pressing national governments for the completion of the Single European Market as the principal cure for countering the (past) Japanese ability to be always a few steps ahead in the high-technology business game. The Round Table of European Industrialists (rent seekers) was successful in eliciting support from governments for the Single Market Programme. When the US announced the 'Star Wars' project in 1983, EU industrialists started to worry. First the Japanese took over a large part of the market for consumer electronics, then the Americans seemed to be en route to domination of the market for advanced industrial goods. Subsequently, the Round Table, created in 1983, pushed for the creation of a transnational industrial policy in the form of EU support for high-technology research projects. In spite of budgetary restrictions, the big EU industrialists were successful again (Curzon Price, 1993, pp. 399–400).

Implementation of EU policy in R&D takes the form of five-year framework programmes[131] which were introduced in 1984. The purpose of these medium-term instruments is to integrate and coordinate all assistance/aid for R&D in the EU.[132] The programmes lay down objectives, priorities and the budget for EU-sponsored R&D. By distributing funds to selected research projects, the EU sets guidelines for specific R&D programmes. Based on the findings of the FAST (Forecasting and Assessment in Science and Technology) programme,[133] the EU introduced about 20 publicly supported programmes for industrial cooperation among EU firms in the R&D stage. Most of the programmes would be beyond the financial capability and will of the participating countries to finance alone. These programmes include the following 'winners':

- A dozen renowned information technology firms from Britain, France, Germany, Italy and the Netherlands wanted to pool resources, share risk and attract subsidies from the EU (although this begs the question of why leading-edge companies should need to form cartels and seek such support). None the less, the pressure group they formed (the Round Table) lobbied both national governments and the European Commission to adopt the European Programme for Research in Information Technology (ESPRIT) to try to 'correct market failures' in R&D. The European Commission was receptive to the idea and together with the Round Table won approval from the national governments. The EU adopted the programme, that is, picked a winner, in 1984. Under the auspices of ESPRIT, the EU funds half of the cost of any project that is in line with the EU terms of reference and that is supported by two or more firms from different EU countries. The other half of the funds has to come from the participating firms and national sources. Eligible projects must be in the field of pre-competitive R&D. So far, the Commission has refused to subsidise joint production in order to avoid criticism from the US about subsidies. Indeed, the Commission has tried to argue that it does not operate a large-scale industrial policy at all, but rather a series of R&D programmes (Curzon Price, 1990, p. 178).
- Research and Development in Advanced Communication for Europe (RACE) is a spillover programme from ESPRIT. Its aim is to advance the telecommunication network in Europe in the future by means that include standardisation and coordination of national telecom services.
- Basic Research in Industrial Technologies in Europe (BRITE) aspires to revitalise traditional industries in the EU. This is to be achieved through the introduction of new technologies in these industries although it is not always obvious what is 'strategic' about the industries. Perhaps the concern here is more about employment than anything else. Public money is spent on projects that financial markets find unattractive.
- The Biotechnology Action Programme (BAP) is small relative to its 'strategic' potential in the future.
- European Collaborative Linkage of Agriculture and Industry through Research (ECLAIR) is like the BAP: relatively small, but with great potential for finding solutions regarding food in the future.

It contributes to the establishment and reinforcement of intersectoral links between agriculture and manufacturing.

- The European Research Cooperation Agency (EUREKA) was established by 17 countries (from the EU and EFTA) on the initiative of the French in 1985. Its formation was a response to the American Strategic Defense Initiative ('Star Wars'). Its objective is the development and production of high-technology goods. It is not confined to pre-competitive R&D as the other programmes are, and other countries may be included in some of its programmes. EUREKA is, however, not an institution of the EU. It has a small secretariat in Brussels and has gained popularity in the business community.

Inter-firm strategic alliances in the development of technology in the EU increased sharply during the 1980s. In addition, the European Commission became quite heavily involved in projects on a cost-sharing basis. Over 70 per cent of private (largely non-subsidised) strategic technology alliances were formed to exploit joint R&D of new core technologies in informatics, new materials and biotechnology. A major field of cooperation was in information technologies, with over 40 per cent of all strategic technology alliances falling into this area (Hagedoorn and Schakenraad, 1993, p. 373). A comparison between established 'private' cooperation in R&D and cooperation sponsored by the EU found that they are very similar. In fact, 'subsidised R&D networks simply add to already existing or emerging private networks and merely reproduce the basic structure of European large firm co-operation' (Hagedoorn and Schakenraad, 1993, p. 387). This being the case, it is difficult to understand why leading and large firms in the EU need subsidies! If the 'official' network largely reproduces the already existing 'private' one, then it is surely largely redundant. The financial resources consumed in promoting cooperation might be better used elsewhere (for instance, on programmes that are not in the field of informatics such as biotechnology or education or infrastructure).

The basic theoretical justification of intervention has always been a need to correct a market imperfection. Incomplete private appropriability of results of R&D may be the issue at stake here. One of the principal conundrums linked with the establishment of a technology policy is whether publicly supported R&D complements or substitutes R&D efforts in private firms. There are theoretical arguments that support either view.

- Public finds are necessary as R&D is costly, uncertain and risky for the private sector. Hence, a public push is necessary. This may be through tax concessions or grants to firms. It may be in the form of guaranteed procurement contracts that signal future demand. The frustrating problem is, however, the lack of systematic evidence that may confirm the obvious contribution of public funds.

- The private sector may be more careful with own R&D funds and selection of projects (than is the public sector) and may know in some cases better than the government which final outcome may 'fly' on the market. If the public sector enters the same kind of R&D, the government may be using (wasting) public funds for something that the firms would do anyway. In addition, firms may be hesitant about public involvement in R&D. At the end of the process, the government may wish to disseminate R&D results. That may endanger the market position of the firm in which innovation took place. It is possible that the government may select projects that are of no or little interest to firms.

Studies and literature surveys arrive at ambiguous conclusions regarding the issue of whether public funding is additional to or replaces private expenditure on R&D (there may be a slight tilt towards complementarity) (David et al., 2000; Garcia-Quevedo, 2004). This continues to create difficulties in economic policy making. Therefore, in some cases public involvement in R&D may be more an issue of belief than of knowledge.

The question of whether replication of R&D networks is the result of a powerful lobby or whether it is necessary to accelerate R&D in the private sector because of significant externalities remains to be answered. Decisions taken at the EU level are easy targets for special lobbies as they are too far removed from the public to monitor. The co-decision procedure between the Council of Ministers and the European Parliament introduced by the Maastricht Treaty was an attempt to overcome this drawback. Although it is a step in the right direction, there is still a danger that EU technology policy may become just a sophisticated new form of protectionism.

The Sixth Framework Programme (2002–06) disposes of €17.5 billion. It aims to contribute to the creation of a true 'European research area' as a kind of internal market for science and technology. It fosters scientific excellence, competitiveness and innovation through the promotion of better cooperation among relevant actors at all levels. This recognises the fact that economic growth increasingly depends on research and innovation, and that many of the present and foreseeable challenges for industry and society can no longer be solved at the national level alone. It is hoped that this programme will prove to be the financial instrument that makes the European research area a reality.

Past framework programmes have helped to develop a culture of scientific and technological cooperation between different EU countries.

The programmes have been instrumental in achieving good research results. This has not, however, created a lasting impact on greater coherence at the European level. The Sixth Programme has therefore been redefined and streamlined with the following objectives:

- concentration of EU efforts on fewer priorities, particularly on areas where cooperation at the European level presents clear added value;
- moving towards progressive integration of activities of all relevant participants working at different levels;
- promotion of research activities designed to have a lasting (structural) impact;
- support of activities that will strengthen Europe's general scientific and technological basis; and
- use of the scientific potential of accession countries preparing for EU entry for the benefit of European science at large.

The priorities of the Sixth Programme include:

- life sciences, genetics and biotechnology for health (€2.2 billion);
- information society technologies (€3.6 billion);
- nanotechnology, multifunctional materials and new production processes (€1.3 billion);
- aeronautics and space (€1.1 billion);
- food quality and safety (€0.7 billion);
- sustainable development, global change and ecosystems (including energy and transport research) (€2.1 billion); and
- citizens and governance in a knowledge-based society (€0.2 billion).

Earlier framework programmes have mainly been implemented through cooperative research projects. In most cases the end of a given research project meant the end of the consortium of research partners. In many cases projects did not reach the necessary 'critical mass' to have a real, structural and long-lasting impact in scientific or in industrial or economic terms. To help solve these problems and to work towards the creation of the European research area, two new instruments have been designed in the Sixth Framework Programme:

- *networks of excellence* in different countries aim to integrate activities of network partners (universities, research centres and firms); and
- *integrated projects* are projects of substantial size, designed to help build up the 'critical mass' in objective-driven research with defined scientific and technological aims and applications.

A great deal of public money has been poured into R&D over the past decade in the EU, but the results have been very slow in coming. Of course, the effects of fundamental R&D cannot be predicted with a high degree of accuracy. As public funds are limited, and as the results of R&D are more important than the origin of the work, companies from foreign countries may take part in the R&D projects of the EU on a case-by-case basis, but without any financial help from the Commission. Production everywhere in the world is becoming more and more 'globalised'. Thus, forcing co-operation in R&D only within the EU may squander taxpayers' money. 'Global' production requires an open (global) industrial and trade policy system.

A changed and improved new industrial strategy of the EU and its member states needs to take into account first and foremost the crucial role played by the development of human capital in the long-term competitiveness of the economy. The creation of a prosperous learning society has to give priority to the creation of human capital, especially skills that create, spread, absorb and extend new technology in production, organisation, marketing and control. In addition, there may be a need for selective intervention in the form of subsidies, promotion of cooperation and information exchange during the pre-commercial phase of R&D projects that may give (oligopolistic) advantages to EU producers relative to foreign rivals. The EU has invested in the past in industries in which there is a high risk of failure and where Japan, the US and from recent times even China are strong. Part of the reason for the relative failure of electronics in the EU during the 1970s is that domestic firms were sheltered from foreign competition. In contrast, in areas where the EU faced global competition, for example commercial aircraft (Airbus), the EU achieved a considerable degree of success.

The growth of knowledge currently doubles every three to four years.[134] This stimulates and drives knowledge-based societies to be involved in a 'war without shooting'. This competition is most obvious across Europe, North America and the Far East. If deemed appropriate, selective intervention in new technologies needs to be aimed at those expanding industries in which EU businesses already have or could create internal resources. This means that EU efforts and funds should be focused not on the replication of industries in which the US,[135] Japan[136] and China[137] are strong (cooperation with them may be a better choice), but primarily where there are grounds for the development of genuine EU technologies and comparative advantages. These may be the development of new production technologies for relatively traditional industries such as food, textiles and furniture, as well as in areas where the EU has strengths. The industries where the EU excels include mobile phones, semiconductors, aeronautics, medical technologies, nanotechnologies, super-fast trains, chemicals and pharmaceuticals, as well as heavy electrical machinery and equipment. The EU is relatively weaker in areas such as information technology, biopharma and biotechnology.

Not only now, but also in the coming decades, there will be an increased overlap between mechanical, electronic, chemical, medical and biotechnology industries. The EU has a reasonable chance of remaining the leader in some of these fields. This may be aided by the problems in the Japanese economy which became apparent at the end of the 1990s. However, there are many dangers in this area. Although there have been important scientific achievements in genetic engineering (for example, cloning of animals), these are often associated with serious ethical, moral, social and religious questions. In addition, serious negative side-effects may emerge from new technology in breeding, biotechnology and genetic engineering, as was the case with 'mad cow disease'[138] in Britain in 1996 and beyond.

Outlook

The competitiveness of a country's goods and services on the international market in modern times is often much more created than inherited. The leader in some lines of production cannot be sure that this position will endure in the long run. Competition is threatening firms from all sides. Being on the top is no longer a state, but rather a process. Therefore, one can find scope in the EU for industrial cooperation and risk sharing. It could be established both in the pre-commercial and during the commercialisation stages of R&D. In this way, inefficient duplication or multiplication of R&D would be eliminated and resources saved and redirected elsewhere. However, the creation of knowledge is not enough to keep a country at the competitive edge. That knowledge needs to be applied in practice with commercial success. Here the US fares much better than the EU. The US system and culture offers wide opportunities to start and restart promising businesses. If sound profit-making ideas fail (for whatever reason) in Boston, there are further chances in Seattle or San Francisco. The Americans treat past business failures like battle scars – as something to be worn with pride. In Europe, the situation is different. If your business start-up fails, you can forget another one for a while, unless you cross the Atlantic.

The elimination of most NTBs on internal EU trade brought by the Single European Market has had its greatest impact on 'sensitive' businesses, and this will continue to be the case. These businesses are those that were protected by high NTBs and which experienced large price distortions, for example, the production of goods that are publicly procured either in the high-technology sector (for example, office machines, telecommunications and medico-surgical equipment) or in traditional manufacturing sectors such as electrical and railway equipment, pharmaceuticals, wine and boiler-making. Businesses protected by relatively modest NTBs will also continue to be affected by market liberalisation and deepening. These include motor vehicles, aerospace equipment, basic chemicals, machine tools for metals and textiles and sewing machines.

Some outsiders feared that the Single European Market would lead to the creation of 'Fortress Europe' as a result of a combination of intra-EU liberalisation and an increase in the existing level of external protection. However, the EU has no such plan, nor would it serve its long-term interests. If the word 'fortress' was mentioned, it was only as a potential bargaining chip with major trading partners. It was expected that the Single European Market would lead, among other things, to increased competition and efficiency, which would reduce prices in the EU. Therefore, even without any change in the existing level of nominal protection, the real level may rise. Any additional increase would be neither necessary nor desirable. On the contrary, increased efficiency prompted the EU to reduce the level of trade protection in the Uruguay Round deal. None the less, the Single Market Programme has influenced the timing and extent of external FDI in the EU. Many foreign TNCs entered the EU in order to become 'internal' residents of the EU prior to full implementation of the Single Market Programme. They wanted to pre-empt any potential moves towards the creation of an EU fortress from the start of 1993.

Potential changes in the rules of origin and local content may, however, discriminate against 'internal' goods with a relatively high external import content. This may be reinforced by a discriminatory application of testing procedures and standards. A fortress mentality may be introduced in the EU through the social(ist) over-regulation of labour issues. If this is done in the future, it could provoke protectionist winds that would make the security of current jobs more important than the long-term efficiency and adjustment of the economy.

Customs union (phase 1 in the EU's integration) offered an incentive to businesses, but its effect was spent by the end of the 1960s. Something novel and more radical was needed. Phase 2 is represented by the formation of the genuine Single European Market, with an unimpeded flow of goods, services and factors, in 1993. This provided the EU with a new momentum. The member countries decided to reintroduce the principle of majority voting (except for fiscal issues, national border controls, working conditions and environmental issues) in order to ease the procedure to implement the Single European Market. In 1999, phase 3 of the integration process, the eurozone, reinforced earlier achievements in integration and removed all possible internal exchange rate variations for participating countries.

The EU member countries realised that the cost of failing to integrate (that is, a 'non-Europe') was too high to be ignored. An EU without internal frontiers (at least for residents of the member countries), as envisaged in the White Paper, could increase GDP in the EU by up to 7 per cent and create 5 million new jobs, if accompanied by supporting national policies (Emerson et al., 1988, p. 165). The 'costs' of these real gains are more freedom for business and less regulation. The opponents of the Single Market Programme were not able to create a more attractive and feasible economic strategy and ultimately gave up the attempt to do so. Only inefficient businesses or those that failed to compete and adjust would lose out in the new situation. As the Single Market Programme (1985–92) was not accompanied by a chain of bankruptcies throughout the EU, this is an indication that the businesses sector has absorbed the change without any serious and negative shocks. However, the programme was merely the first step. One has to bear in mind that it was merely a medium-term strategy. The Maastricht Treaty rearranged the decision-making process in the EU and set the 'agenda' for the eurozone.

Tables 4.13 and 4.14 show annual percentage changes in, respectively, real GDP growth rate and real gross fixed capital formation (investment) in the EU(15) and candidate countries in the 1990–2006 period. Also shown for comparison are the same indicators for the US, Japan, Switzerland and China. Although the actual figures differ for each country in the EU, economic cycles show a certain degree of synchronisation. The most obvious example is 1993, when most of the EU countries were in recession. That was the first year of the Single European Market in the EU. However, it would be unfair to blame negative macroeconomic trends on the failure of the Single Market Programme. Integration is, after all, no more than an instrument to support general national macroeconomic policies. If the policies are right, integration can contribute to their reinforcement. It is still too early to draw any definitive conclusions about the impact of the eurozone, introduced in 1999, on growth. Gross fixed capital formation (investment) shows business interest in the future. A change in this indicator in one period of time may provide signals about the business confidence and the growth rates of output and GDP in the next period. Although the two economic indicators shown in the tables differ among EU countries, the common feature is that their interrelation is almost always strongly positive (signs of slight synchronisation of cycles).

Well, 1992 has come and gone, and the single currency was introduced in the eurozone in 1999, but still the economies of the EU countries have not shown any great expansion despite widespread expectations and predictions of the beneficial effects of the Single European Market. There was even a recession in 1992. Has something gone wrong? Perhaps not. Economic

Table 4.13 Real GDP in EU, candidate and other select countries, 1990–2006 (percentage change over preceding year)

Country	1990	1991	1992	1993	1994	1995	1996	1997	1998	1999	2000	2001	2002	2003	2004*	2005*	2006*
Austria	4.7	3.3	2.3	0.4	2.6	1.6	2.0	1.6	3.9	2.7	3.4	0.7	0.2	0.8	1.9	2.1	2.2
Belgium	3.1	1.8	1.5	−1.0	3.2	2.4	1.2	3.6	2.0	3.2	3.9	0.7	0.9	1.3	2.7	2.5	2.2
Finland	−0.3	−6.3	−3.3	−1.1	4.0	3.8	4.0	6.3	5.3	4.1	6.1	0.7	1.4	1.4	3.1	2.4	2.3
France	2.6	1.0	1.5	−0.9	2.1	1.7	1.1	1.9	3.4	3.2	5.1	1.1	2.3	1.9	2.3	1.5	1.7
Germany	3.2	2.8	2.2	−1.1	2.3	1.7	0.8	1.4	2.0	2.0	2.9	0.8	0.1	−0.1	1.7	1.4	2.0
Greece	0.0	3.1	0.7	−1.6	2.0	2.1	2.4	3.6	3.4	3.6	4.5	4.3	3.6	4.5	3.7	2.7	2.7
Ireland	8.5	1.9	3.3	2.7	5.8	9.9	8.1	10.9	8.8	11.1	9.9	6.9	6.1	3.7	5.6	4.9	4.7
Italy	2.0	1.4	0.8	−0.9	2.2	2.9	1.1	2.0	1.8	1.6	3.0	1.8	0.4	0.3	1.2	1.2	1.5
Luxembourg	5.3	8.6	1.8	4.2	3.8	1.3	3.7	7.7	7.5	6.0	9.0	1.5	2.5	2.9	3.7	3.7	3.5
Netherlands	4.1	2.5	1.7	0.9	2.6	3.0	3.0	3.8	4.3	4.0	3.5	1.4	0.6	−0.9	1.4	1.5	2.0
Portugal	4.0	4.4	1.1	−2.0	1.0	4.3	3.5	3.9	4.5	3.5	3.4	1.7	0.4	−1.2	0.8	1.5	1.7
Spain	3.8	2.5	0.9	−1.0	2.4	2.8	2.4	4.0	4.3	4.2	4.4	2.8	2.2	2.5	2.7	2.5	2.3
Eurozone	3.6	2.6	1.4	−0.8	2.4	2.3	1.5	2.4	2.9	2.9	3.5	1.7	0.9	0.6	2.0	2.0	2.0
Denmark	1.0	1.1	0.6	0.0	5.5	2.8	2.5	3.0	2.5	2.3	2.8	1.6	1.0	0.5	2.0	2.6	2.2
Sweden	1.1	−1.1	−1.7	1.1	4.2	4.0	1.3	2.4	3.6	4.6	4.3	1.0	2.0	1.5	3.6	2.8	2.9
UK	0.8	−1.4	0.2	2.5	4.7	2.9	2.6	3.4	2.9	2.4	3.1	2.0	1.6	2.0	3.1	2.4	2.8
EU(15)	2.5	1.4	1.2	−0.3	2.8	2.5	1.7	2.6	2.9	2.8	3.6	1.8	1.1	0.9	2.0	2.3	2.0
Cyprus	7.6	0.6	9.8	0.7	5.9	6.1	1.6	2.5	5.0	4.8	5.0	4.1	2.1	1.9	3.4	3.8	3.5
Czech R.	–	−11.6	−0.5	0.1	2.2	5.9	4.3	−0.8	−1.0	0.5	3.9	2.6	1.5	3.7	3.8	4.3	4.4
Estonia	–	−10.0	−14.1	−8.5	−1.6	4.3	3.9	9.8	4.6	−0.6	7.8	6.4	7.2	5.1	6.0	5.8	5.6
Hungary	–	−11.9	−3.1	−0.6	2.9	1.5	1.3	4.6	4.9	4.1	5.2	3.8	3.5	3.9	4.0	3.7	4.0
Latvia	–	−10.4	−34.8	−14.9	0.6	−1.6	3.9	8.4	4.8	2.8	6.9	8.0	6.4	7.5	8.0	5.0	5.0
Lithuania	–	−5.7	−21.2	−9.8	6.2	4.7	7.0	7.3	5.1	−1.7	3.9	6.4	6.8	9.7	6.6	5.8	5.6
Malta	6.3	6.3	4.7	4.5	5.7	6.2	4.0	4.8	3.4	4.1	6.4	−2.4	2.6	−0.3	0.7	2.0	2.0
Poland	–	−7.0	−33.9	3.8	44.5	7.0	6.0	6.8	4.8	4.0	4.0	1.0	1.4	3.8	5.4	4.3	4.0
Slovakia	–	−14.6	−6.4	−3.7	5.1	6.5	5.8	5.6	4.2	1.5	2.0	3.8	4.6	4.5	5.5	5.8	5.9
Slovenia	–	−8.9	−5.5	2.8	5.3	4.1	3.8	4.6	3.8	5.2	3.9	2.7	3.3	2.5	4.3	3.9	3.7

New EU(10)	–	−9.6	−2.8	0.2	3.6	5.5	4.7	4.7	3.6	3.1	4.1	2.4	2.4	4.0	–	–	–
EU(25)	–	0.9	0.9	−0.3	2.8	2.7	2.0	2.8	3.0	2.9	3.6	1.8	1.2	1.2	2.3	2.2	2.1
Bulgaria	−9.1	−8.4	−7.3	−1.5	1.8	2.9	−9.4	−5.6	4.0	2.3	5.4	4.1	4.9	4.3	5.5	4.5	4.7
Romania	−5.6	−12.9	−8.8	1.5	3.9	7.1	3.9	−6.1	−4.8	−1.2	2.1	5.7	5.0	4.9	5.0	5.1	–
Croatia	−7.1	−21.1	−11.7	−8.0	5.9	6.8	5.9	6.8	2.5	−0.9	2.9	4.4	5.2	4.3	3.7	3.7	4.2
Turkey	9.3	0.9	6.0	8.0	−5.5	7.2	7.0	7.5	3.1	−4.7	7.4	−7.5	7.9	5.8	4.5	5.0	4.0
Switzerland	3.7	−0.8	−0.1	−0.5	0.5	0.5	0.3	1.7	2.4	1.5	3.6	1.0	0.3	−0.4	1.4	1.6	2.0
United States	1.8	−0.5	3.0	2.7	4.0	2.7	3.6	4.4	4.3	4.1	3.7	0.8	1.9	3.9	3.8	3.3	2.9
Japan	5.2	3.3	1.0	0.3	1.0	1.9	3.4	1.8	−1.1	0.1	2.4	0.2	−0.3	1.3	1.7	1.4	1.1
China	–	8.0	13.6	13.4	12.6	10.5	9.7	8.8	7.8	−4.7	7.4	−7.5	7.9	9.3	9.5	8.4	7.5

Note: * Estimates and projections.

Sources: UNECE (2005), Eurostat (2005) and Economist Intelligence Unit (2005).

Table 4.14 *Real domestic gross fixed capital formation in EU, candidate and other select countries, 1990–2006 (percentage change over preceding year)*

Country	1990	1991	1992	1993	1994	1995	1996	1997	1998	1999	2000	2001	2002	2003	2004*	2005*	2006*
Austria	6.2	6.6	0.6	−0.9	4.6	1.3	2.2	2.0	3.9	2.1	6.5	−2.1	−3.4	6.2	3.2	1.8	2.7
Belgium	8.5	?4.2	1.0	−2.5	0.4	3.4	0.9	7.2	3.0	4.3	4.4	0.3	−3.7	−0.9	3.0	4.0	4.0
Finland	−4.6	−18.6	−16.7	−16.6	−2.7	10.6	8.4	11.9	9.3	3.0	4.1	3.9	−3.1	−2.3	4.3	4.4	4.5
France	3.3	−1.5	−1.6	−6.4	1.5	2.0	–	−0.1	7.0	8.3	7.8	1.9	−1.6	−0.2	3.3	2.7	2.0
Germany	9.0	9.8	4.5	−4.4	4.0	−0.6	−0.8	0.6	3.0	4.1	2.7	−4.2	−6.4	−2.2	−0.7	2.1	2.9
Greece	4.5	4.2	−3.5	−4.0	−3.1	4.1	8.4	6.8	10.6	6.2	8.0	6.5	5.7	13.7	5.0	4.5	4.4
Ireland	13.4	−7.0	–	−5.1	11.8	15.3	16.8	18.1	14.8	14.0	7.6	−1.5	2.8	3.6	7.5	6.1	5.5
Italy	4.0	1.0	−1.4	−10.9	0.1	6.0	3.6	2.1	4.0	5.7	6.9	1.9	1.2	−2.1	2.2	2.0	2.3
Luxembourg	3.4	15.8	−15.1	20.6	–	−1.5	3.9	12.6	11.8	14.0	−3.5	10.0	−1.1	−6.3	3.0	4.0	4.0
Netherlands	2.5	0.4	0.7	−3.2	2.1	3.9	6.3	6.6	4.2	7.8	1.4	−0.1	−4.5	−3.2	0.6	0.9	3.3
Portugal	7.6	3.3	4.5	−5.5	2.7	6.6	5.7	13.9	11.5	7.3	3.8	0.8	−5.1	−9.8	2.3	2.8	3.5
Spain	6.5	1.7	−4.1	−8.9	1.9	7.7	2.1	5.0	9.7	8.8	5.7	3.0	1.7	3.2	4.6	3.0	3.0
Eurozone	5.3	1.4	–	−6.4	2.1	2.9	1.7	2.8	5.6	6.2	5.1	0.1	−2.1	−0.4	3.3	2.0	2.0
Denmark	−2.2	−3.4	−2.1	−3.8	7.7	11.6	3.9	10.9	10.0	1.0	7.1	4.9	4.5	0.1	4.8	4.8	3.2
Sweden	0.2	−8.6	−11.6	−10.3	6.6	9.9	4.5	−0.3	7.8	8.2	5.7	−0.1	−2.6	−1.5	5.5	6.5	6.1
UK	−2.6	−8.2	−0.9	0.3	4.7	3.1	4.7	6.9	12.8	0.6	2.6	2.6	2.7	2.2	6.0	2.8	2.1
EU(15)	4.3	1.0	−0.3	−5.7	2.6	3.2	2.1	3.3	6.6	5.6	5.0	0.5	−1.4	−0.1	4.0	–	–
Cyprus	−2.8	−1.6	16.2	−12.8	−2.5	−1.7	7.4	−4.5	8.0	−1.4	3.8	3.2	8.0	−3.4	5.6	5.2	3.8
Czech R.	–	–	–	–	–	19.3	3.7	−1.2	−10.1	0.3	4.9	5.4	3.4	4.8	10.5	9.0	6.1
Estonia	–	–	–	–	5.3	6.4	14.8	27.4	1.5	−11.1	14.3	13.0	17.2	5.4	7.7	7.0	6.6
Hungary	–	–	–	–	–	–	14.7	4.1	8.4	6.9	7.7	5.0	8.0	3.4	7.8	8.0	8.0
Latvia	–	–	–	–	–	–	1.9	9.3	48.5	16.8	10.2	11.4	13.0	10.9	–	–	–
Lithuania	–	–	–	–	–	–	19.3	18.3	6.8	−8.5	−9.0	13.5	11.1	11.4	20.0	16.0	16.0
Malta	17.9	–	−0.2	11.1	8.5	17.8	−8.4	−4.5	−3.4	4.0	17.5	−8.5	−29.6	41.4	–	–	–
Poland	–	−4.4	2.3	2.9	9.2	16.6	19.7	21.7	14.2	6.8	2.7	−8.8	−5.8	−0.5	5.1	9.0	8.0
Slovakia	–	–	–	32.1	−8.8	17.2	34.5	1.2	5.9	−19.6	−7.2	13.9	−0.6	−1.5	4.0	6.5	6.9
Slovenia	–	–	–	–	–	–	14.3	11.7	10.7	0.9	2.9	–	0.5	2.4	7.3	6.3	5.4

New EU(10)	–	–	–	–	–	–	14.3	11.7	10.7	0.9	2.9	–	0.5	2.4	–	–	–
EU(25)	–	–	–	–	–	–	3.3	4.1	7.0	5.1	4.8	0.4	−1.2	0.2	3.3	3.0	2.7
Bulgaria	–	−20.0	−7.3	−17.5	1.1	16.1	−21.2	−20.9	35.2	20.8	15.4	23.3	8.5	13.8	12.0	9.5	9.0
Romania	−35.6	−31.6	11.0	8.3	20.7	6.9	5.7	1.7	−5.7	−4.8	5.5	10.1	8.2	9.2	–	–	–
Croatia	–	–	−11.5	6.8	−1.0	15.6	37.6	26.4	2.5	−3.9	−3.8	7.1	12.0	16.8	5.5	6.0	5.2
Turkey	15.9	0.4	6.4	26.4	−16.0	9.1	14.1	14.8	−3.9	−15.7	16.9	−31.5	−1.1	10.0	36.0	22.0	8.5
Switzerland	3.8	−2.9	−6.6	−2.7	6.5	1.8	−2.4	1.5	4.5	1.2	4.3	−3.1	0.3	−0.3	5.1	3.2	3.5
United States	−1.8	−6.9	6.5	8.1	9.1	6.1	9.3	9.6	9.1	8.2	6.1	−1.7	−3.1	4.5	10.0	6.3	4.7
Japan	8.1	2.3	−2.4	−2.8	−1.5	0.7	6.4	0.9	−3.9	−0.9	1.9	−1.4	−5.8	0.8	2.0	1.5	1.5
China	–	–	–	–	–	11.0	15.0	9.0	14.5	14.3	10.4	10.4	15.5	20.0	15.4	8.5	8.0

Note: * Estimates and projections.

Sources: UNECE (2005), Eurostat (2005) and Economist Intelligence Unit (2005).

integration, including the operation of the Single European Market and the eurozone, is an ongoing process. The Single European Market is not a project that has clear deadlines after which one may measure the overall effects with only a small margin of error. In addition, it has never been fully implemented, as services markets among the member countries remain split.

While the Single European Market served its purpose in the past decades, the future needs of the EU business demand more flexibility in the labour market[139] and finance, as well as a vision and action in the area of education and R&D to assist in the process of adjustment to threats and to profit from new opportunities. This is the objective and intention of the Lisbon Agenda. Alas, this agenda is falling badly behind schedule. Targets were ambitious and various, but the instruments to achieve them including matching funds and reforms were lacking. This was also recognised in the 2004 report *Facing the Challenge* by Wim Kok on the progress (or lack of it) of the Lisbon strategy. This report argued in favour of a reduction in the number of performance indicators to 14 that focus on jobs and growth (from broad ones of over a hundred that include even clean seas), stronger national policy coordination than is currently the case and constant monitoring of actions and achievements. (Should there be sanctions for the failure to respect the agreed goals even in the shape of a name-and-shame list?) The problem of national policy coordination is hard to solve in the EU for two reasons: there is no central government and, even if there were, it could often be at odds with the governments of member countries.[140]

Research on the effects of the Single European Market suffers from an identification problem. It is a common shortcoming of all studies that deal with the effects of international economic integration. It is hard to know which changes in the economy and the reaction of enterprises are due to the Single European Market and which would have happened anyway. For example, external changes include imports of improved foreign technology (software programs to manage production, inventories, transport and distribution) or 'globalisation' of business and competition. It may take another decade or so until all the effects of the Single Market Programme are fully absorbed by the economies of the EU. Then, this would all be mixed with the introduction of the eurozone and enlargement effects. Perhaps, and again only 'perhaps', the biggest effect on the economies of the EU has already taken place, at the end of the 1980s. Some support for this thesis can be found in the fact that business concentration deals peaked in 1990. Note that the Single European Market was *a*, rather than *the*, reason for change.

In spite of 'grand' expectations regarding employment and growth at the start of the Single Market Programme, as expressed, for example, by Emerson et al. (1988), in practice the benefits have been much more modest, although not negligible. It has been estimated that the programme created between 300 000 and 900 000 jobs, with an extra increase in EU income of 1.1–1.5 per cent over the 1987–93 period (European Commission, 1997b).

Direct intervention in the manufacturing industry by the EU was primarily aimed at declining industries such as steel, shipbuilding and textiles during the 1970s and early 1980s. After 1985, the major emphasis of the policy changed. The EU became much more involved in the expanding high-technology industries through its R&D and technology policies. This should not be taken to mean that the EU is no longer concerned with obsolete 'industries', or that it was not interested in the support and development of advanced industries in the past. On the contrary, EU involvement with both types of manufacturing industries existed in the past, and it continues in the present. What changed was only the order of priorities. None the less, high on the agenda for the future are the following priorities:

- promotion of investment into intangible assets;
- fostering the information society and life-time learning;
- backing good corporate governance;[141]
- advancement of industrial cooperation;
- paying special attention to services, SMEs, energy, bio- and nanotechnologies;
- strengthening of competition; and
- modernisation of public intervention.

4.4.4 SERVICES

Issues

Goods are tangible assets and, as such, are readily defined; the same cannot be said of services. Services have numerous recipients: an individual in the case of a haircut, education, entertainment or transport; a legal entity such as a firm or government in the case of banking or construction; an object such as an aeroplane in the case of guidance, defrosting, repairs or other airport services; or goods in the case of transport and storage. Some services can be provided to more than one recipient. For example, banking, insurance, transport, telecommunication, leasing, data processing and legal advice could be offered to individuals, businesses and governments.

In general, the services sector in the developed market economies contributes more than half to both GDP and employment (about 70 per cent in the EU in 2005). The share of the economy occupied by services has been continuously increasing. This tendency to deindustrialisation has resulted in a shift of emphasis towards the services sector as one of the key solutions to the problems of unemployment and growth. Employment in the manufacturing sector has been declining in the EU since the 1980s, whereas employment in the services sector has been constantly expanding. In 2002, out of 158 million people employed in the EU(15), 43 million (or 27 per cent) were employed in the manufacturing sector, while 110 million (or 70 per cent) were employed in the services sector. Newly created jobs in the services sector more than compensated for job losses in manufacturing. Production of almost all services takes place in every country. However, the same is not true for the manufacturing of cars, lorries, aircraft or steel. This is the direct consequence of high tradability of goods and restricted tradability of services. Hence, the alleged importance of the creation of new jobs in the services sector.

Notwithstanding its importance and impact on the economy, the services sector has been largely neglected in economic analysis. Classical economists such as Adam Smith and Karl Marx neglected services as the residual sector of the economy on the grounds that it does not have durable properties and no facility for physical accumulation or trade. The production and consumption of services is simultaneous and requires a degree of mobility of factors. Therefore, the classical economists turned their attention towards the manufacture of physical goods. In addition, rules relating to trade in services were not negotiated for a long time. However, as world trade in services was constantly increasing, it came as no surprise that services were included in the Uruguay Round Accord and in the WTO. World exports of services was $1795 billion in 2003. This represented a quarter of the $7294 billion trade in goods during the same year.[142]

The services sector of an economy changes its structure and location over time. The traditional services (such as transport, law, medicine, banking and insurance) are enriched by the new and fast-growing ones (such as telecommunications, information, data processing, engineering and management consultancy).

On the 'technical' side, services differ from other economic activities in at least five ways (Buigues and Sapir, 1993, p. xi):

- The production and consumption of services occur at the same time and at the same location. Therefore, they are regarded as non-tradable as they cannot be stored. Because of a relatively low level of internationalisation, the right of establishment (FDI) is essential for the provision of services abroad. Although services account for over two-thirds of the GDP in the EU, their share of total trade is about 20 per cent. This epitomises the non-tradable nature of many services.

On the other hand, services account for over half of all FDI in the EU. Internationalisation of services is lowest in distribution, road transport and construction; average in telecommunications, financial and business services; and relatively high in air transport and hotel chains.

- The quality of services cannot easily be ascertained in advance of consumption. Non-price competitive factors such as reputation often play a key role during the decision-making process by consumers. This is important in longer-term relations such as in financial services. Experience plays a part even in one-off relationships in some cases and places.[143]
- Governments in all countries intervene in services more than in other economic activities, because of market failures. These include imperfect competition in a number of services; asymmetric information between providers and consumers (sellers potentially know more about a service, such as an insurance policy, than do buyers); and externalities. Positive externalities are to be found frequently in the services sector, such as in telecommunications or the Internet. In these areas the value for one user increases with the total number of all users. A negative externality may be found, for example, in financial services, where the failure of one bank may cause problems for others (Sapir, 1993, p. 27). Public intervention influences entry, operation, competition and exit from the sector. Regulation is high and competition low in financial services, air transport and telecommunications. Thus, these industries are served by only a few large companies. Reputation plays a major role in finance and economies of scope are important in air transport, while in telecommunications there are relatively large sunk costs and economies of scale (in most countries a single public firm used to provide the service until the mid-1990s). Competition tends to be higher and regulation easier in road transport, business services, construction and hotels.
- Debates about the (in)ability of the government to intervene (in)efficiently to correct market failures, as well as changes in technology, contributed to an ebb in deregulation in the services sector first in the US at the end of the 1970s, then in Britain during the early 1980s, which subsequently spread to the rest of Europe. All this was also supported by the results of the Uruguay Round.
- Services are characterised by a relatively slow growth of labour productivity. Their rate of productivity growth during the 1970–90 period was half of what it was in the manufacturing sector. There are at least two explanations for such development. First, competition in services is obstructed by a high degree of regulation and, second, the

substitution of capital for labour is more limited in services than in manufacturing. Technological innovations, however, increased labour productivity in telecommunications and air transport during that period.

Differences between services and other economic activities are not confined to the 'technical' side. There is also a social dimension:

- in the 1990s, half of employees in the service sector were women. This is in sharp contrast with the manufacturing sector, in which women account for only one in five jobs;
- there are many more part-time employees in the services sector than in manufacturing;
- temporary contracts are increasing in the services sector;
- there is a relatively high level of non-employees;
- labour unions are not strong in the services sector except in transport and telecommunications; and
- SMEs are the dominant type of business organisation in most service industries.

There are other reasons that make the analysis of services tricky. One is a lack of any profound theory or definition. Services are defined as:

- *indivisibles* because they disappear at the very moment of their production; or
- *unstorables* because they perish as they are produced.[144] Services can be bought and sold, but they cannot be 'dropped on the foot'; or
- *non-tradables* and *non-transportables* because of the above two properties; or
- *the residual sector* of the economy as it does not belong to agriculture, or to mining or to the manufacturing sector.

A wide definition of services states that 'a service is a change in the condition of a person, or a good belonging to some economic unit, which is brought about as a result of the activity of some other economic unit' (Hill, 1977, p. 317). Without a proper definition, the measuring unit is lacking. Trade statistics list thousands of items for goods. Even though the UN Central Product Classification identified more than 600 services products, statistics record only a handful of services (making analysis quite difficult). This reflects the fact that goods have a very high degree of tradability, whereas the tradability of services is low. Hence, the production of services is much more geographically dispersed than is the production of goods.

Although many services are not tradable, progress in information and telecom technology has made many services eligible for international trade. Nevertheless, trade in many services is not recorded. For example, the service part of a good, such as repair and regular maintenance of a car, may be incorporated in the total price of traded goods.

Services may have the following general dimensions:

- *producer*: finance, accounting, consulting . . .
- *distribution*: transport, trade, advertising . . .
- *social*: government, health, security, old-age . . . and
- *personal*: entertainment, restaurants, hotels . . .

This classification is relevant if one wants to employ certain policy instruments to influence the development of the targeted dimension. But even here one may encounter classification, and then policy-related problems. Where to put insurance, marketing, education or postal services?

Apart from transport, financial and telecommunication services, in principle, entry into and exit from a service industry is relatively cheap and easy. However, there are regulatory barriers to such (dis)orderly operation in the service businesses. TNCs release few data on their internal trade in services, whereas other establishments in the sector only reluctantly make this information public, as this can endanger their competitive position. In addition, information can be easily, swiftly and cheaply distributed, which jeopardises property rights. Such a lack of hard statistical information makes trade in services difficult to study.

It is easier to sell goods than services in foreign markets. While barriers to trade in goods can be eliminated at the border, problems for the suppliers of services usually start once they pass the frontier control. Provision of services often requires the right of establishment and national treatment of enterprises. Providers of a service frequently need to be physically present in order to provide a service to their customers.

Impediments to trade in services are not found in the form of tariffs. The principal obstacles can be found in two classes of barriers that may be theoretically obvious but may often be blurred in practice:

- *market access*: regulation of the entry of foreign service providers in the national market (prohibitions, bilateral and regional preferential agreements, local content rules, travel and residency restrictions, recognition of qualifications and experience, standards, insurance and obligatory deposits); and
- *national treatment*: this shows whether a foreign provider of a service is treated the same as the domestic one in the same situation (taxes,

subsidies, charges for public services, buy domestic obligations and campaigns, exchange controls).

Experts may enter and settle in foreign countries, but their qualifications and licences may not be recognised by the host authorities. Public authorities regulate the supply of services to a much higher degree than they do the production of goods. They often regulate public shareholding, quality and quantity of supply, rates and conditions of operation. Fiscal incentives are often given more easily to firms in the manufacturing industry than to those in the services sector. Because of the wide coverage of regulation of industries in the services sector, an easing or a removal of control of the establishment in services can have a much greater impact on trade and investment than would be the case in the trade and production of goods.

More than a decade after its establishment in 1993, the Single European Market is not yet delivering its full benefits to consumers and firms. This is most obvious in services. Belgian electricians have to pay three times the Belgian rate to register with the Luxembourg authorities for a one-day job or Austrian bakers require eight different licences if they want to set up business in Italy.[145] The Single European Market may be weakening. So may be the opportunity to turn the EU into the world's most competitive knowledge-based economy by 2010. Hence, the European Commission intends to be more active in tearing down barriers in the services sector.

Small and open countries that are net importers of goods may prefer not to rely on their domestic manufacturing industry, as this might not operate on an efficient scale. These countries may choose to develop service industries to create proceeds to pay for imports of goods. Thus, the Netherlands has developed trade and transport, Austria tourism, Norway and Greece shipping, while Switzerland and Luxembourg are highly specialised in financial services.

Services and the jobs that they create may be broadly classified into two groups:

- those that require high skills and pay (such as business, financial, engineering, management, consulting, medical and legal advice); and
- those that are geared to consumer and welfare needs.

The suppliers of services in this second group (such as workers in shops, hotels and restaurants) receive poor training and have a high turnover and low pay. Economic development in its post-industrial phase should be aimed at the creation of jobs in the former group, rather than the latter (Tyson, 1987, p. 79).

European Union

Articles 43–8 of the Treaty of Rome grant the right of establishment to EU residents, freedom to supply services throughout the region and freedom of movement for capital. Article 86 states that public enterprises and those with special or exclusive rights to provide services of general economic interest 'shall be subject to . . . the rules on competition, in so far as the application of such rules does not obstruct the performance, in law or in fact, of the particular tasks assigned to them'. Compared with trade in goods, these rights have not yet materialised in practice on a large scale. The major reason for this situation is the existence of various national restrictions (NTBs). In fact, about half of the 282 measures that came from the Single Market Programme related to services such as finance, transport and telecommunications. It was in the financial services (banking and insurance) that the programme advanced most swiftly. This was partly due to the impressive changes in technology (data processing and telecommunications services) and partly a result of international efforts to liberalise trade in services under the auspices of the WTO.

One could ask whether the changes prompted by the Single European Market had the same effects on services as they had on manufacturing. A more apposite question is whether the programme had an impact on the geographical location of services in the EU, as could have happened with manufacturing. In the case of some services that are tradable because of data processing and telecommunications technology, such as accounting, there was some centralisation and reallocation of business. For most others, significant changes are not expected in the short and medium terms. Skilled accountants are able to move around the EU and offer their services, but the Greek islands (tourism) will remain where they are.

The still-evolving legislative framework for the single EU market in services is based on the following four principal elements:

- *Freedom of establishment* Enterprises from other EU countries may not be discriminated against and must receive national treatment in the country of operation. This is important in the services sector because of the need for direct contact between the providers and consumers of services. A single licence is required for the provision of services throughout the EU. This means that a firm that is entitled to provide services in one EU country has the same right in another EU country. The country that issues such a licence is primarily responsible for the control of the licensed firm on behalf of the rest of the EU.
- *Liberalisation of cross-border trade in services* This element increases the possibility of cross-border provision of services without the actual

physical establishment of the business in the host country. A gradual inclusion of and a full permission for cabotage (internal transport service within a country) was one of the key changes. Cabotage in EU air transport was fully liberalised in 1997, and in road transport in 1998.[146]

- *Harmonisation of the national rules* This eases the trans-border establishment of business and the provision of services. This is relevant for telecommunications (technical standards) and financial (solvency) services.
- *Common rules of competition* Restrictive business practices, abuse of the dominant market position and state aid are forbidden or strictly regulated.

Financial services deal with promises to pay. In a world of developed telecommunication services, these promises can move instantaneously all around the globe. Customs posts do not matter in this business. None the less, restrictive rights of establishment may limit the freedom to supply these services. Traditionally, monetary power was jealously protected and saved for domestic authorities. This has changed in recent decades. International mobility of capital can hardly be stopped, therefore countries try to make the best use of it. Financial services not only generate employment and earnings themselves but also, and more importantly, the efficient allocation of resources and the competitiveness of the manufacturing sector depends on a wide choice of efficient and low-cost financial services.

As a result of the First Banking Directive (1977), EU-resident banks are free to open branches throughout the Union, but this is subject to host-country authorisation. Foreign banks cannot compete successfully with local banks, as the costs of establishment differ widely among countries. In addition, foreign banks may be excluded from certain services (securities) which are reserved for local residents. The Second Banking Directive (1989) brought a major breakthrough in the EU banking industry as it introduced the single banking licence. From 1993, member countries of the EU accepted the home-country control principle, as well as a mutual recognition of each other's licensing rules for banks.

The European Parliament approved an ambitious plan in 2002 to unify the EU financial markets by 2005. The intention is to standardise rules for corporate accounting, reporting and oversight in order to allow for greater financial market consolidation and to avoid risks such as those that emerged with the Enron and Andersen corporate scandals in the US in 2002 and Parmalat in the EU in 2003.

Full harmonisation of the banking laws in the EU countries is, however, neither easy nor necessary. Banking laws among the states in the US differ, but this has never been a major handicap to the economic performance of the country. As financial services become globalised, the challenge to the EU and its member countries is to adjust to this change and remain competitive, become mature or lose out to other competitors. In the event that third-country banks wished to benefit from the Single European Market, the Second Banking Directive asked for reciprocal treatment. However, it subsequently became evident that this would be an unrealistic provision in relation to US banks. These banks are not allowed to enter into certain financial operations (such as securities) across the boundaries of federal states. It would be unreasonable to give EU banks operating in the US more favourable treatment than domestic US banks and/or to expect the US to change the domestic rules because of a different regulation in the EU. In the end, the reciprocity provision did not apply to subsidiaries of US banks that were established in the EU prior to 1 January 1993.

The *insurance* business is very special and complex indeed. There are few homogeneous products and there is usually a long-term relation between the parties. If a consumer purchases a bottle of Scotch whisky, he/she still has the pleasure of consuming this drink even if the producer goes out of business. The same is not true for an insurance policy. Control of the insurance business is exercised by regulating entry into the business. Insurers in the EU are granted the general right to establish (locate operations in another partner country), but they are often permitted to solicit business only through local agencies. This is particularly true for compulsory insurance.[147] The rationale for such restrictions can be found in the protection of consumers' interests[148] because of the asymmetric information between the seller and the buyer (the seller may know much more about the policy than the buyer),[149] but it can be employed for the protection of local businesses too. Where a sound case for the protection of local consumers ends and where a barrier to trade in the insurance business and protection of the local industry begins is difficult to determine. Buyers of an insurance policy may appreciate the benefits of relatively tougher regulation, but may not wish to accept the higher costs involved.[150]

Progress in the EU was faster in the non-life than in the life insurance business. The directive (1988) on the freedom to supply non-life insurance distinguished between two kinds of risks. Mass risks (commercial risks) and large risks (transport, marine, aviation) are covered by the home-country regulation of the insurer, whereas personal insurance is covered by national regulations in the country where the policyholder resides.[151] Integration in the insurance business in the EU has not advanced as much as in the field of banking. EU insurance companies are allowed to compete only under the host-country rules, which significantly reduces the opportunity for real competition. In fact, the insurance industry is barely affected by the 'globalisation' of business. Highly protected national insurance markets would require a great deal of harmonisation before real competition could take place and before a 'single EU insurance passport', introduced in 1994, could have a greater impact. The benefit of this 'single passport' is subject to harmonised solvency margin requirements and regulatory supervision among countries.

As part of the implementation of the Single European Market, personal insurance policies have been sold and advertised freely in the EU since 1994. This is not to say that insurers and consumers had reason to rejoice. This is because, first, national tax treatment still favours local companies. These firms have a wide network of tied agents that may not be easily and swiftly replicated by foreign competitors. Second, there are national restraints on the sale of certain types of policies. For example, Italy banned the sale of kidnap insurance because of the concern that it would encourage abductions. The European Commission advocates equal treatment and access for men and women to goods and services. Therefore, in 2003 it proposed to abolish the use of sex as a determining factor in the evaluation of risk. Insurers argue that women live longer than men and, if the insurance industry is deprived of such distinct treatment, their ability to assess risk would weaken and this would increase insurance premiums for women for products such as car insurance.[152]

Uncoordinated national laws can no longer provide the basis for future developments of financial services in the EU. This is increasingly important in the light of increasing globalisation and a loss of an EU-specific dimension in business, especially in banking. If the EU wants to preserve or even increase the existing amount of business and employment that goes with it, it is crucial that it fosters the development of an open and efficient market for financial services. Consumers will gain a wider choice, and better-quality and cheaper financial services, which is essential for the competitiveness of the manufacturing industry and the smooth operation of the whole economy.

The *Debauve* case (1980) dealt with advertising, and showed how complicated cases could be in the services sector. Belgium prohibited advertising on TV. None the less, cable TV programmes that originated in other countries without such restrictions and which were marketed in Belgium contained advertising messages. The issue was whether the Belgian government had the right to ban advertising on channels received in the country, but which originate in other countries. The European Court of Justice concluded that, in the absence of EU action, each member state would regulate and even prohibit advertising on TV on its territory on the grounds of general interest. The question here is what was the 'general interest' in this case? A typical argument for regulation would be the protection of consumers (viewers).

An increase in the choice of channels would not be against the interests of the viewers regardless of whether foreign programmes contain advert breaks. Therefore, the argument that an improvement in the welfare of those in Belgium who wished to watch foreign channels was increased by the ban cannot hold water (Hindley, 1991, p. 279). If Belgian viewers watch foreign programmes (with or without advertising), they will watch fewer domestic channels. Hence, support for the public financing of domestic TV will decrease. An additional reason for the Belgian policy was the protection of the advertising revenue of local newspapers.

One of the fastest-growing and -changing industries in the services sector is *telecommunications*. This is due to the profound technological changes that have taken place since the 1960s, which include communication via satellite, microwaves and digital technology. New goods and services, such as fax machines, electronic mail and mobile phones, also appeared. A total of €450 billion has been invested in the EU information industry. The natural monopoly argument for the provision of long-distance, as well as local, services has vanished.

The EU policy in the telecommunication field was slow and late to appear. During the mid-1980s, the EU was concentrating its efforts on R&D and common standardisation. Subsequently, the aim of having an open network was translated into a directive in 1990. In addition, public contracts that exceed €0.6 million in the industry must be transparent and officially published. Directive 96/19/EC introduced full competition in the telecommunications market in 1998, although Greece, Portugal and Spain were allowed a few years' grace. This means that EU consumers have the right to have a phone connected, to have access to new services, to expect services of a specified quality and to benefit from new methods of solving problems between the consumer and the provider of the service. The obvious benefit was an increase in the number of telecommunication services (often free access to the Internet, huge growth in mobile telecommunications) and a sharp decline in the price of these services.

Business services have high rates of growth too. They include accountancy, auditing, legal, R&D, information, data-processing, computing and various engineering and management consultancy services. Different technical standards, licensing of professionals and government procurement of services represent barriers to the free supply of services throughout the EU. A liberal treatment of these services may reduce their costs and increase the efficiency of business. In a world undergoing continuous changes in technology, markets, laws and so on, consultants who manage to stay at least one step ahead of their clients will survive.

Trade in professional services still faces significant obstacles. The domestic regulation in the accounting business, for instance, is burdened with limitations. They commonly include the following restrictions and requirements:

- qualifications (education and experience);
- recognition of diplomas and certificates (professional competence);
- transparency regarding activities;
- standards for the quality of service (protection of clients);
- professional ethics and insurance/deposit requests;
- obligatory membership in local professional associations;
- limitations in the scope of business;
- control and ownership restrictions;
- residency requirements; and
- limitations regarding the nationality of staff employed.

Outlook

The policy of the EU towards services should be founded on three major freedoms: the freedom to establish business (geographical or spatial liberty); the freedom to offer services; and the freedom to transfer capital. Deregulation in the services sector increased competition, which reduced costs for consumers, increased opportunities and improved the competitive position of the entire economy. Apart from partial deregulation, the promotion of the development of the EU-wide service industries needs to be encouraged. Initial steps towards this objective include recognition of qualifications, a single insurance licence and the opening up of government procurement over a certain (small) threshold to all EU suppliers.

Opening up market for trade and foreign investment in services brings at least two distinct benefits for the domestic economy:

- the competitiveness of the entire economy depends on a free access to efficient services; and
- opening the domestic market for trade in services is the principal means to warrant the efficient operation of the services sector. This move (i) permits an improvement in efficiency because of competition and (ii) makes available services that otherwise may not be available locally.

Although the general interests of a member country do not always conform with the overall interest of the EU, the European Court of Justice has often been reluctant to question national stances. This has limited the effectiveness of Articles 49–55, as well as Article 86 of the Treaty of Rome. While the *Cassis de Dijon* case was applied to internal trade in goods, the application of the same principle to services is waiting for 'better times'. The relatively 'soft' stance of the EU regarding restrictive agreements and abuse of dominant position in services cannot easily be explained only by the properties of services; one also needs to add the influence of entrenched businesses, lobbies and the public protection of specific interests. None the less, it is slowly being realised that regulation that limits competition prevents, rather than stimulates, efficiency in services such as telecommunication, transport and finance.

More than a decade after its establishment in 1993, the Single European Market is not yet delivering its full benefits to consumers and firms. This is most obvious in services that account for over 70 per cent of EU GDP. In order to avoid the weakening of the market, as well as the chance of transforming the EU into the world's most competitive knowledge-based economy by 2010, the European Commission identified in 2002 a set of barriers that impede the free movement in services. These are barriers that deal with the following stages of the business process:

- establishment of the service provider (authorisation, declaration, qualifications of staff);
- use of inputs necessary for the provision of services;
- promotion;
- distribution; and
- after-sales phase (professional liability, insurance, guarantees, maintenance).

The European Commission aims to remove barriers in the services sector and to have a Single European Market for services by 2010.

It is commonly argued that industries that produce tradable goods and services face tough foreign competition and that they tend to attract FDI that is based on modern technologies, as compared with the ones that produce non-tradables. Therefore, these two parts of the economy have different productivity growth. It is higher in the tradables sector. Historical data offer evidence of such developments. On the one hand, the slower rate of productivity growth in non-tradables results in higher relative prices in this part of the economy, while, on the other, the 'law of one price' introduces a tendency of equalisation of prices of tradables among different countries. Higher productivity in the tradables sector increases wages in that part. If there is labour mobility between the two parts of the national economy, this bids up wages throughout the economy. Employers in the non-tradables sector can pay higher wages in this situation only if they increase prices of their goods and services. The general price level in the economy increases (Balassa–Samuelson effect[153]).

As the provision of most services has a local character (because many of them are non-tradable), there will be no big change in the geographical location of their production. Local incumbents have established and operate strong retail networks, and their own reputation (accounting may be an exception) may act as an additional barrier to entry. Therefore national regulation may remain dominant in many industries within the services sector in the future. The structure of ownership, however, may change as local firms enter into the network of large TNCs in the industry. Nevertheless, one should not exaggerate the potential expansion of TNCs in the services sector as most mergers and acquisitions in the sector have a strong national dimension. An international, that is, EU, dimension in the services sector is growing in the insurance industry. Assicurazioni Generali, the biggest insurer in the EU by market capitalisation, earned two-thirds of its premium income from outside Italy, while a third of its equity is reckoned to be in the hands of foreigners.[154]

The impact of the Single European Market on the changing geography of production is much more obvious in the manufacturing sector than in services. This is the consequence of a much higher degree of tradability of goods than is the case with services. The impact on services may not be immediately obvious. It will take a long time to materialise. The Single European Market brought certain benefits to the consumers of services. The most obvious are in telecommunications. However, large-scale benefits may be absent because of important barriers that include the reputation of the already established service firms, past experience, excess capacity and cultural differences. It may be wrong to expect that the genuine internal market will cause an equalisation of prices of services throughout the EU. Prices will only tend to converge because of increased competition. None the less, some price differentials will persist because of differences in productivity and taxation, as well as the needs and preferences of the local markets.

However, some trends are obvious. There is a general trend for the share of services in the economy to expand, while that of the manufacturing industry shrinks. In addition, the services sector of the economy is more spatially dispersed (because of limited tradability) than the manufacturing sector. As personal income increases, there is a disproportional increase in demand for services. At the same time, many manufacturing industries are farming out various services (from cleaning to accounting and design) and relying on external specialist firms to provide them. Finally, as manufacturing in the EU undergoes some degree of spatial reallocation, this will have an impact on the location of services, which may follow their clients in the manufacturing sector.

In its intention to reinvigorate the implementation of the Lisbon Agenda, in 2005 the European Commission proposed a key plan that would liberalise the EU market for services. Provided that they comply with their home market laws and regulations, individuals and firms could provide the same services in other EU member countries. This plan refers particularly to architects, advertisers, car rental companies, employment agencies, healthcare, information technology, security services and travel agents. The expectation is that this would lead to the creation of about 600 000 new jobs, greater productivity and lower prices.

The problem of accepting and applying this plan presents differences in national rules for certain jobs or professions: one EU member country may have strict rules, while another none at all. For example, stone-masonry is strictly regulated in Germany, but not at all in Britain. If the rule of the country of origin is applied throughout the EU, the result can be discrimination against nationals who cannot do certain jobs without specific training and qualifications.[155]

During the mid-term review of the Lisbon Agenda by the European Council in March 2005, the European Commission's plan met strong resistance from France and Germany. The concern is that the plan could introduce 'social dumping' especially in public services and endanger living standards in the more advanced EU countries. Social dumping is a euphemism for cheap immigrant labour (sometimes of substandard education) from central and east European EU member countries. Fears concerning social dumping could be realised.[156] Commenting about the issue, the editorial comment 'Le dumping social' in the *Financial Times*, 26 March 2005, stated:

> However, given the futility of pulling up the drawbridge now that the east European invaders (sorry, fellow EU citizens) are already inside the castle keep, west European protectionists might consider some new tactics. An obvious one is to harmonise upwards. This means getting east Europeans to adopt the Franco-German norms on work, shop and school hours that restrict output, consumption and female participation in the workforce.
>
> And why stop there? It is no good hoping a few World Trade Organization rules can deal with the threat from China and India, the titans of social dumping. They must also be brought into the EU, and told to pull up their standards. Simple really.

The European Council in Brussels (2005) stated: 'In order to promote growth and employment and to strengthen competitiveness, the internal market of services has to be fully operational while preserving the European social model.'[157] This means that the European Council wants to have it both ways: to have their cake and eat it too! Hence, negotiations will continue in the future. Since the decision will be by qualified majority voting, the opposing countries may be outvoted.

4.4.5 CONCLUSION

Consideration of the various problems that arose during the creation and implementation of an industrial policy in the manufacturing and services sectors of a country has given an insight into the magnitude of the problems facing the introduction of schemes across integrated countries. There is at least one forceful argument that favours the introduction of an industrial policy. The neo-conservative school argues that a free market system is the best existing method for solving economic problems. However, this cannot be accepted without reservations. Neither the economic performance of the US prior to the New Deal nor contemporary economic performance in the most successful industrialised countries such as Germany, Japan or Sweden supports this view. Strategic government intervention and comprehensive social welfare programmes, rather than free markets, have been the engines of economic success throughout the advanced industrial world (Tyson and Zysman, 1987b, p. 426). In fact, according to this view, free markets were often no more than 'fine-tuning' policy choices of the government.

A country with a flexible policy towards manufacturing industry in response to market signals (such as Japan during the 1960s and 1970s) or one that shapes the market (France during the 1950s and 1960s or China during and after the 1990s) is better able to adapt to changes than a country that largely resists such changes (such as in Britain in the case of coal and steel production during the 1970s). Industrial policy that ignores market signals and that supports industries with obsolete technologies introduces confusion over future developments and increases the cost of inevitable change. These costs may be much higher in the future than they were in the past because of social rigidities and rapid changes in technology. The success of an industrial policy may be tested by its effectiveness in shifting resources from industries that use ailing technologies, not by how effective it is in preventing this adjustment. However, the problem is that even the most sophisticated national or international institutions and think-tanks do not know exactly what will happen in the future (recall the debt crises in the 1980s, and the impact of Microsoft on the economy).

A policy of picking a winner (a strategic industry with important externalities) *ex ante* may propel the economy of a country in the future. This may have a favourable outcome for the country or the EU if the choice is correct, if this policy is coordinated with the suppliers of inputs and if it is limited to a defined period of time in which the national champion is expected to become self-reliant. The other interventionist approach of rescue (*ex post*) may simply postpone the attrition of the assisted industry and increase the overall costs of change to the society.

The shift out of industries that use obsolete production technologies and into modern ones seems straightforward in theory, but can be quite difficult, costly and slow in practice. This is, of course, a matter of political choice. The inability to do something is different from an unwillingness to do it. During the 1980s, the EU opted for the creation of the Single European Market as the environment that favours change. None the less, its direct industrial policy is in many respects a set of R&D policies coupled with public procurement. Other dimensions of industrial policy are implemented within the domain of competition, trade, regional, education and monetary (stability) policies. It is to be hoped that the 'social dimension' in the future of the EU will remain only as a set of non-obligatory standards and aspirations that will not mislead the EU into the complacency that would kill the urge for continuous change and adjustment for the better.

Britain and Spain were behind the ambitious Lisbon Agenda (2000) for the EU. This rests on the liberal ideas of deregulation that would make the EU economy more flexible and dynamic. Other EU countries did not quite realise what they had agreed to. The European Councils usually set political targets which include deadlines. This is generally a clear-cut part of the exercise. However, it takes much longer for the European Commission and the national governments to jointly legislate and implement policies (most governments try to protect their national interests first). If the principal competitors such as the US (because of the huge budget and trade deficits) or China (because of distortions in the economy and dependency on imported energy and commodities) slow down, the EU may feel less urgency in making painful reforms in its structured labour and product markets.

The shaping of an industrial policy in every country requires detailed and reliable data about the available factors, competition, externalities, changes in the production and management technology, and policies of the major trading partners, as well as about the tax, legal and political environment. Even then, industrial policy prescriptions should be taken with a pinch of salt. At the time when Britain was industrialising, the textile industry was the leader in technology. The capital required to start up a textile firm was much smaller than that required to build a steel mill, which was the leading manufacturing industry when Germany started to industrialise. The problems of development had to be solved by government incentives (intervention) and bank loans. Modern industries require not only capital investment (in many cases this entails reliance on banks) but also, and more importantly, investment in highly qualified personnel. Education policy is always shaped to a large extent by government.

There are justifiable reasons for pessimism about the ability to create and apply an effective and coherent industrial policy in a decentralised country or a group of integrated countries. Many agents and issues need to be taken into account during the decision-making process about uncertain events. Numerous agencies have an impact on industrial policy, including ministries of trade, finance, social affairs, education, regional development, energy, the environment, transport, technology, defence and foreign affairs. Most of these departments exist at the federal, regional and local levels. There are also labour unions, banks, industrial associations and non-governmental organisations. They all have diverse and often conflicting goals. The complexity of representation, coordination, communication, understanding, harmonisation and control of all these players increases exponentially with their number. In spite of all these organisational difficulties, the rewards are worthwhile.[158] However, while numerous agents may, of course, be a source of creativity, in practice they often turn out to be a source of disagreement over the distribution of instruments of industrial policy. The interaction of all these players has an amalgamating effect on the national industrial policy. To reconcile all these diverse demands is a great political challenge.

Evidence from the cases of Japan (1960–90) and Germany may serve as partial examples to other countries in the shaping of national industrial policies. The crucial property of a promising industrial policy is that if it cannot be organised centrally then it ought to coordinate measures taken at lower levels. Without a consensus about the basic objectives of industrial policy among the major players and their commitment to these goals, such a policy will not come about. Exchange of views, mutual understanding, trust, support and, finally, an agreement about the goals and means of industrial policy between governments at all levels, the business community and labour are essential elements of its effectiveness. But this was the situation in the past century. It may be harder to identify social partners in the 21st century. Membership of trade unions is declining. In the time and age of a knowledge-based network economy many do not share trade union ideals. Business associations fare slightly better. In spite of the unrepresentative character of these social partners, they need and rely on one another in spite of their defects. Otherwise there would be an imploding monologue. The deeply rooted social structure in Europe and the EU is built around them. One only has to recall the existence and role of the Economic and Social Committee.

While the EU creates conditions for competition, its member countries implement their own national industrial policies. The divergence in industrial policy philosophies among the member countries and a lack of funds has prevented the EU from playing a more influential role. The variety of uncoordinated national policies has introduced confusion and uncertainty regarding the future actions of the EU. Until the member countries take advantage of a vast Single European Market, they may not profit from the potentials for an increase in the competitive edge in a number of manufacturing industries primarily *vis-à-vis* the US, but also Japan, China and some newly industrialised countries. If it attempts to be durable and successful, an EU industrial policy will require the agreement of the member states regarding their objectives and policy means.

A new philosophy by the European Commission regarding industrial policy is based on the idea that this policy needs to offer primarily a stable macroeconomic environment. The eurozone epitomises this policy stance for the participating countries. In addition, various research programmes will provide an input into the EU industry's competitiveness.

Any 'golden rules' for a respectable industrial policy should include the following elements:

- Any policy should be more about the policy process and less about outcomes.
- The policy should not harm other parts of the economy.
- The spirit of the policy should be continuous and stable.
- The policy instruments should reinforce one another.
- Coordination failure should be eliminated. If technology links the production chain of a particular output, then a simultaneous investment in all segments makes them jointly profitable. A failure to invest in one or more segments in the production chain makes them all unprofitable.
- Inflation should be low, rates of interest positive and exchange rates stable. In such an environment incentives exist for savings and investment.
- Public borrowing should be small in order to give the private sector better opportunities for obtaining investment funds.
- Any intervention should be general and should offer support to industries, rather than individual firms within them.
- There should always be an element of choice among various courses of action, as well as the flexibility to respond to crises and opportunities.
- If support (such as subsidies, procurement contracts, tariffs or quotas) is offered, it should have a timetable and clear benchmarks (for success and failure), and be transparent and of limited duration, after which it should be withdrawn.
- Risk is unavoidable when there are ventures into the unknown. Risk need not be minimised from the outset. Costs should be minimised once a mistake is spotted.
- There should be a reference to investment in human capital. Well-trained labour and an educated management are the most valuable created assets that an economy can have. The policy should create

a 'learning society' that supports and rewards the acquisition of new skills and promotes the flexibility needed for adapting to constant changes in the economy and technology.[159]

- Measures to ease adjustment frictions are often a necessary element. Emphasis should be on all industries (including traditional ones) that use modern technologies.
- A relatively easy international transfer of production from one location to another within a liberal trading system has to be borne in mind. National location-specific advantages (clusters and networks of excellence) for the production of specific goods and services should be cultivated.
- The policy should not neglect the creation of SMEs, which form valuable links throughout the economy, not only with large firms, but also with producers and consumers.
- There should be a consensus among the major players (employers, employees and the government) in the economy about the global economic goals and means for their achievement. These players should also be committed to the achievement of the agreed goals. This implies that the long-term vision of the goals needs to be realistic.
- Innovation in general, and faster innovation than others, in particular, ought to be matched by education and training that will enable the labour force to exploit profitable new opportunities.
- Public support to R&D and innovation should increase the exchange of information among the interested parties.
- As private capital is generally uninterested in investment in certain types of infrastructure, the government should become involved and stimulate public–private partnership.

Although industrial policy is wider than trade or competition policy, the boundaries between them are blurred. Whether an industrial policy increases national GDP compared with what would happen without it can be debated for a long time without reaching a solution that would satisfy everyone. A promising industrial policy should neither shield expanding industries from competition for an excessively long period of time nor prevent the attrition of declining industries for ever. It ought to facilitate the movements of factors from industries that employ obsolete technologies to industries that use modern technologies.

Industrial policy has to be well coordinated at all levels of government with other economic policies that affect the manufacturing and services sectors. Without successful communication, understanding, harmonisation and coordination, intervention in industry will be similar to the work of a brain-damaged octopus. This holds both for single countries and for schemes that integrate countries. None the less, traditional behaviour is sometimes hard to change in reality, even though the need for change is recognised. The EU has chosen the Single European Market and the eurozone as the means for creating conditions for change according to the market criterion of efficiency. It is up to the economic agents to take advantage of these opportunities.

Some results from such a choice have begun to emerge. The industrial structure of the EU countries became more specialised from the early 1980s. This confirms the theoretical expectations of both the standard, neo-classical theory and the new theory of economic integration. A new pattern in the geography of industrial production is emerging in the EU. The major features of this process of divergence in the economic structure of the EU(15) countries include the following (Midelfart-Knarvik et al., 2002, p. 256):

- The process is slow and does not generate great adjustment costs.
- There was a certain convergence among the geography of production in the EU countries towards the EU average during the 1970s, whereas since the early 1980s countries have tended to diverge from the EU average. This is a general sign of increased national specialisation in the EU. The most remarkable national change in the geography of production was the spread of relatively high-technology and high-skill industries to the EU peripheral countries (Ireland and Finland).
- Not all industries follow the same path as a reaction to economic integration. Some of them concentrate, while others spread (contrary to the expectations of neo-classical theory). Several forces, therefore, drive such changes in the structure of production. Strong functional intra-industry linkages (high share of intermediate goods from the same industry and/or the need for a large pool of highly skilled labour and researchers) stimulate agglomeration. Weak functional linkages acts as an incentive to the spread of production.
- While 'economic integration' has made the US geography of industrial production more homogeneous (less specialised) since the 1940s, integration in the EU had as its consequence growing disparity (increasing specialisation) in manufacturing production. This slow process in both regions shows no sign of abating. The unquestionable driving force for this is still not known.
- The slow change in the geography of production has not provoked major adjustment costs in the EU. If this continues, and if it is associated with production linkages and comparative advantages, there will be long-term benefits for everyone.

- Availability of highly skilled and educated workers and engineers is becoming an increasingly important determinant of industrial location.
- Agglomeration tendencies towards the central locations have become more pronounced for industries that use many intermediate inputs.
- High returns to scale are becoming weaker as centripetal (agglomeration) forces.

A man's steps are of the Lord;
How then can a man understand his own way?
Proverbs 20:24

4.5 Spatial location of production and regional policy

4.5.1 INTRODUCTION

Where economic activity will locate in the future is one of the most important and challenging questions in economics. Progress in technology, changes in demand and moves towards a liberal economic policy create new challenges for theorists, policy makers and business executives. As a number of economic activities became 'footloose', highly mobile and internationally connected, one of the most demanding and intricate questions in such a situation is where firms and industries will locate, relocate or stay.

Regional policy dealing with the spatial location of production, as a part of the EU Cohesion Policy,[160] affected the daily life of almost half of the 380 million people who lived in the EU(15). It affects even more people out of the 456 million in the EU(25). The EU regional policy involves various subsidies and development projects, including infrastructure, training and support to SMEs, in order to ease and remedy regional disparities. The objective is to strengthen the output potential of the disadvantaged locations and regions, as well as to reinforce the unity (cohesion) with diversity of the EU.

Annual expenditure from the EU structural funds[161] was about 30 per cent (this is second to the EU expenditure on agriculture) of the overall EU budget of €100 billion during the 2000–06 financial perspective. As a result, European integration has a direct and significant impact on a substantial number of EU citizens and businesses. The importance of the EU regional policy ought to increase in the future not least because of two crucial developments:

- *Eurozone* Member countries can no longer deal with national economic problems using policy instruments such as interest rate, inflation, excessive deficit-financed expenditure or changes in the exchange rate. Potential national balance of payments disequilibria became regional disequilibria in an EMU. Hence, one of the policy instruments to deal with such problems is regional policy.

- *Eastern enlargement* Eight central and east European countries plus Cyprus and Malta joined the EU in 2004. Other countries may also join the group in the future. The eastern enlargement has highlighted regional disparities in the EU. Thus, the EU(15) will continue to assist (as much as the political will and resources permit during the 2007–13 financial perspective) the central and east European EU countries. This assistance will be necessary for quite some time to come in order to ensure that these countries adjust well and with least disturbance to the EU membership.

Various theoretical and policy-oriented aspects that affect the location of production, as well as regional policy, such as competition, industrial and trade policies or the choice of spatial location of foreign-owned firms (TNCs), have already been encountered in this book. The purpose of this section is to present the issues related to the spatial location of firms and industries, the impact of economic integration and the EU regional policy.

The section is structured as follows. First, the issues relating to the location of firms and industries are examined (4.5.2), followed by a brief survey of the theoretical foundations of how firms and industries fit and stay in a certain geographical space (4.5.3). Then follows a simplified explanation of the creation of cities and clusters (4.5.4 and 4.5.5, respectively). The role of historical lock-in effect and expectations is then examined (4.5.6), followed by an exploration of how wars influence then location of production (4.5.7). Theory of spatial location is then discussed (4.5.8), followed by an outline of the theory of regional policy (4.5.9). The next two subsections (4.5.10 and 4.5.11) consider, respectively, objectives and instruments of a regional policy. Then, we examine the impact of economic integration on regions (4.5.12) and various aspects of regional policy in the EU (4.5.13). The conclusion (4.5.14) is that the EU(25) should pay attention to regional and cohesion matters for three reasons. First, in an EMU (eurozone), balance of payments disequilibria are replaced by regional disparities. Second, eastern enlargement deepened the regional problem. Third, there is a constant need for the coordination on all levels of government of various policies that have a regional impact.

4.5.2 ISSUES

Spatial economics (geography of production, that is, the spatial relation among economic units) has been separately analysed as a sub-branch of a number of subjects within economics. It has, however, been treated with different intensity and depth within those research disciplines. Contributions are scattered widely across fields which include: microeconomics, planning, development, economic geography, regional science, urban economics, location theory, industrial organisation, international trade,[162] FDI, transport economics, business economics, innovation studies, public finance, price theory, imperfect competition, labour economics, environment and resource economics. The common research denominator in all these fields was the spatial dimension, which was seen as an opportunity, a medium for interactions and a limitation. As a multidisciplinary research field, new[163] spatial economics has integrated these previously separate research areas. This is in line with the new trend in science which includes merging various methods in research.

In this complex situation, the crucial questions for research, business decisions and economic policy are the following:

- Where will economic activity locate in the future?
- Does international economic integration encourage agglomeration, clustering, spatial concentration of industries, adjoint locations of linked productions and 'thick' market effects? Or, alternatively, does agglomeration encourage economic integration?
- Does this cause convergence or divergence in the geography of production in the participating countries?
- Does this induce convergence or divergence in income in the participating countries?
- How do these forces interact?
- What is the role and effect of public policy (intervention)?
- What will be the properties of economic adjustment (spatial and industry-wise reallocation of resources) to the new situation?
- Where will the 'hot spots' be for the location of business?
- Who will benefit from these developments?

The spatial location of a firm is an issue only in the situation with market imperfections. Without market imperfections such as transport cost (so that location matters),[164] the production location decision becomes irrelevant. This is to say that without market failures, firms can split into units of any size and operate in all locations without any cost disadvantage. Recent empirical research found 'that the degree of production indeterminacy is greatest when trade barriers and trade costs are relatively low' (Bernstein and Weinstein, 2002, p. 73).

According to neo-classical theory, while considering feasible locations for its business in the situation with market imperfections, a firm may either:

- consider cost minimisation (prefer the spatial location with the lowest-cost production function and ignore the demand side); or
- emphasise profit maximisation (demand/revenue and neglect everything else).

In practice, neither of these choices necessarily offers the optimal location in terms of profit. Therefore, when considering possible locations for its business, a firm studies both options simultaneously. The firm attempts to maximise profit, taking into account the operating cost 'penalty' linked with alternative geographical locations.

Apart from these basic, static, 'clean' and direct neo-classical elements, it is essential to employ at least two other approaches in the consideration of spatial location of firms:

- *The behavioural approach* This is employed because of the internal dynamics of a firm. The real situation is charged with imperfections, risks and uncertainties. Therefore, profit optimisation or maximisation may not be the ultimate choice and goal for the firm. In the situation with bounded rationality and imperfect information, firms may choose to have a profit 'satisfactory' behaviour as their business goal.
- *The institution–environment-related approach* Firms make their decisions actively in a dynamic and risky environment in which there are multiple choices and limitations. Firms have to obey laws; fulfil obligations (taxes) and negotiate subsidies with the government; negotiate contracts with suppliers, clients and unions; organise and control production; consider new products, technologies and markets; decide about marketing and prices; and the like. In these circumstances, SMEs often have relatively little leverage, while large firms fare much better.

In the distant past, the resource endowment of a specific location, together with the available technology, was the principal determinant of location for the manufacturing industry. In the new situation, in which most determinants for the spatial location of firms and industries are mobile and man-made, the location determinants for (footloose, mobile and internationally connected) industries and firms include the following considerations:

- *Costs and prices*: availability, substitutability, quality and prices of inputs (raw materials, energy, labour); cost of market access (trade costs); economies of scale; utility costs; infrastructure; transport cost of inputs and output; earlier sunk costs in other locations (not yet depreciated); availability of investment funds; and cost of the project.

- *Demand*: its real and potential size, its growth and consumer preferences.
- *Organisation and technology*: input–output production links; externalities; competition and market structure; location decisions of other competing or supplying firms; technology and the speed of its change; and local R&D resources and capabilities.
- *Policy-related factors*: incentives; taxes; subsidies; public procurement; permissions; and mandatory or voluntary unionisation of labour.
- *Social factors*: spread of literacy and bureaucratisation of the society;[165] system of education of management and training of labour; brain drain; income distribution;[166] general quality of life; and retirement patterns.

Hence, making a decision about the location of a firm or an industry is a complex, uncertain and risky task. It comes as no surprise that the national or regional production geography does not always change very quickly.

4.5.3 THEORIES OF LOCATION

The study of the location of production (spatial economics; economic geography) has a long history. In spite of the general interest, there is no wide consensus in the literature about the factors that influence the location of new businesses. The problem was noted, for example, by Ohlin who wrote that 'the theory of international trade is nothing but *internationale Standortslehre*' (teaching about international location) (Ohlin, 1933, p. 589). In the same vein, Isard wrote that 'location cannot be explained without at the same time accounting for trade and trade cannot be explained without the simultaneous determination of locations. . . . trade and location are the two sides of the same coin' (Isard, 1956, p. 207).

A country's or a region's level of income and its structure of production (size, scope and variety of firms and industries) depend on at least two factors. The first includes a country's endowment of primary and derived stock of factors such as land, labour, capital, infrastructure, technology, as well as production, organisation, entrepreneurial and control skills and competences. The other element is how the country or region interacts with the external environment; in particular, the extent, level and form of its access to the international market for goods, services, capital and knowledge.

Let us now turn to the principal theories of firm location. Acknowledging the arbitrary character of our classification and its limits, we shall look into the issue of how and where firms and industries locate in space, while ignoring the origin, control and ownership of the firm. The issue of foreign ownership and control of firms (TNCs) is considered in the discussion on factor mobility (see Chapter 3).

A starting point in location (spatial) theory and economic geography is the national endowment of primary factors of production. Adam Smith and David Ricardo referred to the geography of production and spatial economics in an indirect way. A country specialises in the production of a good for which it has an absolute advantage in production. Hence, according to Smith, an *absolute advantage* determines the geographical location of production. Ricardo's argument is similar, but in his model a country specialises in the production of goods for which it has a *comparative advantage* in production. Regarding land, the fertile areas are put into cultivation first, while less productive land enters use only as demand for agricultural goods increases.

The models by Smith and Ricardo depend on constant returns to scale and on the assumption that competitive prices guide spatial resource allocation. Hence, free trade allows countries to gain, because they specialise in production that they carry out comparatively well. Such an assumption is challenged by the view that there are in reality important market distortions such as monopolies, externalities (pollution), controlled prices and rigid wages that do not tell the truth about social costs. As such, they send wrong price signals and may lead to the conclusion that trade liberalisation may make matters even worse! Thus some argued that protectionist policies were required for:

- the security of jobs, as was the case during the 1930s and ever since; or
- the safeguard of infant industries, as during the 1950s; or
- rent shifting in oligopolistic markets, as during the 1980s; or
- the safety of the environment and social (labour) standards, as is currently the case.

In addition to these classical models, the standard neo-classical *factor endowment* or *Heckscher–Ohlin* model refers to locational fundamentals. The national endowment of factors (land, capital and labour) and their relative proportion decides the location of production. A relatively abundant national factor of production (compared with other factors) determines what a country produces and exports.[167] Conversely, a country will import goods whose production requires factors that are scarce in the national economy. Considering cases of 'localisation' of industry in one or a few countries, Ohlin (1933, p. 133) simply argued that 'it must be shown that costs of production on the basis of existing factor prices are lower than in other countries: certain factors are cheaper here than abroad, which accounts for that condition'.

In an empirical study of trade patterns of over a hundred economies, Leamer (1984) confirmed that the factor endowment model can explain these trade patterns rather well. This model elegantly assumes that there are no specific factors and that production functions are identical in all countries. As such, it does not give the answer to the whole issue, for it cannot explain intra-industry trade. This type of trade, which includes a large part of trade among developed countries, is not based on differences in factor endowments among them.

The factor endowment model has been one of the two principal single-cause models dealing with specialisation, trade and spatial location of production. The other principal approach takes account of differences in technology, economies of scale and learning by doing. It was conceived by Krugman (1979, 1980) and later developed and expanded both by him and by a host of others. In a nutshell, a variety of causes including history, expectations and changes in technology (not only factor endowment as before) influence a country's specialisation, spatial location of production and, hence, trade patterns. Differences in technology and increasing returns to scale change productivity levels. This in turn alters the bases for specialisation, spatial location of production and trade patterns. In the case where there are both increasing returns to scale and transport costs, there is an incentive to concentrate production. By spatially concentrating production near its largest market, a firm can both profit from economies of scale and minimise transportation costs. Economies of scale have a stronger impact on the location of modern, knowledge-based production than was the case before the Industrial Revolution.

While one cannot dispute the importance of factor proportions for the location of production and some processing of primary resources, this approach cannot explain the location of a footloose, mobile and internationally connected industry. In addition, this model does not consider market structure, economies of scale, demand conditions or trade costs. The Heckscher–Ohlin theory cannot explain the location of an industry in regions with high mobility of factors such as the US and China or in countries with a broadly similar endowment of factors (France and Germany). A common feature in the standard trade theory is that it considers states, while it utterly ignores firms or regions, that is, the distribution of economic activity within a country. This gap is filled by spatial economics.

In their survey of trade theory, Leamer and Levinsohn (1995, p. 1363) stated that 'one rather awkward assumption that cries out for change is that of equal numbers of commodities and factors. After all, we really don't know how to count either.' The existence of more goods than factors, economies of scale, multiple equilibria, trade costs and differences in technology present the principal obstacles for predicting the spatial location of production and specialisation.

Harris (1954) argued that manufacturing firms tend to locate in places where they have favourable access to the market. He showed that the industrialised US regions were also the areas of high *market potential* (a large market attracts producers). The idea is that firms choose to locate in regions that have good market access. However, this access is good in areas in which many other firms already exist and have chosen to settle. There is a self-reinforcing, snowball or herding effect in which the size of the market attracts still more firms. The underlining feature of this approach, like in most models of spatial economics, is that it is based on some kind of economies of scale that rely on a spatial concentration (agglomeration) of certain production activities. Such agglomeration economies represent increasing returns in spatial form.[168] In the case of France, Crozet et al. (2004, pp. 50–51) found that firms from Belgium, Germany and Switzerland initially preferred to locate their operations in the frontier regions, near their home market. However, once they had learned how to operate in France, it became more important to be physically closer to final demand and less relevant to be in locations that share common attributes with the home country.

In the presence of economies of scale and transport costs, countries tend to specialise and export differentiated goods for which they have a relatively large domestic market. It is this large domestic demand or *home market* effect (Linder, 1961; Krugman, 1980) that induces production, rather than domestic factor endowment. The response by firms to strong local demand for a product (and the possibility of making savings in trade costs) is so powerful that the country then exports that product. Countries have a competitive edge in the production of these goods and thus gain an advantage in foreign markets, while they import goods demanded by a minority of the home population. The factor endowment or comparative advantage model would not predict the home market effect. However, economic geography would expect such results. The US, Japan and Germany have the greatest comparative advantage in goods for which their home market is relatively big. These are standardised goods for mass consumption. Empirical investigation by Davies and Weinstein (2003) found support for the existence of home market effects, as well as for the role and importance of increasing returns in determining the production structure in the OECD countries.

At the heart of von Thünen's (1826) location theory are differences in land rents and land uses. This model is primarily concerned with the *location of agricultural production*. While Ricardo focuses on the difference in the fertility of land, von Thünen studies how different agricultural lands around a city (marketplace) bid for various uses. The model assumes a given isolated city (one consuming centre) and surrounding agricultural hinterland, homogeneous land surface, free and costless mobility of labour and identical tastes at all income levels. Land rents are highest in the city. From there, they steadily decline to zero at the outermost limit of cultivation (beyond that limit, land is a free good). Hence the rent in a given location totals the difference between the value of its yield minus the sum of production and transport costs. Under the above assumptions the model explains the kind of crop that would be grown at places located at different distances from the market. In other words, farmers decide on the type of production (expensive to transport vegetables and cheap to transport grain) by taking into account land rent and cost of transport. As transport costs and yields differ among crops, the result is a spontaneous development of concentric circles of production around the city. Land is allocated among different crops in a(n) (optimal) way that minimises production and transport costs of different crops.

Von Thünen's model is based on careful study of farming practices in northern Germany in the early 19th century. Such distribution of farmland is less obvious in the more intricate modern world, but there are certain remnants around large urban centres such as dairy production and gardening. This early model, however, does not consider the role played by economies of scale. There is no answer to the question whether vegetables can be shipped in both directions: towards the city (in exchange for cloth) and towards the outermost limits of cultivation (in exchange for grain). The model is, therefore, suitable for the analysis of a pre-railroad and a pre-industrial society.

The problem with von Thünen's model is to find which good to produce in the given location. In the optimal plant site model by Weber (1909) the branch of industry is given, so the problem is to find the spatial location for production. Weber's model takes the spatial location of markets, raw materials and population as given and assumes that there can be only one location for production. The objective of an individual firm is to *minimise the combined costs of production and delivery*. When the production costs are independent of location, the locational problem relates to the minimisation of transport costs (TC) for inputs and output. This is shown in equation (4.5), where m presents weight of goods in tons, t stands for cost of transport per ton/km, d is distance in kilometres, while i represents a particular good in transport. The key condition in the decision-making process about the spatial location of a firm refers to the minimal TC.[169]

$$TC = \min \sum_{t=1}^{3} m_i t_i d_i. \tag{4.5}$$

When key resources are used on a large scale in certain industries and are highly localised, this may affect the location of the manufacturing industry. These industries would be tempted to locate near resource sites. Hence, this case is 'out of step' with the spatial uniformity and the underlying principle of central-place location for some, but not all, kinds of manufacturing. The problem with the Weber approach to the location of new firms is in the initial linear and static locational needs of a firm, which may alter over time as the firm, industry, technology, consumers' needs, income and tastes, or markets change and evolve. Weber assumes fixed and identical production functions at all locations (elasticities of substitution are zero). But firms always combine inputs and compare alternatives substitutes. This model does not take into account important location-related elements which include the cost of land and labour in the considered locations. There is also the possibility of a historical accident which can be coupled with the economies of scale, lock-in effect and agglomeration.

Moses (1958) extended Weber's work and integrated location theory with the theory of production. Coefficients in production functions were allowed to alter. This approach allowed investigation of the relation between substitution of inputs and geographical location of a firm. Hence, Moses' approach gave different location results from Weber's because it allowed for the existence of economies of scale. The problem with the Weber–Moses transport-only approach to the location of firms is that it does not consider market prices and profit of the firm in the selected location. This is relevant as transport, logistics and overall trade costs often represent only a small share of total costs in most firms.

Geographical remoteness can be a handy scapegoat to some, who may use it to explain why peripheral regions are marginalised in economic and social terms. Hummels (1999) argues that geographical factors remain an important determinant of both trade and location. He suggests furthermore that trade composition patterns and FDI decisions can be sensitive to changes in the relative cost of different transport modes and information transfer. His proposition that international transportation costs have not declined significantly receives some support from Finger and Yeats (1976), who demonstrate that with the process of tariff liberalisation overseen by the GATT/WTO the effective rate of protection in the form of transport costs exceeds that from tariff barriers for many commodities. However, this is a shallow justification for many industries. Because of innovations in transport and communication technologies, these costs are rarely the most important determinant for the location of business. In addition, the cost of 'transport disadvantage' on exports is already included in the local factor prices. Hence, a peripheral location is not an insurmountable obstacle for a number of businesses as demonstrated in the cases of countries such as Japan, Australia, New Zealand, Finland or Ireland.

Christaller (1933) attempted to clarify and explain the rationale for the number, size and spatial distribution of cities (in southern Germany). The inductive analysis of this geographer is based on the idea of market threshold and transport distance. He suggested that cities form a *hierarchy of central places*. This hinges on the supposition that larger cities can sustain a wider variety of activities relative to smaller (low-order) cities and villages. Economies of scale are the source of such uneven distribution of production. The consequence of Christaller's model is that if there are economies of scale, then the size of the market matters for the location of business. The concern here, therefore, is about the most 'national' product, below which are other products. The hidden idea in this model is based on the minimisation of transport costs by rational consumers who make multipurpose trips. In spite of its obvious value for the analysis of urban growth and distribution of services, this rigid application of the impact of market size ignores the consequences of unequal distribution of natural resources, changes in technology and negative externalities that come from agglomeration.

Developing further the central-place theory and the issue of how the economy fits into space, the economist Lösch (1940) started with a useful, but most unrealistic, assumption that there is a perfectly even distribution of raw materials and population. He starts his deductive consideration of the homogeneous economic landscape with a 'local' good and seeks to *minimise transport costs* for a given density of central places. In such a space, centres specialise in different products, hence there is a diversification of economic landscape. An efficient pattern of central places would have the shape of nested hexagonal (honeycomb) market areas with no empty corners.[170] This means that certain economic activities can be done only at a restricted number of locations. It was subsequently demonstrated that there is a wide range of geographical configurations of firms. The spatial arrangements that can satisfy the equilibrium condition include squares, rectangles and regular and irregular hexagons (Eaton and Lipsey, 1976, p. 91). Even though based on unrealistic assumptions, the model of central places need not be disregarded out of hand. A coherent general equilibrium model found some justification for the central-place theory (Krugman, 1993a, p. 298).

While the background theory in Christaller's model of central places is implicit, Lösch's separate approach made it explicit. When they seek to find synchronised locations for many kinds of goods and services they use different arguments. Lösch's model is more appropriate for the analysis of the manufacturing sector, while Christaller's hierarchies are more relevant for the tertiary sector (retail services). In any case, it would seem that Christaller and Lösch both deal with planning problems, rather than with considerations of market results.

The theory of central places points to the factors that need to be examined during the decision-making process about the location of an industry or a firm. These factors are sources of supply, intersections of traffic routes and the centre of gravity.[171] In order to reduce inaccuracies in such a 'technical' process (suitable for the centrally planned system), it is necessary to consider additional elements that are part and parcel of a market-based economy, including actions of other functionally related firms, competitors, consumers and government policies.

The classical German location theory dealt with the locational decisions of firms which are in essence reduced to two issues: homogeneous distribution of natural resources over a flat space and optimum cost of transport. This literature was obsessed with the geometrical shape of market areas in an idealised landscape or with the optimal production site with given resources and markets. It ignored the crucial issue of market structure and competition. This was 'doing things in the wrong order, worrying about the details of a secondary problem before making progress in the main issue' (Krugman, 1992, p. 5). Organisational issues such as institutional reality and policies were put aside. Institution-free theoretical models avoid the problem of the impact of various policies on the location or reallocation of firms and industries.

Perroux (1950, 1955, 1961) introduced a predominantly intuitive concept of *growth poles* in spatial economics. The idea was discussed in the context of controversy between balanced and unbalanced regional growth during the 1950s. Geographical agglomeration, significant production linkages (with the key industry) and strong human contacts are necessary for the growth of a pole. A firm is located in a space consisting of poles. Each pole has both centrifugal and centripetal forces. Hence, each pole has its zone of influence (it both attracts and repels firms) and interacts with other poles. If, however, a certain pole does not have a degree of flexibility and adaptability to new technologies and changes in the market, it will stagnate and decline. For instance, France selected eight urban areas and bolstered their growth during the 1960s in the expectation that such a policy would counteract the growth of Paris. Hence, the policy of spatial concentration of investments was diluted over time as it was coupled with political snags. Many other national 'areas' exerted pressure to be included in the select group of geographical poles for special treatment. The evaluation of the policy of growth poles is beset by difficulties, as it was not vigorously implemented in practice.

Multiple equilibria create a situation for welfare ranking and set up many temptations to try to pick winners. The selection problem, however, remains unresolved as the entire system is unstable. Hence a small *historical accident* (chance, arbitrariness, serendipitous event, a small difference in timing)[172] remains the unique deciding factor that can sway the final outcome (Arthur, 2002, p. 6). If governments want to tip markets towards a preferred solution, then it is timing and, to an extent, instruments that are crucial. There is only a narrow window of opportunity during which the policy may be effective. Otherwise, governments with their limited knowledge, instruments and resources will try to stabilise a 'naturally' unstable and evolving process artificially.

Arthur (1989, 1990a, 1994a, 1994b) argued that certain models of production geography give weight to differences in factor endowment, transport costs, rents and competition. In such cases, the pattern of production locations is an equilibrium outcome. Hence, in these models history does not matter: the locational system is determinate and predictable (Arthur, 1994a, pp. 49–50). However, if one takes increasing returns and multiple equilibria into consideration, the new dynamic model of selection and adoption has four properties that create serious challenges and difficulties in analysis and policy making (Arthur, 1989, pp. 116–17):

- *Multiple equilibria (non-predictability)* *Ex ante* knowledge of firms' preferences and potentials of technologies may not be sufficient to predict the 'market outcome'. The outcome is indeterminate.[173]
- *Potential inefficiency (there is no optimality)* Alternative technologies may compete passively (like certain species in biology) or actively and consciously. Active and strategic competition relies on sponsorship such as aggressive advertisement campaigns in which each rival emphasises its own superiority. Increasing returns (*i*-activities) may imbue the development of technology with inferior long-run aptitude as firms make irreversible investments under uncertainty.[174] Basically, a superior technology may have bad luck in gaining early adherents. For example, the American nuclear industry is dominated by light-water reactors as a consequence of the adoption of such a reactor to propel the first nuclear submarine in 1954. Engineering literature asserts, however, that a gas-cooled reactor would have been a superior choice (Arthur, 1989, p. 126). If the claim by engineers is that Sony's Betamax is a technically superior system for videotape recorders, then the market choice of the VHS (around 1980) did not represent the best outcome.[175] Similar arguments could be used for the triumph of user-unfriendly DOS over Macintosh during the mid-1980s. Another example relates to the 'qwerty' arrangement

for typewriters (a reference to the first six top-line letters on the keyboard). The keyboard was designed at the end of the 1860s by Christopher Latham Sholes, a Milwaukee mechanician, who was more interested in a distribution of keys to prevent jams than in fast strokes. Augustus Dvorak, a professor at the University of Washington, designed the most comfortable, user-friendly and efficient keyboard during the 1920s. The Dvorak keyboard enables a significant increase in typing speed, but it continues to languish in obscurity. Even though it has repeatedly been shown that the 'qwerty' distribution of letters is suboptimal, this system continues to be the standard for keyboards.[176] This shows that the market often chooses what is good at replicating itself, not what is good. Therefore it may be desirable to keep more than one technology alive. This may avoid problems related to monopoly and provide some alternative if things go wrong with the dominant technology; it would be insurance against a possible 'future Chernobyl'.

- *Inflexibility* Once an outcome such as a dominant technology begins to surface it becomes more 'locked in' and persists for a long time. In order to replace an entrenched product or technology, the new one must be superior to the existing one and it must significantly increase consumer convenience. It should be available at a price that takes into account three factors: culture (openness to change); investment of capital and time (learning) in the new good or service (once people learn to use something, they are reluctant to switch to something else); and convenience in use. VCRs were introduced during the 1970s. It has taken three decades to replace them by DVDs and the process is not yet complete. However, Word replaced early text-processing programs such as WordStar, Chi Writer or WordPerfect because it was so much more convenient and powerful that this justified the extra investment in time, money and effort to switch and upgrade.
- *Path dependence (non-ergodicity)*[177] Small, unpredictable, random and arbitrary events (chances, accidents, serendipity), path dependence, even path creation[178] and economies of scale in a non-ergodic system may set in motion mutations in economic structures and routine. These events/facts, like genes in biological evolution, may irreversibly decide behaviour and the direction (path) towards the final outcome.[179] These events are not normalised, or averaged away, or forgotten by the dynamics of the system. Huge sunk costs ensure this irreversible element. There is no homeostasis (habitual return to the initial equilibrium), so the historical CD is played 'only once'. This is a demanding, discrete, uncertain, path-dependent, non-stationary selection and adaptation process in which new knowledge is built on

> previously accumulated knowledge and experience, the results of which are unique and without predestined outcomes. Such an evolutionary view surpasses clear-cut orthodox 'mechanical' economic models in the long-run promise of understanding and (partially) influencing events.

In this model, history matters, but the system's dynamics, increasing returns, multiple equilibria, lock-in effect and path dependence generate theoretical and practical limits to predicting the future spatial location of an industry with a high degree of certitude.

The probability of the location of an industry resulting from a historical accident is shown in highly stylised, graphical form in Figure 4.12. If the distribution of potential locations of an industry is concave (Figure 4.12a), with a single minimum and a corresponding single outcome, the location is not influenced by a historical chance. This type of distribution is exemplified by the mining and steel-making industries, which are usually located close to their source of raw materials. If, however, the distribution is convex (Figure 4.12b), with two minima, then there are two potential outcomes, each resulting in a different location which may depend on historical chance. The third case represents a sphere in which there are *n* solutions for the location of footloose and mobile industries (Figure 4.12c). Hence, multiple equilibria make policy analysis conceptually difficult and uncertain. This type of distribution is exemplified by corner shops, bakeries and petrol stations. However, firms in most industries need to be close to one another (that is, they tend to agglomerate and create towns and cities), not only to be close to common suppliers of inputs, but also to foster competition and to facilitate exchange of information, experience and knowledge, which can be hampered if firms are spatially dispersed.

If agglomeration forces based on increasing returns are unbounded, then a single geographical location monopolises the industry. Which region is selected depends on its spatial attractiveness and the historical accident of

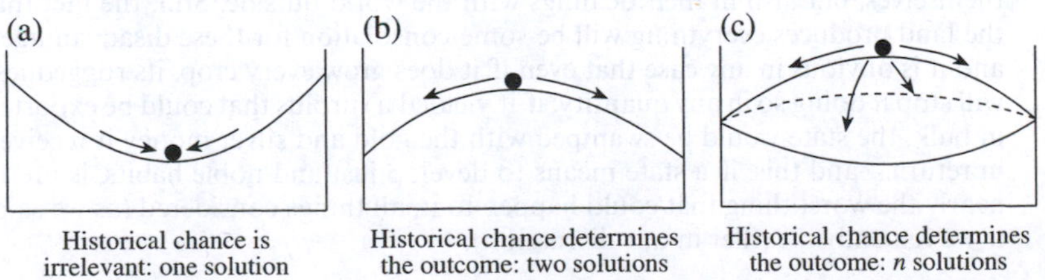

Figure 4.12 Concave (a), convex (b) and spherical (c) distributions of potential industry locations

firm entry, in particular early preferences of first entrants. If, however, agglomeration forces that come from increasing returns are bounded, then various regions may share the industry as if agglomeration economies were absent (Arthur, 1990b, p. 249). Locations with a large number of firms cast an 'agglomeration shadow' in which little or no settlement takes place. This causes separation of an industry. Agglomeration occurs at a certain level of trade costs, while at another level of these costs the spread of activities takes place. With bounded agglomeration economies, neighbouring locations cannot share the industry, but sufficiently separated regions can. In France, for example, Lyon lies between Paris and Marseille. Bounded agglomeration economies caused separation and dispersion. Again, 'which locations gain the industry and which become orphaned is a matter of historical accident' (ibid., p. 247).

4.5.4 CITIES

A city may be thought of in economic terms (with certain qualifications) as the absence of space among people, firms and institutions. It is pertinent to recall Plato's discussion about the location of cities or city-states written in 360 BC in *The Laws* (Book IV) (Plato, 1980, p. 159):

> Then the state will have tolerably healthy prospects of becoming virtuous. If it were going to be founded near the sea and have good harbours, and were deficient in a great number of crops instead of growing everything itself, then a very great saviour indeed and lawgivers of divine stature would be needed to stop sophisticated and vicious characters developing on a grand scale: such a state would simply invite it. As it is, we can take comfort in those eighty stades. Even so, it lies nearer the sea than it should, and you say that it is rather well off for harbours, which makes matters worse; but let's be thankful for small mercies. For a country to have the sea nearby is pleasant enough for the purpose of everyday life, but in fact it is a 'salty-sharp and bitter neighbour' in more senses than one. It fills the land with wholesaling and retailing, breeds shifty and deceitful habits in a man's soul, and makes the citizens distrustful and hostile, not only among themselves, but also in their dealings with the world outside. Still, the fact that the land produces everything will be some consolation for these disadvantages, and it is obvious in any case that even if it does grow every crop, its ruggedness will stop it doing so in any quantity; if it yielded a surplus that could be exported in bulk, the state would be swamped with the gold and silver money it received in return – and this, if a state means to develop just and noble habits, is pretty nearly the worst thing that could happen to it, all things considered (as we said, if we remember, earlier in our discussion).

Urbanisation is one of the important features of modern society. One of the reasons for this development is a declining share of labour relative to capital in agriculture. Footloose industries are less reliant on natural inputs than other types of manufacturing and service industries. In some cases they may place more emphasis on the proximity to final markets which further adds to the urbanisation trend. Another incentive for urbanisation comes from the dependency of many manufacturing and service operations on access to public services, in particular in the countries that are known for intervention. Because of this, lobbyists cluster in politically significant cities such as Brussels or Washington, DC because that is the geographical location where decisions are made, procurement contracts awarded and subsidies distributed.

In the dim and distant past, the creation of wealth largely depended on the local availability of natural resources. A mix of geographical, economic and historical factors shaped industrial development and the location of firms, industries and cities. However, as the economy evolved, wealth creation came to depend more on the accumulated physical assets (mainly equipment and finance).[180] The prosperity of the modern economy depends not only on the physical resources but also and increasingly on intangible assets such as knowledge,[181] information-processing potentials, and organisation and control capabilities.

Regarding the location of cities and clusters, spatial economics distinguishes between first- and second-nature geography. *First nature* refers to the preference of certain locations because of their natural endowments of factors (fresh water, deposits of coal or minerals) or proximity to rivers, estuaries, coasts or natural harbours. *Second nature* geography refers to the actions by human beings to improve and extend the 'first nature'. This deals with economies of scale and interaction among economic agents. Even though cities were initially created to reduce transport and communication costs for people and their goods and ideas (to eliminate physical space between people and firms), many other factors were quite accidental.[182] The most attractive spatial locations for setting up cities, industries and businesses included:

- crossroads;
- estuaries;
- safe natural harbours with a rich hinterland;[183]
- defendable hilltops;
- places with ample fresh water and rich soil; and
- dry cool highlands (free of malaria-carrying mosquitoes).

In the past, the location of a firm or a city was influenced both by the endowment of immobile local resources and by flows of mobile factors.[184] Once the development of a business activity starts in an area and if the economic system is flexible, this area attracts other business activities to the region. This model of uneven development is based on the possibility of meaningful multiple equilibria in the presence of external economies. The point is evident: with external economies, the return on resources in a particular industrial activity is higher when more resources are committed to it (Krugman, 1991a, p. 651). The property of a modern firm is high mobility in its search for profitable opportunities, not only within its region or country, but also internationally. For a footloose firm, the advantages of one location in relation to others are much more man-made than subject to resource endowments.

According to the analysis of spatial economics by Fujita et al. (1999, p. 131), cities exist because firms locate at a cusp in the market potential function made by a concentration of other firms. A growing and spreading agricultural population makes it beneficial for producers to develop new cities. The size of the cities differs (there is a hierarchy) because of differences in industrial externalities and transport costs. Finally, natural advantages (such as the existence of harbours) help as they create natural cusps in market potential. Arthur (1994b, p. 109) argued that the observed pattern of cities cannot be explained only by economic determinants without considering chance events. Cities also grew up where immigrants with certain skills settled, where politicians decided to build railways and canals or where trains stopped for the night.

Over the past century, cities that were based on educated and skilled labour have grown faster than comparable cities with less embodied human capital. Firms in such cities are more productive than elsewhere where labour is less skilled. In addition, cities based on skilled labour and management adapt better to shocks. Accumulated knowledge, its transfer through education and spillovers, as well as talents allow easier adaptation to changes, challenges and opportunities. In addition, the lifestyle in such cities may be more attractive to some people than elsewhere. Some three-quarters of the US population live in the 100km wide coastal belt which includes the Great Lakes and the St Lawrence Seaway.

New possibilities and changes such as the use of the Internet permit modification in working time and place of work for select professions. Certain key employees can work at home in the environment that they enjoy best (presumably non-congested countryside). In this situation, certain office space is liberated in cities which may be transformed into entertainment areas. New country towns may be big enough to create employment on their own.[185] This may be a superior way for the future than to endlessly expand the existing urban areas. If commuting becomes less trendy and acceptable because of congestion, new towns may be developed provided that there are suitable locations. Examples can be found in the creation of Milton Keynes in England in 1970, or Stevenage and Corby during the 1950s.

Why are cities of different sizes? Henderson (1974) argued that there is a trade-off between economies of agglomeration of industries specific to that city and general diseconomies (negative externalities) such as costs related to commuting and high rents which (apart from pollution) do not depend on the structure of the local industry. The optimum city size depends on the maximum welfare of participants in the economy. It does not make much sense to put industries without spillovers (steel production and publishing) in the same city. However, it does make sense to locate the steel and textile industries in close proximity as they employ, respectively, mostly male and mostly female labour. Cities need to be specialised in one or a few industries with related external economies. These external economies, however, vary a great deal across industries. Because of strong links internal to the industry, a financial centre may do best if it includes virtually all financial institutions. The same is not true for the textile or food industry. Hence, the optimal size of a city depends on its role (Fujita et al., 1999, p. 20).[186]

Although Henderson deals with spatial aspects, this type of model is surprisingly 'aspatial', because it says little about the actual location of a city, either in space or relative to other cities. In addition, national trade policy can influence the size of a city, as exemplified by Mexico City. An unintended byproduct of the Mexican import-substitution policy was the expansion of the capital city because of production linkages and economies of scale. Once Mexico started to open its economy during the 1980s, there was a relocation of certain firms away from Mexico City, mainly towards the northern frontier.

4.5.5 CLUSTERS

Industrial clusters often determine what a country exports. Their success establishes the competitive position of a country's goods and services on the international market. Prior to the Industrial Revolution, high transport costs splintered production into many units throughout space. The effects of the Industrial Revolution reduced the cost of transport, but brought high fixed costs that contributed to the development of new and the expansion of existing agglomerations.

A promising point of departure for the analysis of clusters is to consider two basic forces which, through their tension and interplay, influence the spatial distribution (concentration or spread) of firms: the centripetal and centrifugal forces that also help to explain the agglomeration and dispersion forces of the 'core–periphery'[187] development model:

- *Centripetal forces* promote agglomeration. They concentrate production and employment in specific geographical areas. These 'snowball', 'me-too' or herding forces include: market size (concentration of firms and consumers), economies of scale, forward and backward linkages in production, trade costs, increasing returns in transport, existence of suppliers, limited spread of information and embodied knowledge, as well as a 'thick' labour market (especially for certain skills so that employers can find workers and workers can find jobs). Workers can and do invest in industry- and firm-specific productivity-increasing skills, rather than in general ones that they may not need. Centripetal forces take the production system towards the equilibrium.[188]
- *Centrifugal forces* push the other way and test whether the equilibrium is stable. These dispersion (comparative advantage) forces discourage further spatial concentration of business. They favour a geographical spread of firms and include spatial factor immobility, regional or international wage differentials, relative amount of land rents, competition for factors and consumers, commuting costs, pollution, congestion, traffic accidents, crime, allergies, infectious and other diseases, sewage and waste disposal.

The final result depends on the balance between these two forces, on what factors are mobile and what immobile, on barriers to the reallocation of resources, on demand and its change and on public policy. In essence, three outcomes are possible. First, economic activity may spread so that each region, industry and firm becomes more specialised in a certain activity. This type of clustering does not mean polarisation as is exemplified in North America. Second, activity may agglomerate in core regions, leaving others without production potentials and without people. Finally, a long-run polarisation may split the country or an economic grouping into advanced regions with high incomes and low unemployment and depressed regions with low income and high unemployment (Braunerhjelm et al., 2000, pp. 29–30). This final result may turn out to be the creation of a set of growth poles and a set of growth sinks.

A concentration of functionally related business activity within a relatively small area (agglomeration; thick market effects; benefits of co-location; and non-ergodicity) provides firms with collective gains that would not be available if the firms operated in a remote place. These shared benefits or externalities are different from those that are created within and available to a single firm. In essence, clusters create economies that are external to individual firms, but internal to a network of firms in a cluster, which are exchanged and enriched in a non-market way. Hence, a great deal of an individual firm's competitive advantage is outside it, but inside the location where it operates.

A firm locates in an area where there are firms from the same or related industry (in a cluster) because:

- it has production links with other firms;
- it may benefit from the already existing pool of suppliers;
- there are services such as finance, information, consulting and maintenance;
- there may be a pool of trained and experienced labour;
- firms may reduce the cost of transport;
- there may be a concentration of consumers (proximity to the major growing markets is often the most important reason for the selection of a particular location); and
- they may jointly negotiate contracts with transporters and organise export promotion boards and the like.

Manchester (England) in the 19th century provides an example of such a cluster specialising in textile manufacturing. Subsequently, the manufacture and repair of looms, and bleaching, dyeing and finishing facilities also located there. In the course of time, the town set up a technical college in order to train people for the manufacture of machinery, textile design and other skills related to the local industry. All this was supported by marketing organisations such as the Cotton Exchange (Smith, 1981, pp. 60–61). It was a similar story with Reutlingen in Germany. However, even the most recent industries rely on the 'old rule' of geographical concentration (clustering), which is why there is a Silicon Valley in California or a Route 128 in Boston (because of the existence of the best universities in the vicinity).

A more recent example of similar developments in the manufacturing of surgical instruments and certain sports goods can be found in the town of Sialkot (Pakistan), which leads the world in its export of surgical instruments and hand-sewn footballs. This success, as well as that of all other clusters, is based on two factors: first, a demand-driven approach and, second, competition based on collective efficiency (Schmitz, 1998, p. 6). An example of a joint action can be found in the surgical-instruments manufacturing cluster in Tuttlingen (Germany). This cluster produced joint publications on various topics of common interest, including booklets on: quality requirements in the surgical-instrument-making industry; a guide on the correct use of the instruments; and a guide providing customers arriving in Tuttlingen with a list and profile of firms that produce such instruments.

Technical advances in transportation, information technology, organisation and control of production and distribution reduce production time and costs. They 'do away' with distance. 'Globalisation' (integrated international production) creates possibilities for dispersing production and ownership. In such circumstances, already established locations face tougher times anchoring income-generating activities. At the same time, strong centripetal forces ensure that certain spots remain 'sticky places in slippery space' (Markusen, 1996, p. 293). Spatial barriers for the location of businesses are becoming less important, but capital is more sensitive to the choice of location.

Until the 1960s, it seemed to be more efficient to move people to jobs by migration. The footloose element of many modern industries supports production in relatively small and flexible units. Hence, there is an arbitrary and uncertain element (multiple equilibria) in the location of firms that have a footloose industrial character. Locations that are close to consumers save in transport costs of final output, while other locations may save in the cost of production. Due to costs of inputs, economies of scale and forwarding outlays, one business may favour peripheral locations, while another's preference may be for locations nearest to the consumers.

A cluster is a relatively large group (a critical mass) and system (formal and informal) of functionally related specialised firms, knowledge, skills and competences, as well as specialised institutions (standards-setting bodies, schools, universities, research institutes, trade associations), in a particular geographical location. This functional relation among firms may be downstream (suppliers), horizontal (competitors and collaborators), upstream (clients) and/or through the circulation of accumulated knowledge, skills and competences by means of personnel turnover.

Clusters, as spatially limited business incubators, are a part of the new industrial order called 'alliance capitalism', in which continuous collaboration and networking with related knowledge and experience-rich firms are sources of competitiveness. It is also associated with the complex and dynamic 'new economy' based on knowledge and continuous innovation, as firms that operate in clusters are usually innovative. In addition, a vibrant dialogue is constantly taking place among all players in a cluster. The reason why this view fails to define a clear geographical boundary for a cluster is because the structure of a cluster may change over time. Nor does it refer to the specific industrial boundary of a cluster, as this may overlook the complex relationship among different industries that support one another's competitiveness.

Agglomeration and the spatial clustering of firms and industries are motivated by efficiency considerations within a network. They are based on economies of scale in production and transportation, as well as on transaction costs. For example, the Massachusetts General Hospital in Boston is among the largest in the world in terms of R&D funds. Industrial managers are attracted to the R&D department of the hospital because all the specialists and all the needed knowledge are 'within 20 minutes walking' (Lambooy, 1997, p. 298). This cluster of more than 400 firms linked to medical devices is invisible as it is concealed in business categories such as electronic equipment and plastics products.

Agglomeration applies not only to private businesses. Bearing in mind the complexity of action and need for a fast response to changing and uncertain events, Simon Jenkins has noted that 'Britain is a centralised state. Two thirds of the top 100 powerful people in Britain work within 300ft of the Prime Minister and Chancellor of the Exchequer' (*The Times*, 11 December 2002).

Marshall (1890) considered the issue of why it is beneficial for producers from the same industry to be located together. He offered three basic reasons why producers concentrate (form a cluster):

- *Knowledge spillovers*: proximity eases exchange and spread of information.
- Advantages of *thick markets for specialised skills*: firms may easily find the necessary labour and workers may get promotion or work if the current employer does poorly. There is no need to create the human capital from scratch. The 'mysteries of trade' (craft secrets) are no mysteries at all as they are 'in the air' and children learn many of them unconsciously from their parents (vertical cultural transmission).[189] Knowledge, experience and values are 'stored'. In addition, tacit and complex knowledge and shared culture of beliefs and practices is difficult to transfer without labour mobility.
- *Backward and forward linkages* associated with large markets: links may clarify and explain a part of the concentration story only if there are economies of scale. Otherwise, a firm would set up a separate production unit to serve each distinct market. A concentrated industry provides a market for specialised local suppliers of components, as well as private and public suppliers of various services (institutional thickness).

These economies, external to individual firms in a cluster but internal to a network of firms in a cluster, are essential but not sufficient to explain the basic reason for the strength of firms in a cluster. Conscientiously pursued joint action and horizontal and vertical cooperation by firms in a cluster (sharing equipment, developing a new product, various consortia) enhance collective efficiency and improve the competitive advantage of the participating firms. When there is a problem (market failure), it can be resolved by government intervention and/or by private self-help (as was the case in Sialkot, Pakistan) (Schmitz, 1999, pp. 468–70). However, relations between firms in a cluster may take different forms. Take a look, for example, at shoe-producing clusters in Italy and Mexico. While cooperation is more common in Italy, market rules prevail in Mexico.

There are, however, additional reasons for the spatial clustering of firms and industries. They include the following:

- The past arm's-length and hierarchical organisation of a firm can be replaced by a flexible network of business organisation in a cluster, because there is a changed situation in competition and technology. Inter-firm competition is based on innovation.
- Firms may reduce transaction costs.
- The presence of one firm/industry creates a direct or indirect market for another firm/industry. One industry's output is used exclusively as another industry's input (tyres and cars).
- Firms use common services (marketing, storage, accounting, repair, transport).
- Two industries use a common resource.
- Firms may create entry barriers.
- Firms may have the intention to build a shared brand (for example, Solingen knives, Parma cheese and ham; Californian wine).
- Labour markets of two unrelated industries may be complementary: one industry (metal or car assembly) uses male labour, while another (textiles or food processing) employs female labour.
- Firms use common social infrastructure (schools, health, roads).
- The more potential firms that can use the infrastructure, the more likely that infrastructure will be built. Each user in a cluster assists other users in this situation, hence the fixed cost of an infrastructure project (such as educational and training centres, power plant, railway or airport) can be recovered and the project can come close to profitability. These are relatively standard projects, hence the government can readily be involved as specific local knowledge is not always essential for success.

The presence of a relatively large concentration of demanding consumers in an agglomeration, coupled with technologies with economies of scale and agglomeration forces, can bring certain economic advantages through the interrelationship of functionally connected, as well as competing firms. Competition forces firms to employ state-of-the-art technology, hence there are no low-technology industries, but only low-technology firms within various industries.

The clustering of firms selling identical goods (competitors), such as ice cream on the beach, was thought to be welfare inefficient from a social standpoint (Hotelling, 1929, p. 53). However, the clustering of firms often occurs in response to consumers' desires to make comparisons between goods (for example, in shopping malls). Consumers usually visit more than one store prior to making a purchase. Department stores often demand that certain space is made available in shopping malls to small shoe and clothing retailers, to assure clients that the offered goods are balanced by other competitive offers (that is, that a minimum differentiation exists) for comparison. Clustering of *identical* firms can serve a socially useful purpose because they lower transportation costs (Eaton and Lipsey, 1979a, pp. 422–3). The same holds for the clustering of *heterogeneous* firms. A rational consumer would connect purchasing activities such as search, purchase and transport. Multipurpose shopping assists in the lowering of shopping costs (Eaton and Lipsey, 1982, p. 58).

If the firms are similar, they seek comparable if not identical features for the spatial location of business. If this is true, then the outcome may be a cluster in such an industry. For example, the US film industry started a century ago in California, around Los Angeles. The entertainment companies were all looking for comparable locational features such as dry weather and excellent daylight conditions. Although modern filming and lighting technology does not depend on natural light at all, the clustering of the film and entertainment industry in California continued. Homogeneous initial needs of firms created the film cluster rather than the input–output production relations. Hence, functional production links and agglomeration economies are not a necessary condition to create a cluster.

In spite of a few global TV stations such as the BBC or CNN and newspapers such as the *Financial Times*, the *International Herald Tribune* or electronic media, most of the stories that editors publish or broadcast are still local. The proximity of firms in the same industry increases both the visibility of the course of action of competitors and the speed of the spread of information. 'Popular luncheon spots are patronized by executives from several companies, who eye each other and trade the latest gossip. Information flows with enormous speed' (Porter, 1990a, p. 120). This 'cafeteria effect' breaks the spatial boundaries to information flow and gives incentives for the creation of matching improvements by other firms in the cluster. It also offers a partial confirmation that there is a spatial limit to knowledge spillovers. Information may be freely available and transmittable at constant cost notwithstanding distance. However, the charge and trouble for the spread of embodied knowledge, in particular tacit, complex, changeable and 'sticky', increases with the distance.[190]

The high speed of information diffusion is one of the major strengths of clusters. Entrepreneurs often prefer to enter or stay in a cluster even though they may be able to appropriate a higher return on their current innovation elsewhere. The reason for this preference is that the firms in the cluster are not only providers of information, but also recipients (Schmitz, 1999, p. 475). In fields where technology changes often, personal contact may be the preferred way of communication rather than the less timely sources such as professional journals, fairs and conferences. 'Human capital accumulation is a *social* activity, involving *groups* of people in a way that has no counterpart in the accumulation of physical capital' (Lucas, 1988, p. 19; original emphasis). This all supports progress in technology and creation of knowledge.

Personal contacts and informality are essential for the exchange of tacit and complex knowledge:

> *Tacit knowledge*, as opposed to *information* . . . can only be transmitted informally, and typically demands direct and repeated contact. The role of tacit knowledge . . . is presumably the greatest during the early stages of the industry life cycle, before product standards have been established and a dominant design has emerged. (Audretsch, 1998, p. 23; original emphasis)[191]

> Companies that have gone furthest towards linking their global operations electronically report an increase, not a decline in the face-to-face contact needed to keep the firms running well: with old methods of command in ruins, the social glue of personal relations matters more than ever. (*The Economist*, 30 July 1994, p. 11)

Achievements in science and other information may be freely available in various papers, journals or the Internet, but the problem is that only a handful of professionals have the key knowledge and experience to understand that. A big part of science and technology is a 'private good' because it is tacit. Close proximity and a durable social network (behavioural cohesion) shorten the learning curve; informality in contacts and local embeddedness are essential to identify user requirements, proper installation, operation or service of the product.[192] The phrase 'you know what I mean' among members of a professional group in face-to-face communication can be very illuminating.[193] The same holds in relations between suppliers and their clients. What matters in such situations is not only the spatial proximity between the participants, but also their relational closeness together with the sense and logic of belonging to the success of a common project. Therefore, operation of firms within clusters makes firms relatively less sensitive to local taxes. This provides the local authorities with unique opportunities to tax them more heavily than would otherwise be the case.

While close spatial proximity between actors may set favourable conditions for interactive learning and innovation, this is not without perils. Boschma (2005) warns that the negative impact of proximity on innovation may be found in the lock-in effect consisting of routine, the complacency trap and a lack of openness and flexibility. This is related to the following issues:

- *Comprehension* Knowledge building and its extension often ask for different and complementary sources that may trigger new ideas and approaches towards a problem. It also asks for an exchange of information and ideas, as well as for feedback.
- *Organisation* Too much hard hierarchy and organisational closeness may not always recognise and reward (by a bureaucracy) useful ideas.
- *Social embeddedness* Social proximity is necessary and friendly with interactive learning and innovation. The actors share trust based on friendship, common education, experience and/or kinship. This assists in learning and in the exchange of tacit knowledge. But too much closeness creates emotional bonds of loyalty such as friendship and empathy that may introduce negative effects of opportunism.
- *Institutions* Formal (laws) and informal (habits and group norms) institutions provide 'glue' for collective action as they reduce uncertainty and lower transactions costs. Too little institutional proximity is harmful because of the lack of social cohesion and common values. However, too much may introduce inertia and lock-in effects.
- *Geography* There is general agreement in the literature that spatial proximity is relevant for innovation. Knowledge externalities are spatially bounded. Short distances bring people together. This is important for the exchange of tacit knowledge. But too much proximity may be unfriendly with openness for new and fresh ideas.

It is obvious that both too much and too little proximity are detrimental to learning and innovation. Hence, a dynamic context demands a fine balance between the two aspects of proximity. 'To function properly, proximity requires some, but a not too great, distance between actors and organizations' (Boschma, 2005, p. 71).

The principal key to success in clusters of related firms in northern Italy ('Padania') is their ultra-specialisation and family-run type of business. Relatives support one another in business so there is no need for supervision, they constantly upgrade skills and they have opportunities for invention. Common values and objectives, as well as local consensus, are preserved. This reduces the possibility for business sclerosis, so common in large, vertically organised firms. For example, in Lumezzane (near Brescia) which produces two-thirds of the national output of bottle openers, one family specialises strictly in the production of the corkscrews, another has expertise in the covers of the bottle openers and so on. A similar situation can be found in Cadore (near Austria) regarding the production of spectacles. In general, company strategy is friendly with rapid changes, customised products and niche marketing.

A summary of the properties of such industrial districts would include (Garofoli, 1991a, p. 52):

- a high level of division of labour between the firms and closer input–output relations;
- a high level of specialisation which stimulates accumulation of knowledge and introduction of new technologies;
- a high level of skills of workers as a result of a very long-term accumulation of knowledge at a local level;
- a large number of local competitors which leads to the adoption of 'trial and error behaviour' and a fast imitation process;
- efficient local informal (and formal) systems for the exchange of information; and
- an increased emphasis on face-to-face relations.

The existence of the following elements could also be added:

- entrepreneurs;
- innovators;
- financial institutions with venture capital; and
- demanding clients.

The growing importance of intangible assets, particularly intellectual capital together with complexities and changeability of information and uncodified knowledge, increases the importance of knowledge externalities (spillovers) and frequent face-to-face contacts among the relevant players. They need to exchange uncodifiable knowledge, to be involved in interactive learning, to have feedback and suggestions, as well as to have a dialogue about risk and the changing situation in the market and technology. Clear-cut, routine and simple activities based on codified, standardised and teachable knowledge can be managed and controlled from a distance. They can easily be located in regions with lower wages. However, successful handling of more elaborate activities still requires a high degree of exchange of information and face-to-face contacts.[194] This is highly important in complex activities with little or no codified knowledge and where market changes and uncertainty require a fast response (contracts are incomplete). 'Knowledge is the most important resource and learning is the most important process' (Pinch and Henry, 1999, p. 820).

Knowledge externalities are among the key reasons for the existence and success of clusters. Hence, clusters may also be seen as networks for information gathering, fact processing and network creation places. 'Almost every internationally successful Italian industry has several if not hundreds of domestic competitors. Frequently, they are all located in one or two towns. . . . Where domestic rivalry is absent Italian firms rarely succeed internationally' (Porter, 1990a, p. 447).

Toyota in Japan, for example, is cultivating suppliers in its own back yard. Toyota's independent suppliers are on average 94km away from its assembly plants. They make nine deliveries a day. By contrast in North America, GM's suppliers are on average 683km away from plants they serve to which they make fewer than two deliveries a day. One of the results is that Toyota and its suppliers keep inventories that are a quarter the size of GM's.[195] While a just-in-time delivery and logistics method may be technically possible, organisationally feasible and financially desirable for a firm, an area that asks for further research includes the environmental and social costs of this type of logistics. The just-in-time delivery method (as opposed to just-in-case inventory system) is often linked with half loads and more transport journeys than are the more traditional delivery methods.[196]

The existence of competitors in the vicinity serves a useful business and social purpose. If one imagines a cluster in the shape of an input–output matrix for information, then the direct and indirect functional relations are 'diffused' through rows and columns. Competition increases productivity, which is the key ingredient of prosperity. Firms do not pursue every opportunity to ruin rivals. This is contrary to the standard story in every introductory economic textbook.[197] Every firm in a cluster perceives its survival, growth and success in terms of collective growth. These firms learn and prosper collectively. The learning process in a cluster is not only interactive, but also cumulative as it persists over time. Once it exists it does not cease to exist; experience and discovery build on experience and discovery (everyone profits from the past improvements and changes, but not everyone benefits immediately from the current ones). Turnover of labour, technical staff and management among these firms reinforces the transfer of tacit and compound knowledge, cross-fertilising research, collective learning process and regional competitive advantage.

The underlying general operations within a cluster can be seen from another example:

> New York City's garment district, financial district, diamond district, advertising district and many more are as much intellectual centers as is Columbia or

> New York University. The specific ideas exchanged in these centers differ, of course, from those exchanged in academic circles, but the process is much the same. To an outsider, it even *looks* the same: A collection of people in similar activities, each emphasizing his own originality and uniqueness. (Lucas, 1988, p. 38; original emphasis)

Continuous and straight dealings among players allow tacit, complex and accumulated knowledge to be exchanged within a network of players. Social closeness in such cases may be equally, if not more, relevant than the geographical proximity.

Established locations can be vulnerable to 'technological lock-in' in certain cases. New ideas may need new space. 'When IBM developed its own personal computer, the company located its fledgling PC capacity in Boca Ratton, Florida, way outside of the manufacturing agglomeration in the North-east Corridor' (Audretsch, 1998, p. 24). This is an example of a bifurcation point.

Certain industrial regions may become victims of their own past success. Institutional sclerosis, vested interests of large firms, labour unions and public authorities may oppose changes and adjustment to new circumstances. For example, the German Ruhr region was led into the 'trap of rigid specialisation' (Grabher, 1993, p. 275). The Belgian Walloon region is in the same situation. However, it is sometimes overlooked that in certain cases new footloose industries often create their own conditions for growth. For example, new environment-related industries are emerging in the Ruhr (the connection may be the solution of the pollution problem). Formerly coal and steel giants such as Krupp, Thyssen and RAG diversified and invested in environment-related technology, plant engineering and control services. It is estimated that these new activities include about two-thirds of these companies (Hospers, 2004, p. 152). Elsewhere, there is little technological continuity between the textile machinery complex in New England of the 19th century and the current electronics cluster (Boschma and Lambooy, 1999b, p. 394).

The existence of a good university or a research institute is not enough by itself for the overall economic success of an area. During the period of central planning in the former Soviet Union, Akademgorodok (near Novosibirsk) was essentially a town full of research institutes financed by the Soviet Academy of Sciences. It remained an 'isolated island' as it has not developed functional links with industries. During the centrally planned period, the Soviet enterprises depended primarily on the respective ministries and the central plan.

The cluster of high-technology firms around Cambridge (England) offers a different story. The common tacit code of behaviour among such firms in the region includes trust and cooperation. The cluster is based on two local 'collective agents'. They are Cambridge University and consulting firms in R&D. In contrast to most other British universities which have formally regulated links with the industry, Cambridge has rather liberal rules governing such links. In fact, faculty members are allowed to work part-time in the private sector. All this has had a strong and positive spillover effect on the regional cluster of high-technology firms.

Sophia-Antipolis was developed in a vacant space at the end of the 1960s in the south of France. It did not develop around an established university as was the case in Cambridge. Much time and effort, such as the establishment of the University of Nice, was necessary to create the necessary links among the high-technology firms in the Sophia-Antipolis cluster. In general, it is hard to find any plan of action or best practice to promote a cluster that could have instantly recognisable success. However, there is a rare general agreement on one point: to have a commercial success, one needs first to build on and improve already existing competences in the target location. This does not mean that the earlier production has to be continued. However, something (vaguely) related to it may be the starting point. Later on, these local competences may need to be altered, sometimes fundamentally.

There is also the view put forward by Porter:

> [C]lusters often emerge and begin to grow naturally. Government policy had little to do with the beginning of Silicon Valley or the concentration of mechanical firms around Modena, Italy. Once a cluster begins to form, however, government at all levels can play a role in reinforcing it. Perhaps the most beneficial way is through investments to create specialized factors, such as university technical institutes, training centres, data banks, and specialized infrastructure. (Porter, 1990a, p. 655)

In fact, many governments impeded the 'natural' development of clusters on behalf of regional policy and subsidised firms to locate in areas with high unemployment and without supporting infrastructure (rather than to encourage migration of labour from these regions).

Until the 1960s, it was thought that production costs were not sensitive to regional location. It is therefore not surprising that a number of firms located in such areas became 'white elephants' that were demanding and dependent on subsidies to continue operations. The importance of endogenous technological change came to be appreciated only in the following decades, so the policy of regional decentralisation became suspect (Bekar and Lipsey, 2001, p. 1). However, universities have always been established in cities, where there are many children and students. Only relatively recently have universities become established in the countryside.

Governments and large TNCs often have nothing to do with the establishment of clusters such as Silicon Valley, clusters in Italy or the City of London financial district. These clusters were created out of 'thin air' and largely proceeded on 'autopilot'.[198] In most other cases, the role of the government was unclear. However, governments may well support the growth of clusters through the provision of education, infrastructure, tax policy and public procurement, as well as through sponsoring R&D.[199]

If one wants to intervene and to assist the creation of a cluster, then one ought, perhaps, to start to build on some of the existing local specialties and competences, rather than create entirely new ones. This does not mean that the 'same old thing' ought to be perpetuated indefinitely because of necessary adaptations to the industrial structure and adjustment to the changing situation. However, something (vaguely) related to it may be a good start. If the location in question has accumulated knowledge in the production of fertilisers, it would be sensible to start the production of pharmaceuticals rather than TV sets for which there is no accumulated local knowledge and experience (although this may be created at a later stage).

Entrepreneurs find (idea), create (innovation) or respond (to demand) and adapt (commercialise) to business opportunities. The private sector needs to lead the process of a cluster creation, while the government should play a flexible catalytic role that gives grounds and incentives to the self-reinforcing entrepreneurial activity, as a one-size policy does not fit all clusters at all times. There may not be a mechanical transfer of policy instruments from one cluster to another. Positive experiences from other clusters ought to provide more a source of inspiration and less a prescription for general action.

The emergence of a cluster may be based on a historical accident such as the existence of certain skills or raw materials or a crossroads or serendipitous event (such as a discovery in physics or chemistry). Its evolution may enter into the second phase with the agglomeration of firms and the arrival of externalities that may have cumulative features. The next step in the growth of a cluster may include the creation of supporting bodies such as business associations and knowledge-related institutions (schools and research centres). The next stage includes the spread of non-market relations. Firms and institutions create and maintain the spirit of strong non-market collaboration which is external to individual firms but internal to the cluster. Such clusters may be highly specialised and may have success with their output on the market. However, they may easily become victims of their own success. They may fall into a 'trap of rigid specialisation' in the final period of their life. They may be locked in their own technology, specialised output and ethos. If there is another, competing and new good, service or technology elsewhere, which is in demand, then the cluster may decline and disappear. In any case, a cluster is mature when it has at least two properties: (i) a 'thick labour market' that allows both labour and employers (firms) many opportunities and (ii) the ability to withstand and adapt technology, demand and other shocks.

While Boston or Silicon Valley are areas with vibrant life and business culture, Washington, DC is a rather sleepy bureaucratic city. However, it has certain positive features such as people with a higher than average education level and income, as well as a tradition of federally funded R&D. Entrepreneurs in this area self-organised in the early 1980s and started rather ordinary business projects with personal funds (rather than venture capital). The projects included maintenance of computers and their networks, as well as production of medical test kits and reagents for biotechnology. Some of the early start-up firms became successful and the local critical industrial mass grew. Some of these firms went public or were bought by larger ones. Their owners made large fortunes. This fed the 'incubator' of entrepreneurial human capital. Regional universities were alert to the vibrant industrial activity and started offering graduate courses that fitted well with the needs of firms. Johns Hopkins University (Baltimore, Maryland) started offering courses in biotechnology in Silver Spring (50 miles away from the main campus). Similarly, Virginia Tech University (Blacksburg) opened a campus in Falls Church (northern Virginia, some 250 miles from the main campus) within the information technology cluster. Donors enabled universities to recruit top professors (Feldman et al., 2005).

Papageorgiou (1979) demonstrated that agglomerated firms can achieve higher aggregate profit and lower prices per unit of output and generate more demand than more dispersed firms. In addition, firms located in a cluster rich in knowledge tended both to introduce more innovations and to grow faster than more isolated firms (Beaudry et al., 2002, p. 191; Audretsch and Dohse, 2004, p. 23). Relative to the rest of the economy, clusters are likely to have higher productivity and higher profitability, and they may create more new jobs and new firms. On the cost side, land rents tend to increase in and around clusters and so does pollution and congestion. Labour costs can inflate, while institutions and specialisation may suffer from a path-dependence and lock-in effect which may be unconducive to adaptation to changes in technology which is not directly related to the specialisation in the cluster but may easily alter the structure of general demand.

What are the implications for policy towards clusters? Well, new and successful clusters may appear. The examples of Ireland, Finland and the coastal region of China provide evidence for this statement. Economic integration and liberal treatment of trade and FDI may also assist. Many non-spatial policies such as education and training may have a stronger and more important impact than openly 'spatial' policies.

4.5.6 HISTORY AND EXPECTATIONS

Background

As already noted, the Heckscher–Ohlin theory cannot explain why industries locate in regions with a high mobility of factors (US and China) or in countries with a broadly similar endowment of factors (France and Germany). Patterns of regional specialisation and location of firms and industries are often created by a historical accident. In 1894, Karl Marx wrote about capitalist production in *Capital*, Vol. III, Ch. 48, III:

> But in reality this sphere is the sphere of competition, which, considered in each individual case, is dominated by chance; where, then, the inner law, which prevails in these accidents and regulates them, is only visible when these accidents are grouped together in large numbers, where it remains, therefore, invisible and unintelligible to the individual agents in production.[200]

Ohlin noted that 'Chance plays a significant part in determining the localisation of industry . . . A different distribution of inventions would have caused a different localisation' (Ohlin, 1933, p. 137). More recently, Krugman wrote: 'I at least am convinced that there is a strong arbitrary, accidental component to international specialization; but not everyone agrees, and the limitations of the data make a decisive test difficult' (Krugman, 1992, p. 9). In any case, evolutionary dynamics is based to a large extent on chance.

When there are multiple equilibria, various spots for the location of business are substitutable *ex ante* ('putty'). After the investment is made, these locations are not easily substitutable for quite some time ('clay'). Once a business is established at a specific geographical location, it is then 'locked in' through learning, path dependence, sunk costs, circular and cumulative causation[201] effects (for examples of this putty–clay locational model, see Appendix 4A.1). In this sense 'history matters in a way that it does not in neo-classical theory' (Eaton and Lipsey, 1997, p. xxv). Two questions are relevant here:

- Are there inherent differences among locations that create predestination for certain activities?
- How can a small historical accident, a chance (something that is beyond the prior knowledge of an investor), alter the economic fate of an industry, region or country?

Meaningful multiple equilibria exist when firms make independent profit-maximising decisions about output, prices and location. Sources of this multiplicity are pecuniary externalities that originate in (large) fixed costs and imperfect competition. The question is, which equilibrium gets established? Will it be stable in the long run? Since a particular geographical space has only a limited influence on the location of new economic activity (especially footloose industries), what are the options for policy makers in this situation?

On the one hand, there is a belief that the choice is basically resolved by history. Past events set preconditions that move the economy from one steady state to another. This reasoning, found in the traditional literature, argues that history matters because of increasing returns and lumpiness (inseparability) and activity-specific knowledge and capital goods (ibid., pp. x–xi). The same idea is also behind promotional campaigns or 'location tournaments' (David, 1984) among countries to attract international footloose capital (TNCs). The idea is that once an activity starts in a place, it is self-perpetuating and related businesses gravitate towards it. However, this 'self-reinforcing aspect of foreign investment begins to operate only after a certain development threshold has been reached' (Wheeler and Mody, 1992, p. 71). That is, spillovers on the local economy are not a direct consequence of the location of a TNC. Gains that come from these externalities can be achieved only if the local firms have taken on, or can be motivated to take on, new (foreign) technologies and skills. The structure of the local economy, attitude of the private sector and policies of the government that promote change play a key role. In addition, there is evidence in the case of the US foreign investors that 'past investment in the country was a strong predictor of new investment. That persistence was attributed to the favourable effects of agglomeration' (Mody and Srinivasan, 1998, pp. 780–81).

There is, on the other hand, a view that the choice of equilibrium is determined by expectations. This observation is based on the belief 'that there is a decisive element of self-fulfilling prophecy' (Krugman, 1991a, p. 652). Let us consider both these views in turn.

Historical Lock-in Effect

The non-linear probability theory can predict with some certitude the behaviour of systems subject to increasing returns. Suppose that balls of different colours are added on a table. The probability that the next ball will have a specific colour depends on the current proportion of colours. Increasing returns occur when a red ball is more likely to be added when there is already a high proportion of red balls (Arthur, 1990a, p. 98). Equilibrium depends on the initial point and later arrivals. Hence, history as a series of (random) arrivals sets the final result.

The national rate of growth of capital stock (without FDI and foreign loans) depends on home savings and investment. Suppose now that one region/country initially accumulates more capital than the other does. In the following period both regions grow, but the one with more capital grows faster than the one with less capital. As manufacturing capital grows, the relative prices of manufacturing goods fall. After a certain period of time, there is a point where the lagging region's industry cannot compete internationally and it begins to shrink. Once this process begins, the new theory of trade and strategic industrial policy suggests that nothing can stop agglomeration for a long time. Economies of scale may drive prices down in the capital-abundant region and at the same time the lagging region's manufacturing industry disappears. In this model, relatively small beginnings can have large and irreversible final consequences for the manufacturing structure of a country, its trade and the competitiveness of its output (Krugman, 1990a, pp. 99–100).

The dynamics of capital accumulation ensure that the region that starts with a higher capital stock than the other regions ends up with a dominant industrial position. If this is reinforced by a learning process and cumulative causation (strong internal production links where extension of one activity increases the profitability of others), then the existing pattern of comparative advantage is reinforced over time even if the overall structure of the economy has changed. This process-dependent development adds new layers of firms and industries onto the inherited production structure. If output is concentrated within a relatively small area, firms can benefit from economies of scale and linkages (growth of one activity increases the profitability of others). If this area is close to a larger market, there are additional benefits in the form of lower trade (including transport) costs. Hence, the current state of the economy influences, even determines, its future shape.

The investment decisions and trade policy of a country in the current period will have an impact on the shape and direction of the national economy in the future periods. For example, at the end of the 19th century, Argentina and Sweden were relatively comparable backward farming-based economies. At about the same time, Argentina invested in the education of lawyers and priests, while Sweden invested in the education of engineers. The impact of such choices (coupled with other economic policies) on the material standard of living of the two countries is obvious.

Lipsey et al. (2005, p. 414) recently contributed to this debate:

> For example, people may be uncertain as to what changes are needed in the educational system. What is happening to the required skill mix and what kind of new skills are needed and what type of old skills will become redundant? Such

debates raged towards the end of the nineteenth century with Britain and Germany taking very different decisions. The Germans decided to establish trade schools where those who did not go on to formal higher education received an excellent training in some trade. The British concentrated their resources on higher education for a small elite and devoted fewer resources for training the working class in the skills needed in the new factories. This gave Germany a comparative advantage in the production of state-of-the-art but standard consumer durables – an advantage that persisted for over 100 years.

Once the structure of an economy becomes unsustainable, there are certain critical branching points (bifurcations) at which the qualitative behaviour of the economy changes. New production geography either evolves or is triggered. The long-term and dynamic picture of evolution of an economy is not like a ball that smoothly rolls down a slope with a predictable direction and speed. It is more like a cube or, better, a polyhedron that rolls down a slope: full of unexpected developments, accommodating adaptations and sudden turns in direction. Quite bumpy! Thus history-dependent development can follow different paths, hence it is unpredictable both in theory and in practice. A long period of relative stability is broken up by an event of change (equilibrium is punctuated).[202]

These changes, in particular in technology, were (many would argue) the principal sources of growth since the Middle Ages. For example, when water wheels were the principal source of power, the location of many production lines was along rivers and was spatially limited by the length of the drive shaft. The steam engine permitted a huge spatial reallocation of production towards cities, but here again, the length of the shaft restricted the size of the plant. Electricity permitted flexible location of production and the creation of a number of new goods and services. Can you imagine a steam-powered mobile phone? Changes also affected cities. Nearly all big cities are ports. However, it is a long time since New York or Boston ceased to be primarily harbour cities.

There are other examples of punctuated equilibrium. In biology, for instance, many species (crocodiles, crabs, turtles or monotreme animals) remain static for a very long period of time. However, there are crucial, relatively brief and unpredictable moments (bifurcations) when new species arrive and old ones disappear. These include a change in climate 64 million years ago caused by a meteor colliding with the earth, which provoked enormous volcanic activity and fires, water and the atmosphere were polluted, while smoke and dust prevented the penetration of heat from the sun. Hence a very large part of life on earth was frozen, burned, starved or suffocated. This change in climate caused the extinction of the dinosaurs.[203]

More than a century ago, Alfred Marshall spelled out the idea of 'backward-looking dynamics' (or 'external economies' in the modern jargon). In his analysis, factors of production are moving towards those industries in which they earn the highest current rate of return. If there are several meaningful equilibria in which the returns would be equalised, then the initial conditions determine the outcome. History matters, together with factor endowment, tastes and technology (Krugman, 1991a, pp. 653–4).

Marshall also described the concentration of specialised industries in particular localities in the following way:

> When an industry has once chosen a locality for itself, it is likely to stay there long: so great are the advantages which people following the same skilled trade get from near neighbourhood to one another. . . . if one man starts a new idea it is taken up by others and combined with suggestions of their own; and thus becomes the source of yet more new ideas. (Marshall, 1890, p. 332)

Contemporary jargon refers to these processes as 'externalities of innovation'.[204]

Somewhat similar 'first-mover advantages' (to use the term from the analysis of competition) may be found in biology as many elements of the past can be found long after their functions were lost. For example,

> [E]mbryonic birds and mammals still have gill arches, which have been useless for 400 million years. Why are the vestiges not eliminated by natural selection? The usual answer is that *baupläne* and the vestiges are developed early in the embryo and hence are more difficult to modify than features that develop later. The genetic programs controlling embryonic development were formed in the early days and have been frozen ever since. (Auyang, 1998, p. 195)

A similar example can be found in the appendix in the human body. However, a question immediately comes to mind: why cannot newly created adaptive features also be frozen?

One of the chief causes for the localisation of industries can be found in the physical conditions of the area. Metals producers located either near mines or close to sources of abundant and cheap energy. First-rate grit (for grindstones) was found near Sheffield, England, therefore it also became the place for the manufacture of cutlery. Another reason for the localisation of production has been the presence of a royal court. In the Middle Ages many rulers in Europe were constantly changing their place of residence (partly for sanitary reasons). They frequently invited artisans from distant places and settled them in a group near the royal court. Once the court left, if the town survived, in many cases it continued the development of a specialised industry (Marshall, 1890, pp. 329–30). Thus, cities often began to develop around royal courts and bishops' sees (where there was a concentration of consumers).[205] Later on, the administrative, defence and educational dimensions of towns and cities reinforced their function as consumers, but industrial production also started evolving in the cities. Today, many cities produce more value added than they consume.

Recent research has provided some evidence that general government policy can indeed influence the location of firms and industries. From 1947, a number of manufacturing industries in the US migrated to southern states because of the wish to escape unions. This was, however, only one of the reasons for the change in the location of certain businesses in the US. Others included innovation and change in transport (substitution of truck haulage for rail freight which contributed to a spread in production), as well as the advent of air conditioning that 'made the climate in the South relatively more attractive than the climate in the North' (Holmes, 1998, p. 670).

Firms may also use their leverage to reduce costs by intimating to local labour unions that they might move the business elsewhere. Siemens, for example, planned to move two plants from Germany to Hungary in 2004. In return for it not doing that, the employees agreed to work 40 hours a week (instead of the customary 35) with no extra pay.[206] Siemens was not the only firm to try to fight the inflexible German labour market, cut costs and enhance the competitiveness of its output. DaimlerChrysler also threatened to move some production from Germany to South Africa.

Firms cluster together in order to benefit, among other reasons, from the availability of a close network of suppliers. They usually, but not necessarily, cluster in locations with a large local demand. This demand will be large in the areas where most producers choose to locate (a process of circular interdependence or cumulative causation). 'There is a degree of indeterminacy in the location of activities – firms locate where they do because of the presence of other firms, not because of underlying characteristics of the location' (Venables, 1996a, p. 57).[207] For example, there are about 600 tanneries in Arzignano (Vicenza, Italy), most of which employ just a few dozen workers. However, the region produces 40 per cent of Europe's leather supply. The area around Vicenza not only soaks, dyes, stretches, stamps, cuts and ships material used for Gucci handbags, Louis Vuitton luggage, Nike sneakers and BMW car seats, but also produces gold chains, clothing and machine tools, many of them for export.[208] The major problem for a small or a medium-sized enterprise is often not in its 'smallness', but rather in its isolation, which is eased in a cluster.

In such an indeterminate situation should one search for answers to the questions on the geography of production elsewhere? Should it be outside standard economics? Should it be in non-linear dynamics (popularly known as 'chaos theory') which examines unstable behaviour with multiple dynamic equilibria, lock-in effects, bifurcations and extreme sensitivity to initial conditions; or in self-organisation (spontaneous appearance of order)[209] so common in complex systems; or in the new evolutionary economics[210] that has open frontiers, maintains an interdisciplinary dialogue and considers the role of history, technical change, institutions and development of human capital; or in evolutionary biology (evolution and hybridisation)[211] or elsewhere?

'Organisms are vulnerable, but they are not passive; they dig holes, build dams, modify the environment, and create their own niches of survival. Thus organisms and their environment interact, and together they form an ecological system that is better treated as a whole' (Auyang, 1998, p. 61). Humans, however, respond and create novelties intentionally and in certain cases react collectively. Similarly, the effects of externalisation are also pronounced in economics. Consumers' tastes and institutions, both public and private, interact, evolve and alter over time. Consumers, for example, in similar situations make different choices (recall the diversity of breakfast cereals, painkillers, cigarettes, chocolate bars, T-shirts, shoes, cars, cameras or bicycles). Hence, complex systems keep on moving from one pseudo-stable situation to another.

Expectations

Resources move gradually from one location and/or industry to another in response to differences in current earnings. If this shift is only gradual, then there must be certain barriers that increase the cost of the move. If there are costs, then the resource owners will be interested in expected returns in the future, rather than in current returns. However, future returns also depend on the decisions of owners of other factors and their expectations about future earnings.[212] For instance, when a new technology is introduced, multiple equilibria cause expectations of potential action from competitors. In this model, expectations (rather than history) determine the future shape of the economy.

A river may, over centuries, enrich its bed and reinforce the work of natural forces. However, a strong earthquake or a tsunami (a bifurcation point) may instantaneously ruin such a long history. Such was the case with the mechanical and electrical cash registers that were made obsolete by digital ones. Subsequently, optical scanners that read bar codes replaced digital cash registers. These changes were all based on totally different technologies.

Other examples may be found in an almost overnight disappearance of the market for movie cameras after the appearance of video cameras; the redressing of the market for mechanical watches after the invention of digital and quartz ones; a shift from dot matrix to bubble jet and laser printers; or fibre optics that evolved independently of the telecommunication technology. A good encyclopaedia has always been a must if parents want their children to be well educated. The door-to-door salesman selling the *Encyclopaedia Britannica* has been replaced by Microsoft's cheap CD-ROM encyclopaedia Encarta, first produced in 1993. In addition, Amazon is taking business from real-world retail booksellers. Google makes inroads into Microsoft's market. A new product (or service) has to be vastly superior to the well-established product, be it in convenience of use, price, size, shape and/or speed in order to dislodge the entrenched product from the market. Innovation is threatening the existing firms from every side, hence the lock-in effect is not for ever. High business concentration of a cluster/town on a single line of production can leave it highly vulnerable to external shifts in demand and technology. Rational entrepreneurs should allow events to take their natural course. Being a key player and staying on top is not a state, but a process.[213]

Even though they may be important, one may not wish to give an absolute value to external shocks. For example, the nuclear bombs dropped on Hiroshima and Nagasaki in 1945 had no long-run impact on the size of these two cities. 'Within the space of just 20 years, they recovered from the devastation to return to their former place in the constellation of the cities' (Davies and Weinstein, 2002, p. 1283). Similarly, the impact of the bombardment of German cities during the Second World War on the place of the city in the economy and its growth was significant, but temporary (Brakman et al., 2002, p. 28). Sometimes there may be a stronger resilience to shocks in the location-specific fundamentals than one might expect a priori.

A clear example of how expectations shape the national geography of future production can be found if one considers the case of debt in the developing countries.[214] In the 1980s, these countries found themselves unable to repay huge debts owed to the big international banks. Had they all gone into default together, they would have threatened the global economic system. US Secretary of the Treasury Nicholas Brady developed a scheme for refinancing this debt, with the IMF playing the role of the financial policeman of developing countries by linking lines of credit to severe austerity programmes. This was taken to be a victory for the IMF and international institutions. It could have been, but only in the short run.

During the 1970s, the world saw a massive increase in the price of oil and other internationally traded commodities. The conventional wisdom (expectation) was that commodity prices would only go higher. The Club of Rome and other similar observers of history pointed out that the world was running out of scarce resources. The world was compared to a space ship: resources were being exhausted by growing populations and intensified industrial use. It followed that the price of commodities such as oil, copper and wheat could only increase. If this were the case, a rational expectation was that the best business area to invest in was commodities. Correct?

The primary producers of commodities were developing countries that lacked manufacturing capability, but controlled natural resources so much demanded by the industrial world. Any sane investor in the 1970s knew that investing in industries that purchased raw materials was foolish, while investing in production of raw materials was smart. So everyone, particularly the international banking community and the World Bank, began investing billions of dollars in ventures designed to produce raw materials in developing countries from Mexico to Nigeria to the Philippines. As the crucial commodity, namely oil, was expected to cost 40, 50 or even 100 dollars a barrel in the future, the cost of production was not a critical element in decision making about investment. The price of commodities was going up and it was important to get into this business early. All of the technocrats simply knew this and the entire international economic system became skewed towards investing and lending to commodity producers in the developing countries.

As a consequence of the above process, the inevitable happened. It turned out that while the world may have a finite amount of oil or copper, there were still huge untapped reserves and progress to be made in technology (which saves on the use of resources). When these megaprojects in the developing world began to operate, the price of commodities collapsed. When prices fell below the cost of production, projects became unsustainable and bankruptcy ensued. The outcome was the debt crisis. Nicholas Brady and the IMF stepped in to rectify the trouble. The debt crisis, arising from a belief in commodity scarcity, led to an avalanche of investment decisions that has left a legacy of misery. The simplistic and linear projection of the future in which commodity producers dominated industrial commodity consumers was rendered false by the collapse in commodity prices and made irrelevant by another phenomenon in the early 1980s, which is related to Microsoft and similar companies that emerged from nowhere.

Microsoft, and the endless number of other software and related companies that appeared during the 1980s, altered the equation that had obsessed the World Bank and most other serious economic thinkers. The emergence of computing technologies and 'brain imports' in the US meant that it was possible to increase economic growth without having a similar increase in commodity consumption. Microsoft and creators of ideas, after all, produce wealth without consuming commodities in proportion to growth.

A sharp acceleration in productivity growth[215] and increased competition based on knowledge and innovation is at the heart of the 'new economy of permanent prosperity'.[216] In this situation, it was thought in around the mid-1990s that 'old rules' no longer applied. The economy could be closer to full employment without acceleration in inflation. The new situation may have a greater impact on the production of services than on goods. Investments by US firms in shorter-lived assets such as information and communication technology (supposedly important contributors to an increase in productivity) were very high during 1995–2000. After 2000, these investments shrank, but productivity growth accelerated. What is the reason for such growth? Are studies about productivity flawed? These studies may arbitrarily include or exclude depreciation. They may also assume that new computers have a direct and full impact on production from day one, but in reality it takes quite some time to master new equipment.[217] Or, are invisible and intangible activities such as formal and informal computer-related training and reorganisation of business methods more important than measurable investments in new equipment that show only the tip of the iceberg?

These intangible assets helped American companies produce more output with fewer production workers. As far as Europe is concerned, it had the worst performance in industries that are heavy users of information and communication technology, especially the retail trade (where US productivity is growing much more strongly, as is evidenced by retail chains such as Wal-Mart).[218] In addition, US energy consumption in 1997 and 1998 was almost unchanged, while the US economy grew by 9 per cent during those two years.[219] Those economies that are successful in reducing energy consumption per unit of output can, comparatively, benefit a lot from increases in the price of energy in the future; competitors that have not made similar adjustments will suffer.

The extraordinary growth of the US economy has many causes. There is no doubt that the persistent growth of productivity in the US is due to the improvement in efficiency introduced by computing and 'brain imports'. Even Federal Reserve Chairman Alan Greenspan has acknowledged this, while also recognising that it is hard to calculate the impact. This much is apparent. At a time when productivity should be falling, inflation and interest rates soaring and the economy moving towards recession, productivity (driven by the effects of computing, as well as new ideas) is maintaining a long-term growth trend.

At the start of the 1980s, Japan produced cars and cameras at lower prices, smaller in size and of better quality than the US. Two decades later the ability to produce cars, copiers and cameras is much less rewarding profit-wise than the ability to write software. The structure of production has changed almost beyond recognition. The hardware that runs a web server is much less valuable than the non-material intellectual property that resides on the server. Perhaps the Japanese industrial targeting was superior during the age of fax machines, while the US liberal (unplanned) economic system and alert financial markets that force firms to adjust rapidly to shifting markets and changing technology are more appropriate for the age of the Internet (Krugman, 2000, p. 174). To put it bluntly, the Japanese bet on hardware, while the Americans bet on software. The decoupling of value from physical production, its shift to intellectual production, is a millennial shift whose full meaning will not unfold for many generations.

The firms that will define the next twenty years of economic history and production geography are probably completely unknown to anyone today. Uncertainty and risk are very high and the way forward is not always clear. Therefore, it is very difficult to predict with a high degree of confidence where the world's economy is really going. Profound changes that occur little by little (such as the transformation in the economy and in our lives that was brought about by Microsoft) may be noticed only long afterwards. Therefore, the greatest danger and mistake is in 'linear thinking': the belief and expectation that what exists today will also exist tomorrow, but with a higher degree of intensity. Consider what the world looked like in 1980. No scholar ever dreamed or imagined then how the general situation would turn out in reality in 2000. Or go back to 1900–1920, or any other 20-year-period, in particular during the 20th century.

4.5.7 WAR AND THE LOCATION OF FIRMS

Unexpected political events (chance, accidents) such as wars, their start, intensity and length cannot be predicted with a high degree of certitude. None the less, wars decisively influence the development, expansion, location, dislocation and spread of certain industries. There are numerous examples that support such arguments. For instance, as a latecomer in the colonial era and because of post-war external sanctions, Germany had the 'incentive' (was forced by events) to produce various chemicals as substitutes for natural inputs that were not available either in its colonies or through 'normal' trade. Self-sufficiency has often been of vital national importance. Germany's success was remarkable as the country developed world-leading chemical industries[220] and related products such as pumps and sophisticated precision measurement and control instruments. Let us consider other examples:

- After the First World War there was a recession in Seattle (Washington). The economy of the region was based on fishing, production of timber and ship/boat building. At about the same time, demand for aircraft (made of wood) started to emerge. Seattle had unemployed boat-builders and other inputs: workers had the skills to make wooden boats, they could easily build a fully covered boat (the body of an aeroplane), and they also knew how to fix a propeller – all of which led to the emergence of Boeing. The US recognised the huge potential of airmail on a large scale, large purchases of military aircraft and high demand for fast travel, which in turn provided domestic producers with early incentives to lower production and learning costs per aircraft as compared with foreign competitors.

- The first commercially successful motor scooter, the Vespa, was produced by the Italian company Piaggio in 1946, although the idea for it was conceived during the Second World War.[221] During the war, Piaggio, at Pontandera, near Pisa, made aircraft engines. After RAF bombing destroyed the factories, warehouses and roads at the site, it became difficult and tiring to get around the site on foot. The company owner, Enrico Piaggio, asked one of his engineers, Corradino d'Ascanio (who constructed the first fully operational helicopter in 1930) to design a simple and economical two-wheel personal vehicle. D'Ascanio built the prototype using his imagination, the leftovers from small two-stroke motors used to start the aircraft engines, aircraft wheels (note the shape of wheels on a Vespa when you next see one) and whatever else he could find in the warehouse (or what remained of it), such as metal sheets. The vehicle also incorporated a shield on each side to protect the rider's legs from injury. The prototype was ready within a few weeks and, once in production, the Vespa became an immediate hit. It was extremely popular and fashionable in the 1950s and 1960s and was rediscovered by another generation in the 1990s because of increasing traffic congestion in cities.
- The Swiss chemical and heavy industries enjoyed certain benefits during the two world wars. On the one hand, as German industry did not have access to the international market, Swiss entrepreneurs filled the gap where they could. On the other hand, the Swiss benefited from the inflow of funds, talents and invalidation of German patents by the Allies.
- US Caterpillar relocated abroad during the Second World War in order to service machines that were used by the US Army. After the war, the machinery that remained abroad had to be serviced. Hence, Caterpillar became an international company on a larger scale. Coca-Cola also followed the US Army during the Second World War as a morale booster for the soldiers, and also remained abroad. Mars Bars were distributed to armed forces all around the world during the war.[222]

- Sialkot is a provincial town in the Punjab, Pakistan. It had a military garrison and a mission hospital during the British period a century ago. This created a demand for the repair and, later on, production of surgical instruments, tennis rackets and footballs. The area had had a local tradition of producing swords and daggers for several centuries. When the military technology changed, the need for surgical instruments at the local hospital provoked a demand for scalpels. Later on, at around the time of the Second World War, the supply of surgical instruments became a necessary adjunct to the war. Technology and experts were brought from Britain in order to support the production of those goods. Currently, a core of about 300 family-run firms (almost all have fewer than 20 employees) in Sialkot produce a range of 2000 surgical instruments. Together with firms in Germany, they are major world exporters of such instruments. As Sialkot has no airport and as it is located more than 1500 km from the nearest sea port, a private self-help initiative created the Sialkot Dry Port Trust which 'brought the port to Sialkot'. The trust offers a range of collective services such as customs clearance, warehousing and transport. The success of this, as well as all other clusters is based on two factors: first, the demand-driven approach and, second, competition based on collective efficiency. However, the situation in Sialkot is not perfect: the infrastructure is still rather undeveloped; the power supply is inadequate; communications are poor; and roads are ankle deep in mud during the monsoon season. In addition, health and safety standards are insufficient and child labour is a serious problem in Sialkot's football-making industry (Nadvi, 1998).
- Italian motor car racing companies such as Alfa Romeo, Ferrari and Lancia dominated the market in the period immediately after the Second World War. Within a few years, however, a cluster of small firms from around Oxford became another dominant world player. Several fortuitous events prompted this evolution. First, there was a huge surplus of abandoned airfields in southern England after the war. Second, Mercedes withdrew from motor racing in 1955 after an accident in Le Mans in which 183 spectators were either killed or injured. This left room for the British racing car builders. Third, large and vertically integrated manufacturers such as Ferrari and Porsche built cars for their own racing teams, while the British were selling cars to anyone who wanted to buy them. Even though the British were not winning races, they dominated the starting grids with the sheer number of cars. Fourth was the ban on cigarette advertising on British TV in 1965. Tobacco companies became sponsors of motor racing, doling out vast sums of money in return for having their logos

displayed on racing cars. Pinch and Henry (1999) argue that the success of the British constructors may have been influenced by a few accidents, but only marginally. Other more important causes such as accumulated knowledge, its circulation through the companies by means of transfer of personnel, as well as skilled labour, are the true origins of the British success. The British have a tradition of expertise in engines and lubricants, aerodynamics and composite materials. In particular, the national aerospace industry was bigger and more sophisticated after the war than that in Italy. According to Pinch and Henry, this would probably have encouraged the production of racing cars even without the Mercedes crash or the money from cigarette manufacturers.

- Another example of the impact of war on the change in the spatial distribution of production emanates from the end of the 'Cold War' around 1990, when huge defence cuts badly damaged the military aerospace cluster in southern California.

4.5.8 WRAPPING UP THE THEORY OF LOCATION

A century or even half a century ago, economic theory looked at the location of firms and industries in a rather technical and deterministic way. Subjects and causes were separated from objects and effects, and everything ended in equilibrium. Parts of modern spatial economics and the new geography of production consider the location of firms in an evolutionary way, where the state of equilibrium is only a temporary special case and everything is in an unstable organic process of change.

Where a firm or an industry should locate is not a question that has a straightforward answer. Rich nations fear the relocation of firms and industries to low-wage nations; poor nations worry that the production of goods and services will migrate to developed countries; small countries are concerned that businesses will move to large countries; countries that are not integrated with others are afraid that production will migrate to the integrated countries; while all countries are troubled because of reallocation of manufacturing to China, especially following the Asian financial crises of 1997.

In an age of business 'globalisation', one might expect the importance of firm location to be diminishing. Some argue that distance is dead in terms of production and business because of the astonishing changes in communications and computers. 'Time zones and language groups, rather than mileage, will come to define distance' (Cairncross, 2001, p. 5). But this may be relevant only for certain manufacturing and services activities that are simple, routine and have codified (standardised) and teachable knowledge. Trade costs, that is, all costs linked with getting the final good to the consumer (tariffs, quotas, transport, storage, distribution, information, contract enforcement, insurance, exchange and banking) are 'alive and kicking'. The many components of trade costs may rise or fall in a different proportion from distance costs. Trade costs matter not only for economic geography and economic policy, but also for theory as a number of puzzles in international economy rest on their existence.

Geography and local proximity (clusters) of firms that produce similar, competing and/or related products together with supporting institutions still matters for complex activities, with little or no codified knowledge and where market changes and uncertainty require a rapid reaction. Economies of scale, activity-specific backward and forward linkages (indivisible production), accumulated knowledge, innovation, lock-in effects, the existence of sophisticated customers and a fall in transportation costs play relevant roles in the protection of clusters and the absolute advantage of certain locations. 'Global' competitiveness often depends on highly concentrated 'local' knowledge, capabilities and a common tacit code of behaviour which can be found in a spatial concentration (a cluster) of firms.[223] Hence, successful managers must often think regionally and act locally.

The neglect of spatial economics (geography of production) in mainstream economic theory was not because this research field was uninteresting, but rather because the issues were traditionally regarded as intractable. Ricardo's comparative advantage model provided insufficient answers to the problem. New research tools such as increasing returns, production linkages (presence of intermediate goods and services), multiple equilibria (with centrifugal and centripetal forces) and imperfect competition were introduced into the field of spatial economics in the early 1990s. These methodological tools also helped to explain why firms form clusters. Such new developments did not mean the birth of a new subject. Spatial economics has always been important. Even though the ever-increasing demand for quantitative vigour is making such considerations more difficult, the introduction of new analytical tools assisted spatial economics in finding its proper place in mainstream economics and becoming a hot research topic.

The new economic geography differs from the traditional model in several important dimensions. The new model makes the case that production specialisation in a given locality is based not only on certain comparative advantages, but also on a self-reinforcing lock-in effect, path dependence, accumulated knowledge, agglomeration, clustering and linkages (indivisible production). In addition, while the traditional models reason that a reduction in trade costs among locations favours local specialisation, the new economic geography claims that the effect on local specialisation is ambiguous. The final outcome is industry specific and depends on the functional intra-industry production linkages, market structure, consumer preferences (homogeneity of tastes) and factor market (availability and mobility of factors and flexibility in prices). In general, the choice of location for a new investment or a new firm that produces tradable goods and services depends on a complicated interplay of at least three elements: factor intensity; transport intensity; and each in relation to the already established firms and their activities and (re)actions. Remote places do not necessarily need to be poor locations for firms as their remoteness is already reflected in their factor prices (Venables and Limão, 2002, pp. 260–61).

As a reaction to trade liberalisation and economic integration, various industries follow different paths. Depending on the functional intra-industry production links, some industries concentrate (reinforcing absolute advantages of certain locations), while others spread. This is contrary to the expectations of neo-classical theory, which predicts that all industries will be affected in the same way. Different forces, therefore, propel such changes in the spatial structure of production. Strong functional intra-industry linkages (a high share of intermediate inputs from the same industry and/or the need for a large pool of highly skilled labour and researchers) stimulate agglomeration. Where these functional linkages are weak, this acts as an incentive to spread production.

Ultimately, one can reason that there is an important lacuna in our understanding of spatial economics. It is little wonder that there are many disagreements and only some theoretical agreements:

- Starting a new activity in a specific location requires building on and improving already existing accumulated expertise and specialisation of that location (this specialisation needs to be extended, but this does not mean that the earlier production structure has to be continued; something (vaguely) related to it may be the starting point which, later on, needs to be altered, sometimes fundamentally).
- Using policy intervention to influence the location of firms is most effective only very early in the process. There is only a narrow window of opportunity during which the policy may be effective.[224]
- Local education and training has a positive impact on the location of firms and industries.
- Economies of scale and functional linkages in production have some impact on the location of firms and industries.
- Policy should be reviewed periodically and have elements of flexibility.
- Success or failure of a region or a policy sometimes depends on uncontrollable factors and events that are located outside regions themselves.[225]

The analysis of spatial economics depends on special assumptions. It is often a detective-type study and a collection of particular cases. Generality is often abandoned in favour of discovery. This is not surprising as spatial economics is simultaneously charged with some of the most complex and difficult problems in economic theory: multiple equilibria, economies of scale, externalities, imperfect competition (which kind?), linkages and path dependence. None the less, many useful things can be learned from exceptional cases and simplified stories. These examples do not serve the purpose of emulating reality in its entirety, but rather serve as metaphors to illuminate certain important background forces that are at work.

The examination of the issue of location of firms and industries in space is still elastic and highly suggestive (in particular how a historical accident may shape the production geography), rather than conclusive, convincing and general. A coherent and wide-ranging theory of the subject and general prescriptions for the policy are not yet in sight. However, there are various piecemeal approaches driven by anecdotes that contribute to the acquired knowledge and to the raising of new questions and understanding of the issue. This leaves the topic wide open to further theoretical and empirical analysis.[226]

4.5.9 REGIONAL POLICY

A region may be more easily discerned than defined. The definition of a region depends on the problem that one encounters. A region is a geographical phenomenon with distinct borders with others, but it also has political, governmental and administrative features and is an ethnic and social concept with human and cultural characteristics and mores.[227] A region is also an economic concept defined by its endowment factors, their combinations and mobility. Therefore, a region can be defined in theory as a geographical area that consists of adjoining particles with similar unit incomes and more interdependence of incomes than between regions (Bird, 1972, p. 272). North (1955, p. 257) suggested that 'the unifying cohesion to a region, over and beyond geographic similarities, is its development around a common export base. It is this that makes it economically unified and ties the fortunes of the area together.' A region of a country or an economic union may be thought of as an open economy.

There are many causes of regional disequilibria, including (Vanhove and Klaasen, 1987, pp. 2–7):

- market rigidities (such as relatively low mobility of factors);
- geographical factors;

- differences in the availability of resources;
- education of management and training of labour;
- regional economic structure (in some regions industries with ageing technologies, in others industries with modern technologies);
- institutional factors such as the centralisation of public institutions (Paris is an obvious example); and
- national wage setting in spite of differences in productivity and labour market conditions across different regions.

Regional disparities adopt numerous forms. They include not only differences in income levels per capita, rates of growth or rates of unemployment, economies of scale, externalities, output and consumption structures, productivity and access to public services, but also the age structure, population density and the pattern of migration.

The controversy regarding the definition of the 'regional problem' remains. However, several factors together may provide an insight into the issue. These elements include:

- Different regions may grow at uneven rates for a long period of time. This provokes government intervention to reduce that problem.
- Intervention may aim to equalise consumption or GDP per capita among different regions.
- A government may wish to create equal access of the population to an adequate level of public goods and services.
- Public authorities may be interested in having a spatially stable distribution of economic activities and population in order to avoid negative externalities.

Regional policy is basically aimed at influencing economic adjustment in the four (theoretical) types of regions:

- Regions in which agriculture accounts for a relatively high share of production and employment. These are usually underdeveloped rural areas with relatively low levels of income, high levels of unemployment and poorly developed infrastructure.
- Regions whose former prosperity was founded on industries that are now in decline, such as coal, steel, shipbuilding or textiles. These are the regions that failed to keep pace with changes in technology and were unable to withstand external competition (in some cases because of earlier excessive protection). In the case of recession, labour in these regions is the first to be made redundant.
- Regions with a high concentration of manufacturing and resulting congestion and pollution problems. There are benefits from the joint

use of goods and services available in these areas. Regional policy may, however, try to reduce the existing congestion (concentration) and pollution and/or prevent their further increase.

- Frontier regions, which are far from the strongest areas (poles of growth) of a country's or union's economic activity.

Jobs can be located in regions where there are people with suitable qualifications, training and experience. Therefore, regions with unskilled labour cannot be expected to attract any significant number of industries that use modern technologies. By definition, these industries require trained labour and educated management. The location of business near large and/or growing markets saves transport costs. If returns to scale were constant, as neo-classical theory assumes, this could tend to equalise factor owners' rewards in different regions. With economies of scale and other market imperfections (the situation with multiple equilibria), these tendencies may increase rather than decrease regional disequilibria.

Convergence in the level of development among different regions is not a self-sustaining process. It is easier during an economic recovery than during recession. Lagging regions/countries usually have a higher proportion of both 'sensitive industries' and public enterprises than prosperous ones. Therefore, they may be hit harder by a recession and budgetary restrictions (no subsidies and public purchases) than other regions.

The *convergence or neo-classical school* of thought regarding regional matters did not consider either market imperfections such as economies of scale, sunk costs and externalities or institutions that set the organisational environment. This school argued that the 'regional problem' and the spatial location of economic activity are not problems at all. Free trade and unimpeded factor mobility would produce a smooth spatial dispersion of people, skills, technology and economic activity. Of course, in the long term this would equalise factor earnings and living standards in all regions and countries. Apart from transport costs, it should not matter where a tradable good or service is produced. Hence, the spatial location of output is no more than an operational detail. This is because transport, communication and other trade costs have been declining over time because of innovation and increases in productivity. The peripheral regions and countries are expected to gain from trade liberalisation and integration in terms of an increased relocation of industries and trade. Ultimately, there would be a full equalisation in factor prices.

The neo-classical one-sector growth models based on exogenous technological progress anticipate economic convergence among regions. This expectation based on comparative advantages depends on the starting conditions (including the endowment of factors). However, different regions may have different long-run growth rates because of a different starting situation. As technological progress in this model is exogenous, developing countries should grow faster than the developed ones. If, however, technological progress is endogenous, then the convergence school does not give a clear prediction about growth rates and patterns.

This liberal (non-interventionist) attitude in the field of regional policy in the market economies had a certain validity until the economic crisis of the 1930s. With free trade, perfect allocation and use of resources,[228] intervention in regional policy is not necessary because markets clear and bring the economy to equilibrium. Such a convergence approach was not validated by time and experience. In spite of expectations about convergence, even *laissez-faire* governments may consider it necessary and beneficial to intervene as the adjustment process may take too long to be politically acceptable.

The new spatial economics emphasises potentially growing disparities, rather than convergence, among regions and countries. This *divergence school* of thought offered theories that refer to the growing discrepancy among regions. The focus is on a much nearer time horizon compared with the neo-classical school. Explanations are based principally on economies of scale.[229] Together with the new geography of production (spatial economics), divergence theories consider market imperfections and institutions that set rules which streamline liberties and behaviour.[230] This moves theoretical concepts closer to reality. The list of new assumptions includes economies of scale, high fixed costs, trade and adjustment costs, entry and exit barriers,[231] constrained mobility of factors, transport costs, externalities, multiple equilibria, path dependence, the multiplier effect, cumulative causation, non-ergodicity and inflexibility. If applied to intermediate production, these forces can combine and influence one another in such a complex way that their behaviour becomes fickle. They can produce most unpredictable outcomes regarding locations of firms and industries. In many cases history, chance and expectations set the final outcome.

Production and trade in goods are increasingly becoming elaborate and difficult. They depend heavily on sophisticated information and services that are included in the final good and its price. Internal trade within each TNC may account for a large part of the total trade. Hence, national and international markets become more and more incomplete and tough to manage. In addition, the listed new elements that the divergence theory considers exert a strong influence on the location of production, trade and absolute advantages (which widen regional gaps), while local comparative advantages may play a less important role. In this case, competition, liberalisation and economic integration generate concentration (or increase the attractiveness of the already developed areas); they generate economic

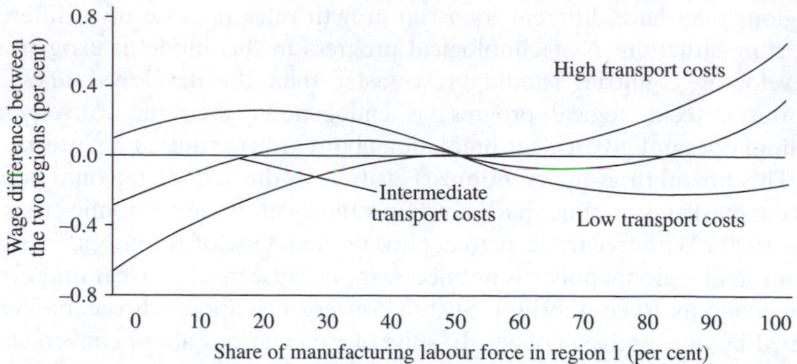

Figure 4.13 Relation between regional manufacturing populations and real wages with varying transport costs

divergence and widening of regional gaps, not economic convergence among regions and countries.

Given that remarkable spatial concentration is the most striking feature of the geography of production, there is clear evidence of some kind of increasing returns to scale (Krugman, 1992, p. 5). New technologies in select industries may overcome some of the obstacles to the spread of production, but not many. Hence, the pattern of regional specialisation and trade can be arbitrary and potential gains from specialisation and trade are likely to be ambiguous.[232]

A lack of R&D, innovation, as well as acquisition and employment of new technological knowledge may be among the principal causes of slow growth in less-developed regions and countries. This weakness may be partially eased by the two-way labour mobility from developed to weaker regions and vice versa. A one-way migration of labour would only depopulate weaker regions, while it could create overcrowding in the prosperous areas.[233] However, structural disparity among the regions does not necessarily mean that there is an income disparity between them. If there are two regions and if each region specialises in a different output activity, then economic structure among them would change, even though the incomes in both regions may still remain comparable.

In a simple model (Figure 4.13), the allocation of manufacturing between two regions determines the difference in real wages between them. Let the horizontal axis represent the share of manufacturing workers residing in region 1 and let the vertical axis show the difference in real wages between the two regions in per cent. The figure shows how various transport costs influence the curve that relates the regional manufacturing population to real wages. Transport costs are taken to epitomise all costs of

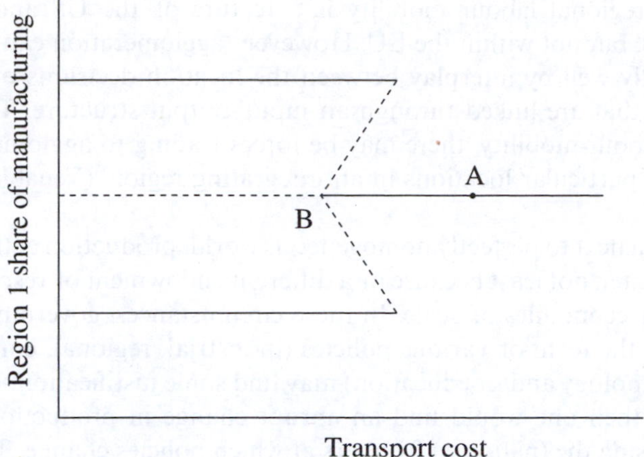

Figure 4.14 Transport costs and equilibria

doing business across geographical space. With high transport costs there is little interregional trade. Regional wages depend mainly on the local conditions in the labour market. If there is an increase in the regional labour supply, competition reduces wages. With low transport costs, there is much interregional trade. A firm can have superior market access if it is located in the region with a higher concentration of workers (consumers). It can also afford to pay higher wages. These higher wages increase the purchasing power as the workers have better access to consumer goods. As the number of residents/workers increases in the region, real wages increase in the same direction. With intermediate transport costs, there is some evening out between centrifugal and centripetal forces (Krugman, 1999, p. 95).

Figure 4.14 shows the situation in which the workers move to the region that offers higher real wages measured by the share of manufacturing labour force in region 1. A set of equilibria depends on transport costs. Solid lines specify stable equilibria, while broken lines show unstable equilibria. If an economy starts with high transport costs, then there is an even distribution of manufacturing between regions 1 and 2, respectively. Point A represents this situation. Then suppose that there is a reduction in transport costs and that production and consumption can be separated (so the concentration of production in one of the two regions becomes possible and likely). The economy reaches point B in this (putty–clay) situation. At this point the process of concentration of manufacturing in one region starts. Which region gets the industry often depends on a small starting difference or on a chance. The economy would spontaneously organise itself into core–periphery geography (ibid., p. 96). A relatively high interregional labour mobility is a feature of the US and Chinese economies, but not within the EU. However, 'agglomeration can be generated equally well by interplay between the location decisions of firms in industries that are linked through an input–output structure. Thus, even without labour mobility, there may be forces leading to agglomeration of activity at particular locations in an integrating region' (Venables, 1996b, p. 356).

Even in a next to perfectly homogeneous world, production activities will tend to cluster, not least because of a different endowment of resources and because of economies of scale. In these circumstances, government intervention in the form of various policies (industrial, regional, competition, trade, technology and/or education) may find some justification. If policies mattered, then one would find an abrupt change in production activity when crossing the (national) frontiers at which policies change. The policy is generally aimed at developing or enhancing the regional or national production potential, competences and capabilities through a (supposedly) superior allocation and use of resources from the national standpoint. The objective of such intervention is to influence the spatial distribution of economic activity, as well as to create and redistribute wealth in order to ease and, eventually, solve the many-sided 'regional problem'.

Governments intervene in regional matters mainly for the following three reasons:

- *Equity* This is a strong social motive based on public pressure on the government to try to achieve and maintain a 'proper' balance, as well as an 'orderly' and just geographical distribution, of national wealth and access to the public in different regions.
- *Efficiency* This is a desire to employ, sustain and increase national economic potentials and capabilities.
- *Strategic behaviour* This gives public authorities a chance to shape comparative advantages and influence the output potential and capabilities of the country.[234]

In the 1960s, the regional problem was usually tackled with supply-side subsidies for the provision of infrastructure and the reallocation of various (public) manufacturing and service industries. Foreign competition, in particular from the newly industrialised countries, placed in jeopardy a number of industries that failed to adjust. As there had been little success with earlier approaches to the regional problem, coupled with austerity programmes in public finances, there was a major change in national regional policies from the 1980s. Outright subsidies were reduced or removed and the policy was supplemented by a system intended to make the lagging regions more self-reliant (support to indigenous development). This included the development of human resources, the attraction of private investors (in particular foreign ones) and the provision of technical services.

There is a great deal of uncertainty regarding the impact of international economic integration on regional matters. One thing, however, should be mentioned here. Having a 'peripheral' location is not an irreversible economic disadvantage. Its impact can be mitigated and even reversed, as has been successfully shown by countries such as Ireland and Finland (or Australia and Japan). The peripheral EU countries became economically more dynamic than the EU 'core' (France, Germany and Italy) from the 1990s (but they also started from a lower base). What matters most for the competitiveness of a country's goods and services on the international market is the efficient creation and employment of and compensation to the most precious economic factor: human capital (heads and hands). However, this asset may depreciate over time through indolence, ageing and vices such as drugs and heavy drinking. Therefore, it needs to be maintained through continuous education and training.

Craig Barrett, the chief executive officer of Intel, referred to economic liberalisation and opening in China, India, the former socialist bloc and other newly emerging countries during the 1990s. He noted that the reform process touched about 3 billion people, 10 per cent of whom are highly skilled workers. 'That's 300 million well-educated people, able to do any job.'[235] To face this and other challenges, Intel would invest heavily in R&D and hire the best and brightest employees wherever the company can find them. Some consider that the external challenges from educated, experienced and productive labour and management could be a threat to skilled workers in America and contest the prosperity of the US economy. This may be an overstatement if one looks at the short and medium terms. It takes time and resources to establish and spread first-rate educational services and equip labour and management with the necessary sophisticated knowledge, training and experience. However, Barrett's statement and Intel's intentions highlight the right issue: the great importance and lasting value of human capital for the prosperity of firms and an economy.

Regional policy was neglected in the EU before its first enlargement in 1973. This was followed by a period of interest in an active regional policy. However, enthusiasm for this policy waned in the 1990s as there were few obvious positive results from intervention. Public intervention in regional issues is still a highly controversial issue. Is there or is there not a self-equilibrating process among the regions in the long term? Is intervention (regional policy) necessary or not? Hence, can regional policy work at all?

National governments introduced regional policies in order to promote growth in weak regions. The policy was based on the assumption that market failures exist. The instruments of the policy included investment aid, direct investment by the state, wage subsidies, tax allowances, licensing and the provision of infrastructure and services. However, since the 1990s, the emphasis of regional policy has moved away from the attraction of extra-regional investment and general subsidies, primarily towards the development of endogenous regional growth and human resources. The national regional policy was transformed in most EU(15) countries into an enterprise and entrepreneurship development policy.

The situation regarding regional policy at the EU level has been ambivalent. On the one hand, cohesion is becoming a *leitmotif* of European integration, hence EU involvement in this issue. On the other hand, market liberalisation and an active regional policy (intervention) do not go hand in hand. Since an automatic market-led adjustment mechanism operates too slowly to be politically acceptable, EU structural funds for regional development and social issues emphasise supply-side intervention. They provide assistance to infrastructure, training and structural adjustment.

Intervention in the form of a regional policy is not a simple task as there are constant changes in technology, taste, competition and demography over time. In spite of intervention in regional affairs over the past decades, a trend appeared during the 1990s in many EU countries towards abandoning or easing regional policies. However, at the EU level, intervention in regional affairs remained enthusiastic, but with questionable results.

4.5.10 OBJECTIVES AND JUSTIFICATION

Regional policy is intervention by the state in order to influence the 'orderly' distribution and 'just' direction of economic activity, as well as to reduce social and economic differences among regions. It was usually a reactive (*ex post*) policy that primarily tried to reduce the existing regional disparities, rather than a policy that primarily prevented the creation of new regional disequilibria.

Trade liberalisation and/or economic integration can easily provoke a country's economic adjustment (geographical, sectoral and professional reallocation of resources). Enhanced competition may force certain regions to embark upon a painful, but potentially rewarding, alteration in the structure of the geography of production (transfer of resources from unprofitable into profitable economic activities). The politicians in the affected regions often blame integration or trade liberalisation for adjustment 'pains'. However, this objection may not always be justified. The most basic reason for a painful adjustment process is often earlier protection. A policy of long and excessive sheltering of the domestic economy reduces the reaction time of local enterprises to international structural pressures and opportunities and, hence, increases the cost of adjustment in the future. Adjustment costs and 'pains' are always present, but the potential benefits from such a change may more than compensate for the effort.

Relatively low wages may attract investment into a region; however, there may be at the same time some agglomeration and concentration tendencies in other regions. If wages are set at a national level, this may act as a structural barrier that works against the lagging regions. In this case, the lack of flexibility in the level of wages among regions despite relative differences in productivity and in the labour market conditions means that the less-developed areas are unable to respond to this situation by reduced wage costs. One cannot know in advance where the balance will tilt. Some developed regions may become more developed, while some less-developed regions/countries may become poorer (if nothing is done to alleviate the situation), but other less-developed regions may move into the group of advanced ones.

The objectives of a regional policy are various, but their common denominator is that they aim to employ the regions' unemployed or under-employed resources and potentials, to locate new ones, to attract missing factors, as well as to increase output and incomes. In congested or polluted areas, this policy restricts the expansion of firms and stimulates exit from the region. In the developing countries, the primary concern is economic development. This is most often coupled with regional imbalances, but their solution is not as high on the agenda as increases in economic potentials and capabilities. In areas of economic integration, the problem of regional (in)equalities is of great concern. Countries are reluctant to lag behind their partners for any length of time. This is of great concern in an EMU, where there are no balance of payments disequilibria, but rather regional disparities. Depressed regions/countries can no longer resort to devaluation as there is a single currency, while advanced regions/countries will not always be willing to finance regional disequilibria without proof that there is structural adjustment and improvement taking place in the regions assisted. With this in mind, a regional policy can be justified on nine counts.

The first justification for a regional policy (intervention that is supposed to assist in the process of economic adjustment), in contrast to free market adjustment, can be found in the structural deficiencies of regions. These include market rigidities, conditions of access to the market and the structure of output. When such imperfections exist, a free market system is 'unable' to achieve a satisfactory equilibrium from the social standpoint in the short and medium terms, so there may be a need for intervention in order to enhance the creation and use of the regional income-generating potentials and capabilities.

Regional imports consists of goods and services. In France, for example, most of the country's regions purchase financial, insurance, legal and other services from Paris. This is not easily quantified. A reduction in a region's exports, for instance, may be obvious from the outset. Regional solutions to these disequilibria are inhibited by rules of competition and by the existence of a single currency. Herein we find the second 'justification' for regional intervention in an economic union.

The third reason may be found in the employment of factors. The neoclassical theory of international trade usually assumes free and full international mobility of factors, which ensures full employment. However, even Adam Smith noted that a man is the most difficult 'commodity' to transport. During recession, the employment situation is tough everywhere, therefore the potential advantages of some regions that are abundant in labour are removed. Reduced mobility of labour prevents the equalisation of discrepancies in economic unions.

Suppose that economic space consists of a core and a periphery. In the case when there are market imperfections, there is a general agreement in theory that at one point in time the core region is likely to dominate the periphery. The disagreement is about the nature, extent, evolution, effects and duration of the core–periphery relation over time.[236] If there is growth in one region, this may create conditions for even higher growth in the same core region and increase inequalities among regions (polarisation or backwash effect). This may, however, also act as a 'locomotive' for development in other peripheral regions as there may be increased markets for food, economies of scale and innovation in other regions (spread effect). In order to adopt the idea that there are benefits from the spread effect, one must assume that there is a complementarity between the regions in question and ignore the fact that the spread effects operate in an asymmetrical way throughout space.

In a situation closer to reality and which includes economies of scale, large sunk costs, externalities and other market failures, adjustment does not happen according to a relatively smooth neo-classical expectation. The regional absorption capacity of new technologies requires an industrial and general culture that incorporates continuous learning, adaptation, spread and development of human capital, as well as flexibility. Therefore, the introduction of new technologies is often uncertain and quite risky, which is why some technologies diffuse quite slowly among the regions. The reallocation of resources induced by the spread effect works at a (much) slower pace than may be politically acceptable, hence the need for intervention.

The fourth rationale can be found in the 'need' for compensation. Two forces created by economic integration affect regional development. The first one, specialisation, leads the backward regions to specialise in labour-intensive production according to their comparative advantage. The second force includes economies of scale, externalities and path dependence. This can lead to a divergence in regional incomes. As integration extends the size of the market, firms take advantage of economies of scale and externalities. The Single Market Programme provided incentives for the concentration of industries with strong internal links. In the case of other regions, the programme reduced trade costs, hence there are potentials for a spread of other industries that may benefit the EU periphery, where labour costs are lower. However, if this does not happen, or takes place very slowly, there is a possibility that some regions may actually be damaged by integration if there are no instruments for compensation, which is another justification for a regional policy.

Subsidies may be one of the tools of a regional policy. However, the distribution of subsidies is always subject to political pressures and mismanagement. The final disbursement of subsidies often reflects more the balance of political powers than the comparative (dis)advantage of a region. At the end of the process, regional policies implemented in such a way may do more harm than good if they diminish local incentives for adjustment and flexibility or, at best, they may have a dubious effect. None the less, public policies in the backward regions, such as support for education, infrastructure and selected public goods, as well as aid for SMEs in the form of loan guarantees for the start-up of a business, have the potential to assist regional development.

The fifth reason is the improved allocation of resources. When the market is imperfect, free market forces usually direct capital towards already developed regions in the short and medium terms. Private investors tend to maximise the speed of the safe return of their invested funds and to minimise investment in infrastructure. Thus, it is understandable why they direct their funds towards already advanced regions. These tendencies of agglomeration (adjoint locations of linked productions), where the developed tend to become more developed while the underdeveloped remain at best where they are, have significant private benefits, but also social costs and benefits. A society may reap the benefits of large-scale efficient production. However, if private entrepreneurs are not impeded in their decision making by government policy, the geographical location of their business may introduce significant social costs such as pollution, congestion and traffic jams in some regions and unemployment and increased social assistance in others.

The sixth reason lies in the improvement of stabilisation (macroeconomic) policy. Regional differences in rates of unemployment may reduce the opportunities to control inflation and introduce a stabilisation policy. The reduction of inflation in some regions may increase unemployment in others. This may not always be the desired outcome. Diversified regions with a variety of employment opportunities will be able to adjust in a less painful way than specialised regions with entrenched market rigidities.

Seventh, a regional policy may reduce public expenditure in the assisted region in the long run. Public support to firms to locate in certain regions may propel economic activity towards these regions. Unemployment may drop, reducing welfare payments and in the long term increasing tax receipts that may be spent on something else. In addition, 'employment' in public administration used to provide a shelter for the unemployed. Such artificial employment may be reduced or even eliminated once the private sector (with superior wages and career prospects) starts thriving in the assisted region.

Eighth, although regional policy is targeted at regions with some disadvantage (underdevelopment, unemployment, obsolete technologies and output structure, congestion or pollution), the benefits of a regional policy are not confined to the assisted area. Other regions, through externalities, enjoy part of the benefit. The beneficial effects of a regional policy extend beyond the assisted area itself, which is why the Germans and Swedes have an interest in helping out the Poles or the Estonians. In general, integration may be reinforced, unwanted migration of labour may be prevented, factors may be employed in a superior way and there are important non-economic gains.

Finally, in addition to the above arguments for regional policy, which mostly deal with 'economic' efficiency, there are political grounds which are at least as important as the economic ones. Solidarity, tolerance and perception of a common future are the core of any social community. The mitigation of economic disparities among the constituent regions may be the necessary reason for the unity of a state or an economic union. This is relevant as the costs and benefits of international economic integration tend to be unequally spread among the participating countries in a situation with market imperfections and multiple equilibria. Arguments of equality require the solution and/or mitigation of intolerable or growing differences in the distribution of wealth among the population which lives in different regions. The national political system does not always take fully into account the needs of backward regions. For example, the national system of setting wages may significantly reduce the wage-cost advantages of many regions, whereas welfare expenditure can contribute to a greater regional equilibrium. Complete equalisation in the standards of living in different regions is neither possible nor desirable because it may reduce incentives for change and improvement. What is needed in regional matters is a continuous adjustment of regional development within commonly agreed guidelines, as well as the protection of the standard of living accepted as desirable by the group.

Regional intervention may be quite costly. In addition, there may be an inefficient replication of effort at various levels of government. Therefore, one may use the coordination advantages argument in favour of an EU regional policy. The EU is best placed to coordinate various national and regional actions, to improve their efficiency and to collect and transfer resources from the prosperous to the weak regions of the EU.

The goals of regional policy, such as balanced growth, equal shares of social and cultural progress of the society, solidarity, regional distinctiveness and stability, are vague and may not be accurately measured. Specific objectives such as job creation, reduction in unemployment, improved housing and development of infrastructure introduce fewer problems in quantification. Care has to be given to select policy tools in order to ensure that the regional policy does not evolve into protection of the present economic structure; rather it needs to assist in continuous structural adjustment of the regions.

4.5.11 INSTRUMENTS

Instruments of regional policy are often directed towards entrepreneurs and factor owners. They can be employed either directly (for example, support to exit from existing technologies or shift towards new technologies or business activities) or indirectly (for example, improvement in infrastructure). Their joint effects may alter and increase employment, investment and output in the assisted regions, at least in the short term.

The dilemma of the state may be whether to stimulate regional development through private investment, to invest directly in production and infrastructure for which there is no interest in the private sector and/or to stimulate public–private partnership. The available policy tools include (i) those that provide incentives and disincentives to firms and labour to move and to locate in or out of specific geographical regions and (ii) those that are intended to alter the level of income in the target regions. Major instruments include:

- tax concessions;
- subsidies: regional allocation of capital, investment, infrastructure, output, social security and income/wage;
- vocational training;
- public procurement and provision of goods, services and infrastructure;

- loan guarantees;
- reduction in interest rates;
- protection of intellectual property;
- decentralisation of government offices, education and health services;
- reductions in energy and public transportation costs;
- free locations;
- licences for the location of business; and
- trade protection.

As seen from this list, the choice of policy tools is rather limited. The secret of success in this situation is not the wide range of instruments, but rather their astute combination and application.

If offered, cash grants may be preferred to reduced tax liabilities as regional policy instruments. Grants apply horizontally and directly to all firms, whereas reduced tax liabilities help only those that are profitable. Trade restrictions are not the wisest instruments of a regional policy. The costs fall on the whole economic union, but they bring benefits to one or only a few regions.

Disincentives for regional expansion in congested areas are a relatively novel feature. In Britain, for example, they appeared in the form of industrial development certificates (1947–81) that had to be obtained prior to expansion or location in non-assisted regions. However, after the second oil shock, as unemployment increased, these certificates were abandoned as an instrument of regional policy. In France, for instance, there were certain constraints on the expansion of manufacturing and service industries in the Paris region. They included a special tax on office floor construction and authorisations for large-scale investments.

The policy of moving workers to jobs views the regional problem as being exclusively one of unemployment. It ignores the fact that other problems in a region may be made worse by this 'forced' mobility of labour. The productive part of the population moves out of the region while the consuming part remains in it. The local tax base may not be able to provide sufficient funds to cover the costs of local health care, schools and other social services. The overall situation may be worsened by the multiplier effect. In advanced regions that receive the migrants, new disequilibria may be created. The additional population increases congestion and rents for a certain type of housing, which may reduce the quality of life there. Education and training are often emphasised as key elements in the solution to the unemployment problem. Although they are necessary, they are not sufficient conditions to fight unemployment. Creating new jobs also requires investment and increased flexibility in the labour markets.

Unemployment rates may be one of the most telling indicators of regional variations. If labour mobility is relatively low, then the movement of jobs to workers may reduce regional disparities in unemployment. One argument against this is that it may increase costs, as alternative locations may not be optimal for the efficient conduct of business. However, as more industries become footloose, these costs to firms may diminish. Improvements in infrastructure, including the training of labour and the education of management together with the spread of timely information, help the location of footloose industries which are at the beginning of their product cycle in the assisted regions.

4.5.12 IMPACT OF INTEGRATION

Gains

First, note that even an announcement and preliminary negotiations about a serious integration deal have a positive and significant impact on the volume and direction of trade and FDI. The period before the eastern enlargement of the EU (2004) provides clear evidence for this observation. The 1993 Copenhagen criteria for EU entry and the publication of *Agenda 2000* (in 1997) represent these announcements and turning points. Elsewhere, the same happened in the case of Mexico before the start of the NAFTA in 1994.

Economic integration may increase the average welfare of consumers in the involved countries in many different direct and indirect ways. The problem is that the benefits accrue to everyone in relatively small instalments and only in the medium and long terms. Some of these gains include:

- secure access to the market of partner countries;
- increased investment opportunities as expectations may be established with an increased degree of security;
- improved efficiency in the use of resources;
- elimination of trade barriers reduces cost of trade;
- increased competition on internal market puts a downward pressure on prices;
- facilitation of exchange of technical information;
- competition forces firms to apply new ideas and technologies;
- due to the enlarged market, producers may better exploit and benefit from economies of scale;
- potential for coordination of certain economic policies;
- improved bargaining position with external partners;

- research and innovation may be stimulated because of tougher competition on a larger market and a possibility of sharing fixed costs in such a market environment;
- the market of the integrated group provides more opportunities for a wider range of goods and services that can be offered to consumers, hence there is an improvement in individuals' utility function; and
- reduction in X-inefficiency which moves the production activities of firms closer to best-practice business organisation.

In spite of these attractive gains, one must always bear in mind that international economic integration is never more than a useful *supporting* tool for sound domestic macro- and microeconomic policies and that it cannot act as their replacement. If these domestic policies are not healthy, integration cannot be their substitute.

Reallocation of Resources and Adjustment Costs

Economic integration affects welfare through increases in product variety and consumption. It was assumed, along the lines of a neo-classical model, that adjustment of production (shifts from unprofitable into profitable activities) is instantaneous and costless. This is a significant weakness of the model. External shocks such as changes in technology, trade liberalisation and economic integration have an immediate impact in the form of increases in efficiency and income. The new employment of labour may be generated at a later stage. Adjustment to these shocks may require both time and government intervention. Gains from shifts in production and trade as a consequence of integration should be reduced by the cost of the adjustment needed to obtain net welfare effects of integration.

Adjustment costs (the social price for change) may be quite high in the uncompetitive economies. Think of the 'pain' and length of time needed for the transition economies of central and eastern Europe to change to a market-type economic system. However, if these countries protect themselves from external trade for too long, such a policy can become an additional obstacle to adjustment. Adjustment costs are borne both by individuals and by society. Private adjustment costs include a reduction in wages, losses in the value of housing and a depreciation of the value of firms' capital. Social costs include lost output from unemployed capital and labour.

The common external protection may discriminate against imports from third countries in such a way that these external economies may adjust more swiftly than would otherwise be the case. In order to avoid the common external protection, the governments of those countries may, among other things, respond by shaping their own geography of production and comparative advantage in higher lines of manufacturing to gain a competitive edge in advanced products and export them to the integrated group of countries. The dynamic models are not as simple, smooth and straightforward as classical models of trade and investment, but they are much closer to real life.

Experiences in the EU, its enlargements, EFTA and successive rounds of tariff reductions under the GATT/WTO have shown that geographical and industrial adjustment takes place relatively slowly and smoothly over a long period of time. In the case of the EU these costs were so much smaller than expected that the elimination of tariffs has advanced at a faster pace than anticipated in the Treaty of Rome. There were intra-industry adjustments, rather than inter-industry ones. The disastrous scenario of throwing home firms out of business on a large scale has not materialised at all. The buffer against such a scenario, as well as the means for the mitigation of adjustment costs, may be found in increased capital mobility and flexible rates of exchange. However, one has to add that the period of the 1960s was characterised by relatively high growth rates and near full employment, which helped the adjustment process.[237]

If freeing trade does not produce pain in the form of pressure and adjustment costs, it probably produces no gain either. The 'compulsory' reallocation of resources is a source of gains. The adjustment cost is a finite, one-time investment. The gains from improved resource allocation present a continuous flow over time. Therefore, there are reasons to believe that the 'pain' is much exaggerated (Curzon Price, 1987, p. 16). Trade liberalisation accelerates competition in participating countries. For this reason, the expectation that international economic integration is beneficial in the long run can be accepted with considerable confidence. Economic adjustment and the alteration in the geography of production is a necessary condition if countries want to maintain the growth of the economy in circumstances of high-risk choices where technology and the situation in the market changes fast. They will have to learn how to live with change in order to reap gains from such a strategy.

Adjustment costs associated with shifts among economic activities include a need for a reallocation of labour. Positions will be lost in some business activities and geographical areas, while they will be created in others. Structural funds for social, regional and industrial issues can act as built-in stabilisers which help the initial losers to recover.

An economic policy of non-interference with market forces has obvious advantages because competition and efficiency are stimulated, consumers' tastes are satisfied and there is a reduction in the costs of government administration and intervention. On the other side of the coin, government intervention may be required because markets are imperfect, firms seldom take into account social costs of production (externalities) and adjustment, and market forces may increase inequality in the regional distribution of income. However, intervention meant to smooth adjustment problems can develop into a deeply rooted protectionism which over time increases costs to everybody. Hence, neither a pure market system nor a paramount government intervention can take account of all private and social costs and benefits of adjustment. While intervention may solve major economic issues, market forces may be more successful in the fine-tuning of the economy.

A country's comparative advantage and geography of production are dynamic concepts. They shift over time. Countries may not be sure that their current production advantages will remain unchanged in the future. International economic integration may be a reliable way for a country to secure wide markets for home goods/services and to obtain sources of supply in the future. Geographical proximity of the partner countries ensures that gains from trade, specialisation and a wider choice of goods are not wasted on transport costs.

Clusters

The production geography of the US is particularly interesting to examine as it is a country without important internal borders and it is so big that it may serve as an example for economic comparison with an integrated Europe. Even a superficial look at the US production geography reveals a high concentration of industries. For example, the following industrial clusters come to mind:

- aviation around Seattle;
- finance on Wall Street;
- insurance in Hartford (Connecticut);
- pharmaceuticals in central New Jersey;
- medical equipment in Minneapolis;
- electronics in Silicon Valley and Boston's Route 128;
- advertising on Madison Avenue in New York City;
- optics related industries in Rochester (New York);
- cars around Detroit;
- paints and coatings in Cleveland (Ohio);
- entertainment in California;
- office furniture in western Michigan;
- orthopaedic devices in Warsaw (Indiana);
- hosiery and home furnishings in North Carolina;

- carpets in Dalton (Georgia);
- wine in Napa Valley (California);
- shoes in Massachusetts; and
- gambling in Las Vegas and Atlantic City.

Development and growth histories differ between Europe and the US. While the US developed, industrialised and grew as an economy under constant but integrated territorial expansion, the same process took place in Europe behind barriers of trade protection, state support and different languages and cultures. As a result, the US has a number of highly developed and specialised regional clusters throughout the country, whereas the same type of specialisation is much less obvious in Europe (Storper et al., 2002, p. 103). European clusters that come to mind include: production of knives in Solingen, watches in Geneva and the Swiss Jura, financial services in London, fashion garments and motorcycles in northern Italy, carpets in Kortrijk (Belgium), pleasure in Paris, flowers in Holland, sex/prostitution[238] in Amsterdam and food manufacturing in York. However, the European car industry has never created a cluster similar to Detroit. A select list of clusters in Italy and Germany is given in Appendix 4A.2.

Once the concentration of business becomes too high, there may be negative externalities for work and private life such as pollution, sewage and waste disposal problems, congestion, allergies, crime and an increase in the price of land and rents.[239] This may have an impact on the spread and decentralisation of businesses and their shift to other regions as firms may wish to leave the 'threatened' regions. However, the EU has on average a less concentrated manufacturing geography and much more segmented markets than the US, as a long-term consequence of various NTBs which increase trade costs.[240] The goal of the Single Market Programme (1985–92) was to eliminate all barriers on internal trade. Hence, if this takes place, the expectation was that the EU industries and its geography of production could resemble those in the US. One should not be deceived into thinking that the EU will ever have a homogeneous market like the one in the US. Most things and ways of doing things (culture) in the US are alike throughout the country (for example, food, customs, services, what towns and settlements look like). In the EU, on the other hand, citizens have distinct national consumer preferences for food and drink. This will persist. In addition, the EU countries have a range of national policies regarding health, safety, social issues and worker representation.

A lesson for the EU is that the Single Market Programme (integration deepening) provided opportunities for a concentration of production in certain hot spots, as well as for rationalisation of business operations. Amiti (1998, 1999) found evidence that this took place in the manufacturing industries which include industrial chemicals, petroleum, textiles, plastics, iron and steel, machinery and transport equipment. These are all industries that are subject to economies of scale and that have a high proportion of intermediate inputs in final output. Hence, this provides some support to the arguments of the new theory of spatial economics. In the 1976–89 period, geographical concentration increased in 30 of 65 recorded industries, concentration fell in 12 industries (the biggest fall was in the manufacturing of concrete for construction), while there was no significant change in the geographical concentration in other industries (Amiti, 1999, p. 580). Midelfart-Knarvik et al. (2002) found that 'between 1970/73 and 1994/97, the general trend towards spatial dispersion is reflected in 29 out of 36 industries' (p. 241) and that there is an 'impression of a spreading out of European manufacturing activity' (p. 241). Aiginger and Pfaffermayr (2004) and Aiginger and Davies (2004) argued that geographical concentration in the EU decreased during the 1990s. This is in line with the second part of the hump-shaped relation between integration and location of production (as trade and transport costs decline, there is a spread of production).

Mora et al. (2004, p. 14) referred to the 1985–95 period and found that 'most sectors had slightly increased their degree of concentration, especially paper and printing products, chemical products, and food, beverages, and tobacco. Services sectors had also increased their concentration level.' In addition, regions close to the EU 'core' and the ones with a diversified economic structure in which high-technology industries and knowledge-based services predominate benefited most from the integration process and improved their relative position in the EU. In contrast, EU regions with a low degree of diversification in production and relying on mature low-technology industries that employ low-skilled labour (therefore highly sensitive to asymmetrical shocks), away from the EU 'core' and dependent on farming, showed the worst relative position in terms of GDP per capita after 15 years of integration. These regions were caught in a 'poverty trap' (ibid., p. 22). If this were the case, then there are important policy lessons not only for the EU(15), but also for the EU(25). On the other hand, a study by the European Commission (1998) observed that an 'examination of data offers mixed evidence for the contention that the single market is leading to a geographical concentration' (p. 67) and that there is 'little evidence of concentration occurring in the EC' (p. 69). Therefore, this topic demands further research and analysis.

Production Geography: with Trade Barriers

International economic integration may influence the geography of production in several ways. There are three in particular, which were neglected in the earlier analysis because of non-linear analytical complications that result from externalities and because they deal with trade costs (Fujita et al., 1999, p. 251):

- With high transport costs and high trade barriers (or autarky), each country is likely to have manufacturing to supply its local consumers.
- With low or no transport and trade costs (free trade), the world gets 'smaller' and markets larger, forward and backward linkages (presence of tradable intermediate goods) dominate and there are possibilities for footloose manufacturing to agglomerate in a single country or a single location (American outcome). There is no need for producers and consumers to be in vicinity as trade is costless. Firms move to the lowest-cost locations.
- With intermediate transport costs concentration becomes possible and necessary. Costs of production may differ among countries depending on country size (market) and economies of scale. Firms in a smaller or peripheral country that produce tradable goods on average depend more on foreign trade than do firms in larger countries. Therefore, if trade is liberalised, firms from the small country may gain more than firms from large countries. However, firms from a large country may exploit economies of scale and have lower costs of production and prices of output than the firms in a small country. Once trade is liberalised and trade costs fall, firms from the large country may capture a large part of the small country's market. Then comes a period of adjustment. Certain firms may relocate in search of low-cost immobile factors (land, labour) and larger markets. In small countries such as Austria, Switzerland or Luxembourg, firms may successfully adjust and penetrate niche markets in a large country.[241] Although the national production geography (distribution of industries) is altered, this does not mean that there will be a divergence in national per capita income. Each country may have a cluster of industries that supply the entire integrated market. However, this case brings with it a range of stable and unstable equilibria (European outcome).

Suppose that transport costs in the real world have a declining path over time. This is a relatively reasonable assumption from the time of Ricardo. One may observe a trend in the narrowing of the income gap between the advanced countries (north) and certain developing countries (south). 'Declining trade costs first produce, then dissolve, the global inequality of nations' (Fujita et al., 1999, p. 260). The problem is that industrialisation and economic development is not a uniform process. It takes place in a series of irregular waves and jumps. Labour-intensive industries are the first ones to leave the industrialised country because of high wages there. The less labour-intensive industries that move at a later stage do so possibly more rapidly than the earlier movers. When upstream industries move, they create potentials for forward and backward production links in the target country which facilitates entry of firms from other downstream industries.

Production Geography: Reduction in Trade Barriers

There is, however, an initiative that may help out the lagging regions in an integrated area. Suppose that the initial reduction of barriers to the movement of goods, services and factors in a common market spurs an inflow of factors to already industrialised areas where they benefit from economies of scale and various externalities. If all barriers to internal trade and factor movements are eliminated or become insignificant, firms may benefit from economies of scale and externalities in other (less-advanced or peripheral) regions where the variable costs of production are potentially lower than in the centre of the manufacturing or service activity (Krugman and Venables, 1990, p. 74; Venables, 1998, p. 3). In this case, the less-developed region or a country that takes part in a common market is likely to benefit on at least two counts:

- it gets firms that benefit from economies of scale; and
- the former regional production structure that was typified by a lack of open competition is altered.

Kim confirmed this type of reasoning for the manufacturing industry in the US during the 1860–1987 period. Industry specialisation rose substantially prior to the turn of the 20th century. At about the same time, the US was developing its transport and communication network in order to become a fully integrated economy. During the inter-war years, the level of regional specialisation 'flattened out', but then fell substantially and continually between the 1930s and 1987. Economic integration made the US regions less specialised today than they were in 1860 (Kim, 1995, pp. 882–6). This trend of dispersion of industries and increasing regional similarity in the US continued throughout the 1990s (Midelfart-Knarvik et al., 2002, p. 253). As we shall see later, economic integration in the EU made the industrial structure in the member countries more specialised and less similar.[242]

In theory, economic integration may, but not necessarily will, bring greater benefits to the regions/countries that lag in their development behind the centre of economic activity. However, if production linkages (forward and backward) are strong (meaning that production is indivisible) and *internal* to an industry such as in chemicals (Basle) or banking and other financial services (London, New York) and imperfect competition prevails, economic integration would trigger agglomeration (clustering) tendencies. Regional policies that aim at spreading these industries are counterproductive. If, however, the linkages are not limited to a relatively narrow industry group, but are strong *across* industries and sectors, integration would produce agglomeration tendencies in select spots. If labour is not mobile, the whole process would tend to open up new and widen the existing regional wage differentials (Venables, 1996a). Although this may produce deindustrialisation tendencies in the peripheral regions, it does not mean that integration is not desirable. For instance, education and regional policies increased the attractiveness of Spain as a location for various manufacturing industries, discovered by the EU and foreign investors. This was particularly obvious following the Spanish entry into the EU in 1986.

Integration of Mexico with the US shifted many manufacturing industries from the area of Mexico City northwards, along the border with the US. This took place not only because there was a growing demand in the US, but also because of the general trade liberalisation policy in Mexico. Once the economy turns outwards, internal production linkages weaken and firms have less incentive to stay in the congested hub.

The textile and clothing industry has been adjusting to the closed or quota-fragmented 'global' textiles market since the 1960s. When exports from one developing country hit the quota ceiling, the textile producers moved to another country to profit from its quota, which is how this 'quota jumping' brought and located textile manufacturing for the first time to countries such as Mauritius.

Policy-induced changes such as the disappearance of quotas on exports of textiles to the US and EU in 2005, as a part of the Uruguay Round deal, speeded up the international reallocation of the textile industry to China. Xiansheng (south of Shanghai) is a flourishing textile export hub that profits enormously from this change. Millions of jobs throughout the world, both developed and developing, are endangered. The textile industry in the developed world was protected for over 30 years with the various agreements that sheltered domestic jobs. None the less, this protective shield did not prevent a steady fall in employment in textiles and clothing. The question is how much longer does this industry need in order to adjust? Can or should it adjust at all?[243]

Certain intentions by the EU and the US to reintroduce restrictions on imports of textiles from China are explicit recognitions that their respective domestic textile industries failed to adjust despite long-term protection and a decade-long advance warning that protection would go in 2005. Severe antidumping duties and obscure methods to calculate them are ill-advised for several reasons. China is among the biggest world importers (it also exports a lot, but the trade balance is only slightly positive). Both the US and the EU argue in favour of free trade. China has a comparative advantage in producing textiles and is using it just as Kuwait did in the production of crude oil. Bearing these facts in mind, what right have the EU and the US to lecture others about the benefits of free trade? What right have they to complain that other countries are too slow to open their markets? Is it hypocritical to blame others for their own failures? The best way to show the benefit of liberal trade to others has always been to lead by example and to be in the forefront of market opening.

Import quotas in the developed world complicated the manufacturing and purchase of clothing and textiles. It makes business sense to rationalise this in the new situation and to buy from a single location, a practice that big retailers prefer. Therefore, China, India and Pakistan may be preferred choices as locations for production and sources of supply. Laura Jones of the US Association of Importers of Textiles and Apparel commented that 'China does not compete just on price: indeed, it is not the lowest-cost producer of some clothing items. Its biggest advantages are its industry's rapid response, reliability, business-like attitude and keen understanding of customer demand. It is very easy to do business there.'[244]

Even though the Multifibre Agreements were condemned as clear protectionism, the system of carving up international markets served many developing countries well. It provided opportunities for less-productive and weaker manufacturers. However, they must now make the adjustment to an open 'global' market. The marginal producers from developing countries have good reason to fear that there will be a relocation of this industry to China. The consequence is that many of them are trying to specialise in select market niches. However, a general problem and weakness in China is a serious shortage of raw materials, including cotton.

If costs of trade are high, industries tend to disperse. When this cost is reduced, agglomeration can take place as demand in distant places can be met by exports. When these trade costs approach zero (as is the case in writing computer software in Bangalore, India or data entry in Manila and the use of the Internet), footloose production may be dispersed and located according to the availability of the specific resource inputs.[245] Globalisation of certain industries (integrated international production) reduces the weight of physical proximity between various production units, as well as between producers and consumers. However, in industries that have strong internal links such as those based on new knowledge (innovation activities are still highly clustered in the world), financial services or chemicals, there is a strong propensity to cluster in spite of 'globalisation' of other businesses.

Deepening of economic integration in the EU through the elimination of NTBs during the introduction and after the establishment of the Single European Market, reduction in the cost of transportation and the eurozone may diminish motives for regional and national self-sufficiency. However, integration may also stimulate agglomeration tendencies and reinforce the core–periphery problem. Production in the EU may resemble that in the US where industrial output (both in manufacturing and in services) is concentrated in distinct geographical locations. Hence, if this takes place in the future, internal EU trade among its member countries will no longer be intra-industry but rather inter-industry in nature. Further reduction of trade costs in the EU may lead to further concentration of production, which is subject to the economies of scale in the already existing core locations, while the periphery may specialise in manufacturing production that does not depend on scale economies. This provides support to the arguments of the new economic geography and trade theories (Brülhart and Torstensson, 1996; Amiti, 1999).

Industry characteristics set the locational response to lower trade costs. Industries that have significant economies of scale and important functional intra-industry production links have a bubble- or hump-shaped relation (∩) between integration and concentration. When there are high trade costs, production is dispersed so industrial concentration is low; as these costs are lowered and reach intermediate level, there is an increase in industrial concentration; as trade costs fall to low levels, there is a decrease in concentration (spread) as industries start to respond to factor markets.[246] These industries are metals, chemicals, machinery and transport equipment. Industries that are not strongly based on economies of scale (textiles, leather and food products) have a monotonously increasing path towards concentration as trade costs decrease because of integration (Forslid et al., 2002, p. 293). This kind of reasoning and regional compensation funds of the group may be used to convince the adversely affected peripheral regions to tolerate the difficult period of transition that may follow trade liberalisation and economic integration (Puga and Venables, 1997, p. 364). Similar arguments may be used in the central and east European EU member countries.

If indigenous entrepreneurs are flexible, then the regional geography of production can be altered within a large integrated area without substantial external assistance or even without a separate regional currency. A clear example is the conversion of New England's production geography from the production of shoes and textiles in the 1960s (coupled with relatively high unemployment) to an economy based on 'high technology' and low unemployment in the 1980s. Centripetal forces may explain relatively low indices of intra-industry trade (agglomeration, clustering) in industries subject to high economies of scale. Conversely, relatively high indices of intra-industry trade (in 'labour-intensive' industries) may suggest the spread of industries. In the case of the EU, Brülhart (1998b, pp. 340–41) suggested that in the 1980–90 period:

- there was no further concentration of already clustered industries that are subject to increasing returns in the central regions;
- there was further concentration of textile-related industries at the periphery; and
- there were certain indicators of a spread of 'high-technology' industries towards the periphery.

Others, however, argue that the outcome may be the reverse of the one just described and that an active regional policy is necessary particularly in an EMU. Emigration of people would discourage an entry of new businesses into such a region. That trend would further weaken the economic position of the region. None the less, such a vicious circle has not taken place in the EU. Even though there are severe problems regarding data, particularly regarding the 1950s and 1960s, certain trends are discernible. What seems likely to be the case in the EU is that regional disparities were slowly narrowing until the early 1970s. This was followed by a decade-long period of widening the regional gaps, and then a mixture of stabilisation and widening between member countries ever since. It is not yet clear what prompted the halt in the convergence process after the 1970s. This does not mean that specific regions are irrevocably stuck in a specific position in the regional ranking order. Evidence is available that there is considerable switching from one position in the regional ranking to another (Armstrong and de Kervenoael, 1997, p. 41; Midelfart-Knarvik et al., 2002). Does this mean that there is a need for a more active cohesion policy in the EU? 'Not necessarily. We still lack evidence on whether existing cohesion policies have been effective in reducing growing regional disparities in the EU' (Midelfart-Knarvik et al., 2003, p. 865).

The economic history of integrated states such as the US points to the fact that integration is associated with regional convergence which predominates over economic divergence in the long run. This process is rather slow, about 2 per cent a year, but it is sustained over a long period (Barro and Sala-i-Martin, 1991, p. 154). General, but very slow, regional convergence has been confirmed by the literature; however, a poor region can expect the gap between its initial level of income and the aggregate to be reduced by only 30–40 per cent at the outside (Canova and Marcet, 1995, pp. 1 and 24). Armstrong (1995, p. 149) found that the convergence rate between 1970 and 1990 was only 1 per cent a year, which is half the rate estimated by Barro and Sala-i-Martin. Thus, a certain convergence process is at work, but it is 'painfully slow' (Armstrong and Taylor, 2003, p. 85).

In a critical survey of the new geographical turn in economics, Martin found that regional convergence is remarkably similar across the US, the EU, Canada, Japan, China and Australia and stated that 'the observed rate of regional convergence is very slow, about 1–2% per annum, and considerably lower than predicted by the simple neoclassical growth model' (Martin, 1999, p. 72). In any case, there are endogenous growth factors (increasing returns) at work and regional policies based on pure transfers of funds are not working unless linked with structural changes and factor mobility.

Carrington (2003, p. 382) argued that growth in each region depends not only on its own characteristics, but also on those of the regions that comprise the neighbourhood to which it belongs (adjoining regions). Applying spatial econometrics to 110 regions of the EU(15), it was found that during the 1990s two opposing forces were exerting their influence across the EU(15). While regions did converge at a rate of about 2 per cent, neighbourhoods of regions diverged at an almost equal rate, leaving a net effect of convergence considerably smaller than the one previously reported in the literature.

As far as the distribution of total production in the EU is concerned, in the period between the 1970s and the 1990s, the EU countries became more specialised. However, EU regions show a mixed pattern. Approximately a half of EU regions became more specialised, while the other half became less specialised. Industrial concentration also varies by industry. Those industries based on high technology and with economies of scale became more spatially concentrated than the others (Combes and Overman, 2004, p. 2857).

The vast majority of EU countries 'experienced a growing difference between their industrial structure and that of their EU partners' (Midelfart-Knarvik et al., 2002, p. 223). These growing divergences in the geography of national production may be the consequence of two factors:

- *The importance of history* This is when countries initially have industries that grow at different rates. Hence a country with a higher proportion of high-growth industries becomes increasingly more specialised than the average or the rest of the group.
- *Differential change* This is when countries move out of a certain type of production and into another.

Midelfart-Knarvik et al. (ibid., p. 221) found that over 80 per cent of the change in the EU during 1980–97 was due to 'differential change', while the rest came from the amplification of initial differences. The most striking feature of this process was a change in the industrial structure of Ireland, Scotland and Finland, where new high-technology industries and the ones subject to increasing returns to scale were established (often with a high FDI component).

The impact of integration on individual industries can also be looked at in the following way. Midelfart-Knarvik et al. (ibid., pp. 232–5) divided industries into five groups and observed their concentration in the 1970/73 and 1990/97 periods. The results of the analysis were as follows:

- *Concentrated industries that remained concentrated over time*: motor vehicles, aircraft, electrical apparatus, chemical and petroleum products. These are the industries with high increasing returns to scale, and which depend on high/medium technology and have a high share of inputs from their own industrial group. In this group, Germany reinforced its position in motor vehicles, to the detriment of Britain and France. In the aircraft industry, Britain, France and Germany remained dominant. However, there was a slight reduction in the shares of Britain and Sweden, while Belgium, France and Spain had slight increases. Britain, Germany and France remained dominant in chemicals, but Britain reduced its share in the petroleum and coal industries.
- *Concentrated industries that became less concentrated*: beverages, tobacco, office and computing machinery, machinery and equipment, and professional instruments. This group of industries relies more on inter- rather than intra-industry linkages, relatively high labour skills, but lower returns to scale than the previous group. A spread of these industries was pronounced in the 1991–97 period. Germany saw a reduction in its dominance in this group. The same trend was also noted for Britain and France. Ireland and Finland were the biggest gainers in this industrial group, but Austria, Italy, Portugal, Spain and Sweden also gained.
- *Dispersed industries that became more concentrated*: textiles, apparel, leather products, furniture and transport equipment. Relatively low technology in this group has low returns to scale and low, too, are the requirements regarding labour qualifications. Britain, France and Germany reduced their shares in this group, while the southern EU countries exhibited growing shares. In transport equipment, however, Germany increased its share by 10 per cent, while Britain and Spain had a combined decrease of 7 per cent.
- *Dispersed industries that remained spread*: food, wood products, paper and its products, printing and publishing, metal products, non-metallic minerals, and shipbuilding. There were no obvious changes in the group. National differences in taste and culture explain such developments for most industries in this group.

- *Residual group*: footwear, industrial chemicals, drugs and medicines, petroleum refineries, rubber and plastic products, pottery and china, glass and its products, iron and steel, non-ferrous metals, railroad equipment, and other manufacturing. This medium-concentrated group did not change much. The only significant change was in drugs and medicines, which became less concentrated. Production spread from Germany and Italy towards Britain, Denmark, Ireland and Sweden.

The change in the production structure data in the EU found certain support in the change in the structure of EU trade. Trade data support the finding that there was a decrease in specialisation during the 1970s. However, the picture is mixed from the beginning of the 1980s. The growing specialisation revealed in the production data is not reflected in the change in the structure of trade. The main reason for this discrepancy is the growing volume of intra-industry trade (ibid., p. 225). In addition, trade data may not be a suitable substitute for the production records. The structure of trade may change as a response to changing demand without any change in production. If there is a change in domestic tastes, then the domestic producers may sell goods on the home market rather than make extra efforts to sell abroad. The structure and volume of trade are altered in this case, while there may be no change in the composition of the domestic output.

Compared with the pre-Single Market Programme, the EU 'problem regions' saw an improved economic performance in the period following the completion of the Single European Market. This improvement was obvious in terms of growth in both employment rates and gross value-added (European Commission, 1997e, p. 5). Concerns that the Single Market Programme would lead to a concentration of economic activity in the 'core' EU countries were not realised. There has been only a limited spread of economic activity to the 'peripheral' EU countries which enjoy certain cost advantages (European Commission, 1998, p. 145). This is consistent with the view that as costs of trade fall for products of certain industries, the periphery may became more attractive for investment as the returns on the capital are greater. However, this development in the EU may also be the consequence of the impact of regional aid (European Commission, 1997e, p. 34).

One of the outcomes of the Single European Market was that certain clusters of firms and industries in the EU became a bit more visible. Relatively high geographical concentration of related firms in relatively small areas eased exchange of information. Following these changes, Frankfurt, London and Paris are now the areas that create jobs faster than the rest of the national economy. However, the problem is in the regions outside a large metropolitan area which still seem to remain 'poor'. Success, like many other things, also appears to cluster.

In spite of all analysis and policy actions, the question remains: do regions converge or not? A relatively large body of literature is still letting us down if we try to formulate a decisive answer to this question. Many research methods are not fully reliable, while not all results are convincing. There may be a general lack of obvious income convergence in the EU. Hence the persistence of the 'regional problem' at the EU level meant a substantial spending of resources to fix it. Whether a long-term transfer of these resources under the auspices of EU structural and cohesion policies were ineffective, misplaced or insufficient shots will remain an important and widely debated issue (Magrini, 2004, pp. 2779–80).

4.5.13 EUROPEAN UNION

Introduction

International economic integration brings multiple equilibria and may, in some cases, aggravate the situation of already weak and peripheral regions in comparison with previous circumstances. This is recognised in part by the existence of national and EU regional policies. None the less, having a peripheral location does not mean that a country is destined to have a poor economic performance. The accumulation and efficient employment of human (and physical) capital is the most important factor in a country's economic performance. Although countries such as Finland, Sweden, New Zealand, Australia and even Japan and South Korea have relatively unfavourable geographical locations regarding major transport routes, the irreversibility of their 'peripheral' geographical position is mitigated and more than compensated for by the accumulation and efficient employment of their national human and physical capital. The expansion of infrastructure and further development of human and physical capital alleviated Spain's location at the fringe of the EU. It is expected that the central and east European countries will do likewise in the future.

The regional policy of an economic union can be justified at least on the grounds of solidarity, unity, harmonisation of national regional policies and the (re)distribution of wealth within the group. Policy coordination at the central level is defended on the grounds that it prevents clashes of different national regional policies with common objectives. The policy needs to ensure, at the very least, that the existing regional problems are not made worse by economic integration, otherwise the less-developed regions/countries will have no incentive to participate in the project.

Evolution

The evolution of the regional policy of the EU can be divided into four broad phases. Regional issues did not feature highly on the agenda among the original six member countries. During the late 1950s and 1960s, only Italy gave weight to the regional problem because of its southern part (Mezzogiorno), which is why regional policy in the EU was practically non-existent until 1973. Following the entry of Britain, Denmark and Ireland in that year, the situation changed. The second phase in the development of the regional policy began after the first enlargement of the EU. Britain was particularly interested in the inclusion of regional issues in the EU. The first tool to apply the policy was the European Regional Development Fund (ERDF). The entry of Greece in 1981, and Spain and Portugal in 1986, increased the desire and need for an EU regional policy. This policy mainly gave benefits to the EU-rim countries (Britain, Greece, Ireland, Italy, Portugal and Spain), just as the CAP favours the 'northern' countries.[247] The third phase started with the reform of policy and the ERDF in 1988. The fourth phase is linked with two events: the creation of the eurozone in 1999 and the eastern enlargement of the EU in 2004.

Following the first enlargement of the EU, the new regional conditions of the EU were officially analysed for the first time in the *Report on the Regional Problems of the Enlarged Community* (the Thomson Report) (European Communities, 1973). The report identified two types of regions in the EU that have problems. First are the farming regions that are located in the periphery of the EU. The Italian Mezzogiorno and Ireland fit into this group. In both regions there is relatively high long-term structural unemployment and dependence on farming. The second type of problem regions are those that have a high proportion of regional output and employment in industries with obsolete technologies and in those with declining demand. These problem regions have a slow rate of shifting resources out of such industries and technologies, as well as a relatively high level of long-term structural unemployment. Some regions in Britain fall into this group. A renegotiation of the British entry and concerns by Italy and Ireland led to the creation of the ERDF in 1975 under Article 308[248] of the Treaty of Rome. However, the ERDF only provides resources for regional development that are *additional* to those available from national funds.

Regional Discrepancies

Differences in economic development among regions exist in every country, but at the EU level they seem much larger. Less-developed regions in one country may have different characteristics from less-developed regions in

Table 4.15 GDP per capita at current prices (€) in the EU and candidate countries, 2002–2004

Country	2002	2003	2004*
EU(25)	21 200	21 400	22 300
EU(15)	24 100	24 400	25 400
New members (10)	6 000	6 000	6 400
Luxembourg	51 100	53 200	56 100
Denmark	34 100	34 900	36 000
Ireland	32 600	33 800	36 000
Sweden	28 800	29 800	31 000
Austria	27 400	27 900	28 700
Finland	27 000	27 500	28 600
Netherlands	27 600	28 000	28 500
United Kingdom	28 000	26 600	28 400
Belgium	25 300	26 000	27 100
Germany	25 500	25 800	26 400
France	24 900	25 300	26 300
Italy	21 100	22 600	23 400
Spain	17 200	18 200	19 300
Cyprus	15 500	15 900	16 900
Greece	12 900	13 900	14 900
Slovenia	11 800	12 300	13 000
Portugal	12 400	12 500	12 800
Malta	10 800	10 700	11 100
Czech Republic	7 700	7 900	8 500
Hungary	6 800	7 200	8 100
Estonia	5 500	5 900	6 500
Slovakia	4 800	5 400	6 100
Poland	5 300	4 900	5 100
Lithuania	4 300	4 700	5 100
Latvia	4 200	4 200	4 700
Candidates			
Romania	2 200	2 300	2 600
Bulgaria	2 100	2 300	2 500
Croatia	5 500	5 700	6 200
Turkey	2 800	3 000	3 400

Note: * Forecasts.

Source: Eurostat (2005).

others, including large variations in income. In addition, congestion in southern Italy is greater than that in the south-west of France. Table 4.15 presents GDP per capita in the EU(25) and candidate countries at market prices in the 2002–04 period in order of decreasing level. This comparison of the relative difference in GDP per capita among countries at current prices may well overestimate the real difference between advanced and weak countries (or regions). The difference within the EU between Luxembourg, the richest country according to this indicator, and Latvia, apparently the least developed, is 11:1. For comparison, on this criterion the difference between Luxembourg and Bulgaria would be 22:1, while the EU(25) average GDP per capita in 2004 was nine times higher than in Bulgaria.

A useful device for overcoming part of the problem associated with the inter-country comparison of GDP at market prices can be found in the use of current purchasing power standard (PPS). This statistical indicator is an artificial currency that reflects differences in national price levels that are not taken into account by exchange rates. It is based on the relative prices of a basket of representative and comparable goods and services among countries. The PPS represents more adequately the real level of the local purchasing power, and it often gives significantly different results from the ones given in current euros, in particular during times of volatility in exchange rates. The PPS is not affected (in the short term) by fluctuations in the exchange market. This problem has disappeared in the case of the countries in the eurozone. Significant differences between data given in current euros and those in the PPS are assigned to differences in price levels in the member countries. If prices in an individual member country are higher than the EU average, then the GDP per capita is higher in current euros than according to the PPS. The reverse is true for the countries whose GDP per capita in current euros is below the EU average. In these countries, the PPS gives a higher value than the GDP in current prices.

Table 4.16 provides data on the differences in GDP per capita in the EU(25) and candidate countries in the 2002–04 period in order of decreasing level in PPS. This kind of presentation changes, to an extent, the picture of the relative wealth of countries in comparison with Table 4.15. According to this indicator, the difference in average real income between the richest EU country, Luxembourg, and the poorest, Latvia, was 'only' 5:1. These measures are an indicator of differences in the level of economic development, whereas disparities in unemployment rates may be an indicator of a relatively poor capacity to adjust to various economic shocks. Differences between the two measures also have implications for the regional problem as they show that local output is below its potential. The ratio between average EU(25) GDP and that in Bulgaria as measured by the PPS is 3.2:1, which is much less dramatic than the difference expressed in current prices.

Table 4.16 GDP per capita at purchasing power standard in the EU and candidate countries, 2002–2004

Country	2002	2003	2004*
EU(25)	21 200	21 400	22 300
EU(15)	23 200	23 300	24 300
New members (10)	11 000	11 300	12 100
Luxembourg	45 000	45 900	48 300
Ireland	28 100	28 300	29 900
Denmark	25 900	26 200	27 200
Austria	26 000	26 100	27 100
Sweden	24 300	24 600	26 900
United Kingdom	24 900	25 300	26 500
Netherlands	25 800	25 800	26 700
Belgium	24 700	25 200	26 300
Finland	24 100	24 300	25 600
France	23 900	23 700	24 700
Germany	23 000	23 100	24 000
Italy	23 100	22 800	23 500
Spain	20 000	20 900	21 800
Greece	16 500	17 300	18 300
Cyprus	17 600	17 400	18 200
Slovenia	15 900	16 400	17 400
Portugal	16 200	16 000	16 400
Malta	15 600	15 800	16 200
Czech Republic	14 300	14 700	15 600
Hungary	12 400	12 900	13 800
Slovakia	10 900	11 100	11 900
Estonia	9 900	10 400	11 300
Poland	9 700	9 800	10 600
Lithuania	9 000	9 800	–
Latvia	8 200	8 800	9 700
Candidates			
Romania	6 100	6 300	6 900
Bulgaria	6 100	6 300	6 900
Croatia	9 300	9 700	10 300
Turkey	5 600	5 900	6 500

Note: * Forecasts.

Source: Eurostat (2005).

There are regional differences within countries too. These discrepancies may be capable of introducing tensions, even dividing the EU. The objective of the EU is to mitigate existing and prevent the creation of new regional imbalances. Even though there are methodological difficulties, the new ranking indicators by Eurostat give data and ranks for 2000.[249] This reveals that the most developed regions in the EU(15) were Luxembourg, Valle d'Aosta (Italy), Trentino-Alto Adige (Italy), Vlaams Brabant (Belgium) and Inner London. This is a different ranking from the one that offers the regional per capita GDP: Inner London, Brussels, Luxembourg, Hamburg and Île de France. The most backward regions by both indicators were Peloponnisos (Greece), Açores (Portugal), as well as a number of other regions in Greece and Portugal.

In a comparison of worker productivity and per capita income, Paci (1997) found that European workers are becoming more similar as differences in their productivity are diminishing. However, European citizens are becoming less equal as disparities in per capita income are not diminishing. Therefore, the EU and national governments have much work to do in order to assist the weaker regions to increase the standard of living of their population (ibid., p. 630).

Action

Regional policies that are carried out at a local level by the member states and their regional authorities can have an advantage over EU regional policy because the local authorities may be better informed about local needs and problems. On the other hand, the EU is better placed to coordinate regional as well as other national policies. In addition, the EU may contribute its own resources and introduce common priorities and standards, and it may take into account regional interests when it reaches certain policy decisions. The EU has to ensure through the use of the rules of competition that the member governments do not distort competition by a 'subsidy war'. Normally, the EU puts a ceiling on the permitted subsidy per establishment and/or job created in various regions.

Established in 1975, the ERDF allocated its expenditure to the member states in fixed quotas as compensation to the countries that contributed more than average to the EU budget. These national quotas were set according to the following four criteria:

- the national average GDP per capita had to be below the EU average;
- the assisted region had to have an above-average dependence on farming or a declining industry;

- there had to be structural unemployment in and/or emigration from the region; and
- EU policies (such as free internal trade) had to have had a detrimental impact on the region.

In other words, to obtain EU funds, the governments of the member states had to submit regional projects to the EU to meet the allocated financial quota and to commit certain funds themselves to these projects. The EU had no leverage on the selection process. It simply reacted to national initiatives. There was also a minuscule non-quota section of the ERDF, which absorbed only 5 per cent of the resources. The EU was able to use these funds freely. This general situation was much criticised and the ERDF was reformed in 1985.

The reformed ERDF divided its funds among the EU member states by indicative ranges instead of fixed quotas as was the case previously. A government is guaranteed to receive the minimum of the range over a period of three years only if it has submitted a sufficient number of suitable projects. The projects submitted are evaluated according to criteria that are consistent with the EU priorities and objectives. The intention is to stimulate a greater number of applications in order to increase competition among various proposals. ERDF support may be up to 55 per cent of public expenditure on regional projects; in addition, it is allowed to co-finance programmes and it may prop up the development of indigenous potential in regions. The ERDF also attempts to mobilise local resources because it is increasingly difficult to attract private investment from wealthy to poor regions. Additional attention is devoted to the coordination of both member countries' regional policies and EU policies that have an impact on regions (agriculture, trade, environment, for example).

A further modification of EU regional policy followed the Single European Act (1987) and the entry of Spain and Portugal, which deepened the EU regional problem. The act introduced a new Title into the Treaty of Rome on Economic and Social Cohesion. Article 158 calls for the promotion of a harmonious development in the EU and 'reducing disparities between the level of development of the various regions'. Article 159 requires the coordination of economic policies among the member countries and authorises the EU to support those actions and other objectives through structural funds. Apart from these grant-awarding funds, loan-awarding institutions such as the European Coal and Steel Community (before its treaty expired in 2002) and the European Investment Bank (EIB) were also involved in regional projects.

Special regional problems emerged in the EU after the entry of Spain and Portugal in 1986. Therefore, during the preparations for this enlargement, the EU introduced the Integrated Mediterranean Programme in 1985. The goal of this coordinated programme was to help the Mediterranean regions of the EU (Greece and the southern regions of Italy and France, with a combined population of about 50 million) to adjust to competition from the two new member countries. The programme disposed of €4.1 billion in grants and €2.5 billion in loans over a period of seven years. It integrated all available sources of finance on the levels of the EU, national, regional and local authorities. In addition, it coordinated other policies of the EU. The programme was aimed at the adjustment not only of agricultural production (olive oil, wine, fruit, vegetables), but also of existing SMEs and the creation of new ones. Alternative employment for jobs lost in agriculture was to be found in services (tourism) and SMEs. Apart from the border regions of Finland, the largely 'unnoticed' entry of three developed countries (Austria, Finland and Sweden) in 1995 has not introduced new regional distortions in the EU.

The modification of regional policy and the ERDF took place in 1988 following the southern enlargement of the EU. It had one basic objective: to improve the coordination of various structural funds in order to support the Single Market Programme. The 1988 reform introduced the following six basic *principles*:

- member countries are to submit plans according to priority objectives;
- there needs to be a partnership between the administration at the local, regional and national levels;
- EU measures play only an additional role;
- there needs to be compatibility with other EU policies such as competition and environment;
- different EU policies need to be coordinated; and
- resources need to be concentrated on the least-developed regions.

At the same time, five priority *objectives* of the regional policy included:

- promotion of the development of the backward regions (Objective 1);
- economic adjustment and conversion of the production structure in the regions that were affected by a large-scale industrial decline (Objective 2);
- a fight against structural unemployment (Objective 3);
- the promotion of youth employment (Objective 4); and
- structural adjustment in agriculture, in particular in the regions affected by the reform of the CAP and fisheries (Objective 5a) and promotion of development in rural areas (Objective 5b).

Another decision in the reform package was to more than double the resources of structural funds from €6.3 billion in 1987 to €14.1 billion in 1993.[250] None the less, these funds had to be additional regional expenditure to that undertaken by national governments. The objective was to ensure that structural policy was a tool with a real impact, to move from an informal project to multiannual programme financing, to increase the predictability of the policy (as the funds were allocated for a period of five years) and to increase partnership with authorities that are involved in regional policy at all levels of government. In practice, all these tasks were quite bureaucratic; the methodology for the designation of regions that had to receive assistance permitted a high degree of political influence, so the coverage of the assisted areas was wider than originally planned, and support was less concentrated (Bachtler and Mitchie, 1993, pp. 722–3).

The provisions that regulate the operation of the structural funds were revised in 1993. The main thrust of the 1988 reform was, none the less, preserved. Alterations included only a simplification of the decision-making procedure and its greater transparency; the planning period over which the structural funds operate was extended to six years (1993–99); the resources for the 1994–99 period totalled €144.5 billion; and there was the inclusion of a few new regions that are eligible for the assistance.

As always when there is a disbursement of funds, the European Commission has to be careful. It has to find a balance between, on the one hand, its aim of having effective policies that do not introduce distortions that may be damaging for the EU in the long term, and subsidy-seeking regions and firms on the other. To be eligible for EU assistance, a disadvantaged region has to have per capita GDP of 75 per cent or less of the EU average. In reality, the application of this official ceiling is quite 'flexible' as aid has also been given to regions with an average income that is 80 per cent of the EU average. As a result, half of the EU(15) population of one of the richest and most-developed regions in the world became eligible for assistance because of the relative drawbacks of the region in which they live.

The regional policy of the EU is simply a supranational policy that is additional to, rather than a partial replacement of, various national regional policies. Its first shortcoming is that the ERDF is modest in relation to regional needs. It should not be forgotten, however, that the regional policy of the EU, and particularly its Cohesion Policy, is relatively new although it is improving over time. Structural funds account for about 35 per cent of the entire EU budget. In these terms, the attempt to reduce disparities between rich and poor countries in the EU is impressive in circumstances of relatively slow growth and general cuts in expenditure. A greater degree of coordination of national economic policies may avoid dissipation of scarce EU funds, which may result in help to the rich in the relatively less-developed regions to the detriment of the poor in the developed ones.

It could appear that there is a tendency to redirect structural spending from rural to urban areas. Regional problems are starting to concentrate in the urban areas of the problem regions. The principal beneficiaries of economic integration in the EU are usually urban areas in the central regions. This process has also created disadvantages in urban areas and in *other* regions of the EU. This is because the EU is a heavily urbanised group of countries.

The impact of the Single European Market on regional disequilibria in the EU is ambiguous. There is an identification problem. First and foremost, one needs to answer difficult questions: what are the short- and long-term effects of the Single European Market on the regions, and what is the impact of the changes on the regional disequilibria that would have happened on their own? If the longer-term effects of the Single European Market include the liberalisation of EU trade, then output may continue to be concentrated in the already advanced regions in order to benefit from positive externalities (this implies a fall in output and wages in the less-advanced regions). However, internal trade liberalisation may reallocate some EU production activities towards the periphery in order to take advantage of lower wages and other production costs there. As the outcome is uncertain in a situation with market imperfections and multiple equilibria, the effects of the Single European Market on the regions will continue to be debated for quite some time.

Traditional forms of national regional policy started to change and to decline in importance from the early 1990s in most of the EU member countries.[251] Denmark, for example, abolished all regional development grants and loans in 1991. The Dutch have restricted their regional assistance to a relatively small part of the country in the north. Owing to budgetary constraints, France had to scale down its regional aid. Germany has severely curtailed regional policy in the western part of the country, while placing priorities in the new eastern *Länder*. Even the less-developed countries such as Greece or Ireland have had to be careful with their regional expenditure because of the restrictions that originated in recession. The new spirit of national regional policies in the EU countries includes (Bachtler and Michie, 1993, pp. 721–2):

- reduction of the importance of regional policy in the northern countries;
- transfer of responsibilities to regional and local levels;
- automatic aid replaced by discretionary assistance; and

- increased involvement of the European Commission in regional matters, in particular through the rules on competition.

Contemporary regional policy also includes the local development of producer services. This feature was gradually incorporated into regional policy only in the second half of the 1980s. None the less, the creation of jobs in new manufacturing businesses, their extension in existing ones or relocation of businesses still account for the major part of regional intervention. The European Commission may authorise investment aid of up to 75 per cent net grant equivalent in the least-developed regions. The same limit is 30 per cent in other areas where aid is allowed. The upper limit for aid in the least-favoured areas is intended to increase the competitiveness of these regions in attracting private investment. In practice, the country that has such regions within its confines may face severe budgetary problems and lack the necessary funds to finance projects in these areas. Hence, the impact of this concession is significantly eroded. In any case, a relatively high proportion of the allowed aid of up to 75 per cent may seriously question the degree of commercial risk borne by the private firm (Yuill et al., 1994, p. 100).

EU regional policy is governed by six key principles (Armstrong and Taylor, 2003, pp. 325–32):

- concentration of assistance on the priority objectives;
- coordination of various EU policies and funds;
- partnership with member state governments, regional and local authorities, private businesses and banks;
- subsidiarity: policy should be carried out at the lowest possible level of government;
- multiannual and multiproject programming; and
- additionality: the EU regional policy should be additional to, rather than a replacement for, national or regional or private expenditure.

The objective of *Agenda 2000* was to offer an overall medium-term plan (2000–06) for the future of the EU. It wanted to prepare the EU for the new millennium when the EU was preparing to enlarge eastwards. As far as regional policy is concerned, for reasons of efficiency and visibility *Agenda 2000* merged earlier objectives for the structural funds into two regional objectives and one pan-EU objective (European Commission, 1997a, pp. 22–5):

- *Objective 1* Backward regions with per capita GDP of 75 per cent of the EU average or below. This covers about 20 per cent of the EU(15) population.

- *Objective 2* Rural and urban reconversion regions. Economic and social restructuring in areas undergoing economic change in manufacturing and services, declining rural areas, urban areas in difficulty and crisis-hit areas depending on fisheries. This covers about 18 per cent of the EU(15) population.
- *Objective 3* Development of human resources in regions not covered by Objectives 1 or 2. This supports training, education and employment.

The 2000–06 financial perspective allocated €213 billion to structural funds to disburse over seven years. *Agenda 2000* also reduced the percentage of the EU(15) disadvantaged population covered by Objectives 1 and 2 from 51 to 35–40 per cent. This is much more in line with the intention to concentrate EU resources on those areas that really need them. In addition, candidate countries (those that joined the EU in 2004) were allocated €45 billion as a pre-accession aid for the 2000–06 period. However, the level of annual assistance to a candidate country cannot exceed 4 per cent of that country's national GDP. This shifting of funds eastwards has aroused some hostility towards such developments as the beneficiary regions and countries (Spain, France) in the EU(15) feel that they are losing out to the eastern regions. Therefore, there are certain moves, particularly by the net contributors to the EU budget, to scale down regional expenditure during the period that will cover the 2007–13 financial perspective.

It is apparent that the European Commission is exerting increasing influence in EU regional matters, mainly through competition rules and funds with an impact on regional markets. National governments also conduct regional policies; however, they are becoming increasingly selective and are making sure that the policy provides value for money. In addition, outright general assistance to the regions is being replaced by transparent grants for capital investment.[252]

There is concern among member countries that the European Commission relies heavily on quantitative indicators in the designation of areas for assistance and that it does not take sufficient cognisance of the specific circumstances of each area. For example, unemployment data in rural areas may hide the 'real' regional problem, as there may be a high level of emigration from those areas. Unemployment rates that are below the national average do not reflect a buoyant local economy, but rather a lack of local job opportunities. The quantitative approach by the European Commission may be justified on the grounds that it must be impartial. The Commission can be questioned on its work by the European Parliament or by the Court of Justice, so it must be able to give reasons for its actions. Although quantitative criteria play an important role in the first phase of the consideration of the problem by the European Commission, the second phase of analysis provides for a greater flexibility and consideration of other, more qualitative elements (Yuill et al., 1994, pp. 98–100).

Three factors account for most of the inequalities in regional levels of income. They deal with differences in total factor productivity, employment level and the share of agriculture in regional income. The suggested regional policy, based on the experience of Ireland from the mid-1980s, relates to the market-oriented approach as 'the best conduit to sustained economic growth and fast convergence in per capita income' (Boldrin and Canova, 2001, p. 211).

In spite of substantial regional expenditure by the EU, Boldrin and Canova showed that neither convergence nor divergence was taking place among the EU(15) regions during the 1980–95 period. The adopted and implemented regional policies, as well as substantial public resources channelled to less-developed regions, do not appear to enhance the capacity of these regions. These funds only redistributed income among regions. With no prospects for change and if income distribution is the principal concern, such transfers will be necessary on a continuous basis. Therefore, there was no evidence that the adopted policies of redistribution of income were the most appropriate. As most regions were growing at a fairly uniform rate, these policies reflected internal political compromises which have little effect on fostering economic growth and convergence in the EU (ibid., pp. 211 and 242).

In spite of substantial expenditure on regional matters by the EU during the 1980s and 1990s, regional inequalities have not narrowed during this period, and by some measures have even widened. 'Income differences across states have fallen, but inequalities between regions within each state have risen. European states have developed increasingly different production structures' (Puga, 2002, p. 400). A similar observation came from Midelfart-Knarvik and Overman (2002, p. 333) who noted that, despite the fact that the EU(15) spent about a third of its overall annual budget on regional matters, there was increasing regional inequality. If the EU regional policy and instruments were successful on the country level, they were less so on the subnational plane.

One Case: Mezzogiorno[253]

Since the early 1950s, Italy has implemented a range of inconsistent regional policies that have failed to enable the Mezzogiorno to catch up with the rest of the Italian economy to any great extent.[254] Public intervention started after the Second World War with the development of a regional infrastructure. Poor transport links may have 'protected' local industries in the backward regions of southern Italy. The building of the *Autostrada del Sole* led to a chain of bankruptcies in the local food, textile and clothing businesses because of a fall in trade costs compared with the rest of the country. The Mezzogiorno started to 'import' cheaper goods from elsewhere in Italy, hence the previously protected local businesses suffered.

Towards the end of the 1950s, the major infrastructure was built, but it was not sufficient to attract firms to invest in the south. At that time regional policy started to offer hefty financial and fiscal incentives to businesses that wanted to locate their activities in the Mezzogiorno. In the late 1960s, public enterprises increased their role in the production geography of the south. At the same time, wage subsidies were employed as a means of industrial policy. In 1968, a national wage agreement laid down a common wage throughout the country. This introduced a major rigidity in the economy of the Mezzogiorno. Private firms abstained from hiring because of wage costs that were not linked to productivity. The south lost wage flexibility to respond to shocks, while public enterprises were overmanned. This type of economy was vulnerable to shocks, as was exemplified in the early 1970s after the increase in the price of oil (Braunerhjelm et al., 2000, p. 72).

The policy reaction to such a geography of production was support to SMEs. However, this policy change came too late to be effective. The gap between the north and the south began to widen from the mid-1970s. During the 1980s, Italian regional policy was restricted to income support (public employment and pensions). Growing taxes and continuous transfers to the Mezzogiorno were frustrating the north of the country. In addition, the European Commission demanded the removal of wage subsidies to firms in the south as they were distorting competition.

The source of the regional problem of the Mezzogiorno lies not necessarily in a lack of funds or infrastructure, but rather in the non-material sphere. One of the major obstacles can be found in the absence of an 'entrepreneurial culture'. In addition, a survey of TNCs that already operate in or have considered investment in the Mezzogiorno revealed that the major obstacles to foreign investors include the existence of criminal organisations and political factors. A lack of infrastructure featured highly only for those TNCs that have not yet established their branches there. Factors that contributed to the attractiveness of the Mezzogiorno included the availability of relatively low-cost labour (both quantity and quality) and the availability of land, as well as various public incentives to locate business operations there.[255]

Dissatisfaction with previous regional policies carried out since the 1950s, pressure from the northern regions and involvement of the European Commission in regional and competition affairs contributed to the introduction of Law 488 in 1992. This law effectively abolished special intervention (*intervento straordinario*) for the Mezzogiorno and extended the coverage of the policy (grant-based support) to the centre-north of Italy. This means that regional policy in Italy is no longer tantamount to a policy directed at the southern part of the country. The abolition of this special treatment for the Mezzogiorno may be considered as one of the most significant developments in regional policies during the past four decades.

One of the policy tools that was used to support industrialisation in the region was law provisions that required public corporations to direct the majority of their investments towards the south. These firms were regarded in the receiving area more as providers of jobs (hence, as supporters of the local demand) than as contributors to the growth of the national economy. As such, a relatively low efficiency of investment in the Mezzogiorno comes as no surprise at all. Because of these 'results' there was growing pressure for a reconsideration of the public policy towards the south, as well as open opposition to the policy from the northern regions of the country.

During the first half of the 1950s, GDP per capita income in the south of Italy was about 55 per cent of that in the north and centre of the country. In the second half of the 1980s the equivalent figure was 57 per cent. In spite of this, the Mezzogiorno cannot be described as a 'poor' region, particularly in terms of consumption. Large transfers of resources from outside the region support the artificially high levels of consumption. Therefore, the Mezzogiorno may be described as a structurally dependent economy (*European Economy*, 1993, pp. 21–2).[256]

4.5.14 CONCLUSION

A country or economic union in which there are differences in the levels of development and/or living standards among constituent regions that do not have at least a tendency towards equalisation cannot be regarded as having a well-integrated economy. Therefore, all countries and economic unions have a certain commitment to reduce regional disequilibria for a few economic and, more importantly, a variety of non-economic reasons. The objectives of EU regional policy are to diminish existing and prevent new regional disparities.

If a regional policy is to be effective, then the authorities at all levels of government have to coordinate their activities in order to influence decisions about the allocation of resources (spatial location of economic activity). In spite of these coercive powers, the regional policies of countries have had relatively limited positive achievements. It should therefore come as no surprise that the achievements of the regional policy of the EU, which often relies more on rules of competition, persuasion and on certain funds than on specific region directed coercion, are scant indeed.

Regional policy has been based on a number of compromises, to the detriment of the purity of principles. Previous attempts to shape regional policy relied mainly on the alleviation of transport and communication costs through the expansion of infrastructure, as well as the mitigation of agglomeration disequilibria. More recently, attention has shifted towards a greater self-reliance for those regions that are lagging in development, as well as the enhancement of enterprise competitiveness in these regions.

Statistical evidence and various surveys of past actions offer little testimony that the EU regional policy has had any significant effect. In the case of France, for example, Crozet et al. (2004, pp. 28 and 51), found that French and EU regional policy investment incentives and structural funds had no significant impact on investors. Elsewhere, the growth of clusters and regions such as northern Italy or Baden-Württemberg was not based on any public action, but rather on inside elements. Public action in regional matters such as those which took place in the Mezzogiorno had very limited success and occasionally could have been harmful.

Enterprise policy and the policy of macroeconomic stability are gradually being used instead of regional policy to tackle the regional (spatial) problems of a country. The new regional (development) policy ought to change the traditional intra- and interregional relations of dependence and hierarchy. This type of rigid structural organisation of firms, industries and institutions (state commands, taxes and shelters; big firms are protected; small and new firms are tolerated but not greatly encouraged; while the family ties and 'old boy' networks connect everything) ought to be replaced by structures that are open for contacts based on affinity, support and perception of common growth and positive-sum games. This new policy should include the following features:

- assistance to innovation and permanent learning;
- aid to increase flexibility to face and adapt to challenges;
- reduction in the traditional financial regional support;
- emphasis on SMEs, business 'incubators' and start-ups of new firms;
- backing of the producers' services; and
- coordination with other policies.

The critics of this policy stance argue that this policy approach lacks the firmness needed to have a direct influence on a given spatial problem.

In contrast to the decentralisation and trimming down of national regional policies, EU regional policy has continued to widen its coverage and scope. It is, however, hard to determine the point at which regional policy distorts competition beyond the interests of the EU. Hence, uncertainty over regional policy will continue in the future. There are many arbitrary elements in the policy, as well as special cases. EU regional policy has revealed its limitations. It is still Byzantine in its complexity. A solution to the regional development problem, as well as to achieving some balance among various regions, is an urgent, difficult, but highly rewarding challenge for the EU(25). Instability in regional policy at national and EU levels seems likely to continue. It is possible that the trend to decentralise the creation and implementation of national regional policy will continue in the future. However, there is a danger in the expansion of regional incentives that compete with one another.

The question arises, however, as to whether regional policy increases or decreases market imperfections. In the second-best world, all answers are possible, but not always desirable. If the costs of such a policy are less than the benefits it brings, then the policy is justified. The rationale for a regional policy that basically redistributes income (equity) must be found in solidarity among regions that constitute countries and/or the EU, as well as the fact that the area of benefit is larger than the assisted region.

Demand, technology and supplies of factors often change. Regions that fail to adjust continuously to the new challenges and opportunities remain depressed and weak. One of the broad objectives of regional policy is to help the redistribution of economic activity among different regions. Its impact cannot be measured easily as it is not a simple task to construct a counterfactual world that would specify what would have happened without this policy. The difference between the actual and counterfactual situation may be attributed to regional policy.

As the central and east European countries brought serious regional disequilibria into the EU in 2004, cohesion will remain one of the major long-term issues in the EU(25). Hence, there are at least three major arguments in favour of the EU regional policy in order to preserve unity with diversity in the EU(25):

- In the absence of policy instruments such as tariffs, NTBs, devaluation or changes in rates of interest, regions that are not able to adjust as fast as the rest of the EU face increases in unemployment and decreases in living standards. In this situation, there is a case for the demand for short-term fiscal transfers at the EU level to ease the adjustment process. The possibility of such transfers in unforeseen cases ought to be permanent in an EMU (eurozone). Otherwise, when in need, the regions that are in trouble may not be sure that other partner countries will provide resources on a case-by-case basis.

The eurozone may not be able to operate efficiently in the long term without an effective regional policy. However, there is high uncertainty regarding the size of the EU(25) structural funds during the 2007–13 period. There are serious political pressures to limit and to scale down the overall EU budgetary expenditure.

- Coordination of national regional policies, as well as other principal economic policies at the EU level can avoid self-defeating divergent regional programmes that are taken in isolation.
- Footloose industries, multiple equilibria, economies of scale and externalities do not guarantee that integration will bring an equitable dispersion of economic activities. Some direction for economic adjustment and allocation of resources in the form of regional policy may be necessary.

The evaluation of regional policy is a demanding and tough task. It is vital to compare policy achievements with goals at the start of the process (for example, the number of created jobs). But that is not enough. An overall social cost–benefit appraisal is necessary. However, data for a thorough assessment of the success of the policy are either imperfect or insufficient or unavailable. Therefore, we are left with the second best, but useful analyses that rely on surveys and econometrics.

Regional policy is another facet of social policy. Hence, the EU faces difficult political choices regarding regional policy. Challenges in this area include the eastern enlargement, monetary union, continuous unemployment, structural change and international competition. Obstacles to a stronger influence in this policy area come from the eurozone restrictions in the monetary and fiscal fields, lack of an automatic federal EU system of transfer of funds, slower growth and little internal migration of labour. However, one has always to bear in mind that the amount of funds at the disposal of a particular policy is not always what matters most. What matters is the amount of funds that are necessary to change a particular type of behaviour in the desired direction. The amount of funds and their astute use to change certain types of behaviour will continue to be a matter for debate long into the future.

Appendix 4A1 Examples of the putty–clay locational model

Relatively modest initial differences between countries or the humble beginnings of an industry or a firm in a region can have irreversible effects for a specific location or region (for a long period of time). Even if two or more potential locations are identical, then the case may be 'solved' by chance. Hence, it may be impossible to predict where a cluster will emerge. But once the industry starts developing, the process of circular interdependence or cumulative causation cuts in and may continue for a long time, even if the structure of the economy has changed. For example, there are interesting stories of why certain firms/industries came to be located where they are today:

- For centuries Basle was an important trading and banking city because of its favourable geographical position. For instance, the Rhine is navigable from Basle. This supported trade and later production specialisation in the textile industry. In neighbouring France, the national patent law of 1844 protected materials, not the production process. A Frenchman, Vergain, invented a red aniline dye (fuchsine) early in 1859. It was used for dyeing textiles and was patented by the dyestuff factory Renard Frères & Franc in April 1859. The patent gave the factory a virtual monopoly to produce it in the country. A few months after the granting of this patent (monopoly to produce), another Frenchman, Jean Gerber-Keller, invented a completely different method for producing the same red dye. However, the law prohibited him from producing this protected dye in France, even though the domestic demand was larger than supply. Hence, he went abroad to Switzerland which, like many other countries, did not have patent laws. Basle was the preferred location because it was a trading and banking centre, salt was available in the vicinity, one could 'safely' unload arsenic into the Rhine, transport and forwarding infrastructure was readily available and the oldest Swiss university, founded in 1460, was located there. Physician and alchemist Theophrastus Bombast von Hohenheim (1493–1541) known as Paracelsus, a precursor of homeopathy, lectured on the link between medical and chemical events, which freed medical thinking. Hence, Basle was a prime and open location to start production of something new. At the same time in France, the (monopolist) producer of the dye, mollycoddled by the system, did not invest further in R&D or improvements in production techniques, while the competitive market structure in Switzerland motivated firms to increase production efficiency. The price of the dye in Switzerland was less than half that in France, so smuggling into France escalated, and the French monopoly subsequently collapsed (Weder, 1995). Production of pharmaceuticals emerged, almost by chance around 1880, when the curative effects of dyes became apparent. The Swiss dye industry could not compete with its German counterpart either on scale of output or on access to raw inputs. Therefore, the Swiss specialised in high-value-added market segments of medicines, pesticides, herbicides, perfumes and flavourings. Highly sophisticated medical and health-care services and equipment followed their expansion throughout the country. Strong incentives came from an inflow of talents and the invalidation of German patents by the Allies following the two world wars, as well as a government policy in education and through the support of R&D. As a relatively small country, Switzerland had to export from the outset. It became specialised and highly competitive in an industry that is not based on natural resources, which are in short supply in Switzerland.

- Towards the end of the Middle Ages, Genevan goldsmiths and jewellers were renowned for their skills, their knowledge of precious metals and the splendour of their products. They were 'expected' to become involved in the new watchmaking industry that started to appear in France, Flanders, England and Germany around 1500. However, the Genevans were so prosperous that they were uninterested in the emerging industry. Nevertheless, two chance events prompted the abrupt appearance of watchmaking in Geneva. First, in 1541, John Calvin issued an edict against luxury, pleasure, elegant clothing and 'useless jewellery'. This limited the activities of the Geneva jewellers and goldsmiths and virtually ended their craft 25 years later when their activities were even more restricted. Second, at about the same time, the persecuted Protestant Huguenots from France and Flanders found sanctuary in Switzerland (Basle, Geneva and Zurich). Some of these refugees brought with them watchmaking knowledge and experience, one of whom was Charles Cusin who settled in Geneva in 1574. As watches performed a 'useful' function, Geneva's jewellers and goldsmiths learned how to make quality, stylish and durable watches in order to find a new source of income. Once the number of watchmakers increased, they instituted their own guild in 1601. Most of the production was sold outside the country as few Swiss were able and willing to afford such watches. None the less, production flourished and the city became congested with watchmakers. It became increasingly difficult and time consuming to obtain a master watchmaker's licence, so many of the apprentices moved to other locations. They mostly clustered in the Swiss Jura (Nyon, Neuchâtel, La Chaux-de-Fonds, Bienne and Basle). In contrast to Geneva, light regulations permitted the production of parts to be subcontracted to the peasants in the mountains, who had limited sources of income, especially during the long winters. These watches were, of course, less sophisticated and cheaper than the ones produced in Geneva, but they found a niche in the market and production expanded. In spite of changes in time measurement technology and hard times during the 1970s and 1980s, the Geneva watchmaking cluster for stylish and the Jura cluster for standard watches weathered the storm, justified their label 'Swiss made' and retained 'global' dominance (Bumbacher, 1995).

- Sassuolo (near Bologna, Italy) is, perhaps, the world capital in the production of ceramic tiles. Pot making started there in the 13th century. Production of ceramic tiles for street names and house numbers began in the 19th century. Immediately after the Second World War, there were only a few ceramic tile producers left in the area. The post-war reconstruction created a boom for all building materials including Italian ceramic tiles. Tiles did well on the market because in the Mediterranean climate they were cool in the hot weather, because wood was scarce and expensive, and because the Italians prefer natural materials to vinyl and carpeting. The principal raw material was kaolin (white) clay. The region was abundant in red clay, hence the white had to be imported from Britain. The equipment kilns and presses were imported (mainly from Germany) in the 1950s and 1960s. From the mid-1960s, the local entrepreneurs learned how to modify the imported equipment for the use of the regionally available red clay. In the 1970s, the Sassuolo area manufacturers became very competitive suppliers of kilns and presses, and they began to export them. A relatively saturated domestic tile market in the 1980s provided the incentive to export ceramic tiles all around the world. Producers were successful in responding quickly to the changing design and other demand conditions which gave them the competitive edge (Porter, 1990a, pp. 210–25).
- Modena (Italy) is an important hub for translations from and into many languages. This area has long been well known for the production and export of agricultural machinery. As the machinery required instruction manuals in various languages, such publications were initiated in Modena; once established, the industry developed and expanded.
- Provided that profitability is maintained, personal factors (that is, whims) can play a role in firm location decision. For example, the

establishment of car production factories in Detroit and Oxford, as in each case the founder of one of the major manufacturers (Ford and Morris, respectively) was born or grew up there. Incidentally, Bill Gates, the founder and chairman of Microsoft, was born in Seattle. Fashion-producing firm Hugo Boss is located in Metzingen (Germany) because Hugo Boss was born there and he wanted to contribute to the development of his home town. Metzingen is situated very close to Reutlingen (near Stuttgart) and there is quite a significant textile industry in the area. Now, not only is there Hugo Boss production and a huge outlet in Metzingen, but others have also established enterprises there, such as Escade and Bally. Hilti, a tool maker, is located in Liechtenstein because its founder Martin Hilti was born there. Bentonville, Arkansas (can you find it on a map?) is the base for Wal-Mart, the world's leading chain of retail shops. This is where Sam Walton, father of Robson Walton, founder of Wal-Mart, grew up. Elsewhere, it has been known for golf-addicted entrepreneurs and business executives to search for locations for their businesses that are close to good golfing facilities.

- 'The systems of paying sailors had strong effects on the formation of human capital to meet the changing location of trade patterns. The English paid their sailors by the voyage while the Italians paid by the day. Although the Italian system was probably well suited to Mediterranean conditions, it caused problems when the Italians entered the Atlantic trade. English sailors would weather tough storms to complete a voyage quickly while Italian sailors would stay in harbour awaiting the most favourable winds. Thus the English sailors endured a process of learning by doing in facing the tougher weather than did the Italians' (Lipsey et al., 2005, p. 173). '[T]he Venetians did not recognize the need to alter their methods of transport and their trading organisations fast enough after the three-masted sailing ship had drastically altered trading routes and arrangements. This hastened the decline that was being brought about by their unfavourable location with respect to the new routes' (ibid., p. 415).
- Policy changes such as the passage of anti-union statutes in the southern states of the US gave certain manufacturing firms the incentive to leave the northern part of the country. This process was supported by another unrelated event: the advent of air conditioning, which made the southern climate more attractive for living and working in than that in the north of the country.
- St Martin's Court is a short street near the English National Opera in London which is full of sellers of second-hand books and prints. Potential customers go there because they expect to find a number of

shops with a wide range of second-hand books, while shop owners locate there because they expect to welcome a stream of clients. A similar reasoning explains the cluster of theatres around Leicester Square and the location of restaurants in Soho. During the Renaissance, Florence was the centre for art in Italy. The clients who lived there were sophisticated, they appreciated art and were able and willing to pay for it. At the same time the artists needed such clients. The densest art expertise in the world can be found along a one-kilometre-long stretch that connects New Bond Street, Old Bond Street and St James's Street in London. The combined turnover of the auction houses Christie's, Sotheby's, Bonhams and Phillips is the largest in the world. In addition, in the same area there are 15 top art dealers. They all tend to flourish during troubled times: periods of calm and political stability have been disastrous for their business, while unpredictable crisis, death, divorce and sorrow are their best friends.

Krugman (1996b) draws an interesting analogy between clusters and the natural evolution process:

> The general attitude of evolutionary theorists seems to be that the Nature can often find surprising pathways to places you would have thought unreachable by small steps; that over a few hundred thousand generations a slightly light-sensitive patch of skin can become an eye that appears to be perfectly designed. . . . [Imagine] a group of frogs sitting at the edge of a circular pond, from which a snake may emerge . . . and that the snake will grab and eat the nearest frog. Where will the frog sit? . . . if there are two groups of frogs around the pool, each group has an equal chance of being targeted, and so does each frog within each group – which means that the chance of being eaten is less if you are a frog in the larger group. Thus if you are a frog trying to maximize your choice of survival, you will want to be a part of the larger group; and the equilibrium must involve clumping of all the frogs as close together as possible.

Does this remind you of the principle of agglomeration? Unlike changes in biology, real-world successful entrepreneurs are smart and often radically change their behaviour within a short period of time in response to challenges, risks and opportunities for business.

Appendix 4A2 Clusters in Italy and Germany

Italy is an often quoted example of a country with distinct manufacturing clusters. A select group of those clusters includes the following:[257]

- motorcycles in Bologna [2370];
- electronics, mainly alarms for cars in Varese [100];
- jewellery in Valenza Po [1400] (Alessandria); Vicenza [1100]; Arezzo [1300] (Florence);
- spectacles in Cadore [930] (Belluno);
- textiles and clothing in Sempione [3900] (Varese);
- textiles around lake Como; Prato [8481] (Florence); Olgiatese [2614] (Varese); Biella [1300] (Piedmont); Valdagno (Pisa);
- clothing in Val Vibrata [1150] (Pescara); Empoli (Florence); Treviso;
- female underwear in Castel Goffredo [280] (Mantova);
- silk in Comasco [2600] (Como);
- wool in Biella;
- knitwear in Carpi [2054] (Modena);
- shoes in Fermo, Montegranaro, Porto Santelpidio, Sanbenedetto, San Benedetto del Trono (Ancona); Lucca, Santa Croce Sull'Arno [1749] (Pisa); Ascoli [3100]; Riviera del Brenta [886] (Padova);
- sports footwear in Montebelluna [623] (Treviso); Asolo (Treviso);
- tannery in Arzignano [600] (Vicenza) and Solofra (Naples);
- ceramic tiles in Sassuolo [199] (Bologna);
- marble in Apuo-Versiliese [1161] (Carrara);
- taps and valves in Alto Cusio [300] (Novara);
- furniture in Brianza Comasca Milanese [6500] (Milan); Cantù [7200] (Milan); Alto Livenza [2000] (Udine); Poggibonsi [1294] (Siena); Bovolone-Cerea [3000] (Verona);
- kitchens in Pesaro [1200];
- chairs and tables in Udine [1200];
- wood machinery in Rimini [1345]; agricultural machinery in Modena [100];
- foodstuffs in Parma [215];
- saucepans and valves in Lumezzane [1008] (Brescia);
- packaging machinery in Bologna; and
- accordions and other musical instruments in Castelfidardo [400] (Ancona).

Clusters in Germany include:

- steel in Dortmund, Essen and Düsseldorf;
- cars in Hanover, Wolfsburg, Stuttgart, Munich, Ingolstadt, Neckarsulm, Bochum, Cologne and Regensburg;
- trains in Berlin, Braunschweig and Nuremberg;
- locksmiths' products in Velbert;
- tools in Remscheid;

- machine tools in Stuttgart;
- cutting tools and cutlery in Solingen;
- precision tools in Enzkreis;
- surgical instruments in Tuttlingen;
- instruments in Hamburg, Berlin and Munich;
- office machines in Hamburg, Hanover, Bremen, Frankfurt, Munich, Leipzig and Berlin;
- printing presses in Heidelberg, Würzburg, Offenbach, Augsburg, Leipzig and Frankenthal;
- chemicals in Leverkusen, Frankfurt and Ludwigshafen;
- pharmaceuticals in Berlin;
- jewellery in Pforzheim;
- hollow glass in Holzminden, Jena, Kronach and Hildburghausen;
- glass blowing and Christmas tree decorations in Lauscha;
- optics in Wetzlar;
- pens and pencils in Nuremberg;
- knitting in Reutlingen; and
- porcelain in Wuppertal, Coesfeld and Tirschenreuth.

Notes

1. Separate countries may, *de facto*, share a common currency. For example, Estonia's Law on Security for the Estonian Kroon (1992), Clause 2, directly linked the exchange rate of the kroon to the German mark. The Estonian central bank was forbidden to devalue the kroon. Devaluation could take place only if the law was changed, for which the usual parliamentary procedure was necessary. There have been no cases so far in history where authorisation for the devaluation of a national currency has been loudly trumpeted by a parliament.
2. Since the 1980s, Chinese labour has exhibited an extraordinary level of mobility from interior to coastal areas.
3. Some Californians may argue, perhaps rightly, that this is not so in the case of their own state.
4. The impact of fiscal policy for the fast fine tuning of the economy should not be exaggerated. A country's fiscal policy is almost as a rule an annual event. It passes through a long parliamentary procedure. Therefore, it is the monetary policy that is continuously at hand to balance the economy. Fiscal policy is not a replacement, but rather a less-flexible supplement.
5. If payroll taxes and various add-on social charges are high, firms are less willing to hire new or even keep existing staff.
6. Estimates are that the annual seigniorage revenue of the US is between $11 and $15 billion (Tavlas, 1997, p. 712). *The Economist* estimated that the annual American seigniorage may be worth some 0.1 per cent of American GDP (14 November 1998, p. 107).
7. If a government cannot or does not want to tax businesses and individuals, it may print money and tax everybody through inflation. Keynes wrote about such an inflation tax that 'a government can live for a long time . . . by printing money. The method is condemned, but its efficacy, up to a point, must be admitted. . . . so long as the public use

the money at all, the government can continue to raise resources by inflation' (Keynes, 1923, p. 23).

8. Following a period of hyperinflation at the start of the 1990s, tiny Montenegro introduced the German mark as its legal tender. At the time of the conversion of the mark to the euro, prices also had to be adjusted. Two German marks were exchanged for one euro. However, a large number of items that were sold on the market for one German mark were sold after the conversion for one euro. Prices of many items effectively doubled. The consequence was an impoverishment of the population and a loss of tourist business.
9. Businesses in the EU yearly convert several trillion euros at an annual cost for the conversion charges of over €15 billion or about 0.4 per cent of the EU's GDP (*European Economy*, 1990a, p. 63). This is the only cost of the monetary non-union that may be relatively easy to quantify.
10. The official foreign currency reserves in the eurozone were €227 billion at the end of 1999. They were €246 billion in December 2000, €236 billion in December 2001, €206 billion in December 2002, €149 billion in December 2003 and €135 billion in November 2004. A reduction in these reserves due to the creation of the monetary union in 1999 is obvious from 2003.
11. Charles de Gaulle once said: 'Treaties, you see, are like girls and roses: they last while they last' (Macleod et al., 1998, p. v).
12. In the early 1980s, firms in the former Yugoslavia were permitted to sell their home-made durable goods to domestic private buyers for hard currency. These buyers received price rebates and priority in delivery. Due to shortages and accelerating inflation, domestic private hard-currency holders increased their purchases in order to hedge against inflation. Growth of this type of home trade relative to the 'normal' trade in the (sinking) domestic currency was increasing. The discrimination of home firms against the domestic currency was spreading. Firms were happy because they received hard currency without the effort required to export, while consumers were happy because they were able to get what they wanted. Subsequently, the domestic sales for hard currency were banned because they reduced the effectiveness of the domestic monetary policy. This is an example of where a weak domestic currency (prior to state intervention) was crowded out from domestic trade by a relatively strong foreign currency (the German mark). Hard currency was not, however, driven out of Yugoslav private savings. About 80 per cent of these savings were in foreign hard currency in Yugoslav banks. This was the way to protect savings from rising home inflation and negative interest rates on savings in the home currency. A new restatement of Gresham's law had in this case the reverse meaning: good money drove out the bad.
13. In 1990, however, 11 years after the creation of the EMS the special (±6 per cent floating band) treatment for the Italian lira ended.
14. Greece and Portugal did not participate in the ERM as they were at a lower level of development relative to the 'core' EU countries, so they wanted time for a gradual adjustment. Thus the EMS was incomplete even in its first phase. A few other countries were out of the ERM, but they joined this part of the EMS later.
15. Belgium and Luxembourg have shared a monetary union since 1921. It has worked relatively well. One reason for such an operation is that one partner dominates the relationship. This monetary union has not brought either a political union or a centralist state. An interesting issue is, however, what happens if tensions arise between partners of a similar weight?
16. A one-dollar reduction in per capita income of a US region causes a reduction in the payment of federal taxes by about 34 cents and, at the same time, an increase in transfers of about 6 cents. Between one-third and one-half of the initial one-dollar shock is absorbed by the federal government (Sala-i-Martin and Sachs, 1992, p. 216).
17. The US is trying to persuade central banks to keep their reserves in US dollars as those reserves may bring in interest. However, the US dollar may easily fluctuate ±20 per cent a year relative to other major currencies. Many central bankers think that the reserves need to be kept in assets which are subject to much greater discipline than is the US dollar.

18. P. Webster, 'Cover-up row over £27 billion secret of Black Wednesday', *The Times*, 4 February 2005.
19. M. Wolf, 'How Britain defeated defeatism', *Financial Times*, 11 February 2005.
20. Ibid.
21. An alternative policy instrument could be (interest-free, one-for-one) deposit requirements.
22. An appraisal of the relative safety of a borrower introduces many problems. The value of assets in the private sector is determined by the net present value of the stream of profit that those assets earn. As for the public assets, there are many that do not yield a financial return (military camps, for example). Their value can be assessed in an indirect way through replacement costs.
23. Exceptions included small states such as Andorra (with Spain), Monaco (with France), Liechtenstein (with Switzerland), Luxembourg (with Belgium), and San Marino and Vatican (both with Italy). In addition, Ireland shared a currency with Britain for a long time.
24. The Austro-Hungarian Empire, Czechoslovakia, the Soviet Union and Yugoslavia.
25. Solidarity in the EU is still quite fragile when principal national interests are at stake. The Bretton Woods currency system collapsed because of similar reasons. Countries refused to forgo control over the domestic money supply for the sake of external equilibrium.
26. The goal of the ECB is to keep the annual inflation over the medium term at the rate of at most 2 per cent.
27. *Financial Times*, 21 November 1997; *The Economist*, 21 November 1998, p. 76.
28. The budget-deficit condition provoked most criticism. A country with a heavy public debt has good reason to have episodes with inflation: it is to reduce the real burden of its debt. Paul de Grauwe argued that France had been more successful than Germany in keeping the domestic budget deficit low over the past 25 years. Yet the franc was weak, while the mark was strong. A low budget deficit is not sufficient to ensure a strong currency. Other factors such as monetary policy are necessary. During the same period France had higher inflation than Germany. Tough monetary policy, rather than strict adherence to the 3 per cent budget-deficit criterion, would make the euro strong (*Financial Times*, 11 July 1997).
29. While annual budget deficits may occur depending on the business cycle, the overall national debt may need to be controlled in a different way from that proposed in the Maastricht Treaty. Instead of putting a cap on public debts (and on the budget deficit) which are, indeed, on various levels among the EU countries, a more effective way may be to install instruments that both discourage trends of growing debts and deficits and encourage their continuous reduction.
30. Competence and credibility are crucial elements for the success of this policy. They are very hard to gain, but easy to lose. Even highly competent institutions such as the Bank of Japan or the World Bank made wrong predictions in certain cases.
31. H. Sinn, 'A shot of inflation would be good for Europe', *Financial Times*, 20 May 2003.
32. Suppose that labour market institutions provide opportunities to extract rents. If this were the case, and if these institutions were to be reformed (deregulated) in such a way as to reduce the size of these rents, then these institutions would become less attractive to labour. A prominent example of such a reform and the labour reaction to it occurred in France in 2003. The issue concerned performing artists. Anyone who worked for at least three months during a year could count on 12 months' unemployment insurance coverage in the following year. Generous indeed. The consequence was a continuous and large deficit in this segment of unemployment insurance (covered by general payroll taxes). None the less, the French government persisted with this system as a means of supporting culture. As always when there is a distribution of such generous 'handouts', certain abuses may take place. A proposal was made to modify the system slightly: basically, in order to qualify for unemployment insurance the person needed to work for four (instead of three) months. The reaction by the artists was robust: a long strike at the start of the summer, with the result that most summer festivals were cancelled.

In spite of the strike and pressure, this 'mild' reform was accepted. In any case, this example reveals the resistance and difficulties encountered in the face of even modest reforms of labour market distortions and rigidities.

33. In 1912 the blueprint for the *Titanic* looked perfect. It was said to be unsinkable. In EMU's case, even the blueprint was full of holes (*The Economist*, 27 July 1996, p. 14).
34. Since the euro replaced the national currencies, most of the internal EU trade has been transacted in euros. Hence, 'international' trade will be smaller. Policy makers in the EU *may* pay less attention to exchange rates than they usually do. If the policy goal is internal stability, rather than stability in the exchange rate, cooperation between the major international players may be weak and the result may be an instability in the currency market.
35. Conversion of the national currencies into the euro was achieved relatively painlessly over the first few months of 2002.
36. Paul de Grauwe, 'The pact should be replaced and not mourned', *Financial Times*, 27 November 2003.
37. European Council, Brussels 23 March 2005, Presidency Conclusions, § 3 and Annex II.
38. European Council, Brussels 23 March 2005, Presidency Conclusions, Annex II, p. 22.
39. European Council, Brussels 23 March 2005, Presidency Conclusions, Annex II, p. 28.
40. 'Furthermore, due consideration will be given to any other factors, which in the opinion of the Member State concerned, are relevant in order to comprehensively assess in qualitative terms the excess over the reference value. In that context, special consideration will be given to budgetary efforts towards increasing or maintaining at a high level financial contributions to fostering international solidarity and to achieving European policy goals, notably the unification of Europe if it has a detrimental effect on the growth and fiscal burden of a Member State' (European Council, Brussels 23 March 2005, Presidency Conclusions, Annex II, p. 34).
41. Paul de Grauwe, 'Europe's instability pact', *Financial Times*, 25 July 2002, p. 11.
42. *The Economist*, 27 September 2003, p. 72.
43. It is difficult to approximate this ratio, but most research would estimate that it is about 85 per cent.
44. See Commission of the European Communities (2002, pp. 31–2).
45. Pensions are becoming one of the principal economic imbalances. However, they are not studied as much as imbalances in trade and in capital flows.
46. France has many retired persons. President Jacques Chirac is a very rare Frenchman over seventy who is still employed full-time.
47. Eurostat (2004). 'Pensions in Europe: expenditure and beneficiaries', *Statistics in Focus*, Theme 8/2004, p. 1.
48. At present, for every 100 persons of working age there are 35 people of retirement age in the EU. Deutsche Bank reported in 2002 that on present demographical trends, by 2050 there would be 75 pensioners for every 100 workers in the EU (*The Economist*, 'A survey of the European Union', 25 September 2004, p. 10).
49. Had Britain been a member of the EU from the outset, the EU farm policy would look very different – perhaps the decades-long and sterile reforms, plus certain costs of this policy, would have been avoided.
50. M. Wolf, 'The benefits of euro entry will be modest (*Financial Times*, 12 May 2003, p. 17).
51. M. Wolf, 'The perfect result for a sceptical nation', *Financial Times*, 9 June 2003.
52. Union monétaire ouest africaine (UMOA). Apart from this monetary union, there was also an economic (trading) community among these African countries, the Economic Community of West Africa (Communauté economique de l'Afrique de l'ouest, CEAO). The CEAO coupled internal trade liberalisation with fiscal compensations. Principal intra-group net exporters (Ivory Coast and Senegal) were contributors to this compensation fund. Financial pressure and economic crises at the end of the 1980s contributed to the collapse of the compensation scheme. That heralded the virtual demise of the CEAO.
53. From 1939 to 1973, the French treasury was in charge of all foreign exchange reserves.

54. Union économique et monétaire ouest africaine (UEMOA).
55. The appreciation of the euro *vis-à-vis* the dollar may continue to create problems for WAEMU exporters.
56. This subject is challenging both for policy makers and for researchers as it combines the most difficult macroeconomic issues. At the same time it is annoying as there are no *ex ante* counterfactual situations against which one may measure costs and benefits of monetary integration.
57. Note that an emu is also a large flightless bird.
58. P. Krugman, *New York Times*, 27 January 2004; 3 February 2004; and 4 March 2005.
59. Both Japan and China were investing huge dollar reserves (export surplus) in the US (treasury bonds) for a simple reason. If the dollar depreciates, so will the value of their enormous dollar holdings; more than $800 billion in Japan and more than $500 billion in China. 'A 10 per cent appreciation of the renminbi means a capital loss of Dollars 50bn for Chinese authorities' (S. Cecchetti, 'Say it softly: the solution is tax increase', *Financial Times*, 23 November 2004). In addition, yield on government bonds continued to be higher in the US than in Japan in 2004. So Japan 'comfortably' paid less interest to its creditors than it was receiving from crediting the US. Both the US and the Asian countries, therefore, entered into an implicit contract and preferred a continuation of this situation that brings benefits to both sides. Informal balance was there, but it is unstable in the long term. Hence the dollar ought to be adjusted principally *vis-à-vis* the Asian currencies, not the euro.

    There is a limit to the extent to which foreigners are willing to finance excessive consumption in the US. It is reached at the point at which the dollar starts to fall. At that point, an increase in US taxes may reduce consumption, including a reduction in the trade deficit. An increase in domestic savings needs to be stimulated too. The fear of US protectionism is looming. However, 'since more than a half of China's exports to the US are produced by foreign-invested factories, the pro-China lobby in Washington has proved more than a match for the protectionists' ('A walking dragon shakes the world', *Financial Times*, 30 December 2004).
60. The dollar will remain the dominant currency in the world economy for some time. The US still has awesome international economic (and other) power and influence. The country has a superior growth rate and prospects compared to the EU. The American huge, open and diversified credit market and institutions have depth and breadth that is still a cut above what is found in both the EU and Japan. In addition, the eurozone countries are fiddling with the monetary integration rules (there is a credibility problem), while in contrast to the eurozone, the US has a centralised fiscal and monetary powers in this domain.
61. During its first two years, the euro was weaker than its creators would have liked it to be. It lost about a third of its value relative to the dollar. This trend was reversed in 2003 mainly because of the huge US trade deficit of $491 billion in that year. The value of the dollar declined, while that of the euro soared (obstructing EU exports).
62. The net annual fiscal transfers from the western part of Germany to the eastern part were about €75 billion throughout the 1990s. They will be necessary for another decade. The danger is that such 'gifts' may stifle local incentives for entrepreneurship and self-reliance; they may also create a structurally dependent economy as is the case with the Italian Mezzogiorno.
63. It may not be easy for 25 or 27 (or even more) people to agree about where to go, say, to the cinema, but just imagine the same number of finance ministers trying to reach agreement about the common rate of interest.
64. Federal is used here in its widest possible meaning.
65. Public authorities may be involved in the supply of goods and services that free markets may not supply at all or may not supply in adequate quantity, quality, geographical location or on time. This public involvement may either be indirect through taxes and subsidies or direct when the government steps in, produces and supplies certain goods and services itself because of their importance (defence, security, fire fighting, statistics, weather forecasts and so on).

66. By offering preferential tax treatment to TNCs, governments may change/improve their competitiveness in relation to other countries or regions.
67. Allocation of resources is production efficient if all producers face the same tax for the same good or service. It is consumption efficient if all consumers face the same tax for the consumption of the same good or service.
68. This implies the expectation that integration is a positive-sum game for everyone.
69. For example, the Roman Catholic cantons formed a league (*Sonderbund*) in 1847. The federal government considered that this was a violation of the constitution. In the civil war of the same year, the league was defeated by the federal government and disbanded. The constitution of 1848 greatly increased federal powers. In 1874 a modified constitution completed the development of Switzerland from a group of cantons to a unified federal state. However, the local communes and cantons still enjoy considerable autonomy in Switzerland. For example, it is the communes within the Swiss cantons that grant individuals Swiss citizenship.
70. Helvets were a tribe that lived in pre-Roman times in what is now known as Switzerland.
71. The Vatican began to employ Swiss mercenaries at the beginning of the 16th century. Their bravery was obvious in 1527 when Charles V of Spain devastated the city. Some 147 Swiss guards died in the fight, but Pope Clement VII was saved. The Swiss guards have been guarding popes ever since. The Vatican *Cohors Helvetica* currently numbers 107.
72. Napoleon was a regular client of Swiss banks.
73. Justinian's Code 5.59.5.2. This Code (AD 528) became the principal source for Roman law.
74. The Hohenzollerns were a dynasty of German rulers, descended from a family of counts from Swabia from the 11th century. They were named after their ancestral castle, Zollern (later Hohenzollern), located near Hechingen, Swabia (now Baden-Württemberg). The Hohenzollerns ruled Prussia and united Germany until the end of the First World War.
75. This type of rule also applies in EU budgetary affairs.
76. Prussia and France became involved in a complicated diplomatic argument over the succession to the throne of Spain. The Spanish government offered the crown to a Hohenzollern (Prussian) prince. The government of Louis Napoleon objected strongly and even began to make certain military threats. The French ambassador to Prussia had a meeting with King William I. The report of this meeting was sent by telegram to Bismarck – the famous Ems Telegram. Bismarck rephrased it in such a way that if it was made public, it would offend both France and Prussia. He sent it to the newspapers and waited for the inevitable reaction. On 19 July 1870 France declared war on Prussia, but on 2 September France admitted defeat. Bismarck had triumphed.
77. Alaska, Arizona, California, Colorado, Connecticut, District of Columbia, Illinois, Indiana, Iowa, Kansas, Massachusetts, New Hampshire, New Jersey, New York, Ohio, Rhode Island and West Virginia. Because of controversy regarding the unitary system of computation of corporate profits, some states are considering abandoning this system.
78. Swiss companies do not have to publish their results unless they are listed or subject to special regulatory duties (for example, banks). One explanation is that they do not need to have a commercial purpose. They can exist for idealistic reasons (for example, to promote fair trade with developing countries) or they may distribute their profits by way of salary or bonuses to limit the withholding tax of 35 per cent on dividends or distribution of accumulated profits on liquidation.
79. Regarding the profitability of Swiss firms, for example, the most astonishing fact 'is the large share of firms with zero rate of return. Nearly half of Swiss firms [do] not report any rate of return' (Feld and Kirchgässner, 2001, p. 5).
80. This assumes that country A grants either an exemption or a full foreign-tax credit.
81. The average level of corporation tax in the 30 richest countries in the world fell from 37.5 per cent in 1996 to 30.9 per cent in 2003 (*Financial Times*, 1 May 2003).
82. Estimates about tax evasion are exceptionally unreliable, but German savers alone are thought to have 'hidden' about €300 billion in the low-tax countries (*Financial Times*, 3 June 2003).

83. In the complex overall EU bargaining in 2003, in return for agreement on this tax matter, Italy demanded and got concessions regarding milk production.
84. Switzerland is estimated to handle one-third of all the money held in private accounts in offshore financial centres. The Swiss Banking Federation claims that Switzerland applied tough legislation to monitor criminal and terrorist funds (*Financial Times*, 3 December 2003).
85. Switzerland will tax interest earned by EU citizens on their bank accounts in Switzerland, with 75 per cent of the proceeds going to the account holders' national tax authorities while the rest would stay with the Swiss authorities to cover running costs.
86. There is also a problem of inflation. Depreciation may be calculated according to historic costs, but how should capital gains be taxed to reflect inflation? The arrival of the euro eliminated this problem for the 12 eurozone countries, while the other countries remain quite tough on inflation.
87. Cnossen (1995) provides a survey of options for the reform of corporate taxes in the EU.
88. For example, language, seniority, xenophobia, social and family ties, as well as propensity to stay in the place of birth and pure choice.
89. The share of direct taxes in total taxes in the EU(25) in 2004 is about a third, indirect taxes contribute another third, while the rest, the last third, belongs to social contributions.
90. The EU adopted a far-reaching, but partial, move towards the origin principle for final consumers (but not for firms). Since 1993, taxation occurs in the place where a good is purchased, rather than where it will be consumed.
91. Apart from making life and travel easier for EU residents, the business community saves too. They were spared the preparation of some 60 million customs and tax documents a year. The abolition of border checks represents a saving of about €8 billion a year to the EU member states (*Business International*, 15 July 1991, p. 237). In 1988, the EU introduced the Single Administrative Document to replace some 30 documents that were required in order to allow goods to move within the EU. This document was not required for internal trade after 1993, but it is used for goods that cross an EU external frontier.
92. The solution to the problem of taxation of e-commerce may include two approaches. The first would be to harmonise taxes on a worldwide basis. The second would be to increase 'policing' of transactions on the Internet. They both have weak points. The first is politically not feasible, while the second may be publicly undesirable. In any case new technologies demand new forms of international fiscal cooperation and a certain reduction in national fiscal sovereignty. Governments struggle to maintain their tax receipts in the light of a potentially expanding underground economy (the one that is not taxed). However, new electronic technologies may enhance, rather than weaken, government tax-collecting capacity. The peril that the e-economy presents is not the erosion of the public tax base, but rather the erosion of privacy. Is more transparency in our lives the price to pay for living in a complex contemporary society?
93. The unanimity rule for tax matters in the EU makes tax unification difficult if not impossible.
94. Regarding budgetary outlays, cereal subsidies would be cut in two steps by 15 per cent; beef prices would be reduced by 20 per cent in three stages (beef farmers would receive direct payment to compensate for 85 per cent of their losses); while the decision on the most contentious area of dairy products was delayed until 2005.
95. European Council, Berlin 1999, Presidency Conclusions, §16 and Table B.
96. European Council, Berlin 1999, Presidency Conclusions, §46.
97. European Council, Berlin 1999, Presidency Conclusions, §67.
98. *Financial Times*, 6 November 2002.
99. European Council, Brussels 2002, Presidency Conclusions, §10.
100. European Council, Berlin 1999, Presidency Conclusions, §16 and Table B.
101. Britain won an arrangement in 1984 enabling it to obtain a refund from the EU budget.
102. 'He said to his brothers, "My money has been put back; here it is in the mouth of my sack!" At this their hearts failed them, and they turned trembling to one another, saying, "What is this that God has done to us?" ' (Genesis 42:28).

103. G. Parker, R. Minder and P. Hollinger, 'Chirac shatters EU unity with attack on British rebate', *Financial Times*, 23 March 2005.
104. European Council, Lisbon 2000, Presidency Conclusions, §5.
105. The EU has always conducted an industrial policy, but its intensity and the cover name were different: state aid, technical standards, company law, competition policy, Single European Market, trade protection, social policy and protection of the environment. In addition, the European Commission changed the name of its Directorate-General for Industrial Policy to Enterprise Directorate-General.
106. Lipsey (1993a, p. 21) first used the term 'massaged-market economies'.
107. 'Strategic' is not taken here to have any military sense, but rather refers to businesses that have important forward and backward links with other industries, as well as strong and positive externalities (spillovers) on the rest of the economy.
108. There is a growing awareness that *most* external economies apply at a regional or metropolitan level, rather than at an international one. Therefore, the fear that external economies would be geographically dissipated abroad is mostly wrong (Krugman, 1993b, pp. 161, 167).
109. Firms also make mistakes and wrong choices. IBM, for example, misjudged the commercial worth of the haloid copying technology it was offered. This technology became the foundation of Xerox.
110. Services employed 69 per cent of the EU(15) labour force in 2001, while the shares of manufacturing and agriculture were 27 and 4 per cent, respectively (Eurostat, 2003).
111. Akio Morita, the chairman of Sony Corporation, argued that 'an economy can be only as strong as its manufacturing base. An economy that does not manufacture well cannot continue to invest adequately in itself. An economy whose only growth is in the service sector is built on sand. Certainly, the service sector is an important and growing economic force. But it cannot thrive on its own, serving hamburgers to itself and shifting money from one side to another. An advanced service economy can thrive only on the strength of an advanced manufacturing economy underlying it . . . The notion of a postindustrial economy that is based principally on services is a dubious one' (Morita, 1992, p. 79).
112. New technologies are less and less sector or industry specific. The same holds for modern firms. Many of them cannot be easily classified in a group of enterprises that belongs to only one industry or sector.
113. A common definition of an SME uses the number of employees as the determining factor. Micro enterprises are taken to be those with up to 10 employees, small ones have less than 50 workers, while medium-sized ones have up to 250 workers.
114. European Commission (2003). *SMEs in Focus: Main Results from the 2002 Observatory of European SMEs*, Observatory of European SMEs 2002, p. 4.
115. In Brussels, the seat of the European Commission and a number of other international organisations, there were several thousand interest (pressure) groups. Those rent-seekers employ around 15 000 lobbyists with the number rising together with the expansion of the Commission's authority and enlargements of the EU. This is roughly one lobbyist (representative of special interest) per employee of the European Commission (M. Karnitschnig, 'Berlin Scandals Highlight an Absence of Regulations; Fancy Addresses for Parties', *Wall Street Journal*, 10 February 2005). In some cases, a very high concentration of lobby services in Washington, DC, made a collection of some (private) interests stronger than those of the government.
116. A lack of natural resources forced Japan to invest in the development of human and technological capital.
117. If one wants to present these long-term dynamic developments in a graphical way, this could be likened to rolling a polyhedron down a slope. This is discussed in Section 4.5.
118. The industrial history of Japan is marked by a concentration of business power, collusion and centralisation in the management of the economy. *Zaibatsu* were large, diversified and internally integrated business groups that operated from the 1870s. The 1947 Anti Monopoly Law enacted by the American Occupation Command broke them

up. The intention was to increase market competition in line with the democratisation of the country. Once occupation ended in 1952, former leading *zaibatsu* (Mitsui, Mitsubishi and Sumitomo) began to re-form in looser organisations known as *keiretsu* (Porter and Sakakibara, 2004, p. 29).

119. Airbus was established in 1970. It is a publicly sponsored consortium of British (British Aerospace, 20 per cent), French (Aérospatiale, 37.9 per cent), German (Deutsche Airbus, 37.9 per cent) and Spanish (CASA, 4.2 per cent) enterprises. It was established without the involvement of the EU and under the French law as a *Groupement d'Intérêt Économique*. The purpose of Airbus is to produce great aeroplanes, fight for orders and satisfy clients before thinking about dividends. The conception of this company is different from Boeing's. As such, Airbus makes no profits or losses in its own right. This means that the accounts of the group were available only to the four shareholders. Unlike Boeing's accounts, which are accessible to the public, Airbus's accounts were concealed from the public and the profit disguised in the accounts of its shareholders. It is, therefore, difficult to assess the commercial success of the best-known consortium in Europe. Why then does Boeing not pressure the US administration to do something about this? As about half of the value built into Airbuses is of US origin, the producers of these components have a strong lobbying power in Washington, DC, and could counter the potential actions of Boeing.

In 2001, 30 years after its creation, Airbus formally became a single integrated company, thus passing another major milestone in its history. The European Aeronautic Defence and Space Company (EADS) was the consequence of the merger between Aérospatiale Matra (France), Daimler Chrysler Aerospace (Germany) and Construcciones Aeronauticas (Spain), and BAE Systems (Britain). They all transferred their Airbus-related assets to the newly incorporated company and, in exchange, became shareholders in Airbus with 80 and 20 per cent, respectively, of the new stock.

120. For example, the Cold War and wars with Korea, Vietnam, Iraq (twice), Yugoslavia and Afghanistan.

121. The policy goal was to acquire the production of war materials. There was little concern about antitrust laws, international competitiveness or competing national objectives (Badaracco and Yoffie, 1983, p. 99). Governments have always affected industrial development through trade policy, public procurement, taxes and subsidies, as well as provision of public goods.

122. One has, however, to remember extreme cases which are not very numerous, but exist everywhere. The most highly paid people are not always highly educated. Many pop singers or sportspeople (often very poor speakers) have a poor education. However, one cluster of educated people who command very high salaries are managers and lawyers (in the countries where law means something).

123. 'French national bureaucracy is tainted less by corruption then by the arrogance of power' (Kay, 2004, p. 7).

124. *Single Market News*, February 1996, p. 13.

125. European Council, Lisbon 2000, Presidency Conclusions, § 5. These objectives continue to be reconfirmed. For example, European Council, Brussels 12 December 2003, Presidency Conclusions, §§ 2 and 14; European Council, Brussels 25 and 26 March 2004, Presidency Conclusions, § 46.

126. Commission of the European Communities, Brussels, 02.02.2005 COM (2005) 24.

127. *Bulletin Quotidien Europe*, 7 February 2003, p. 4.

128. *Financial Times*, 29 and 30 October 2003.

129. *Financial Times*, 14 October 2003.

130. In the US, small, high-technology firms sell as much as half of their output to the federal government and benefit from R&D support. In contrast, public procurement in Europe is effected through a small number of large national suppliers. This suggests that fostering free entry and mobility within flexible industries may be a superior policy choice to supporting a few giants that react to changes with some delay (Geroski and Jacquemin, 1985, p. 177).

131. Nobody in the European Commission uses the term 'five-year plan'. That would remind many of the five-year plans in the former centrally planned economies.
132. The First Framework Programme (1984–87) disposed of a budget of €3.7 billion, the Second (1987–91) had a budget of €6.5 billion, the Third (1991–94) was allocated €8.8 billion, the Fourth (1994–88) received €13.1 billion, while the Fifth (1998–2002) had €14 billion.
133. FAST is a shared-cost programme involving a number of research and forecasting institutes in the EU. It is an instrument for studying future developments, as well as the impact and social uses of science and technology.
134. *European Voice*, 13 November 2003, p. 15.
135. Software, telecommunications, advance materials, semiconductors, biotechnology and defence technology.
136. Electronics and cars.
137. Lower-end mass market consumer goods.
138. Even a layperson would acknowledge that cows are herbivorous animals and should not be expected to eat meat products.
139. In 2005, France made certain moves to introduce flexibility in the 35-hour working week.
140. The Scandinavian countries may exceed the Lisbon Agenda objectives in terms of R&D and education. The Scandinavians give the government about half of the GDP, but they get value for money. Education is working well, there is good social care and investment in R&D is generous. Elsewhere, people eye the government with suspicion because of waste of funds and even corruption.
141. Good corporate governance is essential to avoid scandals and bankruptcies as their consequences always fall on the shoulders of the employed, shareholders and sometimes taxpayers.
142. WTO, 25 October 2004.
143. Do you remember your first (or for that matter even your second or third) taxi ride from the airport in a central or south European country as a foreigner? If you have not yet experienced this pleasure, be assured it is one you will remember. In particular the rate that you will pay.
144. Storage of voice messages may pose a problem in this class.
145. *Financial Times*, 5 May 2003.
146. In spite of the freedom to offer transport services in other EU member countries, cabotage still represents a negligible part of the EU road transport market. In 2001, cabotage represented 0.7 per cent of total road freight transport.
147. The number of road traffic accidents per motor car or per inhabitant is different among countries. Hence, there is a variation in risk. Therefore, differences in insurance premiums among countries will remain in spite of increased competition.
148. 'As patriotism is the last refuge of scoundrels (according to Dr Johnson), the welfare of widows, orphans, and the incompetent is the last refuge of supporters of regulation. Individuals free to make their own decisions will indeed make mistakes. Even if potential buyers are clearly informed of the regulatory regime, some will not understand its significance. Even if large amounts of information are available on that significance, some will not bother to obtain it . . . Protection of the foolish against error provides a rationale for almost infinite extension' (Hindley, 1991, pp. 272–3).
149. Many would say that life is short. One may enjoy it in many interesting ways. If one has a problem with one's glands, why spend time studying endocrinology when there are already experienced experts for this type of medical assistance? A market mechanism to handle asymmetric information is the trust and reputation of the provider of a good or a service.
150. Everyone can appreciate the benefits of a car such as a BMW or a Mercedes. It is quite another matter, however, whether consumers are willing to pay or have the means to pay for such a motor car. A small Fiat may be the limit for many of them.
151. Nobody sells insurance against risks such as divorce, unwanted pregnancy or loss of a job and professional career. Even though statistics are available on these issues, the risk is too high for a profitable business. These are, however, major risks that most people face

every day and for which there is no insurance market. For these risks, we rely on help from our family and friends, our social institutions and the state (Kay, 2004, p. 246).

152. *Financial Times*, 2 November 2003.
153. Balassa (1964) and Samuelson (1964).
154. *Financial Times*, 10 March 2003.
155. *Bulletin Quotidien Europe*, 15 February 2005, p. 4.
156. 'This week saw a Danish-owned Polish construction company fined for paying Polish workers in Denmark below Danish rates, although that practice would still be as illegal under the services directive as before' ('Le dumping social', *Financial Times*, 26 March 2005).
157. European Council, Brussels 23 March 2005, Presidency Conclusions, § 22.
158. Without the highest degree of coordination one would not be able to fly to the Moon and return safely to Earth.
159. Education may be a subsidised input for which the business sector has not paid the full price. None the less, countervailing duties cannot be introduced by foreign partners as education is a long-term activity and cannot be easily and directly valued as is the case with other subsidies, such as those for exports.
160. Economic and social cohesion is defined as 'overall harmonious development' (Article 158 of the Rome Treaty). As cohesion is defined in such a vague way, it can mean different things to different people. It can also mean different things to the same person at various points in time. Does 'overall harmonious development' mean equalisation of income; or equalisation of opportunities; or providing an incentive to remain in the EU?
161. Guidance Section of the Agricultural Fund, European Regional Development Fund, European Social Fund, Cohesion Fund and Financial Instrument for Fisheries Guidance.
162. Trade theory has not come to grips with multiactivity firms and multiplant production, as was the case with the theory of industrial organisation.
163. The word 'new' ought to be qualified here. It refers to the new light that is shed on the known, but scattered and underappreciated, previous research work.
164. Location matters not only in economics. The first lesson in geopolitical theory teaches us the same thing. The behaviour of states is rooted in and influenced by their geographical location. Britain, as an island, has a freedom in geopolitical actions that comes from its geography. This windfall advantage is not available to countries that are boxed in, such as Switzerland or Germany. Their options are constrained.
165. This increases the need for printed matter.
166. Income distribution also affects the location of production. If, for example, income is distributed to a small segment of the population (landowners or owners of capital) who spend it on imports of luxury goods and services, there may not be a spread of development of industries in their area or country. If, however, income is distributed in favour of a large number of families that demand domestically produced goods and services, this may have a positive impact on the location of firms and industries closer to the domestic market.
167. The assumption is that there are no factor movements. Otherwise, the factor abundance proposition has no meaning.
168. The question with agglomeration economies is which geographical spot is going to dominate in production? The analytical challenge and difficulty with agglomeration is that it introduces multiple equilibria.
169. In the case with one market and two deposits of resources, the optimal firm location would fall inside the triangular area which links these three different spots.
170. If one imagines a geometrically even distribution of centres across a flat and homogeneous surface and the corresponding circles (representing ranges of goods) around them, then if one wants to cover all the space with circles, there would be an overlap between the two adjoining circles. If one draws a straight line between the points where the two adjoining circles intersect, one would get a hexagonal market space of identical size around each centre without empty corners, as consumers would purchase goods from the cheapest (nearest) producer.

171. Paris and Madrid have a relatively central geographical location in France and Spain, respectively. The same holds for Munich in Bavaria. In 1998, the capital of Kazakhstan was transferred from Almaty to Astana precisely because the latter city lies at the intersection point of major north–south and east–west transport routes.

One of the reasons why Peugeot-Citroën announced in 2003 that it intends to invest and to locate a large (€700 million) car assembly factory in Trnava, Slovakia (in preference to alternative locations in Poland, the Czech Republic and Hungary) is that this country has good access to transport links and that it is 'in the centre of Europe' (R. Anderson, M. Arnold and J. Reed, 'Peugeot to build new plant in Slovakia', *Financial Times*, 15 January 2003). The factory will start production of about 300 000 small cars from 2006. The management intends to be closer to fast-growing markets in the EU accession countries and to profit from wage rates that are a fifth of those paid in the EU(15) for similar industrial operations.

In 2004, Hyundai selected Slovakia over Poland (known for the aggressive reputation of its labour unions) to build a €700 million car assembly plant in Zilina. This is Hyundai's first car assembly plant in Europe. It would assemble 200 000 cars a year (potentially 300 000 from 2008). The reasons for the decision to locate in Slovakia include wage costs (a quarter of the prevailing rates in western Europe); half the car ownership levels of western Europe; laws that made the labour market flexible; reduced corporate and income taxes; existing network of suppliers (expected to expand further); and membership of the EU. As Volkswagen already produces cars in Slovakia (Bratislava), this 'tiny' (5.4 million people) central European country will become one of the European motor giants. The three Slovak car plants could produce over 800 000 cars a year from 2006, making it the highest per capita car production in the world (R. Anderson and J. Cienski, 'Hyundai picks Slovakia for new €700m car assembly plant', *Financial Times*, 3 March 2004).

Slovakia may produce about 900 000 cars a year from 2008. The automotive industry contributes a quarter to the manufacturing output and a third to exports (this will increase to a half once the two plants are completed). The problem may be in the increasing imbalance in the Slovak industrial structure. Although Slovakia may be the victim of its own success, some of the neighbouring countries (Poland, for example) might have preferred to be faced with such 'troubles' than to lose out to Slovakia.

A looming problem in the central and east European countries is an increase in wages above the improvements in productivity. Having joined the EU, workers in the new member countries want to achieve EU(15) living standards as soon as possible. This will jeopardise the central and east European countries' attraction on account of their relatively low wages. Such an improvement may take a decade, or even a generation, to accomplish.

172. Various judicious marriages (chances or historical accidents) entered into by the Habsburgs created the Austro-Hungarian Empire, which altered the economic space in central and eastern Europe.

Another example of chance can be found in the Treaty of Tordesillas, between Spain and Portugal, which clarified the situation regarding claims on newly discovered territory across the Atlantic Ocean and was intended to pre-empt any misunderstandings following Christopher Columbus's discovery of the New World in 1492. In fact, at first it was not fully realised that Columbus had found something 'big'. Portugal wanted to protect its monopoly of the route to Africa. Pope Alexander IV (Spaniard by birth) intervened to clear up a possible 'confusion' between the two countries. He issued a bull (decree) in 1493 that established an imaginary north–south line through the mid-Atlantic 100 leagues (480 km; 1 league = 4.8 km) west of the Cape Verde Islands. Spain acquired undiscovered non-Christian lands to the west of the line, while Portugal had those to the east. After further explorations, Portugal realised that the Spanish territory was extensive. The Portuguese were discontented and initiated a renegotiation of the partition. The new partition line was established in Tordesillas, a Spanish town, in 1494. The new line ran 370 leagues (1770 km) west of the Cape Verde Islands, which is how Portugal gained possession of Brazil. The partition line was ill-defined, and over several centuries Portugal pushed the Brazilian frontier westwards. Spain raised no objection to this expansion as it was some centuries before longitude could be determined with any degree of accuracy.

The spread of certain products is also based on chance. For example, in 1519 the Aztec king Montezuma offered Hernando Cortez *xocoatl* ('god drink') made from roasted cocoa beans, pimento and corn flour. Subsequently, the recipe was passed on to Spain. In 1615 when the 14-year old Spanish princess Ann of Austria, daughter of king Philip III, married her peer, Louis XIII of France, the Spanish hosts served chocolate to the European nobility. Ann in her turn introduced the confection to the French court – thus chocolate crossed the Pyrenees. At about the same time, the Spanish Inquisition unwittingly instigated another crossing: some of the persecuted Jews fled to Bayonne (France), where they established cocoa-processing plants; others went to the Low Countries.

173. Murphy et al. (1989) discuss multiple equilibria with respect to the process of industrialisation, postulating that a certain critical mass of industries may have to be involved in order for industrialisation to be successful. A parallel could be drawn with location theory. Government policy should be to support the 'take-off' of a particular location, and encourage firms to move to the location.

174. Positive feedback economics may also find parallels in non-linear physics. For example, ferromagnetic materials consist of mutually reinforcing elements. Small perturbations, at critical times, influence which outcome is selected (bifurcation point), and the chosen outcome may have higher energy (that is, be less favourable) than other possible end states (Arthur, 1990a, p. 99).

175. Sony anticipated that its reputation and favourable opinions by the experts about Betamax would be sufficient to impose this standard and to capture the consumer market. Sony also expected that people would primarily use camcorders to make home movies (birthday parties, weddings, family reunions, holidays . . .). Sony was wrong. VHS devices filled the homes chiefly for watching pre-recorded films. For this Betamax was inferior. Hence, Sony abandoned it.

176. Liebowitz and Margolis (1999) sharply criticised the path-dependence claims and lock-in effects. A standard story holds that the most widespread and locked-in 'qwerty' keyboard is much less efficient than the Dvorak keyboard, which was developed more than a half of a century later. Liebowitz and Margolis showed that the Dvorak keyboard offered no advantage over qwerty and that claims for Dvorak's superiority were mainly based on bogus research by someone with a financial interest in the success of the Dvorak keyboard.

Foresight, word of mouth among consumers, consumer journals, money-back guarantees and other marketing efforts all work to prevent lock-in. If everyone knew that a new product was sufficiently better, wouldn't someone find a way to help us switch? Liebowitz and Margolis argued that it was extremely likely that someone would, especially since, in doing so, there would be chances to 'make money'. Competitive advantages in high-technology products are short-lived and temporary. Instead of antitrust actions, policy makers ought to rely on competitive entrepreneurship within the market system.

177. An ergodic system (a pendulum; water – if it is not spilled out – in a glass on a table) ultimately returns to its original steady state, regardless of the disturbances between the starting and ending points in time.

178. Finland was a resource-based (dependent) economy. Within a relatively short period of time towards the end of the 20th century, Finland developed a path towards a knowledge-based economy. Sweden did the same, but many decades earlier.

179. There were no strong a priori reasons why Britain selected the left side of the road while the European continent and the US chose the right. But they did. Other countries opted either for the side of their closest neighbour or the colonial master. Path dependency captured the rest.

180. In the past, the colonial powers obtained natural resources from their colonies. In many cases they prevented the development of manufacturing industry in the colonised countries in order to secure those 'outer markets' for the export of manufactured goods from the colonial master. Thus local competition was eliminated and if any development of

manufacturing activity took place it was usually in port cities and was limited to primary processing.

181. It is difficult to trace knowledge flows, because they are invisible and do not leave a paper trail by which they can be measured and tracked. Hence a theorist may assume what he will (Krugman, 1992, pp. 53–4). Certain traces may be found, however, such as quotations in professional journals.
182. An Italian saint prompted the creation of Brasilia, Brazil's capital, in 1883. He promised great bounties if the interior of the country, mostly the Amazon jungle, was developed. In 1891, a new constitution called for the move. A foundation stone was laid in 1922, but it was not until 1957 that the new capital city project got under way 900km inland. This was a utopian experiment in modern urbanism that was intended to stimulate a quantum leap in the development process. What eventuated was a pedestrian-unfriendly city that lacks a human touch. It is packed with (monstrous) concrete government buildings in various states of decay. Washington, DC was created in the 1790s when President George Washington chose a swamp for the permanent seat of the US government. 'It's not quite so bad now, but . . . once the city's cubicle-dwellers flee to the suburbs, Washington can feel as empty as a bad high-school dance' (K. Iskyan, 'Trading places – What drives a country to switch its capital city?', *Slate*, 1 March 2004).
183. New York and Philadelphia are examples, and even Boston, although its hinterland is smaller. However, why are there no major port cities in the upper south of the east part of the US? The reason is found in the colonial regulation of trade. The Navigation Act of 1660 (and subsequent ones) regulated and reserved exports of colonial articles such as tobacco, sugar, cotton and indigo to England only. Similar restrictions did not apply to trade in wheat, corn, pork, beef, fish and other items. Merchants handled colonial trade from London, rather than from Chesapeake (Virginia). However, the Philadelphia, New York and Boston merchants were free to enter business and export non-colonial commodities to wherever they wanted. They met in coffee shops to exchange information about business opportunities. When Alexandria and Baltimore emerged in the upper south in the 1750s, their activities were based on wheat, rather than tobacco (Kim and Margo, 2004, pp. 2996–7).
184. Relevant factors that influence agglomeration tendencies for producers include the availability of raw materials, energy, labour and capital, while for consumers they include the availability of jobs and education, as well as favourable climate and surroundings.
185. In spite of huge subsidies, a number of towns such as Wittenberge in eastern Germany are dying. They have been unable to stimulate the local economy (K. Connolly, 'Vision of unity fades in German east', *The Daily Telegraph*, 11 September 2004).
186. Zipf's law refers to a special static case of the relation between city population size and its rank among other cities. If this power law with exponent 1 holds, then the largest city is k times as large as the kth largest city. This implies that the largest city is twice as large as the second largest, three times as large as the third one, and so on. The law depends on the existence of labour mobility. The distribution of US city sizes is close to the rank-size rule, while this relation is less obvious in Europe (Midelfart et al., 2003, pp. 860–1).
187. A core region is one that has the capability and potential to create, attract and employ resources and ideas. A periphery region is one that has its economic path determined chiefly by the developments in the core region(s).
188. Urbanisation occurred before advances in modern medicine. Hence, urbanisation contributed to the worsening of health in cities. It is puzzling, then, why there was mass migration of the rural population into cities.
189. Learning from teachers is called oblique transmission, while learning from the members of one's professional group is horizontal transmission.
190. Audretsch and Feldman (1996 and 2004) found evidence that the US industries in which new knowledge spillovers are relevant (semiconductors and computers in California; pharmaceuticals in New Jersey) have a greater propensity to cluster innovative activity than industries where these spillovers are less important. Bottazzi and

Peri (2002) reported that the benefits of R&D in generating innovation were extremely localised.

191. Information is simple structured and unstructured data. Knowledge is the capability to process those data, to analyse and evaluate them and, possibly, to deepen and extend them. Tacit knowledge is something that is within a knowledgeable person, but something that one cannot put in a manual.
192. Personal contacts, face-to-face communication, proximity and trust with a partner are emphasised by Kleinknecht and ter Wengel (1998, pp. 645–6), Porter and Sölvell (1998, pp. 445–6), Sternberg and Tamásy (1999, p. 374), Gordon and McCann (2000, p. 520), Porter (2000a, p. 262), Crafts and Venables (2001, p. 32), Henderson et al. (2001), Venables (2001, p. 24), Audretsch and Feldman (2004), Kay (2004, p. 14), Boschma (2005, p. 69) and many others, but were also well known earlier to Perroux (1955, p. 317 and 1961, p. 152).
193. 'In Britain, the mechanism of financial regulation was for decades described as "the raising of the eyebrows of the governor of the Bank of England". This was a metaphor for informal but powerful expressions of regulatory disapproval. The system was made possible by the common social background of market participants. It ceased to be sustainable when the City of London became a more democratic institution, and when globalization brought into the marketplace foreigners who did not understand what these signals meant, or that failure to observe them would have adverse consequences. So Britain acquired a rule book and an analogue of the Securities and Exchange Commission' (Kay, 2004, p. 14).
194. Has anybody learned to cook a good French or Chinese dish merely by reading a cookbook?
195. *Fortune*, 8 December 1997, p. 43.
196. It has been estimated that empty trucks travelled about 60 billion kilometres in the EU at an approximate annual cost of €45 billion. Better transport organisation could radically reduce these figures (*European Voice*, 29 January 1998, p. 15).
197. Even though Siemens is a dominant firm in the Munich high-technology cluster, it does not threaten or absorb SMEs in the cluster, but rather develops ties with SMEs that are characterised by collaboration (Sternberg and Tamásy, 1999, p. 375).
198. 'The First Industrial Revolution proceeded largely without any systematic intervention from government. Parliament did not help to build a modern financial sector, fund transportation infrastructure in a widespread and coordinated way, provide additional incentives to adopt new technologies, manage fiscal or monetary policy with growth in mind, nor help to train a new labour force with appropriate skills for a new industrial nation. Nonetheless, Britain industrialized relatively quickly.

   'Still, the use of the steam engine, and the rise of urban factories, created pressing policy issues. Many of these were local and specific to single uses of the engine rather than generic to steam power itself. Some were so large as to require broader policy changes. These broad policy issues are so numerous and diverse that we only illustrate them here with two cases. When it entered factories, the steam engine gave employment to men, women, and children, bringing them and their low wages to the attention of middle-class reformers who had been largely unaware of the rural poverty that had existed for millennia. Laws were passed to govern child labour and working conditions. Britain also saw the rise of powerful unions and the many laws governing them' (Lipsey et al., 2005, p. 186).
199. Public policy and administrative areas in which the authorities collect statistics are usually not the same as clusters, which is why it is hard to determine the exact economic significance of clusters with a high degree of reliability.
200. See www.marxists.org/archive/marx/works/1894-c3/ch48.htm.
201. Cumulative causation mixes causes and effects of an event. They are combined in a chain reaction that is increasingly circular, snowballing, herding or perpetually accumulative. This type of self-reinforcement has different labels in economics which include: economies of scale, path dependency, virtuous and vicious circles, as well as threshold effects. The sources of this process are large sunk costs, learning, and network

and coordination effects. Cumulative causation is reinforced by the following four elements: favourable demand conditions, good factor-related setting, strong market competition and fine access to supporting and related industries.

202. Recall the example about industrial policy targeting in Japan in Section 4.4.
203. It is also likely that dinosaurs came into being following an earlier meteor impact 251 million years ago.
204. Because of the availability of wood, Sweden developed its huge pulp and paper industry. Strong links with the suppliers contributed to a similar success for the machinery involved in the paper-production processes.
205. The first 'modern' corporation-like organisation in Europe was the church. Later came the guilds and universities.
206. R. Anderson and R. Atkins, 'The pressure to end the 35-hour week shows that big companies are prepared to take matters into their own hands', *Financial Times*, 23 July 2004.
207. 'Japanese business firms operating in Germany have an unexplainable attraction to Düsseldorf rather than Frankfurt' (Beckmann, 1999, p. 61).
208. L. Hockstader, 'Enterprise belt pulls Italy into Europe', *The International Herald Tribune*, 6 November 1997, p. 13.
209. Consider the applause in a theatre. Soon the audience will spontaneously start clapping at the same tempo. Such self-organisation occurs when many initially uncorrelated actions lock into one another's rhythm and create a strong collective group. Or another example: imagine queues at a supermarket checkout. Which one to join? Clients judge the waiting time according to individual criteria which include: the number of persons in each queue; how full their baskets or trolleys are; how likely it is that those ahead will unload their shopping quickly; who is likely to write a cheque; who will chat with a cashier; and so on. Nobody directs these supermarket clients, but some spontaneous order is established.
210. Mainstream economics deals with decision making within given structures. Evolutionary economics is concerned with decision making and long-term changes of the structure. See the classical article on the issue by Boschma and Lambooy (1999a). For a structuralist-evolutionary approach to economic transformations, see Lipsey et al. (2005).
211. Information in the physical world is transmitted via flows of particles such as electrons or photons and density gradients. In the social world (and to a lesser extent in the biological) 'there are the controls of information flows from the exercise of the *principle of optimum loss of detail* and use of *near-decomposability* within hierarchical structures – and even more so within the intricate interconnections of complicated hierarchical structures that may be embodied in an heterarchical model conceived by a human mind' (Isard, 1996, p. 357; original emphasis). Even though there are difficulties in applying biological analogies to social phenomena, they were widely used in the analysis of firms. Examples include the 'life cycle' theory of the firm, 'viability' of the firm and 'homeostasis' (habitual return to the initial equilibrium) (Penrose, 1952).
212. The relation between expectations and accomplishments is essential for satisfaction.
213. Australians were prevented from selling their wines under French names such as champagne, chablis or claret. So they simply rebranded their products as sparkling wines, cabernet sauvignon and chardonnay. The French were subsequently forced to rebrand obscure labels with various names to compete with the Australians on the British market (*Financial Times*, 28 July 2003).
214. 'IMF's Camdessus misses the point', *Stratfor*, 15 November 1999.
215. Acceleration in productivity (growth in output per hour) is the basis for an increase in living standards and economic progress in the long term.
216. Some even thought that economic cycles were dead.
217. The performance of computer chips at a given price doubles every 18 months (Moore's law). However, this does not mean that the impact of computers on productivity follows this trend in a linear way. It depends who uses computers, how, when and for what purpose: management of stocks or computer games.

218. R. Gordon, 'America wins with a supermarket sweep', *Financial Times*, 19 August 2003.
219. *The Economist*, 19 August 2000, p. 9.
220. The German chemical industry was based on domestic deposits of salt and coal, as well as skills.
221. The first of many attempts to produce a small, economical runaround vehicle early in the 20th century resulted in the Auto-Ped. Introduced in New York in 1915, this looked like a child's scooter: it had no seat and there was a platform for the rider to stand on. A two-horsepower motor gave the Auto-Ped a maximum speed of 55km/h.
222. In an attempt to eliminate textile waste during the Second World War, the US government reduced by one-tenth the amount of fabric allowed for women's swimwear. The chain of events that resulted in the ever-decreasing amount of material necessary for the bikini was set in motion.
223. The Japanese understood this and implemented a policy among domestic rivalry among half a dozen conglomerates. This became the basis for the global competitiveness of their output such as passenger cars and consumer electronics. They also transferred it elsewhere. For example, after the failure of Leyland in the 1980s, Britain developed a relatively dynamic car production and market based to a large extent on local production by Japanese TNCs.
224. Recall the example about Ferguson tractors in Section 4.4, above.
225. Coalmining regions weakened and declined when liquid fuels were used as principal sources of energy.
226. Topics for further research include: spillovers, externalities and linkages as they are so poorly understood; local interactions; monopolistic competition; cross-fertilisation with industrial organisation and urban economics, trade and growth; cost–benefit analysis that can include linkages; services, as research was mainly concentrated on the manufacturing sector; the speed of (exponential?) weakening of the effect of spillovers and information relative to distance, especially in developing countries; and agglomeration and spread of innovative activities.
227. According to the Assembly of European Regions Declaration on Regionalism in Europe, 'The region is the territorial body of public law established at the level immediately below that of the State and endowed with political self-government. The region shall be recognised in the national constitution or in legislation which guarantees its autonomy, identity, powers and organisational structures.' See www.are-regions-europe.org/GB/A1/A16-whatregion.html.
228. The tacit assumption is that there are no transport and adjustment costs.
229. Sources of economies of scale include very high set-up or sunk costs (in fixed capital and R&D); learning effects (the more people learn how to use one Microsoft program, the easier it is for them to learn and adjust to other programs); and network and coordination effects (the more people use mobile phones or electronic banking the greater is the utility of that to all network users).
230. Institutional organisation, social regulation and political intervention may have a significant influence on the location of production.
231. Entry and exit barriers include: huge sunk costs (in project investment and advertising), economies of scale, product differentiation (for example, local market demands a specific brand-name drink), access to distribution channels, R&D, regulation (product quality), marketing, restriction of access to complementary assets and structures (such as a computer reservation system for tickets), reactions of competitors such as predatory pricing, exclusionary pricing, as well as trade, competition and industrial policies.
232. See Brülhart (1998a) for a brief survey of theoretical strands.
233. Evidence from the EU shows that the strongest internal labour mobility took place during the 1960s and the beginning of the 1970s; it came to a halt during the 1990s. However, intra-EU capital mobility increased during the 1980s and has remained strong ever since. Even domestic labour mobility within countries such as Italy was reduced. Labour used to move northwards on a larger scale during the 1950s and 1960s. Not any more. Southerners may easily be overqualified for simple jobs offered in the

north of the country, the cost of living is higher in the north and there is also the attraction of the 'southern way of life'.

234. A strategic industrial (and trade) policy is based on a number of assumptions that include next to perfect information and forecast, as well as on the policy of non-retaliation by the foreign partners.
235. T. Sickinger, 'Outsourcing not bad, Intel chief says', *The Oregonian*, 12 May 2004.
236. Is the core–periphery relation based on the purchase of goods by the core region from the periphery? Or outflow of capital from the core region to the periphery? Or migration of labour (and capital) from the periphery region to the core? Or is there a mix of these possibilities?
237. The shipbuilding industry in Britain and Spain was in decline as it failed to specialise in a market niche as the Finnish industry has done (icebreakers), it was not able to match the production costs in Korea and it lacked the potential for diversification existing in Japan. But this is the story from only one industry, and generalisations about the situation in the whole economy should never be made from a single-industry case study.
238. This has always been an urban 'activity' because cities 'sell' anonymity and limited tolerance.
239. Bangalore (southern India), an important world software and outsourcing hub, may be the victim of its own success. The rapid growth of this city put a strain on its infrastructure. Population is around 6 million, roads are congested and power cuts are frequent. Local software firms are looking to expand elsewhere in India, possibly in Calcutta, Hyderabad, New Delhi and Pune.
240. 'Industries in the US are much more spatially concentrated than in Europe (even controlling for the distribution of population and manufacturing as a whole), suggesting that regional integration in Europe could cause agglomeration at the sectoral level (for example, Germany gets engineering, the UK financial services, and so on)' (Venables, 1999, p. 17; also Brülhart, 1998a, p. 790; Krugman, 1992, p. 72; Midelfart-Knarvik et al., 2002, p. 218; and Krugman and Venables, 1996, p. 960.) Others, however, think differently: 'we think that the results available so far point more towards similarities across the EU and the U.S. than differences. These similarities occur despite underlying differences in mobility and the extent of integration' (Combes and Overman, 2004, pp. 2899–900). It is clear that this is a splendid topic for further research.
241. Casella (1996) discussed the case of reallocation of resources and gains from an enlargement of a trade bloc in small and large countries that already belong to that bloc. She showed that smaller EU countries gained more from the entry of Spain and Portugal into the EU than the large EU countries.
242. Storper et al. (2002, p. 103) argued that the US had a number of highly developed and specialised regional clusters throughout the country; the same type of specialisation is much less obvious in Europe.
243. 'Quotas have inflated clothing prices by creating scarcity and "rents", price premiums that act as taxes on trade. The annual cost to US consumers has been put at Dollars 70bn and has fallen hardest on poor families, which spend a relatively large share of income on clothing. Each job saved by quotas in the US industry is estimated to have cost consumers an average of Dollars 170 000' (G. de Jonquières, 'Clothes on the line', *Financial Times*, 19 July 2004).
244. G. de Jonquières, 'Clothes on the line', *Financial Times*, 19 July 2004.
245. There are, however, certain limits to this type of 'offshoring' and migration of such service jobs towards the developing countries. Tastes and needs change, markets are fickle, hence there will always be a need for a certain local presence, close to consumers. It may be difficult to service such consumers and markets in the EU from Bombay.
246. Ireland, Spain and Sweden as peripheral countries attracted a relatively large number of foreign investors.
247. Federal countries such as the US, Canada, Australia or Switzerland have different regional policies from that of the EU.
248. This is the 'catch-all' article.

249. Eurostat (2003), 'How rich are Europe's regions?', *Statistics in Focus*, Theme 1–06/2003.
250. The European Coal and Steel Community has exerted its own influence on regions that are involved in the coal, iron and steel industries. Loans were given for the retraining and redeployment of workers, as well as for a modernisation of the industry. The EIB has been giving loans for projects in the less-developed regions of the EU.
251. Britain changed its regional policy in 1980. The most important features of this alteration were the following three elements. First, the regional disequilibria started to be seen as a *regional* rather than a *national* issue, one that had to be resolved by indigenous development rather than by a transfer of resources and business activity from elsewhere. Second, direct subsidies for employment were replaced by a system of regional aid programmes based on employment creation through improved competitiveness. Third, the policy became increasingly reliant on employment cost-effectiveness (Wren, 1990, p. 62).
252. Regional support started to include producer services and incentives for the introduction of innovations such as licences or patents.
253. The Mezzogiorno (a name for the southern geographical region relative to the central region of a country) is the area south of Lazio. The population of this region is 21 million.
254. Regional policy in Ireland, another formerly backward EU country, was consistent for over four decades. The policy emphasised the role of markets, selected electronics and pharmaceuticals for special treatment, invested in infrastructure (telecommunications) and more than anything else invested in education (creation of human capital).
255. *Business Europe*, 31 May 1991, p. 3.
256. A similar situation developed in Germany following the *Anschluss* of 1989. During the first decade after reunification, a 'total net resource transfer of about 750 billion € has been transferred to the east' (Sinn and Westermann, 2000, p. 7).
257. The list is based on data for 1996; if available, the number of related firms in the cluster is given in square brackets (although the number of firms in a cluster changes over time, it is given here only as an indication); and a bigger city in the vicinity or province is given in round brackets. Source: 'Quanti sono i distretti industriali in Italia?', *Newsletter Club dei Distretti Industriali* no. 9, November 1998, Club dei distretti industriali Prato, p. 9.

Continue to love each other with true Christian love.
Don't forget to show hospitality to strangers,
for some who have done this have entertained angels without realising it!
Hebrews 13:1–2

5 Integration Schemes

5.1 Introduction

The founders of the GATT recognised the importance and attraction of economic integration between countries. That process can have an identical economic rationale and motivation to integration within a single country that has different regions. Hence, regional economic integration, according to the WTO (1995), does not pose an inherent threat to global integration. None the less, the GATT (Article XXIV) constrains the level of the common external tariff and other trade measures in customs unions. On the whole, these trade measures should not be higher or more restrictive than those of the member countries prior to the integration agreement.

Intra-group trade (as a share of total trade) is relatively high in the EU and North America. That development, however, was not associated with a significant alteration in the relevance of extra-group trade. In spite of various concerns, the WTO (ibid.) did not find conclusive evidence about the emergence of a 'fortress' mentality in integration arrangements. The conclusion was that regional integration was complementary to the multilateral trading system. It was perceived that regional economic integration had, at that time, an overall favourable impact on the pace of global economic integration. However, the period following the start of the Doha

Development Round in 2001 was one of the most prolific regarding the number of notifications of integration deals to the WTO. Therefore, a proliferation of various integration arrangements and various non-tariff barriers (NTBs) in the world may pose an obstacle to deeper multilateral integration in the future under the auspices of the WTO.

The 'traditional' schemes that integrate developing countries, structured along the lines of the neo-classical theory of integration, have not lived up to the great expectations of their founders and most, in fact, failed and collapsed. Most of them can be arbitrarily placed in two broad groups. One is based on the liberalisation of trade, while the rationale of the other is specialisation in production (Mytelka, 1994, pp. 24–5). The former scheme was motivated by pure trade and based on the neo-classical theoretical model. The attention of countries was directed mainly towards the common external trade protection of the integrated countries and to a reduction and elimination of barriers to intra-group trade. It is, then, left to *market forces* to determine the allocation of resources in the region. Attempts to establish a regional agency that organises and/or harmonises industrial policy was largely left out of the arrangement. The organisational structure of these schemes was relatively unsophisticated.[1]

The second simplified theoretical model of integration among the developing countries focused, in practice, on specialisation in production. The stated goals were to increase the relatively low level of development in manufacturing industry, to reap economies of scale, to enhance complementarity in manufacturing, to establish linkages in production and to introduce a certain degree of regional planning. Owing to the relatively backward technologies in production, management and control, as well as to a lack of investment funds, TNCs could be an attractive (initial) choice for bridging that gap. Certain groups sought to reach a coordinated approach towards TNCs. To put it in simple terms, *intervention* was the *leitmotif* in the integration of these countries. However, rather than directing integration energies towards the establishment of production and other business linkages among countries, these groups expended much of their potential on distributing the benefits that might accrue from integration. The groups that suit the model of integration that has as its objective the specialisation in production require a more complex institutional structure than exclusively trade-related models.[2]

The objective of this chapter is to provide no more than a brief reminder of some of the principal international economic integration arrangements in various parts of the world. The most striking absence is the lack of a section on the EU. The reason for this is that this group is so rich in experience, developments, problems and achievements that it is difficult for it to be properly represented in a relatively brief section. In addition, all chapters in this book have a strong EU slant. This is because a number of integration groups, particularly in the developing world, have been attempting to emulate the EU. Therefore, the interested reader is invited to consult economic texts on the issue.[3]

Unfortunately, the international integration schemes were relatively successful only in the developed world. Elsewhere, they either collapsed or, at best, lingered on feebly. Several schemes were referred to for the historical record only. This does not mean that there is no potential for a certain degree of economic integration throughout the (developing) world. In fact, many integration schemes in that group of countries are going through a phase of innovation. However, the new development that may feature high on the agenda in the future is north–south integration as started around South Africa in 1910; and the more recent agreements among the US, Canada and Mexico from 1994, between the EU and Turkey with the 1995 customs union, as well as between the EU and certain countries in the European neighbourhood.

This chapter considers concrete integration schemes.[4] It is structured as follows. Integration experiences in Europe are presented in Section 5.2. Section 5.3 covers the Americas: North American, South American and pan-American past, existing and emerging integration arrangements are presented in sequence. Section 5.4 examines integration schemes in Asia and in the Pacific region. Integration schemes in Africa are referred to in Section 5.5. Finally, Section 6 presents some conclusions about the reasons for the meagre integration achievements among the developing countries.

5.2 Europe

5.2.1 EUROPEAN FREE TRADE ASSOCIATION

As a response to the creation of the European Economic Community (EEC) in 1957, Britain gathered together the 'other six' countries[5] that signed the Stockholm Convention which created the European Free Trade Association (EFTA). The small Secretariat (only around 70 people) did not have any supranational authorities, and it was the only body of EFTA. Agriculture was excluded from the arrangement, so the whole business referred to trade in manufactured goods only. That was not very popular in those countries with a relatively developed agricultural and fisheries sector, such as Denmark, Norway and Portugal. Apart from the elimination of tariffs on internal trade, there was almost no other intervention by EFTA. The market forces were left to do the job of integration. There were no common policies whatsoever. Therefore, the history of EFTA appears to be without significance or event. The important things, that is, market-induced specialisation, happened at such a micro level as to escape the commentator's eye (Curzon Price, 1988, p. 100). However, the group was successful in economic terms. Their average GDP per capita was always (significantly) higher than the same indicator in the EEC.

As a purely commercial arrangement (tariff and quota-free internal trade in manufactured goods), the small, developed, specialised and open EFTA countries did not have a genuine objective of economic integration within the group, but rather the establishment of good commercial relations with the EEC (later EU). The EFTA countries traded much more with the EEC countries than with their partners in EFTA. The reasons are simple. High specialisation and geographical distance between the EFTA countries explain this distribution of trade, which is one of the reasons why there were no serious disputes in internal trade and why economic adjustment to integration in the group was smooth. In other words, the free trade area among the seven EFTA countries was only a means to an end, rather than an objective in itself (Curzon Price, 1987, p. 4). Since the EFTA countries intended to neutralise the impact of the creation of the EEC on EFTA trade, it appears that EFTA succeeded in its aim.

Just one year after the establishment of EFTA, Britain (the most important EFTA member country) submitted its application for full membership of the EEC. Britain realised that it had to be a part of a stronger and larger economic group. EFTA looked stillborn. It had a kind of negative identity, and the remaining members of EFTA took on the mantle of 'not-yet-in-the-EEC'.

The success or failure of any free (preferential) trade area depends to a large extent on how it deals with technical matters such as NTBs and rules of competition.[6] These include restrictive business practices, technical standards, subsidies, dumping, public procurement, rules of origin and dispute settlements. The process of cooperation in EFTA was so smooth and conducted at such a microeconomic level that the entire history of the group seemed to be uneventful (Curzon Price, 1987, 1997). The only exceptions were the departures of Britain, Denmark and Ireland in 1973, and Austria, Sweden and Finland in 1995, to join the EU.

The European Economic Area (EEA) was conceived in 1990[7] as a vehicle for keeping potential new entrants (the EFTA countries) from joining the EU, but it ended up being a waiting room for the new enlargement. The EEA started life as the world's biggest free trade area with over 370 million consumers. It is in essence the virtual entry of the EFTA countries minus Switzerland[8] into the EU, but excluding agriculture, energy, external trade, coal and steel, foreign and security policy. Within the EEA, which is served by an independent EEA Court of Justice, the participating countries enjoy free mobility of goods, services, capital and people (four freedoms), but only for internally produced goods and services.

The small EFTA countries have always had a liberal trade policy for their manufactured goods. These countries obtained from the EEA free entry for their manufactured goods to the largest market in the world. This would increase competition for their businesses and, hence, bring efficiency gains. The EU obtained secure access to wealthy consumers in the EFTA countries and assistance in resisting domestic protectionist appeals as the EFTA countries had a more liberal trade policy than the EU. The EEA was stillborn, since Austria, Finland, Norway and Sweden applied for full membership of the EU in order to get a say in the EU's law-making. These applications were welcomed by the EU, which needed net contributors to its budget.[9] Austria, Finland and Sweden quietly entered the EU in 1995. Norway's voters, however, declined to approve the deal.

5.2.2 CENTRAL EUROPEAN FREE TRADE AGREEMENT

Economic integration in the region of central and eastern Europe continued for the major part of the second half of the 20th century within the Council for Mutual Economic Assistance (CMEA). Majority voting in that group was prohibited. This may be why the CMEA did not have any real powers (endless bilateral negotiations made progress in integration slow). This was also why the Soviets were not able to control fully all member countries. Although market competition did not play a significant role, a certain type of competition between different plans was still present in the group.

'Socialist prices' in CMEA trade were supposed to embody 'equality' in economic relations in contrast to cyclical 'capitalist prices' that represented inequality in economic relations. None the less, the just 'socialist prices' were always calculated on the basis of world market (capitalist) prices. In a system where the major concern was with quantity rather than quality and value in the market, prices did not respond either to costs or to the relation between demand and supply. Therefore, it was hard to understand why CMEA countries spent so much time bargaining over prices or why there was a world market price formula. Bilateral balancing of trade was reducing the extent of external trade and, hence, kept trade at a lower level than in the countries at a similar stage of development with a market-based economic system. Such a trading system was integration unfriendly for the CMEA. Different reforms attempted changes within the socialist system, but that did not lead anywhere. An overhaul of the entire system was necessary. As it was unable to resist the challenge of economic transition towards a market-type economy, the CMEA vanished in 1991. For details about the origin, operation and demise of the CMEA, see Appendix 5A1.

After the collapse of the CMEA, there was a certain external and internal interest in fostering economic links among the central and east European countries that had economies in transition. The Visegrád[10] countries, however, declared joining the EU as their primary objective. Challenges regarding eastern enlargement of the EU are presented in Appendix 5A2. The key problems relating to economic integration in this central European group include the actual interest of the partner countries in integration within this group[11] and the real enthusiasm of the EU to accept them. Hence, the participating countries could see the Visegrád group as a waiting room (vehicle) for entry into the EU (end). In addition, integration may be seen as a means of gaining regional cooperation 'maturity' for joining the EU. The EU could also use the Visegrád group as a safety belt from potential turbulence in other eastern European countries. The EU also 'encouraged' these countries to integrate among themselves, probably to delay their entry into the EU.

The Central European Free Trade Agreement (CEFTA) was created in Krakow in 1992, after member countries signed association agreements with the EU. It was expected that the regional free trade area in manufactured goods would be gradually established in 2001. The impact of CEFTA on the participating countries can be, at best, only marginal. Member countries trade mostly with the EU, while the level of internal CEFTA trade is relatively small (less than 10 per cent of their external trade). This should come as no surprise since modernisation of the CEFTA economies, and a process of economic transition towards a market economy and growth is hardly possible without trade with the developed market economies. Perhaps, internal CEFTA trade would increase if the countries of the group were within the EU, as it did between Spain and Portugal following their entry into the EU.

The possibility of expanding the group to include other countries with economies in transition, the option preferred by the EU, could have been resisted by the original CEFTA countries, as it might have endangered or delayed the accession of the 'original four' to the EU. An expansion of the CEFTA group could be seen by the original four as an alternative to, rather than as instrumental for integration with, the EU. CEFTA, however, did enlarge, to encompass over 100 million consumers when Slovenia joined in 1996, Romania in 1997, Bulgaria in 1999 and Croatia in 2003. The entry of the 'core' CEFTA countries into the EU in 2004 meant the virtual hibernation of CEFTA as Croatia, Bulgaria and Romania had already started the EU entry process.

Following upheavals during the 1990s, south-east European (Balkan) countries, pressed primarily by the EU, started economic cooperation. They concluded 28 bilateral free trade agreements. Although these deals were based on the same general set of rules, they were not uniform. There are differences in the coverage of agricultural goods, public procurement and services (Economic Commission for Europe, 2005, p. 98). Should these existing bilateral deals be harmonised? Would it pay, as the principal trading partner of these countries is the EU? Or, should there be a pan-Balkan free trade area? Or, should CEFTA be enlarged to include all these countries? The CEFTA rules require WTO membership, which is not yet the case for all countries in the Balkans. In any case, all countries in the region have as their goal full EU membership. Hence, all future deals among them will be made according to their stated goal.

5.2.3 NORWAY AND SWITZERLAND

It has been argued in theory that relatively small countries have a need for and an inclination towards international economic integration. Why, then, have relatively small, highly developed and specialised countries such as Norway and Switzerland repeatedly chosen not to join the EU?

In theory, there is an economic rationale for economic integration with the EU in both of those countries. In fact, they have both been 'integrated' with the EU since 1973 through a free trade arrangement for manufactured goods. Such a deal allowed Norway to have its own agriculture, fisheries and natural resources policy. A high-wage Switzerland was protected from an unrestricted inflow of foreign (EU) labour, and its domestic banking secrets and farming were preserved.[12]

The principal reasons in Norway and Switzerland for resisting full and formal integration with the EU are mostly political. A fear of the loss of sovereignty to external forces (no matter how little remained in the economic sphere) looms large in both countries. Diverse institutions, social cleavages and experiences with foreign rulers still present significant obstacles to EU entry in both Norway and Switzerland.

In order to pass through the Swiss direct-democracy political system, any important measure must obtain a double majority (that of the population and that of the number of cantons) in a national referendum. This is very difficult in Switzerland. For example, to relinquish the national control of an exemplary Swiss franc in favour of a central and distant administration of a still unproven euro is highly unlikely in Switzerland for a very long time to come. Then, the minimum agreed VAT rate in the EU is 15 per cent. Many EU countries have introduced a rate double this norm. The Swiss VAT rate

(8.5 per cent) is significantly lower than is the case in the surrounding countries. Therefore, shopping in Switzerland for tax-sensitive goods may continue to be advantageous for the residents of neighbouring EU countries.

Unless there are new and strong overriding political incentives such as security considerations and/or an increased voice in EU affairs, voters in the two countries will continue to favour the status quo. Proponents of EU entry argue that the cost of a policy of staying out of the EU may include a certain loss of R&D, FDI and banking business. However, in the case of Switzerland, they would still have to substantiate their arguments.

Norway and Switzerland are not obliged to adopt the euro. As long as they continue to preserve some of the highest levels of GDP per capita in the world, the domestic voters would need to be presented with stronger and more convincing arguments before they would support full EU entry. It is still possible to be a small country, outside the EU, and to prosper. Therefore, certain EU member countries that may be on the point of leaving the EU (for example, by their own choice or if they do not ratify the Constitutional Treaty) may look at the Norwegian and Swiss model of relations with the EU as a possible future link with the EU. Free access to the Single European Market (bar agriculture) may be obtained and secured, but a country would not be able to vote on the market rules.

5.3 The Americas

5.3.1 NORTH AMERICAN FREE TRADE AGREEMENT

The debate about a free trade agreement between the US and Canada was barely registered in the US. In contrast, however, in Canada the issue provoked one of the largest debates in the history of the country. Canada had five theoretical options regarding its trade future in the mid-1980s:

- First, a continuation with the status quo of gradual moves towards free trade liberalisation through the slow process of multilateral negotiations under the auspices of the GATT. The problem with that approach was that tariffs were declining while the proliferating NTBs were beyond the scope of the GATT until the mid-1990s. Hence, this option was considered to be too risky for Canada.
- Second, an active inward-looking trade and industrial policy. The chances for the success of such a policy were judged to be small, while the risks of foreign (mainly US) retaliation were expected to be high.

- Third, the option of fostering ties with Europe and the developing countries. The experience from this approach was not encouraging. Canada had tried to promote trade with Europe in the early 1970s when the latter had an annual share of 20 per cent in Canadian exports, but in spite of the 'encouragement' of relations, exports to Europe fell to 8 per cent in 1984.
- Fourth, an aggressive policy of multilateralism. Canada should push for negotiations in the GATT and preserve its commercial interest as it would negotiate with the US in a group, rather than go it alone. Lipsey and Smith (1986) were not convinced that for Canada multilateral negotiations with the US were preferable to bilateral ones, and they thought that any gains would be too small for Canada and would come too late.
- Fifth, bilateral trade liberalisation and formal integration[13] with the US. This option, in the form of a free trade area, was the only one that provided a real chance for major improvement in the Canadian economy. Such a deal would secure access for Canadian firms to a market of over 250 million consumers, and it would support economies of scale and a reduction of prices per unit of output. In addition, this would increase the competitiveness of Canadian goods in third markets and, ultimately, it was estimated that the general effect of the deal would be an increase in Canadian living standards of between 4 and 7 per cent (ibid.).

Once the free trade agreement between the US and Canada was signed (1987) and implemented, there were moves to include Mexico in the North American Free Trade Agreement (NAFTA). This was also partly a US reaction to slow progress in multilateral trade-liberalisation negotiations, partly a warning to the negotiating partners, and partly a response to the creation of the Single European Market.

If the US were to enter into a bilateral free trade deal with Mexico and, later, to conclude similar arrangements with other (Latin American) countries, then that would create a hub-and-spoke model of integration (which was undesirable for Canada and other involved countries). The US, as the regional hub, would have a separate agreement with each spoke country. As such, the US would have advantages of negotiating individually with each partner country, as well as being the only country with tariff-free access to the markets of all participants, with locational advantages for FDI. If low-wage Mexico were included in NAFTA, the fear was that it would divert trade.[14] Interestingly enough, such a fear did not feature highly in discussions when Greece, Spain and Portugal were entering the EU, but was of some relevance during discussions about the eastern enlargement of the EU.

What matters in international competition is not how much local labour is paid in terms of purchasing power, but rather how much unit costs of production compare internationally at the ongoing exchange rates. If the level of wages were the determining factor of international trade, then the markets of the US and Canada would be flooded with Mexican goods. Other factors, such as capital stock (its quantity and quality), productivity and the existence and reliability of the supply chain in the target location play more prominent roles. An integration arrangement between the two developed countries (the US and Canada) and one developing country (Mexico)[15] would make the trade and industrial policies of the three countries more outward looking and less focused on uncompetitive import-competing domestic industries (Lipsey, 1990).

The striking feature of NAFTA, created in 1994, is that it is an arrangement that integrates countries with significant differences in per capita income. This is why Mexico was given a 'transition period' of seven years for the elimination of tariffs, which was a bit longer than was the case with Canada and the US. During that period, *maquiladoras*[16] in Mexico were expected to change. NAFTA was concernd that temporary imports from third countries would enter Mexican *maquiladoras* duty free, and then would end up as duty-free imports on the US and Canadian markets. Therefore, Mexico had to charge duty on non-NAFTA imports that have a NAFTA market as their destination. Regardless of whether Mexico lowers or eliminates tariffs on such external imports, the glory days of *maquiladoras* belong to the past because of the Asian factor.

Regarding rules of origin, Mexico and Canada were in favour of a relatively liberal system. Such rules would make a positive impact on Japanese and other FDI in the two countries and the potential exports of goods to the US. Initially, the required local content of goods for liberal treatment in NAFTA was 50 per cent, but that would increase to and stay at 62.5 per cent from 2002.

There are still problems, disputes and irritations within NAFTA regarding issues such as the environment, subsidies, agriculture, sanitary measures and transport (restrictions on Mexican trucking in the US). Some of these disputes have appeared only because of the absence of tariff barriers, which may 'be a sign of the effectiveness of integration under the NAFTA' (Anderson, 2004, p. 662).

NAFTA is not a group such as the EU with free mobility of labour and transfers of various funds. Such integration brings different effects from those of a simple free trade area. If one bears in mind that the entire economy of Mexico is equal to that of Massachusetts, it becomes clear that standard economic arguments (secure larger market, economies of scale and growth) have not played a primary role for the US in this integration group.

The US is very concerned about stability at its southern border. Hence, NAFTA should be seen as a tool that is supposed to help a friendly Mexican government succeed in its reform and development process (Krugman, 1996a, p. 165). None the less, some see an open regional approach by NAFTA regarding new members such as Chile or a few other Latin American states as going some way to assuaging the criticism that NAFTA is undermining the multilateral trading system. Others would argue that a new entrant would just add to the 'spaghetti bowl' of trade relations.

As far as Mexico is concerned, there is a belief that a revival of the US economy can, by itself, also revitalise the Mexican one. While this may pull some weight with Mexico, the US is expanding its trade and investment ties with other countries and regions (China is a robust and successful competitor for Mexico to watch out for). NAFTA has provided Mexico with a strong and reliable economic springboard for the modernisation of its national economy and future prosperity. It has reinforced and stimulated the intensity of trade and investment relations among its members – and that is all it can do for the member countries. Unfortunately, successive Mexican governments have failed to make full use of the potentials made available by NAFTA. They have not (yet) fully attended to the important national issues of crumbling infrastructure, poor education, business-unfriendly taxation, red tape and corruption. These act as important barriers to both domestic and foreign entrepreneurs and investors and prevent them from taking full advantage of the huge possibilities which include open trade with the US (and Canada). Should one reproach the NAFTA integration agreement for this domestic Mexican failure?

Although it may not be headline news (Canada apart) or attracting the attention of the majority of trade analysts, important liberal trade principles are perpetually violated in NAFTA. They are masked by the 'non-sexy' nature of the good in question: softwood lumber.

Canada has an ongoing dispute with the US that has lasted several decades, concerning trade in softwood lumber. The current one started in 1982 when the US lumber producers complained to the US Department of Commerce that Canada gave subsidies to the domestic producers and exporters by charging low 'stumpage fees'. These are charges by the provincial governments for the right to harvest trees on public (Crown) land. In order to solve the problem, the two countries signed a Memorandum of Understanding that referred to trade (Canadian exports) of softwood lumber during 1986–91. Under this deal, Canada agreed to collect a 15 per cent charge on all exports of softwood lumber to the US.

In 1996 the two countries concluded the US–Canada Softwood Lumber Agreement, which regulated exports to the US. In essence, there were no restrictions on exports of softwood lumber to the US, but the first 14.7 billion board feet would enter the US fee-free. Exports between 14.7 and 15.35 billion board feet were subject to an export charge of US$50 per 1000 board feet. Beyond that, exports were subject to an export charge of US$100 per 1000 board feet. A distinctive feature of this deal was that it was entirely administered by Canada: monitoring of exports and collection of all fees (Anderson, 2004, p. 665). The fees collected were kept by Canada. If one forgets about the free trade principle, this was not at all a bad deal for Canada.

The whole deal operated as a 'voluntary export quota'. A tariff would be a preferable solution to such a voluntary quota, but obligations under the WTO and NAFTA made it unworkable. Therefore, the solution came in the form of a voluntary export restraint because that could not be challenged. In a formal sense, this may be legal, but the deal violated the spirit of free trade present in the WTO and NAFTA.

Canadian softwood lumber accounts for 33 per cent of the US market for this commodity. Once the Softwood Lumber Agreement expired in 2001, the US producers complained again and demanded countervailing and anti-dumping duties on imports from Canada. Subsequently, the US Department of Commerce imposed a combined 27 per cent tariff on imports of Canadian lumber.

Canadian producers are more efficient than the Americans in the production of lumber. The Canadians invested heavily to upgrade their mills with the latest technology. Many smaller US mills did not do this and if trade were free, they would go out of business. This is the real reason why the US lumber industry was gunning for the Canadians. This is a textbook example of a comparative advantage, investment in the creation of future advantage and how trade restrictions foster local inefficiency.

According to a draft 2003 agreement, in principle the US would remove the tariff, but Canada would have to reduce its share of the US lumber market to 31 per cent. Over and above that market share, the US would apply a tariff of US$200 for each additional thousand board feet of exports of lumber. At that point the Canadian companies had already paid US$1.6 billion in US duties. Under the Continued Dumping and Subsidy Offset Act (Byrd Amendment), the US passed on part of this amount to the domestic firms.[17] As part of the 2003 draft agreement in principle, the US firms would have to return 52 per cent of the antidumping and countervailing duties paid by importers of softwood lumber, while they could keep the rest. In addition, Canada would have had to withdraw its cases before the WTO against the US which it was winning. Such was the price to be paid in dealings with a big and powerful partner.

The Canadians are not more interventionist; rather they do things in their lumber industry differently from the Americans. Many American producers in their arrogance and/or ignorance think and believe that if others do things differently, then the others must be doing things that are wrong. Perhaps Sweden could argue that south Italian tomato growers have lower energy bills than their Swedish counterparts because they are exposed to southern sunshine. Could they argue in favour of certain protective measures as the Italian producers have a kind of 'subsidy'? Should the Swedes ask the Italian government to tax its domestic tomato growers to put their costs of production on the same footing as the Swedes? Should any (natural) advantage be taxed? In any case the NAFTA market for softwood lumber continues to be distorted either by managed trade or remedial measures.

The impact of NAFTA on trade was positive. More than half of the NAFTA countries' trade was within this group. NAFTA also stimulated FDI into Mexico. This was most obvious in the period before and following the launch of NAFTA. As for the rest, the overall impact of NAFTA has been controversial. TNCs initially supported it because they thought that lower tariffs and lower labour costs in Mexico could help them increase profits. However, the emergence of China after the Asian financial crises of 1997 established it as a superior location for FDI. The US labour unions opposed NAFTA because they feared that it would 'send' jobs to Mexico. Farmers in Mexico opposed it because of the heavy subsidies that their American counterparts receive.

Integration in NAFTA has stalled since 2000. There have been three major problems: the softwood lumber issue; Mexico's debt to the US for Rio Grande water since 1990; and the US ban on Canadian beef because of mad cow disease. However, with the near resolution of these problems, the presidents of Canada, Mexico and the US met in 2005 in order to consider a possible new NAFTA-Plus agreement. The new upgraded deal could include economic, political, security, immigration and energy issues. There are opportunities for gain to all partners, but there are also problems. Mexicans comprise the largest part of legal and illegal immigrants to the US and their home country wants to ensure that they are treated better. The US Congress may be nervous about immigration so this may be a hard sell. On the other hand, the US is interested in investment in Mexican energy. The problem is that Mexico's constitution protects the national ownership of energy resources. Resolving these issues will take some time. None the less, things have started to move again.

5.3.2 THE LATIN AMERICAN FREE TRADE AREA AND THE ANDEAN COMMUNITY

Larger-scale economic integration of countries in Latin America has the longest history among the developing countries. The countries involved include the entire region, with the exception of Cuba. None the less, the integration effort (compared to the achievements of the EU) has confronted many difficulties. On the one hand, within the Latin American Free Trade Area (LAFTA), subregional groups, such as the Andean Pact, were formed in 1969 while integration of the southern countries (Mercosur) is a relatively novel feature. On the other hand, LAFTA was replaced by the Latin American Integration Association (LAIA) in 1980 with no significant effect on any change/improvement in the economic performance of the participating countries. The basic objective of LAIA was to provide a security buffer against the global recession and, in particular, the one that was taking place in Latin America.

The principal instrument of integration was a free trade area. Trade was at the forefront of the arrangement, while other objectives, most notably growth and development, played second fiddle. The Preamble to the Treaty of Montevideo (1960) was long on intentions (it even mentioned the creation of a common market), but short on substance. The signatory countries have not pledged much more than to negotiate liberalisation of trade in the future. This referred to tariffs, but not to NTBs. The heavily protected private sector in Latin American countries was not keen on integration. It wanted to protect the well-entrenched domestic position and did not want to 'rock the boat' with integration and expose itself to an uncertain and risky adjustment. This was one of the reasons for the failure of LAFTA.

A new energy was infused into the scheme in the 1970s, when member countries concluded industrial complementary agreements. Basically, these were arrangements that offered certain tariff concessions only to those countries that participated. The major users and beneficiaries of these agreements, and hence integration, were TNCs since they were the major players in the negotiations and design of the agreements. In addition, there were commercial agreements among firms from participating countries. The role of the governments was merely to ratify, or not, any deals concluded by private businesses.

Since it is basically a free trade area, LAFTA cannot be criticised on the grounds that it has failed to develop, harmonise and apply industrial, regional, social or other economic policies. Perhaps an alternative integration arrangement, with the potential for greater success and fortified with an (effective) enforcement mechanism, ought to include these features. The industrial complementary agreements, the instrument that dealt with manufacturing, were used by foreign TNCs that wanted to penetrate the markets of the participating countries.

The LAFTA Treaty includes a very interesting feature, the super-MFN provision, which provides that any bilateral arrangement reached by any LAFTA country is to be extended to *all* other LAFTA/LAIA member countries. If that is the case, then whatever Mexico achieved in negotiations with the US and Canada regarding NAFTA should be automatically extended, under LAFTA/LAIA, to other central and Latin American countries. The LAFTA/LAIA provisions are, however, not backed by any strong enforcement tool (Whalley, 1992, pp. 130–31).

Although economic integration in Latin America has featured high on the agenda in various discussions since the beginning of the 1960s, at least three real elements have worked against integration. First, the national economic strategies of a number of countries were inward looking. The most obvious example is Brazil, which has a very large domestic market. As such, it might not be, in theory, as interested in integration as the relatively smaller countries. Second, the economic relations of the countries in the region have been complex. These include not only relations among countries of different size and economic potential within the region, but also relations between the Latin American countries and the developed market economies. Third, as a market with substantial potential for growth, TNCs from the US, on the one hand, and from Europe and Japan, on the other, have been competing in the region against each other on protected local, not continental, markets. In any case, regional integration, in particular in trade, among the Latin American countries has, in general, been below expectations.

Attention devoted primarily to the liberalisation of trade in LAFTA was not sufficiently appealing to involve large countries in deeper integration. This was, however, not always the case with the relatively small countries. As a reaction to the 'impotent' LAFTA, a subregional group, the Andean Pact, was formed in 1969.[18] The objective of the members was to create a customs union. The major significance of the Andean Pact, renamed the Andean Community in 1996, may be found in its different approach to integration, as well as the anxiety of the small countries that the large partner countries might economically oust them. The crux of the new arrangement was in industrial development through joint programming. The member countries have, however, been reluctant to extend the concessions to other countries in the LAFTA region. This has, of course, slowed down integration efforts in LAFTA and has also fragmented it (Finch, 1988, pp. 252–3).

The joint programming in the manufacturing industry was supposed to be growth oriented and to pay special attention to the equitable distribution of gains from integration. This was a reaction to the dissatisfaction of the smaller member countries with the uneven distribution of benefits within LAFTA. The developing countries that integrated became experienced enough to give a more prominent role to the issues of coordinated development in their integration schemes.

Treatment of FDI in the Andean Pact received a high priority (Article 27 of the Cartagena Agreement). FDI was regulated by several decisions that were usually quite restrictive. Such a policy reflected the introverted, even autarkic, strategy of the group, which was the major reason why Chile left the pact in 1976. Eliminating the fortress mentality, as well as liberalising trade and FDI did not, for Chile, go hand in hand with pact membership. The unilateral liberalising action by Chile during the Pinochet regime had a positive economic impact on the country. Nogués and Quintanilla (1992, p. 20) argued that unilateral, rather than regional or multilateral, reforms were the most efficient strategies for improving the economic prospects of Latin America. In order to increase the inflow of FDI, the initial restrictive demands of the pact were gradually eased over time.

The Sectoral Programme of Industrial Development aspired to rationalise the industrial structure of the member countries. The programme sought to ensure both the optimal utilisation of resources and even development among the countries. What really happened, however, was quite different from these noble objectives. For example, metal-working and vehicle-producing facilities were allocated to those countries that already housed similar facilities. For industries that were new to the region, the allocations were easier in theory, but little has happened in practice. So the existing structure of production ossified.

The first years of the group brought certain positive economic signs as intra-group trade increased from \$143 million in 1969 to \$213 million in 1974. Subsequently, the standstill, almost collapse, of the Andean Pact was amplified by the failure to distribute benefits equally, since relatively smaller countries had little real say in the decision-making process and strong domestic pressure groups were upset about these developments, a politicisation of integration issues, and inconsistent national economic policies (El-Agraa and Hojman, 1988, pp. 264–5). This is hardly surprising since the governments in many countries in the region have changed frequently. In addition, the Andean countries have been trading very little among themselves. The share of their internal trade was only 5 per cent of their external trade. An extra element came from the inhospitable nature of the terrain which provided formidable barriers for the creation of an integrated system of transport. There were also territorial disputes among the member countries, as well as a war between Peru and Ecuador in 1977. The 1979 oil shock hit hard and the countries in the group were affected in different ways (Venezuela and Ecuador are oil-producing countries). They applied different and conflicting macroeconomic policies that were integration unfriendly. In addition, some member countries, such as Colombia and Venezuela, aspired to follow a policy of closer ties with Mexico, in order to be involved, in one way or another, with NAFTA.

One of the most widely cited attempts to introduce a common policy towards TNCs was Decision 24 (1970) of the Andean Pact. This was the first effort by an integration scheme of developing countries to adopt and implement an organised and collaborative approach towards TNCs. The goal of Decision 24 was not to obstruct inflow of FDI into the region. On the contrary, member countries wanted to encourage such an inflow, but in a 'structured' way that would benefit members of the pact and increase economic efficiency. In addition, they wanted to increase the bargaining power of home firms in relation to foreign TNCs in order to promote an 'equitable' distribution of gains from FDI.

The thrust of a complicated and controversial Decision 24 was the regulation of FDI and transfer of technology. It permitted the establishment of a national screening and registration bureau; outlawed new FDI in utilities and services; prohibited an annual reinvestment of corporate profit of more than 5 per cent without approval; allowed the annual transfer of profit of up to 14 per cent; and compelled TNCs to disclose all data relating to the transferred technology, including those on the pricing of inputs. In addition, the expectation from the divestment stipulation (the most polemic feature) imposed on TNCs was a gradual reduction in foreign ownership of local assets, national capital accumulation and a basis for the development of local technology (Mytelka, 1979, p. 190).

Foreign investors loudly criticised Decision 24 as an unfriendly measure, but in practice they took a more pragmatic and longer-term approach. In spite of stringent conditions for FDI, the flows to the region did not decrease; on the contrary, in some cases they even increased. Far more important instruments for attracting FDI to the region were the size and growth of the local market, as well as national policies and the macroeconomic situation, rather than the potentially stringent Decision 24 and economic integration.

In order to alter economic conditions, the Andean countries began to change their economic philosophy towards export-led policies in the 1980s. They also hoped to reinvigorate the almost defunct integration process and to enhance the inflow of FDI into the region. The group repealed Decision 24 and introduced a more liberal Decision 220 in 1987. This move introduced a set of common rules for FDI, but gave independence to the member states in implementing the policy. Industrial development programmes were abolished and replaced by passing on the integration initiative to the private sector.

Decision 291 replaced Decision 220 in 1991. This represents the biggest turning point in the group since its inception. Decision 291 reversed the alleged dislike of the old approach towards FDI and removed obstacles to the free flow of FDI. It symbolises a total departure of the group from the doubtful import-substitution economic strategy of the pact in favour of a deregulated and export-oriented model of development.[19] The Andean

Pact opened its doors completely to TNCs. The most important feature of Decision 291 was related to the national treatment of TNCs. The intention of the group was to remove obstacles to FDI and promote a free inflow of capital to the region. However, the pact started to 'crumble' in 1997. Peru left the group to join the Asia Pacific Economic Cooperation (APEC) in 1998 and later joined Mercosur as an associate member. Obviously, bigger blocs were more attractive in this case.

5.3.3 THE SOUTHERN COMMON MARKET

Trade conflicts with the US and EU (farm goods) inspired Brazil and Argentina to revitalise their mutual economic relations. This was the background to the decision of Argentina and Brazil to sign 17 partial agreements in 1986 and expedite integration on a bilateral basis. These partial agreements included ones that permit duty-free trade in capital goods and cars. This segmented arrangement, rather than one that liberalises trade across the board, may prove to be quite clumsy to operate since a tit-for-tat negotiation tactic may prevent a free adjustment of the whole economy to a deeper integration.

Such 'integration' of Argentina and Brazil lured Paraguay and Uruguay to join them in 1991 and create the Mercado Común del Sur (Mercosur)[20] by the Treaty of Asuncion. The ambitious goal of this second-generation integration group in Latin America was to create a southern common market, covering 70 per cent of South American territory with over 200 million consumers. It is the third most important trading bloc in the world after the EU and NAFTA. The group's stated objectives were to eliminate tariffs and NTBs on internal trade, to adopt the common external tariff and common trade policy, to coordinate all economic policies and to harmonise laws that would support the process of economic integration. Decisions in Mercosur are reached on the basis of consensus, principally because Brazil does not want to submit its sovereignty to smaller member states. Therefore, the institutional structure of Mercosur is kept to a minimum. The treaty was updated in 1994 to allow Mercosur to negotiate and sign deals with other countries and international organisations.

The first step towards the implementation of the plan was an across-the-board cut in tariff rates on internal trade in 1991. A change of approach to integration in Argentina and Brazil was indeed noteworthy. A set of tailor-made self-contained arrangements was replaced by generally liberalised and integrated trade. An Inter-governmental Common Market Council (which meets twice a year) and a relatively small permanent secretariat in Montevideo are a contrast to the excessive baroque-type structures of previous integration schemes in the region. Although this may be seen as an improvement relative to past integration efforts, the flaw is that even small technical problems may end up consuming the energies of ministers and presidents and may generate a lot of hot air in tit-for-tat bargaining at the highest level. Dispute settlement was to be dealt with by an ad hoc Arbitration Tribunal. However, disagreements were resolved by political means. Presidents usually reached a compromise over issues at stake. Handling disputes in this way tends to have unpredictable outcomes, which introduces risk and uncertainty for investors in the group.

It is Mercosur's intention to move from a free trade area, through a customs union and on to a common market.[21] According to the plan, common external tariffs (rates range from 0 to 20 per cent with an average of 13 per cent) were agreed in 1995. They would be introduced in stages by 2001. The member countries were allowed to exempt about 300 goods from the common external duties on a 'temporary' basis. The local content requirement for preferential treatment in intra-group trade is 60 per cent. Trade in cars is subject to special arrangements, as Brazil wanted to allow time for adjustment to its heavily assisted car manufacturing industry. There are no commitments to free factor mobility, hence a common regional market is still only a dream. There was also a recognised need to coordinate macroeconomic policies. Therefore, economic and monetary union was once stated as a goal, but there has been no progress towards achieving it.

The first integration-related signs and successes were encouraging for the group. Average internal trade in Mercosur as a share of total external trade grew rapidly from 9 per cent in 1990 to 20 per cent in 1995. This trade was also 20 per cent in 2000, but because of crises in subsequent years it fell to 12 per cent in 2003. In spite of rapid expansion of internal trade during the 1990s, there were still important unused potentials for an increase in the regional economic links. One of the obstacles, however, is a deficient transport infrastructure (roads, bridges, different railway gauges). This relative shortage in infrastructure is a consequence of insufficient investment during the 1980s and 1990s, past mistrust among the countries in the region and a deeply rooted legacy of the past protectionism. However, the situation began to be rectified in the early 1990s.

Another stumbling block in the integration process is the confusingly diverse economic policies of the member countries. In addition, Brazil, as a big country, has relatively less inclination towards regional integration than other countries. For Brazil, Mercosur increases the 'local' market by a quarter, while for Argentina the increase is fourfold. Brazil also unilaterally introduced trade barriers. In 1995, as part of the stabilisation programme, it increased tariffs on imported cars to 70 per cent (tariffs on consumer goods were also raised). As Argentina was not initially excluded from those tariffs, this brought Mercosur close to breaking point. Argentina also introduced a 3 per cent 'charge' for the statistical recording of imports from outside Mercosur.

Mercosur, however, became attractive to other countries in the region. Chile and Bolivia joined the Mercosur free trade area in 1996, but not the customs union. Peru also became an associate member. At that time both Argentina and Brazil had their currency pegged to the dollar. To a certain extent, the common external tariff protected the group's industries from external competition. Volatility in exchange rates between the participating countries, however, undermined Mercosur's viability as a customs union. A crucial turning point occurred in 1999 when Brazil devaluated the real (pegged to the dollar since 1994) by 35 per cent and then made it float. This measure was taken in order to handle the economic crisis provoked by Asian and Russian financial turmoil in 1997–98. As a result, Brazil's exports to Argentina soared as the peso was pegged to the dollar from 1991 (without adjustment). This not only replaced the domestic production in Argentina and also in Paraguay and Uruguay, but additionally attracted FDI to Brazil where costs of production were lower than elsewhere in Mercosur. This contributed to the slump in Argentina.

To counter this situation, Argentina unilaterally introduced quotas on a range of Brazilian products, while Brazil withdrew from stalled talks on trade in cars. Internal trade in Mercosur dropped. Since that time Mercosur has made no progress with regard to abandoning the remaining exceptions to free internal trade. In fact, Argentina unilaterally altered its trade tariffs in 2001 (recall that Mercosur is a proclaimed customs union in which countries aspire to have a common external tariff and a common trade policy). This 'temporary' measure abolished duties on imports of capital goods from outside Mercosur and increased tariffs on imports of consumer goods to 35 per cent. In 2004 alone, Argentina introduced import restrictions on Brazilian goods three times. Trade relations in Mercosur are passing through a complicated and frustrating phase. Like many other integration deals in Latin America, Mercosur's strength seems to be dwindling.

It is relatively early to predict whether southern integration is 'irreversible' given the regional history of many integration schemes that did not take off. While Argentina and Chile[22] favour expansion of trade and formal ties with the US, Brazil favours the expansion of Mercosur as a counterweight to the US-dominated Free Trade Area of the Americas (FTAA). As such, Brazil is building strategic commercial and other alliances between Mercosur, on the one side, and the EU and emerging economic powers such as China, India, South Africa and Malaysia, on the other. Colombia, Ecuador and Venezuela are expected to become the new associate members of Mercosur.

Mercosur has introduced at least two positive developments. One is the pledge to create a liberal trade regime. The region became more open to trade (and investment) than was the case for several decades prior to its creation. Many domestic industries and foreign TNCs started to think and act in regional terms. Intra-regional trade increased significantly during the 1990s. The other is the reinforcement of the rule of democratic[23] governments that regarded Mercosur as a long-term project of regional integration among the participating countries. Past military tensions among countries (particularly between Argentina and Brazil) in the region have subsided. However, macroeconomic crises put a stop to Mercosur. Should Mercosur become only a free trade area in the new situation? This is a less ambitious arrangement than a customs union, but perhaps more workable given the circumstances.

If integration-prone approaches continue to develop in the region, then the potential Western Hemisphere Free Trade Area may be a deal between NAFTA (led by the US) and Mercosur (led by Brazil). But would it be a completely new institution or would it be an extension of NAFTA? Interest in the deal could be reinforced if countries such as Brazil grow at relatively high rates without major interruptions. Regional integration can provide a supporting tool for growth, but it will never be a substitute for sound national macroeconomic policies.

The strengthening of Mercosur worries the US. Each time the group increases its scope or coverage, the US initiates an obstructive action. The most obvious case was an offer to Chile to negotiate a free trade deal, just when Chile was about to join Mercosur as a full member. The US refusal to bail out the Argentinian economy (via the IMF) from the debt-repayment crisis in 2002 could be seen in the same light.[24] Mercosur was significantly weakened by the crisis in Argentina, which helped the US aim to 'divide and conquer', as well as to maintain its supremacy over Latin American economies.

The future of Mercosur depends in part on developments linked with the FTAA. If the FTAA expands on a larger and deeper scale, and if Mercosur is confined only to free trade within the group, then the rationale for Mercosur will disappear. Deeper regional integration than a free trade area may provide the way forward for this group.

The leaders of 12 South American countries met in Peru in 2004 and signed an agreement concerning the creation of the South American Community of Nations (SACN). The new grand idea is similar to the EU. In practice, this will mean a long-term merger between Mercosur and the Andean Community. The arrangement is somewhat loose and its institutional structure needs to be worked out in the future.

The new pan-south American free trade area (economic integration) is prompted by several factors. One of them is a certain informal political integration in the region. Left-leaning parties dominate governments in the countries in the region. This new political wave is the consequence of the failure of liberal market policies and democratisation driven by the 'Washington Consensus'.[25] Most people in the region saw the period from the early 1990s as one in which there was a widening gap between the rich and the poor; increasing corruption among the governing elites; and a decline in the welfare state. Voting patterns veered to the left.

The US continues to resist opening a domestic market for South American farm goods and pursues a restrictive immigration policy. In addition, the 'war on terrorism' considerably reduced the US interest in Latin America. If one's own backyard is neglected for too long, someone else may move in. None the less, Colombia, Ecuador and Peru (nominally members of the Andean Community) are negotiating bilateral trade deals with the US. This shows both the priority of national interests over other interests[26] and the insignificance of the Andean Community as a 'northern tier' of southern America. Mercosur is equally split. Instead of discussing trade deals as a group, both Argentina and Brazil signed bilateral trade agreements with China in 2004. Paraguay and Uruguay were dismayed and protested because of this lack of concern for Mercosur. Brazil, as the biggest country in the SACN, could potentially make the biggest political and trade gains in this group.

China is not only a supplier of mass-market manufactured goods, but also a prominent importer of South American commodities. China's weakness is a shortage in raw materials such as oil, gas, minerals and food. Roughly half of China's exports by value represent imported inputs (Tongzon, 2005, p. 204). Just after signing the bilateral trade deal with China in 2004, and the Chinese pledge to invest $20 billion in Argentinian energy and transport, Argentina announced the imposition of trade restrictions against an influx of low-priced Chinese manufactured goods, textiles in particular. Argentina was concerned not to repeat the 'mistake' made by Mexico. Once Mexico started trading with China on a larger scale during the 1990s and early 2000s, hundreds of thousands of jobs in the domestic manufacturing industry were 'lost' to China. On average, Chinese labour is better educated, more advanced in terms of using modern technology and often costs less than half of comparable labour in Latin America. Opposition to a larger-scale liberalisation of trade may slow down economic opening towards China. As China needs South American raw materials, it may be difficult and frustrating to put up with the slow opening of the Latin American markets for its manufactured goods.

South American countries have a new opportunity to work out a regional free trade deal without a large-scale US involvement. The intentions and goals of the new SACN must turn into real action. The lack of a timetable for action reveals two things: the simplicity and flexibility of the SACN, and the lack of confidence (based on experience?) in reaching an agreement. This points to possible unexpected problems in reaching an agreement on an integration deal among countries that are located in a culturally consistent region. The risk is that the SACN can be surpassed by other broader trade negotiations and possible deals. In any case, the pan-south American free trade area fully applied in practice is still a distant dream.

5.3.4 THE CENTRAL AMERICAN COMMON MARKET

The Central American Common Market (CACM),[27] established in 1960, had a misleading name from the outset. The group was similar to a customs union, as factor mobility was not allowed. The common external tariff, however, was introduced in 1970. In spite of a relatively long period of development, the 'real' effect of the CACM group has been quite small.

The member countries intended to industrialise by means of integration. The instrument employed was the creation of a customs union. The market was enlarged, but it was still too small to permit more than a single (monopolistic) firm to operate efficiently in most manufacturing industries. Industrialisation should be accomplished by an import-substitution strategy. Since backward linkages were weak, consumer goods that were produced in the group had substantial import content.

Industrialists have not been a strong pressure group in the region in comparison to land-owners. Therefore, investors have considered returns between the manufacturing industry and agriculture, rather than between different manufacturing industries. If profits were made and if returns justified such a decision, then investment was usually made outside the manufacturing sector. In spite of the initial increase in regional trade, supported by a relatively stable macroeconomic situation, the major cause of CACM failure can be found in the lack of an established structure within which industrialisation of the group can arise (Bulmer-Thomas, 1988, pp. 302–3). In addition, the macroeconomic situation worsened at the end of the 1970s and the introduction of exchange controls led to further disintegration of the group since the goods traded with the CACM partners were not high priority.

A stagnation of the CACM started after the war between El Salvador and Honduras in 1969 and the subsequent exit of Honduras from the scheme. After that, rapid decline of the group followed throughout the 1980s when member countries were faced with oil shocks, budget deficits, unemployment and inflation; they acted unilaterally and restricted even the intra-group trade. The actual role of the CACM moved from economic integration to an arena for soliciting peace.

The small markets of CACM member countries were not attractive to TNCs prior to the establishment of the scheme. After its creation, interest by the TNCs increased. Out of 155 foreign manufacturing subsidiaries at the end of the 1960s, only 10 had established more than one plant in the CACM (UNCTAD, 1983, p. 14). Although such a concentration of sellers might point to the existence of economies of scale and a potential benefit to the integrated countries, in practice the situation was different. TNCs were sourcing components from outside of the area and they were uninterested in exporting output to third countries. If the member countries had chosen an outward-oriented economic strategy, the outcome would perhaps have been different.

Although there are still various impediments to integration in the region, ranging from economic, including most importantly NTBs (there are no CACM tools to eliminate them), to military issues, the CACM continues to function. In fact, at the 1967 conference in Punta del Este (Uruguay) the Latin American presidents decided that LAIA and the CACM would be the basis for a comprehensive Latin American common market by the early 1990s. However, little progress has been made along those lines.

The new surge of interest in integration in the 1990s altered the initial CACM industrial development strategy towards export-led growth. Given the small size of the CACM internal market, member countries accord a high importance to exports outside the group. They have made a thorough evaluation of the possible costs and benefits of the FTAA.

5.3.5 FREE TRADE AREA OF THE AMERICAS

The Enterprise for the Americas Initiative announced by the US in 1990 aspired to support market reforms throughout Latin America. The means for backing these reforms included an increase in trade and FDI and relieving foreign debt, as well as environmental control and improvement. The bilateral framework agreements, quite loose in origin, between the US and almost all Latin American countries, set the agenda for consultations.[28] There is a stated willingness by the US to enter into free trade arrangements with Latin American countries on bilateral bases, although the Latin American group would prefer a multilateral deal. However, a country that is to be considered eligible for free trade has to satisfy ‘indicators of readiness’ which include a stable market and macroeconomic system, outward orientation and a pledge to the multilateral trading system. These framework agreements were, as their name suggests, merely a prelude to what may take place in the (distant) future. Latin American countries have expressed an interest in achieving secure economic links with the US since intra-Latin American trade and FDI are less important for these countries than similar ties with the US. The problem is how much access would they get and for which goods? Another issue is the price to be paid for such access to the US market and for enhanced FDI from this country. This price may include the acceptance of a deal on intellectual property rights.

The Enterprise for the Americas Initiative may have a profound and, even, undermining effect on integration among the Latin American countries. As is well known, many of those countries are much more interested in wide and secure trade access and FDI relations with the US than among themselves. Internal trade within integration groups of the developing countries does not offer even a medium-term alternative to their economic relations with one of the hub partners in the developed world. Mexico is an example of this.

The initiative may be a step towards the Western Hemisphere Free Trade Area (from Alaska to Tierra del Fuego).[29] Although it is not its stated goal, the initiative may evolve into the textbook example of the hub-and-spoke model of international economic integration with dominance by the US. Increased trade with the US may further undermine the relatively low level of trade within the region and increase the dependence on the hub country. With the uncertain future of (democratic) governments in the region and proliferating economic sanctions on an ad hoc basis without any universally applicable criteria for their introduction and lifting (everyone is somewhere a sinner), considerable economic reliance on a big hub partner may be a reason for concern. 'Indicators of readiness' for preferential treatment are a powerful mechanism for discrimination and extraction of concessions. In addition, countries that enter into a preferential deal with the US may present an obstacle to further liberalisation in the region since their initial preferences may be eroded by the expansion of the preferential scheme.

Lipsey (1992a, p. 17) presented arguments why Canada and all Latin American countries should resist the hub-and-spoke model of integration in the western hemisphere:

- As the hub country, the US is the only one with free entry to the markets of all participating countries. On the reverse side of the coin, all other spoke countries have free access only to the US market. The clear beneficiary of such an arrangement is the US.
- Locating a plant in any of the spoke countries offers free access only to the local market and the US. Investment in the US provides free

access to all countries in the arrangement. TNCs will definitely keep that option in mind. The US would be the only beneficiary of such FDI diversion.

- The US is in a better bargaining position than its other partners. Smaller partners may have to forgo many of their spheres of interest and may not wish to 'rock the boat' with their common cause in certain matters simply in order not to jeopardise negotiations and free access to the US market.

The leaders of 34 western hemisphere countries agreed in Miami in 1994 to negotiate a Free Trade Area of the Americas initially projected by 2005 and to apply it by 2015. Many things have changed since that time. Countries that have comprehensive free trade deals with the US (Canada and Mexico), as well as Bolivia, Colombia, Ecuador and Peru, would like the FTAA to be similar to NAFTA, as would the US, since it may dominate in such an arrangement. Others, notably Brazil (which may 'go it alone'), would like to see a less wide-ranging FTAA deal. Brazil may prefer an expansion and deepening of Mercosur where it could dominate.

Many Latin American countries, however, fear that the adjustment cost of free trade with the US would principally fall on them, while the US has certain concerns about the flight of jobs to the low-wage countries (principally to Asia even if there is the FTAA). In addition, the US administration did not get the 'fast track' mandate for this deal. None the less, the Latin American countries can see a huge shift in the location of production towards Asia, in particular China, as well as to India and Vietnam. The Latin American countries consider the FTAA as one of the possible responses to this change in the global manufacturing landscape.

When there is a discriminatory trade liberalisation, then a country gains in static terms from the opening up of partners' markets and 'loses' from its own trade liberalisation. As the US already has low tariffs on average, while these tariffs are high in Latin America, then the US (and Canada) may easily gain more in static terms in the FTAA than may do the Latin American countries. In fact, Latin American countries may gain little in static terms from the FTAA. Dynamic benefits are much more important for them. On the other hand, the US is interested in having politically stable neighbours, which would increase its general security.

The FTAA deal would secure access to the regional, particularly the US, market for manufactured goods (the US would keep trade in farm goods separate); it would protect the countries, as much as possible, primarily from unilateral US protectionist measures; and it would reinforce the drive of the Latin American countries towards the road of reform, modernisation and adjustment. In addition, countries like to be a member of a select club such as NAFTA. At the same time, without certain compensation, the deal could make the Latin American countries highly vulnerable to the economic situation in the US. This may give way to a certain more modest version of the FTAA.

The above considerations dealt with certain theoretical possibilities related to the FTAA. In reality, negotiations have been grounded since 2000 and the whole FTAA idea has been largely ignored throughout Latin America. There are deep differences between the principal actors, Brazil and the US, which contributed to this stalemate. While the US still wants to keep agriculture out of the FTAA, Brazil has no motivation to make any compromise on intellectual property rights, telecommunications and transport. In the meantime the US has pursued a policy of bilateral free trade agreements with individual countries such as Chile (implemented in 2003) and a small group of central American countries, as well as Colombia, Ecuador and Peru. Brazil, on the other hand, has been quite glad to associate with several South American states through Mercosur.

The US will keep the FTAA issue on the agenda as it has not come up with a better substitute. Security is the prime external policy preoccupation of the US. Voters in Latin America do not tend to align with the US on this issue. The fading US interest in the region opens certain possibilities to the EU, China, India and even Russia to step in and expand their economic and certain political influence.

5.4 Asia and the Pacific

5.4.1 ASIA PACIFIC ECONOMIC COOPERATION AND OPEN REGIONALISM

Concerns about 'Fortress North America' prompted by the protectionist lobbies in the US during the 1980s and early 1990s could provoke reactions in the countries of the Pacific region. In spite of the integration of countries at a significantly different level of per capita income and concerns about adjustments in the labour market in the US and Canada, negotiations on NAFTA were relatively quick. The free trade deal eliminated tariffs on internal trade among the three member countries. None the less, restrictive rules of origin are the major means of protection. They are most restrictive for vehicles, textiles and apparel. A trans-Pacific extension of free trade would, perhaps, have taken place if the result of the Uruguay Round had been ambiguous. As that was not the case, reactive regionalism in the Pacific region was not high on the regional agenda.

The 'open regionalism' has its impact on east Asian countries. Economic integration in Europe has been deepening and widening, it is settling in North America and there is a renewed interest in integration in South America. What is the place and future of east Asia in the new wave of international economic integration? If the multilateral trading process does not operate in a satisfactory way for the east Asian countries, should they create a regional trading bloc of their own? The countries in the region would increase their bargaining power *vis-à-vis* other economic groups. Most of the countries in the region followed similar economic strategies and created competitive, rather than complementary, economic structures (but they have a different type and degree of protection). Hence, they have a strong orientation towards extra-regional markets.

Joint bargaining would be beneficial for east Asia. However, an east Asian trading bloc may not materialise in reality. There are several reasons for this. These include a possible tough reaction from North America which could end up in a 'trade war'. If east Asian countries threaten to form a trading bloc in order to influence the trade policy of North America, then such a threat has to be credible. Who is going to lead east Asian countries 'against' North America? Is it Japan, China, South Korea or some other country?[30] Weak political leadership and national resistance to a surrender of trade and industrial policy to a common institution prevent the creation of a regional economic bloc. An east Asia-Pacific group would suffer from a similar problem of effectiveness. Therefore, east Asian countries may wish to continue to support a multilateral trading system.

The emerging Asia Pacific Economic Cooperation (APEC),[31] created in 1989, can be used as a forum for discussing issues related to the liberalisation of regional and global trade (a kind of diluted Asian version of the OECD). Annual meetings are used more and more as high-level political forums to discuss cooperation and security matters, and sometimes to announce certain trade liberalisation measures. There is no procedure to bargain for tariff changes and there are no binding offers and commitments. The APEC relies on unilateral tariff concessions by the members which do not discriminate against non-members. Such a type of 'open regionalism' is practised only within APEC.

The 1994 Jakarta Summit announced a 'grand plan' and a very long-term goal to create a free trade area in the APEC region. The industrialised countries ought to remove trade and investment barriers by 2010, while the less-developed members need to do the same by 2020. 'By then most of the leaders who met in Jakarta will be long out of office, forgotten or dead'[32] were the words of Guy de Jonquières, who questioned the credibility of such commitments. In addition, a number of Asian countries do not accord high importance to liberal trade and economic integration as they developed well without regional arrangements and (fully) open national economies.

A free trade area between the US on the one hand and Japan or China on the other cannot be envisaged for a long time. This would be linked with many hard and controversial issues such as trade in rice, fish, textiles, steel, computers and biotechnology. Many APEC countries are angered by the US curbs on imports of steel, textiles and a basket of other products. In addition, there are important national barriers such as internal business relations, industrial structures, labour issues, relations with the government and distribution systems that are so different that a mere free trade arrangement (in manufactured goods) perhaps may not be sufficient to overcome them. Any real trade-related action in APEC is occurring at a snail's pace. In fact a true economic dialogue in APEC is becoming a thing of the past. Would it be simpler and better to make those trade deals at the WTO? Would the possible Doha Round agreement (or any other WTO trade liberalisation deal) devalue real efforts to free trade (if any) by APEC?

The growth of new institutions reveals that there may be in part certain dissatisfaction with the existing ones. However, if such similar institutions provide 'more of the same', the danger is that time, energy and resources are dissipated on competing activities that may not always work in favour of the region they want to assist.

5.4.2 ASSOCIATION OF SOUTH-EAST ASIAN NATIONS

The geographical location of south-east Asia is at one of the most important natural crossroads of world trade. Countries in the region benefited considerably from this spatial location, in particular from the 16th century, when there was an economic expansion of Europe and India on the one side, and of Japan and China on the other.[33] Subsequently this region developed a vibrant trade with the Americas.[34]

It is hard to imagine an integration scheme that unites such diverse countries as the Association of South-East Asian Nations (ASEAN). The member countries not only vary markedly regarding their size and level of development, but are also heterogeneous due to a host of social issues such as language, history, religion and culture. The approach of ASEAN to integration was in stark contrast to most of the schemes that integrate developing countries. Instead of grand programmes for trade liberalisation, joint production and a vast institutional structure, ASEAN approached integration differently. The institutional structure was light and there were no formal and detailed blueprints for integration. The Bangkok Declaration (1967) merely calls, in a general way, for the participating countries[35] to cooperate in areas of regional interest. This included cooperation to accelerate economic growth, social progress and cultural development in the region. There was no supranational institutional set-up and the activities all followed the principle of unanimity in decision making.

For a decade, ASEAN was only a political (conflict prevention and resolution) organisation. Such a low profile and slow approach to regional economic integration might have worked in support of ASEAN's attempt to establish itself as a regional entity. The diversity among the countries was so immense that, probably, not many other approaches could have survived. The main instruments of cooperation were preferential trade, industrial projects and industrial complementarity.

In spite of the preferences for intra-group trade, the member countries trade mostly with developed countries. None the less, internal trade in the ASEAN countries is by far the largest compared with all other integration groups among the developing countries (over 20 per cent of external trade). This relative level of internal trade may be quite misleading since a notable part of it is directed through Singapore which is not the final destination of goods. In fact, an important share of internal trade is redirected to external markets, in particular to the US.

A further increase in internal trade was expected to be brought by the decisions reached at the Manila Summit (1987). Coverage of the preferential trade arrangements was expanded to include more commodity items, preferences granted were widened and the exclusion lists of 'sensitive items' were limited to 10 per cent of traded goods. Although such a move could enhance links within the region, the ASEAN countries approved at their Singapore Summit (1992) an agreement to create an ASEAN Free Trade Area within the coming 15 years.[36] It was one of their responses to the growing regionalism in the world and uncertain developments in multilateral negotiations about trade liberalisation.

The goals of the ASEAN Free Trade Area include a reduction in the level of tariffs on manufactured goods to a level not higher than 20 per cent in five to eight years, and to a level of up to 5 per cent before the year 2008 (later extended to 2010).[37] Such a (long) timetable is in place because of the accommodation of the demands of the less-developed ASEAN countries (such as Indonesia and the Philippines), as well as national differences on the policy stances regarding different economic sectors and industries within them. Primary farm goods and services are beyond the scope of the free trade regime. A further issue that may frustrate a deeper free trade area is NTBs originating in differences in national taxes, standards and political connections in doing business.[38]

The new free trade area arrangement refers only to manufactured goods. Although everything moves very slowly in ASEAN, the free trade area technique of integration within the region may have a realistic chance of success because of such a disparate membership. With some exceptions, the member countries are among the swiftest growing economies in the world. It makes sense to settle a single production unit with significant economies of scale for standardised goods in a market of about 500 million consumers with growing incomes, rather than to locate seven separate suboptimal units that serve local markets. This may have a profound influence on the inflow of FDI into the region. However, the problem with ASEAN enlargement is that some of the poorest countries in the world joined the group. That may divert energies away from trade liberalisation.

As a more integrated group, the ASEAN countries may have greater leverage in international talks on trade, bearing in mind the splintering of the world market into trade blocs. In addition to the perils of protectionism in the US and the EU, another element that encourages efforts towards tighter integration in ASEAN is the enduring and rapid growth of Asia.

The ASEAN government-to-government industrial projects had as their objective the installation of large-scale capital-intensive ventures. These were perceived to be flexible ventures and, therefore, only the interested ASEAN parties took part in them. The projects for Indonesia and Malaysia (urea), Singapore (diesel engine), Thailand (soda-ash) and the Philippines (superphosphate) were in the first package deal to be considered in 1976. To help these projects get off the ground, the Japanese government promised $1 billion in soft loans. However, the package of projects soon got into various kinds of trouble. Owing to a host of political and economic reasons, one being monopoly rights, only the Indonesian and Malaysian projects were initiated and that was made possible by Japanese assistance (Wong, 1988, p. 323).

The purpose of the ASEAN industrial projects was to introduce grand and state-led industrial projects, while the goal of industrial complementation schemes was to link the existing manufacturing industries (promote complementarity) without government intervention and to serve as a substitute for industrial projects. Since the industrial projects were largely unsuccessful, cooperation energy shifted towards industrial complementarity. None the less, the approval process was so cumbersome that it rendered it unattractive to investors. The Manila Summit (1987) simplified the approval process, increased the margin of tariff preference to 90 per cent for approved products and proposed an increase in the foreign equity participation to 60 per cent. Since the changes were subsequently accepted, there was certain initial interest in the usage of those facilities.

The concept of joint ventures in the group, even though they were among flexible private firms, was attractive in theory. What happened in practice was different. The member countries followed similar industrial strategies and they competed with their goods more than they complemented each other. As such, an across-the-board tariff reduction within the group could jeopardise national industrialisation strategies in spite of a plethora of NTBs that are still in effect. Since ASEAN national strategies took priority over regional ones, the common interest of the group always assumed secondary status, hence the record of joint manufacturing efforts was quite poor. In fact, in the case of ASEAN, regional economic integration played an insignificant part in the economic success of the countries in the region. What mattered first and foremost for that success was the soundness of the national macroeconomic situation, as well as national economic policies that supported trade relations with the principal partners outside ASEAN.

None of the integration projects mentioned provided a leap forward to a deeper integration. The ASEAN group could be seen more as a conflict resolution mechanism than a genuine international economic integration group. The regional market is still largely the sum of separate markets of the member countries. The group has, nevertheless, established a dialogue with major trading partners. With a few exceptions, the member countries have had an open mind and open policy towards FDI. Economic strategy was almost always open towards the rest of the world and the involvement of foreign TNCs was most pronounced in the electronics-related industries in the region. Strong engines of manufacturing growth to the countries in the region came from the involvement of TNCs, initially because of relatively low labour costs. TNCs brought with them not only the necessary manufacturing and management technologies, but also employment and wide international marketing networks. The indigenous business community was receptive to the establishment of sourcing, subcontracting and other links with TNCs, which created potentials for positive externalities for the host country. This was particularly important since the output of the TNCs was basically (in the initial stage) for export, mainly, but not exclusively, to the US. Relatively competition-prone ASEAN industrialists were very receptive towards the positive externalities that came from the involvement of TNCs in their national economies. In fact, the learning, absorption, extension and upgrading process of the business in the new circumstances made them certain that they were capable of competing successfully on the national, regional and international market without protective national or regional economic policies.

The ASEAN Industrial Cooperation Scheme of 1996 is supposed to replace earlier ineffective cooperation plans in manufacturing. This scheme attempts to attract new technology-based FDI. It is open to any investor, but the local ASEAN equity must be at least 30 per cent, while the ASEAN content in output has to be at least 40 per cent. As bait, ASEAN offers a simple and fast administrative approval procedure, as well as big tariff concessions for internal trade and removal of NTBs. Thailand is most active in this scheme, followed by Indonesia, Malaysia and the Philippines. There are also moves to liberalise trade in services (although, this is prompted by the WTO trade liberalisation deals).

In spite of all the integration efforts, national trade policies remained largely independent from each other in the group. In fact, only Brunei and Singapore were free trade nations in the group. Hence, what was the major value added of the group to its member countries? Well, ASEAN (an economic integration enigma) provided a communication channel for member countries in discussions about economic and political relations with major trading partners. In addition, an outward-oriented model of cooperation instead of inward-oriented trade and industrial policies has given ASEAN an international reputation. One of the major lessons that ASEAN can offer to other schemes is that economic 'integration' is no more than a supporting tool for a sound national economic policy (Langhammer, 1991).

The financial crisis[39] in south-east Asia in 1997 contributed to the rise of China as a strong economic driving force in the world. The economic dynamism of China is based on factors that include a huge and growing internal market; low labour costs; increasing manufacturing, engineering and logistic potentials; as well as political stability. China represents for the ASEAN a continuous, strong and growing competitor for the same type of incoming FDI and for the same market for exports (the US and the EU).[40] This diversion of FDI away from the ASEAN countries and the possible creation of the FTAA which may have a similar effect, prompted ASEAN to reconsider its future direction and objectives. One of the opportunities is China, a country that imports food and raw materials.

Since the Asian financial crises in 1997, which slowed down extraordinary growth in most of the countries in the region, ASEAN has held informal meetings with China, Japan and South Korea. The 'ASEAN Plus Three' met initially to discuss monetary issues, but talks began to include other matters too. Certain ideas have been put forward concerning the formalisation of these relations.

The contribution and impact of informal but strong, effective and tightly knit clans and networks of ethnic Chinese in Asia should not be disregarded in integration efforts, trade and FDI in Asia, even though there are no firm data and ways to measure it at present. Estimates are that there are about 60 million ethnic Chinese who live in Asia outside China. Half of them are in the ASEAN countries (Byeong-hae, 2004, p. 508). With the opening up of China for trade and FDI, the 'overseas' Chinese tend to establish and expand business relations with the country with which they have historical, cultural, linguistic and even family ties. This network may play the role of an (informal) accelerator in the integration process.

As far as economic integration is concerned, ASEAN is regarded as slow, bureaucratic and indecisive. Trade, particularly external trade, has always been important for the ASEAN countries. Hence, internal ASEAN integration and trade should perhaps function like strong external trade relations. The still fragmented internal market and bureaucracy are significant obstacles to doing business in ASEAN. With no free factor flows, China is a more favourable location for FDI than ASEAN. Hence, 'ASEAN Plus Three' may be a way to make this region more economically viable in the future. In fact, the ASEAN leaders and China decided during the 2000 summit to enhance economic cooperation and integration with the goal of creating an ASEAN–China free trade area. This may bring economic benefits to all parties involved, but it may also cause serious challenges, as China is already a formidable competitor in trade and a strong magnet for FDI on its own account. China may, however, be a good market for ASEAN raw materials including food and a promising source of FDI. Hence the basic relations may be complementary.[41]

Regional organisations that integrate countries in the region have been slow to evolve and grow roots of any significance. Therefore, countries in the region face a conundrum. Which of the two regional organisations will bring them bigger benefits? Is it an enlarged ASEAN or APEC? ASEAN is based on non-intervention,[42] consensus building and weak institutional structure with slow and difficult decision-making procedures. APEC with its openness is elastic and accessible, but ambiguous. On the economic side, both of them are regarded as ineffective and weak. Note that the reason for their establishment was, just like the EU, inter-state conflict prevention (this aspect receives full marks with regard to achievements).

Integration in the region was applied through trade and FDI before the 1997 financial crises. In the following years when FDI shifted to China, monetary cooperation and fostering of regional production networks gained prominence. Hence, bringing China (and other countries) into a kind of regional arrangement, as well as cooperation in the monetary sphere in the region, need a higher profile. This regional nature is relevant as such an organisation would know and appreciate regional needs and possibilities better than a global institution that imposes one size on all.

The leaders of 10 ASEAN counties met in 2003 and agreed on a new ambitious course for the organisation. In the light of slow trade liberalisation progress in the WTO and no real trade-related evolution in APEC, the leaders agreed to transform ASEAN into a group with a free flow of goods, services and investment by 2020. An arrangement, similar to the

EU, may provide these countries with market access assurance, which in turn could contribute to a better employment of internal resources, which could more readily attract FDI. Singapore and Thailand are exploring ways to inspire the other ASEAN partners to speed up the process, fearing that 2020 is too far away in the light of external and challenging factors such as China and the possible FTAA. If this takes place, a possible '10 minus X principle' may dilute ASEAN as a relatively cohesive organisation (recall that ASEAN was created to act as a unified bloc). As ASEAN lost its initial international clout, this possible dilution may be the price to be paid in order to face the economic challenge from China. In this set-up, less-developed countries such as Cambodia, Laos and Vietnam will lag behind the faster-moving ASEAN core. Time will tell whether these aspirations will be applied and whether this is enough to improve ASEAN's economic performance.

5.4.3 AUSTRALIA AND NEW ZEALAND

Integration arrangements between Australia and New Zealand have escaped attention by many in Europe and North America. These two high-income countries specialise in primary commodities – Australia in mining and agriculture, New Zealand in agriculture and forestry – and they have had a free trade agreement since 1966. It was replaced by the agreement on Closer Economic Relations (CER) Treaty in 1983. Free trade in goods within the group was achieved in 1990, five years ahead of the deadline specified in the agreement. In addition, there has been internal free trade in almost all services since 1989. The two countries have strong and developed cooperation in areas that include mutual recognition (goods that can be legally sold in one country can be sold in the other; a person who is licensed to practise an occupation in one country has the right to do the same in the other); open skies; harmonisation of customs policies and procedures,[43] food standards and business law; and avoidance of double taxation.

Market forces will drive the economies of Australia and New Zealand towards deeper integration, hence the two countries may proceed in the future towards some kind of single market. A single currency, however, is not yet advocated. As all big companies from Australia do business in New Zealand and vice versa, there is a market-induced drive to improve co-ordination in competition policy, in particular authorisations of mergers and acquisitions. In addition, there are moves afoot to strengthen commercial and FDI relations with the ASEAN countries, first formally established in 1995, and the establishment of a free trade area between the two groups by 2010 is being considered.

5.5 Africa

5.5.1 EAST AFRICAN COMMUNITY

Paradoxically, economic integration in the East African Community (EAC) (1967–77) among Kenya, Tanzania and Uganda can be observed not as a way towards regional integration, but rather as a step towards disintegration of the countries in the region. These countries were 'integrated' before they achieved independence. However, the colonial era arrangement could not be expected to continue without alteration, as there was an issue about the distribution of benefits of integration (basically the location of firms and industries). Tanzania and Uganda felt that regional integration favoured the more industrialised Kenya.

In theory, a regional EAC transfer tax was supposed to provide certain protection to industries in the less-developed countries in the group. In practice, it encouraged subscale replication of industries in the EAC countries, which contributed to relatively high unit costs of production. The East African Development Bank was supposed to complement the financing of projects that would make the industries of the countries complementary. The countries, however, made little progress regarding their industrial planning which was supposed to contribute to the fair sharing of benefits of integration. Regional differences were exacerbated by ideological problems as Kenya was 'capitalist' and welcomed foreign investors while Tanzania was 'socialist' and resisted it (unless they came from the socialist bloc). Economic integration in the group was perceived as a zero-, even a negative-sum game. In those circumstances, the EAC faded away as no interest was shown by the participants in keeping it alive (Hazlewood, 1988).

5.5.2 CENTRAL AFRICAN CUSTOMS AND ECONOMIC UNION

The major novelty brought by the Central African Customs and Economic Union (Union douanière et économique de l'Afrique centrale: UDEAC)[44] in trade relations with its members was the single tax (*taxe unique*). Goods manufactured in UDEAC and sold in more than one of its member states were subject to a single tax that was always lower than the customs duty. The single tax was supposed to provide incentives for industrialisation in this economic union.

The UDEAC countries started to compete with one another in order to attract foreign investors with incentives that included duty-free imports of capital goods and other inputs. TNCs entered the region and dominated the manufacturing industries there. They segmented local markets, linked those markets with inputs from the developed countries and created an oligopolistic, even monopolistic, local market structure. A replication of manufacturing in small batches in the countries of the group increased the costs of production, but TNCs were able to pass these high costs of production on to consumers in the form of higher prices. A lack of any coherent industrial planning at both domestic and regional levels, uneven distribution of benefits and an absence of an effective regional financial institution may be the primary culprits for the weak progress of integration in UDEAC (Mytelka, 1984).

The UDEAC countries decided to breathe new life into the situation. Therefore, in 1998 they established the Economic and Monetary Community of Central Africa. This transformed institution aimed to create an economic and a monetary union, as well as to harmonise industrial projects.

5.5.3 ECONOMIC COMMUNITY OF WEST AFRICAN STATES

Nigeria was the country that spearheaded the creation of the Economic Community of West African States (ECOWAS)[45] in 1975 as a means of reducing French influence in the region. In addition, Nigeria, a noted exporter of oil, planned to use the group as a way of increasing its own economic and political authority in the region. The ambitious goal was to create a common market. The ECOWAS countries are a mix of diverse, mainly, but not exclusively, anglophone and francophone countries. As the production structure of the countries in the region is generally characterised by the production of very similar goods, it comes as no surprise that internal trade in ECOWAS was unimportant for participating countries.

The Fund for Co-operation, Compensation and Development, although conceived as a means for the promotion of a fair and equitable distribution of benefits of integration, had very limited effect on the group because of the financing problem. In the short and medium terms, real progress in economic development in a situation of severe poverty may not depend much, or primarily, on the integration arrangement, but rather on the discovery and exploitation of natural resources and the consequent ample inflow of FDI.[46] Useful industrial, regional and social policies may be necessary for the alleviation of the rough times linked to the distribution of the costs and benefits of integration.

The existence of smaller integration groups within ECOWAS such as the Mano River Union,[47] the Economic Community of West Africa[48] (a French tool to check the influence of Nigeria in the region from 1973) and the

Senegambian Confederation made decision making difficult. The member countries were not always convinced that ECOWAS offered a better arrangement than the smaller and cosier integration groups. A policy of trade liberalisation in the absence of supporting regional and industrial policies in ECOWAS was mainly responsible for keeping the group only at the blueprint stage (Robson, 1983). A revision of the ECOWAS treaty of 1993 brought no visible change in the life of ECOWAS.

There are constant behind-the-scene differences and tensions between the largest and English-speaking country Nigeria and the French-speaking group, notably Ivory Coast. This may continue to contribute to the slow progress in economic integration in ECOWAS. In fact, the francophone countries established the West African Economic and Monetary Union (WAEMU)[49] in 1994 in order to solve their own economic and monetary integration affairs. The other six ECOWAS members (the Gambia, Ghana, Guinea, Liberia, Nigeria and Sierra Leone) signed a treaty in 2000 to establish a second monetary union in the area, the West African Monetary Zone (WAMZ). They set the following convergence criteria (inspired by the Maastricht Treaty): a budget deficit of at most 4 per cent of GDP; the central bank may finance the budget deficit up to 10 per cent of the previous year's tax receipts; inflation should not be more then 5 per cent; and hard currency reserves ought to cover at least six months of imports. They also envisaged the West African Monetary Institute as a provisional institution that would evolve into the West African Central Bank, which would manage a common currency, the eco, from 2003. Progress to achieve these goals has been absent. Therefore, the WAMZ countries decided in 2002 to postpone the deadline for two years. Even the July 2005 deadline was missed because of the lack of convergence towards the stated criteria. In addition, the IMF was against the WAMZ, because the group would be dominated by Nigeria whose imbalances would be translated into monetary instability throughout the WAMZ.

From the early 1990s, ECOWAS was quite active and successful in the area of regional security. Examples include Liberia in 1990, Sierra Leone in 1997, Guinea Bissau in 1998 and Liberia in 2003. However, factors that work against a deeper integration in the ECOWAS include: suspicion between the English- and the French-speaking member countries; distrust regarding Nigeria as the biggest and strongest country in the group; political instability in the region; as well as the lack of financial resources.

5.5.4 SOUTH AFRICAN CUSTOMS UNION

The Southern African Customs Union (SACU), the oldest operating customs union in the world, was created in 1910 between South Africa and its neighbours (Botswana, Lesotho, Swaziland and Namibia).[50] It was underpinned by a monetary arrangement in which the South African rand was the dominant currency. This arrangement between a 'developed' (according to many criteria applied for African countries) and several developing countries had as one of its consequences trade diversion. In particular, South Africa was not the cheapest source of supply for many items imported by its partners in the deal.

SACU has a system for the redistribution of customs revenue. This is supposed to favour the less-developed countries and to compensate them for the costs of polarisation in the location of industries and the loss of fiscal discretion. In spite of the problems of trade diversion and a polarisation of economic activity towards South Africa, even during the apartheid days, the SACU members maintained an interest in keeping and strengthening the scheme. New political realities in the post-apartheid South Africa gave SACU a fresh impetus. The 2000 reform introduced the following bodies:

- *Council of Ministers*: the supreme decision-making body; decisions must be unanimous.
- *Commission*: the administrative body, comprising senior officials.
- *Tribunal*: an independent body that reports to the Council of Ministers and deals with tariff setting and antidumping measures.
- *Secretariat*: deals with day-to-day operations.

The revenue allocation among SACU members, according to the reform implemented in 2004, is calculated on the basis of three components, two based on the member country share in the customs and excise pools plus a development component.

A regular and stable inflow of resources is important for countries that depend a lot on customs revenue such as Lesotho and Swaziland. Roughly half of government income comes from this source in either country. The new revenue-sharing formula treats customs and excise duties separately. South Africa, as the principal intra-regional exporter, supplies most of the funds (about 80 per cent). Most of the excise pool (85 per cent) is distributed in proportion to the share of the member country's GDP, while the rest goes to the poorest countries. Member countries meet towards the end of each year to determine the size of the funds to be distributed during the following fiscal year. In the case of disagreement, a panel of experts would resolve the problem. This is supposed to provide a certain security and stability in the inflow of funds to the less-developed partners.

SACU started negotiations with the US about a free trade agreement in 2003. The US insisted on a comprehensive deal that would also cover FDI, labour and intellectual property issues. The SACU countries thought that the deal should be limited to trade in agricultural and manufactured goods and services. Apart from South Africa, the SACU countries were unwilling to go deeply into (costly) labour rights that may be more suited to developed countries. These developing countries prefer flexibility in labour relations as even bad jobs at low wages may be better than no jobs at all. In addition, they do not have a common FDI system. As such, it is difficult to negotiate with the US, as the Americans may not realise that the benefits of FDI in one country would spill over on the entire group market. Therefore, these talks have been limited. However, SACU members are considering the possibilities of making trade deals with Mercosur and India.

5.5.5 SOUTHERN AFRICAN DEVELOPMENT COMMUNITY

The Southern African Development Coordination Conference had its origin during the apartheid years in South Africa. It was created in 1980 by Angola, Botswana, Lesotho, Malawi, Mozambique, Swaziland, Tanzania, Zambia and Zimbabwe to promote regional cooperation and to reduce these 'front-line' states' dependence on South Africa. Regional 'cooperation' in transport and communication was initially at the heart of the activities. Trade became an issue at a later stage, in 1992 when these countries created the Southern African Development Community (SADC). Following political changes, South Africa joined the SADC in 1995. Mauritius entered in 1995, and Congo and Seychelles in 1997.[51] The first agreements in the SADC concerned sharing river water during droughts and facilitation of trade in hydroelectric power. Then came an improvement in transport links among the member countries. In 1997 the SADC decided to create a free trade area and to implement it over a period of seven years. However, the ratification process of this deal has been slow.

The intention of the group to be involved in deeper regional integration will require an alignment of trade and other economic policies with other schemes that operate in the region. It is possible that various subregional groups of countries may proceed with integration at different speeds. If the South African economy exhibits strong growth, it may have a similar 'locomotive' role on the economies of neighbouring countries to that of the US on Mexico. In fact, following South Africa's entry, the countries in the region started trading with it, but not with each other. However, if there continues to be a strong trade dependence of SADC countries on South Africa as has been the case, then a slowdown in the hub economy would have a negative impact on the spokes in the group. There are plans to create a SADC free trade area by 2008.

5.5.6 COMMON MARKET FOR EASTERN AND SOUTHERN AFRICA

The Preferential Trade Area for Eastern and Southern African States (PTA),[52] was established in 1984. It was expected to be the principal vehicle for economic integration among the countries in the region. Apart from trade, the objectives included promoting cooperation in the areas of manufacturing, agriculture, monetary affairs, as well as transport and communication services. The PTA started to reduce tariffs on a select number of goods that were traded internally. A preferential treatment of trade in goods was granted only to those that were produced in facilities that were majority owned by the residents of the PTA countries. However, internal trade liberalisation proved to be unrealistic in practice as there were often no other sources of public revenue (apart from customs duties). There were inconsistent interpretations of rules of origin, the removal of NTBs was resisted by vested interests, while political stability conducive to regular investment, specialisation and trade was often absent.

A novelty brought by the PTA was the establishment of a clearing house, which handled a sizeable proportion of settlements in regional trade. Such an arrangement was important as the countries in the region did not have convertible currencies.

The PTA failed to deliver obvious benefits to the member countries, hence it was replaced by a much more ambitious Common Market for Eastern and Southern Africa (COMESA)[53] in 1994. An additional goal of the new arrangement is the creation of a monetary union. There are few grounds to expect that it will fare better than ECOWAS (Robson, 1997, p. 350). Internal trade has always accounted for about 5 per cent of the total trade of the group.

There is a weak commitment to COMESA objectives by its member countries. An absence of common FDI rules acted as a hindrance to an inflow of investment and, consequently, to intra-group trade. Mozambique and Tanzania withdrew from COMESA in 1997, while Namibia did the same in 2003. South Africa decided not to join. Hence, membership of the SADC is more appealing to the countries that have South Africa as their principal trading partner.

5.5.7 AFRICAN EXPERIENCE

Sadly, Africa has for a long time been a 'bad news continent'. In spite of many attempts to integrate on a regional scale, overlapping membership in various groups, as well as investing of scarce resources into those enterprises (building of institutions, customs systems, industrial projects and so on) the economies of most African countries remained detached from each other. The total GDP of all sub-Saharan African countries was $393 billion[54] in 2002 (measured in constant 1995 US dollars).[55] As a matter of comparison, this was less than the total Dutch GDP of $505 billion but more than Belgium's $321 billion in the same year. Suppose now that the Dutch or Belgian economies were each splintered into 47 independent countries with different nations, administration, currencies, taxation, armies and poor transport and communications infrastructure. The management of such entities can represent a problem and a headache. If one adds to those factors ethnic tensions, territorial disputes and often different languages, the integration and development tasks may be immense.

The principal reasons for the poor results of integration arrangements in Africa include a low level of economic development of the countries (they have few goods to trade), import-substitution policies and constant problems with the distribution of gains from integration. If these are taken together, it is not surprising that intra-regional trade has always been very small, just a few per cent of their total trade. Economic integration in the region may be fruitful in the future if the countries abandon their past economic policies and introduce transparent and market-oriented policies that are supported by best practice in corporate and state governance. Other types of integration policies have already been tried out in the region with results that were at best disappointing.

A degree of structured and well-thought-out protection may be needed for some time, even though the developed countries preach to the developing countries about the benefits of a liberal system. However, the developed countries tend to forget that they had protected economies of their own before they reached their current (high) level of development. Perhaps looking to the north, as Mexico did, or south towards South Africa, may offer better economic results, even though such an approach may be sometimes criticised on the political grounds that this may reintroduce some of the old colonial type of links. Project-based cooperation among African states, as well as stronger economic relations with the 'northern' countries (based on free access of 'sensitive' products to northern markets), may be beneficial to both regions.

At the 1999 summit of the Organisation of African Unity (OAU) all African states announced the creation of the African Union. A year later, in Lomé (Togo) they adopted the Constitutive Act of the African Union which replaced the 38-year-old and ineffective OAU. After two-thirds of the 53 member states had ratified this act, the African Union was launched in 2002. It is located in Addis Ababa and is expected to do better than its predecessor. The African Union is modelled on the EU. Its list of objectives includes a standard and demanding wish list of aims such as solidarity and unity among the participating states; respect of national sovereignty and contribution to peace and stability;[56] acceleration of cooperation, integration and sustainable growth and development of the participating countries; harmonisation of economic policies; a single currency; and rising living standards of the population which includes a fight against diseases.

To implement these goals, some of them quite costly, the organisation needs resources. The member states decided during the 2004 annual summit to pledge 0.5 per cent of GDP to fund the African Union. This would permit the organisation to increase its staff and to carry on with policies, notably the New Partnership for Africa's Development. The general problem is that many members fail to pay their membership dues, even though external donors such as the EU and the US help the organisation to an extent. Another problem is that governments lacked any real commitment to many of the previously announced initiatives and failed to take appropriate action.

Another general problem is that the Abuja Treaty (1991), which created the African Economic Community among the same states, had very similar goals. The final Abuja goal, the creation of the United States of Africa, was to be achieved in many stages over a transition period of up to 34 years. The supporting institutions bear a striking similarity to those in the EU. Having in mind the acceleration of the implementation of these objectives, the African Union effectively incorporated the African Economic Community. While all this may be necessary to reduce infighting and split loyalties, one has immediate concerns about the actual capacity (and will) to carry it out. Perhaps a much less ambitious and scaled-down, but workable arrangement for the near future would be a superior approach to integration in Africa. Among the leaders who made those pledges, who will recall in three decades what was agreed way back in the distant 1990s? In any case, even if the grandiose goals are not fulfilled, the African Union can serve a useful purpose of providing a necessary forum for discussions of pan-African issues.

5.5.8 ARAB COUNTRIES

Integration among the Arab countries in North Africa and the Middle East is characterised by the frequent creation (high-level pronouncements by statesmen) and the even more habitual breakdown or attrition of integration deals. On the face of it this might be surprising, since all these countries share a common language and religion.[57]

The distribution of natural wealth (minerals) is very uneven among the Arab countries. In theory, however, there are a number of fusing elements among the countries that may, potentially, facilitate the integration process. The Arab League was founded in 1945 to maintain and reinforce relations among the Arab states. The objective of the Arab Monetary Fund created in 1977 was to help to integrate economies and expand trade among the Arab countries. The success has been rather limited. None the less, the League launched a proposal to establish an Arab Free Trade Area in 2007.

Numerous attempts to integrate these countries have got nowhere, principally because of stark political differences.[58] This is discouraging for non-resource-related FDI that seeks wider markets such as integration can provide. TNCs have been active in the region almost exclusively in the exploitation of one natural resource – hydrocarbons.

5.6 Conclusion

Integration groups among the developing countries were not propelled by high and/or fast-growing internal trade or FDI. Intra-group trade played a minor role in these schemes. This is even truer for intra-regional FDI. The main instrument of integration in many schemes among the developing countries, as structured in the past, was some kind of trade liberalisation. It was very hard to move integration efforts beyond the opening stage. The opening up of the regional market, although on a limited scale, was an instrument that prompted a certain involvement of TNCs in the groups. The only exception is the Andean Community where the core of the arrangement was to structure this involvement of TNCs in the region, even though the success of the policy has not materialised. Only in ASEAN were countries able to take a common and FDI-friendly joint stance towards foreign TNCs from the outset. TNCs have been contributing to the local fixed capital formation and technology in production and management. They also brought wide international marketing networks that were export friendly and that supported the general ASEAN trade openness. The Asian financial crises in 1997 and the emergence of China's economy as one of the principal international economic factors shifted business interest towards this country.

The soundness of the national economic policy and macroeconomic stability has always played an important role in attracting FDI, rather than a country's participation in the regional integration scheme. Therefore, an exploration of the paths taken for north–south integration, as took place in the NAFTA, SADC and EU eastern enlargement provides a promising research area for the future. The presence of a strong and stable partner provided firm grounds for the survival and evolution of the scheme.

In the near future it is unlikely that intra-regional trade (as structured so far) will provide a strong fuel for growth in the developing world. Perhaps the convertibility of national currencies will boost the stimulus for trade, investment and payments. This requires only an astute national macroeconomic policy over a longer period of time.

Developing countries, in particular in Latin America and in Africa, have been attempting economic integration for almost half a century with little success. Reasons for the failures, unfulfilled expectations or very weak positive results from integration among the developing countries include the following:

- Absence of preconditions for a promising integration (certain macroeconomic and political stability, lack of goods and services that are in demand by partner countries, high administrative and other trade costs).
- Absence of local entrepreneurs and institutions (particularly in Africa) to support their own creation and expansion, as well as those that can attract TNCs on a larger scale.
- Lack of true dedication of member countries to integration (restrictive domestic economic systems are not easily abandoned; administration wants to control domestic agents and does not create a monetary and fiscal environment in which they may compete internationally; emphasis on import substitution).
- Insufficient institutional capacity to handle integration, to settle disputes, to ascertain and distribute gains and potential costs of integration (particularly sharing of common revenue and distribution of projects).
- Poor infrastructure, particularly one necessary to provide a link between developing countries.
- Absence of a firm, stable and determined (perhaps relatively developed) core country that would provide a lead, stability, resources and security to the arrangement.
- Deep political problems.[59]
- Growing number of often overlapping[60] integration schemes which may have conflicting objectives; there has been much infighting and competition for the loyalty of member countries (countries become enthusiastic about a certain integration deal, but as soon as there is a problem in its implementation, they try to create another and more elaborate one to be enthused about).

- Inadequate external support, particularly regarding trade access to other markets including those in the developed world. The EU has a passion for preferential (that is, discriminatory) trade agreements. These were often used as carrots and sticks in trade relations. Almost 80 African, Caribbean and Pacific (ACP) developing countries (mostly former colonies) benefited from ACP conventions that offered trade concessions and aid from the EU. However, in certain respects these conventions had a negative effect on the beneficiary countries. ACP exporters were assured of access to the EU markets so they did not lobby their own governments to open domestic markets as a quid pro quo for access to foreign markets. The domestic political engine behind trade liberalisation (export lobbies) was destroyed. To make things worse, just before independence, 'subsidiaries of EC firms constituted the core of the modern industrial sector in ACP countries, and became the major beneficiaries of growing ACP protection – enjoying considerable monopoly rents when things were still going well, and benefiting from subsidies granted by the ACP host countries (and often financed by EC member-state aid funds) when things turned bad' (Messerlin, 2001, p. 204). In addition, the EU proposed new economic partnership agreements with the ACP countries. These new agreements are supposed to replace the current trade and aid deal that expires in 2008. The EU wants to use such agreements to split the ACP countries into six regional groups. These countries have weak bargaining power and high dependence on the EU for market access and aid. They would succumb to EU demands even though this may not always be in accord with their best interest.[61]

A simple look at these reasons immediately reveals the source of these obstacles: politics. Organised power holders such as the military and the urban 'elite' are able to extort 'favours' from those in a country with weak democratic institutions. They are simply unwilling to relinquish easily such levers of power (including corruption) to accumulate wealth for themselves and share it (even partially) with other external agents. The way forward should include redressing the above features.

In the past, economic integration among the developing countries has had few successes. 'If a certain level of integration cannot be made to work, the reaction of policy-makers has typically been to embark on something more elaborate, more advanced and more demanding in terms of administrative requirements and political commitment' (Robson, 1997, p. 348). Their attempts to replicate the EU failed because of the absence of the preconditions for such integration.

Appendix 5A1 Council for Mutual Economic Assistance[62]

INTRODUCTION

The Council for Mutual Economic Assistance (CMEA) or Comecon existed for four decades. Regrettably it did not live up to its potential or to the expectations of its members. This situation was due to the following two reasons. First, the former USSR was territorially the largest country in the world. As such it had a vast domestic market which permitted diversification in production so that international trade was (presumably) not a key factor in its economic prosperity. Second, such a situation in the CMEA was also due to central planning which worked out detailed tasks regarding production, investments, prices and trade. Foreign trade flows were not due to differences in absolute and comparative costs among countries, but, rather, they were only an extension of the plan. Many of the impediments to trade which are studied in the theory of international economic integration (tariffs, quotas, taxes) did not appear in the CMEA system.

A communiqué announced the establishment of the CMEA in 1949. The statute of this group was, however, delivered a decade after the communiqué. The main objectives of this institution were the continuous increase in the welfare of the people in all CMEA member countries, as well as the gradual equalisation of the level of economic development among the member countries. Other goals (development and improvement of economic cooperation, development of socialist economic integration and acceleration of economic and technical progress) are means to achieving the main objective. The principles upon which the CMEA was founded were the sovereign equality of all member countries, voluntary membership, socialist internationalism, mutual benefit and fraternal assistance.

This appendix is structured as follows. First it examines the basic features of the CMEA. This is followed by a consideration of factor mobility. Separate attention is accorded to the socialist prices in trade and trade flows. Reforms of the CMEA system are then presented, followed by conclusions about the demise of the group.

BASIC FEATURES

Majority voting within the CMEA was prohibited. This was the real reason why the CMEA did not have any real power, as well as why the former USSR had not succeeded in completely controlling all CMEA member countries. The group's institutional set-up was complicated. There were many CMEA bodies. The CMEA intended to compensate for the lack of real power by means of a formidable institutional structure. Decision making in this bureaucratic labyrinth was very slow because every country could block any proposals by dissenting.

It was after the promulgation of the CMEA statute that 'The Basic Principles of International Socialist Division of Labour' were accepted in 1962. These principles set down guidelines for future cooperation among the CMEA countries. During the 1950s there was considerable disequilibria in the economies of the CMEA countries. On the one hand, there were shortages of consumer goods, while on the other, there was a glut of producer goods. This situation brought open dissatisfaction in Hungary in 1956 which was 'pacified' by Soviet intervention. Little attention had been paid to specialisation until that time. On the basis of the Basic Principles, the socialist division of labour was applied through the coordination of economic plans and specialisation in production on the basis of the employment of disposable factors in each country. As a relatively less-developed country in the CMEA, Romania did not want to accept this kind of specialisation, for under this pattern its industrial development would be impeded.

Romanian opposition to the introduction of supranational planning within the CMEA was supported by Hungary and Czechoslovakia. The last two countries were implementing reforms directed towards a socialist system in which the market played an important role. A relative dilution of the CMEA was prevented by the intervention of the Warsaw Pact in Czechoslovakia in 1968. After that event the former USSR had to find a way to close ranks within the CMEA.

The Comprehensive Programme of Socialist Economic Integration was presented and accepted in 1971. This programme was basically a list of proposals which refer to a number of issues in economics and science, over a long period of time (15–20 years). The pivotal clause within the Comprehensive Programme is joint planning and joint investment projects in the priority sectors (raw materials and energy, machine industry, food, consumer goods industries and transport). If a CMEA country was not interested in decision making with respect to an issue, then the decision or recommendation would not refer to the country in question. This principle of 'interested party' was applied in the CMEA structure as protection against the introduction of supranationality.

Competition takes place among firms in market economies. In centrally planned economies competition existed among different plans which were offered to the central decision-making body. At an earlier stage, the adjustment of national plans meant only an exchange of information for bilateral trade negotiations. This was changed so that the procedure began three years before the end of the five-year period covered by the plan. This allowed time for the planners to change and supplement their investment plans. The adjustment of plans among the CMEA countries was done on the basis of mutual prognoses, consultations, planning of the interested countries in certain fields, exchange of experience and planning principles. The intention was to consciously link bilateral and multilateral measures for the development of cooperation in economics, science and technology.

Planning, as a process in which the future of a certain field is consciously shaped, has a theoretical advantage because mistakes and costs which can cause 'blind market forces' are deliberately avoided. The politicisation of integration, however, reduced the advantages of planning, and the speed of integration was much slower than in the market model. Endless bilateral negotiations made the integration progress very slow. This could easily be a sign that countries did not welcome it with enthusiasm (on such terms).

During the negotiation process about common projects, negotiators from the member countries appraised costs and benefits of the project in question, compared projects with alternatives, estimated concessions given to and received from partners and, finally, compared possible projects with national priorities in development. This was a complicated and time-consuming task (Robson, 1987, p. 218).

There have been about 20 common projects, most of them in energy and raw materials. Common investments were made in the country which was endowed with a substantial amount of mineral resources. Consequently, most common projects were located in the former USSR. The most important projects were found in a common infrastructure for energy which was the greatest source of pride in the CMEA, for they represented genuine integration. The Druzhba oil pipeline was 5500 km long and linked oil wells in the former USSR with consumers in the former German Democratic Republic, Poland, Hungary and the former Czechoslovakia. The Soyuz gas pipeline was 2750 km long and supplied European countries with natural gas from the USSR. The Mir was a huge electric grid that linked the CMEA countries from Mongolia to eastern Europe. Other important common projects included the production of cellulose and asbestos in the former USSR, the production of cobalt and nickel in Cuba and cotton spinning in Poland.

Most of these projects were directed towards the production and transport of primary products from the former USSR. This was how the European CMEA member countries compensated the former USSR for the supply of resources which could be easily sold on the international market for hard currency. Investments of the European member countries in the former USSR were made in the form of the export of goods, labour and know-how. European member countries of the CMEA protested at the low interest rates which they received, payments in kind and high costs of projects. However, the security of supplies from the former USSR in the future compensated for these concerns.

FACTOR MOBILITY

Mobility of capital within the CMEA framework was of little importance. If the funds moved, then it was due to the interest of the countries to which the funds belonged. From the point of view of normative economics, the funds should move from those countries which have a surplus of capital (in which profit and interest rates are relatively lower) to those countries which have a shortage of capital (in which profit and interest rates are relatively higher) and in which there is confidence that the invested funds will be recovered. Capital mobility within and outside the CMEA, however, had a political dimension. The CMEA countries, just like governments in the west, 'exported' capital everywhere they wanted to win friends and exert political influence.

The International Investment Bank (IIB) was established in 1970 in order to finance the common investments necessitated by the 'socialist division of labour'. It gave medium- and long-term loans which were in most cases of benefit to all CMEA member countries. The capital of the bank was 1 billion transferable roubles. The IIB was also entitled to take funds from the international capital market. In the beginning Romania did not want to participate in the IIB, because decisions were made in the bank according to majority vote (each country had one vote), but subsequently joined. This decision-making process was in contrast to the operation of all other CMEA bodies. None the less, there was a lack of interest in the active operation of the bank. This can be explained by the need of the relatively advanced countries of the CMEA for investments in their own economy. In this situation the relatively advanced countries did not want to help, to any great extent, the development of relatively less-advanced CMEA countries. In addition, the rates of interest on the one hand, and profitability, supply and demand of funds on the other, were not connected.

According to CMEA opinion, labour movements were inherent to capitalism. These flows were of very little significance in the CMEA, although there were differences among member countries in the relative level of wages due partly to the relative abundance or shortage of labour. Labour flows between the relatively backward countries of the CMEA towards the relatively advanced ones (from Bulgaria to the former USSR, from Poland to the former German Democratic Republic) were observed. In 1989–90 (the fall of the Berlin Wall) there was a massive outflow of population from the CMEA, in particular from the former German Democratic Republic to the Federal Republic of Germany before reunification in 1989.

The exchange of scientific and technical information between the CMEA member countries was very well developed, at least formally. It was based on the critique of capitalism in which private owners control scientific achievements and prevent a wide application of new ideas in order to make super-normal profit. However, there was a problem in financing research in the CMEA. Relatively advanced countries had little incentive to share the fruits of their achievements with other users because of the high costs and uncertainty of research which they bore alone. Recipients of the scientific information had neither the interest nor the funds to take part in research when they could get the results of such research free from others. Therefore, the CMEA countries tried to compensate for their relative backwardness in technology by purchasing western equipment and licences.

PRICES IN TRADE

Eastern European theorists maintained throughout the 'socialist period' that capitalism was in crisis and that it had a destabilising cyclical effect and caused speculative movements of prices. On these grounds, the CMEA endeavoured to find its own socialist prices (which embodied 'equality' in economic relations) in contrast to capitalist prices (which represent inequality). In the socialist centrally planned system of economic autarky a concern with quantity rather than value was dominant.

Fluctuations in prices could endanger the planned nature of the CMEA economies. The economic results of this system were measured in metres, litres and tonnes, not in money, which was only an accounting unit. Prices in this system responded neither to costs of production nor to the relation of supply and demand. Nor did they reflect the relative abundance or shortage of goods and services. They were set arbitrarily and were used for accounting purposes only. Hence, they did not play any role in the allocation of resources. The gap between prices and the cost of production was caused by relatively low prices for producers' goods, low rates of interest and taxes which burdened consumer goods. The system of prices in the CMEA member countries gave neither a satisfactory nor a rational denominator for the production of goods and services. It was much more suited to a large closed economy than to a small developed and specialised country which pursues a policy of openness in trade and investment.

Domestic rationality in production can be tested by comparison with prices on the world market. It is not a simple self-comparison, but rather a comparison with the most efficient and competitive world producers. Trade and comparison with the most advanced world economies could give a positive signal and impetus to economic development in the region. The CMEA member countries conducted negotiations about volume and structure of trade, and bargained over prices (terms of trade). Every country's administration decided its own prices, so prices among the states could not be compared directly. In their internal trade, the CMEA countries hoped to 'clear' the world market (capitalist) prices of cyclical and speculative movements and used the five-year weighted averages. Following the sharp increase in the world market price for oil, the prices for intra-CMEA trade, on the basis of a Soviet request, were delivered every year from 1976 (instead of every five years). The bases were world market prices from the preceding five years.

This system of prices did not cause problems for basic and standardised goods (raw materials); however, problems arose regarding manufactured goods. For example, should a Bulgarian computer be worth as much as a Japanese one? Such a system of 'just and equivalent socialist prices' in trade within the CMEA was very slow to bring the beneficial effects which come from the world market. At the same time, it isolated the CMEA from the abrupt and disadvantageous effects which came in the form of sharp increases in prices which distort planning. It could also give rise to perverse situations. Prices for oil in the CMEA were rising between 1982 and 1986 while they were decreasing on the world market.

The CMEA member countries used current world market prices in trade with third countries, while in their internal trade they used prices which were reached after bilateral negotiations on the basis of historic world prices as explained above. These bilateral negotiations were quite tough as it was no easy task to obtain the world market price for each particular good. Commodity exchanges deal with only a limited number of goods. In addition, the bulk of world trade is covered by long-term contracts which do not necessarily have a close relation to current world market prices. Prices played no role in the allocation of resources in the centrally planned system. Therefore, it is hard to understand why the CMEA countries spent so much time bargaining over prices or why there was a world market price formula.

The CMEA price system enabled the former USSR in the 1955–59 period to charge prices that were 15 per cent higher for exports to the CMEA partner countries, while on the import side the former USSR paid to the same partners prices that were 15 per cent lower for the same or similar import goods than those paid to western countries (Mendershausen, 1959; 1960). On these grounds the former USSR could take advantage of the CMEA member countries because of its monopolistic position. Such a result can be questioned on several grounds. Econometric problems arise regarding the comparison of data, price, quantity and quality of goods. In addition, the former USSR had to accept higher prices from western partners in order to attract them for trade. At the same time the former USSR had to offer relatively lower prices for exports in order to penetrate the western markets and earn the necessary hard currency to pay for imports.

If the terms of trade were favourable to the former USSR until the 1960s, after that period the situation altered. The former USSR exported mainly primary goods and energy to its CMEA partners while the partners exported industrial goods in exchange. Relative prices of manufactured goods rose in relation to prices for primary goods, so that the terms of trade were working against the former USSR within the CMEA. This tendency was manifested in 1975 when the Soviets insisted on a change in the pricing system. These potential losses from trade, or subsidies to the CMEA partners, took place when the former USSR exported energy and raw materials below the world market price and when it imported manufactured goods at prices higher than those which prevailed on the world market for goods of similar quality. The former USSR may have consciously directed such subsidies to the CMEA partner countries in order to prevent or stimulate policy changes in these countries. One of the crucial factors which induced Britain and France to decolonise was the need by their colonies to be subsidised. However, it appears that the Soviets in the past compensated for possible losses in trade within the CMEA by using their political influence.

Various studies found the existence of Soviet subsidies to CMEA partners. Where they disagreed was in the magnitude of these subsidies. The accumulated Soviet subsidies over the 1973–84 period due to divergent price developments on the CMEA and world markets amounted to 18.8 billion transferable roubles (Dietz, 1986) which is three times less than in another estimate even for 1980 (Marrese and Vanous, 1983). Yet another study reported Soviet aid in all forms to eastern Europe of around $134 billion between 1971 and 1980 (Bunce, 1985). The major source of these subsidies was the price (and its change) of energy.

The leaders in the former USSR did not want its population to be aware that the CMEA partners were being subsidised. Socialist cooperation was supposed to be founded on 'equality'. Therefore, it was unnecessary to compensate partners for their friendship. In addition, Soviet citizens would not be happy to learn that their country subsidised other partner countries with higher living standards. At the same time, east European political leaders did not want their population to know that national sovereignty was being 'sold' in return for the Soviet subsidies to help the running of their economies (Marrese, 1986, p. 311).

Prices were relatively stable in the CMEA countries and direct inflation did not exist. None the less, producer prices differed from consumer prices due to bonuses, subsidies and taxes. These 'additives' can create quite a significant gap between the two kinds of prices, although the planners attempted to keep consumer prices fixed. Inflation of a kind, however, existed. It appeared in the form of shortages, cutting off electricity supplies, restrictions on foreign travel, long queues in shops, low quality of goods and the like. The solution to the price problem in the CMEA countries was to be found in domestic reforms which would introduce the system of production according to market needs. By doing this, one would avoid the absurd situation in which Soviet sewing machine producers received bonuses for fulfilling their plan, although there were piles of sewing machines in the shops which nobody wanted to buy!

TRADE

Trade, FDI, reallocation of resources and specialisation (division of labour) represent the core of international economic integration. Because of the non-market formation of prices within the CMEA, the trade data expressed in monetary values which were released by the CMEA were generally useless for international comparisons, as well as for calculations of trade creation and trade diversion. Of course, this did not hold for data which referred to litres, metres or tonnes.

The CMEA could not be seen as a customs union. Indirectly, customs protection was replaced by a complicated system of direct control of foreign trade quotas which were set by the plan. State ownership of the means of production, state foreign trade monopoly and a high degree of self-sufficiency removed the need for the existence of customs duties.

Customs duties might have some justification when they protect an infant industry for a limited period of time; when they reduce consumption of imported goods in order to curtail and redirect home consumption; and when the proceeds are needed for the budget in the short term. Since the state could get funds from enterprises without obstacles and directly protect/promote firms and industries, there was no need for customs duties in the centrally planned system. In the 1970s the CMEA countries started introducing tariffs. The main reason for this move was the creation of the base for negotiation and concessions in trade from the west.

Intra-CMEA trade has been characterised by bilateralism (the most protectionist trading system) during the entire life of this organisation. Bilateralism is a kind of exchange control. It is usually introduced when countries face severe payment problems for which the more subtle kinds of intervention are not sufficient to achieve the desired policy objectives (van Brabant, 1980, p. 128). If the bilaterally negotiated price for a good is too high for a country, then this country tries to produce the good at home. If this option is expensive, then the country purchases it from western countries. Either action is integration averse. The goal of bilateral balancing was economic independence. In the case of deficit, the currencies of the CMEA countries were not accepted internationally, and they had few reserves, while the opportunities to arrange *ex post* loans were limited. These countries did not want to become too dependent on unplanned capital imports which might jeopardise their major policy objective, independence (ibid., p. 114). Therefore, the level of trade of the CMEA countries was lower than was the case for market economies at a comparable level of development.

Bilateral balancing in trade among the CMEA member countries used to be a routine occurrence. Since the mid-1970s and the energy crisis, this has not been the case in trade between the former USSR and all other CMEA member countries. The former USSR became a creditor of these countries. These disequilibria in trade enabled the former USSR to 'favour' (large 'credits') some countries or 'punish' (small 'credits') others.

A specific CMEA trade took place in 'hard' and 'soft' goods. Hard goods in the CMEA were either deficient goods (food) or those that could be sold easily for hard currency (raw materials). These goods became an accepted means of payment because of their scarcity. Countries which were abundant in raw materials (the former USSR and to an extent Poland and Romania) were under pressure from the other CMEA countries. Countries which had 'soft' (manufactured) goods tried to swap them for as many 'hard' goods as possible. Sellers of 'hard' goods requested in return better-quality 'soft' ones. As a rule, however, hard goods were traded for hard goods and soft goods were traded for soft goods. Note that money did not fit into this barter. Holders of money were not even sure that their national currency was fully convertible into the home goods and services they wanted.

REFORMS

A permanent increase in welfare (consumption by kind and volume) of the citizens of the CMEA member countries was the rationale for the existence of the CMEA. With an increase in economic development, consumers (public and private) demanded improvements in the quality and increase in the choice of goods and services. This required an improvement in the operation of the economy. The rate of growth has continuously fallen in the CMEA countries since the 1960s. One reason is found in the relatively low starting base of the CMEA countries in the post-war period, with the exception of Czechoslovakia and the former East Germany. The other reason was the exhaustion of the effects of extensive economic development. This development model relied on increases in employment, investment and the plentiful use of raw materials. Such a model had its full justification in the CMEA at the time, but its achievements were limited to one-time positive effects. Such a development model offered little opportunities for development in the long term.

An increase in the rate of growth, prevention of its fall or, at least, maintaining this rate at the current level, together with the introduction of intensive economic development (based on increases in productivity and efficiency in production, that is, better use of inputs per unit of output), were the reasons for reform of the centrally planned system in the CMEA countries. In order to reverse unfavourable domestic economic flows, the CMEA countries looked westwards for loans and modern technology. In a situation of forced full employment, additional loans increased the quantity of money, so the existing economic disproportions become more pronounced.

The central plan is not capable of harmonising infrastructure, production and the trade of each good and service out of the millions that circulate within every economy. Nor has it been able to take account of changing consumer preferences, world market prices, new technology, new mineral discoveries and weather conditions. The consequences of central planning systems included shortages of goods, services and spare parts, poor quality of output, delays in delivery, separation of producers from consumers and lack of interest in their interrelationship, lack of direct competition which stimulates innovation, as well as protection from the impact of the world market. These shortcomings can be redressed to a large extent by a kind of self-regulating market system. Of course, the immediate and, possibly, short-term reaction would be a change in prices, inflation, economic cycles and unemployment.

The interlacing of trade ties between integrated partners is a measure of the degree of integration. Bilateralism in trade and inconvertibility of currencies in the CMEA reflected a disconnection among the CMEA partners, which, within four decades, have developed neither competition nor large-scale cooperation. The exceptions include the field of energy. The CMEA has not lived up to its potential in a great many areas. Hence, the controversial thesis by Sobell (1984) that the CMEA was a highly integrated scheme cannot be accepted.

Production for the foreign market is harder than for the domestic market. A firm's production in the CMEA was not subordinated to consumer demand, but rather to the central plan. Firms produced not in order to make a profit, but rather to fulfil the plan targets. Their existence was not imperilled by import competition. When the plan was fulfilled, the firm received bonuses. These favours were much more easily obtained through negotiations with the central planning administration about the production targets than through efforts in exports.

Attitudes towards reforms differed among the countries. This was due not only to the shape of the economy, but also to the country's objectives and the ability of its leaders to carry them out. Hungary tried to soften the rigid central planning system in 1968. However, the legacy from the old way of conducting the economy was such that, even after the reform, the state still controlled over 80 per cent of the GNP. The dominant role of the state sector and control of the economy prevented the operation of market forces and may be a major factor for the economic crisis. The Hungarian model of reform was interesting to study, but not to follow.

Poland tried to reform its economy during the 1970s by a heavy investment programme. It took loans from the west. The technical capacity of the economy was transformed, but the economic system remained the same. This led to investments in a number of projects that turned out to be unprofitable. Protectionism and a lack of competition, owing to the system of central planning, was to blame for the wrong investment choices. A profound economic crisis in Poland in the late 1980s was due to an increase in the rates of interest and an inability of projects to service foreign hard currency debt. The result was high inflation and crisis.

The leaders of the CMEA countries considered ways for improving the operation of the CMEA on a number of occasions during the 1980s. They identified priority industries for cooperation and development. These industries included food, energy, transport, consumer goods and science and technology. The problem was that these industries had priority in the preceding two decades too. The centrally planned economic system was unable to solve these issues and presented a hindrance to the economic development and prosperity of the CMEA member countries.

Perestroika in the former USSR was a step towards a greater openness of the economy and society in the mid-1980s. But the citizens began to be nervous about its achievements. What they saw were longer queues, soaring inflation, a decline in real income and a rationing of meat and dairy products. They felt that they were worse off than before and disregarded dubious statistics which sometimes offered a different statistical conclusion.

Market-type reforms which started in eastern Europe and the former USSR in the late 1980s aimed at discovering the sources of competitive advantage which are found in developed market economies. They should start with innovative small private firms. In many developed countries, the average size of the firm is becoming smaller, not bigger. SMEs create the necessary web among different parts of the economy. The lack of SMEs came from the basic weakness of the centrally planned system. In the situation where shortages prevailed and without the confidence that the planned and agreed quantities of inputs would be delivered in time, the only way to obtain, in a reliable way, the necessary inputs was to make them oneself (and to stockpile). Firms did not have the choice between make and buy. Such a situation increased prices per unit of output, reduced competitiveness and weakened links among firms.

The enterprises in eastern Europe and the former USSR had very soft budget constraints. They were taking loans without any fear of going bust. If the projects were profitable, enterprises and management would receive bonuses and medals. If they were unprofitable, the government was always there to bail them out. Proprietors of firms in a market economy, the shareholders, are interested not only in the income-generating capacity of their assets, but also, and equally important, in the market value of their assets. A mistaken judgement about investment will be instantaneously reflected in the market value of the shares. This was missing in the CMEA countries. Since workers in the centrally planned economies did not have shares in their firms, they were afraid of investment in new technology that would make them redundant. Hence, driven by their short-term income-maximising goals, they demanded that the management and the state increase their wages, rather than invest in new technology to respond to a change in demand. Even if they did have shares, there was no reliable stock market to trade them on.

CONCLUSION

Various piecemeal reforms within the framework of the central planning system in eastern Europe and the former USSR had very limited success. Central planning is quite tough and it successfully resisted profound reforms. This became obvious at the end of 1989 when an overhaul of the whole economic system resulted in its replacement by a kind of market-type economy.

The CMEA decided in 1990 to abolish coordination of national plans and multilateral cooperation. These were the most important functions of the whole organisation. In 1991 all CMEA trade was conducted at 'world prices' in convertible currencies. Not much, then, was left of the CMEA, and the group vanished in the same year.

Appendix 5A2 Eastern enlargement of the European Union

INTRODUCTION

The objective of this appendix is to take a brief look at issues related to the eastern enlargement of the EU. Eight countries with economies in transition,[63] the Czech Republic, Estonia, Hungary, Latvia, Lithuania, Poland, Slovakia and Slovenia, and two market economies, Cyprus and Malta, concluded[64] terms for full membership with the EU and joined in May 2004. Bulgaria and Romania are scheduled to join the EU in 2007. Croatia and Turkey are negotiating entry conditions.

The appendix is structured as follows. It begins by looking at the economic structure of the new EU members and the entry criteria. This is followed by an analysis of EU enlargement costs and benefits. Then come certain reflections about the disillusionment on both sides of the story regarding the enlargement. The controversial issue of the potential EU entry of Turkey is covered in a special section. The conclusion is that the final operational entry conditions set by the European Council in Brussels (2002) are such that this enlargement may be relatively cheap for the EU in financial terms, but much costlier and slower for the accession countries than expected by politicians, both in the EU and in the new member countries. The reasons for this include the voting rules in the enlarged EU, self-imposed limits for the EU's expenditure and increasing standards that come from the ever-expanding *acquis communautaire* that are costly to introduce, apply and enforce. The new member countries will need to invest a considerable amount of effort, funds and time of their own to comply with the requirements for full membership.

ECONOMIC STRUCTURE OF THE 10 NEW MEMBER COUNTRIES

The 10 new member countries brought 74 million additional consumers into the EU (2004). If Bulgaria, Croatia, Romania and Turkey were included, then this would increase to 176 million. However, some of those countries are so small that the EU economy would barely register their entry. As for the level of development measured by GDP per capita in purchasing power standard (PPS), the new member countries are at a far lower level of development than the EU(15) average (Table 5A2.1). However, there are three distinct groups of newcomers. Cyprus and Slovenia are in

Table 5A2.1 GDP per capita at purchasing power standard and population in the EU and candidate countries in 2004

Country	GDP per capita, PPS*	Population in millions
EU(25)	22 300	456.8
EU(15)	24 300	383.0
New members	12 100	74.1
Cyprus	18 200	0.7
Slovenia	17 400	2.0
Malta	16 200	0.4
Czech Republic	15 600	10.2
Hungary	13 800	10.1
Slovakia	11 900	5.4
Estonia	11 300	1.4
Poland	10 600	38.2
Lithuania	9 800	3.5
Latvia	9 700	2.3
Candidates		
Romania	6 900	21.7
Bulgaria	6 900	7.8
Croatia	10 300	4.5
Turkey	6 500	69.0

Note: * Estimates.

Source: Eurostat (2005).

the group of relatively developed new member countries. In descending order, the other groups consist of Malta, the Czech Republic and Hungary; then come Slovakia, Estonia, Poland, Lithuania and Latvia. Bulgaria, Romania and Turkey have a quarter of EU(15) average GDP. If there were no changes in the EU policy, most of the newcomers would be eligible for a large share of EU regional funds. This is particularly relevant for Poland, Romania and Turkey because of their large population and relative 'backwardness' measured by the GDP per capita. However, the European Council in Brussels (2002) confirmed earlier budgetary restrictions and put new limits on EU expenditure.

The economic structure of the new member countries shows that services are the predominant economic sector (Table 5A2.2). The same is true for the EU(15). However, there are concerns regarding agriculture. The contribution of this sector to the GDP in the new member and candidate countries is higher than is the case in the EU(15). In Bulgaria, Romania and Turkey, it is more than five times, respectively, the EU(25) average.

Table 5A2.2 Structure of GDP in the EU and candidate countries in 2004 (%)

Country	Structure of GDP (%)		
	Agriculture[1]	Manufacturing[2]	Services
EU(25)	1.9	19.6	78.5
EU(15)	1.8	19.4	78.8
New members			
Cyprus	3.9	11.0	85.1
Czech Republic	2.5	29.2	68.3
Estonia	4.0	19.3	76.7
Hungary	2.9	22.1	75.0
Latvia	3.9	15.3	80.8
Lithuania	5.6	23.2	71.2
Malta	2.2	20.9	76.9
Poland	2.6	21.7	75.7
Slovakia	3.6	24.5	71.9
Slovenia	2.3	26.8	70.9
Candidates			
Romania	11.7	28.4	59.9
Bulgaria	10.0	22.3	67.7
Croatia	8.2	23.4	68.4
Turkey	11.7	24.7	63.6

Notes:
1. Agriculture, hunting, forestry and fishing.
2. Excluding construction.

Source: Eurostat (2005).

The unemployment problem in the new member countries is uneven (Table 5A2.3). Poland and Slovakia had unemployment rates that were more than twice as high as the EU(15) average in 2004. The problem is that Poland is a large economy in the group of newcomers. As for the sectoral structure of employment, almost a fifth of the labour force in Poland is in agriculture (this is more than four times the EU(15) average). Some 18 per cent of Poland's labour employed in agriculture contributes 2.6 per cent to the GDP. This compares with figures of 3.7 and 1.8 per cent, respectively, in the EU(15). If farm labour in Poland migrates to cities, this may increase the productivity of Polish farming. However, if there are no new jobs in manufacturing and services sectors to absorb such an inflow, significant societal tensions may develop. A third of the Romanian and Turkish labour force is employed in agriculture. This is largely semi-subsistence farming and its share is almost 10 times the EU(15) average.

Table 5A2.3 Unemployment rate and share of agriculture in total employment in the EU and candidate countries, 2004 (%)

Country	Unemployment rate	Agriculture in total employment
EU(25)	9.0	5.0
EU(15)	8.0	3.7
New members		
Cyprus	5.0	5.1
Czech Republic	8.3	4.4
Estonia	9.2	4.9
Hungary	5.9	5.2
Latvia	9.8	13.0
Lithuania	10.8	16.2
Malta	7.3	2.0
Poland	18.8	17.6
Slovakia	18.0	5.0
Slovenia	6.0	9.6
Candidates		
Bulgaria	11.9	10.6
Romania	7.1	32.6
Croatia	18.7	16.5
Turkey	10.3	33.0

Source: Economic Commission for Europe (2005); Eurostat (2005).

A relatively active labour market policy (safety regulation), which is a feature of the economies in the EU countries, may harm the new member and candidate countries in the short term. Nobody questions the social and other features of high labour protection standards, but these standards are often expensive to apply and maintain. This may hinder the creation of new firms, as well as protection of existing marginal jobs. The general EU labour market rigidities may slow down the painful and ongoing transition and adjustment processes in the accession countries.

ENTRY CRITERIA

'Any European state may apply to become a Member of the Union' (Article O of the Maastricht Treaty).[65] That is the only Maastricht Treaty based (necessary) condition for a country to be considered for full membership of the EU. In addition, there are several other sufficient, economic and political requirements for entry. These were formally defined during the

European Council in Copenhagen (1993). The potential candidate country must fulfil three sets of conditions. It must have a functioning market economy, a democratic political system and accept, apply, enforce and adhere to the *acquis communautaire*.

First, the broad *economic* conditions: a country must have a functioning market economy. Apart from the Czech Republic and Slovakia, not a single transition country had a fully functioning market economy even before they became centrally planned countries (van Brabant, 1996). Entry into the EU, in particular an early entry by transition economies, could cause a serious external shock. Their economies are not yet fully adjusted to the market-based economic system and their manufacturing and service sectors are still too fragile to absorb the expensive *acquis communautaire*. Early entry into the EU without full macroeconomic stabilisation and modernisation of the output structure may be painful for them. Countries that are passing through the 'transition phase' would not be able to withstand the strict rules governing competition with EU producers in most industries.[66] Transition fatigue is already apparent in these countries and is evidenced by the return of the 'recycled' communists to office.

The second set of broad conditions relates to *politics*. The prospective entrant must have a stable democratic political system; that is, a multiparty parliament, rule of law and respect for human and minority rights. It also includes good neighbourly relations and no territorial disputes. With regard to the last criterion, not one transition country passes the test, and the northern part of Cyprus is still occupied. Nor do certain EU countries fare well here: consider Northern Ireland or Gibraltar. However, their advantage is that they are already in the EU.

The EU is interested in resolving pressing problems in the region. There are some signs that the prospect of EU membership may ease some tensions, as happened with Hungary and Romania in 1996, Greece and Turkey in 2000, Serbia and Montenegro with Croatia in 2003 or Armenia and Turkey in 2005. The possibility of joining the EU and a specific invitation in the form of a positive feasibility study by the European Commission is a strong and effective foreign policy tool for the imposition of EU-type discipline which is used by this organisation. The EU should also assist accession countries in order to create a peaceful and prosperous neighbourhood for itself in the future. The question has not been whether central and east European countries need to be incorporated into the EU. The question has always been the cost to the EU(15) of expanding their club, as well as how long the enlargement would take.

The third set of conditions is associated with *organisational and administrative* issues. This relates to the *acquis communautaire* or the Community patrimony (the whole body of established EU laws, policies and practices), which must be fully accepted by the accession countries. The belief that skilful national diplomacy and bargaining may provide better deals for the accession countries is false. Entry into the EU is just the beginning, not the end, of the story. The *acquis communautaire* consists of around 80 000 pages of EU legislation. The only possibility for negotiations concerned the length of the adjustment period and, potentially, the size of funds that may help to apply it. *Agenda 2000* (1997), the EU's plan for action in the medium term, is clear on this point. The new EU member countries are required to accept, apply and enforce the *acquis communautaire* upon accession. In order to safeguard the EU internal competition rules, those measures that relate to the Single European Market should be applied immediately upon accession.[67] However, there may be certain transition measures for a limited period. Many EU firms are against any transition period that may be given to their competitors from the accession countries because they fear social and environmental dumping from the east.

The EU is already a multispeed organisation. Countries that are in the EMU form one tier, with Britain, Denmark and Sweden forming another. Even within the EMU, large countries (France, Germany and Italy) succeeded in 2002 in persuading the European Commission to bend the rules of the Stability and Growth Pact (1996) which require eurozone countries to keep their national budgets within strict limits. As a result the European Commission postponed the target date for achieving budgetary balance from 2004 to 2006. Another EU tier includes the countries that are members of the Schengen Agreement on the free movement of foreigners. Creating yet another tier by conceding derogations or opt-outs to the accession countries would complicate the operation of the EU and imperil free competition in the Single European Market. Hence, according to *Agenda 2000* and subsequent official statements this should not happen.[68] An accession country's record in the implementation of existing commitments was used by the EU as one measure by which to judge the country's capacity to take on the obligations of full membership.[69] There may be another internal group of EU countries that have ratified the EU constitution and those that have not.

The fourth, tacit, requirement for the EU entry relates to *finances*. This means that an enlargement should not imperil the EU's financial resources, nor should widening of the EU risk deepening of the integration process. If there were no changes in the EU policies and if accession countries entered the unreformed EU(15), various early estimates stated that the annual transfers from the EU to those countries would cost the EU budget around €50 billion a year.[70] That is about half of the entire annual budget for EU(15). The European Council in Brussels (2002) set the final operational financial rules that made eastern enlargement of the EU relatively cheap for the EU as will be seen below.

In order to assist prospective transition countries, the European Council in Essen (1994) outlined the 'pre-accession strategy' of the EU. The key element is the assistance offered to the select group of transition countries. The prospective member countries committed themselves, among other things, to approximate their legislation to that of the EU. The gap in the political, economic and social organisation and development between the EU and the potential new members has to narrow, otherwise the new members may not assume the full set of obligations and enjoy all the benefits of membership. Europe Agreements, a structured dialogue and the PHARE programme are the major tools of the 'pre-accession strategy'.[71] In addition, the European Council in Cannes (1995) endorsed the White Paper, a reference document that can guide the prospective member countries through the labyrinth of EU legislation in order to make the task of accession simpler. Additionally, in order to ease entry, the EU opened the Technical Assistance Information Exchange Office (TAIEX) in 1996, providing a one-stop shop where information and technical/legal advice on EU legislation, enforcement and infrastructure can be obtained.

The British and the Danes entered the EU (or the European Economic Community as it was then called) in 1973 on the false assumption that EU business was all about economics, and not about politics. That is the root of subsequent opt-outs for these two countries from new legislation. All the broad and necessary conditions for entry into the EU reveal that the EU has very high discretionary powers and flexibility to select would-be members, as well as to set the time, pace and conditions for entry. In any case, any offers and incentives to enter the EU are effective foreign policy tools for the EU, especially those from the Copenhagen European Council (1993). One Brussels official stated that 'Once a country applies to join the EU, it becomes our slave.'[72]

COSTS AND BENEFITS

New Member Countries

Accession countries from central and eastern Europe share political, security and economic reasons for joining the EU. Politically, these countries still have a young and potentially fragile democratic system. Fragility comes from unfulfilled grand hopes that the change for the better towards a market-type democratic system can take place in a relatively short period of time and at a relatively acceptable cost. Although the immediate threat of an armed conflict in Europe is not highly likely (even though there are hot spots such as the Balkan peninsula, the Aegean Sea or Cyprus), there is still apprehension regarding the division of 'spheres of influence' between the west and Russia. The central, eastern European and Baltic states only recently obtained their freedom from the 'eastern bloc'. They have concerns both about preserving their independence from the east and about 'losing' it to the west.

With regard to the economic issues, there are important gains for the accession countries from entry into the EU:

- The major benefit is secure access to the huge EU market. This is particularly relevant for the goods that are politically 'sensitive' for the EU (agricultural products, textiles, steel, chemicals), as the accession countries have comparative advantage in the production of those goods. Entry would mean a kind of 'insurance policy' that the EU trade regime would credibly remain open for their exports.
- The second gain in theory would be the possibility of labour migration into the rest of the EU following the specified adjustment period. This may be a two-edged sword. If the educated and the experienced leave the accession countries, the productivity in the 'accession region' would suffer and funds for the education of experts would be lost. A relatively tight labour market in the rest of the EU(15) would, however, prevent such a scenario occurring. In addition, experience has shown that labour migration (wars apart) takes place chiefly when labour cannot find employment in its country of origin.
- A third benefit from entry includes access to the structural and other EU funds.

This would all give an impetus to strengthen the market system (van Brabant, 1996).

Structural aid and the geography of production

None of the potential gains from entry into the EU are without risks. In some cases, the costs are quite serious. Central and east European countries still have fragile economies that would be exposed to the chill wind of fierce competition in the Single European Market. Adjustment problems are well known even for relatively advanced transition economies, as evidenced by the problems experienced in the former East Germany after the *Anschluss* of 1989. Gross annual transfers from the western part of the reunified Germany to the east were around DM 180 billion (€90 billion) during the 1990s (Table 5A2.4). Such massive aid to the former East Germany will be necessary for at least another five years in order to try to adjust its economy and partly catch up with the rest of the country. If the eastern part of the reunited Germany needs such massive annual transfers of around 4 per cent

Table 5A2.4 Annual public financial transfers[1] from western to eastern Germany, 1991–99 (DM bn)

Transfer	1991	1992	1993	1994	1995	1996	1997	1998[2]	1999[3]
Gross	139	152	168	168	185	187	183	189	194
Net	106	115	129	125	140	140	136	141	144

Notes:
Data for 1998 and 1999 = Bundestags-Drucksache 13/11472, p. 11.
1. Including social insurance.
2. Partly estimated.
3. According to the draft budget.

Source: Herausgeber BMI, *Jahresbericht der Bundesregierung zum Stand der Deutschen Einheit*. Berlin, 1998.

Table 5A2.5 Convergence indicators for East Germany 1991, 1996 and 1998 (West Germany = 100)

Indicator	1991	1996	2000
Average monthly wages			
Gross	48.3	76.7	77.2*
Net	54.8	84.2	86.1*
Productivity			
Total economy	34.3	66.8	68.2
Manufacturing	23.9	63.6	69.5
Construction	48.8	75.7	67.8
GDP per capita at current prices	32.8	54.0	59.9

Note: * 1998.

Sources: Economic Commission for Europe (1997). *Economic Survey for Europe in 1996–1997*. New York: United Nations, p. 30. Wirtschaftsdaten neue Bundesländer, Bundesministerium für Wirtschaft und Technologie. Berlin, 2001.

of the German GDP,[73] one shudders to think about the volume of potential transfers that will be needed by other accession countries.[74]

There have been certain positive results during this 'catch-up' process as exemplified in the doubling of productivity (Table 5A2.5). The convergence road was principally based on shrinking employment and emigration rather than on higher investment and output. The financial cost of such a catch-up process was immense and continuing. This is the root of the difficult budgetary position of Germany. The question remains as to whether such massive aid will be necessary in the medium and long terms. Aid may kill local incentives to adjust and it may create a structurally dependent economy out of the former East Germany as happened with the Italian Mezzogiorno. Welfare standards have been raised in the former East Germany and, consequently, wages have increased above productivity. Similarly, the Italian social system prevented wages from falling to competitive levels in the Mezzogiorno. As a result, both southern Italy and the former East Germany have high unemployment and dependency on public transfers.

Bearing all these issues in mind, one may ask whether the accession countries are not, perhaps, aspiring to do too much too soon. Where are the funds to accommodate the adjustment of the central and east European countries to come from? The Maastricht criteria for the EMU and the Stability and Growth Pact require budgetary cuts throughout the EU. The Cannes Summit (1995) allocated 'only' €6.7 billion to the PHARE Programme for the 1995–99 period. Therefore, most of the funds will have to come from the accession countries themselves or from foreign loans.

As for the 2000–06 period, there is a decision to keep the spending limit for all EU activities at the current level of 1.27 per cent of the total GDP of the 15 member countries. This limit is combined with strict constraints on the national public expenditure that are related to the EMU. However, Agenda 2000 earmarked €45 billion for the 2000–06 period (a kind of mini Marshall Plan) to be used as pre-accession aid to the accession countries. During that time, accession countries will be granted €1 billion a year as structural aid plus €0.5 billion a year for agricultural development.[75]

Negotiations about the financing of EU(25) expenditure (Financial Perspective 2007–13) are much more difficult than was the case in the past. The EU(15), in particular the eurozone member governments, argue against an expansion of the EU budget at a time when they are making unprecedented efforts at home to cut spending in order to keep within the rules of the EMU. To make things harder, this new perspective will have to include also the cost of entry of Bulgaria and Romania, expected in 2007.

In theory, economic integration may, but will not necessarily, bring greater benefits to the regions/countries that lag behind the centre of economic activity in their development. However, if production linkages (forward and backward) are strong and internal to an industry such as in chemicals or financial services, and if imperfect competition prevails, economic integration will trigger agglomeration tendencies. If those linkages are not limited to a relatively narrow industry group, but are strong *across* industries and sectors, integration will produce agglomeration tendencies in select spots. If labour is not mobile, the whole process will tend to open up new and widen the existing regional wage differentials (Venables, 1996a). Although this may produce deindustrialisation tendencies in the peripheral regions, it does not mean that integration is not desirable. For instance, education and regional policies increased the attractiveness of Spain, Finland or Ireland as locations for various manufacturing industries, as discovered by EU and foreign investors.

As for the structure of industrial geography of production in the EU and relying on the study by Midelfart-Knarvik et al. (2002, p. 256), the observation is that the EU countries became more specialised from the early 1980s than was previously the case. This confirms the theoretical expectations of standard, neo-classical and new theories of economic integration. A new pattern of industrial production is emerging in the EU. The major features of this divergence process in the geography of industrial production in the EU are that this process is slow and does not provoke great adjustment costs; the most remarkable change in the geography of production was the spreading of relatively high-technology and high-skill industries towards the EU periphery (Ireland and Finland); and the availability of highly skilled and educated workers is becoming an increasingly important determinant for industrial location.

Acquis communautaire

Economic transition towards a market-type system is in itself a lengthy and costly process. Furthermore, to accept and to apply a continuously evolving *acquis communautaire* is costly not only for the new members, but also for the countries that are already in the EU. Being less developed, the accession countries both have a lower financial, technical and administrative capacity, and require a greater degree of reform to incorporate and 'digest' the EU rules. So many things are highly regulated (standardised) in the EU, from the length of ladders for window cleaners to the quality of water and cheese to the size of apples. This includes not only health, environment and consumer protection, but also safety at work and social standards. Many of these items do not directly increase productivity. With an out-of-date capital stock, there is a dilemma in the accession countries: should they invest scarce capital first into upgrading output potential or do something else or both (in what proportion)?[76]

The cyanide spill in Romania (2000) was the worst ecological disaster since the Chernobyl nuclear accident (1986). It reminded everyone about the gravity of the problem in the accession countries.[77] The environmental dimension of the *acquis communautaire* has 320 pieces of 'green' legislation. To apply all those laws could cost the 10 transition accession countries as much as €110 billion over a decade.[78] Table 5A2.6 provides information on the parts of these harmonisation costs which deal with water, air and waste standards in six selected accession countries. The EU would offer some financial support to these countries in order to ease the burden of meeting the entry criteria, but most of the funds would have to come from the new

Table 5A2.6 What would it cost six new member countries to reach the EU environmental standards? (€ bn)

Country	Water	Air	Waste (maximum)	Total investment (maximum)	Total € per capita
Poland	18.1	13.9	3.3	35.2	927
Hungary	6.6	2.7	4.4	13.7	1306
Czech R.	3.3	6.4	3.8	12.4	1427
Slovakia	1.9	1.9	1.6	5.4	760
Estonia	1.5	n.a.	n.a.	1.5	n.a.
Slovenia	n.a.	0.7	1.1	1.8	n.a.

Source: Parlement européen, 'La politique de l'environnement et l'élargissement', *Fiche thématique* no. 17, Luxembourg, 23 March 1998, p. 15.

member countries themselves.[79] Can these costs be compensated for by the potential benefits that would come from the entry? If so, how can one measure that? How long would it take? Is such an investment justified at this moment? Public opinion polls in transition countries rank concern for the environment much lower than health care, education, security and the economy.

The benefit side of these investments is hard to measure and is unfortunately often forgotten. Safe water free of toxins or pollutants, pure air and secure handling of waste would contribute both to an improvement in quality of life and savings in resources. For example, it is estimated that by cutting air pollution, all new member countries could avoid between 43 000 and 180 000 cases of chronic bronchitis and between 15 000 and 34 000 cases of premature death. The cumulative value of these benefits to the new member countries until 2020 is estimated to be in the range of €134–681 billion.[80] Having to 'import' expensive *acquis communautaire*, central and east European member countries expect an inflow of FDI as compensation.

Even though the European Commission noted in its annual enlargement reports (2003) that accession countries have made meaningful progress in the adjustment of their economies in relation to the EU(15), serious flaws still persist. They include weaknesses in administrative capacity,[81] excessive public expenditure, underperforming judicial systems, public-sector internal auditing and widespread corruption. Poland, a country that presents the biggest eastern enlargement challenge, for example, slowed down all reforms and did little to reduce public expenditure and deficit throughout 2003. However, even the EU's administrative capacity is far from perfect. In 2005, for the eleventh successive year, the EU Court of Auditors was able to certify the legality and regularity of only 5 per cent of the EU expenditure (mainly relating to internal administration). The rest, that is, 95 per cent, was not given a positive statement of assurance owing to the number of errors that were found.[82]

All these data reveal that a number of new member countries are not only considerably worse off than EU(15) members, but they still constitute a distinct structural class by themselves. The difference in income per capita as well as investment needed to comply with the *acquis communautaire* between the new member countries and that of the EU(15) is not only structural, but also huge.

Economic and monetary union

The theory of international monetary integration is based on criteria which include factor mobility, openness of the economy, similar rates of unemployment, diversification of the economic structure, coordination of economic policies and comparable rates of inflation between the integrating countries. The Maastricht Treaty brought conditions for the EMU that are not known in the theory of monetary integration. A sceptic might say that this is why the eurozone may work. In any case, if transaction costs remain significant and if there is a danger from the exchange risk, then the EMU might give stability and an additional impetus to the expansion of intra-EU trade.

Let us recall the Maastricht criteria for the EMU:

- a high degree of price stability (low inflation);
- a sound public finance position (budget deficit of maximum 3 per cent of the GDP);
- national debt of less than 60 per cent of GDP;
- no devaluation within the exchange rate mechanism for at least the two preceding years; and
- the national interest rate needs to be within the 2 per cent margin of the three best-performing countries.

The criteria for the EMU may create some barriers for accession to the EU. *Agenda 2000* and subsequent documents state that each accession country is required to accept, apply and enforce the *acquis communautaire* upon accession. In order to safeguard the EU competition rules, those measures that relate to the Single European Market should be applied immediately upon accession.[83] Being out of the EMU, a new member country's currency may be the target for a speculative attack on the currency market that the country may not be able to withstand.[84] The country may alter the rate of exchange. By doing so, trade flows and free competition in the Single European Market could be jeopardised. Hence the need for the accession

Table 5A2.7 Government deficit(−)/surplus(+) in the EU and candidate countries, 1997–2004 (% of GDP)

Country	1997	1998	1999	2000	2001	2002	2003	2004*
EU(25)		−1.7	−0.8	0.8	−1.2	−2.3	−2.8	−3.0
EU(15)	−2.4	−1.6	−0.7	1.0	−1.1	−2.1	−2.7	–
Eurozone	−2.6	−2.2	−1.3	0.2	−1.7	−2.4	−2.7	–
New members								
Cyprus	−5.3	−4.3	−4.5	−2.4	−2.4	−4.6	−6.4	−3.6
Czech R.	−2.5	−5.0	−3.6	−3.7	−5.9	−6.8	−12.6	−4.7
Estonia	1.9	−0.3	−3.7	−0.6	0.3	1.4	3.1	1.4
Hungary	−6.8	−8.0	−5.6	−3.0	−4.4	−9.2	−6.2	−5.1
Latvia	−0.2	−0.6	−4.9	−2.8	−2.1	−2.7	−1.5	−1.2
Lithuania	−1.1	−3.0	−5.6	−2.5	−2.0	−1.5	−1.9	−1.9
Malta	−10.7	−10.8	−7.6	−6.2	−6.4	−5.9	−9.7	–
Poland	−4.0	−2.1	−1.4	−0.7	−3.8	−3.6	−3.9	−5.3
Slovakia	−5.5	−4.7	−6.4	−12.3	−6.0	−5.7	−3.7	−3.9
Slovenia	−1.9	−2.2	−2.1	−3.5	−2.8	−2.4	−2.0	−1.9
Candidates								
Bulgaria	−0.3	1.7	0.4	−0.5	0.2	−0.8	−0.1	1.7
Romania	−4.5	−3.2	−4.5	−4.4	−3.5	−2.0	−2.0	−1.2
Croatia	–	–	–	–	–	–	−6.2	−5.0
Turkey	−13.0	−12.0	−19.0	−6.0	−29.8	−12.6	−8.8	−7.3

Note: * Estimates.

Source: Eurostat (2005) and Economist Intelligence Unit (EIU) (2005).

countries to join the eurozone. The three EU(15) member countries that are currently out of the eurozone should not be taken as best precedents for the accession countries. The three are already fully adjusted EU members with stable and developed economies. It would be difficult to manage the EU(25) economy when slightly under half of the EU uses the euro while the rest does not.

If the macroeconomic situation remains stable in the future, many accession countries may not have great difficulty in satisfying most (inflation apart) of the loosely interpreted Maastricht criteria for the EMU (Tables 5A2.7–10, respectively).[85] All new member countries have growing economies, which is a very positive development. The problem is to maintain this positive differential growth rate over and (well) above the EU(15) rate for a long period in order to catch up with the average EU level of development. A relatively stable catch-up process with the EU may well require a rate of inflation that may be over and above the norms required

Table 5A2.8 National debt in the EU and candidate countries, 1997–2003 (% of GDP)

Country	1997	1998	1999	2000	2001	2002	2003
EU(25)	–	67.5	66.7	62.9	62.1	61.6	63.3
EU(15)	71.0	68.9	67.9	64.1	63.3	62.7	64.3
Eurozone	74.9	74.2	72.7	70.4	69.5	69.4	70.7
New members							
Cyprus	–	61.6	62.0	61.6	64.3	67.4	70.9
Czech R.	12.2	12.9	13.4	18.2	25.3	28.8	37.8
Estonia	6.4	5.6	6.0	4.7	4.4	5.3	5.3
Hungary	64.2	61.9	61.2	55.4	53.5	57.2	59.1
Latvia	–	9.8	12.6	12.9	14.9	14.1	14.4
Lithuania	15.2	16.5	23.0	23.8	22.9	22.4	21.6
Malta	51.5	64.9	56.8	56.4	62.2	62.7	71.1
Poland	44.0	39.1	40.3	36.8	36.7	41.1	45.4
Slovakia	33.1	34.0	47.2	49.9	48.7	43.3	42.6
Slovenia	23.2	23.6	24.9	27.4	28.1	29.5	29.5
Candidates							
Bulgaria	105.1	79.6	79.3	73.6	66.2	53.2	46.2
Romania	16.5	18.0	24.0	23.9	23.2	23.3	21.8
Croatia	–	–	–	–	–	–	–
Turkey	53.0	50.0	67.4	57.4	105.2	94.3	87.4

Source: Eurostat (2005).

by the EMU. This is a very real conflict between the demand for accelerated growth and the EMU demand for stability both in prices (deflationary bias) and in the exchange rate. Long-run growth projections predict that it may take about 30 years (one generation) for most of the central and eastern European countries to catch up with the income levels in 'low-income' EU countries (Table 5A2.11).[86] With average income per capita about half the EU(15) average, central and east European countries need relatively fast and continuous economic growth. For them this may be a much more important sign of national economic success than an early eurozone entry.

Monetary policy in the central and east European countries may gain in general credibility and stability inside the eurozone, but different growth priorities and asymmetric shocks relative to other eurozone countries may introduce tensions within the EMU. While the eurozone may serve the interest of many of the 12 participating member countries fairly well, this may not be the case for an EMU of perhaps 27 or more member countries. This difficulty is compounded by the Governing Council's voting system in

Table 5A2.9 Growth rate of GDP in the EU and candidate countries, 1997–2006 (% change over preceding year)

Country	1997	1998	1999	2000	2001	2002	2003	2004*	2005*	2006*
EU(25)	2.8	3.0	2.9	3.6	1.8	1.2	1.2	2.3	2.2	2.1
EU(15)	2.6	2.9	2.8	3.6	1.8	1.1	0.9	2.0	–	–
Eurozone	2.4	2.9	2.9	3.5	1.7	0.9	0.6	2.0	2.0	2.0
New members										
Cyprus	2.5	5.0	4.8	5.0	4.1	2.1	1.9	3.4	3.8	3.5
Czech R.	−0.8	−1.0	0.5	3.9	2.6	1.5	3.7	3.8	4.3	4.4
Estonia	9.8	4.6	−0.6	7.8	6.4	7.2	5.1	6.0	5.8	5.6
Hungary	4.6	4.9	4.1	5.2	3.8	3.5	3.9	4.0	3.7	4.0
Latvia	8.4	4.8	2.8	6.9	8.0	6.4	7.5	8.0	5.0	5.0
Lithuania	7.3	5.1	−1.7	3.9	6.4	6.8	9.7	6.6	5.8	5.6
Malta	4.8	3.4	4.1	6.4	−2.4	2.6	−0.3	0.7	2.0	2.0
Poland	6.8	4.8	4.0	4.0	1.0	1.4	3.8	5.4	4.3	4.0
Slovakia	5.6	4.2	1.5	2.0	3.8	4.6	4.5	5.5	5.8	5.9
Slovenia	4.6	3.8	5.2	3.9	2.7	3.3	2.5	4.3	3.9	3.7
Candidates										
Bulgaria	−5.6	4.0	2.3	5.4	4.1	4.9	4.3	5.5	4.5	4.7
Romania	−6.1	−4.8	−1.2	2.1	5.7	5.0	4.9	5.0	5.1	–
Croatia	6.8	2.5	−0.9	2.9	4.4	5.2	4.3	3.7	3.7	4.2
Turkey	7.5	3.1	−4.7	7.4	−7.5	7.9	5.8	4.5	5.0	4.0

Note: * Estimates and projections.

Sources: European Commission for Europe (2005), Eurostat (2005) and Economist Intelligence Unit (2005).

which each participating country has one vote. A reduction in the weight of small countries in the decision making process may be necessary in the future (de Grauwe, 2002).

Agriculture

Farm gate prices in the central and east European countries were on average within a range of 40 to 80 per cent of the EU level which was guaranteed by the Common Agricultural Policy towards the end of the 1990s.[87] If the unreformed CAP prices were to apply directly in the new member countries, that would give a strong boost to the output of both crop (cereals, oilseeds and sugar) and livestock production, as well as milk. At the same time, an increase in the price of farm goods in the accession countries could provoke social tensions. Indeed, price hikes have severely affected social groups such as the retired and the unemployed, following EU entry.

Table 5A2.10 Annual rate of inflation in the EU and candidate countries, 1997–2004 (%)

Country	1997	1998	1999	2000	2001	2002	2003	2004
EU(25)	2.6	2.1	1.6	2.4	2.5	2.1	1.9	2.1
EU(15)	1.7	1.3	1.2	1.9	2.2	2.1	2.0	2.0
Eurozone	1.7	1.2	1.1	2.1	2.4	2.3	2.1	2.1
New members								
Cyprus	3.3	2.3	1.1	4.9	2.0	2.8	4.0	1.9
Czech R.	8.0	9.7	1.8	3.9	4.5	1.4	−0.1	2.6
Estonia	9.3	8.8	3.1	3.9	5.6	3.5	1.4	3.0
Hungary	18.5	14.2	10.0	10.0	9.1	5.2	4.7	6.8
Latvia	8.1	4.3	2.1	2.6	2.5	2.0	2.9	6.2
Lithuania	8.8	5.0	0.7	0.9	1.3	0.4	−1.1	1.1
Malta	3.9	3.7	2.3	3.0	2.5	2.6	1.9	2.7
Poland	15.0	11.8	7.2	10.1	5.3	1.9	0.7	3.6
Slovakia	6.0	6.7	10.4	12.2	7.2	3.5	8.5	7.4
Slovenia	8.3	7.9	6.1	8.9	8.6	7.5	5.7	3.6
Candidates								
Bulgaria	1082.6	18.7	2.6	10.3	7.4	5.8	2.3	6.1
Romania	154.9	59.1	45.8	45.7	34.5	22.5	15.3	11.9
Croatia	3.7	5.2	3.5	5.4	4.7	1.8	2.2	2.1
Turkey	85.4	84.6	65.0	55.2	54.3	44.9	25.4	10.6

Sources: Eurostat (2005), European Commission for Europe (2005) and Economist Intelligence Unit (2005).

It is difficult to convince the new member countries not to increase farm production, unless they can see clear signs that the CAP is undergoing reform. One thing is clear: enlargement of the EU could not easily proceed without a prior change in the CAP. A profound reform of the CAP would test the EU's commitment to enlargement.

The eastern enlargement also introduces the practical problem of how to operate country-specific transitional arrangements. If, for example, alignment of the prices of agricultural products between the EU and Hungary takes place at a different rate from alignment of prices in Poland, it will be necessary to impose tariffs, not only between the accession countries and the EU(15), but also between the accession countries themselves.

Introduced in the 1960s, the CAP was an instrument for ensuring security in food supplies and a means for protecting farmers' income. As food shortages were eliminated, as the EU started to dispose of surpluses of agricultural output and as farmers' income was generally safeguarded against unfavourable developments, the EU concern shifted towards food safety and

Table 5A2.11 Period needed to reach 75% of the EU(15) average GDP per capita

Country	Annual growth rate		Period needed to reach 75% of EU GDP per capita in years
	Assumption from 2004	Average achieved 1995–2002	
Bulgaria	5.0	0.5	40
Cyprus	3.8	3.6	1
Czech Republic	3.9	1.7	19
Estonia	5.1	4.9	23
Hungary	4.1	3.9	24
Latvia	6.0	5.6	24
Lithuania	5.0	3.9	28
Malta	3.7	3.3	25
Poland	3.7	3.9	50
Romania	5.0	0.4	44
Slovakia	4.5	3.7	22
Slovenia	3.7	3.9	7
Turkey	4.5	2.9	61

Source: *European Economy* (2003b, p. 10).

protection of the environment. This last concern is of great importance, as the accession countries have a legacy of serious environmental damage.

Reform of the CAP represented one of the most serious challenges for the EU. It would have consequences for the EU internal operation, for external economic relations and for enlargement. A reform plan, proposed in mid-2002, would break the link between intervention and production. Farm subsidies would be linked to rural conservation. In addition, export subsidies would be significantly reduced. However, this idea to reform the CAP was postponed by France (with Germany's support) until 2006 when the new Financial Perspective (2007–13) is to be finalised. In addition, Britain, Germany, the Netherlands and Sweden are particularly concerned about future farm spending. These countries would like to see a certain reform of the CAP before the EU offers potentially generous subsidies to farmers in the accession countries. This is important as the EU(15) has about 7 million farmers, while central and east European countries would bring an additional 3.8 million.[88] The lobbying and voting power of farmers in the enlarged EU would increase in theory, but in practice it may be difficult to organise them because of their different interests and priorities. In any case, enlargement without a reform of the CAP would not be affordable for the EU.

France and Germany were the driving force behind the European Council in Brussels (24–25 October 2002) deal that brought the 'adjustment' (limit) of the future CAP payments in the light of the forthcoming enlargement. From 2006, total CAP subsidies would have a ceiling. This would keep payments static at current levels during the 2007–13 period, with a possibility of a modest inflation-proof increase of 1 per cent per year. In real terms, these payments would almost certainly decline steadily. Subsidies to farmers in new member countries would be limited to only 25 per cent of those paid to farmers in the EU(15) in 2004. However, the payments to all EU farmers would be gradually brought into parity by 2013. EU(15) farmers would lose from this deal over the coming decade, and this would hit the influential French lobby hard. Therefore, France has made a significant enlargement-related concession. Farmers in the new member countries have lost their illusions about hefty subsidies from Brussels, but most others would gain: in particular, EU consumers and potential exporters to the EU.

European Union

The European Union is generally interested in enlargement for various political, security, ecological and economic reasons. Key EU values would be secured in countries that desperately want them. However, what the central and east European countries would actually contribute to the EU's economy is less easy to discern. One negative organisational aspect of the enlargement process is that the EU may become cumbersome and potentially ungovernable. The enlarged EU may become an extended free trade area. In addition, the entry of eight central and east European countries plus Cyprus and Malta increased the EU population by 20 per cent, while the volume of the EU's GDP increased by only 4.9 per cent at current prices (roughly comparable to the Dutch GDP) and 9.6 per cent at PPS (roughly comparable to the Spanish GDP). The entry of Turkey would increase the EU(25) population by 15 per cent, while the volume of the EU(25) GDP would increase by only 2.4 per cent at current prices and 4.5 per cent at PPS (Table 5A2.12).

Is the 'eastern' market, with relatively cheap labour and possibilities for FDI,[89] an opportunity or a threat for the EU(15)? Germany, the country with the highest unemployment rate since the 1930s, and Austria fear that eastern enlargement would set off an annual inflow of more than 300 000 immigrants (OECD, 2003b, p. 85). This would amount to over 3 million over a decade. Workers from the central and east European countries will have preference in the EU labour market over others who come from non-EU countries. However, there is a five-year transition period, which may be

Table 5A2.12 Total GDP at current prices and in purchasing power standard in the EU and candidate countries in 2004

Country	€ billion	€ billion PPS
EU(25)	10 208.0	10 208.0
EU(15)	9 730.8	9 311.4
New members	477.0	893.5
Cyprus	12.4	13.4
Czech Republic	86.9	158.8
Estonia	8.8	15.2
Hungary	81.4	139.0
Latvia	10.9	22.3
Lithuania	17.7	33.8
Malta	4.4	6.5
Poland	195.9	405.6
Slovakia	32.6	64.1
Slovenia	26.0	34.8
Candidates		
Bulgaria	19.7	53.5
Romania	56.7	150.3
Croatia	27.5	45.8
Turkey	244.5	464.1
10 new members as % of EU(15)	4.9	9.6
Turkey as % of EU(25)	2.4	4.5

Source: Eurostat (2005).

extended for another two years by the EU(15), before these workers are free to work anywhere in the EU. With the exception of Britain, Sweden and Ireland, all EU(15) member countries have applied their right to impose transitional arrangements which restrict freedoms to work and stay for the nationals from central and east European member countries until 2011.

However, although citizens of the new EU member countries are not permitted to seek work freely in the EU(15) until 2011, firms from these countries are not barred from doing business anywhere in the EU. Some of them have started to provide services. This has provoked dismissals in German slaughterhouses in 2005. Low-paid central and eastern European contractors from Poland and the Czech Republic have replaced local employees. These eastern service firms must, of course, comply with the host-country rules on consumer protection, as well as standards that deal with social issues, health and the environment. The German trade unions are particularly concerned that the eastern firms are using business freedom provisions to circumvent labour mobility restrictions and trade in cheap labour (social dumping). There is an anxiety in Germany that services such as construction, nursing and hospitality could soon experience the same trend.[90]

When Spain and Portugal entered the EU they had a seven-year transition period before full labour mobility was granted. However, when this did occur, there was no large labour migration flow to the rest of the EU partner countries. In any case, there are no expectations of any significant labour migrations from central and eastern Europe towards the rest of the EU. These new member countries will also be affected by the general European demographic trends from about 2010.

The potential economic and political gains for the EU need to be combined with at least two potential economic costs that are often mentioned.

- The first is the need to finance the adjustment of the new member countries to the *acquis communautaire* and to the Maastricht criteria for the eurozone.[91] In a situation with serious austerity measures in the EU countries, the question is where would the funds come from? The European Council in Brussels (2002) put a cap on all EU expenditure in order to make enlargement cheap for the EU in financial terms.
- The second 'cost'(?) could come from the (potential) loss of jobs and business in the 'sensitive' manufacturing industries and in agriculture in the EU because of the penetration of goods from the east. There may be strong lobby pressure on policy makers in certain countries to slow down eastern enlargement and/or request compensation from the EU. This second 'cost' may be exaggerated. As a result of the signing of Europe agreements, 'sensitive' manufactured goods from the accession countries entered the EU mainly free of tariff and quantitative restrictions. The major continuing barriers are chiefly antidumping measures. In addition, exports of sensitive products from the accession countries to the EU have not expanded relative to other products since the 1980s. Hence, one should not expect a surge in new member countries' exports of sensitive manufactured products to the EU as a consequence of accession.

The production structure in the new member countries within each of the three broad economic sectors is very different from the structure in the EU(15). If the gains from trade depend on the extent of these differences, the (private) gains should be correspondingly large. Hence, a surge of 'sensitive' imports from the new member countries by the EU may be welcome. The job losses in the sensitive sectors will be more than compensented for by expansion in the non-sensitive sectors. This approach is hotly disputed by politicians and well-entrenched lobbies, but if economists have just one thing to say about adjustment 'costs', then this would be it.

Such debates about the employment effect of trade liberalisation (in the countries with developed and stable economies) are based on 'a fallacy of composition, that the effect of productivity increase *in a given industry* on the number of jobs *in that industry* is very different from the effect of a productivity increase *in the economy as a whole* on the *total* number of jobs' (Krugman, 1998a, pp. 16–7, original emphasis). The negative impact of jobs going 'south' on a large scale has not materialised in practice and the net effect on the US job market might even have been positive.

In the medium term, southern EU countries need not fear the eastern enlargement of the EU and the potential 'exodus' of jobs to central and eastern Europe because of lower wages there. If there is no adjustment 'pain' for these southern countries, there may also be little 'gain' from enlargement. If firms were looking only for low-cost production locations, then China and India may be superior long-term choices to countries in central and eastern Europe. If relatively low wages were the only determining factor for the location of production, then the EU would have already been flooded with cheap goods from those countries. Factors such as productivity, the capital stock, size and growth of the market, supply chain and institutional stability often play a more decisive role for investors than mere differences in nominal wages. But this may change in the future in the new member and accession countries. For example, Peugeot-Citroën announced in 2003 that it intended to invest and to locate a large (€700 million) car assembly factory in Slovakia. The factory would start production of about 300 000 small cars in 2006. The management intended to be closer to fast-growing markets in accession countries and to profit from wage rates that are a fifth of the rates paid in the EU(15) for similar operations. Earlier plants established by western companies in central and eastern Europe were often only additions to their existing plants in the west. This Peugeot-Citroën factory would serve as a replacement plant.[92] Even though similar stories can be cited, the 'eastern region' is still too small to make a significant impact on total production and real income elsewhere in the EU.

The most important argument about the employment impact of the eastern enlargement has, unfortunately, not yet made its way into the public consciousness. It also wrong-footed certain academic debates. The eastern enlargement may create new jobs or at least maintain the existing 'higher quality' jobs in the EU. Isolated and highly publicised stories about the closure of a firm due to the enlargement are not typical for the whole EU economy. Those stories should be seen in the context of a bigger picture. Following the start of the eurozone in the majority of EU(15) countries, the average unemployment rate over the coming years will be to a large extent at the level chosen by the European Central Bank, which may pay little or no regard to the situation in the EU trade balance with the accession countries. This is important if one bears in mind that the total annual merchandise trade of the new member countries with the EU(15) in recent years is twice as much as the EU(15) trade with 'small' Switzerland alone.

Spain, France and Austria (with tacit support from a number of other countries) were cautious about the eastern enlargement. Spain has two national fears that can be substantiated. First, there may be an inflow of cheap fruit and vegetables from the east into the EU(15) which would put Spain's market share of these goods at risk. Second, expenditure from generous structural funds would be directed eastwards to the detriment of beneficiaries in Spain. Following EU enlargement, Spain will cease to qualify for much of the relatively generous EU regional aid that it has been accustomed to receive. Indeed, Spain may even become a net contributor to the EU budget. Therefore, Spain has a vested interest in keeping EU expenditure under strict control. France had reservations about the overall capacity (among other things) of the central and east European countries to undertake all the obligations that are required for EU membership.

It should be recalled that European integration started in the early 1950s, not for economic reasons, but rather to preserve peace. The political goal was to make war between Germany and France impossible through economic means. The southern enlargements of the EU, although costly in financial terms, had the objective of stabilising democracy in Greece, Spain and Portugal following a period of dictatorship (even though these 'revolutions towards democracy' were not led by Brussels). Identical arguments could be used regarding the eastern enlargement of the EU. As for Cyprus, reunification of the country and a reduction in tensions in the eastern Mediterranean region may be among the goals. Stability and predictability at the eastern border is in the interest of the EU. If the EU wants to play a more prominent role in world geopolitics, then eastern enlargement had to take place. Enlargement is not a charity. It is in the EU's self-interest. Ecological and certain economic factors also apply. In addition, modernisation of the central and east European countries may create and keep high-technology jobs in manufacturing and services in the EU(15).

DISILLUSIONMENT

The Treaty of Nice (2001) is popularly portrayed as the act that allowed the new EU enlargement, but the member countries of the EU(15), in particular the large member countries, preserved a certain influence in the new voting structure. However, the Byzantine voting system will put the EU(25+) on track for a crash as far as quick action is concerned. No bloc of member countries, indeed no two blocs, would be able to force through any policy, but almost any single bloc could veto any policy. And there is no shortage of topics that would face harsh conflicts of interest. Hence, one may predict that the basic (economic) policy structure of the EU would remain as it is.

Consideration of the issues of the timing and terms of the new EU enlargement has been highly speculative. Entry depends on the political will (and the funds) of the EU countries. However, the funds and the political will existed even when Spain and Portugal were negotiating entry with the EU during the 1980s, but their entry took several years longer than expected and almost an additional decade to get to full speed with the rest of the EU. In addition, the Iberian enlargement of the EU was technically and economically much simpler than the accession of central and east European transition countries.

The overriding goal of the EU is to safeguard the efficient operation of its Single European Market. This means that a multispeed EU should be avoided as much as possible. Thus, there should be a sufficiently long pre-accession period tailored to the individual conditions of each new country in order to absorb the *acquis communautaire*. This would eliminate the need for the unnecessary post-entry transition period. However, all this is highly speculative as the *acquis communautaire* will be very different in the future from what it was when enlargement negotiations started in 1998 (or much earlier when these countries applied for EU membership). In 2004 alone, the *acquis communautaire* was 'enriched' by 2279 new regulations. To make matters worse, more and tougher rules are on the horizon. It is true that most of them have a limited time duration. However, the accession countries face a continuous race against ever-shifting goalposts. This would not be a problem for Cyprus as Agenda 2000 did not expect any major obstacle regarding the adoption, implementation and enforcement of the *acquis communautaire* in the southern part of the country.[93]

When the EU last accepted 'poor countries' (Spain and Portugal in 1986), the European Community, as it was then called, was not a single market for goods, services, capital and labour. The EU deepened integration and the eurozone was introduced in 1999. Even though Spain and Portugal were 'poor' countries, they were market economies. With this in mind, the chance of even the most advanced central and east European countries accepting, implementing and enforcing the *acquis communautaire* in full seemed a bleak prospect.

Countries such as Norway and Switzerland would be warmly welcomed by the EU. However, the EU has few general economic incentives and limited funds to accept countries with economic structures that are significantly different from its own. Such an attitude may seem hypocritical since the west has spent almost half a century encouraging countries in the east to join the free market and democratic world. Central and east European countries also had to exercise a degree of patience. Jovanović (1997b, p. 368) argued that even if all goes well from the vantage point of 1997, that is, if entry negotiations are successfully finalised, including ratification in all involved countries and a post-entry adjustment period of around a decade, it would take the most advanced central and east European countries some 15–20 years to become full members of the EU.

A clear message to central and east European countries came from the top echelons of the European Commission's DG for Enlargement in 2000.[94] These countries should not attach too much importance to the date of EU entry, but rather focus on the essential issue: the quality of the accession, that is, a respect for the entry criteria. To set a firm date for entry might be a mistake. This might lock the EU into a promise it might regret. The enlargement should take place in such a way as to be beneficial both to the existing EU(15) member countries and to the central and east European countries. In addition, the EU has to remain strong after enlargement.

The European Commission would recommend access only if the accession country could respect rights and duties from the first day of accession.[95] Such transparent messages contributed to a drop in enthusiasm among the accession countries for rapid entry. The Convention on the Future of Europe (2002–03) on the institutional reform of the EU raised new doubts among the central and east European countries. The candidates feared that the accession would be made subject to new conditions or that plots against them were being hatched. Expectation fatigue was taking its toll. None the less, the European Commission considered that Cyprus, the Czech Republic, Estonia, Hungary, Latvia, Lithuania, Malta, Poland, Slovakia and Slovenia would be ready for EU membership from May 2004. Bulgaria and Romania have 2007 as their possible date for accession (European Commission, 2002a, p. 33–4).

Was it necessary to move so fast with the eastern enlargement? It may be true that the central and east European countries had 'no other way' but to join the EU. It is also true that they survived a 'big boom' adjustment following the transition process. However, the 'big boom' was a one-time affair. Integration in the EU is a constantly evolving process. Unless the central and east European countries are well prepared, they may face similar problems to those that Germany encountered with the absorption of the eastern part of the country.[96]

Can the central and east European countries repeat the economic and development success of 'peripheral' Ireland (even other peripheral countries such as Finland, Spain and Portugal after their respective accessions)? The peripheral EU countries became economically more dynamic than the EU 'core' (France, Germany and Italy). However, Ireland is a relatively small country (population 3.7 million). Its story resembles those of Singapore or Hong Kong. Ireland created a business-friendly environment for new technology firms and FDI. A relatively small amount of FDI could have a powerful impact on a small economy such as Ireland. In addition, over a long period, Ireland unlike Greece used EU funds for infrastructure projects of lasting value. Greece, on the other hand, lagged behind other EU countries for years following its EU entry. There is a serious concern that with Poland on board, the EU may be burdened with a much larger version of Greece for years to come. In any case, following the Irish example, the central and east European EU countries introduced lower company taxes than the core EU countries.

A near absence of public debate in the EU about enlargement left most people in ignorance about the tectonic political and economic changes that this involved. For most of them, this was a remote abstraction and a done deal. Enlargement should not be done surreptitiously as was the case with the creation of the eurozone. That was an important reason for the Irish rejection of the Treaty of Nice in 2001. This can easily serve as an argument that the enlargement process is going too fast and that public opinion is not supporting it. Ireland was the only EU country to offer its citizens the privilege (or is this a democratic right?) of being consulted directly on the Treaty. The rest, that is, 99 per cent, of EU citizens were not given the opportunity to express their views directly on this crucial issue.

COST OF ENLARGEMENT

What will the financial cost of enlargement be for the EU(15)? Since *Agenda 2000* (1997) and the European Council in Berlin (1999), there has been an overall cap on the total receipts that any EU member state may get from the EU: 4 per cent of the recipient country's GDP. As the total GDP of the 10 new member countries is rather small (4.9 per cent of the total EU GDP in 2004 at current prices), the actual cost of enlargement for the EU need not be excessive and could be relatively small.

The European Council in Copenhagen (12–13 December 2002) and previously in Brussels (2002)[97] reconfirmed its Berlin (1999)[98] decision that the ceiling for enlargement-related expenditure set out for the years 2004–06 must be respected. That is to say that total EU expenditure must be consonant with its own resources, which are limited to 1.27 per cent of the combined EU GDP of all member countries. Therefore, the EU has very little room for manoeuvre in which to enlarge its funds. During the three-year period from 2004 to 2006, 'of the €25.1 billion in payments for the period, €14.1 billion will be covered by new member states' contributions, so that the net cost for the EU15 would be €10.3 billion' (*Enlargement Weekly*, 28 January 2003). Consequently, the actual annual net 'cost' of the eastern enlargement will be €3.4 billion or less than €10 per EU(15) citizen.[99] Tough negotiations and horse trading started in 2005 in order to define the new financial perspective for the 2007–13 period . If one recalls the CAP adjustment deal, full equality of the 10 new member countries with the rest of the EU(15) will not come before 2013. Before that, the new member countries will in certain respects be second-class citizens. In any case, the EU(25) entered a much more difficult phase of integration in 2004 than most people imagine, not forgetting the symptoms of enlargement fatigue.

The fact that public transfers to agriculture are to be limited on regional policy grounds is surely a good thing. Aid has never helped anyone in the medium and long terms, even though one can easily make emotional cases for assistance. The central and east European countries need private investment, not public aid. Many would argue that public investment is a 'good thing'. If devoted to infrastructural public goods, it can be. But much gets lost on the way. The administrative capacity of public officials in the central and east European countries to handle projects in a new way still needs to be strengthened.[100] There are fears that much EU aid goes to the general budget, allowing local ex-communists to pursue policies for which there is little or weak democratic support and accountability, as well as to prop up lame-duck firms, rather than to assist promising projects which require assistance only in their initial phase.

The European Council in Brussels (2002) brought in two safeguard clauses – one regarding the internal market and the other in the area of justice and home affairs – of up to three years' duration after accession. These measures may be invoked even *before* accession and the 'duration of such measures may extend beyond the three-year period'.[101] Hence, the message, in plain English, from the European Council to the accession countries was: 'Welcome to our club. But from today we are watching you closely to see whether you are applying and enforcing "our" rules. Any mistake and you will pay for that. And do not forget, your dreams of big handouts will remain just that. Dreams.' What an unfriendly message regarding investment, particularly private investment, in and towards the accession countries! If there is any 'mishap' in central and eastern Europe, an introduction of EU safeguards may easily jeopardise returns on an investment.

TURKEY IN THE EU: EUTHANASIA OR THE REJUVENATION OF EUROPE?

The issue of Turkish aspirations for full membership of the EU is a highly polarising, sensitive and controversial matter both politically and economically.[102] An obvious peril for Turkey is to regard EU membership as a panacea and no-cost, no-risk solution for all its domestic ills. Turkey may be welcome in the EU family, but it has to make sure that its European identity and credentials are crystal clear.

First and foremost, Turkey and the EU have had a functioning customs union in manufactured goods and processed agricultural products since 1995. Hence, almost all trade gains between the EU and Turkey are already well in place. Interestingly, the major beneficiary of this customs union is most likely to be the EU. Most of the Turkish manufactured exports to the EU were liberalised even before the customs union deal, which simply formalised trade relations in manufactured products. On the other hand, Turkey had to open its market to imports from the EU. Second, the EU(25) is no longer the honey pot it once was during the time of the EU(9) or even the EU(12). This was belatedly discovered in the cold light of day with bitterness and disappointment by the central and east European countries within the EU(25). What they saw and expected when they applied for membership was not at all what they got when they joined the EU.

The EU signed an association agreement with Turkey in 1963. Turkey applied for full EU membership in 1987 and was given the status of candidate country in 1999. After 41 years of waiting, entry negotiations started in October 2005. This negotiation process may easily last a decade even if there are no political interruptions in Turkey and in the EU. One of the biggest obstacles to the accession process is in Turkey itself. Many in Turkey may understand the accession process as pure negotiations about a detailed and 'boring' Single European Market. In other areas, they may consider giving concessions in one area (Cyprus) and expecting EU concessions in another. Accepting, implementing and enforcing the *acquis communautaire* goes far beyond economics and includes democratic and religious freedoms, as well as human and minority rights.

Apart from the general Copenhagen criteria for EU membership, there are also others. Many of them can be quite unpredictable and whimsical. Turkey is a special, indeed a very special, Euro-Oriental country. The obvious conditions, negotiation items and pressure issues would include the following:

- *Genocide* Even though some may argue that this deals with the past, the issue of genocide will feature high on the agenda. For example,

German statesmen and politicians at the highest level have explicitly and officially given their apologies for the genocide committed during the Second World War. The country is still paying compensation to victims. As such, Germany has passed through a moral catharsis (*Vergangenheitsbewältigung*) and is fully accepted into the family of countries that share common European values. Turkey will be asked do the same. The genocide committed by Turkey against its indigenous inhabitants, the Armenian Christians, in 1915 left 1.5 million Armenians dead.[103] Turkey will be asked to come to terms with this (as the Germans have).[104] An international commission might be a good starting point.[105] In order to address the issue of the Armenian genocide, Recep Tayyip Erdogan, the Prime Minister of Turkey, has called for an unbiased study by historians.[106]

- *Expansionism* Germany, for example, relinquished the expansionist Nazi-type pan-German ideas that are a threat to peace. This is most obvious and important in relations with Poland (Germany's eastern border). Turkey's statesmen, politicians and government institutions will be asked to clearly and publicly renounce the pan-Turkish ideas asserted even by the latest generation of its statesmen such as Suleiman Demirel and Turgut Ozal about a Turkey 'from the Chinese Wall to the Adriatic sea'. Such alarming ambitions[107] raise concerns and fears about the re-establishment of the Ottoman Empire (1350–1918). Austrians still have a strong collective memory of hardships suffered during the Turkish sieges of Vienna (1529–1683) and fear that this may be repeated. Many of them wonder whether the 1683 victory over the Ottoman Empire was in vain.[108] The Balkan countries, all working towards full EU membership, share similar concerns as they still feel the consequences of centuries of Turkish occupation. There are also constant Turkish claims and provocations regarding Greek territory.[109] Following tense top-level negotiations in December 2004, it was decided that negotiations for Turkey's entry into the EU would begin on 3 October 2005. *Al-Ahram Weekly* reported:

> Erdogan returned to Turkey to a hero's welcome, feted by the Turkish media and greeted at Istanbul airport by thousands of members of his Justice and Development Party (JDP) carrying banners proclaiming him 'The Conqueror of Europe'.[110]

This would boost the domestic popularity of the pro-Islamic JDP in the next elections. Regardless of the EU's political declarations, it is a fact that ever since the Muslim invasion of Spain in 711 and the Crusades in the Middle Ages, Europe has had uncomfortable relations with the Arab and Muslim world.[111] Their cultures and destinies have been following different paths.

- *Cyprus* Turkey will be asked to withdraw all (35 000) occupation forces[112] from Cyprus, which, as an EU member country, must be recognised in its entirety.[113] In addition, illegally seized property in Cyprus must be returned to its original owners.
- *Turkish-speaking countries* Following the dissolution of the former Soviet Union, Azerbaijan, Kazakhstan, Kyrgyzstan, Turkmenistan and Uzbekistan emerged as independent Turkish-speaking states with a total population of over 60 million. In 2005, Kazakhstan invited Turkey to assist the five central Asian states[114] to form an economic union. This is an exceptional opportunity for Turkey. The five countries are apprehensive about stronger relations either with Russia, their former master; or with China, a country that is short on natural resources and is actively seeking external sources; or with the west, which promotes 'democracy', a lethal medicine for the local rulers. Turkey fits well into this situation and identifies closely with their concerns, because it is different from other exporters of political influence. Turkey shares a common heritage with the five, it is not keen on an export of 'democratic revolutions', it is relatively geographically distant and it has applied to join the EU. Turkey has the accumulated know-how to 'integrate' and run a big multi-ethnic empire. One economic benefit for Turkey may be the creation of new and the strengthening of existing east–west transport corridors. Having in mind the re-established strong relations with some Balkan countries, in a certain sense Turkey could return to its Ottoman heritage.[115] Would Turkey also bring the citizens of all these countries into the EU because of dual-nationality agreements with Turkey?
- *Culture and religion* Relations between Europe and the Muslim world are passing through a delicate phase. If Turkey is permitted to join the EU, this could confirm the fact that Islam is compatible with EU values and culture.[116] However, once in the EU, Turkey would be expected to accept and implement the EU's 'conduct of behaviour'. This could be regarded as a direct threat to and attack on international Islamic solidarity, which could create problems.

> Turkey is becoming a re-religious society at the point where it is trying to join a post-religious Europe. Many urban Turks today, far from being westernised as is commonly believed or at least hoped in Europe, want to join the EU without diluting Turkey's social and religious values.[117]

Kemal Ataturk's controls and vision of a modern Turkey have been relaxed. Turkish Prime Minister Erdogan ('The conqueror of Europe') and Foreign Minister Abdullah Gul 'are distinctly more religious than any of their predecessors'.[118] Hence, it may be laborious, but not impossible, to bring together EU values and Turkish society. The process may, however, inflame passions on either side. What if instead of building bridges with the Muslim world, the Turkish entry provokes Islamophobia in Europe? Rather than 'exporting' democracy and stability, the EU may import instability. The protector of democracy and the secularity of the Turkish state has been the army command (surprising by EU standards), even if this has provoked occasional *coups d'état*. With regard to Prime Minister Erdogan and the ruling Justice and Development Party (AKP), *The Economist* commented:

> Most of the Kemalists in Istanbul and Ankara suspect that he has a hidden agenda which, once revealed, will show the AK Party in its true colour: an intense Islamic green. They sincerely believe that it is merely using the prospect of EU membership to reduce the power of the armed forces before turning the country into an Islamic state, something akin to Iran. . . . EU membership will never actually come about. Somewhere along the way it will be vetoed. And then Turkey will be left in the hands of the AK Party, and all the good works of Ataturk and his republican successors will be undone.[119]

Could or should the EU take this risk? Are the French and Dutch 'no' votes on the EU Constitutional Treaty just first stumbling-blocks on the way to Turkish and all other EU enlargements? And as for Turkey, could the transformation of its society provoke strong resistance at home?

- *Jobs* There are also evident anxieties in the EU (especially Austria, Germany and France) about large-scale migrations of Muslims into Europe and a 'clash of civilisations'. One can discount this view on the grounds that it is too ideological and incorrect, but there is a technical side to it. Many in the EU have expressed fears about freely roaming crowds of unemployed Turks who take jobs and reduce the wages of the locals.
- *Human, democratic and minority rights* The 1923 Treaty of Lausanne protects Turkey's Armenian, Greek and Jewish inhabitants. During the entry negotiations, Turkey will be asked to improve its rather poor human rights record, in particular regarding Kurds and others, as well as women.[120] The Kurdish minority in Turkey is about 12 to 15 million strong. Calls for regionalisation and autonomy within Turkey are therefore quite powerful.[121] However, this may easily be regarded and opposed in Turkey as a call for the disintegration of the country.
- *Frontier control* Turkey has extensive land borders with Armenia (268 km), Azerbaijan (9 km), Bulgaria (240 km), Georgia (252 km),

Greece (206 km), Iran (499 km), Iraq (352 km) and Syria (822 km). It is immensely difficult and costly to police it effectively. Turkey has to demonstrate that it can apply and maintain EU standards regarding this issue because some of Turkey's southern and eastern neighbours are larger sources of illegal immigration into the EU.

Doubts or Opportunities?

These are all thorny and important issues that need to be dealt with. In addition, by 2015, Turkey would be the most populous EU state. It would have the biggest single voting power in the EU.[122] This would have an enormous consequence for the voting process and operation of the entire EU. Valéry Giscard d'Estaing (France), chairman of the European Convention, observed:

> The European Convention sought a clearer definition of the foundations of this entity: the cultural contributions of ancient Greece and Rome, Europe's pervasive religious heritage, the creative enthusiasm of the Renaissance, the philosophy of the Age of the Enlightenment and the contributions of rational and scientific thought. Turkey shares none of these. This is not meant to be pejorative. Turkey has developed its own history and its own culture, which deserve respect. However, the foundations of Europe's identity, so vital to the cohesion of the EU today, are different. Turkey's accession would change the nature of the European project . . .
>
> If the only solution Europe can come up with is allowing entry to the Union or antagonising its partners, the EU is doomed to slide into a regional version of the UN, designed for meeting, dialogue and certain specific co-operative projects. It would have no identity, no common will and no role to play. The world would evolve without Europe.[123]

Giscard d'Estaing argued in favour of a privileged partnership agreement with Turkey, rather than full membership. Otherwise, the EU may implode. There is even some support in Turkey for this less complicated and workable relationship with the EU. The question is: can Turkey justify the time and effort required to make so many necessary, painful, unpopular and expensive adjustments to satisfy the demanding *acquis communautaire*,[124] which is concerned not only with a change in the law, but also with a change in habits? Would a deal that avoids centralised regulation of many factors in the EU be a superior choice for either party?

Turkey, with its well-established and fully operational customs union with the EU, may well be envied by other countries for having such a business privilege at its fingertips. Surprisingly, Turkey has failed to fulfil a role for the EU similar to the one that Mexico plays for the US. The reason is that Turkey attracts only a small fraction of FDI compared with Mexico. After the establishment of the customs union with the EU in 1995 and

Table 5A2.13 Foreign direct investment in Mexico and Turkey, annual inflows 1994–2003 ($m)

Country	1994	1995	1996	1997	1998	1999	2000	2001	2002	2003
Mexico	10 973	9 526	9 186	12 831	12 332	13 206	16 586	26 776	14 754	10 783
Turkey	608	885	722	805	940	783	982	3 266	1 037	575

Source: UNCTAD (2004).

contrary to all expectations and predictions, FDI to Turkey fell for a year (Table 5A2.13). In general, corruption, red tape and a lack of protection of intellectual property rights are the principal reasons for this weak performance in comparison with Mexico.

New Dynamics of European Relations and Future EU Enlargements

Whether to let Turkey into the EU is not a straightforward matter. It is not high on the EU's list of priorities.[125] Even the European Commission has publicly revealed divisions on the issue during 2004. Frits Bolkestein (Netherlands) was against the entry of Turkey for historical, political and religious reasons. Franz Fischler (Austria) was opposed to entry not only because of the lack of 'long-term secular and democratic credentials', but also because the financial cost of applying the CAP in Turkey would not be tenable. It would cost the EU €11.5 billion a year. However, Chris Patten (UK) was positive about Turkish entry and argued in favour of an increase in EU farm and structural spending.[126]

Turkey, Ukraine, the Balkans and other east European countries prefer freedom and democracy to dictatorship, success and wealth to poverty, new ways and opportunities to sanctions, peace and prosperity to war. They want to join the EU club that shares and extends those values and achievements, and hope to benefit from their membership. Britain has been championing Turkey's entry, as well as other EU enlargements, principally because of the British aversion to the closely knit federal EU. As a champion of EU enlargements Britain should be willing to finance in part the new entrants' membership costs.[127] Ironically, Britain is perhaps least entrenched in the EU as it is neither in the eurozone nor party to the Schengen agreement (through choice rather than ineligibility). Britain, and even some central and east European EU member states that fear a soviet-style command structure from Brussels, may prefer a wider, not deeper, future EU. However, in the mega-enlarged EU structure Turkey may become another awkward player like Britain or even Poland.

Regardless of how this issue is resolved, the fact is that Turkey has never enjoyed whole-hearted relations with its neighbours. Therefore, political or any other integration with any of its neighbours (save perhaps for Azerbaijan) seems highly unlikely in the foreseeable future.

With regard to possible future enlargements of the EU there is the inevitable issue of Russia (and Ukraine) to consider. It is hard to conceive what Sweden, Ireland or Poland have in common with Turkey. In these terms, Russia and Ukraine are much more 'European' than Turkey can ever be. This is particularly important in the light of the strong and repeated demands to include a reference to the EU's 'Christian roots' in the Constitutional Treaty.[128] In fact, it is hard to imagine in the long term a strong, sovereign and independent Europe without Russia. With Russia in the EU, Europe could be free from any transatlantic or Middle Eastern blackmail regarding energy.[129] The amount of hydrocarbons is finite. The direction and control over pipelines might soon become a modern equivalent of the colonial disputes of the nineteenth century, so Europe ought to be safe here. Apart from energy-related security and independence, so necessary for the EU because of its vulnerability, Russia can offer huge market potential, and certain types of high technology, as well as contributing to defence systems.[130]

For over three centuries, Germany and Russia have enjoyed a long and fruitful relationship, not only with regard to commerce, but also among the nobility, intellectuals and the military elite. The First World War and the Bolshevik Revolution curbed the process,[131] while the Second World War and its aftermath temporarily interrupted it. As Germany redevelops its post-Cold War international identity and interests, it is patching up its (natural) geopolitical ties. With the elevation of Chancellor Gerhard Schröder to power in 1998, Germany stopped walking around and apologising. It started to develop its own foreign policy. This process was helped by the lack of interest shown by the US towards both Germany and France, especially since the 2003 war with Iraq.[132] Even though it is much more expensive than building overland, Germany started to construct a direct undersea gas pipeline beneath the Baltic with Russia in 2005. This would bypass Poland, Germany's EU and NATO partner country. Poland was dismayed about this.

Germany has been generous with loans to Russia and is relatively comfortable on the issue of human rights. Along with many in Europe it wants to see a stable Russia. It realises that the collapse of Russia would be dangerous for the continent because of possible spillovers, while a stable, democratic, prosperous and terrorist-free Russia may be a promising economic and geopolitical partner. Germany is no longer looking at Russia as a threat, but rather as a stable partner and a key element in Germany's long-term future (as a supplier of resources and a market for goods). Russia already supplies most of Germany's energy needs, and is eager to receive German goods, FDI and technology. Hence, such a partner is worth courting, not antagonising. This is reinforced by the German wish to foster a geopolitical partner that can counteract divisions between Germany and the US, as well as discords within the EU. Therefore, Ukraine, which is unfriendly towards Russia, is an obstacle to German geopolitical interests. France does not need Russia (all that much): Russia is too far away to be geopolitically useful and French policy has always been to have the maximum possible energy independence.[133] Be that as it may, the more EU firms become involved in large and lucrative projects in Russia, the less their governments will be interested in Russia's disintegration. Indeed, in May 2005, the EU–Russia summit adopted four broad road maps for cooperation between the partners (economic integration; external security; freedom and justice; and education and research).

Where and how EU–Turkey accession negotiations will evolve is anyone's guess. Discussions about an enlargement of the EU that may involve Turkey are largely academic at this point in time. This is because it is difficult to know what the EU will look like in 10, even five, years from now. Anything is possible, perhaps, *except* that the EU will still be the same. Could anyone in 1989 even imagine how the world and the EU would look 10 or 15 years down the road?

It is very hard to predict what the EU will look like in a decade: its membership, the coverage and depth of its policies, dynamism of negotiations, ratification of enlargement, response to demographical factors, developments in the eurozone, openness, general priorities, energy situation, to mention just a few. It is almost certain that the EU will look very different from what it is in 2005. But this is only as far as the EU is concerned. With regard to Turkey, we should optimistically assume that there will be no glitches in the pro-EU reform process; that EU standards of democracy will be introduced and maintained; that there will be no wars;[134] and that the Turks still want to join the EU. Perhaps the EU in 10 or 20 years may not be as appealing to Turkey as it is in 2005.

It is a complicated matter even now to create a common and coherent EU(25) foreign and defence policy because France has its enduring ambitions, Britain has its longstanding interests and concerns, Germany has its growing needs, while central and eastern Europe are dealing with the legacy of the soviet communist past. Given the political and military weight of Turkey, its interests and ambitions, a common foreign policy would be unimaginable in an even more enlarged EU. One may perhaps start thinking again in terms of France, Germany, Britain and others, rather than in terms of Europe. De Gaulle once said: 'Treaties, you see, are like girls and roses: they last while they last' (Macleod et al., 1998, p. v). The EU might easily be transformed into the world's largest and most comprehensive free trade area with some elements of policy coordination. This would be a huge achievement in its own right. Britain would argue that this is a worthwhile goal for the future EU. In this situation, one of the possible options for the EU is to offer Turkey a special or 'privileged partnership' status. This offers an alternative solution to full membership.

No full public debate in the EU(25) has yet taken place on Turkey's entry. EU citizens (and voters) need to know what benefits Turkish entry would bring them. If the entry is presented by the elite as a done deal without wide public debate and consultation with the people (voters), their resistance and hostility may shatter the project even in advance, during the ratification of the Constitutional Treaty.

In spite of public statements by various EU governments and the European Commission that Turkey is welcome in the EU, polls reveal that the EU public displays serious misgivings about letting such a big, poor and culturally and religiously different country into the EU club.[135] If Turkey were in the EU, then it would be hard to say 'no' to countries such as Armenia, Azerbaijan, Georgia, Moldova and, of course, to Russia, Ukraine and Belarus.

In any case, the issue *is not* whether Turkey will join the EU. It will in one way or another, but not before about 2015. The real issue *is* what kind of EU would Turkey be joining at that time. If the EU(25) countries ratify some version of the Constitutional Treaty (following the French and Dutch 'no' vote in 2005), then the EU will be a fairly consistent group. If this were not the case, a multi-speed EU might accept Turkey in some of its 'outer' circles. The entry of Turkey would not bring the EU extra efficiency or growth; it would not create extra new jobs. Its basic objective may be to provide opportunities and to support a neighbouring country in its reform and general stabilisation process according to EU criteria. Once in the EU, Turkey may easily find that the EU is perhaps no longer the group that it originally wanted to join. This might already have happened in the case of the central and east European countries which joined the EU in 2004.

CONCLUSION

European integration has always been based on the political decision to secure peace and freedom in Europe. That is the purpose of the EU, although many observers have forgotten it. European integration is intended to mitigate the impact of old rivalries and replace them by mutual economic advantage and social prosperity. The EU has a splendid record regarding the promotion of economic and political reform in its neighbourhood, as well as concerning enlargements. The reward for successful reform is membership. The EU results are superior to those achieved by the US in the southern part of its continent (the American 'reward' is only a specific free trade deal). The EU spreads its values of peace, democracy, solidarity, human rights, rule of law, stability and prosperity to the countries that join and that apply to join. The eastern enlargement did not bring the EU extra efficiency or growth; it did not create extra new jobs. Its basic objective was to give a certain support to friendly countries and governments in their reform and general stabilisation process.

The Treaty of Nice changed the voting system in the enlarged EU. It makes the introduction of new policies and rapid reaction to new challenges very difficult, while it makes the blocking of new initiatives relatively swift and easy. In addition, the EU limited its total expenditure in advance of enlargement. Some welcome the eastern enlargement as they think that this will water down the EU into an extended free trade area. Others are depressed because they consider that enlargement is being done in a rush, without adequately prepared candidates and without a duly consolidated EU. The cost of implementing the *acquis communautaire* is staggering, and this represents one good reason why the central and east European countries should think again. A very long transition period might be the only reasonable alternative solution, but it is too late for such thoughts now.

When full integration of central and east European countries with the EU was first discussed at the beginning of the 1990s and when it was just a remote possibility, everyone was enthusiastic about it. The closer the date of entry approached, the more this enthusiasm evaporated and certain serious doubts were expressed. Some say that the EU carried out its promise that many now wish had never been made. At least not that quickly. The general mood is one of worry, rather than of cheer. The leaders failed to explain to their citizens the benefits of this enlargement. Others rejoice: enlargement, as such, is a very good thing as it marks the end of the east–west divide in Europe. But, if European integration is such a profound, favourable and necessary process, can one explain why Europe consisted of 32 countries in 1990, while it now has 48? Festivities and glamorous speeches cannot, however, disguise the distrust and discontent that hovers beneath the surface. They cannot mask the sombre fact that almost all EU(15) countries slammed their doors to the free movement of labour from central and east European member countries. Would this all play into the hands of eurosceptics? Would the basic geopolitical principle that nations always act first in their own self-interest continue to prevail in the EU?

European integration has always been in the hands of national elites. This is why the treaties on which European integration is based are complicated and incomprehensible to the man in the street. When the national elites decide to defend Europe from various challenges, in particular external ones (coming from both the west and the south), public enthusiasm to deepen and to enlarge the EU may regain momentum. The major priority for the national elites in the EU countries must now be to reclaim popular understanding and backing for the process of European integration. Therefore, the enlargements of the EU and a certain European Constitution deserve support, but the speed of these changes is not so important as mistakes could be paid for with a longer-term loss of confidence in European integration. *Festina lente*! (Make haste, slowly!)

Notes

1. Schemes that fit into this group include the Latin American Free Trade Area, the Latin American Integration Association, the Southern Common Market, the Economic Community of West African States and the Preferential Trade Area for Eastern and Southern African States.
2. Schemes that fit into this group include the Andean Pact, the Central American Common Market, the East African Community and some aspects of ASEAN.
3. Dent (1997); Tsoukalis (1997); El-Agraa (1998); Hitiris (1998); Swann (2000); Molle (2001); Baldwin and Wyplosz (2004); Jovanović (2005a).
4. For select readings on some of these groups, see UNCTAD (1996b), El-Agraa (1997), Jovanović (1998) and Page (2000).
5. Apart from Britain there were Austria, Denmark, Norway, Sweden and Switzerland. Portugal joined the group a little later, but took part in the establishment of the organisation. Iceland joined in 1970. Finland became an associate member in 1961, while it entered the group in 1986 as a full member.
6. EFTA created the Portugal Fund in 1975, which gave soft loans to this less-developed country following the end of the dictatorship.
7. The EEA entered into force in 1994.
8. The Swiss declined to approve it in a referendum in 1992.
9. The neutrality of most of the EFTA countries was seen to be an obstacle to those countries joining the EU. None the less, the concept became quite flexible (except in Switzerland) after the dissolution of the east European bloc.
10. The town in Hungary where the leaders of the Czech Republic, Hungary, Poland and Slovakia met in 1991 and agreed to start negotiations on the establishment of a free trade area.
11. The Czech and Slovak republics split in 1993. One may ask whether their real interest lies in getting together again.
12. On average, agricultural policies in Norway and Switzerland were more expensive and trade distorting than the Common Agricultural Policy of the EU. So much for the financial aspect. However, there are some issues that do not (or should not) pass through the market, for example, gains regarding national security and preservation of the deeply embedded national culture that involves farming.
13. Of the total Canada–US trade, 80 per cent was free of tariffs and an additional 15 per cent was subject to tariffs of 5 per cent or less.
14. In spite of strong opposition in the early 1990s by the US presidential candidate Ross Perot regarding the free trade agreement between the US and Mexico and a possible loss of jobs in the American economy ('giant sucking sound' of jobs moving south (*The Economist*, 18 September 1993, p. 51)), only 117 000 Americans have applied for the benefits offered to workers displaced by the free trade agreement. If compared with the 1.5 million who lose their jobs each year from factory closures, slack demand and

corporate restructuring (*The Economist*, 5 July 1997, p. 17), the cost of adjustment to the agreement by the US does not seem too high. Free trade with Mexico might have destroyed some jobs in the American textile industry which is 'labour intensive', but it created new ones in electronics, aeronautics and writing software.

15. Mexico joined the OECD in 1994.
16. '*Maquiladora*' is in-bond manufacturing or assembly for re-export. This method of production was first established in 1965 under Mexico's Border Industrialisation Programme. It flourished during the 1990s and was located primarily along the US border. It was the most productive part of the whole national economy and accounted for the biggest part of Mexico's total exports. A fall in US demand, hardening of border controls especially from 2001 and competition from Asian manufacturers revealed Mexico's dwindling competitive advantages as a location for FDI and a source of imports for manufactured goods. Although the wages paid in *maquiladoras* are still far lower than comparable ones in the US, they are higher than those paid in China and south-east Asia. This does not mean that *maquiladoras* will disappear altogether. Mexico's proximity to the US lowers transport costs, which may be relevant in certain industries. Therefore, *maquiladoras* will remain in Mexico, but they are likely to be more specialised in scope and reduced in range.
17. The WTO Appellate Body found in 2003 that the Byrd Amendment was inconsistent with the WTO principles. And as it was not repealed, the WTO allowed trade sanctions against imports from the US from May 2005.
18. The Cartagena Agreement among Bolivia, Colombia, Chile, Ecuador, Peru and Venezuela established the Andean Pact. For some time it was regarded as the model for economic integration among the developing countries.
19. The merits of import-substitution strategies of growth have been debated for a long time. Neo-liberals dispute their value. Others measure the success of such a strategy by rates of growth. Although Brazil followed an import-substitution strategy, its average annual rate of growth during the 1950s and 1960s was about 7 per cent.
20. Mercosur in Portuguese.
21. A cynic might exclaim: 'Yet another Latin American grand plan destined for oblivion!'
22. Chile withdrew its application for full Mercosur membership, preferring to start (in 2000) negotiations for a free trade deal with the US.
23. Trans-border links among national political parties still have to be developed.
24. Argentina's foreign debt is over $100 billion.
25. The term, 'Washington Consensus' was coined to express the neo-liberal policy advice given (or imposed) by the Washington-based international financial institutions (principally the World Bank and the IMF) to unlucky Latin American countries from 1989 (and before). These policies include fiscal discipline; channelling of public expenditure priorities towards health care, primary education and infrastructure rather than investment in production (for this loans need to come from Washington and Wall Street); tax reform (to lower marginal rates and broaden the tax base); interest rate liberalisation; a competitive exchange rate; trade and FDI liberalisation; privatisation; deregulation of the economy (to reduce and eliminate barriers to entry and exit); corporate governance; and protection of property rights. The term is used in debates on trade and development as synonymous with neo-liberalism and globalisation that (*i*) never changed Latin American countries from being vulnerable exporters of commodities to exporters of higher-technology products and (*ii*) led them into crisis and misery because they were driven to follow advice that paid little attention to distribution and fairness. In addition, loans and their reprogramming were such that the debtor countries would 'never stop repaying them'.
26. Basic geopolitical law states that countries first and foremost act in their national self-interest.
27. Guatemala, Honduras, Nicaragua and El Salvador. Costa Rica joined in 1962.
28. Abolition of tariffs and NTBs, protection of FDI and intellectual property rights, as well as settlement of disputes.
29. The exception is Cuba unless there is a change to democracy as defined by the US.

30. East Asia is beginning to feel the tilt in the balance of power in the post-Cold War era. The US is no longer as strongly involved in this region as it once was. The countries in the region are competing to maintain the upper hand over their neighbours and hope that they may partially fill the power vacuum left by the US.
31. Australia, Brunei, Canada, South Korea, China (1991), Chile (1994), Hong Kong, Indonesia, Japan, Malaysia, Mexico (1993), New Zealand, Papua New Guinea (1993), Peru (1998), the Philippines, Russia (1998), Singapore, Thailand, US and Vietnam (1998). Years in brackets give the date of entry.
32. G. de Jonquières, 'Different aims, common cause', *Financial Times*, 18 November 1994, p. 16.
33. China was 'closed' during the 15th century, and Japan during the 16th.
34. In general, south-east Asia exported spices, while it imported cloth from India, silk from China, ceramics from Japan and silver from the Americas.
35. Indonesia, Malaysia, the Philippines, Singapore and Thailand. Brunei joined ASEAN in 1984, Vietnam in 1995, Laos and Myanmar in 1997 and Cambodia in 1999.
36. A more 'compact' integration agreement in the form of a customs union might not be very realistic in the near future because of enormous differences in the level of income (per capita) and approaches to economic policy.
37. The deadline for 'new' members (Vietnam, Laos, Myanmar and Cambodia) is 2018.
38. The preferential trading agreement covers 15 000 items in ASEAN. Countries are granted the right to exclude 'sensitive' items from such a preferential trade. Contrary to expectations the preferential regime has not had a strong impact on internal trade. Intra-ASEAN trade takes 20 per cent of trade of the member countries. Out of that volume of trade less than 1 per cent is affected by preferential treatment. Many regional preferences were without real substance. For example, the Philippines grants preferential access to snowploughs (*Business Asia*, 2 September 1991, p. 304).
39. The origin of the crises was in the reckless expansion of bad loans.
40. FDI is not diverted towards China only from ASEAN. China also attracted the location of subsidiaries of TNCs away from Mexico and central and eastern Europe. Many Latin American countries need to find an effective response to such a changing global geography of production.
41. Some neo-conservatives think that resource-poor China may be a threat to peace as was the case with Japan during the 1930s. However, they do not explain what China would gain from going to war. China untiringly and peacefully reintegrated Hong Kong and Macao into the homeland after many years. Taiwan is next. China's prosperity increasingly depends on a stable, smooth and open international trading system. Any disruption would damage China's development prospects. China is successfully 'conquering' the world with certain of its manufactured products.
42. There have been discussions regarding how to deprive Myanmar (ex-Burma) of its scheduled chairmanship of ASEAN in 2006. The reason is a lack of democratic reforms in the country which may harm relations with the EU and the US. This pressure may be withstood by Myanmar because of its growing attraction for FDI: China and South Korea won exploration and development contracts for natural gas (the biggest export item). Other ASEAN countries, as well as India, are also investing in Myanmar.
43. There is no common external tariff. 'Averaging' of tariffs could present problems as they are lower in New Zealand than in Australia.
44. UDEAC was created in 1964 by Cameroon, the Central African Republic, Chad, Congo, Equatorial Guinea and Gabon.
45. Benin, Burkina Faso, Cape Verde, the Gambia, Ghana, Guinea, Guinea Bissau, Ivory Coast, Liberia, Mali, Mauritania, Niger, Nigeria, Senegal, Sierra Leone and Togo.
46. Foreign aid may also assist, but only in the short term and in exceptional circumstances such as natural disasters. Long-term aid has always had a profound negative impact on the recipient because it creates a dependence mentality and removes incentives to change and adjust.
47. Liberia and Sierra Leone created this group in 1973. The aim was to create a customs union and free mobility of persons. The group was open to other countries so Guinea

joined in 1980. The countries signed a Non-Aggression Treaty in 1986. However, all three countries have suffered political trouble since then, which has contributed to distrust among the countries. The Mano River Union had very few achievements.

48. Communauté économique de l'Afrique de l'ouest (CEAO). The CEAO tried to integrate Benin, Burkina Faso, Guinea Bissau, Ivory Coast, Mali, Niger, Senegal and Togo. The scheme was dissolved in 1994 when the same group of countries created the West African Monetary and Economic Union.
49. Union économique et monétaire ouest africaine (UEMOA).
50. The agreement was revised in 1969.
51. Seychelles withdrew in 2003 as it could not adhere to the SADC protocols.
52. Angola, Burundi, Comoros, Djibouti, Eritrea, Ethiopia, Kenya, Lesotho, Madagascar, Malawi, Mauritius, Mozambique, Namibia, Rwanda, Seychelles, Somalia, Sudan, Swaziland, Tanzania, Uganda, Zambia and Zimbabwe.
53. Angola, Burundi, Comoros, Congo, Djibouti, Egypt, Eritrea, Ethiopia, Kenya, Madagascar, Malawi, Mauritius, Namibia, Rwanda, Seychelles, Sudan, Swaziland, Uganda, Zambia and Zimbabwe.
54. South Africa's share in this total was 46 per cent ($182 billion).
55. World Bank database (2004).
56. Unlike the former OAU, the African Union has a Peace and Security Council that may sanction military action in member states in cases such as genocide, unlawful change of government or large-scale abuse of human rights.
57. There is a similar structure in Latin America, where progress has been very slow.
58. These differences include, for example, which country will lead the Arab world and attitudes towards the Anglo-American led war with Iraq and other problems in the Middle East.
59. The South Asian Preferential Trading Arrangement (SAPTA) was formed in 1994 by Bangladesh, Bhutan, India, Maldives, Pakistan and Sri Lanka. The stated goal was the establishment of a free trade area by 2005. In 1997, SAPTA decided to implement its final goal earlier, in 2001. However, serious political (including military) tensions between India and Pakistan about Kashmir prevented any real progress. There are also other regional rivalries and tensions which include India and Sri Lanka (over Tamil independence) and Nepal and India (trade and transit).
60. The more complex the system becomes, the more administrative resources it absorbs and the more it becomes prone to uncertainty, smuggling and corruption. Many working hours can be lost by firms, by customs, by forgers of origin certificates, by checkers of these forgeries and so on. If these countries accept the MFN treatment, this will be more efficient from the resource-allocation point of view, as well as cheaper to run (Curzon Price, 1996b, pp. 73–4).
61. 'The great hypocrisy is for America, Europe and the Far East to offer aid yet continue de facto economic sanctions on trade. There was no mention this week of the 20 per cent tariff on South-East Asian textiles or the refusal to end food subsidies and import controls. There was no mention of what would do most for the world's poor, a revival of imperial preference in the form of Third World preference. This does not happen because spending taxes on aid is cheap but confronting domestic trade lobbies is politically painful.

    The tsunami response has given us a glimpse of the wider, poorer world as it really is, selfish, short-term and chaotic. No amount of aid will end Indonesia's misrule of Aceh province or Sri Lanka's wretched civil war against the Tamils. No fine words can justify Britain spending more on "humanitarian" war in Iraq (some £6 billion) than the entire world is offering to tsunami victims' (S. Jenkins, 'A tidal wave of hypocrisy', *The Times*, 7 January 2005).
62. The presentation of integration efforts among the formerly centrally planned economies is outlined mainly for historical and educational purposes, in order to avoid past mistakes.
63. The Czech Republic, Estonia, Hungary, Poland and Slovenia started accession negotiations on 31 March 1998, while Bulgaria, Latvia, Lithuania, Romania and Slovakia started negotiations on 15 March 2000.

64. The Treaty of Accession was signed in Athens on 16 April 2003 and subsequently duly ratified.
65. The unresolved question is what is a European state? Is it a member of the UN Economic Commission for Europe (include among others the US, Canada, Israel, Turkmenistan and Uzbekistan)? Does religion matter? Is a European state a member of the Council of Europe?
66. 'Several commissioners, led by Frits Bolkenstein, who is responsible for the internal market, commented that many of the candidate countries would not be ready to withstand the pressures of competition once they joined' (*Financial Times*, 10 October 2002, p.1).
67. European Commission (1997a), p. 52; *Bulletin Quotidien Europe*, 12 November 2001.
68. European Commission (1997a, pp. 44, 51 and 134); *Bulletin Quotidien Europe*, 12 November 2001.
69. European Commission (1997a, p. 45).
70. An early short survey of select studies is given by Baldwin (1995b).
71. There were concerns that the accession countries do not all have the institutional capacity to absorb the financial opportunities provided by the PHARE programme. To obtain funds (aid), the acceding country has to make reforms and submit sensible projects to the EU. As the submitted Polish projects were ill-prepared, the EU cut €34 million off the planned aid of €212 million for that country for 1998 (*The Economist*, 6 June 1998, pp. 37–8). As this was the first time ever that funds to a PHARE programme assisted country had been cut, this sent a strong signal to the accession countries that they should undergo a serious institutional overhaul if they wanted to meet the high EU criteria.
72. 'Outgrowing the Union', a survey of the EU, *The Economist*, 25 September 2004, p. 9. One example of this is as follows 'Britain has advised Croatia that it may wish to suspend its membership application to prevent a humiliating rebuff and resubmit it when progress has been made on arresting General Gotovina, an official told *The Times*. . . . The Croatians say that the West's tough stand smacks of hypocrisy. Operation *Storm* had the support of the United States and Europe. Yet now Washington and Brussels are pressing Croatia to arrest their former ally for it' (A. LeBor, 'Croatia acts against fugitive "hero"', *The Times*, 15 March 2005).

    However, there is another reason for Britain to be tough on Croatia: 'Another factor explaining MI6's energetic activity in Croatia is that recent years have seen ample gun-running operations between Croatia and the Real IRA. Indeed, an investigation by Scotland Yard's anti-terrorist branch, the Irish Garda and the Croatian police established that the missile used in the Real IRA rocket attack on MI6's headquarters at Vauxhall in London in 2000 was of Croatian provenance. The same year the armoury found at a Real IRA arms depot in County Meath in the Irish Republic was sourced to Croatia' (I. Traynor, 'The fugitive who stands in the way of Croatia's EU entry', *The Guardian*, 18 March 2005).
73. Economic Commission for Europe (2003, p. 37); G. Parker, 'Sweeping rewrite of EU stability pact agreed', *Financial Times*, 21 March 2005.
74. If the rules on regional aid from the EU were not changed, then such aid to the accession transition countries would transfer resources that are equal to 10–20 per cent of the new members' GDP. That is far more than the 3.5 per cent of GDP that Greece received in 1996 (*The Economist*, 3 August 1996, p. 28). Agenda 2000 limited the level of annual structural and cohesion aid to 4 per cent of the recipient country's GDP (European Commission, 1997, p. 25). This was reconfirmed by the European Council in Berlin (1999) in § 46. Given the relatively small size of the economies of the accession countries, this rule would tightly limit the amount of funds they could get from the EU.
75. European Commission (1997a, pp. 25 and 53).
76. The NATO entry, achieved with little public debate, may harden both the economic adjustment and the EU accession. Most of the investment in the military forces is not

producing direct value added which can be consumed or exported. Investment in this sector crowds out investment in other, market-oriented sectors because of the need to coordinate and to harmonise with other NATO partners and standards. Hungary, for example, met less than a third of its NATO commitments three years after NATO entry in 1999. If Hungary is considered to be a successful country in transition, then one may question the ability of Bulgaria and Romania to meet the NATO challenge (*The Times*, 18 November 2002). If this continues, the Americans would control the still fragile democracies in the new member countries; guide political, military and other types of European integration; and be even closer to the oil-rich Caspian and Middle Eastern regions.

77. Agenda 2000 states that the environment is a major challenge for enlargement (European Commission, 1997a, p. 49).
78. *The European Voice*, 28 May 2003, p. 14.
79. Compliance with those standards refers to all member countries of the EU. For example, the privatised British water industry is expected to spend around $60 billion between 1989 and 2004 to bring its water supply network into line with EU directives (*Financial Times*, 6 October 1997, p. 18).
80. *Uniting Europe*, 10 December 2001.
81. This may be one of the consequences of having badly underpaid officials in the public sector.
82. *Financial Times*, 6 November 2002.
83. European Commission (1997a, p. 52).
84. When the Polish government presented its 2004 budget (€9.9 billion deficit) to parliament, the Polish zloty hit its lowest level ever against the euro (*Financial Times*, 30 September 2003).
85. Some of the Maastricht criteria were loosely interpreted, as national debt was over 120 per cent of the GDP in 1997 both in Belgium and in Italy, but both countries were permitted to enter the EMU from the start in 1998, even though the Maastricht norm is 60 per cent.
86. See also Fisher et al. (1998, p. 28); Economic Commission for Europe (2002, p. 183).
87. *European Economy*, 1997a, p. 8.
88. The rural working-age population in Poland is growing annually by 100 000. To create alternative jobs for many existing and newly arriving farmers may be like pushing water uphill (*Financial Times*, 10 June 2003).
89. Central and eastern Europe received $21 billion in FDI in 2003. The primary beneficiaries were Poland ($4.2 billion), the Czech Republic ($2.6 billion) and Hungary ($2.5 billion). While relatively low wages could have been an advantage for the central and east European countries in the past, they are becoming less and less so. For example, real wages in Hungary are on the rise. This may be one of the reasons why FDI outflow from Hungary was $1.6 billion in the same year (UNCTAD, 2004, pp. 371 and 375). Investors are leaving for China.
90. B. Benoit, 'Germany seeks to stem flow of cheap labour', *Financial Times*, 17 February 2005.
91. The total direct expenditure of the EU on enlargement in the 1990–2006 period is estimated to be €69.5 billion (*Uniting Europe*, 14 July 2003, p. 7). In relative terms and over a period of 17 years this cost does not seem to be excessive compared with the EU GDP.
92. *Financial Times*, 15 January 2003.
93. European Commission (1997a), p. 54.
94. *Bulletin Quotidien Europe*, 15 March 2000.
95. *Bulletin Quotidien Europe*, 29 March 2000; 12 November 2001.
96. On the political side, there are still problems which include divided Cyprus and the Beneš Decrees (1946) in Czechoslovakia under which 2.5 million Germans were deported and deprived of their property.
97. European Council, Brussels 2002, Presidency Conclusions, § 10.
98. European Council, Berlin 1999, Presidency Conclusions, § 16 and Table B.

99. The 'net benefit' for Spain, for instance in 2001, amounted to €7.7 billion or €192 per EU citizen (*Uniting Europe*, 23 December 2002, p. 6).
100. The European Commission confirmed in July 2003 that some of the €22 billion allocated to accession countries for the 2004–06 period may remain unused unless adequate administrative structures are set up quickly (*Enlargement Weekly*, 22 July 2003).
101. European Council, Brussels 2002, Presidency Conclusions, § 8.
102. Although it has never been the public position of the EU, there are influential voices that reflect the serious privately expressed anxiety of many officials that the EU is storing up trouble by embracing Turkey. The worry is that if Turkey enters the EU, then the biggest EU country could be 'south-east European'. For example, a prominent Christian Democrat in the European Parliament, Wilfried Martens, said: 'The EU is in the process of building a civilisation in which Turkey has no place.' In addition, eminent Dutch politicians have expressed doubts about the Turkish application 'because there are too many of them, and they are too poor – and they are Muslims' (*The Economist*, 15 March 1997, p. 31). Or, Valéry Giscard d'Estaing, Chairman of the Convention on the Future of Europe, said that Turkey's membership would represent 'the end of the European Union . . . Those who are pushing hardest for the enlargement in the direction of Turkey are adversaries of the EU' (G. Parker, 'Giscard attacks Turkey's attempt to join EU', *Financial Times*, 8 November 2002). A former senior American official declared that 'the US has done everything but slap the German government across the face in an effort to get the EU to agree to Turkish membership' (A. Lieven, 'EU must face up to a fractured future', *Financial Times*, 2 February 2003).
103. There was a precursor to these atrocities in 1894–96, which left 300 000 Armenians dead.
104. Croatia may also be asked to do likewise because of its Nazi past and atrocities during the Second World War in the Jasenovac Nazi death camp, which numbers among the top Nazi camps according to the number of people murdered. For further information see: www1.yadvashem.org/odot_pdf/Microsoft%20Word%20-%205930.pdf; www.yad-vashem.org/; and www.jasenovac.org/libraries/viewdocument.asp?DocumentID=145.
105. Armenians are seeking recognition of the killings as genocide. Seven EU member countries (Belgium, Cyprus, Greece, France, Italy, Poland and Sweden) have already recognised them as such and Germany, Slovakia and the Netherlands are considering the issue (L. Kirk, 'Armenian massacre hangs over Turkey', *EU Observer*, 25 April 2005).
106. H. Mahony, 'Turkey calls for study into Armenia genocide claims', *EU Observer*, 9 March 2005.
107. Recall that the European Coal and Steel Community, a precursor of the EU, was conceived first and foremost as an organisation that would prevent 'bloody conflicts'.
108. Austria is one of the countries that are planning to hold a referendum about Turkish membership of the EU.
109. One immediately thinks of the islands of Imia and Gavdos.
110. G. Jenkins, 'Europe eyes Turkey', *Al-Ahram Weekly*, 23–29 December 2004.
111. The fall of Constantinople in 1453 with the conversion of St Sophia (Aya Sophia) Christian church into a mosque and the slowdown of trade in spices from the Molucca islands gave strong incentives to explore other, westward, ways of sailing to India (which led to the discovery of America).
112. Syria had a 29-year military presence in Lebanon. The last 15 years represented an effective occupation. Rafiq Hariri, the former prime minister, was assassinated on 14 February 2005. 'His death was blamed on Syria, which denied the accusations. But intense international pressure for an end to Syria's grip over its tiny neighbour has forced Damascus to withdraw its 15 000 troops' (K. Ghattas, 'Syria prepares to withdraw last troops from Lebanon today', *Financial Times*, 25 April 2005). Following a 'bit of persuasion' by the US (and France and others), Syria withdrew its troops from Lebanon in a matter of weeks. Hence, a swift withdrawal of occupation troops is perfectly feasible if there is a persuasive 'incentive'.

113. Turkish readiness to sign a protocol that would extend its customs union with the EU(15) to the EU(25) is a positive step in this process. This is important as ships registered in Cyprus (one of the largest fleets in the world) could dock in Turkey.
114. Kazakhstan, Kyrgyzstan, Tajikistan, Turkmenistan and Uzbekistan. Apart from the Iran-affiliated Tajikistan, all the other countries share a common Turkish regional heritage.
115. The US welcomes any step that weakens the Russian influence in the region. The EU would welcome such cooperation as Turkey may be a useful intermediary between Europe and central Asia. This could also divert Turkish energies away from Europe for some time.
116. The western military interventions in Bosnia-Herzegovina (1995) and in and around Kosovo and Metohija (1999) were 'on behalf of Muslims, though many Muslims seem to forget it' (*The Economist*, 19 February 2005, p. 24).
117. V. Boland and D. Dombey, 'A government led by a devout Muslim shows how migration to the cities is bringing rural values to the fore', *Financial Times*, 5 October 2004.
118. *The Economist*, 'A survey of Turkey', 19 March 2005, p. 6.
119. *Ibid.*, p. 8.
120. The treatment of women in Turkey will be an issue during entry negotiations. 'The prime minister was born to a poor family in Istanbul, went to a religious high school, toyed with being a professional footballer, became mayor of the city in the 1990s and is said to pray at least three times a day. Emine, his wife, wears a headscarf and is therefore banned from state functions. She has been to the White House but she has yet to be invited to the presidential palace in Ankara' (V. Boland and D. Dombey, 'A government led by a devout Muslim shows how migration to the cities is bringing rural values to the fore', *Financial Times*, 5 October 2004).
121. The Turkish government was accused in March 2005 of misleading the EU about progress made in resettling nearly 400 000 people displaced by the civil war between the army and the Kurds during the 1980s and 1990s (V. Boland, 'Turkey accused of misleading EU over resettlement', *Financial Times*, 7 March 2005). Elsewhere, Croatia overran the UN protected zone and expelled 300 000 of its Serb citizens, almost 10 per cent of the country's population, during operation *Storm* in 1995. This issue (return of people and restitution of property) may feature prominently in Croatia's EU entry negotiations.
122. And, as a point of interest, once Turkey joins the EU, Mount Ararat (5156m) will become the EU's highest mountain.
123. V. Giscard d'Estaing, 'A better European bridge to Turkey', *Financial Times*, 25 November 2004.
124. H. Unal, 'Turkey would be better off outside the EU', *Financial Times*, 17 December 2004.
125. The top EU priorities are institutional and constitutional arrangements; protection of the Single European Market and the eurozone; assimilation of the eastern enlargement; and security.
126. *Bulletin Quotidien Europe*, 8 September 2004, p. 4 and 16 September 2004, p. 3; Q. Peel, 'The case for letting in Turkey', *Financial Times*, 16 September 2004, p. 21; *Enlargement Weekly*, 21 September 2004.
127. 'The budget summit fiasco has left Poland feeling bitter that richer EU members – particularly Britain, until now a close Polish ally – were unwilling to be generous to the much poorer countries that entered the Union last year' (B. Benoit, J. Blitz and J. Cienski, 'Poles hit out at national egoism', *Financial Times*, 20 June 2005).
128. The loudest voices came from the Czech Republic, Italy, Lithuania, Malta, Poland, Portugal and Slovakia. It is not insignificant that on 8 April 2005, up to 3 million people spontaneously flocked to Rome for the funeral of Pope John Paul II (doubling the city's population for a few days). Cardinal Josef Ratzinger, the new pope, took the name Benedict XVI after St Benedict who was proclaimed by Pope Paul VI in 1964 as the 'patron and protector of Europe'. The choice of this name is more than symbolic

as it represents the unity of Europe. In addition, St Benedict founded the most famous monastery in the whole of western Christendom at Monte Cassino in 529. The non-Europeans destroyed this monastery unnecessarily in 1944 (since the German troops arrived there only *after* its destruction).

129. Most of the oil resources in the Middle East are under the direct management and control of US corporations or the US Army.
130. 'Russia is offering its newest missile defense system to protect Europe from "rogue" missiles. Because of the system's unparalleled qualities and Europe's need for defense, the European Union will probably accept the offer sometime soon' ('Can missile defense buy Russian–EU harmony?', *Stratfor*, 4 March 2005).
131. The Treaty of Rapallo (1922) ended diplomatic isolation and fostered cooperation between Soviet Russia and Weimar Germany.
132. Gerhard Schröder openly and publicly questioned the relevance of NATO in February 2005.
133. A discussion topic may be to consider what happens once the Germans have more in common with Russia than with France ('Geopolitical diary', *Stratfor*, 24 February 2005).
134. Some Syrians claim the southern Turkish region of Hatay. There is an unpredictable dynamic of developments in Iraq and Kurdistan. If Kurds in Iraq get substantial autonomy and powers, what type of relationship will they have with their brethren in the neighbouring countries? There are also many in Turkey who consider Kirkuk as a place that should always have been Turkish. The relations between Turkey and Iran have traditionally been frosty. Therefore, if negotiations for EU entry are unsuccessful, Turkey may have difficulty finding an ally among its neighbours, apart from Azerbaijan. Even though the Ottoman occupation of the Middle East ended in 1918, the population in the region still have anti-Turkish sentiments.
135. Austria, Cyprus and Greece are the most obvious examples. The Scandinavian countries attach great weight to the human rights record. In addition, Ljubljana (Slovenia) is the only EU capital without a mosque.

For we dare not class ourselves or compare
ourselves with those who commend themselves.
But they, measuring themselves by themselves, and
comparing themselves among themselves, are not wise.
We, however, will not boast beyond measure, but
within the limits of the sphere which God appointed us,
a sphere which especially includes you.
2 Corinthians 10:12–13

6 Measurement of the Effects of International Economic Integration

6.1 Introduction

It is no strange thing in economics to discover that the evolution of the theory on a particular topic and the development of empirical research and measurement of it have pursued rather different courses. It is difficult to imagine a better example of this divergence than the study of the effects of international economic integration (Mayes, 1988, p. 42). Various studies have attempted to measure these effects. Some of them aimed to show the advance in integration as the interlacing of trade ties among countries and static effects. Others wanted to ascertain the increase in welfare and the dynamic effects. Yet another group of studies strove to quantify the distribution of the costs and benefits of integration. However, the theory of international economic integration encountered in this book is so complex that, at present, it cannot be taken on econometrically with any great precision.

Before the time of Viner (1950), it was often assumed that tariffs reduce welfare. Hence, any reduction in tariffs could increase it. Viner showed that such expectations cannot always be substantiated. In addition, the second-best character of economic integration makes a priori problematical any discovery of the welfare effects of integration. Proponents of integration argue that regional trade integration deals are steps (building blocks) towards universal free trade, while opponents disagree and state that these agreements are stumbling blocks.

There are also important methodological problems linked with the issue of identification. There are several things taking place simultaneously. These include, to mention just a few, trade liberalisation, increase in competition, change in income, modification in tastes, fluctuation in exchange rates, external shocks, innovation and transformation in technology. How to separate and measure them with a reasonable degree of certainty? That is one of the reasons why empirical research has not provided firm conclusions regarding the effects of economic integration. Others include the complexity of relations. It is hard to predict and quantify the outcome in a given time in the future without knowing the uncertain process of transformation of elements along the time path.

This chapter goes over the issue of quantification of effects of international economic integration, and is structured as follows. This introduction is followed by a review of influential models and studies (Section 6.2). The conclusion (Section 6.3) is that the effects of integration are interwoven with many others in the economy. There are still significant methodological difficulties to ascertain and separate the effects that are due only to integration.

6.2 Models

Econometric models which attempt to measure the effects of international economic integration can be divided into two groups: *ex ante* and *ex post*. The former are often founded on a simple extrapolation of trends. These models cannot be based on reliable data, but rather on estimations. The problem represents the fact that there are no reliable data on future developments, in particular on external shocks and on a change in behaviour. It is assumed that the future flow of foreign trade is a function of income, production, relative prices, change in the level of trade barriers, and substitutability among import sources, as well as between imports and domestic production.

The *ex post* models attempt to measure a hypothetical situation (the counterfactual world or anti-monde) which may represent what could have happened with trade in a situation without integration. The difference between the actual and expected imports of each of the participating countries represents trade creation, while the same difference in imports from outside countries shows trade diversion. These variations may be attributed to autonomous changes in prices, changes in income and competition, reductions in barriers to trade and to errors.

Econometric estimation is harder than meteorology or seismology. In the words of John Kay:

> But we can identify earthquake zones even if we cannot predict earthquakes and we can look forward to summer even if we cannot forecast the weather on June 4 next. Seismologists tell us where not to build our houses, and meteorologists help us know where to sell sun cream and when to take an umbrella. Useful economic knowledge is of a similar kind. . . . But when someone tells you that the dollar will appreciate in the second quarter of next year, or what the level of the S & P will be at the end of 2004, they do not know what they are talking about. If they did, they would not be making these predictions. But if you stop asking economists to forecast the future, there are other interesting things they can tell you.[1]

The models may single out a reduction or removal of trade barriers as the most important reason for the change in the pattern of trade. This may not be the most reliable method of assessing the effects of integration. Trade may have been diverted from third countries because of FDI which has replaced imports, not only because of changes in tariff structure. Instead of comparing the actual behaviour with what would have happened without integration and attributing all the difference to integration, one should rather compare what a model predicts with integration with what it predicts without integration (Mayes, 1988, p. 45). By doing that, the possible biases may be reduced. None the less, one can be fully certain neither about what would have happened without integration, nor about the influence of integration on the economic policies of member countries.

Most of the 'early' quantitative studies measure trade creation, trade diversion and output effects mainly in the context of the EU. An early influential study found that trade among the member countries of the EU was 50 per cent higher in 1969 than would have been the case without integration (Williamson and Bottrill, 1973, p. 139). Another study found that there was a 25 per cent increase in both exports and imports in EFTA in the 1959–65 period (EFTA, 1969, p. 10).

There is considerable agreement among various studies that trade creation outweighs trade diversion. The disagreement arises regarding the magnitude of this difference. The net effect of trade flows is usually positive (trade creating), but is relatively small. This is obvious from surveys by Mayes (1978)[2] and El-Agraa (1989). In spite of their relative magnitude (smallness) the perceived static gains always lend support to a number of economists' and some politicians' arguments in favour of integration. Alternatively, if these measured gains are so small, why should a country enter an integration agreement that necessitates making significant changes in the national economy?

Economic integration, just like free trade, may be welfare improving. However, economists have a hard time explaining these benefits to the general public (even to some fellow economists). This is in part due to the conflict between those who suffer adjustment costs in the short run (the unemployed and shareholders of closed firms) and long-term gainers (consumers and shareholders of efficient firms). Another part of the problem deals with the relative ambiguity or smallness in the measured gains from integration agreements. These quantitative results are due to several elements. They include the following:

- Some countries that take part in integration may trade a relatively small part of their goods and services within the group. That is most obvious in the schemes that integrate developing countries (see Table 2.13: Intra-trade of regional and trade groups).
- The degree of trade liberalisation within different groups, including the level and influence of non-tariff barriers (NTBs) and their harmonisation, may vary. The freedom offered to commerce by the rules of origin presents an important example.
- Comparative advantages and complementarities in the economies of countries that are in the integrated group *vis-à-vis* each other, as well as *vis-à-vis* the rest of the world, play an important role in the accuracy of measurement of gains.
- Intra-group competition rules and taxation influence potential gains.
- Mere trade creation/diversion effects do not properly represent changes in welfare. The total effect of regional economic integration is a blend of various effects of integration in the long run. Countries might not embark upon international economic integration because of clear balances in trade with partners, but rather to reap the dynamic benefits of integration such as an enhancement in opportunities for specialisation, economies of scale and increased welfare and development. Hence, the net trade creation/diversion effect cannot give an answer to the question of why countries integrate.[3]

Traditional general equilibrium models reported small welfare gains from integration, that is, less than 1 per cent of GNP in the EU (Lipsey, 1960, p. 511).[4] Subsequent analysis considered imperfect competition and economies of scale. Brada and Méndez (1988) estimated two dynamic effects of integration: levels of investment and growth in productivity in six integration groups. Faster productivity effects were found only in two, while increased investment levels were discovered in five schemes. The modest dynamic gains discovered reflected the cumulative effects of about two decades of integration. Therefore, according to these authors, dynamic gains could not explain the rapid growth of west European countries during the 1960s, nor be a strong justification for external countries to join the existing groups, nor be used as arguments for the creation of new ones.

The first generation of computable general equilibrium (CGE) models attempted to incorporate constant returns to scale and perfect competition, and evaluate the effects of integration or trade liberalisation deals. The second-generation models included economies of scale and imperfect competition. This is because of the cost impact on the changing scale of production and because of the 'love of variety'. The third-generation models attempt to capture inter-temporal effects of integration and investment on productivity growth.[5]

A complex general equilibrium model that considered economies of scale and imperfect competition was offered by Harris (1984a) and applied to Canada. Although it had limitations that included only one fixed factor (labour) and one internationally mobile factor (capital), Harris considered situations both with and without product differentiation. The findings were that trade liberalisation provoked intra-industry adjustment and a reallocation of resources and that trade liberalisation gave incentives for the expansion of economies of scale as a response to access to larger markets and competitive pressure from abroad.

Various studies of the potential effects of the Canada–US free trade agreement (1988) estimated a relatively modest long-run increase in the Canadian real income, between 1 and 3 per cent (Government of Canada, 1988, pp. 30–32). The only exception was the study by Harris and Cox (1985) which estimated an increase of 9 per cent. However, that study was prepared in 1984 and was based on outdated estimates of tariff rates, economies of scale and NTBs.

The explanation for the relatively modest trade-creating effects of economic integration in Europe and North America could be found in the already high trade among partners prior to integration. The estimated modest gains from integration had two impacts on public debate about the issue. The internal dimension is that if the gains were so meagre, why should one bother to integrate? The external dimension is that when the effects of integration are so small, then there is little need for retaliation by third countries. However, a principal benefit of the deal for Canada was security of access to the US market. Similarly in Europe, the main economic integration gain is the assurance of secure access to a large and rich EU market.

Clausing (2001) found that the Canada–US Free Trade Agreement had a substantial effect on trade between the two countries. Tariff liberalisation was responsible for over half of the $42 billion increase in US imports from Canada in the 1989–94 period. The highest increase in trade was in those goods that had the largest reduction in tariffs. There was also little evidence of any trade diversion. This means that Canada–US integration was not at the expense of other countries. This, however, does not mean that such a group-specific conclusion has a universal value and application. Each integration deal must be judged on its own merits.

Focusing attention on economic integration in Europe and in North America, Egger (2004, p. 164) drew two conclusions: that joining a trade bloc does not have any short-term impact on trade volumes, and that there is a substantial long-term trade-creation effect.

The intuition behind gravity models of trade is found in physics. Attraction or gravity force (total trade) between two objects (countries) depends on their respective masses (size of their economies) and the spatial distance between them. These gravity models[6] use factors that include country size, income and population to mirror demand and supply (the bigger the country, the smaller the interaction with the outside world); common borders and physical distance to reflect transport and overall trade costs; common language (to describe cultural affinity); and artificial trade barriers. Some explain regional pattern and concentration of trade and integration as a result of low transport costs (low natural obstacles, hence they are 'natural' trading partners such as the US and Canada), while others argue that they are the outcome of discriminatory (preferential) trading deals. In general, gravity models give us little guidance about the suitability of preferential trade deals. The spaghetti-bowl mix of preferential trade relations may provide an incentive to go towards a simple and lean multilateral liberalisation of trade.

The 1985 'White Paper' set out the Single European Market Programme in the EU. The EU acted first, and only afterwards attempted to assess the potential impact of its action. Cecchini (1988) analysed the effects of completing the EU internal market. This should be achieved by the elimination of both NTBs and fragmented national markets by the end of 1992. The EU also published 'The economics of 1992' (Emerson et al., 1988). This project estimated the impact of the removal of all trade barriers on internal trade, freedom to provide services, economies of scale, and the effect of competition on corporate behaviour and public procurement in the EU. As such, it became a valuable benchmark for subsequent research and comparison. The major results of Emerson et al.'s project can be summarised as follows:

- The estimated partial equilibrium economic gains were between €175 and 255 billion in 1988 prices. Most of those gains would come in the form of savings from the elimination of customs formalities and technical barriers to trade, liberalisation of public procurement, economies of scale, freedom to provide services, reduction in X-inefficiency, as well as a downward convergence in prices.

- The above would increase EU GNP by 5 per cent of the 1988 level. If economic policies were coordinated, then the increase in GNP might be in the range between 2.5 and 6.5 per cent in the medium term.
- The extra non-inflationary economic growth would create up to 5 million new jobs in the medium term.

Such gains, which might occur under certain conditions (accommodating economic policy), even though they have a one-time character, were hard to resist. There was no widespread opposition to the completion of the Single European Market, because opponents to the plan could not offer an alternative strategy (and calculate its effects) that would make up for the losses forgone from preserving the status quo.

The results of the above study may well be underestimations as they excluded certain types of continuing and likely dynamic benefits. These indirect effects are difficult to measure. They include technological innovations which depend on the existence of competition; the impact of the growth of GNP on long-term savings and investment; the dynamic effects of economies of scale, learning by doing and know-how would be most obvious in the fast-growing high-technology industries where market segmentation seriously limited the scope for these gains and jeopardised performance in the future; and the large EU market would induce EU enterprises to change their business behaviour in that they would foster the emergence of truly European companies and business strategies which are better suited to secure a superior place in competition both within and out of the EU.

Medium- and long-term effects of integration depend on several variables. They include the following:

- changes in the structure and volume of production and trade in goods and services between the partners;
- changes in the balance of trade;
- created and lost jobs in the integrated countries;
- changes in wage rates;
- alterations in the real rates of exchange;
- changes in prices;
- accumulation effects (human and physical capital);
- creation of new goods and services;
- FDI;
- retaliation by the 'injured' countries/regions; and
- changes in GNP.

To ascertain all this, one needs a number of equations and many assumptions about unknown parameters (elasticities and cross-elasticities of demand and supply, substitution rate between capital and labour, or expenditure functions). This also requires high-powered econometric models, which makes results and interpretations vulnerable. Very often only the authors of the models (and a few others) understand the exercise (Hufbauer and Schott, 1992, p. 51). This restrains constructive dialogue and contributes to intellectual autarky and misunderstandings regarding policy implications.

NTBs contribute to an increase in costs that accrue from the non-competitive segmentation of the market. They encourage import substitution and discourage rationalisation of investments. The anticipated benefits that would come from their elimination include increased competition, with its parallel effects of improved efficiency, increased gains coming from economies of scale and a consequent reduction in unit costs of production for an enlarged market, as well as increased specialisation. The outcome of this process would be an increase in average living standards.

The greatest benefits of the Single Market Programme in the EU are not expected from one-off effects, as studies by Cecchini/Emerson suggest. They would come from continuous dynamic influences. Baldwin (1989) argued that Cecchini/Emerson (C/E in Figure 6.1) significantly *underestimated* the dynamic effects of the programme, for they concentrated on the impact of the single market on the level of output. The one-time efficiency gains from the programme would be translated into a substantial 'medium-term growth bonus' (B in Figure 6.1).[7] A rise in savings and investment, due to the initial 2.5 to 6.5 per cent growth in GNP, would increase EU capital stock. The medium-term growth bonus might evolve into a long-term one,

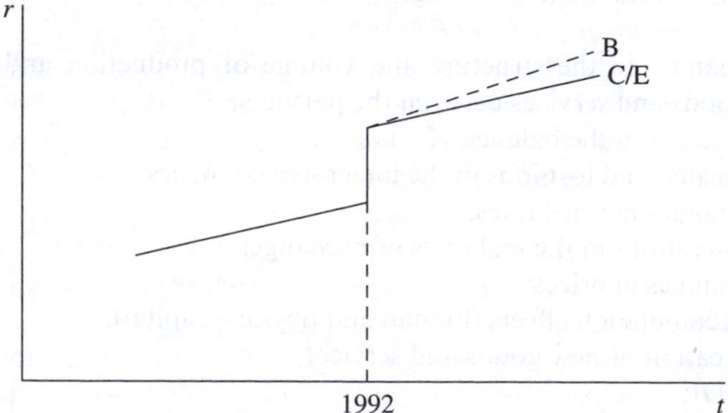

Figure 6.1 Potential growth effect of the Single European Market

adding permanently between 0.2 and 0.9 per cent to the EU long-term growth rate. The static part of it would be spread over five to seven years following completion of the Single European Market at the start of 1993. It may take about 10 years for the realisation of half of the medium-term 'growth bonus'. Baldwin concluded that the most important impact of the Single Market Programme might be on growth of the EU, not on its effect on resource allocation. If this analysis is correct, then the gains of the programme may be between 13 and 33 per cent of EU GNP. This type of analysis, along the lines suggested by Romer (1986), could be discouraging for all critics who argued that the Cecchini/Emerson results were too high.

Contrary to the view of Baldwin, Peck (1989) thought that the estimates by the European Commission of the potential gains of the Single Market Programme were *overestimates*. His own assessment of the gains of the programme was that it may increase GDP of the EU by 2 per cent. Hence, the computation by the European Commission overestimated the potential gains by a factor of 2 or 3 (ibid., p. 289). In addition, he referred to the argument that it was difficult to increase significantly the growth rate of an economy.

Smith and Venables (1988) also studied the possible effects of the programme on economic welfare. Increased competition and a fuller exploitation of economies of scale due to the change in the size of firms were expected to raise welfare in the EU. The partial equilibrium model calibrated to 10 separate industries included imperfect competition, economies of scale and differentiated products. The results of both Cournot and Bertand behaviour were presented, although the authors regarded Cournot competition as a more satisfactory model. Simulations were carried out both where there was a fixed number of firms and where entry in and exit from an industry was possible. The results showed that the gains from integration could be quite significant for certain industries as they exceeded 4 per cent of base consumption.

A general equilibrium model for the estimation of the impact of the Single Market Programme was developed by Gasiorek et al. (1992). Their starting point was that the partial equilibrium models were potentially misleading as they did not capture the impact of a change in one industry on others in imperfectly competitive markets. Another limitation of the partial equilibrium models was that they assumed horizontal input-supply curves. In the general equilibrium model, Gasiorek et al. considered 8 countries and 5 factors (8×5 model) and cases when markets are both segmented and integrated. If one ignored restrictive assumptions of the model that gave a crude approximation of the real world and an imperfect set of data, the results supported the view that intra-EU liberalisation of trade had pro-competitive effects that could make a substantial contribution to welfare.

Most of the welfare gains were attributable to the competition effect and economies of scale, although this was partly offset by a loss in variety, trade diversion and deterioration in terms of trade with the third countries as certain benefits of lower costs of the EU goods were passed on to foreign consumers.

A Communication from the European Commission based on replies from 13 000 enterprises offered an *ex post* assessment of the impact of the Single Market Programme (European Commission, 1997a). The findings included solid evidence of the positive effects of the Single European Market:

- growing competition between firms in both manufacturing and services;
- an accelerated pace of industrial restructuring;
- a wider range of goods and services available to the public sector, industrial and domestic consumers at lower prices, particularly in newly liberalised services such as transport, financial services, telecommunications and broadcasting;
- faster and cheaper cross-frontier deliveries resulting from the absence of cross-border controls on goods;
- greater inter-state mobility of workers, as well as students and retired people;
- between 300 000 and 900 000 more new jobs created than would be the case without the programme;
- an extra increase in EU income of 1.1–1.5 per cent over the 1987–93 period;
- inflation rates 1.0–1.5 per cent lower than would be the case in the absence of the programme; and
- an increase in economic convergence and cohesion between different EU regions.

The model estimated that the GDP for the EU(12) in 1994 was in the range of 1.1–1.5 per cent above the level that would have prevailed in the absence of the Single European Market. That was a gain in the range of €60–80 billion – this was as if an income the size of Portugal's economy (€75 billion in 1994) had been added to the EU(12). The gains came from the increase in competition/efficiency and the rise in total factor productivity (each accounting for about half of the total effect) (*European Economy*, 1996, pp. 166–7). The elimination of trade barriers reduced the segmentation of the national market, increased competition and decreased costs (and prices).

The above quantitative findings were 'disappointing' compared with the earlier official estimations and expectations when the Single Market

Programme was launched. These data from the European Commission are (for whatever reason) more in line with the expectations of Peck (1989) than in accord with any other *ex ante* estimation.[8]

Several arguments may be put forward to explain these relatively 'small' results, including the following:

- Although the programme was 'formally' implemented and the Single European Market introduced from 1993, the process of 'digestion' of all the changes and adjustment to new opportunities still needs additional time. In spite of the large wave of (defensive) mergers and acquisitions around 1990, the exploitation of new opportunities for output and business in an enlarged market (free of NTBs) needs more time, perhaps a decade or two. This is relevant both for the manufacturing sector and, even more important, for services.
- The reunification of Germany and related adjustment difficulties and costs have affected the economic performance of the EU.

The welfare effects of the integration of a group of countries on external countries are quite important and debatable. Usually, there was a simple observation of exports of these countries to the integrated group. This is a poor indicator of welfare. If welfare is equated with consumption, then the more these countries export, the fewer goods and services are left for them to consume. However, imports by and terms of trade of third countries with the integrated group are superior indicators of effects on welfare in external countries. An enlarged variety of goods and services available in domestic consumption is one of the principal benefits that trade brings. The problem is that estimation of the terms-of-trade effect is more problematical than the approximation of trade quantities. These challenges and problems were put succinctly by Winters (1997, p. 134):

> We have virtually no hard evidence on how regional integration affects economic welfare in the rest of the world. The reasons are that, to date, we have largely failed to measure the effects that theory shows to matter, and that much of what we have measured hardly matters at all. The theoretical and empirical analyses of this important issue are far apart, and the practical difficulties of doing the latter correctly are formidable in terms of both finding data and extracting their message. Nonetheless, we should try.

The methodological problems that appear concern the choice of assumptions: the base year and length of time series before and after integration. The structure of domestic production and foreign trade changes throughout time: new goods and services appear, old ones disappear while tastes and income change. The quality of goods and services changes over time and technology becomes more productive. Capacity utilisation within broadly defined sectors escapes scrutiny. All these issues jeopardise generalisations about the long-term structure and pattern of production, trade and investment. Asymmetrical business cycles make comparisons of prices among countries questionable. Some of the trade flows (traditional trade or unique commodities) are independent of international economic integration. The same holds for the spatial location of firms and industries with strong intra-industry functional production linkages (finance and certain chemicals). Hence, inter-temporal estimates are very complex and demanding indeed.

While trade creation indicates new imports of goods from partner countries and a reduction by the same quantity of domestic production, trade diversion indicates a reduction of imports from (and production in) third countries, as well as new imports and production in partner countries. Therefore, a comprehensive measurement of the effects of integration requires not only analysis of trade data, but also data on production (El-Agraa, 1989, p. 346).

Changes other than international economic integration need to be considered too. These refer to a reduction of tariffs and NTBs to trade under the auspices of the GATT/WTO. These modifications are not always a direct consequence of the creation of the EU or the EFTA or NAFTA, although regional integration deals contributed to the multilateral negotiations about the reductions in tariffs and NTBs. It is widely accepted that the Dillon (1959–62), Kennedy (1963–67) and Tokyo (1973–79) Rounds of trade negotiations were attempts by the US and other developed market economies to reduce the discriminating effect that came from the creation and enlargement of the EU. Other alterations include the introduction of convertibility in the late 1950s and an increase in US investment in western Europe. Hence, formal integration is not the only reason for an increase in economic and investment activity.

Assumptions about unchangeable market shares for the purpose of the extrapolation of trends means that technology, competition, costs, tastes, elasticities and economic policy are given and fixed. The availability and comparability of data may also be criticised. Actual production and trade does not mean that all potentials are fully utilised. Unfortunately, there is no model that accurately measures unused potential.

Customs duties are made public, but their implementation is often formidable. Only part of the reduction in tariffs is passed on to the consumers in the form of lower prices. The prices of imported goods are often set (by means of various taxes and price discrimination policies of firms[9]) with reference to competing home goods if they exist. Technology and inputs for the standardised products are available to all producers, but the final goods are often produced and distributed at different costs. The answer to this question may easily be found in differences in location-related X-inefficiency.

Adjustment to integration is not instantaneous. Integration and growth-induced forces are interlaced. Integration-induced effects may dominate the more sudden the integration. Growth-induced effects may dominate over a longer time. The more gradual the integration and the longer the period of observation, the more the effects will be mixed up (Lipsey, 1976, p. 38). Part of the answer to this problem may be found in models inspired by the work of Romer (1986).

6.3 Conclusion

Econometrics has advanced a great deal since the 1960s, but it is still unable to solve some important methodological issues. The problem is bolstered by the complexity and fickleness of the modern economy. Has it grown in such a way and is it changing so fast that it has become immeasurable? It is, however, recognised that it is better to measure in some way, even with all the limitations of modelling, than not to measure at all. 'Given our present ignorance any information would be useful' (Winters, 1997, p. 145). Hence, there is a substantial space for the improvement and extension of our knowledge and understanding of this challenging research area.

The analysis has revealed that there are serious drawbacks in the econometric modelling and interpretation of the results of international economic integration. All models should be viewed with a certain degree of suspicion as they rely on a number of restrictive assumptions and there is also a complexity of causes and effects. One wonders if slightly different assumptions might not have produced a completely different econometric result. The final outcome of all estimations is always a blend of various effects. The whole analysis, therefore, suffers from an identification problem, that is, how to distinguish between the effects of integration and the various other influences. This has so far been unfortunate for econometrics, not for the effects of international economic integration.

Baldwin (1993) investigated the problems of the measurement of dynamic effects of international economic integration. Some politicians and many economists believe that economic integration is an engine of growth. The available estimates of the effects of integration do not fully justify these expectations. While the static effects of economic integration were believed to produce more output from a given set of inputs, the dynamic effects were assumed to affect the accumulation of factors. The measurement of both effects is tricky, in particular in the case of the dynamic effects, as it takes decades to accumulate factors and to reach a new theoretical steady-state equilibrium.

Economic integration does not affect all industries and all participating countries in an identical way. Problems are also amplified by our lack of a full understanding of what governs investment in human and physical capital in the short and medium terms. The same holds for savings. The variable impact of integration on different industries and countries is one of the principal drawbacks of the quantitative estimates. In general, economic integration is expected to have the strongest impact on the competitive behaviour and productivity in traded goods and industries characterised by economies of scale and easy spatial mobility. These are activities that employ a lot of human and physical capital, hence economic integration has the potential to increase the return on capital.

There is, sometimes, conflicting evidence regarding the effects of integration, in particular, regarding the Single Market Programme. For example, Neven (1990) concluded that the programme was relatively unimportant to the northern EU member countries since they have already used most of the potential for large-scale production. Alternatively, Smith and Venables (1988) and Cecchini/Emerson believed that the potential for economies of scale was significant throughout the EU. This puzzle reveals that there does not yet exist a full understanding of the determinants of trade and production patterns in the EU and that the analyses of integration will remain speculative (Norman, 1990, p. 52).

A meaningful comparison of the gap in prices for a good in different parts of an integrated area ought to reflect not only the trade costs, as was traditionally the case, but also the consumption pattern in different countries. The problems of measurement become immense because income, tastes, traditions and climate may be very different even within the confines of a single country. The greater the diversity of the integrated countries, the harder the test.

A pragmatic way to encounter the effects of international economic integration may be to follow the structure of home consumption (proportions of home-made goods, the ones imported from partner countries and goods from third countries). Another way may be to compare the relative prices of equal goods and services on the markets of the integrated countries. In a homogeneous and relatively well-integrated area such as the US with no differences in tastes, similarity in income and (to an extent) climate, these prices may differ only for costs of transport.

The magnitude of the effects of international economic integration will be debated for a long time. It is widely accepted that integration increases potentials for economic gains. The actual and perceived distribution of costs and benefits of these effects matters a lot. However, when one participant gains from integration it does not mean that others lose. It is essential that every participant gains more in the long term than he/she is able to gain when acting alone. The crucial problem and big difficulty is a search for simple, clear and straightforward answers to complicated and controversial questions related to the effects of integration. Such results and answers may not be obtained. 'The theory of economic integration (from Viner (1950) onwards) tells us that the effects of membership are ambiguous but gives little guidance on these questions' (Venables, 2003, p. 747). Therefore, the results may be easily abused and distorted in the policy debate.

In spite of significant improvements in techniques to measure the effects of integration, the studies presented reveal an important puzzle: our lack of full understanding of the determinants, operation and effect of integration on production, investment, trade and consumption. Until this is solved, the nature of the analysis and measurement of the effects of integration will remain speculative. Attempts to solve these problems, in particular the dynamic effects, will be on the research agenda for the future.

Notes

1. J. Kay, 'Economic forecasting will never be an exact science', *Financial Times*, 29 October 2003, p. 23.
2. If one removed barriers to trade such as tariffs, quotas and biased public procurement, one might reasonably expect an increase in trade (trade creation). If such domestic barriers were removed from commerce with foreign country A, but not with country B, as is the case in customs unions, imports from country A may increase at the expense of the imports from country B (trade diversion). Mayes considered three types of quantitative models. First were residual (*ex post*) models. They compared various hypothetical situations (often referred to as the anti-monde of what would have happened had the integration not taken place) to the actual situation. Second were simple analytic (*ex ante*) models that tried to predict the course of developments in the near future. Third were the dynamic models. The process of integration takes place over time and is not limited to the simple static effects of trade creation and diversion. However, analytical tools were, at the time, modest for such a complex econometric exercise.
3. A non-market-based economic system and integration in the former CMEA created controversies. Dietz (1986) attempted to estimate effects of trade in the CMEA. One view was that in this group the Soviet Union, at that time, used political clout in order to obtain economic advantages in trade relations with east European countries. Another one was that the Soviet Union was heavily subsidising these countries through the CMEA pricing system. These gains/losses included the difference in the world market price (most notably for energy) and the internal CMEA price for the same good. The finding was that the Soviet Union gave subsidies to its CMEA partners, but these were much smaller than the ones estimated in earlier studies.
4. Balassa (1967) employed an *ex post* model for the comparison of income elasticities of import demand in intra- and extra-area trade, for periods that preceded and followed integration in the EU. There was evidence of trade creation and no indication of trade diversion.

5. See Lloyd and MacLaren (2004) for a detailed survey.
6. A major gravity study of trade in integration groups was done by Frenkel (1997). Greenaway and Milner (2002) provided a survey of literature about gravity models.
7. In theory, the principal factors conducive to the growth rate of per capita GDP are a high level of education, a high-quality health system, low fertility, low public expenditure, favourable terms of trade, low inflation and the rule of law (Barro, 1997, pp. 119–29).
8. See Sapir (1996) for another assessment of the effects of the Single Market Programme.
9. Different pricing of the same model of a car in various member countries of the EU is a prime example of such a policy.

O Lord, I know the way of man is not in himself;
it is not in man who walks to direct his own steps.
O Lord, correct me, but with justice;
not in Your anger, lest You bring me to nothing.
Jeremiah 10:23–4

7 Conclusions

Free trade and an unimpeded movement of factors is the first-best policy in a world that does not have any distortions. This is only a hypothetical situation. The real situation is full of market imperfections that may be corrected to an extent by the employment of an economic policy (intervention). The rationale for international economic integration (an introverted economic strategy, to a degree) and trade liberalisation agreements can be found in the case where market imperfections exist. When one distortion (for example, a universal tariff of a country) is replaced by another (for example, the common external tariff of a customs union) the net effect may be obscure.

Theory about regional economic integration is the analysis of second-best situations. It is, therefore, not surprising that general theoretical principles and consensus about motivations, desirability and results of international economic integration and trade liberalisation agreements may not be found. What matters, however, is not solely the predictions of theory, but rather what happens in real life: a proliferation of trade liberalisation and integration agreements.

A customs union or any regional trading bloc may be seen as a compromise between two groups of protagonists promoting seemingly irreconcilable principles of economic policy: free-traders and protectionists. Having made the compromise in a regional group, the former are happy about the abolition of barriers on intra-bloc trade, while the latter are glad about the continuation of barriers against extra-bloc imports. Does it make any sense to ask who has made the greater concession in reaching the compromise? The question makes sense indeed, and the answer depends on the height of the trade barriers abolished and that of the barriers retained (Machlup, 1979, p. 102).

Reasonable prospects for gains that international economic integration provides can be summarised as follows:

- Integration extends, improves, makes credible and secures the markets for a country's goods and services against abrupt changes in the trade policy of partners in the future. Hence, integration can be seen as an 'insurance policy' against sudden and unilateral economic actions by partners in the deal. Although this is one of the principal gains, it should not be taken as the 'end of the story'. The Single Market Programme (1985–92) has shaken and deepened the EU market, but it has failed to accelerate growth.[1] Additional measures such as defragmentation of national services markets, flexibility in the labour market, as well as a more vigorous R&D and education and training were suggested as necessary.
- Wider and secure markets increase investment opportunities for both domestic firms and TNCs. Business expectations may be established with an increased degree of security.
- There is an improvement in the allocation and the efficiency of use of resources and capabilities due to increased competition, specialisation and returns to scale. This increases the efficiency of the manufacturing and services sectors, hence average standards of living increase.
- Integration arrangements exist because trade barriers can be adapted according to the preferences of the countries involved.
- Integration partners have a greater degree of mutual understanding and trust, which is often lacking on the global scale. A relatively small number of participants may create close relations, make monitoring of the deal easier and more friendly. Positive cooperation within the group may potentially help the exchange of favours, an agreement can be reached with few problems and (perhaps) disputes may be settled faster and more efficiently than is the case in multilateral institutions.
- Integration assists in the creation of new technologies, goods and services.
- Integration reduces the cost of a national import-substitution policy.
- Integration makes it difficult to reverse domestic market liberalisation reforms. Examples are central and east European countries in the EU and Mexico in NAFTA.

- International action limits, to an extent, the possibility for unnecessary public intervention in the economy because it extends the scope of economic policy across several countries.
- Relatively larger markets have a potentially greater capacity for coping with various distortions than smaller markets, because larger markets may more easily offset the impact of both favourable and unfavourable effects. Vulnerability to external shocks can be reduced.
- International coordination of economic policies.
- Creation of the potential for monetary stability.
- Improvement in bargaining positions with external partners (an example is the EU).
- Terms-of-trade effects and gains to exporters provide benefits from preferential trading agreements that are not available from unilateral trade liberalisation policies.
- Stimulation of economic growth.
- Trade creation and trade diversion.

Given the above motives for regional integration, it is not necessary to resort exclusively to non-economic reasons for economic integration. However, there are still many unanswered and emerging questions regarding international economic integration. Appendix 7A1 provides a brief list of research topics for the future.

It is hard to forecast with any degree of accuracy how the effects of integration will turn out in practice. In the short term, just after the lifting of barriers to trade, production, GDP and commerce may increase[2] while some prices may fall. In addition, some increase in unemployment may occur in the short run because of intensified competition and the unfinished adjustment and reallocation process. In the medium and long terms, structural adjustment and improved allocation of resources takes place, economies of scale occur, retraining and mobility of labour reduces unemployment because new and better jobs are being created. Market rigidities are being eased as agents change their behaviour due to increased opportunities and challenges for business and competition. It is in this context that the dynamic effects of integration materialise.

One of the difficulties of international economic integration and trade liberalisation agreements is that their gains accrue in the long run to everybody, but in relatively small instalments. The costs of integration and trade liberalisation may be more easily identified. They affect certain visible and loud segments of business and labour, but their effects may have only a relatively short-term impact on the national economy. The coordination of economic policies, which may be brought by regional integration, has the potential to exercise its full beneficial effects only in the long run. These joint economic policies should not be abandoned even if they do not bring the desired results in the short run. Enhanced competition stimulates R&D, while economies of scale exert a downward pressure on costs and prices. This creates conditions for non-inflationary growth. None the less, it is unclear how this would happen in practice. It may occur through increased output with unchanged inflation or less price inflation or, and most likely, a mixture of both. One real problem is that the gains of international economic integration may not be easily comprehended and appreciated by non-economists.

External countries may experience unfavourable effects from integration. Trade diversion is an example. But if integrated countries grow at a faster rate than in the case without integration, their income may increase and, by such acceleration, the integrated countries may expand their trade with outside countries. In spite of fears of a 'Fortress Europe' following the completion of the Single European Market at the end of 1992, EU imports from third countries continued to grow.

When there are economies of scale, changes in technology, sunk costs, imperfect competition, path dependency and/or FDI, it is select intervention in the form of economic policy (for example, development of human resources through education and training; qualified protection for a limited period of time; investment/production subsidies) which may successfully correct those market imperfections. The theory of strategic trade and industrial policy which takes into account market imperfections, supplements the smooth and straightforward conclusions of neo-classical theory. Under certain assumptions, free trade may be an attractive economic policy. In more realistic conditions, however, judicious intervention (of which integration is a part) may fare even better. This is only a possibility, not a definite outcome, as the 'lone-wolf' development strategies of Switzerland, Norway, Taiwan, South Korea, Singapore, Hong Kong or Sweden (until it joined the EU in 1995) have shown. Still, these countries were quite open for trade. However, their economic performance may be the exception, rather than the general rule. None the less, in 'normal' circumstances countries grow richer together, not at each other's expense. Hence the need for cooperation (if not integration) on a larger international scale.

Trade is not a zero-sum game. David Hume wrote in his essay 'Of the jealousy of trade' in 1752 a message that is at least as relevant today as it was during his time and much earlier:[3]

> I will venture to assert, that the increase of riches and commerce in any one nation, instead of hurting, commonly promotes the riches and commerce of all its neighbours; and that a state can scarcely carry its trade and industry very far, where all the surrounding states are buried in ignorance, sloth, and barbarism. . . . I shall

> therefore venture to acknowledge, that, not only as a man, but as a British subject, I pray for the flourishing commerce of Germany, Spain, Italy and even France[4] itself. I am at least certain, that Great Britain, and all those nations, would flourish more, did their sovereigns and ministers adopt such enlarged and benevolent sentiments towards each other.

A relatively big and integrated market is not a guarantee in itself that international economic integration will bring both satisfactory and desired economic outcomes. This evidence can be found in the cases of Russia and India, as well as China (perhaps until the 1990s). Contrasting evidence can be traced in the impressive experience of individualistic development of the small countries mentioned. A country's prosperity does not depend on its size and natural resources, since the most important assets are human resources (heads and hands), as well as the political and regulatory (institutional) framework. None the less, relatively larger markets may have the potential for a greater capacity in coping with the various distortions than smaller markets, because they may more easily offset the impact of both favourable and unfavourable effects. This presents the case in favour of integration. Although all countries are not under the same kind of pressure to adjust, joint action by countries may offer attractive economies of scale in economic policy relative to the situation where each country acts alone.

Large developed countries depend to a lesser degree on external relations than do small countries. In theory, these countries may have a diversified economic structure which allows for a kind of autarkic economic policy, while such a policy for small countries in a situation with economies of scale, changing technology and situation in the market, as well as other externalities such as a high international mobility of capital, does not have an economic rationale. Without secure and free access to a market wider than the national one, a relatively limited domestic market and demand in small countries often prevents the employment of the most efficient technology, even if trade barriers are prohibitive. If some production takes place, the consequences include short production runs, high prices and a lower standard of living. The efficient operation of many modern technologies requires secure access to the widest market, which does not exist in small and, sometimes, medium-sized countries. That is why large economies such as the US, Germany, France or Brazil get involved in economic integration. The elimination of tariffs, NTBs, restrictions on factor mobility, as well as the international coordination of economic policies and integration, can be solutions to this problem of country size. The goal is to widen, improve and secure access to markets by the participating countries.

The traditional (static) model of preferential trading areas considered the effect of a reduction in tariffs on welfare. It concluded that the elimination or lowering of tariffs increased competition which, in turn, could lead to an improvement in welfare. The new theory focuses on the dynamic effects of integration. In the case of perfect competition, a narrow range of outcomes is obvious. However, in the situation characterised by imperfect competition, economies of scale, international capital mobility and multiple equilibria, there can be many outcomes. There are no unconditional expectations that all countries will gain from integration and trade, even less that they will gain equally.

The objective of this book is not to give *carte blanche* to intervention; it is much more modest than that. The goal is to explore prospects for a structured framework for analysis that may advise on choices and challenges, as well as on possible policy responses. This book argues that, in a situation with market imperfections, 'smart' intervention (integration is a part of it), under certain conditions, may have a more favourable welfare outcome than the 'free' play of market forces. It has always been shoddy economics to argue that free trade is an all-time favourable policy option for all participants. There are always those that gain and others, usually a minority, that lose in the long term. In addition, even gains from integration are not always equally or satisfactorily distributed among the beneficiaries.

The views expressed in this book do not supplant the neo-classical economic model, but rather enrich it with another possibility that needs to be considered during the policy-making process. Unfortunately, any theoretically respectable case for intervention may often find support for the wrong reasons. Intervention is capable of provoking a chain of retaliations and counter-retaliations that may impoverish everybody.

A move from a fragmented to an integrated market can create some of the most striking results of economic integration. However, integration does not affect all industries equally. The industries that are most directly affected are those that produce traded goods and services with increasing returns to scale. Links between integration, trade, FDI and geography of production are complex and vary with the types of integration as various types permit different freedoms to factor mobility and introduction of joint economic policies.

According to the classical trade theory, a reduction in trade costs is expected to bring benefits via an increase in a country's specialisation. The neo-classical theory predicts that national specialisation will mirror differences in comparative advantage. Countries trade in order to take advantage of their differences. The 'new economic geography' and 'spatial economics' and the 'new trade' theories argue that countries specialise in production and trade according to the potential for greater economies of scale even if these countries are of the same size and have identical endowment of factors.

An additional point of interest for the 'new school' is the impact of economies of scale on spatial agglomeration of production. The specialisation process (reallocation of resources) is, however, not without adjustment costs. These costs are lower in the case of intra-industry trade than when the adjustment has an inter-industry dimension. This aspect needs to be taken into consideration when ascertaining the net effect. The two 'new' approaches to economic theory study production linkages. These theories confirm that, depending on the strength of the functional production linkages, regional, national or international geography of production may change in response to the alteration in trade costs. This change in the costs of trade may originate in changes in marketing, transport, data processing and communication technology, as well as in bilateral, regional or international institutional reductions in trade barriers.

Regional economic integration is not an enterprise without risks of adjustment. On those grounds some countries may accept protectionism as an attractive alternative to integration. In the short run, national protectionism may offer some advantages over a relatively outward-oriented economic policy that includes integration. Such a choice is defensive in its nature. International markets and technology continuously increase their speed of change. To maintain the status quo by endless protection is the surest way to economic disaster in the long run, when every country will face the need to adjust. If economic policy provides a friendly environment with continuous adjustment, then the costs of relatively continuous and sometimes fairly smooth shifts may be smaller than the big-bang adjustment which may occur after a long period of protection. An example of such a shock may be found in the long, difficult, costly and uncertain transition process towards a market-type economy in a number of countries of central and eastern Europe. However, the eight successful formerly socialist and centrally planned economies joined the EU in 2004. This provoked a regional domino effect in integration. Other countries are reforming, applying and lining up to join the EU.

'Free competition' within the group is not likely to destroy all business in some of the participating countries. Two instruments prevent such a disastrous scenario. First is the adjustment period (before or after the entry of the group) to new circumstances. This will gradually enable firms to reallocate resources. A country with serious adjustment problems may seek free access to the markets of partner countries some time before it offers the same concession to these partners. The exchange rate is the second safety valve which will prevent such a 'catastrophe'. The experience of the EU, EFTA, NAFTA and various rounds of trade-liberalisation negotiations under the auspices of GATT/WTO showed that economic adjustment to integration and trade liberalisation took place smoothly. Trade, production, economic growth and employment had an increasing trend in the long term. If structural problems did occur, then they were due to increases in prices for oil, competition from the newly industrialising countries or, most often, a poor national macroeconomic policy, rather than integration.

There was (and perhaps still is) confusion about external trade policy, including integration, on the aggregate level of employment. Sometimes the champions of integration may try to 'oversell' their case. Trade and integration alter the structure of employment within different economic sectors and the overall standard of living, that is, the kind and pattern of jobs available, rather than whether they are available at all (their total number). Trade normally stimulates reallocation of capital and jobs from lower- towards higher-productivity industries and sectors. The result of trade and integration is not necessarily more jobs, but rather better jobs.

A change in the national production and employment pattern is one of the chief reasons for promoting trade and integration. As long as the newly created jobs roughly balance lost ones, the general influence of integration on total employment will be small. There is a tendency for some (politicians) to blame international economic integration and trade for every domestic economic failure and disillusionment, no matter how weak the link may be between the two. A relatively high and stubborn unemployment rate in the EU is due mainly to rigid national labour markets, not to European integration. Apart from the monetary policy in the eurozone countries, primary policy tools to cope with the problem of unemployment are at the national, not EU, level. Perhaps, without integration, unemployment would be even higher.

International economic integration limits, to an extent, the possibility for unnecessary public intervention in the economy because it extends the scope of economic policy to at least two countries. The result is increased competition which may create more efficient manufacturing and services sectors. An additional benefit of integration is that it reduces the cost of a national import-substitution policy. However, integration is not a cure for all economic ills. It is only a supporting tool that increases the intensity of (good) overall national economic policy. One has to be realistic in expectations as integration facilitates market access and creates opportunities for increased competition on an enlarged market. Economic progress also depends on an astute macroeconomic policy and similar policies in education (investment in human capital that is supposed to solve problems), R&D, investment in capital goods, as well as the interest of firms to take advantage of the newly created environment.

In spite of various economic arguments in favour of integration, there are still a number of controversies as the real and full dynamic gains and costs of integration are still not known. If regional integration is here to stay for a long time,[5] what are the disposable means to make these trading blocs complementary with the multilateral trading system? The situation in the first decade of the new millennium is much different from that in the 1960s when south–south integration deals were operated in an inward-looking environment. Many of the integration schemes among the developing countries as structured in the past were mistakes that are not worth repeating. The potential for the expansion of intra-regional trade was simply not there.[6]

The theory of international economic integration has been basically Euro-centric as Europe is the area where regional integration has had its most significant impact since the 1950s. The application of this theory to the case of developing countries may be enhanced by cost–benefit analysis. The classical theory may find that customs unions among the developing countries could be trade diverting. This may often be the case during the initial integration and adjustment phases. The reason is the fact that the developing countries may be higher-cost suppliers for a number of (but not for all) goods and services than are industrialised and newly developed countries. The *existing* structure of production and trade does not provide a rationale for economic integration among many developing countries. It is, however, the potential for *change* in this structure which could provide the rationale for integration among the developing countries. Integration and adequate intervention (economic policy) may offer attractive gains.

Earlier integration arrangements among developing countries have had at best very limited results. In certain cases, they were a waste of time and resources. The potential for a bigger economic change in the future may be found in north–south integration as was the case with Mexico, which integrated with the US and Canada.[7] The developing countries may have, in general, relatively high tariffs. Integration with developed countries that have relatively lower tariffs may be a move that is prone to relatively faster trade liberalisation than could be the case when highly protected developing countries integrate among themselves. This may also increase pressure on the developed north to liberalise trade in farm goods and even permit international labour mobility. In the meantime, new integration arrangements may develop in which the parties are already integrated groups. The examples include deals between the EU and Mercosur, SACU and SADC or CACM and the Caribbean group.

Integration between partners at different levels of development took place in the EU when this group accepted Greece in 1981, Spain and Portugal in 1986, and a select group of central and east European countries in 2004. A certain kind of economic 'cooperation' in the Pacific region may take place in the coming decades among countries at different levels of economic development. In addition, some 'stronger economic links' across the Mediterranean may be discussed in the (distant) future.

Countries throughout the world have revived their interest in regional economic integration since the early 1990s. Regional free trade arrangements are expanding all around the world. This is especially true from 1995 (when the WTO came into existence). However, past attempts at integration have been achieved with very different degrees of success in relation to the stated objectives, expectations and potential. One of the possible explanations for the slowness in economic integration may be traced to the non-acceptance of supranationality. Small countries, in particular, have to learn that it is much less a matter of actual economic sovereignty and integration, and much more a choice between one or another form of interdependence.

While there is general agreement about the advantages, value and importance of a multilateral approach to international trade, there are differences in opinion regarding international trade liberalisation (integration) arrangements. Do they help or hinder the multilateral trading system under the auspices of the WTO? Are regional trade liberalisation agreements and integration effective substitutes for badly operating multilateral trade liberalisation processes and institutions? A fierce debate among economists and policy makers started during the 1990s.[8] It revealed sharp divisions, which comes as no surprise as we consider a second-best situation. Proponents of integration argue that regional trade liberalisation arrangements and regional integration are steps (building blocks) towards universal free trade through growth and many other favourable effects. Opponents disagree, stating that these deals are stumbling blocks, and offer a long list of arguments which were itemised at the beginning of this book.

Let us also recall that if there are so many serious objections to regional trade agreements and little hard quantitative evidence about their clear beneficial effects, wherein lies their fatal fascination and justification? Why do they proliferate? In the real world, bilateral or regional trading agreements may be a response to tremendous and uncertain resource costs related to multilateral negotiations and multilateral deals. It may be simpler, faster, cheaper and more tangible to put into practice a regional integration deal than to wait interminably for an uncertain multilateral trade arrangement and its benefits. Static and usually short-term costs in terms of trade diversion do not give the full picture of the costs of regional deals for third countries.[9] Long-term dynamic effects may be much more important and beneficial for everyone. The choice that policy makers face in reality is not between multilateral agreements and economic integration, but rather between a potentially beneficial economic integration with select partners (now) or no such arrangement at all.

Whether regional economic integration can result in multilaterally liberal trade cannot be proved.[10] Integration may, however, start this process.

The bottom line may be uncertain: are the new integration programmes the outcome of the success of multilateralism or its failure?

One should not forget important ideological factors and political, especially security, gains that bring integration agreements. Some of them, the EU is one example,[11] were primarily created in order to make war between France and Germany impossible. Economic integration was just a vehicle towards that objective. Politics and strong and sustained commitment (or a lack of it) to the letter and spirit of the agreed goals are often the primary reason for the success, slow progress or failure of an integrating group. In addition, many integration deals go well beyond mere trade, so that arguments about substantial costs that integration brings are only a possibility, not a certainty.[12] Many quantitative studies about the effects of integration on world welfare have questionable and ambiguous results.

An inevitable question is whether integration/regionalism is a good or a bad thing. The answer to this depends on a further question: for whom? For the multilateral trading system it may be bad. For individual countries this may not be the case in the short term. Many countries have little confidence in a multilateral trading system. In general, regional integration arrangements in themselves have been neither liberal nor 'illiberal'. Their impact on trade depended on the provisions of the scheme, the way in which they evolved and the potential collision with the trade policies of third countries. The pace of post-1960s trade liberalisation trends and the entry of the GATT/WTO into new fields such as agriculture and services might have been slower in the absence of the challenge posed by the evolution and impact of the EU. Hence, regional integration in Europe has been 'friendly' to multilateral trade liberalisation.[13] The creation and existence of the EU expedited the multilateral process that began several trade-liberalisation rounds from the end of the 1950s (but note the distorting production and trade effects of the CAP). It remains to be seen whether this will continue to be the case in the new millennium.

Existing WTO rules on integration arrangements have not been an appropriate means of handling the reality and variety of integration deals. This weakness should be a topic for negotiation. The WTO noted:

> The rules, which require RTAs to be transparent and to provide for deep internal trade liberalization and neutrality *vis-à-vis* non-parties' trade, have been subject to diverging interpretations for nearly half a century, and opened the door to a situation of great ambiguity with respect to the relationship between RTAs and the multilateral trading system. (WTO, 2003, pp. 12–3).

In spite of proliferating trade liberalisation agreements, well beyond the will and imagination of the founders of the GATT, the GATT/WTO has shown its strength and durability. Since 1995, there have been major international liberalisation deals in telecommunication and financial services; China joined the WTO in 2001 and there was a resolution of a number of disputes in trade. The MFN clause[14] is resilient as countries prefer, all other things being equal, to buy from the cheapest source of supply. The GATT/WTO membership continues to widen, while the coverage of its rules has an expanding path. It remains to be seen whether this situation will continue.

Even though regional integration appears to have been supporting multilateral trade liberalisation, rather than preventing it, we should sound a warning note. Integration reduced incentives to take global welfare into account. Hence, it is still a matter for debate whether the member countries of the EU would have been on a higher or lower level of protection without the EU. The decision-making process in Brussels makes the EU prone to yielding to various lobbies such as farming or certain industries. The common policy of the EU was often set in such a way as to reflect that of the most protectionist member country. Hence, the impact of the EU on the international trading system has not been entirely benign.

Dr Samuel Johnson's (1709–84) remark 'Like a dog walking on his hind legs. It is not well done, but you are surprised to find it done at all' aptly describes integration arrangements among countries. International economic integration increases the conditions and potentials for improvements in economic welfare. However, countries have to organise themselves both individually and collectively to reap these benefits. National economic policies concerning investment, industrial change, R&D, mobility of people and knowledge, and investment in human capital (education) that develops and extends skills, experience and organisational competencies of the most important factor are crucial for the efficiency side of the economy; and regional and social matters, on the equity[15] side, are absolutely crucial for the success, evolution, cohesion and survival of integration schemes.[16]

The main conclusion is that a certain type of international economic integration may often be a desirable economic strategy especially for small and medium-sized countries in a world of risks and uncertainties emanating from continuous changes in both technology and the market situation. Integration can enlarge and secure foreign markets for a variety of a country's goods and services in the future and, hence, mitigate the inevitable costs of adjustment to change, especially if this change is big and/or abrupt. The opponents of integration for small countries would have to ask themselves whether the loss of the market and other potentials for expanded business is worth the 'gain' of retaining the sovereign right to continue with a (bad) home economic policy that is insulated from international influences.

International economic integration is not an economic policy choice that would intimidate small and medium-sized countries. The only thing that these countries would lose from the integration process is the illusion that international economic integration is a bad policy choice on a purely economic and 'technical' basis. However, does international economic integration jeopardise the culture, deep-rooted traditions, local tastes, established social values, customary networks and past hierarchies in the countries that integrate? Is integration 'globalising', unifying and standardising everything? Does it make life simpler, better, easier, safer, more exciting and interesting or does it make it more depressing, insecure and boring? There are no satisfactory answers to such questions. It is also difficult to imagine what one can have in the world without a certain degree of openness and integration. None the less, these questions should be asked to clarify our understanding. Furthermore, there is considerably more to life than technical efficiency in the allocation of resources, economies of scale and mechanical expansion in production,[17] reduction in prices, economic equilibrium and more money.

Appendix 7A1 Research topics for the future

Obviously this book does not provide the last word on the topic of international economic integration. The modest goal (and hope) was that it would shed some light and direction through the mist that obscures the future, as well as being an inspiration and incentive for further intellectual forays into the issue. There are so many dilemmas and puzzles regarding international economic integration that anyone embarking upon studying these issues should have no fear that the circle is closed and that their research efforts will be in vain.

The objective of this appendix is to provide a select list of possible research areas for the future in the field of international economic integration. Many of these issues relate to some of the most complex and difficult problems in economic theory: multiple equilibria, economies of scale, externalities, imperfect competition (which kind?), linkages and path dependence. These research topics could include the following:

- The evolution, development, life cycle and duration of integration groups should be studied, together with the effects of proliferation of integration arrangements.
- Relations between regionalism and multilateral solutions to the trade and investment problems offer another challenging research topic.

Is there a way to prevent the creation and evolution of regional blocs that inhibit global liberalisation?

- Spillovers, externalities and linkages are poorly understood and ascertained. Their speed and force is alleged to (exponentially?) weaken with spatial distance, especially in developing countries. Investigation of their effects (costs and benefits) provoked by international economic integration is needed.
- Is simple economic integration and liberalisation in an enlarged market sufficient for an increase in competitiveness? What are the corporate strategies regarding economic integration? How will they change over time? Is business consolidation (mergers and acquisitions) a necessary consequence of an enlarging and integrating market? Will it be reversed in the future? What is the impact of integration on concentration ratios? What is the *ex post* impact of the Single European Market on consumers? (That is, have prices fallen or not increased? By how much?) What would be the *ex ante* effect of the Single European Market in services?
- Another research issue is a consideration of economic integration between countries on different levels of development (north–south): integration between the EU on the one hand, and Turkey, transition economies or developing countries, on the other. Is integration, such as a free trade area between the US, Canada and Mexico, without special treatment for the weaker country, a good thing? What are the potential and expected effects of the FTAA? What are the chances of deeper integration between South Africa and its neighbours?
- Another global theme for research is the impact of integration on various industries. Integration has had the strongest impact on higher value-added industries with significant economies of scale and strong technological intra-industry production links. This, however, should be studied in greater detail, in particular, its relevance for developing countries.
- Is monopolistic competition altered (how?) by international economic integration? Does integration bring about agglomeration or spread of production, employment and innovative activities? Related to these issues is analysis and evaluation in the area of mergers and acquisitions.
- Regional disparities and spatial location of firms and industries, their structure, volume and pattern of production offer enormous opportunities to study economic behaviour and the changes provoked by international economic integration. This could be complemented by the issue of the relation between demography and migration on the

one hand, and changing market space that the output of firms should cover, on the other.

- There is still a query regarding the location of firms and economic integration. The fact that integration has brought about a change in the location of economic activity, on the one hand, and the growth rate in the economic activity, on the other, is another research topic.
- Since regional policies had very limited results in the past, is it necessary to have such a policy at the level of an integration scheme? If not, how should economic and monetary union among countries that are on different levels of economic development be reconciled? Can the solution of the 'regional problem' be left exclusively to market forces? How to cope with the regional problem of a group that has countries at very different levels of development? What are the implications of north–south integration?
- Does international economic integration encourage agglomeration, clustering, spatial concentration of industries, adjoint locations of linked productions and 'thick' market effects? Or, alternatively, does agglomeration encourage economic integration? Does this cause convergence or divergence in the geography of production and income in the participating countries?
- What are the properties of economic adjustment (spatial and sectorwise reallocation of resources) to integration? How do these forces interact?
- Where will the 'hot spots' be for the location of business? Who will benefit from these developments?
- The following quotations highlight another issue: 'Industries in the US are much more spatially concentrated than in Europe (even controlling for the distribution of population and manufacturing as a whole), suggesting that regional integration in Europe could cause agglomeration at the sectoral level (for example, Germany gets engineering, the UK financial services, and so on)' (Venables, 1999, p. 17). Others, however, think differently: 'we think that the results available so far point more towards similarities across the EU and the U.S. than differences. These similarities occur despite underlying differences in mobility and the extent of integration' (Combes and Overman, 2004, pp. 2899–900). What a splendid topic for further research and analysis.
- The question of whether replication of R&D networks is the result of a powerful lobby or whether it is necessary to accelerate R&D in the private sector because of significant externalities remains to be re-examined and answered.

- In the case of integration among developing countries, should primary consideration be given to free mobility of labour and capital in their integration attempts and, only then, to the movement of goods and services?
- One should not forget the development of the theory of public choice. What do the voters want regarding economic integration and what are they prepared to pay for in terms of taxes, prices and security of employment? Does that public choice change over time? How do you adjust integration arrangements to accommodate these changes?
- What are the ways of resolving difficulties in integrating diverse financial market structures (for example, instruments of supervision and regulation) when countries decide to form a monetary union? In the absence of some degree of harmonisation, is it possible to create incentives for regulatory arbitrage in which financial institutions migrate to the relatively more lax regulatory jurisdictions within the group?
- The US has a huge and mounting foreign debt, the biggest in the world's history. Hence, there will be an erosion of confidence in the stability of the dollar. What would be the effect of a massive switch in international reserves from unstable dollars to stable or unstable euros?
- Monetary integration between the EU and candidate countries is a promising research area. The same holds for capital market integration and international monetary stability. Should monetary integration precede EU entry? Why?
- There are also unresolved issues regarding fiscal federalism, tax harmonisation and tax competition in integration groups. This issue may be more problematical if the members are at different levels of development.
- The future of the inflow of foreign labour into the EU is highly uncertain. On the one hand, an ageing population will demand extra expenditure by the state. On the other, an inflow of foreign labour to rectify demographic trends may relieve the pressure of labour shortages. But an inflow from where? An 'orderly' inflow from the countries in transition or a 'disorderly' inflow from the Islamic and unstable countries which are experiencing a demographic 'explosion' such as the south Mediterranean countries and Turkey? Some background research on how to cope with such developments is still lacking. Would the answer to the problem be to foster jobless growth based on an increase in productivity built on knowledge and innovation in the EU?

- A possible claim that immigration is beneficial for the country of destination in net terms should be tested and proved in each situation.
- Integration issues related to FDI, such as competition, competitiveness, the attraction of TNCs, sectoral distribution, new technology and trade, offer research topics that will not be easily exhausted.
- What is the impact of international economic integration on SMEs?
- What is the impact of economic integration and the deepening of an internal market on the penetration of external suppliers?
- Is there a need for the harmonisation of regulations in an integrating group of countries, or can/should one leave competition regarding, for example, labour, tax or environment issues within national regulations? Would such competition be helpful or harmful? How and why?
- As for the services sector, the question is whether a liberal regulatory framework within a group of countries is sufficient to cause the integration of this sector. If not, is something else necessary? Why?
- High and ever-increasing environmental standards will continue to introduce NTBs to trade. How to cope with that problem? Is it a mutual recognition of national standards in the EU or should the highest standards be imposed throughout the group? If the highest standards are to be imposed, then certain countries may face financial difficulties in implementing them. Who should/is willing to pay for that? The national taxpayers, the taxpayers of the standard-imposing country and/or the group from its common resources?
- An empirical examination of the issue of who gains more in an integrated group is necessary before more reliable conclusions can be drawn. Trade theory says that larger countries do not gain asymmetrically more from integration (or an enlargement of the existing group) than smaller countries do. Who gains from integration (more), why and how? Should one rectify these developments? Up to what point? Why and how?
- In addition to liberal internal trade within an integration group, there are also other important effects of international economic integration. These may include trans-border investment (capital mobility), learning spillovers (mobility of ideas) and labour mobility. Such effects may reinforce, soften or aggravate the impact of freer trade in a group that integrates countries. These effects and related policies call for further research.
- In spite of significant improvements in techniques for measuring the effects of international economic integration, our lack of a full understanding of the determinants, operation and effect of integration on trade, production, investment and consumption continues to

be a problem. Until this is solved, the nature of the analysis and measurement of the effects of integration will remain speculative. Attempts to solve these measurement problems, in particular the dynamic ones, should be on the research agenda in the future as they may have important policy implications.

- Last, but not least, there is the question of regional integration and the multilateral rules for trade and investment. Almost all countries in the world are and will be involved in a certain type of integration arrangement. Integration is now here to stay. The challenge is to strengthen the complementarity between regional economic integration and the WTO, and to prevent regional groups from turning into blocs that inhibit global liberalisation. Researchers and practitioners will have to find ways of ensuring that integration and the multilateral process continue to reinforce each other in the decades to come.

Notes

1. Part of the responsibility for this shortcoming can be found in the excessive costs related to German reunification from 1989.
2. Some food prices increased in the central and east European countries following entry into the EU in 2004.
3. I pray that in all respects you may prosper and be in good health, just as your soul prospers (3 John 2).
4. As far as France itself is concerned, this has always been quite an effort for an Englishman, and vice versa.
5. Haberler noted as early as 1964 that 'We live in the age of integration' (Haberler, 1964, p. 1). If this is so, can anyone explain how and why Europe had 32 countries in 1990, while it now has 48?
6. As China continues to be a magnet for FDI and location of production, especially following 1997, the economic relevance of various schemes that integrate developing countries for the attraction of FDI is somehow weakened.
7. The EU–Turkey customs union and the Cotonou Agreement between the EU and developing countries still need to prove themselves.
8. See further, Lipsey and Smith (1989), Krugman (1991b, 1995b), Bhagwati (1995), Snape (1996), Frenkel (1997), Bagwell and Staiger (1998), Bhagwati et al. (1998), Ethier (1998), Baldwin et al. (1999), Krueger (1999), Laird (1999), Panagariya (1999, 2000), McLaren (2002) and Limão (2005). The answer to the dilemma may be found most likely in the middle ground between those two extreme positions.
9. Lowering of tariffs under the auspices of GATT/WTO reduced large-scale chances for trade diversion.
10. Lipsey and Smith (1989, p. 334) argued that 'the Canada–US agreement clearly conforms with the GATT practice under Article XXIV and, indeed, appears consistent with the original spirit of the architects of the multilateral trading system'.
11. ASEAN is another example.
12. The distorting effects of the EU's CAP.
13. Blackhurst and Henderson (1993, p. 412). In addition, Renato Ruggiero, Director-General of the WTO, wrote in a comment to the *International Herald Tribune* (28 November 1996) that 'regional agreements have been a generally positive force for

liberalization'. Krugman (1995b, pp. 181–2) asked whether the GATT could really have done much better in the absence of moves towards regional free trade areas: 'This did not seem too plausible . . . the situation would not be better, and could easily have been worse, had the great free trade agreements of recent years never happened.'

14. The MFN has recently been renamed the least favoured nation (LFN) clause. The EU applies the MFN (LFN) tariffs to only nine of its trading partners. However, the volume of trade is huge as these partners include the US, Japan and China. 'The US is just as bad in using bilateral deals as a political reward' ('Trading up', *Financial Times*, 18 January 2004). The drift towards politically motivated trade relations is dangerous for the multilateral trading system.
15. The equity side of economic life is provoked by the polarisation effect due to market imperfections and it arises from the desire of the 'losers' to share the benefits of integration.
16. An effective dispute settlements system also looms large for the success of the integration scheme.
17. The crisis in the quantity, quality and safety of agricultural output is a good reminder of the perils.

And further, my son, be admonished by these.
Of making many books there is no end,
and much study is wearisome to the flesh.
Ecclesiastes 12:12

Bibliography

Abugattas, L. (2004). 'Swimming in the spaghetti bowl: challenges for developing countries under the "new regionalism"', Policy Issues in International Trade and Commodities Study Series, No. 27, UNCTAD.

Adams, G. (1983). 'Criteria for US industrial policy strategies', in *Industrial Policies for Growth and Competitiveness* (eds G. Adams and L. Klein). Lexington, MA: Lexington Books, pp. 393–418.

Adams, G. and A. Bolino (1983). 'Meaning of industrial policy', in *Industrial Policies for Growth and Competitiveness* (eds G. Adams and L. Klein). Lexington, MA: Lexington Books, pp. 13–20.

Adams, G. and L. Klein (1983). 'Economic evolution of industrial policies for growth and competitiveness: overview', in *Industrial Policies for Growth and Competitiveness* (eds G. Adams and L. Klein). Lexington, MA: Lexington Books, pp. 3–11.

Aiginger, K. and S. Davies (2004). 'Industrial specialisation and geographic concentration: two sides of the same coin?', *Journal of Applied Economics*, pp. 231–48.

Aiginger, K. and M. Pfaffermayr (2004). 'The Single Market and geographic concentration in Europe', *Review of International Economics*, pp. 1–11.

Altshuler, R., H. Grubert and T. Newlon (1998). 'Has U.S. investment abroad become more sensitive to tax rates?', NBER Working Paper No. 6383, National Bureau of Economic Research, Cambridge, MA.

Amin, A. and A. Malmberg (1992). 'Competing structural and institutional influences on the geography of production in Europe', *Environment and Planning*, pp. 401–16.

Amiti, M. (1998). 'New trade theories and industrial location in the EU: a survey of evidence', *Oxford Economic Papers*, pp. 45–53.

Amiti, M. (1999). 'Specialization patterns in Europe', *Weltwirtschaftliches Archiv*, pp. 573–93.

Anderson, G. (2004). 'The Canada–United States softwood lumber dispute: where politics and theory met', *Journal of World Trade*, pp. 661–99.

Anderson, K. and R. Blackhurst (1993). 'Introduction and summary', in *Regional Integration and the Global Trading System* (eds K. Anderson and R. Blackhurst). New York: Harvester Wheatsheaf, pp. 1–15.

Ando, K. (1998). 'The Single European Market and the location strategy of foreign car multinationals', Discussion Paper No. 249, Department of Economics, University of Reading.

Anson, J., O. Cadot, A. Estevadeordal, J. de Melo, A. Suwa-Eisenmann and B. Tumurchudur (2004). 'Rules of origin in North–South preferential trading arrangements', Ecole des Hautes Etudes Commerciales de l'Université de Lausanne, mimeo.

Aristotelous, K. and S. Fountas (1996). 'An empirical analysis of inward foreign direct investment flows in the ECU with emphasis on the market enlargement hypothesis', *Journal of Common Market Studies*, pp. 571–83.

Armington, P. (1969). 'A theory of demand for products distinguished by place of production', *International Monetary Fund Staff Papers*, pp. 159–78.

Armstrong, H. (1995). 'Convergence among regions of the European Union, 1950–1990', *Papers in Regional Science*, pp. 143–52.

Armstrong, H. (1996). 'European Union regional policy: sleepwalking to a crisis', *International Regional Science Review*, pp. 193–209.

Armstrong, H. and R. de Kervenoael (1997). 'Regional economic change in the European Union', in *The Coherence of EU Regional Policy* (eds J. Bachtler and I. Turok). London: Jessica Kingsley, pp. 29–47.

Armstrong, H. and J. Taylor (2003). *Regional Economics and Policy*. Oxford: Blackwell.

Arthur, B. (1988). 'Competing technologies: an overview', in *Technical Change and Economic Theory* (eds G. Dosi, R. Nelson, G. Silverberg and L. Soete). London: Pinter, pp. 590–607.

Arthur, B. (1989). 'Competing technologies, increasing returns, and lock-in by historical events', *Economic Journal*, pp. 116–31.

Arthur, B. (1990a). 'Positive feedbacks in the economy', *Scientific American*, February, pp. 92–9.

Arthur, B. (1990b). 'Silicon Valley locational clusters: when do increasing returns imply monopoly?', *Mathematical Social Sciences*, pp. 235–51.

Arthur, B. (1994a). 'Industrial location patterns and the importance of history', in *Increasing Returns and Path Dependence in the Economy* (ed. B. Arthur). Michigan: University of Michigan Press, pp. 49–67.

Arthur, B. (1994b). 'Urban systems and historical path dependence', in *Increasing Returns and Path Dependence in the Economy* (ed. B. Arthur). Michigan: Michigan University Press, pp. 99–110.

Arthur, W.B. (2002). 'How growth builds upon growth in high-technology', Annual Sir Charles Carter Lecture. Belfast: Northern Ireland Economic Council.

Audretsch, D. (1989). *The Market and the State*. New York: New York University Press.

Audretsch, D. (1993). 'Industrial policy and international competitiveness', in *Industrial Policy in the European Community* (ed. P. Nicolaides). Dordrecht: Martinus Nijhoff, pp. 67–105.

Audretsch, D. (1998). 'Agglomeration and the location of innovative activity', *Oxford Review of Economic Policy*, pp. 18–29.

Audretsch, D. and D. Dohse (2004). 'The impact of location on firm growth', CEPR Discussion Paper No. 4332, Centre for Economic Policy Research, London.

Audretsch, D. and M. Feldman (1995). 'Innovative clusters and the industry life cycle', CEPR Discussion Paper No. 1161, Centre for Economic Policy Research, London.

Audretsch, D. and M. Feldman (1996). 'R&D spillovers and the geography of innovation and production', *American Economic Review*, pp. 630–40.

Audretsch, D. and M. Feldman (2004). 'Knowledge spillovers and the geography of innovation', in *Handbook of Regional and Urban Economics* (eds J. Henderson and J. Thisse). Amsterdam: Elsevier, pp. 2713–39.

Auyang, S. (1998). *Foundations of Complex-system Theories in Economics, Evolutionary Biology and Statistical Physics*. Cambridge: Cambridge University Press.

Bachtler, J. (1995). 'Policy agenda for the decade', in *An Enlarged Europe: Regions in Competition?* (eds S. Hardy, M. Hart, L. Albrechts and A. Katos). London: Jessica Kingsley, pp. 313–24.

Bachtler, J. and R. Michie (1993). 'The restructuring of regional policy in the European Community', *Regional Studies*, pp. 719–25.

Bachtler, J. and R. Michie (1995). 'A new era in EU regional policy evaluation? The appraisal of the structural funds', *Regional Studies*, pp. 745–51.

Bachtler, J. and I. Turok (1997). *The Coherence of EU Regional Policy*. London: Jessica Kingsley.

Badaracco, J. and D. Yoffie (1983). 'Industrial policy: it can't happen here', *Harvard Business Review*, November–December, pp. 97–105.

Bagwell, K. and R. Staiger (1998). 'Will preferential agreements undermine the multilateral trading system?', *Economic Journal*, pp. 1162–82.

Balassa, B. (1964). 'The purchasing power parity doctrine: a reappraisal', *Journal of Political Economy*, pp. 584–96.

Balassa, B. (1967). 'Trade creation and trade diversion in the European Common Market', *Economic Journal*, pp. 1–17.

Balassa, B. (1973). *The Theory of Economic Integration*. London: George Allen & Unwin.

Balassa, B. and L. Bauwens (1988). 'The determinants of intra-European trade in manufactured goods', *European Economic Review*, pp. 1421–37.

Baldwin, R. (1989). 'The growth effects of 1992', *Economic Policy*, pp. 248–70.

Baldwin, R. (1993). 'On the measurement of dynamic effects of integration', *Empirica*, pp. 129–45.

Baldwin, R. (1995a). 'A domino theory of regionalism', in *Expanding Membership of the European Union* (eds R. Baldwin, P. Haaparanta and J. Kiander). Cambridge: Cambridge University Press, pp. 25–48.

Baldwin, R. (1995b). 'The eastern enlargement of the European Union', *European Economic Review*, pp. 474–81.

Baldwin, R. (1997a). 'Review of theoretical developments on regional integration', in *Regional Integration and Trade Liberalization in SubSaharan Africa* (eds A. Oyejide, I. Elbadawi and P. Collier). Basingstoke: Macmillan, pp. 24–88.

Baldwin, R. (1997b). 'The causes of regionalism', *World Economy*, pp. 865–88.

Baldwin, R., D. Cohen, A. Sapir and A. Venables (eds) (1999). *Market Integration, Regionalism and the Global Economy*. Cambridge: Cambridge University Press.

Baldwin, R. and P. Martin (2004). 'Agglomeration and regional growth', in *Handbook of Regional and Urban Economics* (eds J. Henderson and J. Thisse). Amsterdam: Elsevier, pp. 2671–711.

Baldwin, R. and A. Venables (1995). 'Regional economic integration', in *Handbook of International Economics* (eds G. Grossman and K. Rogoff). Amsterdam: Elsevier, pp. 1597–646.

Baldwin, R. and C. Wyplosz (2004). *The Economics of European Integration*. London: McGraw-Hill.

Baptista, R. and P. Swann (1998). 'Do firms in clusters innovate more?', *Research Policy*, pp. 525–40.

Barro, R. (1997). *Determinants of Economic Growth*. Cambridge, MA: MIT Press.

Barro, R. and X. Sala-i-Martin (1991). 'Convergence across states and regions', *Brookings Papers on Economic Activity*, pp. 107–82.

Bartik, T. (1991). *Who Benefits from State and Local Economic Development Policies?*, Kalamazoo: Upjohn Institute.

Bauer, P. (1998). 'Eastward enlargement – benefits and costs of EU entry for the transition countries', *Intereconomics*, January/February, pp. 11–19.

Bayliss, B. and A. El-Agraa (1990). 'Competition and industrial policies with emphasis on competition policy', in *Economies of the European Community* (ed. A. El-Agraa). New York: St. Martin's Press, pp. 137–55.

Beaudry, C., S. Breschi and P. Swann (2002). 'Clusters, innovation and growth', in *Multinational Firms* (eds J. Dunning and J. Mucchielli). London: Routledge, pp. 190–213.

Beckmann, M. (1999). *Lectures on Location Theory*. Berlin: Springer.

Begg, I. and D. Mayes (1994). 'Peripherality and Northern Ireland', *National Institute Economic Review*, pp. 90–100.

Bekar, C. and R. Lipsey (2001). 'Clusters and economic policy', Simon Fraser University, Vancouver, mimeo.

Belderbos, R. (1997). 'Antidumping and tariff jumping: Japanese firms' DFI in the European Union and the United States', *Weltwirtschaftliches Archiv*, pp. 419–57.

Berglas, E. (1979). 'Preferential trading theory: the *n* commodity case', *Journal of Political Economy*, pp. 315–31.

Bernstein, J. and D. Weinstein (2002). 'Do endowments predict the location of production? Evidence from national and international data', *Journal of International Economics*, pp. 55–76.

Bhagwati, J. (1995). 'U.S. trade policy: the infatuation with free trade areas', in *The Dangerous Drift to Preferential Trade Agreements* (eds J. Bhaghwati and A. Krueger). Washington, DC: American Enterprise Institute, pp. 1–18.

Bhagwati, J., D. Greenaway and A. Panagariya (1998). 'Trading preferentially: theory and policy', *Economic Journal*, pp. 1128–48.

Bhagwati, J. and E. Tironi (1980). 'Tariff change, foreign capital and immiserization', *Journal of Development Economics*, pp. 71–83.

Bianchi, P. (1995). 'Small and medium-sized enterprises in the European perspective', *International Journal of Technology Management,* Special Issue, pp. 119–30.

Bird, R. (1972). 'The need for regional policy in common market', in *International Economic Integration* (ed. P. Robson). Harmondsworth: Penguin Books, pp. 257–77.

Blackhurst, R. and D. Henderson (1993). 'Regional integration arrangements, world integration and GATT', in *Regional Integration and the*

Global Trading System (eds K. Anderson and R. Blackhurst). New York: Harvester Wheatsheaf, pp. 408–35.

Blais, A. (1986). 'Industrial policy in advanced capitalist democracies', in *Industrial Policy* (ed. A. Blais). Toronto: University of Toronto Press, pp. 1–53.

Blomström, M. and A. Kokko (1997). 'Regional integration and foreign direct investment', Policy Research Working Paper No. 1750, World Bank, Washington, DC.

Blomström, M. and A. Kokko (1998). 'Multinational corporations and spillovers', *Journal of Economic Surveys*, pp. 247–77.

Blomström, M. and A. Kokko (2003). 'The economics of foreign direct investment incentives', Stockholm School of Economics Working Paper No. 168, Stockholm.

Blonigen, B. (1997). 'Firm-specific assets and the link between exchange rates and foreign direct investment', *American Economic Review*, pp. 447–65.

Boldrin, M. and F. Canova (2001). 'Inequality and convergence in Europe's regions: reconsidering European regional policies', *Economic Policy*, pp. 207–53.

Bordo, M. and L. Jonung (1999). 'The future of the EMU: what does the history of monetary unions tell us?', NBER Working Paper No. 7365, National Bureau of Economic Research, Cambridge, MA.

Borrus, M. and J. Zysman (1997). 'Wintelism and the changing terms of global competition: prototype of the future?', BRIE Working Paper No. 96B, University of California, Berkeley.

Boschma, R. (2005). 'Proximity and innovation: a critical assessment', *Regional Studies*, pp. 61–74.

Boschma, R. and J. Lambooy (1999a). 'Evolutionary economics and economic geography', *Evolutionary Economics*, pp. 411–29.

Boschma, R. and J. Lambooy (1999b). 'The prospects of an adjustment policy based on collective learning in old industrial regions', *GeoJournal*, pp. 391–9.

Bottazzi, L. and G. Peri (2002). 'Innovation and spillovers in regions: evidence from European patent data', CEPR Working Paper No. 215, Centre for Economic Policy Research, London.

Brada, J. and J. Méndez (1988). 'An estimate of the dynamic effects of economic integration', *Review of Economics and Statistics*, pp. 163–8.

Brainard, W. and J. Tobin (1992). 'On the internationalization of portfolios', *Oxford Economic Papers*, pp. 533–65.

Brakman, S., H. Garretsen and M. Schramm (2002). 'The strategic bombing of German cities during World War II and its impact on city growth', CESifo Working Paper No. 808, Munich.

Brander, J. (1987). 'Shaping comparative advantage: trade policy, industrial policy and economic performance', in *Shaping Comparative Advantage* (eds R. Lipsey and W. Dobson). Toronto: C.D. Howe Institute, pp. 1–55.

Brander, J. (1995). 'Strategic trade policy', in *Handbook of International Economics* (eds G. Grossman and K. Rogoff). Amsterdam: Elsevier, pp. 1395–455.

Brander, J. and B. Spencer (1985). 'Export subsidies and international market share rivalry', *Journal of International Economics*, pp. 83–100.

Braunerhjelm, P. and K. Ekholm (eds) (1998). *The Geography of Multinational Firms*. Boston, MA: Kluwer.

Braunerhjelm, P., R. Faini, V. Norman, F. Ruane and P. Seabright (2000). *Integration and the Regions of Europe: How the Right Policies Can Prevent Polarization*. London: CEPR.

Brenner, T. (2004). *Local Industrial Clusters: Existence, Emergence and Evolution*. London: Routledge.

Brülhart, M. (1998a). 'Economic geography, industry location and trade: the evidence', *World Economy*, pp. 775–801.

Brülhart, M. (1998b). 'Trading places: industrial specialization in the European Union', *Journal of Common Market Studies*, pp. 319–46.

Brülhart, M. and R. Elliott (1998). 'Adjustment to the European single market: inferences from intra-industry trade patterns', *Journal of Economic Studies*, pp. 225–47.

Brülhart, M. and R. Elliott (1999). 'A survey of intra-industry trade in the European Union', in *Intra-Industry Trade and Adjustment: The European Experience* (eds M. Brülhart and R. Hine). Basingstoke: Macmillan, pp. 98–117.

Brülhart, M. and R. Hine (eds) (1999). *Intra-Industry Trade and Adjustment: The European Experience*. Basingstoke: Macmillan.

Brülhart, M. and J. Torstensson (1996). 'Regional integration, scale economies and industry location in the European Union', CEPR Discussion Paper No. 1435, Centre for Economic Policy Research, London.

Buigues, P. and A. Jacquemin (1992). 'Foreign direct investment and exports in the Common Market', paper presented at the conference 'Japanese direct investment in a unifying Europe', INSEAD, Fontainebleau, 26–27 June, mimeo.

Buigues, P. and A. Jacquemin (1994). 'Foreign direct investment and exports to the European Community', in *Does Ownership Matter?* (eds M. Mason and D. Eucarnation). Oxford: Clarendon Press, pp. 163–97.

Buigues, P. and A. Sapir (1993). 'Market services and European integration: issues and challenges', *European Economy Social Europe*, No. 3, pp. ix–xx.

Bulmer-Thomas, V. (1988). 'The Central American Common Market', in *International Economic Integration* (ed. A. El-Agraa). Houndmills: Macmillan, pp. 284–313.

Bulmer-Thomas, V. (1998). 'The Central American Common Market: from closed to open regionalism', *World Economy*, pp. 313–22.

Bumbacher, U. (1995). 'The Swiss watch industry', in *Studies in Swiss Competitive Advantage* (eds M. Enright and R. Weder). Bern: Peter Lang, pp. 113–51.

Bunce, V. (1985). 'The empire strides back: the evolution of the eastern bloc from a Soviet asset to a Soviet liability', *International Organization*, pp. 1–46.

Byeong-hae, S. (2004). 'Towards a new regionalism in east Asia', *Journal of Economic Integration*, pp. 499–518.

Cairncross, F. (2001). *The Death of Distance 2.0*. London: Texere.

Canova, F. and A. Marcet (1995). 'The poor stay poor: non-convergence across countries and regions', CEPR Discussion Paper No. 1265, Centre for Economic Policy Research, London.

Cantwell, J. and L. Piscitello (2005). 'Recent location of foreign-owned research and development activities by large multinational corporations in the European regions', *Regional Studies*, pp. 1–16.

Canzoneri, M. and C. Rogers (1990). 'Is the European Community an optimal currency area? Optimal taxation versus the cost of multiple currencies', *American Economic Review*, pp. 419–33.

Carlaw, K. and R.G. Lipsey (2002). 'Externalities, technological complementarities and sustained economic growth', *Research Policy*, pp. 1305–15.

Carlén, B. (1994). 'Road transport', EFTA Occasional Paper No. 49, Geneva, pp. 81–111.

Carliner, G. (1988). 'Industrial policies for emerging industries', in *Strategic Trade Policy and the New International Economics* (ed. P. Krugman). Cambridge, MA: MIT Press, pp. 147–68.

Carlton, D. (1983). 'The location and employment choices of new firms: an econometric model with discrete and continuous endogenous variables', *Review of Economics and Statistics*, pp. 440–49.

Carrington, A. (2003). 'A divided Europe? Regional convergence and neighbourhood spillover effects', *Kyklos*, pp. 381–94.

Casella, A. (1996). 'Large countries, small countries and the enlargement of trade blocs', *European Economic Review*, pp. 389–415.

Caves, R. (1996). *Multinational Enterprise and Economic Analysis*. Cambridge: Cambridge University Press.

Cecchini, P. (1988). *The European Challenge 1992: The Benefits of a Single Market*. Aldershot: Wildwood House.

CEPR (1992). *Is Bigger Better? The Economics of EC Enlargement*. London: Centre for Economic Policy Research.
CEPR (1994). *The Location of Economic Activity: New Theories and Evidence*. London: CEPR.
Chakrabarti, R. and B. Scholnick (2002). 'Exchange rate expectations and foreign direct investment flows', *Weltwirtschaftliches Archiv*, pp. 1–21.
Chandler, A., P. Hagström and Ö. Sölvell (eds) (1998). *The Dynamic Firm*. Oxford: Oxford University Press.
Chang, H. (1994). *The Political Economy of Industrial Policy*. London: Macmillan.
Christaller, W. (1933). *Die Zentralen Orte in Süddeutschland*. Jena: Gustav Fischer. (Translated from German by C. Baskin, *Central Places in Southern Germany* (1966), Englewood Cliffs: Prentice-Hall.)
Cini, M. and L. McGowan (1998). *Competition Policy in the European Union*. Basingstoke: Macmillan.
Clark, G., M. Feldman and M. Gertler (eds) (2000). *The Oxford Handbook of Economic Geography*. Oxford: Oxford University Press.
Clark, S. (2000). 'Tax incentives for foreign direct investment: empirical evidence on effects and alternative policy options', *Canadian Tax Journal*, pp. 1139–80.
Clausing, K. (2000). 'Customs unions and free trade areas', *Journal of Economic Integration*, pp. 418–35.
Clausing, K. (2001). 'Trade creation and trade diversion in Canada–United States Free Trade Agreement', *Canadian Journal of Economics*, pp. 677–96.
Clausing, K. and C. Dorobantu (2005). 'Re-entering Europe: does European Union candidacy boost foreign direct investment?', *Economics of Transition*, pp. 77–103.
Clegg, J. and S. Scott-Green (1999). 'The determinants of new FDI capital flows into EC: a statistical comparison of the USA and Japan', *Journal of Common Market Studies*, pp. 597–616.
Cline, W. (1995). 'Evaluating the Uruguay Round', *World Economy*, pp. 1–23.
Cnossen, S. (1986). 'Tax harmonization in the European Community', *Bulletin for International Fiscal Documentation*, pp. 545–63.
Cnossen, S. (1990). 'The case for tax diversity in the European Community', *European Economic Review*, pp. 471–9.
Cnossen, S. (1995). 'Reforming and coordinating company taxes in the European Union', paper presented at the conference 'Changing role of the public sector: transition in the 1990s', Lisbon, 21–24 August.
Cnossen, S. (2001). 'Tax policy in the European Union: a review of issues and options', *FinanzArchiv*, pp. 466–558.
Cobham, D. (1989). 'Strategies for monetary integration revisited', *Journal of Common Market Studies*, pp. 203–18.

Cockfield, A. (1994). *The European Union: Creating the Single Market*. London: Wiley.

Coffey, P. (1982). *The Common Market and Its International Economic Policies*. Amsterdam: Europa Institute.

Combes, P. and H. Overman (2004). 'The spatial distribution of economic activities in the European Union', in *Handbook of Regional and Urban Economics* (eds J. Henderson and J. Thisse). Amsterdam: Elsevier, pp. 2845–909.

Commission of the European Communities (1992). *The Future Development of the Common Transport Policy*. Brussels: European Union.

Commission of the European Communities (2002). Communication from the Commission to the Council, the European Parliament, the European Economic and Social Committee and the Committee of the Regions: Joint Report by the Commission and the Council on Adequate and Sustainable Pensions. Brussels, 17 December 2002, COM(2002) 737 final.

Commission of the European Economic Community (1961). *Memorandum on the General Lines of the Common Transport Policy* (Schaus Memorandum). Brussels: European Economic Community.

Cooper, C. and B. Massel (1965). 'A new look at customs union theory', *Economic Journal*, pp. 742–7.

Corden, W. (1972). *Monetary Integration*. Essays in International Finance, Princeton, NJ: Princeton University Press.

Corden, W. (1984). 'The normative theory of international trade', in *Handbook of International Economics* (eds R. Jones and P. Kenen). Amsterdam: North Holland, pp. 63–130.

Cossentino, F., F. Pyke and W. Sengenberger (eds) (1996). *Local and Regional Response to Global Pressure: The Case of Italy and Industrial Districts*. Geneva: International Labour Organisation.

Crafts, N. and A. Venables (2001). 'Globalization in history: a geographical perspective', Centre for Economic Performance, London School of Economics, London.

Crandall, R. and C. Winston (2003). 'Does antitrust policy improve consumer welfare? Assessing the evidence', *Journal of Economic Perspectives*, pp. 3–26.

Crozet, M., T. Mayer and J. Mucchielli (2004). 'How do firms agglomerate? A study of FDI in France', *Regional Science and Urban Economics*, pp. 27–54.

Culem, C. (1988). 'The location determinants of direct investments among industrialized countries', *European Economic Review*, pp. 885–904.

Curzon Price, V. (1981). *Industrial Policies in the European Community*. London: Macmillan.

Curzon Price, V. (1987). *Free Trade Areas? The European Experience*. Toronto: C.D. Howe Institute.

Curzon Price, V. (1988). 'The European Free Trade Association', in *International Economic Integration* (ed. A. El-Agraa). London: Macmillan, pp. 96–127.

Curzon Price, V. (1990). 'Competition and industrial policies with emphasis on industrial policy', in *Economics of the European Community* (ed. A. El-Agraa). New York: St. Martin's Press, pp. 156–86.

Curzon Price, V. (1991). 'The threat of "Fortress Europe" from the development of social and industrial policies at European level', *Aussenwirtschaft*, pp. 119–38.

Curzon Price, V. (1993). 'EEC's strategic trade-cum-industrial policy: a public choice analysis', in *National Constitutions and International Economic Law* (eds M. Hilf and E. Petersmann). Deventer: Kluwer, pp. 391–405.

Curzon Price, V. (1994). 'The role of regional trade and investment agreements', paper presented at the conference 'Policies dealing with the EU–LDC relations in view of the transition in central and eastern European countries', The Netherlands Economic Institute, Rotterdam, 16–17 May.

Curzon Price, V. (1996a). 'Residual obstacles to trade in the Single European Market', *Euryopa*, Institut européen de l'Université de Genève.

Curzon Price, V. (1996b). 'The role of regional trade and investment agreements', in *Transition in Central and Eastern Europe* (eds A. Kuyvenhoven et al.). Dordrecht: Kluwer, pp. 69–88.

Curzon Price, V. (1997). 'The European Free Trade Association', in *Economic Integration Worldwide* (ed. A. El-Agraa). London: Macmillan, pp. 175–202.

Curzon Price, V. (2002). 'Everything but arms', Institute of European Studies, University of Geneva, mimeo.

d'Arge, R. (1969). 'Note on customs unions and direct foreign investment', *Economic Journal*, pp. 324–33.

d'Arge, R. (1971a). 'Customs unions and direct foreign investment', *Economic Journal*, pp. 352–5.

d'Arge, R. (1971b). 'A reply', *Economic Journal*, pp. 357–9.

Davenport, M. (1995). 'Fostering integration of countries in transition in central and eastern Europe in the world economy and the implications for the developing countries', Geneva: UNCTAD/ITD 7, 31 October.

David, P. (1984). 'High technology centers and the economics of locational tournaments', Stanford University, mimeo.

David, P., B. Hall and A. Toole (2000). 'Is public R&D a complement or substitute for private R&D? A review of econometric evidence', *Research Policy*, pp. 497–529.

Davies, R. and D. Weinstein (2002). 'Bones, bombs and break points: the geography of economic activity', *American Economic Review*, pp. 1269–89.

Davies, R. and D. Weinstein (2003). 'Market access, economic geography and comparative advantage: an empirical test', *Journal of International Economics*, pp. 1–23.

de Ghellinck, E. (1988). 'European industrial policy against the background of the Single European Act', in *Main Economic Policy Areas of the EEC – towards 1992* (ed. P. Coffey). Dordrecht: Kluwer, pp. 133–56.

de Grauwe, P. (1975). 'Conditions for monetary integration – a geometric interpretation', *Weltwirtschaftliches Archiv*, pp. 634–46.

de Grauwe, P. (1991). 'The 1992 European integration program and regional development policies', in *Trade Theory and Economic Reform: North, South and East* (eds J. de Melo and A. Sapir). Cambridge, MA: Basil Blackwell, pp. 142–53.

de Grauwe, P. (1994). 'Towards EMU without the EMS', *Economic Policy*, pp. 149–85.

de Grauwe, P. (1995). 'The economics of convergence towards monetary union in Europe', CEPR Discussion Paper No. 1213, Centre for Economic Policy Research, London.

de Grauwe, P. (2002). 'The challenge of the enlargement of the Euroland', paper presented at the conference 'EU enlargement: endgame economic issues', Jean Monnet European Centre of Excellence, University of Genoa, 15 November.

de Grauwe, P. (2003). *Economics of Monetary Union*. Oxford: Oxford University Press.

de Grauwe, P. and G. Kouretas (2004). 'EMU: current state and future prospects – Editorial', *Journal of Common Market Studies*, pp. 679–87.

de Grauwe, P. and M. Polan (2003). 'Globalisation and social spending', CESifo Working Paper No. 885, Munich.

de Grauwe, P. and M. Sénégas (2003). 'Monetary policy in EMU when the transmission is asymmetric and uncertain', CESifo Working Paper No. 891, Munich.

de la Fuente, A. and X. Vives (1995). 'Regional policy and Spain: infrastructure and education as instruments of regional policy', *Economic Policy*, April, pp. 13–51.

de Melo, J., F. Miguet and T. Müller (2002). 'The political economy of migration and EU enlargement: lessons from Switzerland', University of Geneva, mimeo.

Defraigne, P. (1984). 'Towards concerted industrial policies in the European Community', in *European Industry: Public Policy and*

Corporate Strategy (ed. A. Jacquemin). Oxford: Clarendon Press, pp. 368–77.

Dell'Aringa, C. and F. Neri (1989). 'Illegal immigrants and the informal economy in Italy', in *European Factor Mobility* (eds I. Gordon and A. Thirlwall). New York: St. Martin's Press, pp. 133–47.

Delors, J. (1989). *Report on Economic and Monetary Union in the European Community*. Brussels: European Community.

Demopoulos, G. and N. Yannacopoulos (1999). 'Conditions for optimality of a currency area', *Open Economies Review*, pp. 289–303.

Demopoulos, G. and N. Yannacopoulos (2001). 'Monetary unions, adjustment mechanisms and risk sharing: can market forces replace fiscal policy in the European Union?', Discussion Paper No. 135, Athens University of Economics and Business.

Dent, C. (1997). *The European Economy*. London: Routledge.

Dertouzos, M., R. Lester and R. Solow (1990). *Made in America*. New York: Harper Perennial.

Deutscher Bundestag (1999). *Jahresbericht 1999 der Bundesregierung zun Stand der Deutschen Einheit* (1999 Annual Report on the State of German Unity), Drucksache 14/1825, 10 October.

Devarajan, S. and J. de Melo (1987). 'Evaluating participation in African monetary unions: a statistical analysis of the CFA zones', *World Development*, pp. 483–96.

Devereux, M. and R. Griffith (1998). 'Taxes and location of production: evidence from panel of US multinationals', *Journal of Public Economics*, pp. 335–67.

Dicken, P., M. Forsgren and A. Malmberg (1995). 'The local embeddedness of transnational corporations', in *Globalization, Institutions and Regional Development in Europe* (eds A. Amin and N. Thrift). Oxford: Oxford University Press, pp. 23–45.

Dickerson, A., H. Gibson and E. Tsakalotos (1997). 'The impact of acquisitions on company performance: evidence from a large panel of UK firms', *Oxford Economic Papers*, pp. 344–61.

Dietz, R. (1986). 'Soviet foregone gains in trade with the CMEA six: a reappraisal', *Comparative Economic Studies*, pp. 69–94.

Donges, J. (1980). 'Industrial policies in West Germany's not so market-oriented economy', *The World Economy*, pp. 185–204.

Dosi, G. (1988). 'Sources, procedures and microeconomic effects of innovation', *Journal of Economic Literature*, pp. 1120–71.

Dosi, G. (1997). 'Opportunities, incentives and collective patterns of technological change', *Economic Journal*, pp. 1530–47.

Dosi, G., K. Pavitt and L. Soete (1990). *The Economics of Technical Change and International Trade*. New York: Harvester Wheatsheaf.

Dowd, K. and D. Greenaway (1993a). 'Currency competition, network externalities and switching costs: towards an alternative view of optimum currency areas', *Economic Journal*, pp. 1180–89.

Dowd, K. and D. Greenaway (1993b). 'A single currency for Europe?', *Greek Economic Review*, pp. 227–44.

Drabek, Z. and D. Greenaway (1984). 'Economic integration and intra-industry trade: the EEC and CMEA compared', *Kyklos*, pp. 444–69.

Drysdale, P. and R. Garnaut (1993). 'The Pacific: an application of a general theory of economic integration', in *Pacific Dynamism and the International Economic System* (eds F. Bergsten and M. Noland). Washington: Institute for International Economics, pp. 183–223.

Dunning, J. (1988). *Explaining International Production*. London: Unwin Hyman.

Dunning, J. (ed.) (1993). *The Theory of Transnational Corporations* (The United Nations Library on Transnational Corporations). London: Routledge.

Dunning, J. (1994a). 'MNE activity: comparing the NAFTA and the European Community', in *Multinationals in North America* (ed. L. Eden). Calgary: University of Calgary Press, pp. 277–308.

Dunning, J. (1994b). 'Globalization: the challenge for national economic regimes', Discussion Paper No. 186, Department of Economics, University of Reading.

Dunning, J. (1995). 'Think again Professor Krugman: competitiveness does matter', *International Executive*, pp. 313–24.

Dunning, J. (1997). 'The European Internal Market Programme and inbound foreign direct investment', *Journal of Common Market Studies*, (Part I) pp. 1–30, (Part II) pp. 189–223.

Dunning, J. (1998a). 'Location and the multinational enterprise: a neglected factor?', *Journal of International Business Studies*, pp. 45–66.

Dunning, J. (1998b). 'Globalization, technological change and the spatial organization of economic activity', in *The Dynamic Firm* (eds A. Chandler et al.). Oxford: Oxford University Press, pp. 289–314.

Dunning, J. (1998c). 'Regions, globalization and the knowledge economy: the issues stated', Rutgers University, New Brunswick, NJ, mimeo.

Dunning, J. (1999). 'The eclectic paradigm as an envelope for economic and business theories of MNE activity', Discussion Paper No. 263, Department of Economics, University of Reading.

Dunning, J. and P. Robson (1987). 'Multinational corporate integration and regional economic integration', *Journal of Common Market Studies*, pp. 103–24.

Easson, A. (2001). 'Tax incentives for foreign direct investment', *International Bureau of Fiscal Documentation Bulletin*, (Part I) pp. 266–74, (Part II) pp. 365–75.

Eaton, C. and R. Lipsey (1975). 'The principle of minimum differentiation reconsidered: some new developments in the theory of spatial competition', *Review of Economic Studies*, pp. 27–49.

Eaton, C. and R. Lipsey (1976). 'The non-uniqueness of equilibrium in the Löschian location model', *American Economic Review*, pp. 77–93.

Eaton, C. and R. Lipsey (1979a). 'Comparison shopping and the clustering of homogeneous firms', *Journal of Regional Science*, pp. 421–35.

Eaton, C. and R.G. Lipsey (1979b). 'The theory of market pre-emption: the persistence of excess capacity and monopoly in growing spatial markets', *Economica*, pp. 149–58.

Eaton, C. and R. Lipsey (1982). 'An economic theory of central places', *Economic Journal*, pp. 56–72.

Eaton, C. and R. Lipsey (1997). *On the Foundations of Monopolistic Competition and Economic Geography*. Cheltenham, UK and Lyme, USA: Edward Elgar.

Eaton, J., E. Gutierrez and S. Kortum (1998). 'European technology policy', *Economic Policy*, pp. 405–38.

Economic Commission for Europe (1949). 'European steel trends in the setting of the world market'. Geneva: United Nations, [E/]ECE/112–[E/]ECE/STEEL/42.

Economic Commission for Europe (1994). *Economic Survey of Europe in 1993–1994*. New York: United Nations.

Economic Commission for Europe (1996). *Economic Bulletin for Europe*. New York: United Nations.

Economic Commission for Europe (1997). *Economic Survey of Europe in 1996–1997*. New York: United Nations.

Economic Commission for Europe (1998). *Economic Survey of Europe 1998*. No. 3. New York: United Nations.

Economic Commission for Europe (2000). *Economic Survey of Europe 2000*. No. 1. New York: United Nations.

Economic Commission for Europe (2002). *Economic Survey of Europe 2002*. No. 1. New York: United Nations.

Economic Commission for Europe (2003). *Economic Survey of Europe 2003*. No. 1. New York: United Nations.

Economic Commission for Europe (2005). *Economic Survey of Europe 2005*. No. 1. New York: United Nations.

Economic Policy Committee (2000). Progress report to the Ecofin Council on the Impact of ageing populations on public pension systems. Brussels, 6 November, EPC/ECFIN/518/00-EN-Rev.1.

EFTA (1969). 'The effects of EFTA on the economies of member states', *EFTA Bulletin* (January).

EFTA (1993). *Pattern of Production and Trade in the New Europe*. Geneva: EFTA.

Egger, P. (2004). 'Estimating regional trading bloc effects with panel data', *Review of World Economics*, pp. 151–66.

Eichengreen, B. (1993a). 'European monetary unification', *Journal of Economic Literature*, pp. 1321–57.

Eichengreen, B. (1993b). 'Labour markets and European monetary unification', in *Policy Issues in the Operation of Currency Unions* (eds P. Mason and M. Taylor). Cambridge: Cambridge University Press, pp. 130–62.

El-Agraa, A. (1985). 'General introduction', in *The Economics of the European Community* (ed. A. El-Agraa). Oxford: Philip Allan, pp. 1–8.

El-Agraa, A. (ed.) (1988). *International Economic Integration*. Houndmills: Macmillan.

El-Agraa, A. (1989). *The Theory and Measurement of International Economic Integration*. New York: St Martin's Press.

El-Agraa, A. (1997). 'UK competitiveness policy vs. Japanese industrial policy', *Economic Journal*, pp. 1504–17.

El-Agraa, A.M. (ed.) (1998). *The European Union*. London: Prentice-Hall.

El-Agraa, A. (2004). 'The enigma of African economic integration', *Journal of Economic Integration*, pp. 19–45.

El-Agraa, A. and D. Hojman (1988). 'The Andean Pact', in *International Economic Integration* (ed. A. El-Agraa). Houndmills: Macmillan, pp. 257–66.

Ellison, G. and E. Glaeser (1997). 'Geographic concentration in U.S. manufacturing industries: a dartboard approach', *Journal of Political Economy*, pp. 889–927.

Ellison, G. and E. Glaeser (1999). 'The geographic concentration of industry: does natural advantage explain agglomeration?', *American Economic Review* (Papers and Proceedings), pp. 311–16.

Emerson, M., M. Auejan, M. Catinat, P. Goybet and A. Jacquemin (1988). 'The economics of 1992', *European Economy*, March.

Enright, M. (1998). 'Regional clusters and firm strategy', in *The Dynamic Firm* (eds A. Chandler et al.). Oxford: Oxford University Press, pp. 315–42.

Enright, M. and R. Weder (eds) (1995). *Studies in Swiss Competitive Advantage*. Bern: Peter Lang.

Ethier, W. (1998). 'The new regionalism', *Economic Journal*, pp. 1149–61.

Euro Papers (2001). 'The economic impact of enlargement', Enlargement Papers No. 4.

European Commission (1992). *The Future Development of the Transport Policy*. Brussels: European Commission.

European Commission (1997a). *Agenda 2000 for a Stronger and Wider Union*. Luxembourg: European Communities.

European Commission (1997b). *The Impact and Effectiveness of the Single Market*. Luxembourg: EU.

European Commission (1997c). *The Single Market Review: Impact on Competition and Scale Effects*. London: Kogan Page.

European Commission (1997d). *Trade Creation and Trade Diversion*. London: Kogan Page.

European Commission (1997e). *Regional Growth and Convergence*. London: Kogan Page.

European Commission (1998). *Foreign Direct Investment*. London: Kogan Page.

European Commission (2000). *The Community Budget: The Facts in Figures*. Luxembourg: European Communities.

European Commission (2001). *European Transport Policy for 2010: Time to Decide*. Luxembourg: European Communities.

European Commission (2002a). *Towards the Enlarged Union: Strategy Paper and Report of the European Commission on the Progress towards Accession by Each of the Candidate Countries*. Brussels, 9 October, COM(2002) 700 final.

European Commission (2002b). *Report on United States Barriers to Trade and Investment*. European Commission: Brussels.

European Commission (2003). *European Union Competition Policy: XXXIInd Report – 2002*. Luxembourg: European Communities.

European Commission (2004a). *European Union Competition Policy: XXXIIIrd Report – 2003*. Luxembourg: European Communities.

European Commission (2004b). *Structures of the Taxation Systems in the European Union*. Luxembourg: European Communities.

European Communities (1973). *Report on the Regional Problems of the Enlarged Community* (Thomson Report). Brussels: European Community.

European Communities (1985). *Completing the Internal Market (White Paper)*. Brussels: European Communities.

European Communities (1991). *XXth Report on Competition Policy*. Brussels: European Communities.

European Communities (1993). *The Community Budget: The Facts in Figures*. Luxembourg: European Community.

European Economy (1989). *International Trade of the European Community*. No. 39.

European Economy (1990a). *One Market? One Money*. No. 44.

European Economy (1990b). *Social Europe*. Special Edition.
European Economy (1991). *The Economies of EMU*. Special Edition No. 1.
European Economy (1993). *The Economic and Financial Situation in Italy*. No. 1.
European Economy (1994a). *Competition and Integration; Community Merger Control Policy*. No. 57.
European Economy (1994b). *EC Agricultural Policy for the 21st Century*. No. 4.
European Economy (1996). *Economic Evaluation of the Internal Market*. No. 4.
European Economy (1997a). 'The CAP and enlargement', Reports and Studies No. 2.
European Economy (1997b). 'Towards a Common Agricultural and Rural Policy for Europe', Reports and Studies No. 5.
European Economy (2003a). 'Economic forecasts for the candidate countries Spring 2003', Enlargement Papers No. 15.
European Economy (2003b). 'Key structural challenges in the acceding countries: The integration of the acceding countries into the Community's economic policy co-ordination processes', Occasional Papers No. 4, July.
European Economy (2003c). 'Main results of the April 2003 fiscal notifications presented by the candidate countries', Enlargement Papers No. 17.
European Economy (2003d). 'Structural features of economic integration in an enlarged Europe: patterns of catching-up and industrial specialisation', Economic Papers No. 181.
Feld, L. and G. Kirchgässner (2001). 'The impact of corporate and personal income taxes on the location of firms and on employment: some panel evidence from Swiss cantons', CESifo Working Paper No. 455, Munich.
Feld, L. and G. Kirchgässner (2004). 'Sustainable fiscal policy in a federal system: Switzerland as an example', Discussion Paper No. 2004–09, Department of Economics, University of St. Gallen, Switzerland.
Feldman, M., J. Francis and J. Bercovitz (2005). 'Creating a cluster while building a firm: entrepreneurs and the formation of industrial clusters', *Regional Studies*, pp. 129–41.
Finch, M. (1988). 'The Latin American Free Trade Association', in *International Economic Integration* (ed. A. El-Agraa). Houndmills: Macmillan, pp. 237–56.
Finger, J., K. Hall and D. Nelson (1982). 'The political economy of administered protection', *American Economic Review*, pp. 452–66.
Finger, J. and A. Yeats (1976). 'Effective protection by transportation costs and tariffs: a comparison of magnitudes', *Quarterly Journal of Economics*, pp. 169–76.

Finger, M. (1975). 'A new view of the product cycle theory', *Weltwirtschaftliches Archiv*, pp. 79–99.

Fisher, S., R. Sahay and C. Végh (1998). 'How far is eastern Europe from Brussels?', IMF Working Paper WP/98/53, Washington, DC.

Flam, H. and E. Helpman (1987). 'Industrial policy under monopolistic competition', *Journal of International Economics*, pp. 79–102.

Fleming, M. (1971). 'On exchange rate unification', *Economic Journal*, pp. 467–86.

Folkerts-Landau, D. and D. Mathieson (1989). *The European Monetary System in the Context of the Integration of European Financial Markets*. Washington, DC: IMF.

Ford, S. and R. Strange (1999). 'Where do Japanese manufacturing firms invest within Europe and why?', *Transnational Corporations*, pp. 117–42.

Forslid, R., J. Haaland and H. Midelfart-Knarvik (2002). 'A U-shaped Europe? A simulation study of industrial location', *Journal of International Economics*, pp. 273–97.

Freeman, C. (1994). 'The economics of technical change', *Cambridge Journal of Economics*, pp. 463–514.

Frenkel, J. (1997). *Regional Trading Blocs in the World Economic System*. Washington, DC: Institute for International Economics.

Frenkel, J. and A. Rose (1998). 'The endogeneity of the optimum currency area criteria', *Economic Journal*, pp. 1009–25.

Fretz, D., R. Stern and J. Whalley (eds) (1985). *Canada/United States Trade and Investment Issues*. Toronto: Ontario Economic Council.

Friedman, J., D. Gerlowski and J. Silberman (1992). 'What attracts foreign multinational corporations? Evidence from branch plant locations in the United States', *Journal of Regional Science*, pp. 403–18.

Frischtak, C. (2004). 'Multinational firms' responses to integration of Latin American markets', *Business and Politics*, www.bepress.com/bap/vol6/iss1/art5.

Fujita, M. and R. Ishii (1998). 'Global location behavior and organizational dynamics of Japanese electronics firms and their impact on regional economies', in *The Dynamic Firm* (eds A. Chandler et al.). Oxford: Oxford University Press, pp. 343–83.

Fujita, M., P. Krugman and A. Venables (1999). *The Spatial Economy*. Cambridge, MA: MIT Press.

Fujita, M. and T. Mori (1996). 'The role of ports in the making of major cities: self-agglomeration and hub-effect', *Journal of Development Economics*, pp. 93–120.

Fujita, M. and J. Thisse (1996). 'Economics of agglomeration', *Journal of the Japanese and International Economies*, pp. 339–78.

Garcia-Quevedo, J. (2004). 'Do public subsidies complement business R&D? A meta-analysis of the econometric evidence', *Kyklos*, pp. 87–102.

Garofoli, G. (1991a). 'Industrial districts: structure and transformation', in *Endogenous Development and Southern Europe* (ed. G. Garofoli). Aldershot: Avebury, pp. 49–60.

Garofoli, G. (1991b). 'Endogenous development and southern Europe: an introduction', in *Endogenous Development and Southern Europe* (ed. G. Garofoli). Aldershot: Avebury, pp. 1–13.

Gasiorek, M., A. Smith and A. Venables (1992). '1992: trade and welfare – a general equilibrium model', in *Trade Flows and Trade Policy after 1992* (ed. A. Winters). Cambridge: Cambridge University Press, pp. 35–62.

Gavin, B. (2001). *The European Union and Globalisation*. Cheltenham, UK and Northampton, MA, USA: Edward Elgar.

Geroski, P. (1987). 'Brander's "Shaping comparative advantage": some comments', in *Shaping Comparative Advantage* (eds R. Lipsey and W. Dobson). Toronto: C.D. Howe Institute, pp. 57–64.

Geroski, P. (1988). 'Competition and innovation', in Commission of the European Communities, *Studies on the Economics of Integration*. Brussels: European Community, pp. 339–88.

Geroski, P. (1989). 'European industrial policy and industrial policy in Europe', *Oxford Review of Economic Policy*, pp. 20–36.

Geroski, P. and A. Jacquemin (1985). 'Industrial change, barriers to mobility, and European industrial policy', *Economic Policy*, pp. 170–218.

Gittelman, M., E. Graham and H. Fukukawa (1992). 'Affiliates of Japanese firms in the European Community: performance and structure', paper presented at the conference 'Japanese direct investment in a unifying Europe', INSEAD, Fontainebleau, 26–27 June, mimeo.

Gleiser, H., A. Jacquemin and J. Petit (1980). 'Exports in an imperfect competition framework: an analysis of 1,446 exporters', *Quarterly Journal of Economics*, pp. 507–24.

Goldberg, M. (1972). 'The determinants of U.S. direct investment in the E.E.C.: a comment', *American Economic Review*, pp. 692–9.

Goldstein, A. (1998). 'Mercosur at seven: goals, achievements and outlook', *Economia Internazionale*, pp. 349–81.

Gordon, I. and P. McCann (2000). 'Industrial clusters: complexes, agglomeration and/or social networks?', *Urban Studies*, pp. 513–32.

Görg, H. and D. Greenaway (2004). 'Much ado about nothing? Do domestic firms really benefit from foreign direct investment?', *World Bank Research Observer*, pp. 171–97.

Görg, H. and F. Ruane (1999). 'US investment in EU member countries: the internal market and sectoral specialization', *Journal of Common Market Studies*, pp. 333–48.

Görg, H. and E. Strobl (2001). 'Multinational companies and productivity spillovers: a meta analysis', *Economic Journal*, pp. F723–F739.

Görg, H. and E. Strobl (2003). 'Multinational corporations, technology spillovers and plant survival', *Scandinavian Journal of Economics*, pp. 581–95.

Government of Canada (1988). *The Canada–U.S. Free Trade Agreement: An Economic Assessment*. Ottawa: Department of Finance.

Grabher, G. (1993). 'The weakness of strong ties: the lock-in of regional development in the Ruhr area', in *The Embedded Firm* (ed. G. Grabher). London: Routledge, pp. 255–77.

Graham, E. (1978). 'Transatlantic investment by multinational firms: a rivalistic phenomenon?', *Journal of Post Keynesian Economics*, pp. 82–99.

Graham, E. and P. Krugman (1995). *Foreign Direct Investment in the United States*. Washington, DC: Institute for International Economics.

Greenaway, D. and C. Milner (1987). 'Intra-industry trade: current perspectives and unresolved issues', *Weltwirtschaftliches Archiv*, pp. 39–57.

Greenaway, D. and C. Milner (2002). 'Regionalism and gravity', *Scottish Journal of Political Economy*, pp. 574–85.

Greenaway, D. and J. Torstensson (1997). 'Back to the future: taking stock on intra-industry trade', *Weltwirtschaftliches Archiv*, pp. 248–69.

Greenaway, D. and J. Torstensson (2000). 'Economic geography, comparative advantage and trade within industries: evidence from the OECD', *Journal of Economic Integration*, pp. 260–80.

Gremmen, H. (1985). 'Testing the factor price equalization theorem in the EC: an alternative approach', *Journal of Common Market Studies*, pp. 277–86.

Grilli, E. (1993). *The European Community and the Developing Countries*. Cambridge: Cambridge University Press.

Gros, D. (1989). 'Paradigms for the monetary union of Europe', *Journal of Common Market Studies*, pp. 219–30.

Grubel, H. (1970). 'The theory of optimum currency areas', *Canadian Journal of Economics*, pp. 318–24.

Grubel, H. (1984). *The International Monetary System*. Harmondsworth: Penguin Books.

Grubel, H. and P. Lloyd (1975). *Intra Industry Trade*. London: Macmillan.

Gual, J. (1995). 'The three common policies: an economic analysis', in *European Policies on Competition, Trade and Industry* (eds P. Buigues, A. Jacquemin and A. Sapir). Aldershot, UK and Brookfield, US: Edward Elgar, pp. 3–48.

Guillaumont, P. and S. Guillaumont (1989). 'The implications of European monetary union for African countries', *Journal of Common Market Studies*, pp. 139–53.

Haberler, G. (1964). 'Integration and growth of the world economy in historical perspective', *American Economic Review*, pp. 1–22.

Haberler, G. (1977). 'Survey of circumstances affecting the location of production and international trade as analysed in theoretical literature', in *The International Allocation of Economic Activity* (eds B. Ohlin, P. Hesselborn and P. Wijkman). London: Macmillan, pp. 1–24.

Hagedoorn, J. (1998). 'Atlantic strategic technology alliances', in *The Struggle for World Markets* (ed. G. Boyd). Cheltenham, UK and Lyme, USA: Edward Elgar, pp. 177–91.

Hagedoorn, J. and J. Schakenraad (1993). 'A comparison of private and subsidized R&D partnerships in the European information technology industry', *Journal of Common Market Studies*, pp. 373–90.

Hague, D. (1960). 'Report on the proceedings: summary record of the debate', in *Economic Consequences of the Size of Nations* (ed. E. Robinson). London: Macmillan, pp. 333–438.

Hamilton, B. and J. Whalley (1986). 'Border tax adjustment and US trade', *Journal of International Economics*, pp. 377–83.

Hanson, G. (1998). 'North American economic integration and industry location', *Oxford Review of Economic Policy*, pp. 30–44.

Hanson, G. (2001). 'Should countries promote foreign direct investment?', G-24 Discussion Paper, New York: UNCTAD.

Harris, C. (1954). 'The market as a factor in the localization of industry in the United States', *Annals of the Association of American Geographers*, pp. 315–48.

Harris, R. (1984a). *Trade, Industrial Policy and Canadian Manufacturing*. Toronto: Ontario Economic Council.

Harris, R. (1984b). 'Applied general equilibrium analysis of small open economies with scale economies and imperfect competition', *American Economic Review*, pp. 1016–32.

Harris, R. (1985). *Trade, Industrial Policy and International Competition*. Toronto: University of Toronto Press.

Harris, R. and D. Cox (1985). 'Summary of a project on the general equilibrium evaluation of Canadian trade policy', in *Canada–US Free Trade* (ed. J. Whalley). Toronto: University of Toronto Press, pp. 157–77.

Hartog, J. and A. Zorlu (2002). 'The effect of immigration on wages in three European countries', IZA Discussion Paper No. 642, Institute for the Study of Labour, Bonn.

Hay, D. (1993). 'The assessment: competition policy', *Oxford Review of Economic Policy*, pp. 1–26.

Hayek, F. (1978). *New Studies in Philosophy, Politics, Economics and the History of Ideas*. London: Routledge & Kegan Paul.

Hazlewood, A. (1988). 'The East African Community', in *International Economic Integration* (ed. A. El-Agraa). Houndmills: Macmillan, pp. 166–89.

Head, K. and T. Mayer (2004). 'The empirics of agglomeration and trade', in *Handbook of Regional and Urban Economics* (eds J. Henderson and J. Thisse). Amsterdam: Elsevier, pp. 2609–69.

Heinemann, F. (2002). 'The political economy of eastern enlargement', *Rivista di Politica Economica*, pp. 359–83.

Henderson, J. (1974). 'The sizes and types of cities', *American Economic Review*, pp. 640–56.

Henderson, J., Z. Shalizi and A. Venables (2001). 'Geography and development', *Journal of Economic Geography*, pp. 81–106.

Herin, J. (1986). 'Rules of origin and differences between tariff levels in EFTA and in the EC', Occasional Paper No. 16, EFTA, Geneva.

Hermann-Pillath, C. (2000). 'Indeterminacy in international trade: methodological reflections on the impact of non-economic determinants on the direction of trade and absolute advantage', *Aussenwirtschaft*, pp. 251–89.

Herzog, H. and A. Schlottmann (eds) (1991). *Industry Location and Public Policy*. Knoxville, TN: University of Tennessee Press.

Hill, T. (1977). 'On goods and services', *Review of Income and Wealth*, pp. 315–38.

Hillman, D. and D. Gibbs (1998). *Century Makers*. London: Weidenfeld & Nicolson.

Himphrey, J. and H. Schmitz (1996). 'The triple C approach to local industrial policy', *World Development*, pp. 1859–77.

Hindley, B. (1991). 'Creating an integrated market for financial services', in *European Economic Integration* (eds G. Faulhaber and G. Tamburini). Boston, MA: Kluwer, pp. 263–88.

Hitiris, T. (1998). *European Union Economics*, London: Prentice-Hall Europe.

Holden, M. (1998). 'Southern African economic integration', *World Economy*, pp. 457–69.

Holmes, T. (1998). 'The effects of state policies on the location of manufacturing: evidence from state borders', *Journal of Political Economy*, pp. 667–705.

Holzman, F. (1976). *International Trade under Communism*. New York: Basic Books.

Hospers, G. (2004). 'Restructuring Europe's rustbelt', *Intereconomics*, pp. 147–56.

Hotelling, H. (1929). 'Stability in competition', *Economic Journal*, pp. 41–57.

Hufbauer, G. and J. Schott (1992). *North American Free Trade*. Washington, DC: Institute for International Economics.

Hume, D. (1752). *Essays: Moral, Political and Literary*, 'Of the jealousy of trade' (Part II). www.angelfire.com/pa/sergeman/issues/foreign/jealousy.html.

Hummels, D. (1999). 'Have international transportation costs declined?', University of Chicago, Graduate School of Business, mimeo. www.mgmt.purdue.edu/faculty/hummelsd/research/decline/declined.pdf.

Hymer, S. (1976). *The International Operations of National Firms: A Study of Direct Foreign Investment*. Boston, MA: MIT Press.

Iqbal, Z. and M. Khan (eds) (1998). *Trade Reform and Regional Integration in Africa*. Washington, DC: IMF.

Isard, W. (1954). 'Location theory and trade theory: short run analysis', *Quarterly Journal of Economics*, pp. 305–20.

Isard, W. (1956). *Location and Space-Economy*. Cambridge, MA: Technology Press of MIT and London: Chapman & Hall.

Isard, W. (1977). 'Location theory, agglomeration and the pattern of world trade', in *The International Allocation of Economic Activity* (eds B. Ohlin, P. Hesselborn and P. Wijkman). London: Macmillan, pp. 159–77.

Isard, W. (1996). *Commonalities in Art, Science and Religion: An Evolutionary Perspective*. Aldershot: Avebury.

Isard, W. and M. Peck (1954). 'Location theory and international and interregional trade theory', *Quarterly Journal of Economics*, pp. 97–114.

Jacquemin, A. (1984). *European Industry: Public Policy and Corporate Strategy*. Oxford: Clarendon Press.

Jacquemin, A. (1990a). 'Mergers and European policy', in *Merger and Competition Policy in the European Community* (ed. P. Admiraal). Oxford: Basil Blackwell, pp. 1–38.

Jacquemin, A. (1990b). 'Horizontal concentration and European merger policy', *European Economic Review*, pp. 539–50.

Jacquemin, A. (1991). 'Collusive behaviour, R&D and European competition policy', in *European Economic Integration* (eds G. Faulhaber and G. Tamburini). Boston, MA: Kluwer, pp. 201–35.

Jacquemin, A. (1996). 'Les enjeux de la competitivite européenne et la politique industrielle communautaire en matière d'innovation' (What is at stake with the European competitiveness and the industrial policy in the field of innovation), *Revue du Marché – commun et de l'Union européenne*, March, pp. 175–81.

Jacquemin, A., P. Lloyd, P. Tharakan and J. Waelbroeck (1998). 'Competition policy in an international setting: the way ahead', *World Economy*, pp. 1179–83.

Jacquemin, A. and J. Marchipont (1992). 'De nouveaux enjeux pour la politique industrielle de la Communauté' (New challenges for the industrial policy of the Community), *Revue d'économie politique*, pp. 69–97.

Jacquemin, A. and L. Pench (1997). *Europe Competing in the Global Economy*. Cheltenham, UK and Lyme, USA: Edward Elgar.

Jacquemin, A. and A. Sapir (1991). 'The internal and external opening-up of the Single Community Market: efficiency gains, adjustment costs and new Community instruments', *International Spectator*, pp. 29–48.

Jacquemin, A. and A. Sapir (1996). 'Is a European hard core credible? A statistical analysis', *Kyklos*, pp. 105–17.

Jacquemin, A. and D. Wright (1993). 'Corporate strategies and European challenges post-1992', *Journal of Common Market Studies*, pp. 525–37.

Jansen, M. (1975). *History of European Integration 1945–75*. Amsterdam: Europa Institute.

Jarillo, J. and J. Martínez (1991). 'The international expansion of Spanish firms: towards an integrative framework for international strategy', in *Corporate and Industry Strategies for Europe* (eds L. Mattsson and B. Stymne). Amsterdam: Elsevier, pp. 283–302.

Johnson, C. (1984). 'The idea of industrial policy', in *The Industrial Policy Debate* (ed. C. Johnson). San Francisco: Institute for Contemporary Studies, pp. 3–26.

Johnson, H. (1973). 'An economic theory of protectionism, tariff bargaining and the formation of customs unions', in *Economics of Integration* (ed. M. Krauss). London: George Allen & Unwin, pp. 64–103.

Johnson, H. (1977). 'Technology, technical progress and the international allocation of economic activity', in *The International Allocation of Economic Activity* (eds B. Ohlin, P. Hesselborn and P. Wijkman). London: Macmillan, pp. 314–27.

Johnson, H. and M. Krauss (1973). 'Border taxes, border tax adjustment, comparative advantage and the balance of payments', in *Economics of Integration* (ed. M. Krauss). London: George Allen & Unwin, pp. 239–53.

Jovanović, M. (1992). *International Economic Integration*. London: Routledge.

Jovanović, M. (1995). 'Economic integration among developing countries and foreign direct investment', *Economia Internazionale*, pp. 209–43.

Jovanović, M. (1997a). *European Economic Integration*. London: Routledge.

Jovanović, M. (1997b). 'Probing leviathan: the eastern enlargement of the European Union', *European Review*, pp. 353–70.

Jovanović, M. (1998a). *International Economic Integration: Limits and Prospects*. London: Routledge.

Jovanović, M. (ed.) (1998b). *International Economic Integration: Critical Perspectives on the World Economy – Theory and Measurement* (Volume I). London: Routledge.

Jovanović, M. (ed.) (1998c). *International Economic Integration: Critical Perspectives on the World Economy – Monetary, Fiscal and Factor Mobility Issues* (Volume II). London: Routledge.

Jovanović, M. (ed.) (1998d). *International Economic Integration: Critical Perspectives on the World Economy – General Issues* (Volume III). London: Routledge.

Jovanović, M. (ed.) (1998e). *International Economic Integration: Critical Perspectives on the World Economy – Integration Schemes* (Volume IV). London: Routledge.

Jovanović, M. (1998f). 'Does eastern enlargement mean the end of the European Union?', *International Relations*, pp. 23–39.

Jovanović, M. (1999). 'Where are the limits to the enlargement of the European Union?', *Journal of Economic Integration*, pp. 467–96.

Jovanović, M. (2000a). 'Eastern enlargement of the European Union: sour grapes or sweet lemon?', *Economia Internazionale*, pp. 507–36. http://papers.ssrn.com/ sol3/papers.cfm?abstract_id=261059.

Jovanović, M. (2000b). 'Economic integration and location of industries', in *Economic Interests and Cultural Determinants in European Integration* (ed. B. Schefold). Bolzano: European Academy, pp. 169–204.

Jovanović, M. (2001a). *Geography of Production and Economic Integration*. London: Routledge.

Jovanović, M. (2001b). 'Why eastern enlargement of the European Union won't be fast', in *Europe: What Kind of Integration? (Europa: Verso Quale Integrazione?)* (ed. G. Casale). Milan: Franco Angeli, pp. 140–67.

Jovanović, M. (2003a). 'Spatial location of firms and industries: an overview of theory', *Economia Internazionale*, pp. 23–81. http://papers.ssrn.com/ sol3/ papers.cfm?abstract_id=451800.

Jovanović, M. (2003b). 'Local vs. global location of firms and industries', *Journal of Economic Integration*, pp. 60–104. http://papers.ssrn.com/sol3/ papers.cfm?abstract_id=394760.

Jovanović, M. (2003c). 'Eastern enlargement of the EU', in *The Economics of Enlargement* (ed. F. Praussello). Milan: Franco Angeli, pp. 39–73.

Jovanović, M. (2004a). 'Eastern enlargement of the EU: a topsy-turvy endgame or permanent disillusionment?', *Journal of Economic Integration*, pp. 830–68. http://papers.ssrn.com/sol3/papers.cfm? abstract_id=650165.

Jovanović, M. (2004b). 'Economic integration and spatial location of production', Department of Economics and Finance Working Paper No.

12/2004, University of Genoa, http://papers.ssrn.com/sol3/papers.cfm?abstract_id=647382.
Jovanović, M. (2005a). *The Economics of European Integration: Limits and Prospects*. Cheltenham, UK and Northampton, MA, USA: Edward Elgar.
Jovanović, M. (2005b). 'Turkey in the European Union: euthanasia or the rejuvenation of Europe?'. paper presented at the conference 'Turkey, EU and the US: high stakes, uncertain prospects', Intercollege, Nicosia, 13–14 May.
Jovanović, M. (2005c). 'Spatial location of firms and industries: is local superior to global?', in *Contemporary Issues in Urban and Regional Economics* (ed. L. Yee). New York: Nova Scientific Publishers, pp. 1–53.
Jovanović, M. (ed.) (2006). *Economic Integration and Spatial Location of Firms and Industries*, two volumes. Cheltenham, UK and Northampton, MA, USA: Edward Elgar (forthcoming).
Kahnert, F., P. Richards, E. Stoutjesdijk and P. Thomopoulos (1969). *Economic Integration among Developing Countries*. Paris: OECD.
Karsenty, G. and S. Laird (1986). 'The generalized system of preferences: a quantitative assessment of the direct trade effects and of policy options'. UNCTAD Discussion Paper 18. Geneva: UNCTAD.
Kay, J. (1990). 'Tax policy: a survey', *Economic Journal*, pp. 18–75.
Kay, J. (2004). *Culture and Prosperity*. New York: HarperCollins.
Kemp, M. and H. Wan (1976). 'An elementary proposal concerning the formation of customs unions', *Journal of International Economics*, pp. 95–7.
Kenen, P. (1969). 'Theory of optimum currency areas: an eclectic view', in *Monetary Problems of the International Economy* (eds R. Mundell and A. Swoboda). Chicago: Chicago University Press, pp. 41–60.
Keuschnigg, C. and W. Kohler (2000). 'Eastern enlargement of the EU: a dynamic general equilibrium perspective', in *Using Dynamic General Equilibrium Models for Policy Analysis* (eds G. Harrison, S. Hougard Jensen, L. Haagen Pedersen and T. Rutherford), Amsterdam: Elsevier, pp. 119–70.
Keynes, J. (1923). *A Tract on Monetary Reform*. London: Royal Economic Society.
Kim, S. (1995). 'Expansion of markets and the geographic distribution of economic activities: the trends in U.S. regional manufacturing structure, 1860–1987', *Quarterly Journal of Economics*, pp. 881–908.
Kim, S. and R. Margo (2004). 'Historical perspectives on U.S. economic geography', in *Handbook of Regional and Urban Economics* (eds J. Henderson and J. Thisse). Amsterdam: Elsevier, pp. 2981–3019.

Kimura, Y. (1996). 'Japanese direct investment in the peripheral regions of Europe: an overview', in *Japan and the European Periphery* (ed. J. Darby). Basingstoke: Macmillan, pp. 13–36.

Kleinknecht, A. and J. ter Wengel (1998). 'The myth of economic globalisation', *Cambridge Journal of Economics*, pp. 637–47.

Knickerboker, F. (1973). *Oligopolistic Reaction and Multinational Enterprise*. Boston, MA: Harvard University Press.

Kojima, K. (1996). *Trade, Investment and Pacific Economic Integration*. Tokyo: Bunshindo.

Kok, W. (2004). *Facing the Challenge*. Luxembourg: European Communities.

Komiya, R. (1988). 'Introduction', in *Industrial Policy of Japan* (eds R. Komiya, M. Okuno, K. Suzumura). Tokyo: Academic Press, pp. 1–22.

Krätke, S. (1999). 'Regional integration or fragmentation? The German–Polish border region in a new Europe', *Regional Studies*, pp. 631–41.

Krauss, M. (1972). 'Recent developments in customs unions theory: an interpretative survey', *Journal of Economic Literature*, pp. 413–36.

Krauss, M. (ed.) (1973). *The Economics of Integration*. London: George Allen & Unwin.

Kravis, I. and R. Lipsey (1982). 'The location of overseas production and production for export by U.S. multinational firms', *Journal of International Economics*, pp. 201–23.

Kreinin, M. (1964). 'On the dynamic effects of a customs union', *Journal of Political Economy*, pp. 193–5.

Kreinin, M. (1969). 'Trade creation and trade diversion by the EEC and EFTA', *Economia Internazionale*, pp. 273–80.

Krueger, A. (1999). 'Are preferential trading arrangements trade-liberalising or protectionist?', *Journal of Economic Perspectives*, pp. 105–24.

Krugman, P. (1979). 'Increasing returns, monopolistic competition and international trade', *Journal of International Economics*, pp. 469–79.

Krugman, P. (1980). 'Scale economies, product differentiation and the pattern of trade', *American Economic Review*, pp. 950–59.

Krugman, P. (1987). 'The narrow moving band, the Dutch disease, and the competitive consequences of Mrs. Thatcher', *Journal of Development Economics*, pp. 41–55.

Krugman, P. (1990a). *Rethinking International Trade*. Cambridge, MA: MIT Press.

Krugman, P. (1990b). 'Protectionism: try it, you'll like it', *International Economy*, June/July, pp. 35–9.

Krugman, P. (1991a). 'History versus expectations', *Quarterly Journal of Economics*, pp. 651–67.

Krugman, P. (1991b). 'Increasing returns and economic geography', *Journal of Political Economy*, pp. 483–9.

Krugman, P. (1991c). 'Is bilateralism bad?', in *International Trade and Trade Policy* (eds E. Helpman and A. Razin). Cambridge, MA: MIT Press, pp. 9–23.

Krugman, P. (1992). *Geography and Trade*. Cambridge, MA: MIT Press.

Krugman, P. (1993a). 'On the number and location of cities', *European Economic Review*, pp. 293–8.

Krugman, P. (1993b). 'The current case for industrial policy', in *Protectionism and World Welfare* (ed. D. Salvatore). Cambridge: Cambridge University Press, pp. 160–79.

Krugman, P. (1993c). 'First nature, second nature, and metropolitan location', *Journal of Regional Science*, pp. 129–44.

Krugman, P. (1993d). 'Lessons of Massachusetts for EMU', in *Adjustment and Growth in the European Monetary Union* (eds F. Torres and F. Giavazzi). Cambridge: Cambridge University Press, pp. 241–61.

Krugman, P. (1995a). 'A reply to Professor Dunning', *International Executive*, pp. 325–7.

Krugman, P. (1995b). 'The move toward free trade zones', in *International Economics and International Economic Policy: A Reader* (ed. P. King). New York: McGraw-Hill, pp. 163–82.

Krugman, P. (1996a). *Pop Internationalism*. Cambridge, MA: MIT Press.

Krugman, P. (1996b). 'What economists can learn from evolutionary theorists', A talk given to the European Association for Evolutionary Political Economy, November, http://web.mit.edu/krugman/www/.

Krugman, P. (1996c). 'The Adam Smith Address: what difference does globalization make?', *Business Economics*, pp. 7–10.

Krugman, P. (1996d). 'Urban concentration: the role of increasing returns and transport costs', *International Regional Science Review*, pp. 5–30.

Krugman, P. (1997). 'What should trade negotiators negotiate about?', *Journal of Economic Literature*, pp. 113–20.

Krugman, P. (1998a). 'What's new about the new economic geography', *Oxford Review of Economic Policy*, pp. 7–17.

Krugman, P. (1998b). *The Accidental Theorist and other Dispatches from the Dismal Science*. New York: Norton.

Krugman, P. (1998c). 'Space: the final frontier', *Journal of Economic Perspectives*, pp. 161–74.

Krugman, P. (1999). 'The role of geography in development', in *Annual World Bank Conference on Development Economics 1998* (eds B. Pleskovic and J. Stiglitz). Washington, DC: World Bank, pp. 89–107.

Krugman, P. (2000). 'Can America stay on top?', *Journal of Economic Perspectives*, pp. 169–75.

Krugman, P. (2003). *The Great Unraveling*. New York: Norton.

Krugman, P. and A. Venables (1990). 'Integration and the competitiveness of peripheral industry', in *Unity with Diversity in the European Economy: the Community's Southern Frontier* (eds C. Bliss and J. Braga de Macedo). Cambridge: Cambridge University Press, pp. 56–75.

Krugman, P. and A. Venables (1995). 'Globalization and the inequality of nations', *Quarterly Journal of Economics*, pp. 857–80.

Krugman, P. and A. Venables (1996). 'Integration, specialization, and adjustment', *European Economic Review*, pp. 959–67.

Lahiri, S. (1998). 'Controversy: regionalism versus multilateralism', *Economic Journal*, pp. 1126–7.

Laird, S. (1999). 'Regional trade agreements: dangerous liaisons?', *World Economy*, pp. 1179–200.

Lall, S. (1994). 'The east Asian miracle: does the bell toll for industrial strategy?', *World Development*, pp. 645–54.

Lambooy, J. (1997). 'Knowledge production, organisation and agglomeration economies', *GeoJournal*, pp. 293–300.

Lambooy, J. and R. Boschma (2001). 'Evolutionary economics and regional policy', *Annals of Regional Science*, pp. 113–31.

Lancaster, K. (1980). 'Intra-industry trade under perfect monopolistic competition', *Journal of International Economics*, pp. 151–75.

Langhammer, R. (1991). 'ASEAN economic co-operation: a stock taking from a political economy point of view', *ASEAN Economic Bulletin*, pp. 137–50.

Langhammer, R. and U. Hiemenz (1990). *Regional Integration among Developing Countries*. Tübingen: J.C.B. Mohr.

Leamer, E. (1984). *Sources of International Comparative Advantage*. Cambridge, MA: MIT Press.

Leamer, E. and J. Levinsohn (1995). 'International trade theory: the evidence', in *Handbook of International Economics* (eds G. Grossman and K. Rogoff). Amsterdam: Elsevier, pp. 1339–94.

Levin, R., A. Klevorick, R. Nelson and S. Winter (1987). 'Appropriating the returns from industrial research and development', *Brookings Papers on Economic Activity*, pp. 783–820.

Liebowitz, S. and S. Margolis (1999). *Winners, Losers & Microsoft – Competition and Antitrust in High Technology*. Oakland: Independent Institute.

Limão, N. (2005). 'Preferential trade agreements as stumbling blocks for multilateral trade liberalization: evidence for the US', CEPR Discussion Paper No. 4884, Centre for Economic Policy Research, London.

Lin, Y. (1935). *My Country and My People*. New York: John Day and Regnal & Hitchcock.

Linder, S. (1961). *An Essay on Trade and Transformation*. Uppsala: Almquist & Wiksell.

Lipsey, R.E. (1999). 'The role of foreign direct investment in international capital flows', NBER Working Paper No. 7094, National Bureau of Economic Research, Cambridge, MA.

Lipsey, R.E. (2004). 'Home- and host-country effects of foreign direct investment', in *Challenges to Globalisation – Analyzing the Economics* (eds R. Baldwin and A. Winters). Chicago: Chicago University Press, pp. 333–79.

Lipsey, R.G. (1957). 'The theory of customs unions: trade diversion and welfare', *Economica*, pp. 40–46.

Lipsey, R.G. (1960). 'The theory of customs unions: a general survey', *Economic Journal*, pp. 496–513.

Lipsey, R.G. (1976). 'Comments', in *Economic Integration Worldwide, Regional, Sectoral* (ed. F. Machlup). London: Macmillan, pp. 37–40.

Lipsey, R.G. (1985). 'Canada and the United States: the economic dimension', in *Canada and the United States: Enduring Friendship, Persistent Stress* (eds C. Doran and J. Stigler). New York: Prentice-Hall, pp. 69–108.

Lipsey, R.G. (1987a). 'Models matter when discussing competitiveness: a technical note', in *Shaping Comparative Advantage* (eds R. Lipsey and W. Dobson). Toronto: C.D. Howe Institute, pp. 155–66.

Lipsey, R.G. (1987b). 'Report on the workshop', in *Shaping Comparative Advantage* (eds R.G. Lipsey and W. Dobson). Toronto: C.D. Howe Institute, pp. 109–53.

Lipsey, R.G. (1990). 'Canada at the US–Mexico free trade dance: wallflower or partner?', *Commentary 20*. Toronto: C.D. Howe Institute.

Lipsey, R.G. (1991). 'The case for trilateralism', in *Continental Accord: North American Economic Integration* (ed. S. Globerman). Vancouver: Fraser Institute, pp. 89–123.

Lipsey, R.G. (1992a). *An Introduction to Positive Economics*. London: Weidenfeld & Nicolson.

Lipsey, R.G. (1992b). 'Global change and economic policy', in *The Culture and the Power of Knowledge* (eds N. Stehr and R. Ericson). New York: De Gruyter, pp. 279–99.

Lipsey, R.G. (1993a). 'Globalisation, technological change and economic growth', Annual Sir Charles Carter Lecture. Northern Ireland Economic Development Office, Belfast.

Lipsey, R.G. (1993b). 'The changing technoeconomic paradigm and some implications for economic policy', Canadian Institute for Advanced Research, Vancouver.

Lipsey, R.G. (1993c). 'Canadian trade policy in relation to regional free trade agreements: CAFTA, NAFTA and WHFTA', Canadian Institute for Advanced Research, Vancouver.

Lipsey, R.G. (1994). 'Markets, technological change and economic growth', Canadian Institute for Advanced Research, Vancouver.

Lipsey, R.G. (1997). 'Globalization and national government policies: an economist's view', in *Governments, Globalization and International Business* (ed. J. Dunning). Oxford: Oxford University Press, pp. 73–113.

Lipsey, R.G., K. Carlaw and C. Bekar (2005). *Economic Transformations: General Purpose Technologies and Long Term Economic Growth*. Oxford: Oxford University Press.

Lipsey, R.G. and K. Lancaster (1956–57). 'The general theory of the second best', *Review of Economic Studies*, pp. 11–32.

Lipsey, R.G. and M. Smith (1986). *Taking the Initiative: Canada's Trade Options in a Turbulent World*. Toronto: C.D. Howe Institute.

Lipsey, R.G. and M. Smith (1987). *Global Imbalances and US Policy Responses*. Toronto: C.D. Howe Institute.

Lipsey, R.G. and M. Smith (1989). 'The Canada–US free trade agreement: special case or wave of the future?', in *Free Trade Areas and U.S. Trade Policy* (ed. J. Schott). Washington: Institute for International Economics, pp. 317–35.

Lipsey, R.G. and R. York (1988). *Evaluating the Free Trade Deal: A Guided Tour through the Canada–US Agreement*. Toronto: C.D. Howe Institute.

Lloyd, P. (1982). '3 × 3 theory of customs unions', *Journal of International Economics*, pp. 41–63.

Lloyd, P. and D. MacLaren (2004). 'Gains and losses from regional trading agreements: a survey', *Economic Record*, pp. 445–67.

Loertscher, R. and F. Wolter (1980). 'Determinants of intra-industry trade: among countries and across industries', *Weltwirtschaftliches Archiv*, pp. 280–93.

Lösch, A. (1938). 'The nature of economic regions', *Southern Economic Journal*, pp. 71–8.

Lösch, A. (1940). *Die Räumliche Ordnung der Wirtschaft*. Jena: Gustav Fischer. (Translated from German by W. Woglom and W. Stolper, *The Economics of Location* (1973), New Haven, CT: Yale University Press.)

Lowe, N. and M. Kenney (1999). 'Foreign investment and the global geography of production: why the Mexican consumer electronics industry failed', *World Development*, pp. 1427–43.

Lucas, R. (1988). 'On the mechanics of economic development', *Journal of Monetary Economics*, pp. 3–42.

Ludema, R. and I. Wooton (2000). 'Economic geography and the fiscal effects of regional integration', *Journal of International Economics*, pp. 331–57.

Lundgren, N. (1969). 'Customs unions of industrialized west European countries', in *Economic Integration in Europe* (ed. G. Denton). London: Weidenfeld & Nicolson, pp. 25–54.

Lunn, J. (1980). 'Determinants of US direct investment in the EEC', *European Economic Review*, pp. 93–101.

Lunn, J. (1983). 'Determinants of US direct investment in the EEC', *European Economic Review*, pp. 391–3.

MacDougall, G. (1977). *Report of the Study Group on the Role of Public Finance in European Integration*. Brussels: European Community.

Machlup, F. (1979). *A History of Thought on Economic Integration*. London: Macmillan.

Macleod, I., I. Hendry and S. Hyett (1998). *The External Relations of the European Communities*. Oxford: Clarendon Press.

Magrini, S. (2004). 'Regional (di)convergence', in *Handbook of Regional and Urban Economics* (eds J. Henderson and J. Thisse). Amsterdam: Elsevier, pp. 2741–96.

Maksimova, M. (1976). 'Comments on paper types of economic integration by B. Balassa', in *Economic Integration Worldwide, Regional, Sectoral* (ed. F. Machlup). London: Macmillan, pp. 32–6.

Malmberg, A. (1996). 'Industrial geography: agglomeration and local milieu', *Progress in Human Geography*, pp. 392–403.

Malmberg, A., Ö. Sölvell and I. Zander (1996). 'Spatial clustering, local accumulation of knowledge and firm competitiveness', *Geografiska Annaler*, pp. 85–97.

Maloney, M. and M. Macmillen (1999). 'Do currency unions grow too large for their own good?', *Economic Journal*, pp. 572–87.

Mansfield, E. and E. Reinhardt (2003). 'Multilateral determinants of regionalism: the effects of GATT/WTO on the formation of preferential trading arrangements', *International Organisation*, pp. 829–62.

Marer, P. and J. Montias (1988). 'The Council for Mutual Economic Assistance', in *International Economic Integration* (ed. A. El-Agraa). London: Macmillan, pp. 128–65.

Margalioth, Y. (2003). 'Tax competition, foreign direct investments and growth: using the tax system to promote developing countries', *Virginia Tax Review*, pp. 157–98.

Markusen, A. (1996). 'Sticky places in slippery space: a typology of industrial districts', *Economic Geography*, pp. 293–313.

Markusen, J. (1983). 'Factor movements and commodity trade as complements', *Journal of International Economics*, pp. 342–56.

Markusen, J. (1984). 'Multinationals, multi-plant economies and the gains from trade', *Journal of International Economics*, pp. 205–26.

Markusen, J. and J. Melvin (1984). *The Theory of International Trade and Its Canadian Applications*. Toronto: Butterworths.

Markusen, J. and A. Venables (1998). 'Multinational firms and the new trade theory', *Journal of International Economics*, pp. 183–203.

Markusen, J. and A. Venables (2000). 'The theory of endowment, intra-industry and multi-national trade', *Journal of International Economics*, pp. 209–34.

Marrese, M. (1986). 'CMEA: effective but cumbersome political economy', *International Organization*, pp. 287–327.

Marrese, M. and J. Vanous (1983). *Soviet Subsidization of Trade with Eastern Europe: A Soviet Perspective*. Berkeley: Institute of International Studies, University of California.

Marshall, A. (1890). *Principles of Economics*. London: Macmillan.

Martin, R. (1999). 'The new geographical turn in economics: some critical reflections', *Cambridge Journal of Economics*, pp. 65–91.

Mayes, D. (1978). 'The effects of economic integration on trade', *Journal of Common Market Studies*, pp. 1–23.

Mayes, D. (1988). 'The problems of quantitative estimation of integration effects', in *International Economic Integration* (ed. A. El-Agraa). London: Macmillan, pp. 42–58.

Mayes, D. (ed.) (1997). *The Evolution of the Single European Market*. Cheltenham, UK and Lyme, USA: Edward Elgar.

McAfee, R., H. Mialon and M. Williams (2004). 'When are sunk costs barriers to entry? Entry barriers in economic and antitrust analysis', *American Economic Review*. pp. 461–65.

McCann, P. (ed.) (2002). *Industrial Location Economics*. Cheltenham, UK and Northampton, MA, USA: Edward Elgar.

McFetridge, D. (1985). 'The economics of industrial policy', in *Canadian Industrial Policy in Action* (ed. D. McFetridge). Toronto: University of Toronto Press, pp. 1–49.

McKay, D. and W. Grant (1983). 'Industrial policies in OECD countries: an overview', *Journal of Public Policy*, pp. 1–12.

McKinnon, R. (1963). 'Optimum currency area', *American Economic Review*, pp. 717–25.

McKinnon, R. (1994). 'A common monetary standard or a common currency for Europe? The fiscal constraints', *Rivista di Politica Economica*, pp. 59–79.

McKinnon, R. (2004). 'Optimum currency areas and key currencies: Mundell I versus Mundell II', *Journal of Common Market Studies*, pp. 689–715.

McLaren, J. (2002). 'A theory of insidious regionalism', *Quarterly Journal of Economics*, pp. 571–608.

Meade, J. (1968). *The Pure Theory of Customs Unions*. Amsterdam: North-Holland.

Meade, J. (1973). 'The balance of payments problems of a European free-trade area', in *The Economics of Integration* (ed. M. Krauss). London: George Allen & Unwin, pp. 155–76.

Mendershausen, H. (1959). 'Terms of trade between the Soviet Union and smaller communist countries 1955–57', *Review of Economics and Statistics*, pp. 106–18.

Mendershausen, H. (1960). 'Terms of Soviet-satellite trade: a broadened analysis', *Review of Economics and Statistics*, pp. 152–63.

Mennis, B. and K. Sauvant (1976). *Emerging Forms of Transnational Community*. Lexington, MA: Lexington Books.

Messerlin, P. (1996). 'Competition policy and antidumping reform: an exercise in transition', in *The World Trading System: Challenges Ahead* (ed. J. Schott). Washington, DC: Institute for International Economics, pp. 219–46.

Messerlin, P. (2001). *Measuring the Cost of Protection in Europe*. Washington, DC: Institute for International Economics.

Micco, A., E. Stein and G. Ordoñez (2003). 'The currency union effect on trade: early evidence from EMU', *Economic Policy*, pp. 317–43.

Midelfart-Knarvik, K. and H. Overman (2002). 'Delocation and European integration', *Economic Policy*, pp. 323–59.

Midelfart-Knarvik, K., H. Overman, S. Redding and A. Venables (2002). 'The location of European industry', *European Economy*, Special report No.2/2002, pp. 213–69.

Midelfart, H., H. Overman and A. Venables (2003). 'Monetary union and the economic geography of Europe', *Journal of Common Market Studies*, pp. 847–68.

Mishan, E. (1976). 'The welfare gains of a trade diverting customs union reinterpreted', *Economic Journal*, pp. 669–72.

Mody, A. (2004). 'Is FDI integrating the world economy?', *World Economy*, pp. 1195–222.

Mody, A. and K. Srinivasan (1998). 'Japanese and U.S. firms as foreign investors: do they march to the same tune?', *Canadian Journal of Economics*, pp. 778–99.

Molle, W. (1991). *The Economics of European Integration*. Aldershot: Dartmouth. Reprinted Aldershot: Ashgate, 2001.

Molle, W. and A. van Mourik (1988). 'International movements of labour under conditions of economic integration: the case of western Europe', *Journal of Common Market Studies*, pp. 317–42.

Mongelli, F. (2002). 'New views on the optimum currency area theory: what is EMU telling us?', Working Paper No. 138, European Central Bank, Frankfurt.

Mora, T., E. Vaya and J. Suriñach (2004). 'The enlargement of the European Union and the spatial distribution of economic activity', *Eastern European Economics*, pp. 6–35.

Moran, T. (1998). *Foreign Direct Investment and Development*. Washington, DC: Institute for International Economics.

Morita, A. (1992). 'Partnering for competitiveness: the role of Japanese business', *Harvard Business Review*, May–June, pp. 76–83.

Moses, L. (1958). 'Location and the theory of production', *Quarterly Journal of Economics*, pp. 259–72.

Moss Kanter, R. (2003). 'Thriving locally in the global economy', *Harvard Business Review*, pp. 119–28.

Mundell, R. (1957). 'International trade and factor mobility', *American Economic Review*, pp. 321–35.

Mundell, R. (1961). 'A theory of optimum currency areas', *American Economic Review*, pp. 321–5.

Mundell, R. (1973). 'Uncommon arguments for common currencies', in *The Economics of Common Currencies* (eds H. Johnson and A. Swoboda). London: George Allen & Unwin, pp. 114–32.

Mundell, R. (1994). 'European monetary union and the international monetary system', *Rivista di Politica Economica*, pp. 83–128.

Murphy. K., A. Shleifer and R. Vishny (1989). 'Industrialization and the Big Push', *Journal of Political Economy*, pp. 1003–26.

Mytelka, L. (1979). *Regional Development in a Global Economy*. New Haven, CT: Yale University Press.

Mytelka, L. (1984). 'Competition, conflict and decline in the Union Douanière et Économique de l'Afrique Centrale (UDEAC)', in *African Regional Organizations* (ed. D. Mazzeo). Cambridge: Cambridge University Press, pp. 131–49.

Mytelka, L. (1994). 'Regional co-operation and the new logic of international competition', in *South–South Co-operation in a Global Perspective* (ed. L. Mytelka). Paris: OECD, pp. 21–54.

Nadvi, K. (1998). 'International competitiveness and small firm clusters – evidence from Pakistan', *Small Enterprise Development*, pp. 12–24.

Narula, R. (1999). 'Explaining the growth of strategic R&D alliances by European firms', *Journal of Common Market Studies*, pp. 711–23.

Nelson, R. (1999). 'The sources of industrial leadership: a perspective on industrial policy', *De Economist*, pp. 1–18.

Nelson, R. and S. Winter (1982). *An Evolutionary Theory of Economic Change*. Cambridge, MA: Harvard University Press.

Neven, D. (1990). 'EEC integration towards 1992: some distributional aspects', *Economic Policy*, pp. 14–46.

Nicolaides, P. (ed.) (1993). *Industrial Policy in the European Community*. Dordrecht: Martinus Nijhoff.

Nicolaides, P. (1994). 'Why multilateral rules on competition are needed', *Intereconomics*, pp. 211–18.

Nicolaides, P. (1999). 'The economics of enlarging the European Union: policy reform versus transfers', *Intereconomics*, January/February, pp. 3–9.

Nicolaides, P. and A. van der Klugt (eds) (1994). *The Competition Policy of the European Community*. Maastricht: EIPA.

Nogués, J. and R. Quintanilla (1992). 'Latin America's integration and the multilateral trading system', paper presented at the World Bank Conference on New Dimensions in Regional Integration, Washington, 2–3 April 1992.

Norman, V. (1990). 'Discussion of D. Neven's paper', *Economic Policy*, pp. 49–52.

Norman, V. (1995). 'The theory of market integration: a retrospective view', in *35 Years of Free Trade in Europe: Messages for the Future* (ed. E. Ems). Geneva: European Free Trade Association, pp. 19–37.

North, D. (1955). 'Location theory and regional economic growth', *Journal of Political Economy*, pp. 243–58.

OECD (2003a). *OECD Economic Outlook*, No. 73. Paris: OECD.

OECD (2003b). *Trends in International Migration (SOPEMI 2002)*. Paris: OECD.

OECD (2003c). *OECD Science, Technology and Industry Scoreboard 2003*. Paris: OECD.

OECD (2005). *OECD Science, Technology and Industry Scoreboard 2005*. Paris: OECD.

Ohlin, B. (1933). *Interregional and International Trade*. Cambridge, MA: Harvard University Press.

O'Keefe, T. (1996). 'How the Andean Pact transformed itself into a friend of foreign enterprise', *International Lawyer*, pp. 811–24.

Ottaviano, G. (1999). 'Integration, geography and the burden of history', *Regional Science and Urban Economics*, pp. 245–56.

Ottaviano, G. (2003). 'Regional policy in the global economy: insights from new economic geography', University of Bologna, mimeo.

Ottaviano, G. and D. Puga (1998). 'Agglomeration in the global economy: a survey of the "new economic geography"', *World Economy*, pp. 707–31.

Ottaviano, G. and J. Thisse (1999). 'Integration, agglomeration and the political economics of factor mobility', CEPR Discussion Paper No. 2185, Centre for Economic Policy Research, London.

Ottaviano, G. and J. Thisse (2004). 'Agglomeration and economic geography', in *Handbook of Regional and Urban Economics* (eds J. Henderson and J. Thisse). Amsterdam: Elsevier, pp. 2563–608.

Oyejide, A., I. Elbadawi and P. Collier (eds) (1997). *Regional Integration and Trade Liberalization in SubSaharan Africa*. Basingstoke: Macmillan.

Ozawa, T. (2004). 'The Hegelian dialectic and evolutionary economic change', *Global Economy Journal*, vol. 4, article 7.

Paci, R. (1997). 'More similar and less equal: economic growth in the European regions', *Weltwirtschaftliches Archiv*, pp. 609–34.

Paci, R. and S. Usai (1999). 'The role of specialisation and diversity externalities in the agglomeration of innovative activities', University of Cagliari and University of Sassari, mimeo.

Pack, H. (2000). 'Industrial policy: growth elixir or poison?', *World Bank Research Observer*, pp. 47–67.

Pack, H. and K. Saggi (1997). 'Inflows of foreign technology and indigenous technological development', *Review of Development Economics*, pp. 81–98.

Page, S. (2000). *Regionalism among Developing Countries*. Basingstoke: Macmillan.

Palmeter, D. (1993). 'Rules of origin in customs unions and free trade areas', in *Regional Integration and the Global Trading System* (eds K. Anderson and R. Blackhurst). New York: Harvester Wheatsheaf, pp. 326–43.

Palmeter, D. (1995). 'Rules of origin in a western hemisphere free trade agreement', in *Trade Liberalization in the Western Hemisphere*. Washington, DC: Inter-American Development Bank, pp. 191–206.

Panagariya, A. (1999). 'The regional debate: an overview', *World Economy*, pp. 477–511.

Panagariya, A. (2000). 'Preferential trade liberalization: the traditional theory and new developments', *Journal of Economic Literature*, pp. 287–331.

Panagariya, A. (2002). 'EU preferential trade arrangements and developing countries', *World Economy*, pp. 1415–32.

Panić, M. (1988). *National Management of the International Economy*. London: Macmillan.

Panić, M. (1991). 'The import of multinationals on national economic policies', in *Multinationals and Europe 1992* (eds B. Bürgenmeier and J. Mucchelli). London: Routledge, pp. 204–22.

Panić, M. (1998). 'Transnational corporations and the nation state', in *Transnational Corporations and the Global Economy* (eds R. Kozul-Wright and R. Rowthorn). Basingstoke: Macmillan, pp. 244–76.

Papageorgiou, G. (1979). 'Agglomeration', *Regional Science and Urban Economics*, pp. 41–59.

Pautler, P. (2001). 'Evidence on mergers and acquisitions', Bureau of Economics, Federal Trade Commission, Washington, DC, mimeo.

Peck, M. (1989). 'Industrial organization and the gains from Europe 1992', *Brookings Papers on Economic Activity*, pp. 277–99.

Pelkmans, J. (1980). 'Economic theories of integration revisited', *Journal of Common Market Studies*, pp. 333–53.

Pelkmans, J. (1984). *Market Integration in the European Community*. The Hague: Martinus Nijhoff.

Pelkmans, J. and P. Robson (1987). 'The aspirations of the White Paper', *Journal of Common Market Studies*, pp. 181–92.

Pelkmans, J. and A. Winters (1988). *Europe's Domestic Market*. London: Routledge.

Penrose, E. (1952). 'Biological analogies in the theory of the firm', *American Economic Review*, pp. 804–19.

Perroux, F. (1950). 'Economic space: theory and applications', *Quarterly Journal of Economics*, pp. 89–104.

Perroux, F. (1955). 'Note sur la notion de "pôle de croissance"' (A note on the notion of a pole of growth), *Économie Appliquée*, pp. 307–20.

Perroux, F. (1961). *L'Économie du XXe Siècle* (Economics of the 20th Century). Paris: Presses Universitaires de France.

Petith, H. (1977). 'European integration and the terms of trade', *Economic Journal*, pp. 262–72.

Pfann, G. and H. van Kranenburg (2002). 'Tax policy, location choices and market structure', IZA Discussion Paper No. 499, Institute for the Study of Labour, Bonn.

Pinch, S. and N. Henry (1999). 'Paul Krugman's geographical economics, industrial clustering and the British motor sport industry', *Regional Studies*, pp. 815–27.

Pinder, J. (1969). 'Problems of European integration', in *Economic Integration in Europe* (ed. G. Denton). London: Weidenfeld and Nicolson, pp. 143–70.

Pinder, J. (1982). 'Causes and kinds of industrial policy', in *National Industrial Strategies and the World Economy* (ed. J. Pinder). London: Croom Helm, pp. 41–52.

Pinder, J., T. Hosomi and W. Diebold (1979). *Industrial Policy and International Economy*. New York: The Trilateral Commission.

Pitelis, C. and R. Sugden (eds) (1991). *The Nature of the Transnational Firm*. London: Routledge.

Plasschaert, S. (1994). 'Introduction: transfer pricing and taxation', in *Transnational Corporations: Transfer Pricing and Taxation* (ed. S. Plasschaert). London: Routledge, pp. 1–21.

Plato (360 BC) (1980). *The Laws*. Harmondsworth: Penguin Books.
Pomfret, R. (1986). 'The trade-diverting bias of preferential trading arrangements', *Journal of Common Market Studies*, pp. 109–17.
Pomfret, R. (1997). *The Economics of Regional Trading Arrangements*. Oxford: Clarendon Press.
Porter, M. (1990a). *The Competitive Advantage of Nations*. New York: Free Press.
Porter, M. (1990b). 'The competitive advantage of nations', *Harvard Business Review*, pp. 73–93.
Porter, M. (1994). 'The role of location in competition', *Journal of the Economics of Business*, pp. 35–9.
Porter, M. (1996). 'Competitive advantage, agglomeration economies, and regional policy', *International Regional Science Review*, pp. 85–94.
Porter, M. (1998a). 'Clusters and the new economics of competition', *Harvard Business Review*, pp. 77–90.
Porter, M. (1998b). 'Location, clusters, and the "new" microeconomics of competition', *Business Economics*, pp. 7–13.
Porter, M. (2000a). 'Locations, clusters and company strategy', in *The Oxford Handbook of Economic Geography* (eds G. Clark et al.). Oxford: Oxford University Press, pp. 253–74.
Porter, M. (2000b). 'Location, competition and economic development: local clusters in a global economy', *Economic Development Quarterly*, pp. 15–34.
Porter, M. and M. Sakakibara (2004). 'Competition in Japan', *Journal of Economic Perspectives*, pp. 27–50.
Porter, M. and Ö. Sölvell (1998). 'The role of geography in the process of innovation and the sustainable competitive advantage of firms', in *The Dynamic Firm* (eds A. Chandler et al.). Oxford: Oxford University Press, pp. 440–57.
Posner, M. (1961). 'International trade and technical change', *Oxford Economic Papers*, pp. 323–41.
Prais, S. (1981). *Productivity and Industrial Structure*. Cambridge: Cambridge University Press.
Pratten, C. (1971). *Economies of Scale and Manufacturing Industry*. Cambridge: Cambridge University Press.
Pratten, C. (1988). 'A survey of the economies of scale', in *Studies on the Economics of Integration*, Research on the Costs of Non-Europe, vol. 2, Brussels: European Communities, pp. 11–165.
Praussello, F. (2002). 'The stability of EMU in the aftermath of the EU eastwards enlargement', paper presented at the conference 'EU Enlargement: Endgame Economic Issues', Jean Monnet European Centre of Excellence, University of Genoa, 15 November.

President's Commission on Industrial Competitiveness (1985). *Global Competition: The New Reality* (Volumes 1 and 2). Washington, DC: US Government Printing Office.

Prest, A. (1983). 'Fiscal policy', in *Main Economic Policy Areas of the EEC* (ed. P. Coffey). The Hague: Martinus Nijhoff, pp. 58–90.

Puga, D. (2002). 'European regional policies in light of recent location theories', *Journal of Economic Geography*, pp. 373–406.

Puga, D. and D. Trefler (2002). 'Knowledge creation and control in organizations', NBER Working Paper No. 9121, National Bureau of Economic Research, Cambridge, MA.

Puga, D. and A. Venables (1997). 'Preferential trading arrangements and industrial location', *Journal of International Economics*, pp. 347–68.

Puga, D. and A. Venables (1998). 'Trading arrangements and industrial development', *The World Bank Economic Review*, pp. 221–49.

Puga, D. and A. Venables (1999). 'Agglomeration and economic development: import substitution vs. trade liberalisation', *Economic Journal*, pp. 292–311.

Purvis, D. (1972). 'Technology, trade and factor mobility', *Economic Journal*, pp. 991–9.

Pyke, F., G. Becattini and W. Sengenberger (eds) (1990). *Industrial Districts and Inter-firm Co-operation in Italy*. Geneva: International Labour Organisation.

Pyke, F. and W. Sengenberger (eds) (1992). *Industrial Districts and Local Economic Regeneration*. Geneva: International Labour Organisation.

Quah, D. (1996a). 'Empirics for economic growth and convergence', *European Economic Review*, pp. 1353–75.

Quah, D. (1996b). 'Regional convergence clusters across Europe', CEPR Discussion Paper No. 1286, Centre for Economic Policy Research, London.

Rauch, J. (1993). 'Does history matter only when it matters little? The case of city-industry location', CEPR Discussion Paper No. 4312, Centre for Economic Policy Research, London.

Read, R. (1994). 'The EC internal banana market: the issues and the dilemmas', *The World Economy*, pp. 219–35.

Reich, R. (1982). 'Why the U.S. needs an industrial policy', *Harvard Business Review*, January/February, pp. 74–81.

Reich, R. (1990). 'Who is us?', *Harvard Business Review*, January/February, pp. 53–64.

Reuber, G. (1973). *Private Foreign Investment in Development*. Oxford: Clarendon Press.

Richter, S. and L. Tóth (1994). 'Perspectives for economic cooperation among the Visegrád Group countries', Vienna Institute for

International Economic Studies – Wiener Institut für Internationale Wirtschaftsvergleiche (wiiw) no. 156, November.

Riezman, R. (1979). 'A 3×3 model of customs unions', *Journal of International Economics*, pp. 341–54.

Robson, P. (1968). *Economic Integration in Africa*. London: George Allen & Unwin.

Robson, P. (ed.) (1972). *International Economic Integration*. Harmondsworth: Penguin Books.

Robson, P. (1980). *The Economics of International Integration*. London: George Allen & Unwin.

Robson, P. (1983). *Integration, Development and Equity*. London: George Allen & Unwin.

Robson, P. (1987). *The Economics of International Integration*. London: George Allen & Unwin.

Robson, P. (1997). 'Integration in Sub-Saharan Africa', in *Economic Integration Worldwide* (ed. A. El-Agraa). London: Macmillan, pp. 348–67.

Robson, P. (1998). *The Economics of International Integration*. London: Routledge.

Rodas-Martini, P. (1998). 'Intra-industry trade and revealed comparative advantage in the Central American Common Market', *World Development*, pp. 337–44.

Rodrik, D. (2004). 'Industrial policy for the twenty-first century', Faculty Research Working Paper, RWP 04-047, John F. Kennedy School of Government, Harvard University, Cambridge, MA.

Romer, P. (1986). 'Increasing returns and long-run growth', *Journal of Political Economy*, pp. 1002–37.

Romer, P. (1994). 'New goods, old theory and the welfare costs of trade restrictions', *Journal of Development Economics*, pp. 5–38.

Rose, A. (2000). 'One money, one market: the effect of common currencies on trade', *Economic Policy*, pp. 9–45.

Rose, A. (2004). 'Do we really know that the WTO increases trade?', *American Economic Review*, pp. 98–114.

Rosenberg, N., R. Landau and D. Mowery (eds) (1992). *Technology and the Wealth of Nations*. Stanford, CA: Stanford University Press.

Rubin, S. (1970). 'The international firm and the national jurisdiction', in *The International Corporation* (ed. C. Kindleberger). Cambridge, MA: MIT Press, pp. 179–204.

Ruding Committee (1992). *Conclusions and Recommendations of the Committee of Independent Experts on Company Taxation*. Luxembourg: European Communities.

Rugman, A. (1985). 'The Behaviour of US Subsidiaries in Canada: Implications for Trade and investment', in *Canada/United States Trade and Investments Issues* (eds D. Fretz, R. Stern and J. Whalley). Toronto: Ontario Economic Council, pp. 460–73.

Rugman, A. (2002). 'Multinational enterprises and the end of global strategy', in *Multinational Firms* (eds J. Dunning and J. Mucchielli). London: Routledge, pp. 3–17.

Rugman, A. and R. Hodgetts (2001). 'The end of global strategy', *European Management Journal*, pp. 333–43.

Rugman, A. and A. Verbeke (1998). 'Multinational enterprise and public policy', *Journal of International Business Studies*, pp. 115–36.

Rugman, A. and A. Verbeke (2003). 'Regional and global strategies of multinational enterprises', Kelley School of Business, Indiana University, Bloomington, IL, mimeo.

Sabrianova Peter, K., J. Svejnar and K. Terrell (2004). 'Distance and the efficiency frontier and FDI spillovers', IZA Discussion Paper No. 1332, Institute for the Study of Labour, Bonn.

Sadiq, K. (2001). 'Unitary taxation – the case for global formulary apportionment', *International Bureau of Fiscal Documentation Bulletin*, pp. 275–86.

Sakakibara, E. and S. Yamakawa (2003). 'Regional integration in east Asia: challenges and opportunities', World Bank Policy Research Paper No. 3078 (Part One) and No. 3079 (Part Two), World Bank, Washington, DC.

Sala-i-Martin, X. (1994). 'Regional cohesion: evidence and theories of regional growth and convergence', CEPR Discussion Paper No. 1075, Centre for Economic Policy Research, London.

Sala-i-Martin, X. (1996). 'Regional cohesion: evidence and theories of regional growth and convergence', *European Economic Review*, pp. 1325–52.

Sala-i-Martin, X. and J. Sachs (1992). 'Fiscal federalism and optimum currency areas: evidence for Europe from the United States', in *Establishing a Central Bank: Issues in Europe and Lessons from the US* (eds M. Canzoneri, V. Grilli and P. Mason). Cambridge: Cambridge University Press, pp. 195–219.

Samuelson, P. (1964). 'Theoretical notes on trade problems', *Review of Economics and Statistics*, pp. 145–54.

Sapir, A. (1992). 'Regional integration in Europe', *Economic Journal*, pp. 1491–506.

Sapir, A. (1993). 'Structural dimension', *European Economy Social Europe*, No. 3, pp. 23–39.

Sapir, A. (1996). 'The effects of Europe's Internal Market Program on production and trade: a first assessment', *Weltwirtschaftliches Archiv*, pp. 456–75.

Sapir, A., P. Aghion, G. Bertola, M. Hellwig, J. Pisani-Ferry, D. Rosati, J. Viñals and H. Wallace (2003). *An Agenda for a Growing Europe*. Brussels: European Commission.

Sapir, A., P. Buigues and A. Jacquemin (1993). 'European competition policy in manufacturing and services: a two speed approach?', *Oxford Review of Economic Policy*, pp. 113–32.

Sarris, A. (1994). 'Consequences of the proposed common agricultural policy reform for the southern part of the European Community', *European Economy*, No. 5, pp. 113–32.

Scaperlanda, A. (1967). 'The EEC and US foreign investment: some empirical evidence', *Economic Journal*, pp. 22–6.

Scaperlanda, A. and R. Balough (1983). 'Determinants of US direct investment in Europe', *European Economic Journal*, pp. 381–90.

Scaperlanda, A. and E. Reiling (1971). 'A comment on a note on customs unions and direct foreign investment', *Economic Journal*, pp. 355–7.

Schatz, K. and F. Wolter (1987). *Structural Adjustment in the Federal Republic of Germany*. Geneva: International Labour Organisation.

Schiff, M. (2000). 'Multilateral trade liberalization and political disintegration', World Bank Policy Research Paper No. 2350, World Bank, Washington, DC.

Schmalensee, R. (1988). 'Industrial economics: an overview', *Economic Journal*, pp. 634–81.

Schmitz, H. (1998). 'Fostering collective efficiency', *Small Enterprise Development*, pp. 4–11.

Schmitz, H. (1999). 'Collective efficiency and increasing returns', *Cambridge Journal of Economics*, pp. 465–83.

Schmitz, H. and K. Nadvi (1999). 'Clustering and industrialization: introduction', *World Development*, pp. 1503–14.

Scitovsky, T. (1967). *Economic Theory and Western European Integration*. London: George Allen & Unwin.

Sellekaerts, W. (1973). 'How meaningful are empirical studies on trade creation and diversion?', *Weltwirtschaftliches Archiv*, pp. 519–53.

Servan-Schreiber, J. (1969). *The American Challenge*. New York: Athenaeum.

Sharp, M. and K. Pavitt (1993). 'Technology policy in the 1990s: old trends and new realities', *Journal of Common Market Studies*, pp. 129–51.

Sharp, M. and G. Shepherd (1987). *Managing Change in British Industry*. Geneva: International Labour Organisation.

Sidjanski, D. (2000). *The Federal Future of Europe*. Ann Arbor, MI: University of Michigan Press.

Sidjanski, D. (2001). 'The federal approach to the European Union or the quest for an unprecedented European federalism', Research and Policy Paper No. 14, Notre Europe, Paris.

Siebert, H. (ed.) (1995). *Locational Competition in the World Economy*. Tübingen: J.C.B. Mohr.

Simon, J. (1996). 'Some findings about European immigration', *International Regional Science Review*, pp. 129–37.

Sinn, H. (2004). 'EU enlargement, migration and the new constitution', *CESifo Working Paper* No. 1367, Munich.

Sinn, H. and F. Westermann (2000). 'Two Mezzogiornos', *CESifo Working Paper* No. 378, Munich.

Sleuwaegen, L. and K. de Backer (2001). 'Multinational firms, market integration and trade structure', *Weltwirtschaftliches Archiv*, pp. 379–403.

Smarzynska Javorcik, B. (2004). 'Does foreign direct investment increase the productivity of domestic firms? In search of spillovers through backward linkages', *American Economic Review*, pp. 605–27.

Smith, A. (1839). *An Inquiry into the Nature and Causes of the Wealth of Nations*. Edinburgh: Adam & Charles Black.

Smith, A. and A. Venables (1988). 'Completing the internal market in the European Community', *European Economic Review*, pp. 1501–25.

Smith, D. (1981). *Industrial Location – An Economic Geographical Analysis*. New York: John Wiley.

Smith, D. and R. Florida (1994). 'Agglomeration and industrial location: an econometric analysis of Japanese-affiliated manufacturing establishments in automotive-related industries', *Journal of Urban Economics*, pp. 23–41.

Snape, R. (1996). 'Trade discrimination – yesterday's problem?', *Economic Record*, pp. 381–96.

Sobell, V. (1984). *The Red Market – Industrial Co-operation and Specialisation in Comecon*. Aldershot: Gower.

Sternberg, R. and C. Tamásy (1999). 'Munich as Germany's no. 1 high technology region: empirical evidence, theoretical explanations and the role of small firm/large firm relations', *Regional Studies*, pp. 367–77.

Storper, M., C. Yun-chung and F. de Paolis (2002). 'Trade and location of industries in the OECD and European Union', *Journal of Economic Geography*, pp. 73–107.

Straubhaar, T. (1988). 'International labour migration within a common market: some aspects of EC experience', *Journal of Common Market Studies*, pp. 45–62.

Straubhaar, T. and K. Zimmermann (1993). 'Towards a European migration policy', *Population Research and Policy Review*, pp. 225–41.

Swann, D. (1978). *The Economics of the Common Market*. Harmondsworth: Penguin Books.

Swann, D. (1996). *European Economic Integration: The Common Market, European Union and Beyond*. Cheltenham, UK and Brookfield, USA: Edward Elgar.

Swann, D. (2000). *The Economics of Europe*. London: Penguin.
Swann, P., M. Prevezer and D. Stout (eds) (1998). *The Dynamics of Industrial Clustering*. Oxford: Oxford University Press.
Tanzi, V. and H. Zee (2000). 'Tax policy for emerging markets: developing countries', *National Tax Journal*, pp. 299–322.
Tavlas, G. (1993a). 'The theory of optimum currency areas revisited', *Finance and Development*, June, pp. 32–5.
Tavlas, G. (1993b). 'The "new" theory of optimum currency areas', *The World Economy*, pp. 663–85.
Tavlas, G. (1997). 'The international use of the US dollar: an optimum currency area perspective', *World Economy*, pp. 709–47.
Teich, A. (2003). 'R&D in the Federal Budget: frequently asked questions' *AAAS Report XXVI: Research and Development FY 2002*. Washington, DC: American Academy of Arts and Sciences, www.aaas.org/spp/rd/xxvi/chap1.htm.
Tharakan, M., D. Greenaway and J. Tharakan (1998). 'Cumulation and injury determination of the European Community in antidumping cases', *Weltwirtschaftliches Archiv*, pp. 320–39.
Thomsen, S. and P. Nicolaides (1991). *The Evolution of Japanese Direct Investment in Europe*. New York: Harvester Wheatsheaf.
Thygesen, N. (1987). 'Is the EEC an optimal currency area?', in *The ECU Market* (eds R. Levics and A. Sommariva). Toronto: D.C. Heath, Lexington Books, pp. 163–89.
Tinbergen, J. (1954). *International Economic Integration*. Amsterdam: Elsevier.
Tironi, E. (1982). 'Customs union theory in the presence of foreign firms', *Oxford Economic Papers*, pp. 150–71.
Tongzon, J. (2005). 'ASEAN–China free trade area: a bane or boon for ASEAN countries?', *World Economy*, pp. 191–210.
Tovias, A. (1982). 'Testing factor price equalization in the EEC', *Journal of Common Market Studies*, pp. 375–88.
Tovias, A. (1990). 'The impact of liberalizing government procurement policies of individual EC countries on trade with nonmembers', *Weltwirtschaftliches Archiv*, pp. 722–36.
Trebilcock, M. (1986). *The Political Economy of Economic Adjustment*. Toronto: University of Toronto Press.
Trimbath, S. (2002). *Mergers and Acquisitions: Changes across Time*. Boston, MA: Kluwer.
Tsoukalis, L. (1997). *The New European Economy Revisited.* Oxford: Oxford University Press.
Tyson, L. (1987). 'Comments on Brander's "Shaping comparative advantage": creating advantage, an industrial policy perspective', in *Shaping*

Comparative Advantage (eds R. Lipsey and W. Dobson). Toronto: C.D. Howe Institute, pp. 65–82.

Tyson, L. (1991). 'They are not us. Why American ownership still matters', *The American Prospect*, Winter, pp. 37–49.

Tyson, L. (1992). *Who Is Bashing Whom? Trade Conflict in High-technology Industries*. Washington, DC: Institute for International Economics.

Tyson, L. and J. Zysman (1987a). 'American industry in international competition', in *American Industry in International Competition* (eds J. Zysman and L. Tyson). Ithaca, NY: Cornell University Press, pp. 15–59.

Tyson, L. and J. Zysman (1987b). 'Conclusion: what to do now?', in *American Industry in International Competition* (eds J. Zysman and L. Tyson). Ithaca, NY: Cornell University Press, pp. 422–7.

Ul Haq, M. (1980). 'Beyond the slogan south–south co-operation', *World Development*, pp. 743–51.

UNCTAD (1983). *The Role of Transnational Enterprises in Latin American Economic Integration Efforts: Who Integrates with Whom, How and for Whose Benefit?* New York: United Nations.

UNCTAD (1992). *World Investment Report: Transnational Corporations as Engines of Growth*. New York: United Nations.

UNCTAD (1993). *World Investment Report: Transnational Corporations and Integrated International Production*. New York: United Nations.

UNCTAD (1994). *World Investment Report: Transnational Corporations, Employment and the Workforce*. New York: United Nations.

UNCTAD (1995a). 'Incentives and foreign direct investment', TD/B/ITNC/Misc. 1, 6 April.

UNCTAD (1995b). *World Investment Report: Transnational Corporations and Competitiveness*. New York: United Nations.

UNCTAD (1996a). *Sharing Asia's Dynamism: Asian Direct Investment in the European Union*. New York: United Nations.

UNCTAD (1996b). *Handbook of Economic Integration and Cooperation Groupings of Developing Countries*. New York: United Nations.

UNCTAD (1997). *World Investment Report: Transnational Corporations, Market Structure and Competition Policy*. United Nations: New York.

UNCTAD (1998). *World Investment Report: Trends and Determinants*. United Nations: New York.

UNCTAD (1999a). *World Investment Report: Foreign Direct Investment and the Challenge of Development*. United Nations: New York.

UNCTAD (1999b). *Investment-Related Trade Measures*. New York: United Nations.

UNCTAD (2000). *World Investment Report: Cross-border Mergers and Acquisitions and Development*. United Nations: New York.

UNCTAD (2001). *World Investment Report: Promoting Linkages*. New York: United Nations.
UNCTAD (2002). *World Investment Report: Transnational Corporations and Export Competitiveness*. United Nations: New York.
UNCTAD (2003). *World Investment Report: FDI Policies for Development – National and International Perspectives*. United Nations: New York.
UNCTAD (2004). *World Investment Report: The Shift Towards Services*. United Nations: New York.
UNCTC (1990). *Regional Economic Integration and Transnational Corporations in the 1990s: Europe 1992, North America and Developing Countries*. New York: United Nations.
UNCTC (1991a). *The Impact of Trade-related Investment Measures on Trade and Development*. New York: United Nations.
UNCTC (1991b). *World Investment Report: The Triad in Foreign Direct Investment*. New York: United Nations.
UNCTC (1991c). *Government Policies and Foreign Direct Investment*. New York: United Nations.
United Nations (2000). 'Replacement migration: is it a solution to declining and ageing populations?' ESA/P/WP.160, 21 March.
Vaitsos, K. (1978). 'Crisis in regional economic cooperation (integration) among developing countries: a survey', *World Development*, pp. 719–69.
van Aarle, B. (1996). 'The impact of the Single Market on trade and foreign direct investment in the European Union', *Journal of World Trade*, pp. 121–38.
van Brabant, J. (1980). *Socialist Economic Integration*. Cambridge: Cambridge University Press.
van Brabant, J. (1996). 'Remaking Europe – the accession of transition economies', *Economia Internazionale*, pp. 507–31.
van Brabant, J. (2001). 'EU widening and deepening – are these goals reconcilable?', *Most*, pp. 113–41.
van Mourik, A. (1987). 'Testing the factor price equalisation theorem in the EC: an alternative approach', *Journal of Common Market Studies*, pp. 79–86.
Vanhove, N. and L. Klaasen (1987). *Regional Policy: A European Approach*. Aldershot: Avebury.
Vaubel, R. (1990). 'Currency competition and European monetary integration', *Economic Journal*, pp. 936–46.
Venables, A. (1985). 'Trade and trade policy with imperfect competition: the case of identical products and free entry', *Journal of International Economics*, pp. 1–19.
Venables, A. (1994). 'Economic integration and industrial agglomeration', *Economic and Social Review*, pp. 1–17.

Venables, A. (1995). 'Economic integration and the location of firms', *American Economic Review* (Papers and Proceedings), pp. 296–300.
Venables, A. (1996a). 'Localization of industry and trade performance', *Oxford Review of Economic Policy*, pp. 52–60.
Venables, A. (1996b). 'Equilibrium locations of vertically linked industries', *International Economic Review*, pp. 341–59.
Venables, A. (1998). 'The assessment: trade and location', *Oxford Review of Economic Policy*, pp. 1–6.
Venables, A. (1999). 'Regional integration agreements', World Bank Policy Research Working Paper No. 2260, World Bank, Washington, DC.
Venables, A. (2001). 'Geography and international inequalities: the impact of new technologies', Centre for Economic Performance, London School of Economics, London.
Venables, A. (2003). 'Winners and losers from regional integration agreements', *Economic Journal*, pp. 747–61.
Venables, A. and N. Limão (2002). 'Geographical disadvantage: a Heckscher–Ohlin–von Thünen model of international specialisation', *Journal of International Economics*, pp. 239–63.
Vernon, R. (1966). 'International investment and international trade in the product cycle', *Quarterly Journal of Economics*, pp. 190–207.
Viner, J. (1950). *The Customs Union Issue*. London: Stevens & Sons.
Viner, J. (1976). 'A letter to W.M. Corden', *Journal of International Economics*, pp. 107–8.
von Thünen, J. (1826). *Der Isolierte Staat in Beziehung auf Landtschaft und Nationalökonomie*. Hamburg: Perthes. (Translated from German by C. Wartenberg, *Von Thünen's Isolated State* (1966), Oxford: Pergamon Press.)
Wallis, K. (1968). 'The EEC and United States foreign investment: some empirical evidence re-examined', *Economic Journal*, pp. 717–19.
Walz, U. (1998). 'Does an enlargement of a common market stimulate growth and convergence?', *Journal of International Economics*, pp. 297–321.
Wasylenko, M. (1991). 'Empirical evidence on interregional business location decisions and the role of fiscal incentives in economic development', in *Industry Location and Public Policy* (eds H. Herzog and A. Schlottmann). Knoxville, TN: University of Tennessee Press, pp. 13–30.
Weber, A. (1909). *Über den Standort der Industrien*. Tübingen: J.C.B. Mohr. (Translated from German by C. Friedrich, *Theory of the Location of Industries* (1962), Chicago: University of Chicago Press.)
Weder, R. (1995). 'The Swiss dyestuff industry', in *Studies in Swiss Competitive Advantage* (eds M. Enright and R. Weder). Bern: Peter Lang, pp. 24–60.

Werner, P. (1970). *Report to the Council and the Commission on the Realization by Stages of Economic and Monetary Union in the Community*. Luxembourg: European Community.

Whalley, J. (ed.) (1985). *Canada–United States Free Trade*. Toronto: University of Toronto Press.

Whalley, J. (1987). 'Brander's "Shaping comparative advantage": remarks', in *Shaping Comparative Advantage* (eds R. Lipsey and W. Dobson). Toronto: C.D. Howe Institute, pp. 83–9.

Whalley, J. (1990). 'Non-discriminatory discrimination: special and differential treatment under the GATT for developing countries', *Economic Journal*, pp. 1318–28.

Whalley, J. (1992). 'CUSTA and NAFTA: can WHFTA be far behind?', *Journal of Common Market Studies*, pp. 125–41.

Wheeler, D. and A. Mody (1992). 'International investment location decisions: the case of U.S. firms', *Journal of International Economics*, pp. 57–76.

Wilkinson, B. (1985). 'Canada/US free trade and Canadian economic, cultural and political sovereignty', in *Canadian Trade at a Crossroads: Options for New International Agreements* (eds D. Conklin and T. Chourchene). Toronto: Ontario Economic Council, pp. 291–307.

Wilkinson, B. (1997). 'NAFTA in the world economy: lessons and issues for Latin America' in *Western Hemisphere Trade Integration* (eds R.G. Lipsey and P. Meller). Basingstoke: Macmillan, pp. 30–57.

Wilkinson, C. (1984). 'Trends in industrial policy in the EC: theory and practice', in *European Industry: Public Policy and Corporate Strategy* (ed. A. Jacquemin). Oxford: Clarendon Press, pp. 39–78.

Williamson, J. and A. Bottrill (1973). 'The impact of customs unions on trade in manufactures', in *The Economics of Integration* (ed. M. Krauss). London: George Allen & Unwin, pp. 118–51.

Winters, A. (1987). 'Negotiating the abolition of non-tariff barriers', *Oxford Economic Papers*, pp. 465–80.

Winters, A. (1994). 'The EC and protection: the political economy', *European Economic Review*, pp. 596–603.

Winters, A. (1997). 'Regionalism and the rest of the world: theory and estimates of the effects of European integration', *Review of International Economics*, pp. 134–47.

Wong, J. (1988). 'The Association of Southeast Asian Nations', in *International Economic Integration* (ed. A. El-Agraa). London: Macmillan, pp. 314–28.

Wonnacott, P. (1987). *The United States and Canada: The Quest for Free Trade*. Washington, DC: Institute for International Economics.

Wonnacott, P. and R. Wonnacott (1981). 'Is unilateral tariff reduction preferable to a customs union? The customs union of the missing foreign tariffs', *American Economic Review*, pp. 704–13.

Woodward, D. (1992). 'Locational determinants of Japanese manufacturing start-ups in the United States', *Southern Economic Journal*, pp. 690–708.

World Bank (1993). *The East Asian Miracle*. New York: Oxford University Press.

Wren, C. (1990). 'Regional policy in the 1980s', *National Westminster Bank Quarterly Review*, pp. 52–64.

WTO (1995). *Regionalism and the World Trading System*. Geneva: World Trade Organization.

WTO (2002). *Trade Policy Review: European Union*. Geneva: WTO.

WTO (2003). 'The changing landscape of RTAS', Seminar on Regional Trade Agreements and the WTO, 14 November.

WTO (2004). *Trade Policy Review: European Communities*. Geneva: WTO.

Yamada, T. and T. Yamada (1996). 'EC integration and Japanese foreign direct investment in the EC', *Contemporary Economic Policy*, pp. 48–57.

Yamawaki, H. (1991). 'Discussion', in *European Integration: Trade and Industry* (eds A. Winters and A. Venables). Cambridge: Cambridge University Press, pp. 231–3.

Yamawaki, H. (1993). 'Location decisions of Japanese multinational firms in European manufacturing industries', in *European Competitiveness* (ed. K. Hughes). Cambridge: Cambridge University Press, pp. 11–28.

Yannopoulos, G. (1990). 'Foreign direct investment and European integration: the evidence from the formative years of the European Community', *Journal of Common Market Studies*, pp. 236–59.

York, R. (1993). *Regional Integration and Developing Countries*. Paris: OECD.

Yuill, D., K. Allen, J. Bachtler, K. Clement and F. Wishdale (1994). *European Regional Incentives, 1994–95*. London: Bowker.

Zimmermann, K. (1994). 'European migration: push and pull', *Proceedings of the World Bank Annual Conference on Development Economics 1994*. Washington, DC: World Bank, pp. 313–42.

Zimmermann, K. (1995). 'Tackling the European migration problem', *Economic Perspectives*, pp. 45–62.

Zysman, J. (1983). *Governments, Markets and Growth*. Ithaca, NY: Cornell University Press.

Zysman, J. and A. Schwartz (1998). 'Reunifying Europe in an emerging world economy: economic heterogeneity, new industrial options, and political choices', *Journal of Common Market Studies*, pp. 405–29.

Index